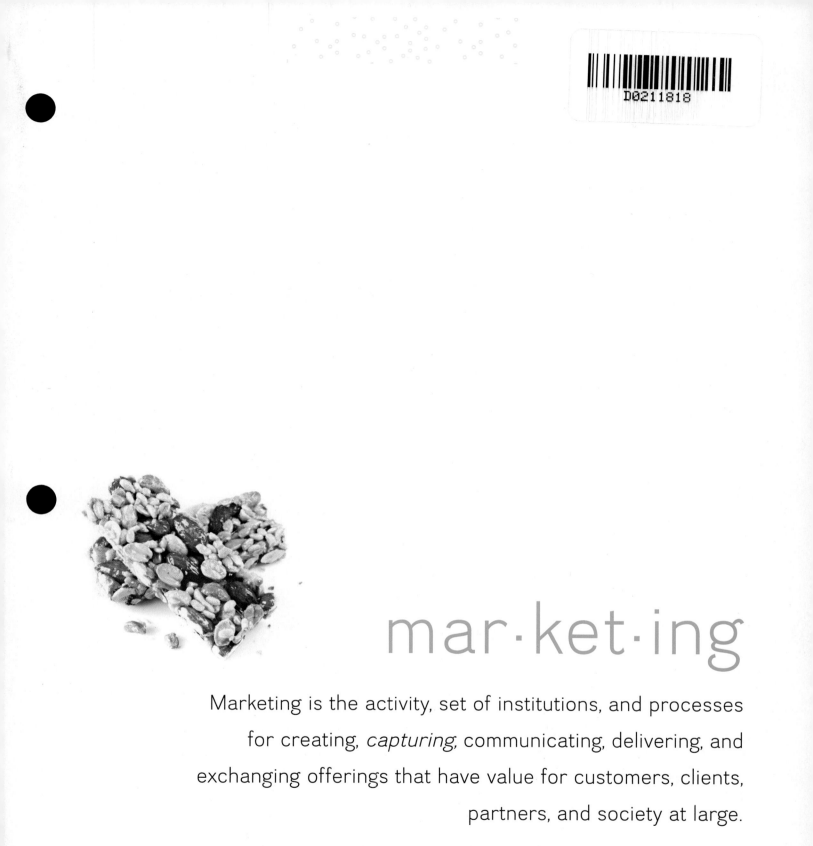

mar·ket·ing

Marketing is the activity, set of institutions, and processes for creating, *capturing,* communicating, delivering, and exchanging offerings that have value for customers, clients, partners, and society at large.

The definition of marketing, established by the American Marketing Association, October 2007. Word in italics was added by authors.

Marketing

Seventh Edition

Dhruv Grewal, PhD
Babson College

Michael Levy, PhD
Babson College

MARKETING, SEVENTH EDITION

Published by McGraw-Hill Education, 2 Penn Plaza, New York, NY 10121. Copyright ©2020 by McGraw-Hill Education. All rights reserved. Printed in the United States of America. Previous editions ©2018, 2016, and 2014. No part of this publication may be reproduced or distributed in any form or by any means, or stored in a database or retrieval system, without the prior written consent of McGraw-Hill Education, including, but not limited to, in any network or other electronic storage or transmission, or broadcast for distance learning.

Some ancillaries, including electronic and print components, may not be available to customers outside the United States.

This book is printed on acid-free paper.

2 3 4 5 6 7 8 9 LWI 21 20 19

ISBN 978-1-260-08771-0 (bound edition)
MHID 1-260-08771-9 (bound edition)
ISBN 978-1-260-42825-4 (loose-leaf edition)
MHID 1-260-42825-7 (loose-leaf edition)

Executive Portfolio Manager: *Meredith Fossel*
Product Developer: *Kelsey Darin*
Senior Marketing Manager: *Nicole Young*
Lead Content Project Manager: *Christine Vaughan*
Senior Content Project Manager: *Danielle Clement*
Senior Buyer: *Laura Fuller*
Senior Designer: *Matt Diamond*
Senior Content Licensing Specialist: *Ann Marie Jannette*
Cover images: *(granola bars)* © *Roman Samokhin/Getty Images;*
(packaging) © *BUTENKOV ALEKSE/Shutterstock*
Compositor: *Aptara®, Inc.*

All credits appearing on page or at the end of the book are considered to be an extension of the copyright page.

Library of Congress Cataloging-in-Publication Data

Names: Grewal, Dhruv, author. | Levy, Michael, 1950- author.
Title: Marketing / Dhruv Grewal, PhD, Babson College, Michael Levy, PhD,
    Babson College.
 Description: Seventh edition. | New York, NY : McGraw-Hill Education, [2020]
 Identifiers: LCCN 2018043778 | ISBN 9781260087710 (alk. paper) | ISBN
    1260087719 (alk. paper)
 Subjects: LCSH: Marketing.
 Classification: LCC HF5415 .G675 2020 | DDC 658.8—dc23 LC record
 available at https://lccn.loc.gov/2018043778

The Internet addresses listed in the text were accurate at the time of publication. The inclusion of a website does not indicate an endorsement by the authors or McGraw-Hill Education, and McGraw-Hill Education does not guarantee the accuracy of the information presented at these sites.

mheducation.com/highered

To our families for their never-ending support.

To my wife, Diana, my daughter, Lauren, my son-in-law, Chet, and my son, Alex.

—Dhruv Grewal

To my wife, Marcia, my daughter, Eva, and my son-in-law, Alex.

—Michael Levy

about the authors

Dhruv Grewal

©Morse Photography

Dhruv Grewal (PhD, Virginia Tech) is the Toyota Chair in Commerce and Electronic Business and a professor of marketing at Babson College. His research and teaching interests focus on direct marketing and e-commerce, marketing research, the broad areas of value-based marketing strategies, services and retailing, and pricing. He is listed in Thomson Reuters' 2014 World's Most Influential Scientific Minds list (only 8 from the marketing field and 95 from economics and business are listed). He is an Honorary Distinguished Visiting Professor of Retailing and Marketing, Center for Retailing, Stockholm School of Economics; an Honorary Distinguished Visiting Professor of Retailing and Marketing, Tecnológico de Monterrey; a GSBE Extramural Fellow, Maastricht University; a Global Chair in Marketing at University of Bath; and has been a Visiting Scholar at Dartmouth. He has also served as a faculty member at the University of Miami, where he was a department chair.

Professor Grewal was ranked first in the marketing field in terms of publications in the top-six marketing journals during the 1991–1998 period and again for the 2000–2007 period, and ranked eighth in terms of publications in *Journal of Marketing* and *Journal of Marketing Research* during the 2009–2013 period. He was also ranked first in terms of publications and third in citations for pricing research for the time period 1980–2010 in 20 marketing and business publications. He has published over 150 articles in *Journal of Marketing, Journal of Consumer Research, Journal of Marketing Research, Journal of Retailing, Journal of Consumer Psychology, Journal of Applied Psychology,* and *Journal of the Academy of Marketing Science,* as well as many other journals. He has over 45,000 citations based on Google Scholar. He currently serves on numerous editorial review boards, such as *Journal of Marketing* (area editor), *Journal of the Academy of Marketing Science* (area editor), *Journal of Marketing Research, Academy of Marketing Science Review, Journal of Interactive Marketing, Journal of Business Research, Journal of Public Policy & Marketing,* and the advisory board for *Journal of Retailing.* He has also served on the boards of *Journal of Consumer Psychology* and *Journal of World Business.* He also received Best Reviewer Awards (*Journal of Retailing,* 2008, *Journal of Marketing,* 2014), Outstanding Area Editor (*Journal of Marketing,* 2017, *Journal of the Academy of Marketing Science,* 2016), and a Distinguished Service Award (*Journal of Retailing,* 2009).

Professor Grewal was awarded the 2017 Robert B. Clarke Outstanding Educator Award (Marketing Edge, formerly DMEF),

2013 university-wide Distinguished Graduate Alumnus from his alma mater Virginia Tech, the 2012 Lifetime Achievement Award in Pricing (American Marketing Association Retailing & Pricing SIG), the 2010 Lifetime Achievement Award in Retailing (American Marketing Association Retailing SIG), the 2005 Lifetime Achievement in Behavioral Pricing Award (Fordham University, November 2005), and the Academy of Marketing Science Cutco/Vector Distinguished Educator Award in May 2010. He is a Distinguished Fellow of the Academy of Marketing Science. He has served as VP Research and Conferences, American Marketing Association Academic Council (1999–2001) and as VP Development for the Academy of Marketing Science (2000–2002). He was coeditor of *Journal of Retailing* (2001–2007).

He has won a number of awards for his research: 2018 William R. Davidson *Journal of Retailing* Best Paper Award (for paper published in 2016); 2017 *Journal of Interactive Marketing* Best Paper Award (for paper published in 2016); 2016 *Journal of Marketing* Sheth Award; 2016 William R. Davidson *Journal of Retailing* Best Paper Award (for paper published in 2014); 2015 Louis W. Stern Award (American Marketing Association Interorganizational SIG); Babson College Faculty Scholarship Award (2015); William R. Davidson *Journal of Retailing* Best Paper Award 2012 (for paper published in 2010); 2011 Best Paper Award (La Londe Conference for Marketing Communications and Consumer Behavior); 2011 Louis W. Stern Award (American Marketing Association Interorganizational SIG); William R. Davidson *Journal of Retailing* Honorable Mention Award 2011 (for paper published in 2009); Babson College Faculty Scholarship Award (2010); William R. Davidson *Journal of Retailing* Best Paper Award 2010 (for paper published in 2008); William R. Davidson *Journal of Retailing* Honorable Mention Award 2010 (for paper published in 2008); 2017 Best Paper Award, Connecting for Good Track, Winter AMA Conference; Stanley C. Hollander Best Retailing Paper, Academy of Marketing Science Conference 2002, 2008, and 2016; M. Wayne DeLozier Best Conference Paper, Academy of Marketing Science 2002 and 2008; Best Paper, CB Track, Winter AMA 2009; Best Paper, Technology & e-Business Track, AMA Summer 2007; Best Paper Award, Pricing Track, Best Services Paper Award (2002), from the American Marketing Association Services SIG presented at the Service Frontier Conference, October 2003; Winter American Marketing Association Conference 2001; Best Paper Award, Technology Track, Summer American Marketing Association Educators' Conference 2000; and University of Miami School of Business Research Excellence Award for 1991, 1995, 1996, and 1998. He has also been a finalist for the 2014 *Journal of Marketing* Harold H. Maynard Award, the 2012 Paul D. Converse Award, and the 2005 Best Services Paper Award from the Services SIG.

Professor Grewal has coedited a number of special issues including *Journal of Public Policy & Marketing* "Pricing & Public Policy" (Spring 1999); *Journal of the Academy of Marketing Science*, "Serving Customers and Consumers Effectively in the 21st Century: Emerging Issues and Solutions" (Winter 2000); *Journal of Retailing*, "Creating and Delivering Value through Supply-Chain Management" (2000); *Journal of Retailing*, "Branding and Customer Loyalty" (2004); *Journal of Retailing*, "Service Excellence" (2007); *Journal of Retailing*, "Customer Experience Management" (2009); and *Journal of Retailing*, "Pricing in a Global Arena" (2012).

He cochaired the 1993 Academy of Marketing Science Conference; the 1998 Winter American Marketing Association Conference "Reflections & Future Directions for Marketing"; Marketing Science Institute Conference (December 1998) "Serving Customers and Consumers Effectively in the 21st Century: Emerging Issues and Solutions"; the 2001 AMA doctoral consortium; the American Marketing Association 2006 Summer Educator's Conference; the 2008 Customer Experience Management Conference; the 2010 Pricing Conference; the 2011 DMEF research summit; the 2012 AMA/ACRA First Triennial Retailing Conference; the 2013 Pricing & Retailing Conferences; the 2014 Shopper Marketing conference at SSE; and the 2015 AMA/ACRA Second Triennial Retailing Conference.

Professor Grewal has also coauthored *Marketing* (publisher McGraw-Hill, 1e 2008; 2e 2010—Awarded Revision of the Year, McGraw-Hill Corporate Achievement Award with Connect-Marketing in the category of Content and Analytical Excellence; 3e 2012; 4e 2014; 5e 2016; 6e 2018); *M Series: Marketing* (publisher McGraw-Hill, 1e 2009, 2e 2011, 3e 2013, 4e 2015, 5e 2017, 6e 2019); *Retailing Management* (publisher McGraw-Hill, 9e 2014, 10e 2018—is the leading textbook in the field); and *Marketing Research* (publisher Houghton Mifflin Co., 1e 2004, 2e 2007). He was ranked #86 for Books in Business and Investing by Amazon in 2013.

Professor Grewal has won many awards for his teaching: 2005 Sherwin-Williams Distinguished Teaching Award, Society for Marketing Advances; 2003 American Marketing Association, Award for Innovative Excellence in Marketing Education; 1999 Academy of Marketing Science Great Teachers in Marketing Award; Executive MBA Teaching Excellence Award (1998); School of Business Teaching Excellence Awards (1993, 1999); and Virginia Tech Certificate of Recognition for Outstanding Teaching (1989).

He has taught executive seminars/courses and/or worked on research projects with numerous firms such as Dell, ExxonMobil, IRI, RadioShack, Telcordia, Khimetrics Profit-Logic, McKinsey, Ericsson, Motorola, Nextel, FP&L, Lucent, Sabre, Goodyear Tire & Rubber Company, Sherwin-Williams, and Asahi. He has delivered seminars in the United States, Europe, Latin America, and Asia. He has served as an expert witness or worked as a consultant on numerous legal cases. He serves on the Board of Directors of Babson Global, and on the Board of Trustees of Marketing Edge.

Michael Levy

©*Karen Rubin Photography*

Michael Levy, PhD (Ohio State University), is the Charles Clarke Reynolds Professor of Marketing Emeritus at Babson College and CEO of RetailProf LLC. He received his PhD in business administration from The Ohio State University and his undergraduate and MS degrees in business administration from the University of Colorado at Boulder. He taught at Southern Methodist University before joining the faculty as professor and chair of the marketing department at the University of Miami.

Professor Levy received the inaugural ACRA Academic Lifetime Achievement Award presented at the 2015 AMA/ACRA (American Marketing Association/American Collegiate Retailing Association) Triennial Conference; and was recognized for 25 years of dedicated service to the editorial review board of the *Journal of Retailing* in 2011. He won the McGraw-Hill Corporate Achievement Award for Grewal–Levy *Marketing 2e* with Connect in the category of excellence in content and analytics (2010); Revision of the Year for *Marketing 2e* (Grewal–Levy) from McGraw-Hill/Irwin (2010); the 2009 Lifetime Achievement Award, American Marketing Association, Retailing Special Interest Group (SIG); the Babson Faculty Scholarship Award (2009); and the Distinguished Service Award, *Journal of Retailing* (2009) (at winter AMA).

He was rated as one of the best researchers in marketing in a survey published in *Marketing Educator* (Summer 1997). He has developed a strong stream of research in retailing, business logistics, financial retailing strategy, pricing, and sales management. He has published over 50 articles in leading marketing and logistics journals, including the *Journal of Retailing, Journal of Marketing, Journal of the Academy of Marketing Science*, and *Journal of Marketing Research*. He has served on the editorial review boards of the *Journal of Retailing, Journal of the Academy of Marketing Science, International Journal of Physical Distribution and Materials Management, International Journal of Business Logistics, ECR Journal*, and *European Business Review*, and has been on the editorial advisory boards of *European Retail Research and the European Business Review*. He is coauthor of *Retailing Management*, 10e (2019), the best-selling college-level retailing text in the world. Professor Levy was coeditor of the *Journal of Retailing* from 2001 to 2007. He cochaired the 1993 Academy of Marketing Science conference and the 2006 summer AMA conference.

Professor Levy has worked in retailing and related disciplines throughout his professional life. Prior to his academic career, he worked for several retailers and a housewares distributor in Colorado. He has performed research projects with many retailers and retail technology firms, including Accenture, Federated Department Stores, Khimetrics (SAP), Mervyn's, Neiman Marcus, ProfitLogic (Oracle), Zale Corporation, and numerous law firms.

New to the Seventh Edition

Some exciting new additions to the Seventh Edition!

The seventh edition of *Marketing* sees significant changes. As always, every example, fact, and key term has been checked, updated, and/or replaced. What follows are major changes in the text, chapter-by-chapter.

Chapter 1: Overview of Marketing starts with a discussion of how different brands are marketing meal replacement bars, such as protein, whole food, and snack bars, to emphasize the text's cover—how marketing adds value to the meal replacement bar market. Examples using these bars are placed throughout the chapter. There are three new Adding Value boxes: the product line extension of Baby Dove, kids recycling and selling products on e-commerce platforms, and Amazon's new cashless stores. A new Ethical & Societal Dilemma box discusses gender inequality in the coffee market. At the end of the chapter is a new section that sets up the rationale for each of the special boxes included in the text. Finally, we conclude with a new case study highlighting KIND Bars' marketing strategy, a nice tie-back to the opener and the cover concept.

Chapter 2: Developing Marketing Strategies and a Marketing Plan begins with a discussion of PepsiCo's Frito-Lay snack brand, and this product line is used in examples throughout the chapter. We also introduce a new Adding Value box highlighting Sally Beauty's updated loyalty program.

Chapter 3: Digital Marketing: Online, Social, and Mobile has seen a line-by-line revision to reflect the rapid changes in digital marketing. We have added a new section that discusses the 7C framework for online marketing: core goals, context elements (design and navigation), content, community, communication, commerce, and connection. The chapter starts by highlighting the success that L'Oréal has experienced with its innovative digital marketing efforts. There are two new Ethical & Societal Dilemma boxes: Facebook's emphasis on personal posts over public content, and how Google and YouTube are helping advertisers avoid controversy. A new Adding Value box on Amazon's marketing universe appears. There is also a new Social & Mobile Marketing box that discusses P&G's responsibility in the "Tide Pod Challenge."

Chapter 4: Conscious Marketing, Corporate Social Responsibility, and Ethics begins by highlighting how sustainability is at the core of Unilever's development of its Love Beauty and Planet line. We showcase how firms must consider pertinent issues when implementing their marketing strategy using TOMS shoes. There are two new Adding Value boxes, one about a philanthropic partnership between Elbi and David Yurman, and another about Patagonia's challenge to keep conscious marketing a guiding principle in the face of growing its business. A new Ethical & Societal Dilemma box describes how Google has banned the advertising of financial products that may do more harm than good. We end the chapter with a new case study on Daily Table, a nonprofit, membership-based grocery store that serves lower-income areas.

Chapter 5: Analyzing the Marketing Environment has gone through a major revision. There is an entirely new section that describes how the physical environment of the store affects the immediate marketing environment. The Social Trends section includes new subsections about sustainability and the utilization and distribution of food. There is also a new section on technological advances and how they influence the marketing environment. The chapter begins with a discussion of a how Tesla is responding to customer needs by introducing the Model 3, its first affordable electric car. A new example using Verizon and Sprint shows how competitors affect the marketing environment. There are two new Ethical & Societal Dilemma boxes: The first examines how the electric car is leading to shifts in the auto industry. The second discusses the backlash General Mills faced when it introduced its all-natural Trix cereal. A new Social & Mobile Marketing box describes Pokémon Go. We also include a new example highlighting how women might be the next big market for the gaming industry. A new example examines the response of many companies to the United States leaving the Paris Accord, and highlights how companies are responding to the environment. Finally, the chapter ends with a new case study on the rise of the electric car.

Chapter 6: Consumer Behavior has also undergone a significant revision. The Noncompensatory section now discusses choice architecture, nudges, defaults, and opt out and opt in. The Learning and Memory section now discusses the information encoding stage, information storage stage, and retrieval stage. The Situational Factors section now includes information on the sensory situation, which discusses how the five senses (visual, auditory, olfactory, tactile, and taste) affect marketing. The opener ties in the openers for Chapters 3 and 4 to discuss how consumer behavior influenced L'Oréal's new vegan hair dyes. There are two new Ethical & Societal Dilemma boxes: The first is on CVS' focus on customer health, while the second is about how "certified" may not mean safe. There are also three new Adding Value boxes: The first is about Pirch's functional showrooms. The second focuses on how La Croix has entered customers' evoked set using social media, and the third highlights how brands are meeting customer demands for healthy snacks with salty alternatives. Finally, the fourth is about Taco Bell's vile deep-fried taco that everyone seems to love. There is also a new Social & Mobile Marketing box about the partnership between Snapchat and Rent the Runway. The chapter ends with a new case study on Amazon's, Google's, and Apple's connected home devices.

Chapter 7: Business-to-Business Marketing starts with an interesting discussion on LinkedIn and its new "native video" feature. A new Marketing Analytics box about the artificial intelligence chip being manufactured by Intel with Facebook's help is included. A new Ethical & Societal Dilemma box concerns whether Facebook should be able to block competing advertisers. There is also a new Adding Value box about how Intel is prompting problem recognition with a new advertising campaign featuring Lady Gaga. Finally, a new Social & Mobile Marketing box examines Snapchat's use of advertising.

Chapter 8: Global Marketing has a new opener highlighting Apple's global strategy. There is a new Social & Mobile Marketing box about how a social media campaign helped save Nigeria's national currency. There are two new Adding Value boxes: The first explains why Whirlpool is raising prices in foreign markets, while the second describes Starbucks' foray into Italy. There are also two new Ethical & Societal Dilemma boxes. The first examines how fast-food chains are entering no-beef markets, while the second examines how advertising and privacy regulations are causing concern for Google in France. A new example featuring Uber and Spotify is used to highlight strategic alliances.

Chapter 9: Segmentation, Targeting, and Positioning opens with how lululemon is targeting male customers. There are two new Adding Value boxes: The first highlights how Nintendo is targeting a more mature market with its Nintendo Switch, while the second examines Under Armour's advertising campaign for extreme runners. There is a new Social & Mobile Marketing box about how teens love to share on social media. A new Ethical & Societal Dilemma box examines how Sanderson Farms targets a market that doesn't mind antibiotics in its poultry. A new example uses the NFL to highlight how brands can use differentiated targeting strategies. A P&G example is used to showcase micromarketing.

Chapter 10: Marketing Research begins with a discussion of how American Express uses analytics to better serve customers and businesses. There are two new Adding Value boxes: The first examines the use of data analytics in the restaurant industry, while the second is about how universities are using research to determine what students want to see in their fitness centers. There are also two new Marketing Analytics boxes: The first highlights Under Armour's "connected fitness" program, while the second discusses how big data are used to predict box office revenues. Finally, a new Ethical & Societal Dilemma box discusses the ethical concerns of Roomba's collecting personal data.

Chapter 11: Product, Branding, and Packaging Decisions begins with a new opener on Aston Martin's branding strategy. There is also a new Adding Value box about how B&G Foods is bringing back the Jolly Green Giant mascot. New examples include how Häagen-Dazs ice cream has increased its product depth and P&G's use of sustainable packaging.

Chapter 12: Developing New Products begins with a discussion of GE's FirstBuild independent innovation arm. A new Adding Value box discusses Mars' Goodness Knows brand's marketing campaign, which films people trying to do something new. There is also a new Ethical & Societal Dilemma box on privacy concerns surrounding smart toys. The shape of the product life cycle is highlighted with a new example featuring Microsoft's Xbox Kinect. The chapter ends with a new case study on how Mattel is reinventing itself.

Chapter 13: Services: The Intangible Product includes an opening vignette that describes how Lyft is innovating the ride-sharing industry by partnering with Taco Bell for its new "Taco Mode." Three new Adding Value boxes appear: The first discusses how a start-up company, Cabin, is delivering a service innovation with its hotels on wheels, the second outlines how virtual reality is enabling travelers to virtually test drive their next vacation; and the third examines how luxury resorts are teaming up with auto manufacturers. A new Social & Mobile Marketing box looks at customer responses to Starbucks' mobile app—while efficient, some customers prefer the old days when baristas wrote misspelled names on the cups, followed by a smiley face. A new example showcases the tech company Motley Fool's peer-to-peer employee recognition system. A new section is outlined in Exhibit 13.6 that discusses the various ways in which technology is augmenting the human effort. A new case study examining artificial intelligence in customer service closes the chapter.

Chapter 14: Pricing Concepts for Capturing Value describes new pricing strategies at Kroger in the opening vignette, including the pricing of its different private brands, digital pricing shelf tags, the use of dynamic pricing, and in-store mobile applications. An Adding Value box examines the trade-off that Taco Bell customers apparently do not make with regard to trading off price and value. How dynamic pricing is used to price tickets for Major League Baseball is examined in a new Marketing Analytics box.

Chapter 15: Strategic Pricing Methods and Tactics opens with an examination of Tiffany & Co.'s unsuccessful product line expansion. A new Adding Value box describes the price drop at Whole Foods following its acquisition by Amazon. The chapter also includes new examples featuring UberXL and Apple.

Chapter 16: Supply Chain and Channel Management opens with a new vignette highlighting Nike's supply chain. There is a new Adding Value box about how grocers are developing their own dairy farms, forming a vertically integrated marketing channel. There are two new Ethical & Societal Dilemma boxes: The first examines the pros and cons associated with driverless trucking, while the second discusses how technology advances adversely affect retail workers. The importance of supply chain management is highlighted in a new example about Brown Betty Dessert Boutique.

Chapter 17: Retailing and Omnichannel Marketing begins with a discussion of the implications of Amazon's acquisition of Whole Foods. The 4Ps of retailing have been expanded to the 6Ps with the addition of *presentation* and *personnel*. Target's private-label expansion is examined in a new Adding Value box. A Social & Mobile Marketing box examines Sephora's clever and risqué tactics. The chapter ends with a new case study about how Ashley Stewart, a once-struggling apparel brand catering to African American women, became the largest plus-size retailer in the United States.

Chapter 18: Integrated Marketing Communications opens with a description of how Toyota is creating ads to spice up the Camry's image and appeal to different demographic groups. There is a new Social & Mobile Marketing box on how BuzzFeed's Tasty, the division responsible for producing the site's vastly popular and widely viewed videos, is revolutionizing marketing. A new Adding Value box appears highlighting how Eggo has leveraged its role in the TV show *Stranger Things*.

Chapter 19: Advertising, Public Relations, and Sales Promotions starts with examinations of Volkswagen's nostalgic campaign. Exhibit 19.2 showcases new examples of emotional appeals in advertising. There are two new Ethical & Societal Dilemma boxes. The first examines some old advertising campaigns that would shock today's viewers, like the one that attempts to get mothers to give chewing gum to their toddlers. The second describes how Volkswagen is trying to put its emissions standards scandal behind it with its new "Think New" advertising campaign. A new example compares the advertising campaigns of the new Hyundai Kona and the Subaru Outback. The Mastercard end-of-chapter case study has been updated to include its most recent "Start Something Priceless" campaign.

Chapter 20: Personal Selling and Sales Management includes a new Marketing Analytics box on how technology and data are changing sales management. A new Adding Value box describes how Tupperware is empowering Indonesian women.

We are pleased to welcome you to the seventh edition of *Marketing*! Since the first edition, we have been committed to emphasizing a basic, yet essential, theme: **Marketing adds value.** This theme comes through not only in our instructional features but also in our covers. With each edition's cover, we have featured a product that, because of marketing, has become more valuable in the eyes of consumers than it might have otherwise become. Last edition we featured chocolate; in previous editions we featured coffee, water, and jeans. For this seventh edition, we feature energy bars. These are all familiar products that started out as commodities but became high-value branded products because of marketing.

How We Show That Marketing Adds Value

As with previous editions of *Marketing,* we continue to emphasize how marketing has evolved into its present-day, integral business function of creating value. We also focus on how firms maintain value and rely on value for establishing lasting relationships with their customers.

To keep students engaged with this theme, we offer the following features:

- **Adding Value**—illustrate how companies add value not only in providing products and services but also in making contributions to society.

- **Ethical & Societal Dilemmas**—emphasize the role of marketing in society.

- **Marketing Analytics**—feature companies that rely on sophisticated data analytics to define and refine their approaches to their customers and their markets.

- **Marketing Digitally**—illustrate how marketers successfully use digital media in their marketing campaigns and efforts.

- **Social & Mobile Marketing**—discuss how social media are used in marketing products.

How We Teach the Basics of Marketing

We understand that for students to appreciate discussions of how marketing adds value, they must first develop a basic understanding of key marketing principles and core concepts. In this effort, we believe students learn best when they see how a subject relates to them. Throughout this edition and all those prior, we provide numerous examples of how students engage in marketing activities every day of their lives—either as consumers or sellers of a product or service. In addition to providing the traditional study and reinforcement tools of most principles of marketing products, we also offer ways to help students think critically about and apply core concepts:

Chapter-Opening Vignettes focus on some of the marketplace challenges faced by such well-known companies as KIND and Kashi bars, L'Oréal, Kroger, PepsiCo, and others.

Marketing Applications encourage students to apply what they have learned to marketing scenarios that are relevant to their lives.

End-of-Chapter Cases help students develop analytical, critical-thinking, and technology skills.

Progress Checks throughout each chapter give students the opportunity to stop and consider whether their understanding of key concepts is progressing as it should.

Auto-Graded Application Exercises in Connect (such as video cases, case analyses, and click and drags) challenge students to apply marketing concepts to real-life marketing scenarios, which fosters their critical-thinking skills in lecture and beyond.

Why We Believe in the Value of Marketing

Beyond teaching a principles of marketing course and developing a product to be taught, we also want to impress upon our students why marketing in and of itself is valuable. Marketing creates enduring and mutually valuable relationships between companies and their consumers. Marketing identifies what customers value at the local level in order to make it possible for firms to expand at the global level. Without marketing, it would be difficult for any of us to learn about new products and services. In fact, an understanding of marketing can help students find jobs after they finish school. If we can inspire this understanding of the value of marketing in our students, then we will have succeeded in demonstrating how *marketing adds value . . .* to their education, their careers, and their lives.

Dhruv Grewal,
Babson College

Michael Levy,
Babson College

Effective, efficient studying.

Connect helps you be more productive with your study time and get better grades using tools like SmartBook, which highlights key concepts and creates a personalized study plan. Connect sets you up for success, so you walk into class with confidence and walk out with better grades.

©Shutterstock/wavebreakmedia

> **"**I really liked this app—it made it easy to study when you don't have your text-book in front of you.**"**
>
> —Jordan Cunningham,
> Eastern Washington University

Study anytime, anywhere.

Download the free ReadAnywhere app and access your online eBook when it's convenient, even if you're offline. And since the app automatically syncs with your eBook in Connect, all of your notes are available every time you open it. Find out more at **www.mheducation.com/readanywhere**

No surprises.

The Connect Calendar and Reports tools keep you on track with the work you need to get done and your assignment scores. Life gets busy; Connect tools help you keep learning through it all.

13	14
Chapter 12 Quiz	Chapter 11 Quiz
Chapter 13 Evidence of Evolution	Chapter 11 DNA Technology
	Chapter 7 Quiz
	Chapter 7 DNA Structure and Gene...
	and 7 more...

Learning for everyone.

McGraw-Hill works directly with Accessibility Services Departments and faculty to meet the learning needs of all students. Please contact your Accessibility Services office and ask them to email accessibility@mheducation.com, or visit **www.mheducation.com/about/accessibility.html** for more information.

Asset Alignment with Bloom's Taxonomy

Principles of Marketing

We Take Students Higher

As a learning science company we create content that supports higher order thinking skills. Interactive learning tools within *McGraw-Hill Connect* are tagged accordingly, so you can filter, search, assign, and receive reports on your students' level of learning. The result—increased pedagogical insights and learning process efficiency that facilitate a stronger connection between the course material and the student.

The chart below shows a few of the key assignable marketing assets with *McGraw-Hill Connect* aligned with Bloom's Taxonomy. Take your students higher by assigning a variety of applications, moving them from simple memorization to concept application.

Asset Alignment with Bloom's Taxonomy

	SmartBook	iSeeit! Videos	Video Cases/Analytics	Marketing Analytics	Marketing Plan Prep	Mini Simulation
Create						
Evaluate						✔
Analyze			✔	✔	✔	✔
Apply			✔	✔	✔	✔
Understand	✔	✔	✔	✔	✔	✔
Remember	✔	✔	✔	✔	✔	✔

Higher Order Thinking Skills ↑
Lower Order Thinking Skills ↓

SmartBook

- Adaptively aids students to study more efficiently by highlighting where in the chapter to focus, asking review questions and pointing them to resources until they understand.

iSeeit! Videos

- Short, contemporary videos provide engaging, animated introductions to key course concepts. Available at the chapter level. Perfect for launching lectures and assigning pre- or post-lecture.

Video Cases & Case Analyses

- Mini-cases and scenarios of real-world firms accompanied by questions that help students analyze and apply marketing theory and other core concepts.

Marketing Analytics

- These newest auto-graded, data analytics activities challenge students to make decisions using metrics commonly seen across Marketing professions. The goal of this activity is to give students practice analyzing and using marketing data to make decisions.

Marketing Plan Prep

- These exercises use guided activities and examples to help students understand and differentiate the various elements of a marketing plan.

Mini Simulation

- Marketing Mini Sims help students apply and understand the interconnections of elements in the marketing mix by having them take on the role of Marketing Manager for a backpack manufacturing company.
- Mini Sims can be assigned by topic or in its entirety.

acknowledgments

Throughout the development of this text, several outstanding individuals were integrally involved and made substantial contributions. First, we thank Elisabeth Nevins and Jenny Esdale for their important assistance in doing research for the book, writing examples, and preparing the manuscript for publication. Our McGraw-Hill editorial and production staff also deserve recognition for their patient and professional support: notably executive brand manager, Meredith Fossel; the support, expertise, and occasional coercion from our product developer, Kelsey Darin; with an eye to detail, lead content project manager, Christine Vaughan; our bridge to corporate intellectual property experts, content licensing specialist, Ann Marie Jannette; senior designer, Matt Diamond, who always makes our books look great; senior marketing manager, Nicole Young, who helps present our best face forward to our adopters; our ever-diligent copyeditor, Sharon O'Donnell; our eagle-eyed proofreader, Becky Komro; our eye-to-the-aesthetic and pedagogy photo editor, David Tietz; and to Kelly Luchtman at Lightfellow for her continuing hard work on video production.

Ancillary materials have become increasingly more integral to the success of any classroom experience. We are privileged to have had a superb team working with us on 7e: Kathleen Gruben (Instructor's Manual); Courtney Worsham (Test Bank/Quizzes review); Leroy Robinson (Connect Application Exercises); Barbara Conte and Sandra Robertson (PowerPoint Presentations); Lois Olson (LearnSmart review); Cathy Currin, UMass, Dartmouth (end-of-chapter exercises); Holt Wilson, Central Michigan University (input on Chapter 14); and Ruth Gilleran, Babson College (input on Chapter 3).

Our colleagues in industry have been invaluable in providing us with case, video, advertising, and photo materials.

Over the years, we have had the opportunity to work with many talented and insightful colleagues. We have benefited from our research and discussions with them. Some of these colleagues are: Anne L. Roggeveen, Victoria Crittenden, Anjali Bal, Lauren S. Beitelspacher, Krista Hill, Rajendra Sisodia, Bala Iyer, and Ruth Gilleran (Babson College); Ruth Bolton, Steve Brown, and Terry Bristol (Arizona State University); Ramon Avila (Ball State University); Joan Lindsey-Mullikin and Norm Borin (Cal Poly, San Luis Obispo); Ko de Ruyter (Cass Business School); Larry D. Compeau (Clarkson University); Don Lehmann and Keith L. Wilcox (Columbia); Praveen Kopalle, Scott Neslin, and Kusum Ailawadi (Dartmouth); Rajneesh Suri (Drexel); Rajesh Chandrashekaran (Fairleigh Dickinson University); Gopal Iyer and Tamara Mangleburg (Florida Atlantic University); Anthony Miyazaki and Walfried Lassar (Florida International University); Martin Mende and Maura Scott (Florida State University), Hooman Estelami (Fordham University); Ronnie Goodstein (Georgetown); V. Kumar (Georgia State University); Scott Motyka (KGI); K. Sivakumar (Lehigh University); Martin Wetzels and Dominik Mahr (Maastricht University); Yu Ma (McGill University); Maria Elena Vazquez Lira (Monterrey Tec); Douglas M. Lambert and Walter Zinn (Ohio State University); Wagner Kamakura (Rice); Thomas Rudolph (St. Gallen University); Jens Nordfält (Stockholm School of Economics); Zhen Zhu (Suffolk University); Venkatesh Shankar and Manjit Yadav (Texas A&M); Julie Baker, Mark Houston, and William Cron (Texas Christian University); Rodney C. Runyan (Texas State University); Kristy Reynolds (University of Alabama); Merrie Brucks and Ajith Kumar (University of Arizona); Dinesh Gauri (University of Arkansas); Nancy M. Puccinelli (University of Bath); Cheryl Nikata (University of Illinois, Chicago); David Hardesty (University of Kentucky); Arun Sharma, A. Parasuraman, R. Krishnan, Howard Marmorstein, Anuj Mehrotra, and Michael Tsiros (University of Miami); Francisco Villarroel Ordenes (University of Massachusetts, Amherst); A. C. Samli (University of North Florida); Monika Kukar Kinney and Kent Monroe (University of Richmond); Abhijit Guha (University of South Carolina); Valerie Folkes (University of Southern California); Stephanie Noble (University of Tennessee); Robert Peterson (University of Texas at Austin); Carolyn Costley (University of Waikato); Rob Palmatier (University of Washington); Abhijit Biswas and Sujay Dutta (Wayne State University); and M. Joseph Sirgy (Virginia Tech).

We would like to thank the following instructors for providing feedback to shape the seventh edition. A special thank you to:

Nancy Abram
University of Iowa

Christopher Anicich
California State University, Fullerton

Robert W. Battle
Nassau Community College

Kimberly D. Grantham
University of Georgia

Jeffrey Harper
Texas Tech University

Fred Hurvitz
Pennsylvania State University

Robert McMillen
James Madison University

Lars Perner
University of Southern California

Lisa C. Troy
Texas A&M University

Frank R. Veltri
University of Oregon

James E. Zemanek, Jr.
East Carolina University

For their contributions to previous editions of *Marketing*, we gratefully acknowledge:

Wendi Achey
Northampton Community College

Praveen Aggarwal
University of Minnesota, Duluth

Ebru Ulusoy Akgun
University of Maine

Maria Aria
Camden County College

Dennis Arnett
Texas Tech University

Audrey Ashton-Savage
Peter T. Paul College of Business and Economics, University of New Hampshire

Gerard Athaide
Loyola College of Maryland

Timothy W. Aurand
Northern Illinois University

Laurie Babin
University of Louisiana at Monroe

Nisreen Bahnan
Salem State University

Ainsworth Bailey
University of Toledo

Aysen Bakir
Illinois State University

Joyce Banjac
Myers University

Harvey Bauman
Lees McRae College

Oleta Beard
University of Washington

Sandy Becker
Rutgers Business School

Hannah Bell-Lombardo
Bryant University

Ellen Benowitz
Mercer County Community College

Gary Benton
Western Kentucky University

Joseph Ben-Ur
University of Houston at Victoria

Patricia Bernson
County College of Morris

Harriette Bettis-Outland
University of West Florida

Parimal Bhagat
Indiana University of Pennsylvania

Amit Bhatnagar
University of Wisconsin, Milwaukee

Jan Bingen
Little Priest Tribal College

John Bishop
University of South Alabama—Mobile

Nancy Bloom
Nassau Community College

Claire Bolfing
James Madison University

Karen Bowman
University of California

Tom Boyd
California State University—Fullerton

Nancy Boykin
Tarleton State University

Cathy Brenan
Northland Community and Technical College

Martin Bressler
Houston Baptist University

Claudia Bridges
California State University

Glen H. Brodowsky
California State University, San Marcos

Greg Broekemier
University of Nebraska Kearney

Gary Brunswick
Northern Michigan University

Alan J. Bush
University of Memphis

John Buzza
Monmouth University

Linda Calderone
SUNY, Farmingdale

Nathaniel Calloway
University of Maryland, University College

Rae Caloura
Johnson & Wales University

Michaelle Cameron
St. Edwards University

Catherine Campbell
University of Maryland

Carlos Castillo
University of Minnesota, Duluth

Eve Caudill
Winona State University

Carmina Cavazos
University of Saint Thomas

Lindell Chew
Linn University of Missouri

Dorene Ciletti
Duquesne University

Melissa Clark
University of North Alabama

Terry Clark
Southern Illinois University—Carbondale

Joyce Claterbos
University of Kansas

Gloria Cockerell
Collin County College

Paul Cohen
Florida Atlantic University

Linda Jane Coleman
Salem State University

Mark E. Collins
University of Tennessee

Clare Comm
University of Massachusetts, Lowell

Sherry Cook
Southwest Missouri State University

Stan Cort
Case Western Reserve University

Keith Cox
University of Houston

Ian Cross
Bentley College

Geoffrey Crosslin
Kalamazoo Valley Community College

Kevin Joseph Cumiskey
Eastern Kentucky University

Brent Cunningham
Jacksonville State University

Clayton L. Daughtrey
Metropolitan State College of Denver

Charlene Davis
Trinity University

Joseph DeFilippe
Suffolk County Community College

George Deitz
University of Memphis

Kathleen DeNisco
Erie Community College

Tilokie Depoo
Monroe College

Laura Dix
Ferris State University

Monique Doll
Macomb Community College

Kimberly Donahue
Indiana University–Purdue University at Indianapolis

Jim D'Orazio
Cleveland State University

Michael Dore
University of Oregon

James Downing
University of Illinois–Chicago

Michael Drafke
College of DuPage

Leon Dube
Texas A&M University

Colleen Dunn
Bucks County Community College

John Eaton
Arizona State University–Tempe

Kellie Emrich
Cuyahoga Community College

Nancy Evans
New River Community College

Keith Fabes
Berkeley College

Tina Facca
John Carroll University

Joyce Fairchild
Northern Virginia Community College

David J. Faulds
University of Louisville

Larry Feick
University of Pittsburgh

Karen Flaherty
Oklahoma State University–Stillwater

Leisa Flynn
Florida State University

William Foxx
Auburn University

Alan Friedenthal
Kingsborough Community College

Douglas Friedman
Penn State University

Jerome Gafford
University of North Alabama

Stanley Garfunkel
Queensborough Community College

S. J. Garner
Eastern Kentucky University

David Gerth
Nashville State Community College

Peggy Gilbert
Missouri State University

Kelly Gillerlain
Tidewater Community College

George Goerner
Mohawk Valley Community College

Jana Goodrich
Penn State Behrend

Robin Grambling
University of Texas at El Paso

Kimberly D. Grantham
University of Georgia

James I. Gray
Florida Atlantic University

Kelly Gredone
Bucks County Community College

Tom Greene
Eastern Washington University

Michael Greenwood
Mount Wachusett Community College

Barbara Gross
California State University–Northridge

David Grossman
Florida Southern College

Hugh Guffey
Auburn University

Reetika Gupta
Lehigh University

John Hafer
University of Nebraska at Omaha

Allan Hall
Western Kentucky University

Joan Hall
Macomb Community College

Daniel E. Hallock
University of North Alabama

Clark Hallpike
Elgin Community College

James E. Hansen
University of Akron

Don Hanson
Bryant University

Jeffrey Harper
Texas Tech University

Dorothy Harpool
Wichita State University

Lynn Harris
Shippensburg University

Dana L. E. Harrison
East Tennessee State University

Reba Heberlein
Madison Area Technical College

Linda Hefferin
Elgin Community College

Charlane Held
Onondaga Community College

Lewis Hershey
Fayetteville State University

Jonathan Hibbard
Boston University

Tom Hickman
Loyola University

Robbie Hillsman
University of Tennessee–Martin

Nathan Himelstein
Essex County College

Adrienne Hinds
Northern Virginia Community College at Annandale

John Hobbs
University of Oklahoma

Don Hoffer
Miami University

Craig Hollingshead
Texas A&M University, Kingsville

Donna Hope
Nassau Community College

Tarique Hossain
California State Polytechnic University

James Gorman Houston
University of Alabama

Ronald Hoverstad
University of the Pacific

Kris Hovespian
Ashland University

James Hunt
University of North Carolina Wilmington

Shane Hunt
Arkansas State University

Julie Huntley
Oral Roberts University

Sean Jasso
University of California–Riverside

Carol Johanek
Washington University, St. Louis

Doug Johansen
University of North Florida

Candy Johnson
Holyoke Community College

Maria Johnson
Macomb Community College, Clinton Township

Keith Jones
North Carolina A&T University

Janice Karlen
CUNY–LaGuardia Community College

Eric J. Karson
Villanova University

Rajiv Kashyap
William Paterson University

Josette Katz
Atlantic Cape Community College

Garland Keesling
Towson University

Mayuresh M. Kelkar
Salem State University

Imran Khan
University of South Alabama–Mobile

Todd Korol
Monroe Community College

Dennis Lee Kovach
Community College of Allegheny County

Kathleen A. Krentler
San Diego State University

Dmitri Kuksov
Washington University–St Louis

Jeff Kulick
George Mason University

Michelle Kunz
Morehead State University

Ann T. Kuzma
Minnesota State University, Mankato

John Kuzma
Minnesota State University at Mankato

Sandie Lakin
Hesser College

Jamie Lambert
Ohio University

Timothy Landry
University of Oklahoma

Don Larson
Ohio State University

Felicia Lassk
Northeastern University

J. Ford Laumer
Auburn University

Marilyn Lavin
University of Wisconsin, Whitewater

Kenneth Lawrence
New Jersey IT

Freddy Lee
California State University, Los Angeles

Rebecca Legleiter
Tulsa CC Southeast Campus

Hillary Leonard
University of Rhode Island

Natasha Lindsey
University of North Alabama

Guy Lochiatto
Massachusetts Bay Community College

Paul Londrigan
Mott Community College

Terry Lowe
Heartland Community College

Dolly Loyd
University of Southern Mississippi

Harold Lucius
Rowan University

Alicia Lupinacci
Tarrant Community College

Stanley Madden
Baylor University

Lynda Maddox
George Washington University

Moutusi Maity
University of Wisconsin, Whitewater

Cesar Maloles
California State University, East Bay

Karl Mann
Tennessee Tech University

Patricia Marco
Madison College

Cathy Martin
University of Akron

Mary Christene Martin
Fort Hays State University

Melissa Martin
George Mason University

Carolyn Massiah
University of Central Florida

Tamara Masters
Brigham Young University

Erika Matulich
University of Tampa

Bob Mayer
Mesa State College

Nancy McClure
University of Central Oklahoma

Maria McConnell
Lorain County Community College

Dennis Menezes
University of Louisville, Louisville

Mohan Menon
University of South Alabama

Joyce L. Meyer
The University of Alabama

Michelle Meyer
Joliet Junior College

Ivor Mitchell
University of Nevada Reno

Mark Mitchell
University of South Carolina

Steven Moff
Pennsylvania College of Technology

Rex Moody
University of Colorado

Melissa Moore
Mississippi State University

Linda Morable
Richland College

Farrokh Moshiri
University of California–Riverside

Dorothy Mulcahy
Bridgewater State College

James Munch
Wright State University–Dayton

Brian Murray
Jefferson Community College

Suzanne Murray
Piedmont Technical College

James E. Murrow
Drury University

Susan Myrden
University of Maine

Noreen Nackenson
Nassau Community College

Sandra Blake Neis
Borough of Manhattan Community College

John Newbold
Sam Houston State University

Keith Niedermeier
University of Pennsylvania

Steve Noll
Madison Area Technical College

Martin Nunlee
Syracuse University

Hudson Nwakanma
Florida A&M University

Matthew O'Hern
University of Oregon

Lois Olson
San Diego State University

Beng Ong
California State University, Fresno

Daniel Onyeagba
Argosy University, Atlanta

Karen Overton
Houston Community College

Deborah L. Owens
University of Akron

Esther Page-Wood
Western Michigan University

Richard Pascarelli
Adelphi University

Terry Paul
The Ohio State University

Michael Pearson
Loyola University

Jerry Peerbolte
University of Arkansas–Fort Smith

Glenn Perser
Houston Community College

Diane Persky
Yeshiva University

Susan Peters
California State Polytechnic University at Pomona

Renee Pfeifer-Luckett
University of Wisconsin at Whitewater

Frank Alan Philpot
George Mason University

Gary Pieske
Minnesota State Community and Technical College

Jeff Podoshen
Temple University

Carmen Powers
Monroe Community College

Mike Preis
University of Illinois—Champaign

Susan Price
California Polytechnic State University

Lori Radulovich
Baldwin-Wallace College

Bruce Ramsey
Franklin University

Rosemary Ramsey
Wright State University

Srikumar Rao
Long Island University

Kristen Regine
Johnson & Wales University

Joseph Reihing
Nassau Community College

Jean Marc Rejaud
Fashion Institute of Technology

William Rice
California State University—Fresno

Patricia Richards
Westchester Community College

Eric Rios
Eastern University

Janet Robinson
Mount St. Mary's College

Harper Andrew Roehm, Jr.
University of North Carolina—Greensboro

Ann Renee Root
Florida Atlantic University

Tom Rossi
Broome Community College

Heidi Rottier
Bradley University

Juanita Roxas
California State Polytechnic University

Donald Roy
Middle Tennessee State University

Linda Salisbury
Boston College

Nick Sarantakes
Austin Community College

Shikhar Sarin
Boise State University

Carl Saxby
University of Southern Indiana

Diana Scales
Tennessee State University

Dwight Scherban
Central Connecticut State University

James Schindler
Columbia Southern University

Jeffrey Schmidt
University of Oklahoma—Norman

Laura Shallow
St. Xavier University

Donald Shemwell
East Tennessee State University

Dan Sherrell
University of Memphis

Philip Shum
William Paterson University

Lisa Simon
California Polytechnic State University, San Luis Obispo

Rob Simon
University of Nebraska—Lincoln

Erin Sims
DeVry University at Pomona

Lauren Ruth Skinner
University of Alabama at Birmingham

Karen Smith
Columbia Southern University

Lois J. Smith
University of Wisconsin

Julie Z. Sneath
University of South Alabama

Brent Sorenson
University of Minnesota—Crookston

James Spiers
Arizona State University—Tempe

Geoffrey Stewart
University of Louisiana

John Striebich
Monroe Community College

Randy Stuart
Kennesaw State University

James Swanson
Kishwaukee College

James Swartz
California State Polytechnic University

Robert R. Tangsrud, Jr.
University of North Dakota

Robert Scott Taylor
Moberly Area Community College

Steve Taylor
Illinois State University

Sue Taylor
Southwestern Illinois College

Sharon Thach
Tennessee State University

Mary Tharp
University of Texas at San Antonio

Frank Tobolski
Lake in the Hills

Louis A. Tucci
College of New Jersey

Sue Umashankar
University of Arizona

Deborah Utter
Boston University

Ven Venkatesan
University of Rhode Island at Kingston

Bronis Verhage
Georgia State University

Deirdre Verne
Westchester Community College

Steve Vitucci
Tarleton University Central Texas

Keith Wade
Webber International University

Suzanne Walchli
University of the Pacific

Wakiuru Wamwara-Mbugua
Wright State University—Dayton

Bryan Watkins
Dominican University, Priory Campus

Ron Weir
East Tennessee State University

Ludmilla Wells
Florida Gulf Coast University

Thomas Whipple
Cleveland State University

Tom Whitman
Mary Washington College

Kathleen Williamson
University of Houston—Clear Lake

Elizabeth Jane Wilson
Suffolk University

Phillip Wilson
Midwestern State University

Doug Witt
Brigham Young University

Kim Wong
Albuquerque Tech Institute

Letty Workman
Utah Valley University

Courtney Worsham
University of South Carolina

Brent Wren
University of Alabama—Huntsville

Alex Wu
California State University—Long Beach

Joseph Yasaian
McIntosh College

Poh-Lin Yeoh
Bentley College

Paschalina Ziamou
Bernard M. Baruch College

We would like to thank all the professors who were instrumental in guiding our revision of not only the text, but also Connect and other ancillary materials

Ivan Abel
St. John's University

Wendi Achey
Northampton Community College

Praveen Aggarwal
University of Minnesota, Duluth

Keanon Alderson
California Baptist University

Rosalyn Amaro
Florida State College at Jacksonville

Maria Aria
Camden County College

Jill S. Attaway
Illinois State University

Michelle Barnhart
Oregon State University

Robert Belenger
Bristol Community College

Tom Bilyeu
Southwestern Illinois College

Mark Blake
York College of Pennsylvania

Maurice Bode
Delgado Community College

Jean M. Brown
University of Alabama in Huntsville

Gary Brunswick
Northern Michigan University

Desislava Budeva
Ramapo College of New Jersey

Melissa Burnett
Missouri State University

Susan Carder
Northern Arizona University

Ella Carter
Bowie State University

Debi Cartwright
Truman State University

Haozhe Chen
East Carolina University

Angeline Close
The University of Texas at Ausin

Kevin Coulson
Emporia State University

Brad Cox
Midlands Technical College

Brent Cunningham
Jacksonville State University

Datha Damron-Martinez
Truman State University

Beth Deinert
Southeast Community College

David DiRusso
Millersville University

Michael Dotson
Appalachian State University

Colleen Dunn
Bucks County Community College

Diane Edmondson
Middle Tennessee State University

Burcak Ertimur
Fairleigh Dickinson University

David J. Faulds
University of Louisville

Amy Feest
Tunxis Community College

Kathleen Ferris-Costa
Bridgewater State University

Troy A. Festervand
Middle Tennessee State University

Paul Fombelle
Northeastern University

John Fraedrich
Southern Illinois University–Carbondale

Theresa E. Frame
Horry Georgetown Technical College

Sheila Fry
Champlain College

Jerome Gafford
University of North Alabama

Tao (Tony) Gao
Northeastern University

Lance Gentry
Colorado State University–Pueblo

Nabarun Ghose
The University of Findlay

Connie Golden
Lakeland Community College

Lisa Goolsby
Southern Adventist University

Deborah M. Gray
Central Michigan University

Susan Greer
Horry-Georgetown Technical College

Cynthia Grether
Delta College

Mike Griffith
Lone Star College–Kingwood

Barbara Gross
California State University, Northridge

Chiquan Guo
The University of Texas–Pan American

Jamey Halleck
Marshall University

Richard Hanna
Northeastern University

David Eric Hansen
Texas Southern University

Jeffrey Harper
Texas Tech University

Perry Hidalgo
Gwinnett Technical College

Monica Hodis
St. John Fisher College

Diane Holtzman
Richard Stockton College of New Jersey

Donna Hope
Nassau Community College

Gorman Houston
University of Alabama

Erika Hovland
Temple University

Vince Howe
University of North Carolina, Wilmington

Miriam Huddleston
Harford Community College

James B. Hunt
University of North Carolina, Wilmington

Eva Hyatt
Appalachian State University

Roxanne Jackson
Vance-Granville Community College

Grace Jebakumari Johnson
University of Wisconsin–Milwaukee

Victoria Jones
University of North Carolina, Wilmington

Sungwoo Jung
Columbus State University

Vishal Kashyap
Xavier University

Mark Kay
Montclair State University

Sylvia Keyes
Bridgewater State University

Tina Kiesler
California State University, Northridge

Brian Kinard
University of North Carolina, Wilmington

John Kinnett
Columbus State University

Peter Knight
University of Wisconsin, Parkside

Michael W. Kroff
Montana State University

Ann T. Kuzma
Minnesota State University, Mankato

Theodore Labay
Bishop State Community College

Donald W. Larson
The Ohio State University

James R. Lashley
Bowie State University

E. Scott Lathrop
Whitman School of Management, Syracuse University

Debra Laverie
Texas Tech University

Cary LeBlanc
Assumption College

David M. Lee
Sam Houston State University

Andrea Licari
St. John's University

Junsang Lim
Virginia State University

Bryan D. Little
Marshall University

Guy Lochiatto
MassBay Community College

Ruth Lumb
Minnesota State University, Moorhead

Anne Weidemanis Magi
University of South Florida

David Matthews
SUNY Adirondack (Adirondack Community College)

Fredric Mayerson
Kingsborough Community College

Myke McMullen
Long Beach Community College

Rajiv Mehta
New Jersey Institute of Technology

Sanjay S. Mehta
Sam Houston State University

Jeffrey Meier
Fox Valley Technical College

Michael Mejza
University of Nevada, Las Vegas

Robert Meyer
Parkland College

Elizabeth Miller
Boston College

Iris Mohr
St. John's University

Josefer Montes
Walla Walla University

Dorothy J. Mulcahy
Bridgewater State University

Jay Mulki
Northeastern University—Boston

Benjamin Muller
Portland Community College

Gergana Nenkov
Boston College

John Newbold
Sam Houston State University

Hudson Nwakanma
Florida A&M University

Matt O'Hern
University of Oregon

Richard B. Osborn
York College of Pennsylvania

Rodney Oudan
Worcester State University

Lauren Paisley
Genesee Community College

Mahatapa Palit
Borough of Manhattan Community College

Janet Parish
Texas A&M University

Raymond A. Parkins, Jr.
Florida State College at Jacksonville

Ed Petkus
Ramapo College of New Jersey

Julie M. Pharr
Tennessee Tech University

Rajani Ganesh Pillai
North Dakota State University

Sampath Ranganathan
University of Wisconsin—Green Bay

Mohammed Rawwas
University of Northern Iowa

Virginia Reilly
Ocean County College

John E. Robbins
Winthrop University

Ann R. Root
Florida Atlantic University

Robert Rouwenhorst
University of Iowa

Donald P. Roy
Middle Tennessee State University

Alberto Rubio-Sanchez
University of the Incarnate Word

Catherine Ruggieri
St. John's University, New York

Doreen Sams
Georgia College & State University

Robin Schallie
Fox Valley Technical College

Douglas Scott
State College of Florida

Christine Seel
Delaware Valley College

Daaim Shabazz
Florida A&M University

Abhay Shah
Colorado State University—Pueblo

Rick Shannon
Western Kentucky University

Kenneth Shaw
State University of New York, Oswego

Robert Simon
University of Nebraska—Lincoln

Peter D. Simonson
North Dakota State University

David Smith
Bemidji State University

Dennis Spector
Naugatuck Valley Community College

Vernon R. Stauble
San Bernardino Valley College

Susan Steiz
Norwalk Community College

Geoffrey Stewart
University of Louisiana

Karen L. Stewart
Richard Stockton College of New Jersey

Susan Stone
Shippensburg University of Pennsylvania

Ray Stroup, Jr.
University of Louisiana at Lafayette

James Swenson
Minnesota State University, Moorhead

Steven Taylor
Illinois State University

Ramendra Thakur
University of Louisiana—Lafayette

Norman Thiel
Walla Walla University

Dennis Tootelian
California State University, Sacramento

Philip Trocchia
University of South Florida, St. Petersburg

Sven Tuzovic
Pacific Lutheran University

Leo Vasquez
San Bernardino Valley College, San Bernardino

Franck Vigneron
California State University Northridge

Doug Wilson
University of Oregon—Lundquist College of Business

Roger Wilson
Fairmont State University

Doug Witt
Brigham Young University

Mike Wittmann
The University of Southern Mississippi

Van R. Wood
Virginia Commonwealth University

Jefrey R. Woodall
York College of Pennsylvania

Kim Wong
Central New Mexico Community College

Ashley Wright
Spartanburg Community College

Elle Wu
Louisiana State University

Charles Wyckoff
Riverside Community College

Ge Xiao
Wilkes University

Jim Zemanek
East Carolina University

Lin Zhang
Truman State University

We express our thanks to all faculty who have contributed to the development of digital learning content:

Lauren Spinner Beitelspacher
Babson College University

Barbara Black
University of Miami

Thomas Byrnes
North Carolina State University

Donna Haeger
Monroe Community College

Todd Korol
Monroe Community College

Melissa Martin
George Mason University

Leroy Robinson
University of Houston, Clear Lake

John Striebich
Monroe Community College

Lois Olson
San Diego State University

A special thank you to Steven A. Taylor of Illinois State University, Elizabeth Jane Wilson of Suffolk University, Kevin Bertotti of iTVk, and Becky and Patrick of We Write Good for their efforts in authoring and producing the iSee it! videos in Connect.

We'd also like to thank the team at Hurix—Sumesh Yoganath, Namrata Gunjal, and Ashwin Srivastav—for their contributions, as well as Sue Sullivan of Editors, Inc.

brief contents

table of contents

©HandmadePictures/iStock/
Getty Images

©Steven Senne/AP Images

©Tharanat Sardsri/Shutterstock

©McGraw-Hill Education

©Eakrat/Shutterstock

©Michael Gordon/Shutterstock

©Denys Prykhodov/Shutterstock

©VCG via Getty Images

©Jonathan Weiss/Shutterstock

©Nada Sertic/Shutterstock

SECTION 4   VALUE CREATION   331

©Jim Young/AFP/Getty Images

12 DEVELOPING NEW PRODUCTS   360

Courtesy of GE FirstBuild

13 SERVICES: THE INTANGIBLE PRODUCT   394

©Photopat/Alamy Stock Photo

©Lam Yik Fei/The New York Times/ Redux Pictures

©Stephen Lovekin/Getty Images for 20th Century Fox

SECTION 6   VALUE DELIVERY: DESIGNING THE CHANNEL AND SUPPLY CHAIN   477

©Michael Nagle/Bloomberg via Getty Images

©Gado Images/Alamy Stock Photo

SECTION 7 VALUE COMMUNICATION 539

18 INTEGRATED MARKETING COMMUNICATIONS 540

©Justin Sullivan/Getty Images

©James Davies/Alamy Stock Photo

©Christian Charisius/dpa/ picture-alliance/Newscom

ASSESSING THE MARKETPLACE

Section One: Assessing the Marketplace contains five chapters. Following an introduction to marketing in Chapter 1, Chapter 2 focuses on how a firm develops its marketing strategy and a marketing plan. A central theme of that chapter is how firms can effectively create, capture, deliver, and communicate value to their customers. Chapter 3 is devoted to understanding how to develop social and mobile marketing strategies. In Chapter 4, conscious marketing is introduced, and corporate social responsibility is woven into the overarching conscious marketing framework. Then the role of the stakeholders in conscious marketing, both internal and external to the firm, is examined. An ethical decision framework is developed and presented. Finally, Chapter 5, Analyzing the Marketing Environment, focuses on how marketers can systematically uncover and evaluate opportunities.

LEARNING OBJECTIVES

After reading this chapter, you should be able to:

LO1-1 Define the role of marketing.

LO1-2 Detail the evolution of marketing over time.

LO1-3 Describe how marketers create value for a product or service.

CHAPTER 1

OVERVIEW
OF MARKETING

On your way to class today, did you grab a bite to eat? If you're like many students, you did not have enough time or the ingredients needed to prepare a fresh meal and sit down to eat it. Instead, you might have pulled an energy bar from your cupboard or snagged one from the coffee shop on the way to campus. Why do so many people lean on these energy bars—pressed rectangles of various grains, fruits, nuts, and so forth—rather than other options as meal replacements or snacks throughout the day?

Your individual answers might vary, but the overriding answer has a lot to do with marketing. Companies that produce and sell energy bars work hard to position them as appealing, convenient, tasty, healthy, socially responsible, and energy-dense foods that can help nearly any consumer meet his or her consumption needs. By making a product that can satisfy virtually every demand a consumer might have, these marketers ensure that their offerings provide value.

Consider, for example, the umbrella term often used to describe these prepared foods. By highlighting the term *energy*, marketers inform consumers that they can expect a boost when they eat one of these products. But energy really is just another word for calories; every food item a human being ever consumes provides energy.[1] Still, with this emphasis, the marketing surrounding energy bars offers a valuable promise to consumers, namely, that they will be energized and able to continue on with their day after they eat one.

Beyond this basic premise, various brands leverage other elements to communicate the value of their products. According to one classification, this market consists of five general types: meal replacement bars, protein bars, whole food bars, snack bars, and others.[2] Other classifications are even more specific, reflecting more detailed, unique benefits, such as paleo, gluten-free, low-carb, low-calorie, and workout recovery options.[3]

For example, the brand name adopted by Phyter bars refers to their unique contents: phytonutrient-dense vegetable and fruit purees.[4] KIND puts its healthy bars' promised benefits even more obviously in its brand name. With a positioning that suggests that consuming these bars supports a healthy lifestyle, KIND's marketing department emphasizes its natural ingredients—along with its commitment to being "kind" and proactively seeking the good of the world overall (as we discuss further in the case study that concludes this chapter).[5]

In establishing an even more specific promise of natural ingredients, Kashi's emphasis is largely on the organic contents of its products, as well as its efforts to encourage expanded organic production of wheat and other ingredients. For farmers, switching from conventional to organic methods is costly and time-consuming. To position itself as the organic option in this market, Kashi has developed a program to help farmers make the transition, then publicizes this information widely to ensure customers regard it as an appealing choice.[6]

But other brands are less interested in healthy or natural offerings and more oriented to appealing to consumers' sense of pleasure. For example, Fiber One bars might promise the healthy benefit of more fiber, but General Mills also works hard to communicate their products' great taste. The bars themselves, and the pictures on the boxes, sport heavy "drizzles" of chocolate, as well as pretzels, salty nuts, and candy pieces mixed in with the grains and fruits.[7] Even confectionary brands such as Snickers and Mars offer entries in this market, placing what are essentially candy bars in store aisles next to more protein-dense offerings.[8]

The pictures on the boxes are not the only packaging elements that are critical to the appeal of energy bars. By designing the products as single-serve, relatively small portions, the companies provide convenience benefits for consumers.[9] They can be tucked easily into a backpack or suitcase. Most of them contain preservatives, such that they can sit in a pantry or desk drawer for months without going bad.

That may be exactly why you grabbed one on your way to class today: It was readily available from your kitchen and easy to stick in your bag. A banana or apple, as well as a conventional candy bar, might offer some similar benefits and convenience. Yet the value established by good marketing, which helps consumers see the appeal of energy bars, makes it more likely that you opted for one of these snacks instead.

L01-1 Define the role of marketing.

WHAT IS MARKETING?

Unlike other subjects you may have studied, marketing already is very familiar to you. You start your day by agreeing to do the dishes if your roommate will make the coffee. But doing the dishes makes you late for class, so you dash out the door and make a quick stop to fill up your car with gas and grab an energy bar for breakfast. You attend a class that you have chosen and paid for. After class, you pick up lunch at the cafeteria, which you eat while reading a book on your iPad. Then you leave campus to have your hair cut and take in a movie. On your bus ride back to school, you pass the time by buying a few songs from Apple's iTunes. In each case, you have acted as the buyer and made a decision about whether you should part with your time and/or money to receive a particular product or service. If, after you return home, you decide to sell some clothes on eBay that you don't wear much anymore, you have become a seller. In each of these transactions, you were engaged in marketing.

The American Marketing Association (AMA) states that marketing is "the activity, set of institutions, and processes for creating, *capturing,* communicating, delivering, and exchanging offerings that have value for customers, clients, partners, and society at large."[10] Good marketing is not a random activity; it requires thoughtful planning with an emphasis on the ethical implications of any of those decisions on society in general. That is, good marketing should mean doing good for the world at large, while also benefiting the firm and its customers. To achieve these long-term goals, firms develop a marketing plan (Chapter 2) that specifies the marketing activities for a specific period of time. The marketing plan also is broken down into various

EXHIBIT 1.1 Core Aspects of Marketing

Marketing affects various stakeholders.

Marketing is about satisfying customer needs and wants.

Marketing

Marketing can be performed by individuals and organizations.

Marketing creates value through product, price, place, and promotion decisions.

Marketing entails an exchange.

components—how the product or service will be conceived or designed, how much it should cost, where and how it will be promoted, and how it will get to the consumer. In any exchange, the parties to the transaction should be satisfied. In our previous example, you should be satisfied or even delighted with the power bar you selected, and Kashi or KIND should be satisfied with the amount of money it received from you. Thus, the core aspects of marketing are found in Exhibit 1.1. Let's see how these core aspects look in practice.

Marketing Is about Satisfying Customer Needs and Wants

Understanding the marketplace, and especially consumer needs and wants, is fundamental to marketing success. In the broadest terms, the marketplace refers to the world of trade. More narrowly, however, the marketplace can be segmented or divided into groups of people who are pertinent to an organization for particular reasons. For example, the entire world needs to eat, but makers of energy bars first identify people who might consume their products (which excludes, for example, babies). Then they divide that marketplace into various categories: busy people who want a convenient snack, as well as those who replace entire meals with energy bars; elite athletes who seek high-calorie contents; health-conscious consumers who demand high levels of protein and low sugars; snackers who instead demand great taste, without worrying too much about the nutrition label; and even socially conscious buyers who believe that purchasing an organic product gives them a way to help farmers. If you manufacture and sell energy bars, you need to know for which marketplace segments your product is most relevant, then make sure you build a marketing strategy that targets those groups. If instead you are the maker of Dove beauty products, you introduce an extended range of products to appeal to more of the various groups, as Adding Value 1.1 explains.

Adding Value 1.1 The Baby Dove Product Line Extension and Its Context[i]

For years, Dove marketed only cleaning and personal care products for women. A few years ago, it added the Dove Men+Care line, and today, it is expanding into products for babies, including wipes, lotions, and baby washes. Although the extension certainly seems like a reasonable move, it also might constitute a competitive strategy, designed to take advantage of the struggles of other big names in the baby care market.

Dove is well known for its moisturizing products, so it argues that an extension that leverages this expertise for a different type of consumer is utterly appropriate. In addition, it gained recent experience with product line extensions when it introduced its lines of products for men. Much of the advertising Dove already uses (targeting both male and female consumers) features families too, such that it does not seem like much of a stretch to focus on the babies that already appear in the ads.

Moreover, the approach Dove is taking when introducing the new product lines resonates with its long-standing efforts to support consumers' sense of self-worth. The marketing communications used to introduce the new products strongly emphasize the idea that there is no "perfect parent" and that there are innumerable, appropriate ways to take care of a baby. Dove is there to help in all those situations, never to make parents feel as if they are failing to do their jobs well enough. Similarly, in advertising to male consumers, Dove seeks to acknowledge and recognize modern men's caregiving roles, so it can link these communications to its baby care products too.

Dove seeks to acknowledge and recognize modern men's caregiving roles, so it can link these communications to its baby care products.

Source: Unilever

These discussions and rationales make it seem like the product line extension is a no-brainer. But history also shows that many companies struggle to gain a foothold in markets for baby care products. For example, Huggies has great name recognition for diapers, but it was unable to get parents to purchase bath products under that brand. As Dove moves its baby products into more and more markets, both domestically and abroad, it hopes that the consistency of its approach will lead to success instead.

EXHIBIT 1.2   Exchange: The Underpinning of Seller–Buyer Relationships

Communications
and delivery

Goods/services
producers
(sellers)

Money and
information

Customers/
consumers (buyers)

Marketing Entails an Exchange

Marketing is about an exchange—the trade of things of value between the buyer and the seller so that each is better off as a result. As depicted in Exhibit 1.2, sellers provide products or services, then communicate and facilitate the delivery of their offering to consumers. Buyers complete the exchange by giving money and information to the seller. Suppose you learn about the new Phyter bar from a friend's tweet or a foodie newsletter to which you subscribe.[11] To learn more, you might visit the company's website, where you learn that the bars are available mainly in stores in the Chicagoland area, but you can order a box for delivery. To complete the order, you have to give the company your billing and address information, which represents another exchange. If you sense that you are giving up too much in the exchange, because it takes too long to fill in all your billing information for every individual site you visit, you might prefer to search for another energy bar option on Amazon, where you place orders all the time, so you do not have to enter your credit card number or other information again. Furthermore, Amazon creates a record of your purchase, which it uses, together with your other purchase trends, to create personalized recommendations of other luscious treats that you might like. Thus, Amazon uses the valuable information you provide to facilitate future exchanges and solidify its relationship with you.

Marketing is about an exchange—you give your time, information, and money to Phyter, and they give you a great energy bar.

©McGraw-Hill Education

Marketing Creates Value through Product, Price, Place, and Promotion Decisions

Marketing traditionally has been divided into a set of four interrelated decisions and consequent actions known as the marketing mix, or four Ps: product, price, place, and promotion (as defined in Exhibit 1.3).[12] The four Ps are the controllable set of decisions or activities that the firm uses to respond to the wants of its target markets. But what does each of these activities in the marketing mix entail?

Product: Creating Value The first of the four Ps is product. Although marketing is a multifaceted function, its fundamental purpose is to create value by developing a variety of offerings, including goods, services, and ideas, to satisfy customer needs. Energy bars have gained traction in the market because consumers had needs that were not being met by existing offerings, such as cold cereal, fruit, or traditional candy bars. The first bars were designed for astronauts; in the 1960s, people thrilled with the space race snapped up

EXHIBIT 1.3 The Marketing Mix

Pillsbury Space Food Sticks, right alongside their Tang.[13] But the more modern iterations started off with PowerBar marketed as dense nutrition options for marathoners and other extreme athletes who have to consume massive amounts of calories to maintain their body mass. As PowerBar flew off the shelves, competitors such as Clif Bar and Balance Bar entered the market. People liked the idea of eating like an elite athlete, even if they were not one.[14] This market continued to grow, so new brands designed new products that would appeal to different audiences. Weight Watchers produced a bar that it touted, mostly to women, as a diet aid. Moving away from the space-age image of the first bar, Lärabar and RXBAR promise all-natural, "real" food ingredients.[15] Thus the many different product versions in the general category of energy bars each create value in specific ways (as we discussed in the opener to this chapter), whether by offering convenience, taste, or a sense of healthiness.[16]

Goods are items that you can physically touch. A KIND or Kashi bar, a Rolex watch, Nike shoes, Pepsi-Cola, a Frappuccino, Kraft cheese, Tide, an iPad, and countless other products are examples of goods. Goods primarily function to fulfill some need, such as satiating hunger or cleaning clothing. But their ultimate value stems from what they provide—and how they are marketed—in terms of convenience (e.g., energy bars instead of a cooked breakfast), status (e.g., Rolex instead of Timex watch), performance (innovative Nike sneakers), taste, and so forth.

Unlike goods, services are intangible customer benefits that are produced by people or machines and cannot be separated from the producer. When people buy tickets—whether for airline travel, a sporting event, or the theater—they are paying not for the physical ticket stub but, of course, for the experience they

A watch is a watch is a watch, right? Wrong! All watches are goods, and they tell the time. But Rolex is marketed as a status brand.
©Casimiro PT/Shutterstock

JetBlue has enhanced its customer experience by enabling its fliers to peruse Amazon content or invest in a Prime membership.

©aradaphotography/Shutterstock

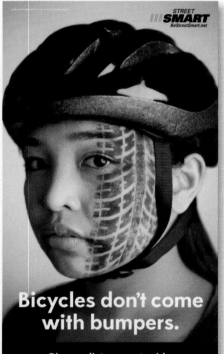

When you attend a Bruno Mars concert, you are paying for a service.

©Rich Polk/Clear Channel/Getty Images

Bicycles don't come with bumpers.

Give cyclists room to ride.

Marketing creates value by promoting ideas, such as bicycle safety.

Source: Street Smart, a public safety campaign of Metro, the District of Columbia, Maryland, and Virginia.

gain. For example, JetBlue offers Wi-Fi–enabled flights at no charge as a service to customers.[17] It also realized that many passengers used this service to visit shopping websites, so it expanded its service offerings, in partnership with Amazon, to make it easy for fliers to peruse Amazon content or invest in a Prime membership. Hotels, insurance agencies, and spas provide services too. Getting money from your bank, whether through an ATM or from a teller, is another example of using a service. In this case, cash machines usually add value to the banking experience because they are conveniently located, fast, and easy to use.

Many offerings in the market combine goods and services. When you go to an optical center, you get your eyes examined (a service) and purchase new contact lenses (a good). If you attend a Bruno Mars concert, you can be enthralled by the world-class performance. To remember the event, you might want to pick up a shirt or a souvenir from the concert. With these tangible goods, you can relive and remember the enjoyment of the experience over and over again.

Ideas include thoughts, opinions, and philosophies; intellectual concepts such as these also can be marketed. Groups promoting bicycle safety go to schools, give speeches, and sponsor bike helmet poster contests for the members of their primary market—children. Then their secondary target market segment, parents and siblings, gets involved through their interactions with the young contest participants. The exchange of value occurs when the children listen to the sponsors' presentation and wear their helmets while bicycling, which means they have adopted, or become "purchasers" of, the safety idea that the group marketed.

Price: Capturing Value The second of the four Ps is price. Everything has a price, although it doesn't always have to be monetary. Price, therefore, is everything the buyer gives up—money, time, and/or energy—in exchange for the product.[18] Marketers must determine the price of a product carefully on the basis of the potential buyer's belief about its value. For example, JetBlue Airways can take you from New York to Denver. The price you pay for that service depends on how far in advance you book the ticket, the time of year, and whether you want to fly coach or business class. If you value the convenience of buying your ticket at the last minute for a ski trip between Christmas and New Year's Day and you want to fly business class, you can expect to pay four or five times as much as you would for the cheapest available ticket. That is, you have traded off a lower price for convenience. For marketers, the key to determining prices is figuring out how much customers are willing to pay so that they are satisfied with the purchase, while the seller still achieves a reasonable profit.

Place: Delivering the Value Proposition The third P, place, represents all the activities necessary to get the product to the right customer when that customer wants it. For Starbucks, for example, that means expanding its storefronts constantly and proactively, so that it is easy for caffeine junkies to find their fix. Creative locations, such as kiosks at the baggage claim in airports or small booths in grocery stores, represent the chain's effort to improve its offering on this dimension of the marketing mix.

Place also deals specifically with retailing and marketing channel management, also known as supply chain management. Supply chain management is the set of approaches and techniques that firms employ to efficiently and effectively integrate their suppliers, manufacturers, warehouses, stores, and other firms involved in the transaction (e.g., transportation companies) into a seamless value chain in which merchandise is produced and distributed in the right quantities, to the right locations, and at the right time, while minimizing systemwide costs and satisfying the service levels required by the customers. Many marketing students initially overlook the importance of marketing channel management because a lot of these activities are behind the scenes. But without a strong and efficient marketing channel system, merchandise isn't available when customers want it. Then customers are disappointed, and sales and profits suffer.

Promotion: Communicating the Value Proposition The fourth P is promotion. Even the best products and services will go unsold if marketers cannot communicate their value to customers. Promotion is communication by a marketer that informs, persuades, and reminds potential buyers about a product or service to influence their opinions and elicit a response. Promotion generally can enhance a product's or service's value. When the publisher of the well-known Babar books wanted to celebrate the 80th anniversary of the series, it initiated a $100,000 campaign. Working in collaboration with toy stores and bookstores, the campaign did not just suggest people buy the books and read about an elephant king. Instead, it embraced a sense of nostalgia and evoked a simpler time, in which grandparents might read pleasant stories to their grandchildren.[19]

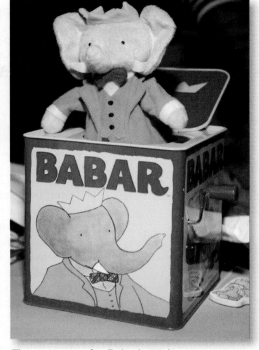

The promotion for Babar's 80th anniversary was not only designed to sell books; it also embraced a sense of nostalgia for the beloved character.

©Anthony Behar/Sipa USA/Newscom

Marketing Can Be Performed by Individuals and Organizations

Imagine how complicated the world would be if you had to buy everything you consumed directly from producers or manufacturers. You would have to go from farm to farm buying

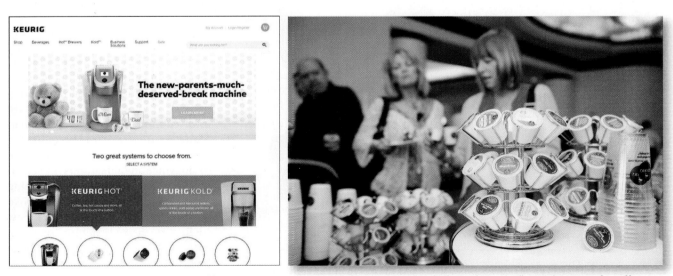

When Keurig sells its machines and coffee to you on its website (left), it is a B2C sale, but when it sells similar items for office use, it is a B2B transaction (right).

(Left): Source: Keurig Green Mountain, Inc.; (right): ©Sergi Alexander/Getty Images

EXHIBIT 1.4   Marketing Can Be Performed by Individuals and by Organizations

Manufacturer (makes monitors) → B2B → Retailer (sells PCs & monitors) → B2C → Consumer A → C2C → Consumer B

your food and then from manufacturer to manufacturer to purchase the table, plates, and utensils you need to eat that food. Fortunately, marketing intermediaries such as retailers accumulate merchandise from producers in large amounts and then sell it to you in smaller amounts. The process by which businesses sell to consumers is known as business-to-consumer (B2C) marketing; the process of selling merchandise or services from one business to another is called business-to-business (B2B) marketing. When Keurig sells its machines and coffee to you on its website, it is a B2C sale, but when it sells similar items for office use, it is a B2B transaction. Through various Internet sites such as eBay and Etsy, consumers market their products and services to other consumers. This third category, in which consumers sell to other consumers, is consumer-to-consumer (C2C) marketing, and the appeal of this channel continues to grow, as Adding Value 1.2 describes. These marketing transactions are illustrated in Exhibit 1.4.

Individuals can also undertake activities to market themselves. When you apply for a job, for instance, the research you do about the firm, the résumé and cover letter you submit with your application, and the way you dress for the interview and conduct yourself during it are all forms of marketing activities. Accountants, lawyers, financial planners, physicians, and other professional service providers also constantly market their services one way or another.

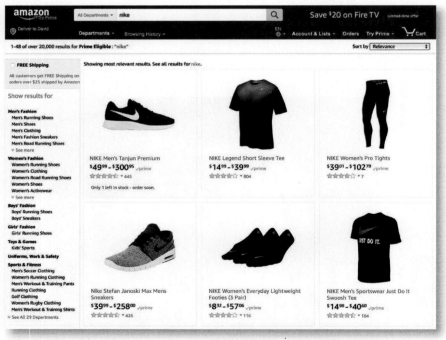

Nike is now sold on Amazon. Amazon gets to sell Nike in return for policing nonauthorized Nike sellers.

Source: Amazon.com, Inc.

Marketing Affects Various Stakeholders

Most people think of marketing as a way to facilitate the sale of products or services to customers or clients. But marketing can also affect several other stakeholders (e.g., supply chain partners, society at large). Partners in the supply chain include wholesalers, retailers, or other intermediaries such as transportation or warehousing companies. All of these entities are involved in marketing to one another. Manufacturers sell merchandise to retailers, but the retailers often have to convince manufacturers to sell to them. After many years of not being able to purchase products from Nike on Amazon, the two giants are now trading partners. In return for being able to sell the much-sought-after brand, Amazon has agreed to no longer allow unauthorized sellers to sell Nike products.[20]

Adding Value 1.2 | **The Kids Are Marketing All Right: Recycling and Selling on E-Commerce Platforms[ii]**

Rather than waiting for retailers to stock the fashions they want or for their parents to give them enough money to purchase the latest fashion, teenagers have embraced a recycling economy in e-commerce settings. Functioning as both sellers and buyers, the young consumers have prompted the emergence of retail platforms that reflect their unique competencies and needs.

On the Poshmark app, for example, teens can earn credits for products they sell. They are not required to provide a credit card, as is standard on many other e-commerce sites. Then they can use the credits to buy other items available on the site. Poshmark also offers social networking capabilities and an intuitive process for uploading photos and descriptions of the items for sale. To facilitate the supply chain, it allows sellers to print out shipping labels, ready to slap onto a box getting mailed to a buyer.

The consumers on such sites enjoy the distinctiveness they can achieve. Rather than going to the mall to buy the same things that everyone else is wearing, they can find unique, one-of-a-kind items. Accordingly, a recent survey suggests that more teenaged consumers shop resale and recycling sites than shop at once popular retail chains such as Abercrombie & Fitch.

When these buyers shift to selling mode, they also obtain several notable advantages. An obvious one is the chance to make money. One New York teen has leveraged his sense of fashion by selling rare sneakers effectively and frequently enough to earn more than $100,000 last year. He notes his fervent anticipation to purchase a luxury car—as soon as he is old enough to drive, that is.

Beyond the direct earnings, the young resellers gain valuable experience with sales, marketing, and retailing. Many of them customize products, such as one savvy seller who buys out-of-fashion merchandise at a low cost, then cuts, dyes, and decorates the items to make them more stylish.

Teenagers have embraced a recycling economy by using apps like Poshmark.

Source: Poshmark

Thus a $10 pair of blue jeans was transformed into an acid-washed pair of pink denim shorts with frayed hems, which she sold for $75.

Interviews with some of these entrepreneurs indicate their growing understanding of the four Ps of marketing: They recommend finding distinctive products that can set the wearer apart; promoting the offerings using vivid descriptions, pricing them to sell quickly, and uploading new offerings at times when buyers are most likely to make a purchase (e.g., evening hours, after school).

The "Milk Life" and "Body by Milk" marketing campaigns create a high level of awareness for the milk industry.

(Left): Courtesy of Lowe Campbell Ewald and MilkPEP, (right): ©Jonathan Ferrey/Getty Images

Marketing also can aim to benefit an entire industry or society at large. Ethical & Societal Dilemma 1.1 details how one coffee company is seeking to improve the lives of women throughout the world. On a broader level, the dairy industry as a whole targets its "Milk Life" and "Body by Milk" campaigns at different target segments, including parents, their children, and athletes. Through this campaign, the allied milk producers have created high levels of awareness about the benefits of drinking milk, including the high levels

Ethical & Societal Dilemma 1.1 — Making a Family Business More Valuable by Addressing Gender Inequality in the Coffee Market[iii]

Worldwide, the coffee supply chain is dominated by women—not that most marketing in this industry would indicate that. Rather than the conventional images of a male farmer walking a burro along rows of coffee beans in fields, the reality is that women perform approximately 70 percent of the work involved in getting beans to market and into consumers' cups. Together with the misleading imagery, gender inequality throughout the supply chain has meant that in many places, female farmers are underpaid, excluded from negotiations, or limited in the competitive moves they are allowed to make.

For one small, family-owned gourmet coffee company in Minnesota, that situation led to the inspiration for a new way to market its products. As the second generation of the family took over the company, Alakef Coffee Roasters, from her parents, Alyza Bohbot first determined that she did not want simply to keep doing what her parents had done, because she believed that brand had reached a plateau. It was not growing anymore, and its marketing and branding had remained the same for years.

Upon taking over, Bohbot decided to attend a conference of the International Women's Coffee Alliance. There she heard a story of a farmer from Colombia who lost her farm after her husband died because women were not allowed to make decisions about property. With this growing recognition of the gender inequality that marked her industry, Bohbot realized that she could turn a negative into a positive. The company initiated a new brand, City Girl Coffee, dedicated to ensuring the empowerment and employment of women throughout the supply chain. It purchases beans only from cooperatives and farms that are owned or managed by women. In addition, it donates 5 percent of its profits to nonprofit industry groups that are committed to supporting women.

In line with these initiatives, City Girl is unapologetically feminine in its marketing. Beyond the brand name, the packaging is bright pink. The logo depicts a clearly feminine figure on a scooter, and the mission statement asserts straightforwardly, "We are bringing awareness and equality to the coffee industry."

of protein, potassium, and calcium it provides. The focus is largely on how drinking milk for breakfast fits in with a healthy lifestyle that helps people maintain their focus, weight, and muscle mass. Even the industry's charitable campaigns resonate with this notion: The Great American Milk Drive, run in conjunction with Feeding America, seeks to ensure that local food banks are sufficiently stocked with this nutritious, frequently requested item. Such campaigns benefit the entire dairy industry and promote the health benefits of drinking milk to society at large.

PROGRESS CHECK

1. What is the definition of marketing?
2. Marketing is about satisfying _____ and _____.
3. What are the four components of the marketing mix?
4. Who can perform marketing?

THE IMPORTANCE OF MARKETING OVER TIME

LO1-2 Detail the evolution of marketing over time.

Firms spend billions of dollars in the United States and worldwide on marketing initiatives. Without such spending, and the marketing jobs associated with it, the global economy would plummet. If all ad spending on television and on streaming services such as Hulu were to disappear, consumers would wind up paying around $1,200 per year to access about a dozen channels each. Some currently available channels that appeal to relatively small, niche audiences likely would not be able to survive, though, so the options would shrink overall. Removing all marketing spending would also affect many websites. For example, Facebook is so widespread and popular it likely could make up for any lost advertising revenues by charging users about $12 per year, and most users probably would be willing to pay that rate. However, the charges would severely limit Facebook's spread into less developed nations, where $12 is more than many people earn in a period of two weeks. Other sites, such as BuzzFeed, would likely disappear altogether.[21]

But marketing didn't get to its current level of prominence among individuals, corporations, and society at large overnight.[22] To understand how marketing has evolved into its present-day, integral business function of creating value, let's look for a moment at some of the milestones in marketing's short history (see Exhibit 1.5).

EXHIBIT 1.5	Marketing Evolution: Production, Sales, Marketing, and Value

Turn of the century   1920   1950   1990   Turn of the 21st century

Production   Sales   Marketing   Value-based marketing

Photos (left to right): ©Ryan McVay/Getty Images; ©CMCD/Getty Images; ©Lawrence Manning/Getty Images; ©Ryan McVay/Getty Images; ©McGraw-Hill Education/Mark Dierker, photographer

Production-Oriented Era

Around the turn of the 20th century, most firms were production oriented and believed that a good product would sell itself. Henry Ford, the founder of Ford Motor Company, once famously remarked, "Customers can have any color they want so long as it's black." Manufacturers were concerned with product innovation, not with satisfying the needs of individual consumers, and retail stores typically were considered places to hold the merchandise until a consumer wanted it.

Sales-Oriented Era

Between 1920 and 1950, production and distribution techniques became more sophisticated; at the same time, the Great Depression and World War II conditioned customers to consume less or manufacture items themselves, so they planted victory gardens instead of buying produce. As a result, manufacturers had the capacity to produce more than customers really wanted or were able to buy. Firms found an answer to their overproduction in becoming sales oriented: They depended on heavy doses of personal selling and advertising.

Market-Oriented Era

After World War II, soldiers returned home, got new jobs, and started families. At the same time, manufacturers turned from focusing on the war effort toward making consumer products. Suburban communities, featuring cars in every garage, sprouted up around the country, and the new suburban fixture, the shopping center, began to replace cities' central business districts as the hub of retail activity and a place to just hang out. Some products, once in limited supply because of World War II, became plentiful. And the United States entered a buyers' market—the customer became king! When consumers again had choices, they were able to make purchasing decisions on the basis of factors such as quality, convenience, and price. Manufacturers and retailers thus began to focus on what consumers wanted and needed before they designed, made, or attempted to sell their products and services. It was during this period that firms discovered marketing.

Value-Based Marketing Era

Most successful firms today are market oriented.[23] That means they generally have transcended a production or selling orientation and attempt to discover and satisfy their customers' needs and wants. Before the turn of the 21st century, better marketing firms recognized that there was more to good marketing than simply discovering and providing what consumers wanted and needed; to compete successfully, they would have to give their customers greater value than their competitors did. (The importance of value is appropriately incorporated into the AMA definition of marketing.)

Value reflects the relationship of benefits to costs, or what you *get* for what you *give*.[24] In a marketing context, customers seek a fair return in goods and/or services for their hard-earned money and scarce time. They want products or services that meet their specific needs or wants *and* that are offered at a price that they believe is a good value. A good value, however, doesn't necessarily mean the product or service is inexpensive. If it did, luxury goods manufacturers would go out of business. There are customers willing to pay asking prices for all types of goods at all price levels because, to those individuals, what they get for what they give is a good value. This point is central to the marketing strategy adopted by Whole Foods, as Adding Value 1.3 explains.

A creative way to provide value to customers is to engage in value cocreation.[25] In this case, customers can act as collaborators to create the product or service. When clients work with their investment advisers, they cocreate their investment portfolios; when Nike allows customers to custom design their sneakers, they are cocreating.

During the past couple of decades, as a way to build value marketers have used a relational orientation because they have realized that they need to think about their customers in terms of relationships rather than transactions.[26] To build relationships, firms focus on the lifetime profitability of the relationship, not how much money is made during each transaction. Thus, Apple makes its innovations compatible with existing products to encourage consumers to maintain a long-term relationship with the company across all their

Adding Value 1.3   The Meaning of Best Value: Whole Foods' Purpose-Based Marketing[iv]

Some analysts looking at Whole Foods' dwindling sales numbers and decreased earnings would feel the solution to these issues is obvious: The grocery chain should lower its prices so that consumers consider the company and its products more valuable. It did, in fact, lower its prices after it was acquired by Amazon, but those reductions have almost vanished recently. Whole Foods rejects that notion, though, arguing instead that value means far more than prices. And it has several ideas in mind to prove that it is right.

To start, it introduced a new Responsibly Grown sourcing program, which identifies all fresh produce and flowers according to their environmental impact.

Whole Foods' Responsibly Grown rating program identifies all fresh produce and flowers according to their environmental impact.

©Justin Sullivan/Getty Images

The program is stringent in its demands. When vendors exert minor environmental impacts, they are rated good; those producers that go further by, for example, minimizing wasteful plastic usage or ensuring conservation areas for bees, earn a ranking better. The producers identified as the best address a vast range of responsibility initiatives, from working conditions for farmers to conservation efforts to clean energy to renewable resources and so on. For example, one criterion asks farmers how many earthworms live in the soil on their farms.

This produce-oriented initiative follows Whole Foods' existing efforts, such as its Eco-Scale rating system applied to cleaning products and separate programs to determine the sustainability and responsibility associated with animal and fish products. Furthermore, it has considered introducing labels that indicate whether any particular food item contains any genetically modified ingredients.

In parallel with these new initiatives, Whole Foods developed a revised advertising campaign, with a prominent tagline that reminds shoppers that "Values matter." The commercials emphasize that by shopping at Whole Foods, consumers can be confident that their food has been sourced responsibly and fairly. For example, any beef purchased in the stores has been raised by responsible ranchers who give the cows "room to roam."

By promoting the idea that "value is inseparable from values," Whole Foods seeks to remind shoppers of all that it provides, in exchange for a somewhat higher price point. In particular, it promises that they can make their food choices confidently, buoyed by a range of information that Whole Foods will make available to them at all times.

---

electronic needs. This relationship approach uses a process known as **customer relationship management (CRM)**, a business philosophy and set of strategies, programs, and systems that focus on identifying and building loyalty among the firm's most valued customers. Firms that employ CRM systematically collect information about their customers' needs and then use that information to target their best customers with the products, services, and special promotions that appear most important to them.

In the next section, we explore the notion of value-based marketing further. Specifically, we look at various options for attracting customers by providing them with better value than the competition does. Then we discuss how firms compete on the basis of value. Finally, we examine how firms transform the value concept into their value-driven activities.

PROGRESS CHECK

1. What are the various eras of marketing?

Apple makes its new products compatible with existing ones to maintain a long-term relationship with its customers.
©Spencer Platt/Getty Images

LO1-3 Describe how marketers create value for a product or service.

HOW DOES MARKETING CREATE VALUE, AND HOW DO FIRMS BECOME MORE VALUE DRIVEN?

Value stems from four main activities that value-driven marketers undertake. We describe them in the remainder of this chapter, and these four activities also are reflected in the contents of the boxes that appear throughout this book: Adding Value, Marketing Analytics, Ethical & Societal Dilemma, Superior Service, and Social & Mobile Marketing. First, to ensure that their offerings are valuable, firms leverage all the various elements of marketing and work to build relationships with partners and customers to introduce their product, service, or idea to the marketplace at just the place and time that customers want it. Second, they gather vast information about customers and competitors, then analyze it and share it across their own organization and with other partner firms, such as those that provide promotion and social media services. Third, they strive to balance the benefits and costs of their offerings for not just themselves and their customers, but also their communities and society as a whole. Fourth, they take advantage of new technologies and connect with their customers using the latest social media channels.

Adding Value

As we have consistently noted, value is central to marketing. Thus the first element we describe appears frequently throughout the book, in boxes that we call Adding Value. Value-oriented marketers constantly measure the benefits that customers perceive against the cost of their offerings. They use available customer data to find opportunities to satisfy their customers' needs better, keep down costs, and develop long-term loyalties. For example, as Adding Value 1.4 describes, Amazon continually looks for ways to make it more convenient for shoppers to obtain the products it sells and thus to keep them coming back.

Marketing Analytics

Modern marketers rely on sophisticated data analytics to define and refine their approaches to their customers and their markets. The growth of big data and the associated challenges are inescapable, so the Marketing Analytics boxes in this textbook detail their implications for a wide range of organizations and firms, as well as their customers. In particular, companies such as Starbucks, CVS, Kroger, Netflix, and Amazon collect massive amounts of data

Adding Value 1.4　　Is There Cash Value of No Cash? Amazon Thinks So[v]

Amazon has determined that consumers rarely use cash anymore, so it is increasingly seeking technology-supported, seamless innovations to eliminate it altogether, whether online or in physical stores—along with most of the human staffers who previously were required to take the dollar bills and make change. In Amazon's technologically advanced experimental Go store, located in its Seattle headquarters, customers can shop for groceries without ever pulling a payment form out of their pockets. As they enter the store, they scan their phone to identify themselves. Then cameras mounted throughout the store track and monitor their movements, including whether they place particular items in their shopping baskets. After completing their shopping trip, they simply walk out, and their account gets charged for the items they have selected.

This sophisticated operation continues to deal with various challenges, though, which is part of why Amazon has opened the Go store only to employees thus far. For example, the monitors have difficulty following individual customers when the store is very crowded. The underlying software does not rely on facial recognition, to avoid privacy concerns, so each shopper is represented simply as a three-dimensional figure. Specifying each individual customer thus is difficult if they are bunched together in a crowd.

In addition, the software has not quite perfected its ability to recognize precisely which product a customer has selected. Tubs of sour cream and cottage cheese look pretty much the same to a video monitor, for example. Human shopping habits complicate this effort even further, in that when people grab products from the shelf, their hands often cover the label information that might allow the program to determine precisely which item they have chosen.

The Amazon experimental Go store is so high-tech that it doesn't even take cash.
©Rocky Grimes/Shutterstock

For now at least, store personnel are still required for some functions, such as to check identification when shoppers want to buy age-restricted products like alcohol. But conceivably, such tasks could be performed by advanced technology in the near future, implying the possibility of daily shopping experiences totally devoid of human service providers. Such experiences might be far in the future, especially considering the bugs in the system and shoppers' continued appreciation for friendly interactions with human salesclerks. Still, Amazon has an "unwritten rule" that any new innovation must offer the promise of being expandable on a vast scale—a novel idea cannot be just a one-time goof, to see if it can be done. Thus the likelihood that Amazon Go stores will spread, adding value in various locations, seems high.

---

about how, when, why, where, and what people buy, and then analyze those data to inform their choices. Marketing Analytics 1.1 gives an extended account of how Starbucks uses its data to make critical decisions about one of the four Ps: the place to locate its stores.

Social and Mobile Marketing

Marketers have steadily embraced new technologies such as social and mobile media to allow them to connect better with their customers and thereby serve their needs more effectively. The Social & Mobile Marketing boxes that crop up in each chapter aim to provide timely views on some of the most prominent examples. Businesses take social and mobile media seriously and include these advanced tools in the development of their marketing strategies, though as Social & Mobile Marketing 1.1 explains, even these efforts might not be sufficient to keep up with consumers' rapidly changing demands. Yet 97 percent of marketers assert that they use social media tools for their businesses.[27] That's largely because approximately 4.2 billion people link to some social media sites through their mobile devices.[28]

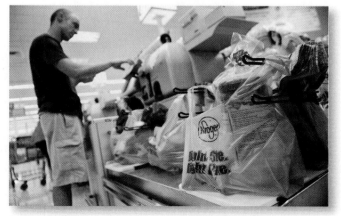

Kroger collects massive amounts of data about how, when, why, where, and what people buy, and then analyzes those data to better serve its customers.
©Daniel Acker/Bloomberg/Getty Images

Marketing Analytics 1.1   Location, Location, Analytics: Starbucks' Use of Data to Place New Stores[vi]

By now, nearly everyone on the planet recognizes the green mermaid logo that proudly sits atop every Starbucks sign, poster, and cup. The ubiquitous coffee giant maintains more than 22,000 locations in more than 66 countries. But its growth has not been without a few stumbles and bumps in the road. For example, in the last decade, hundreds of newly opened stores had to be closed because of their poor performance. In analyzing how the company got to that point, Patrick O'Hagan, Starbucks' manager of global market planning, explained that many of the stores never should have opened. However, the staff in charge of these location choices had been inundated with so much data, they were unable to use them to make profitable decisions. Thus, the Starbucks story reveals a great deal about the importance of data analytics.

Starbucks began using Esri's geographic information system (GIS) technology as far back as the 1990s. But it has perfected its applications of the GIS-provided predictive analytics only recently. Currently, it is using the information gleaned from the technology to plan 1,500 new locations. With the system's ArcGIS Online tool, Starbucks obtains a graphical summary of the GIS data in map form. These data include both location information and demographic details, which the software analyzes according to pertinent criteria. The applications allow Starbucks' staff to pinpoint ideal locations that are likely to attract substantial traffic and thus boost chainwide sales such that "ArcGIS allows us to create replicable consumer applications that are exactly what they need." Because the GIS technology is accessible through desktops as well as mobile devices, location experts in the field also can combine the high-tech insights with their real-world observations.

Starbucks uses geographic information system (GIS) technology to pinpoint ideal locations and determine which kinds of stores to open in those locations.

©Bhandol/Alamy Stock Photo

Not only does the GIS technology help Starbucks determine the ideal locations for new stores, but it also can enable the company to decide which kinds of stores to open. For example, many of the 1,500 planned new stores will feature drive-through windows; others will be smaller stores, strategically placed to provide the greatest customer convenience. The new approach already has been proving effective, according to results that show that the most recently opened stores, particularly those in the Americas, consistently are producing great returns and exceeding hurdle rates.

Marketers are increasingly connecting with their customers via mobile devices.

© Tanya Constantine/Getty Images

Yet even with this astounding penetration, only 20 percent of the world's population uses Facebook—which means 80 percent still has not signed up.[29] The United States and United Kingdom may be approaching saturation, but there is still huge growth potential for social networks. Before users can sign up for Facebook, they need access to high-speed Internet. Other countries continue to experience higher Facebook growth rates as they gain greater Internet access and as Facebook becomes available in more languages (around 140 currently). The global average Internet penetration rate hovers below 50 percent, with massive populations in Africa and Asia still limited in their access.[30]

Beyond social media sites, online travel agencies such as Expedia, Travelocity, Orbitz, Priceline, and Kayak have become the first place that users go to book travel arrangements. In 2015, almost 150 million bookings, representing 57 percent of all travel bookings, were made on the Internet. Sixty-five percent of same-day bookings were made from mobile devices.[31] Customers who book hotels using travel agencies become loyal to the agency that gives them the lowest prices rather than to any particular hotel brand. So hotels are using social media and mobile applications to lure customers back to their specific brands by engaging in conversations with them on Facebook and allowing fans of the page

Social & Mobile Marketing 1.1   What Comes Around: Marketing Today[vii]

The signs of the growth of mobile advertising, at the expense of other digital forms such as desktops and laptops, have long been evident. But the speed with which this shift is occurring is taking many marketers by surprise because it is virtually unprecedented. Consider some of the numbers: In 2009, mobile Internet ad spending was $1.3 billion, whereas in 2018 it is projected to be $125 billion. Within just a couple of years, mobile advertising will be a bigger market than digital advertising.

Both forms are similar, in the sense that they are clearly distinct from traditional marketing and seek to reach technologically savvy shoppers. But they require unique approaches and marketing plans because a campaign that works well on a user's desktop computer might not function effectively on a tablet or smartphone. Furthermore, mobile marketing offers functionalities and advertising tactics that digital ads cannot provide. For example, mobile advertising allows brands and marketers to send timely, location-based communications to consumers at the moment they enter a store or begin a search for a nearby restaurant on their phones.

Another trend occurring apace with this shift is the rise of ad-blocking technology. Apple now allows users to install software to block banner ads in digital channels. Although consumers indicate that they would like the ability to block advertising in mobile settings as well, marketing messages contained within apps continue to be prevalent. In this sense, advertisers might seek to expand and improve their mobile marketing to avoid the barriers that consumers can implement on their desktops. In the longer term, though, the shift to more mobile marketing likely implies the need for new forms of communication, including game-oriented, social content, and informational advertising that does not really look like advertising at all.

to book their hotel reservations through Facebook. Some hotel chains have mobile applications that allow customers to make changes to their reservations, shift check-in and check-out times, and add amenities or services to their stays. The hotels know a lot about their customers because they collect information about their previous visits, including the type of room they stayed in, their preferences (from pillows to drinks consumed from the minibar), and the type of room service they prefer.

Several restaurant chains are exploiting location-based social media applications.[32] By using location-based apps on their mobile phones, customers can use, for example, HappyCow to find nearby vegetarian restaurants or Yelp to find restaurants that are well rated by users.

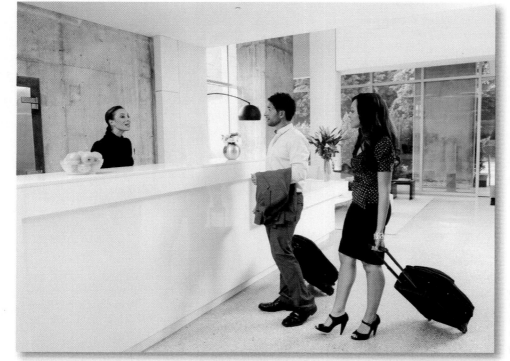

Make travel arrangements online either through Facebook or your mobile app and check-in is a breeze.

©Erik Isakson/Getty Images

Buffalo Wild Wings attracts young and tech-savvy customers to its restaurants by offering contests and games through mobile devices.

©dcwcreations/Shutterstock

Buffalo Wild Wings suggests that its diners check in to its locations using their phones. The target customers for this chain are young and tech savvy, and with its in-house games and sports broadcasts, Buffalo Wild Wings is uniquely situated to encourage customers to connect and bring along their friends. It offers contests and encourages frequent visits to win. Customers can earn free chicken wings or soft drinks within their first three visits. Buffalo Wild Wings' Game Break allows customers to play fantasy-style and real-time games for prizes, whether they are in-store using a tablet or anywhere at all on their smartphones.[33]

Ethical and Societal Dilemma

Should marketing focus on factors other than financial profitability, like good corporate citizenry? Many of America's best-known corporations seem to think so—they have undertaken various marketing activities such as developing greener products, making healthier food options and safer products, and improving their supply chains to reduce their carbon footprint. At a more macro level, firms are making ethically based decisions that benefit society as a whole, while also considering all of their stakeholders, as the grocers in Ethical & Societal Dilemma 1.2 exemplify. This revised view of the responsibilities and roles of marketers reflects a concept we refer to as *conscious marketing,* which we cover in more detail in Chapter 4.

Socially responsible firms recognize that including a strong social orientation in business is a sound strategy that is in both its own and its customers' best interest. It shows the consumer marketplace that the firm will be around for the long run and can be trusted with the marketplace's business. In a volatile market, investors view firms that operate with high

Ethical & Societal Dilemma 1.2   Free Fruit for Children: What Could Go Wrong?[viii]

Childhood obesity is a serious, global problem. For parents, shopping with hungry kids who demand sugary snacks sometimes might seem like an equally vexing challenge. In an effort to help resolve both concerns, several grocery store chains are offering a new kind of appealing giveaway. Specifically, these grocers set up stands that display a range of fruits, with signs offering the produce for free to children under a certain age.

The idea is that a banana or apple at the start of the shopping trip can keep kids from getting hungry and cranky, thus making the shopping experience more pleasant for their parents. The fruit options are more healthful and less troublesome than other options, such as the free cookies or doughnuts that some in-store bakeries provide for young shoppers. Because the fruit is free, it also offers notable benefits over packaged chocolate bars, fruit snacks, or granola bars that parents might open in the aisles before they check out.

The fruit giveaway experiments have expanded globally, with chains in the United States, United Kingdom, and Australia all taking part. Although many responses have been positive, including parents' praise for stores that help them encourage healthful eating by their children, others question the tactic. The key complaint has been hygiene, in that there are

Should grocery stores offer free fruit to children?

©Hero Images Inc./Alamy Stock Photo

few options for washing fruit such as apples, peaches, and pears before children bite down. Still, the generally positive responses have led at least one chain to estimate that it will give away approximately 1 million pieces of fruit over the next year.

levels of corporate responsibility and ethics as safe investments. Similarly, firms have come to realize that good corporate citizenship through socially responsible actions should be a priority because it will help their bottom line in the long run.[34]

PROGRESS CHECK

1. Does providing a good value mean selling at a low price?
2. How are marketers connecting with customers through social and mobile media?

Reviewing Learning Objectives

LO1-1 Define the role of marketing.

Formally, marketing is "the activity, set of institutions, and processes for creating, *capturing,* communicating, delivering, and exchanging offerings that have value for customers, clients, partners, and society at large."[35] But marketing has a prominent role in every person's daily life, whether he or she is exchanging money for conventional products, exchanging personal information for services, or exchanging time for a cause that gives him or her a good feeling. It includes a vast range of stakeholders, including not just the firm and the customer but also other members of the supply chain, communities, and society as a whole. Furthermore, the foundation of all marketing can be summarized in the four Ps, such that marketing defines the product, price, place, and promotion that firms use to get their offerings into consumers' hands.

LO1-2 Detail the evolution of marketing over time.

Marketing has evolved from a production- or sales-oriented approach, in which firms told people what they could and should buy, to a market- and value-oriented perspective. In this more recent view, firms look to their markets to tell them what they need to produce and provide, in a way that creates value for them and their customers.

LO1-3 Describe how marketers create value for a product or service.

Value stems from at least four main activities that value-driven marketers undertake and are reinforced throughout the book:

- Adding value, such that they leverage various elements of marketing and work to build relationships with partners and customers to ensure that they introduce their product, service, or idea to the marketplace at just the place and time that customers want it.
- Marketing analytics, which companies use to gather vast amounts of information about customers and competitors, then analyze it and share it across their own organization and with partner firms.
- Social and mobile marketing, to take advantage of new technologies and connect with customers using the latest social media channels.
- Ethical and societal dilemmas, such that firms engage in conscious marketing that takes into account the benefits and costs of their actions for all stakeholders.

Key Terms

- business-to-business (B2B) marketing, 10
- business-to-consumer (B2C) marketing, 10
- consumer-to-consumer (C2C) marketing, 10
- customer relationship management (CRM), 15

- exchange, 6
- four Ps, 6
- goods, 7
- ideas, 8
- marketing, 4
- marketing channel management, 9
- marketing mix, 6
- marketing plan, 4

- relational orientation, 14
- service, 7
- supply chain management, 9
- value, 14
- value cocreation, 14

Marketing Digitally

1. Visit the websites for KIND (www.kindsnacks.com), Kashi (www.kashi.com), and Snickers and Mars (www.snickersandmarsproteinbars.com) bars. What value do these manufacturers provide customers? How are their value propositions different?

2. Go to Facebook.com and navigate to the "About" section. What is Facebook's mission? How could marketers use Facebook, and what other social media tools could they use? What are the drawbacks marketers might face when using Facebook to communicate with their customers?

3. Visit Mondelēz International's website (www.mondelez-international.com) and then click on the "Brand Family" link. In what major categories does Mondelēz have brands? Can you identify related categories in which the company should compete?

Marketing Applications

1. Do you know the difference between needs and wants? When companies that sell coffee develop their marketing strategy, do they concentrate on satisfying their customers' needs or wants? What about a utility company, such as the local power company or a humanitarian agency, such as Doctors without Borders?

2. People can apply marketing principles to finding a job. If the person looking for a job is the product, describe the other three Ps.

3. What is the difference between a good and a service? When you buy a music subscription on Pandora, are you buying a good or a service? Would your answer be different if you bought an MP3 album on Amazon?

4. One of your friends was recently watching TV and saw an advertisement that she liked. She said, "Wow, that was great marketing!" Was the ad, in fact, marketing?

5. Using the four Ps, discuss how Kashi creates value for customers with its Kashi bars.

6. Explain how a $45 Timex watch and a $10,000 Rolex watch deliver value to respective target markets? Which factors account for the dramatic difference in watch prices?

7. Assume you have been hired into the marketing department of a major consumer products manufacturer such as Nike. You are having lunch with some new colleagues in other departments—finance, manufacturing, and logistics. They are arguing that the company could save millions of dollars if it just got rid of the marketing department. Develop an argument that would persuade them otherwise.

8. Why do marketers like those at Apple find it important to embrace societal needs and ethical business practices? Provide an example of a societal need or ethical business practice that Apple is addressing.

Quiz Yourself

1. Which of the following is *not* a function of marketing's value creation process?
   a. Capturing value
   b. Delivering value
   c. Communicating value
   d. Exchanging value
   e. All of these are part of marketing's value creation process.

2. Value creation is the central activity of marketing. Which is not a benefit to the firm from engaging in value creation and the ongoing process of identifying value-adding options for consumers?
   a. The firm is able to satisfy consumer needs.
   b. The firm is able to expand.
   c. The firm is able to build brand loyalty.
   d. The firm is able to sell fewer products.
   e. All of these are benefits to the firm.

(Answers to these two questions can be found in the Quiz Yourself Answer Key section at the end of the chapter.)

KIND BARS FOR A KINDER WORLD

Among the many energy and snack bars we have discussed, KIND (www.kindsnacks.com) stands out for its largely successful efforts to apply nearly every aspect of good marketing presented in this chapter. Its products offer substantial value by satisfying modern consumers' needs and wants through an exchange. Its promotions are unique and compelling, and it has established its place on store shelves and through mobile channels. Furthermore, the company embraces a conscious marketing perspective, while also using its customer data to develop new innovations and promotions.

Consider, to start, how KIND provides product solutions to satisfy customers. As a central corporate ethic, it asserts that people should not be forced to eat any ingredient that they cannot pronounce. It excludes artificial sweeteners and preservatives, so for modern consumers who embrace a healthy lifestyle, it markets a product that they can trust to contain only "natural" ingredients.[36]

As it has learned more about what consumers want, it also has expanded its product offerings. Beyond its initial snack bars, KIND now markets fruit snacks and protein bars. For these selections, its marketing remains consistent, promising more natural alternatives to conventional versions of these items.[37] The fruit snacks, which are vastly popular among children, contain no added sugars, preservatives, or genetically engineered ingredients, for example.

To introduce such products to the market, KIND embraces diverse and clever promotional tools as well. To tout its fruit snacks, it installed a three-story-high mountain made up of 45,485 pounds of sugar in Times Square, along with statues of children made out of sugar. The mountain represented the added sugar that U.S. children consume every five minutes; each statue consisted of 64 pounds of sugar, or the average amount that an eight-year-old child consumes each year.[38]

To get people to try its new protein bar, KIND took a different tack because its target audience was different. Its extensive analysis of market data showed KIND that when people considered buying a protein bar or thought about switching brands, they often searched for phrases like "best tasting protein bar" or "protein bars that aren't gross."[39] So it developed a product based primarily on nuts, which it argues will always and inherently taste better than synthetic or processed food blends. Then it undertook a promotion designed primarily to get people to try its new product: It offered the first 10,000 visitors to its website who requested one a free KIND protein bar—as well as a bar from a competing company of their choice.[40] Thus the consumers received both a KIND Bar and, for example, a Clif Bar, and the company encouraged them to evaluate both options and post their reviews.

But the online channel represents just one of the places that KIND has leveraged to market its protein bars. Soon after its online promotion, it hosted taste test events in various big

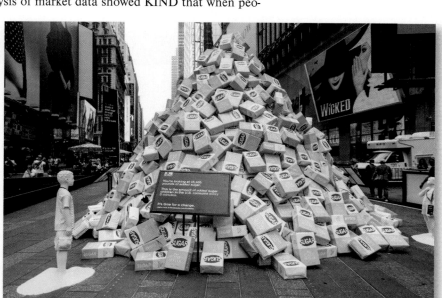

To tout its healthy fruit snacks, Kind installed a three-story-high mountain made up of 45,485 pounds of sugar in Times Square, along with statues of children made out of sugar. The mountain represented the added sugar that U.S. children consume every five minutes; each statue consisted of 64 pounds of sugar, or the average amount that an eight-year-old child consumes each year.

©Brazil Photo Press/Getty Images

cities across the United States, in which it similarly handed out samples of both its own and its competitors' offerings. It described the promotion not as a way to sell more products, but rather as a route to help consumers learn about a better-tasting bar.

Such espoused interest in consumers' best outcomes is prominent throughout KIND's marketing, which consciously embraces the company's goal and responsibility to "make the world a little kinder."[41] It defines kindness (and thus its brand) as more active than simply being nice. To manifest this initiative, it supports various causes. The KIND Foundation granted awards worth approximately $1.1 million to seven people who acted in ways to improve their communities. The company's CEO wrote a book, *Do the KIND Thing*, and all proceeds from the sales of that text are donated to kindness initiatives.[42] The company also prints and issues #kindawesome cards, which it delegates its employees to hand out to random people they find engaging in kind action. The recipients receive special codes on the cards that allow them discounts on KIND products.

These are not the only tactics it uses, though. First-time visitors to its website encounter a button they can click, inviting them to receive a discount on their first offer. In exchange for the price cut, they simply need to fill in their e-mail address—which of course means that KIND has gathered that information and can use it to track its sales and consumer preferences better, so that it can develop additional new products to meet those consumers' needs and wants.

And thus it comes full circle. By exemplifying nearly all the elements of marketing that this chapter describes, KIND is achieving success in a market that continues to grow, in competition with other brands that seek to establish their own positions in the marketplace.

Questions

1. Describe the target market for KIND bars? In your discussion explain:
    - What types of people does KIND sell to?
    - How does KIND appeal to those different groups of people?
2. Outline KIND's four Ps.
3. Does KIND act in a socially responsible manner? Explain your answer.

Endnotes

1. Lisa Drayer, "Are Energy Bars Healthy?," CNN, August 25, 2017.
2. "Nutritional Bars Market Insights 2017–2023," *Industry Today*, February 9, 2018.
3. Patricia Bannan, "The Top 12 Energy Bars for Every Occasion (Post-Workout, Gluten-Free and More)," Livestrong.com, February 23, 2018.
4. Abby Reisner, "These Aren't Your Typical Energy Bars," Tasting Table, February 20, 2018.
5. "Do the Kind Thing for Your Body, Your Taste Buds, and the World," KIND, www.kindsnacks.com/about-us.
6. Heather Clancy, "Kashi Steps Up Purchases from Farms Transitioning to Organic," GreenBiz, February 27, 2017; "One Box at a Time: Kashi Expands Product Portfolio to Support Organic Farmland," *Cision PR Newsletter*, February 22, 2017.
7. Eric Schroeder, "Bars: Boom or Bust?," *Food Business News*, November 27, 2017.
8. "Nutritional Bars Market Insights 2017–2023," *Industry Today*, February 9, 2018.
9. Ibid.
10. Source: The American Marketing Association, www.marketingpower.com.

11. Reisner, "These Aren't Your Typical Energy Bars."
12. The idea of the four Ps was conceptualized by E. Jerome McCarthy, *Basic Marketing: A Managerial Approach* (Homewood, IL: Richard D. Irwin, 1960).
13. Jaya Saxena, "Energy Bars Tell the Story of a Nation Obsessed with Food," *Man Repeller*, January 10, 2018.
14. Drayer, "Are Energy Bars Healthy?"
15. Saxena, "Energy Bars Tell the Story of a Nation Obsessed with Food."
16. Bannan, "The Top 12 Energy Bars for Every Occasion."
17. Martha C. White, "Airlines Use Wireless Networks to Replace Seat-Back Catalogs," *The New York Times*, February 1, 2015.
18. Dhruv Grewal, Anne L. Roggeveen, and Lauren S. Beitelspacher, "How Retailing Cues Influence Shopping Perceptions and Behaviors," in *The Routledge Companion to Consumer Behavior*, ed. Michael Solomon and Tina Lowrey (New York: Informa UK Limited, 2017), pp. 291–303.
19. Stuart Elliot, "A New Coronation for the King of Elephants," *The New York Times*, November 13, 2012.
20. Dennis Green, "Nike Is Finally Going to Start Selling on Amazon for One Simple Reason," *Business Insider*, June 29, 2017.

21. Simon Dumenco, "Ad Age Imagines a World without Ads—and It's Not Cheap," *Advertising Age,* September 28, 2015.

22. Peter C. Verhoef et al., "A Cross-National Investigation into the Marketing Department's Influence within the Firm: Toward Initial Empirical Generalizations," *Journal of International Marketing* 19 (September 2011), pp. 59–86.

23. George S. Day, "Aligning the Organization with the Market," *Marketing Science Institute* 5, no. 3 (2005), pp. 3–20.

24. Abhijit Guha et al., "Framing the Price Discount Using the Sale Price as the Referent: Does It Make the Price Discount More Attractive?," *Journal of Marketing Research* (2018).

25. Anne L. Roggeveen, Michael Tsiros, and Dhruv Grewal, "Understanding the Co-Creation Effect: When Does Collaborating with Customers Provide a Lift to Service Recovery?," *Journal of the Academy of Marketing Science* 40, no. 6 (2012), pp. 771–90.

26. Robert Palmatier et al., "Relationship Velocity: Towards a Theory of Relationship Dynamics," *Journal of Marketing* 77 no. 1 (2013), pp. 13–20; Anita Luo and V. Kumar, "Recovering Hidden Buyer–Seller Relationship States to Measure the Return on Marketing Investment in Business-to-Business Markets," *Journal of Marketing Research* 50, no. 1 (2013), pp. 143–60.

27. Harsh Ajmera, "Social Media Facts, Figures, and Statistics 2013," *Digital Insights,* http://blog.digitalinsights.in.

28. Kadie Regan, "10 Amazing Social Media Growth Stats from 2015," *Social Media Today,* August 10, 2015, www.socialmediatoday.com/social-networks/kadie-regan/2015-08-10/10-amazing-social-media-growth-stats-2015.

29. U.S. Census Bureau, "U.S. and World Population Clock," April 7, 2016, www.census.gov/popclock/.

30. "Internet Usage Statistics," November 30, 2015, Internet World Stats, www.internetworldstats.com/stats.htm.

31. "Internet Travel Hotel Booking Statistics," March 3, 2015, Statistic Brain Research Institute, www.statisticbrain.com/internet-travel-hotel-booking-statistics/.

32. Alex Heath, "8 Apps Every Food Lover Needs," June 29, 2015, www.businessinsider.com/the-best-food-apps-2015-6; www.foodspotting.com/about; www.happycow.net/.

33. www.bdubsgamebreak.com/Home/About.

34. Philip Kotler, "Reinventing Marketing to Manage the Environmental Imperative," *Journal of Marketing* 75 (July 2011), pp. 132–35; Katherine White, Rhiannon MacDonnell, and John H. Ellard, "Belief in a Just World: Consumer Intentions and Behaviors toward Ethical Products," *Journal of Marketing* 76 (January 2012), pp. 103–18.

35. American Marketing Association.

36. "Do the Kind Thing for Your Body, Your Taste Buds, & the World."

37. Tanya Dua, "Kind Snacks Is Venturing Outside of Nutrition Bars for the First Time Ever—and It Should Terrify Welch's," *Business Insider,* August 22, 2017.

38. Ibid.

39. Patty Odell, "KIND Challenges Competitors with Taste Tests," *Chief Marketer,* January 17, 2018.

40. Tanya Dua, "Kind Is Sending Out Its Competitors' Products to 10,000 Consumers in an Edgy Marketing Stunt," *Business Insider,* January 17, 2018.

41. "Make the World a Little Kinder," KIND, www.kindsnacks.com/our-mission.

42. Ibid.

i. Jack Neff, "Unilever Gives Birth to Baby Dove as Johnson's Tries to Bounce Back," *Advertising Age,* April 5, 2017; Sheila Shayon, "Unilever's Baby Dove Woos Imperfect Moms and Mums," Brandchannel, April 5, 2017; Ellen Thomas, "Baby Dove to Launch in U.S.," *Women's Wear Daily,* April 5, 2017; "Welcome to the World of Baby Dove," www.dove.com.

ii. Khadeeja Safdar, "Young Consumers Tap Online Market for Recycled Apparel," *The Wall Street Journal,* February 16, 2016.

iii. Dan Hyman, "Giving a Family Business a Jolt with a Coffee That Empowers Women," *The New York Times,* December 20, 2017. See also City Girl Coffee, www.citygirlcoffee.com.

iv. Hayley Peterson, "Amazon Is Raising Prices at Whole Foods after Its Highly-Publicized Cuts," *Business Insider,* December 5, 2017; Stephanie Strom, "Whole Foods to Rate Its Produce and Flowers for Environmental Impact," *The New York Times,* October 15, 2014; Stuart Elliot, "Whole Foods Asks Shoppers to Consider a Value Proposition," *The New York Times,* October 19, 2014, www.nytimes.com.

v. Laura Stevens, "Amazon's Cashierless 'Go' Convenience Store Set to Open," *The Wall Street Journal,* January 21, 2018; George Anderson, "Starbucks and Amazon Go Cashless in Seattle," *RetailWire,* January 25, 2018.

vi. Barbara Thau, "How Big Data Helps Chains Like Starbucks Pick Store Locations—An (Unsung) Key to Retail Success," *Forbes,* April 24, 2014, www.forbes.com; Mikal Khoso, "Data Analytics in the Real World: Starbucks," *Northeastern University Level,* March 4, 2016, www.northeastern.edu/levelblog/2016/03/04/data-analytics-in-the-real-world-starbucks/; Malcolm Wheatley, "Data-Driven Location Choices Drive Latest Starbucks Surge," *Data Informed,* January 10, 2013, http://data-informed.com/data-driven-location-choices-drive-latest-starbucks-surge/.

vii. Miriam Gottfried, "Publishers Face Moving Target in Mobile," *The Wall Street Journal,* July 7, 2015; eMarketer, September 2014.

viii. Tom Ryan, "Does It Pay for Grocers to Give Free Fruit to Kids?," *RetailWire,* February 4, 2016.

Quiz Yourself Answer Key

1. Which of the following is *not* a function of marketing's value creation process?

   Answer: (e) All of these are part of marketing's value creation process.

2. Value creation is the central activity of marketing. Which is not a benefit to the firm from engaging in value creation and the ongoing process of identifying value-adding options for consumers?

   Answer: (d) The firm is able to sell fewer products.

LEARNING OBJECTIVES

After reading this chapter, you should be able to:

LO2-1 Define a marketing strategy.

LO2-2 Describe the elements of a marketing plan.

LO2-3 Analyze a marketing situation using SWOT analyses.

LO2-4 Describe how a firm chooses which consumer group(s) to pursue with its marketing efforts.

LO2-5 Outline the implementation of the marketing mix as a means to increase customer value.

LO2-6 Summarize portfolio analysis and its use to evaluate marketing performance.

LO2-7 Describe how firms grow their business.

CHAPTER 2

DEVELOPING MARKETING STRATEGIES AND A MARKETING PLAN

The corporate name of the company that produces and sells popular food and beverage brands such as Gatorade, Frito-Lay, Tropicana, Quaker, and Mountain Dew—PepsiCo—signals which of the products in its portfolio have been the most important historically. The company began by selling carbonated beverages, but today it earns most of its revenues and enjoys most of its growth in snack, not drink, categories.

This development reflects PepsiCo's careful analysis of the market and efforts to ensure that it continues to attract a wide range of consumers by offering many types of products. Noting consumer trends, such as increasing interest in healthy options, demands for more variety in flavors, and growing globalization in consumption, the U.S.-based company has sought to leverage its expertise to get its products into the hands of consumers. It also continues to innovate and expand in its efforts to circumvent competition and hold on to its market share.

For example, finding opportunity in the growing groups of consumers who search for healthy options,

even when they are consuming usually guilt-inducing snacks, PepsiCo offers a "guilt-free" group of products, spanning baked potato chips, lower-sodium tortillas, and chips made of beans.[1] Going beyond product innovations, the company also pursues value through novel packaging, such as smaller packages that help consumers limit their calorie or sodium consumption.[2] In these efforts, it seeks to provide unique and appealing "platforms" for snackers who might be interested in virtually any type of tasty treat, from salty chips to hearty crackers to spicy Cheetos to chocolate-covered granola bars.

Such versatility and diversity represent key strengths of the broad corporate brand. It counts approximately 3,000 different flavor profiles among its intellectual property, which it refers to as its "flavor bank." These valuable resources enable PepsiCo to introduce unique, distinctive flavors for its Lay's potato chips, from Everything Bagel with Cream Cheese in the U.S. market to Salmon Teriyaki in Asian markets. To enhance the benefits of such resources, it also leverages these strengths in marketing efforts that get people talking, such as its highly popular annual "Do Us a Flavor" contest that encourages fans to pick their favorite flavors among the unusual options that PepsiCo comes up with that year.[3]

Of course, it is not the only company seeking to appeal to such consumers. Carbonated beverages remain an important part of the company's product portfolio, and in these segments, Coca-Cola and Dr Pepper Snapple are actively in pursuit of more market share. All three corporations have increased their juice and sports drink offerings, especially as sales of carbonated beverages continue their downward trend.

Such threats are an inherent aspect of the highly competitive food and beverage market, where companies also confront rising costs.[4] Overall, modern consumer goods and grocery retailing scenarios are challenging. As PepsiCo's chair and chief executive officer Indra Nooyi recently acknowledged, "Over my several decades in business I have never seen this combination of sustained headwinds across most economies, combined with high volatility across global financial markets."[5]

PepsiCo also has struggled with some formulations, such as the use of aspartame in Diet Pepsi. Studies suggesting its harmful effects led consumers to call for its removal from the recipe. But when PepsiCo did so, fans also complained about the taste of the reformulated version. In response, it now maintains several diet colas, in an attempt to appeal to multiple audiences.[6] Another weakness stems from its long-standing image as a company that produces less-than-healthy snack options. As it has tried to expand its organic offerings, it has met with some resistance. Although sales in this sector finally are starting to increase, it has had to adjust its growth projections downward when those sales did not expand fast enough to keep shareholders happy.[7]

All these factors are reinforced and intensified by PepsiCo's international presence in more than 200 countries. In these various national markets, it leverages its massive "flavor bank" to appeal to consumers who might prefer Yorkshire Pudding or Tikka Masala, rather than salt and vinegar, when they chow down on some potato chips. It also enjoys the power of recognizable brand names and the ability to deliver its products throughout the world. However, even as the company has noted productivity gains in many international markets, it also has admitted that unfavorable currency exchanges and wider macroeconomic factors have led to reduced profits in international markets.[8]

In the face of these challenges and promises, PepsiCo maintains a highly positive outlook. Its guiding philosophy, whether it is developing new products or expanding into new markets, looks for the bright side while attempting to mitigate any dark sides. As the company's principal scientist Elizabeth Roark explained, in reference to healthy snack innovations, "We're really looking to not only decrease the negatives but also increase the positives and transform our portfolio in a positive direction."[9]

 LO2-1 Define a marketing strategy.

WHAT IS A MARKETING STRATEGY?

A marketing strategy identifies (1) a firm's target market(s), (2) a related marketing mix (its four Ps), and (3) the bases on which the firm plans to build a sustainable competitive advantage. A sustainable competitive advantage is an advantage over the competition that is not easily copied and can be maintained over a long period of time. A competitive advantage acts like a wall that the firm has built around its position in a market. This wall makes it hard for outside competitors to contact customers inside—otherwise known as the marketer's target market. Of course, if the marketer has built a wall around an attractive market, competitors will attempt to break down the wall. Over time, advantages will erode because of these competitive forces, but by building high, thick walls, marketers can sustain their advantage, minimize competitive pressure, and boost profits for a longer time. Thus, establishing a sustainable competitive advantage is key to long-term financial performance.

For Pepsi, this wall involves the bricks of a strong brand and a loyal customer base, which were built on the foundation of its strong innovative capabilities. Customers around the world know Pepsi and consider it a primary "go-to" brand if they want a refreshing drink. This positioning reflects Pepsi's careful targeting and marketing mix implementation.

In terms of the four Ps (as we described them in Chapter 1), Pepsi already has achieved *product* excellence with its signature colas, Pepsi and Diet Pepsi. It also is constantly adding new products to its product line, like Caleb's Kola, which features African Kola nuts, cane sugar, and unique spices, along with a slight citrus flavor. The drink is named after Caleb Bradham, the pharmacist who first started selling "Brad's Drink" in 1893 in his North Carolina drugstore.[10] Furthermore, the Pepsi brand is owned by a parent company, PepsiCo, that also owns many of the top snack brands; other cola lines; and additional beverage products such as Lay's, Quaker, Mountain Dew, and Naked—among dozens of others.[11] To market its products, it relies on an extensive distribution network that *places* its familiar and appealing brands in stores in more than 200 countries.[12] Its pricing also is competitive and strategic. For example, customers can readily access a quick drink from a Pepsi soda fountain at a higher price by volume, or they can pay a little less per liter and buy larger, two-liter bottles to store and consume at home. Central to its promotion efforts are Pepsi's celebrity endorsements. Pepsi partners with some of the world's biggest musicians, including Katy Perry, Beyoncé, and Elton John,[13] and sponsors major sports events and leagues, such as the Super Bowl, as well as the NBA and WNBA, NHL, and NFL.[14] Also, to enable up-and-coming artists to more easily reach their fans, Pepsi sponsors its "Sound Drop" music platform that partners with MTV, Shazam, and iHeartMedia.[15]

EXHIBIT 2.1 Macro Strategies for Developing Customer Value

There are four macro, or overarching, strategies that focus on aspects of the marketing mix to create and deliver value and to develop sustainable competitive advantages, as we depict in Exhibit 2.1:[16]

- **Customer excellence:** Focuses on retaining loyal customers and excellent customer service.
- **Operational excellence:** Achieved through efficient operations and excellent supply chain and human resource management.
- **Product excellence:** Having products with high perceived value and effective branding and positioning.
- **Locational excellence:** Having a good physical location and Internet presence.

Customer Excellence

Customer excellence is achieved when a firm develops value-based strategies for retaining loyal customers and provides outstanding customer service.

Retaining Loyal Customers Sometimes the methods a firm uses to maintain a sustainable competitive advantage help attract and maintain loyal customers. For instance, having a strong brand, unique merchandise, and superior customer service all help solidify a loyal customer base. In addition, having loyal customers is, in and of itself, an important method of sustaining an advantage over competitors.

Loyalty is more than simply preferring to purchase from one firm instead of another.[17] It means that customers are reluctant to patronize competitive firms. Loyal customers drink Pepsi even if Coca-Cola goes on sale. More and more firms realize the value of achieving customer excellence by focusing their strategy on retaining loyal customers. PepsiCo doesn't think in terms of selling a single case of Mountain Dew for $15; instead, it focuses on satisfying customers who buy various bottles or cans to keep in their homes all the time, including Mountain Dew for the kids, Diet Pepsi for the adults, and Pepsi for guests. It also considers whether those consumers might want some salty snacks to go with their beverages and how it can help them combine those desires through the purchase of multiple PepsiCo products. Even if we just consider cola purchases, it is reasonable to imagine that a household of cola consumers might buy 50 cases of carbonated beverages every year for something like 20 years. In this case, the consumer is not a $15 customer who bought a single case; by combining all purchases for the family over the years, we determine that this household represents a $15,000 customer! Viewing customers with a lifetime value perspective rather than on a transaction-by-transaction basis is key to modern customer retention programs.[18] We will examine how the lifetime value of a customer is calculated in Chapter 10.

Another method of achieving customer loyalty creates an emotional attachment through loyalty programs. These loyalty programs, which constitute part of an overall customer relationship management (CRM) program, prevail in many industries, from airlines to hotels to movie theaters to retail stores. With such programs, firms can identify members through the loyalty card or membership information the consumer provides when he or she makes a purchase. Using that purchase information, analysts determine which types of merchandise certain groups of customers are buying and thereby tailor their offering to better meet the needs of their loyal customers. For instance, by analyzing their databases, banks develop profiles of customers who have defected in the past and use that information to identify customers who may defect in the future. Once it identifies these customers, the firm can implement special retention programs to keep them.

Providing Outstanding Customer Service Marketers also may build sustainable competitive advantage by offering excellent customer service,[19] though consistency in this area can prove difficult. Customer service is provided by employees, and, invariably, humans are less consistent than machines. Firms that offer good customer service must instill its importance in their employees over a long period of time so that it becomes part of the organizational culture.

Disney's My Magic system enables users to swipe their MagicBand wristbands to get on rides, make purchases, and open their hotel room door.

©parrysuwanitch/123RF

Disney offers excellent examples of both of these types of customer excellence. First, Disney's My Magic system enables visitors to swipe their MagicBand wristbands to get on rides, make purchases, and open their hotel room door. They can also use the mobile app to get dinner reservations or check in for rides throughout the park and its grounds. The system also enables Disney to collect a remarkable amount of information about what each guest is doing at virtually every moment of his or her visit to its theme parks.[20]

Second, its customer service is virtually unparalleled. Visitors to Disney parks are greeted by "assertively friendly" staff who have been extensively trained to find ways to communicate positively with customers and provide better service. The training includes information about how to recognize the signs that a visitor is lost, so the Disney employee can offer help locating a destination. It also highlights the need to communicate frequently and collaboratively about every aspect of the park, so a custodian at one end of the Magic Kingdom likely knows what time a restaurant on the other side opens.[21]

Although it may take considerable time and effort to build such a reputation for customer service, once a marketer has earned a good service reputation, it can sustain this advantage for a long time because a competitor is hard-pressed to develop a comparable reputation. Adding Value 2.1 details how Sally Beauty's loyalty program helps retain loyal customers.

Adding Value 2.1   Beautiful Loyalty: Sally Beauty's Updated Loyalty Program[i]

For the loyalty program at Sally Beauty, everything starts with an e-mail address. It may end with consistent customer engagement, sophisticated data analysis, and increased sales, but the first step in the process is ensuring that it can reach customers directly and effectively.

Therefore, when customers enter one of the retailer's 3,000 stores or visit its online sites, they receive an invitation to purchase a $5 membership into the program, with the promise that they will receive a $5 coupon via e-mail. Thus, the company learns customers' e-mail addresses immediately, enabling it to share information about itself that might engage these shoppers on a more emotional level.

Such tactics represent the retailer's attempt to counteract some downward sales trends and move beyond price promotions, to compel more engagement and loyalty from shoppers. In addition to restructuring the company to find some cost efficiencies, it hopes to rely more on loyalty, and less on one-time discounts, to keep shoppers coming back to its stores. Instead, it promises 15 percent discounts for the rest of the month, as long as the consumer spends at least $25 in that month.

Then, with the data it gathers, it takes a careful look at what the customer buys. As an example, the company's chief marketing officer (CMO) notes that if a customer purchases hair dye, that person is likely going to need color-safe conditioner, perhaps a touch-up tool, and then another box of dye in about six weeks. Therefore, Sally Beauty times special offers and incentives accordingly, sending e-mail messages and coupons at just the moment the customer is likely to be looking to purchase those items. It plans to add targeted advertising too, such that a banner advertisement that pops up when a loyal customer accesses the website would feature a model whose hair color matches the color that the customer bought most recently.

Beyond such immediate information, Sally Beauty works to leverage the data it gathers from its loyalty program to design new offerings that will appeal to the demographics and preferences exhibited by its loyal customers. In the CMO's own words, "We're at a place where everything is driven by the customer and driven by data."

Sally Beauty works hard at obtaining and keeping loyal customers by providing outstanding customer service.

Source: Sally Beauty Supply LLC

©Craig Barritt/Getty Images

Operational Excellence

Firms achieve operational excellence, the second way to achieve a sustainable competitive advantage, through efficient operations, excellent supply chain management, and strong relationships with suppliers.

All marketers strive for efficient operations to get their customers the merchandise they want, when they want it, in the required quantities, and at a delivered cost that is lower than that of their competitors. By so doing, they ensure good value to their customers, earn profitability for themselves, and satisfy their customers' needs.

Firms achieve efficiencies by developing sophisticated distribution and information systems as well as strong relationships with vendors. Like customer relationships, vendor relations must be developed over the long term and generally cannot be easily offset by a competitor.[22]

You are likely aware of, and perhaps have taken advantage of, Amazon's Prime shipping program that offers, for $99 a year, free two-day shipping on all orders. Perhaps you have paid for overnight delivery with Amazon, or if you live in 1 of the 11 cities in the United States that offer it, you may have paid for same-day shipping. With attractive shipping options like these, how are other online retailers able to compete? Operational excellence is required for Amazon to execute this program effectively. Not only does it need to have the technology to coordinate the personal buyers, but it needs to have an effective human resource hiring program that selects and trains employees capable of going the extra mile to please its customers.[23]

Product Excellence

Product excellence, the third way to achieve a sustainable competitive advantage, occurs by providing products with high perceived value and effective branding and positioning. Some firms have difficulty developing a competitive advantage through their merchandise and service offerings, especially if competitors can deliver similar products or services easily. However, others have been able to maintain their sustainable competitive advantage by investing in their brand itself; positioning their product or service using a clear, distinctive brand image; and constantly reinforcing that image through their merchandise, service, and

IBM is one of Bloomberg Businessweek's *top global brands.*

©drserg/Shutterstock

promotion. For example, with its new product introductions, such as Caleb's Kola,[24] the company clearly is seeking to reinforce and emphasize its historical legacy and image as a provider of excellent, refreshing, distinctive beverages. Top global brands—such as Apple, Google, Microsoft, Coca-Cola, Amazon, Samsung, Toyota, Facebook, Mercedes, and IBM—are all leaders in their respective industries, at least in part because they have strong brands and a clear position in the marketplace.[25]

Locational Excellence

Locational excellence is particularly important for retailers and service providers. Many say, "The three most important things in retailing are location, location, location." For example, most people will not walk or drive very far when looking to buy a cup of coffee. A competitive advantage based on location is sustainable because it is not easily duplicated. Starbucks has developed a strong competitive advantage with its location selection. The high density of stores it has established in some markets makes it very difficult for a competitor to enter that market and find good locations. After all, if Starbucks has a store on the corner of a busy intersection, no other competitor can take that location and will instead have to settle for a less worthy spot.

Multiple Sources of Advantage

In most cases, a single strategy, such as low prices or excellent service, is not sufficient to build a sustainable competitive advantage. Firms require multiple approaches to build a "wall" around their position that stands as high as possible.

Southwest Airlines consistently has positioned itself as a carrier that provides good service at a good value—customers get to their destinations on time for a reasonable price without having to pay extra for checked luggage. At the same time, its customers know not to have extraordinary expectations, unlike those they might develop when they purchase a ticket from Singapore Airlines. They don't expect food service or seat assignments. But they do expect—and even more important, get—on-time flights that are reasonably priced. By developing its unique capabilities in several areas, Southwest has built a very high wall around its position as the premier value player in the airline industry, which has resulted in a huge cadre of loyal customers.

PROGRESS CHECK

1. What are the various components of a marketing strategy?
2. List the four macro strategies that can help a firm develop a sustainable competitive advantage.

THE MARKETING PLAN

LO2-2 Describe the elements of a marketing plan.

Effective marketing doesn't just happen. Firms like Pepsi carefully plan their marketing strategies to react to changes in the environment, the competition, and their customers by creating a marketing plan. A marketing plan is a written document composed of an analysis of the current marketing situation, opportunities and threats for the firm, marketing objectives and strategy specified in terms of the four Ps, action programs, and projected or pro forma income (and other financial) statements.[26] The three major phases of the marketing plan are planning, implementation, and control.[27]

Although most people do not have a written plan that outlines what they are planning to accomplish in the next year, and how they expect to do it, firms do need such a document. It is important that everyone involved in implementing the plan knows what the overall objectives for the firm are and how they are going to be met. Other stakeholders, such as investors and potential investors, also want to know what the firm plans to do. A written marketing plan provides a reference point for evaluating whether or not the firm has met its objectives.

A marketing plan entails five steps, depicted in Exhibit 2.2. In Step 1 of the planning phase, marketing executives, in conjunction with other top managers, define the mission and/or vision of the business. For the second step, they evaluate the situation by assessing how various players, both in and outside the organization, affect the firm's potential for success. In the implementation phase, marketing managers identify and evaluate different opportunities by engaging in a process known as segmentation, targeting, and positioning (STP) (Step 3). They then are responsible for implementing the marketing mix using the four Ps (Step 4). Finally, the control phase entails evaluating the performance of the marketing strategy using marketing metrics and taking any necessary corrective actions (Step 5).

As indicated in Exhibit 2.2, it is not always necessary to go through the entire process for every evaluation (Step 5). For instance, a firm could evaluate its performance in Step 5, then go directly to Step 2 to conduct a situation analysis without redefining its overall mission.

EXHIBIT 2.2   The Marketing Plan

We first discuss each step involved in developing a marketing plan. Then we consider ways of analyzing a marketing situation, as well as identifying and evaluating marketing opportunities. We also examine some specific strategies marketers use to grow a business. Finally, we consider how the implementation of the marketing mix increases customer value.

Step 1: Define the Business Mission

PepsiCo's mission statement emphasizes the global nature of its products, whereas Coke's evokes emotions like happiness.

(Left): ©Bloomberg/Getty Images; (right): Source: The Coca-Cola Company

The mission statement, a broad description of a firm's objectives and the scope of activities it plans to undertake,[28] attempts to answer two main questions: What type of business are we? What do we need to do to accomplish our goals and objectives? These fundamental business questions must be answered at the highest corporate levels before marketing executives can get involved. Most firms want to maximize stockholders' wealth by increasing the value of the firms' stock and paying dividends.[29] Let's look at the two very different mission statements of PepsiCo and Coca-Cola:

- **PepsiCo's Mission Statement:** "To provide consumers around the world with delicious, affordable, convenient and complementary foods and beverages from wholesome breakfasts to healthy and fun daytime snacks and beverages to evening treats."[30]

- **Coke's Mission Statement:** "To refresh the world. . . . To inspire moments of optimism and happiness. . . . To create value and make a difference."[31]

For both of these firms, marketing is primarily responsible for enhancing the value of the company's offering for its customers and other constituents, whether in pursuit of a profit or not. Another key goal or objective often embedded in a mission statement relates to how the firm is building its sustainable competitive advantage.

However, owners of small, privately held firms frequently have other objectives, such as achieving a specific level of income and avoiding risks. Nonprofit organizations such as the "Pink Ribbon" campaign instead have nonmonetary objectives:

Pink Ribbon is a nonprofit organization that supports breast cancer patients, survivors, and their families.
©Steve Thorne/Getty Images

- **Pink Ribbon International's Mission Statement:** "Pink Ribbon is organized exclusively for charitable, educational and scientific purposes. We provide information, resources and support. We promote research into the causes, prevention, treatment and a possible cure."[32]

Step 2: Conduct a Situation Analysis

L02-3 Analyze a marketing situation using SWOT analyses.

After developing its mission, a firm would perform a situation analysis using a SWOT analysis that assesses both the internal environment with regard to its **S**trengths and **W**eaknesses and the external environment in terms of its **O**pportunities and **T**hreats. In addition, it should assess the opportunities and uncertainties of the marketplace due to changes in **C**ultural, **D**emographic, **S**ocial, **T**echnological, **E**conomic, and **P**olitical forces (CDSTEP). These factors are discussed in more detail in Chapter 5. With this information, firms can anticipate and interpret change, so they can allocate appropriate resources.

One of PepsiCo's strengths is its portfolio of celebrity endorsers such as Beyoncé (left) and David Beckham (right).
(Left): ©Wenn US/Alamy Stock Photo; (right): ©Clive Brunskill/Getty Images

EXHIBIT 2.3   Examples of Elements in a SWOT Analysis

		Environment		Evaluation	
		Positive		**Negative**	
Pepsi	**Internal**	**Strengths**		**Weakness**	
		Brand product portfolio		Relies heavily on Walmart	
		Strong celebrity endorsers		Relatively lower brand awareness	
		Many products are complementary to each other		Public scrutiny over practices	
		Dedication to charitable and social projects		Low profit margins	
		Large marketing budget			
	External	**Opportunity**		**Threats**	
		Health food segments		Water scarcity	
		Expansions due to acquisitions		Changes to labeling regulations	
		Ready-to-drink tea and coffee market growth		Increasing exchange rate of U.S. dollar	
		Bottled water		Health concerns may reduce product demands	
Coca-Cola	**Internal**	**Strengths**		**Weakness**	
		High market share		Low diversification	
		Strong brand		Few healthy beverages	
		Strong global presence			
		Excellent customer loyalty			
		Supply chain			
	External	**Opportunity**		**Threats**	
		Emerging countries		Water scarcity	
		Diversifying products		Potential market saturation	
		Bottled water		Changes to labeling regulations	
				Increasing competitors	

Sources: SWOT analysis of Pepsi, Strategic Management Insight, March 16, 2016, www.strategicmanagementinsight.com/swot-analyses/pepsico-swot-analysis.html; Hitesh Bhasin, "SWOT of Cola Cola," Marketing91, November 21, 2017, www.marketing91.com/swot-coca-cola/.

One of PepsiCo's Global Citizenship Initiatives is its S.M.A.R.T. program that identifies which Pepsi/Frito-Lay products are healthier. S.M.A.R.T. stands for five steps that encourage active living and better food choices: Start with a healthy breakfast; Move more; Add more fruits, vegetables, and whole grains; Remember to hydrate; and Try lower-calorie or lower-fat foods.

©Kayte Deioma/Zumapress/Newscom

Consider how PepsiCo might conduct a SWOT analysis, as outlined in Exhibit 2.3. We focus on PepsiCo here, but we also recognize that its marketing managers might find it helpful to perform parallel analyses for competitors, such as Coca-Cola.

A company's strengths (Exhibit 2.3, upper left) refer to the positive internal attributes of the firm. In this example, the strengths we might identify include PepsiCo's diversified product portfolio and celebrity endorsements. Pepsi has signed some of the world's most recognized musicians and athletes as spokespersons, from Beyoncé to Michael Jordan and David Beckham.[33] Building on this forte, it launched its own music program, Out of the Blue, that debuted during a Grammy Awards ceremony. The program aimed to connect fans with their favorite artists by giving away extravagant trips to major music festivals, concerts, and other fabulous experiences.[34] Another strength comes from its efforts to benefit society, such as the PepsiCo Foundation's Global Citizenship Initiatives, which encourage healthy lifestyles, clean water, and waste reduction, among other positive goals.[35]

Yet every firm has its weaknesses, and PepsiCo is no exception. Weaknesses (Exhibit 2.3, upper right) are negative attributes of the firm. Furthermore, PepsiCo has much lower global brand awareness and market share than does its main rival, Coca-Cola.[36] Also, PepsiCo's Aquafina water brand relies on a public water source. It has faced public criticism and negative press that jeopardizes its market position and has had to acknowledge that Aquafina is simply tap water in a bottle.[37]

Opportunities (Exhibit 2.3, lower left) pertain to positive aspects of the external environment. Among PepsiCo's opportunities is the rising demand for healthy food and drink options, as we indicated in the opening vignette. That is, the increasing interest in healthier options gives PepsiCo new opportunities to expand its product lines, introduce innovative new colas that appeal to people's preferences for premium options, and offer healthier options as well. For example, even with the public sourcing controversy, PepsiCo's bottled water brand, Aquafina, and its other health options have seen significant growth.[38] Another notable opportunity for PepsiCo is the growth in global markets for snacks and beverages. In particular, it has invested strongly in Brazil, India, and China, as well as in sub-Saharan Africa.[39] If these efforts are successful, PepsiCo can enjoy substantial growth while also reducing its nearly exclusive reliance on the U.S. market. There are multiple ways to take advantage of opportunities, though; Adding Value 2.2 describes how Coca-Cola is taking another approach to address the external environment and provide value to its customers.

Adding Value 2.2 — Small Coke Cans: Are Consumers Paying More for Less, or Are They Just Paying to Get What They Want?[ii]

When Coca-Cola checked its sales data recently, it found consistently over the past few quarters that sales of smaller containers, such as 7.5-ounce cans, were growing fast, while traditional packages kept suffering stagnant or even decreasing sales. The evidence has prompted the beverage company to revisit its approach, such that its goal is not just to sell Coke but rather to sell Cokes.

What's the difference? Consumer trends have led more people to request and purchase small containers of cola, so that they can limit their intake and achieve healthier lifestyles. In particular, parents wanted the smaller containers so that they could allow their children to have a treat without loading them up with more sugar and caffeine than would be good for the kids. Therefore, they sought to be able to buy a 12-pack of small cans or bottles rather than a 6-pack of the traditional 12-ounce packages. The volume of actual beverages being purchased might not change, or even might decline. But the number of packages being bought increases. As a result, approximately 14 percent of Coca-Cola's product mix now consists of the small servings—a move that also reflects the company's effort to live up to its pledge to reduce the number of calories people consume through carbonated beverages. As the president of Coca-Cola North America explained, "Having a 20 oz. bottle of Coca-Cola is pointless if half of it is never consumed."

In addition to revising its perspective on what customers actually want, Coke has reinvented its pricing approach. It enjoys a beneficial new price platform due to the switch. The cost to consumers for the small cans is approximately the same as that for the larger packages, meaning that shoppers pay approximately the same amount of money for substantially less product. But for the most part, shoppers appear willing to do so because the smaller packaging meets their needs and represents a clear response to their requests. The 17 percent sales growth in the small-size categories affirms this willingness.

Consumers are demanding smaller containers of cola to limit their intake and achieve healthier lifestyles. So, Coke provides the smaller cans on the right.
©Matt Rourke/AP Images

As a result of "more people, enjoying more Coke, more often, for a little more money," Coca-Cola also has increased its revenues, despite decreased volume sales. Customer research showed that consumers often equate finishing a drink with their sense of refreshment. Leaving customers wanting more, by giving them smaller containers, thereby helps encourage repurchase and consumption intentions while still making those consumers feel happier and more refreshed. The threat of cannibalization certainly remains pertinent, such that the sales growth in small packages might only come at the cost of lost sales of larger ones; yet the company appears confident that it is on the right path, ready to offer the "perfect pour" of carbonation.

Finally, threats (Exhibit 2.3, lower right) represent the negative aspects of the company's external environment. Water scarcity is a significant concern because the production of cola demands substantial amounts of water.[40] In addition, increased attention to labeling and nutrition facts could threaten to undermine PepsiCo's appeal.[41] Finally, competition in the snack-food market continues to increase, not just among the existing members of the market but also by new entrants that are coming up with innovative, alternative snacks to appeal to consumers' specific preferences.[42] These are just some of the threats that PepsiCo is facing.

LO2-4 *Describe how a firm chooses which consumer group(s) to pursue with its marketing efforts.*

Step 3: Identify and Evaluate Opportunities Using STP (Segmentation, Targeting, and Positioning)

After completing the situation analysis, the next step is to identify and evaluate opportunities for increasing sales and profits using segmentation, targeting, and positioning (STP). With STP, the firm first divides the marketplace into subgroups or segments, determines which of those segments it should pursue or target, and finally decides how it should position its products and services to best meet the needs of those chosen targets (more details on the STP process can be found in Chapter 9).

Segmentation Many types of customers appear in any market, and most firms cannot satisfy everyone's needs. For instance, among Internet users some do research online, some shop, some look for entertainment, and many do all three. Each of these groups might be a market segment consisting of consumers who respond similarly to a firm's marketing efforts. The process of dividing the market into groups of customers with different needs, wants, or characteristics—who therefore might appreciate products or services geared especially for them—is called market segmentation.

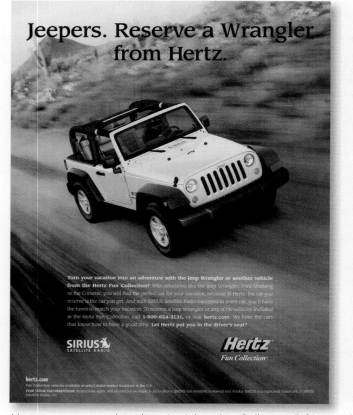

Hertz targets several markets. Its Adrenaline Collection (left) appeals to single people and couples wanting to have fun, while its Prestige Collection (right) appeals to its business customers and families who prefer a luxurious ride.

Source: The Hertz Corporation

EXHIBIT 2.4	Hertz Market Segmentation Illustration				
	Segment 1	**Segment 2**	**Segment 3**	**Segment 4**	**Segment 5**
Segments	Single thrill seekers and gear heads on vacation	Business customers and families who prefer a luxurious ride	Environmentally conscious customers	Families	Commercial customers
	Adrenaline Collection	Prestige Collection	Green Collection	SUV/Minivan/4x4	Commercial Van/Truck
Cars Offered	Corvette ZHZ	Infiniti QX56	Toyota Prius	Toyota RAV4	
	Chevrolet Camaro	Cadillac Escalade	Ford Fusion	Ford Explorer	Ford Cargo Van

Let's look at Hertz, the car rental company. The example in Exhibit 2.4 reveals some of the segments that Hertz targets. With the Adrenaline Collection, Hertz offers up the Chevrolet Camaro or Corvette to appeal to thrill seekers and gear heads on vacation. Its Prestige Collection features various Cadillac and Infiniti models, targeting business customers and families who prefer a luxurious ride. With its Green Collection of cars such as the Toyota Prius and Ford Fusion, and even some electric vehicle options in selected locations, Hertz appeals to environmentally conscious customers. It also offers commercial vans for service customers with its Commercial Van/Truck Collection.[43] Thus, Hertz uses a variety of demographics—gender, age, income, interests—to identify customers who might want the Prestige, Green, and Adrenaline Collections, but it also applies psychological or behavioral factors, such as a need to move possessions across town, to identify likely consumers of its commercial vans.

Targeting After a firm has identified the various market segments it might pursue, it evaluates each segment's attractiveness and decides which to pursue using a process known as target marketing or targeting. For example, Hertz realizes that its primary appeal for the SUV/Minivan/4x4 collection centers on young families, so the bulk of its marketing efforts for this business is directed toward that group.

Soft drink manufacturers also divide their massive markets into submarkets or segments. Coca-Cola, for instance, makes several different types of Coke, including regular, Coke II, and Cherry Coke. Among its diet colas, it targets Coke Zero Sugar to men and Diet Coke to women because men prefer not to be associated with diets. It also markets Sprite to those who don't like dark colas, Fruitopia and Minute Maid for more health-conscious consumers, and Dasani bottled water for purists.

Positioning Finally, when the firm decides which segments to pursue, it must determine how it wants to be positioned within those segments. Market positioning involves the process of defining the marketing mix variables so that target customers have a clear, distinctive, desirable understanding of what the product does or represents in comparison with competing products. Hertz positions itself as a quality car (and truck) rental company that is the first choice for each of its target segments. In its marketing communications, it stresses that customers will get peace of mind when they rent from Hertz, the market leader in the car rental business, and be able to enjoy their journey (e.g., leisure consumers) and reduce travel time (e.g., business consumers).[44]

To segment the coffee-drinker market, Starbucks uses a variety of methods, including geography (e.g., college campuses versus shopping/business districts) and benefits (e.g., drinkers of caffeinated versus decaffeinated products). After determining which of those segments represent effective targets, Starbucks positions itself as a firm that develops a variety of products that match the wants and needs of the different market segments—espresso drinks, coffees, teas, bottled drinks, pastries, and cooler foods.

After identifying its target segments, a firm must evaluate each of its strategic opportunities. A method of examining which segments to pursue is described in the Growth Strategies section later in the chapter. Firms typically are most successful when they focus on opportunities that build on their strengths relative to those of their competition. In Step 4 of the marketing plan, the firm implements its marketing mix and allocates resources to different products and services.

LO2-5

Outline the implementation of the marketing mix as a means to increase customer value.

Step 4: Implement Marketing Mix and Allocate Resources

When the firm has identified and evaluated different growth opportunities by performing an STP analysis, the real action begins. It has decided what to do, how to do it, and how many resources should be allocated to it. In the fourth step of the planning process, marketers implement the actual marketing mix—product, price, place, and promotion—for each product and service on the basis of what they believe their target markets will value. At the same time, marketers make important decisions about how they will allocate their scarce resources to their various products and services.

Product and Value Creation Products These products include services and constitute the first of the four Ps. Because the key to the success of any marketing program is the creation of value, firms attempt to develop products and services that customers perceive as valuable enough to buy. Dyson fans and fan heaters draw in and redirect surrounding air without potentially dangerous or fast-spinning blades or visible heating elements. Although more expensive than conventional fans and space heaters, these sculpturally beautiful appliances are perceived by consumers to be a valuable alternative to products that haven't significantly changed since the early 1900s.

Price and Value Capture Recall that the second element of the marketing mix is price. As part of the exchange process, a firm provides a product or a service, or some combination thereof, and in return, it gets money. Value-based marketing requires that firms charge a price that customers perceive as giving them a good value for the product they receive. Clearly, it is important for a firm to have a clear focus in terms of what products to sell, where to buy them, and what methods to use in selling them. But pricing is the only activity that actually brings in money and therefore influences revenues. If a price is set too high, it will not generate much volume. If a price is set too low, it may result in lower-than-optimal margins and profits. Therefore, price should be based on the value that the

Dyson creates value with its innovative products (left). It can therefore charge significantly more than the price charged for conventional fans (right).

(Left): Source: Dyson, Inc.; (right): ©Stockbyte/PunchStock/Getty Images

Dyson invoked two of the four Ps, price and place, by making a select number of fans available on Groupon at a heavily discounted price.

©digitallife/Alamy Stock Photo

customer perceives. Dyson fans can retail for $150 or more; conventional fans retail for around $25. Customers can decide what they want from their fan and choose the one at the price they prefer.

Place and Value Delivery For the third P, place, after it has created value through a product and/or service, the firm must be able to make the product or service readily accessible when and where the customer wants it. Dyson therefore features fans prominently on its website, but also makes sure to place them on Amazon and in Bed Bath & Beyond stores. In these locations, consumers previously found other Dyson products, and they likely would look for fans there too.

Promotion and Value Communication Integrated marketing communications (IMC) represents the fourth P, promotion. It encompasses a variety of communication disciplines—advertising, personal selling, sales promotion, public relations, direct marketing, and online marketing including social media—in combination to provide clarity, consistency, and maximum communicative impact.[45] Using the various disciplines of its IMC program, marketers communicate a *value proposition,* which is the unique value that a product or service provides to its customers and how it is better than and different from those of competitors.

To increase its exposure, Dyson offers promotions for its products not only on its website but also on promotion websites such as coupon.com and Groupon. That is, it makes a select number of products available on several promotion channels at a discounted price to encourage people to try the innovations.

Step 5: Evaluate Performance Using Marketing Metrics

The final step in the planning process includes evaluating the results of the strategy and implementation program using marketing metrics. A metric is a measuring system that quantifies a trend, dynamic, or characteristic. Metrics are used to explain why things happened and also project the future. They make it possible to compare results across regions, strategic business units (SBUs), product lines, and time periods. The firm can determine why it achieved or did not achieve its performance goals with the help of these metrics. Understanding the causes of the performance, regardless of whether that performance exceeded, met, or fell below established goals, enables firms to make appropriate adjustments. Procter & Gamble uses performance metrics to test its new geolocation method of reaching users of the popular social networking app Snapchat, as Social & Mobile Marketing 2.1 reveals.

Social & Mobile Marketing 2.1

Making Snapchat More Strategic: How CoverGirl Uses Geotargeting to Leverage the Marketing Potential of a Fun App[iii]

Companies know well that social media apps can be great for their marketing communications, enabling them to reach lots of customers in a fun and engaging way. But while some apps offer detailed data about how consumers behave, many others do not provide any such insights because their primary goal is helping users have fun.

Take Snapchat for example. It allows visitors to overlay photo filters, but it has no capacity to calculate or show advertisers who is using its branded overlays or what consumers do after adopting such a filter. All it can tell them is how many people used the focal filter, which is not nearly enough information to be used to make any marketing decisions.

Recognizing that Snapchat lacked a user-friendly dashboard or summary statistics that might provide it with straightforward insights and marketing data, Procter & Gamble (P&G) decided that it needed to do the analytical work on its own. It devised an innovative marketing strategy: It would release *Star Wars*–themed lines of cosmetics under its CoverGirl brand, available only in Ulta retail stores. At the same time, it would allow Snapchat users to apply a related filter to their photos, all coinciding with the release of *Star Wars: The Force Awakens*. The social media move was likely to enhance brand awareness by revealing to users that the *Star Wars*–linked products even existed. But P&G also wanted to increase sales. To measure these effects, it implemented a detailed, careful experiment.

First, it created geofilters that reflected the locations of the 868 Ulta stores in which the new eye and lip cosmetic product lines were available. If a consumer was located near one of these stores and also visited Snapchat to post a photo, she encountered the option to use a filter that featured logos for Ulta, CoverGirl, and *Star Wars,* as well as a frame that surrounded the picture with what looked like lightsaber rays. However, P&G did not make the filter available for every store that carried the makeup products. By strategically limiting the application of the campaign, it created what was essentially a control sample: stores whose consumers could not have seen the Snapchat-affiliated advertising campaign whose sales could be compared with those that had the campaign.

Second, it gathered data about how many Snapchat users saw a related ad on the social media site, how many times they swiped to look at the filter, and how many times they used that filter. Then it correlated these data with sales information available from Ulta stores that prompted the geolocated

Through the Snapchat platform, P&G's CoverGirl brand developed a Star Wars*–themed cosmetics line that is available only in Ulta stores. If a consumer was located near an Ulta store that had the cosmetics line, and also posted a photo on Snapchat, she could use a filter that featured logos for Ulta, CoverGirl, and* Star Wars, *as well as a frame that surrounded the picture with what looked like lightsaber rays.*
©Mim Friday/Alamy Stock Photo

campaign and those that did not. By combining these data, P&G could obtain a pretty clear idea of how many of the sales stemmed from the Snapchat campaign because they took place in a focal store, versus how many sales would have occurred without the advertising, according to the sales data for similar but nongeolocation-linked stores.

Third, P&G compared the results of this social media campaign, timed to link with a major movie release, against a similar campaign that it conducted in 2013, in relation to the arrival of a new *Hunger Games* film in theaters. In that previous effort, though, it relied on traditional television advertising and a brand-linked Tumblr blog instead of Snapchat. Although the company declined to release exact numbers, it determined that the new Snapchat strategy was more efficient, more effective, and less costly. Thus P&G might have invented the analytics that make it possible to calculate the returns on Snapchat campaigns, but the method holds great promise for any marketer willing to undertake similar efforts in social media channels.

Typically, managers begin by reviewing the implementation programs, and their analysis may indicate that the strategy (or even the mission statement) needs to be reconsidered. Problems can arise both when firms successfully implement poor strategies and when they poorly implement good strategies.

Who Is Accountable for Performance? At each level of an organization, the business unit and its manager should be held accountable only for the revenues, expenses, and profits that they can control. Thus, expenses that affect several levels of the organization (such as

Ethical & Societal Dilemma 2.1 | Volkswagen's "Dieselgate" Scandal[iv]

The automotive market really was rocked by scandal when the U.S. Environmental Protection Agency discovered that many of the cars that Volkswagen (VW) had sold in the United States contained faulty software, apparently installed purposefully. The purpose of the software was to detect the amount of emissions produced by the cars' diesel engines—information that is critical to regulators that enforce emissions standards, as well as to consumers who seek environmentally friendly transportation options. But when the cars underwent emissions tests, the software tweaked their performance, making it seem better than it was normally.

Instead, when driven under normal conditions, the diesel-engine cars were emitting approximately 40 times the legal limit imposed on nitrogen oxide pollutants. That is, the vehicles were polluting illegally, and then the integrated software was falsifying the data, so that no one could even identify the damage.

Consumers protest Volkswagen's falsification of its cars' emissions.
©John MacDougall/Getty Images

But the evidence came to light, forcing VW to admit that approximately 11 million cars worldwide, sold over the course of nearly a decade, had been outfitted with the emissions-cheating software. The cars in question came with multiple brand names in the VW portfolio, including not just the VW brand but also Skoda, SEAT, and Audi. Soon thereafter, the company came under scrutiny again when it admitted to finding an irregularity in tests measuring carbon dioxide emissions that could affect an additional 800,000 vehicles, though subsequent investigations led VW to reduce that estimate to only 36,000 cars being affected.

In handling the situation, VW has provided examples of both what to do and what not to do. The company quickly instituted several internal changes, mainly designed to increase the amount of oversight and thereby prevent such unacceptable practices in the future. In implementing both structural and management changes, VW also replaced a number of key executives. Top executives also firmly asserted that the scandal was the result of poor choices by a relatively small group of middle managers, not indicative of a wider corporate ethical lapse.

The scandal has had powerful and drastic effects on the performance of the world's biggest car manufacturer. Sales in the United States dropped by nearly one-quarter, compared with same-month sales for the previous year, immediately following the scandalous announcement. The drop—resulting both from consumers' perception that the brand is not trustworthy and from the loss of sales that followed from the company pulling the affected engines off the market—is a particular concern for VW today because the automotive industry as a whole is on track to post record sales. In addition, VW could owe an estimated $18.2 billion in fines related to the scandal, not to mention the further legal and reputational costs it is likely to accrue. Yet the company's chief executive remains remarkably confident, noting that "Although the current situation is serious, this company will not be broken by it." Only time will tell if he is right.

the labor and capital expenses associated with operating a corporate headquarters) shouldn't be arbitrarily assigned to lower levels. In the case of a store, for example, it may be appropriate to evaluate performance objectives based on sales, sales associate productivity, and energy costs. If the corporate office lowers prices to get rid of merchandise and therefore profits suffer, then it's not fair to assess a store manager's performance based on the resulting decline in store profit.

Performance evaluations are used to pinpoint problem areas. Reasons performance may be above or below planned levels must be examined. If a manager's performance is below planned levels, was it because the sales force didn't do an adequate job, because the economy took a downward turn, because competition successfully implemented a new strategy, or because the managers involved in setting the objectives aren't very good at making estimates? The manager should be held accountable only in the case of the inadequate sales force job or setting inappropriate forecasts. When the fault is difficult to assign, the company faces a serious challenge, as Ethical & Societal Dilemma 2.1 explains

Promotional discounts are one way General Mills is trying to save the cereal industry.

©Joe Raedle/Getty Images

in relation to Volkswagen's attempts to respond to the scandal surrounding falsified emissions data for diesel engines in its cars.

When it appears that actual performance is going to be below the plan because of circumstances beyond the manager's control, the firm can still take action to minimize the harm. Similar to the soft drink industry, the cereal industry has been beset by a number of setbacks due to trends in the wider consumer environment. People seek to cut carbohydrates out of their diets, but cereal is mostly carbs. Many consumers are recognizing their allergies to gluten, but many cereals include wheat as a main ingredient. In response, the largest cereal maker General Mills (GM) has called on its competitors to step up their marketing efforts to save the industry. Leading the way, it has increased its advertising budget and offers promotional discounts on some of its most popular cereal brands, including Cheerios.[46]

In remarkable cases such as this, marketing managers must ask themselves several relevant questions: How quickly were plans adjusted? How rapidly and appropriately were pricing and promotional policies modified? In short, did I react to salvage an adverse situation, or did my reactions worsen the situation?

Performance Objectives, Marketing Analytics, and Metrics

Many factors contribute to a firm's overall performance, which makes it hard to find a single metric to evaluate performance.[47] One approach is to compare a firm's performance over time or to competing firms, using common financial metrics such as sales and profits. Another method of assessing performance is to view the firm's products or services as a portfolio. Depending on the firm's relative performance, the profits from some products or services are used to fuel growth for others.

With its extensive data, Google claims that it can use a combination of metrics to predict the performance of a major motion picture up to a month prior to the date it opens in theaters. Using search volume for the movie title in combination with several other metrics, such as the season and whether the movie is a sequel, Google promises a 94 percent accurate prediction of box office performance. Other proprietary metrics include the volume of clicks on search ads. If, for example, one movie prompted 20,000 more paid clicks than another film, it will bring in approximately $7.5 million more in revenues during its opening weekend. Beyond the implications for opening weekend, Google asserts that weekday searches in the weeks leading up to the release offer better predictors of continued revenues. That is, if a film fan searches for a movie title on a Tuesday, she or he is more likely to hold off on seeing the movie rather than rushing out during opening weekend.[48] Google's extensive analytics abilities support its competitive tactics in other markets too, as Marketing Analytics 2.1 describes.

Financial Performance Metrics

Some commonly used metrics to assess performance include revenues, or sales, and profits. For instance, sales are a global measure of a firm's activity level. However, a manager could easily increase sales by lowering prices, but the profit realized on that merchandise (gross margin) would suffer as a result. An attempt to maximize one metric may therefore lower another. Thus, managers must understand how their actions affect multiple performance metrics. It's usually unwise to use only one metric because it rarely tells the whole story.

In addition to assessing the absolute level of sales and profits, a firm may wish to measure the relative level of sales and profits. For example, a relative metric of sales or profits is its increase or decrease over the prior year. In addition, a firm may compare its growth in sales or profits relative to other benchmark companies (e.g., Coke may compare itself to Pepsi).

The metrics used to evaluate a firm vary depending on (1) the level of the organization at which the decision is made and (2) the resources the manager controls. For example, although the top executives of a firm have control over all of the firm's resources and

Marketing Analytics **2.1**   The First Name in Predictive Analytics: Google[v]

In the world of analytics, Google has made a significant name for itself because, from the moment it was established, Google has put predictive analytics at the heart of the company. As the most widely used search engine, Google needs to be able to predict which websites and pages a person is seeking, based on just a few keywords. Google is so successful at this method that few users even bother going to the second page of the results list in a Google search. Google now offers Google Analytics for companies to help improve their online presence by providing insights into customers' web searching behavior. In addition, Google has started using its analytics for more than just its search engine. They were critical to the development of Android software, Apple's biggest competitor in the smartphone domain. Now with the help of its sophisticated analytics, Google is taking on Apple in another domain as well: cars.

In Google's 2015 Android boot camp, the company officially introduced its Android Auto dashboard interface, which will face off against Apple's CarPlay. Data analytics have played a big role in the development of these systems. Study after study has shown how dangerous it is to drive while using one's phone. Data even show that driving while using a smartphone is equatable to driving while under the influence of alcohol. These startling results have spurred top phone system manufacturers' interest in creating dashboard platforms. When Google debuted Android Auto, it was clear that extensive analytics went into the development of every feature.

For example, Google developed a driver distraction lab to learn what tasks people do frequently when driving. These data informed which functions would be included and how

Data analytics have played a big role in developing Google's Android Auto dashboard interface to help keep drivers safe while using electronic dashboard functions.

©David Paul Morris/Bloomberg via Getty Images

they would work in the Android Auto system. According to Google's studies, no action should take longer than two seconds, so every function of Android Auto must be "glanceable." In addition, the interface does not include any "back" or "recent" buttons. Not only are social media apps blocked, but texting is accessible only through voice commands. With these improvements in the connection between phones and cars, data analytics are helping make the world both more convenient and safer.

resulting expenses, a regional sales manager has control over only the sales and expenses generated by his or her salespeople.

Let's look at Pepsi's sales revenue and profits (after taxes) and compare them with those of Coca-Cola (Exhibit 2.5).

EXHIBIT 2.5 Performance Metrics: Coke vs. Pepsi

Dollars (in billions)

	Coke		Pepsi	
	Net sales	Net profit	Net sales	Net profit
2014	46	7.1	66.7	6.6
2015	44.3	7.3	63.1	5.5

■ 2014   ■ 2015

LO2-6 Summarize portfolio analysis and its use to evaluate marketing performance.

Portfolio Analysis In portfolio analysis, management evaluates the firm's various products and businesses—its "portfolio"—and allocates resources according to which products are expected to be the most profitable for the firm in the future. Portfolio analysis is typically performed at the **strategic business unit (SBU)** or **product line** level of the firm, though managers also can use it to analyze brands or even individual items. An SBU is a division of the firm itself that can be managed and operated somewhat independently from other divisions and may have a different mission or objectives. For example, Goodyear is one of the largest tire firms in the world, selling its products on six continents and with sales of approximately $18 billion. Its four SBUs are organized by geography: North American; Europe, Middle East, African; Latin American; and Asia-Pacific.[49]

A product line, in contrast, is a group of products that consumers may use together or perceive as similar in some way. One line of product for Goodyear could be car, van, sport-utility vehicle (SUV), and light truck tires; another line could be high-performance tires or aviation tires.

One of the most popular portfolio analysis methods, developed by the Boston Consulting Group (BCG), requires that firms classify all their products or services into a two-by-two matrix, as depicted in Exhibit 2.6.[50]

The circles represent brands, and their sizes are in direct proportion to the brands' annual sales. The horizontal axis represents the relative market share. In general, **market share** is the percentage of a market accounted for by a specific entity[51] and is used to establish the product's strength in a particular market. It is usually discussed in units, revenue, or sales. A special type of market share metric, **relative market share**, is used in this application because it provides managers with a product's relative strength compared with that of the largest firm in the industry.[52] The vertical axis is the **market growth rate**, or the annual rate of growth of the specific market in which the product competes. Market growth rate thus measures how attractive a particular market is. Each quadrant has been named on the basis of the amount of resources it generates for and requires from the firm.

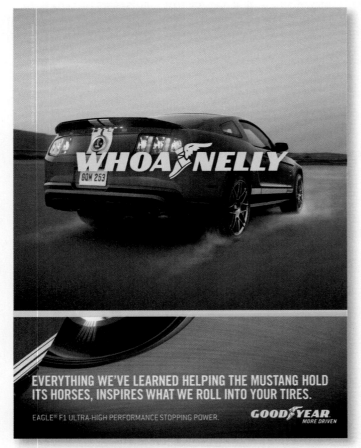

Goodyear, one of the largest tire firms in the world, organizes its strategic business units by geography. This ad for high-performance tires, one of Goodyear's many product lines, was designed for its North American SBU.

Source: The Goodyear Tire & Rubber Company

Stars Stars (upper left quadrant) occur in high-growth markets and are high market share products. That is, stars often require a heavy resource investment in such things as promotions and new production facilities to fuel their rapid growth. As their market growth slows, stars will migrate from heavy users of resources to heavy generators of resources and become cash cows.

Cash Cows Cash cows (lower left quadrant) are in low-growth markets but are high market share products. Because these products have already received heavy investments to develop their high market share, they have excess resources that can be spun off to those products that need it. For example, the firm may decide to use the excess resources generated by Brand C to fund products in the question mark quadrant.

Question Marks Question marks (upper right quadrant) appear in high-growth markets but have relatively low market shares; thus, they are often the most managerially intensive products in that they require significant resources to maintain and potentially increase their market share. Managers must decide whether to infuse question marks with resources generated by the cash cows, so that they can become stars, or withdraw resources and eventually phase out the products. Brand A, for instance, is currently a question mark, but by infusing it with resources, the firm hopes to turn it into a star.

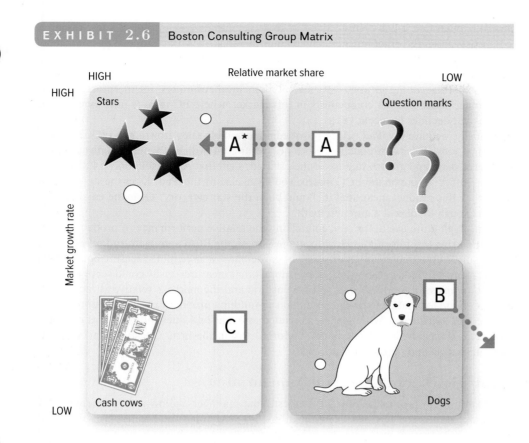

| EXHIBIT 2.6 | Boston Consulting Group Matrix |

Dogs Dogs (lower right quadrant) are in low-growth markets and have relatively low market shares. Although they may generate enough resources to sustain themselves, dogs are not destined for "stardom" and should be phased out unless they are needed to complement or boost the sales of another product or for competitive purposes. In the case depicted in Exhibit 2.6, the company has decided to stop making Brand B.

Now let's look at Apple and some of its products.[53] The four that we will focus our attention on are iPhone, iPod, iMac Desktop, and iPad.

Let's consider each of these products and place them into the BCG matrix based on the data. The iPhone has clearly been the star, with a steady growth rate of 35 percent each quarter.

The iPod tells a different story. With a staggering absolute market share consistently above 75 percent, its relative market share is 100 percent. More than 300 million iPods have been sold in a little over 10 years, so this product definitely has been important for Apple. Unfortunately, the MP3 market is contracting, and sales of iPods have slowed to their lowest level. Combine the lack of growth with a large relative market share and it is likely that the iPod is a cash cow for Apple.[54] Even if Apple continues to introduce a few new versions, it needs to recognize the threat that the iPod could transform into a dog, such that ultimately it might be wise to halt its production.[55]

Although popular with graphic designers, the growth rate of the iMac Desktop has

In which Boston Consulting Group quadrant do these products fit?
©Krisda/Shutterstock

slowed enough that it has even declined in some recent quarters. Although some disagreement exists about the exact rate of decline, it appears that sales have dropped by up to about 3 percent in recent years. It also has a small relative market share in the desktop market, such that the iMac tentatively could be classified as a dog. But Apple should not get rid of the iMac because doing so would risk alienating its loyal customers. Furthermore, Apple is performing better than its competitors in this market, where PC makers have experienced double-digit declines in recent years.[56]

Finally, we have the iPad, which provided an incredible sales growth rate of 333 percent in the first year after its introduction. Sales peaked in 2014, with 67.99 million units sold. But its market share and growth rate have since slowed, such that Apple sold only 54.85 million units in 2015.[57] Where on the BCG matrix would you classify the iPad? Does the still excellent market for this product mean that it should be in the star category? Or is the erosion of its growth enough to make it a question mark?

Although quite useful for conceptualizing the relative performance of products or services and using this information to allocate resources, the BCG approach, and others like it, is often difficult to implement in practice. In particular, it is difficult to measure both relative market share and industry growth. Furthermore, other measures easily could serve as substitutes to represent a product's competitive position and the market's relative attractiveness. Another issue for marketers is the potential self-fulfilling prophecy of placing a product or service into a quadrant. Whether it is classified as a star or a question mark has profound implications on how it is treated and supported within the firm. Question marks require more marketing and production support.

Strategic Planning Is Not Sequential

The planning process in Exhibit 2.2 suggests that managers follow a set sequence when they make strategic decisions. Namely, after they've defined the business mission, they perform the situation analysis, identify strategic opportunities, evaluate alternatives, set objectives, allocate resources, develop the implementation plan, and, finally, evaluate their performance and make adjustments. But actual planning processes can move back and forth among these steps. For example, a situation analysis may uncover a logical alternative that perhaps was not included in the mission statement, which would mean that the mission statement would need to be revised. The development of the implementation plan also might reveal that insufficient resources have been allocated to a particular product for it to achieve its objective. In that case, the firm would need to either change the objective or increase the resources; alternatively, the marketer might consider not investing in the product at all.

Now that we have gone through the steps of the marketing plan, let's look at some growth strategies that have been responsible for making many marketing firms successful.

PROGRESS CHECK

1. What are the five steps in creating a marketing plan?
2. What tool helps a marketer conduct a situation analysis?
3. What is STP?
4. What do the four quadrants of the portfolio analysis represent?

LO2-7 Describe how firms grow their business.

GROWTH STRATEGIES

Firms consider pursuing various market segments as part of their overall growth strategies, which may include the four major strategies in Exhibit 2.7.[58] The rows distinguish those opportunities a firm possesses in its current markets from those it has in new markets, whereas the columns distinguish between the firm's current marketing offering and that of a new opportunity. Let's consider each of them in detail.

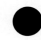

Market Penetration

A market penetration strategy employs the existing marketing mix and focuses the firm's efforts on existing customers. Such a growth strategy might be achieved by attracting new consumers to the firm's current target market or encouraging current customers to patronize the firm more often or buy more merchandise on each visit. A market penetration strategy generally requires greater marketing efforts, such as increased advertising and additional sales and promotions, or intensified distribution efforts in geographic areas in which the product or service already is sold.

To further penetrate its current customer base, the superhero entertainment giant, Marvel, has expanded its movie offerings. In collaboration with several production companies, as well as talented directors and well-known star actors, Marvel has helped bring the X-Men, Spiderman, Iron Man, and other popular characters to the big screen, where they confront some relevant, modern-day topics such as discrimination, environmental destruction, and international wars—before ultimately kicking tail and saving the city. These films have grossed massive profits.[59] Marvel has further increased its market penetration by expanding the distribution of its films. Today, Marvel movies can be seen in theaters, accessed on Xfinity, and viewed on DVDs available in discount stores, grocery stores, and a host of other stores, including book and comic stores.

Market Development

A market development strategy employs the existing marketing offering to reach new market segments, whether domestic or international. Marvel pursues such a market development strategy when it enhances the viewing of its movies in global markets. For example, the release of *Black Panther* proved to be one of the biggest movies of all time, grossing more than $1 billion worldwide, about half of which were international sales.[60] These phenomenal results highlight the importance of expanding into new market segments.

Product Development

The third growth strategy option, a product development strategy, offers a new product or service to a firm's current target market. For example, Marvel has launched several successful series on Netflix, including *Jessica Jones, The Defenders, Iron Fist,* and *Luke Cage.*[61] Unlike traditional network providers, Netflix (and its competitors, such as Hulu or Amazon) allows viewers to binge watch entire series in one sitting. Binge watching has become a phenomenally successful pastime for couch potatoes worldwide. Netflix has 69 million subscribers worldwide,

| EXHIBIT 2.7 | Markets/Products and Services Strategies |

PRODUCTS AND SERVICES

	Current	New
Current	Market penetration	Product development
New	Market development	Diversification

MARKETS

Marvel pursues a market development strategy by releasing Black Panther *globally.*

©Moviestore collection Ltd/Alamy Stock Photo

Pursuing a product development strategy, Marvel has launched several series on Netflix including The Defenders.

©Netflix/Photofest

including 43 million in the United States alone, making it an outstanding new service channel for Marvel character lovers. By developing series designed for this format, Marvel can connect with its customers in a new and important way.

Diversification

A diversification strategy, the last of the growth strategies from Exhibit 2.7, introduces a new product or service to a market segment that currently is not served. Diversification opportunities may be related or unrelated. In a related diversification opportunity, the current target market and/or marketing mix shares something in common with the new opportunity.[62] In other words, the firm might be able to purchase from existing vendors, use the same distribution and/or management information system, or advertise in the same newspapers to target markets that are similar to their current consumers. Marvel has pursued related diversification with its home décor, for example. Collectibles and T-shirts have long been a staple of the comic market, but Marvel also has diversified its offerings, expanding to include lamp shades and throw pillows.[63]

In contrast, in an unrelated diversification, the new business lacks any common elements with the present business. Unrelated diversifications do not capitalize on either core strengths associated with markets or with products. Thus, they would be viewed as very risky. For instance, if Marvel ventured into the child day care service industry, it would be an unrelated diversification because it is so different from its core business and therefore very risky.

PROGRESS CHECK

1. What are the four growth strategies?
2. What type of strategy is growing the business from existing customers?
3. Which strategy is the riskiest?

Reviewing Learning Objectives

LO2-1 Define a marketing strategy.

A marketing strategy identifies (1) a firm's target market(s), (2) a related marketing mix (four Ps), and (3) the bases on which the firm plans to build a sustainable competitive advantage. Firms use four macro strategies to build their sustainable competitive advantage: *Customer excellence* focuses on retaining loyal customers and excellent customer service. *Operational excellence* is achieved through efficient operations and excellent supply chain and

human resource management. *Product excellence* entails having products with high perceived value and effective branding and positioning. Finally, *locational excellence* entails having a good physical location and Internet presence.

LO2-2 Describe the elements of a marketing plan.

A marketing plan is composed of an analysis of the current marketing situation, its objectives, the strategy for the four Ps, and appropriate financial statements. A marketing plan represents the output of a three-phase process: planning, implementation, and control. The planning phase requires that managers define the firm's mission and vision and assess the firm's current situation. It helps answer the questions "What business are we in now, and what do we intend to be in the future?" In the second phase, implementation, the firm specifies, in more operational terms, how it plans to implement its mission and vision. Specifically, to which customer groups does it wish to direct its marketing efforts, and how does it use its marketing mix to provide good value? Finally, in the control phase, the firm must evaluate its performance using appropriate metrics to determine what worked, what didn't, and how performance can be improved in the future.

LO2-3 Analyze a marketing situation using SWOT analyses.

SWOT stands for strengths, weaknesses, opportunities, and threats. A SWOT analysis occurs during the second step in the strategic planning process, the situation analysis. By analyzing what the firm is good at (its strengths), where it could improve (its weaknesses), where in the marketplace it might excel (its opportunities), and what is happening in the marketplace that could harm the firm (its threats), managers can assess their firm's situation accurately and plan its strategy accordingly.

LO2-4 Describe how a firm chooses which consumer group(s) to pursue with its marketing efforts.

Once a firm identifies different marketing opportunities, it must determine which are the best to pursue. To accomplish this task, marketers go through a segmentation, targeting, and positioning (STP) process. Firms segment various markets by dividing the total market into those groups of customers with different needs, wants, or characteristics who therefore might appreciate products or services geared especially toward them. After identifying the different segments, the firm goes after, or targets, certain groups on the basis of the firm's perceived ability to satisfy the needs of those groups better than competitors, and do so profitably. To complete the STP process, firms position their products or services according to the marketing mix variables so that target customers have a clear, distinctive, and desirable understanding of what the product or service does or represents relative to competing products or services.

LO2-5 Outline the implementation of the marketing mix as a means to increase customer value.

The marketing mix consists of the four Ps—product, price, place, and promotion—and each P contributes to customer value. To provide value, the firm must offer a mix of products and services at prices its target markets will view as indicating good value. Thus, firms make trade-offs between the first two Ps, product and price, to give customers the best value. The third P, place, adds value by getting the appropriate products and services to customers when they want them and in the quantities they need. The last P, promotion, informs customers and helps them form a positive image about the firm and its products and services.

LO2-6 Summarize portfolio analysis and its use to evaluate marketing performance.

Portfolio analysis is a management tool used to evaluate the firm's various products and businesses—its "portfolio"—and allocate resources according to which products are expected to be the most profitable for the firm in the future. A popular portfolio analysis tool developed by the Boston Consulting Group classifies all products into four categories. The first, stars, are in high-growth markets and have high market shares. The second, cash cows, are in low-growth markets but have high market share. These products generate excess resources that can be spun off to products that need them. The third category, question marks, are in high-growth markets but have relatively low market shares. These products often utilize the excess resources generated by the cash cows. The final category, dogs, are in low-growth markets and have relatively low market shares. These products are often phased out.

LO2-7 Describe how firms grow their business.

Firms use four basic growth strategies: market penetration, market development, product development, and diversification. A market penetration strategy directs the firm's efforts toward existing customers and uses the present marketing mix. In other words, it attempts to get current customers to buy more. In a market development strategy, the firm uses its current marketing mix to appeal to new market segments, as might occur in international expansion. A product development growth strategy involves offering a new product or service to the firm's current target market. Finally, a diversification strategy takes place when a firm introduces a new product or service to a new customer segment. Sometimes a diversification strategy relates to the firm's current business, such as when a women's clothing manufacturer starts making and selling men's clothes, but a riskier strategy is when a firm diversifies into a completely unrelated business.

Key Terms

- control phase, 33
- customer excellence, 29
- diversification strategy, 50
- implementation phase, 33
- integrated marketing communications (IMC), 41
- locational excellence, 32
- market development strategy, 49
- market growth rate, 46
- market penetration strategy, 49
- market positioning, 39
- market segment, 38

- market segmentation, 38
- market share, 46
- marketing plan, 33
- marketing strategy, 28
- metric, 41
- mission statement, 34
- operational excellence, 32
- planning phase, 33
- product development strategy, 49
- product excellence, 32
- product line, 46

- related diversification, 50
- relative market share, 46
- segmentation, targeting, and positioning (STP), 38
- situation analysis, 35
- strategic business unit (SBU), 46
- sustainable competitive advantage, 28
- SWOT analysis, 35
- target marketing/targeting, 39
- unrelated diversification, 50

Marketing Digitally

1. The mission statement for The Estée Lauder Companies is "'Bringing the best to everyone we touch'. By 'The best', we mean the best products, the best people and the best ideas. These three pillars have been the hallmarks of our Company since it was founded by Mrs. Estée Lauder in 1946. They remain the foundation upon which we continue to build our success today." Harley-Davidson, Inc.'s mission statement is more straightforward: "We fulfill dreams through the experience of motorcycling, by providing to motorcyclists and to the general public an expanding line of motorcycles and branded products and services in selected market segments." (Both statements taken from www.missionstatements.com/fortune_500_mission_statements.html) These different perspectives also reflect the quite different positioning adopted by each company. Visit the websites of each manufacturer and review the descriptions of the company, its mission,

and its values. Do you believe these two disparate mission statements reflect what the firms do and how they are portrayed in the media? Justify your answer.

2. Price comparison sites such as trivago.com and pricegrabber.com have been created for a variety of products and services. These sites allow consumers to see the prices from a variety of vendors and let them choose the lowest-priced option without visiting different websites. What are the benefits of these sites to the firm? What are the benefits to consumers?

3. Black and Decker (www.blackanddecker.com) and DeWalt (www.dewalt.com) are owned by the same parent company, and both sell similar products. Visit each of their websites and identify what markets each brand targets. Next, discuss how the two companies use the marketing mix differently to target these unique target markets.

Marketing Applications

1. How have PepsiCo and Coca-Cola created sustainable competitive advantages for themselves?

2. Using your school library or Google, locate a SWOT analysis for a brand you currently use. For each section, list an additional item that was not part of the initial analysis and discuss why you included this item.

3. How does Coca-Cola segment its market? Describe the primary target markets for Coca-Cola. How does it position its various offerings so that it appeals to these different target markets?

4. How does your university add value to students through the implementation of the four Ps?

5. Dyson successfully sells its fans and heaters for $150 to $400, whereas most conventional fans sell for around $25. Explain the value it creates and how this affects the price it can charge.

6. Of the four growth strategies described in the chapter, which is the riskiest? Which is the easiest to implement? Why?

7. Choose three companies. You believe the first builds customer value through product excellence, the second through operational excellence, and the third through customer excellence. Justify your answer.

8. You are in the job market and have received offers from three very different firms. Develop a marketing plan to help market yourself to prospective employers.

Quiz Yourself

1. The four fundamental growth strategies help firms identify growth opportunities in the marketplace. The strategies are based on two dimensions: new and current markets, and new and existing products and services. For example, market penetration is the strategy where the firm attempts to grow by having its existing market consume more of its existing products. On the other hand, the growth strategy that involves the firm attempting to grow by attracting a new market to its existing products is called what?
   a. Product development
   b. Market development
   c. Diversification
   d. Market penetration
   e. Product penetration

2. Markets must be segmented for any marketing strategy to be effective. This is because from the identified segments, the firm will choose one or more target markets. The choice of target market will then determine how which of these concepts are designed?
   a. Four Ps (product, price, place, promotion)
   b. SWOT analysis (strengths, weaknesses, opportunities, threats)
   c. STP (segmentation, targeting, positioning)
   d. GM (gross margin)
   e. SBU (strategic business unit)

(Answers to these two questions can be found in the Quiz Yourself Answer Key section.)

Chapter Case Study

THE COFFEE WARS

In the coffee and breakfast market, Starbucks vigorously competes with the likes of Dunkin' Donuts and, more recently, McDonald's. Independent coffeehouses and smaller regional chains, seen by many as more hip and less commercial, also continually nip at Starbucks' heels. However, the "coffee war" between Starbucks and Dunkin' Donuts is particularly fierce in the areas in which they compete head to head, even though each chain has its geographic strongholds—Dunkin' in the East and Starbucks in the West.[64] Part of the reason for this infamous battle might be the dominance of these two brands: Together, Starbucks and Dunkin' Donuts control well over half of the coffee market in the United States.[65] Moreover, Starbucks can claim some victories over Dunkin' Donuts, considering that its net revenues and stock prices have risen continuously since 2009.[66] By 2014, its global revenues had reached a record-setting $16.4 billion, and in 2015, its stock surged by more than 50 percent for the year.[67]

Starbucks' ubiquitous stores—from long-standing locations in U.S. cities and towns to international expansion into a vast range of new nations—are easy to locate and visit. A recent count showed that the chain maintains more than 22,000 stores, spanning 67 countries.[68] By making sure its stores, with their familiar siren logo, are easy to find, Starbucks guarantees that most people can readily find a place to get their coffee fix. For the vast majority of buyers, an addictive Salted Caramel Mocha, or just a great cup of black coffee, is convenient to find and very familiar.

There are plenty of jokes about how Starbucks manages to charge upwards of $5 for a jolt of caffeine, but a quick glance at its marketing methods and strategies helps explain why it can do so. The products it sells are appealing to customers and fulfill their needs: They taste good, are available readily and conveniently, and offer the benefit of helping them wake up to start their day (or stay awake for a long night of studying). Thus the exchange of money for coffee—or tea or juice or yogurt or a nice pastry—is a good value for consumers, despite the relatively high cost.

Starbucks also connects with fans through social marketing channels, including its popular My Starbucks Idea site. The site is an innovative approach to developing new products. Customers share ideas about everything "Starbucks," from store designs to new drink recipes. They can also join one of the many discussions in the customer forums. The site connects customers to its Twitter and Facebook sites too, and it also links users to its mobile apps. New capabilities available through the apps allow consumers to order their preferred beverage in advance and pay for their drinks or other products, then pop into the store to grab their purchases without ever having to wait in line.

When it comes to Starbucks' competition with Dunkin' Donuts, history shows that the two early morning giants actually had coexisted nicely for many years: Dunkin' Donuts made the donuts, and Starbucks brewed the coffee. Starting in 2000 though, Dunkin' Donuts slowly started encroaching on the upscale coffee market with the Dunkaccino. It also joined the "espresso revolution" in 2003, before formally declaring in 2006 its explicit intent to enter a head-to-head competition with Starbucks.[69]

Along with expanding its menu to feature specialty espresso drinks, Dunkin' Donuts launched a smartphone app that competes directly with Starbucks' widely popular version. In particular, the new Dunkin' Donuts app aims to extend the battle to the mobile field. It offers not just mobile ordering but also mobile delivery services, called DoorDash. The delivery service began in Dallas, Texas; plans are in place to expand it to other major U.S. cities.[70]

Although Dunkin' Donuts still trails Starbucks as a global company—with only 3,100 stores in 30 countries[71]—it uses this relatively small size and regional feel strategically, leveraging these attributes to adjust flexibly and integrate itself with local communities. Accordingly, it has ranked tops in the market for customer loyalty since 2007.[72] This focus on loyalty also resonates with the company's chosen sponsorship efforts. It lends its support to professional sports teams with strong local and national followings, including all the major league Boston-area teams (Red Sox, Patriots, Celtics, and Bruins), the Dallas Cowboys, New York's Yankees and Mets, and the Tampa Bay Rays. Expanding on the strategy, both abroad and to less famous leagues, Dunkin' Donuts partners with the Liverpool Football Club and the National Women's Hockey League.

Through these partnerships with sports teams, Dunkin' Donuts encourages consumers to interact more closely with it. For example, New England customers receive inducements to become DD Perks members and use its mobile app. With its "Pats Win, You Win" promotion, DD Perks members who pay through the app receive a free cup of coffee each time the New England Patriots win a game. The popular, vastly successful promotion has continued for several seasons, during which the Patriots continue winning lots of games, thus bringing lots of excited fans into Dunkin' Donuts stores.[73]

The competition between these two brands is well established and likely to continue, especially as Dunkin' Donuts continues to move away from being exclusively a donut shop and toward becoming a more coffee-centered business. As big new competitors such as McDonald's and Taco Bell enter the breakfast, coffee, and espresso markets, both Starbucks and Dunkin' Donuts are likely to continue coming up with new ways to maintain their existing customer base, then expand it in the United States and abroad.

Questions

1. Perform a SWOT analysis for Starbucks and Dunkin' Donuts. Based on your analysis, in which company would you invest? Justify your answer.

2. Which growth strategies have been pursued by Starbucks and Dunkin' Donuts in the past? Which strategies do you believe will be most successful for the two firms in the future? Why?

3. Which marketing metrics would be most helpful for an executive in charge of developing new products for a coffee chain?

Endnotes

1. Jennifer Kaplan, "PepsiCo Turns to Premium Snacks to Fuel Growth," *Bloomberg*, July 11, 2017.

2. Monica Watrous, "Inside PepsiCo's Snacks Strategy," *Food Business News*, February 11, 2016.

3. Monica Watrous, "How Frito-Lay Is Making Its Products Healthier," *Food Business News*, November 20, 2017.

4. PepsiCo, "PepsiCo Reports Third Quarter 2017 Results; Updates 2017 Financial Targets," October 4, 2017, www.pepsico.com/docs/album/q32017/q3_2017_fullrelease_jsyg3eavndrdgwab.pdf?sfvrsn=2.

5. Watrous, "Inside PepsiCo's Snacks Strategy."

6. Kaplan, "PepsiCo Turns to Premium Snacks to Fuel Growth."

7. Watrous, "Inside PepsiCo's Snacks Strategy"; PepsiCo, "PepsiCo Reports Third Quarter 2017 Results."

8. Watrous, "Inside PepsiCo's Snacks Strategy."

9. Watrous, "How Frito-Lay Is Making Its Products Healthier."

10. Ben Bouckley, "PepsiCo Launches Craft Cola: Caleb's Kola Promises 'Amazing Freshness,'" Beverage Daily.com, October 8, 2014.

11. PepsiCo, "The PepsiCo Advantage," www.pepsico.com/docs/album/Investor/barclays_bts_presentation.pdf?sfvrsn=0.

12. PepsiCo, "Who We Are," www.pepsico.com/Company.

13. Allison Aubrey, "This Is How Much Celebrities Get Paid to Endorse Soda and Unhealthy Food," *NPR*, June 7, 2016, www.npr.org/sections/thesalt/2016/06/07/481123646/this-is-how-much-celebrities-get-paid-to-endorse-soda-and-unhealthy-food; Robert Klara, "Why Celebrities Want to Be in PepsiCo's Ads," *Advertising Age*, June 8, 2015.

14. Beth Kowitt, "PepsiCo Nabs NBA Sponsorship Rights from Coca-Cola," *Fortune*, April 13, 2015; E. J. Schultz, "Coke Takes Over from Pepsi as MLB Sponsor," *Advertising Age*, March 31, 2017.

15. PepsiCo, "Pepsi Launches the Sound Drop to Identify and Support the Next Generation of Breaking Artists in Partnership with iHeartMedia, Shazam and MTV," August 24, 2016, www.pepsico.com/live/pressrelease/pepsi-launches-the-sound-drop-to-identify-and-support-the-next-generation-of-bre08242016.

16. Michael Treacy and Fred Wiersema, *The Discipline of Market Leaders* (Reading, MA: Addison-Wesley, 1995). Treacy and Wiersema suggest the first three strategies. We suggest the fourth—locational excellence.

17. V. Kumar et al., "Establishing Profitable Customer Loyalty for Multinational Companies in the Emerging Economies: A Conceptual Framework," *Journal of International Marketing* 21 (March 2013), pp. 57–80; Yuping Liu-Thompkins and Leona Tam, "Not All Repeat Customers Are the Same: Designing Effective Cross-Selling Promotion on the Basis of Attitudinal Loyalty and Habit," *Journal of Marketing* 77 (September 2013), pp. 21–36.

18. Michael Schrage, "What Most Companies Miss about Customer Lifetime Value," *Harvard Business Review*, April 18, 2017; V. Kumar and Werner Reinartz, "Creating Enduring Customer Value," *Journal of Marketing* 80, no. 6 (2016), pp. 36–68; Melea Press and Eric J. Arnould, "How Does Organizational Identification Form? A Consumer Behavior Perspective," *Journal of Consumer Research* 38 (December 2011), pp. 650–66.

19. Valarie A. Zeithaml, Mary Jo Bitner, and Dwayne D. Gremler, *Services Marketing: Integrating Customer Focus across the Firm*, 7th ed. (New York: McGraw-Hill Education, 2017).

20. https://disneyworld.disney.go.com/plan/my-disney-experience/my-magic-plus/; Brooks Barnes, "At Disney Parks, a Bracelet Meant to Build Loyalty (and Sales)," *The New York Times*, January 7, 2013.

21. Carmine Gallo, "Customer Service the Disney Way," *Forbes*, April 14, 2011; Justyna Polaczyk, "Be Like Disney: Best Customer Service Training Ideas," *Live Chat*, February 15, 2016; Todd van Luling, "Here's One Thing You've Never Noticed about Disney Parks," *Huffington Post*, July 13, 2015.

22. Diane M. Martin and John W. Schouten, "Consumption-Driven Market Emergence," *Journal of Consumer Research* 40 (February 2014), pp. 855–70. Also see articles in special issue edited by John T. Mentzer and Greg Gundlach, "Exploring the Relationship between Marketing and Supply Chain Management: Introduction to the Special Issue," *Journal of the Academy of Marketing Science* 38, no. 1 (2010), pp. 1–4.

23. Hilary Stout, "In War for Same-Day Delivery, Racing Madly to Go Last Mile," *The New York Times*, November 23, 2013, www.nytimes.com.

24. E. J. Schultz, "Can Caleb's Kola Help Pepsi Restore the 'Cool' to Cola?," *Advertising Age*, December 8, 2014.

25. http://interbrand.com/best-brands/best-global-brands/2017/ranking/#?listFormat=ls.

26. "Marketing Plan," *American Marketing Association Dictionary,* www.marketingpower.com.

27. Anastasia, "The Strategic Marketing Process: A Complete Guide," *Cleverism,* February 4, 2015, www.cleverism.com/strategic-marketing-process-complete-guide/; Donald Lehman and Russell Winer, *Analysis for Marketing Planning,* 7th ed. (Burr Ridge, IL: McGraw-Hill/Irwin, 2008).

28. E. O. Ekpe, S. I. Eneh, and B. J. Inyang, "Leveraging Organizational Performance through Effective Mission Statement," *International Business Research* 8, no. 9 (2015), pp. 135–41; Nancy J. Sirianni et al., "Branded Service Encounters: Strategically Aligning Employee Behavior with the Brand Positioning," *Journal of Marketing* 77 (November 2013), pp. 108–23; Andrew Campbell, "Mission Statements," *Long Range Planning* 30 (1997), pp. 931–33.

29. Gene R. Laczniak and Patrick E. Murphy, "Stakeholder Theory and Marketing: Moving from a Firm-Centric to a Societal Perspective," *Journal of Public Policy & Marketing* 31 (Fall 2012), pp. 284–92; Alfred Rappaport, *Creating Shareholder Value: The New Standard for Business Performance* (New York: Wiley, 1988).

30. PepsiCo, "Our Mission & Values," www.pepsico.com/Purpose/Our-Mission-and-Values; Coca-Cola, "Mission, Vision & Values," www.coca-colacompany.com/our-company/mission-vision-values/.

31. Coca-Cola, "Mission, Vision & Values."

32. Pink Ribbon International, http://pinkribbon.org/about/our-organization/.

33. Robert Klara, "Why Celebrities Want to Be in PepsiCo's Ads: A 'Symbiotic Relationship' with Stars Like Beckham, Beyoncé and Jordan," *Adweek,* June 8, 2015, www.adweek.com/news/advertising-branding/why-celebrities-want-be-pepsicos-ads-165217.

34. "Pepsi Launches New Music Platform 'Out of the Blue' to Debut during the 57th Annual Grammy Awards," *PR Newswire,* February 4, 2015, www.prnewswire.com/news-releases/pepsi-launches-new-music-platform-out-of-the-blue-to-debut-during-the-57th-annual-grammy-awards-300031079.html.

35. www.pepsico.com/sustainability/Philanthropy.

36. StreetAuthority, "Coke vs. Pepsi: By the Numbers," *Nasdaq,* March 24, 2014, www.nasdaq.com/article/coke-vs-pepsi-by-the-numbers-cm337909.

37. RT, "PepsiCo Admits Public Source Origins of Its Aquafina Bottled Water," www.rt.com/usa/319980-aquafina-tap-water-origins/.

38. Kate Taylor, "The Future of Coke and Pepsi Depends on This Unlikely Beverage," *Business Insider,* April 24, 2016; Trefis Team, "Non-Carbonated Beverages Spearhead Growth for PepsiCo's North America Business," *Forbes,* December 10, 2015, www.forbes.com/sites/greatspeculations/2015/12/10/non-carbonated-beverages-spearhead-growth-for-pepsi-cos-north-america-business/.

39. www.pepsico.com/Company/Global-Divisions.

40. PepsiCo, "PepsiCo Exceeds Global Water Stewardship Goals," August 29, 2016; Brian Dumaine, "The Water Conservation Challenge of Coke vs. Pepsi," *Fortune,* August 20, 2015, http://fortune.com/2015/08/20/coca-cola-vs-pepsi/.

41. Martin Caballero, "FDA Issues Draft Guidance on New Nutrition Facts Label," *BevNET,* January 4, 2017, www.bevnet.com/news/2017/fda-issues-draft-guidance-new-nutrition-facts-label; Ilan Brat and Mike Esterl, "FDA Proposes Placing Sugar Guide on Food Labels," *The Wall Street Journal,* July 24, 2015, www.wsj.com/articles/fda-proposes-listing-added-sugar-on-food-labels-1437774370.

42. Angelica LaVito, "Millennials Like Small Food Companies, but Big Brands Aren't Dead—Yet," *CNBC,* June 15, 2017; Stephanie Strom, "Small Food Brands, Big Successes," *The New York Times,* August 24, 2015, www.nytimes.com/2015/08/26/dining/start-up-food-business-changing-appetites.html?_r=0.

43. www.hertz.com/rentacar/productsandservices/productsandservicesRegions.do.

44. https://images.hertz.com/pdfs/VMVWeb.pdf; www.adweek.com/aw/content_display/creative/new-campaigns/e3i21cea1586d-d4edf5d50f9a17e7f18bf3.

45. Terence A. Shimp, *Advertising Promotion and Other Aspects of Integrated Marketing Communication,* 8th ed. (Mason, OH: South-Western, 2008); T. Duncan and C. Caywood, "The Concept, Process, and Evolution of Integrated Marketing Communication," in *Integrated Communication: Synergy of Persuasive Voices,* ed. E. Thorson and J. Moore (Mahwah, NJ: Erlbaum, 1996); see also various issues of the *Journal of Integrated Marketing Communications,* http://jimc.medill.northwestern.edu.

46. Nathalie Tadena, "Cheerios Is King of Commercial Spending among Cereal Brands," *The Wall Street Journal,* July 17, 2014, http://blogs.wsj.com/cmo/2014/07/17/cheerios-is-king-of-commercial-spending-among-cereal-brands/.

47. Ofer Mintz and Imran S. Currim, "What Drives Managerial Use of Marketing and Financial Metrics and Does Metric Use Affect Performance of Marketing-Mix Activities?," *Journal of Marketing* 77 (March 2013), pp. 17–40.

48. Kirsten Acuna, "Google Says It Can Predict Which Films Will Be Huge Box Office Hits," *Business Insider,* June 6, 2013.

49. Goodyear, "Annual Report 2014."

50. This discussion is adapted from Roger A. Kerin, Steven W. Hartley, and William Rudelius, *Marketing,* 10th ed. (Burr Ridge, IL: McGraw-Hill/Irwin, 2011).

51. P. Farris et al., *Marketing Metrics: 50+ Metrics Every Executive Should Master* (Upper Saddle River, NJ: Pearson, 2006), p. 17.

52. Relative market share = Brand's market share ÷ Largest competitor's market share. If, for instance, there are only two products in a market, A and B, and product B has 90 percent market share, then A's relative market share is 10 ÷ 90 = 11.1 percent. If, on the other hand, B only has 50 percent market share, then A's relative market share is 10 ÷ 50 = 20 percent. Farris et al., *Marketing Metrics,* p. 19.

53. Apple Inc., "Form 10-K 2011 Annual Report," October 30, 2013.

54. Sherilynn Macale, "Apple Has Sold 300M iPods, Currently Holds 78% of the Music Player Market," *The Next Web,* October 4, 2011, http://thenextweb.com; Chris Smith, "iPad Tablet Market Share Down to 57 Percent," *Techradar.com,* February 16, 2012, www.techradar.com; Ken Yeung, "Apple Sold 4.6M Macs and 3.49M iPods in Q4 FY2013," *The Next Web,* October 28, 2013, http://thenextweb.com.

55. "iPhone, iPad and iPod Sales from 1st Quarter 2006 to 4th Quarter 2015 (in Million Units)," *Statista,* December 4, 2015, www.statista.com/statistics/253725/iphone-ipad-and-ipod-sales-comparison/.

56. Katie Collins, "Apple Mac Sales Down, but the Broader PC Market Is Even Worse," *CNET,* October 9, 2015, www.cnet.com/news/apple-mac-sales-reportedly-hit-two-year-ow/.

57. Chuck Jones, "Morgan Stanley Survey Shows Strong Demand for Apple's iPhone and Expects Growth in 2016," *Forbes,* September 6, 2015, www.forbes.com/sites/chuckjones/2015/09/06/morgan-stanley-survey-shows-strong-demand-for-apples-iphone-and-expects-growth-in-2016/.

58. Roger Kerin, Vijay Mahajan, and P. Rajan Varadarajan, *Contemporary Perspectives on Strategic Market Planning* (Boston: Allyn & Bacon, 1991), Chap. 6; Susan Mudambi, "A Topology of Strategic Choice in Marketing," *International Journal of Market & Distribution Management* (1994), pp. 22–25.

59. Devin Leonard, "Calling All Superheroes," *Fortune,* May 23, 2007; Box Office Mojo, "X-Men (2000)," www.boxofficemojo.com/movies/?id=xmen.htm.

60. "'Black Panther' Surpasses $1 Billion in Sales After China Debut," *Bloomberg,* March 10, 2018.

61. Patrick Cavanaugh, "Netflix Orders a Second Season of 'Marvel's Daredevil,'" *Marvel.com,* April 21, 2015; Todd Spangler, "Netflix, Marvel Pick 'Luke Cage' Showrunner, Cheo Hodari Coker," *Variety,* March 31, 2015.

62. A. A. Thompson et al., *Crafting and Executing Strategy,* 18th ed. (New York: McGraw-Hill/Irwin, 2012).

63. Marvel, "Home Décor," http://shop.marvel.com/home-decor/.

64. Alvin Chang and Matt Carroll, "Split Country: Dunkin' vs. Starbucks," *Boston Globe*/Boston.com (n.d.).

65. Christine Champagne and Teressa Iezzi, "Dunkin' Donuts and Starbucks: A Tale of Two Coffee Marketing Giants," *Fast Company Co Create,* August 21, 2014, www.fastcocreate.com/3034572/coffee-week/dunkin-donuts-and-starbucks-a-tale-of-two-coffee-marketing-giants.

66. Starbucks, "Fiscal Year 2015 Annual Report," http://investor.starbucks.com.

67. Justin Bariso, "The Strategy That Led Starbucks's Stock Price to Jump 50 Percent," *Inc.,* December 7, 2015, www.inc.com/justin-bariso/what-you-can-learn-from-starbucks-continued-success.html.

68. Starbucks, "Starbucks Company Profile," https://news.starbucks.com/uploads/documents/AboutUs-Company_Profile-Q32015-8.6.2015.pdf.

69. Champagne and Iezzi, "Dunkin' Donuts and Starbucks."

70. "Dunkin' Donuts Tests On-the-Go Ordering and Delivery Service in Select Markets," Dunkin' Donuts Newsroom, November 18, 2015, http://news.dunkindonuts.com/news/dunkin-donuts-tests-on-the-go-ordering-and-delivery-service-in-select-markets-3105177.

71. "Global Presence," www.dunkindonuts.com/dunkindonuts/en/company/global.html.

72. "Dunkin' Donuts," Dunkin' Brands, http://dunkinbrands.com/about/donuts.

73. Frank O'Laughlin, "Dunkin' Donuts to Give Away Free Coffee When Patriots Win," *Woburn Patch,* September 8, 2015, http://patch.com/massachusetts/woburn/dunkin-donuts-give-away-free-coffee-when-patriots-win-0.

i. Drew Neisser, "How Sally Beauty Gave Its Loyalty Program a Stunning Makeover," *Advertising Age,* April 5, 2017; "Sally Beauty," www.sallybeauty.com; Jim Tierney, "Sally Beauty Looks to Ramp Up Customer Loyalty, Engagement Initiatives," Loyalty360, February 3, 2017.

ii. Seb Joseph, "Coca-Cola Has an Internal Strategy Called 'Marketing in Smaller Sizes' to Make People Buy Its Soda More Often for More Money," *Business Insider,* November 18, 2015; Rachel Arthur, "Coca-Cola Sees Big Success with Small Pack Sizes, Celebrating a 'Tremendous Amount of Positive Growth,'" BeverageDaily.com, July 23, 2015; Brooke Metz, "Less Is More: For Coca-Cola, Small Packs Mean Big Business," July 22, 2015, www.coca-colacompany.com/stories/less-is-more-for-coca-cola-small-packs-mean-big-business/; Associated Press, "Coke, Pepsi, Pledge to Shrink Can and Bottle Sizes to Cut Calories," *CBC News,* September 23, 2014, www.cbc.ca/news/health/coke-pepsi-pledge-to-shrink-can-and-bottle-sizes-to-cut-calories-1.2775467.

iii. Tim Peterson, "How P&G Is Tying Snapchat Ads to In-Store Sales," *Advertising Age,* November 18, 2015.

iv. William Boston, Hendrink Varnhot, and Sarah Sloat, "Volkswagen Blames 'Chain of Mistakes' for Emissions Scandal," *The Wall Street Journal,* December 10, 2015; Russell Hotten, "Volkswagen: The Scandal Explained," *BBC News,* December 10, 2015; Alex Davis, "Volkswagen's US Sales Plummet 25 Percent as Dieselgate Rolls On," *Wired,* December 1, 2015; Stephen Edelstein, "Used VW Prices Fall More, with No End to Diesel Scandal in Sight," *Green Car Reports,* December 9, 2015, www.greencarreports.com/news/1101315_used-vw-prices-fall-more-with-no-end-to-diesel-scandal-in-sight.

v. Aaron M. Kessler and B. X. Chen, "Google and Apple Fight for the Car Dashboard," *The New York Times,* February 22, 2015, www.nytimes.com; Tim Stevens, "2014's Battle for Dashboard Supremacy: Apple's CarPlay vs. Google's OAA vs. MirrorLink," *CNET,* March 4, 2014, www.cnet.com/news/2014s-battle-for-dashboard-supremacy-apples-carplay-vs-googles-oaa-vs-mirrorlink/.

Quiz Yourself Answer Key

1. The growth strategy that involves the firm attempting to grow by attracting a new market to its existing products is called what?

   Answer: (e) Product penetration

2. The choice of target market will determine how which of these concepts are designed?

   Answer: (a) Four Ps (product, price, place, promotion)

WRITING A MARKETING PLAN

Have a plan. Follow the plan, and you'll be surprised how successful you can be. Most people don't have a plan. That's why it's easy to beat most folks.

—Paul "Bear" Bryant, football coach, University of Alabama

WHY WRITE A MARKETING PLAN?[1]

As a student, you likely plan out much in your life—where to meet for dinner, how much time to spend studying for exams, which courses to take next semester, how to get home for winter break, and so on. Plans enable us to figure out where we want to go and how we might get there.

For a firm, the goal is not much different. Any company that wants to succeed (which means any firm whatsoever) needs to plan for a variety of contingencies, and marketing represents one of the most significant. A marketing plan—which we defined in Chapter 2 as a written document composed of an analysis of the current marketing situation, opportunities and threats for the firm,

marketing objectives and strategy specified in terms of the four Ps, action programs, and projected or pro forma income (and other financial) statements—enables marketing personnel and the firm as a whole to understand their own actions, the market in which they operate, their future direction, and the means to obtain support for new initiatives.[2]

Because these elements—internal activities, external environments, goals, and forms of support—differ for every firm, the marketing plan is different for each firm as well. However, several guidelines apply to marketing plans in general; this appendix summarizes those points and offers an annotated example.

MARKETING PLAN VERSUS BUSINESS PLAN

Of course, firms consider more than marketing when they make plans and therefore commonly develop business plans as well. Yet as this book highlights, marketing constitutes such an important element of business that business plans and marketing plans coincide in many ways.[3] Marketing plans as well as business plans generally encompass:

1. Executive summary.
2. Company overview.
3. Objectives or goals, usually according to strategic plan and focus.
4. Situation analysis.
5. Customer segmentation, target marketing, and positioning analysis.
6. Marketing strategy.
7. Financial projections.
8. Implementation plan.
9. Evaluation and control metrics.
10. Appendix

A business plan also includes details about R&D and operations, and both may feature details about other key topics, depending on the focus of the company and the plan.

STRUCTURE OF A MARKETING PLAN

This section briefly describes each of the elements of a marketing plan.[4]

Executive Summary

The executive summary essentially tells the reader why he or she is reading this marketing plan—what changes require consideration, what new products need discussion, and so forth—and suggests possible actions to take in response to the information the plan contains.

Company Overview

The company overview provides a brief description of the company, including perhaps its mission statement, background, and competitive advantages.

Objectives/Goals

The objectives/goals section offers more specifics about why readers are reading the marketing plan. What does the company want to achieve, both overall and with this particular marketing plan?

Situation Analysis

Recall from the chapter text that a situation analysis generally relies on SWOT considerations; the situation section, then, describes the strengths, weaknesses, opportunities, and threats facing the company.

STP Analysis

The analysis proceeds by assessing the market in which the company functions, the products it currently offers or plans to offer in the future, and the characteristics of current or potential customers.

Marketing Strategy

The marketing strategy may be very specific, especially if the plan pertains to, for example, a stable product in a familiar market, or it may be somewhat open to varied possibilities, such as when the firm plans to enter a new market with an innovative product.

Financial Projections

On the basis of the knowledge already obtained, the marketing plan should provide possible developments and returns on the marketing investments outlined in the marketing strategy.

Implementation Plan

The implementation plan includes the timing of promotional activities, when monitoring will take place, and how expansions likely will proceed.

Evaluation and Control Metrics

The firm must have a means of assessing the marketing plan's recommendations; the marketing plan therefore must indicate the methods for undertaking this assessment, whether quantitatively or qualitatively.

Appendix

The final section(s) offers additional information that might be of benefit, such as a list of key personnel; data limitations that may influence the findings; and suggestions of the plan, relevant legislation, and so forth.

INFORMATION SOURCES[5]

When writing a marketing plan, you likely can turn to a variety of your firm's in-house information sources, including annual reports, previous marketing plans, published mission statements, and so on. In addition, various sources offer suggestions and examples that may provide you with direction and ideas. A reference librarian can help you find many of these sources, which likely are available through your university's library system.

- Knowthis.com—"a knowledge source for marketing," www.knowthis.com/tutorials/principles-of-marketing/how-to-write-a-marketing-plan/21.htm.
- *Encyclopedia of American Industries*—introduces industry structure; arranged by SIC and NAICS codes.
- Standard & Poor's NetAdvantage—surveys of more than 50 industries, with financial data about companies in each industry.
- Investext Plus—brokerage house reports.
- IBISWorld—marketing research on thousands of industries; classified by NAICS code.
- *Statistical Abstract of the United States*—a vast variety of statistics on a wealth of topics.
- U.S. Bureau of the Census—detailed statistical data gathered every 10 years on all aspects of the U.S. population.
- County Business Patterns: U.S. Bureau of the Census—payroll and employee numbers for most NAICS codes.
- Consumer Expenditure Survey: U.S. Bureau of Labor Statistics—income and expenditures by household, classified by various demographics.
- *The LifeStyle Market Analyst*—lifestyle information about geographic areas, lifestyle interest groups, and age and income groups.
- MediaMark Reporter—information about demographics, lifestyles, product and brand usage, and advertising media preferences.
- Scarborough Arbitron—local market consumer information for various media in 75 local markets for consumer retail shopping behavior, product consumption, media usage, lifestyle behavior, and demographics.

- *Simmons Study of Media & Markets*—products and consumer characteristics; various media audiences and their characteristics.
- *Sourcebook America*—demographic data, including population, spending potential index, income, race, and Tapestry data, presented by state, county, DMA, and zip code, as well as business data by county and zip code.
- *Rand McNally Commercial Atlas and Marketing Guide*—maps and tables showing demographic, industrial, transportation, railroad, airline, and hospital data.
- "Survey of Buying Power," Sales and Marketing Management—current state, county, city, and town estimates of population by age, retail sales by store group, effective buying income, and buying power index.
- Annual & 10-K reports from *Thomson One Banker, Edgar,* and *LexisNexis*—business descriptions, product listings, distribution channels, possible impact of regulations and lawsuits, and discussions of strategic issues.
- MarketResearch.com Academic—marketing research reports on a variety of consumer products.
- Mintel Reports Database—marketing research reports focusing on consumer products, lifestyles, retailing, and international travel industry.

LINGUISTIC AND VISUAL SUGGESTIONS

Again, recall that all marketing plans differ because all firms differ. However, just as rules exist that dictate what makes for good writing, some rules or guidelines apply to all well-written marketing plans.

- Maintain a professional attitude in the writing and presentation.
- Keep descriptions and summaries concise. Get to the point.
- Use standard English in a professional tone.
- Proofread the entire plan multiple times to catch grammatical, spelling, or other such errors that could dampen the professionalism of the writing.
- Adopt a businesslike tone; avoid flowery or jargon-filled writing.
- Employ active voice rather than passive voice, and present tense rather than past tense whenever possible (e.g., "We plan to achieve 30 percent growth in two years" rather than "The plan was that 30 percent growth would be achieved by the firm within two years").
- Be positive.
- Avoid meaningless adjectives (e.g., "Our goal is tremendous growth").
- Be specific; use quantitative information whenever possible.
- Insert graphics to convey important concepts succinctly, including photos, graphs, illustrations, and charts.
- Avoid using so many visual elements that they clutter the plan.
- Lay out the plan clearly and logically.
- Organize sections logically using multiple levels of headings distinguished clearly by font differences (e.g., bold for first-level heads, italics for second-level heads).
- Consider the use of bullet points or numbered lists to emphasize important points.
- Exploit modern technology (e.g., graphics software, page layout software, laser printers) to ensure the plan looks professional.
- Adopt an appropriate font to make the text easy to read and visually appealing—avoid using anything smaller than 10-point font at a minimum.
- Avoid unusual or decorative fonts; stick with a common serif type to make the text easy to read.
- Consider binding the report with an attractive cover and clear title page.
- Generally, aim for a plan that consists of 15–30 pages.

Endnotes

1. This appendix was written by Tom Chevalier, Britt Hackmann, and Elisabeth Nevins Caswell, in conjunction with the textbook authors (Dhruv Grewal and Michael Levy) as the basis of class discussion, rather than to illustrate either effective or ineffective marketing practice.

2. www.knowthis.com (accessed May 16, 2008); see also "Marketing Plan Online," www.quickmba.com (accessed May 16, 2008); "Marketing Plan," www.businessplans.org (accessed May 18, 2008).

3. Roger Kerin, Steven Hartley, and William Rudelius, *Marketing* (New York: McGraw-Hill/Irwin, 2008), p. 53.

4. Roger A. Kerin, Steven W. Hartley, and William Rudelius, *Marketing*, 12th ed. (Burr Ridge, IL: McGraw-Hill Education, 2015); www.knowthis.com (accessed May 16, 2008).

5. This listing of sources largely comes from the Babson College Library Guide, www3.babson.edu, May 12, 2008 (accessed May 15, 2008). Special thanks to Nancy Dlott.

6. This marketing plan presents an abbreviated version of the actual plan for PeopleAhead. Some information has been changed to maintain confidentiality.

7. Publishers' and Advertising Directors' Conference, September 21, 2005.

8. Mintel International Group, "Online Recruitment–US," January 1, 2005, www.marketresearch.com (accessed September 1, 2005).

9. Corzen Inc., May 1, 2004, www.wantedtech.com (accessed May 17, 2004).

10. Mintel International Group, "Online Recruitment–US."

PEOPLEAHEAD MARKETING PLAN ILLUSTRATION[6]

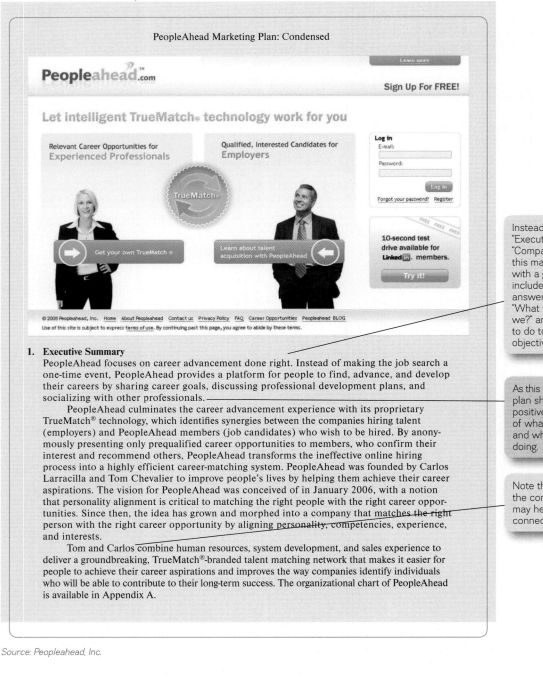

PeopleAhead Marketing Plan: Condensed

Instead of using separate "Executive Summary" and "Company Overview" sections, this marketing plan begins with a general overview that includes both aspects and answers the key questions: "What type of business are we?" and "What do we need to do to accomplish our objectives?" (see Chapter 2).

1. Executive Summary

PeopleAhead focuses on career advancement done right. Instead of making the job search a one-time event, PeopleAhead provides a platform for people to find, advance, and develop their careers by sharing career goals, discussing professional development plans, and socializing with other professionals.

As this plan does, a marketing plan should start with a positive, upbeat assessment of what the company does and what it hopes to continue doing.

PeopleAhead culminates the career advancement experience with its proprietary TrueMatch® technology, which identifies synergies between the companies hiring talent (employers) and PeopleAhead members (job candidates) who wish to be hired. By anonymously presenting only prequalified career opportunities to members, who confirm their interest and recommend others, PeopleAhead transforms the ineffective online hiring process into a highly efficient career-matching system. PeopleAhead was founded by Carlos Larracilla and Tom Chevalier to improve people's lives by helping them achieve their career aspirations. The vision for PeopleAhead was conceived of in January 2006, with a notion that personality alignment is critical to matching the right people with the right career opportunities. Since then, the idea has grown and morphed into a company that matches the right person with the right career opportunity by aligning personality, competencies, experience, and interests.

Note the personalization of the company founders, which may help readers feel connected to the company.

Tom and Carlos combine human resources, system development, and sales experience to deliver a groundbreaking, TrueMatch®-branded talent matching network that makes it easier for people to achieve their career aspirations and improves the way companies identify individuals who will be able to contribute to their long-term success. The organizational chart of PeopleAhead is available in Appendix A.

Source: Peopleahead, Inc.

2. Strategic Objectives

2.1. Mission

PeopleAhead's mission is to help individuals with career advancement and improve the human capital in companies. The site will act as a networking platform for professionals and career matching as opposed to job and resume-posting searches.

> The paragraph provides a general outline of the firm's objectives; the bulleted list offers more specific goals, and the subsequent sections go into more detail about the various factors that may influence these objectives.

2.2. Goals

- Use brand-matching technology: TrueMatch®
- Build critical mass of users.
- Drive traffic to the Web site through marketing blitzes.
- Utilize word-of-mouth advertising from satisfied users.

2.3. Business Summary

- **Business customers:** This group provides PeopleAhead's revenues. Customers purchase contact information about the Top Ten PROfiles gleaned from the individual member base that have been sorted and ranked by the TrueMatch® technology. PeopleAhead will focus on small and medium businesses (see Market Segmentation section), because these entities are underserved by large competitors in the online recruitment market, and because research shows that this demographic has a less efficient recruitment process that would benefit most readily from PeopleAhead's services. Within this segment, customers include HR managers who are responsible for the sourcing of candidates, functional area managers who require new talent for their team, and executives whose business objectives rely on human capital and efficiency of operations.

> By referring to another section, the plan makes clear where it is heading and enables readers to cross-reference the information.

- **Individual members:** This group does not pay for services but is the main source of data points for PeopleAhead's TrueMatch® system. PeopleAhead will focus on building a base of individual members who range from recent graduates to individuals with 5–7 years of continuous employment. Ideal members are those who are currently employed or will be graduating within nine months and are "poised" to make a career change. These individuals can utilize the services to the fullest extent and are valuable candidates for business customers.

> The plan acknowledges both a general, potential target market and the ideal targets.

2.4. Competitive Advantage

- **TrueMatch® offers a branded technology,** marketed to both business customers and individual candidates for its "black box" value proposition, which establishes PeopleAhead as the category leader for recruitment-matching software. This technology provides a point of differentiation from competitors, which may have technically similar matching software but constantly need to reinforce their marketing messages with explanations of their value proposition.

> As Chapter 2 suggests, the plan notes PeopleAhead's sustainable competitive advantage as part of its overall mission statement.

- **For individual candidates,** PeopleAhead will be the favored career advancement platform online, where individuals enthusiastically create a history and have connections (invited friends, coworkers, and mentors) in place that will make PeopleAhead a staple among their favorite Web sites. PeopleAhead delivers TrueMatch® career opportunities, professional development plans that let people establish a professional record, and valuable career advancement tools, including automatic position feedback, "recommend-a-friend," and team-based career networking.
- **For business customers,** PeopleAhead makes online sourcing and qualification of candidates quick and efficient by prequalifying potential candidates, seeking recommendations for hard-to-find individuals, and delivering only the Top 10 most highly qualified candidates who have

preconfirmed interest in the available position. PeopleAhead will be the most effective candidate-company matching platform available in the market, delivering prequalified, preconfirmed candidates.

3. Situation Analysis—Online Recruitment

Online recruitment is the system whereby companies use the Web to locate and qualify prospective candidates for available positions. The methods employed by online recruitment service providers to serve this market range from resume aggregation to assessment test application to linking strategies. However, the common underlying objective is to locate candidates who would not be found by traditional recruitment methods and use computing power to qualify candidates quickly and with more accuracy than would be possible manually.

3.1. Industry Analysis

Large online recruitment Web sites make this a tedious process by requiring companies to search through many resumes manually to find the right candidate. Other sites solicit recommendations for positions. However, resumes are often "enhanced," such that almost all candidates appear qualified, and information found in the resume or provided through a recommendation is simply not sufficient to make an educated hiring decision. Companies need more information and intelligent tools that make this screening process more accurate.

3.1.1. Market Size

The market size for both member segments in 2005 was as follows:

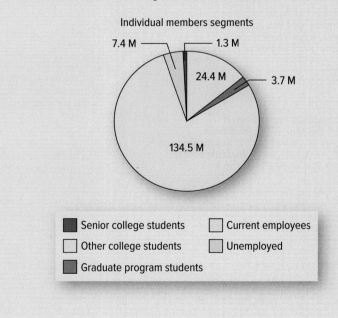

Individual members segments

7.4 M — 1.3 M

24.4 M — 3.7 M

134.5 M

- ■ Senior college students   □ Current employees
- □ Other college students   ▨ Unemployed
- ■ Graduate program students

In discussing both the external market and the internal advantages of PeopleAhead, the plan carefully distinguishes between individual job candidates and businesses, thus differentiating the focus and objectives according to this segmentation.

Figures provide a visually attractive break in the text and summarize a lot of information in an easy-to-read format.

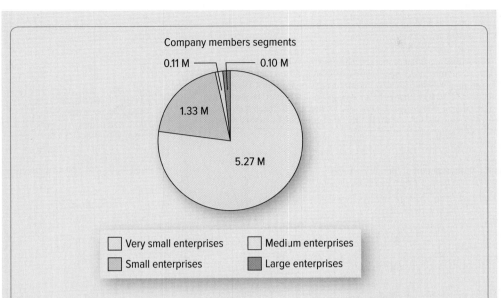

Company members segments

0.11 M ———   ——— 0.10 M

1.33 M

5.27 M

☐ Very small enterprises   ☐ Medium enterprises
☐ Small enterprises   ■ Large enterprises

The most critical issue in examining market size is the relationship between the number of companies and the number of workers employed, because sales are based on the number of positions (profiles purchased), not the number of companies that use the service.

The following figure shows the number of people employed by each enterprise market segment as of January 2006, according to the U.S. Department of Labor. This segment information will be useful in defining PeopleAhead's target market.

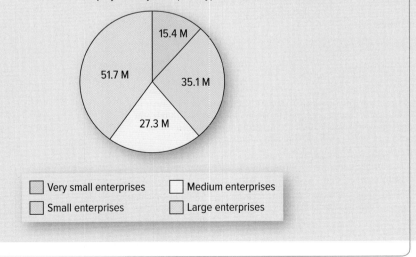

Employment by enterprise type

15.4 M

51.7 M

35.1 M

27.3 M

☐ Very small enterprises   ☐ Medium enterprises
☐ Small enterprises   ☐ Large enterprises

3.1.2. Market Growth

PeopleAhead will operate in the online recruitment market. The growth of this industry is subject to two primary constraints: U.S. economic health and online recruitment advertisement adoption rates. Understanding these constraints will help identify PeopleAhead's opportunity. General indicators suggest the U.S. economy (GDP) will grow at an average annual rate of 4% for the next decade.[7] Online recruitment advertising is expected to grow by 35% per year to reach $7.6 billion by 2010.[8] Not only is the market expanding, but it is exhibiting rapid adoption by new entities, as the following graph shows.[9]

Another visually attractive graph summarizes complicated information easily. The use of high-quality color can add a professional feel to a marketing plan.

Recruitment advertisement industry growth

Total recruitment advertisement

Total online recruitment market

Main competitors: Monster, CareerBuilder, and Yahoo/HotJobs

3.1.3. Market Needs

- **The right person for the right position:** The right employee for one company or position is not the same for all others. Not only must companies locate intelligent individuals with relevant experience, but they also prefer people who are aligned with the position requirements in terms of personality, competencies, and fit with the company culture.

- **Prescreening qualification tools:** Increasing the number of candidates through online recruitment can be advantageous, but it can also be a hindrance. When sourcing candidates, recruiters need tools that help them qualify applicants.

- **Time savings:** Companies need to complete the online sourcing and qualification of candidates quickly. Leaving positions unfilled can cause critical performance gaps to emerge within the company.

3.1.4. Market Trends

The methods by which online recruitment service providers deliver candidates has been undergoing a migration from resume aggregation and search services like Monster and CareerBuilder to new Web 2.0 methodologies that include passive recruitment, "meta tagging," and social networking.

The underlying objective of these Web 2.0 services is to allow individuals to remain on a few, trusted Web sites while enabling companies to access those individuals for financial purposes. In parallel, the focus is moving from aggregation of unique visitors toward engaging existing users more intensively. Internet users are growing familiar with sites that encourage socializing, collaborating, and distributing private information online to help improve network benefits and need to be engaged to maintain contact.

3.2. SWOT Analysis

	Positive	Negative
Internal	**STRENGTHS** • Industry best practices: The networking model used by PeopleAhead draws on the industry accepted best practices contact protocols drawn from multiple industries, including online feedback, recruitment, and social networking and offline professional networking. TrueMatch® software aligns business objectives with appropriate candidates. • Team expertise: The combined talents of the founders include human resources, system development, sales, and marketing. • Web development expertise: PeopleAhead has partnered with an award-winning European software development provider. This company provides quality usually reserved for high-budget projects, at terms that are favorable for a start-up company.	**WEAKNESSES** • Absence of industry "influentials": As a start-up, PeopleAhead does not currently have resources to attract influential industry managers. • Inability to guarantee critical mass: As is true of many Internet companies, the business must solve the "chicken and egg" puzzle to build critical mass. • Verifying efficiency of matching capabilities: In theory, the system has an absolute guarantee of effectivity; computations make decisions rather than humans. However, the matching capabilities must be verified as accurate to gain widespread acceptance. • Broad target market: Because PeopleAhead is targeting a wide range of businesses, the product being developed has not been "customized" ideally for each segment.
External	**OPPORTUNITIES** • Service gap: Recruiters are not pleased with current online recruitment vendors. • Industry gap: Job turnover is every 3.5 years per person. • Demand for productive candidates. • Online recruitment advertising: Growing by 35% per year, to reach $7.6 billion by 2010.[10]	**THREATS** • Convergence: Existing competitors may form strategic alliances and establish powerful positions before PeopleAhead can establish itself. • Inability to protect model: Very little intellectual property created by Web sites is protected by law. Although PeopleAhead will pursue aggressive

(continued)

Before engaging in a firm-specific SWOT analysis (see Chapter 2), this marketing plan assesses the external market environment further and thus establishes a basis for the subsequent SWOT analysis.

Using a table and bullet points, the plan summarizes a lot of information succinctly and clearly.

Note that the analysis uses outside sources to support its claims.

External   **OPPORTUNITIES**

THREATS

- Fragmented business models: Online recruitment is fragmented by recruitment methodology: active (people who need jobs), passive (people who are not looking but would move if enticed), poised (people unsatisfied with jobs they have), and network (finding people of interest based on who or what they know).

IP protection strategies, the model could be copied or mimicked by competitors.
- Inadequate differentiation: Inability to explain our differentiation would relegate PeopleAhead to (unfair) comparisons with competitors. Without differentiation, PeopleAhead will not be able to create scale through network effects.

3.3. Competition

Most online recruitment Web sites compete in the active recruitment market, including Monster, CareerBuilder, and Yahoo/HotJobs. The pervasive segment includes job seekers who actively look for jobs, post their resumes, and search for jobs on company Web sites. Most active recruiters offer free services to users and charge companies on a fee basis. Companies can post jobs and search for candidate resumes in the database (average fee for local searches is $500 and nationwide is $1,000). In this first-generation online recruitment business model, competitors face the challenge to make the process more user-friendly and reduce the effort required to make these sites deliver results.

- **Monster:** Monster.com is the sixteenth most visited Web site in the United States, with more than 43 million professionals in its viewer base. Monster earns revenue from job postings, access to its resume database, and advertisements on Web sites of partner companies.
- **Careerbuilder:** Careerbuilder.com has experienced 75% growth for the past five years. This job post/resume search company uses its media ownership to attract passive candidates from partner Web sites. It achieves growth through affiliate partnerships that host job searches on affiliated Web pages, such as Google, MSN, AOL, *USA Today,* Earthlink, BellSouth, and CNN. Job posting is the primary activity, sold together with or separately from resume searches.
- **Passive recruitment:** The second generation of online recruitment locates candidates who are not necessarily looking for jobs but who could be convinced to move to a new position if the right opportunity was presented. The most recognized competitors in this category include Jobster, LinkedIn, and H3 (Appendix B).

3.4. Company Analysis

PeopleAhead's mission is simple: improve people's lives through career advancement. PeopleAhead recognizes that career advancement means many things to many people and provides a fresh perspective on career networking that is flexible yet powerful:

- **Users are not alone:** Finding a job is not easy. Why search solo? PeopleAhead unites groups of friends, coworkers, and mentors to create natural, team-based career discovery.
- **Job posting is not natural:** People spend countless hours searching job listings and posting resumes, only to be overlooked because their writing style or resume format does not match an overburdened recruiter's preference. Good people, not resumes, make great companies. PeopleAhead's TrueMatch technology matches the right people with the right position. No posting, no applying—just good, quality matches.

If PeopleAhead chooses to adopt a competitor-based pricing strategy (see Chapter 14), detailed information about how other recruitment firms work will be mandatory.

Information about competitors' revenues, customers, growth, and so forth often is available publicly through a variety of sources.

For information that may not belong in the main text, an appendix offers an effective means to provide detail without distracting readers.

This section offers the "product" component of the market/product/customer analysis. Because PeopleAhead's product is mostly a service (see Chapter 13), it focuses on some intangible features of its offering.

- **Professionals being professionals:** There is a place online for social networking, pet networking, and music networking. So why is there no outlet for career networking online—the activity that consumes the majority of our professional lives? PeopleAhead is a place where professionals share their experiences, achievements, and objectives with other professionals that care and can be found by employers who value their professionalism.

3.5. Customer Analysis

PeopleAhead's R&D efforts show that the impetus to improve recruitment effectivity is pervasive and that unmet needs revolve around a few core issues: the ability to find qualified talent, establishing a fit between the candidate and the company culture, verifying the candidate's career progression, and working quickly and cost effectively. The following customer characteristics represent ideal attributes that align with PeopleAhead's service offering. This information might be used in conjunction with the Marketing Strategy.

3.5.1. Business Customer

- **Industry:** Because companies that value human capital are more likely to take a chance on a start-up that promotes professional development, the broadly defined professional services industry, including insurance, banking, and consulting, is the primary focus.
- **Functional area:** PeopleAhead's system identifies "people" people, so positions that require human interaction are more aligned with system capabilities than those with stringent skill requirements, sets such as programming or accounting.
- **Size:** Large businesses (>1,000 employees) have high volume requirements and demand vendors with proven track records; small businesses (<25 employees) hire fewer people and may not justify acquisition costs. PeopleAhead aligns best with medium-sized customers.
- **Hiring need:** PeopleAhead serves two types of searches very well: those with too many applicants and those with too few applicants. By drawing applicants that most systems overlook and delivering only the most qualified applicants, the system assures the right candidate is identified quickly.

3.5.2. Individual Member

- **Background:** People who value professional development and are familiar with computer networking technologies; most are likely college educated, motivated by career success, and aware of their professional competencies/deficiencies.
- **Situation:** Members should have a professional development plan to share with others who can help them achieve their objectives—likely people who are inquisitive about their professional future and not content with their current situation. The common industry terminology for this group of people is "poised candidates."
- **Outlook:** Proactive people who research, plan, self-educate, and talk about their career. Probably the clearest example of proactivity is a student who devotes time, effort, and financial resources toward career advancement.

The last—and some would say most important—piece of the analysis puzzle: customers.

Although the introduction to this appendix and the plan's organization suggest that analyses of competitors, products, and customers are separate, as this plan shows, a firm usually cannot address one without considering the other. Here, in the "customer" section, the plan notes what its competitors fail to do and therefore why it offers a more valuable service.

Understanding a target customer is not just about numbers. PeopleAhead tries to consider what customers think and feel when searching for jobs too.

4. Marketing Strategy

4.1. Market Segmentation

4.1.1. Business Customers

- **Small enterprises.** Businesses with 10–99 employees. Companies with fewer than 10 employees are categorized as "Very Small Enterprises" and will not be a primary target market.
- **Medium enterprises.** Businesses with 100–1,000 employees.

4.1.2. Individual Members

- **Senior college students.** Students in the process of searching for a first career.
- **Graduate program students.** Mid-career candidates searching for new career opportunities, such as internships, part-time during enrollment, or full-time after graduation.
- **Current employees.** Persons who are currently employed but are poised to locate better career opportunities.
- **Unemployed.** Persons searching for jobs not included in previous segments.

4.2. Target Market

PeopleAhead plans to focus resources on small to medium enterprises (SMEs) in the New England metro market, including Boston, Providence, Hartford, Stamford, Norwalk, Worcester, and Springfield. Online recruitment companies compete for national recruitment spending, but most job seekers are locally based, so market penetration is possible by covering a single geographical location. By maintaining this focus, PeopleAhead will be better equipped to build a critical mass of users that represent the job-seeking population and thus improve both users' and customers' experience, customer service, and the use of financial resources.

4.3. User Positioning

To the proactive professional, PeopleAhead is career advancement done right—providing a platform to discover, plan, and advance careers by uniting friends, coworkers, and mentors with companies searching for the right talent.

5. Marketing Mix

5.1. Products/Services Offered

The first planned offering is **group profiling:** users self-associate with groups to share development plans. Access to groupings is permission based and similar to social networking. Members will be able to share professional experiences with people they know. Group profiling may prompt "voyeur" networking, such that members join to view the profiles of the people they know.

PeopleAhead will then open **group profiling to business customers,** who will be granted access to groups of members to target people they want to hire.

The next added feature will be **user feedback** on professional development plans. People-Ahead will track data from successful member profile matches to provide feedback for members who have not been matched successfully.

The plan continues with the same segmentation throughout. Here the plan discusses targeting and what makes each segment attractive.

By already identifying key markets in the previous section, the plan provides a foundation for a more specific targeting statement in this section.

The final step in the STP process: Positioning for the segmented, targeted market.

PeopleAhead's mission

Given its own section in this plan, a discussion of the marketing mix constitutes a key element of the strategic planning process (see Chapter 2).

According to well-known marketing concepts, the marketing mix consists of the four Ps: product (service here), price, place (distribution here), and promotion.

The product (service) offering must establish the value for consumers: Why should they expend effort or resources to obtain the offering?

5.2. Price

In addition to a basic pricing schedule, PeopleAhead will offer bulk pricing and contract pricing to business customers to satisfy unique customer needs. The pricing model is expected to remain constant, but customer feedback will be analyzed to ensure alignment with their requirements.

Continuing the new customer acquisition plan, PeopleAhead will encourage new trials by offering promotional pricing to new customers.

5.3. Distribution

- **PeopleAhead Challenge:** The PeopleAhead Challenge will act as a primary user acquisition strategy. Selection will be focused on successful target segments demanded by customers.
- **Direct sales:** Direct customer contact is the preferred method of communication during the first six months. Telesales is the anticipated eventual sales model, due to reduced costs and quicker customer sales cycle, but it limits intimacy between the customer and PeopleAhead. During the initial stages, intimacy and excellent customer service are more highly desired than reduced cost, and direct sales achieves that objective.
- **Industry events:** Attendance at HR industry and recruitment events will supplement direct sales efforts.
- **Challenge groups:** Word-of-mouth distribution by PeopleAhead members.

> Making the product (service) available where and when consumers want it may seem somewhat easier for PeopleAhead because of the vast development of the Internet; however, the firm still needs to consider how it can ensure people know where and how to access its offering.

5.4. Promotion

- **Public profiling:** When the product is ready, with proper precautions for protecting competitive advantages, PeopleAhead can increase its Web presence. Strategies include contributing articles to recruitment publishers, writing op/ed pieces, public profiling of the founders on Web sites like LinkedIn, Ziggs, and zoominfo, and blogging.
- **Blogger community testimonials:** Influential users of blogs will be invited to try the system and be granted "exclusive" access to the inner workings of the site. A subsequent linking blitz will put opinion pieces in front of recruiters, job seekers, and the investment community.
- **Strategic alliances:** PeopleAhead offers a product that complements the services offered by many large organizations. Partner opportunities exist with

  a. Universities, colleges, academic institutions
  b. Professional associations, clubs, industry affiliation groups
  c. Online associations, groups, blogs
  d. Professional services firms, outplacement firms, and executive search firms

Strategic alliances serve multiple purposes: They can help PeopleAhead increase public exposure, increase the user base, expand product offerings, and increase revenue opportunities. These benefits will be considered and partnerships proposed prior to the official launch. For strategic purposes, PeopleAhead prefers to focus on product development in the near term (3 months) and then reassess potential alliances after system efficacy has been proven.

> The plan offers a specific time frame, which recognizes the potential need to make changes in the future, as the market dictates.

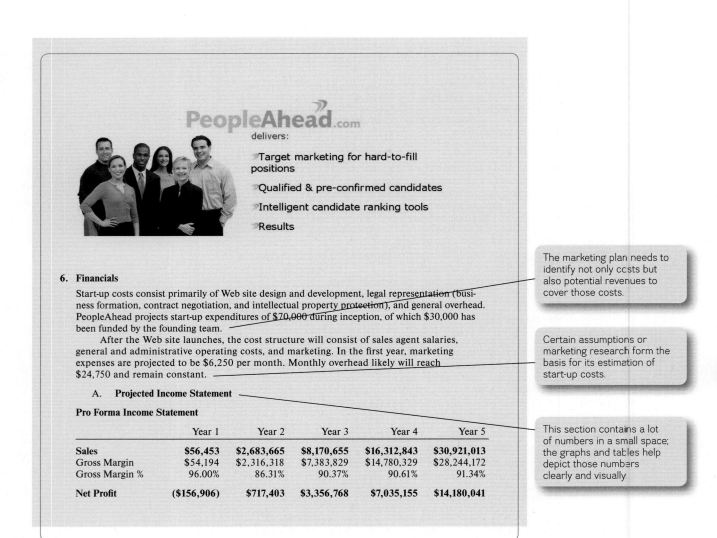

PeopleAhead.com delivers:

» Target marketing for hard-to-fill positions

» Qualified & pre-confirmed candidates

» Intelligent candidate ranking tools

» Results

6. Financials

Start-up costs consist primarily of Web site design and development, legal representation (business formation, contract negotiation, and intellectual property protection), and general overhead. PeopleAhead projects start-up expenditures of $70,000 during inception, of which $30,000 has been funded by the founding team.

   After the Web site launches, the cost structure will consist of sales agent salaries, general and administrative operating costs, and marketing. In the first year, marketing expenses are projected to be $6,250 per month. Monthly overhead likely will reach $24,750 and remain constant.

   A.   **Projected Income Statement**

Pro Forma Income Statement

	Year 1	Year 2	Year 3	Year 4	Year 5
Sales	**$56,453**	**$2,683,665**	**$8,170,655**	**$16,312,843**	**$30,921,013**
Gross Margin	$54,194	$2,316,318	$7,383,829	$14,780,329	$28,244,172
Gross Margin %	96.00%	86.31%	90.37%	90.61%	91.34%
Net Profit	**($156,906)**	**$717,403**	**$3,356,768**	**$7,035,155**	**$14,180,041**

The marketing plan needs to identify not only costs but also potential revenues to cover those costs.

Certain assumptions or marketing research form the basis for its estimation of start-up costs.

This section contains a lot of numbers in a small space; the graphs and tables help depict those numbers clearly and visually.

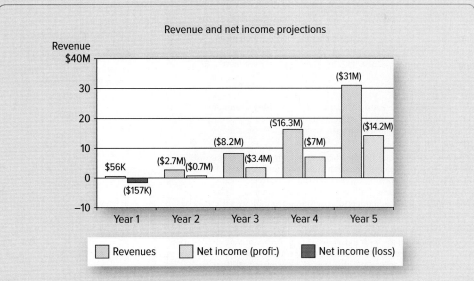

Revenue and net income projections

Revenue
$40M

($31M)
30
20   ($16.3M)   ($14.2M)
10   ($2.7M)   ($8.2M)   ($7M)
$56K   ($0.7M)   ($3.4M)
0
($157K)
−10
Year 1   Year 2   Year 3   Year 4   Year 5

☐ Revenues   ☐ Net income (profit)   ■ Net income (loss)

7. Implementation Plan

The launch of PeopleAhead will use a phased approach, beginning with building brand awareness. Brand awareness should be developed through the founders' visible presence at professional events, online searches, membership in professional associations, networking, and strategic alliances. This visibility will help gain investment capital.

7.1. Objective—Growth

- During the first six months of commercial availability, the primary objective is to expand both the user and customer base to maintain a 100:1 user to customer ratio.
  - **Business customers:** Sign 24 regular customers and 72 occasional customers. Execute 117 position matches.
  - **Individual members:** Convert 10,000 people to PeopleAhead members.

7.2. Marketing Objectives—Growth

- **PeopleAhead Challenge:** Pursue groups that were effective during beta trial and represent a cohesive set of profiles. Expand and refine the Challenge to reflect lessons learned.

- **Increase member networking activity:** Increase user numbers through networking initiated by existing members. Improve user experience to promote networking.

- **Increase profile completeness:** Increase user engagement with platform.

- **Generate traffic.**

- **Public relations campaign (PR):** Increase awareness of PeopleAhead brand through concentrated PR efforts directed at the target market of customers and users.

> This plan divides the objectives into three categories: overall objective, marketing, and financial. Although this is a marketing plan, it must also include other aspects that influence marketing, such as financial status.

7.3. Financial Objectives

- **Efficient marketing expenditures:** 9,000 target users (10,000 year-end total − 1,000 during beta) × $5.00 target acquisition cost = $45,000 budget.
- **Revenue:** $482.50 per position × 117 positions = $56,452.50 revenue.

7.4. Key Success Factors

- **Economical marketing to relevant constituents:** PeopleAhead needs to establish communication (distribution) channels that pinpoint relevant constituents in a manner consistent with mission values. Limited by resources, chosen channels must aggregate many relevant eyes with free, minimal, or deferred costs involved.
- **Crafting of brand identity:** The contrast between PeopleAhead and competitors lies not only in product differentiation but also in the company's mission statement and delivery. One-time job search is available from thousands of online recruitment sources. Social networking has been covered from diverse angles, attracting many different audiences. The challenge is to associate www.PeopleAhead.com and TrueMatch technology with "career advancement done right." The goal is to become the only company that a person thinks of for long-term career discovery, advancement, and development.
- **Efficient value delivery:** The base of customers (both individual and business) needs to receive the proposed value in a timely manner, with consideration given to quality versus quantity of results, alignment with existing objectives, and overall experience with the PeopleAhead brand.
- **Critical mass of business customers and individual users:** The matching process requires that both customers and users exist in the system from the outset of commercialization. This need brings to the forefront the "chicken and egg" scenario; establishing either customers or users requires the other constituent to exist already. The exact number that constitutes "critical mass" ranges from 100 users per position to 10 users per position, depending on compatibility between each constituency.
- **System effectivity:** The ability of PeopleAhead's TrueMatch software to provide relevant candidate recommendations is critical. The effectiveness of the software depends on the algorithms that match users with positions and the networking protocol that initiates recommendations between users and the people they know. Proposing an inappropriate match could jeopardize the credibility of the system.
- **Intellectual property (IP) strategy:** PeopleAhead is engaged in two primary segments of online enterprise: online recruitment and social networking. Existing competitors have made many efforts to protect their methodologies through U.S. patents. However, precedent has not been established for the legal assertions made by these companies. As a result, PeopleAhead will assume an offensive IP strategy, consisting of diligent IP infringement review, patent application where appropriate, and aggressive trade secret protection of best practices.
- **Financial support:** The founders' investment is sufficient to form the business core and take delivery of PeopleAhead's Web site and software. Financial support will be required to fund operations, execute the IP strategy, and secure customers and users to meet financial targets. Without funding, PeopleAhead will not be able to proceed beyond the product development stage.
- **Sales process:** PeopleAhead's business model requires the acquisition of both business customers who have available positions and users who will be matched with those

By offering quantitative, direct goals, PeopleAhead ensures that it can measure its progress toward those goals.

positions. These two constituents may be reached through different sales processes without overlap.

8. Evaluation & Control

PeopleAhead will evaluate user profiles to identify sets of profiles that are valuable to new business customers, which will aid in the selection of subsequent target market customers.

8.1. Business Customers

Face-to-face meetings, phone conversations, and e-mail survey contacts with people from a range of industries, company sizes, and functional areas provide a means to (1) build relationships with prospective customers, (2) understand customer needs, and (3) ensure alignment between PeopleAhead's product and customers' recruitment preferences. A summary of the key findings is listed here:

- **Employee fit:** Will the applicant fit our corporate culture? Will the applicant fit with the team we're considering? Will the applicants' competencies fit with the position requirements?

- **Pay for performance:** Objections to recruitment services focus not on price (though it is a consideration) but rather on lack of performance.

- **Unqualified applicants:** Many people who want a job apply, whether they are qualified or not. Recruiters then must scan resumes and weed out unqualified applicants instead of getting to know the qualified applicants.

- **Hard costs vs. soft costs:** Most companies track the recruitment costs of hiring providers, but few measure the time costs of hiring, opportunity costs of hiring the wrong employee, or productivity costs of leaving a position unfilled. Recruitment performance must be easy to measure. Value selling is difficult in the human resources departments.

- **Valuable recommendations:** Most recruiters use online recruitment as a necessary but ineffective means of candidate sourcing, secondary to recommendations. Recommendations include the recommender's judgment of the candidate's fit with the available position.

8.2. Individual Members

Periodic surveys of various prospective users of online recruitment services indicate (1) current services, (2) methods that work well, and (3) biggest problems with online recruitment providers. The following is a qualitative summary of the key findings:

- **Willingness to try:** Careers are important to people; they are averse to spending time uploading resume information to online recruitment Web sites only because of the lack of perceived value. They will spend time when the career opportunities are perceived as valuable.

- **Frustration:** Job seekers are frustrated with available online recruitment providers. Networking is the favored method for career advancement.

- **Lack of differentiation:** Regardless of the qualifications a job seeker possesses, it is difficult to make them evident in a traditional resume.

- **Motivation shift over time:** Early professionals are motivated by financial rewards. Mid-career professionals recommend people because it helps the people they know. Late-career professionals hope to improve their own job search opportunities.

Appendix A. Organizational Chart of PeopleAhead

Appendix B. Competition: Passive Recruiters

The evaluation section retains the segmentation scheme established previously between business customers and individual members.

Additional useful information that might clutter the plan should appear in an appendix, but is not included in this illustration.

©Tharanat Sardsri/Shutterstock

LEARNING OBJECTIVES

After reading this chapter, you should be able to:

LO3-1 Describe the 4E framework of digital marketing.

LO3-2 Examine the seven critical elements of online marketing.

LO3-3 Understand the drivers of social media engagement.

LO3-4 Understand various motivations for using mobile applications.

LO3-5 Recognize and understand the components of a digital marketing strategy.

CHAPTER 3

DIGITAL MARKETING: ONLINE, SOCIAL, AND MOBILE

igital marketing and social media have revolutionized how companies communicate with, listen to, and learn from customers. The influence is far-reaching, whether firms are selling online or in stores, providing services or products, or dealing primarily with consumers or business customers. Modern listening and analysis tools allow firms to identify salient, pertinent trends and customer input, such that they can provide personalized assistance to meet customers' needs.

There may be nothing more personal than people's personal appearance. Accordingly, L'Oréal works hard to leverage the power of digital marketing to ensure that "we are . . . useful wherever our customers need us," providing tips and tools to help them select hair color products, find makeup tips, and interact with others for inspiration.[1] Noting that digital and mobile channels enable anyone to play around with images of themselves with various hairstyles or colors, L'Oréal has sought to integrate these options with its existing marketing, while also being at the forefront of new technology-enabled options.[2] With the Makeup Genius app, it enables people to scan their own faces, then obtain recommendations for different cosmetic products or mixes of shades.[3] The app considers approximately 60 facial characteristics, but it also tracks what consumers do when they are using it. In turn, it can provide personalized, customized recommendations. With these insights, L'Oréal gains critical, detailed information about what the approximately 20 million users of the app want and need.

Leveraging these data represents a second key development that L'Oréal pursues with its digital marketing efforts. With the realization that most customers start searching online, the company is collaborating with Google to determine which specific questions they have when they start their search.[4] The insights they gain reveal that a key target audience are people who want to try contouring but lack the time or dedication to spend hours learning how to do it. The launch of the company's

Maybelline Master Contour line of products therefore coincides with the release of a series of videos on YouTube that provides quick tips, promising people they could get a great contour in just three simple steps. The distinct videos in the series are personalized to people with various skin types and colors, such that it makes the intimidating process of contouring easier and more appealing and accessible to the approximately 9 million people who watched the videos.

By showing customers videos of people who look like them, L'Oréal also embraces a third benefit of digital marketing, in that it places them in a sort of narrative or story, enabling them to imagine themselves with great contours, a stylish haircut, and a perfect lipstick color, for example. In modern marketing contexts, consumers' attention often is limited, so L'Oréal embraces the appeal of bumper ads—short messages that appear before a chosen video.[5] By giving viewers rapid but clear insights into what its products can do for them, L'Oréal engages them and encourages them to learn more. In this sense, it designs these short marketing communications specifically, then if needed, expands them into longer forms, rather than the other way around.[6] With this omnichannel approach, it reflects the interests, habits, and preferences of modern consumers.

Such personalization is central to L'Oréal's entire strategy. For example, it also is pursuing technology-supported options that enable it literally to match each person's skin tone with individually formulated foundation choices.[7] With digital marketing, it can go further and broader in all these efforts to provide value to consumers.

LO3-1 Describe the 4E framework of digital marketing.

THE 4E FRAMEWORK FOR DIGITAL MARKETING

As we will see throughout this book, digital marketing is becoming integral to every integrated marketing strategy and omnichannel communication tactic. **Digital marketing** pertains to all online marketing activities, which includes all digital assets, channels, and media, spanning not just online but also social media and mobile marketing.[8] Among the online marketing activities associated with digital marketing, website design, blogging, and search engine optimization are prominent.

Subsumed within the domain of digital media the term social media refers to online and mobile technologies that create and distribute content to facilitate interpersonal interactions, with the assistance of various firms that offer platforms, services, and tools to help consumers and firms build their connections. Through these connections, marketers and customers share information of all forms—from personal assessments and thoughts about products or images, to uploaded personal pictures, music, and videos.

The changes and advances in online, social media, and mobile technologies have created a perfect storm, forcing firms to change how they communicate with their customers. Traditional ways to market products, using brick-and-mortar stores, traditional mass media (e.g., print, television, radio), and other sales promotional vehicles (e.g., mail, telemarketing), are no longer sufficient for many firms. The presence of online, social media, and mobile marketing is steadily expanding relative to these more traditional forms of integrated marketing channels and communications.

The changing role of traditional media, sales promotions, and retail, coupled with the new online, social media, and mobile media and technology, has led to a different way of thinking about the objectives of digital marketing: the 4E framework (see Exhibit 3.1):

- Excite customers with relevant offers.
- Educate them about the offering.
- Help them experience products, whether directly or indirectly.
- Give them an opportunity to engage with the firm's digital marketing activities.

EXHIBIT 3.1   The 4E Framework for Digital Marketing

Excite the Customer

Marketers use many kinds of digital offers to excite customers, including mobile applications ("apps") and games to get customers excited about an idea, product, brand, or company. Firms actively use social networks such as Facebook, Pinterest, and WhatsApp to communicate deals that are likely to excite consumers, such as when the Red Letter Days encouraged Facebook and Twitter followers to post pictures with their mother and tell why she deserved a day off for a chance to win a free lunch at a top London restaurant.[9]

To excite customers, an offer must be relevant to its targeted customer. Relevancy can be achieved by providing personalized offers, which are determined through insights and information obtained from customer relationship management (CRM) and/or loyalty programs. To obtain these insights and information, the firm might use online analytic tools such as Google Analytics.

Qwertee has created many different ways to win free tees that include liking them on Facebook and following them on Google+, Pinterest, or Instagram. Retweet or share their comments for another chance for you to win a tee and in exchange Qwertee wins the chance at earning more customers.

Source: Quertee

Qwertee   TODAY'S TEES   TEE SHOP   PRINTS   VOTE   WIN/FREE   TALK   HELP

WIN FREE TEES!

We give away no fewer than 30 FREE TEES every week, here's how you can win...

Qwertee Weekly Free Tee Winners!!!!
Hey Guys! Here's where you can find all our new winners each week, they are announced each Friday night along with the new tees at 10pm GMT. **click here for more**

1 **Newsletter**
- We give a FREE TEE to a newsletter subscriber EVERY WEEK. Just sign up on the right now!
- We also give you a free €1/£1/$1 discount code off your next order when you sign up
- If you sign up to our daily mails (see tickbox) also you'll get another €1/£1/$1 discount code
- Newsletter readers also get all the latest news, sneak peeks of upcoming designs, InsanITEE Sales, etc!

Enter Your Email:

Sign Up for Newsletter Now!
Also sign up for Daily Update Mail, Get €1/£1/$1 discount code and never miss a tee!

2 **Facebook**
- "Like" us on the right. We give away a FREE TEE to a Facebook fan every weekend so you have a chance to win EVERY WEEK!
- "Like", "Share" and "Comment" on our posts. We give a FREE TEE to one lucky "Like'r EVERY DAY and separately EVERY WEEK!

3 **Twitter**

Tweets by @qwertee

- "Follow" us on Twitter to the right. We give away a FREE TEE to a Twitter follower every weekend so follow us now for a chance to win EVERY WEEK!
- ReTweet Our Tweets! Every time you ReTweet one of Qwertee's tweets about a new tee etc gives you another chance to win a FREE TEE that weekend.

4 **Google +**
- "Follow" us on the right. We give away a FREE TEE to a Google+ fan every weekend so you have a chance to win EVERY WEEK!
- "+1" and "Share" our posts. We give a FREE TEE to one lucky "Share'r EVERY WEEK!

The Minnesota Timberwolves excited Facebook fans by offering a chance to win tickets by posting pictures of a dunk to its Pinterest page.

©Genevieve Ross/AP Images

In some cases, location-based software and applications help bring the offer to the customers when they are in the process of making a purchase decision. For instance, Staples may provide a loyal customer a relevant coupon, based on previous purchases through his or her mobile phone, while the customer is in the store—a very relevant and hopefully exciting experience. As Ethical & Societal Dilemma 3.1 details, efforts to ensure relevant, exciting content have driven Facebook to reconsider how it presents content, potentially to consumers' benefit.

Educate the Customer

An imperative of well-designed digital marketing offers is that they have a clear call to action to draw customers through their computers, tablets, and mobile devices into online websites or traditional retail stores. When potential customers arrive at the websites or stores, the marketer has a golden opportunity to educate them about its value proposition and communicate the offered benefits. Some of this information may be new, but in some cases, education is all about reminding people what they already know. Therefore, by engaging in appropriate education, marketers are expanding the overlap of the benefits that they provide with the benefits that customers require.

Especially for efforts to market ideas, this second E of the 4E framework can be a means to improve people's well-being, along with selling the underlying concept. For example, in an effort to educate women about how to perform breast self-exams, the #KnowYourLemons campaign posted pictures of a dozen lemons, to teach people about 12 shapes and lumps they

To educate women about how to perform breast self-exams, the #KnowYourLemons campaign posted pictures of a dozen lemons, to teach people about 12 shapes and lumps they should be looking for when they check themselves for cancer each month.

Source: Worldwide Breast Cancer

Ethical & Societal Dilemma 3.1

What Really Drives Facebook: Benefiting Users or Something Else?

When Mark Zuckerberg went on Facebook on January 11, 2018, he had more to share than what he'd had for dinner. In a lengthy post, he announced changes to the way that the content on users' News Feeds would be prioritized. He promised that visitors to Facebook would see more personal content from friends and family, and less public content from businesses, brands, and media sources.

The underlying reason for the change, Zuckerberg maintained, was to benefit users. The post cited research showing that social media are good for people's well-being, as long as they enable them to feel connected. But passively watching videos and perhaps liking a post here or there, without any sort of interaction, actually might be harmful to people and their interpersonal relations. So, if Facebook prioritizes personal content, it believes it can "encourage meaningful interactions between people" and "make sure that Facebook is time well spent." The rationale makes an ethical argument: Zuckerberg asserts that Facebook is putting the well-being of users ahead of financial or performance goals. He explicitly acknowledges that "by making these changes, I expect the time people spend on Facebook and some measures of engagement will go down." The company's vice president in charge of the News Feed added to this insight, noting that Facebook makes changes to its algorithms all the time, but it was announcing this change in advance. Because the change would lead to clear differences in users' experiences, Facebook felt a responsibility to make sure people were aware of the shifts in advance.

What is less clear is how these changes will affect brand communications and marketing efforts. Certainly, some metrics of reach and measures of success will diminish; if brands' posts appear further down in people's News Feeds, they are less likely to attract likes or clicks. Accordingly, brands may need to shift their measurements, to focus more on how many shares or comments they prompt. With Facebook's new algorithms, content that gets shared or that sparks long, detailed comments in response will move up in the News Feed because those activities imply interest among users. Thus, brands need to get consumers to do more than like their

Is Mark Zuckerberg imagining a Facebook world that would enable its users to see more relevant content, or one that facilitates unethical marketers to engage in clickbait or inappropriate tactics to get clicks?

©Bloomberg/Getty Images

posts; they need to provide content so compelling and exciting that it sparks them to comment or share.

But even this revised approach still leaves room for unethical marketers to engage in clickbait or inappropriate tactics to get a reaction. The social media platform assigns higher rankings to reputable publications, yet many people enjoy the sort of silly, gossip-laced posts available from less reputable sources. Facebook acknowledges that, even with all its massive data and constant efforts to tweak the system, no optimization effort will be perfect. The changing face of news, media, and social interactions also means that it has to find a precise, constantly changing balance between requiring appropriate materials and avoiding censorship. As the News Feed vice president explained, "A lot of the problems that we're trying to tackle are complicated and will take a long time. And that's not a way of trying to absolve ourselves of any responsibility, it's more with trying to communicate that we are really committed to getting this right."

---

should be looking for when they check themselves for cancer each month. It appeared on Facebook, supporting vibrant images that meant that even people with limited literacy skills could understand the message. From that page, interested visitors could click a link to a microsite with more detailed and scientific information, but with a simple picture of lemons and some humorous content, the Worldwide Breast Cancer organization was able to market its preventive message effectively by educating people about a key indicator of women's health. The nonprofit organization also garnered massive increases in donations to support its efforts.[10]

Experience the Product or Service

Although most of the top videos on YouTube are funny, silly, or otherwise entertaining, the site's most useful contributions may be the vivid information it provides about a firm's goods and services—how they work, how to use them, and where they can be obtained. YouTube and similar sites can come relatively close to simulating real, rather than virtual, experiences. Such benefits are very common for products that have long been sold online—so much so that

Sephora maintains its own YouTube channel with dedicated videos that encourage customers to experience specific product lines, such as the "Kat Von D playlist."

©Steve Jennings/Getty Images

Wayfair engages customers with its "View in Room" feature within its mobile app that enables customers to select an item from its catalog and then, by using the camera within the app, visualize the item in their home or office.

Source: Wayfair LLC

we might forget that it used to be difficult to assess these products before buying them. But today, consumers can download a chapter of a new book to their tablet before buying it. They can try out a software option for a month before buying it. They often view tutorials on everything from how to purchase caviar to how cowboy boots are made. Being able to experience a product or service before buying it has expanded the market significantly.

For other offerings, such as services, digital marketing again offers experience-based information that was not previously available unless consumers bought and tried the product or service. Sephora has perfected the art of customer service in-store, online, and in social media. Customers know they can find beauty advice and makeovers in Sephora stores. But they can also visit Sephora.com for information. The community section contains over 60,000 conversations among Sephora customers, and to facilitate these conversational experiences, Sephora suggests a featured topic each week, asking contributors to indicate their favorite eyebrow products, for example. The how-to section contains video tutorials by customers who offer testimonials about their experiences, as well as from beauty professionals who describe how viewers can achieve similar experiences with their hair, nail, makeup, and skincare beauty tools.[11] For customers seeking an experience in other settings, Sephora also maintains its own YouTube channel featuring not only all the tutorial videos but also dedicated videos that encourage them to experience specific product lines, such as tutorials featuring products from Too Faced and Bobbi Brown."[12]

Engage the Customer

In a sense, the first three Es set the stage for the last one: engaging the customer. With engagement comes action, the potential for a relationship, and possibly even loyalty and commitment. Through social media tools such as blogging and microblogging, customers actively engage with firms and their own social networks. Such engagement can be positive or negative. Positively engaged consumers tend to be more profitable consumers. Such promising outcomes are part of why Gucci, when it wanted to engage with a younger audience, used a meme-based campaign and sought to leverage the popular catchphrase "that feeling when . . . " by creating a #TFWGucci hashtag. A meme reference to Arthur (the aardvark) was up to the moment, such that the 2 million cool kids who understood the reference and liked the post on Instagram sensed a closeness to the brand that they might not have imagined previously.[13]

Another creative example of customer engagement comes from Wayfair, which sells close to 10 million products for the home, including everything from furniture to bedding. Its "View in Room" feature within its mobile app enables customers to select an item from its catalog and then, by using the camera within the app, visualize the item in their home or office.[14]

But negative engagement has the potential to be even more damaging than positive engagement is beneficial. Many companies also seek to leverage the viral appeal of hashtag campaigns, sometimes without thinking through the potential consequences. When McDonald's launched a Twitter

Buy it
Buy it in just a few taps, right on Pinterest

Pay with Apple Pay™ or credit card

campaign to highlight its supply chain, using the hashtag #McDStories, the vagueness of the hashtag allowed consumers to move the conversation in a very different direction, sharing horror stories about their negative experiences eating at the fast-food chain.[15]

Furthermore, social media engagement is moving past talking with companies, as the Wheel of Social Media Engagement that we discuss in a subsequent section reveals. After years of watching users express their deep desire to purchase the products highlighted on their sites, the social media powerhouses Pinterest and Instagram are adopting new initiatives to facilitate purchase transactions. "Buy buttons" enable users to click on a featured post or picture to initiate a sales process. On Instagram, the button is similar in function to the Facebook buy button. Advertisers on the site can include buy buttons in their ads, and when users click, the button links them to an external website where they can complete their purchase. The process is a little different on Pinterest. The presence of "buyable" pins signals to users that they may click on the link to receive detailed information about available colors, sizes, and other information. If they choose to purchase, the order goes directly to the merchant without ever taking the user off the Pinterest site. In a recent survey, 93 percent of Pinterest users—or pinners—noted that they would like to use the site to make their purchases. However, these links are unpaid thus far, so Pinterest will not earn any revenues on the transaction. Both Instagram and Facebook instead can leverage advertising dollars to support their buying capabilities.[16]

To engage its customers, Pinterest uses "buyable" pins, which signal users that they may click on the link to receive detailed information about products.

Source: Pinterest

> ## PROGRESS CHECK
>
> 1. What are the 4Es?
> 2. What social media elements work best for each of the 4Es?

ONLINE MARKETING

LO3-2 Examine the seven critical elements of online marketing.

As a primary element of digital marketing, online marketing might be the most familiar and well-established. And it continues to grow rapidly, expanding into innovative new marketing activities in various electronic channels, such as websites and thought-sharing sites, which are more widely known as blogs. Nearly all manufacturers, retailers, and service providers in operation today have created and maintain websites, blogs, and a social media presence (such as on Facebook or Twitter) to enable customers to interact with them over the Internet. Arguably the most powerful and influential online marketer in the United States, the

Adding Value 3.1   How Amazon's Website Creates an Entire Marketing Universe[ii]

Across nearly every product and service category, marketers and advertisers are experiencing a revolution in the way they conduct business, revising their own marketing strategies and core goals to ensure that they fit with Amazon's platforms, capabilities, and restrictions.

For example, product manufacturers increasingly devise sophisticated campaigns for the product pages on Amazon's main site. The expanded, detailed information and editorial content seek to provide browsers with more insights into the offering, and attractive photographs give the pages the feel of glossy magazine spreads. Noting that 56 percent of shoppers start their product searches on Amazon, such initially appealing communications are critical to the advertisers' future success.

To encourage more consumer reviews, marketers also have come up with innovative incentives. Company representatives of firms selling on Amazon are carrying their portable devices in stores while they are doing new product tests, so if a willing customer enjoys the new product, he or she can not only purchase the item but also review it, on the spot, on its Amazon page.

Amazon's influence spreads far beyond its increasingly important URL. New marketing innovations are emerging for the Echo service, such that Alexa can prompt consumers to purchase various items. The device might suggest replenishment of a previously ordered item, facilitate the purchase of a tool that the shopper is missing for a DIY project that she or he has asked Alexa to provide instructions for completing, or even recommend alternatives to consistently purchased products and brands. Through its expanding applications, Alexa also can suggest service recommendations and place to-go orders at nearby restaurants.

On Amazon's new commercially oriented social network Spark (which seeks to combine the recommendations of Pinterest with the ease of Instagram), it remunerates influential social media actors for posting their submissions, suggestions, and reviews. On their feeds, users can tag the products that appear in their posts, linking to the sale page on Amazon. Followers then can click through to make their purchases.

In response to these growing opportunities, various consulting firms are developing departments dedicated expressly to optimizing brands' presence across Amazon. Such firms can work with Amazon's Media Group, which itself is a dedicated advertising arm that promises to help partners improve their standing in the "Amazon ecosystem," such as by revealing when consumers view their product pages, what location on the page prompts a click, and which customers buy. On its Marketing Services page, Amazon offers examples and short case studies detailing previous success stories of small companies that leveraged its power and thus earned massive returns by selling vast amounts of their products.

However, these sophisticated algorithms also can threaten to undermine any firms that are unprepared. For example, if a manufacturer asks Amazon to promote one of its products but then cannot keep up with demand, it will be penalized and is unlikely ever to receive such preferential treatment by the retailer again.

Another concern arises with regard to consumer privacy. If Amazon is granting advertisers in-depth information gleaned from its channels, will Alexa inappropriately guide buyers to purchase Brand X over Brand Y, regardless of whether it is a better option for the consumer?

But despite these issues, the trends by which Amazon is reinventing marketing appear inevitable. Since so many consumers now start their product searches on Amazon, if marketers fail to access shoppers there, they may not be able to succeed anywhere.

firm that strives to be "earth's most customer-centric company; to build a place where people can come to find and discover anything they might want to buy online"[17] is Amazon, the subject of Adding Value 3.1.

Firms use these primary online channels for a variety of goals that reflect the 4Es: informational websites that educate consumers, entertaining websites that excite them, transactional e-commerce channels to help them experience the products they sell, culminating in websites that engage with consumers. With regard to e-commerce, online, and omnichannel retailing, we provide additional details in Chapter 17; when it comes to informational, educational goals, we provide an extended discussion in Chapter 18.

As firms go about developing their online marketing efforts through their websites and blogs, they can turn to the 7C framework for online marketing (Exhibit 3.2).[18] This framework encompasses seven critical elements that marketers must consider carefully when devising an online marketing strategy and designing websites and blogs to target and appeal to both potential and current customers.

Core Goals

The basis of any marketing strategy is its goals. In general, the primary goal of any website is to engage its users by encouraging them to spend time viewing and interacting with its content. More specifically, however, the goal may be to engage the customer in commerce,

EXHIBIT 3.2 The 7C Online Marketing Framework

as exemplified by Walmart's site (www.walmart.com). Alternatively, it may be to educate the customer (or potential customer) about the product, such as by introducing a new offering using appealing, engaging content, like Hasbro's Hanazuki line and related digital content (www.hasbro.com/en-us/brands/hanazuki).

Specifically, Hasbro has embraced online marketing to reflect its core goals. To introduce this new brand called Hanazuki, it developed an entire series, just like it did when it launched My Little Pony. But whereas shows featuring the ponies appeared on television, the Moonflowers who appear in Hanazuki are available on the brand's own website and YouTube, anytime that viewers want to watch.[19] Then the advertising appearing in conjunction with the online series was matched to its content (as we discuss in the third C of the 7C framework), rather than reflecting more traditional approaches. With this online marketing approach, the company also could assess how well it was engaging and connecting with (the seventh C) customers in real time, so then it also adjusted its communications (the fifth C) to their preferences, such as adding music at specific points.

Context Elements

The second element of website design involves the traditional contextual elements, such as design (e.g., color, font) and navigation. These contextual elements must be in alignment with the target market(s). Because Walmart's core goal is to encourage purchases, its commerce-oriented website features a simple look and feel, which help consumers browse and find the products they want easily—similar to Amazon.com (its primary online competitor). In contrast, the Hanazuki page is filled with animation, movement, and bright colors, encouraging visitors to take their time exploring the different characters, watching videos, downloading apps, and perhaps shopping too. Looking closely at the design and color schemes of the websites shown here, notice that Walmart's home page aligns with its adult target market, while Hanazuki's bright, bold colors and large font are in line with its female, preteen target market.

Content

The information content on the site (text, graphic, video, and audio) is critical to being successful with the 4Es of digital marketing discussed earlier in this chapter. Marketers must continually monitor the information content they share digitally to ensure that the information is relevant to their target market(s) and creates excitement, such that they will be interested in engaging more, with both the website and the firm.[20] By providing the right content, the firm anticipates visitors' questions and attempts to answer those questions through its content. The home page is particularly important in this regard. When visitors land on this page, the firm's purpose must be clear; if not, visitors will quickly exit the site.

    It is critical that the content aligns with the target market and that content is not always directly about the firm's products or services. For example, following is a Facebook post from Alex and Ani. Notice the nature of the post. The company is not showcasing its jewelry per se, but rather providing a motivational quote that resonates with young females, its primary target market. Likewise, examine the Fidelity tweet that appeared during April when income taxes are due. Fidelity is not pushing one of its product offerings, but instead is providing much desired advice on how to lower one's tax bill. While the goal of e-commerce is to convert website visitors to paying customers, firms should resist the temptation to continually and exclusively sell, sell, sell.

    In the modern, online environment, every online channel helps customers interact with the firm. Therefore, firms not only have to present the content to feature rich information, but they also need to devise appropriate keywords to describe that content. When a user

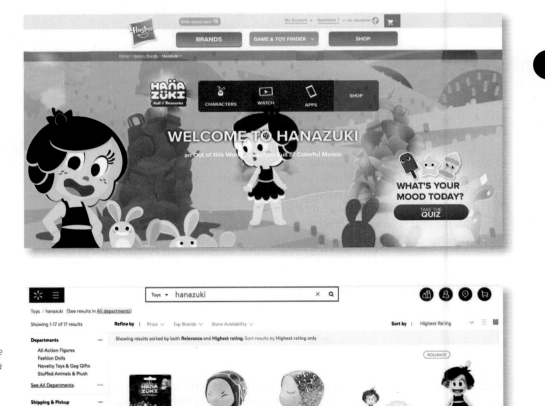

The Hasbro site (top) is focused on selling the Hanazuki brand or experience and thereby driving sales on a more subconscious level. Compare this to the Walmart website (bottom), which is more traditionally focused on selling Hanazuki merchandise with little concern for the brand itself.

(Top) Source: Hasbro.com; (bottom) Source: Wal-Mart Stores, Inc.

The content of these messages must resonate with its target market, but need not always showcase merchandise or services, as in the Facebook post from the jewelry firm, Alex and Ani (top) and the Fidelity Tweet prior to the April income tax deadline (bottom).

(Top) Source: Alex and Ani, LLC/Facebook; (bottom) Source: FMR LLC./Twitter

enters a keyword in a search engine like Google, an organic search ensues that determines the ranking that appears on the search engine's page. These rankings are not based on money obtained by firms appearing in the search. The more relevant the key term, the higher the ranking will be on the search engine's page.

But because consumers often consider only the first few entries in a list of search results, search engine marketing is becoming an important component in any firm's digital marketing strategy to improve a key term's position on the search engine's page. Search engine marketing (SEM) is an activity used in online searches to increase the visibility of a firm by using paid searches to appear higher up in search results. Paid search is similar to conventional advertising because firms pay to appear higher up in the search results, and also often pay an additional fee every time a user clicks on their entry.[21]

Community

Firms also use their websites and blogs actively to allow their customers to interact, socialize, share information, and create a sense of community by posting comments, reviews, responses, images, videos, and suggestions for new products or services.

Basketball player Steph Curry may be more influential on Twitter than the firms he tweets about, like Under Armour.

©Visual China Group/Getty Images

Thought-sharing sites are particularly effective for creating a sense of community, whether they take the form of personal, corporate, professional, or micro blogs. The different types of blogs have varying degrees of efficacy with regard to the 4E framework of digital marketing depicted in Exhibit 3.1.

Whereas they previously might have been confined to a journal or diary, kept hidden in a person's room, blogs (from "weblog") or microblogs (e.g., Twitter) allow people to share their thoughts, opinions, and feelings with the entire world. Personal blogs are created by and usually for individuals, with relatively few marketing implications.

But for firms, corporate blogs created by the companies themselves are central to their digital marketing efforts. These blogs can *educate* customers as they discuss their products or services, and create *excitement* when they promote special offers. Although they do not have control over customers' posts, and sometimes the customers' posts are negative, this two-way dialog with end users is very *engaging*. For example, the American Express Open Forum site invites business experts to share their wisdom in various posts. Because the information is so engaging and educational, the site draws many visitors, and though American Express does not create the content (or, hopefully, have to pay for it), it retains editorial control.[22] Corporate blogs can also post videos that are not only educational, but also help customers simulate the *experience* of using the product or service.

Professional blogs instead are written by people with some particular expertise, who review and give recommendations on products and services. Marketers often offer free products or provide modest remuneration to top-rated professional bloggers in the hopes of getting a good product or service review. Marketers have less control over professional bloggers than they do their own corporate blogs. But consumers seem to trust professional bloggers' reviews—except when they realize that professional bloggers are being compensated for positive reviews. Similar to corporate blogs, professional blogs can be *exciting* and *educational* by exposing customers to the nuances of different products or services. They are also excellent *experience*-creating mechanisms when, for instance, these bloggers post videos of themselves or others using the products or experiencing the service. These factors taken together with customers' ability to post responses to the blogs make this community development mechanism very *engaging*.

Influential bloggers can make all the difference. Steph Curry is great on the basketball court, but his activities on the web help establish his reputation as a reliable source of information, leading brands as varied as Under Armour and Brita to seek him out to share information about their products.[23] Under Armour might have half a million Twitter followers,[24] but Steph Curry has 3.4 million.[25] As part of his partnership, in his Twitter profile and cover pictures, Curry sports Under Armour gear. In parallel, Under Armour's Twitter cover picture features Curry prominently.[26]

Another way to build a community is by crowdsourcing, in which users submit ideas for a new product or service, and/or comment and vote on the ideas submitted by others. For example, LEGO allows individuals to upload ideas for new LEGO products.

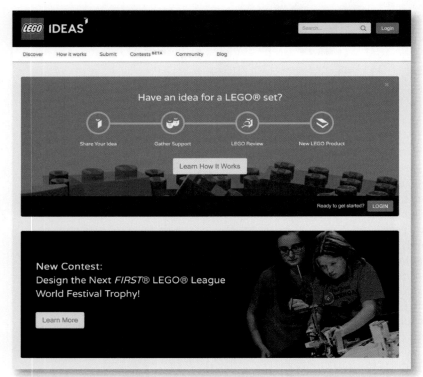

LEGO uses crowdsourcing in which individuals upload ideas for new LEGO products. A portion of the sales of the chosen products are shared with whoever submitted the design.

Source: The LEGO Group

The ideas receiving a large number of votes are reviewed by LEGO's product design team, and if approved, a portion of the sales are shared with whoever submitted the design.[27]

Communication

Digital communities rely on clear, helpful, meaningful content (the third C). The communication vehicles that appear on any website or blog determine how effectively the firm can interact with, educate, and engage site visitors. Virtually all websites provide a mechanism for customers to communicate with them through live chat, instant message, telephone, or e-mail. The various types of blogs described in the previous section also can engage consumers by providing a compelling platform for two-way communications. In particular, Twitter continues to evolve as the preferred method for many people to interact with firms, to inform them about concerns or complaints. A thorough discussion of these methods of communicating digitally with customers is found in Chapter 18.

Commerce[28]

When it comes to actual purchases, consumers exhibit varying preferences for the types of digital marketing tools they want to use. Some consumers rely on websites; others want a mobile app that enables them to shop quickly. Yet despite the predominate use of apps for checking social media or the weather, desktop usage is greater, and conversion rates are higher, for online purchases.[29] Many people might start searching online but then visit a physical store in person for their actual purchase. The most loyal customers use multiple channels. Customers thus demand that firms offer them a range of options, consistently and constantly, so that they can pick and choose the channel from which to purchase at any specific time.

Sephora, the specialized beauty product retailer, has developed innovative methods for capitalizing on this desire. Although it has long maintained a good reputation for its interactive website, the company remains in constant pursuit of a strategy that enables it to reach both current and potential new customers through the most channels at the most frequent times. Its mobile app, Sephora to Go, encourages customers to sign up for the loyalty program and create a Beauty Insider account, which grants them a mobile version of their loyalty card. They can check their loyalty points at any time, as well as redeem them however they wish. Furthermore, users of the Sephora to Go app can engage in any activity they would pursue in stores. The close alignment across these channels provides a seamless experience. Downloadable bar codes also are available, which can be scanned in stores. Moreover, the in-store signs encourage brick-and-mortar shoppers to take advantage of the benefits they can gain from interacting with the retailer, either online or through mobile apps. The company recognizes that "the majority of Sephora's clients are cross-channel shoppers," so it wants consumers to go ahead and use their phones while in the stores. In return, Sephora has enjoyed a 150 percent increase in the amount of mobile shopping its customers undertake.[30]

To stimulate sales, Sephora encourages customers to sign up for its loyalty program and create a Beauty Insider account, a mobile version of its loyalty program.
Source: Sephora

Warby Parker connects customers with four call-to-action buttons: inviting visitors to get started, order frames to try on at home, take a quiz, and shop online.

Source: Warby Parker

Connection

The final E of the 4E framework involves engagement; but it also might be called connection. A good website or blog engages customers and provides them with a call to action—whether to buy, post, review, comment, or share. Call-to-action buttons such as Buy Now, Learn More, or Show Your Support encourage visitors to delve deeper into a website, to explore other pages and, in general, spend more time on the site. The Warby Parker website includes four call-to-action buttons that invite visitors to get started ordering frames to try on at home, to take a quiz, or to shop online.[31]

These online marketing activities are geared to get customers to interact and engage with the firm continuously and in a positive manner (e.g., purchase, repurchase, share positive word of mouth). We discuss engagement and connection strategies, according to the "listen, analyze, and do" framework, in the last section of this chapter.

PROGRESS CHECK

1. Describe the components of the 7C online marketing framework.
2. Differentiate between organic and paid search.

LO3-3 Understand the drivers of social media engagement.

THE WHEEL OF SOCIAL MEDIA ENGAGEMENT[32]

Marketers recognize the importance of engaging customers; social media engagement offers a profitable way to engage customers by taking into account their current behavior while also setting the stage for future behavior. The growth of social media and their effects in turn stems from several related factors.

A unifying framework, the Wheel of Social Media Engagement, comprises these fundamental drivers of social media engagement as five related effects, as Exhibit 3.3 shows. In the Wheel of Social Media Engagement, we propose that the hub is a repository of past and

EXHIBIT 3.3   The Wheel of Social Media Engagement

```
                    Information

        Timeliness              Connected

                  Engagement

          Dynamic           Network
```

current social media engagements, and the circles around the wheel are the five effects that drive social media, as detailed next.

The Information Effect

The information effect is the outcome of digital marketing in which relevant information is spread by firms or individuals to other members of their social network. Information—whether because it is funny, cute, instructive, surprising, or interesting—is the key to turning the wheel. But the relevance of the information, and therefore its impact, depends on its context and the receiver. Marketers work hard to provide information that is somehow contextually relevant, such as interjecting a humorous advertisement into a social network of users who like to joke around and share funny pictures.

As we think further about the information effect and the incredible magnitude of information being conveyed through reviews, Facebook posts, tweets, Snaps, and so on, it raises the question: What can and should marketers do with all of it? The amount of information available can be overwhelming, even for the best marketers. Even when they know a lot about potential customers, marketers continue to find it challenging to create appeals that consumers embrace and to leverage the information they obtain from consumers in ways that encourage shoppers to purchase from them.

For example, BMW gained in-depth information about visitors to a popular Chinese social media site. Using those data, which included income and prior purchase behaviors, it determined which visitors were likely to be luxury car buyers

BMW gains information about visitors to a Chinese social media site to target advertising to them.

Source: BMW Group China

and targeted advertising at them. That sounds great, except that other visitors, who were not targeted, protested vehemently. By not showing them luxury car ads, they asserted, the car brand and the social media site combined to make them feel like "losers."[33]

The Connected Effect

The connected effect is an outcome of social media that satisfies humans' innate need to connect with other people. This connection in social media is bidirectional: People learn what their friends are interested in, but they also broadcast their own interests and opinions to those friends. Humans seek connections to other people, and social media have provided them with a new, easy, and engaging way to do so. In particular, people can connect by sharing different types of information, whether their location, the food they have consumed, exercises they have completed, or a news article that they find interesting. And they achieve this connection by checking in, posting a picture to Instagram, uploading a video to YouTube, or sharing a link to an article they have liked on Facebook. Brands like Mr. Clean seek to leverage this effect. The detergent company's digital marketing in the weeks before Valentine's Day implied that romance could be sparked if people would share household chores with their spouses, a promise that is both universal and appealing.[34]

The need to connect with others has been a powerful evolutionary force throughout human history, driving communities as well as civilizations, including our modern technology civilization. Today, humans are less physically connected because they shop online and have products delivered instead of interacting with the local shopkeeper, and they telecommute instead of working in an office with colleagues. But social media empower them to connect in novel ways. Some connections involve existing friends and colleagues; others refer to acquaintances who might not have been connected in an offline world or with firms, brands, or news outlets that were not available before social media created the link.

This increased connection allows consumers to seek social approval for themselves and provide social approval to others. For example, consumers click to express their liking of various posts by members of their social networks. However, the increased forms of connections created by this effect also might threaten to annoy users who start looking at their smartphones every time they ding. Markets for filters could emerge to help consumers categorize posts and updates in ways that reflect their own preferences. Furthermore, whereas different platforms currently serve distinct purposes (e.g., Facebook for personal and LinkedIn for business), these social media outlets might seek to grow by encouraging users to visit their platform exclusively, then sort the various purposes from that point.

The Network Effect

The connected effect enhances human interaction on a one-to-one basis and enables the impact of the interaction to expand exponentially. The network effect is the outcome of social media engagement in which every time a firm or person posts information, it is transferred to the poster's vast connections across social media, causing the information to spread instantaneously. That is, when a person or company posts something on social media, other people or firms in their network might repost it, as when one "shares" on Facebook. The credibility and influence of the original poster and the network partners that choose to share the post will determine the ultimate influence of the post. From a marketing perspective, people who discuss products are more likely to buy them.[35]

One way companies extend their network effects is by paying celebrities or pseudo-celebrities with large followings (i.e., bigger networks), hiring them to write posts about or upload pictures with their products. CoverGirl may have fewer than

If Katy Perry tweets a close-up of her eyelashes, lengthened using her favorite CoverGirl mascara, CoverGirl will have instantly reached all her millions of followers.

©Harry Durrant/Getty Images

2,000 Twitter followers,[36] but one of its Cover-Girls, Katy Perry, has more than 80 million.[37] If Katy Perry tweets a close-up of her eyelashes, lengthened using her favorite CoverGirl mascara, CoverGirl will have instantly reached all her millions of followers. The message here is clear: By using influencers as brand ambassadors, a firm can use the power of digital marketing to exponentially spread its message.

The Dynamic Effect

The impact of the dynamic effect of social media engagement is twofold. First, it describes the way in which information is exchanged to network participants through back-and-forth communications in an active and effective manner. This back-and-forth exchange promotes engagement, which makes consumers more likely to buy. The dynamic nature of social media is a very efficient way to get information or to resolve disputes, and can provide the firm

Coca-Cola engages customers in a timely manner by offering moviegoers a free Coke at the moment they walk into a movie theater.
©SeongJoon Cho/Bloomberg/Getty Images

with insights into how to best provide a product or service in the future. Customers can communicate their level of satisfaction with an issue and suggest further actions to be taken.

Second, the dynamic effect expands the impact of the network effect by examining how people flow in and out of networked communities as their interests change.[38] Consider a social network community that is concerned with power or energy bars. As it evolves and matures, its members develop varied interests—some want to know where to buy the best power bars, while others are concerned about the bars' health benefits. New people join the community, while others leave; and people's interests change, causing them to seek out new and different information. Because the community is dynamic, power bar social media sites can specialize to meet the needs of their varied constituents. From a marketing perspective, this dynamic effect is very powerful. Marketers can provide very specific information, which should be well received by the interested parties.

The Timeliness Effect

The timeliness effect of social media engagement is concerned with the firm being able to engage with the customer at the right place and time—that is, 24/7 from any location. To be effective, firms must, in fact, respond quickly or the timeliness effect benefit diminishes. Such benefits can be especially necessary when the marketing involves ethical issues, as Social & Mobile Marketing 3.1 reveals. Responding in a timely manner can positively impact customers' buying intentions: 24 percent of Twitter users who fail to get a quick response say they would not buy as much from the company in the future, and 35 percent of users who receive fast responses note that they would buy more.[39] Further, 70 percent of Twitter users expect a response from companies—53 percent of them within an hour! Among customers who tweet a complaint, the number who expect responses within an hour jumps to 72 percent. Responding quickly can pay off far better than a slow response in that nearly 50 percent of consumers recommend brands that respond quickly.[40]

Many customers enjoy the timely interactions with firms when they engage with them at the point of purchase. To reach customers at the right time, Coca-Cola relies on beacon technology—that is, technology that allows companies to detect where customers (who have enabled the feature) are at each moment through their smartphones.[41] Its pilot campaign offered moviegoers a free Coke at the moment they walked into the theater if they had already downloaded the appropriate app from the brand.[42]

As the Wheel of Social Media Engagement shows, intimate connections can arise between a firm and customers. Firms increasingly are not only investing time and money in creating

Social & Mobile Marketing 3.1

Just Don't Eat the Detergent! Who Is Responsible for Consumers' Risky Behaviors?[iii]

The Tide Pod challenge may be about the dumbest thing available on social media. But it's also extremely risky and quite serious, as dozens of teenagers suffer damage to their health when they intentionally ingest the small packets of detergent, despite extensive warnings on the packaging to avoid just that behavior.

Faced with a public relations nightmare, Tide has taken to social media, which is also the source of inspiration for most of the people eating the Pods, then uploading videos of themselves doing so. The company pleads with teens not to eat the detergent. It has also released a public service announcement to highlight the dangers, and it has asked other advocacy groups to help it discourage the practice. It brought in New England Patriots' Rob Gronkowski to issue a skeptical video that it posted on Twitter, Facebook, and YouTube. Then on various social media platforms, it has asked the providers to remove content depicting the dangerous behaviors.

But ultimately, there is little that Tide can do if teens, aware of the risks and dangers, choose to consume a product that clearly is not designed for human consumption. Most of them appear driven by a desire for Internet notoriety. This desire is powerful; whereas in 2017, there were 53 cases of accidental ingestions of detergent, in just the first month of 2018, poison

Whose fault is it that people, mostly young people, are eating detergent pods in the Tide Pod challenge?

©Kristoffer Tripplaar/Alamy Stock Photo

control centers reported 40 cases, many of which were not accidental. That figure represents only people who sought help for the ill effects of eating the detergent; many others simply waited out the nausea, vomiting, and gastrointestinal suffering at home.

engagement, but also in capturing engagement data. Social media posts contain rich information that a well-equipped company can mine to understand its customers better. As a consequence, firms are striving to make profitable customers even more profitable through increased engagement. The power of the Internet, mobility, computing, and analytics that harness the power of social connections all have led to a leapfrog advance in the potential to create meaningful engagement with customers. According to the Wheel of Social Media Engagement, understanding how to engage effectively with consumers thus is important for marketing managers.

PROGRESS CHECK

1. What are the five drivers of social media engagement described in the Wheel of Social Media Engagement?

LO3-4 Understand various motivations for using mobile applications.

GOING MOBILE AND SOCIAL

In the United States, 77 percent of adults own a smartphone and more than half of them make purchases on these devices.[43] Almost 200 billion apps were downloaded globally in 2017,[44] and customers spent more than $86 billion,[45] even though nearly 93 percent of apps downloaded are free.[46] Mobile app downloads are expected to grow to 353 billion annually by 2021.[47] Thus, mobile marketing is significant and growing.

As Exhibit 3.4 illustrates, there are seven primary needs that apps meet: the need to find "me time," socialize, shop, accomplish, prepare, discover, and self-express. The numbers in the inner circle represent the percentage of all interactions with mobile and social media; whereas the numbers in the outer circle represent the average minutes per month per user, and includes email, SMS messages, and voice calls.

- The most popular need is all about entertainment and relaxation—that is, "me time." People spend nearly half their time on their smartphones seeking fun, whether by playing Candy Crush Saga or watching *Stranger Things* through their Netflix app.

- Because apps enable people to stay connected with friends both near and far, specialized entrants are growing to meet people's need to *socialize*. For example, in China, the social networking app Weixin (pronounced way-SHEEN) allows users to send videos, photos, messages, web links, status updates, and news; it has been released as WeChat for non-Chinese users. Weixin has had a faster adoption rate than either Facebook or Twitter has, with more than 300 million users in only three years.[48] In 2016 Weixin users spent an average of

With more than 500 million downloads, Candy Crush Saga clearly fulfills for many people an important need for unproductive "me time."

©Blaize Pascall/Alamy Stock Photo

EXHIBIT 3.4 Seven Primary Motivations for Mobile App Usage

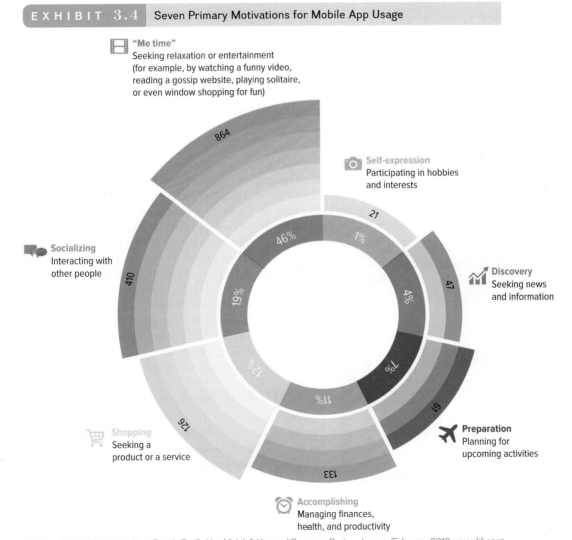

"Me time"
Seeking relaxation or entertainment (for example, by watching a funny video, reading a gossip website, playing solitaire, or even window shopping for fun)

Self-expression
Participating in hobbies and interests

Socializing
Interacting with other people

Discovery
Seeking news and information

Shopping
Seeking a product or a service

Preparation
Planning for upcoming activities

Accomplishing
Managing finances, health, and productivity

Source: "Vision Statement: How People Really Use Mobile," *Harvard Business Review,* January/February 2013, www.hbr.org.

Growing faster than Twitter and Facebook, Weixin has 300 million users, mainly in China, and allows people to send videos, photos, messages, web links, status updates, and news to friends.

©Imaginechina/AP Images

66 minutes a day on the app, surpassing Facebook's 50 minutes. Furthermore, although only 10 percent of users had over 200 contacts in 2016, almost 50 percent had more than 200 contacts in 2017.[49]

- Shoppers want to *shop* anytime they choose. In a process that facilitates 24/7 shopping called showrooming, a customer visits a store to touch, feel, and even discuss a product's features with a sales associate, and then instantly compares the prices online to see whether a better deal is available. Using the showrooming Amazon app, if the Amazon price is better, the customer can buy the product online with a single click.

- On the flip side of the need for fun, the need to *accomplish* means that people seek to manage their finances, improve their health, or become more productive through apps.[50] MyFitnessPal allows users to track their daily exercise, calories, and weight loss, and its social component enables people to post their successes. This app also can interact with Fitbit, Jawbone UP, and iHealth Wireless Scales.[51]

- Calendars, flight trackers, and trip planning apps help consumers meet their need to *prepare*.[52] For example, Google Trips helps people plan vacations by storing and organizing all their travel information, such as flight itineraries and hotel reservations. In addition it offers customized tours and maps for when you get to your destination. Google Trips links with your Gmail account to gather your travel information and stores it offline so you have access to it even if you don't have access to Wi-Fi.[53]

- When people seek information due to their need to *discover,* they now turn to weather and news apps. Flipboard produces a full-screen magazine, aggregating multiple news and entertainment sources to provide top stories, entertainment, local news, and business news personalized to your interests. Its social component also allows readers to send selected stories to friends.[54]

- Finally, people have diverse interests and tastes and thus a need for apps that allow them to *express themselves.* Tapatalk aggregates tens of thousands of interest groups into a single app, making it easy to connect aficionados of just about any interest or hobby.[55]

As you can see from this discussion, apps can meet several needs at once. Sharing an interesting story with friends via Flipboard can meet the needs of discovery and socialization. Consider the person who purchases Chinese food via GrubHub's app on her ride home; she's not only shopping, but she's also avoiding making dinner to get some extra me time. With this information in mind, apps (and advertising within those apps) can be designed and targeted in ways that better apply the 4Es. This is especially true if the app requires a user to create a profile. At that point, the user moves from obscurity to someone advertisers are willing to pay organizations to reach. For example, IBM, owners of the Weather Channel app, does not know much about its users since the app is simply downloaded. On the other hand, Puma knows its users' gender, birthday, height, weight, and exercise preferences, because its Pumatrac workout app captures this information.

Not only does Flipboard aggregate all of the news important to you in one place, its unique format also gives the app the look and feel of a printed magazine.

©Alliance Images/Alamy Stock Photo

App Pricing Models

A key decision for firms producing apps is what to charge for them. There are four basic ways of generating revenue from apps—ad-supported apps, freemium apps, paid apps, and paid apps with in-app purchases.

Ad-supported apps are free to download, but ads appear on the screen. They generate revenues while users interact with the app. Although there are many of these types of apps, the majority of app revenue is generated from the remaining three pricing models, discussed next.

Freemium apps are apps that are free to download but include in-app purchases that enable the user to enhance an app or game. In Candy Crush Saga, you get five lives to play in the game. When you lose a life, it takes 30 minutes in real-life time to get that life back. This is where in-app purchases come in. For just $0.99, you can get all five lives back immediately so you can keep playing.[56] Candy Crush Saga is estimated to earn the developer about $1 million *a day* in revenue from in-app purchases.[57]

Paid apps charge the customer an up-front price to download the app ($0.99 is the most common), but offer full functionality once downloaded. Similar to the freemium model, paid apps with in-app purchases require the consumer to pay initially to download the app and then offer the ability to buy additional functionality.

PROGRESS CHECK

1. What are the seven types of customer motivations for using mobile apps?
2. What are the four options for pricing mobile apps?
3. What are some of the most popular types of mobile applications?

HOW DO FIRMS ENGAGE THEIR CUSTOMERS?

LO3-5 Recognize and understand the components of a digital marketing strategy.

Now that we have an understanding of various digital marketing options at the firm's disposal, it is important to determine how firms should go about engaging customers through online, social, and mobile media. The three-stage process found in Exhibit 3.5 involves *listening* to what customers have to say, *analyzing* the information available through various touchpoints, and implementing (or *doing*) social media tactics to excite customers.

Listen

From a marketing research point of view, companies can learn a lot about their customers by listening to (and monitoring) what they say on their social networks, blogs, review sites, and so on. Similar to being at a party or in class, it is best to listen before engaging in a conversation. Listening can help marketers determine their digital marketing objectives. If no one is talking about a product or brand, then stimulating brand awareness or excitement may be required. The older brand, Old Spice (circa 1938), wasn't getting much attention until it initiated the campaign illustrated below.

If the conversation is negative, firms should respond immediately, possibly using a social media platform like Twitter, so that customers and the firm can communicate directly and quickly to resolve an issue. If the conversation is positive, listening will help the firm understand

---

EXHIBIT 3.5   Social Media Engagement Process

Listen → Analyze → Do

By listening to (and monitoring) digital media, Old Spice realized it needed a new message like the "Smell Like a Man" campaign.

Source: Procter & Gamble

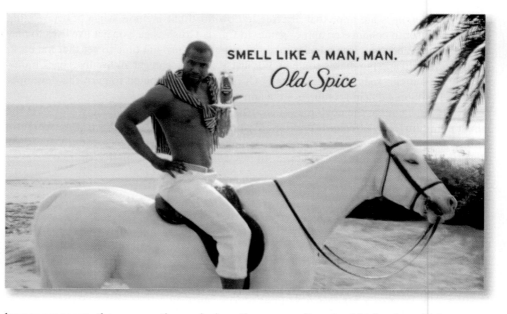

how to propagate the conversation and where the conversation should take place. If, for example, potential customers are talking primarily on LinkedIn, the firm should be there. If they are talking within an online community, perhaps a wine site, then the firm should be there, with the objective of subtly directing the community to the firm's website.

Using a technique known as sentiment analysis, marketers can analyze the content found on sites such as Facebook, Twitter, and online blogs and reviews to assess the favorableness or unfavorableness of the sentiments. Sentiment analysis allows marketers to analyze data from these sources to collect consumer comments about companies and their products. The data are then analyzed to distill customer attitudes and preferences, including reactions to specific products and campaigns. Scouring millions of sites with sentiment analysis techniques provides new insights into what consumers really think. Companies plugged into this real-time information and these insights can become nimbler, allowing for numerous quick changes such as a product rollout, a new advertising campaign, or reactions to customer complaints.

Salesforce.com's Radian6 website analyzes customer sentiment for its customers, which enables them to identify opinion trends that might warrant an online corporate response.

©salesforce.com, inc. Used with permission.

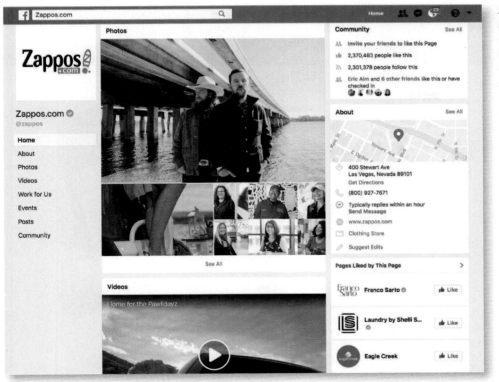

Zappos takes the information it gathers from listening to customers to design strategies that emphasize what they like most.

Source: Zappos.com, Inc

Several companies specialize in monitoring social media. For example, Radian6 from Salesforce.com offers sentiment analysis that helps its clients such as adidas, T-Mobile, and Yeti Coolers engage with their customers.[58] Using sentiment analysis techniques, it processes a constant stream of online consumer opinions from blogs, Facebook, and other networking sites. The Salesforce.com tools for managing consumer sentiment data allow companies to identify opinion trends that might warrant an online corporate response. It is also useful for identifying influencers, from where they are talking to which specific content is liked and shared the most.

Other companies perform their own analyses, effectively leveraging their existing capacities for listening to customers. Zappos is known for its remarkable customer service; accordingly, it attracts plenty of buzz about its offerings from happy customers. In its social media campaigns, it takes the information it gathers from listening to customers to design strategies that emphasize what they like most.[59]

Analyze

Fortunately, the companies that help facilitate listening also provide analytic tools to assess what customers are saying about the firm and its competitors. There are three main categories of analysis used for understanding data collected from social media.[60]

First, it is important to determine the amount of traffic using their sites, visiting their blogs, or tweeting about them. A measure used for this purpose is the number of hits (i.e., total requests for a page). More useful, however, is the number of unique visitors and page views. If, for instance, Sam visits a site once, but Sol visits it five times, there are six hits, two unique visitors, and Sam has one page view, while Sol has five page views—Sol is potentially a more important customer than Sam.[61]

Second, although knowing how many people are using a firm's social media is important, it is even more critical to learn who those visitors are, what they are doing, and what engages and excites them. For example, eHarmony works hard to understand what its clients want, both in a service provider and in a mate, as Marketing Analytics 3.1 details. To analyze these factors, marketers use metrics such as the bounce rate, which refers to the percentage of times a visitor leaves the site almost immediately, such as after viewing only one page. The bounce rate is

Marketing Analytics 3.1

Finding a Perfect Match: How eHarmony Leverages Users' Data to Identify Dates—and Their Consumption Patterns[iv]

Some of the same information that enables eHarmony, the online dating service, to connect romantic partners is exactly the same sort of detail that enables eHarmony, the marketer, to communicate most effectively with its clients and prospective customers. The company is upfront in revealing that it collects a lot of data about users—that collection is one of its selling points. By gathering so much insightful information about users, it can better match them with their perfect mates. As a result, it possesses massive amounts of information—approximately 125 terabytes of data, according to one estimate.

To leverage those data for its own benefit, eHarmony switched from an external data analysis service and brought the process in-house. Its sophisticated data analytics enable the firm's team to determine which communications media sparked responses from which users and when. Whereas previously it struggled to grasp when and why people became loyal customers depending on the channel they used to access its services, today the team gains real-time alerts about whether this person used a smartphone to access its app, or if that person relied on a tablet to visit its website. It carefully calculates the return on its investment in each media buy, according to the lifetime value of each customer, classified according to the route this customer used to access the service, as well as where and when she or he did so.

By enhancing the efficiency of its efforts, eHarmony was able to cut its marketing budget by approximately $5 million. Furthermore, clients' requests for additional information have dropped by around 75 percent, because eHarmony now knows in advance what sorts of details they want and provides it to them predictively.

These data also inform the personalized service the company provides. For example, eHarmony has learned that users who click onto the website through a display ad are more flexible in terms of their requirements in a potential mate. In contrast, users who purchase the service after seeing a televised advertisement are much more particular and specific with regard to the range of ages they will consider in a partner. For users who rely on the eHarmony app, the company

eHarmony uses its clients' data for matchmaking and more precise target marketing.
©iPhone/Alamy Stock Photo

offers a shorter questionnaire but a wider range of potential dates, because these users tend to be younger and more open-minded when it comes to dating.

Its confidence in its data analytics capabilities is pushing eHarmony's future moves as well. In addition to adding a Spanish-language service, it plans to grow internationally. With a commitment to add one new country each quarter for the next several years, eHarmony is also learning all sorts of new things about its clients. Did you know, for example, that people outside the United States are more willing to date a smoker than are members of the U.S. dating site?

---

similar to walking into a store, taking a quick look, and leaving. So, the higher the bounce rate, the less effective the site. Analyzing which pages are the most frequent entry and exit locations provides direction on how to make a website more effective. Similarly, following visitors' **click paths** shows how users proceed through the information—not unlike how grocery stores try to track the way shoppers move through their aisles. A firm can use frequent entry and exit locations and click paths to improve the way users navigate through the site so they can more quickly find what they are looking for. One of the most important data analysis tools is the **conversion rate**, a measure that indicates what percentage of visitors or potential customers act as the marketer hopes, whether by clicking, buying, or donating. Not only does it measure how well the site is achieving its goals, it can also signal a serious problem. For instance, a sudden drop in the conversion rate may signal a navigation problem or even a broken navigation path.

Third, some companies want to analyze data that come from other sites, such as measuring where people have come from to get to the company's site. Did they search through

Google or Amazon? Did they receive a referral from a friend? Which keywords did they use to find the firm? As mentioned earlier, firms can use keyword analysis to determine what keywords people use to search on the Internet for their products and services. With this information, they can refine their websites by choosing keywords to use on their site that their customers use. These keywords should be placed on the website pages, in the page titles, and in the website's URLs. Then they can assess the return on investment (ROI) made by improving the site. This would be done by calculating the incremental profit increase divided by the investment on the site improvement. For digital marketing, it is more challenging to determine ROI than for more traditional marketing applications because the revenue generated by the digital media is often not directly related to the expenditure. So, instead of traditional ROI measures, firms often examine questions such as: Does having more Twitter followers correlate with having higher sales? Do the company's Facebook fans buy more than nonfans do?[62]

These analyses require well-trained marketing managers, marketing analytic software, and sometimes help from consulting specialists (e.g., IBM, SAS, PricewaterhouseCoopers). But almost everyone seems to be turning to Google Analytics these days because it offers a sophisticated, in-depth form of analysis, all for free. For example, by simply signing on to Google Analytics and embedding the tracking code into a website, a firm can view the origin of its traffic. In particular, it can view if the origin is from an Internet search, a social media platform like Instagram or Twitter, or a third-party site. With these data, it can determine which outlets have been successful, and provide clues to direct future marketing efforts. A firm can also determine the physical location of its visitors, which pages they visited, and how long they stayed on each page. Additionally, the firm can analyze user demographic and interest data collected from their browser cookies or from their search activities if they are logged in to a Google account. Finally, Google Analytics is also highly customizable.[63]

Do

Even the greatest analysis has little use if firms fail to implement what they have learned from analyzing their social and mobile media activity. That is, social media may be all about relationships, but ultimately, firms need to use their connections to increase their business.[64] They might launch a new Facebook campaign, actively blog, or provide mobile offers.

YouTube still earns more daily video views than Facebook does, and being second is not a position that Facebook enjoys. Accordingly, it has launched a new platform for videos called "Watch." Watch marks Facebook's first attempt to make its video streaming a standalone platform. It has its own logo and dedicated space on the Facebook app and website. To incentivize advertisers, Facebook promotes Facebook videos above other content. As a result, Facebook videos get 10 times more shares than YouTube uploads.[65] However, in addition to running the communications on Facebook, the advertiser also can run them on its own websites, insert them into traditional channels (e.g., television), or pay the content provider to run the videos on its site. Such links can benefit advertisers, which obtain high-quality marketing communications designed specifically for a social media platform. They also help content providers find new clients and outlets for their creativity. But for Facebook, the benefits might be even more critical: By requiring that the videos run through its platform, it nearly inevitably increases the number of daily views it can attract from consumers.[66]

Mercedes-Benz bypassed Facebook for LinkedIn for its social media campaign since its professional audience is more in line with Mercedes' target customer base, as Adding Value 3.2 explains.

To illustrate how firms might go about undertaking such campaigns, consider the steps involved in developing and implementing a digital marketing campaign using Facebook (Exhibit 3.6).[67] These steps are not unlike the steps used in any integrated marketing communications (IMC) program. (See Chapter 18 for more details.) Assume a marketer is developing a Facebook marketing campaign for a new product that his or her firm has designed.

1. **Identify strategy and goals.** The firm has to determine exactly what it hopes to promote and achieve through its campaign. Does it want to increase awareness of the product? Is it hoping more potential customers might visit and "like" its Facebook page? Is its focus

Adding Value 3.2   Mercedes-Benz Is LinkedIn[v]

With all of the social networking sites available now, it can be difficult for marketers to decide which one to use to connect with their target demographic. Facebook undoubtedly has the most users of all social networking sites, so it might seem like the smartest choice when launching a social media campaign. However, if looking to target a specific audience, the number of users on Facebook might in and of itself be a reason not to turn to the social networking giant as a platform for a marketing campaign.

For example, when the luxury auto brand Mercedes-Benz needed to target affluent potential customers with the launch of its new E- and C-Class models, it turned to LinkedIn. Although LinkedIn has a smaller network, its users spend more online—more than 2.5 times as much as an average U.S. consumer—which likely signals their relative affluence.

Mercedes' LinkedIn ad campaign used sponsored updates and display ads with product videos. With the sponsored updates, Mercedes could reach more customers and gain real-time insights, according to sophisticated analytics, to improve its future content. Furthermore, the company was able to target professionals and senior executives and drive them to the company's website.

The high level of engagement that customers exhibited with this campaign in turn inspired Mercedes to employ LinkedIn's platform for a giveaway contest, in which the top prize was a new C-Class car. The "Driven to Perform" contest was unique; users nominated others in their LinkedIn network, based on their professional achievements and how they embodied the sophistication of

To inspire a high level of involvement, Mercedes employed LinkedIn's platform to give away a new C-Class car.
©Harold Cunningham/Getty Images

the Mercedes brand. In this sense, it represented a perfect fit with LinkedIn, which already provides a function that enables users to recommend or praise colleagues for their professional skills. The contest thus did not require LinkedIn users to change their behaviors; it simply leveraged those behaviors to target the ideal customers for Mercedes-Benz.

mainly on increasing sales of the product? Depending on what the company aims to achieve, it might focus on developing a Facebook page, creating a Facebook app, or hosting a Facebook event.

2. **Identify target audience.** The next step is to determine whom the firm is targeting. Facebook enables the firm to perform targeting that is based on location, language, education, gender, profession, age, relationship status, likes/dislikes, and friends or connections. The marketers' aim is to find an audience big enough that they reach all those who might adopt their product, but not so big that they end up trying to appeal to someone way outside their target audience as Exhibit 3.7 illustrates. For firms with multiple target markets, this analysis should be performed iteratively because both the marketing messages and digital channels likely will be different among and between the segments.

EXHIBIT 3.6   How to Do a Digital Marketing Campaign

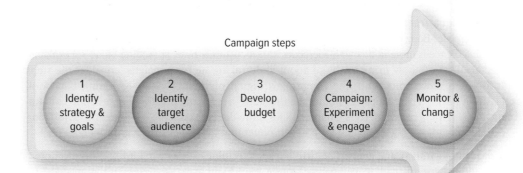

Campaign steps

1 Identify strategy & goals

2 Identify target audience

3 Develop budget

4 Campaign: Experiment & engage

5 Monitor & change

EXHIBIT 3.7	Example Facebook Targeting Choices

2. Targeting

Location

Country: (?) [New York]
- ○ Everywhere
- ○ By State/Province (?)
- ◉ By City (?)

Demographics

Age: (?) [24 ⬍] – [35 ⬍]

Demographics

Age: (?) [24 ⬍] – [35 ⬍]
☐ Require exact age match

Sex: (?) ◉ All   ○ Men   ○

Interests

Precise interests: (?) [Cooking]

Switch to Broad Category Targeting (?)

Estimated Reach (?)

266,920 people
- who live in the United States
- who live within 50 miles of New York, NY
- between the ages of 24 and 35 inclusive
- who are in the category Cooking

Source: Facebook

3. **Develop the budget.** Budgeting is key. Facebook allows advertisers to set a daily budget: Once their costs (usually per click) reach a certain level, the ad disappears for the rest of the day. Of course, this option can be risky if the firm is getting great feedback, and all of a sudden, a compelling ad disappears. Therefore, similar to the campaign content, budgets demand nearly constant review. For example, if a competitor lowers its price significantly, it might be necessary to follow suit to avoid being excluded from customers' consideration sets. In addition to an advertising and content development budget, money should be allocated for digital marketing—management tools that allow the marketing staff to post content to multiple platforms and to schedule posts throughout the week. Hootsuite's autoscheduling feature is particularly useful in this regard. It posts content based on when its algorithms have determined the majority of a firm's target market is online.

4. **Develop the campaign: Experiment and engage.** Now that the firm knows whom it is targeting, the next step is to develop the communications, including the copy and images. Here again, the process is not very different from any other IMC campaign. There should be a call to action that is clear and compelling. Strong, eye-catching images and designs are important. And the campaign must appeal to the right customers. However, an aspect that is more critical with social media than with other forms of IMC is that the images and messages need to be updated almost constantly. Because people expect changing content online, it would be inappropriate to run the same campaign for several months, as the firm might if it were advertising on television, for example.

5. **Monitor and change.** The final step is to review the success of the campaign and make changes as necessary. After analyzing their digital marketing analytics as well as their website traffic data, firms should make the necessary changes to increase their brand presence online and improve their digital conversion rate. Too often, companies collect, store, and analyze data but do not make the necessary changes to increase the ROI from their online activities.

Reviewing Learning Objectives

 LO3-1 **Describe the 4E framework of digital marketing.**

The 4E framework recognizes that marketers must excite customers with relevant offers; educate them about the offering; help them experience products, whether directly or indirectly; and give them an opportunity to engage.

LO3-2 **Examine the seven critical elements of online marketing.**

Online marketing now has a long history and is fairly established with marketing activities in various electronic channels, such as websites and blogs. There are numerous types of blogs, ranging from corporate, professional, personal, and micro.

LO3-3 **Understand the drivers of social media engagement.**

The Wheel of Social Media Engagement highlights five factors that focus on the uniqueness of social media in driving engagement. The five spokes of the wheel are the information effect, connected effect, network effect, dynamic effect, and timeliness effect.

LO3-4 **Understand various motivations for using mobile applications.**

As mobile users increase in number and diversity, the applications developed to appeal to them are spreading as well. Although there are well over a million apps, they meet seven basic customer motivations: for "me time" and to socialize, shop, accomplish, prepare, discover, and self-express. By meeting a multiple of these motivations, companies can attract large numbers of customers. When choosing how to charge for apps, firms have four options: ad-supported, freemium, paid apps, and paid apps with in-app purchases.

LO3-5 **Recognize and understand the components of a digital marketing strategy.**

Firms engage with customers through social and mobile media using a three-step process. First, they listen to the customer using techniques like sentiment analysis. Second, they analyze the data collected in the first step using metrics like the bounce rate, click paths, and conversion rates. Finally, they use this information to develop tactics to engage their customers in a way very similar to the process described in Chapter 18.

Key Terms

- ad-supported apps, 98
- beacon technology, 95
- blog, 90
- bounce rate, 101
- click path, 102
- conversion rate, 102
- connected effect, 94
- corporate blog, 90
- crowdsourcing, 90
- digital marketing, 80
- dynamic effect, 95

- freemium apps, 99
- hit, 101
- in-app purchase, 99
- information effect, 93
- keyword, 88
- keyword analysis, 103
- microblog, 90
- network effect, 94
- organic search, 89
- page view, 101
- paid apps, 99

- paid apps with in-app purchases, 99
- paid search, 89
- personal blog, 90
- professional blog, 90
- search engine marketing (SEM), 89
- sentiment analysis, 100
- showrooming, 98
- social media, 80
- timeliness effect, 95

Marketing Digitally

1. Go to https://ads.google.com to learn how to build ads and measure performance. What are some of the things that Google suggests someone consider when creating advertisements? What kinds of analytic tools does Google offer to its clients?

2. Go to HubSpot.com and check out its top case studies. How do these case studies provide insights into how listening and analytics can help firms improve their social media marketing?

3. Learn about Tide's "#TideAd" social media campaign on YouTube by searching for advertisements that use the hashtag. Which of the 4E components does this campaign leverage?

4. A student who graduates with a marketing degree likely has a good foundation for jobs that utilize social media. Go to Monster.com and search for jobs in your area using the keyword "social media." Would you be interested in pursuing one or more of these positions? Why or why not?

Marketing Applications

1. Which component of the 4E framework does Red Bull's digital media strategy leverage most frequently?

2. Using the components of the 4E framework, outline how an entrepreneur marketing low-sugar candy might apply it to his or her marketing mix efforts.

3. Suppose an herbal tea company introduced a new product called Mint-Enhanced Tea—a mint and lemon herbal tea. How should it go about creating excitement using various social and mobile media tools?

4. If you were marketing a new running shoe, what sort of mobile applications might enhance your marketing efforts?

5. Assume you work for a large consumer packaged-goods firm that has discovered that its latest line of snack foods is moving very slowly off store shelves. Recommend a strategy for listening to what consumers are saying on blogs, review sites, and the firm's website. Describe how your strategy might provide insights into consumers' sentiments about the new product line.

6. As an intern for Starbucks, you have been asked to develop a social media campaign for a new latte. The objective of the campaign is to increase awareness and trial of this new line. Use the listen–analyze–do framework to outline a new campaign.

7. You were just hired by a company that wants to produce apps that help people become healthier by exercising, eating well, and reducing stress. On which customer motivations would you recommend the company focus? Describe the app you would design, the customer motivations it meets, and why your app is the right design for your potential customers.

8. The company loves the idea for the app you suggested in the previous question, but is concerned about how it will make money on the app. Suggest a pricing model for the app and discuss why this model will maximize profits.

Quiz Yourself

1. Downloading a chapter of a new book before buying it or listening to a few seconds of a song before purchasing it are examples of which aspect of the 4E framework?
   a. Engage the customer
   b. Excite the customer
   c. Experience the product
   d. Employ the product
   e. Educate the customer

2. When developing a social media campaign, what is critical and unique about the copy and images used on social media compared to other forms of IMC?
   a. They need to be humorous.
   b. They need to be updated almost constantly.
   c. They should feature only young actors.
   d. They must appear in color (as opposed to black and white).
   e. They must appeal to a diverse multicultural audience.

(Answers to these two questions can be found in the Quiz Yourself Answer Key section.)

Chapter Case Study

IMAGES, SALES, BRANDS: HOW RED BULL USES VARIOUS DIGITAL AND SOCIAL MEDIA TECHNIQUES TO ACHIEVE ALL ITS OBJECTIVES

It isn't as if the digital social media strategy adopted by Red Bull—the energy drink that "gives you wings"—is a trade secret. Granted, the private company has a policy that discourages employees from giving interviews. But its overall strategy is clear from its actions and their outcomes. The success it has accrued from this strategy therefore isn't a matter of doing things differently from anyone else. It's a function of doing them better.

To begin, Red Bull distinguishes its goals for leveraging contacts. Is it hoping for more brand exposure, or is it pursuing sales increases? Depending on its focus, it adopts distinct, appealing methods that are specific and unique to each digital and social media platform. Then it implements these tactics consistently and comprehensively to increase the chances that they will be widely shared and recognized.

Sponsored by Red Bull, Felix Baumgartner's jump reached speeds of Mach 1.25.

©Jay Nemeth/Zumapress/Newscom

Name Recognition

Perhaps one of the most famous Red Bull events was when Felix Baumgartner (purposefully) fell to Earth from 127,852 feet up, and broke all sorts of records. His jump was from the highest height ever achieved by a human. During the 4-minute, 20-second freefall, he also reached greater speeds—up to Mach 1.25, faster than the speed of sound—than anyone else ever has. The event was a breakthrough on various levels. Baumgartner's pressure suit was the first version to be able to protect the human body in space but still enable maneuverability. To address the threat of ebullism (i.e., when liquid in the body evaporates due to high altitudes, causing a person's blood to literally boil), Baumgartner and his team derived new medical techniques with widespread applications. His parachute also adopted a new "reefed" design to reduce drifting, with clear implications for airdrops of materials and supplies.[68]

In reporting on all these remarkable feats, Baumgartner's name was mentioned frequently—though not as frequently as the project that sponsored his jump and all the technology that went into supporting it: the Red Bull Stratos project. Every official mention of the event included the full name, such that *Red Bull Stratos* often appeared as a single term. It was not just the Stratos project. It was the Red Bull Stratos project.

And what a project it was, leading to the creation of not just scientific advances but also a remarkable video. That video, taken from the camera mounted on Baumgartner's helmet, features vast, picturesque views of Earth and the sense of plummeting. Red Bull immediately made it available for people to check out at their leisure. But the real targets—the people whom Red Bull hoped would be most engaged by the video and the stunt in general—were extreme sports fanatics. These folks willingly put their bodies at risk on a regular basis to perform some cool stunt to cause their friends to marvel. For them, there may be no better stunt than having some guy fall from space.[69] In full awareness of this appeal, Red Bull made sure that the video was prominent on its website and YouTube channel. On the day of the jump itself, approximately 8 million viewers streamed the video live and in real time. Also on that day, the number of subscribers to Red Bull's YouTube channel increased by a remarkable 87,801.[70]

On Twitter, recognizing that 140 characters was not nearly enough to communicate the awesomeness of the stunt, it simply used hashtags and links to connect followers to the video, whether through YouTube or on a Red Bull site. Although Red Bull's main Twitter feed did not exhibit any notable differences, the dedicated Red Bull Stratos Twitter feed prompted more than 20,000 mentions in tweets by others on that day.

The Red Bull Stratos Facebook page featured several photos during and after the jump. Just one shot of a landed Baumgartner, still in his space suit and on his knees beside his reefed parachute, prompted more than 20,000 comments, more than 50,000 shares, and nearly half a million likes.[71]

The example of the Red Bull Stratos project and its attendant coverage through digital and social media suggests several things Red Bull did well. It knew its audience and its own goals, and it understood how different channels could help it attain those goals. To ensure that it appealed to the target audience, it engaged them in an exciting, never-before-tried daredevil experience. Moreover, it shared the scientific lessons learned through the project to give those who wanted it an education. But it also spent a lot of money to get Baumgartner to space and back down again. And that meant it needed to translate some of the brand awareness it developed into sales. Luckily for Red Bull, its social media strategy also has room for that effort.

Performance

Red Bull does not just send athletes to space. It also sponsors them on the pitch, in the form of the New York Red Bull MLS team, which plays in Red Bull Arena in Harrison, New Jersey. In one recent game, the team's star forward Thierry Henry scored yet another goal.

Afterward, he leaned, with his right arm up against the goal post and left hand on his hip. The pose, caught on camera, almost immediately became a Twitter meme as amateur photo editors placed him against a variety of backgrounds.[72]

The team was quick to move on this social media coup. It rapidly posted the photo to its website and encouraged fans to vote for it as their favorite shot of the season. Immediately above and below the encouragement to engage with the brand also appeared links that would allow fans to purchase tickets for a full season, half season, or individual games.[73]

Beyond these fun, consumer-oriented efforts, Red Bull makes sure that it has advanced capabilities for supporting the retail vendors that sell its products. For example, all its mobile sales representatives are equipped with their own tablet computers, loaded with proprietary mobile software. Thus, on visits to retail sites and vendors, the salespeople can provide the latest inventory information. They also present detailed analytics to show vendors how best to position their coolers of Red Bull products and how to line up the cans in the display case to encourage sales.[74]

Combining the Uses of Digital and Social Media

When you are as good at engaging and exciting people as Red Bull is, the next step might be to make digital social media your main focus. In a sense, it has transformed itself into a media company that just happens to sell energy drinks. Red Bull continues to sponsor extreme sporting events and stunts; it also has its own record label, which finds, pursues, and produces artists who make high-energy music.[75] On the dedicated Red Bull Records YouTube channel, it highlights these artists, then pairs their output with some of its sponsored events. For example, it creates playlists for skydiving events and X-fighters, featuring not just its own artists but also other popular musicians.[76]

Furthermore, Red Bull offers a slew of applications for smartphones and tablets, including the RedBull.com app, which presents content similar to that on Facebook and Instagram, along with a customizable feed.[77] In addition, Red Bull offers several gaming apps featuring snowboarding, biking, and car and airplane racing games, along with a "Mind Gamers" puzzle. At the same time, it provides a radio app and Red Bull TV;[78] the Red Bull TV app can be downloaded on mobile devices or streamed directly to consumers' televisions through Apple TV, Chromecast, Xbox, or PlayStation. The various channels available through this app include not just the expected coverage of all types of extreme sports but also channels dedicated to music, festivals, and original films—one of which documents the Red Bull Stratos mission, of course.[79]

This move toward a greater focus on different media channels is well in line with Red Bull's long-standing social media strategy. For example, it maintains a plethora of Facebook pages and Twitter accounts for various events and locations, yet virtually none of them ever feature pictures of its drinks. Instead, they offer exciting in-sport shots or humorous images. Fans can—and do—comment, but Red Bull rarely responds. Its primary goal appears to be establishing an edgy, entertaining, exciting image as a lifestyle brand, which it feels confident will translate ultimately into product sales.[80]

Questions

1. What social and mobile media tools is Red Bull using?

2. Evaluate Red Bull's social media marketing strategy using the 4E framework.

3. How should Red Bull assess the effectiveness of these campaigns? Describe how it should respond to insights gained by this assessment.

Endnotes

1. Marie Gulin-Merle, "L'Oréal's Digital Transformation," *Think with Google*, April 2017, www.thinkwithgoogle.com/marketing-resources/loreal-mobile-digital-marketing-strategy/.

2. Alexandra Gibbs and Tania Bryer, "L'Oréal CEO: Beauty's Future Will Be More about Technology, Quality, Formulation and Individualization," *CNBC*, January 12, 2018, www.cnbc.com/2018/01/12/loreal-ceo-jean-paul-agon-on-the-beauty-industrys-outlook-and-rise-of-digitalization.html.

3. Alanna Petroff, "Why Is L'Oréal Buying a Technology Company?," *CNNMoney*, March 16, 2018, http://money.cnn.com/2018/03/16/technology/loreal-modiface-technology-ai-artificial-intelligence/index.html.

4. Gulin-Merle, "L'Oréal's Digital Transformation."

5. Ibid.

6. Kim Larson, "How L'Oréal, a Century-Old Company, Uses Experimentation to Succeed in the Digital Age," *Think with Google*, August 2017, www.thinkwithgoogle.com/marketing-resources/data-measurement/loréal-cosmetics-beauty-brand-experimentation/.

7. Gibbs and Bryer, "L'Oréal CEO."

8. HubSpot, *Digital Marketing for Beginners*, https://offers.hubspot.com/beginners-guide-to-digital-marketing; Rob Stokes, *E-marketing: The Essential Guide to Marketing in a Digital World*, 6th ed., 2017, www.redandyellow.co.za/textbook/.

9. "Most Famous Social Network Sites Worldwide as of January 2018, Ranked by Number of Active Users (in Millions)," *Statista*, January 2018, www.statista.com/statistics/272014/global-social-networks-ranked-by-number-of-users/; Dan Hughes, "The 5 Best Social Media Campaigns of 2017 (So Far)," *Digital Marketing Institute*, April 4, 2017, https://digitalmarketinginstitute.com/blog/2017-4-4-the-5-best-social-media-campaigns-of-2017-so-far.

10. Digital Marketing Institute, "7 of the Most Impactful Digital Campaigns of 2017 . . . So Far," https://digitalmarketinginstitute.com/the-insider/14-06-17-7-of-the-most-impactful-digital-campaigns-of-2017; www.facebook.com/knowyourlemons.

11. www.sephora.com.

12. www.youtube.com/user/sephora.

13. Digital Marketing Institute, "7 of the Most Impactful Digital Campaigns of 2017."

14. https://investor.wayfair.com/investor-relations/press-releases/press-releases-details/2016/Wayfair-Mobile-App-Lets-Shoppers-Visualize-Furniture-and-Decor-in-Their-Homes-before-They-Buy/default.aspx.

15. Seth Fendley, "7 Hilarious Twitter Brand Hashtag Fails," *HubSpot*, March 12, 2015, http://blog.hubspot.com/marketing/hilarious-twitter-brand-hashtag-fails.

16. Matthew Stern, "Social Sites Move to Boost Retail Sales," *RetailWire*, June 5, 2015, www.retailwire.com/discussion/18327/social-sites-move-to-boost-retail-sales.

17. www.thebalance.com/amazon-mission-statement-4068548.

18. Dhruv Grewal, Joan Lindsey-Mullikin, and Jeanne Munger, "Loyalty in e-Tailing: A Conceptual Framework," *Journal of Relationship Marketing* 2, no. 3/4 (2003), pp. 31–49; https://arxiv.org/abs/1801.04829; J. Rayport and B. Jaworski, *Introduction to E-Commerce* (McGraw-Hill: New York, 2001).

19. Victor Lee, "Hasbro Shares Its Content Strategy behind Launching a Brand on YouTube," *Think with Google*, June 2017, www.thinkwithgoogle.com/advertising-channels/video/youtube-content-strategy-hasbro-hanazuki/.

20. Sarah Steiner, "The Marketer's SEO Playbook, 2017 Edition," *Marketing News*, February 1, 2017, www.ama.org/publications/MarketingNews/Pages/marketers-seo-playbook-2017.aspx.

21. Benjamin Edelman and Zhenyu Lai, "Design of Search Engine Services: Channel Interdependence in Search Engine Results," *Journal of Marketing Research* 53, no. 6 (2016) pp. 881–900.

22. Eric Siu, "30 Companies with the Best Digital Marketing Campaigns," *Single Grain*, www.singlegrain.com/digital-marketing/best-online-marketing-companies/.

23. Kate Stanford, "The Secret to Successful Influence Marketing? Letting Go of Control," *Think with Google*, August 2017, www.thinkwithgoogle.com/advertising-channels/video/millennial-social-influencer-endorsement-marketing/.

24. https://twitter.com/UnderArmour.

25. https://twitter.com/StephenCurry30.

26. https://twitter.com/UnderArmour.

27. https://ideas.lego.com/dashboard (accessed April 2018).

28. Dhruv Grewal, *Retail Marketing Management: The 5Es of Retailing Today* (Thousand Oaks, CA: Sage Publications, 2018).

29. www.smartinsights.com/mobile-marketing/mobile-marketing-analytics/mobile-marketing-statistics/ (accessed April 2018).

30. Lauren Johnson, "Sephora Magnifies Mobile Ambitions via In-Store Signage, Updated App," *Mobile Commerce Daily*, August 23, 2013.

31. www.warbyparker.com/ (accessed April 2018).

32. This section draws heavily from Anne L. Roggeveen and Dhruv Grewal, "Engaging Customers: The Wheel of Social Media Engagement," *Journal of Consumer Marketing* 33, no. 2 (March 2016).

33. Peter Schrank, "A Brand New Game: As People Spend More Time on Social Media, Advertisers Are Following Them," *The Economist*, August 29, 2015.

34. Hughes, "The 5 Best Social Media Campaigns of 2017."

35. Dhruv Grewal et al., "Mobile Advertising: A Framework and Research Agenda," *Journal of Interactive Marketing* 34 (May 2016), pp. 3–14; Elizabeth M. Aguirre et al., "Personalizing Online, Social, and Mobile Communications: Opportunities and Challenges," *Journal of Consumer Marketing* 33, no. 2 (2016), pp. 98–110.

36. https://twitter.com/covergirl.

37. http://twittercounter.com/pages/100?version=1&utm_expid=102679131-65.MDYnsQdXQwO2AlKoJXVpSQ.1&utm_referrer=http%3A%2F%2Fwww.google.com%2Furl%3Fsa%3Dt%26rct%3Dj%26q%3D%26esrc%3Ds%26source%3Dweb%26cd%3D3%26ved%3D0ahLKEwiv9Pr4ipbKAhUKbj4KHUnPCkkQFggoMAI%26ur.

38. "Social Media and Dynamic Social Communities," SAM (Socializing Around Media), http://samproject.net/social-media-and-dynamic-social-communities/.

39. Pamela Vaughan, "72% of People Who Complain on Twitter Expect a Response within an Hour," *HubSpot*, July 23, 2014, http://blog.hubspot.com/marketing/twitter-response-time-data.

40. Ibid.

41. H. O. Maycotte, "Beacon Technology: The Where, What, Who, How and Why," *Forbes*, September 1, 2015, www.forbes.com/sites/homaycotte/2015/09/01/beacon-technology-the-what-who-how-why-and-where/.

42. Seb Joseph, "Coca-Cola Has Taken a Step Closer to Using Beacons to Turn Location-Based Marketing on Its Head," *The Drum*, August 13, 2015, www.thedrum.com/news/2015/08/13/coca-cola-has-taken-step-closer-using-beacons-turn-location-based-marketing-its-head.

43. Lee Rainie and Andrew Perrin, "10 Facts about Smartphones as the iPhone Turns 10," *Pew Research Center*, June 28, 2017, www.pewresearch.org/fact-tank/2017/06/28/10-facts-about-smartphones/.

44. "Number of Mobile App Downloads Worldwide in 2016, 2017 and 2021 (in Billions)," *Statista*, January 2018, www.statista.com/statistics/271644/worldwide-free-and-paid-mobile-app-store-downloads/.

45. Sarah Perez, "Global App Downloads Topped 175 Billion in 2017, Revenue Surpassed $86 Billion," *TechCrunch*, January 17, 2018, https://techcrunch.com/2018/01/17/global-app-downloads-topped-175-billion-in-2017-revenue-surpassed-86-billion/.

46. "Number of Free Mobile App Downloads Worldwide from 2012 to 2017 (in Billions)," *Statista*, January 2018, www.statista.com/statistics/241587/number-of-free-mobile-app-downloads-worldwide/.

47. "Number of Mobile App Downloads Worldwide in 2016, 2017 and 2021 (in Billions)," *Statista*, January 2018, www.statista.com/statistics/271644/worldwide-free-and-paid-mobile-app-store-downloads/.

48. "WeChat vs. Weixin: For China Marketing You Need an Official Weixin Account," *Chozan*, September 6, 2017, https://chozan.co/2017/09/06/wechat-vs-weixin/; David Barboza, "A Popular Chinese Social Networking App Blazes Its Own Path," *The New York Times*, January 20, 2014.

49. He Wei, "WeChat Becomes Work Tool," *The Telegraph,* May 24, 2017, www.telegraph.co.uk/news/world/china-watch/technology/wechat-popularity-in-china/.

50. "Vision Statement: How People Really Use Mobile," *Harvard Business Review,* January/February 2013, https://hbr.org/2013/01/how-people-really-use-mobile/ar/1.

51. www.myfitnesspal.com/; Adda Bjarnadottir, "The 5 Best Calorie Counter Websites and Apps," *Healthline,* May 29, 2017, www.healthline.com/nutrition/5-best-calorie-counters.

52. "Vision Statement: How People Really Use Mobile."

53. https://get.google.com/trips/; Lori Zaino, "5 Best Apps for Planning Your Next Vacation," *The Points Guy,* February 1, 2017, https://thepointsguy.com/2017/02/5-best-vacation-apps/.

54. https://flipboard.com/; Casey Newton, "Flipboard Comes to the Web, and It's Beautiful," *The Verge,* February 10, 2015, www.theverge.com/2015/2/10/8008905/flipboard-comes-to-the-web.

55. www.tapatalk.com/; Microsoft + Startups, "Tapatalk Brings Online Forums out of the Internet Dark Ages," *Medium,* February 28, 2017, https://medium.com/@MicrosoftforStartups/tapatalk-brings-online-forums-out-of-the-internet-dark-ages-ea6ca239bf9d.

56. https://candycrushsaga.com/en/; "Candy Crush Saga," iTunes, https://itunes.apple.com/us/app/candy-crush-saga/id553834731?mt=8.

57. Motek Moyen, "Activision Blizzard: Steady Revenue Stream from King's Old Candy Crush Game," *Seeking Alpha,* January 25, 2017; "Candy Crush Saga," *Think Gaming,* https://thinkgaming.com/app-sales-data/2/candy-crush-saga/.

58. www.salesforce.com.

59. Siu, "30 Companies."

60. Laura S. Quinn and Kyle Andrei, "A Few Good Web Analytics Tools," *TechSoup,* May 19, 2011, www.techsoup.org.

61. Willem van Heerden, "The 6 Most Important Web Metrics to Track for Your Business Website," Linkedin.com, July 18, 2017.

62. Christina Warren, "How to Measure Social Media ROI," *Mashable,* October 27, 2009, http://mashable.com/2009/10/27/social-media-roi/.

63. "iNoobs: What Is Google Analytics?," http://inspiredm.com; www.google.com/analytics/features/index.html; www.advanced-web-metrics.com; Kevin Ryan, "What Can the Average Marketer Learn from Google Creative Lab?," *Advertising Age,* April 19, 2013.

64. Amy Porterfield, "3 Steps to an Effective Social Media Strategy," *Social Media Examiner,* March 1, 2012, www.socialmediaexaminer.com.

65. John Koetsier, "Facebook: Native Video Gets 10X More Shares Than YouTube," *Forbes,* March 13, 2017, www.forbes.com/sites/johnkoetsier/2017/03/13/facebook-native-video-gets-10x-more-shares-than-youtube/#679d70da1c66.

66. Brendan Ghan, "Facebook Watch Will Overtake YouTube as the Biggest Video Platform. Here's Why," *Mashable,* December 5, 2017, https://mashable.com/2017/12/05/how-facebook-watch-will-overtake-youtube-as-biggest-video-platform/#N62fQPXqM5qW.

67. Andy Shaw, "How to Create a Facebook Ad Campaign," *Social Media Tips,* September 23, 2011, http://exploringsocialmedia.com/how-to-create-a-facebook-ad-campaign/.

68. Red Bull Stratos, "Scientific Data Review," www.redbullstratos.com.

69. Rick Mulready, "The Secret to Red Bull's Media Success Is There Is No Secret," November 6, 2013, http://rickmulready.com.

70. SocialBakers, "Red Bull Stratos on Social Media," www.socialbakers.com.

71. Ibid.

72. Jack Bell, "Red Bulls' Henry Strikes a Pose, and Starts a Trend," *The New York Times,* September 21, 2013.

73. www.newyorkredbulls.com/.

74. Clint Boulton, "Red Bull Eyes 'SoLoMo' Software to Grow Business," *The Wall Street Journal,* April 30, 2012.

75. http://redbullrecords.com/.

76. www.youtube.com/user/redbullrecords.

77. www.redbullmediahouse.com/company/news/article/redbull-com-now-available-as-a-mobile-app.html; www.redbull.com/us-en/redbullcom-mobile-app-launch.

78. https://itunes.apple.com/us/developer/red-bull/id319400189.

79. https://itunes.apple.com/us/app/red-bull-tv/id364269164?mt=8.

80. David Moth, "How Red Bull Uses Facebook, Twitter, Pinterest, and Google+," *eConsultancy.com,* February 21, 2013, http://econsultancy.com.

i. Elizabeth Winkler, "What Facebook's Feed Change Means for the News," *The Wall Street Journal,* January 22, 2018; Mark Zuckerberg, Facebook post, January 11, 2018; Fred Vogelstein, "Facebook's Adam Mosseri on Why You'll See Less Video, More from Friends," *Wired,* January 13, 2018; Paul Ramondo, "Facebook Zero: The Changing News Feed and What Marketers Need to Know," *Social Media Examiner,* January 22, 2018.

ii. Sapna Maheshwari, "As Amazon's Influence Grows, Marketers Scramble to Tailor Strategies," *The New York Times,* July 31, 2017; Jack Marshall, "Amazon Lures Publishers to New Social Network by Paying Them to Post," *The Wall Street Journal,* July 19, 2017; Lauren Johnson, "Amazon Is Opening Up Its Ads Business, and Marketers See a Big Opportunity to Shake Up Search," *Adweek,* September 13, 2017; "Amazon Marketing Services," https://advertising.amazon.com/amazon-marketing-services.

iii. Sharon Terlep, "P&G Trying to Stop 'Dangerous' Tide Pods Challenge, CEO Says," *The Wall Street Journal,* January 22, 2018; Imani Moise and Sharon Terlep, "P&G Grapples with How to Stop a Tide Pods Meme," *The Wall Street Journal,* January 20, 2018.

iv. Kate Kaye, "eHarmony's Love for Data Goes beyond Dating: It's Good for Marketing Too," *Advertising Age,* February 18, 2015, http://adage.com; Samuel Greengard, "eHarmony Enhances Its Relationship with Big Data," *Baseline,* February 2, 2015, www.baseline.com; "IBM Big Data & Analytics Helps eHarmony Identify More Compatible Matches in Real Time," *IBM Big Data & Analytics Hub,* September 8, 2014, www.ibmbigdatahub.com.

v. LinkedIn Marketing Solution, "Mercedes-Benz USA Gets More Mileage from Shareable Content with Sponsored Updates from LinkedIn," https://business.linkedin.com/content/dam/business/marketing-solutions/global/en_US/site/pdf/cs/LinkedIn-MercedesBenz%20SU-CaseStudy-130919.pdfl; Andrew Adam Newman, "Mercedes Looks for Up-and-Comers on LinkedIn," *The New York Times,* July 14, 2014, http://www.nytimes.com/2014/07/18/business/media/mercedes-looks-for-up-and-comers-on-linkedin.html; We Are Social, and IAB Singapore, "Leading Social Networks Worldwide."

Quiz Yourself Answer Key

1. Downloading a chapter of a new book before buying it or listening to a few seconds of a song before purchasing it are examples of which aspect of the 4E framework?

   Answer: (c) Experience the product

2. When developing a social media campaign, what is critical and unique about the copy and images used on social media compared to other forms of IMC?

   Answer: (b) They need to be updated almost constantly.

©Editorial Image, LLC

LEARNING OBJECTIVES

After reading this chapter, you should be able to:

LO4-1 Define conscious marketing.

LO4-2 Describe what constitutes marketing's greater purpose.

LO4-3 Differentiate between conscious marketing and corporate social responsibility.

LO4-4 Describe the ways in which conscious marketing helps various stakeholders.

LO4-5 Explain how conscious leadership can produce a conscious culture in the firm.

LO4-6 Describe how ethics constitutes an integral part of a firm's conscious marketing strategy.

LO4-7 Identify the four steps in ethical decision making.

CHAPTER 4

CONSCIOUS MARKETING, CORPORATE SOCIAL RESPONSIBILITY, AND ETHICS

In the modern market, thousands of beauty and personal care products vie to be perceived as the most natural or most organic. In many cases those claims are overstated. The shampoo may be made from the same ingredients as "regular" shampoo. It's just that the bottle features pictures of natural wildflowers, for example.

In developing its Love Beauty and Planet line, Unilever has gone well beyond such a superficial approach, ensuring that a sustainability philosophy underlies every element of the products sold under that brand. From the product formulations to the packaging to the promotions used, Unilever has embraced a sustainable and environmental focus as a core element to the very essence of the brand.[1] Consider the four Ps (which we introduced in Chapter 1) as they apply to Love Beauty and Planet.

Product The products under the Love Beauty and Planet label promise to be ethically sourced and made from natural ingredients.[2] Its perfumes are vegan and never tested on animals.[3] But many brands make similar claims. To distinguish itself and establish its sustainability credentials, Unilever also has pursued innovative benefits. For example, a novel technology integrated into the hair conditioner allows it to be rinsed out of users' hair faster. (The molecules scatter when hit by water, pushing the product out of hair more quickly.) As a result, consumers can take shorter showers, which conserves water.[4] Another innovation, a showerless cleansing mist, makes it possible for people to freshen up without using any water whatsoever.

Price Although the innovative, all-natural products are priced higher than conventional shampoos, conditioners, and cleansers, Love Beauty and Planet is not a luxury brand with astronomical prices that make it impossible for everyday consumers to embrace the sustainability initiative. Instead, the price points around $6–$9 seek to encourage like-minded consumers to try the products but still feel good about their purchases.[5] The brand also highlights that the price reflects its voluntary, self-imposed carbon tax. That is, for every carbon ton produced to manufacture Love Beauty and Planet products, Unilever will contribute an extra $40 to the Carbon Tax Fund.[6] Thus its pricing strategy explicitly acknowledges and demonstrates how and why the sustainable products cost a little more than conventional versions.

Place Unilever is a massive international conglomerate, but for Love Beauty and Planet, it relies on somewhat limited distribution channels, such as e-commerce and drugstores that already have a reputation for selling natural and organic products. The goal is to help consumers who find such options appealing discover the products on their own. Rather than pushing Love Beauty and Planet on every store shelf, it will be something special that sustainability-conscious consumers can take pride in finding.[7] By the same token, if it proves popular, Unilever has relationships in place with major retailers so it can ensure consumers' ready access to the responsible products.

Promotion To get consumers interested and convince them to investigate the innovative offering, Love Beauty and Planet also will use packaging that matches its sustainable philosophy. But it also isn't stopping at using colors or images conventionally associated with sustainability. All the bottles are made from completely recycled plastic and are fully recyclable themselves. In another innovation, Unilever designed labels that can be removed easily, so that there is less threat of contamination in the recycling process.[8]

Although the Love Beauty and Planet line offers a coherent sustainability initiative, Unilever also has committed itself to environmental responsibility across its portfolio. It has published the Unilever Sustainable Living Plan, enumerating its dedication to reducing the environmental impact of its products by half within the next few decades (along with improving the health of society and ensuring the livelihoods of the people who work for it, as two other prongs of the plan).[9] It explicitly aims to separate the growth of the business from growing damage to the environment through a conscious approach to production and distribution. That sort of conscious pursuit of environmental responsibility spans every element of Love Beauty and Planet, suggesting that Unilever is offering consumers truly ethical sustainability and a way to feel good about their consumption—as well as a means to smell nice.

Which is the more important corporate objective: making a profit or protecting customers, employees, and the broader needs of society and the environment?[10] This question underlies a primary dilemma that marketers have long faced. At one point, they might have argued that profit was the primary goal of any firm. But over time, firms—and society as a whole—came to agree that corporations have social responsibilities to a range of stakeholders that they must meet.

Doing so can be harder than it sounds, especially because the goals of different shareholder groups often can be at odds. For example, employees in the coal industry want to keep their jobs; consumers want cheap energy; society wants clean, sustainable energy; and shareholders who own stock in a coal company want to earn profits. But those goals often come in conflict because coal will never be a clean or sustainable energy, so to satisfy society, shareholders by definition would lose their source of income. Accordingly, some industries and companies resist the idea that they need to acknowledge the impact of their actions on others. However, in the long term, if customers believe they can no longer trust a company or that the company is not acting responsibly, they will no longer support that company by purchasing its products or services or investing in its stock.

Ultimately then, modern firms and their marketing efforts must address these notions. For corporate leaders, their firm's ability to balance the needs of various stakeholders—while building and maintaining consumer trust by conducting ethical, transparent, clear transactions that have a positive impact on society and the environment—must be of paramount importance. It is the role of the firm's leadership to weigh the trade-offs among stakeholders and establish a culture that encourages the company to function in a responsible, ethical way.[11] Throughout history, regardless of the objectives they embrace, companies and marketers have needed to be ethical in their actions if they hope to survive.

As these corporate social responsibilities have grown, and ideas about how they should be implemented have expanded, the progression in thinking has moved to encompass the relatively more recent concept of conscious marketing. This chapter details these developments over time, in an effort to describe and explain what conscious marketing means and how it depends on ethics and corporate social responsibility. We start by defining conscious marketing and its four main components (a higher purpose, stakeholders, conscious leadership and culture, and ethics). In particular, we explain why behaving consciously is so important to successful marketing. We then examine how a firm can balance the sometimes disparate needs of various stakeholders to create an offering that sustains the company financially in the long term while also benefiting society and the environment (i.e., the triple bottom line). Then we turn our attention to the leaders who establish a conscious marketing culture in the firm. Coming full circle, we describe how conscious marketing can be integrated into a firm's marketing strategy and marketing plan (from Chapter 2). Finally, we consider ethics as a crucial component of conscious marketing. To help you make ethical marketing decisions, we also provide a framework for ethical decision making.

CONSCIOUS MARKETING

 LO4-1 Define conscious marketing.

Conscious marketing entails a sense of purpose for the firm that is higher than simply making a profit by selling products and services. It encompasses four overriding principles:[12]

1. **Recognition of marketing's greater purpose.** When the marketing function recognizes that the purpose of business should be more than just making profits—whether the purpose is to be more environmentally responsible, as Unilever is, or ensure employment opportunities for local communities, or provide goods for the citizens of poor nations—the actions it undertakes change in focus. The resulting engagement improves inputs as well as outcomes of marketing actions for everyone involved, as Adding Value 4.1 demonstrates.

2. **Consideration of stakeholders and their interdependence.** Conscious marketers consider how their actions will affect the expansive range of potential stakeholders, which are the broad set of people who might be affected by a firm's actions, including not just corporate shareholders and customers but also past, current, and prospective employees and their families; supply chain partners; government agencies; the physical environment; and members of the communities in which the firm operates (defined either locally or on a global scale). Marketers increasingly acknowledge that to serve as many stakeholders as possible and avoid inflicting severe damage on any others, they must give up their exclusive focus on maximizing profits.[13] Rather, they engage in conscious marketing, such that they attend to the broad implications of their actions. By considering these impacts as a foundation for any marketing decisions, conscious marketers achieve the most benefits for the largest numbers of stakeholders while also ensuring that they avoid causing significant harm to any group. For example, when Walmart issued new standards for farms that supply it with livestock products, the effects were felt by the supply chain partners who might need to adjust their practices, competitors that might need to adopt similar protections, consumers who can take more assurance that the animals raised for their food will not have been fed antibiotics, and animal welfare groups that call the new standards "a step in the right direction."[14]

When Walmart issued new standards for livestock products that were raised on food without antibiotics or artificial growth hormones, it considered multiple stakeholder groups including the ranchers that supply the food, its customers, and animal welfare groups.

©Rudmer Zwerver/Shutterstock

It isn't every day that a luxury jeweler is linked to charitable micro-funding initiatives. But in its efforts to connect with younger consumers, the high-end jewelry brand David Yurman has taken a creative new approach and partnered with the charitable app Elbi—which itself was founded by Natalia Vodianova, one of the models who appears in some of David Yurman's marketing campaigns. The outcome promises to benefit the brand, the charity, consumers, and beneficiaries of the charitable efforts.

First, David Yurman can connect better with Millennials, in a new and innovative way, thereby building brand recognition in an age group that typically lacks enough discretionary income to purchase fancy jewelry. The resulting, recognizable brand image also is based in social philanthropy. That is, by introducing itself to young consumers through its partnership with Elbi, David Yurman can expand its conscious marketing image. The brand has selected seven specific causes, all associated with children's charities, that it will support in conjunction with this particular brand partnership.

Second, for Elbi, the connection increases attention and clicks on its site. The social sharing approach seeks to generate micro-donations through clicks, which then go to support three different charities each day. Through the partnership, David Yurman promises to contribute $1 for each transaction on its website, as well as donating a bracelet that users could win.

Third, with each donation or activity, users earn points that they can redeem for luxury prizes, including handbags and electronics, as well as the exciting jewelry. Millennial shoppers can sense that they are doing good through their consumption, fulfilling their need to contribute positively to the world, even if they cannot afford to make a monetary donation themselves. In turn, the charities associated with the app receive more support, which goes to their intended audiences.

To promote this new partnership between Elbi and David Yurman, the marketing campaign features the model who also founded the Elbi app. It embraces the conscious marketing notions of togetherness and family, showing both adults and children playing and enjoying life, adorned with the brand's jewelry. With this whimsical approach, the marketing links

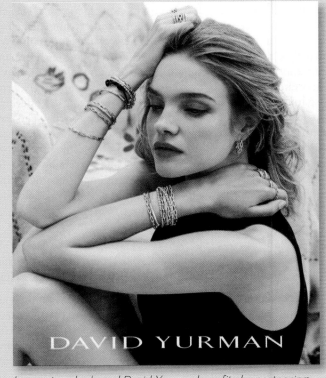

Luxury jewelry brand David Yurman benefits by partnering with the charitable app founded by Natalia Vodianova, who is pictured in this David Yurman ad.

Source: David Yurman

clearly to the seven causes selected by David Yurman as recipients of the benefits of the partnership, all of which have an emphasis on helping children. Finally, by airing the resulting spots in traditional channels, as well as movie theaters and on the brand's social media sites David Yurman hopes to capture the attention of younger consumers, ensuring that their first impression of this luxury brand is a positive one.

3. **The presence of conscious leadership, creating a corporate culture.** A conscious marketing approach implies that the firm's leaders are dedicated to the proposition of being conscious at all levels of the business, throughout its entire culture. For example, Elon Musk, the visionary head of a range of innovative companies (e.g., Tesla, SpaceX, Solar City, Hyperloop), explains, "I like to be involved in things that change the world."[15] Therefore, regardless of whether his firm is selling electric vehicles, investigating realistic options for building renewable public transportation systems, or seeking to colonize space, the vision remains the same: to change the world for the better. The resulting conscious culture remains dedicated to the notion that the choices the firm makes reflect its conscious consideration of stakeholders, in line with its higher purpose and in accordance with the leader's ideals. As a result, every member of the firm embodies the ideas of conscious marketing, and every stakeholder affected by that marketing can recognize the higher principles involved.

4. **The understanding that decisions are ethically based.** Conscious marketers must make decisions that are based on sound marketing ethics. Business ethics is concerned with distinguishing between right and wrong actions and decisions that arise in a business setting, according to broad and well-established moral and ethical principles that might arise in a business setting, and any special duties or obligations that apply to persons engaged in commerce. Marketing ethics, in contrast, examines ethical situations that are specific to the domain of marketing, including societal, global, or individual consumer issues. They can involve societal issues such as the sale of products or services that may damage the environment, global issues such as the use of child labor (see Chapter 8), or individual consumer issues such as misrepresenting a product in advertising or marketing dangerous products.

Elon Musk, the head of SpaceX, wants to be involved in things that change the world.

©Patrick T. Fallon/Bloomberg/Getty Images

MARKETING'S GREATER PURPOSE: CORPORATE SOCIAL RESPONSIBILITY AS AN ELEMENT OF CONSCIOUS MARKETING

 Describe what constitutes marketing's greater purpose.

As we noted previously, the notion of conscious marketing has evolved over time. At one point, a popular view held that the only responsibility of a business was to its shareholders, so its only purpose was to make a profit.[16] In many parts of the world, that view has been supplanted with the idea that companies must consider their responsibilities to a wider range of stakeholders who make up society. Although there are many and varied definitions of corporate social responsibility (CSR),[17] firms generally acknowledge that, in addition to economic and legal duties, they have responsibilities to society. These responsibilities are not mandated by any law or regulation but instead are associated with the demands, expectations, requirements, and desires of various stakeholders. For example, one definition describes CSR as context-specific actions and policies, taking stakeholders' expectations into account, to achieve what is referred to as the triple bottom line: economic, social, and environmental performance.[18]

Today, virtually all large and well-known companies engage in some form of CSR. The available initiatives are vast in their spread, from establishing charitable foundations to supporting and associating with existing nonprofit groups to supporting the rights of minority groups to adopting responsible marketing, sales, and production practices. Exhibit 4.1 provides several illustrations of the CSR programs undertaken by major firms.

EXHIBIT 4.1	Sampling of Major Companies' CSR Programs
Company	**Illustration of CSR Program**
Amazon.com	Developed nonprofit Simple Pay Donation system to help nonprofits raise money easily
BMW	Light Up Hope and BMW Children's Safety programs
Coca-Cola	Spent $102 million through the Coca-Cola campaign focusing on water stewardship, healthy and active lifestyles, community recycling, and education
FedEx	Transported more than 67 planes' worth of aid to disaster victims
General Electric	Ecomagination campaign, GE Volunteers Foundation
Google	Google.org funds pro-profit entrepreneurship in Africa, Google China Social Innovation Cup for College Students
McDonald's	99 percent of fish come from MSC-fisheries, transitioning to sustainable food and packaging sources, Ronald McDonald House charities
Procter & Gamble	Live, Learn, and Thrive improves the lives of children worldwide
Southwest Airlines	Employees donate volunteer hours to Ronald McDonald Houses throughout the United States
Starbucks	Develops ecologically friendly growing practices, LEED certified stores

Source: Adapted from http://money.cnn.com/magazines/fortune/most-admired/.

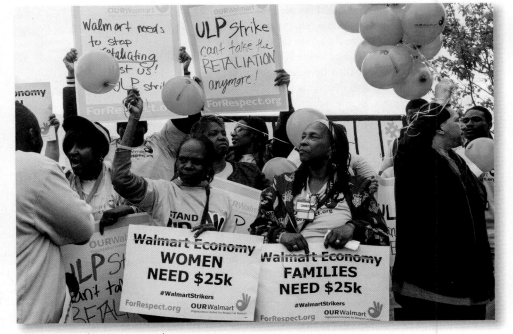

Walmart employees protest low wages.
©Marie Kanger Born/Shutterstock

EXHIBIT 4.2	How Conscious Marketing Differs from CSR[22]
Corporate Social Responsibility	**Conscious Marketing**
Independent of corporate purpose or culture	Incorporates higher purpose and a caring culture
Reflects a mechanistic view of business	Takes a holistic, ecosystem view of business as a complex adaptive system
Often grafted onto traditional business model, usually as a separate departm ent or part of PR	Social responsibility is at the core of the business through the higher purpose and viewing the community and the environment as stakeholders
Sees limited overlap between the business and society, and between business and the planet	Recognizes that business is a subset of society, and that society is a subset of the planet

LO4-3 Differentiate between conscious marketing and corporate social responsibility.

Although CSR is an important element of conscious marketing, it is not the same thing. Becoming a conscious marketing organization is a complex effort, and for some firms, it may prove virtually impossible to achieve. When marketers work in controversial or polluting industries such as tobacco or fossil fuels, their central activities largely bar them from becoming conscious marketers. However, they might engage in CSR in an effort to mitigate the damage that their products cause, such as when cigarette companies sponsor public information campaigns or oil companies plant trees to balance out their carbon footprint.[19] In addition, these companies might undertake efforts in other sectors, such as donating time in local communities or guaranteeing fair wages, because they recognize the importance of such socially responsible efforts.

Walmart offers an interesting example in this discussion. The retail giant has been widely criticized as the worst-paying company in the United States.[20] Yet it also engages in extensive CSR programs across the triple bottom line. It has committed to reducing its carbon footprint (environmental performance), donates more than $1 billion in cash and in-kind items to charitable causes per year (social performance), and still earns strong profits (economic performance).[21]

Thus, though conscious marketing and CSR have some clear connections, they also differ in critical ways, as Exhibit 4.2 summarizes.

PROGRESS CHECK

1. What are the criteria for being a conscious marketer?
2. Is Walmart a conscious marketer or is it a practitioner of CSR?

THE STAKEHOLDERS OF CONSCIOUS MARKETING

Among the key differences between conscious marketing and CSR, we can highlight the unique view on shareholders that is absolutely critical to conscious marketing. That is, when companies embrace conscious marketing, they appeal not only to their shareholders but also to all of their key stakeholders (Exhibit 4.3), including their own employees, consumers, the marketplace, and society at large. The choices they make with regard to what they produce and how, and then how they seek to sell those offerings, take a broad range of elements into consideration.

A prominent example appears in the supply chain for processed foods (e.g., cereals, salad dressings). For decades, most of these foods have contained ingredients made from plants whose DNA has been manipulated in a laboratory, for example, to help produce weather frosts better and produce a greater yield of crops. Such genetically modified organisms, or GMOs, appear in many of the foods that U.S. consumers eat daily. The U.S. Food and Drug Administration does not require GMO food

Whole Foods has committed to issuing labels, by 2018, on all GMO-containing foods it sells.
©Ralph Barrera/MCT/Newscom

product labeling,[23] so legally, food manufacturers do not have to identify which of their products contain GMOs. Although there is ample evidence that GMOs aren't harmful, the demand for such options is still growing.[24] Many consumers express a preference to know GMO information, primarily because they have concerns about their potential negative health effects. Fearful that GMO labels will hurt sales, many food manufacturers seem to be fighting GMO labeling, as Marketing Analytics 4.1 describes. Despite the fact that removing GMOs may increase production costs, companies such as General Mills have removed them from some of their products, and grocers such as Whole Foods have committed to issuing GMO labels by 2018.[25]

In this example, the stakeholders have contrasting preferences and demands, and they are diverse—they include farmers, consumers, manufacturing companies, shareholders, retailers,

EXHIBIT 4.3 Key Conscious Marketing Stakeholders

- Employees
- Their families

- Current customers
- Potential customers

Employees

Customers

Marketplace

Society

- Partners
- Competitors

- Community
- Environment

Marketing Analytics 4.1   How Kellogg's Uses Analytics to Address GMO Concerns[ii]

Analytics are a valuable tool for helping manufacturers understand the relationship their customers have with their brands. For example, Kellogg's recently suffered its first sales and profit decreases in decades. The unprecedented drop in these key metrics prompted the company to revamp its brand, cleanly and clearly. But what exactly did it need to change? Using advanced analytics, Kellogg's realized that one of its brands was getting creamed on social media: Reports showed that Kashi, which Kellogg's has promoted as an all-natural option, contained genetically modified organisms (GMOs). Consumers were furious, and they made their opinions clear on various social media.

In response, Kellogg's undertook a complete overhaul in an attempt to redefine its brands' core purpose. It consolidated its 42 separate company websites into a single umbrella site. And it made social media a focal point in its brand overhaul. To manage this social media reinvention, Kellogg's hired a computer whiz to serve as its director of digital and social media strategy. The strategy first went into effect in the United Kingdom. To encourage trial of its Krave cereal, it released the hashtag "#KravetheSmiler," then awarded prizes to customers who used the hashtag. Throughout the campaign, Kellogg's constantly gathered data, including daily summaries of tweets that featured the hashtag, the daily top tweeters, how many tweets per hour they received, and so forth.

The well-planned campaign worked: Kellogg's received more than 35,000 tweets about Krave cereal. Using specially designed algorithms, Kellogg's could quickly comb through all

Kellogg's used social media to introduce and gather data about its new Krave cereal.
©studiomode/Alamy Stock Photo

the data and award prizes fairly and effectively. Although the campaign improved customer relations, the more important result might have been the way it provided Kellogg's with new insights and data. With this information, Kellogg's is likely to be able to replicate this success in other social media campaigns. For example, it could identify the products in which consumers would be willing to allow GMOs and those in which they absolutely would reject GMOs. Analytics also might show Kellogg's how to seed communication campaigns to give consumers accurate information about GMOs' actual threats and benefits. Thus far, though, its implementation of careful data-based strategies has boosted the return on investment for Kellogg's brands—in some cases, up to six times more than previous methods ever achieved.

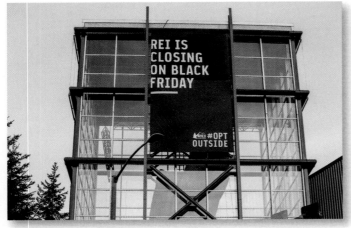

REI closes on Black Friday, the day after Thanksgiving, so its employees can enjoy time outdoors with their families.
©Suzi Pratt/Getty Images

and the environment. Let's consider five stakeholder categories in more depth to understand the meaning and effects of conscious marketing in the modern marketing arena, as well as how conscious marketing ultimately can benefit firms that undertake it.

Employees

Perhaps the most basic responsibility of a firm is to employees: to ensure a safe working environment free of threats to their physical safety, health, or well-being. In some cases, this basic level of safety seems insufficient to ensure responsibility to workers. For example, more firms today realize that happy employee families make happy and productive employees, so they are offering new benefits and options, such as on-site daycare[26] or flextime arrangements. When REI thought more consciously about its practices, it determined that living up to its higher purpose—that is, helping people enjoy outdoor adventures—meant closing its stores on Thanksgiving and the day after, popularly known as Black Friday. Although closing meant that REI lost some sales, the conscious culture in the firm emphasized that employees should be enjoying time outdoors with their families too.[27]

Walt Disney's VoluntEAR program is one of the best CSR programs in the world.
©Deshakalyan Chowdhury/Stringer/ Getty Images

Customers

Especially as changes in the marketing environment emerge, firms must consider the effects on their current customers as well as future customers they have targeted. Conscious marketing programs must take such shifts and trends into account and react to them quickly. Some trends receiving substantial attention in modern times include respecting and protecting privacy in an electronic world and ensuring the healthiness of products, especially those aimed at children. When conscious marketing takes on such pertinent issues, it often increases consumer awareness of the firm, which can lead to better brand equity and sales in the long run. The Walt Disney Company appears to be a strong proponent: In one year, Disney gave more than $400 million to charity. It has also donated 23.1 million books and its employees have donated 2.9 million hours of their time through Disney's VoluntEAR program since 2012. Reflecting its higher purpose of ensuring the happiness and enjoyment of children, Disney has partnered with Give Kids the World, and its employees have renovated 88 vacation villas that the charitable organization offers to the families of children with life-threatening illnesses, so that they can take life-affirming vacations.[28]

Marketplace

When one firm in the industry leads the way toward conscious marketing, its partners and competitors often have no choice but to follow—or run the risk of not doing business or being left behind. To address issues such as global warming, water scarcity, and energy, GE uses a program it calls ecomagination. Reflecting the company's higher purpose, ecomagination encompasses a business strategy composed of four commitments: to double investments in clean research and development (R&D), increase revenues from ecomagination products, reduce greenhouse gas emissions, and inform the public about these issues.[29] The initiative for the program came from conscious leaders who recognized that the energy field had great potential to exert long-lasting effects on the world. When confronted with such initiatives, other energy companies are forced to make a decision: continue as they have been doing or adopt more responsible practices themselves. In either case, the initiating firm enjoys an advantage by gaining a reputation for being on the cutting edge of CSR efforts.

Society

Firms expend considerable time and energy engaging in activities aimed at improving the overall community and the physical environment, which suggests their increasing recognition

GE is the industry leader in CSR with its ecomagination program.

Source: General Electric Company

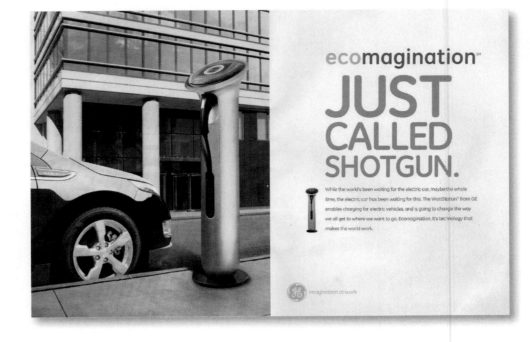

of the importance of a broad range of varied stakeholders. Broader society, a key stakeholder, demands that companies act responsibly, companies cannot ignore this, a lesson that Patagonia learned well, as Adding Value 4.2 describes. A firm that fails to act responsibly causes damage to all the preceding stakeholders as well as to itself. For example, reports that the artificial sweeteners in diet sodas might have ill effects, such as long-term weight gain and possible links to developing cancer, have led customers to alter their buying habits. Specifically, sales of diet soda have dropped 6.8 percent in a year, more than three times the decline in regular soda sales. Even though organizations such as the American Diabetes Association and the U.S. Food and Drug Administration have affirmed that diet sodas are safe, the broader shift in societal opinions demands that beverage companies seek new options. In particular, many companies are researching the potential use of stevia, a plant with naturally sweet properties, to replace the artificial versions.[30]

Environment

A special category that combines considerations of all these stakeholders is sustainability. According to the U.S. Environmental Protection Agency, "Sustainability is based on a simple principle: Everything that we need for our survival and well-being depends, either directly or indirectly, on our natural environment." Therefore, sustainable actions, including sustainable marketing, allow "humans and nature [to] exist in productive harmony, that permit fulfilling the social, economic and other requirements of present and future generations."[31] When marketing is truly sustainable, it can benefit all stakeholders: employees, customers, the marketplace, and society. We discuss sustainable, or "green," marketing further in Chapter 5.

PROGRESS CHECK

1. What is the difference between conscious marketing and corporate social responsibility?
2. Provide a specific example of a conscious marketing firm that considers the needs of each of its stakeholders.

Adding Value **4.2**   Are Growth and Conscious Marketing Contradictory? The Challenge for Patagonia[iii]

Hikers, adventurers, and even just folks who want a good jacket have long trusted Patagonia to provide high-quality gear that will stand up to the elements, last for years, and allow them to feel good about their socially responsible consumption. These habits are largely based on Patagonia's clear promise to customers: It vows to "Build the best product, cause no unnecessary harm, use business to inspire and implement solutions to the environmental crisis."

But sometimes missions are easier to state than they are to fulfill. For Patagonia, the challenge has been that it builds such good products that the company is growing. Growth creates expanded supply chain needs. For example, Patagonia spent three years developing a new woolen long underwear line that proved extremely popular with customers in cold weather climates. Thus, its demand for wool expanded, leading the company to enter into a contract with a network of 160 different wool suppliers from South America. Such an expansive network makes it extremely difficult to monitor all the practices of all the farms raising the sheep that provide the wool. But if Patagonia also promises to cause no harm, then it must be responsible for that monitoring, as PETA pointed out when it captured video of terrible animal abuses at some of the farms that provided the wool for Patagonia. The brand agreed; it dropped its contract with the wool supply network, halted production on its new long underwear line, and sought new sources for wool. But how many sales did it lose in the process?

By establishing its broad mission, Patagonia essentially promises to be socially responsible on every level, even if it is not primarily an animal welfare organization, for example. Thus, when evidence surfaced that the geese that supplied down for its jackets also were sources of foie gras for a totally separate company, observers held Patagonia responsible. In this case, its supply chain in no way encouraged the force-feeding of the geese. Whether fat or thin, geese provide the down that Patagonia was purchasing. But it was supporting, even if indirectly, a practice that many people regard as ethically indefensible, creating another challenge for the company.

Nor are the challenges limited to animal welfare concerns. Labor issues affect Patagonia, as they do most clothing brands that outsource their production to global factories. For Patagonia, a key ethical challenge arose when it discovered that workers had been required to pay bribes before they could get work in its Taiwanese factories. Although Patagonia responded by reimbursing the workers for any of the unethical bribes they were forced to pay, the incident raised renewed awareness of the difficulty associated with keeping track of the ethical practices adopted in each factory or farm around the world.

Patagonia has implemented new, more stringent standards and policies in its supply chain, including a collaborative effort to establish a "Responsible Wool Standard" for the entire industry. Yet the conscious marketing issues appear poised to become even more difficult and intense, because Patagonia still is making the best products it can. Its profits have tripled in the past few years, meaning that it needs to keep expanding its supply chains to ensure it has enough products to satisfy these customers, seeking the best options that it has promised them.

Patagonia's Mission Statement

Build the best product, cause no unnecessary harm, use business to inspire and implement solutions to the environmental crisis.

As Patagonia expands, it is often difficult to live up to its mission statement.

Source: Patagonia

LO4-5 Explain how conscious leadership can produce a conscious culture in the firm.

INTEGRATING CONSCIOUS MARKETING THROUGHOUT THE FIRM: LEADERSHIP AND CULTURE

For new firms founded on conscious marketing principles, their leaders, who are also their founders, establish the standard from the very start. But even if an existing firm seeks to move toward a conscious approach to marketing, it can adopt decision rules (as we discuss in the next section) and norms that encourage consciousness throughout its entire corporate culture. For example, to ensure that conscious marketing is infused into all levels of the firm, it can be integrated into each stage of the marketing plan (introduced in Chapter 2), as we detail here. In their constant pursuit of conscious marketing, firms can address relevant questions at each stage of the strategic marketing planning process. For instance, in the planning stage, the firm will decide what level of commitment to its ethical policies and standards it is willing to declare publicly and how the firm plans to balance the needs of its various stakeholders. In the implementation stage, the tone of the questions switches from "can we?" serve the market with the firm's products or services in a conscious marketing manner to "should we?" be engaging in particular marketing practices. The key task in the control phase is to ensure that all potential conscious marketing issues raised during the planning process have been addressed and that all employees of the firm have acted ethically.

Planning Phase

With strong leadership, marketers can introduce conscious marketing at the beginning of the planning process by including statements in the firm's mission or vision statements (recall our discussion of various mission statements in Chapter 2). For instance, the mission statement for natural skin care company Burt's Bees is to "create natural, Earth-friendly personal care products formulated to help you maximize your well-being and that of the world around you,"[32] which reflects not only what is good for its customers but for society in general. Google's well-known code is simple in its phrasing, "Do the right thing," but often complex in its application, as Ethical & Societal Dilemma 4.1 explains.

For General Electric, the complexity of its organization and the wealth of ethical issues it faces necessitated an entire booklet, "The Spirit and the Letter." This booklet presents not only a statement of integrity from the CEO and a code of conduct, but also details policies for dealing with everything from international competition laws to security and crisis management to insider trading. In addition, GE publishes an annual citizenship report to determine the scope of its impacts, "produced for the benefit of all stakeholders, including GE employees—the people whose actions define GE every day."[33]

Newman's Own's mission takes a fairly straightforward perspective: Its simple but powerful purpose was to sell salad dressing (initially; it expanded later to many other product

Since 1982, Newman's Own has given more than $490 million to charities such as Newman's Hole in the Wall Gang camps for children with life-threatening diseases.

(Left): ©Food Collection/Alamy Stock Photo; (right): ©Lamperti Francois-Xavier/Abaca/Newscom

Ethical & Societal Dilemma 4.1

Defining Dangerous Advertising: Google Bans Financial Products That May Do More Harm Than Good[iv]

Google's company motto is well known: "Do the right thing." In the ongoing discussion about what that means, the search engine has taken a new step and banned advertising by payday loan companies from its sponsored search results. Although the companies still might appear in the list of organic results, they will no longer appear in the prized positions at the top and side of the page.

It is no accident that a Google search on "jeans," (left) yields ads, whereas a search for payday loans (right) does not. In attempting to abide by its corporate motto, "Do the right thing," Google has banned payday loan advertising from its sponsored search results.

Source: Alphabet Inc.

For Google's purposes, the definition of payday loan companies refers to those lenders that demand repayment of the loan within 60 days and that charge annual percentage rates that exceed 36 percent. Many policymakers have expressed concerns about the practices of such companies, which tend to target consumers who have low or unstable sources of income and relatively poor credit ratings. When faced with an emergency that they cannot pay for, consumers often might search for solutions online—where they are likely to find promises from the loan companies that offer ready access to funds. The "slick" advertising highlights the ease of the loan process but rarely makes the extremely high interest rates and demanding repayment timelines sufficiently transparent.

In turn, some of the most vulnerable consumers, who struggle to pay their regular bills, wind up entering into a debt cycle in which a loan for a few hundred dollars ultimately winds up costing them thousands, through compounded interest and penalties. In its attempt to protect its users from such "deceptive or harmful financial products," Google has placed unethical payday lenders in the same category as tobacco and gun sellers, which Google also bans from sponsored advertising on its site.

Some loan industry representatives claim the ban is too widespread, such that it restricts not just unethical lenders but also legitimate businesses that provide credit to people who would be unable to obtain a traditional bank loan. Furthermore, the ban might be considered a form of censorship, especially considering that payday loans are legal and do not involve the direct health threats that are associated with the other types of banned advertisers.

But a report by the Pew Charitable Trusts also reveals that payday loans obtained online, which account for about one-third of the market, often charge even higher interest rates than the loans that consumers receive in the physical store locations. One estimate indicates that the annual percentage rates exceed 300 percent in many cases. Consumer advocates thus have called for other search engines to ban the advertisements as well, even as they pressure regulatory bodies to impose more limits on the kinds of advertising that the payday loan companies can spread.

lines) and use the proceeds to benefit charities. This simple idea began with the leadership of Paul Newman, the late actor who whipped up a batch of salad dressing to give as holiday gifts one year. When he and a friend decided to check with a local grocer to see if it would be interested in the product, they found they could sell 10,000 bottles in two weeks. Thus Newman's Own Foundation, the nonprofit organization, grew quickly; today, dozens of products with the Newman's Own and Newman's Own Organic brands are sold in countries around the world, from coffee to popcorn to dog food. Profits from Newman's Own—more than $490 million since 1982—have been donated to thousands of charities, especially Newman's Hole in the Wall Gang camps for children with life-threatening diseases.[34] The unique mission of the company and the entrepreneurial flair of the founders, along with their conscious leadership, made this nonprofit a smashing, ongoing success. Employees of Newman's Own have the great satisfaction of giving back to society, various charities benefit from the donations, and customers enjoy good food with a clear conscience.

Implementation Phase

In the implementation phase of the marketing strategy, when firms are identifying potential markets and ways to deliver the four Ps to them, firms must consider several pertinent issues. TOMS Shoes is well known as a socially conscious company, which gives one pair of shoes to someone in need in poor countries for each pair it sells. Its ethics is also prominent in its marketing strategy. In every aspect of its marketing campaigns its mission is displayed as prominently as the brand itself, ensuring that the brand and mission are inseparable. One of its most famous marketing campaigns is its "One Day Without Shoes." The social media campaign asks consumers to post pictures of their bare feet with the event hashtag, and for every photo the company will donate a pair of shoes. In 2016 the event led to TOMS donating over 27,000 shoes and reached 3.5 million people online.[35]

In other situations, an implementation can have unforeseen benefits. A conscious marketer might predict some of those benefits, but as Social & Mobile Marketing 4.1 explains, sometimes positive situations that arise for an entire population can lead to more conscious practices by firms.

Once the strategy is implemented, controls must be in place to be certain that the firm has actually done what it has set out to do. These activities take place in the next phase of the strategic marketing planning process: the control phase.

Control Phase

During the control phase of the strategic marketing planning process, managers must be evaluated on their actions from a conscious marketing perspective. Systems must be in place to check whether each conscious marketing issue raised in the planning process was actually successfully addressed. Systems used in the control phase must also react to change. The emergence of new technologies and new markets ensures that new potentially troubling issues continually arise. In particular, people expect to be able to move normally in public spaces without their location being recorded for subsequent use. Yet marketers regularly collect data on people's location through purchase transactions and posts on social and mobile sites such as Facebook, Twitter, Instagram, Pinterest, and YouTube. Additionally, several retailers' credit card systems have been violated, resulting in the theft of consumer data of millions of people, the most egregious of which were the estimated

TOMS Shoes is well known as a socially conscious company, which gives one pair of shoes to someone in need in poor countries for each pair it sells.

©jackie ellis/Alamy Stock Photo

Social & Mobile Marketing 4.1

How Mobile Phones and Payments Have Created a Viable New Market at the Bottom of the Pyramid[v]

We might imagine that the greatest spread of mobile technology is among middle-class and wealthy consumers who demand the most advanced phones with innumerable gadgets and added features. But in truth, the biggest jumps might be coming from the opposite side of the economic divide—namely, from some of the poorest consumers in the world.

For people living in extreme poverty, basic, functional phones offer a vast opportunity for consumption. In sub-Saharan Africa, for example, consumers rely on text messages to communicate with distant contacts because texts are less expensive than phone calls.

More notably, mobile payment services allow these consumers to load as little as a dollar on their phones, which they can then use to pay for services that improve their quality of life. One woman described her ability to pay less than 50 cents daily to receive electricity from a solar panel provider. In the past, taking such small daily payments would have been too much work and too inefficient for the service provider. By linking to a mobile payment system, neither the consumer nor the supplier needs to engage in additional effort. And if the consumer isn't able to load enough onto her phone on one day, she can go without electricity until she can reload her mobile account with funds, without risk of harming her credit or losing access to her account. As one Kenyan investment firm, which helps poor consumers gain access to micro-insurance and savings plans, explains, "If you're taking a dollar off a million people, that's a reasonable revenue stream, but it wasn't possible to do that without the mobile phone."

Among these consumers, bank accounts are unusual, so the mobile payment systems allow them to load funds with the assistance of agents that work in local gas stations and stores. Once the funds are loaded, they can pay for groceries at the point of sale by tapping their phones, or they can send funds electronically. This latter functionality is critical because for many Africans, making a trip to pay a bill might mean an entire day of lost labor due to travel times.

In sub-Saharan Africa, consumers rely on text messages to communicate with distant contacts because texts are less expensive than phone calls.

©Jake Lyell/Alamy Stock Photo

These benefits have turned Africa into the source of some astounding innovations, especially for microbusiness concepts. Sub-Saharan Africa accounts for about 70 percent of the world's poor population, but nearly 65 percent of these households have access to at least one mobile phone. In addition, Africa is the fastest-growing mobile market in the world.

Mobile payments are being introduced in other impoverished areas as well. India has a large impoverished population. Out of the 1.2 billion people living in the country, 600 million people do not have access to basic necessities such as drinking water and toilets. However, there are 1 billion cell phone subscribers in the country, making the number of people with access to a cell phone significantly higher than the number of those with bank accounts. To push for financial inclusion of the impoverished population, a network is being put in place to allow for digital payments possible across the country.

143 million at Equifax (the credit rating company) in 2017, 145 million at eBay in 2014, and 110 million at Target in 2013.[36] Although most experts blamed the thefts on U.S.-based credit card companies' reticence to adopt a more secure type of credit card that is used in Europe and elsewhere, the retailers and their customers suffer the consequences.

Many firms have emergency response plans in place just in case they ever encounter a crisis that would negatively impact their conscious marketing philosophy. Conscious marketers adopt such contingency plans from the start, reflecting their conscious leadership and conscious culture. In this sense, conscious marketing remains an ongoing crucial component of the strategic marketing planning process and should be incorporated into all the firm's decision making down the road.

PROGRESS CHECK

1. What ethical questions should a marketing manager consider at each stage of the marketing plan?

LO4-6 Describe how ethics constitutes an integral part of a firm's conscious marketing strategy.

MARKETING ETHICS AS A CONSCIOUS MARKETING PRINCIPLE

Decision making according to conscious marketing might sound easy, but as this chapter has shown, it is often difficult to balance the needs and preferences of various stakeholders. A key component for making any conscious marketing decision can be very personal in that individuals must decide whether their actions are right or wrong based on their moral principles. In other words, are they making ethically correct decisions? As noted earlier in this chapter, like CSR, marketing ethics is an integral component of a conscious marketing initiative. To begin our discussion, we examine the nature of ethical and unethical marketing decisions and the difference between marketing ethics and CSR.

The Nature of Ethical and Unethical Marketing Decisions

People are expected to know what is and is not ethical behavior based on their ability to distinguish right from wrong in a particular culture. Consider product recalls of toys, for example. How can certain manufacturers engage in such egregious behavior as using lead paint on toys or including magnets that can be swallowed in toys marketed toward young children? What makes people take actions that create so much harm? Are all the individuals who contributed to that behavior just plain unethical?

There are no ready answers to such philosophical questions. But when asked in a survey whether they had seen any unethical behavior among their colleagues, chief marketing officers responded that they had observed employees participating in high-pressure, misleading, or deceptive sales tactics (45 percent); misrepresenting company earnings, sales, and/or revenues (35 percent); withholding or destroying information that could hurt company sales or image (32 percent); and conducting false or misleading advertising (31 percent).[37] Did all the marketers in these situations view their actions as unethical? Probably not. There may have been extenuating circumstances. In marketing, managers often face the choice of doing what is beneficial for them and possibly the firm in the short run and taking a conscious marketing perspective by doing what is right and beneficial for the firm and society in the long run.

For instance, a manager might feel confident that earnings will increase in the next few months and therefore believe it benefits himself, his branch, his employees, and his shareholders to exaggerate current earnings just a little. Another manager might feel considerable pressure to increase sales in a retail store, so she brings in some new merchandise, marks it at an artificially high price, and then immediately puts it on sale, deceiving consumers into thinking they are getting a good deal because they view the initial price as the real price. These decisions may have been justifiable at the time and to some stakeholders, but they have serious long-term consequences for the company and are therefore not in concert with a conscious marketing approach.

To avoid such potentially unethical behaviors, conscious marketing seeks to align the short-term goals of each employee with the long-term, overriding goals of the firm. To align personal and corporate goals, firms need to have a strong ethical climate exemplified by the actions of corporate leaders and filtered through an ethically based corporate culture. There should be explicit rules for governing transactions; these rules should include a code of ethics and a system for rewarding and punishing inappropriate behavior. The American Marketing Association (AMA) provides a detailed, multipronged "Statement of Ethics" that can serve as a foundation for marketers,

What is the "real" price? Did the manager bring the sweatshirts in at an artificially high level and then immediately mark them down?

©Alexander Mazurkevich/Shutterstock

emphasizing that "As marketers . . . we not only serve our organizations but also act as stewards of society in creating, facilitating and executing the transactions that are part of the greater economy."[38]

Ethics and Corporate Social Responsibility

Although both fall under the conscious marketing umbrella, it is important to distinguish between ethical marketing practices and corporate social responsibility programs. When a firm embraces conscious marketing, it implements programs that are socially responsible, and its employees act in an ethically responsible manner. (See Exhibit 4.4, upper left quadrant.) None of the other quadrants in Exhibit 4.4 embodies conscious marketing principles.

A firm's employees may conduct their activities in an ethically acceptable manner, but it may not be considered socially responsible because its activities have little or no impact on anyone other than its closest stakeholders: its customers, employees, and stockholders. It does not engage in programs that better society or the environment as a whole (Exhibit 4.4, upper right quadrant).

Employees at firms that are perceived as socially responsible can nevertheless take actions that are viewed as unethical (Exhibit 4.4, lower left quadrant). For instance, a firm might be considered socially responsible because it makes generous donations to charities, but if it is simultaneously involved in questionable sales practices it cannot be seen as ethical. The worst situation, of course, is when firms behave both unethically and in a socially unacceptable manner (Exhibit 4.4, lower right quadrant).

Customers may be willing to pay more if they can be assured the companies truly are ethical.[39] According to recent studies 87 percent of Americans will buy products because the company supported social issues they cared about and 76 percent will refuse to buy products from companies that were opposed to issues important to them. The trend has been tied to the rise of the "ethical consumer" and the evolution of the social contract "between many Americans and businesses about what goes into making the products we buy."[40]

Embracing conscious marketing is one way to enforce this social contract. However, even in the most conscious of firms, individual members may face challenges in their efforts to act ethically. Therefore, a framework for ethical decision making can help move people to work toward common ethical goals.

EXHIBIT 4.4   Ethics versus Social Responsibility

	Socially Responsible	Socially Irresponsible
Ethical	Both ethically and socially responsible	Ethical firm not involved with the larger community
Unethical	Questionable firm practices, yet donates a lot to the community	Neither ethically nor socially responsible

A Framework for Ethical Decision Making

Exhibit 4.5 outlines a simple framework for ethical decision making. Let's consider each of the steps.

LO4-7 Identify the four steps in ethical decision making.

Step 1: Identify Issues The first step is to identify the issue. Imagine the use (or misuse) of data collected from consumers by a marketing research firm. One of the issues that might arise is the way the data are collected. For instance, are the respondents told about the real purpose of the study? Another issue

EXHIBIT 4.5   Ethical Decision-Making Framework

Step 1	Step 2	Step 3	Step 4
Identify issues	Gather information and identify stakeholders	Brainstorm and evaluate alternatives	Choose a course of action

With its sustainability and transparency efforts, Philips takes a global view of its stakeholders.

Source: Koninklijke Philips N.V.

might be whether the results will be used in a way that might mislead or even harm the public, such as selling the information to a firm to use in soliciting the respondents.

Step 2: Gather Information and Identify Stakeholders
In this step, the firm focuses on gathering facts that are important to the ethical issue, including all relevant legal information. To get a complete picture, the firm must identify all the individuals and groups that have a stake in how the issue is resolved.

As we detailed previously, stakeholders typically include the firm's employees, suppliers, the government, customer groups, stockholders, and members of the community in which the firm operates. Beyond these, many firms now also analyze the needs of the industry and the global community, as well as one-off stakeholders such as future generations and the natural environment. In describing its sustainability and transparency efforts, for example, the electronics firm Philips notes that it tries to communicate with and consider "anyone with an interest in Philips."[41]

Step 3: Brainstorm and Evaluate Alternatives
After the marketing firm has identified the stakeholders and their issues and gathered the available data, all parties relevant to the decision should come together to brainstorm any alternative courses of action. In our example, these might include halting the marketing research project, making responses anonymous, instituting training on the AMA Code of Ethics for all researchers, and so forth. The company leaders and managers then can review and refine these alternatives, leading to the final step.

Step 4: Choose a Course of Action
The objective of this last step is to weigh the various alternatives and choose a course of action that generates the best solution for the stakeholders, using ethical practices based on a conscious marketing approach. Management—ideally, conscious leaders—ranks the alternatives in order of preference, clearly establishing the advantages and disadvantages of each. It is also crucial to investigate any potential legal issues associated with each alternative. Of course, any illegal activity should be rejected immediately.

To choose the appropriate course of action, marketing managers will evaluate each alternative by using a process something like the sample ethical decision-making metric in

EXHIBIT 4.6 Ethical Decision-Making Metric

	Decision						
	Yes		Maybe			No	
Test	1	2	3	4	5	6	7
The Publicity Test Would I want to see this action that I'm about to take described on the front page of the local paper or in a national magazine?							
The Moral Mentor Test Would the person I admire the most engage in this activity?							
The Admired Observer Test Would I want the person I admire most to see me doing this?							
The Transparency Test Could I give a clear explanation for the action I'm contemplating, including an honest and transparent account of all my motives, that would satisfy a fair and dispassionate moral judge?							
The Person in the Mirror Test Will I be able to look at myself in the mirror and respect the person I see there?							
The Golden Rule Test Would I like to be on the receiving end of this action and all its potential consequences?							

Source: Adapted from The Art of Achievement: Mastering the 7 Cs of Business and Life, *Andrews McMeel Publishing LLC, 2002.*

Exhibit 4.6. The conscious marketer's task here is to ensure that he or she has applied all relevant decision-making criteria and to assess his or her level of confidence that the decision being made meets those stated criteria. If the marketer isn't confident about the decision, he or she should reexamine the other alternatives. Using Exhibit 4.6, you can gauge your own ethical response. If your scores tend to be in the "Yes" area (columns 1 and 2), then the situation is not ethically troubling for you. If, in contrast, your scores tend to be in the "No" area (columns 6 and 7), it is ethically troubling, and you know it. If your scores are scattered or are in the "Maybe" area (columns 3, 4, and 5), you need to step back and reflect on how you wish to proceed. In using such an ethical metric or framework, decision makers must consider the relevant ethical issues, evaluate the alternatives, and then choose a course of action that will help them avoid serious ethical lapses.

Next, let's illustrate how the ethical decision-making metric in Exhibit 4.6 can be used to make ethical business decisions.

Myra Jansen, the head cook at Lincoln High School in Anytown, USA, has had enough. Reports showing that children rarely eat enough vegetables have combined with studies that indicate school kids have a limited amount of time to eat their lunches. The combination has led to increasing obesity rates and troublesome reports about the long-term effects. Myra has therefore decided that the Tater Tots and hot dogs are out. Vegetables and healthy proteins are in.

The problem, of course, is getting the kids to eat raw vegetables, plant proteins, and lean meat. For many teenagers, recommending that they eat healthy food at lunch is akin to calling detention a play date. But Myra has a plan: She's going to reformulate various menu items using different ingredients and just never tell the students. Thus the regular hot dogs will be replaced with turkey or soy dogs. The Tater Tots will contain more nutrient-dense sweet potatoes instead of the vitamin-deficient regular spuds they used to be made out of. She is convinced she can make such switches for most of the menu items, and none of the children need to know.

If schools want children to eat more healthy foods, should they switch to healthier options without telling them, or tell them even though the children might reject the changes?

©asiseeit/E+/Getty Images

Most of the kitchen staff members are on board with the idea and even have suggested other possible menu switches that would benefit the students by ensuring that they receive a well-balanced meal at school. School board members, when apprised of the idea, got very excited and praised Myra for her innovative thinking. But the community liaison for the school, Salim Jones, whose job it is to communicate with parents and other members of the community, is not so sure. Salim is nervous about how students will react when they learn that they have been deceived. He also has two small children of his own, one of whom has a severe wheat allergy. Thus the Joneses are extremely cautious about eating out, always asking for a detailed, specific list of ingredients for anything they order.

Using his training in ethical decision making, Salim sits down to evaluate his alternatives, beginning with identifying possible options available to the school district as well as the various stakeholders who might be affected by the decision. He comes up with the following list:

1. Switch out the food without telling students.
2. Leave menus as they are.
3. Switch out the food ingredients but also tell students exactly what is in each item in the cafeteria.

To make a clear recommendation to the board about what would be the best ethical choice, Salim decides to evaluate each alternative using a series of questions similar to those in Exhibit 4.6.

Question 1: Would I want to see this action described on the front page of the local paper? The school board's reaction caused Salim to think that the larger community would appreciate the effort to improve students' health. Thus, option 1 appears best for these stakeholders, and possibly for society, which may reduce the prevalence of obesity among these students. However, he shudders to think about how angry students might be if they learned they had been tricked. They also likely are accustomed to their menu as it is, and therefore, they would prefer option 2.

Question 2: Would the person I admire most engage in this activity, and would I want him or her to see me engage in this activity? For most of his life, Salim has held up Mahatma Gandhi as his ideal for how to act in the world. For Gandhi, truth was an absolute concept, not something that could be changed depending on the situation. Therefore, Salim believes Gandhi would strongly disapprove of option 1. However, Gandhi also worried about the ethics of eating and avoided food choices that had negative effects on society, so he might reject option 2 as well.

Question 3: Can I give a clear explanation for my action, including an honest account of my motives? In thinking about his children, Salim realizes that he is prioritizing their needs more than he is the needs of other children, such as those who struggle with weight issues. That is, he worries that his daughter might unknowingly be exposed to wheat in a school cafeteria, so he prefers option 3.

Question 4: Will I be able to look at myself in the mirror and respect what I see? By bringing up the ethics of this decision, even when it seems as if everyone else has agreed with it, Salim feels confident that he has taken the right first step. The option chosen is still important, but it is a group decision, and Salim thinks he is doing his part.

Question 5: Would I want to be on the receiving end of this action and its consequences? Salim struggles most with this question. He remembers the kind of junk foods he chose when he was in college and the **20 pounds** he put on as a result. He wishes now that his parents had given him rules to follow about what to eat at school. But he also remembers how rebellious he was and knows that he probably would not have followed those rules. And at the same time, he hates the idea that someone could give him food to eat with falsified ingredients.

On the basis of this exercise, Salim decides that he wants to recommend option 3 to the school board. When he does so, Myra Jansen protests loudly: "This is ridiculous! I know better what kids should be eating, and I know too that some community liaison has no idea what they are willing to eat. You've got to trick them to get them to eat right."[42] Another school board member agrees, noting, "They're just kids. They don't necessarily have the same rights as adults, so we are allowed to decide what's best for them. And hiding the healthy ingredients to get the kids to eat healthy foods is what's best."

So what does the school board decide?

PROGRESS CHECK

1. Identify the steps in the ethical decision-making framework.

Reviewing Learning Objectives

L04-1 Define conscious marketing.

Conscious marketing involves a sense of purpose for the firm that is more than simply making a profit by selling products and services. It consists of four main principles: a greater purpose, consideration of stakeholders, conscious leadership and culture, and ethics.

L04-2 Describe what constitutes marketing's greater purpose.

Marketers must recognize that the purpose of business is more than making profits. The actual purpose might vary, such as providing necessary products, ensuring employment opportunities, or achieving greener production methods, but in all of these cases, the engagement improves the inputs as well as the outcomes of marketing actions.

L04-3 Differentiate between conscious marketing and corporate social responsibility.

Although CSR is an important element of conscious marketing, they are different from one another. CSR implies a focus on the triple bottom line of good performance according to economic, environmental, and social criteria. Thus good CSR can support and help promote conscious marketing. But conscious marketing goes beyond just CSR to refer to the overall meaning and purpose of the company and its marketing.

L04-4 Describe the ways in which conscious marketing helps various stakeholders.

To describe the ways, we first have to identify the various stakeholders of a company—namely, employees, customers, the marketplace, society, and the environment:

- *Employees:* A firm committed to conscious marketing treats its employees with decency and respect. For many employees, working for an irresponsible firm would be antithetical to their own morals and values.
- *Customers:* When companies exhibit conscious marketing principles, customers know that they can trust the firms to provide healthy, ethically acceptable products and services. Many customers also feel better about buying from a company that engages in responsible practices, which provides them with the additional value of feeling good about buying from that company.
- *Marketplace:* An industry improves its practices and avoids scandals when it ensures that the participating firms act responsibly and appropriately in all areas.
- *Society:* This stakeholder is local, national, or global communities who benefit when conscious marketers give thought to how their practices might influence values or connections, such as providing aid to underprivileged communities.
- *Environment:* The benefits of conscious marketing might include cleaner air and water as well as healthier product options.

L04-5 Explain how conscious leadership can produce a conscious culture in the firm.

Conscious marketing should be integrated into the very foundation of the firm by its leaders, such as in the firm's mission statement. Then top management must follow through and commit to supporting CSR, a strong ethical climate in the organization, and conscious marketing principles. When considering their strategy, conscious marketing firms ask not only "can we implement a certain policy?" but also "should we do it?" If any action is not ethical or socially responsible, the conscious firm will make changes to its marketing strategy.

 Describe how ethics constitutes an integral part of a firm's conscious marketing strategy.

Being a part of an ethically responsible firm should be important to every employee, but it is particularly important to marketers because they interact most directly with customers and suppliers and make decisions about how their products impact society and the environment. Thus marketing issues present a multitude of ethical questions and opportunities to handle.

 Identify the four steps in ethical decision making.

First, firms identify the ethical issue in question. Second, the firm gathers relevant information about the issue and the individuals and groups that have a stake in how the issue is resolved. Third, all parties relevant to the issue brainstorm alternative courses of action. Finally, the various alternatives are examined, and the course that generates the best alternative for the stakeholders is chosen. Firms can model their ethical policies after a well-established code of ethics like the one provided by the American Marketing Association. When making ethically sensitive decisions, firms can utilize a metric such as the ethical decision-making metric in Exhibit 4.6.

Key Terms

- business ethics, 117
- conscious marketing, 115
- corporate social responsibility (CSR), 117

- marketing ethics, 117
- stakeholders, 115

- triple bottom line, 117

Marketing Digitally

1. TOMS' mission has grown over time as the firm has grown, from the simple "Get One/Give One" proposition to now including other causes and greater commitments. Visit www.toms.com/improving-lives and explore how TOMS' social entrepreneurship has grown and how it communicates the message to its customers. How do you feel these efforts help TOMS build brand loyalty among its customers?

2. An increasing number of firms are stating their strong commitment to corporate social responsibility initiatives. The Corporate Social Responsibility Newswire Service keeps track of these various initiatives and posts stories on its website about what various corporations are doing. Go to www.csrwire.com and choose one story. Write a description of the corporation and the initiative.

Marketing Applications

1. Distinguish among conscious marketing, CSR, and marketing ethics.

2. Develop an argument for why a cosmetics manufacturer should build and maintain an ethical climate.

3. A clothing company gives generously to charities and sponsors donation drives to help lower-income teen girls get reasonably priced prom dresses. It also locates its manufacturing plants in countries with few labor laws, such that it does not know whether children are working in its factories, and works to prevent union activity among its employees in the United States. Evaluate this company from an ethical and social responsibility perspective.

4. Based on the evaluation you developed for question 3, provide responses to the ethical decision-making metric

from Exhibit 4.6. Provide a rationale for your score for each question.

5. Seventh Generation produces a line of cleaning and personal care products that are chemical-free and natural. Explore the Seventh Generation website and identify ways the firm lives up to the four principles of conscious marketing. In what ways does the firm go beyond these principles?

6. Amazon's purchase of Whole Foods Market had many consumers concerned that being owned by a very large firm would change the conscious marketing culture at Whole Foods. Visit www.wholefoods.com to see if the four principles of conscious marketing are still present. What impact do you believe Amazon's purchase of Whole Foods has had on the firm's socially responsible reputation? Do you believe that the concern surrounding the purchase is warranted? Why or why not?

Quiz Yourself

1. In what way does corporate social responsibility differ from conscious marketing?
    a. There is no difference.
    b. Conscious marketing is one part of corporate social responsibility.
    c. Corporate social responsibility is one part of conscious marketing.
    d. Corporate social responsibility uses different elements of the firm.
    e. Conscious marketing cannot be measured.

2. If a firm's sales force pressures potential customers to purchase services they cannot afford or need, but they require that sales force to work one week a year for Habitat for Humanity, that firm is
    a. Unethical yet socially responsible.
    b. Ethical and socially responsible.
    c. Neither ethical nor socially responsible.
    d. Ethical but not involved in helping the community.

(Answers to these two questions can be found in the Quiz Yourself Answer Key section.)

Chapter Case Study

McGraw Hill Education **connect**

DAILY TABLE

The growing social trends surrounding organic foods and healthy eating have helped companies such as Whole Foods and Trader Joe's become power players in the grocery market. But the high price of organic food remains a hurdle to expanding this market, especially to include lower-income families. Trader Joe's has positioned itself as a lower-cost option, yet the prices it charges still keep it out of reach of many working families. In response, the company's former president, Doug Rauch, decided to open a new kind of health food store in 2015. Daily Table, a nonprofit, membership-based grocery store, sells fresh produce and prepackaged meals at affordable prices.[43] It operates one store in Dorchester, Massachusetts, a moderate- to low-income suburb of Boston. It has expansion plans sighted for New York, Los Angeles, Detroit, and San Francisco.[44]

The innovative approach to groceries seeks to address several elements of the "food paradox" simultaneously. First, hunger is a major problem worldwide, as well as in the United States. One in six Americans can be categorized as hungry, and according to the U.S. Department of Agriculture, nearly 50 million Americans—including 7.9 million children—are "food insecure." Yet nearly one-third of the nation's annual food supply, or 133 billion pounds, goes uneaten. Grocery stores that offer high-quality food tend to cater to wealthier consumers, and they discard more than $165 billion worth of food annually, often simply because it has minor aesthetic flaws or blemishes. According to the Environmental Protection Agency, food waste is the single biggest source of waste in municipal landfills.

Not only are people from low-income sectors at risk of going hungry, but they also lack reliable access to nutritious and affordable food. In turn, they often suffer health problems related to their poor diets, including diabetes, heart disease, anemia, and so forth. Some communities don't have access to traditional grocery stores, thus smaller family-owned stores often fill this gap and may sell overripe produce. However, as the only healthy option available, those retailers can mark up the prices, such that the food sells at double the price it would go for in conventional grocery stores. That is, the people who most desperately need healthy food cannot access it.[45]

To address all these issues at once, Daily Table works with conventional supermarkets and restaurants to recover food that otherwise would go to waste. These relationships benefit both parties; the supermarket or restaurant reduces the margins of its losses by up to half, and Daily Table receives inventory for its shelves. It also visits local farms and fisheries to source excess produce and fish. For example, when New England enjoyed a bumper crop of apples in a recent season, Daily Table partnered with the nonprofit Boston Area Gleaners to obtain more than 10,000 pounds of excess fruit that otherwise would have rotted. The apples, brought from local farms, sold for $0.49 a pound. The fish wholesaler and distributor John Nagle Co. brings its excess cuts of fresh fish to Daily Table every few weeks. Daily Table can then sell the swordfish, ahi tuna, and salmon, which can cost as much as $30 a pound, for as little as $5.99 a pound.[46]

Such prices certainly are appealing, but they might not be enough to overcome perhaps the greatest competition Daily Table faces: namely, the fast-food chains that provide fast, plentiful, easy food service options for lower-income families. To enhance its competitive standing, Daily Table therefore introduced prepared meals, starting at $1.79, with sides ranging from $0.50 to $1.00. The grab-and-go, ready-to-eat meals are ideal for some families, though for others, Daily Table also encourages purchases of convenient, ready-to-cook meals. Some of the tasty ready-to-cook meals also get prepared in the stores' kitchens, on-site. Rather than the high-fat, high-sodium choices at fast-food restaurants, these alternatives give consumers greater access to wider choices of fresh food, rich in nutrients.[47]

Beyond these choices, Daily Table also works to ensure that it provides its primary customers with a sense of dignity. Low-income consumers often sense a stigma associated with visiting food pantries or soup kitchens. Daily Table thus cannot risk leading customers to feel as if they are receiving charity when they shop there. For example, though its prices are vastly discounted, it charges for all the food it sells. This strategy has another benefit, in that it increases the chances that Daily Table can survive as a self-sustaining business. In another tactic to avoid the stigma of charity, Daily Table's store environment looks like any other trendy supermarket, with clean aisles, wooden crates to display the fresh produce, a friendly vibe, and windows that look into the kitchen area.[48]

Finally, it identifies its valued customers as members. To ensure it primarily serves the community in surrounding neighborhoods, Daily Table established membership standards. The first time customers visit, they must share some basic information to receive their (free) membership. On subsequent visits, they provide their zip code and phone number, which confirms their membership, without any need for a physical membership card. Checking for whether customers are from the local neighborhood may raise some privacy concerns, but Daily Table assures customers that no such information is ever shared with outside institutions.[49]

Still, Daily Table has faced some challenges, as well as some criticisms. The first introduction of the concept led to concerns that it would sell expired produce that conventional supermarkets could not sell by law. According to this view, the store is a sort of dumping ground for food rejected by the rich and affluent, discarded and left as crumbs for the poor.[50] In response, Daily Table cites a report from the Natural Resources Defense Council and Harvard Law School that reveals that "sell by" and "best by" dates on food actually provide little relevant information because the dates are mostly unregulated. Therefore, Daily Table calls its food "rescued" instead of "expired."[51] Regardless of what it is called, selling officially expired food creates several legal and regulatory challenges for Daily Table. By working with regulatory authorities, it acquires the necessary permits, though the back-and-forth interactions with bureaucratic institutions often hinder the smooth functioning of its business model. The retailer also largely depends on grants and donations to keep its prices low. The resulting financial constraints require Daily Table to rely on word-of-mouth marketing; many consumers still have not heard of it.

Questions

1. How does Daily Table compare to Whole Foods and the conventional supermarket where you shop on the four principles of conscious marketing?

2. How does Daily Table address the needs of each of the different stakeholder groups: employees, customers, marketplace, society, and environment?

Endnotes

1. Jack Neff, "Why Unilever Needs Love Beauty and Planet," *Advertising Age*, December 11, 2017.

2. Alyssa Hardy, "Unilever Launches Sustainable Drugstore Brand Love Beauty Planet," *Teen Vogue*, December 13, 2017.

3. Neff, "Why Unilever Needs Love Beauty and Planet."

4. Aimee Lutkin, "Unilever's New Beauty Line Is Good for Your Face and the Planet," *Green Matters*, December 12, 2017.

5. Neff, "Why Unilever Needs Love Beauty and Planet."

6. Hardy, "Unilever Launches Sustainable Drugstore Brand."

7. Neff, "Why Unilever Needs Love Beauty and Planet."

8. Lutkin, "Unilever's New Beauty Line."

9. Unilever, "Sustainable Living," www.unileverusa.com/sustainable-living/.

10. Theodore Levitt, *Marketing Imagination* (Detroit, MI: Free Press, 1983).

11. See John Mackey and Raj Sisodia, *Conscious Capitalism: Liberating the Heroic Spirit of Business* (Boston, MA: Harvard Business Review Press, 2014).

12. The first three principles draw on Raj Sisodia, "Conscious Capitalism: A Better Way to Win," *California Management Review* 53 (Spring 2011), pp. 98–108.

13. Gene R. Laczniak and Patrick E. Murphy, "Stakeholder Theory and Marketing: Moving from a Firm-Centric to a Societal Perspective," *Journal of Public Policy & Marketing* 31 (Fall 2012), pp. 284–92.

14. Stephanie Strom, "Walmart Pushes for Improved Animal Welfare," *The New York Times*, May 22, 2015.

15. Andrew Khouri and Samantha Masunaga, "Tesla's Elon Musk and His Big Ideas: A Brief History," *Los Angeles Times*, May 1, 2015.

16. The most famous proponent of this view was Milton Friedman. See, for example, *Capitalism and Freedom* (Chicago: University of Chicago Press, 2002); or *Free to Choose: A Personal Statement* (Orlando, FL: Harcourt, 1990).

17. For a broad discussion of the range of CSR definitions, see "Communicating Corporate Social Responsibility," University Catholique de Louvain, www.edx.org/course/communicating-corporate-social-louvainx-louv12x.

18. H. Aguinis, "Organizational Responsibility: Doing Good and Doing Well," in *APA Handbook of Industrial and Organizational Psychology*, Vol. 3, ed. S. Zedeck (Washington, DC: American Psychological Association, 2011), pp. 855–79.

19. For a collection of articles discussing such challenges, see the "Special Issue on Corporate Social Responsibility in Controversial Industry Sectors," *Journal of Business Ethics* 110, no. 4 (November 2012).

20. Thomas C. Frohlich, Michael B. Sauter, and Sam Stebbins, "Companies Paying Americans the Least," 247WallSt.com, September 3, 2015.

21. Ibid.

22. This table was adapted from Mackey and Sisodia, *Conscious Capitalism*.

23. U.S. Food and Drug Administration, "Guidance for Industry: Voluntary Labeling Indicating Whether Foods Have or Have Not Been Derived from Genetically Engineered Plants," November 2015, www.fda.gov/food/guidanceregulation/guidancedocumentsregulatoryinformation/ucm059098.htm.

24. Hadley Malcolm, "Non-GMO Demand Growing Despite Report That Says GMOs Are Safe," *USA Today*, May 18, 2016, www.usatoday.com/story/money/2016/05/18/gmo-report-not-likely-to-change-minds-over-gmo-concern/84501686/.

25. www.generalmills.com/News/Issues/on-biotechnology; A. C. Gallo, "It's Non-GMO Month: Our Progress on GMO Transparency," *Whole Foods*, October 10, 2016, www.wholefoodsmarket.com/blog/its-non-gmo-month-our-progress-gmo-transparency; Laura Parker, "The GMO Labeling Battle Is Heating Up—Here's Why," *National Geographic*, January 11, 2014; Stefanie Strom, "Major Grocer to Label Foods with Gene-Modified Content," *The New York Times*, March 8, 2013; Amy Harmon and Andrew Pollack, "Battle Brewing over Labeling of Genetically Modified Food," *The New York Times*, May 24, 2012.

26. Rana Florida, "The Case for On-Site Day Care," *Fast Company*, October 1, 2014.

27. Aaron Katersky and Susannah Kim, "Slew of Retailers Say No to Black Friday," *ABC News*, October 27, 2015.

28. https://thewaltdisneycompany.com/philanthropy/; www.gktw.org/help/bio/disney.php; http://disneyparks.disney.go.com/blog/galleries/2014/01/disney-cast-members-create-an-extreme-village-makeover-for-give-kids-the-world/#photo-5.

29. www.ge.com/about-us/ecomagination; "GE Launches New Ecomagination Healthcare Products, Opens Renewable Energy HQ," GreenBiz, February 2, 2010, www.greenbiz.

30. United Press International, "Diet Soda Sales: Flat Would Be Better," December 9, 2013, www.upi.com.

31. U.S. Environmental Protection Agency, "What Is Sustainability?," www.epa.gov/sustainability/basicinfo.htm.

32. www.burtsbees.com.

33. See, for example, General Electric, "2014 Performance," www.gecitizenship.com; General Electric, "The Spirit and the Letter," http://integrity.ge.com.

34. http://newmansownfoundation.org/about-us/total-giving.

35. Blake Mycoskie, TOMS Shoes; Dan Shewan, "Ethical Marketing: 5 Examples of Companies with a Conscience," *WordStream,* September 20, 2017, www.wordstream.com/blog/ws/2017/09/20/ethical-marketing; Charlotte Rogers, "How Toms Engaged 3.5 Million People in One Day," *Marketing Week,* June 29, 2016, www.marketingweek.com/2016/06/29/how-footwear-brand-toms-engaged-3-5-million-people-in-one-day-using-tribe-power/.

36. Taylor Armerding, "The 16 Biggest Data Breaches of the 21st Century," *CSO,* October 11, 2017, www.csoonline.com/article/2130877/data-breach/the-16-biggest-data-breaches-of-the-21st-century.html.

37. www.cmomagazine.com. This survey was conducted in 2006; more recent reports suggest that 41 percent of respondents to a 2013 survey reported having seen ethical misconduct overall, and 26 percent of these general employees considered the misconduct to represent a repeated pattern of behavior. See Ethics Resource Center, "2013 National Business Ethics Survey," www.ethics.org.

38. American Marketing Association, "Statement of Ethics," April 8, 2014, https://archive.ama.org/archive/AboutAMA/Pages/Statement%20of%20Ethics.aspx.

39. Nielsen, "Global Customers Are Willing to Put Their Money Where Their Heart Is When It Comes to Goods and Services Committed to Social Responsibility," June 17, 2014, www.nielsen.com/us/en/press-room/2014/global-consumers-are-willing-to-put-their-money-where-their-heart-is.html; Michael Connor, "Survey: U.S. Consumers Willing to Pay for Corporate Responsibility," *Business Ethics,* March 29, 2010, http://business-ethics.com.

40. www.conecomm.com/research-blog/2017-csr-study; Richard Stengel, "Doing Well by Doing Good," *Time,* September 10, 2009, www.time.com.

41. "2011 World's Most Ethical Companies," Ethisphere, http://ethisphere.com/2011-worlds-most-ethical-companies.

42. Myra Jansen.

43. Daily Table, "About Us," http://dailytable.org/about-us/our-story/.

44. Ibid.

45. Ron Mott, "Daily Table Supermarket Specializes in Food Past Its Prime," *NBC News,* June 29, 2015, www.nbcnews.com/nightly-news/food-past-its-prime-supermarket-specializes-expired-food-n383826; Yvonne Abraham, "Waste Not, Hunger Not," *Boston Globe,* June 13, 2015, www.bostonglobe.com/metro/2015/06/13/dorchester-daily-table-emporium-cleverly-reuses-food-waste/bhZZSacW4xqaij5UrkeKbM/story.html.

46. Lindsay Abrams, "'Expired' Food Is Good for You: A Supermarket Exec's Bold Business Gamble," *Salon,* January 20, 2014, www.salon.com/2014/01/20/expired_food_is_good_for_you_a_supermarket_execs_bold_business_gamble/.

47. Taryn Luna, "Nonprofit Grocery Store Set to Open in Dorchester," *Boston Globe,* May 22, 2015, www.bostonglobe.com/business/2015/05/21/nonprofit-daily-table-grocery-store-set-open-dorchester/CBzBHC1RsEOVCSgOFa0p9O/story.html.

48. Mark Winne, "The Daily Table: Is This What We Really Need?," *Beacon Broadside,* June 30, 2015, www.beaconbroadside.com/broadside/2015/06/the-daily-table-is-this-what-we-really-need.html; Mott, "Daily Table Supermarket Specializes in Food Past Its Prime."

49. Daily Table, "Membership," http://dailytable.org/become-a-member/; Steve Holt, "Whether You Call It 'Rescued' or 'Expired,' Old Food Is a Tough Sell," *TakePart,* June 11, 2015, www.takepart.com/article/2015/06/11/rescued-food-grocery.

50. Brad Tuttle, "Former Trader Joe's Exec Opens Super Cheap Nonprofit Supermarket," *Time Money,* June 4, 2015; Steve Holt, "Did Doug Rauch Just Fix Food Deserts and Food Waste?," *Edible Boston,* www.edibleboston.com/blog/did-doug-rauch-just-fix-food-deserts-and-food-waste?rq=Daily%20Table.

51. Abrams, "'Expired' Food Is Good for You"; www.businessinsider.com/trader-joes-exec-launches-daily-table-2015-6.

i. Martha C. White, "Selling Jewelry with a Crowdfunding App and Dash of Social Sharing," *The New York Times,* December 18, 2016; Joy Sewing, "Jewelry Designer David Yurman on Cowboys, Yoga, and Happiness," *Houston Chronicle,* November 29, 2016; Kristin Tice Studeman, "Natalia Vodianova, Supermodel Supermom, Can Do It All," *W Magazine,* October 13, 2016.

ii. Hannah Tregear, "Case Study/Kellogg's: Kellogg's Boosts Social Media Campaign ROI," *Brandwatch,* November 23, 2013, www.brandwatch.com/wp-content/uploads/2013/11/Brandwatch_CS_Kelloggs.pdf; Jennifer Rooney, "Kellogg's Completes Major Brand Overhaul," *Forbes,* May 10, 2012, www.forbes.com/; E. J. Schultz, "Media Maven Bob Arnold Leads Kellogg into Digital-Buying Frontier," *Advertising Age,* September 23, 2013, http://adage.com; Larisa Bedgood, "5 Compelling Reasons to Ramp Up Your Digital Marketing Strategy," SmartData Collective, March 18, 2015, http://smartdatacollective.com/lbedgood/305186/5-compelling-reasons-ramp-your-digital-marketing-strategy.

iii. Erica E. Phillips, "Patagonia's Balancing Act: Chasing Mass-Market Appeal While Doing No Harm," *The Wall Street Journal,* August 17, 2016; Jamie Feldman, "Patagonia Just Made Another Major Move to Save the Earth and Your Wallet," *Huffington Post,* January 30, 2017; Patagonia's clear promise to customers.

iv. Christine Hauser, "Google to Ban All Payday Loan Ads," *The New York Times,* May 11, 2016; Hannah Kuchler, "Google Bans Payday Lender Advertising," *Financial Times,* May 11, 2016; David Mayer, "Why Google Was Smart to Drop Its 'Don't Be Evil' Motto," *Fast Company,* February 9, 2016.

v. Heidi Vogt, "Making Change: Mobile Pay in Africa," *The Wall Street Journal,* January 2, 2015; Leslie Shaffer, "Consumer Companies Struggle to Tap Aspirational Middle-Class India," *CNBC,* November 25, 2015, www.cnbc.com/2015/11/25/consumer-companies-struggle-to-tap-aspirational-middle-class-india.html; "How Digital Revolution Can Push Financial Inclusion," *CNBC,* December 7, 2015, www.moneycontrol.com/news/economy/how-digital-revolution-can-push-financial-inclusion_4472241.html.

Quiz Yourself Answer Key

1. In what way does corporate social responsibility differ from conscious marketing?

   Answer: (c) Corporate social responsibility is one part of conscious marketing.

2. If a firm's salesforce pressures potential customers to purchase services they cannot afford or need, but they require that salesforce to work one week a year for Habitat for Humanity, that firm is

   Answer: (a) Unethical yet socially responsible.

APPENDIX 4A

UNDERSTANDING ETHICS USING SCENARIOS

In this appendix, we present nine ethical scenarios designed to assist you in developing your skills at identifying ethical issues. There is no one right answer to the dilemmas below, just as there will be no correct answers to many of the ethical situations you will face throughout your career. Instead, these scenarios can help you develop your ethical reasoning skills as well as your sensitivity toward ethical issues. As mentioned throughout the chapter, Exhibit 4.6 provides an ethical decision-making metric to assist you in evaluating the following and all such ethical dilemmas you may face.

Scenario 1: R.J. Reynolds: Promotions to the Youth Market

Tobacco giant R.J. Reynolds sent a set of coasters featuring its cigarette brands and recipes for mixed drinks with high alcohol content to young adults, via direct mail, on their 21st birthdays (the legal age for alcohol consumption). The alcohol brands in the recipes included Jack Daniels, Southern Comfort, and Finlandia Vodka. The reverse side of the coaster read, "Go' til Daybreak, and Make Sure You're Sittin'." The campaign, called "Drinks on Us," clearly promoted abusive and excessive drinking. This campaign was eventually stopped because the cigarette company did not have permission to use the alcohol brands.

The Federal Drug Administration (FDA) has been given the authority to regulate tobacco, including banning certain products, limiting nicotine, and blocking labels such as "low tar" and "light" that could wrongly imply certain products are less harmful.[1] The law doesn't let the FDA ban nicotine or tobacco entirely. A committee has been formed to study several issues, including dissolvable tobacco products, product changes, and standards, and report back to the FDA. Of particular interest is the increase in the share of smokers using menthol cigarettes from 31 percent to almost 34 percent in four years, with more pronounced increases among young smokers. It also showed that among black smokers, 82.6 percent used menthol cigarettes, compared with 32.3 percent for Hispanic smokers and 23.8 percent for white smokers.[2] A ban on cigarettes with flavors such as clove, chocolate, or fruit took effect in 2009 because they are believed to appeal to youth.

After graduation, you have an offer to work in either marketing or sales at R.J. Reynolds, the tobacco company that sells many popular brands of cigarettes. The pay and benefits are very competitive. The job market is tight, and if you don't get a job right away, you will have to live with your parents. Should you take the job?

Scenario 2: Car Manufacturer Gives Bribes for Contracts

A car and truck manufacturer just found out that two of its overseas business units have been engaging in bribery over a 10-year period of time. The company paid $56 million in bribes to more than 20 countries to gain government contracts for their vehicles.[3] The company is now paying millions in criminal and civil charges because of its violation of the Foreign Corrupt Practices Act (FCPA), and it admits to earning more than $50 million in profits based on its corrupt transactions. The car company recorded the bribe payments as commissions, special discounts, or necessary payments. Should the manufacturer discontinue its operations with the countries that were unlawfully bribed to buy its cars? Are financial fines sufficient to repair the problem? How can companies be sure the commissions they earn are true commissions and not a bribe?

Scenario 3: Retailers Lack Ethical Guidelines

Renata has been working at Peavy's Bridal for nearly a year now. Her sales figures have never been competitive with those of her coworkers, and the sales manager has called her in for several meetings to discuss her inability to close the sale. Things look desperate; in the last meeting, the sales manager told her that if she did not meet her quota next month, the company would likely have to fire her.

In considering how she might improve her methods and sales, Renata turned to Marilyn, the salesperson in the store who had the most experience. Marilyn has been with Peavy's for nearly 30 years, and she virtually always gets the sale. But how?

"Let me tell you something sweetie," Marilyn tells her. "Every bride-to-be wants one thing: to look beautiful on her wedding day so that everyone gasps when they first see her. And hey, the husband is going to think she looks great. But let's be honest here—not everyone is all that beautiful. So you have to convince them that they look great in one, and only one, dress. And that dress had better be the most expensive one they try, or they won't believe you anyway! And then you have to show them how much better they look with a veil. And some shoes. And a tiara . . . you get the picture! I mean, they need all that stuff anyway, so why shouldn't we make them feel good while they're here and let them buy from us?"

Should she follow Marilyn's advice and save her job?

Scenario 4: Giving Credit Where Credit Isn't Due

A catalog retailer that carries home and children's items, such as children's furniture, clothing, and toys, was seeking a way to reach a new audience and stop the declining sales and revenue trends it was suffering. A marketing research firm hired by the retailer identified a new but potentially risky market: lower-income single parents. The new market seemed attractive because of the large number of single parents, but most of these homes were severely constrained in terms of their monetary resources.

The research firm proposed that the retailer offer a generous credit policy that would allow consumers to purchase up to $500 worth of merchandise on credit without a credit check, provided they signed up for direct payment of their credit account from a checking account. Because these were high-risk consumers, the credit accounts would carry extremely high interest rates. The research firm believed that even with losses, enough accounts would be paid off to make the venture extremely profitable for the catalog retailer.

Should the retailer pursue this new strategy?

Scenario 5: The Jeweler's Tarnished Image

Sparkle Gem Jewelers, a family owned and operated costume jewelry manufacturing business, traditionally sold its products only to wholesalers. Recently, however, Sparkle Gem

was approached by the charismatic Barb Stephens, who convinced the owners to begin selling through a network of distributors she had organized. The distributors recruited individuals to host jewelry parties in their homes. Sparkle Gem's owners, the Billing family, have
been thrilled with the revenue generated by these home parties and started making plans for
the expansion of the distributor network.

However, Mrs. Billing just received a letter from a jewelry party customer, who
expressed sympathy for Mrs. Billing's loss. Confused, Mrs. Billing contacted the letter
writer, who told her that Barb Stephens had come to the jewelry party at her church and
told the story of Sparkle Gem. According to Stephens' story, Mrs. Billing was a young
widow struggling to keep her business together after her husband had died on a missionary
trip. The writer had purchased $200 worth of jewelry at the party and told Mrs. Billing that
she hoped it helped. Mrs. Billing was stunned. She and her very-much-alive husband had
just celebrated their 50th wedding anniversary.

What should Mrs. Billing do now?

Scenario 6: No Wonder It's So Good

Enjoy Cola is a new product produced by ABC Beverage and marketed with the slogan
"Relax with Enjoy." Unlike other colas on the market, Enjoy does not contain caffeine and
therefore is positioned as the perfect beverage to end the day or for a slow-paced weekend
and as a means to help consumers relax and unwind. The market response has been tremendous, and sales of Enjoy have been growing rapidly, especially among women.

ABC Beverage decided not to list on the ingredients label that Enjoy contains a small
amount of alcohol, because it is not required to do so by the government unless the alcohol
content is more than 1 percent.

Mia Rodriguez, the marketing director for Enjoy, only recently learned that Enjoy contains small amounts of alcohol and is troubled about ABC's failure to disclose this information on the ingredients list. She worries about the impact of this omission on consumers
who have alcohol sensitivities or those who shouldn't be consuming alcohol, such as preg-
nant women and recovering alcoholics.

What should Rodriguez do? What would you do in her position?

Scenario 7: Bright Baby's Bright Idea

Bartok Manufacturing produces a line of infant toys under the Bright Baby brand label. The
Consumer Product Safety Commission (CPSC) recently issued a recall order for the Bright

Baby car seat gym, a very popular product. According to the CPSC, the gym contains small parts that present a choking hazard. The CEO of Bartok Manufacturing, Bill Bartok, called an executive meeting to determine the firm's strategy in response to the recall.

Mike Henderson, Bartok's CFO, stated that the recall could cost as much as $1 million in lost revenue from the Bright Baby line. Noting that there had been no deaths or injuries from the product, just the potential for injury, Henderson proposed that the remaining inventory of car seat gyms be sold in regions where the CPSC's rules do not apply. Sue Tyler, the marketing director for Bartok, recommended that the product be repackaged and sold under a different brand name so that the Bright Baby name would not be associated with the product. Bartok, though a bit leery of the plan, agreed to go along with it to avoid the monetary losses.

What would you have recommended to the CEO?

Scenario 8: Money from Mailing Lists[4]

Sports Nostalgia Emporium sells autographed sports memorabilia online. Recently, the director of marketing, John Mangold, started using a mailing list he had purchased from Marketing Metrix, a marketing research firm that sells consumer information. Mangold relies on such purchased mailing lists to grow the company and sends printed catalogs to thousands of people each month. The mailing lists he gets from Marketing Metrix are much more effective than other mailing lists and generate almost twice as much revenue.

In a recent conversation with a sales representative from Marketing Metrix, Mangold discovered the reason its lists were so effective: Marketing Metrix tracks the online behavior of consumers and uses that information to create targeted lists. The mailing lists that Mangold has been using consist of consumers who visited the websites of Sports Nostalgia Emporium's competitors. Based on what he can discern, Mangold believes that these consumers are not aware that someone is collecting information about their online behavior, along with their names and addresses, and selling it to other firms.

Should Mangold continue to use the Marketing Metrix mailing list? If so, should he tell his new customers how he got their names and addresses? Do consumers need to give consent before firms can collect information about their behavior?

Scenario 9: The Blogging CEO[5]

David Burdick is the CEO of ACME Bubblegum, a successful public company. As one of the cofounders of the company, Burdick has enjoyed speaking and writing about the success of ACME Bubblegum for several years. Typically, he speaks at conferences or directly to the press, but recently he has been blogging about his firm anonymously. Specifically, he defended a recent advertising campaign that was unpopular among consumers and pointedly attacked one of ACME Bubblegum's competitors. Burdick deeply enjoys his anonymous blogging and believes that none of his readers actually know that he works for ACME Bubblegum.

Should Burdick be allowed to praise his company's performance anonymously online? Should he be allowed to attack his competitors without disclosing his relationship with the company? How would you feel if the CEO of a company at which you shopped was secretly writing criticisms of his or her competition? How would you feel if you knew a writer for your favorite blog was actually closely involved in a company that the blog community discussed?

Endnotes

1. Michael Felberbaum, "Panel to Examine Menthol Cigarettes' Impact," Associated Press, March 29, 2010.

2. Ibid., based on a study by the Substance Abuse and Mental Health Services Administration in November 2009.

3. Department of Justice, Office of Public Affairs, "Daimler AG and Three Subsidiaries Resolve Foreign Corrupt Practices Act Investigation and Agree to Pay $93.6 Million in Criminal Penalties," press release, April 1, 2010; Michael Connor, "Daimler Agrees to Pay $185 Million to Settle Bribery Charges," *Business Ethics*, March 26, 2010, http://businessethics.com.

4. Emily Steel, "How Marketers Hone Their Aim Online," *The Wall Street Journal*, June 19, 2007, p. B6.

5. "Mr. Mackey's Offense," *The Wall Street Journal*, July 16, 2007, p. A12.

©Eakrat/Shutterstock

LEARNING OBJECTIVES

After reading this chapter, you should be able to:

 LO5-1 Outline how customers, the company, competitors, corporate partners, and the physical environment affect marketing strategy.

 LO5-2 Explain why marketers must consider their macroenvironment when they make decisions.

 LO5-3 Identify various social trends that impact marketing.

 LO5-4 Examine the technological advances that are influencing marketers.

CHAPTER 5

ANALYZING THE MARKETING ENVIRONMENT

It's finally here! But then again, don't get too excited. These are the mixed messages coming from Tesla as the first models of the long-promised Model 3 sedan roll off the production line. The Model 3, with its base price of $35,000, represents an accessible version of the innovative company's famous (and thus far, very expensive) electric cars. After multiple delays and missed deadlines, the sedans are finally entering into actual production, such that the environmentally conscious but less wealthy customers who put their names on waiting lists are receiving delivery.

But even as excitement mounts about the fulfillment of this promise, Tesla's founder Elon Musk is cautioning that the months ahead will be marked by challenges related to its production capacities. Currently, Tesla has an estimated 500,000 reservations for Model 3 sedans. Musk anticipates that the company can produce 10,000 cars per week—if everything goes right in the supply chain. But with the recognition that everything going right is rare, Musk also has suggested that the first six months of production will be "manufacturing hell" and warned people not to get their hopes up too high. External observers, noting that the company produced only 30 cars in the month of Musk's announcement, and 75 the month after that,

suggest that even these cautions do not go far enough. Most indications suggest that Tesla is nowhere close to its target production volume.

This balance between encouraging excitement to sell more cars and dampening expectations to avoid a service failure remains a difficult one, though Tesla has walked the tightrope for years. Early predictions suggested the Model 3 would be ready years ago, so consumers have grown a little accustomed to being disappointed in their expectations of the company. But the company's production capacity has finally caught up with its technology, even as these technological advances continue to spread throughout and alter the broader automotive market. Some observers even call the Model 3 a "breakthrough offering"—perhaps not the first electric vehicle, but the one that will irrevocably change the marketing environment.

Although Tesla seeks to expand its reach more widely by introducing this more affordable version of its electric car, it also needs to avoid eliminating the market for its more expensive models, such as the existing Model S or the Model X sport-utility vehicle. This specific balance is complicated by the broader goals that Musk has established for his company. That is, Tesla seeks to make electric cars (including those produced by brands other than Tesla) the norm in the vehicle market and eventually drive out gasoline-powered automobiles. Doing so requires it to attract a vast number of consumers, not just those who can afford the luxury versions of its products.

At the same time, Tesla cannot ignore the impacts of competitors. Most major carmakers have announced plans to introduce electric or improved hybric models of their popular brands. Volvo has promised that all its new cars will be hybrids or electric vehicles by 2019. Chevrolet already sells the fully electric Bolt, and though its range (at 238 miles) is not as great at Tesla's (310 miles), it already is selling thousands of these currently available cars to customers every month.[1]

LO5-1 Outline how customers, the company, competitors, corporate partners, and the physical environment affect marketing strategy.

A MARKETING ENVIRONMENT ANALYSIS FRAMEWORK

As the opening vignette illustrates, marketers continue to find changes in what their customers demand or expect and adapt their product and service offerings accordingly. By paying close attention to customer needs and continuously monitoring the business environment in which the company operates, a good marketer can identify potential opportunities.

Exhibit 5.1 illustrates factors that affect the marketing environment. The centerpiece, as always, is consumers. Consumers may be influenced directly by the immediate actions of the focal company, the company's competitors, the corporate partners that work with the firm to make and supply products and services to consumers, and the physical environment. The firm, and therefore consumers indirectly, is influenced by the macroenvironment, which includes various impacts of culture; demographics; and social, technological, economic, and political/legal factors. We discuss each of these components in detail in this chapter and suggest how they might interrelate.

Because the consumer is the center of all marketing efforts, value-based marketing aims to provide greater value to consumers than competitors offer. Therefore, the marketing firm must consider the entire business process, all from a consumer's point of view.[2] Consumers' needs and wants, as well as their ability to purchase, depend on a host of factors that change and evolve over time. Firms use various tools to keep track of competitors' activities and consumer trends, and they rely on various methods to communicate with their corporate partners and understand their physical environment. Furthermore, they monitor their

EXHIBIT 5.1 Understanding the Marketing Environment

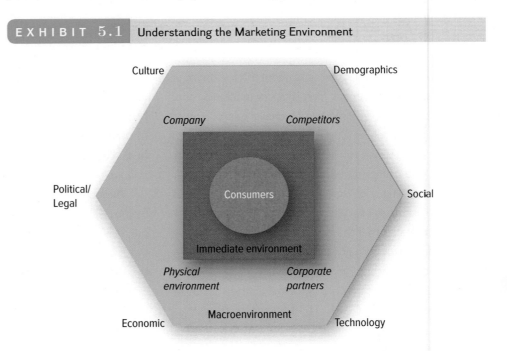

macroenvironment to determine how such factors influence consumers and how they should respond to them. Sometimes, a firm can even anticipate trends.

THE IMMEDIATE ENVIRONMENT

Exhibit 5.2 illustrates the factors that affect consumers' immediate environment: the company's capabilities, competitors, corporate partners and physical environment.

Company Capabilities

In the immediate environment, the first factor that affects the consumer is the firm itself. Successful marketing firms focus on satisfying customer needs that match their core competencies. The primary strength of Corning is its ability to manufacture glass. The company initially made its name by producing the glass enclosure to encase Thomas Edison's lightbulb. But by successfully leveraging its core competency in glass manufacturing while also recognizing marketplace trends toward mobile devices, Corning shifted its focus. As a result, Corning is one of the leading producers of durable, scratch-resistant glass on the faces of smartphones and tablets. More than 4.5 billion mobile devices feature its Gorilla Glass.[3] Marketers can use analyses of their external environment, like the SWOT analysis described in Chapter 2, to categorize any opportunity as attractive or unattractive. If it appears attractive, they also need to assess it in terms of their existing competencies.

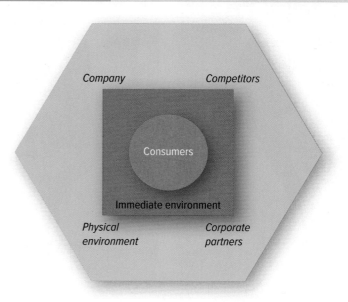

| EXHIBIT 5.2 | Understanding the Immediate Environment |

Competitors

Competition also significantly affects consumers in the immediate environment. It is therefore critical that marketers understand their firm's competitors, including their strengths, weaknesses, and likely reactions to the marketing activities that their own firm undertakes.

For example, in one of the most competitive markets, the wireless network industry, two of the current ruling competitors are Verizon and Sprint. As Verizon works to maintain its dominance and Sprint works to gain market share, they have recently directly targeted each other in their advertisements. In particular, in 2016 Sprint hired a new spokesperson, Verizon's famous 2002 "can you hear me now" ex-spokesperson. In the ad he proudly states, "I used to ask if you could hear me now with Verizon. Not anymore." In response, Verizon states, "They're using our 2002 pitchman because they're finally catching up to where we were in 2002."[4] Furthermore, Verizon has also enlisted a new spokesperson, Thomas Middleditch, the star of HBO's hit show *Silicon Valley,* who proclaims the benefits of Verizon and then literally drops the mic.[5] These efforts represent the companies' recognition of what their closest competitor is doing. But at the same time, each company touts its benefits over its competitors because the ultimate goal, of course, is to appeal to consumers.

Corporate Partners

Few firms operate in isolation. For example, automobile manufacturers collaborate with suppliers of sheet metal, tire manufacturers, component part makers, unions, transport companies, and dealerships to produce and market their automobiles successfully. Parties that work with the focal firm are its corporate partners.

Consider an example that demonstrates the role these partners play and how they work with the firm to create a single, efficient manufacturing system. Unlike most outdoor clothing manufacturers that use synthetic, nonrenewable materials, Nau makes modern urban+outdoor apparel from renewable sources such as sustainably harvested eucalyptus

Nau works with its corporate partners to develop socially responsible outdoor (left) and urban (right) apparel.

(left): ©Philipp Nemenz/Cultura/Getty Images; (right): ©PeopleImages/E+/Getty Images

and recycled plastic bottles. It was founded by a team of entrepreneurs who left companies such as Nike and Patagonia. To develop rugged and beautiful clothing from sustainable materials, these founders turned to manufacturing partners around the world to develop new fabrics that are performance-driven and technical. One example of an innovative fabric used in Nau's jackets is a blend of recycled polyester and organic cotton that is coated and bonded to recycled polyester knit. The result is a water-resistant, breathable technical soft shell material that is ideal for outdoor activities. To complement the new fabrics, the company uses only organic cotton and wool from "happy sheep," provided by partners in the ranching industry that embrace animal-friendly practices. Furthermore, Nau donates 2 percent of the profit from every sale to charities, such as Conservation Alliance and Mercy Corps. So far it has donated over $200,000 to Mercy Corps alone.[6] Not only does Nau represent the cutting edge of sustainability and green business, it also clearly demonstrates how "going green" can prompt companies to work more closely with their partners to innovate.[7]

Physical Environment

The physical environment includes land, water, air, and living organisms (flora and fauna).[8] Products and services are influenced by how they are used in the physical environment, and in turn they can also influence the physical environment. Concerns about adverse changes to the physical environment—such as depletion of the ozone layer, increased emissions, pollutants in water systems, rapidly increasing deforestation, and irreversible reductions in wildlife and their habitats—have reached epic proportions. Globally, worries and concerns about the sustainability of the planet have led to demands for companies and consumers to avoid harming the environment and depleting these natural resources.

In response, a historic agreement of 193 world leaders produced 17 Global Goals of Sustainable Development (Exhibit 5.3).[9] These goals seek to preserve the physical environment and protect the planet. They also are likely to bring about important social changes (e.g., eliminating poverty, achieving prosperity for all) that might be facilitated by technological advances and shifts in the ways firms (and their societies) operate. These goals largely can be addressed through a physical environmental lens, focused on climate action, affordable and clean energy, sustainable production/consumption, and protections of life on land and water.

In Europe, Nissan and ENEL provide a way for drivers with the battery-powered Nissan Leaf car models to sell the energy contained in their vehicles back to the grid.

©Steve Lagreca/Shutterstock

Energy Trends Firms are actively engaging in sustainable practices in terms of how they go about manufacturing products and provisioning services, as well as the types of products and services that they offer. Consider the vehicle market as an example, where Tesla and Uber are radically altering people's driving behaviors. Electric cars and ride-sharing options already are helping reduce carbon emissions and improving the physical environment.

Novel options also add value, such as smart grids that increase the efficiency of energy consumption. In

EXHIBIT 5.3 Global Goals of Sustainable Development

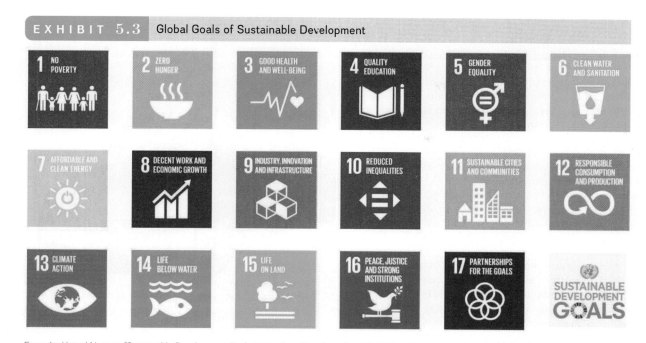

a joint European venture, Nissan and ENEL, an Italian multinational manufacturer and distributor of electricity and gas, provide a way for drivers with the battery-powered Nissan Leaf car models to sell the energy contained in their vehicles back to the grid.[10] This example combines an innovative product manufacturer—Nissan leads the electric vehicle market thus far—with a well-established service provider, in that ENEL already had operations in place to reclaim energy from car batteries. By working together, the companies give consumers a means to purchase battery power when they need it but supply that power back to the grid when they don't, promising the potential for reduced emissions, diminished pollution, and an estimated $2.85 billion savings in electricity costs for consumers by 2030.[11] As Ethical & Societal Dilemma 5.1 notes, carmakers might benefit more generally if they can shift their production capabilities to cleaner and electric engines.

Greener Practices and Greener Consumers When they undertake green marketing strategic efforts, firms work to supply customers with environmentally friendly, sustainable merchandise and services.[12] As we noted in Chapter 4, sustainability is a critical ethical consideration for marketers. Many consumers, concerned about everything from the purity of air and water to the safety of beef and salmon, believe that each person can make a difference in the environment. For example, nearly half of U.S. adults now recycle their soda bottles and newspapers, and European consumers are even more green. Germans are required by law to recycle bottles, and the European Union does not allow beef raised on artificial growth hormones to be imported.

Demand for green-oriented products has been a boon to the firms that supply them. Marketers encourage consumers to replace older versions of washing machines and dishwashers with water- and energy-saving models and to invest in phosphate-free laundry detergent and mercury-free and rechargeable batteries. New markets emerge for recycled building products, packaging, paper goods, and even sweaters and sneakers, as well as for more efficient appliances, lighting, and heating and cooling systems in homes and offices. To promote their greener practices, nearly 500 firms have joined the Tropical Forest Alliance (TFA) 2020,[13] which seeks to reduce the deforestation caused by the production of many consumer products that rely on palm oil, soy, tree pulp, and paper. Brands owned by Unilever and Mondelēz, two corporate partners in TFA, commit to finding ways to support regional production processes that not only limit deforestation but also

Ethical & Societal Dilemma 5.1   Even Paris Is Going Electric: The Trends Leading to Shifting Norms in the Auto Industry[i]

In Europe, diesel engines have long been the standard for automobiles. Embracing the engines allowed European nations to highlight their manufacturing capacity and support an industry that contributed significantly to their national economies. Such efforts were particularly notable for France, home to not only such famous brands as Renault and Citroën but also to the Paris Motor Show, an every-other-year event that draws a massive international crowd.

The most recent Paris Motor Show was a little different though. In particular, far fewer diesel engines were on display. In their place, carmakers touted their electric and hybrid models. What led to the radical change? There are several notable influences.

First, it constitutes a response to recent emissions scandals, in which Volkswagen was found to have inserted technology into its diesel engines that fraudulently made it seem as if the engines issued lower emissions than they actually did. Faced with consumer skepticism, as well as growing recognition that diesel is not as clean as it might have seemed, carmakers simply are avoiding mentioning the term or their use of these engines.

Second, environmental conditions make it impossible to ignore the need for cleaner fuels. In Paris in particular, the air quality is so poor that regulations ban older cars (manufactured before 1997), with their inefficient motors, from driving on city streets during daytime hours (8:00 a.m.–8:00 p.m.). Faced with such realities, and the resulting customer demand for alternatives, including electric and hybrid options, car manufacturers are moving their own practices and production lines more toward environmentally friendly vehicles.

BMW is going a little green with its i8 hybrid model. You can save a lot of money on gas, but you'll have to shell out at least $140,000 to do so.

©Joby Sessions/T3 Magazine via Getty Images

Third, even if some automobile companies might prefer to keep producing their best-selling diesel engines, they simply cannot ignore the advantages that their international competitors might be achieving by innovating the ways they power their cars. Across the world, companies such as BMW, Mercedes-Benz, Mitsubishi, General Motors, Toyota, and Infiniti are expanding the range of electric automobiles available, from sport-utility vehicles to luxury cars.

help ensure the living standards of farmers in tropical nations. Such commitments appeal to consumers, but they also may help ensure stable supply chains and potentially reduce production costs. Jumping on the green bandwagon, Kohl's has made over 1,000 of its 1,160 stores Energy Star certified and even has on-site solar panels at over 150 of its locations.[14]

But not all green products and initiatives are inexpensive, and the resulting business model is complicated. Are green practices really good for business? Some green options are more expensive than traditional products and initiatives. Are consumers interested in or willing to pay the higher prices for green products? Are firms really interested in improving the environment? Or are they disingenuously marketing products or services as environmentally friendly, with the goal of gaining public approval and sales rather than actually improving the environment? This type of exploitation is common enough that it even has produced a term to describe it: greenwashing. Consumers need to question whether a firm is spending significantly more money and time advertising its green credentials or describing how it helps the environment, rather than actually spending these resources on developing and expanding environmentally sound practices.

PROGRESS CHECK

1. What are the components of the immediate environment?

MACROENVIRONMENTAL FACTORS

 LO5-2 Explain why marketers must consider their macroenvironment when they make decisions.

In addition to understanding their customers, the company itself, their competition, and their corporate partners, marketers must understand the macroenvironmental factors that operate in the external environment. These factors are culture, demographics, social trends, technological advances, economic situation, and political/legal environment, or CDSTEP, as shown in Exhibit 5.4.

Culture

We broadly define culture as the shared meanings, beliefs, morals, values, and customs of a group of people.[15] Transmitted by words, literature, and institutions, culture is passed down from generation to generation and learned over time. You participate in many cultures: Your family has a cultural heritage, so perhaps your mealtime traditions include eating rugelach, a traditional Jewish pastry, or sharing corned beef and cabbage to celebrate your Irish ancestry on St. Patrick's Day. In addition, your school or workplace shares its own common culture. In a broader sense, you also participate in the cultural aspects of the town and country in which you live. The challenge for marketers is to have products or services identifiable by and relevant to a particular group of people. Our various cultures influence what, why, how, where, and when we buy. Two dimensions of culture that marketers must take into account as they develop their marketing strategies are the culture of the country and that of a region within a country.

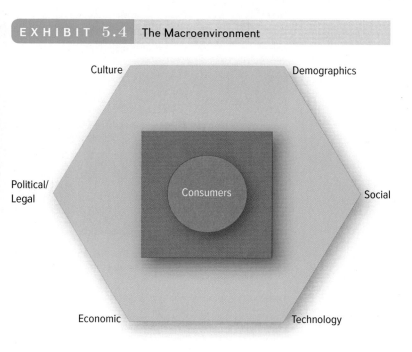

EXHIBIT 5.4 The Macroenvironment

Country Culture The visible nuances of a country's culture, such as artifacts, behavior, dress, symbols, physical settings, ceremonies, language differences, colors, tastes, and food preferences, are easy to spot. But the subtler aspects of country culture generally are trickier to identify and navigate. Sometimes the best answer is to establish a universal appeal within the specific identities of country culture. Disney and other global firms have successfully bridged the cultural gap by producing advertising that appeals to the same target market across countries. The pictures and copy are the same. The only thing that changes is the language.

Regional Culture The region in which people live in a particular country has its own regional culture that affects many aspects of people's lives, including their dietary tastes and preferences. For national and global restaurant chains, it is particularly important to cater to these preferences. But implementing completely different menus for each region would create significant strains on supply chains. To resolve this dilemma, McDonald's keeps the staple elements of its menu consistent throughout the United States, but it offers slightly different variations to appeal to specific regions.[16] In the southern and southwestern regions of the United States, McDonald's offers a Hot 'n Spicy variant of the McChicken sandwich that is not available other areas.[17] Such variation is relatively easy for McDonald's to offer because the only real difference between the Hot 'n Spicy McChicken and the regular McChicken is the spicy breading on the chicken patty. Furthermore, McDonald's has pledged to continue personalizing offerings according to regional tastes,[18] even expanding menus in select areas with completely new items. For example, in Maine, McDonald's menu includes a lobster roll; in parts of New York, New Jersey, and Pennsylvania, it features mozzarella sticks; and in Hawaii—which arguably gets

Some firms, like Disney, bridge the cultural gap by using very similar advertising in different countries, as illustrated by these two ads for The Avengers. *The left photo is for the Russian market; the right photo is for the Chinese market.*

©Walt Disney Studios Motion Pictures/Photofest

the most regional U.S. customization—McDonald's offers breakfasts of Spam, eggs, and rice. The chain can sustain these vastly different menu items by turning to local sources for the ingredients in the relevant regions[19]

Demographics

Demographics indicate the characteristics of human populations and segments, especially those used to identify consumer markets. Typical demographics such as age (which includes generational cohorts), gender, race, and income are readily available from marketing

To accommodate regional cultures, McDonald's offers regional specialties such as Spam for breakfast in Hawaii (left) and lobster rolls in Maine (right).

(Left): ©Phil Mislinski/Getty Images; (right): ©Felix Choo/Alamy Stock Photo

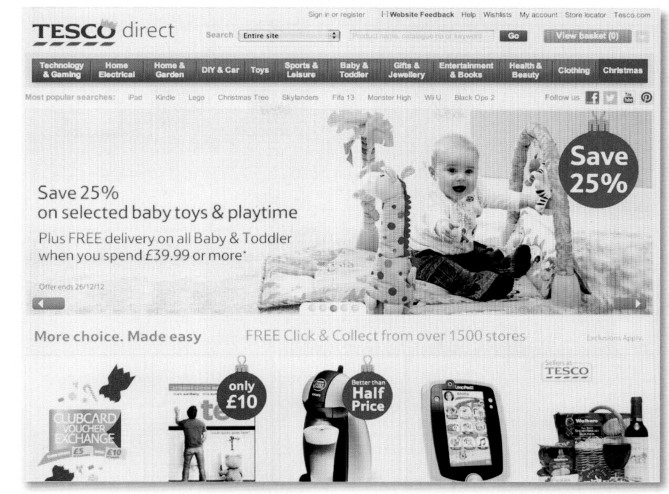

Tesco uses the demographic information it collects from its 16 million cardholders to create 9 million different versions of its newsletter that offers customized discounts.

©NetPhotos/Alamy Stock Photo

research firms such as IRI. Many firms undertake their own marketing research as well. For example, with its Clubcard loyalty program, UK-based grocery chain Tesco collects massive amounts of data about shoppers who visit its stores. It uses this information to target offers. For Tesco's 16 million cardholders, 9 million different versions of its newsletter offer customized discounts for, say, cosmetics to young female shoppers.[20] It also uses these data to cut food waste, such that by analyzing location and customer data, Tesco can create a sales forecast and stock stores appropriately.[21]

Demographics thus provide an easily understood snapshot of the typical consumer in a specific target market, as the next few sections detail.

Generational Cohorts Consumers in a generational cohort—a group of people of the same generation—have similar purchase behaviors because they have shared experiences and are in the same stage of life. Applying age as a basis to identify consumers is quite useful to marketers, as long as it is used in conjunction with other consumer characteristics. For example, most media are characterized by the consumers who use them.[22] Age groups can identify appropriate media in which firms should advertise. Although there are many ways to cut the generational pie, we describe four major groups, as listed in Exhibit 5.5.

Members of Generation Z (Gen Z) are also known as Digital Natives because people in this group were born into a world that already was full of electronic gadgets and digital technologies such as the Internet and social networks.[23] These technologies are being developed

EXHIBIT 5.5 Generational Cohorts

Generational cohort	Gen Z	Gen Y	Gen X	Baby Boomers
	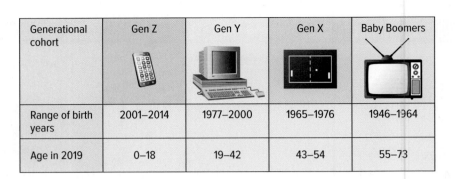			
Range of birth years	2001–2014	1977–2000	1965–1976	1946–1964
Age in 2019	0–18	19–42	43–54	55–73

and adopted at an unprecedented rate, creating novel marketing possibilities and channels, as Social & Mobile Marketing 5.1 details. Whereas it took 38 years for the radio to be adopted by 50 million people and 13 years for television, it only took 2 years for the same number of consumers to sign up for Facebook.

Social & Mobile Marketing 5.1　What Can Pokémon Go Do for Marketers?[ii]

Here's a quick question: If you could make a $10 investment and increase your retail sales by an estimated 75 percent, would you? The answer seems simple, and hundreds of retailers have adopted the promising approach. But there are others that actively avoid and even ban the investment on their property. What could prompt such divergent reactions? Pokémon Go, of course.

After the app launched, Pokémon Go rapidly was downloaded by tens of millions of consumers. These players actively seek out Pokéstops and Pokégyms, many of which are located in malls and stores, in addition to public settings such as parks and landmarks. Accordingly, some retailers have entered into sponsorship agreements, drawing hundreds of customers in search of rare Pokémon in their stores. For one New York pizzeria, investing just $10 to make its location a Pokéstop increased its sales by 75 percent in just one weekend's time.

For malls, the promise seems even greater. Malls depend heavily on foot traffic metrics; the more people walking through the mall, the higher rents they can charge to tenants. Faced with years of declining performance, many malls are embracing the virtual reality promise and inviting players in, with the hope that they will look up from their phones at least once in a while to notice the retail offerings on display around them. One T-Mobile store took the link even further, hanging an attention-grabbing sign in the windows of its mall location that encouraged consumers to get a new phone that would help them use the Pokémon Go app more effectively.

Yet some retailers dismiss the connection to the app as bad for business. People's general annoyance at the players who often fail to pay much attention to the real world around them might represent a negative effect on other consumers in the store setting. Nonplayers thus might avoid a store that actively invites more Pokémon-glazed wanderers and get in the way of their efficient shopping tasks.

As a retail store or mall manager, would you want Pokémon seekers playing in your spaces?

©Volkan Furuncu/Anadolu Agency/Getty Images

Still, the vast success of the app suggests that even if the immediate fad fades, the application of augmented and virtual reality has some interesting implications for retailers. For example, one Woolworths in Australia used each Pokémon capture in its store as a reason to connect on Facebook with the player who caught the Pokémon. Augmented reality advertisements similarly could appear on shoppers' phones in stores, giving them realistic and in-depth insights into the products for sale.

Moreover, the popularity of the simple, straightforward game app may offer some lessons to retailers that dream of having similar levels of engagement with their customers. Developing strong game apps that are specific to a retailer might cost more than $10, but the returns might be unsurpassable too.

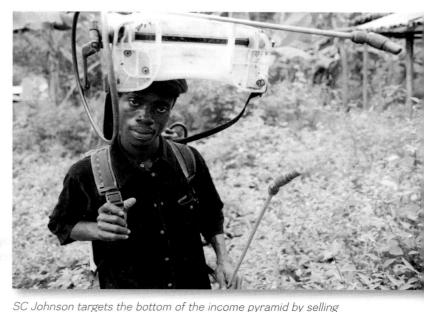

Digital Natives are always connected.

©Alberto Pomares/E+/Getty Images

SC Johnson targets the bottom of the income pyramid by selling pest control products in Ghana.

©Danita Delimont/Alamy Stock Photo

Members of Generation Y (Gen Y), also called Millennials, include the more than 60 million people born in the United States between 1977 and 2000. As the children of the Baby Boomers, this group is the biggest cohort since the original post–World War II boom. It also varies the most in age, ranging from teenagers to adults who have their own families.[24]

The next group, Generation X (Gen X), includes people born between 1965 and 1976 and represents some 41 million Americans. Vastly unlike their Baby Boomer parents, Xers are the first generation of latchkey children (those who grew up in homes in which both parents worked), and 50 percent of them have divorced parents.

After World War II, the birthrate in the United States rose sharply, resulting in a group known as the Baby Boomers, the 78 million Americans born between 1946 and 1964. Now that the oldest Boomers are collecting Social Security, it is clear that this cohort will be the largest population of 50-plus consumers the United States has ever seen.

Income Income distribution in the United States has grown more polarized—the highest-income groups are growing, whereas many middle- and lower-income groups' real purchasing power keeps declining. Although the trend of wealthy households outpacing both poor and middle classes is worldwide, it is particularly prominent in the United States. For 2016, the average (median) yearly income of the richest 5 percent of the population was $225,252 or more, the average (median) yearly income for the United States as a whole was $59,039, and the poorest 25 percent of the population earned $24,002 or less per year.[25] Furthermore, the number of people who earn less than the poverty line annually ($24,300 for a family of four in 2016) dropped only 0.8 percent since 2015. However, it is the second consecutive decline since 2014.[26] The wealthiest 10 percent control 76 percent of Americans' total net worth; in comparison, the bottom 50 percent control only 1 percent.[27] The increase in wealthy families may be due to the maturing of the general population, the increase in dual-income households, and the higher overall level of education. It also may prompt some ethical concerns about the distribution of wealth. However, the broad range in incomes creates marketing opportunities at both the high and low ends of the market.

Although some marketers choose to target only affluent population segments, others have had great success delivering value to middle- and low-income earners. Consider, for example, SC Johnson, the parent company of many familiar household brands such as Glade, Ziploc, Windex, and Raid. SC Johnson has long been working at the bottom of the

income pyramid; in the 1960s it began establishing locations in impoverished countries. Its most successful project has been in Ghana, where SC Johnson uses a direct-sales model and coaches to sell and teach customers about the benefits of pest control products and how to use them. Furthermore, SC Johnson sells these products in refillable containers and bundles them with air fresheners, in an effort to boost sales.[28]

Education Studies show that higher levels of education lead to better jobs and higher incomes.[29] According to the U.S. Bureau of Labor Statistics, employment that requires a college or secondary degree accounts for nearly half of all projected job growth in the near future. Moreover, average annual earnings are higher for those with degrees than for those without. Young adults who did not graduate from high school have an average annual salary of about $25,000, high school grads earn $30,500, and those with bachelor's degrees earn around $50,000.[30]

For some products, marketers can combine education level with other data such as occupation and income and obtain pretty accurate predictions of purchase behavior. For instance, a full-time college student with a part-time job may have relatively little personal income but will spend his or her disposable dollars differently than would a high school graduate who works in a factory and earns a similar income. Marketers need to be cognizant of the interaction among education, income, and occupation.

To encourage female gamers, in Bandai Namco Entertainment's recent "Bonnie-and-Clyde" tournament, teams comprised of one male and one female player battled one another for prize money.

©Gorodenkoff/Shutterstock

Gender Years ago gender roles appeared clear, but those male and female roles have been blurred. In particular, women today outperform men scholastically, earn higher grades on average, and graduate from both high school and college at greater rates. Perhaps unsurprisingly, recent studies also show that approximately 38 percent of married women in the United States earn more than their husbands do.[31] Furthermore, women are also becoming more prominent in politics. The percentage of seats in Congress held by women has been increasing steadily in recent years. In 2017 women made up almost 20 pecent of the U.S. Congress.[32] These shifts in status, attitudes, and behaviors affect the way many firms need to design and promote their products and services. More firms are careful about gender neutrality in positioning their products and attempt to transcend gender boundaries, especially through increased interactions with their customers.

The gaming industry has historically targeted male gamers; however, about 42 percent of gamers are female.[33] Even though many women are playing video games, only about 15 percent of professional competition viewers are female. Efforts to increase women's participation in e-sports go back more than a decade, though only recently have publishers and event organizers devoted substantial attention to targeting female competitors and consumers. For example, in Bandai Namco Entertainment's recent "Bonnie-and-Clyde" tournament, teams comprised of one male and one female player battled one another for prize money. The e-sports company Oxent also holds annual women's-only tournaments for popular games such as Counter-Strike.[34]

Ethnicity Because of immigration and increasing birthrates among various ethnic and racial groups, the United States continues to grow more diverse. Approximately 80 percent of all population growth in the next 20 years is expected to come from African American, Hispanic, and Asian communities. Minorities now represent approximately one-quarter of the population; by 2050 they will represent about 50 percent, with nearly 23 percent of the

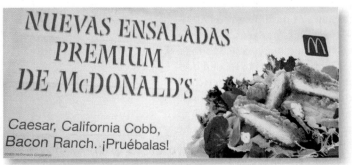

NUEVAS ENSALADAS PREMIUM DE McDONALD'S

Caesar, California Cobb, Bacon Ranch. ¡Pruébalas!

The Hispanic market is so large in some areas of the United States that some firms, like McDonald's, develop entire marketing programs just to meet its needs.

©Ethel Wolvovitz/The Image Works

population Hispanic, and by 2055 there will not be an ethnic minority in the United States.[35] Many foreign-born Americans and recent immigrants tend to concentrate in a handful of metropolitan areas, such as New York, Los Angeles, San Francisco, and Chicago.

Among the different groups, Hispanic buying power was projected to reach $1.3 trillion in 2015, a cumulative increase of around 25 percent compared with 2010.[36] The 50 million Hispanic consumers in the United States have increasing influences on mainstream U.S. culture. Many families have been in the United States for multiple generations, and the consumer behavior of these highly acculturated Hispanics differs little from that of other groups of Americans.

In 2016, African American U.S. households had a mean (average) yearly income of over $49,000. They also tend to be younger, such that 58 percent are between the ages of 15 and 49 years (a key age demographic for many marketers). Thirty-two percent of black households earn more than $75,000, and it is expected that a majority of black Americans now live in the suburbs.[37] Asian Americans make up only about 5.6 percent of the U.S. population,

Entertainment site BuzzFeed has successfully engaged with Asian Americans by posting a mix of content including comedy and hard-hitting pieces that speak directly to them.
©digitallife/Alamy Stock Photo

but they also represent the fastest-growing minority population, growing 46 percent from 2000 to 2010, having more schooling, and being more likely to be professionally employed or own a business.[38] Furthermore, Asian Americans have a lot of spending power, with an average household income 28 percent higher than the U.S. median. Many companies have not yet been able to effectively reach this segment. However, entertainment site BuzzFeed has successfully engaged with Asian Americans by posting a mix of content including comedy and hard-hitting pieces that speak directly to them, outlining a way in which other marketers can tap into this market.[39]

Social Trends

L05-3 Identify various social trends that impact marketing.

Various social trends appear to be shaping consumer values in the United States and around the world, including a greater emphasis on sustainability, health and wellness considerations, and more efficient utilization and distribution of food. Three other social trends are relevant as well: Energy trends and green marketing are discussed in the previous section on the physical environment, while privacy concerns are examined later in the technological advances section.

Sustainability The UN Sustainable Development Goals highlight social issues associated with meeting basic needs, such as ensuring consistent, universal access to sufficient food, clean water, health care, and sanitary living conditions, mainly by eliminating extreme poverty.[40] But they also extend to social structures, of which firms and marketers are an inherent part. To market their sincere efforts to ensure sustainability, companies can rely on certifications from various agencies, including obtaining the International Fairtrade Certification Mark.[41] The fairtrade mark is a certification that is granted to products that are determined to promote sustainable farming and provide higher prices and improved social and environmental standards for producers, typically in developing countries.[42]

The fairtrade mark is a certification that is granted to products that are determined to promote sustainable farming and provide higher prices and improved social and environmental standards for producers, typically in developing countries.
©Peter Titmuss/Alamy Stock Photo

Get your kids to eat better
without ever raising your voice.

Childhood obesity is a growing issue and a big concern. And we're doing something to combat it. Our SUBWAY FRESH FIT FOR KIDS™ meal fits into the American Heart Association's approach to a healthy lifestyle. And best of all, it's a fast, tasty way to give kids a "better for them" meal. Finally there's fast food you can feel good about.

American Heart Association | Proud sponsor of the American Heart Association's Jump Rope for Heart.

This Subway ad speaks directly to the issue of childhood obesity and responds to the new advertising guidelines adopted by marketers. The SUBWAY FRESH FIT FOR KIDS™ meal, which meets the American Heart Association's criteria for a heart-healthy meal, provides a nutritional choice for customers wanting a quick-service food alternative for their children.

Source: Subway Franchise Advertising Fund Trust

Such trends create challenges for other marketers, though. For example, discussions of struggles in the fast fashion industry often cite consumers' concerns about the sustainability of these production processes. If a shirt costs only $5, buyers might come to realize that it is unlikely to have supported a living wage for the laborers who helped make it. They also might start to question the ethics of replacing an entire wardrobe each season.[43]

Health and Wellness Health concerns, especially those pertaining to children, are prevalent, critical, and widespread. In the past 20 years, child obesity has doubled and teenage obesity has tripled in the United States, leading to skyrocketing rates of high blood pressure, high cholesterol, early signs of heart disease, and type 2 diabetes among children. The U.S. Centers for Disease Control and Prevention (CDC) also estimates that approximately 87.5 percent of U.S. adults are obese, and the incidence of diabetes has reached 7.2 percent—with much higher rates for people still undiagnosed or classified as having prediabetes.[44] It is also increasing at alarming rates in other countries and among consumers who adopt more Western diets. Although governments and many consumers have become more concerned about the health problems associated with obesity, Ethical & Societal Dilemma 5.2 explains that consumers continue to make unhealthy food choices.

New advertising guidelines therefore require marketers to produce food in reasonably proportioned sizes. Advertised food items must provide basic nutrients, have less than 30 percent of their total calories from fat, and include no added sweeteners. The advertising also cannot be aired during children's programming, and companies cannot link unhealthy foods with cartoon and celebrity figures. For example, the SUBWAY FRESH FIT FOR KIDS™ offerings meet the American Heart Association's criteria for heart-healthy meals, because they feature lean protein, fruits, vegetables, grains, and milk, with fewer than 500 calories.[45] The company also has partnered with Disney in a *Star Wars*–related television ad promoting healthy meals.[46]

Consumers' interest in improving their health also has opened up several new markets and niches focused on healthy living. For example, consumer spending on yoga classes, mats, and clothing has increased from $10 billion to $16 billion in just four years.[47] Yoga studios actually combine multiple modern trends: As the economy sours, people face increasing stress, which they hope to reduce through yoga. In addition, yoga studios are relatively inexpensive to open and operate, so entrepreneurs and consumers appreciate the value for the money they offer. And of course, Americans remain consistently on the lookout for exercise mechanisms that can help them shed pounds and match media images of

Ethical & Societal Dilemma 5.2 | Consumers Insist on Healthy Foods—Until You Mess with the Color of Their Trix[iii]

What trend watchers and marketing researchers tell us, over and over, is that consumers are seeking healthier food options. But when General Mills tried to change the formula for its Trix cereal, using natural and vegetable options rather than artificial dyes to create the coloring of the sugar-laden product, people rejected the switch wholeheartedly. And so, "Trix Classic" will return to store shelves, with the bright colors and strong fruit flavors that generations of children have come to love, even as the naturally colored option remains an alternative choice on shelves.

For General Mills, offering the original recipe seemed mandatory. On social media and the company website, consumers complained so bitterly that it knew it would lose them if it only offered the "depressing" naturally colored version. Using turmeric, beets, and purple carrots as ingredients to manufacture its cereal, General Mills came up with a colored but drab version, vastly unlike the vibrant version achieved through artificial dyes. The clearly visible difference prompted people to mourn the loss of a childhood favorite, worry that their own children would never have the fun of eating Trix, and accuse General Mills of selling "basically a salad" instead of a cereal.

But the switch back to artificial ingredients also creates a dilemma for the company, which vowed several years ago to eliminate all artificial flavors and colors from its cereal products. By switching back to keep customers happy, General Mills also is going back on a commitment it publicized widely, which may annoy an entirely different set of consumers. Thus, General Mills continues to sell the natural version too, in the hopes that its presence will be enough to appease these cereal eaters.

Although this latter group of consumers who prefer natural ingredients is influential, and sales of products that bar artificial dyes and flavorings are growing faster than those of other segments, food manufacturers clearly cannot ignore the substantial population of folks who love food produced with artificial means—always have, always will. Even if about half of North American consumers indicate that they avoid artificial colors in their foods due to health concerns, they also appreciate a sense of balance: I'll eat healthy most of the time, so that I can consume some unhealthy foods when I want to indulge in some nostalgia or have a sweet treat. Processed foods thus continue to sell well to consumers who see no need to consider an organic kale chip when Pringles already taste great, or who enjoy Apple Jacks cereal over organic alternatives because the preservatives it contains help the food stay crisper in milk for longer.

Accordingly, General Mills is not the only food manufacturer to face problems. When Coca-Cola began sweetening some of its drinks with the plant-based sweetener Stevia, customers complained that the levels of sweetness were not the same. Other companies have had better luck; Kraft changed the recipe for its famous macaroni and cheese to eliminate an artificial yellow dye. It did so without announcing the change, and it ensured that it could replicate the signature neon color of the meal even without the dye. Then, when it made the change public, consumers already knew that they had tried the new recipe and, in most cases, never noticed a difference.

But for most makers of processed foods, especially those that resonate strongly with consumers' sense of nostalgia and childhood memories, changing things represents a grave risk. At the same time, ignoring the demands for healthier production methods could be risky too. It turns out, as a spokesperson for General Mills noted in what may perhaps be the understatement of the century, consumers "don't all want the same thing."

Some consumers prefer Trix colored with natural ingredients (left), whereas others prefer "Trix Classic" (right).

(Left): ©Michael Neelon/Alamy Stock Photo; (right): ©McGraw-Hill Education

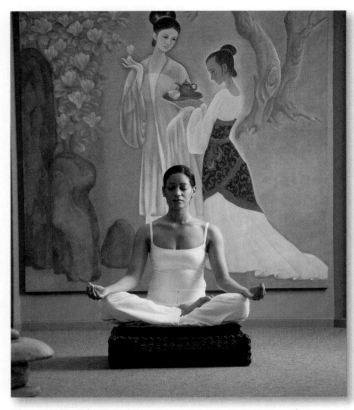

The practice of yoga is growing as more consumers embrace healthy lifestyles.

©Plush Studios/Blend Images LLC.

athletic prowess and beautiful bodies. Thus competition is growing in this industry, and some studios have begun to combine their basic yoga classes with additional offers to attract clients such as food services, acupuncture, and massages, or by teaming up with other fitness centers.[48] Health and wellness concerns have also spurred a number of mobile apps, many of which help customers get or stay in shape by tracking exercise, calorie intake, and sleep cycles.

Efficient Utilization and Distribution of Food

In many ways, food has always defined social trends that are central to people's lives and environments. It also constitutes a major market in any economy, with niches devoted to specialized options such as organic food. Beyond the food products themselves, trends associated with food and eating establish markets for diet-related products, ranging from snack packages that come in smaller servings to apps that help consumers count their calories and steps. One of the UN Sustainable Development Goals is to reduce hunger, and reducing food waste is critical to that effort. So some firms are focusing on reducing food waste throughout the value chain. Specifically, there are laws that encourage restaurants and grocery stores to donate food to charities such as food banks. But 40 percent of all food in the United States goes uneaten. In 2010, grocery stores and restaurants threw out almost $47 billion worth of food, much of which was not past its expiration date or otherwise uneatable. This is not the case in France, however. A recently passed law requires grocery stores to donate food to charity that would otherwise be tossed.[49]

Furthermore, retailers such as Whole Foods have committed to expanding their efforts to eliminate food deserts, defined as areas and neighborhoods in which consumers, usually of lower socioeconomic strata, have limited or no access to healthy, affordable, fresh food options. For example, Chicago's Englewood neighborhood suffers from vacant buildings and a heartbreakingly high crime rate, and its residents earn an average of just more than $20,000 annually. Their access to fresh produce is limited; neighborhood convenience stores sell mostly highly processed, packaged foods. When Whole Foods opened a store in Englewood, it undertook a careful analysis to ensure the success of the location. In particular, representatives interviewed local residents to determine what they would want to find at a new grocery store, then stocked the shelves accordingly and committed to charging lower prices on certain staple foods, including eggs and dairy.[50]

Technological Advances

Technological advances have accelerated vastly, improving the value of products and services. Consumers have constant access to the Internet, through services such as Wi-Fi, mobile hotspots, 4G, and LTE. Smartphones using the iOS or Android systems allow for greater computing, data

Although there are laws that encourage restaurants and grocery stores to donate food to charities such as food banks, 40 percent of all food in the United States goes uneaten.

©Joe Raedle/Getty Images

storage, and communication capabilities. Tablet computers, starting with the iPad, and wearable technology, such as the Apple Watch, have extended mobile computing even further by offering mobile interfaces in environments that traditionally have limited access. These examples of advanced technology make consumers increasingly dependent on the help they receive from the providers of the technology. As Marketing Analytics 5.1 details, Netflix relies on its advanced technological capabilities not just to suggest which movies we should watch but also to develop new content that it is confident we will like.

LO5-4 Examine the technological advances that are influencing marketers.

Mobile devices enhance customers' experience by making it easier to interact with the manufacturer or retailer or other customers, and they add a new channel of access, which makes customers more loyal and more likely to spend more with a particular retailer. The Starbucks application allows customers to order their favorite coffee and snack online and pay through their mobile device, all while earning rewards points. As Adding Value 5.1 summarizes, even more new and exciting technologies are entering the market. Such offerings largely are based on three cutting-edge technology formats: artificial intelligence, robotics, and the Internet of Things.

Artificial Intelligence Firms increasingly are experimenting with **artificial intelligence (AI)** solutions, which rely on computer systems to perform tasks that require human intelli-

Marketing Analytics **5.1** When the Best Is Good Enough: Netflix's Stellar Predictive Analytics[iv]

Netflix's data analytics are groundbreaking. In academic circles, its influence has been called a "scientific renaissance" because of the techniques the streaming service has pioneered in its efforts to handle the massive amounts of data it deals in and process payments from across the globe. The power and precision of Netflix's predictive analytics have become such common knowledge that even Netflix pokes fun at itself. In one April Fool's joke, it revised its recommended television and movie categories to include classifications such as "TV Shows Where Defiantly Crossed Arms Mean Business!" Netflix gathers data about every aspect of the viewing process, including not just the basics, such as customer ratings, searches, time of day and week, and location, but also customer behaviors that take place during the movie, such as rewinds, fast-forwards, pauses, and how long they let the credits roll. Going even a step further, Netflix analyzes every hue of color contained in the cover art of the options that it offers and can create a profile of the average color of titles viewed by each customer.

Netflix clearly relies on such customer data to create its hallmark personalized suggestions. But in 2010, Netflix chose not to enhance its ability to personalize any further. In 2009, a team of mathematicians created a new algorithm that would have improved Netflix's personalization by 10 percent in response to a company-sponsored contest. But Netflix never implemented the improved algorithm. Why? There simply wasn't enough value to be gained from it. Various studies show that, even for the most personal choices, including their love lives, people often forgo what they know already for the thrill of what's new. Thus, Netflix decided that it could deliver more value to its customers by offering something new rather than a personalized version of what they wanted yesterday. Accordingly, it has changed its strategy and its uses of predictive analytics to focus more on creating original content.

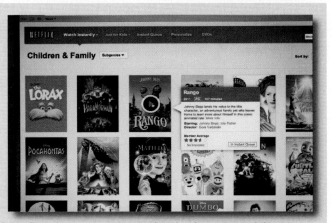

Netflix relies on its advanced technological capabilities not just to suggest which movies we should watch but also to develop new content that it is confident we will like.
©Victor J. Blue/Bloomberg/Getty Images

Netflix challenges traditional approaches to content development by using data to help make new shows as well as production decisions. This approach has almost guaranteed the success of the shows, as evidenced by the release of the third season of the award-winning series *House of Cards*. Before this release, the show experienced an unprecedented increase in fans on Facebook and Twitter, approximately double the increase that occurred prior to the start of the second season. This jump was especially notable because a show's social growth usually slows after its first or second season. Even though the third season initially brought some mixed reviews, many viewers already had finished watching the entire season just a week or so after its release.

Adding Value 5.1   Are We There Yet? Google's Moves to Get Us Closer to Driverless Cars[v]

Self-driving cars were the central focus at the 2016 Consumer Electronics Show (CES). Google's self-driving cars have been the most widely talked-about product, in part because its driverless car program, which began in 2009, is the oldest. Its self-driving cars currently being tested include modified Lexus SUVs as well as Google-designed prototype vehicles. Google's self-driving cars have logged a significant amount of mileage, with an average of 30,000–40,000 miles driven each month (the average American drives about 13,500 miles a year). Currently Google is in talks with Ford to produce the self-driving cars—Google gets Ford's manufacturing expertise; Ford gets the self-driving technology.

Although Google has the most advanced driverless car program, the latest report shows that there is still plenty of work to be done before the cars are completely driverless. From September to November 2014, Google reported 341 self-driving disengagements, where the driver had to take over control of the car. More than 270 of these disengagements were reportedly due to lapses in the technology; only 69 were due to the test drivers opting to take control. On average there was one disengagement experienced every 1,244 miles. However, these numbers are significantly better than with other self-driving cars. For example Bosch's model had one disengagement every 41 miles, Nissan experienced a disengagement every 14 miles, Mercedes-Benz disengaged every 1 to 2 miles, and Volkswagen disengaged once every 57 miles. A Tesla was involved in a fatal accident when the car was in self-driving mode.

Automakers such as Toyota are collaborating with companies such as Apple and Google to create self-driving cars.
©Karen Bleier/AFP/Getty Images

The Google car might not be ready yet, but it seems to be leading the pack and improving rapidly. The 2015 reports of self-driving disengagement show a considerable drop from the 2014 reports, down to just one human intervention every 5,318 miles. Furthermore, Google recognizes these disengagements as an important aspect of its testing. Driver interventions give Google critical data and insight into the strengths and weaknesses of its software, allowing the company to make improvements. Google is undoubtedly one of the best companies at using data, and as seen by the rapid decline in driver intervention, its self-driving cars may soon be ready for the general public.

gence, such as speech recognition, decision making, or translations. Such experimentation reflects the already vast spread of AI in consumers' pockets, such as through their smartphones that run Apple's Siri, and in their homes, as exemplified by Amazon's Alexa. In some ways, AI remains at an early stage of development, but marketers also recognize that customers already prefer to search on their phones rather than interact with a salesperson. With its On Call mobile app, Macy's leverages the abilities of IBM's Watson and smartphone location services to help customers navigate stores.[51] The app can recognize language, so customers can ask questions, using natural phrases in English or Spanish, and the responses likely determine which products they consider, how readily they find them in stores, and so forth.[52]

Some recent tests, conducted by The North Face with an innovative Expert Personal Shopper program, suggest the great promise of AI for retailing in particular. This program seeks to determine exactly what consumers seek at the first moment they click onto The North Face's website or mobile channel—just like a salesclerk might do when greeting a consumer walking into a North Face store. By asking questions with progressively increasing detail, the program (powered by IBM's famous Watson) selects several items that might meet a shopper's needs and presents them onscreen. The two-way communication seeks to feel natural and organic, rather than imposing selections on the shopper. But before it achieves this status or devises accurate recommendations, the program first must learn about all the products available. A sophisticated search assistant is little help if it can't recognize the meaning of product descriptions to be able to match items with consumers' wants. In addition, it needs to integrate external information that might be pertinent: For a consumer searching for a jacket to wear on a ski trip to Vermont in December, for example, the Fluid program needs to know what the average temperatures are at that time

The North Face is using artificial intelligence with its Expert Personal Shopper program in which it seeks to determine what customers are looking for when they click onto its website or mobile channel. By asking questions, the program selects several items that might meet a shopper's needs and presents them onscreen.

Source: The North Face

and place. But as these lessons get learned, this experiment might predict the future of retailing. The 50,000 customers who worked with a beta version of the software remained on the site for an average of two minutes longer than they did without the assistant. They also gave it high ratings for its functionality, and 75 percent of them noted that they would use it again.[53]

Robotics Robots in all shapes, sizes, and forms are entering the marketplace and performing work that previously was the responsibility of human workers. They already are commonly in distribution and fulfillment centers to fill orders for stores or individual customers. Retailers also are experimenting with delivering products using drones or driverless cars.[54] Walmart has installed Cash360 machines in nearly all its stores. The machines count cash drawers more quickly than human workers could and make immediate deposits, increasing the efficiency of the stores' accounting operations.[55] But it is not limiting robots to the back office; the superstore has announced plans to roll out two-foot-tall, shelf-scanning robots that patrol stores, looking for items that are out of stock or goods that are incorrectly priced or missing tags. The information each robot collects then gets compiled and reported to management, so that human associates can better target their efforts to keep things running smoothly. By automating these repetitive and predictable tasks, Walmart hopes to free up its human staff to provide better customer service and handle tasks that cannot be easily outsourced to robotic labor.[56] The shelf-scanning robot program also continues to be tweaked in response to feedback from customers and associates, so that the robots are used as effectively as possible. The hope is that the program can be implemented and expanded to an even greater number of stores in the future. Walmart also is seeking input from other retailers that might test similar robots in their own stores. For example, updates to the existing program might allow the robots to be programmed to skip busy aisles or stop when approached by a customer, to help avoid inconvenience and accidents. With more stock on the shelves and human associates freed up to better meet the needs of customers, Walmart believes it is poised for success with its new robotic program, when it comes to both the bottom line and the perceptions of customers.[57]

Service firms also are using humanoid robots—that is, robots that have humanlike features—at their information desks, such as a department store in Tokyo,[58] or to serve

Retailers are experimenting with delivering products using drones.
©Ulrich Baumgarten via Getty Images

The next time you disembark at the Munich, Germany, airport, you may be greeted by Josie Pepper, a robot that will answer your questions in English about restaurants, shops, and flight operations.

©EyesWideOpen/Getty Images

food, such as at a Pizza Hut in Asia.[59] The customer service representative in the department store has a name (Aiko Chihira) and a backstory that specifies some of her demographics (e.g., 32 years of age). She also is lifelike enough that she fools some consumers into believing she is real, as she bows in welcome and answers their questions. The pizza order taker is Pepper, a popular robot that looks like a playful robot, rather than a human, and that has found positions not only in restaurants but also in various hotels and coffee shops. Such developments result from not only the desire to reduce the costs of service (i.e., no longer needing to pay servers) as well as some evidence that consumers tend to order more food when they are served by robots.[60]

Internet of Things Firms like iRobot have a long history of developing robotic machines that help consumers undertake daily chores in the house, such as vacuuming. But other home appliances are joining and extending this trend, producing the new notion of the Internet of Things (IoT). The IoT emerges when multiple "smart devices" with Internet-connected sensors, such as refrigerators, dishwashers, and coffee machines, combine the data they have collected to help both consumers and companies consume more efficiently.[61] Bosch Home Connect ovens, Samsung smart washers and dryers, Nest thermostats, Ring video doorbells, and SimpliSafe's security system all promise to help consumers take care of their homes and needs more effectively, usually by linking to apps on people's smartphones. Sensors in smart vehicles can gather driving and engine performance data to schedule service appointments when the car needs an oil change and also might alert drivers to the threat of critical engine failures or risky driving conditions.[62]

Furthermore, the IoT delivers insightful data to retailers and manufacturers that they can use to optimize their inventories, predict the need for maintenance services, and so forth.[63] An innovation called the Smart Retail Solution combines dedicated software, wireless devices, and electronic kiosks that function as points of sale to gather data from consumers, identify tagging or pricing errors, and follow up on employees' activities to make sure they are performing the tasks that still require human intervention.[64]

Privacy Concerns More and more consumers worldwide sense a loss of privacy. At the same time that the Internet has created an explosion of accessibility to consumer information, improvements in computer storage facilities and the manipulation of information have led to more and better security and credit check services. In recent years

The Internet of Things (IoT) emerges when multiple "smart devices" with Internet-connected sensors, such as Samsung smart refrigerators, combine the data they have collected to help both consumers and companies consume more efficiently.

©David Becker/Getty Images

there have been a number of hacking scandals. However, the largest one came to light in October 2017, when Yahoo announced that all 3 billion of its accounts had been hacked in 2013. Yahoo states that the information that was hacked did not include bank account or credit card data but it did include security questions and backup e-mail addresses, making other accounts of those who were hacked also vulnerable. Although companies continuously develop new ways to keep customer information safe, some observers suggest hackers are just getting more effective.[65]

Every time a consumer surfs the web and clicks on a site, online marketers can place "cookies" on that user's computer, showing them where the user starts, proceeds, and ends the online encounter—as well as what the user buys and doesn't buy. For many consumers, such close access to their behaviors is an unacceptable invasion of privacy. Realizing consumers are upset about this issue, the marketing industry as a whole has sought to find solutions and self-regulations that would calm customers, satisfy cautious regulators, and still enable marketing firms to gain access to invaluable information about consumer behaviors. But the online marketing industry simply has not been able to agree on how to police itself. It looks like it may be up to Congress to address this growing issue. In 2017 a bill aiming to improve customer privacy, the Consumer Privacy Protection Act of 2017, was introduced to Congress. It remains to be seen if it will pass, and if so, if it would be effective.[66]

Economic Situation

Marketers monitor the general economic situation, both in their home country and abroad, because it affects the way consumers buy merchandise and spend money. Some major factors that influence the state of an economy include the rate of inflation, foreign currency exchange rates, and interest rates.

U.S. tourists are flocking to other countries such as the UK to shop because the value of the dollar is high compared to other currencies like the pound sterling.
©Samir Hussein/Getty Images Entertainment/Getty Images

Inflation refers to the persistent increase in the prices of goods and services. Increasing prices cause the purchasing power of the dollar to decline; in other words, the dollar buys less than it used to.

In a similar fashion, foreign currency fluctuations can influence consumer spending. For instance, in the summer of 2002 the euro was valued at slightly less than US$1. By 2008, it had risen to an all-time high of $1.60, but in late 2017, the euro was once again slightly less than $1.[67] When the euro is more expensive than the dollar, merchandise made in Europe is more costly for Americans, but European shoppers enjoy bargains on U.S. products. When the dollar is worth more than the euro, American-made products become more costly for European consumers, but U.S. buyers can get great deals in Europe.

Interest rates represent the cost of borrowing money. When customers borrow money from a bank, they agree to pay back the loan, plus the interest that accrues. The interest, in effect, is the cost to the customers or the fee the bank charges those customers for borrowing the money. Likewise, if a customer opens a savings account at a bank, he or she will earn interest on the amount saved, which means the interest becomes the fee the consumer gets for loaning the money to the bank. If the interest rate goes up, consumers have an incentive to save more because they earn more for loaning the bank their money; when interest rates go down, however, consumers generally borrow more.

How do these three important economic factors—inflation, foreign currency fluctuations, and interest rates—affect firms' ability to market goods and services? Shifts in the three economic factors make marketing easier for some and harder for others. For instance, when inflation increases, consumers probably don't buy less food, but they may shift their expenditures from expensive steaks to less expensive hamburgers. Grocery stores and inexpensive restaurants win, but expensive restaurants lose. Consumers also buy less discretionary merchandise, though off-price and discount retailers often gain ground at the expense of their full-price competitors. Similarly, the sales of expensive jewelry, fancy cars, and extravagant vacations decrease, but the sale of low-cost luxuries, such as personal care products and home entertainment, tends to increase.

Political/Legal Environment

The political/legal environment comprises political parties, government organizations, and legislation and laws. Organizations must fully understand and comply with any legislation regarding fair competition, consumer protection, or industry-specific regulation. Since the turn of the 20th century, the government has enacted laws that promote both fair trade and competition by prohibiting the formation of monopolies or alliances that would damage a competitive marketplace, which fosters fair pricing practices for all suppliers and consumers.

The government enacts laws focused on ensuring that companies compete fairly with one another. Although enacted in the early part of the 20th century, these laws remain the backbone of U.S. legislation protecting competition in commerce: The 1890 Sherman Antitrust Act prohibits monopolies and other activities that would restrain trade or competition and makes fair trade within a free market a national goal; the 1914 Clayton Act supports the Sherman Act by prohibiting the combination of two or more competing corporations through pooling ownership of stock and restricting pricing policies such as price discrimination, exclusive dealing, and tying clauses to different buyers; and the 1936 Robinson-Patman Act specifically outlaws price discrimination toward wholesalers, retailers, or other producers and requires sellers to make ancillary services or allowances available to all buyers on proportionately equal terms. These laws have been used specifically to increase competition. For example, the telephone and energy industries were deregulated, which resulted in massive conglomerates such as Ma Bell (the nickname for AT&T) being broken into smaller, competing companies.

Legislation has also been enacted to protect consumers in a variety of ways. First, regulations require marketers to abstain from false or misleading advertising practices that might mislead consumers, such as claims that a medication can cure a disease when in fact it causes other health risks. Second, manufacturers are required to refrain from using any harmful or hazardous materials (e.g., lead in toys) that might place consumers at risk. Third, organizations must adhere to fair and reasonable business practices when they communicate with consumers. For example, they must employ reasonable debt-collection methods and disclose any finance charges, and they are limited with regard to their telemarketing and e-mail solicitation activities. A summary of the most significant legislation affecting marketing interests appears in Exhibit 5.6.

EXHIBIT 5.6   Consumer Protection Legislation

Year	Law	Description
1906	Federal Food and Drug Act	Created the Food and Drug Administration (FDA); prohibited the manufacture or sale of adulterated or fraudulently labeled food and drug products.
1914	Federal Trade Commission Act	Established the Federal Trade Commission (FTC) to regulate unfair competitive practices and practices that deceive or are unfair to consumers.
1966	Fair Packaging and Labeling Act	Regulates packaging and labeling of consumer goods; requires manufacturers to state the contents of the package, who made it, and the amounts contained within.
1966	Child Protection Act	Prohibits the sale of harmful toys and components to children; sets the standard for child-resistant packaging.
1967	Federal Cigarette Labeling and Advertising Act	Requires cigarette packages to display this warning: "Warning: The Surgeon General Has Determined That Cigarette Smoking Is Dangerous to Your Health."
1972	Consumer Product Safety Act	Created the Consumer Product Safety Commission (CPSC), which has the authority to regulate safety standards for consumer products.
1990	Children's Television Act	Limits the number of commercials shown during children's programming.
1990	Nutrition Labeling and Education Act	Requires food manufacturers to display nutritional contents on product labels.
1995	Telemarketing Sales Rule	Regulates fraudulent activities conducted over the telephone. Violators are subject to fines and actions enforced by the FTC.
2003	Controlling the Assault of Non-Solicited Pornography and Marketing Act of 2003 (CAN-SPAM Act)	Prohibits misleading commercial e-mail, particularly misleading "subject" and "from" lines.
2003	Amendment to the Telemarketing Sales Rule	Establishes a National Do Not Call Registry, requiring telemarketers to abstain from calling consumers who opt to be placed on the list.
2003	Do Not Spam Law	Laws created to reduce spam or unwarranted e-mails.
2010	Financial Reform Law	Created the Consumer Financial Protection Bureau whose aim is to enforce appropriate consumer-oriented regulations on a number of financial firms such as banks, mortgage businesses, and payday and student lenders. It also set up the Financial Services Oversight Council to act as an early warning system.

Responding to the Environment

As the examples throughout this chapter show, many companies engage in tactics and marketing strategies that attempt to respond to multiple political, regulatory, economic, technical, and social developments and trends in the wider environment. For example, in 2016, in response to the threats of climate change, the United Nations ratified the Paris Accord. Countries participating in this accord agreed to reduce greenhouse gas emissions as they see best fit, limiting the atmosphere to rise 2°C in this century.[68] Although the United States officially left the accord in 2017, many businesses officially committed themselves to uphold the accord. Companies that have dedicated themselves to these emission reductions include Apple, Google, Facebook, Microsoft, Target, and Campbell Soup.[69] In a constantly changing marketing environment, the marketers that succeed are the ones that respond quickly, accurately, and sensitively to their consumers.

In response to the threats of climate change, the United Nations ratified the Paris Accord, which agreed to reduce greenhouse gas emissions.

©geniusksy/Shutterstock

PROGRESS CHECK

1. What are the six key macroenvironmental factors?
2. Differentiate between country culture and regional culture.
3. What are some important social trends shaping consumer values and shopping behavior?

Reviewing Learning Objectives

LO5-1

Outline how customers, the company, competitors, corporate partners, and the physical environment affect marketing strategy.

Everything a firm does should revolve around the customer; without the customer, nothing gets sold. Firms must discover their customers' wants and needs and then be able to provide a valuable product or service that will satisfy those wants or needs. If there were only one firm and many customers, a marketer's life would be a piece of cake. But because this situation rarely occurs, firms must monitor their competitors to discover how they might be appealing to their customers. If a firm does not monitor its competitors, the firm's customers might soon belong to its competitors. Though life certainly would be easier without competitors, it would be difficult, if not impossible, without corporate partners. Good marketing firms or departments work closely with suppliers, marketing research firms, consultants, and transportation firms to coordinate the extensive process of discovering what customers want and finally getting it to them when and where they want it. Finally, the purchases people make are influenced by their physical environment. In particular people are

concerned about adverse changes to their environment such as global warming and pollution. Firms are responding to these concerns with new products and services. For instance, electric cars and ride-sharing services are designed to save energy. And greener practices have spurred environmentally friendly, sustainable merchandise. Each of these activities—discovering customer needs, studying competitors' actions, working with corporate partners, and developing products and services that help improve the physical environment—helps add value to firms' products and services.

LO5-2

Explain why marketers must consider their macroenvironment when they make decisions.

What are the chances that a fast-food hamburger restaurant would be successful in a predominantly Hindu neighborhood? Not good. Marketers must be sensitive to such cultural issues to be successful, and they must also consider customer demographics—age, income, market size, education, gender, and ethnicity—to identify specific customer target groups. In any society, major social trends influence the way people live. In no other time in history has technology moved so rapidly and had such a pervasive influence on the way we live. Not only do marketers help identify and develop technologies for practical, everyday uses, but technological advances help marketers provide consumers with more products and services more quickly and efficiently. The general state of the economy influences how people spend their discretionary income. When the economy is healthy, marketing success comes relatively easily. But when the economy gets bumpy, only well-honed marketing skills can yield long-term successes. Naturally, all firms must abide by the law, and many legal issues affect marketing directly. These laws pertain to competitive practices and protecting consumers from unfair or dangerous products.

 L05-3 Identify various social trends that impact marketing.

Social trends have a tremendous impact on what consumers purchase and consume. Understanding these trends—sustainability, health and wellness, and how to more efficiently utilize and distribute food—can help marketers serve their customers better.

L05-4 Examine the technological advances that are influencing marketers.

Technological advances in products and services continue to change the way we live, from more "thoughtful" coffeemakers to the potential for self-driving cars and trucks in the not-so-distant future. At the cutting edge of these technologies is artificial intelligence, which relies on computers to perform humanlike tasks. A more physical technology is found in robotics, which are machines that can perform human tasks, like a machine that can "roll around" a store checking for out-of-stock merchandise, or one that takes your food order at a restaurant. Finally, the Internet of Things refers to products such as home appliances that work more efficiently and are able to perform more tasks by being connected to the Internet. How these and other technologically advanced products and services will diffuse into the marketplace is certainly not clear. What is clear, however, is that technology will continue to play an increasingly important part in the products and services we use every day.

Key Terms

- artificial intelligence (AI), 161
- Baby Boomers, 155
- country culture, 151
- culture, 151
- demographics, 152
- Digital Native, 153
- economic situation, 165
- food deserts, 160
- foreign currency fluctuations, 165
- Generation X (Gen X), 155
- Generation Y (Gen Y), 155
- Generation Z (Gen Z), 153
- generational cohort, 153
- green marketing, 149
- greenwashing, 150
- inflation, 165
- interest rates, 165
- Internet of Things (IoT), 164
- macroenvironmental factors, 151
- Millennials, 155
- physical environment, 148
- political/legal environment, 165
- regional culture, 151

Marketing Digitally

1. Seventh Generation is the leading brand of nontoxic, environmentally safe household products in the United States. Visit its website (www.seventhgeneration.com) and review the philosophy behind the business. Next, review the site to identify the products the company offers. Briefly summarize some of the consumer trends you think are reflected. Describe the ways in which Seventh Generation's products address the wants and needs of its customers.

2. Visit The Cool Hunter (www.thecoolhunter.net) and identify examples that would provide marketers insights regarding social trends.

3. Visit and explore the Peloton website (www.onepeloton.com). What demographic, social, and technical trends impact this firm's ability to succeed?

Marketing Applications

1. Assume you are going to open a new store selling fitness products. Describe it. Who are your competitors? What would you do to monitor your competitors' actions? Who are your customers? What are you going to do to appeal to them? What are your social responsibilities, and how will you meet them?

2. How would your approach to buying a computer differ from your parents' approach? What about buying an outfit to wear to a party? How can firms use their knowledge of different age or generational cohorts to market their products and services better?

3. How can firms use customer demographics like income, market size, education, and ethnicity to market to their customers better?

4. Today, marketers cannot ignore consumers' concerns about the environmental impact of the firm's activities.

What are some of the environmental concerns consumers have regarding marketing activities? How can marketers address these concerns?

5. Identify some recent technological innovations in the marketplace and describe how they have affected consumers' everyday activities.

6. Digital storefronts such as Etsy allow small producers to have a presence in the online marketplace. What benefits do these online storefronts offer small producers? What benefits do they offer consumers?

7. Several social trends were discussed in the chapter. For each of these trends, choose a retailer or service provider that you believe has seized the moment by grasping the importance of the trend and successfully marketing to its customers as a result.

8. Identify a company that you believe does a particularly good job of marketing to different cultural groups. Justify your answer.

9. Examine the consumer protection legislation in Exhibit 5.6. Which law do you believe has had the biggest impact on society in general? Which has had the largest impact on you personally? Justify your answer.

10. A small shoe store stocks a line of handmade sandals from Spain. In determining the selling price, the owners must monitor the euro. Explain how the value of the euro impacts the selling price.

Quiz Yourself

1. Why is understanding the macroenvironmental forces that create the marketing environment critical for a firm?
   a. These forces influence consumer behavior.
   b. These forces are controllable by a firm.
   c. These forces are uncontrollable by a firm.
   d. These forces remain stable.
   e. These forces determine profitability.

2. How does identifying trends in the marketplace help marketers' strategic planning efforts?
   a. It informs about trends that may impact sales.
   b. It shows how the market is changing.
   c. It provides insight on how to best reach consumers.
   d. It reveals what consumers desire from the market.
   e. All of the above help marketers' strategic planning efforts.

(Answers to these two questions can be found in the Quiz Yourself Answer Key section.)

Chapter Case Study   ▇ connect˙

THE RISE OF THE ELECTRIC CAR

One of the most notable social trends affecting consumer behavior is the idea of going green. As climate change and environmental concerns increase in their seriousness and impact, consumers seek to buy green products that might help mitigate or combat the problem. In response, many companies are developing new green products—including electric cars. The first electric car actually was built in 1891, but it lost popularity when Henry Ford introduced the gas-powered Model T. Electric cars regained consumers' interest as Toyota developed its Prius in the late 1990s. The original Prius actually was a hybrid, powered by both gas and electricity; its success prompted other companies such as Honda, General Motors (GM), Ford, and Chevrolet to innovate their own hybrid models, as well as some all-electric versions. By the early 2000s, though, all the major automakers had terminated their all-electric programs. It was not until 2006, when Tesla Motors revealed its Roadster, that a modern version of the all-electric car became a distinct and appealing possibility.[70]

Tesla remains the gold standard for electric cars. The Model S all-electric sedan is the top-ranked ultra-luxury vehicle. Yet its high price has kept the brand from being a very widely purchased car. For example, a new Tesla Model S 75D starts at $75,700, and models with longer ranges without recharging start at $98,700.[71] Even if more customers might want to purchase an all-electric car, few of them can afford a Tesla. In response, Tesla innovated a less expensive entry model, the Model 3, that starts around $35,000.[72] In parallel, other companies have released their more economical all-electric options: the Chevrolet Bolt starts around $37,000 and offers a battery life comparable to that of the Tesla Model S.[73]

General Motors also recently decided to compete with Tesla directly. One of Tesla's greatest advantages has been its over-the-air software, which automatically and regularly updates the cars' software when they are plugged in overnight. Recognizing that it already installs OnStar

Launched in China by General Motors, the inexpensive Baojun electric car is designed to overcome the problems of congestion in cities.

©Imaginechina via AP Images

as a safety service standard on any GM vehicle, GM has found a large fleet of connected cars at its disposal already. Therefore, it plans to use OnStar as a means to compete directly with Tesla's software.[74]

Furthermore, GM's latest all-electric car seeks to do more than address just the problem of climate change; it wants to help drivers overcome the problem of congestion in cities. Its all-electric E100 will cost only $14,000 before incentives; with the incentives, the paid price drops to close to $5,000.[75] But it is being launched only in China, under the company's Baojun brand. The Chinese car market is the largest in the world, and the electric car segment is the largest growing segment in China, due in part to the subsidies and incentives offered by the national and local governments.[76] Accordingly, China already makes up 40 percent of the worldwide electric car market.[77] The E100 has been designed specifically to meet the needs of consumers living in Chinese cities, in that it is compact, seating only two adults, and easy to maneuver in the heavily populated streets. Furthermore, its top speed is 62 miles per hour, and its battery can last for about 96 miles, and then takes only about 7.5 hours to charge. It might not be an ideal option for someone living in a rural area who needs to travel long distances, but it is perfect for a city dweller.[78] Finally, although the car does not cost much to own, the E100 still provides some key luxuries: the interior features a digital dashboard, a seven-inch touchscreen center console, and Wi-Fi capabilities.[79]

Within the week of its announcement, more than 5,000 people had registered to buy the first 200 models of the E100, spurring the company to make another 500 cars available quickly. Although the E100 will be available only in the Guangxi region of China in the immediate term, GM plans to expand its availability throughout the country as soon as possible.[80]

Questions

1. Discuss how specific environmental issues examined in this chapter impact the development and sale of electric cars.

2. Which market do you believe will be more successful, Tesla in the United States or GM's E100 in China? Defend your answer.

Endnotes

1. Tim Higgins, "Tesla Model 3 Arrives as Elon Musk Warns of 'Manufacturing Hell,'" *The Wall Street Journal*, July 29, 2017; Ben Levisohn, "How Tesla's Model 3 Is Like Apple's iPhone. Really," *Barron's*, September 12, 2017; Matthew DeBord, "Tesla Is Taking a Long Time to Ramp Up Production for the Model 3—Here's Why," *Business Insider*, September 13, 2017.

2. Peter F. Drucker, *The Essential Drucker* (New York: HarperCollins, 2001).

3. "Consumer Electronics Glass Technology," Corning, www.corning.com/worldwide/en/industries/consumer-electronics.html.

4. Lisa Eadicicco, "Verizon's 'Can You Hear Me Now?' Guy Works for Sprint Now," *Time*, June 6, 2016.

5. Chris Matyszczyk, "Verizon Gets 'Silicon Valley' Star to Drop the Mic on Rivals," *CNET*, February 14, 2017, www.cnet.com/news/verizon-unlimited-plan-silicon-valley-thomas-middleditch/.

6. www.nau.com.

7. Ibid.

8. www.thoughtco.com/the-four-spheres-of-the-earth-1435323. The four spheres of the earth are the lithosphere or geosphere that deals with the mantle and crust of the earth, the hydrosphere that deals with the water on the surface or in the atmosphere, the biosphere that deals with all living organisms, and the atmosphere that surrounds the earth.

9. www.globalgoals.org/#the-goals; www.un.org/sustainabledevelopment/sustainable-development-goals/.

10. Business and Sustainable Development Commission, "Nissan and ENEL Case Study," http://report.businesscommission.org/case-studies/nissan-enel-case-study; "Nissan and ENEL Launch First Smart Grid Trials," *Nissan Insider*, http://nissaninsider.co.uk/nissan-and-enel-launch-first-smart-grid-trials.

11. Ibid.

12. This definition of green marketing draws on work by Jacquelyn A. Ottman, *Green Marketing: Opportunity for Innovation* (Chicago: NTC Publishing, 1997).

13. Business and Sustainable Development Commission, "Tropical Forest Alliance (TFA) 2020," http://report.businesscommission.org/case-studies/tropical-forest-alliance-2020-case-study.

14. Kohl's, "2016 Corporate Social Responsibility Report," http://corporate.kohls.com/content/dam/kohlscorp/non-press-release-pdfs/2017/Kohls-2016-CSR-Report.pdf.

15. Del I. Hawkins and David L. Mothersbaugh, *Consumer Behavior: Building Marketing Strategy*, 11th ed. (Burr Ridge, IL: McGraw-Hill/Irwin, 2009); Philip Cateora and John Graham, *International Marketing*, 16th ed. (Burr Ridge, IL: McGraw-Hill/Irwin, 2012).

16. Katie Little, "Hot McDonald's Items You (Probably) Can't Order," *CNBC*, July 30, 2015, www.cnbc.com/2015/04/16/hot-mcdonalds-items-you-probably-cant-order.html.

17. "Fast Food Review: Hot 'n Spicy McChicken from McDonald's," *GrubGrade*, March 7, 2011, www.grubgrade.com/reviews/fast-food-review-hot-n-spicy-mcchicken-from-mcdonalds/.

18. Little, "Hot McDonald's Items You (Probably) Can't Order."

19. Emily Shah, "10 Ways McDonald's Is Changing Its Menu," *The Fiscal Times*, August 3, 2016; Little, "Hot McDonald's Items You (Probably) Can't Order"; www.mcdonalds.com/us/en-us/product/spam-eggs-and-rice.html.

20. www.tesco.com.my/html/clubcard_about.aspx?ID=6&PID=68&ULID=6,68; Lindsay Cook, "Which Loyalty Cards Are Best to Have in Your Wallet?," *Financial Times,* March 24, 2016; "The Top Customer Loyalty Programs and Why They Work," *Consumer Strategist*, March 3, 2015, www.consumerstrategist.com/top-customer-loyalty-programs/.

21. Bernard Marr, "Big Data at Tesco: Real Time Analytics at the UK Grocery Retail Giant," *Forbes,* November 17, 2016; Mark van Rijmenam, "Tesco and Big Data Analytics, a Recipe for Success?," *DataFloq*, December 22, 2014, https://datafloq.com/read/tesco-big-data-analytics-recipe-success/665.

22. Geoffrey E. Meredith, Charles D. Schewe, and Janice Karlovich, *Defining Markets, Defining Moments: America's 7 Generational Cohorts, Their Shared Experiences, and Why Businesses Should Care* (New York: Wiley, 2002).

23. "Consumers of Tomorrow: Insights and Observations about Generation Z," Grail Research, June 2010.

24. Suzy Menkes, "Marketing to the Millennials," *The New York Times*, March 2, 2010; Pamela Paul, "Getting Inside Gen Y," *American Demographics* 23, no. 9; Sharon Jayson, "A Detailed Look at the Millennials," *USA Today*, February 23, 2010.

25. Jessica Semega, Kayla Fontenot, and Melissa Kollar, "Income and Poverty in the United States: 2016," U.S. Census Bureau, September 2017.

26. Ibid.; "Computation for the 2016 Poverty Guidelines," April 25, 2016, U.S. Department of Health & Human Services.

27. Jeanne Sahadi, "The Richest 10% Hold 76% of the Wealth," *CNNMoney*, August 18, 2016.

28. Erik Simanis and Duncan Duke, "Profits at the Bottom of the Pyramid," *Harvard Business Review*, October 2014, https://hbr.org/2014/10/profits-at-the-bottom-of-the-pyramid.

29. www.census.gov; www.infoplease.com.

30. National Center for Education Statistics, "Annual Earnings of Young Adults," 2017, https://nces.ed.gov/programs/coe/indicator_cba.asp.

31. Ester Bloom, "Millennial Women Are 'Worried,' 'Ashamed' of Out-Earning Boyfriends and Husbands," *CNBC*, April 19, 2017.

32. Center for American Women and Politics, "Women in Elective Office 2017," www.cawp.rutgers.edu/current-numbers.

33. Statista, "Distribution of Computer and Video Gamers in the United States from 2006 to 2017, by Gender," 2017, www.statista.com/statistics/232383/gender-split-of-us-computer-and-video-gamers/.

34. Gregory Schmidt, "Esports Sees Profit in Attracting Female Gamers," *The New York Times,* December 21, 2016.

35. Elena Holodny, "There Will No Longer Be a Racial or Ethnic Majority in the US by 2055," *Business Insider*, September 28, 2015; Jeffrey S. Passel and D'Vera Cohn, "U.S. Population Projections: 2005–2050," Pew Research Center, http://pewhispanic.org.

36. Julie Jargon, "Pizza Chain Seeks Slice of Bicultural Pie," *The Wall Street Journal*, December 30, 2010, http://online.wsj.com.

37. U.S. Census Bureau, "U.S. Census Bureau, Current Population Survey, 2017 Annual Social and Economic Supplement," www.census.gov/data/tables/time-series/demo/income-poverty/cps-finc/finc-02.html; Todd Wasserman, "Report: Shifting African American Population," *Adweek*, January 12, 2010, www.adweek.com; U.S. Census Bureau, "Annual Social and Economic Supplement to the Current Population Survey," www.census.gov.

38. Asia Matters for America, "Asian Population—US & State Data," www.asiamattersforamerica.org/asia/data/population/states.

39. Yuriy Boykiv, "How BuzzFeed Is Winning with Asian-Americans," *Advertising Age*, August 5, 2015.

40. Business and Sustainable Development Commission, "Better Business, Better World," http://report.businesscommission.org/report.

41. Andria Cheng, "'Fair Trade' Becomes a Fashion Trend," *The Wall Street Journal,* July 7, 2015.

42. https://wfto.com/fair-trade/definition-fair-trade.

43. Tom Ryan, "Is Fast-Fashion Slowing Down?," *RetailWire*, June 22, 2016.

44. Centers for Disease Control and Prevention, "National Diabetes Statistics Report, 2017," www.cdc.gov.

45. www.subway.com/subwayroot/about_us/Social_Responsibility/NutritionalLeadership.aspx.

46. Dan Galbraith, "Subway Partners with Disney on Star Wars–Themed Fresh Fit For Kids Meal Promotion," *The Packer*, December 21, 2015.

47. "2016 Yoga in America Study Conducted by Yoga Journal & Yoga Alliance," Yoga Alliance, January 13, 2016, www.yogaalliance.org/2016YogaInAmericaStudy.

48. "Pilates & Yoga Studios in the US: Market Research Report," *IBISWorld*, November 2016; Candy Osborne, "The 6 Biggest Challenges Yoga Studios Face Today," *Medium*, January 28, 2017; Catherine Clifford, "Yoga: The Booming Business of Zen," *CNNMoney*, October 18, 2011, http://money.cnn.com.

49. George Dvorsky, "Why the US May Never Pass a Food Waste Law Like France," Gizmodo, February 2, 2016.

50. Heather Haddon and Shibani Mahtani, "Whole Foods Sets Up Shop in Low-Income Neighborhoods," *The Wall Street Journal*, October 9, 2016.

51. Rachel Arthur, "Macy's Teams with IBM Watson for AI-Powered Mobile Shopping Assistant," *Forbes*, July 20, 2016.

52. Dhruv Grewal and Scott Motyka, "The Evolution and Future of Retailing and Retailing Education," *Journal of Marketing Education* 40, no. 1 (2018).

53. National Retail Foundation, "It's Time for a Conversation on Artificial Intelligence: How The North Face Uses AI to Create Natural Conversations with Online Shoppers," January 18, 2016, https://medium.com/nrf-events/it-s-time-for-a-conversation-on-artificial-intelligence-30aea7d73f69#.tqi8g4jc9.

54. Grewal and Motyka, "The Evolution and Future"; Jenny Van Doorn et al., "Domo Arigato Mr. Roboto: Emergence of Automated Social Presence in Organizational Frontlines and Customers' Service Experiences," *Journal of Service Research* 20, no. 1 (2017), pp. 43–58.

55. Sarah Nassauer, "Robots Are Replacing Workers Where You Shop," *The Wall Street Journal*, July 19, 2016; Brian Baskin, "Next Leap for Robots: Picking Out and Boxing Your Online Order," *The Wall Street Journal*, July 25, 2017.

56. George Anderson, "Walmart Puts Robots to Work with Humans in More Stores," *RetailWire*, October 27, 2017.

57. Ibid.

58. Elise Hu, "She's Almost Real: The New Humanoid on Customer Service Duty in Tokyo," *NPR*, May 14, 2015, www.npr.org/sections/alltechconsidered/2015/05/14/403498509/shes-almost-real-the-new-humanoid-on-customer-service-duty-in-tokyo.

59. Sophie Curtis, "Pizza Hut Hires Robot Waiters to Take Orders and Process Payments at Its Fast-Food Restaurants," *The Mirror*, May 25, 2016, www.mirror.co.uk/tech/pizza-hut-hires-robot-waiters-8045172.

60. Martin Mende et al., "Service Robots Rising: How Humanoid Robots Influence Service Experiences and Food Consumption" (working paper, 2018).

61. Grewal and Motyka, "The Evolution and Future"; Jayavardhana Gubbi et al., "Internet of Things (IoT): A Vision, Architectural Elements, and Future Directions," *Future Generation Computer Systems* 29, no. 7 (2013), pp. 1645–60.

62. Dhruv Grewal and Bala Iyer, "The Age of Smart Products and Service: Changing Expectations," *Journal of Service Research* 20, no. 1 (2017), pp. 95–96.

63. Grewal and Motyka, "The Evolution and Future."

64. IBM, "IoT Applications Spanning across Industries," *Internet of Things* blog, April 28, 2017, www.ibm.com/blogs/internet-of-things/iot-applications-industries/.

65. "Yahoo Says All Three Billion Accounts Hacked in 2013 Data Theft," Reuters, October 3, 2017; Alina Selyukh, "Every Yahoo Account That Existed in Mid-2013 Was Likely Hacked," *NPR*, October 3, 2017.

66. www.ftc.gov/news-events/media-resources/protecting-consumer-privacy; www.congress.gov/bill/115th-congress/house-bill/4081; John Bussey, "Taming the Spies of Web Advertising," *The Wall Street Journal*, August 8, 2013.

67. www.irs.gov/.

68. "The Paris Agreement," United Nations, http://unfccc.int/paris_agreement/items/9485.php.

69. Camila Domonoske, "Mayors, Companies Vow to Act on Climate, Even as U.S. Leaves Paris Accord," *NPR*, June 5, 2017.

70. *PBS*, "Timeline: History of the Electric Car," PBS.org, October 30, 2009, www.pbs.org/now/shows/223/electric-car-timeline.html.

71. Kristen Korosec, "How a Chevy Bolt Just Beat a Tesla Model S," *Fortune*, August 3, 2017, http://fortune.com/2017/08/03/chevy-bolt-tesla-model-s/.

72. www.tesla.com.

73. Korosec, "How a Chevy Bolt Just Beat a Tesla Model S."

74. Matthew DeBord, "GM Is Targeting Tesla in an Area Where Tesla Dominates All Other Automakers," *Business Insider*, July 25, 2017, www.businessinsider.com/gm-new-tech-framework-for-over-the-air-updates-challenge-tesla-2017-7.

75. Peter Valdes-Dapena, "GM Is Selling a $5,000 Electric Car in China," *CNNMoney*, August 8, 2017, http://money.cnn.com/2017/08/07/autos/gm-china-electric-car/index.html.

76. Tycho De Feijter, "5 Stunning Facts about the Chinese Car Market You Need to Know," *Forbes*, May 16, 2016, www.forbes.com/sites/tychodefeijter/2016/05/16/five-things-you-need-to-know-about-the-chinese-car-market/#107fcf763025.

77. Valdes-Dapena, "GM Is Selling a $5,000 Electric Car in China."

78. Ibid.; Thomas Tamblyn, "GM Just Unveiled a $5,000 Electric Car for China," *Huffington Post* (UK), August 11, 2017, www.huffingtonpost.co.uk/entry/gm-just-unveiled-a-5000-electric-car-for-china_uk_598c7421e4b0449ed5085f9a.

79. Tamblyn, "GM Just Unveiled a $5,000 Electric Car for China."

80. Ibid.; Michael Holder, "GM Unveils Low-Cost Electric Car," *Business Green*, August 11, 2017, www.businessgreen.com/bg/news/3015508/gm-unveils-low-cost-electric-car-in-china.

i. Jerry Garrett, "In a Switch for Paris Show, Automakers Turn from Diesel," *The New York Times*, September 22, 2016; Hannah Elliott, "The Paris Motor Show Is Light on Luxury, Heavy on Green Cars," *Bloomberg*, September 28, 2016; www.mondial-automobile.com/en/visiteurs/.

ii. Glenn Taylor, "Pokémon Go Showcases Potential of Augmented Reality in Retail," *RetailWire*, July 18, 2016; Chirag Kulkarni, "15 Ways Geolocation Is Totally Changing Marketing," *Fortune*, February 6, 2017.

iii. Annie Gasparro, "Silly Rabbit! Original Trix with Artificial Colors Is Back after Customers Revolt," *The Wall Street Journal*, September 21, 2017; Caitlin Dewey, "Consumers Loved 'All-Natural'—Until Trix Cereal Lost Its Neon-Bright Glow," *The Washington Post*, September 23, 2017; Monica Watrous, "Clean Label Not Always the Best Strategy," *Food Business News*, September 26, 2017.

iv. Scott M. Fulton III, "Netflix Has an Exchange So Complex That It Has Triggered a Scientific Renaissance," *The New Stack*, February 24, 2015, http://thenewstack.io/netflix-exchange-complex-triggered-scientific-renaissance/; Ben Kunz, "Why Netflix Walked Away from Personalization," ThoughtGadgets, January 4, 2014, www.thoughtgadgets.com/whynetflix-walked-away-from-personalization/; Amol Sharma, "Amazon Mines Its Data Trove to Bet on TV's Next Hit," *The Wall Street Journal*, November 1, 2013, www.wsj.com/; Derrick Harris, "Netflix Analyzes a Lot of Data about Your Viewing Habits," Gigaom, June 14, 2012, https://gigaom.com/2012/06/14/netflix-analyzes-a-lot-of-data-about-your-viewing-habits/; Phil Simon, "Big Data Lessons from Netflix," *Wired*, March 11, 2014, www.wired.com/; Marianne Zumberge, "'House of Cards' Sees Unusual Social-Media Spike ahead of Season 3," *Boston Herald*, February 27, 2015, www.bostonherald.com/.

v. John Greenough, "Self-Driving Cars Took Center Stage at CES," *Business Insider*, January 14, 2015, www.businessinsider.com/self-driving-cars-ces-2016-01; www.google.com/selfdrivingcar/where/; Alyssa Newcomb, "Google Self-Driving Cars: What We Learned from Latest Report," *ABC News*, January 14, 2015, http://abcnews.go.com/Technology/google-driving-cars-learned-latest-report/story?id=36285705; U.S. Department of Transportation Federal Highway Administration, "Average Annual Miles per Driver by Age Group," www.fhwa.dot.gov/ohim/onh00/bar8.htm; Samantha Masunaga, "Self-Driving Cars Aren't Ready Yet: Here's How Often Human Drivers Need to Grab the Wheel," *Los Angeles Times*, January 14, 2016, www.latimes.com/business/autos/la-fi-hy-self-driving-cars-20160113-story.html; Bill Vlasic and Neal E. Boudette, "Self-Driving Tesla Was Involved in Fatal Crash, U.S. Says," *The New York Times*, June 30, 2016.

Quiz Yourself Answer Key

1. Why is understanding the macroenvironmental forces that create the marketing environment critical for a firm?

   Answer: (a) These forces influence consumer behavior.

2. How does identifying trends in the marketplace help marketers' strategic planning efforts?

   Answer: (e) All of the above help marketers' strategic planning efforts.

UNDERSTANDING THE MARKETPLACE

The three chapters in Section Two, Understanding the Marketplace, focus on three levels of marketing: to individual consumers; from business to business; and on the global playing field. Chapter 6, Consumer Behavior, discusses why individual consumers purchase products and services. The consumer decision process is highlighted. Chapter 7, Business-to-Business Marketing, explores the whys and hows of business-to-business buying. Finally, Chapter 8, Global Marketing, focuses on global markets. Thus, the three chapters in Section Two move from creating value for the individual consumer, to creating value for the firm or business, to creating value on the global level.

_DISCOVER
A NEW WAY
TO COLOR

#EMPOWEREDBYNATURE

Botanēa
100% HERBAL HAIRCOLOR
WITH PROFESSIONAL RESULT

VEGAN

Blends greys.
Reveals natural color and luminous shine.
Fully respects hair.

EXCLUSIVELY IN YOUR SALON

L'ORÉAL
PROFESSIONNEL
PARIS

L'Oreal has introduced a new line of completely plant-based, vegan hair dyes to appeal to consumers that do not wish to apply harsh chemicals to their heads every few weeks.

Source: L'Oreal

LEARNING OBJECTIVES

After reading this chapter, you should be able to:

LO6-1 Articulate the steps in the consumer buying process.

LO6-2 Describe the difference between functional and psychological needs.

LO6-3 Describe factors that affect information search.

LO6-4 Discuss postpurchase outcomes.

LO6-5 List the factors that affect the consumer decision process.

LO6-6 Describe how involvement influences the consumer decision process.

CHAPTER 6

CONSUMER BEHAVIOR

When it comes to dyeing their hair, people have some specific preferences. For those who do it at home in their bathrooms, these preferences are so specific that effective retailers even anticipate precisely when shoppers will need a new box of dye to hide their gray hair or which color-safe shampoos they are likely to buy about 10 days after they undergo the beauty process.[1] Accordingly, they can issue coupons and incentives to push beauty patrons to make specific purchases from their stores.

Such signals make for compelling insights for not just retailers but also manufacturers that seek to sell to these beauty-conscious, environmentally conscious, trend-conscious consumers. As we discussed in the opener to Chapter 4, many brands are pursuing an all-natural or organic image;[2] in this chapter, we consider in more detail some of the reasons that they might be doing so. The ultimate driver of brands' choices and marketing strategies is how consumers behave: what they are doing and what kinds of products and services they demand to support those behaviors.

For example, many people, and especially younger consumers, have grown wary of applying harsh chemicals to their heads every four to six weeks, whether at home or with the help of a professional at a salon. In response, L'Oréal—the company known for creating the chemical technology that first allowed people to go platinum blonde[3]—has launched a new line of completely plant-based, vegan dyes.[4] The product line, which takes the brand name Botanëa, relies on natural elements such as indigo to impart vibrant color to hair strands. Such options are not only natural but also "retro" in a sense, because many cultures have long used plants such as henna or indigo to dye clothing and hair and in early cosmetics products.[5]

However, the development process has been slow, as L'Oréal seeks to find plants that can produce the vast range of colors that consumers demand for their hair. Accordingly, the plant-based line initially was introduced only in salons, not on drugstore shelves. In particular, the current formulations require users to mix the product using precise measurements, and the company realizes that such precision behaviors might be more than most consumers are willing to undertake just to use a box of home-treatment hair color.[6]

The move also reflects how consumer trends have affected L'Oréal's business overall. For example, the rise of selfie culture has meant that more people—and again, especially younger consumers—tend to wear cosmetics more regularly in their attempts to present a positive image at all times. Thus, the company has enjoyed growth in its cosmetics sector. But sales of its hair dye lines have stagnated, not just because people seek to avoid chemicals but also in response to a fashion trend that embraces gray hair as an attractive choice.[7]

To go along with its natural hair dyes, L'Oréal also has introduced a line of vegan hair care options, under the brand name Source. This move suggests its determination to retain its global market leadership in the styling products sector. In addition, it reflects the company's recognition that it is not just the harsh chemicals that people seek to avoid; consumers also are embracing natural options more broadly for all of their health and beauty needs.[8]

Beyond product alternatives, L'Oréal also has reacted to the changing ways that many consumers purchase their cosmetics, moving increasingly into specialty retailer channels such as Sephora, rather than relying solely on traditional department store counters or drugstore displays.[9]

Thus across the board, L'Oréal's strategic marketing choices reflect its awareness and assessment of how consumers are behaving—including what kind of hair dye they want, where they want it, and how they want to care for their new color.

We are all consumers, and we take this status for granted. But we are also complex and irrational creatures who cannot always explain our own choices and actions. This inability makes the vitally important job of marketing managers even more difficult, in that they must be able to explain consumers' behavior to give marketers as clear an understanding of their customers as possible.

To understand consumer behavior, we must ask *why* people buy goods or services. Using principles and theories from sociology and psychology, marketers have been able to decipher many consumer choices and develop basic strategies for dealing with consumer behavior. Generally, people buy one product or service instead of another because they perceive it to be the better value for them; that is, the ratio of benefits to costs is higher for a particular product or service than for any other.

However, benefits can be subtle and less than rationally assessed, as we shall see. Consider Lauren Smith, who is thinking of buying a new outfit for a job interview. She requires something fashionable but professional looking and doesn't want to spend a lot of money. In making the decision about where she should buy the outfit, Lauren asks herself:

- Which alternative gives me the best overall value—the most appropriate yet fashionable outfit at the lowest price?
- Which alternative is the best investment—the outfit that I can get the most use of?

Because Lauren might have several reasons to choose a particular store or outfit, it is critical for companies such as Banana Republic or Macy's to key in on the specific benefits that are most important to her. Other factors that might influence Lauren go beyond her conscious awareness, which means that the retailers need to be even more well versed in her decision process than she is.[10] For example, when trying on a dress, Lauren might be influenced by the way that same dress looks on a salesperson or a mannequin in the store. Only then can they create a marketing mix that will satisfy Lauren.

In this chapter, we explore the process that consumers go through when they buy products and services. Then we discuss the psychological, social, and situational factors that influence this consumer decision process. Throughout the chapter, we emphasize what firms can do to influence consumers to purchase their products and services.

THE CONSUMER DECISION PROCESS

The consumer decision process model represents the steps that consumers go through before, during, and after making purchases.[11] Because marketers often find it difficult to determine how consumers make their purchasing decisions, it is useful for us to break down the process into a series of steps and examine each individually, as in Exhibit 6.1.

Need Recognition

The consumer decision process begins when consumers recognize they have an unsatisfied need and they would like to go from their actual, needy state to a different, desired state. The greater the discrepancy between these two states, the greater the need recognition

EXHIBIT 6.1

The Consumer Decision Process

Need recognition

Information search

Alternative evaluation

Purchase and consumption

Post-purchase

will be. For example, your stomach tells you that you are hungry, and you would rather not have that particular feeling. If you are only a little hungry, you may pass it off and decide to eat later. But if your stomach is growling and you cannot concentrate, the *need*—the difference between your actual (hungry) state and your desired (not hungry) state—is greater and you'll want to eat immediately to get to your desired state. Furthermore, your hunger conceivably could be satisfied by a nice, healthy salad, but what you really want is a bowl of ice cream. Wants are goods or services that are not necessarily needed but are desired. Regardless of the level of your hunger, your desire for ice cream will never be satisfied by any type of salad. Consumer needs like these can be classified as functional, psychological, or both.[12]

Functional Needs Functional needs pertain to the performance of a product or service. For years, BMW has made functionally superior motorcycles. BMW's K1600 model has an inline six-cylinder motor, something previously available only in BMW automobiles, combined with a stiff aluminum frame. Thus it offers remarkable power on a lightweight bike, enabling it to outperform the best luxury touring bikes in terms of comfort as well as serious sporty motorcycles in terms of speed. Of course, not everyone in need of a transportation function needs the power and speed of a BMW. A bicycle, a motor scooter, or a car can perform this function as well. It just depends on the specific needs of the purchaser.

LO6-1 Articulate the steps in the consumer buying process.

Psychological Needs Psychological needs pertain to the personal gratification consumers associate with a product and/or service.[13] Purses, for instance, provide a functional need—to transport wallets and other personal items and keep them organized and safe. So why would anyone pay more than $5,000 for a purse that does not perform these tasks any better than a $100 purse? Because they seek to satisfy psychological needs. For example, Dior offers evening clutches costing between $1,650 and $7,700. The most expensive Minaudière purse features aged, gold-toned metal and embroidered suede lambskin.[14] These bags are often seen on the red carpet, such as when Charlize Theron showed up at the 2017 Oscars carrying a Dior Minaudière clutch.[15] Even though these bags are not known for being particularly practical, strong demand for Dior bags persists among women who love exciting (and expensive) purses.

LO6-2 Describe the difference between functional and psychological needs.

These examples highlight that most goods and services seek to satisfy functional as well as psychological needs, albeit to different degrees. Whereas the functional characteristics of a BMW K1600 are its main selling point, it also maintains a fashionable appeal for bikers and comes in several

Does a Dior Minaudière clutch like this one carried by Charlize Theron at the 2017 Oscars satisfy psychological or functional needs?
©Jim Ruymen/UPI/Newscom

What needs does a BMW K1600 satisfy?
©Bill Pugliano/Getty Images

Ethical & Societal Dilemma 6.1   CVS Makes Changes to Focus on Customer Health[i]

In the past few years, CVS Health Corp. has made moves to promote shoppers' health, including removing tobacco products from its stores. The change cost the chain $2 billion in annual sales, but CVS has stood firmly by the tobacco ban and sought to leverage its ethical stance by setting itself apart from competitors as the healthier alternative to other pharmacy chains.

Ultimately the tobacco ban did not drive customers away, so CVS is planning to expand on its positive image, as well as its underlying goals to make its customers healthier, by targeting candy, low-protection sunscreen, and foods containing artificial trans-fats next. In four test stores, the retailer has moved candy and other snack foods to the back of the store, where they are less visible. The chain will no longer carry any sun protection products with SPF ratings lower than 15.

Finally, CVS will stop stocking foods with artificial trans-fats more than a year before a new FDA ban on such ingredients takes effect. At the same time, it will be increasing the number of healthier food options available through its private-label brand, Gold Emblem; overall, it anticipates increasing healthy food options in its stores by 50 percent. This change will be accompanied by changes to the store layout, such that several new aisles will heavily showcase the healthier food items, along with beauty products. This move away from its old strategy—namely, being a convenient store for virtually anything—signals its effort to show customers that the company stands for something specific: health.

CVS' largest competitor Walgreens has taken note of these planned changes, but it does not necessarily plan to follow suit. Rather, Walgreens continues to sell tobacco products, even as it also promotes smoking cessation aids. Furthermore, the company will continue to stock candy and snack foods in the usual store locations, though it has plans to offer a greater selection of fresh fruits and vegetables. The Walgreens loyalty program also provides rewards to customers when they demonstrate that they are engaging in exercise and health monitoring behaviors. With these changes, Walgreens believes it is granting consumers the option to make healthier choices, while still allowing them to decide what is best for themselves when it comes to their consumption.

Ultimately, the issue may be moot: Both chains report that retail sales make up less and less of their overall revenue. The pharmacy and in-store health care clinics currently account for more than half of the revenues earned by both pharmacy

retailers, and this trend is expected to continue. Accordingly, CVS is also making moves to emphasize health in its pharmacy departments. It is imposing stronger regulations on opioid painkillers, a strategic move in response to pressures from health insurance and health care providers trying to crack down on prescription abuse and ensure patients receive the medications they need, in amounts that are appropriate.

The real impact that these changes will have on the bottom line may be up to the consumer. Will CVS be applauded for putting customer health over profit, or will consumers feel that these new restrictions are an overreach of the chain's influence on their day-to-day lives? Only time will tell if the candy aisle will remain at the back of the store.

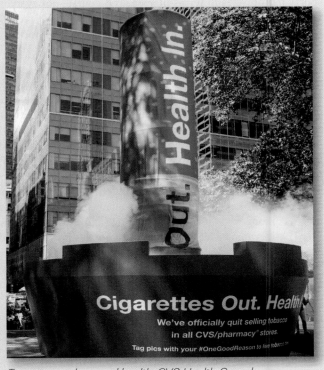

To promote shoppers' health, CVS Health Corp. has removed tobacco products from its stores.

©Donato Sardella/Getty Images for CFDA/Vogue

colors to match buyers' aesthetic preferences. Dior purses satisfy psychological needs that overshadow the functional needs, though they still ultimately serve the function of carrying personal items.

Successful marketing requires determining the correct balance of functional and psychological needs that best appeal to the firm's target markets, as described in Ethical & Societal Dilemma 6.1.

Search for Information

The second step, after a consumer recognizes a need, is to search for information about the various options that exist to satisfy that need. The length and intensity of the search

Adding Value 6.1   Trying Out a Shower in the Store: Pirch's Functional Showrooms[ii]

Consumers can test cosmetics, try on pants, and lie on mattresses for a few moments before purchasing them, and such trial runs are critical for many purchase decisions. But when it comes to home remodeling, home improvement stores and design showrooms alike generally force shoppers just to imagine how a product on a shelf might look in a room that they have spent thousands of dollars to redesign or build. One high-end chain seeks to overcome that challenge by making sure everything it sells, from showerheads to stoves, is completely functional in stores. With the assertion that it wants customers to feel like guests in the homelike setting of its showroom, it invites people to give those items a try before they leave.

The Pirch chain of eight stores thus is notably different. Although it sells dishwashers and ranges, it presents them like art instead of appliances. Begun in California, it recently opened a New York store, with 32,000 square feet. In addition to the artistic sensibility and soft lighting, the store is unique in its inclusion of massive gas lines and water pipes—needed to make sure everything works as it would in the customers' homes.

Those homes might not be quite as large as the showroom, but they also are unlikely to be one-bedroom apartments. Pirch's prices clearly establish it as a high-end retailer, targeting wealthy clients who might spend $157,000 on a gas range or $11,427 for a bathtub. It also regards and describes its mission somewhat differently than traditional retailers might. For example, Pirch's preferred terminology suggests that it "curates" the products in its stores, rather than selling or carrying them. Employees attend the "Elements" training seminar, a

Trying out things is an important part of the external search process for some products. But how many times do you get to try out a showerhead right in the store before you buy, like you can at Pirch stores?

©Yana Paskova/The New York Times/Redux Pictures

weeklong course that ensures they understand the guest-oriented retail philosophy, including its organizing principles—verbs that suggest what customers should do in its stores: "dream, play, choose," as well as "live joyfully."

Living joyfully might be exactly what it is like to take a shower in the middle of a showroom to select from among the 30 different showerhead fixtures. Or maybe it is simply the best way for customers to get exactly the bathing experience they want.

---

are based on the degree of perceived risk associated with purchasing the product or service. If the way your hair is cut is important to your appearance and self-image, you may engage in an involved search for the right salon and stylist. Alternatively, an athlete looking for a short buzz cut might go to the closest, most convenient, and cheapest barber shop. Regardless of the required search level, there are two key types of information search: internal and external.

Internal Search for Information In an internal search for information, the buyer examines his or her own memory and knowledge about the product or service gathered through past experiences. For example, every time Lauren wants to eat salad for lunch, she and her friends go to Sweetgreen, but if she's craving dessert, she heads straight to The Cheesecake Factory. In making these choices, she relies on her memory of past experiences when she has eaten at these restaurant chains.

External Search for Information In an external search for information, the buyer seeks information outside his or her personal knowledge base to help make the buying decision. Consumers might fill in their personal knowledge gaps by talking with friends, family, or a salesperson. They can also scour commercial media for unsponsored and (it is hoped) unbiased information, such as that available through *Consumer Reports,* or peruse sponsored media such as magazines, television, or radio. One of the most effective and long-standing ways to search for information is to do so right in the store. The appliance retailer Pirch even encourages people to test out showerheads in the store before installing them in their homes, as Adding Value 6.1 reports. But perhaps the most common sources of external information these days are online search engines, such as Google and Bing.

Lauren liked the picture of Zendaya wearing a ruffled turtleneck in a magazine so much that she resorted to online channels to purchase it.

©Andrew Burton/Getty Images

 LO6-3 Describe factors that affect information search.

The Internet provides information in various ways.[16] For example, while reading a popular magazine, Lauren saw Zendaya, one of the lead actors of *The Greatest Showman,* wearing a fantastic outfit that included a ruffled turtleneck. She pulled out her phone, went on Instagram, and found a popular fan account that posts all of Zendaya's outfits. She found the post from the CFDA/Vogue Fashion Fund Show, which in turn told her where to purchase the item she loved. The turtleneck was designed by Teresa Helbig, but it was extremely expensive. However, Lauren is a savvy shopper, so when she searched for "Teresa Helbig pink, ruffled turtleneck" on Google, she found that she could get it at a lower price from another retailer. Satisfied with that purchase, she continued to flip through the magazine and saw Reese Witherspoon wearing a pair of adorable True Religion jeans. This time she navigated directly to Shopzilla.com, searched for True Religion jeans, and found those very jeans on the first page, on sale on Amazon.com.[17] Lauren went to the Amazon store, entered her measurements, and the website returned recommendations for jeans that would be a good fit for her.[18]

All these examples are external searches for information. Lauren used the television show's dedicated site to find a style she liked; she referred to a magazine for additional style tips; and, using the web, she found jeans that would be a perfect fit for her. All these events took place without Lauren ever leaving her home to go to the store or try on dozens of pairs of pants.

Factors Affecting Consumers' Search Processes It is important for marketers to understand the many factors that affect consumers' search processes. Among them are the following three factors: perceived benefits versus perceived costs of search, the locus of control, and the actual or perceived risk.

The Perceived Benefits versus Perceived Costs of Search Is it worth the time and effort to search for information about a product or service? For instance, most families spend a lot of time researching the housing market in their preferred area before they make a purchase because homes are a very expensive and important purchase with significant safety and enjoyment implications. They likely spend much less time researching which inexpensive dollhouse to buy for the youngest member of the family.[19]

The Locus of Control People who have an internal locus of control believe they have some control over the outcomes of their actions, in which case they generally engage in more search activities. With an external locus of control, consumers believe that fate or other external factors control all outcomes. In that case, they believe it doesn't matter how much information they gather; if they make a wise decision, it isn't to their credit, and if they make a poor one, it isn't their fault. People who do a lot of research before purchasing individual stocks have an internal locus of control; those who purchase mutual funds are more likely to believe that they can't predict the market and probably have an external locus of control. These beliefs have widespread effects. For example, when people believe that they can choose their own consumption goals (internal locus of control), they work harder to achieve them than if those goals feel imposed upon them (external locus of control).[20]

Actual or Perceived Risk Five types of risk associated with purchase decisions can delay or discourage a purchase: performance, financial, social, physiological, and psychological. The higher the risk, the more likely the consumer is to engage in an extended search. Marketers may seek to minimize these risks and make the search easier, as Social & Mobile Marketing 6.1 describes in relation to Rent the Runway.

Performance risk involves the perceived danger inherent in a poorly performing product or service. An example of performance risk is the possibility that Lauren Smith's new interview outfit is prone to shrinking when dry cleaned.

Social & Mobile Marketing 6.1   Using Snapchat to Reduce Risk at Rent the Runway[iii]

For the fashion rental retailer Rent the Runway, getting a customer's order right is critical on multiple levels. Most customers place their order less than a week before the event for which they need the rental fashions. And those events tend to be fancy, high-profile events, such that the customers want to look their very best in a luxury, designer gown. Faced with these high service demands, Rent the Runway is turning to social media to find new ways to connect with customers before they place their orders, thus increasing the chances that the dress will fit on the day of the big event.

Rent the Runway promises designer gear for women who want to look great at a party or event to which they have been invited, but who don't have the time, money, or desire to pay for an expensive ball gown or cocktail dress that they might never wear again. Because of the unique demands and needs of these shoppers, Rent the Runway already allows customers to order the next size of the same outfit, to make sure that one of them will fit. They also can request two different dresses in the same order, for a flat handling fee.

But such efforts were not quite enough. Panicked customers who realized only too late that the bodice of a dress was too tight or that the hem trailed on a particular skirt were unhappy, even though the company already offered extensive customer service assistance by phone. Noting that customers were contacting the company not just through e-mail and phone calls but also through Snapchat, to share pictures and videos, Rent the Runway decided to try something totally different. It now encourages customers to upload pictures or videos of themselves, how they move, and what kinds of clothing they like to the corporate site.

In the meantime, Rent the Runway has recruited a pool of models from among its own employees. Approximately 250 workers from the customer service department at its corporate headquarters have agreed to help and offer themselves as sort of living mannequins, with varied body types that generally offer matches with customers' bodies. Thus, when the customer uploads a video, provides her body type information, and explains what she's looking for, the company solicits the assistance of a model with a similar body type. This model

Rent the Runway reduces perceived and actual risk by utilizing "models" from its staff to show customers how a particular outfit would look on their body type.

©IPGGutenbergUKLtd/Getty Images

then tries on the chosen outfit and offers a review of minor details that might make a difference, such as how easy it is to sit in a skirt or how low the neckline falls.

The customer and customer service representative then engage in a conversation, covering the customer's detailed questions and concerns. The plan is for service representatives to spend about 10 minutes with each customer, ensuring that the product ordered is the best option for this shopper.

With its broad sample of employees, Rent the Runway has thus far been able to match every customer to a model who can wear the dress and post the resulting information to the customer's Snapchat account. If it can keep up the conversation, it seems poised to achieve even higher levels of satisfied—and well-dressed—customers.

Financial risk is risk associated with a monetary outlay and includes the initial cost of the purchase as well as the costs of using the item or service.[21] Lauren is concerned not only that her new outfit will provide her with the professional appearance she is seeking but also that the cost of dry cleaning will not be exorbitant. Retailers recognize that buying professional apparel can be a financial burden and therefore offer guarantees that the products they sell will perform as expected. Their suppliers are also well aware that dry cleaning is expensive and can limit the life of the garment, so many offer easy-to-care-for washable fabrics.

Social risk involves the fears that consumers suffer when they worry others might not regard their purchases positively. When buying a fashionable outfit, consumers like Lauren consider what their friends would like. Alternatively, because this job interview is so important, Lauren might make a conscious effort to assert a distinctive identity or make a statement by buying a unique, more stylish, and possibly more expensive outfit than her friends would typically buy. She also hopes to impress her prospective boss rather than her pals with her choice.

Physiological risk could also be called safety risk. Whereas performance risk involves what might happen if a product does not perform as expected, physiological (or safety) risk refers to the fear of an actual harm should the product not perform properly. Although physiological risk is typically not an issue with apparel, it can be an important issue when buying other products, such as a car, a topic covered in Ethical & Societal Dilemma 6.2. External agencies and government bodies publish safety ratings for cars to help assuage this risk. Consumers compare the safety records of their various choices because they recognize the real danger to their well-being if the automobile they purchase fails to perform a basic task, such as stopping when the driver steps on the brakes or protecting the passengers in the cabin even if the car flips.

Finally, psychological risks are those risks associated with the way people will feel if the product or service does not convey the right image. Lauren Smith, thinking of her outfit purchase, read several fashion magazines and sought her friends' opinions because she wanted people to think she looked great in the outfit—and she wanted to get the job!

Recent research suggests that psychological risks might help explain why consumers often think that "bigger is better." In particular, this research helps explain why some enjoy buying large-sized menu items at restaurants. Especially when consumers feel powerless or more vulnerable, they equate larger sizes—whether in televisions, houses, or menu items—with improved status.[22]

Evaluation of Alternatives

Once a consumer has recognized a problem and explored the possible options, he or she must sift through the choices available and evaluate the alternatives. Alternative evaluation often occurs while the consumer is engaged in the process of information search. For example, Lauren Smith would rule out various stores because she knows they won't carry the style she needs for the job interview. Once in the right kind of store, she would try on lots of outfits and eliminate those that do not fit, do not look good on her, or are not appropriate attire for the occasion. Consumers forgo alternative evaluations altogether when buying habitual (convenience) products; you'll rarely catch a loyal Pepsi drinker buying Coca-Cola.

Attribute Sets Research has shown that a consumer's mind organizes and categorizes alternatives to aid his or her decision process. Universal sets include all possible choices for a product category, but because it would be unwieldy for a person to recall all possible alternatives for every purchase decision, marketers tend to focus on only a subset of choices. One important subset is retrieval sets, which are those brands or stores that can be readily brought forth from memory. Another is a consumer's evoked set, which comprises the alternative brands or stores that the consumer states he or she would consider when making a purchase decision. If a firm can get its brand or store into a consumer's evoked set, it has increased the likelihood of purchase and therefore reduced search time because the consumer will think specifically of that brand when considering choices.

Lauren Smith knows that there are a lot of apparel stores (universal set). However, only some have the style that she is looking for, such as Macy's, The Gap, and Banana Republic (retrieval set). She recalls that Macy's is where her mother shops and The Gap is a favorite of her younger sister. But she is sure that Banana Republic and Macy's carry business attire she would like, so only those stores are in her evoked set.

When consumers begin to evaluate different alternatives, they often base their evaluations on a set of important attributes or evaluative criteria. Evaluative criteria consist of salient, or important, attributes about a particular product. For example, when Lauren is looking for her outfit, she might consider things such as the selling price, fit, materials and construction quality, reputation of the brand, and the service support that the retailer offers. At times, however, it becomes difficult to evaluate different brands or stores because there are so many choices,[23] especially when those choices involve aspects of the garment that are difficult to evaluate, such as materials and construction quality.

Consumers use several shortcuts to simplify the potentially complicated decision process: determinant attributes and consumer decision rules. Determinant attributes are product or service features that are important to the buyer and on which competing

Ethical & Societal Dilemma **6.2**

"Certified" May Not Mean Safe: New FTC Ruling Creates Confusion for Used Car Buyers[iv]

To help boost consumer confidence in used cars, many manufacturers tout the benefits of their "certified" used car resale programs. However, the extent of repairs required for such a car to gain certified status has never been defined by well-established, accepted, industry-wide standards. The Federal Trade Commission (FTC) also recently issued a new ruling about used cars with certified status, with a specific reference to safety recalls, which may contribute to creating even more consumer confusion and potential danger.

Specifically, under the new ruling, used car dealers may now advertise that the pre-owned cars have been inspected and repaired, even if that particular car model was subjected to a safety recall for a problem that has not been fixed. In lieu of fixing the safety issues prior to sale, dealers instead must notify buyers that the car they are thinking about purchasing might be subject to a recall and provide information about how to check for recalls that might apply to their particular vehicle. They also are prohibited from advertising it as "safe."

Politicians and consumer groups, including the Consumers Union, the Center for Auto Safety, and the Consumer Federation of America, were quick to criticize the new FTC ruling, arguing that the new rules would endanger the lives and safety of buyers who lack the time, ability, or willingness to conduct extensive research into safety recalls that may apply to their new purchase. The ruling also is at odds with the position of the National Highway Traffic Safety Administration, which has called for all used car dealers to identify and fix any item on a car that is subject to a safety recall prior to its resale. However, this Administration lacks any authority to order or require such fixes, so used car dealers are not under any obligation to perform the repairs. Finally, it conflicts with the rules for new cars, which may not be sold if any of their features are subject to a safety recall.

The FTC had defended its decision, arguing that its ruling will empower consumers, who now have a choice to purchase a used car from a dealership that confirms which safety recall–

Although criticized by many groups, including Consumers Union, the FTC nonetheless has ruled that used car dealers may advertise that pre-owned cars have been inspected and repaired, even if that particular car model was subjected to a safety recall for a problem that has not been fixed.

©B Christopher/Alamy Stock Photo

related repairs and replacements have been made, rather than one that does not. According to the FTC, this distinction will incentivize more used car dealerships to perform the repairs required to address the issues associated with recalls.

The reaction of the industry to the new ruling remains to be seen, and a recently filed lawsuit asked the U.S. Court of Appeals to overturn the FTC's position. Unfortunately though, a history of high-profile cases in which automobile manufacturers actively concealed crucial safety or pollution emission information suggests the potential for misleading tactics. In this case, the FTC ruling could have effects opposite those it intended, by making the car-buying process even more difficult and confusing for consumers seeking a safe and reliable used car.

Macy's is part of the retrieval set of stores available to women for business apparel, but Banana Republic is in the evoked set for young women looking for business apparel.

(Left): ©Ron Antonelli/Bloomberg via Getty Images; (right): ©Sang Tan/AP Images

Adding Value 6.2 — How La Croix Has Entered Consumers' Evoked Set Using Social Media That Highlights Its Determinant Attributes[v]

Sometimes, things just come together for a brand. At the same time that people began really looking for alternatives to heavily sweetened, calorie-laden colas, National Beverage, which owns and markets the La Croix brand of sparkling water, hit on a social media campaign that stresses determinant attributes that would appeal effectively to Millennial consumers, and enter their retrieved choice set and ultimately their evoked set. The result has been a massive expansion of the brand's profits, and popularity.

Although National Beverage does not separate its reported profit by brand, its annual profits have more than doubled in the last couple of years. This financial success stems largely from an increase in brand awareness, which is necessary to enter consumers' retrieval and evoked sets. La Croix in particular is virtually everywhere these days, and especially on people's social media feeds. For its Instagram-related marketing efforts, the brand targets "micro-influencers," which it defines as users who have thousands of followers, rather than going after famous names with millions of followers. With this approach, it creates a more organic feeling to promotional posts, in that these micro-influencers can be more convincing when they include pictures of themselves drinking La Croix at their summer picnic or during their work break.

Furthermore, it encourages consumers to tag La Croix in relation to their experiences and to post recipes for drinks stressing the determinant attributes—lightly flavored and calorie-free carbonated water. These experiences often reference the health-related claims that La Croix can make about specific attributes, namely, that it has no calories, sugar, or artificial sweeteners. Such experience-oriented marketing makes it seem as if virtually everyone is drinking La Croix, and doing so without negative effects on their health or wellness.

What determinant attributes are salient to La Croix's Millennial customers?

©McGraw-Hill Education/Evelyn Nicole Kirksey, photographer

But many of the posts also refer vaguely to the ethereal attribute of La Croix that seemingly encompasses the mild flavor, refreshing carbonation, and also the intangible benefits of the brand and the image that it evokes.

This ethereal attribute is part of the set of determinant attributes too; the attractive packaging of the cans notes that the sophisticated flavors (e.g., kiwi sandia, peach-pear) are created by ingredients that include "natural essence oils." Its price point reiterates and reinforces this positioning. That is, at about $6 per 12 pack, the brand is more expensive and thus more exclusive than colas, but still affordable enough that Millennials can enjoy it as an everyday luxury.

But even as Millennials claim the fizzy essence as their own, National Beverage is making sure that other consumer cohorts are familiar with La Croix too—even if they don't know too much about it. As one 56-year-old rancher and La Croix enthusiast explained, "I know what flavors I like but I have no idea what kinds of chemicals are in there and I don't care. I know it tastes good."

---

brands or stores are perceived to differ.[24] Because many important and desirable criteria are equal among the various choices, consumers look for something special—a determinant attribute—to differentiate one brand or store from another. Determinant attributes may appear perfectly rational, such as health and nutrition claims offered by certain foods and beverages, or they may be more subtle and psychologically based, such as the stitching on the rear pockets of those True Religion jeans that Reese Witherspoon was wearing. Adding Value 6.2 highlights how determinant attributes are used to evaluate soft drinks.

Consumer Decision Rules Consumer decision rules are the set of criteria that consumers use consciously or subconsciously to quickly and efficiently select from among several alternatives. These rules are typically either compensatory or noncompensatory.

Compensatory A compensatory decision rule assumes that the consumer, when evaluating alternatives, trades off one characteristic against another, such that good characteristics compensate for bad characteristics.[25] For instance, Hanna Jackson is looking to buy breakfast cereal and is considering several factors such as taste, calories, price, and natural/organic claims. But even if the cereal is priced a little higher than Hanna was planning to spend, a superb overall rating offsets, or compensates for, the higher price.

Although Hanna probably would not go through the formal process of making the purchasing decision based on the multi-attribute model described in Exhibit 6.2, this exhibit

	Taste	Calories	Natural/Organic Claims	Price	Overall Score
EXHIBIT 6.2 Compensatory Purchasing Multi-Attribute Model for Buying Cereal					
Importance Weight	0.4	0.1	0.3	0.2	
Cheerios	10	8	6	8	8.2
Post	8	9	8	3	7.1
Kashi	6	8	10	5	7.2

Photos: ©Michael J. Hruby

illustrates how a compensatory model would work.[26] Hanna assigns weights to the importance of each factor. These weights must add up to 1.0. So, for instance, for Hanna, taste is the most important, with a weight of 0.4, and calories are least important, with a weight of 0.1. She assigns weights to how well each of the cereals might perform, with 1 being very poor and 10 being very good. Hanna thinks Cheerios has the best taste, so she assigns it a 10. Then she multiplies each performance rating by its importance rating to get an overall score for each cereal. The rating for Cheerios in this example is the highest of the three cereals [(0.4 × 10) + (0.1 × 8) + (0.3 × 6) + (0.2 × 8) = 8.2)]. This multi-attribute model allows the trade-off between the various factors to be incorporated explicitly into a consumer's purchase decision.

Noncompensatory Sometimes, however, consumers use a noncompensatory decision rule in which they choose a product or service on the basis of one characteristic or one subset of a characteristic, regardless of the values of its other attributes.[27] So although Cheerios received the highest overall score of 8.2, Hanna might still pick Kashi because she is particularly sensitive to claims of natural or organic contents, and this brand earned the highest score on this attribute (i.e., a 10).

Choice Architecture Consumers' decisions, when they consider alternative options, can be influenced by the choice architecture surrounding the evaluation. The choice architecture represents an effort to influence consumers through the design of the environments in which they make their choices. A notable example would be a choice architecture that encourages consumers to purchase impulse products, or products that are purchased without planning, such as fragrances and cosmetics in department stores and magazines in supermarkets. The prime store locations for selling this type of merchandise are heavily trafficked areas such as 10 feet beyond the entrance on the right side of the store and areas near escalators and cash wraps. By putting impulse products in these areas, the store has created a choice architecture that encourages customers to buy.

This tactic constitutes a "nudge." A nudge is one element of the choice architecture that alters behavior in a predictable way, without forbidding other options or significantly changing any economic incentives.[28] In the store, customers have the option of bypassing merchandise at the front of the store or at the cash wrap. Thus, even as the choice architecture nudges them to purchase because of their convenient location, the choice of whether or not to buy is still theirs.[29]

Another element of a choice architecture is a default, which deals with a "no-action" condition by imposing a choice on a person who fails to make a decision or does not actively opt for a different alternative. Internet marketers in the United States use this option to encourage people to receive their messages. Personal information in the United States is generally viewed as being in the public domain, and Internet marketers can use it any way they desire. U.S. consumers must explicitly tell these firms not to use their personal information—they must explicitly opt out. The EU perspective is that consumers own their personal information, so firms must get consumers to agree explicitly to share this personal information. This agreement is referred to as opt in.[30] The United States' opt out convention nudges them into viewing firms' Internet messages. But to be excluded completely from viewing the messages, they would have to explicitly opt out.[31] Considering the growing consensus that personal information must be collected fairly and purposefully, and that the data should be relevant, accurate, and secured, firms should find ways to assure customers that information about them is held securely and not passed on to other companies without the customers' permission. Once a consumer has considered the possible alternatives and evaluated the pros and cons of each, he or she can move toward a purchase decision.

Purchase and Consumption

After evaluating the alternatives, customers are ready to buy. However, they don't always patronize the store or purchase the brand or item on which they had originally decided. It may not be available at the retail store, for example. Retailers therefore turn to the conversion rate to measure how well they have converted purchase intentions into purchases. One method of measuring the conversion rate is the number of real or virtual abandoned carts in the retailer's store or website.

When it realized that approximately two-thirds of decisions about home improvements are made by women, Home Depot embarked on a strategy to increase its conversion rate by appealing more to women. It has implemented in-store renovations to ensure that female consumers not only visit its stores but also make their purchases there rather than from its main rival, Lowe's. In particular, whereas Home Depot once purposefully embraced a sort of construction site feel, with wheeled pallets and jumbled displays of nuts and bolts, the renovated stores feature better lighting and cleaner product displays. In addition, greeters at the entrance help people find what they need. In addition to the greeters, Home Depot is enhancing customer service by mounting devices throughout stores to enable shoppers to check prices or find particular items, and it is providing more training to employees, encouraging them to provide more effective assistance to shoppers who might be less familiar with hardware and home improvement projects.

To make sure that shoppers can find everything they want and therefore don't have the desire to shop elsewhere, Home Depot is expanding its product lines to feature familiar

When Home Depot realized that the majority of home improvement decisions are made by women, it implemented changes from its traditional construction site feel (left) to include cleaner product displays (right).

(Left): ©Capture +/Alamy Stock Photo; (right): ©Paul Bersebach/Zumapress/Newscom

names such as Martha Stewart and include more décor and convenience items for the household. The idea is that a trip to Home Depot can be a family event because it carries items for parents of either gender, as well as small projects for kids. If these family members want to install their new purchases on their own, Home Depot offers do-it-yourself workshops in stores as well as video tutorials online. If they want to have the product installed by professionals, Home Depot provides a list of qualified, rated subcontractors available for the work. Thus the retailer seeks to become the sole source for all its customers' home improvement needs, from the smallest project to the largest remodeling.[32]

EXHIBIT 6.3 Components of Postpurchase Outcomes

Postpurchase

The final step of the consumer decision process is postpurchase behavior. Marketers are particularly interested in postpurchase behavior because it entails actual rather than potential customers. Satisfied customers, whom marketers hope to create, become loyal, purchase again, and spread positive word of mouth, so they are quite important. There are three possible postpurchase outcomes, as illustrated in Exhibit 6.3: customer satisfaction, postpurchase cognitive dissonance, and customer loyalty (or disloyalty).

LO6-4 Discuss postpurchase outcomes.

Customer Satisfaction Setting unrealistically high consumer expectations of the product through advertising, personal selling, or other types of promotion may lead to higher initial sales, but it eventually will result in dissatisfaction if the product fails to achieve high performance expectations. (For a related discussion about communication gaps, see Chapter 13.) This failure can lead to dissatisfied customers and the potential for negative word of mouth.[33] Setting customer expectations too low is an equally dangerous strategy. Many retailers fail to put their best foot forward. For instance, no matter how good the merchandise and service may be, if a store is not clean and appealing from the entrance, customers are not likely to enter.

Marketers can take several steps to ensure postpurchase satisfaction:

- Build realistic expectations, not too high and not too low.
- Demonstrate correct product use—improper usage can cause dissatisfaction.
- Stand behind the product or service by providing money-back guarantees and warranties.
- Encourage customer feedback, which cuts down on negative word of mouth and helps marketers adjust their offerings.
- Periodically make contact with customers and thank them for their support. This contact reminds customers that the marketer cares about their business and wants them to be satisfied. It also provides an opportunity to correct any problems. Customers appreciate human contact, though it is more expensive for marketers than are e-mail or postal mail contacts.

Postpurchase Cognitive Dissonance Postpurchase cognitive dissonance is an internal conflict that arises from an inconsistency between two beliefs or between beliefs and behavior. For example, you might have buyer's remorse after purchasing an expensive television because you question whether this high-priced version offers appreciably better quality than does a set of similar size but at a lower price—or whether you need a television at all, considering your ability to stream content through your computer. Postpurchase cognitive dissonance generally occurs when a consumer questions the appropriateness of a purchase after his or her decision has been made.

Postpurchase cognitive dissonance is especially likely for products that are expensive, are infrequently purchased, do not work as intended, or are associated with high levels of risk. Marketers direct efforts at consumers after the purchase is made to address this issue.[34] General Electric sends a letter to purchasers of its appliances, mentioning the high quality that went into the product's design and production, thus positively reinforcing the message that the customer made a wise decision. Some clothing manufacturers include a tag on their garments to offer the reassurance that because of their special manufacturing process, perhaps designed to provide a soft, vintage appearance, there may be variations in color that have no effect on the quality of the item. After a pang of dissonance, satisfaction may then set in.

Let's check back in with our friend Lauren to recognize these effects. After Lauren purchased her interview outfit at Macy's, she tried it on for some of her friends. Her boyfriend said he loved it, but several of her girlfriends seemed less impressed. Lauren thought it made her look more mature. Because of these mixed signals, some dissonance resulted and manifested itself as an uncomfortable, unsettled feeling. To reduce the dissonance, Lauren could:

- Take back the outfit.
- Pay attention to positive information, such as looking up ads and articles about this particular designer.
- Seek more positive feedback from friends.
- Seek negative information about outfits made by designers not selected.

Customer Loyalty In the postpurchase stage of the decision-making process, marketers attempt to solidify loyal relationships with their customers. They want customers to be satisfied with their purchases and buy from the same company again. Loyal customers will buy only certain brands and shop at certain stores, and they include no other firms in their evoked set. As we explained in Chapter 2, such customers are therefore very valuable to firms, and marketers have designed detailed analytics software and customer relationship management (CRM) programs specifically to acquire and retain them.

Undesirable Consumer Behavior Although firms want satisfied, loyal customers, sometimes they fail to attain them. Passive consumers are those who don't repeat purchase or recommend the product to others. More serious and potentially damaging, however, is negative consumer behavior such as negative word of mouth and rumors.

Negative word of mouth occurs when consumers spread negative information about a product, service, or store to others. When customers' expectations are met or even exceeded, they often don't tell anyone about it. But when consumers believe that they have been treated unfairly in some way, they usually want to complain, often to many people. The Internet and social media have provided an effective method of spreading negative word of mouth to millions of people instantaneously through personal blogs, Twitter, and corporate websites. In turn, some firms rely on listening software offered by companies such as Salesforce.com (as we discussed in Chapter 3), then respond to negative word of mouth through customer service representatives—whether online, on the phone, or in stores—who have the authority to handle complaints. Many companies also allow customers to post comments and complaints to proprietary social media sites.

For example, Whirlpool set up Facebook pages for its appliance brands Maytag, KitchenAid, and Whirlpool. Customers may share their thoughts on these sites without fear that their negative feedback will be deleted from the site. Whirlpool believes that it should keep the bad comments to

Stores collect customer information for their CRM programs from their loyalty cards.

©Mark Lennihan/AP Images

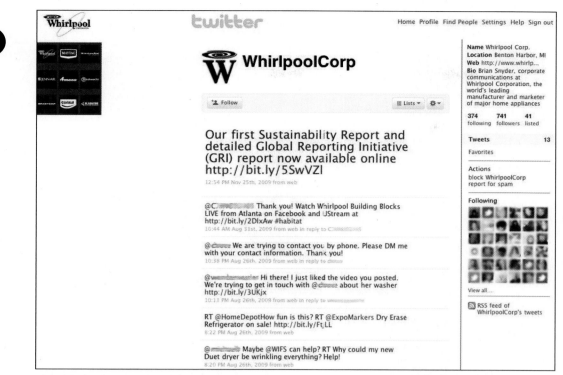

Whirlpool posts good as well as bad comments on Twitter. It believes that posting negative comments opens up discussions and emphasizes the proactive measures the company is taking to remedy service or product failures.

Source: Whirlpool

open up discussions and emphasize the proactive measures the company is taking to remedy service or product failures.[35] If a customer believes that positive action will be taken as a result of the complaint, he or she is less likely to complain to family and friends or through the Internet. (A detailed example of word of mouth appears in Chapter 13.)

PROGRESS CHECK

1. Name the five stages in the consumer decision process.
2. What is the difference between a need and a want?
3. Distinguish between functional and psychological needs.
4. What are the various types of perceived risk?
5. What are the differences between compensatory and noncompensatory decision rules?
6. How do firms enhance postpurchase satisfaction and reduce cognitive dissonance?

FACTORS INFLUENCING THE CONSUMER DECISION PROCESS

LO6-5 List the factors that affect the consumer decision process.

The consumer decision process can be influenced by several factors, as illustrated in Exhibit 6.4. First are psychological factors, which are influences internal to the customer, such as motives, attitudes, perception, learning and memory, and lifestyle. Second are social factors, such as family, reference groups, and culture, that influence the decision process. Third are situational factors, such as the specific purchase situation, a sensory situation, or temporal

EXHIBIT 6.4   Factors Affecting the Consumer Decision Process

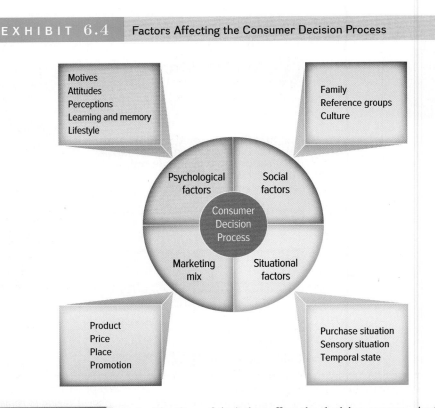

state (the time of day) that affect the decision process. And fourth are the elements of the marketing mix, which we discuss throughout this book.

Every decision people make as consumers will take them through some form of the consumer decision process. But, like life itself, this process does not exist in a vacuum.

Psychological Factors

Although marketers can influence purchase decisions, a host of psychological factors affect the way people receive marketers' messages. Among them are motives, attitudes, perception, learning and memory, and lifestyle. In this section, we examine how such psychological factors can influence the consumer decision process.[36]

Motives In Chapter 1 we argued that marketing is all about satisfying customer needs and wants. When a need, such as thirst, or a want, such as for a Diet Pepsi, is not satisfied, it motivates us, or drives us, to get satisfaction. So, a motive is a need or want that is strong enough to cause the person to seek satisfaction.

People have several types of motives. One of the best-known paradigms for explaining these motive types, developed by Abraham Maslow more than 70 years ago, is called Maslow's hierarchy of needs.[37] Maslow categorized five groups of needs: physiological (e.g., food, water, shelter), safety (e.g., secure employment, health), love (e.g., friendship, family), esteem (e.g., confidence, respect), and self-actualization (people engage in personal growth activities and attempt to meet their intellectual, aesthetic, creative, and other such needs). The pyramid in Exhibit 6.5 illustrates the theoretical progression of those needs.

Physiological needs deal with the basic biological necessities of life—food, drink, rest, and shelter. Although for most people

In this ad, Subway satisfies the physiological need for food while letting the consumer know that healthy eating can also be delicious.

Source: Subway IP Inc.

in developed countries these basic needs are generally met, there are those in developed as well as less developed countries who are less fortunate. However, everyone remains concerned with meeting these basic needs.[38] Marketers seize every opportunity to convert these needs into wants by reminding us to eat at Subway, drink milk, sleep on a Beautyrest mattress, and stay at a Marriott.

Safety needs pertain to protection and physical well-being. The marketplace is full of products and services that are designed to make you safer, such as airbags in cars and burglar alarms in homes, or healthier, such as vitamins and organic meats and vegetables.

Love needs relate to our interactions with others. Haircuts and makeup make you look more attractive, deodorants prevent odor, and greeting cards help you express your feelings toward others.

Esteem needs allow people to satisfy their inner desires. Yoga, meditation, health clubs, and many books appeal to people's desires to grow or maintain a happy, satisfied outlook on life.

Finally, self-actualization occurs when you feel completely satisfied with your life and how you live. You don't care what others think. You drive a Ford Fusion because it suits the person you are, not because some celebrity endorses it or because you want others to think better of you.

Which of these needs apply when a consumer makes a purchase from Starbucks? On the surface, Starbucks satisfies physiological needs by providing food and drink. But Starbucks also satisfies safety needs, such as those related to healthier living, by publishing the calorie, fat, and sugar contents of all of its products and offering healthy alternatives, such as a spinach, feta, and egg white breakfast wrap.[39] Furthermore, Starbucks satisfies love needs through its powerful focus on creating relationships with customers: Baristas call each customer by his or her name, and the store environment encourages customers to sit for a while, talk, and work together while enjoying their beverages. For many customers, Starbucks' in-store environment even encourages them to better themselves. The music at low volume as well as warm beverages create an ideal setting in which to read a book or work on a project, such that it helps people satisfy their esteem needs. Good marketers add value to their products or services by nudging people up the needs hierarchy and offering information on as many of the pyramid of needs as they can.

Attitude We have attitudes about almost everything. For instance, we like this class, but we don't like the instructor. We like where we live, but we don't like the weather. An attitude is a person's enduring evaluation of his or her feelings about and behavioral tendencies toward an object or idea. Attitudes are learned and long lasting, and they might develop over a long period of

EXHIBIT 6.5 Maslow's Hierarchy of Needs

Self-actualization
Esteem
Love
Safety
Physiological

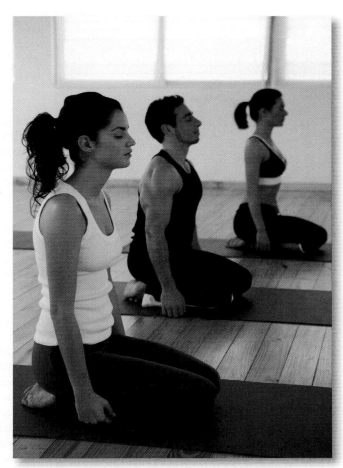

Yoga satisfies esteem needs by helping people satisfy their inner desires.

©GoGo Images/age fotostock

Which category of Maslow's hierarchy of needs is satisfied by a visit to Starbucks?

©Jean Baptiste Lacroix/WireImage/Getty Images

time, though they can also abruptly change. You might like your instructor for much of the semester—until she returns your first exam. The one thing attitudes have in common for everyone is their ability to influence our decisions and actions.

An attitude consists of three components. The cognitive component reflects our belief system, or what we believe to be true; the affective component involves emotions,[40] or what we feel about the issue at hand, including our like or dislike of something; and the behavioral component pertains to the actions we undertake based on what we know and feel. For example, Matt and Lisa Martinez see a poster for the latest *Avengers* movie. The ad lists quotes from different movie critics who call it a great and exciting film. Matt and Lisa therefore come to believe that the critics must be correct and that the new *Avengers* movie will be a good movie (cognitive component). Later they catch an interview with Robert Downey Jr., who talks about making the movie and his enjoyment playing Tony Stark (Iron Man). Therefore, Matt and Lisa start to believe the movie will be fun and engaging because they appreciate action adventures and have enjoyed previous Marvel films (affective component). After weighing their various options—which include numerous other movies, other entertainment options such as attending a concert instead, or just staying home—Matt and Lisa decide to go see the movie (behavioral component).

Ideally, agreement exists among these three components. But when there is incongruence among the three—if Matt and Lisa read positive reviews and like action films but do not find Robert Downey Jr. an appealing actor—cognitive dissonance might occur. Matt and Lisa might decide their reviews and their liking of action films will outweigh their dislike of Robert Downey Jr. and go see the movie. If they then find the movie unenjoyable because he is a primary star, they may feel foolish for having wasted their money.

Such dissonance is a terrible feeling that people try to avoid, often by convincing themselves that the decision was a good one in some way.[41] In this example, Matt and Lisa might focus on the special effects and the romantic elements of the movie while mentally glossing over the parts that featured the actor they did not enjoy. In this way, they can convince themselves that the parts they liked were good enough to counterbalance the part they didn't like, and thus they make their moviegoing experience a positive event overall.

Based on positive reviews (cognitive component) and positive feelings (affective component), many movie watchers will go see the latest Avengers *movie (behavioral component) and come away with a positive attitude.*

©BFA/Alamy Stock Photo

Although attitudes are pervasive and usually slow to change, the important fact from a marketer's point of view is that they can be influenced and perhaps changed through persuasive communications and personal experience. Marketing communication—through salespeople, advertisements, free samples, or other such methods—can attempt to change what people believe to be true about a product or service (cognitive) or how they feel toward it (affective). Because of these effects, marketers have an ethical responsibility to communicate truthfully. If the marketing communication is successful, the cognitive and affective components work in concert to affect behavior. Continuing with our example, suppose that prior to viewing the movie ad, Matt and Lisa thought they wanted to see *Fast and Furious,* but when they heard such good things about *Avengers,* they decided to see it instead. The ad positively influenced the cognitive component of their attitude toward *Avengers,* making it consistent with their affective component.

Perception Another psychological factor, perception, is the process by which we select, organize, and interpret information to form a meaningful picture of the world. Perception in marketing influences our acquisition and consumption of goods and services through our tendency to assign meaning to such things as color, symbols, taste, and packaging. Culture, tradition, and our overall upbringing determine our perception of the world. For instance, Lisa Martinez has always wanted an apartment in the Back Bay neighborhood of Boston because her favorite aunt had one, and they had a great time visiting for Thanksgiving one year. However, from his past experiences Matt has a different perception. Matt thinks Back Bay apartments are small, expensive, and impractical for a couple thinking about having children—though they would be convenient for single people who work in downtown Boston. In recent years, however, the city of Boston, working with developers to create larger, modern, and more affordable apartments and using promotion to reposition the perception of apartments in the Back Bay for young couples, has labored to overcome the long-standing negative perceptual bias that Matt and many others hold.[42]

Learning and Memory

Learning Learning refers to a change in a person's thought process or behavior that arises from experience and takes place throughout the consumer decision process. After Lauren Smith recognized that she needed an outfit for her job interview, she started looking for ads and searching for reviews and articles on the Internet. She learned from each new piece of information, so her thoughts about the look she wanted in an outfit were different from those before she had read anything. She liked what she learned about the clothing line from Macy's. She learned from her search, and it became part of her memory to be used in the future, possibly so she could recommend the store to her friends.

Memory Consumers' memories influence their decision making. Memories consist of information that has been acquired and stored in the brain, to be available and utilized when needed. There are three stages of memory that influence consumers' decision making: information encoding, information storage, and information retrieval. In the information encoding stage, consumers transform information that they receive about products and services into storable information. For example, Lauren sees a televised advertisement for Tommy Hilfiger blazers that are available at Macy's and adds that information to the information she associates with the high quality and fashion available at Macy's and for Tommy Hilfiger residing in her memory. Next, the information storage stage refers to how that knowledge gets integrated and stored with what consumers already know and remember (e.g., about blazers and Tommy Hilfiger). Finally, in the retrieval stage, consumers access desired information. If Lauren is looking for blazers or giving advice to a friend who wants to buy a professional outfit, she can retrieve the information about Tommy Hilfiger and other related designers that she has encoded and stored in her memory. This learned information that is stored in memory assists with future decisions.

Learning and memory affect attitudes as well as perceptions. Lauren's attitudes shifted throughout the buying process. The cognitive component came into play for her when she learned Macy's had one of the most extensive collections of career apparel available in her area. Once she was in the store and tried on some outfits, she realized how much she liked the way she looked and felt in them, which involved the affective component. Then she made her purchase, which involved the behavioral component. Each time she was exposed to information about the store or the outfits, she learned something different that affected her perception, and this information was stored in her memory. Before she tried them on, Lauren hadn't realized how easy it would be to find exactly what she was looking for; thus, her perception of Macy's selection of career clothing changed through learning. The memory of this learned perception could be drawn upon to make future buying decisions or provide advice to others.

Lifestyle Lifestyle refers to the way consumers spend their time and money to live. For many consumers, the question of whether the product or service fits with their actual lifestyle (which may be fairly sedentary) or their perceived lifestyle (which might be outdoorsy) is an important one. Some of the many consumers sporting North Face jackets certainly need the high-tech, cold weather gear because they are planning their next hike up Mount Rainier and want to be sure they have sufficient protection against the elements. Others, however, simply like the image that the jacket conveys—the image that they might be leaving for their own mountain-climbing expedition any day now—even if the closest they have come has been shoveling their driveway.

A person's perceptions and ability to learn are affected by his or her social experiences, which we discuss next.

Social Factors

The consumer decision process is influenced from within by psychological factors but also by the external social environment, which consists of the customer's family, reference groups, and culture.[43] (Recall Exhibit 6.4.)

Family Many purchase decisions are made about products or services that the entire family will consume or use. Thus, firms must consider how families make purchase decisions and understand how various family members might influence these decisions.

When families make purchase decisions, they often consider the needs of all the family members. In choosing a restaurant, for example, all the family members may participate in the decision making. In other situations, however, different members of the family may take

on the purchasing role. For instance, the husband and teenage child may look through car magazines and *Consumer Reports* to search for information about a new car. But once they arrive at the dealership, the husband and wife, not the child, decide which model and color to buy, and the wife negotiates the final deal.[44]

Influencing a group that holds this much spending power is vitally important. Traditional food retailers are already caught in a squeeze between Walmart, which lures low-end customers, and specialty retailers such as Whole Foods, which targets the high end. Knowing how children influence food-buying decisions is a strategic opportunity for traditional supermarkets and their suppliers to exploit.

Reference Groups A reference group is one or more persons whom an individual uses as a basis for comparison regarding beliefs, feelings, and behaviors. A consumer might have various reference groups, including family, friends, coworkers, or famous people the consumer would like to emulate. These reference groups affect buying decisions by (1) offering information and (2) enhancing a consumer's self-image.[45]

Children can have a strong influence on purchasing decisions.
©Stockbroker/Purestock/SuperStock

Reference groups provide information to consumers directly through conversation, either face-to-face or electronically, or indirectly through observation. For example, Lauren received valuable information from a friend about where she should shop for her interview outfit. On another occasion, she heard a favorite cousin who is a fashionista praising the virtues of shopping at Macy's, which solidified her decision to go there.

With the increasing popularity of blogs, such as Geeky Girl Reviews, more and more people also get recommendations for products from their favorite bloggers. When you follow a blog about kittens, you might notice that the author posts a scathing review of a particular cat tree or strongly recommends a product that encourages kittens to use their litter boxes. Because this blogger offers insights you appreciate, you go out to buy the litter box product but avoid adding that cat tree to your shopping cart. In realizing the vast influence of this reference group, companies today offer prominent bloggers free products and sometimes even pay them to write positive reviews.[46]

Consumers can identify and affiliate with reference groups to create, enhance, or maintain their self-image. Customers who want to be seen as earthy might buy Birkenstock sandals, whereas those wanting to be seen as high fashion might buy Dior bags.

Reference groups are a powerful force, especially among young consumers. For example, the primary way teenagers have expressed their personalities has long been through their fashion choices, which has made them an appealing market for retailers such as Forever 21, H&M, and American Eagle. The teen market is also using social media, smartphones, and various apps to communicate and express their self-image. As a consequence teens seek out places that offer free Wi-Fi, such as fast-food restaurants, coffee shops, and casual eateries.[47]

Culture We defined culture in Chapter 5 as the shared meanings, beliefs, morals, values, and customs of a group of people. As the basis of the social factors that affect your

If you aspire to a high fashion image, carry a Dior Minaudière clutch.

©Jim Ruymen/UPI/Newscom

Situational factors may influence your purchase decisions. If you are buying jewelry for yourself, you might browse the clearance counter at Kay Jewelers (left). But if you are buying a gift for your best friend's birthday, you may go to Tiffany & Co (right).

(Left): ©Andriy Blokhin/Shutterstock; (right): ©Victor J. Blue/Bloomberg/Getty Images

buying decisions, the culture or cultures in which you participate are not markedly different from your reference groups. That is, your cultural group might be as small as your reference group at school or as large as the country in which you live or the religion to which you belong. Like reference groups, cultures influence consumer behavior. For instance, the culture at Lauren's college is rather fashion conscious. This influences, to some extent, the way she spends, how she dresses, and where she shops.

Situational Factors

Psychological and social factors typically influence the consumer decision process the same way each time. For example, your motivation to quench your thirst usually drives you to drink a Coke or a Pepsi, and your reference group at the workplace coerces you to wear appropriate attire. But sometimes situational factors, or factors specific to the situation, override or at least influence psychological and social issues. These situational factors are related to the purchase and sensory situation as well as to temporal states.[48]

Purchase Situation Customers may be predisposed to purchase certain products or services because of some underlying psychological trait or social factor, but these factors may change in certain purchase situations. For instance, Samantha Crumb considers herself a thrifty, cautious shopper—someone who likes to get a good deal. But her best friend is having a birthday, and she wants to get her some jewelry. If she were shopping for herself, she might seek out the clearance merchandise at Macy's. But because it is for her best friend, she went to Tiffany & Co. Why? She wanted to purchase something fitting for the special occasion of having a birthday.

Sensory Situation When a consumer enters a store, various sensory aspects influence his or her decisions. When leveraged in concert with other aspects of the retail environment and retail strategy, the five senses can strongly influence consumer decision processes. We discuss each of the five senses and their main impacts on consumer choice.[49]

Visual For most people, the first sense triggered in a new setting is the visual sense. Visual sense refer to the colors, lighting, brightness, size, shape, and setup of a retail space and the products within it.[50] Dylan's Candy Bar, owned by designer Ralph Lauren's daughter Dylan, operates large candy stores in New York City, Los Angeles, Miami, Chicago, and East Hampton and sells its confections in stores around the globe. No other candy store can claim over 2 million visitors a year and maintain a position on New York City's top

10 tourist attractions. Yes, its candy is great, but its presentation is spectacular. Like a modern version of Willy Wonka's chocolate factory, visitors feast on eye candy such as candy-embedded staircases, kaleidoscopic candy wallpaper, dripping chocolate shelves, candy cane columns, and an oversized lollipop tree. All these visual cues make it "retail-tainment" at its best.[51]

Auditory Retailers often rely on the influences evoked through auditory senses. For example, retailers might select the music that plays in their stores in an effort to appeal to target markets and make the shopping experience more enjoyable, which should keep customers in the stores longer.[52] Abercrombie & Fitch uses loud music to appeal to its young customers[53]; Target plays upbeat, positive music in urban locations to fit its customer base; and Starbucks uses calm music to create a "Sunday morning" atmosphere, even during the week.[54] Background music in a store generally increases customers' positive feelings toward the store.[55]

Olfactory The sense of smell, or the olfactory senses, is another essential component that can positively influence consumer behavior in retail and service settings. Cinnabon, for example, strategically places its ovens so the smell of cinnamon rolls attracts customers.[56] Abercrombie & Fitch sprays its men's fragrance, Fierce, in the store to promulgate its image of "lifestyle . . . packed with confidence and a bold, masculine attitude."[57] Other stores, however, such as the cosmetics store Lush, avoid scents in their stores so as not to overwhelm their customers.

Tactile The tactile sense (or sense of touch) is the first one that humans develop. Marketers and retailers seek to give consumers opportunities to interact with the merchandise in this innate way, such as when clothing retailers make their cashmere sweaters and scarfs readily accessible, encouraging shoppers to pick up and feel the products.

Taste The last element, taste sense, can be influenced by marketers and is of tantamount importance in restaurants and for food and beverage retailers, as seen in Adding Value 6.3.

If Lauren were to go shopping with a much older friend, and walked into an Abercrombie & Fitch store, they would experience loud music, a pleasant, masculine scent, and subtle lighting. Lauren may love the ambiance, thus increasing her propensity to linger in the store and ultimately buy; in contrast, her older friend may be put off by these sensory stimuli, but be more comfortable at J.Jill with its softer country pop music, lack of scent, and true-to-life lighting. The appropriate mix of sensory stimuli thus depends on the store's target market.[58]

Dylan's Candy Bar draws in over two million visitors a year, partially because it is so visually appealing.
©Bryan Bedder/Getty Images

Doublemint Gum changed its packaging after 100 years to appeal to a younger audience, while still being attractive to its older customers.
©Mahathir Mohd Yasin/Shutterstock

Adding Value 6.3   Meeting Consumers' Demands for Healthy While Also Fulfilling Their Cravings for Salty[vi]

We keep reading and writing about how consumers are seeking healthier food options, and there is no denying that it is true. Reflecting people's efforts to avoid sugar and fat, companies that rely on confectionary sales, such as Hershey's, have suffered sales declines and pressures. But even as they avoid sugars, it appears that consumers still can't get enough salty snacks, so the strategy for food companies is to expand their product lines to include such addictive treats. Rather than limiting itself to Kisses, for example, Hershey Co. recently acquired the company that makes SkinnyPop popcorn, as well as the chip brands Paqui and Tyrrell's. This expansion follows a previous acquisition of Krave Pure Foods, which produces beef jerky products. Thus Hershey is moving beyond sweet to savory, hoping that the variety can appeal to a broad range of consumers. It asserts that the acquisition will grant it more flexibility for continuing to expand its chocolate business but also establish a competitive advantage in retail settings and with customers. Hershey predicts sales will grow by 5–7 percent in the coming year.

Campbell Soup Co. already had a range of products in its assortment, but it similarly has been undertaking various acquisitions to respond to consumer trends. Noting that even as sales of soup declined, its Goldfish brand of crackers held strong, so the company saw a clear way forward. In purchasing Snyder's-Lance Inc., the fifth-ranked healthy snack maker, it brings brands like Pop Secret, Snyder's pretzels, and Cape Cod potato chips into its portfolio. Most Snyder's-Lance products explicitly contain no trans-fats; its portfolio also includes dairy-free cheese and naturally sweetened products. Nor is Campbell's limiting its options to just salty snacks. It also acquired the organic soup label Pacific Foods, and it made a substantial investment in a prepackaged meal service called Chef'd.

Because some consumers are avoiding sugar and fat, Hershey's has developed salty snacks like these.
©McGraw-Hill Education

The real driver in these acquisitions is clearly the persistent trends in what consumers want to satisfy their palates. Even as the U.S. packaged food market is losing billions of dollars in revenue, popcorn, pretzels, and chips still remain strong sellers. Salty snack sales even have increased in the past four years, and the pre-popped popcorn market in particular has seen significant growth. People may be seeking meals dominated by fresh foods, such as by avoiding packaged cereals, but when it comes to snack time, they appear happy to make use of the convenient, tasty options provided by bagged snacks. They also might assume that salt is less of a risk than sugar or fat, despite consistent evidence that too much salt consumption can impose serious health risks. That is, even if potato chips and pretzels are not exactly healthy, U.S. consumers still express substantial demand for them as a good option for on-the-go snacks.

The way consumers shop, respond to various sensory stimuli, and make decisions also depends on whether they are shopping in a brick-and-mortar store or online.[59] For example, if Lauren wants to buy a new outfit from Nordstrom, she might visit a physical retail store to obtain it or else purchase the outfit online. If she shops in the physical store, she confronts multiple situational factors that will likely influence her purchase decisions, such as the salespeople, the presence and actions of other shoppers, the music in the store, the smells coming from the perfume counters, the lighting around her, the feel of the clothes, and so forth. However, if Lauren were to search for the outfit on Nordstrom's website, she can no longer physically interact with any products or people, which naturally leads to a different perception of the products she might consider purchasing. In particular, online shopping induces sensory distance, decreases the vividness of the process, and increases some of the perceived risks of purchase. For example, she cannot try on the outfit to ensure a good fit before purchasing.[60] Yet online shopping offers different benefits; consumers do not need to deal with crowds or find parking, the search costs are lower, and the transaction generally can be completed more quickly and efficiently. Different types of products likely appear more appealing or preferable, depending on whether the consumer is shopping online or offline, where different types of sensory information might play a role.

Temporal State Our state of mind at any particular time can alter our preconceived notions of what we are going to purchase. For instance, some people are morning people, whereas others function better at night. Therefore, a purchase situation may have different appeal levels depending on the time of day and the type of person the consumer is. Mood swings can alter consumer behavior.[61] Suppose Samantha received a parking ticket just prior to shopping at Tiffany & Co. It is likely that she would be less receptive to the salesperson's influence than if she came into the store in a good mood. Her bad mood might even cause her to have a less positive postpurchase feeling about the store. Because retailers cannot affect what happens outside the store very much, they should do everything possible to make sure their customers have a positive shopping experience once they are in the store.

The factors that affect the consumer decision process—the marketing mix, psychological factors, social factors, and situational factors—are all affected by the level of consumer involvement, the subject of the next section.

PROGRESS CHECK

1. What are some examples of specific needs suggested by Maslow's hierarchy of needs?

2. Which social factors likely have the most influence on (a) the purchase of a new outfit for a job interview and (b) the choice of a college to attend?

3. What situational factors do firms use to influence consumer purchase behavior?

INVOLVEMENT AND CONSUMER BUYING DECISIONS

LO6-6 Describe how involvement influences the consumer decision process.

Consumers make two types of buying decisions, depending on their level of involvement: extended problem solving or limited problem solving (which includes impulse purchases and habitual decision making). Involvement is the consumer's degree of interest in the product or service.[62] Consumers may have different levels of involvement for the same type of product. One consumer behavior theory, the elaboration likelihood model illustrated in Exhibit 6.6, proposes that high- and low-involvement consumers process different aspects of a message or advertisement.

If both types of consumers viewed ads for career clothing, the high-involvement consumer (e.g., Lauren, who is researching buying an outfit for a job interview) will scrutinize all the information provided (price, fabric quality, construction) and process the key elements of the message more deeply. As an involved consumer, Lauren likely ends up judging the ad as truthful and forming a favorable impression of the product, or else she regards the message as superficial and develops negative product impressions (i.e., her research suggests the product is not as good as it is being portrayed).

In contrast, a low-involvement consumer will likely process the same advertisement in a less thorough manner. Such a consumer might pay less attention to the key elements of the message (price, fabric quality, construction) and focus on elements such as brand name (Macy's I·N·C) or the presence of a celebrity endorser. The impressions of the low-involvement consumer are likely to be more superficial.

Extended Problem Solving

The buying process begins when consumers recognize that they have an unsatisfied need. Lauren Smith recognized her need to buy a new outfit for a job interview. She sought information by asking for advice from her friends, reading fashion magazines, and conducting research online. She visited several stores to determine which had the best options for her. Finally, after considerable time and effort analyzing her alternatives, Lauren purchased an outfit at Macy's. This process is an example of extended problem solving, which is common when the customer perceives that the purchase decision entails a lot of risk. The potential risks associated with Lauren's

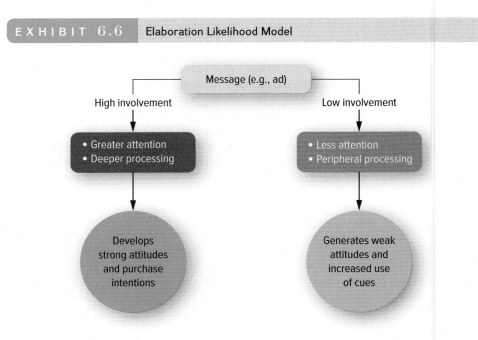

EXHIBIT 6.6   Elaboration Likelihood Model

Message (e.g., ad)

High involvement

- Greater attention
- Deeper processing

Develops strong attitudes and purchase intentions

Low involvement

- Less attention
- Peripheral processing

Generates weak attitudes and increased use of cues

decision to buy the outfit include financial (did I pay too much?) and social (will my potential employer and friends think I look professional?) risks. To reduce her perceived risk, Lauren spent a lot of effort searching for information before she actually made her purchase.

Limited Problem Solving

Limited problem solving occurs during a purchase decision that calls for, at most, a moderate amount of effort and time. Customers engage in this type of buying process when they have had some prior experience with the product or service and the perceived risk is moderate. Limited problem solving usually relies on past experience more than on external information. For many people, an apparel purchase, even an outfit for a job interview, could require limited effort.

A common type of limited problem solving is **impulse buying**, a buying decision made by customers on the spot when they see the merchandise.[63] When Lauren went to the grocery store to do her weekly shopping, she saw a display case of popcorn and Dr Pepper near the checkout counter. Knowing that some of her friends were coming over to watch a movie, she stocked up. The popcorn and soda were an impulse purchase. Lauren didn't go through

Typically, fashion apparel purchases (left) require extended problem solving, whereas grocery shopping normally requires limited problem solving (right).

(Left): ©Jeff Greenough/Blend Images/Getty Images; (right): ©DreamPictures/Getty Images

the entire decision process; instead, she recognized her need and jumped directly to purchase without spending any time searching for additional information or evaluating alternatives. The grocery store facilitated this impulse purchase by providing easily accessible cues (i.e., by offering the popcorn and soda in a prominent display, at a great location in the store, and at a reasonable price).

Some purchases require even less thought. Habitual decision making describes a purchase decision process in which consumers engage in little conscious effort. On her way home from the grocery store, for example, Lauren drove past a Jack in the Box and swung into the drive-through for a couple of tacos and Diet Coke—just as millions of other people do every day, according to Adding Value 6.4. She did not ponder the potential benefits of going to Wendy's instead for lunch. Rather, she simply reacted to the cue provided by the sign and engaged in habitual decision making. Marketers strive to attract and maintain habitual purchasers by creating strong brands and store loyalty (see Chapters 11 and 12) because these customers don't even consider alternative brands or stores.

Picking up a hamburger at a drive-thru fast-food restaurant like In-N-Out Burger requires little thought. It is a habitual decision.
©Michael Gordon/Shutterstock

Adding Value 6.4 | "Vile and Amazing": How a Taco That Consumers Despise and Also Cannot Get Enough of Gives Jack in the Box a Sustainable Advantage[vii]

We all know that fast food is not the healthiest choice, and yet most consumers rely on these options at some point, whether for convenience, consistency, or cost reasons. But there are also certain menu items that people actively seek out for the unique benefits they provide, transforming an easy convenience item into a sought-after prize.

The contradiction might be nowhere more evident than in the Jack in the Box taco, a menu item initially introduced by the burger-oriented chain in the 1950s. Unlike conventional fast-food tacos, Jack in the Box stuffs the tortilla with ground beef before freezing the individual tacos to ship to stores. Once they arrive, workers complete an order by dropping the entire tortilla into the fryer, then top it with a slice of American cheese, some hot sauce, and lettuce. It is utterly weird, and for those who have never tried it, it seems deeply unappealing.

Even those who try it tend to question its appeal, and yet they seem unable to resist. Jack in the Box sells more tacos than any other menu item, which is especially remarkable for a burger chain. It even sells approximately as many tacos as McDonald's sells Big Macs—about 1,055 of them every minute of the day.

The odd combination of soggy interior (created because the meat is already in the taco shell when it gets fried) and crunchy edge evokes comparisons to an envelope of wet cat food but also a nearly obsessive desire for the small, inexpensive tacos. Diners can get two tacos for just 99¢. They also can get them delivered; in partnership with the DoorDash delivery service, Jack in the Box promises that fans can get tacos as late as 3:00 a.m., a time when people tend to be a little less picky about what they are eating anyway.

Millions habitually flock to Jack in the Box for their taco fix—a tortilla stuffed with ground beef, frozen, and then deep-fried, topped with American cheese, hot sauce, and lettuce. Yummy or yucky, it has been a big seller for more than 60 years.
©H.S. Photos/Alamy Stock Photo

Famous fans include Selena Gomez (whose friends built her a Jack in the Box taco cake for her birthday), Chrissy Teigen, and Chelsea Handler. The legion of fans also include restaurateurs who try to copy the fried treat for their own stores. One higher-end restaurant serves three of its version of the tacos for $18. But Jack in the Box appears unconcerned about the threat of copycats taking some of its business. The chain's director of product marketing assures consumers that "We are always imitated but never duplicated."

PROGRESS CHECK

1. How do low- versus high-involvement consumers process the information in an advertisement?
2. What is the difference between extended versus limited problem solving?

Reviewing Learning Objectives

LO6-1 Articulate the steps in the consumer buying process.

The consumer buying process consists of five main steps: First, during need recognition, consumers simply realize they have an unsatisfied need or want that they hope to address. Second, they begin to search for information to determine how to satisfy that need. Third, during the alternative evaluation stage, they assess the various options available to them to determine which is the best for their purposes. Fourth, the purchase stage involves obtaining and using the product. Finally, consumers enter the postpurchase stage, during which they determine whether they are satisfied or dissatisfied with their choice.

LO6-2 Describe the difference between functional and psychological needs.

Functional needs pertain to the performance of a product or service. Psychological needs pertain to the personal gratification consumers associate with a product and/or service.

LO6-3 Describe factors that affect information search.

The information search that people undertake varies depending on both external and internal factors. Among the former, the type of product or service dictates whether people can make an easy, quick decision or instead must undertake significant research to find the best purchase option. A person's perceptions of the benefits versus the costs of the search also determine how much effort they undertake. These perceptions often relate closely to their perception of the risk involved in their purchase. Finally, people's locus of control, whether external or internal, strongly influences their information search actions.

LO6-4 Discuss postpurchase outcomes.

Marketers hope that after their purchase, consumers are satisfied and pleased with their purchase, which can lead to customer loyalty, a positive postpurchase outcome. However, consumers also may suffer postpurchase dissonance, or buyer's remorse.

LO6-5 List the factors that affect the consumer decision process.

The elements of the marketing mix (product, price place, and promotion) have significant effects, of course. In addition, social factors, such as family, reference groups, and culture, influence not only what a consumer buys but also how a consumer goes about making a purchase decision. The psychological factors that influence purchase decisions include motives, attitudes, perceptions, learning, and lifestyle. Finally, the situational factors such as the specific purchase situation, a sensory situation, or temporal state (time of day) can alter people's decision process.

LO6-6 Describe how involvement influences the consumer decision process.

More involved consumers, who are more interested or invested in the product or service they are considering, tend to engage in extended problem solving. They gather lots of information, scrutinize it carefully, and then make their decisions with caution, to minimize any risk they may confront. In contrast, less involved consumers often engage in limited problem solving, undertake impulse purchases, or rely on habit to make their purchase decisions.

Key Terms

Marketing Digitally

1. Visit the Amazon website (www.amazon.com) and describe the benefits it offers to consumers. Click on the "Try Prime" button. Which kinds of need appeals does Amazon use to encourage shoppers to join? Trace how you might go through the steps in the consumer decision process to make a purchase on Amazon. In which steps does Amazon excel, and where could it improve?

2. Customers use a variety of methods to provide feedback to companies about their experiences. Planetfeedback.com was developed as one such venue. Visit its website (www. planetfeedback.com) and identify the types of feedback that customers can provide. Look over the feedback for Verizon by typing "Verizon" in the company search space. Summarize some of the most recent comments. What is the ratio of positive to negative comments about Verizon during the last year or so? Describe the effects these comments might have on customer perceptions of Verizon.

3. Different companies emphasize different aspects of attitude in making decisions. Explore the Microsoft (www. microsoftstore.com) and Apple (store.apple.com) stores online. Discuss the primary attitude components they are targeting and how the two stores differ.

4. Companies often emphasize either the functional or psychological needs their products fulfill. Go to *Car and Driver*'s website (www.caranddriver.com) and identify a luxury car company that emphasizes functional needs and one that emphasizes psychological needs.

Marketing Applications

1. Does buying Kashi cereal satisfy a consumer's functional or psychological needs? How might this information help a Kashi brand manager better promote the product?

2. When consumers buy a new notebook computer, what sort of information search (internal versus external) would they conduct? If you were a marketing manager for Sony, how would you use this information?

3. Explain the factors that affect the amount of time and effort a consumer might take when choosing an oral surgeon to get his or her wisdom teeth removed. How would your answer change if the consumer were looking for a dentist to get a cleaning? How should the office manager for a dental practice use this information?

4. When evaluating different alternatives for a Saturday night outing at a fine restaurant, explain the difference between the universal set, the retrieval set, and the evoked set. From which set of alternatives will the consumer most likely choose the restaurant?

5. What can retailers do to make sure they have satisfied customers after the sale is complete?

6. Tazo makes a blend of exotic green teas, spearmint, and rare herbs into a tea called Zen. Using Maslow's hierarchy of needs, explain which need(s) is (are) being fulfilled by this tea.

7. Think about your last purchase either online or in a retail store. Were you presented with a nudge? If yes,

what was the nudge? Did you make the purchase? If not, which item could have been presented to you as a nudge? Why did you choose this item?

8. Trek has designed a new off-road bicycle designed to stand up to the rugged conditions of trail riding. Develop a theme for an advertising strategy that covers all three components of attitude.

9. What can a marketer do to positively influence a situation in which a consumer is ready to buy but has not yet done so?

10. Choose a retailer you visit frequently and identify how at least two factors of the sensory situation may affect your behavior.

Quiz Yourself

1. Which of the following is *not* an example of a functional need?
   a. Physical warmth
   b. Food
   c. Shelter
   d. Love
   e. Water

2. Which of the following is a characteristic of a highly involved consumer?
   a. Greater interest in the product
   b. Spending more time researching the product
   c. Engaging in extensive problem solving
   d. Making a very thoughtful choice
   e. All of these activities characterize highly involved consumers.

(Answers to these two questions are provided in the Quiz Yourself Answer Key section.)

Chapter Case Study

connect

BATTLE OF THE TITANS: AMAZON ECHO VS. GOOGLE HOME (AND DON'T FORGET ABOUT APPLE)

The newest battleground for the tech giants is being fought over smart home devices. Amazon's Echo was the first to hit the market in 2014; the smart speaker responds to voice commands and serves an ever-growing range of purposes, such as music streaming, news updates, Internet searches for information, grocery lists, joke telling, takeout orders from local restaurants, and answers to general questions.[64] Furthermore, in homes with other smart features, Echo and its voice personification Alexa allow users to control compatible lights, fans, thermostats, garage doors, sprinklers, and locks with simple voice commands.[65] By 2017, Alexa even gained the ability to call or send texts to the contacts in users' linked smartphones through Echo.[66]

Google's competing Google Home device did not even hit the shelves until April 2017.[67] In some ways, Google Home is more advanced and "smarter" than Echo. For example, its web browsing capabilities are more advanced because it relies on Google's stellar search engine, whereas Echo is limited to Wikipedia and Bing. Google Home also can sync its audio playback with other devices and Google Cast speakers,[68] providing better playback and the option to insert linked devices throughout the house, such that even customers with big homes can engage in constant interactions with the central device. If a user moves from the downstairs family room, where a Google Home device is playing music, to the upstairs bedroom, as long as there is another device there those elements sync and the user does not miss a beat of the song. Amazon's Echo does not have such a capability.

Overall, though, the two devices have similar functionalities, with some notable differences in the quality of the services they provide. Perhaps the biggest difference is how "smart" the devices really are when it comes to responding to users' requests. In a study conducted by the digital agency 360i, Google Home was six times more likely to answer requests correctly than was Echo. In this study, the researchers asked each device a series of 3,000 questions. Although they did not publish the questions they asked, the superiority of Google Home likely stems from Google's access to its advanced search engine. In addition, Google Home recognizes more colloquial command words. For example, if a consumer asks Google Home what movies are playing at the nearby theater, then asks how long it will take to get "there," Google Home understands that "there" refers to the theater, whereas Echo would need the user to cite the specific theater name or location.[69]

Yet in other areas, Amazon's device takes the lead. Echo is compatible with more smart devices, including about a half a dozen other smart home devices, whereas Google Home is compatible with only three.[70] Regardless of which brand of smart device people use in their homes to control things like lights or appliances, they thus can likely use Echo to help control those operations. Furthermore, when it comes to e-commerce, Google cannot come close to comparing with Amazon for product searches or purchases.[71] The vast customer insights maintained by Amazon help it power Echo, such that it is much better at enabling consumers to search for, find, and purchase the precise products they want at the very moment they realize they need something.

With its earlier entrance, Amazon also has a leg up on the market already; Echo dominates, with an approximately 70 percent market share.[72] Among people who already use voice assistants—such as Siri on their iPhones or Cortana on their personal computers—the three-year head start on Echo means that they likely have already made their purchase, and they are no longer in the market that might be served by Google Home. Moreover, almost half of all U.S. consumers do not currently use voice assistants,[73] and these customers do not seem interested in buying one for their homes.

Another hurdle in the market stems from customers' privacy concerns. Such smart devices are always on and listening for commands. Some customers are uneasy with the presence of a device that is always listening to them. Although the companies offer assurances that customers are not being recorded if they are not directly giving commands, and it is possible to disable the microphone and delete past commands, customers remain wary.[74]

As the first to market, Amazon was able to set the price level for this type of device. Echo currently costs about $180. When Google entered, it priced Google Home at $130.[75] However, Amazon also has released a smaller, cheaper version, Echo Dot, that costs only $50. This new device was a huge hit on Amazon's most recent Prime Day, sold at a special price of $35, which made it the top selling item on Amazon that day.[76] In response, Google cut the cost of Google Home to $100.[77]

Even as this seeming head-to-head competition persists and intensifies, some other tech companies are starting to venture onto the battlefield. Apple introduced its smart speaker

Who will win the smart home device battle: Amazon Echo (left), Google Home (center), or Apple HomePod (right)?

(Left): ©Charles Brutlag/Alamy Stock Photo; (center): ©Zapp2Photo/Shutterstock; (right): ©pianodiaphragm/Shutterstock

home device, HomePod, in January 2018.[78] Along with the functions provided by Google Home and Echo, Apple's entry features a special focus on music and sound quality. Even its name is evocative of the revolutionary iPod, which changed the way people listen to music. Priced around $349, it is the most expensive option. But for devoted Apple customers, a high price tag rarely turns the tide.

Questions

1. Trace how you might go through the steps in the consumer decision process if you were thinking of buying a smart home device.

2. Identify the four determinant attributes that set apart the Amazon, Google, and Apple smart home devices. Use those attributes to develop a compensatory purchasing model similar to the one in Exhibit 6.2. Based on your importance and performance ratings, which product would you buy?

3. Which device features examined in this chapter might have the greatest impact on consumers' propensity to buy one of these products?

4. Which risk factors might impact consumers' propensity to buy one of these products?

5. After purchasing one of these products, why might you experience postpurchase cognitive dissonance? What might the seller do to help you resolve this dissonance?

Endnotes

1. Drew Neisser, "How Sally Beauty Gave Its Loyalty Program a Stunning Makeover," *Advertising Age*, April 5, 2017.

2. Jack Neff, "Why Unilever Needs Love Beauty and Planet," *Advertising Age*, December 11, 2017.

3. Robert Williams, "Platinum Blonde Creator L'Oréal Goes Vegan with New Hair Dye," *Bloomberg*, December 13, 2017.

4. Sarah White, "L'Oréal Turns to Plant-Based Hair Dye as Natural Cosmetics Thrive," Reuters, December 13, 2017.

5. Jill Ettinger, "L'Oréal Goes Retro (and Vegan) with Natural Henna-Based Hair Dye," *EcoSalon*, December 14, 2017, http://ecosalon.com/loreal-vegan-henna-hair-dye/.

6. White, "L'Oréal Turns to Plant-Based Hair Dye."

7. Williams, "Platinum Blonde Creator L'Oréal Goes Vegan."

8. Ibid.

9. Khadeeja Safdar and Sharon Terlep, "As Sephora Adds Products, Rivalry Heats Up at Its Stores," *The Wall Street Journal*, January 8, 2017.

10. Jennifer J. Argo and Darren W. Dahl, "Standards of Beauty: The Impact of Mannequins in the Retail Context," *Journal of Consumer Research* 44, no. 5 (2017), pp. 974–90; Morgan K. Ward and Darren W. Dahl, "Should the Devil Sell Prada? Retail Rejection Increases Aspiring Consumers' Desire for the Brand," *Journal of Consumer Research* 41, no. 3 (2014), pp. 590–609; Kate L. White, Darren W. Dahl, and Robin J. Ritchie, "When Do Consumers Avoid Imperfections? Superficial Packaging Damage as a Contamination Cue," *Journal of Marketing Research* 53, no. 1 (2016), pp. 110–23.

11. For a detailed discussion of customer behavior, see David Mothersbaugh and Delbert Hawkins, *Consumer Behavior: Building Marketing Strategy*, 13th ed. (New York: McGraw-Hill Education, 2016).

12. Rafay A. Siddiqui, Frank May, and Ashwani Monga, "Time Window as a Self-Control Denominator: Shorter Windows Shift Preference toward Virtues and Longer Windows toward Vices," *Journal of Consumer Research* 43, no. 6 (2016), pp. 932–49; Elke Huyghe et al., "Clicks as a Healthy Alternative to Bricks: How Online Grocery Shopping Reduces Vice Purchases," *Journal of Marketing Research* 54, no. 1 (2017), pp. 61–74; Peggy J. Liu et al., "Vice-Virtue Bundles," *Management Science* 61 no. 1 (2015), 204–28; Ran Kivetz and Yuhuang Zheng, "The Effects of Promotions on Hedonic versus Utilitarian Purchases," *Journal of Consumer Psychology* 27, no. 1 (2017), pp. 59–68; Anne L. Roggeveen et al., "The Impact of Dynamic Presentation Format on Consumer Preferences for Hedonic Products and Services," *Journal of Marketing* 79, no. 6 (2015), pp. 34–49.

13. Francine E. Petersen, Heather J. Dretsch, and Yuliya K. Loureiro, "Who Needs a Reason to Indulge? Happiness Following Reason-Based Indulgent Consumption," *International Journal of Research in Marketing*, 2017; Felix Septianto, "Work More and Indulge More: Exploring the Self-Licensing Effect of Hard Work on Likelihood to Purchase Hedonic Products," *Journal of Retailing and Consumer Services* 34 (2017), pp. 235–39; Ann Kronrod, Amir Grinstein, and Luc Wathieu, "Enjoy! Hedonic Consumption and Compliance with Assertive Messages," *Journal of Consumer Research* 39, no. 1 (2011), pp. 51–61.

14. www.dior.com/.

15. Amanda Mull, "The Best Red Carpet Clutches of the 2017 Academy Awards," *Purse Blog*, February 27, 2017, www.purseblog.com/celebrities/2017-academy-awards-red-carpet-clutches/.

16. Anindya Ghose, Panagiotis G. Ipeirotis, and Beibei Li, "Examining the Impact of Ranking on Consumer Behavior and Search Engine Revenue," *Management Science* 60, no. 7 (2014), pp. 1632–54; Girish Mallapragada, Sandeep R. Chandukala, and Qing Liu, "Exploring the Effects of 'What' (Product) and 'Where' (Website) Characteristics on Online Shopping Behavior," *Journal of Marketing* 80, no. 2 (2016), pp. 21–38; Kinshuck Jerath, Liye Ma, and Young-Hoon Park, "Consumer Click Behavior at a Search Engine: The Role of Keyword Popularity," *Journal of Marketing Research* 51, no. 4 (2014), pp. 480–86.

17. www.shopzilla.com/.

18. www.amazon.com/.

19. Greg M. Allenby, Jaehwan Kim, and Peter E. Rossi, "Economic Models of Choice," in *Handbook of Marketing Decision Models* (Cham, Switzerland: Springer, 2017), pp. 199–222; Lan Luo, Brian T. Ratchford, and Botao Yang, "Why We Do What We Do: A Model of Activity Consumption," *Journal of Marketing Research* 50 (February 2013), pp. 24–43.

20. Gabriela N. Tonietto and Selin A. Malkoc, "The Calendar Mind-set: Scheduling Takes the Fun Out and Puts the Work In," *Journal of Marketing Research* 53, no. 6 (2016), pp. 922–36; Kaitlin Woolley and Ayelet Fishbach, "The Experience Matters More Than You Think: People Value Intrinsic Incentives More Inside Than Outside an Activity," *Journal of Personality and Social Psychology* 109, no. 6 (2015), p. 968; Juliano Laran and Chris Janiszewski, "Work or Fun? How Task Construal and Completion Influence Regulatory Behavior," *Journal of Consumer Research* 37, no. 6 (2010), pp. 967–83.

21. Jos M. Magendans, Jan M. Gutteling, and Sven Zebel, "Psychological Determinants of Financial Buffer Saving: The Influence of Financial Risk Tolerance and Regulatory Focus," *Journal of Risk Research* 20, no. 8 (2016), pp. 1076–93.

22. Huachao Gao, Karen P. Winterich, and Yinlong Zhang, "All That Glitters Is Not Gold: How Others' Status Influences the Effect of Power Distance Belief on Status Consumption," *Journal of Consumer Research* 43, no. 2 (2016), pp. 265–81; Lukasz Walasek, Sudeep Bhatia, and Gordon D. Brown, "Positional Goods and the Social Rank Hypothesis: Income Inequality Affects Online Chatter about High-and Low-Status Brands on Twitter," *Journal of Consumer Psychology*, 2017.

23. Leilei Gao and Itamar Simonson, "The Positive Effect of Assortment Size on Purchase Likelihood: The Moderating Influence of Decision Order," *Journal of Consumer Psychology* 26, no. 4 (2016), pp. 542–49; Alexander Chernev, Ulf Böckenholt, and Joseph Goodman, "Choice Overload: A Conceptual Review and Meta-Analysis," *Journal of Consumer Psychology* 25, no. 2 (2015), pp. 333–58.

24. The term *determinance* was first coined by James Myers and Mark Alpert nearly three decades ago; www.sawtoothsoftware.com.

25. Ibid.

26. Naomi Mandel et al., "The Compensatory Consumer Behavior Model: How Self-Discrepancies Drive Consumer Behavior," *Journal of Consumer Psychology* 27, no. 1 (2017), pp. 133–46; Richard Lutz, "Changing Brand Attitudes through Modification of Cognitive Structure," *Journal of Consumer Research* 1, no. 1 (1975), pp. 125–36.

27. Lucas Bremer, Mark Heitmann, and Thomas Schreiner, "When and How to Infer Heuristic Consideration Set Rules of Consumers," *International Journal of Research in Marketing* 34, no. 2 (2017), pp. 516–35.

28. Richard H. Thaler and Cass R. Sunstein, *Nudge: Improving Decisions about Health, Wealth, and Happiness* (New Haven, CT: Yale University Press, 2008).

29. Brian Wansink and A. S. Hanks, "Slim by Design: Serving Healthy Foods First in Buffet Lines Improves Overall Meal Selection," *PLoS ONE* 8, no. 10 (2013), p. e77055. doi.org/10.1371/journal.pone.0077055.

30. www.ftc.gov/tips-advice/business-center/guidance/ how-comply-privacy-consumer-financial-information-rule-gramm.

31. Annamaria Lusardi, Punam A. Keller, and Adam M. Keller, "New Ways to Make People Save: A Social Marketing Approach," Report No. w14715 (National Bureau of Economic Research, 2009); Brigitte C. Madrian and Dennis F. Shea, "The Power of Suggestion: Inertia in 401(k) Participation and Savings Behavior," *Quarterly Journal of Economics* 116, no. 4 (2001), pp. 1149–87.

32. James M. Kerr, "How Appealing to Women Has Helped The Home Depot," ManagementIssues.com, October 3, 2014.

33. Na Young Jung and Yoo-Kyoung Seock, "Effect of Service Recovery on Customers' Perceived Justice, Satisfaction, and Word-of-Mouth Intentions on Online Shopping Websites," *Journal of Retailing and Consumer Services* 37 (2017), pp. 23–30; Marsha Richins, "Negative Word-of-Mouth by Dissatisfied Consumers: A Pilot Study," *Journal of Marketing 47*, no. 1 (1983), pp. 68–78.

34. Sterling A. Bone et al, "'Mere Measurement Plus': How Solicitation of Open-Ended Positive Feedback Influences Customer Purchase Behavior," *Journal of Marketing Research* 54, no. 1 (2017), pp. 156–70; Hyunju Shin et al., "Employing Proactive Interaction for Service Failure Prevention to Improve Customer Service Experiences," *Journal of Service Theory and Practice* 27, no. 1 (2017), pp. 164–86.

35. www.facebook.com/whirlpoolusa; Jack Neff, "Case Study: How Whirlpool Heated Up Sales by Warming Up 'Cold Metal,'" *Advertising Age*, June 8, 2015; Randall Stross, "Consumer Complaints Made Easy. Maybe Too Easy," *The New York Times*, May 28, 2011, www.nytimes.com.

36. For a more extensive discussion on these factors, see Mothersbaugh and Hawkins, *Consumer Behavior*.

37. A. H. Maslow, *Motivation and Personality* (New York: Harper & Row, 1970).

38. Yukti Sharma and Reshma Nasreen, "Perceived Consumer-Centric Marketing-Mix at the Urban Bottom of the Pyramid: An Empirical Study of Non-Core Food Items," *International Journal of Information, Business and Management* 10, no. 1 (2018), pp. 89–107; Charlene Bebko, "Implications of the Unique Characteristics of Social Causes," *Journal of Business and Behavioral Sciences* 29, no. 1 (2017), pp. 18–33.

39. www.starbucks.com/menu/nutrition/35-under-350.

40. For recent research on the link between emotions and consumer behavior, see the "Emotions and Consumer Behavior" special issue of *Journal of Consumer Research* 40 (February 2014).

41. Sumit Banerjee, "Consumer Post Purchase Cognitive Dissonance," *International Journal of Advanced Research in Computer Science and Management Studies* 5, no. 10 (2017), pp. 86–89; Leonard Lee, On Amir, and Dan Ariely, "In Search of Homo Economicus: Cognitive Noise and the Role of Emotion in Preference Consistency," *Journal of Consumer Research* 36, no. 2 (2009), pp. 173–87.

42. www.bostonbackbay.com/.

43. For more discussion on these factors, see Mothersbaugh and Hawkins, *Consumer Behavior: Building Marketing Strategy*, Michael Levy, Barton A. Weitz, and Dhruv Grewal, *Retailing Management*, 10th ed. (New York: McGraw-Hill Education, 2019), Chapter 4; Tae-Im Han and Leslie Stoel, "Explaining Socially Responsible Consumer Behavior: A Meta-Analytic Review of Theory of Planned Behavior," *Journal of International Consumer Marketing* 29, no. 2 (2017), pp. 91–103.

44. Kátia Eloisa Bertol et al., "Young Children's Influence on Family Consumer Behavior," *Qualitative Market Research: An International Journal* 20, no. 4 (2017), pp. 452–68; Juliano Laran, "Goal Management in Sequential Choices: Consumer Choices for Others Are More Indulgent Than Personal Choices," *Journal of Consumer Research* 37, no. 2 (August 2010), pp. 304–14.

45. Machiel Reinders and Jos Bartels, "The Roles of Identity and Brand Equity in Organic Consumption Behavior: Private Label Brands versus National Brands," *Journal of Brand Management* 24, no. 1 (2017), pp. 68–85; Mandel, "The Compensatory Consumer Behavior Model."

46. Tamar Weinberg, "How to Work with Influencers: The Ultimate Guide," *HubSpot*, August 8, 2017; see sites that recruit bloggers

to do paid reviews: www.sponsoredreviews.com and www.payperpost.com.

47. Mark Matousek, "These Are the 10 Clothing Brands That Teens Are Obsessed With," *Business Insider*, October 17, 2017; Steve Henderson, "Spending Habits by Generation," *U.S. Department of Labor Blog*, November 3, 2016; Alexandra Sheehan, "20+ Unique Ideas to Boost Foot Traffic to Your Retail Store," *Shopify*, December 22, 2016; Elizabeth A. Harris and Rachel Abrams, "Plugged-In over Preppy: Teenagers Favor Tech over Clothes," *The New York Times*, August 27, 2014, www.nytimes.com.

48. For an expanded discussion on these factors, see Mothersbaugh and Hawkins, *Consumer Behavior*. For some interesting experiments involving consumers' physical positioning and its effects on behavior, see Herb Sorensen et al., "Fundamental Patterns of In-Store Shopper Behavior," *Journal of Retailing and Consumer Services* 37 (2017), pp. 182–94; John Murray, Jonathan Elms, and Christoph Teller, "Examining the Role of Store Design on Consumers' Cross-Sectional Perceptions of Retail Brand Loyalty," *Journal of Retailing and Consumer Services* 38 (2017), pp. 147–56.

49. Charles Spence et al., "Store Atmospherics: A Multisensory Perspective," *Psychology & Marketing* 31, no. 7 (2014), pp. 472–88.

50. Philip Kotler, "Atmospherics as a Marketing Tool," *Journal of Retailing* 49, no. 4 (1973), pp. 48–64.

51. www.dylanscandybar.com/info/About_Us.html.

52. Spence et al., "Store Atmospherics."

53. Humayun Khan, "How Retailers Manipulate Sight, Smell, and Sound to Trigger Purchase Behavior in Consumers," *Shopify*, April 25, 2016, www.shopify.com/retail/119926083-how-retailers-manipulate-sight-smell-and-sound-to-trigger-purchase-behavior-in-consumers.

54. Dan DeBaun "Now Playing at More Target Stores: Background Music," *Minneapolis/St. Paul Business Journal*, June 9, 2017, www.bizjournals.com/louisville/news/2017/06/09/now-playing-at-more-target-stores-background-music.html.

55. Spence et al., "Store Atmospherics."

56. Haley Peterson, "How Stores Use Scents to Manipulate You into Spending More Money," *Business Insider*, May 21, 2014.

57. Khan, "How Retailers Manipulate Sight, Smell, and Sound."

58. Dipayan Biswas et al., "Shining Light on Atmospherics: How Ambient Light Influences Food Choices," *Journal of Marketing Research* 54, no. 1 (2017), pp. 111–23.

59. Elke Huyghe et al., "Clicks as a Healthy Alternative to Bricks."

60. P. Huang, N. H. Lurie, and S. Mitra, "Searching for Experience on the Web: An Empirical Examination of Consumer Behavior for Search and Experience Goods," *Journal of Marketing* 73, no. 2 (2009), pp. 55–69.

61. Valerie Vaccaro et al., "Pleasant Music's Relationship to Congruence, Consumer Behavioral Intentions, Unplanned Purchase, and Time Spent in Retail and Service Environments," *Journal of International Management Studies* 17, no. 2, (2017), pp. 35–48; Isabel Wellbery, Franziska Roth, and Thomas Fortmann, "Beyond Retail Therapy: Can the Relationship between Affective Data & Consumer Behavior Be Utilized to Develop User-Directed E-Commerce Personalization?," in *Communications in Computer and Information Science*, vol. 713, ed. C. Stephanidis, *HCI International 2017–Posters' Extended Abstracts, HCI 2017* (Cham, Switzerland: Springer, 2017).

62. Banwari Mittal, *Consumer Behavior* (Cincinnati, OH: Open Mentis, 2008); J. Paul Peter and Jerry C. Olson, *Consumer Behavior and Marketing Strategy*, 9th ed. (Burr Ridge, IL: McGraw-Hill Education, 2010).

63. Timothy J. Gilbride, J. Jeffrey Inman, and Karen M. Stilley, "The Role of Within-Trip Dynamics in Unplanned versus Planned Purchase Behavior," *Journal of Marketing* 79, no. 3 (2015), pp. 57–73; Daniel Sheehan and Koert Van Ittersum, "In-Store Spending Dynamics: How Budgets Invert Relative Spending Patterns," *Journal of Consumer Research*, 2018; Yuping Liu-Thompkins and Leona Tam, "Not All Repeat Customers Are the Same: Designing Effective Cross-Selling Promotion on the Basis of Attitudinal Loyalty and Habit," *Journal of Marketing* 77 (September 2013), pp. 21–36.

64. Amazon, "Amazon Echo," www.amazon.com/p/feature/ofoyqn-7wjy2p39a.

65. Amazon, "Amazon Echo-Black," www.amazon.com/dp/B00X4WHP5E.

66. Amazon, "Alexa Calling & Messaging," www.amazon.com/b?node=16713667011; Todd Haselton, "The Amazon Echo Just Made Home Phones Cool Again. Here's How to Make Calls with Alexa," *CNBC*, May 11, 2017, www.cnbc.com/2017/05/11/how-to-make-calls-with-amazons-alexa.html.

67. Laura Hautala, "Google Home to Sell for $129, Launches on November 4," *CNet*, October 5, 2016, www.cnet.com/au/news/google-home-to-sell-for-129-launches-on-november-4/.

68. Jim Martin, "Google Home vs. Amazon Echo," *Tech Advisor*, June 27, 2017, www.techadvisor.co.uk/review/digital-home/google-home-vs-amazon-echo-3648158/.

69. Martin, "Google Home vs. Amazon Echo"; John Patrick Pullen, "Google Outsmarts Amazon Alexa in 3,000 Question Quiz," *Fortune*, June 23, 2017, http://fortune.com/2017/06/23/google-home-amazon-alexa-smarter/.

70. Martin, "Google Home vs. Amazon Echo."

71. Pullen, "Google Outsmarts Amazon Alexa in 3,000 Question Quiz."

72. Ibid.

73. Nick Vega, "Amazon's Echo Dot Is Outselling Google Home—But Many Consumers Aren't Convinced They Need a Voice Assistant," *Business Insider*, June 29, 2017, www.businessinsider.com/amazons-echo-dot-smart-speaker-outselling-google-home-by-large-margin-2017-6.

74. Tony Bradley, "How Amazon Echo Users Can Control Privacy," *Forbes*, January 5, 2017, www.forbes.com/sites/tonybradley/2017/01/05/alexa-is-listening-but-amazon-values-privacy-and-gives-you-control/#16264ad47ee6.

75. Jenny McGrath, "Is There an Echo in Here? Amazon Alexa vs. Google Home vs. Apple HomePod," *Yahoo Tech*, June 13, 2017, www.yahoo.com/tech/echo-amazon-alexa-vs-google-214958334.html.

76. Nat Levy, "Amazon Echo Devices Are Top Prime Day Sellers, Doubling Last Year's Total in the U.S.," *GeekWire*, July 11, 2017, www.geekwire.com/2017/amazon-echo-devices-top-prime-day-sellers-doubling-last-years-total-u-s/; Connie Chen, "The Echo Dot Came Out on Top as the Best-Selling Product from Amazon Prime Day 2017," *Business Insider*, July 12, 2017, www.businessinsider.com/echo-dot-best-selling-product-amazon-prime-day-2017.

77. Jake Swearingen, "Google Slashes Prices on Google Home and Chromecast," *NYMag, Select all*, July 10, 2017, http://nymag.com/selectall/2017/07/google-home-chromecast-and-chromecast-audio-on-sale.html.

78. Serenity Caldwell, "Should You Buy a HomePod?," *iMore*, January 24, 2018.

i. Sharon Terlep, "Why Your Local CVS Is Hiding the Candy and Tanning Oil," *The Wall Street Journal*, June 28, 2017; Phil Wahba, "Your Local CVS Drugstore Is about to Look Very Different," *Fortune*, April 19, 2017; Bruce Japsen, "CVS Health Increases Restrictions on Opioids," *Forbes*, September 11, 2017.

ii. Jason Barron, "SoHo's Gilded Home Store: Where Money Flows Like Water," *The New York Times*, May 20, 2016; Dennis Green and Sarah Jacobs, "This Luxury Appliance Store Lets

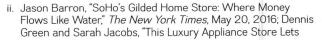

You Take a Bath or Cook a Pizza before Deciding to Buy Its Products—and It Could Be the Future of Retail," *Business Insider*, May 25, 2016; Tom Ryan, "PIRCH Could Top Apple for Retail Experience," *Forbes*, June 1, 2016; www.pirch.com/home.

iii. Hilary Milnes, "Rent the Runway Snapchats Customers the Right Fit," *Glossy*, August 15, 2016; Valentina Zarya, "A Newly-Profitable Rent the Runway Raises Another $60 Million," *Fortune*, December 28, 2016; www.renttherunway.com.

iv. Christopher Jensen, "Buyer Beware: 'Certified' Used Cars May Still Be under Recall," *The New York Times*, December 16, 2016; Christopher Jensen, "Groups Sue FTC, Charge Agency Has Failed to Protect Consumers from Used Car Recall Danger," *Forbes*, February 6, 2017; Ron Lieber, "How to Buy a Used Car in an Age of Widespread Recalls," *The New York Times*, January 27, 2016.

v. Laura Entis, "Here's Why It Feels Like You're the Only Millennial Not Drinking La Croix," *Fortune*, July 21, 2017; Rob Copeland,

"La Croix Fizzy Water Is Everyone's Favorite. No One Knows What's in It," *The Wall Street Journal*, September 13, 2017; "La Croix," www.lacroixwater.com/corporate/.

vi. "With Acquisitions, Campbell, Hershey Bet That Salty Snacks Will Reignite Sales," *Advertising Age*, December 18, 2017; Craig Giammona, "Campbell, Hershey Bet That Salty Snacks Will Reignite Sales," *Bloomberg*, December 18, 2017; Gayathree Ganesan and Uday Sampath Kumar, "Hershey, Campbell Bet Nearly $6 Billion on Healthy Snacks Makers," *Reuters*, December 18, 2017; Monica Watrous, "Hershey Setting the Stage for a Stronger Year," *Food Business News*, February 2, 2018.

vii. Russell Adams, "Americans Eat 554 Million Jack in the Box Tacos a Year, and No One Knows Why," *The Wall Street Journal*, January 3, 2017; Bill Peters, "Jack in the Box Finds a 'Forgiving' Late-Night-Delivery Customer," *Investor's Business Daily*, January 10, 2017; www.jackintheboxinc.com.

Quiz Yourself Answer Key

1. Which of the following is **not** an example of a functional need?

   Answer: (d) Love

2. Which of the following is a characteristic of a highly involved consumer?

   Answer: (e) All of these activities characterize highly involved consumers.

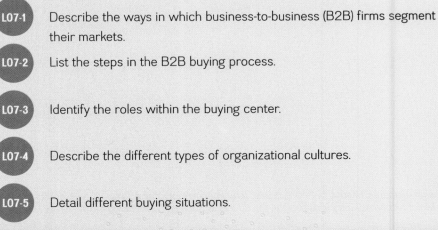

LEARNING OBJECTIVES

After reading this chapter, you should be able to:

LO7-1 Describe the ways in which business-to-business (B2B) firms segment their markets.

LO7-2 List the steps in the B2B buying process.

LO7-3 Identify the roles within the buying center.

LO7-4 Describe the different types of organizational cultures.

LO7-5 Detail different buying situations.

CHAPTER 7

BUSINESS-TO-BUSINESS MARKETING

To reach their buyers, business-to-business (B2B) companies rely on a vast range of channels, from trade shows and conferences to industry publications and direct mailing. But these traditional modes are, of course, increasingly being surpassed by modern forms of communication, especially those facilitated by online and social media. But unlike consumer markets, in which companies try to reach individual customers, B2B markets require one company to find another one that will want to purchase its products or services, so that the buyer can produce whatever offerings that it ultimately will sell to its customers.

Accordingly, the online and social media sites in use by B2B companies differ somewhat as well. That is, a supplier still might maintain a presence on Facebook and Twitter, but a buyer may prefer something other than the often less professional context of those sites to complete a multimillion-dollar purchase that is critical to the continued survival of the business. Sites that have developed a more serious image, such as LinkedIn, thus recognize the room in the market that may enable them to become the primary link by which sellers find buyers and vice versa.

LinkedIn is well known for connecting businesspeople; as the largest network of business professionals, with global reach, it counts approximately 530 million members, including at least one executive from all of the *Fortune* 500 companies.[1] Its promise for networking, whether individually or for the company, is virtually unsurpassed. Such networking entails several key groups:

- *Customers and prospective customers.* LinkedIn allows a firm or its representatives to introduce themselves to possible buyers, using a credible and easily accessible format. The Q&A option on LinkedIn pages also allows customers to ask questions and suppliers to demonstrate their expertise.

- *Investors.* The LinkedIn page offers tangible evidence of the firm's existence and its promise, which is critical information for outsiders who might be willing to invest in its development.

- *Suppliers.* By starting their own group on LinkedIn, B2B buyers might better identify which suppliers in the market are best matched with their needs and most interested in providing the resources they need.

- *Employees and prospective employees.* LinkedIn is a great source for finding employees who are diligent, professional, interested, and qualified. Furthermore, if a firm retains its links to former employees, it can gain a good source of referrals—assuming those employees left on good terms.

- *Analysts.* The job of an analyst is to find detailed information about a company and then recommend it, or not, to the market. LinkedIn gives firms a means to provide that information in a credible but still firm-controlled context.

Such benefits have been available to users since approximately 2003, when the site first launched. But thus far, they have been able to post videos only by linking to another site, such as YouTube. As a key player in the industry, though, LinkedIn continues to innovate (especially after being purchased by Microsoft in 2016).[2] Along these lines, it has added a new feature that enables companies to upload their own video documentaries of their products, speeches by their leaders, or any other aspects that they want to communicate to their B2B markets.

In this "native video" option, as visitors scroll through their LinkedIn feeds, the videos play automatically but without sound. They can click to turn on the sound, assuming they are interested enough in what the visuals are showing. LinkedIn suggests several main uses for native video, such as showing off the company's great corporate culture to appeal to potential job seekers, inviting likely conference attendees to visit their booth at a trade show, offering tutorials on using their products, or giving behind-the-scenes insights into a particular project or service.[3]

The initial rollout of the feature was limited to select users, but its effectiveness has encouraged LinkedIn to pursue further expansions. For example, the tests revealed that users shared the videos approximately 20 times more than static content (e.g., text posts, images).[4] Along with such information, LinkedIn collects data about who watches each video. If a network member watches the video multiple times, such that this user can be designated a top viewer, LinkedIn also gathers more comprehensive insights about where that person is located, his or her job title and employer, and so forth.

Such analytics are a key value proposition for LinkedIn users too. For B2B sales forces, data that show who has watched a video, from what company and in what role, suggest promising sales leads and networking opportunities.[5] When a video introducing a new service garners a lot of views from members of the same company, the supplier has a clear indication that this company represents a good sales prospect. Of course, obtaining these data requires a premium membership, rather than the free version available to any user.[6]

For companies that specialize in content, the new option also gives them a completely new means to reach their audiences.[7] Media companies or influencers have a more direct route to their followers, rather than having to go through an external video-sharing site. The videos also promise the potential of a larger audience because past evidence suggests that once a site adds video capabilities, users visit it more often and stay longer. Considering that LinkedIn currently averages relatively short visits from users (i.e., 2 minutes per day, versus 50 minutes for Facebook), encouraging visitors to stay longer could help B2B firms establish a more in-depth and meaningful conversation.[8]

Business-to-business (B2B) marketing refers to the process of buying and selling goods or services to be used in the production of other goods and services for consumption by the buying organization and/or resale by wholesalers and retailers. Therefore, a typical B2B marketing transaction involves manufacturers (e.g., GE, Levi's, Siemens, IBM, Ford) selling to wholesalers that, in turn, sell products to retailers. B2B transactions can also involve service firms (e.g., UPS, Oracle, Accenture) that market their services to other businesses but not to the ultimate consumer (e.g., you). The distinction between a B2B and a business-to-consumer (B2C) transaction is not the product or service itself; rather, it is the ultimate user of that product or service. Another key distinction is that B2B transactions tend to be more complex and involve multiple members of both the buying organization (e.g., buyers, marketing team, product developers) and the selling organization (e.g., sellers, R&D support team), whereas B2C often entails a simple transaction between the retailer and the individual consumer.

The demand for B2B sales is often derived from B2C sales in the same supply chain. More specifically, **derived demand** reflects the link between consumers' demand for a company's output and the company's purchase of necessary inputs to manufacture or assemble that particular output. For example, if more customers want to purchase staplers (a B2C

Ethical & Societal Dilemma 7.1

To Block or Not to Block: The Competing and Compelling Interests of Advertisers, Users, and Facebook[i]

Facebook is, obviously, a social media site. But it also is an advertising platform that links advertisers to consumers, and in this role, a recent move has stakeholders on all sides up in arms.

As a platform, Facebook has to mediate the interests of advertisers that pay it to place their ads on the site versus the interests of users who don't want their social interactions interrupted by various product and service advertisements. These contradictory goals have prompted technical developments in support of both efforts. For example, ad blocking software helps consumers limit the number of advertisements that pop up as they browse websites, including Facebook. In turn, anti–ad blocking software entered the scene, offering a means to alter the signals that the blocking software uses to identify something as an advertisement. Thus the advertising gets around the ad blocking software because it doesn't look like advertising anymore, at least to the algorithm used by existing software.

Facebook is the latest and most prominent adopter of the anti–ad blocking software, suggesting that in this case, it is prioritizing the needs of its advertisers over the desires of its consumers. When users visit Facebook through their computers (the technology is different for mobile access), even if they have sophisticated ad blocking software installed, they will confront ads.

To explain its move, Facebook notes that even if advertising seems annoying, it serves a critical function for the overall social media platform: It pays for everything. If users want to keep using Facebook for free, the company needs to find some other source of revenue. But if the consumers block all the ads, then advertisers have no motivation to pay to appear on Facebook, ultimately disrupting the entire structure that enables most media sites to exist. As one analyst put it, "Ad blocking is a detriment to the entire advertising ecosystem."

Some digital content publishers also are experimenting with anti–ad blocking software, including *Forbes, Wired,* and *The New York Times.* Some options seek to solicit the help of users, such as by asking them to "whitelist" their specific site. This step tells the ad blocking software to give a free pass to the ads on a particular site. To convince users to agree, one publisher noted, "We need to spell this out clearly to our users. The journalism they enjoy costs real money and needs to be paid for."

Advertisers have praised the moves, noting that by facilitating their marketing communications, Facebook and other platforms are enabling the market to survive. However, companies that write and sell the ad blocking software regard the move as unacceptable and cite as evidence the limitations it places on consumers' ability to define what they will see on their computers. Furthermore, some privacy advocates argue that the ad blocking software can serve another function, as a means to limit the amount of tracking that websites can do. If the blocks on ad blocking become strong enough, such privacy protections would disappear too.

Together with these technological efforts to resolve the demands of its various stakeholders, Facebook added new options to allow users to indicate their advertising preferences, which it asserts are sufficient to keep customers happy. As a firm that provides a service to consumers, Facebook appears to be taking a big risk. As a business that supports other businesses, it might have no other option.

---

transaction), a company that produces them must purchase more metal from its supplier to make additional staplers (a B2B transaction). In some cases, though, the participants in B2B transactions come in conflict, so providers such as Facebook face a dilemma, namely, Ethical & Societal Dilemma 7.1.

Similar to organizations that sell directly to final consumers in B2C transactions, B2B firms focus on serving specific types of customer markets by creating value for those customers. Recognizing the growing demand for ever-increasing smartphone connectivity in cars, both Apple (with its CarPlay) and Google (with its Android-based Open Automotive

Apple (left) and Google (right) both offer smartphone connectivity for specific car manufacturers.

(Left): ©Jae C. Hong/AP Images; (right): ©Martin Leissl/Bloomberg via Getty Images

Marketing Analytics 7.1

Intel Inside AI: The Deep-Learning, Artificial Intelligence Chip Being Developed in Collaboration with Facebook[ii]

Intel Corporation already has made a name for itself in computer processors, but now it is aiming to establish an even bigger presence in the artificial intelligence (AI) market. After acquiring the chip company Nervana, Intel has teamed up with Facebook to leverage the social media firm's technology expertise. Specifically, recognizing an urgent and substantial need among its business clients, Intel is actively developing a new chip that will enable and encourage continued advances in artificial intelligence. This promised chip will be able to support deep learning—the sort of artificial intelligence that is able to identify specific elements, such as particular objects in a photograph, that has thus far has eluded the ability of computers.

In developing the chip, Intel has relied on its own expertise but also the input of key customers and partners, most of which see vast potential for deep learning. Initially, the chip will be available only to these partners, such as Facebook. The partners then will provide feedback, leading to revisions that seek to perfect the chip before it hits the wider market. Facebook's partnership is critical because it has conducted its own extensive research already. It also can apply the AI techniques readily to its social media platform for the premarket tests.

By enabling computers to study vast amounts of data, learn from them, and then apply that knowledge to new tasks, the new chip, called the Nervana neural network processor, promises new advancements in various goals that companies have

set. For example, it could increase the accuracy and precision of automated medical diagnoses, enhance the capacities of driverless cars, produce more accurate weather forecasts, and allow investigators to spot and prevent fraud in financial transactions. Today, these sorts of predictions, involving innumerable variables, are difficult to make with any confidence. But most technology companies hope to change that; estimates indicate that the artificial intelligence market will be worth $9 billion by 2020.

With the Nervana processor, Intel promises that computing can take place faster because it takes shortcuts, similar to those that the human brain follows. Furthermore, it designed the chip to be able to collaborate with other chips, so that companies can "stack" their computing power by leveraging the capacities of multiple Nervana processors at the same time.

It is not the only entrant to this market, of course. Google reportedly is working on developing its own chips to facilitate deep learning. In addition, a company called Nvidia designed chips to review and process graphics, then realized that they also functioned well and efficiently on various other deep-learning tasks. Thus far, Nvidia dominates the market for deep-learning hardware and software, but clearly Intel hopes to change that position. By leveraging its connections with and knowledge of some of its best business clients, it may be able to do just that.

Alliance) are making deals to integrate their operating systems into cars. Ferrari, Audi, Mercedes-Benz, Volvo, and more all offer CarPlay in select models, and it can also be added as an aftermarket system; Google's platform is compatible with select models from Cadillac, Honda, Hyundai, General Motors, and more.[9]

Also, like B2C firms, many B2B companies find it productive to focus their efforts on key industries or market segments. Marketing Analytics 7.1, for example, describes how Intel is working with Facebook and other social media partners to develop a new artificial intelligence chip that will identify elements of an object, such as a photo. Although the average large corporation has more than 175 social media accounts, small-business owners often struggle to maintain a single social media account on each of the major networks.[10] Enter the B2B firm Constant Contact.[11] This firm provides a centralized dashboard for small businesses to manage their social media accounts as well as templates for posts and help on creating social media campaigns. Constant Contact could target businesses of any size, but it has become one of the leaders in small-business social media management by narrowing its efforts on this key market segment.[12]

In this chapter, we look at the different types of B2B markets and examine the B2B buying process, with an eye toward how it differs from the B2C buying process we discussed in Chapter 6. Several factors influence the B2B buying process, and we discuss these as well.

B2B MARKETS

L07-1 Describe the ways in which business-to-business (B2B) firms segment their markets.

The most visible types of B2B transactions are those in which manufacturers and service providers sell to other businesses. However, resellers, institutions, and governments also may be involved in B2B transactions. Therefore, in the next sections we describe each of these B2B organizations (see Exhibit 7.1).

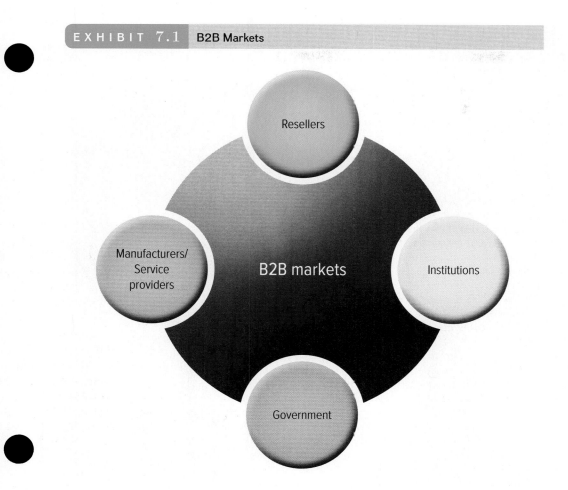

EXHIBIT 7.1 | B2B Markets

Manufacturers and Service Providers

Manufacturers buy raw materials, components, and parts that allow them to make and market their own goods and ancillary services. For example, the German-based Volkswagen Group, the largest auto manufacturer in Europe, owns and distributes the Audi, Bentley, Bugatti, Lamborghini, SEAT, Skoda, Scania, VW, and VW Commercial Vehicles brands.[13] Whereas purchasing agents formerly spent 70 percent of their time searching for, analyzing, validating, and forwarding information about parts and components, today they can use the VW Group's ONE.Konzern Business Plattform to communicate with suppliers for all transactions, from procurement to logistics.[14] Purchasing agents receive product descriptions directly from suppliers online, which means search processes that used to take two hours now require about nine minutes. Users of the system receive alerts of potential parts shortages before they occur and thus can focus on efficiencies instead of redundant paperwork.

IBM provided the consulting services necessary to design the Volkswagen Group's system. IBM, which was once a major manufacturer of

German-based Volkswagen Group, the largest auto manufacturer in Europe, owns and distributes numerous brands.
©Oliver Hardt/AFP/Getty Images/Newscom

Adding Value 7.1   The "Alfonso Versant" Fashion Show: Creating Excitement for a New Xerox Printer[iii]

Fuji Xerox enjoys a strong reputation as a steady provider of equipment to business customers—but steady also can mean boring. Drumming up excitement for new products in its core market, document management, isn't exactly easy. Therefore, when a New Zealand branch of Fuji Xerox launched its new HD printer, the Versant 2100, it decided to get creative and host a fashion show, designed and produced fully through the use of the new printer.

Noting that the name Versant had a high fashion ring to it, the Fuji Xerox team decided to make up a designer, Alfonso Versant. It sent out glossy lookbooks of the designer's fashions, all printed on the Versant 2100. The direct-mail campaign also included invitations to a fashion show, sent to business customers that might consider purchasing the products. These customers all were in the business of printing high-quality materials themselves, so the key was to demonstrate the remarkable and added-value capabilities of the Versant 2100. In support of this effort, Fuji Xerox solicited designs for a fashion show from fashion school students, who had to produce everything they designed by using only materials that came out of the Versant 2100. Highlighting the varieties of paper the printer could use, the students integrated not just traditional paper but also tissue paper and card stock in their designs.

Thus the direct-mail campaign with the lookbook of designs clearly highlighted what the Versant 2100 could do, appealing to business customers who wanted to be able to promise their own customers that they could undertake complex print jobs easily and professionally. The lookbook included some traditional information about the printer too, but the main focus was on the creative and fun products that the project would produce. By the time the fashion show rolled around, Fuji

To introduce the HD printer, the Versant 2100, Xerox made up a designer named Alfonso Versant and solicited designs for a fashion show from fashion school students, who had to produce everything they designed by using only materials that came out of the Versant 2100.

Courtesy of MarketingSherpa and Fuji Xerox

Xerox was able to showcase 14 dresses and demonstrate how its new printer could offer value to its customers—while also achieving the added social benefit of collaborating with students to give them some real-world experience.

Overall, the event was a huge success for Fuji Xerox. Three months after the event, the New Zealand branch had surpassed its sales targets by a remarkable 240 percent; it alone accounted for 34 percent of total sales in the Asia-Pacific region, even though New Zealand makes up less than 1 percent of the region in area.

---

computers and related products, now generates 90 percent of its profits from its software, consulting, and financing businesses—all of which are considered services. Like Volkswagen Group, it requires a host of B2B products and services to support these businesses. For instance, the airlines that IBM consultants and service providers rely on to shuttle them around the globe also use a mix of products such as airplanes and fuel as well as consulting, legal, and other services.

Resellers

Resellers are marketing intermediaries that resell manufactured products without significantly altering their form. For instance, **wholesalers** and **distributors** buy Xerox products and sell them to retailers (B2B transaction), then retailers resell those Xerox products to the ultimate consumer (B2C transaction). Alternatively, these retailers may buy directly from Xerox. Thus, wholesalers, distributors, and retailers are all resellers. Retailers represent resellers and engage in B2B transactions when they buy fixtures, capital investments, leasing locations, financing operations, and merchandise for their stores. To appeal to resellers and keep them interested in what it has to offer, Xerox works hard to ensure that its innovative products appeal to them and their customers. Adding Value 7.1 explains how it is promoting its HD printer technology to enhance its value, its commercial customers' value, and in the end, the consumers' value.

Institutions

Institutions such as hospitals, educational organizations, and religious organizations also purchase all kinds of goods and services. A public school system might have a $40 million annual budget for textbooks alone, which gives it significant buying power and enables it to take advantage of bulk discounts. However, if each school makes its own purchasing decisions, the system as a whole cannot leverage its combined buying power. Public institutions also engage in B2B relationships to fulfill their needs for capital construction, equipment, supplies, food, and janitorial services.

Government

In most countries, the central government is one of the largest purchasers of goods and services. For example, the U.S. federal government spends nearly $4 trillion annually on procuring goods and services.[15] The Department of Defense was slated to receive $582.7 billion in fiscal year 2017, and

The U.S. Department of Defense spends more than $500 billion a year on everything from nuts and bolts to cybersecurity.
©Rawpixel.com/Shutterstock

$6.7 billion of that amount was to be dedicated to working with cybersecurity firms to help the U.S. government protect against cyberterrorism attacks.[16] Thus the government, and the Department of Defense in particular, represents a spending force to be reckoned with.

Across these various B2B markets, purchasing methods might vary with the range of options being pursued. iPads are playing increasing roles in educational institutions and businesses, which suggests that institutions need to start making thoughtful purchasing decisions about them too.

PROGRESS CHECK

1. What are the various B2B markets?

THE BUSINESS—TO—BUSINESS BUYING PROCESS

As noted in the previous section, the B2B buying process is unique (Exhibit 7.2): It both parallels the B2C process and differs in several ways. Both start with need recognition, but the information search and alternative evaluation steps are more formal and structured in the B2B process. Typically, B2B buyers specify their needs in writing and ask potential suppliers to submit formal proposals, whereas B2C buying decisions are usually made by individuals or families and do not need formal proposals. Thus, for an individual to buy a tablet computer, all that is required is a trip to the store or a few minutes online and perhaps some preliminary research about iPads versus competitors.

L07-2 List the steps in the B2B buying process.

EXHIBIT 7.2   Business-to-Business Buying Process

Need recognition → Product specification → RFP process → Proposal analysis, vendor negotiation, and selection → Order specification → Vendor performance assessment using metrics

The first step in the B2B decision process is to recognize that the university needs to purchase 1,200 tablets.

©duckycards/iStock Photos

For a school to buy thousands of tablet computers, however, it must complete requisition forms, accept bids from manufacturers, and obtain approval for the expenditure. The final decision rests with a committee, as is the case for most B2B buying decisions, which often demand a great deal of consideration. Finally, in B2C buying situations, customers evaluate their purchase decision and sometimes experience postpurchase cognitive dissonance. But formal performance evaluations of the vendor and the products sold generally do not occur in the B2C setting, as they do in the B2B setting. Let's examine all six stages in the context of a university buying tablets for its incoming first-year students to use as resources.

Stage 1: Need Recognition

In the first stage of the B2B buying process, the buying organization recognizes, through either internal or external sources, that it has an unfilled need. Sellers actively work to prompt such need recognition, as detailed in Adding Value 7.2. Hypothetical University wants to ensure that its students are well educated and able to participate in a technologically connected workforce. It also seeks to grant them affordable access to required educational resources, from textbooks to library access to administrative tasks. The administration of the university also has reviewed research suggesting that portable devices, including tablet computers, can enhance students' in-class learning because they can directly and constantly interact with the materials and take notes in conjunction with the lecture and text, rather than only hearing information or seeing it on a whiteboard. The tablets also support innovative learning methodologies, such as the use of interactive clickers in lecture-based courses. Using this information, the university has determined it will issue a tablet to each of the 1,200 new first-year students.

Stage 2: Product Specification

After recognizing the need and considering alternative solutions, including laptop computers, the university wrote a list of potential specifications that vendors might use to develop their proposals. The school's specifications include screen size, battery life, processor speed, how the device connects to the Internet, and delivery date. In addition, the board of directors of the university has requested that a bundle of educational apps be preloaded on the tablets, that all other apps be removed, and that each tablet come equipped with a screen protector, power cord, cover, stand, keyboard, and headphones. The school hopes to obtain a four-year service contract that includes replacement within 24 hours for any tablets that are returned to the vendor for servicing.

Stage 3: RFP Process

The request for proposals (RFP) is a common process through which organizations invite alternative vendors or suppliers to bid on supplying their required components or specifications. The purchasing company may simply post its RFP needs on its website or work through various B2B web portals or inform its preferred vendors directly. Because the university does not have a preferred vendor for tablets yet, it issues an RFP and invites various tablet suppliers, technology companies, and other interested parties to bid on the contract.

Smaller companies may lack the ability to attract broad attention to their requests, so they might turn to a web portal, an Internet site whose purpose is to be a major starting point for users when they connect to the web. Although there are general portals such as Yahoo! or MSN, B2B partners connect to specialized or niche portals to participate in online information exchanges and transactions. These exchanges help streamline procurement or distribution processes. Portals can provide tremendous cost savings because they

Adding Value 7.2   What Isn't Intel Inside?[iv]

As one of the best examples of a successful branding effort, Intel created awareness and familiarity with its "Intel Inside" slogan, alerting business customers and consumers alike that the company offered high-quality computer chips to support various brands of computers. But as Intel sought to gain recognition for the other projects that it can support, it had become something of a victim of its own success. Everyone knew the "Intel Inside" phrase, leading to a common, and incorrect, assumption that chips were all that the company produced.

Therefore, its latest branding efforts target potential business partners in diverse industry sectors, far beyond the computer manufacturers with which it has long collaborated. For example, in partnership with Lady Gaga—a brand unto herself, who also heads the House of Gaga creative agency—Intel helped create a virtual skin that the entertainer "wore" during her tribute to David Bowie at the Grammys. The projection onto Gaga's face made it appear as if her makeup were changing in real time. The effect would have been impossible without Intel's expertise, a capability that Intel is promoting widely among its other business customers as an example of what it can do.

The promotions generally are featured in short videos that are available through Intel's online publication, so that it can offer them up readily to potential partners. The videos highlight collaborations and advances in various fields, including fashion, science, and medicine. For example, one video describes how a scientist investigating declining bee populations relied on Intel's microcomputing technology to create tiny "backpacks" that could track the bees' movement. Another video shows the creation of a dress decorated by mechanical butterflies that flutter away and return as the wearer moves, prompted by Intel technology.

But the examples are not all about bugs. They also feature life-changing tools, such as a low-cost Braille printer that relies on an Intel chip and a mom who created a glove that could provide advance warning when her epileptic son was about to suffer a seizure.

To promote problem recognition and extend its brand beyond its "Intel Inside" slogan, Intel partnered with Lady Gaga to create a virtual skin that made her face appear as if her makeup were changing in real time at her tribute to David Bowie at the Grammys.

©Larry Busacca/Getty Images for NARAS

In conjunction with these targeted promotions, Intel has revised its overall branding strategy. Rather than just "Intel Inside," the tagline on all its advertising now encourages customers—whether business partners or consumers—to "experience what's inside." Rather than a high-quality chip, Intel wants to be known for the cool stuff that its technology and expertise can produce.

eliminate periodic negotiations and routine paperwork, and they offer the means to form a supply chain that can respond quickly to the buyer's needs.

Small- to medium-sized companies looking for skilled service workers also can use portals such as Guru.com, started to help freelance professionals connect with companies that need their services, whether those services entail graphic design and cartooning or finance and accounting advice. Currently, more than 1.5 million professionals list their offerings on this service-oriented professional exchange, in over 3.7 million services. Guru.com thus provides value to both companies and freelancers by offering not only a site for finding each other but also dispute resolution, escrow for payments, and a means to rate freelancer quality.[17]

Stage 4: Proposal Analysis, Vendor Negotiation, and Selection

The buying organization, in conjunction with its critical decision makers, evaluates all the proposals it receives in response to its RFP. Hypothetical University reviews all proposals it receives, together with the board of directors, representatives from the teachers' union, and members of the student government. Many firms narrow the process to a few suppliers, often those with which they have existing relationships, and discuss key terms of the

| EXHIBIT 7.3 | Evaluating a Vendor's Performance | | |

(1) Key Issues	(2) Importance Score	(3) Vendor's Performance	(4) Importance × Performance (2) × (3)
Customer Service	0.40	5	2.0
Issue Resolution	0.20	4	0.8
Delivery	0.10	5	0.5
Quality	0.30	3	0.9
Total	1.0		4.2

sale, such as price, quality, delivery, and financing. The university likely considers the bid by the company that installed computers in its library, assuming that provider performed well. Some firms have a policy that requires them to negotiate with several suppliers, particularly if the product or service represents a critical component or aspect of the business. This policy keeps suppliers on their toes; they know that the buying firm can always shift a greater portion of its business to an alternative supplier if it offers better terms.

The university evaluates proposals on the basis of the amount of experience the vendor has with tablet computers and similar technology products because it wants to make sure that its investment is reliable in the short term and flexible enough to accommodate new apps or updates. In addition, the school wants to be sure the technology will remain relevant in the longer term and not become obsolete. The vendor's ability to meet its specifications also is important because if the processor is too slow, students are unlikely to make use of the devices. The vendor's financial position provides an important indication of whether the vendor will be able to stay in business.

Stage 5: Order Specification

In the fifth stage of the B2B buying process, the firm places its order with its preferred supplier (or suppliers). The order includes a detailed description of the goods, prices, delivery dates, and, in some cases, penalties for noncompliance. The supplier then sends an acknowledgment that it has received the order and fills it by the specified date. In the case of the school's tablets, the terms are clearly laid out regarding when and how the vendor is expected to perform any preventive maintenance, who the contact person is for any problems with delivery or the tablets themselves, and under what circumstances the vendor will be expected to provide a replacement for a malfunctioning tablet. Issues such as maintenance and replacement are important because the university does not plan to keep any inventory of extra tablets on hand.

Stage 6: Vendor Performance Assessment Using Metrics

Just as in the consumer buying process, firms analyze their vendors' performance so they can make decisions about their future purchases. The difference is that in a B2B setting, this analysis is typically more formal and objective. Let's consider how Hypothetical University might evaluate the tablet vendor's performance, as in Exhibit 7.3, using the following metrics: customer service, issue resolution, delivery (based on promised delivery date), and quality.

1. The buying team develops a list of issues that it believes are important to consider in the vendor evaluation.

2. To determine the importance of each issue (column 1), the buying team assigns an importance score to each (column 2). The more important the issue, the higher its score, but the importance scores must add up to 1. In this case, the buying team believes that customer service and quality are most important, whereas issue resolution and delivery are comparatively less important.

3. In the third column, the buying team assigns numbers that reflect its judgments about how well the vendor performs. Using a 5-point scale, where 1 equals poor performance and 5 equals excellent performance, the university decides that the tablet vendor performs quite well on all issues except product quality.

4. To calculate an overall performance score in the fourth column, the team combines the importance of each issue and the vendor's performance scores by multiplying them. Because the tablet vendor performed well on the most important issues, when we add the importance/performance scores in column 4, we find that the overall evaluation is pretty good—4.2 on a 5-point scale.

THE BUYING CENTER

In most large organizations, several people are responsible for buying decisions. These **buying center** participants can range from employees who have a formal role in purchasing decisions (i.e., the purchasing or procurement department) to members of the design team who will specify the equipment or raw materials needed for employees who will be using a new machine that is on order. All these employees are likely to play different roles in the buying process, which vendors must understand and adapt to in their marketing and sales efforts.

L07-3 Identify the roles within the buying center.

We can categorize six buying roles within a typical buying center (see Exhibit 7.4). One or more people may take on a certain role, or one person may take on more than one of the following roles: (1) **initiator**, the person who first suggests buying the particular product or service; (2) **influencer**, the person whose views influence other members of the buying center in making the final decision; (3) **decider**, the person who ultimately determines any part of or the entire buying decision—whether to buy, what to buy, how to buy, or where to buy; (4) **buyer**, the person who handles the paperwork of the actual purchase; (5) **user**, the person who consumes or uses the product or service; and (6) **gatekeeper**, the person who controls information or access, or both, to decision makers and influencers.[18]

EXHIBIT 7.4 Buying Center Roles

In the buying center, the medical device supplier is the influencer, whereas the doctor is the initiator.

©Siri Stafford/Iconica/Getty Images

To illustrate how a buying center operates, consider purchases made by a hospital. Where do hospitals obtain their X-ray machines, syringes, and bedpans? Why are some medical procedures covered in whole or in part by insurance, whereas others are not? Why might your doctor recommend one type of allergy medication instead of another?

The Initiator—Your Doctor When you seek treatment from your physician, he or she initiates the buying process by determining the products and services that will best address and treat your illness or injury. For example, say you fell backward off your snowboard and, in trying to catch yourself, you shattered your elbow. You require surgery to mend the affected area, which includes the insertion of several screws to hold the bones in place. Your doctor promptly notifies the hospital to schedule a time for the procedure and specifies the brand of screws she wants on hand for your surgery.

The Influencer—The Medical Device Supplier, the Pharmacy For years your doctor has been using Mendell bone screws, a slightly higher-priced screw. Her first introduction to Mendell bone screws came from the company's sales representative, who visited her office to demonstrate how Mendell bone screws were far superior to those of its competition. Your doctor recognized Mendell bone screws as a good value. Armed with empirical data and case studies, Mendell's sales rep effectively influenced your doctor's decision to use that screw.

The Decider—The Hospital Even though your doctor requested Mendell bone screws, the hospital ultimately is responsible for deciding whether to buy Mendell bone screws. The hospital supplies the operating room, instrumentation, and surgical supplies, and, therefore, the hospital administrators must weigh a variety of factors to determine whether the Mendell bone screw is not only best for the patients but also involves a cost that is reimbursable by various insurance providers.

The Buyer The actual buyer of the screw will likely be the hospital's materials manager, who is charged with buying and maintaining inventory for the hospital in the most cost-effective manner. Whereas Mendell bone screws are specific to your type of procedure, other items, such as gauze and sutures, may be purchased through a group purchasing organization (GPO), which obtains better prices through volume buying.

The User—The Patient Ultimately, the buying process for this procedure will be greatly affected by the user, namely you, and your broken elbow. If you are uncomfortable with the procedure or have read about alternative procedures that you prefer, you may decide that Mendell bone screws are not the best treatment.

The Gatekeeper—The Insurance Company Your insurer may believe that Mendell bone screws are too expensive and that other screws deliver equally effective results and therefore refuse to reimburse the hospital in full or in part for the use of the screws.

In the end, the final purchase decision must take into consideration every buying center participant.

Organizational Culture

LO7-4 Describe the different types of organizational cultures.

A firm's organizational culture reflects the set of values, traditions, and customs that guide its employees' behavior. The firm's culture often comprises a set of unspoken guidelines that employees share with one another through various work situations. For example, Walmart buyers are not allowed to accept even the smallest gift from a vendor, not even a cup of coffee. This rule highlights its overall corporate culture: It is a low-cost operator whose buyers must base their decisions only on the products' and vendors' merits.

At General Electric (GE), the culture aims to ensure that members and partners regard B2B as a source of innovation, not a "boring-to-boring" proposition. Rather than lament the

To excite its customers, GE publishes the series "Drone Week," in which a drone visits a GE facility every day, and streams it live on Facebook.

Source: General Electric Company

relatively less glamorous process of B2B, GE has "decided we are geeky and we are proud of it."[19] Therefore, rather than turning to some of the more conventional uses of Instagram, GE relies on the social media site to communicate with "its people," those followers it affectionately refers to as #AVgeeks. What GE offers to its business customers is mainly advanced technology and scientifically based products and services. But those sorts of offerings are exactly what get geeks excited, so it offers content that they can share with other geeks, as well as with their own customers. GE was one of the first adopters of Facebook Live, publishing the series "Drone Week," in which a drone visited a GE facility every day, and streaming it live on Facebook. GE has also been innovative in its use of Snapchat, publishing Snapchat stories from its leadership event "Minds + Machines" using Snap "Spectacles."[20]

Organizational culture also can have a profound influence on purchasing decisions. Corporate buying center cultures can be divided into four general types: autocratic, democratic, consultative, and consensus (as illustrated in Exhibit 7.5). Knowing which buying center culture is prevalent in a given organization helps the seller decide how to approach that particular client, how and to whom to deliver pertinent information, and to whom to make sales presentations.

In an autocratic buying center, even though there may be multiple participants, one person makes the decision alone, whereas the majority rules in a democratic buying center. Consultative buying centers use one person to make a decision but solicit input from others before doing so. Finally, in a consensus buying center, all members of the team must reach a collective agreement that they can support a particular purchase.

Cultures act like living, breathing entities that change and grow, just as organizations do. Even within some companies, culture may vary by geography, by division, or by functional department. Whether you are a member of the buying center or a supplier trying to sell to it, it is extremely important to understand the buying center's culture and the roles of the key players in the buying process. Not knowing the roles of the key players could waste a lot of time and even alienate the real decision maker.

Building B2B Relationships

In B2B contexts there are a multitude of ways to enhance relationships, and these methods seem to be advancing and evolving by the minute. For example, blogs and social media can build awareness, provide search engine results, educate potential and existing clients about products or services, and warm up a seemingly cold corporate culture. Fiberlink offers document and mobile enterprise management services. To make its offerings and content more engaging, it launched a series of fun webinars and video campaigns filled with pop culture references. One webinar, "Game of Phones," used comparisons from the popular HBO series *Game of Thrones* to highlight the different mobile operating systems and detail how Fiberlink's

EXHIBIT 7.5   Organizational Buying Culture

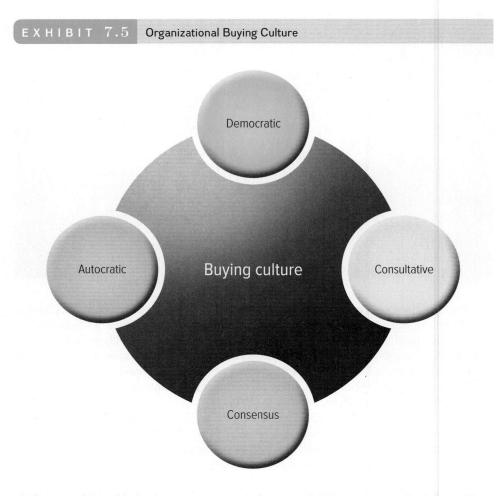

platform could enable business customers to leverage their content on all of them. Thus Apple, as the current market leader, was presented as the House Lannister; Android was the House Targaryen because the factors that kept it on the sidelines also have helped it gain power; and Windows was House Stark because it is "full of battle scars." The engaging campaign allowed the company to generate 20 percent more new leads than previous campaigns had achieved.[21]

An expert who offers advice and knowledge about products increases brand awareness, and a blog is a great medium for this information. Web analytics, such as traffic on the website and the number of comments, can offer tangible evaluations, but a better measure is how often the blog gets mentioned elsewhere, the media attention it receives, and the interaction, involvement, intimacy, and influence that it promotes.

The LinkedIn.com social network is mainly used for professional networking in the B2B marketplace. Twitter, the microblogging site, is also valuable for B2B marketers because they can communicate with other businesses as often as they want. Snapchat also is providing new opportunities, as Social & Mobile Marketing 7.1 shows. Companies such as HootSuite make it easier for companies using Twitter to manage their followers, update their posts, track analytics, and even schedule tweets, just as they would to manage a traditional marketing campaign.[22]

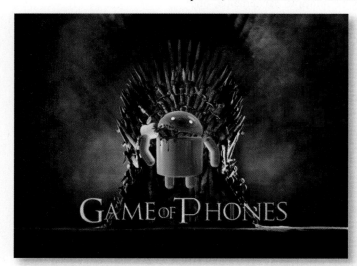

To make its offerings more engaging, Fiberlink launched a series of fun webinars and video campaigns, like this one that "plays" with the popular HBO series Game of Thrones.

Source: Mobile Nations

Social & Mobile Marketing 7.1

Snapchat as an Advertising and Content Platform: The Latest Experiments in Television[v]

When Snapchat seeks new business, it promises advertisers and corporate users that it is the social media channel that is best suited to playing video and most likely to get those videos before the eyes of the young consumers whom marketers are desperate to reach. The argument appears to have convinced AMC, the network that aims to get its fans hooked on its latest series, *Preacher*.

For a week before the premiere of the new show on AMC, the first five minutes of the opening episode were available on Snapchat. For the first 24 hours after this promotional release, Snapchat was the only place viewers could find the highly anticipated video. At the end of the week, the video came down, but by that time, the entire episode was queued up to play on the network.

The carefully planned timing thus actively sought to increase the hype about *Preacher*, a dark, supernatural comedy based on an even darker comic series and produced by, among others, Seth Rogan. The premise is odd and challenging—not unlike *The Walking Dead*, AMC's hit zombie series. Thus, the network had some experience and insights into the ways in which it could connect with and appeal to its target audience. For example, as it learned just how dedicated fans were to *The Walking Dead*, AMC developed *Talking Dead*, an hourlong talk show that features cast members chatting with fans and celebrities about the previous week's narrative episode.

As AMC's executive vice president of marketing explained, the network thus has some good insights into its target marketing, including the recognition that "For millennials, the thrill of discovery is really important. Our hope is to turn our fans into evangelists by getting 'Preacher' to them ahead of the premiere."

To increase its business, Snapchat works closely with its B2B customers like the AMC network, producers of Preacher, *by releasing the first five minutes of the premier episode a week early.*
©AMC/Photofest

These cross-platform experiments also are not limited to traditional broadcasters trying out social media options. Flipping this innovative approach on its head, Netflix has agreed to sell its own series, *Narcos*, to a traditional network. That is, the first season of *Narcos* was available exclusively through the streaming service. But this first season soon will appear as traditional programming on the Univision network, in advance of the premiere of the second season on Netflix. With this move, Netflix is testing the proposition that allowing people to watch some of its shows through their basic cable package will encourage them to sign up for the streaming service, so they can continue watching a new favorite.

When executives confront an unfulfilled business need, they normally turn to **white papers** prepared by potential B2B marketers.[23] White papers are a promotional technique used by B2B sellers to provide information about a product or service in an educational context, thereby not appearing like a promotion or propaganda. The goal of white papers is to provide valuable information that a potential B2B buyer can easily understand and that will help the company address its problems with new solutions. For instance, say a B2B seller has a technologically advanced solution for an inventory problem. Because the executives of the potential B2B buying firm are not technologically oriented, the B2B seller creates a white paper to explain the solution in nontechnological terms so that the buying firm's executives can understand and appreciate the solution before they consider a purchase.

PROGRESS CHECK

1. What are the six buying roles?
2. What are the types of cultures that exist in buying centers?

THE BUYING SITUATION

LO7-5 Detail different buying situations.

The type of buying situation also affects the B2B decision process. Most B2B buying situations can be categorized into three types: new buys, modified rebuys, and straight rebuys (see Exhibit 7.6). To illustrate the nuances among these three buying situations, consider how colleges and universities develop relationships with some of their suppliers. Most universities negotiate with sports apparel manufacturers, such as Nike, Reebok, and New Balance, to establish purchasing agreements for their sports teams. Those with successful sports teams have been very successful in managing these relationships, to the benefit of both the team and the company.[24] Large universities that win national championships, such as the University of Alabama or University of Southern California (USC), can solicit sponsorships in exchange for free athletic equipment, whereas less popular teams or smaller schools typically must accept an upfront sponsorship and then agree to buy from that vendor for a specified period of time. In exchange for this sponsorship, the vendors gain the right to sell apparel with the university logo and require the school's team to purchase only their equipment. Many apparel companies make a significant portion of their revenue through sponsorship deals that grant them the right to sell apparel with popular university logos.

In a new buy situation, a customer purchases a good or service for the first time,[25] which means the buying decision is likely to be quite involved because the buyer or the buying organization does not have any experience with the item. In the B2B context, the buying center is likely to proceed through all six steps in the buying process and involve many people in the buying decision. Typical new buys might range from capital equipment to components that the firm previously made itself but now has decided to purchase instead. For example, a small college might need to decide which apparel company to approach for a sponsorship. For smaller colleges, finding a company that will sponsor multiple sports teams—such as women's soccer as well as men's basketball—is a priority, though it also must balance other considerations such as the length of the contract. Some vendors offer perks to attract new buyers; New Balance offers teams that sign up for long-term contracts custom fittings for their players' shoes. Each season, a sales team from New Balance visits the school and custom fits each player to achieve the best fit possible.

Another example of a new buy occurs in the fashion industry, where runway shows offer wholesale buyers an opportunity to inspect new lines of clothing and place orders. Designer sales often occur during private meetings with buyers, both before and after runway shows. Buyers meet with the designers, discuss the line, and observe a model wearing the clothing. The buyer's challenge, then: determine which items will sell best in the retail stores he or she represents while trying to imagine what the item will look like in regular, as opposed to model, sizes. Buyers must also negotiate purchases for orders that may not be delivered for as long as six months. Buyers

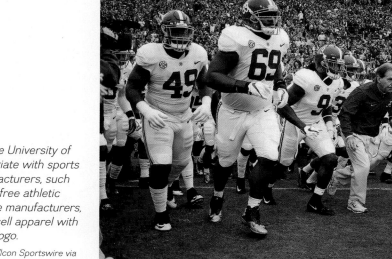

Schools like the University of Alabama negotiate with sports apparel manufacturers, such as Nike, to get free athletic equipment. The manufacturers, in turn, get to sell apparel with the university logo.

©Scott Donaldson/Icon Sportswire via Getty Images

can suggest modifications to make the clothing more or less expensive or more comfortable for their customers. Buyers and designers recognize the significant value of this relationship, which occasionally prompts buyers to purchase a few items from a designer even if those items do not exactly fit the store's core customers' tastes. Doing so ensures that the buyer will have access to the designer's collection for the next season.[26]

In a *modified rebuy*, the buyer has purchased a similar product in the past but has decided to change some specifications such as the desired price, quality level, customer service level, options, and so forth. Current vendors are likely to have an advantage in acquiring the sale in a modified rebuy situation as long as the reason for the modification is not dissatisfaction with the vendor or its products. The Ohio State University's sports department might ask adidas to modify the specifications for its basketball shoes after noticing some improvements made to the adidas shoes used by the University of Michigan.

Straight rebuys occur when the buyer or buying organization simply buys additional units of products that had previously been purchased. Many B2B purchases are likely to fall in the straight rebuy category. For example, sports teams need to repurchase a tremendous amount of equipment that is not covered by apparel sponsorships, such as tape for athletes' ankles or weights for the weight room. The purchase of bottled water also typically involves a straight rebuy from an existing supplier.

| EXHIBIT 7.6 | Buying Situations |

These varied types of buying situations call for very different marketing and selling strategies. The most complex and difficult is the new buy because it requires the buying organization to make changes in its current practices and purchases. As a result, several members of the buying center will likely become involved, and the level of their involvement will be more intense than in the case of modified and straight rebuys. In new buying situations, buying center members also typically spend more time at each stage of the B2B buying process, similar to the extended decision-making process that consumers use in the B2C process. In comparison, in modified rebuys the buyers spend less time at each stage of the B2B buying process, similar to limited decision making in the B2C process (see Chapter 6).

In straight rebuys, however, the buyer is often the only member of the buying center involved in the process. Like a consumer's habitual purchase, straight rebuys often enable the buyer to recognize the firm's need and go directly to the fifth step in the B2B buying process, skipping the product specification, RFP process, proposal analysis, and supplier selection steps.

Thus, in various ways B2B marketing both differs from and mirrors the consumer behavior (B2C) process we detailed in Chapter 6. The differences in the six stages of the buying process make sense in view of the many unique factors that come into play. The constitution of the buying center (initiator, influencer, decider, buyer, user, and gatekeeper), the culture of the purchasing firm (autocratic, democratic, consultative, or consensus), and the context of the buying situation (new buy, modified rebuy, straight rebuy) all influence the B2B buying process in various ways, which means that sellers must be constantly aware of these factors if they want to be successful in their sales attempts.

PROGRESS CHECK

1. How do new buy, straight rebuy, and modified rebuy differ?

Reviewing Learning Objectives

L07-1 Describe the ways in which business-to-business (B2B) firms segment their markets.

All firms want to divide the market into groups of customers with different needs, wants, or characteristics who therefore might appreciate products or services geared especially toward them. On a broad level, B2B firms divide the market into four types: manufacturers or service providers, resellers, institutions, and government. Manufacturers and service providers purchase materials to make their products and components and offer expertise to help run their businesses, such as computer and telephone systems. Resellers are primarily wholesalers, distributors, or retailers that sell the unchanged products. Institutions include nonprofit organizations such as hospitals, schools, or churches. Finally, governments purchase all types of goods and services; in the United States, defense is among the largest expenditures.

L07-2 List the steps in the B2B buying process.

Similar to the B2C buying process, the B2B process consists of several stages: need recognition; product specification; the RFP process; proposal analysis, vendor negotiation, and selection; order specification; and vendor performance assessment using metrics. The B2B process tends to be more formalized and structured than the customer buying process.

L07-3 Identify the roles within the buying center.

The initiator first suggests the purchase. The influencer affects important people's perceptions and final decisions. The decider ultimately determines at least some of the buying decision—whether, what, how, or where to buy. The buyer handles the details of the actual purchase. The user consumes or employs the product or service. The gatekeeper controls information and access to decision makers and influencers. In B2B situations, it is likely that several people, organized into a buying center, will be involved in making the purchase decision. The vendor must understand the relationships among the participants of the buying center to be effective. A firm's organizational culture can also influence the decision process. For instance, if a firm is trying to sell to a young, high-tech computer component manufacturer, it might be well advised to send salespeople who are fluent in technology-speak and can easily relate to the customer.

L07-4 Describe the different types of organizational cultures.

Firm culture consists of unspoken guidelines that employees share through various work situations. They generally can be classified as autocratic, in which one person makes most decisions; democratic, where the majority rules; consultative, in which one person makes decisions based on the input of others; or consensus, which requires all members of the team to reach collective agreement.

L07-5 Detail different buying situations.

The buying process depends to a great extent on the situation. If a firm is purchasing a product or service for the first time (i.e., new buy), the process is much more involved than if it is engaging in a straight rebuy of the same item again. A modified rebuy falls somewhere in the middle, such that the buyer wants essentially the same thing but with slightly different terms or features.

Key Terms

- autocratic buying center, 223
- business-to-business (B2B) marketing, 212
- buyer, 221
- buying center, 221
- consensus buying center, 223
- consultative buying center, 223
- decider, 221
- democratic buying center, 223
- derived demand, 212
- distributor, 216
- gatekeeper, 221
- influencer, 221
- initiator, 221
- modified rebuy, 226
- new buy, 226
- organizational culture, 222
- request for proposals (RFP), 218
- reseller, 216
- straight rebuy, 227
- user, 221
- web portal, 218
- white papers, 225
- wholesaler, 216

Marketing Digitally

1. LinkedIn has grown into a platform that firms use for a variety of business needs. Choose a firm of interest and explore the content on its LinkedIn page. How is the firm that you selected using LinkedIn to attract customers, suppliers, or employees?

2. Siemens offers a multitude of products and services to many industries. Go online to learn more about its products and market-specific solutions (https://www.siemens.com/global/en/home.html). Choose a market-specific solution and describe how a potential customer might go through the business-to-business buying process to purchase this product or service from Siemens.

Marketing Applications

1. Provide an example of each of the four types of B2B organizations.

2. What are the major differences between the consumer buying process discussed in Chapter 6 and the B2B buying process discussed in this chapter? Use buying iPads for personal use versus buying more than 100 iPads for a firm to illustrate the key points.

3. Assume you have written this textbook and are going to attempt to sell it to your school. Identify the six members of the buying center. What role would each play in the decision process? Rank them in terms of how much influence they would have on the decision, with 1 being most influential and 6 being least influential. Will this ranking be different in other situations?

4. Now provide an example of the three types of buying situations that the bookstore at your school might face when buying textbooks.

5. Finally, discuss for which types of products the bookstore would do a straight rebuy and for which it would pursue a modified rebuy.

6. Mazda is trying to assess the performance of two manufacturers that could supply music systems for its vehicles.

Performance Evaluation of Brands

Issues	Importance Weights	Manufacturer A's Performance	Manufacturer B's Performance
Sound	0.4	5	3
Cost	0.3	2	4
Delivery time	0.1	2	2
Brand cachet	0.2	5	1
Total	1		

Using the information in the accompanying table, determine which manufacturer Mazda should use.

7. Describe the organizational culture at your school or job. How would knowledge of this particular organization's culture help a B2B salesperson sell products or services to the organization?

8. You have just started to work in the purchasing office of a major pharmaceutical firm. The purchasing manager has asked you to assist in writing an RFP for a major purchase. The manager gives you a sheet detailing the specifications for the RFP. While reading the specifications, you realize that they have been written to be extremely favorable to one bidder. How should you handle this situation?

Quiz Yourself

1. Knowing the culture of the organizational buying center can help salespeople identify what type of approach to use. For example, if you know that a firm has a central decision maker who seeks input from others, then that firm has which type of buying center?
   a. Autocratic
   b. Democratic
   c. Consultative
   d. Consensus
   e. None of the above

2. In which process are vendors invited to submit bids based on firm specifications?
   a. Rebuy
   b. New product purchase
   c. Request for proposals
   d. Straight rebuy
   e. Modified rebuy

(Answers to these two questions can be found in the Quiz Yourself Answer Key section.)

Chapter Case Study

STAPLES: THE BIG-BOX RETAILER THAT'S REALLY A B2B POWERHOUSE

Probably every reader of this book has visited a Staples store or its website at least once, needing to stock up on back-to-school supplies, grab a roll of packing tape, or take a look at the newest printers available in the market. Clearly, selling to individual consumers is important to Staples. But some of its greatest growth, and some of its most important marketing efforts, relate to its Staples Advantage division, which provides business customers with services and support.

This support may be most valuable for small businesses, which often lack the resources to manage all their various functions on their own. Most straightforwardly, Staples Advantage provides companies with the behind-the-scenes supplies that are necessary to keep the doors open: coffee machines, sugar, and creamer to stock employee break rooms; janitorial supplies and floor mats that keep the place looking clean; paper towels and soap dispensers in restrooms; and office equipment to ensure that workers can keep their files organized and their workspaces productive. To facilitate these offerings, Staples has begun equipping all its B2B sales associates in the field with iPads that are loaded with a virtual assistant. Thus, rather than relying on their recall or a bulky product catalog, they can depend on the virtual tool to determine which type of furniture polish will save their business clients the most money while still enabling them to keep all their surfaces free of dirt.[27]

To appeal even more to these small-business owners and provide them with not just office supplies but also ideas on how to run their offices, Staples has introduced the Quick Wins app. The app tracks the small businesses' performances on a range of measures, including social media engagement, website traffic, and financial metrics, all in one place. In this case, the innovative offering is a clear response to customer demand. Through its research, Staples determined that approximately 41 percent of its small-business customers expressed their need for help with these measures of performance, but they also did not know which metrics were most important or how to measure them accurately. Worried about their ability to keep up with the information, respondents to Staples' surveys also noted that they would prefer for all the information to be available in one easy-to-read dashboard. In helping business customers track key data regularly, Staples promises to develop customized, specific suggestions for how the business customers can expand their firms and increase business. Furthermore, through the Quick Wins app, users can interact with other small-business owners, seeking answers and support from their peers.[28]

Once they determine their performance, small-business owners likely identify sources of improvement. Pursuing such improvements often requires new investments, especially monetary ones—a resource that small-business owners usually lack. Therefore, Staples' latest service introduction is Lendio, an online financing arm that facilitates loans for these customers. Accessing the loan forms through Staples' main website, business customers can provide the necessary information.[29] Lendio then forwards the information to a relevant lender and maintains the financing agreement. In just a few months, Lendio had facilitated close to $1.5 million in loans to small firms, such as Bubba Nubb's Lunch Wagon, which used the loan to equip its food truck, or Hitt Medical Writing, which spent the money to hire new employees and expand its capacity to provide content to medical publications.[30]

By spreading and expanding its B2B offerings, Staples effectively protects against upheaval in any one market. Sales that it categorizes as B2B account for approximately one-third of its $23 billion in annual revenue. The revenues earned through Lendio, for example, are still just a tiny percentage of those totals, but by adding this service, Staples achieves two critical goals. First, it establishes itself as a source for such services, so the contributions to its bottom line might grow over time. Second, it makes sure that it is available for every need that a business customer might imagine. By doing so, it becomes a true partner that businesses turn to so that they can serve their own customers.

Questions

1. Imagine a small business that has long bought its office supplies from Staples. It reads about Lendio and considers whether to solicit a loan. What kind of buying situation has this small business entered?

2. What attributes should this small business use to evaluate Staples as vendor? What about Lendio? Using those attributes for Staples and Lendio, perform two separate vendor analyses.

Endnotes

1. LinkedIn, "About Us," www.linkedin.com/company/linkedin? src=or-search&veh=www.google.com%7Cor-search.

2. Pete Davies, "Introducing LinkedIn Video: Show Your Experience and Perspective," *LinkedIn Official Blog,* August 22, 2017, https://blog.linkedin.com/2017/august/22/Introducing-LinkedIn-Video-Show-Your-Experience-and-Perspective.

3. George Slefo, "LinkedIn Debuts 'Native Video,' Looks More Like Facebook," *Advertising Age,* August 22, 2017.

4. Ibid.

5. Davies, "Introducing LinkedIn Video."

6. Robert Elder, "LinkedIn Video Sharing Could Be a Revelation," *Business Insider,* July 14, 2017.

7. Brian Peters, "What Marketers Need to Know about LinkedIn," Entrepreneur.com, December 28, 2017.

8. Elder, "LinkedIn Video Sharing Could Be a Revelation."

9. www.apple.com/ios/carplay/available-models/; www.android.com/intl/en_ca/auto/.

10. Corey Eridon, "The Average Large Company Has 178 Social Media Accounts," *HubSpot,* January 10, 2012, http://blog.hubspot.com.

11. www.constantcontact.com.

12. Ibid.

13. www.volkswagenag.com.

14. www.vwgroupsupply.com/one-kbp-pub/en/kbp_public/home-page/homepage.html.

15. www.cbo.gov/topics/budget.

16. "Department of Defense (DoD) Releases Fiscal Year 2017 President's Budget Proposal," Department of Defense Press Operations, February 9, 2016, www.defense.gov/News/News-Releases/News-Release-View/Article/652687/department-of-defense-dod-releases-fiscal-year-2017-presidents-budget-proposal/.

17. www.guru.com.

18. These definitions are provided by www.marketingpower.com (the American Marketing Association's website). We have bolded the key terms.

19. E. J. Schultz, "GE Tells the Secret of Making Geeky Cool," *Advertising Age,* October 5, 2013, http://adage.com.

20. Charlotte Rogers, "GE's CMO on Redefining B2B Marketing at the 'Pretty Damn Cool' Brand," *Marketing Week,* January 11, 2017, www.marketingweek.com/2017/01/11/general-electric-cmo-redefining-marketing/.

21. Erin Hogg, "Case Study—B2B Content Marketing: Video Campaign Leveraging Pop Culture Lifts New Leads Generated 20%," *MarketingSherpa,* February 4, 2015, www.marketingsherpa.com/article/case-study/video-campaign-leverages-pop-culture.

22. www.hootsuite.com.

23. Tracey Peden, "The Use of White Papers in Today's B2B Market," *Marketing Resources Blog,* May 28, 2013, http://blog.ubmcanon.com/bid/285080/.

24. Michael Krause, "How Does Oregon Football Keep Winning? Is It the Uniforms?," *Grantland,* August 30, 2011, www.grantland.com.

25. Fabiana Ferreira et al., "The Transition from Products to Solutions: External Business Model Fit and Dynamics," *Industrial Marketing Management* 42, no. 7 (2013), pp. 1093–1101; Mark W. Johnston and Greg W. Marshall, *Contemporary Selling: Building Relationships, Creating Value* (New York: Routledge, 2013); Barton A. Weitz, Stephen B. Castleberry, and John F. Tanner, *Selling: Building Partnerships,* 6th ed. (Burr Ridge, IL: McGraw-Hill/Irwin, 2005), p. 93.

26. Leslie Kaufman, "Stone-Washed Blue Jeans (Minus the Washed)," *The New York Times,* November 1, 2011, www.nytimes.com.

27. Robert Hackett, "Staples, Never Stationary," *Forbes,* March 9, 2015.

28. Mike Troy, "Staples' New Digital Tool to Help Small Biz," *Retailing Today,* January 4, 2016.

29. See www.staples.com/sbd/cre/business-loans/.

30. Paul Demery, "Staples Connects Growing Businesses with Its Online Financing Service," *Internet Retailer,* May 28, 2015, www.internetretailer.com/2015/05/28/staples-connects-growing-businesses-its-online-financing-se.

i. Mike Isaac, "Facebook Blocks Ad Blockers, but It Strives to Make Ads More Relevant," *The New York Times,* August 9, 2016; Jack Marshall, "Facebook Will Force Advertising on Ad-Blocking Users," *The Wall Street Journal,* August 9, 2016; Mark Scott, "Use of Ad-Blocking Software Rises by 30% Worldwide," *The New York Times,* January 31, 2017.

ii. Ted Greenwald and Jack Nicas, "Facebook Pitches In on Intel's Coming Artificial Intelligence Chip," *The Wall Street Journal,* October 18, 2017; Jonathan Vanian, "Intel and Facebook Are Collaborating on Artificial Intelligence Technology," *Fortune,* October 17, 2017; Aaron Tilley, "Facebook Is Helping Intel Build Its First AI Chip," *Forbes,* October 17, 2017.

iii. Kayla Cobb, "Case Study—Event Marketing: Fuji Xerox Achieves 240% of Sales Target via a Fashion Show," *MarketingSherpa,* September 16, 2015, www.marketingsherpa.com/article/case-study/b2b-achieves-target-with-fashion-show#; Courtney Eckerle, "Fuji Xerox Launches New B2B Product with a Fashion Show," *MarketingSherpa Blog,* December 29, 2015, http://sherpablog.marketingsherpa.com/marketing/fuji-xerox-fashion-show/; www.xerox.com/about-xerox/75th-anniversary/enus.html.

iv. Rob Walker, "Intel Tells Stories That Go Beyond Chips," *The New York Times,* June 26, 2016; Adrianne Pasquarelli, "Intel's Agency Inside," *Advertising Age,* January 23, 2017.

v. Mike Isaac, "AMC Unveils 'Preacher' Clip in Snapchat," *Business Insider,* May 16, 2016; Shalina Ramachandran, "Netflix Original Series 'Narcos' to Air on Univision," *The Wall Street Journal,* May 17, 2016; Jeanine Poggi, "What Advertisers Really Need to Know about Cross-Platform TV Measurement," *Advertising Age,* January 16, 2017.

Quiz Yourself Answer Key

1. Knowing the culture of the organizational buying center can help salespeople identify what type of approach to use. For example, if you know that a firm has a central decision maker who seeks input from others, then that firm has which type of corporate buying center culture?

   Answer: (c) Consultative

2. In which process are vendors invited to submit bids based on firm specifications?

   Answer: (c) Request for proposals

©VCG via Getty Images

LEARNING OBJECTIVES

After reading this chapter, you should be able to:

LO8-1 Describe the components of a country market assessment.

LO8-2 Understand the marketing opportunities in BRIC countries.

LO8-3 Identify the various market entry strategies.

LO8-4 Highlight the similarities and differences between a domestic marketing strategy and a global marketing strategy.

CHAPTER 8
GLOBAL MARKETING

Expanding into global markets is nearly a necessity for most modern companies, especially those that seek to put their products and services in as many people's hands as possible. Take Apple for example. The goal of the tech giant is essentially to drive every other technology provider out of the market. It wants consumers to rely solely on iPhones for all their smartphone needs (and Apple Watches for their connected timepieces, and iPads for their tablets, and so on).

To make that happen, Apple has had to pursue international markets almost from its beginning. But doing so creates a wealth of challenges, along with the opportunities that arise.

Among the most notable challenges is deciding how to market products in different markets. Is it best to use a single, consistent strategy around the globe, or should marketing campaigns be targeted, such that they vary in different locales? For many years, Apple chose the former route. Its strong brand image and appealing advertising might appear in different languages—in a strategy known as localizing—but the message remained similar across the board. It sought a reputation as a sophisticated, tech-savvy, and cool product to own, whether the consumer buying it was in New York City or New Delhi or Mexico City.[1]

Today, though, it has shifted gears and created a wider array of marketing communications to target individual markets with dedicated appeals. For example, the "Meu Bloco na Rua" (loosely translated as "My Block on the Street") campaign plays only in Brazil, touting the latest iPhone in a Carnival-themed string of advertising. At the same time, it has shifted more of its focus to online and mobile marketing channels, rather than television, to ensure that it can reach every corner of the globe at no extra cost.[2]

Another key factor in global expansions relates to the prices that people are willing or able to pay across different nations. Whereas consumers in developed economies might be ready to shell out close to $1,000 for the latest iPhone, such a price point is utterly out of reach for millions of people who live in poverty or near poverty. Yet these millions of consumers are a critical target market because smartphones have saturated the developed markets. There are not many new customers in the United States or Europe to attract; if Apple is to become truly ubiquitous, it needs to find new buyers in India, China, Brazil, throughout Africa, and so forth.

In particular, Apple needs to convince the more than 2 billion potential consumers in China and India, with their rising incomes and purchasing power, that they want to start off with an iPhone, not a competitive Android product, then keep them coming back.[3] History shows that once a consumer has committed to a particular phone and platform, she or he is less likely to switch to a different platform. Thus, a first-mover advantage is critical in global markets.

But in this effort, Apple has hit something of a roadblock. It continues to maintain its high price points, whether in developed, developing, or underdeveloped economies. There are several reasons to do so, including the effort to maintain its sophisticated, aspirational image. In addition, one analyst estimated that raising the average sale price on an iPhone by $10 would increase Apple's profit by $723 million, even if it never added another customer (but retained all its current ones).[4]

Still, if the goal is global dominance, Apple's price points might put it at a disadvantage. There are many competitors seeking the same consumers, and in 2016, its sales in China dropped a substantial 16 percent as people jumped ship and adopted Android phone models. These data are especially remarkable considering that in just 2015, many observers were arguing that Apple's brilliant entry strategy for China—in which it partnered with a national mobile network and thus gained immediate access to 760 million subscribers—would be the key to its persistent and consistent success.[5]

Perhaps it can learn from its experience in its efforts to enter India, though. For example, it has opened around 100 stores throughout India, using a franchise model that can rely on the Apple brand but still provide local expertise. It also has started discussions with government officials to open manufacturing plants in the nation, which would enable it to avoid some duties on products that thus far have had to be imported into the country.[6] It is pursuing a similar deal in Indonesia, where it invested $44 million to create a research and development center that it hopes will lead the government to allow it to sell there.[7]

Still, the challenges remain. Designing promotions and pricing structures so that they can span the globe and appeal to consumers in various nations continues to vex companies like Apple, which also have no choice but to pursue those consumers in global markets.

Increasing globalization affects not only massive U.S. corporations that actively search out new markets but also small- and medium-sized businesses that increasingly depend on goods produced globally to deliver their products and services. Few people think about how globalization affects their daily lives, but take a minute to read the labels on the clothing you are wearing right now. Chances are that most of the items, even if they carry U.S. brand names, were manufactured in another part of the world.

In the United States, the market has evolved from a system of regional marketplaces to national markets to geographically regional markets (e.g., Canada and the United States together) to international markets and finally to global markets. **Globalization** refers to the processes by which goods, services, capital, people, information, and ideas flow across national borders. Global markets are the result of several fundamental changes such as reductions or eliminations of trade barriers by country governments, the decreasing concerns of distance and time with regard to moving products and ideas across countries, the standardization of laws across borders, and globally integrated production processes.[8]

Each of these fundamental changes has paved the way for marketing to flourish in other countries. The elimination of trade barriers and other governmental actions, for instance, allows goods and ideas to move quickly and efficiently around the world, which in turn facilitates the quick delivery of goods to better meet the needs of global consumers.

These replicas of Shanghai, China, buildings are made completely out of LEGOs. How do LEGOs get from their manufacturer in Denmark to toy stores in China?

©VCG via Getty Images

As a consequence, consumers have easy access to global products and services. When we walk into a toy store, we expect to find LEGO brand toys from Denmark. In the local sporting goods store we anticipate finding running shoes made in China by the German firm adidas. In the grocery store, we demand out-of-season produce such as blueberries from Chile in January. Or consider how a $12 digital camera for your keychain, made in Taiwan, could be produced, transported halfway around the world, and sold for so little money at your local Target. These are the questions we will be examining in this chapter.

We begin by looking at how firms assess the potential of a given market, with particular attention to the BRIC countries (Brazil, Russia, India, and China). Next we examine how firms make decisions to go global and choose how and what they will sell globally. Then we explore how to build the marketing mix for global products.

ASSESSING GLOBAL MARKETS

LO8-1 Describe the components of a country market assessment.

Because of globalization, marketers are presented with a variety of opportunities, which means that firms must assess the viability of various potential market entries. As illustrated in Exhibit 8.1, we examine four sets of criteria necessary to assess a country's market: economic analysis, infrastructure and technological analysis, governmental actions or inactions, and sociocultural analysis. Information about these four areas offers marketers a more complete picture of a country's potential as a market for products and services.

EXHIBIT 8.1   Components of a Country Market Assessment

- General economic environment
- Market size and population growth
- Real income

- Transportation
- Channels
- Communication
- Commerce

Economic analysis using metrics

Infrastructure and technology

Sociocultural analysis

Governmental actions

- Power distance
- Uncertainty avoidance
- Individualism
- Masculinity
- Time orientation

- Tariff
- Quota
- Exchange control
- Trade agreement

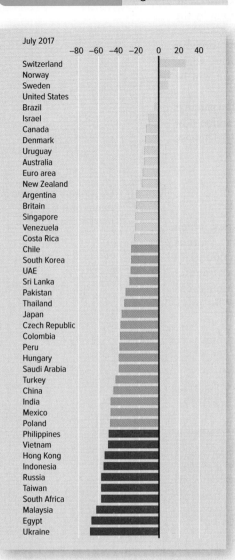

Source: The Economist, "The Big Mac Index," July 13, 2017,
www.economist.com/content/big-mac-index.

Economic Analysis Using Metrics

The greater the wealth of people in a country, generally, the better the opportunity a firm will have in that particular country. A firm conducting an economic analysis of a country market must look at three major economic factors using well-established metrics: the general economic environment, the market size and population growth rate, and real income.

Evaluating the General Economic Environment

In general, healthy economies provide better opportunities for global marketing expansions, and there are several ways a firm can use metrics to measure the relative health of a particular country's economy. Each way offers a slightly different view, and some may be more useful for some products and services than for others.

To determine the market potential for its particular product or service, a firm should use as many metrics as it can obtain. One metric is the relative level of imports and exports. The United States, for example, suffers a trade deficit, which means that the country imports more goods than it exports.[9] For U.S. marketers this deficit can signal the potential for greater competition at home from foreign producers. Firms would prefer to manufacture in a country that has a trade surplus, or a higher level of exports than imports, because it signals a greater opportunity to export products to more markets.

The most common way to gauge the size and market potential of an economy, and therefore the potential the country has for global marketing, is to use standardized metrics of output. Gross domestic product (GDP), the most widely used of these metrics, is defined as the market value of the goods and services produced by a country in a year. Gross national income (GNI) consists of GDP plus the net income earned from investments abroad (minus any payments made to nonresidents who contribute to the domestic economy).[10] In other words, U.S. firms that invest or maintain operations abroad count their income from those operations in the GNI but not the GDP.

Another frequently used metric of an overall economy is the purchasing power parity (PPP), a theory that states that if the exchange rates of two countries are in equilibrium, a product purchased in one will cost the same in the other, if expressed in the same currency.[11] A novel metric that employs PPP to assess the relative economic buying power among nations is *The Economist*'s Big Mac Index, which suggests that exchange rates should adjust to equalize the cost of a basket of goods and services, wherever it is bought around the world. Using McDonald's Big Mac as the market basket, Exhibit 8.2 shows that the cheapest burger is in Ukraine, where it costs $1.70, compared with an average American price of $5.30. In Switerland, the same burger costs $6.74. This index thus implies that the Ukrainian hryvnia is 68 percent undervalued, whereas the Swedish krona is about 27.2 percent overvalued, in comparison with the U.S. dollar.[12]

These various metrics help marketers understand the relative wealth of a particular country, though they may not give a full picture of the economic health of a country because they are based solely on material output. Nor is a weak dollar always a bad thing. For U.S. exporters, a weak dollar means greater demand for their products in foreign countries because they can sell at a lower price. Although an understanding of the macroeconomic environment is crucial for managers facing a market entry decision, of equal importance is the understanding of economic metrics of market size and population growth rate.

Evaluating Market Size and Population Growth Rate

The global population has been growing dramatically since the turn of the 20th century. But from a marketing perspective, this growth has never been equally dispersed. Today, many less developed nations by and large are experiencing rapid population growth, while many developed countries are experiencing either zero or negative population growth. The countries with the highest purchasing power today may become less attractive in the future for many products and services because of stagnated growth. And the BRIC countries are likely to be the source of most market growth.

In response, consumer goods companies are paying close attention to the strong demand in BRIC nations. Procter & Gamble (P&G), which enjoyed a strong early advantage in the Chinese market, is looking to gain more market share by offering more premium products.[13] P&G also is expanding aggressively into India and Brazil. In Brazil, P&G's hair care products have gained more market share than any other global competitor.[14] In India, big-name Western firms are competing for market share of laundry products.[15]

Another aspect related to market size and population growth pertains to the distribution of the population within a particular region: Is the population located primarily in rural or urban areas? This distinction determines where and how products and services can be delivered. Long supply chains, in which goods pass through many hands, are often necessary to reach rural populations in less developed countries and therefore add to the products' cost. India's 1.2 billion people live overwhelmingly in rural areas, although the population is moving toward urban areas to meet the demands of the growing industrial and service centers located in major cities such as Bangalore and New Delhi. This population shift, perhaps not surprisingly, is accompanied by rapid growth in the middle class. Furthermore, relatively careful banking policies and minimal dependence on exports have helped protect India from the global financial crisis. The business impacts of these combined trends of increasing urbanization, a growing middle class, a degree of protectionism by the central government, and a youthful populace make India an absolutely enormous market for consumer goods.

To increase consumption of Coca-Cola in rural India, the company lowered its price to the equivalent of about 40 cents per bottle.
©Rob Elliot/AFP/Getty Images

Evaluating Real Income Firms can make adjustments to an existing product or change the price to meet the unique needs of a particular country market. Such shifts are particularly common for low-priced consumer goods. In settings in which consumers earn very low wages, the market is known as the bottom of the pyramid. That is, there is a large, impoverished population that still wants and needs consumer goods but cannot pay the prices that the fewer, wealthier consumers in developed nations can. To increase consumption of Coca-Cola in rural India, the company lowered its price to the equivalent of about 40 cents per bottle.[16] Textbook publishers sell paperback versions of U.S. books for a fraction of their U.S. price to countries where students would not otherwise be able to afford a textbook.

But pricing adjustments aren't only for inexpensive products. Fashion and jewelry manufacturers also make downward adjustments to their prices in countries where the incomes of their target markets cannot support higher prices. Nor is price the only factor that companies adjust to appeal to lower-income markets. Haier sells washing machines that also have the capacity to wash vegetables to Chinese consumers who confront limited access to resources such as water and electricity.[17]

For the Chinese market, Haier sells washing machines that can wash both clothes and vegetables.

Courtesy of Haier America

Analyzing Infrastructure and Technological Capabilities

The next component of any market assessment is an infrastructure and technological analysis. Infrastructure is defined as the basic facilities, services, and installations needed for a community or society to function, such as transportation and communications systems, water and power lines, and public institutions such as schools, post offices, and prisons.

Marketers are especially concerned with four key elements of a country's infrastructure: transportation, distribution channels, communications, and commerce. First, there must be a system to transport goods throughout the various markets and to consumers in geographically dispersed marketplaces—trains, roads, refrigeration. Second, distribution channels must exist to deliver products in a timely manner and at a reasonable cost. Third, the communications system, particularly media access, must be sufficiently developed to allow consumers to find information about the products and services available in the marketplace. Fourth, the commercial infrastructure, which consists of the legal, banking, and regulatory systems, allows markets to function. In the next section, we focus on how issues pertaining to the political and legal structures of a country can affect the risk that marketers face in operating in a given country.

Analyzing Governmental Actions

Governmental actions, as well as the actions of nongovernmental political groups, can significantly influence firms' ability to sell goods and services because they often result in laws or other regulations that either promote the growth of the global market or close off the country and inhibit growth.

Tariffs A tariff, also called a duty, is a tax levied on a good imported into a country. In most cases, tariffs are intended to make imported goods more expensive and thus less competitive with domestic products, which in turn protects domestic industries from foreign competition. In other cases, tariffs might be imposed to penalize another country for trade practices that the home country views as unfair.[18] When tariffs are reduced, it is meant to bolster foreign trade. For example, in 2017 many U.S. companies announced new deals with China totaling $250 billion. Later that year China cut tariffs on U.S. consumer goods and medicine by almost 10 percent, indicating China wanted to open up its markets more to American companies.[19]

Quotas A quota designates a minimum or maximum quantity of a product that may be brought into a country during a specified time period. China, for instance, had a plan to allow at least 2.285 million barrels per day of crude oil from independent refineries to be imported (the quota) without a tariff, increasing the profitability of smaller independent companies.[20] It will then monitor consumption closely to protect domestic refineries. If demand exceeds supply, it increases the quota, but the level depends on annual consumption and production rates.[21]

Tariffs and quotas can have fundamental and potentially devastating impacts on a firm's ability to sell products in another country—a lesson that the United Kingdom is discovering in the aftermath of its Brexit vote, as Adding Value 8.1 explains. Tariffs artificially raise prices and therefore lower demand, and quotas reduce the availability of imported merchandise. Conversely, tariffs and quotas benefit domestically made products because they reduce foreign competition.

In the past, Chinese customers seeking luxury goods, such as Chanel, would fly to Europe to shop because the prices were lower there. But Chanel is raising its retail prices in Europe while cutting them in China to encourage its Chinese customers to buy at home, like at this Chanel store in Shanghai.

©VCG via Getty Images

Exchange Control Exchange control refers to the regulation of a country's currency exchange rate, the measure of how

Adding Value 8.1 The Spin Cycle of International Currency: Whirlpool Raises Appliance Prices in Foreign Markets[i]

The washers, dryers, dishwashers, and other appliances that Whirlpool sells around the world also are produced in worldwide factories. For example, the appliances it sells in the United Kingdom are manufactured in other European nations, largely to take advantage of the geographic proximity and the lack of trade tariffs associated with exporting to another member of the European Union. Except that following the "Brexit" vote, England is no longer part of the European Union, which means that the favorable trade agreements no longer hold. To make up the difference, Whirlpool plans to increase the prices it charges to its British customers.

But Brexit is not the sole reason for the price change. The company had planned to raise prices even before the referendum because the British pound, similar to the Russian ruble, already had been plummeting. These weak currencies make it harder for the manufacturer to earn the necessary profits; the changing value of the currencies is essentially equivalent to an increase in costs for manufacturers.

For example, in Russia, Whirlpool already manufactures appliances within the country, so it can avoid tariff concerns. But the weak ruble means that it earns less on each product it sells. In response, it claims it has no option but to raise prices to offset these losses.

Initial evidence suggests that it is justified; in the first quarter after the effects of the Brexit vote became manifest, Whirlpool reported that its earnings in the United Kingdom fell by approximately $40 million. In the same period, sales volumes in Europe, Africa, and the Middle East dropped by 6.7 percent.

Along with its price increases, Whirlpool has sought to lower its operating costs, including restructuring some of its European manufacturing facilities to cut about 500 jobs. It also is working to increase its sales in other markets, like the United States, where it does not face currency challenges. But in a global market, it needs sales in every country to produce at least some profits, so it continues to make tough choices.

much one currency is worth in relation to another.[22] A designated agency in each country, often the central bank, sets the rules for currency exchange. In the United States, the Federal Reserve sets the currency exchange rates. In recent years the value of the U.S. dollar has changed significantly compared with other important world currencies. When the dollar falls, it has a twofold effect on U.S. firms' ability to conduct global business. For firms that depend on imports of finished products, raw materials that they fabricate into other products, or services from other countries, the cost of doing business goes up dramatically, as Social & Mobile Marketing 8.1 describes in Nigeria. At the same time, buyers in other countries find the costs of U.S. goods and services to be much lower than they were before.

Prices are nearly always lower in the country of origin because there are no customs or import duties to pay, and international transportation expenses are less than domestic ones. For many products, the price difference might not be significant. But for luxury items that cost thousands of euros (or tens of thousands of Chinese yuan), buying overseas thus has long been a habit for consumers. As the euro dropped, international shopping excursions have become especially appealing for consumers from China, where the yuan remains strong. As a result, for Chinese shoppers seeking Italian designer clothing or French handbags, it literally is worth the cost of flying to Milan and Paris and buying the items there rather than shopping in Shanghai. But that's not what the luxury fashion houses want, so they are revising their pricing schemes. Chanel announced it would raise its retail prices in Europe but cut them in China, in an attempt to level the playing field, so that the same handbag would cost approximately the same amount wherever people buy it.[23] As economies and currencies continue their constant rising and falling relative to one another, marketers must keep revising their pricing strategies to reflect the current international conditions.

Trade Agreements Marketers must consider the trade agreements to which a particular country is a signatory or the trading bloc to which it belongs. A trade agreement is an intergovernmental agreement designed to manage and promote trade activities for a specific region, and a trading bloc consists of those countries that have signed the particular trade agreement.[24] Together, the following major trade agreements cover two-thirds of the world's international trade: the European Union (EU), the North American Free Trade Agreement

Social & Mobile Marketing 8.1

Can a Hashtag Save a National Currency? Using Twitter to Help Nigeria[ii]

When oil prices fell, the nation of Nigeria—the largest oil producer in Africa—suffered a massive blow to its economy. Even as it was losing revenue, its currency dropped precipitously in value, and its national stock markets plummeted. Such developments would be disastrous anywhere, but they are particularly painful in Nigeria, where consumers express deep-seated preferences for imported products, including not only Japanese cars and Italian handbags but also most of the vegetables and produce that they eat.

In response to the crisis, a new social media campaign encourages people to seek out and buy more local products. With a government-sponsored hashtag, #BuyNaijaToGrowTheNaira, it aims to increase people's sense of patriotism and thereby lead them to buy local items, which in turn should prompt growth in local trade and manufacturing, with benefits for the entire economy.

In response to lower currency values, a Nigerian social media campaign encourages people to purchase locally made items like these dresses.
©Pius Utomi Ekpei/AFP/Getty Images

Along with the social media campaign on Twitter, legislators have passed regulations that require government agencies to search for local providers before considering purchases from international sellers. With this rule in place, some manufacturers have a nearly guaranteed market for their products.

But the biggest stumbling block to this plan might not be the level of demand; it might have to do with the supply. Nigeria's manufacturing sector is relatively weak, such that businesses claim they cannot simply buy the items they need from local providers, whether those needs involve security systems and technology or coffee and tea. This paradox is evident even in Nigeria's biggest source of revenue: It produces more oil than any other African nation, and yet it still imports a majority of the oil it uses from elsewhere.

In this sense, virtual reality runs hard up against the actual reality. People can retweet the hashtag innumerable times, but unless there is action to back up the viral campaign, nothing can change.

(NAFTA), Central America Free Trade Agreement (CAFTA), Mercosur, and the Association of Southeast Asian Nations (ASEAN).[25] These trade agreements are summarized in Exhibit 8.3. The EU represents the highest level of integration across individual nations; the other agreements vary in their integration levels.

EXHIBIT 8.3   Trade Agreements

Name	Countries
European Union	There are 28 member countries of the EU: Austria, Belgium, Bulgaria, Croatia, Cyprus, Czech Republic, Denmark, Estonia, Finland, France, Germany, Greece, Hungary, Ireland, Italy, Latvia, Lithuania, Luxembourg, Malta, Netherlands, Poland, Portugal, Romania, Slovakia, Slovenia, Spain, Sweden, and the United Kingdom. There are five official candidate countries to join the EU: Macedonia, Serbia, Turkey, Montenegro, and Albania. Bosnia and Herzegovina and Kosovo are also potential candidates.
NAFTA	United States, Canada, and Mexico.
CAFTA	United States, Costa Rica, the Dominican Republic, El Salvador, Guatemala, Honduras, and Nicaragua.
Mercosur	Full members: Argentina, Brazil, Paraguay, Uruguay, and Venezuela.
ASEAN	Brunei Darussalam, Cambodia, Indonesia, Laos, Malaysia, Myanmar, Philippines, Singapore, Thailand, and Vietnam.

Source: Information about EU members is from http://europa.eu/about-eu/countries/./index_en.htm.

Adding Value 8.2   Can Starbucks Give Italy's Espresso Culture a Jolt?[iii]

The 74th country in which Starbucks will open shops is also the first place that anyone ever had the idea for Starbucks. As the chain's well-known origin story has noted, Howard Schultz loved the espresso culture in Italy and sought to bring it to the United States. But the version of this culture and experience that has made Starbucks into a global juggernaut is quite different from the traditional version of espresso consumption in Italy, raising questions about just how successful this specific international expansion will be.

In particular, in Italy, an espresso break means heading over to a small bar, where consumers receive small cups, with saucers, of the strong coffee, consumed quickly while standing up. They might chat for a few moments about the weather, the football league, or politics, but after a few minutes, the bar owner will shoo them out the door to make room for the next consumers.

The experience at Starbucks is totally different of course, and for some traditionalists, the expectation that Italians would linger over sweetened drinks with made-up names, served in paper cups, is not just absurd but also a little horrifying. Paper cups!

However, some evidence suggests that there is room for both traditional bars and third space venues like Starbucks. Arnold Coffee is a four-store chain that has adopted the Starbucks model, offering free Wi-Fi, bagels and brownies, and cinnamon caffè lattes. Even its motto highlights its distinction, laying claim to offering "The American Coffee Experience." Especially for younger consumers, as one student explained, "The experience at the traditional Italian bar, downing an espresso in two seconds, isn't what I'm looking for. I need a place like this to study or meet friends or just relax."

That is precisely what Starbucks offers, so the company expresses confidence in the expansion. At the same time, it is making some nods to local preferences. Starting in its first Milan store, Starbucks will emphasize espresso more than it does in other international locations, where coffee drinkers prefer something a little lighter. It also will rely on local farmers to source milk and some of its food options. In terms of

How ironic! Starbucks borrowed heavily from the Italian coffee experience and "Americanized" it to be successful in the United States and elsewhere in the world. Now it is opening its American version of the Italian coffee experience back in Italy. Will it work? Arnold Coffee thinks so. Arnold already offers "The American Coffee Experience" in its Italian stores.
©Alessia Pierdomenico/Getty Images

expansion, Starbucks is opening several stores with an Italian licensee, and a Roastery, which is one of its larger, higher-end stores where customers can see the entire coffee-making process from roasting to brewing. It seems like only a matter of time before the mermaid logo will appear on corners of cities throughout Italy, next to the espresso bars that line the streets today.

Analyzing Sociocultural Factors

Understanding another country's culture is crucial to the success of any global marketing initiative. Culture, or the shared meanings, beliefs, morals, values, and customs of a group of people, exists on two levels: visible artifacts (e.g., behavior, dress, symbols, physical settings, ceremonies) and underlying values (thought processes, beliefs, and assumptions).[26] Visible artifacts are easy to recognize, but businesses often find it more difficult to understand the underlying values of a culture and appropriately adapt their marketing strategies to them, a challenge that Starbucks is taking very seriously in its effort to penetrate the Italian espresso market (see Adding Value 8.2).[27]

For example, though the opening of China's market to foreign brands has been a boon, it also represents a very risky proposition for firms that forget to take their international expansion seriously enough. And, when Porsche filmed an advertisement in which its vehicles ran over the Great Wall of China, Chinese consumers were left more confused than intrigued. The ancient site had little in common with Porsche's own storied history. It also had little to do with Uncle Ben's rice or FedEx, but that did not stop those brands from

Entering the Chinese market can be difficult. This Porsche ad left more Chinese consumers confused than intrigued because the Great Wall of China has little in common with Porsche.
Source: Porsche AG

featuring the Great Wall in their advertising either. By the same token, hiring Western spokespeople who are unfamiliar to Chinese audiences to introduce a brand offers few benefits. Marks & Spencer paid substantial sums to hire Oscar winner Emma Thompson to appear in Chinese advertisements, but because few Chinese consumers knew who she was, those investments were likely wasted.[28]

To address or avoid such issues, one important cultural classification scheme that firms can use is Geert Hofstede's cultural dimensions concept, which sheds more light on these underlying values. Hofstede initially proposed that cultures differed on four dimensions, but he has added two more dimensions in recent years.[29] Despite some arguments for using other models,[30] Hofstede's cultural dimensions offer a foundation for most research into culture:

1. **Power distance:** willingness to accept social inequality as natural.

2. **Uncertainty avoidance:** the extent to which the society relies on orderliness, consistency, structure, and formalized procedures to address situations that arise in daily life.

3. **Individualism:** perceived obligation to and dependence on groups.

4. **Masculinity:** the extent to which dominant values are male oriented. A lower masculinity ranking indicates that men and women are treated equally in all aspects of society; a higher masculinity ranking suggests that men dominate in positions of power.

5. **Time orientation:** short- versus long-term orientation. A country that tends to have a long-term orientation values long-term commitments and is willing to accept a longer time horizon for, say, the success of a new product introduction.

6. **Indulgence:** the extent to which society allows for the gratification of fun and enjoyment needs or else suppresses and regulates such pursuits.[31]

To illustrate two of the six dimensions, consider the data and graph in Exhibit 8.4. Power distance is on the vertical axis and individualism is on the horizontal axis. Several Latin American countries, including Brazil, cluster high on power distance but low on individualism; the United States, Australia, Canada, and the United Kingdom, in contrast, cluster high on individualism but low on power distance. Using this information, firms should expect that if they design a marketing campaign that stresses equality and individualism, it will be well accepted in English-speaking countries, all other factors being equal, but not be as well received in Latin American countries.

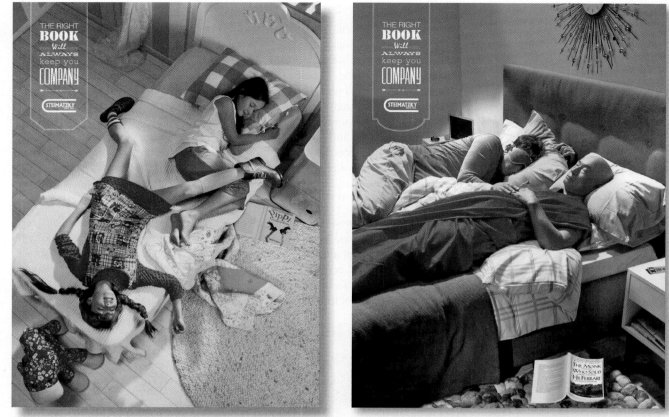

Ads from Steimatzky, the oldest and largest bookstore chain in Israel, illustrate marketing along one of Hofstede's cultural dimensions: one is highly feminine (left) and the other masculine (right).

Source: Agency: ACW Grey Tel-Aviv, Israel; Production Company: We Do Production; Photographer: Shai Yehezkelli.

Another means of classifying cultures distinguishes them according to the importance of verbal communication.[32] In the United States and most European countries, business relationships are governed by what is said and written down, often through formal contracts. In countries such as China and South Korea, however, most relationships rely on nonverbal cues, so that the situation or context means much more than mere words. For instance, business relationships in China often are formalized by just a handshake, and trust and honor are often more important than legal arrangements.

Overall, culture affects every aspect of consumer behavior: why people buy; who is in charge of buying decisions; and how, when, and where people shop. After marketing managers have completed the four parts of the market assessment, they are better able to make informed decisions about whether a particular country possesses the necessary characteristics to be considered a potential market for the firm's products and services. In the next section, we assess the market potential in the BRIC countries.

EXHIBIT 8.4 **Country Clusters**

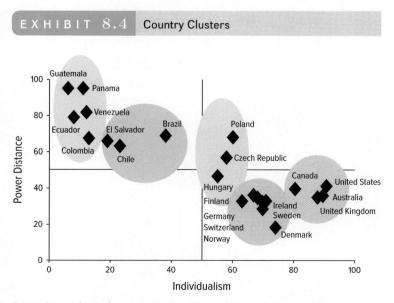

Source: Geert Hofstede, Gert Jan Hofstede, and Michael Minkov, *Cultures and Organizations, Software of the Mind*, Third Revised Edition, McGraw-Hill 2010, ISBN: 0-07-166418-1. ©Geert Hofstede B.V. quoted with permission.

LO8-2 Understand the marketing opportunities in BRIC countries.

The Appeal of the BRIC Countries

Changes in technology, especially communications, have been a driving force for growth in global markets for decades. The telegraph, radio, television, computers, and the Internet have increasingly connected distant parts of the world. Today, communication is instantaneous. Sounds and images from across the globe are delivered to televisions, radios, and computers in real time, which enables receivers in all parts of the world to observe how others live, work, and play.

Perhaps the greatest change facing the global community in recent years has been the growth and expansion of four countries that together have come to be known as the BRIC countries: Brazil, Russia, India, and China. Some commentators suggest adding South Africa, to make BRICS, because of that nation's remarkable transformation into a functioning democracy.[33] The inspiring changes to South Africa suggest its increasing promise as a market, but its relatively smaller size leads us to focus on the four BRIC nations, which seem to have the greatest potential for growth. Let's examine each in turn.

Brazil[34] Long a regional powerhouse, Brazil's ability to weather, and even thrive during, economic storms has transformed it into a global contender. Currently, Brazil is the world's eighth largest economy.[35] Although a recent recession caused the country to have a negative growth rate in 2016, there was a 0.2 percent growth rate in 2017 and it is expected to continue to grow slowly in 2018.[36] Still, Brazil's impressive economic growth in the 21st century largely can be attributed to the expansion of its literate population and the impositions of social programs that have allowed more than half of the 201 million Brazilians to enter the middle class.[37] This large South American democracy also welcomes foreign investors both politically and economically.

Russia[38] The relations between the United States and Russia are a little more complicated than for Brazil. Since the fall of the former Soviet Union, Russia has undergone multiple upturns and downturns in its economy. However, its overall growth prospects appear promising, especially as a consumer market. Long denied access to consumer goods, the well-educated population of 143 million exhibits strong demand for U.S. products and brands. In particular, the number of Russian Internet users, presently at 83 million,[39] is growing at a rate of approximately 10 percent annually,[40] and is already Europe's largest Internet market.[41] The country became part of the World Trade Organization (WTO) in 2012 to improve trade relations with other countries.[42] In 2015 it ranked as one of the top countries in terms of retail growth; even though economic and political issues challenge its retail growth prospects, the market simply is too big for most firms to disregard.[43] Yet Russia still faces an aging population and low birthrates. If these trends persist, Russia's population could decline by one-third in the next half century. At the same time, corruption is widespread, creating ethical dilemmas for firms trying to market their goods and services. Furthermore, international sanctions on Russia, in response to its occupation of Ukraine and its involvement in the Middle East, and fluctuations in oil prices threaten the country with a financial crisis.[44]

Like other countries in which McDonald's thrives, Brazil has a strong and growing middle class.

©Bloomberg/Getty Images

In which of the BRIC countries does each of these classic structures reside?

©Steve Allen/Getty Images

©McGraw-Hill Education/Barry Barker, photographer

©Travelif/iStock Exclusive/Getty Images

©Martin Child/Getty Images

India[45] With more than 1.2 billion people, or approximately 15 percent of the world's population, together with expanding middle and upper classes, India is one of the world's fastest-growing markets. India also has one of the youngest populations in the world, with a median age of 27.9 years.[46] Its young inhabitants increasingly are adopting global attitudes while living in growing urban centers and shopping at large malls. The well-educated, modern generation is largely fluent in English, and the highly skilled workforce holds great attraction for firms that hope to expand using local talent, especially in technical fields.

India's retail environment is still dominated by millions of small stores and lacks modern supply chain management facilities and systems.[47] Recent changes by the Indian government, however, have the potential to significantly modernize the retail landscape. For example, foreign retailers that carry multiple brands, such as Walmart, are now allowed to own up to 51 percent of joint ventures in India, and retailers that carry only their own brand, such as adidas and

Recent changes in India have the potential to modernize the retail landscape. adidas, for example can now own 100 percent of its Indian business.

©Brent Lewin/Bloomberg via Getty Images

Reebok, can now own 100 percent of their Indian businesses, prompting brands such as Skechers to plan on opening 400–500 more outlets in India in the next five years.[48] India is also projected to become the fastest-growing e-commerce market in the world, with e-commerce sales forecasted to reach $120 billion by 2020.[49]

China[50]

For most of the 20th century, China experienced foreign occupation, civil unrest, major famine, and a strict one-party Communist regime. However, since 1978, China's leadership, while maintaining communist political ideals, has embraced market-oriented economic development, which has led to startlingly rapid gains. For many Chinese, recent developments have dramatically improved their living standards and their levels of personal freedom. Increasing liberalization in the economy has prompted a large improvement in China's Global Retail Development Index (GRDI); it enjoyed the greatest retail growth in 2014. Even as growth in its gross domestic product has slowed, China maintains a thriving retail market, likely to reach the $8 trillion mark soon and surpass the United States as the world's largest.[51]

Yet the country continues to suffer from drastically unequal economic distribution, which has led to a significant migrant workforce that subsists on part-time, low-paying jobs. These workers were hit hard by the global financial crisis, which reduced demand for Chinese exports for the first time in years. Government regulations limiting families to one child have negatively impacted the Chinese population. As a result, growth of the 1.4 billion-strong Chinese population has slowed and is therefore aging, but the median age is still slightly younger than in the United States, which is at 37.4 years old. Although the Chinese government has amended the policy to allow for two children per family, these trends will impact how products and services are purchased for many years.[52]

In the next section, we detail the market entry decision process, beginning with a discussion of the various ways firms might enter a new global market.

China's population has been aging as a result of its one-child policy, and will likely continue to do so for many years, even though the government has recently rescinded the policy and will now allow two children per couple.

©Tang Ming Tung/Getty Images

CHOOSING A GLOBAL ENTRY STRATEGY

LO8-3 Identify the various market entry strategies.

When a firm has concluded its assessment analysis of the most viable markets for its products and services, it must then conduct an internal assessment of its capabilities. As we discussed in Chapter 2, this analysis includes an assessment of the firm's access to capital, the current markets it serves, its manufacturing capacity, its proprietary assets, and the commitment of its management to the proposed strategy. These factors ultimately contribute to the success or failure of a market expansion strategy, whether at home or in a foreign market. After these internal market assessments, it is time for the firm to choose its entry strategy.

A firm can choose from many approaches when it decides to enter a new market, which vary according to the level of risk the firm is willing to take. Many firms actually follow a progression in which they begin with less risky strategies to enter their first foreign markets and move to increasingly risky strategies as they gain confidence in their abilities and more control over their operations, as illustrated in Exhibit 8.5. We examine these different approaches that marketers take when entering global markets, beginning with the least risky.

EXHIBIT 8.5 Global Entry Strategies

Control

- Direct investment
- Joint venture
- Strategic alliance
- Franchising
- Exporting

Risk

Exporting

Exporting means producing goods in one country and selling them in another. This entry strategy requires the least financial risk but also allows for only a limited return to the exporting firm. Global expansion often begins when a firm receives an order for its product or service from another country, in which case it faces little risk because it has no investment in people, capital equipment, buildings, or infrastructure. By the same token, it is difficult to achieve economies of scale when everything has to be shipped internationally. The Swiss watchmaker Rolex sells relatively small numbers of expensive watches all over the world. Because its transportation costs are relatively small compared with the cost of the watches, the best way for it to service any market is to export from Switzerland.

Franchising

Franchising is a contractual agreement between a firm, the **franchisor**, and another firm or individual, the **franchisee**. A franchising contract allows the franchisee to operate a business—a

Rolex exports its watches to countries all over the world from its factory in Switzerland.

©Jeafish Ping/Shutterstock

KFC and Pizza Hut are successful global franchisors.
(Left): ©Yang zheng/AP Images; (right): ©Zhou junxiang/AP Images

retail product or service firm or a B2B provider—using the name and business format developed and supported by the franchisor. Many of the best-known retailers in the United States are also successful global franchisors, including McDonald's, Pizza Hut, Starbucks, Domino's Pizza, KFC, and Holiday Inn, all of which have found that global franchising entails lower risks and requires less investment than does opening units owned wholly by the firm. However, when it engages in franchising, the firm has limited control over the market operations in the foreign country, its potential profit is reduced because it must be split with the franchisee, and, once the franchise is established, there is always the threat that the franchisee will break away and operate as a competitor under a different name.

Strategic Alliance

Strategic alliances refer to collaborative relationships between independent firms, though the partnering firms do not create an equity partnership; that is, they do not invest in one another. For example, the music streaming service Spotify, with headquarters in Sweden, and the ride-sharing app Uber, with headquarters in San Francisco, have a strategic alliance, which allows Uber customers to use Spotify to control the music during their ride, although each company still operates independently. In fact, Uber has alliances with other music services, such as Pandora. Because not all Uber drivers have Spotify and not all Spotify listeners use Uber, this alliance allows each company to reach new potential customers.[53]

Joint Venture

A **joint venture** is formed when a firm entering a market pools its resources with those of a local firm. As a consequence, ownership, control, and profits are shared. In addition to sharing financial burdens, a local partner offers the foreign entrant greater understanding of the market and access to resources such as vendors and real estate.

Some countries require joint ownership of firms entering their domestic markets, as is the case with the new regulations affecting multi-line retailers entering India, though many of these restrictions have loosened as a result of WTO negotiations and ever-increasing globalization pressures. Problems with this entry approach can arise when the partners disagree or if the government places restrictions on the firm's ability to move its profits out of the foreign country and back to its home country.

Spotify and the ride sharing app Uber have a strategic alliance that allows Uber customers to use Spotify to control the music during their ride.

(Left): ©tanuha2001/Shutterstock; (right): ©Emmanuel Dunand/AFP/Getty Images

Direct Investment

Direct investment requires a firm to maintain 100 percent ownership of its plants, operation facilities, and offices in a foreign country, often through the formation of wholly owned subsidiaries. This entry strategy requires the highest level of investment and exposes the firm to significant risks, including the loss of its operating and/or initial investments. A dramatic economic downturn caused by a natural disaster, war, political instability, or changes in the country's laws can increase a foreign entrant's risk considerably. Many firms believe that in certain markets, these potential risks are outweighed by the high potential returns. With this strategy, none of the potential profits must be shared with other firms. In addition to the high potential returns, direct investment offers the firm complete control over its operations in the foreign country.

Although we often tend to think of direct investment flowing from more to less developed economies, the dynamic international market means that sometimes it goes the other way. The computer maker Lenovo started in China but has since expanded its operations. In addition to purchasing IBM's PC division and Motorola's handset business unit, it established parallel headquarters in both Beijing and North Carolina.[54]

As we noted, each of these entry strategies entails different levels of risk and rewards for the foreign entrant. But even after a firm has determined how much risk it is willing to take, and therefore how it will enter a new global market, it still must establish its marketing strategy, as we discuss in the next section.

China-based Lenovo purchased U.S.-based IBM's PC division and Motorola's handset business unit, and has parallel headquarters in both Beijing and North Carolina.

Courtesy of Lenovo

PROGRESS CHECK
1. Which entry strategy has the least risk and why?
2. Which entry strategy has the most risk and why?

LO8-4 Highlight the similarities and differences between a domestic marketing strategy and a global marketing strategy.

CHOOSING A GLOBAL MARKETING STRATEGY

Just like any other marketing strategy, a global marketing strategy includes two components: determining the target markets to pursue and developing a marketing mix that will sustain a competitive advantage over time. In this section, we examine marketing strategy as it relates specifically to global markets.

Target Market: Segmentation, Targeting, and Positioning

Global segmentation, targeting, and positioning (STP) are more complicated than domestic STP for several reasons. First, firms considering a global expansion have much more difficulty understanding the cultural nuances of other countries. Second, subcultures within each country also must be considered. Third, consumers often view products and their role as consumers differently in different countries.[55] A product, service, or even a retailer often must be positioned differently in different markets.

Even when an STP strategy appears successful, companies must continually monitor economic and social trends to protect their position within the market and adjust products and marketing strategies to meet the changing needs of global markets. In this sense, global marketing is no different from local or national marketing.

When any firm identifies its positioning within the market, it then must decide how to implement its marketing strategies using the marketing mix. Just as firms adjust their products and services to meet the needs of national target markets, they must alter their marketing mix to serve the needs of global markets.

Global Product or Service Strategies There are three potential global product strategies: (1) sell the same product or service in both the home-country market and the host country,

Campbell's research found that Russians eat a lot of soup, and they want time-saving preparation help. So it developed broths to enable cooks to prepare soups with their own flair.

Source: Campbell Soup Company

referred to as glocalization; (2) sell a product or service similar to that sold in the home country but include minor adaptations; and (3) sell totally new products or services. The strategy a firm chooses depends on the needs of the target market. The level of economic development, as well as differences in product and technical standards, helps determine the need for and level of product adaptation. Cultural differences such as food preferences, language, and religion also play a role in product strategy planning. Respecting such differences is an important ethical choice too, as burger restaurants have learned as they seek ways to access the Indian consumer market, according to Ethical & Societal Dilemma 8.1.

Same Product or Service The most typical method of introducing a product outside the home country is to sell the same product or service in other countries. As discussed in this chapter's opener, when Apple launched the iPhone 6 and 6 Plus, it did not customize them for global consumers, although they were available in 115 countries. This approach has helped Apple establish a strong identity as a brand. No matter where you live,

Ethical & Societal Dilemma 8.1

Burger Wars in India: Fast-Food Chains Are Finding Creative Ways to Enter a No-Beef Market[iv]

In the Hindu religion, the predominant belief system in India, cows are sacred, and eating beef is strictly forbidden. This foundational belief may make it seem as if hamburger joints would never be able to gain a foothold in India. But the massive growth and potential of the nation's consumer market has proved irresistible, leading the restaurants simply to get a little more creative in their offerings.

Wendy's first Indian store features mutton and veggie burgers, and the buns are sprinkled with local flavors such as turmeric, coriander, and chilies. But the menu is not the only thing that sets the Indian Wendy's apart. Servers bring meals to customers at their tables, on china plates, and the store environment is more like a casual restaurant than a traditional fast-food outpost. The burger chain has two

Fast-food chains like McDonald's adapt to the no-beef culture in India with vegetarian and chicken options.
©Douglas E. Curran/AFP/Getty Images

stores in India so far, but it plans to go "location by location," opening new stores slowly and carefully to ensure their success. Ultimately, the Indian franchise hopes that Wendy's India will be as big as Wendy's USA.

The road to success will not be smooth, though. Wendy's is not the only prominent chain seeking access to Indian consumers. McDonald's entered relatively early and is currently the market leader, but it has not stopped there. It recently announced plans to create burger-type versions of popular Indian dishes such as masala dosa. More recent entries by Burger King, Carl's Jr., Fatburger, and Johnny Rockets have

prompted predictions of a burger war. Not to be left out, even Dunkin' Donuts stores in India serve some type of burger because doughnuts have not proved popular enough.

The flavors and ingredients contained in the versions of burgers offered by the different chains are widely varied. Some rely on chicken offerings, with smoky chipotle flavoring, barbeque bacon additions, or a tandoori-style preparation. Others integrate other types of meat, but some are purely vegetarian. Thus the burger wars feature some notable differentiation across the combatants. Whether any or all of them will emerge victorious remains to be seen.

you have a similar view of the Apple brand. However, although Apple products are universal, the customer service offered in Apple stores is localized to the region, which helps create customer loyalty.[56]

Similar Product or Service with Minor Adaptations Campbell Soup discovered that even though Russia and China are two of the largest markets for soup in the world, cooks in those countries have unique demands. Chinese consumers drink 320 billion bowls of soup each year, and Russian buyers consume 32 billion servings, compared with only 14 billion bowls of soup served in the United States. However, Chinese cooks generally refuse to resort to canned soup; the average Chinese consumer eats soup five times each week, but he or she also takes great pride in preparing it personally with fresh ingredients. In contrast, Russian consumers, though they demand very high quality in their soups, had grown tired of spending hours preparing their homemade broths. To identify opportunities in these markets, Campbell sent teams of social anthropologists to study how Chinese and Russian cooks prepare and consume soup. When it faced further hurdles, it entered into a joint venture with the Swire soup company in China. But its efforts in Russia never panned out, forcing Campbell to withdraw after around four years. That is, even with extensive, devoted efforts by an industry giant, global marketing remains a challenge.[57]

Referred to as glocalization, some firms also standardize their products globally but use different promotional campaigns to sell them. The original Pringles potato chip product remains the same globally, as do the images and themes of the promotional campaign, with limited language adaptations for the local markets, although English is used whenever possible. However, the company does change Pringles' flavors in different countries, including paprika-flavored chips sold in Italy and Germany.[58]

Totally New Product or Service The level of economic development and cultural tastes also affects global product strategy because it relates directly to consumer behavior. For example, although you are likely to know Heinz for its tomato ketchup, as you traveled the globe you would find it sells many unique products in different countries. If you taste the ketchup in the Philippines, you'll be surprised to find it's made with bananas instead of tomatoes (and sold under Heinz's Jufran label). In many East Asian countries, Heinz competes by selling soy sauce. The size of the package varies by country as well. Whereas in the United States big bottles of condiments are sold, in poorer countries, such as Indonesia, condiments such as soy sauce are sold in single-serve packets for a few pennies.[59]

Pringles sometimes changes flavors to reflect local tastes and demand; for example, these paprika-flavored chips are sold in Italy and Germany.

©Whitebox Media/Mediablitzimages/ Alamy Stock Photo

Global Pricing Strategies Determining the selling price in the global marketplace is an extremely difficult task.[60] Many countries still have rules governing the competitive marketplace, including those that affect pricing. In most European countries retailers can't sell below cost, and in others they can't advertise "before" prices if the product hasn't been sold at that price for two weeks. For firms such as Walmart and other discounters, these restrictions threaten their core competitive positioning as the lowest-cost provider in the market. Other issues, such as tariffs, quotas, antidumping laws, and currency exchange policies, can also affect pricing decisions.[61]

Competitive factors influence global pricing in the same way they do home-country pricing, but because a firm's products or services may not have the same positioning in the global marketplace as they do in their home country, market prices must be adjusted to reflect the local pricing structure. Spain's fashion retailer Zara, for instance, is relatively inexpensive in the EU but is priced about 40 percent higher in the United States, putting it right in the middle of its moderately priced competition.[62] Zara is dedicated to keeping production in Spain, but it also must get its fashions to the United States quickly, so it incurs additional transportation expenses, which it passes on to its North American customers. Finally, as we discussed previously in this chapter, currency fluctuations affect global pricing strategies.

Global Distribution Strategies Global distribution networks form complex value chains that involve wholesalers, exporters, importers, and different transportation systems. These additional intermediaries typically add cost and ultimately increase the final selling price of a product. As a result of these cost factors, constant pressure exists to simplify distribution channels wherever possible.

The number of firms with which the seller needs to deal to get its merchandise to the consumer determines the complexity of a channel. In most developing countries, manufacturers must go through many types of distribution channels to get their products to end users, who often lack adequate transportation to shop at central shopping areas or large malls. Therefore, consumers shop near their homes at small, family-owned retail outlets. To reach these small retail outlets, most of which are located far from major rail

Zara is relatively inexpensive in its home country, Spain, but is more expensive in North America because of transportation expenses and currency fluctuations.

©Denis Doyle/Bloomberg via Getty Images

stations or roads, marketers have devised a variety of creative solutions. For example, Tupperware parties offer an acceptable way for women in Indonesia—where the traditional culture discourages women's participation in the workforce—to sell and distribute the plastic food storage containers, benefiting both the firm and these entrepreneurs.[63]

Global Communication Strategies The major challenge in developing a global communication strategy is identifying the elements that need to be adapted to be effective in the global marketplace. For instance, literacy levels vary dramatically across the globe. Consider again the BRIC nations: In India, approximately 71 percent of the adult population is literate, compared with 86 percent in Brazil, more than 90 percent in China, and more than 99 percent in Russia.[64] Media availability also varies widely; some countries offer only state-controlled media. And adver-

Tupperware provides an acceptable way for women in Indonesia to make money, because the traditional culture discourages women's participation in the workforce.

©Lam Yik Fei/The New York Times/Redux Pictures

tising and privacy regulations differ too, leading to some contested choices, as Ethical & Societal Dilemma 8.2 explains.

Differences in language, customs, and culture also complicate marketers' ability to communicate with customers in various countries. Language can be particularly vexing for advertisers. For example, in the United Kingdom a thong is only a sandal, whereas in the United States it can also be an undergarment. To avoid the potential embarrassment that language confusion can cause, firms spend millions of dollars to develop brand names that have no preexisting meaning in any known language, such as Accenture (a management consulting firm) or Avaya (a subsidiary of Lucent Technologies, formerly Bell Labs).

Within many countries there are multiple variants on a language or more than one language. For example, China has three main languages: the written forms produce meaning through the characters used, but the spoken forms depend on tone and pronunciation. Some firms choose names that sound similar to their English-language names, such as Nike, whose Chinese brand name is pronounced *nai-ke*. Others focus on the meanings of the char-

acters, such that Citibank is known as *hui-qi-yinhang*, which means "star-spangled banner bank." Still other firms, such as Mercedes-Benz, have adapted their names for each language: *peng-zee* in Cantonese for Hong Kong, *peng-chi* in Mandarin for Taiwan, and *ben-chi* in Mandarin for mainland China. Naming is a constant challenge in China, especially to avoid the threat that a brand name evokes unwanted connotations, such as when Microsoft realized that the sound of its search engine name, Bing, meant "virus" in China—not the best image for an online company![65]

Even with all these differences, many products and services serve the same needs and wants globally with little or no adaptation in their form or message. Firms with global appeal can run global advertising campaigns and simply translate the wording in the advertisements and product labeling.

Other products require a more localized approach because of cultural and religious differences. In a classic advertisement for Longines watches, a woman's bare arm

Nike's Chinese brand name is pronounced nai-ke, *which is very similar to the English pronunciation, and means "Enduring and Persevering."*

©Shiho Fukada/Redux Pictures

Ethical & Societal Dilemma 8.2   Do European Rights Apply to the Online Universe? Google's Battle with France[v]

The European Union has ruled that its citizens have a basic "right to be forgotten." When they request that search engines remove links associated with searches for their names, the engines are required to do so. For example, if a business executive sought to remove a link between her or his name and a website featuring some embarrassing video of her or his sixth birthday party, search engines would sever that link. The page remains online, but there is no connection between the search for the person's name and that particular page.

The rule has been in place for just a couple of years, and the implications are becoming increasingly clear, but also increasingly contested. In France, the office in charge of privacy regulations has notified Google that, according to its reading of the law, Google must apply the right to be forgotten worldwide, for all European residents, regardless of where the search occurs. Currently, a person in another country, using the Internet to search for a European name, still might access a link to a site that the subject has tried to "forget" in Europe. The French regulators assert that this ability undercuts the EU mandate and holds Google responsible for the violation.

Google contests this reading and is arguing, before France's administrative high court, the Conseil d'État, that applying European law globally represents a violation of international law. It also cautions that allowing the EU to apply its standards worldwide would open the door to other nations that might want to limit search in potentially more troublesome or ethically

Maintaining personal privacy on Google is more complicated in France than in the United States.
©Joel Saget/AFP/Getty Images

questionable ways. Google already has faced difficult questions about how to deal with censorship laws in repressive countries. In its court briefings, it warns that if France can impose its regulations on the Internet globally, then repressive dictatorships could attempt to impose their own standards, to the detriment of transparency and the free flow of information.

France, unsurprisingly, disagrees. Arguing that the right to be forgotten is not censorship—because the pages still remain, even if the links do not—the privacy minister asserts that the goal is to protect citizens, not censor them.

and hand appear, with a watch on her wrist. The advertisement was considered too risqué for Muslim countries, where women's bare arms are never displayed in public, but the company simply changed the advertisement to show a gloved arm and hand wearing the same watch.

Even among English speakers, there can be significant differences in the effectiveness of advertising campaigns. Take the popular "What Happens in Vegas Stays in Vegas" advertising campaign, which has been very successful and spawned numerous copycat slogans in the United States. Essentially, the U.S. mass market thought the provocative campaign pushed the envelope, but just far enough to be entertaining. However, when the Las Vegas tourism group extended its advertising to the United Kingdom, it found that the ad campaign was not nearly as effective. After conducting focus groups, the group found that British consumers did not find the advertisements edgy enough for their more irreverent British tastes. In response, the advertising agency began studying British slang and phrases to find ways to make the campaign even sexier and more provocative.[66]

PROGRESS CHECK

1. What are the components of a global marketing strategy?
2. What are the three global product strategies?

Reviewing Learning Objectives

LO8-1 **Describe the components of a country market assessment.**

First, firms must assess the general economic environment. For instance, countries with a trade surplus, strong domestic and national products, growing populations, and income growth generally are relatively more favorable prospects. Second, firms should assess a country's infrastructure. To be successful in a particular country, the firm must have access to adequate transportation, distribution channels, and communications. Third, firms must determine whether the proposed country has a political and legal environment that favors business. Fourth, firms should be cognizant of the cultural and sociological differences between their home and host countries and adapt to those differences to ensure successful business relationships.

LO8-2 **Understand the marketing opportunities in BRIC countries.**

Technology, particularly in the communication field, has facilitated the growth of global markets. Firms can communicate with their suppliers and customers instantaneously, easily take advantage of production efficiencies in other countries, and bring together parts and finished goods from all over the globe. Four countries that provide tremendous marketing opportunities are the BRIC nations—Brazil, Russia, India, and China. These countries have large populations that are increasingly interested in the latest goods and services.

LO8-3 **Identify the various market entry strategies.**

Firms have several options for entering a new country, each with a different level of risk and involvement. Direct investment is the riskiest but potentially the most lucrative. Firms that engage in a joint venture with other firms already operating in the host country share the risk and obtain knowledge about the market and how to do business there. A strategic alliance is similar to a joint venture, but the relationship is not as formal. A less risky method of entering a new market is franchising, in which, as in domestic franchise agreements, the franchisor allows the franchisee to operate a business using its name and strategy in return for a fee. The least risky method of entering another country is simply exporting.

LO8-4 **Highlight the similarities and differences between a domestic marketing strategy and a global marketing strategy.**

The essence of a global marketing strategy is no different from that of a domestic strategy. The firm starts by identifying its target markets, chooses specific markets to pursue, and crafts a strategy to meet the needs of those markets. However, additional issues make global expansion more problematic. For instance, should the product or service be altered to fit the new market better? Does the firm need to change the way it prices its products in different countries? What is the best way to get the product or service to the new customers? How should the firm publicize its product or service offering in various countries?

Key Terms

- bottom of the pyramid, 237
- direct investment, 249
- duty, 238
- exchange control, 238
- exchange rate, 238
- exporting, 247
- franchisee, 247
- franchising, 247

- franchisor, 247
- globalization, 234
- glocalization, 250
- gross domestic product (GDP), 236
- gross national income (GNI), 236
- infrastructure, 237
- joint venture, 248

- purchasing power parity (PPP), 236
- quota, 238
- strategic alliance, 248
- tariff, 238
- trade agreements, 239
- trade deficit, 236
- trade surplus, 236
- trading bloc, 239

Marketing Digitally

1. For many small businesses, the idea of entering a foreign market is intimidating. The U.S. government and most state governments now offer assistance designed specifically for small-business owners. Visit the website of the Massachusetts Export Center (www.mass.gov/export/) and examine the types of services it provides. Click on the "Export Statistics" link. To what five countries did Massachusetts export the most? Are you surprised?

2. McDonald's operates restaurants around the globe. To see how products vary, visit some of McDonald's international websites (www.mcdonalds.ie, www.mcdonalds.it, and www.mcdonalds.com.mx). Which product differ-ences did you notice? Now, visit McDonald's U.S. website (www.mcdonalds.com) to compare the similarities and differences between the international and U.S.-based websites.

Marketing Applications

1. What is globalization? Why is it important for marketers to understand what globalization entails?

2. Moots is a high-end bicycle manufacturer located in Steamboat Springs, Colorado. Assume the company is considering entering the Brazilian, Chinese, and Indian markets. When conducting its market assessment, what economic factors should Moots consider to make its decision? Which market do you expect will be more lucrative for Moots? Why?

3. Now consider the political, economic, and legal systems of China, India, and Brazil. Explain why you think one country might be more hospitable to Moots than the others.

4. Colgate-Palmolive sells its products in many countries throughout the world. How would you expect its marketing strategy to differ in various countries, compared with that in the United States? Consider various areas across the globe in formulating your answer.

5. How would Colgate-Palmolive vary its marketing strategies for product lines in low-income, emerging markets? Discuss using each of the elements of the marketing mix.

6. What are some examples of companies that use a glocalization strategy?

7. Choose a firm that currently manufactures and sells its products or services only in the United States. Choose and defend a global entry strategy for the firm.

Quiz Yourself

1. What is the most common way to measure the current size and market potential of a country?
   a. Gross domestic product
   b. Gross national income
   c. Purchasing power parity
   d. Trade deficit
   e. Trade surplus

2. Many firms begin global expansion by moving from less risky ventures initially to riskier ventures in later years.

Which of the following global entry strategy progressions would characterize that type of evolution?
   a. Direct investment to strategic alliance
   b. Strategic alliance to exporting
   c. Exporting to strategic alliance
   d. Joint venture to strategic alliance
   e. Direct venture to joint venture

(Answers to these two questions can be found in the Quiz Yourself Answer Key section.)

Chapter Case Study   McGraw Hill Education connect

MCDONALD'S—A GLOBAL GIANT

From the Maharaja Mac in India to the Prosperity Burger prepared especially for Chinese New Year celebrations, McDonald's has built a global fast-food empire under its golden arches. Only 33.5 percent of McDonald's revenue now comes from sales in the United States, and most of its international growth has come from the surging economies of Brazil, Russia, China, and India.[67] A pioneer in overseas franchising, McDonald's has spared no effort in its attempts to penetrate foreign markets. In China, it currently has more than 2,400 stores and is building partnerships with local companies that will help open 1,500 more over the next several years.[68] In Brazil, it created Latin America's first environmentally certified fast-food restaurant. A vast market defined by stark cultural differences, India has required a more modest approach that would allow McDonald's to develop its real estate and supply infrastructure, train the local workforce and management at its famed Hamburger

University, and adjust the menu for vegetarian customers.[69] There are currently 400 McDonald's locations in India; in 2016, it introduced its first Big Mac–branded vegetarian burger, the Veg Maharaja Mac.[70]

But McDonald's growth strategy relies on more than just added locations. In crowded cities, with real estate prices too high to build drive-through restaurants, the company has hired droves of motorbike drivers to bring Big Macs to customers. This nimble delivery approach is now a mainstay in cities from Beijing to Kuwait City. Mobile ordering and payments, for either curbside pickup or table service, also will be available in 20,000 restaurants in the United States and abroad by 2018.[71]

Fast-food restaurants enjoy some segment-specific benefits as they pursue such international expansion. Unlike retail brands, such as Walmart or Carrefour, restaurants pose fewer perceived competitive threats. Local eateries can exist side-by-side with a McDonald's in a way that a mom-and-pop grocer cannot survive if an international hypermarket moves in next door.[72] But even considering the massive growth in rapidly transitioning economies, Europe still generates the bulk of foreign sales for McDonald's. In France, for example, "MacDo" restaurants attract crowds that line up outside for a bite of lunch. But lunch might mean something a little different in this case: French McDonald's offer menus that feature Camembert cheese on the burgers, Heineken, a McBaguette, and macarons for dessert.[73] At one time, the secret to McDonald's success was "lockstep" consistency—namely, that a meal in Memphis tasted the same as it did in Moscow or Madrid. But the novelty of the American hamburger stand has worn off in the new

McDonald's France has its own version of the "I'm lovin' it" slogan.
©Bill Ryall/William Ryall

millennium, as has McDonald's ability to export American culture as its staple commodity. A cheeseburger, fries, and Coke don't register the same level of excitement when the café next door and the bistro down the block are also serving burgers. More and more, the key to McDonald's future appears to be found in the DNA of the places it inhabits, like the sweet potato soft serve now available in Hong Kong.[74] And thus, the fast-food giant that has long represented the globalization of taste suddenly has found itself in a very unlikely position: as a defender of local cuisine.[75]

The kosher burger has been a hit in Israel, and Indian consumers seem to appreciate the opening of McDonald's first vegetarian restaurant. However, most new growth comes from Russia, where the company has 609 locations and holds the largest market share in terms of total sales. Even as fast-food competitors face potential market saturation in the United States, Russian demand for quick burgers appears insatiable.[76] Driving this Russian appetite has been the growth of a newly affluent middle class with money to spend to dine out. Infrastructure development in Russia also has been a boon to McDonald's as cities open malls with food courts, highways are constructed with drive-through locations, and specialty suppliers of frozen food and packaging have appeared.

In the early years of Russian expansion, few private businesses existed to supply the ingredients McDonald's needed to produce Big Macs and fries. The company solved the problem by building an enormous food processing plant outside Moscow. But it also worked to cultivate relationships with local Russian vendors and contractors, to which it eventually could outsource its supply chain. Today, a grower who began selling cucumbers to McDonald's in 1990 has become the Pickle King of Russia, dominating the processed foods market.[77]

Even when faced with some politically sensitive challenges—such as suspicious inspections by Russian agencies that alleged code violations in several McDonald's stores, seemingly

McDonald's is successful in Israel because of its kosher offerings.

©David Silverman/Getty Images

in response to the strained relations between the Russian and U.S. governments[78]— McDonald's has continued with its plans to expand in the country. In 2016 it spread into Siberian regions, opening 20 new restaurants, and plans further expansion in the future.[79] International enrollment in Hamburger University thus shows no signs of slowing.

To achieve this international growth, McDonald's is relying not only on integrating local flavors but also on leveraging technology to make meals totally customizable. In the United Kingdom, Australia, and Canada, self-order touchscreen kiosks have been popular with consumers. Adding customization means more menu items, though, so service times have become a concern. But McDonald's believes it can deal with this issue because the self-service kiosks not only give customers more control but also make it easier to order and receive meals. Once a customer has placed a customized order, he or she can take a seat and wait for the food to be delivered to the table, enhancing the experience by offering more conventional restaurant service, with the convenience of a fast-food outlet. Sales from these kiosks have accounted for one-quarter of sales in the locations where they are available. Accordingly, McDonald's has begun implementing them in the United States as well.[80]

Questions

1. Which sociocultural factors have informed McDonald's global expansion?

2. Describe some of the global marketing strategies that McDonald's uses or might consider using to spread throughout the world.

3. Explain McDonald's global marketing strategy. Compare McDonald's strategy in the United States (www.mcdonalds.com/us/en/home.html) to McDonald's strategy in India (www.mcdonaldsindia.com).

Endnotes

1. Patrick Coffee, "Apple Shifts Global Marketing Strategy, Restructures Its Relationship with TBWA/Media Arts Lab," *Adweek*, February 17, 2017.

2. Ibid.

3. Tim Culpan, "Chindia Needs One More Thing from Apple," *Bloomberg Businessweek*, September 13, 2017.

4. Shira Ovide, "Think You Won't Pay $1,000? Apple's Prices Are Going Up Anyway," *Bloomberg Businessweek*, September 12, 2017.

5. Reem Nasr, "Apple's Success in China Can Teach US Firms a Lot," *CNBC*, January 29, 2015.

6. Harsh Chauhan, "Apple Makes a Smart Move to Expand in This Huge Market," *The Motley Fool*, April 1, 2017.

7. "Apple Is Focusing More on Emerging Markets," *Business Insider*, December 21, 2016.

8. Pierre-Richard Agenor, *Does Globalization Hurt the Poor?* (Washington, DC: World Bank, 2002); "Globalization: Threat or Opportunity?," International Monetary Fund, www.imf.org.

9. www.census.gov.

10. https://stats.oecd.org/glossary/detail.asp?ID=1176.

11. http://siteresources.worldbank.org/DATASTATISTICS/ Resources/GNIPC.pdf; Arthur O'Sullivan, Steven Sheffrin, and Steve Perez, *Macroeconomics: Principles and Tools,* 8th ed. (Upper Saddle River, NJ: Prentice Hall, 2013).

12. *The Economist*, "The Big Mac Index," July 13, 2017, www.economist.com/content/big-mac-index.

13. Phil Wahba, "How P&G Plans to Fix Its China Business," *Fortune*, February 18, 2016.

14. Data Mark, "P&G Grows More Than Rivals in Conditioners and Hair Treatments in Brazil," May 19, 2017, www.datamark.com.br/en/ news/2017/5/p-g-grows-more-than-rivals-in-conditioners-and-hair-treatments-in-brazil-229567/.

15. Sagar Malviya, "P&G Fails to Reverse India Tide; Sales Dive," *The Economic Times*, November 30, 2017, https://economic-times.indiatimes.com/industry/cons-products/fmcg/pg-fails-to-reverse-india-tide-sales-dive/articleshow/61870702.cms;

Jack Neff, "Emerging Market Growth War Pits Global Brand Giants against Scrappy Local Rivals," *Advertising Age*, June 13, 2011, http://adage.com.

16. www.numbeo.com/cost-of-living/country_result.jsp?country= India; "Coca-Cola Tackles Rural Indian Market" (video), *The Wall Street Journal*, May 3, 2010.

17. *Vision Times*, "A Chinese Washing Machine Can Clean Both Clothes and Vegetables," September 6, 2017, www.visiontimes. com/2017/09/06/rural-chinese-washing-machines-used-to-clean-vegetables-and-gourds.html.

18. Wayne Ma, "China Levies 6.5% Tariff on U.S. Solar-Panel Materials," *The Wall Street Journal*, September 18, 2013, www. online.wsj.com.

19. *Investor's Business Daily*, "Trump Notches Another Win on Trade as China Slashes Tariffs," November 24, 2017, www. investors.com/politics/editorials/trump-notches-another-win-on-trade-as-china-slashes-tariffs/.

20. Chen Aizhu and Meng Meng, "China Sets 2018 Non-state Crude Oil Import Quota 55 Percent Higher Than 2017," Reuters, November 7, 2017.

21. www.cbp.gov/trade/quota/guide-import-goods/administration; Leslie Josephs, "U.S. Unlikely to Raise Sugar-Import Quota," *The Wall Street Journal*, February 19, 2013, http://online.wsj.com.

22. "Exchange Rate," http://en.wikipedia.org/wiki/Exchange_rate.

23. Jason Chow and Nadya Masidlover, "Chanel Acts on Prices as Euro Worsens Gray Market," *The Wall Street Journal*, March 17, 2015.

24. https://ustr.gov/trade-agreements: provides information on U.S. trade agreements.

25. www.unescap.org.

26. Johny Johansson, *Global Marketing*, 5th ed. (New York: McGraw-Hill/Irwin, 2008).

27. Philip R. Cateora, Mary C. Gilly, and John L. Graham, *International Marketing*, 17th ed. (New York: McGraw-Hill, 2015); Danielle Medina Walker and Thomas Walker, *Doing Business Internationally: The Guide to Cross-Cultural Success*, 2nd ed. (Princeton, NJ: Trade Management Corporation, 2003).

28. Angela Doland, "Six Cringeworthy Blunders Brands Make in China," *Advertising Age*, July 8, 2014, http://adage.com.

29. For a website dedicated to Hofstede's research, see www. geert-hofstede.com/.

30. Rosalie L. Tung and Alain Verbeke, eds., "Beyond Hofstede and GLOBE: Improving the Quality of Cross-Cultural Research," *Journal of International Business Studies* 41 (Special Issue, 2010).

31. Note that the time orientation and indulgence dimensions are relatively more recent additions to the categorization. See Geert Hofstede, "Dimensions of National Cultures," www. geerthofstede.eu/dimensions-of-national-cultures.

32. James W. Carey, *Communication as Culture*, rev. ed. (New York: Routledge, 2009).

33. *The Economist*, "Why Is South Africa Included in the BRICS?," March 29, 2013, www.economist.com/blogs/economist-explains/.

34. "Brazil," U.S. Department of State, www.state.gov; CIA, *The World Factbook*, www.cia.gov/library/publications/the-world-factbook/.

35. Prableen Bajpai, "The World's Top 10 Economies," *Investopedia*, July 7, 2017, www.investopedia.com/articles/investing/022415/worlds-top-10-economies.asp.

36. Ibid.

37. Asher Levine, "Brazil's 'New Middle Class' Struggles as Economy Plunges," Reuters, October 12, 2015, www.reuters.com/article/us-brazil-economy-fears-idUSKCN0S61QF20151012.

38. "Russia," U.S. Department of State, www.state.gov; CIA, *The World Factbook*.

39. eMarketer, "Number of Internet Users in Russia from 2013 to 2019 (in Millions)," *Statista*, February 4, 2016, www.statista. com/statistics/251818/number-of-internet-users-in-russia/.

40. "Russia," Internet Live Stats, www.internetlivestats.com/internet-users/russia/.

41. "Internet in Europe Stats," Internet World Stats, January 8, 2016, www.internetworldstats.com/stats4.htm#europe.

42. World Trade Organization, "Members and Observers," www. wto.org/english/thewto_e/whatis_e/tif_e/org6_e.htm.

43. Marianne Wilson, "China Is Top Emerging Retail Market," *The New York Times*, June 1, 2015.

44. Liz Stark and Maegan Vazquez, "US to Maintain Russia Sanctions until it Withdraws from Ukraine, Tillerson Says," *CNN*, December 7, 2017; U.S. Department of State, "Ukraine and Russia Sanctions," www.state.gov/e/eb/tfs/spi/ukrainerussia/; Kenneth Rogoff, "Russia's Future Looks Bleak without Economic and Political Reform," *The Guardian*, July 5, 2017; Paul Gregory, "A Russian Crisis with No End in Sight, Thanks to Low Oil Prices and Sanctions," *Forbes*, May 14, 2015, www.forbes.com/sites/paulroderick gregory/2015/05/14/a-russian-crisis-with-no-end-in-sight-thanks-to-low-oil-prices-and-sanctions/3/#5502e1f66d5e.

45. "India," U.S. Department of State, www.state.gov; CIA, *The World Factbook*.

46. CIA, *The World Factbook*, www.cia.gov/library/publications/the-world-factbook/fields/2177.html.

47. "Retail Industry in India," *India Brand Equity Foundation*, December 2017, www.ibef.org/industry/retail-india.aspx.

48. Ibid.

49. Ibid.

50. "China," U.S. Department of State, www.state.gov; CIA, *The World Factbook*.

51. Wilson, "China Is Top Emerging Retail Market."

52. CIA, *The World Factbook*, www.worldometers.info/world-population/china-population/; Laurie Burkitt, "Tapping China's 'Silver Hair' Industry," *The Wall Street Journal*, January 19, 2015, www.wsj.com; Laurie Burkitt, "China's Aging Future," *The Wall Street Journal*, January 19, 2015, www.wsj.com/video; Steven Jiang and Susannah Cullinane, "China's One-Child Policy to End," *CNN*, October 30, 2015.

53. Nicki Kamau, "Successful Strategic Alliances: 5 Examples of Companies Doing It Right," Allbound, August 16, 2016, www. allbound.com/blog/successful-strategic-alliances-5-examples-of-companies-doing-it-right.

54. www3.lenovo.com/us/en/lenovo/; Tim Bajarin, "How a Chinese Company Became a Global PC Powerhouse," *Time*, May 4, 2015; Juro Osawa and Lorraine Luk, "How Lenovo Built a Tech Giant," *The Wall Street Journal*, January 30, 2014, http://online.wsj.com.

55. Cateora et al., *International Marketing*.

56. Francoise Hovivian, "Globalization: Apple's One-Size-Fits-All Approach," *Brand Quarterly*, December 19, 2014, www.brand-quarterly.com/globalization-apples-one-size-fits-approach.

57. Julie Jargon, "Can M'm, M'm Good Translate?," *The Wall Street Journal*, July 9, 2007, p. A16; Brad Dorfman and Martinne Geller, "Campbell Soup in Joint Venture to Expand in China," Reuters, January 12, 2011, www.reuters.com; Julie Jargon, "Campbell Soup to Exit Russia," *The Wall Street Journal*, June 29, 2011, http://online.wsj.com.

58. www.pringles.it/.

59. Bill Johnson, "The CEO of Heinz on Powering Growth in Emerging Markets," *Harvard Business Review*, October 2011.

60. Silvia Fabiana et al., eds., *Pricing Decisions in the Euro Era: How Firms Set Prices and Why* (Oxford: Oxford University Press, 2007); Cateora et al., *International Marketing*.

61. https://europa.eu/youreurope/business/sell-abroad/free-competition/index_en.htm; David Griner, "9 Sneaky Marketing Tricks We Fall for Every Time We Shop," *Adweek*, August 6, 2014; Fabiana et al., eds., *Pricing Decisions in the Euro Era*.

62. Sarah Morris, "How Zara Clothes Turned Galicia into a Retail Hotspot," Reuters, October 31, 2011, www.reuters.com.

63. Joe Cochrane, "Tupperware's Sweet Spot Shifts to Indonesia," *The New York Times*, February 28, 2015, www.nytimes.com.

64. CIA, *The World Factbook*.

65. Michael Wines, "Picking Brand Names in Asia Is a Business Itself," *Advertising Age*, November 11, 2011, www.nytimes.com; Brand Channel, www.brandchannel.com.

66. Joan Voight, "How to Customize Your U.S. Branding Effort to Work around the World," *Adweek*, September 3, 2008.

67. McDonald's, "Revenue of McDonald's Corporation Worldwide from 2013 to 2016, by Region (in Billion U.S. Dollars)," *Statista*, 2017, www.statista.com/statistics/219453/revenue-of-the-mcdonalds-corporation-by-geographic-region/.

68. Elzio Barreto, "McDonald's Unloads Its Business in China," *Business Insider*, January 9, 2017, www.businessinsider.com/mcdonalds-unloads-china-business-2017-1.

69. "McDonald's Best Practices," http://bestpractices.mcdonalds.com; Annie Gasparro, "Yum Splits India into Separate Division, Names New International CEO," *The Wall Street Journal*, November 23, 2011.

70. Milly Montgomery and Rishi Iyengar, "Closed until Further Notice: Most McDonald's Restaurants in India's Capital," *CNNMoney*, June 29, 2017, http://money.cnn.com/2017/06/29/news/india/mcdonalds-india-delhi-stores-closed/index.html; McDonald's, "Our Story," www.mcdonaldsindia.com/our_story.html.

71. Julie Jargon, "For Food Delivery, China Calls McDonald's," *The Wall Street Journal*, December 12, 2011, http://online.wsj.com; McDonald's, "McDonald's Unveils New Global Growth Plan," March 1, 2017, http://news.mcdonalds.com/Corporate/news-stories/McDonald-s-Unveils-New-Global-Growth-Plan.

72. Neha Thirani Bagri, "A Growing Taste for U.S. Fast Food in India," *The New York Times*, January 8, 2014, http://india.blogs.nytimes.com/.

73. Hannah Fleishman, "13 Businesses with Brilliant Global Marketing Strategies," *HubSpot*, July 29, 2015, http://blog.hubspot.com/blog/tabid/6307/bid/33857/10-Businesses-we-admire-for-brilliant-global-marketing.aspx.

74. Charles Passy, "How Fast Food Chains Cook Up New Menu Items," *The Wall Street Journal*, August 24, 2015; McDonald's, "What a Twist! McDonald's Hong Kong Launches Sweet Potato Sensation Ice Cream," January 22, 2016, http://news.mcdonalds.com/Corporate/Feature-Stories-Articles/2016/What-a-twist-McDonald-s-Hong-Kong-Launches.

75. Matt Goulding, "Why the French Secretly Love the Golden Arches," *Slate*, August 2013, www.slate.com.

76. Ravi Krishnani, "McDonald's in Russia: Defeated Communism with a 'Happy' Meal," *Business Today*, www.businesstoday-eg.com; McDonald's Europe Virtual Press Office, press brief, www.mcdpressoffice.eu; "Russia's Fast Food Market: Resilient & Robust," *ITE Food & Drink*, March 14, 2017, www.food-exhibitions.com/Market-Insights/Russia/Russia-fast-food-market-resilient-robust.

77. Andrew E. Kramer, "Russia's Evolution, Seen through Golden Arches," *The New York Times*, February 2, 2010, www.nytimes.com.

78. "For First Time Ever, McDonald's Closes a Restaurant in Russia," *The Moscow Times*, April 14, 2015, www.themoscowtimes.com/business/article/for-first-time-ever-mcdonalds-closes-a-restaurant-in-russia/519066.html.

79. Olga Razumovskaya, "McDonald's Extends Reach in Russia," *The Wall Street Journal*, August 21, 2015, www.wsj.com/articles/mcdonalds-extends-reach-in-russia-1440174904; Maria Kiselyova and Olga Sichkar, "In Russia, McDonald's 'Golden Arches' Have a Russian Shine," Reuters, February 2, 2017, www.reuters.com/article/us-mcdonalds-russia-idUSKBN15H1E0.

80. Stephanie Strom, "McDonald's Introduces Screen Ordering and Table Service," *The New York Times*, November 17, 2016, www.nytimes.com/2016/11/18/business/mcdonalds-introduces-screen-ordering-and-table-service.html.

i. Bob Tita, "Whirlpool to Boost U.K., Russian Prices to Offset Weakening Currencies," *The Wall Street Journal*, July 22, 2016; Andrew Tangel, "Whirlpool to Restructure Dryer Manufacturing in Europe," *The Wall Street Journal*, January 24, 2017; Richa Naidu, "Whirlpool Profit Misses Expectations as Brexit Hits Sales," Reuters, January 26, 2017.

ii. Emmanuel Akinwotu, "Nigerians Told to #BuyNaija as the Economy Battles Falling Oil Prices," *The Guardian*, March 16, 2016; Heenali Patel, "Nigerians Are Using a Twitter Hashtag to Help Their Country's Economy," *CNN*, February 12, 2016; Yomi Kazeem, "Nigerian Leaders Hope a Twitter Campaign to Buy Local Can Save Its Currency," *Quartz Africa*, February 15, 2016.

iii. Dan Liefgreen and Chiara Albanese, "Can Starbucks Sell Espresso Back to Italians?," *Bloomberg*, June 16, 2016; Lucia Maffei, "Starbucks to Open in Italy, Home of Espresso, in 2018. Italian Cafes Say Bring It," *The Salt: What's on Your Plate*, February 28, 2017.

iv. Angela Doland, "How Wendy's Is Building a Beefless Burger Brand for India," *Advertising Age*, May 29, 2015; "When Fast Food Gets an Indian Twist," *BBC News*, January 17, 2017; "Coming Soon at McDonald's: A Masala Dosa Burger and Anda Bhurji," *Business Standard*, January 11, 2017.

v. Sam Schechner, "Google Appeals French 'Right to Be Forgotten' Order," *The Wall Street Journal*, May 19, 2016; Alex Hern, "Google Takes Right to Be Forgotten Battle to France's Highest Court," *The Guardian*, May 19, 2016; Stephanie Bodoni, "Google Argues Privacy Right Is Wrong in Clash with French Czar," *Business Standard*, January 27, 2017.

Quiz Yourself Answer Key

1. What is the most common way to measure the current size and market potential of a country?

   Answer: (a) Gross domestic product

2. Many firms begin global expansion by moving from less risky ventures initially to riskier ventures in later years. Which of the following global entry strategy progressions would characterize that type of evolution?

   Answer: (c) Exporting to strategic alliance

TARGETING THE MARKETPLACE

Section Three, Targeting the Marketplace, contains two chapters. Chapter 9 focuses on segmentation, targeting, and positioning. In this chapter, we examine how firms segment the marketplace, then pick a target market, and finally position their goods/services in line with their customers' needs and wants. Chapter 10, on marketing research, identifies the various tools, techniques, and metrics that marketers use to uncover customers' needs and wants and to ensure that they create goods and services that provide value to their target markets.

©Jonathan Weiss/Shutterstock

LEARNING OBJECTIVES

After reading this chapter, you should be able to:

LO9-1 Outline the different methods of segmenting a market.

LO9-2 Describe how firms determine whether a segment is attractive and therefore worth pursuing.

LO9-3 Articulate the differences among targeting strategies: undifferentiated, differentiated, concentrated, or micromarketing.

LO9-4 Determine the value proposition.

LO9-5 Define positioning, and describe how firms do it.

CHAPTER 9

SEGMENTATION, TARGETING, AND POSITIONING

Glowing reports of the successful expansion by lululemon into menswear mainly focus on how the brand—long known primarily for the yoga pants it designed for women—has broadened its market by targeting men too. But in reality, the success of the strategy derives from more than a simple gender-based segmentation. That is, lululemon does more than derive products for and market to men or women. It establishes segments within these categories that enable it to identify precise needs and desires, then provide greater value by meeting those needs for each specific segment of buyers.

Let's start with the basic gender segmentation. When it comes to athletic gear, whether for working out or just lounging around, the physical differences between women and men make this segmentation evident. Women need sports bras and prefer yoga pants that are flattering and functional. Accordingly, lululemon constantly seeks to introduce different models and versions of both tops and bottoms for women, to keep them buying.[1]

But men don't need bras, and their wants and needs when it comes to pants also differ from those of women. lululemon's most popular men's pant, and its "best-kept secret," reflects those desires. That is, the ABC pant promises a significantly improved level of comfort for wearers (we will leave it to you to figure out the slightly risqué meaning of ABC).[2]

But as it sought to increase sales, the brand also realized there was more room for expansion among the segment of men who work out and need athletic gear. Accordingly, it initiated a new design round, creating outerwear pieces that were novel and innovative and thus could support the requirements of various outdoor enthusiasts.[3] For example, the Einn Shell and the Surge Thermo Vest are designed to work together, for people in really cold climates, or separately, for those in warmer areas. Each piece also allows wearers to increase or decrease the warmth provided by their gear with simple adjustments. Thus the vest design puts more warmth at the chest but provides more breathability in the back, and a snap located right at the sternum level can be easily opened (if the wearer gets hot) or closed (once the cold temperatures start getting in). For segments of guys who sweat a lot, for example, such options can be invaluable.

Beyond the designs, its marketing tactics resonate with various segments of male consumers. A series of advertisements, under a campaign titled "Strength to Be," encourage men to reconsider what it means to be strong by presenting diverse opinions from a range of people. The goal is to encourage men to move beyond simple notions of physical strength. According to one of the company's brand directors, lululemon aims to "empower people to blaze their own trail, rather than conform to traditional stereotypes and archetypes."[4]

Thus the marketing communication moves beyond conventional or limited views of masculinity. For example, the spot featuring the Olympic boxer Orlando Cruz certainly displays his muscles, but the focus is on the strength he displayed in being the first professional boxer to come out as gay while still fighting.[5] Another spot in the campaign, featuring the community organizer Ibn Ali Miller, suggests that being a "real man" requires a desire to be better, along with a sense of humility and humanity. The advertisement shows Miller working out (e.g., crunches, sit-ups), then transitions seamlessly into depictions of him performing a ritual Islamic *salah*, or prayer in which he prostrates himself.

Furthermore, lululemon recognizes that segmentation can refer to more than just who a person is or how she or he self-identifies. Thus it has expanded its efforts to reach customers who prefer to shop through its website and improved the site's navigability.[6] With these efforts, it also can reach new segments of consumers in Asia, including Chinese consumers who already shop more frequently online and through mobile channels than do their U.S. or Canadian counterparts.[7] These consumers also are exhibiting increasing interest in health and wellness, in response to Chinese government–provided health plans that encourage people to exercise more. In support of this global targeting, lululemon made its presence very visible on Alibaba on the most recent Singles' Day (November 11, when young Chinese people celebrate their single status, often by purchasing extravagant or fun gifts for themselves), earning unprecedented foreign sales as a result.[8]

Even the supply chain for the company is receiving a segmentation approach. To enhance efficiencies and get products to all segments of consumers faster, it separates its supply chain into unique segments, each of which can be ramped up to increase supply as needed. Then the fabrics that are most popular in various geographic locations get sent to the most appropriate and proximal manufacturing facilities.[9]

As a result of these varied tactics to enhance its segmentation and targeting, lululemon has exceeded recent predictions of its performance. The sales bumps occur across the board but mainly come from the menswear items. For example, a remarkable 21 percent of purchases by men came from new customers in a recent quarter.[10] The appeal to these guys—who previously assumed that lululemon was only for women—is strategic and targeted. And it seemingly is working too: In a recent survey, men expressed far more positive views of the brand than they had previously, and more of them had made purchases from it.[11]

We learned in Chapter 1 that marketing is about satisfying consumers' wants and needs. Chapter 2 noted how companies analyze their markets to determine the different kinds of products and services people want. But it is not sufficient just to produce such an offering. Firms must also position their offerings in the minds of customers in their target market in such a way that these consumers understand why the thing the company is providing meets their needs better than other competitive offerings do.

This process requires a marketing plan, as we discussed in Chapter 2. You should recall that the third step of this plan is to identify and evaluate opportunities by performing an STP (segmentation, targeting, and positioning) analysis. This chapter focuses on that very analysis.

Outline the different methods of segmenting a market.

THE SEGMENTATION, TARGETING, AND POSITIONING PROCESS

In this chapter, we discuss how a firm conducts a market segmentation or STP analysis (see Exhibit 9.1). We first outline a firm's overall strategy and objectives, methods of segmenting the market, and which segments are worth pursuing. Then we discuss how to choose a target market or markets by evaluating each segment's attractiveness and, on the basis of this evaluation, choose which segment or segments to pursue. Finally, we describe how a firm develops its positioning strategy.

Although the STP process in Exhibit 9.1 implies that the decision making is linear, this need not be the case. For instance, a firm could start with a strategy but then modify it as it gathers more information about various segments' attractiveness.

Step 1: Establish the Overall Strategy or Objectives

The first step in the segmentation process is to articulate the vision or objectives of the company's marketing strategy clearly. The segmentation strategy must be consistent with and derived from the firm's mission and objectives as well as its current situation—its strengths, weaknesses, opportunities, and threats (SWOT). Botticelli's objective, for instance, is to increase sales in a mature industry. The company, which sells olive oil, pasta, pasta sauces, and roasted red peppers,[12] knows its strengths are its reputation for using quality ingredients.[13] However, a weakness is that it may not currently have a product line that appeals to those who like Italian food but not the traditional options that are high in carbohydrates and heavy sauces. Identifying this potentially large and profitable market segment, and doing so before many of its mainstream competitors do, offers a great opportunity. However, following through on that opportunity could lead to a significant threat: competitive retaliation. Botticelli's recent choice to pursue health-conscious and vegan customers with a vegan-friendly Bolognese sauce made with soy is consistent with its overall strategy and objectives.[14]

Now let's take a look at methods for segmenting a market.

Step 2: Use Segmentation Methods

The second step in the segmentation process is to use a particular method or combination of methods to segment the market. This step also develops descriptions of the different segments, which helps firms better understand the customer profiles in each segment. With this information, firms can distinguish customer similarities within a segment and dissimilarities

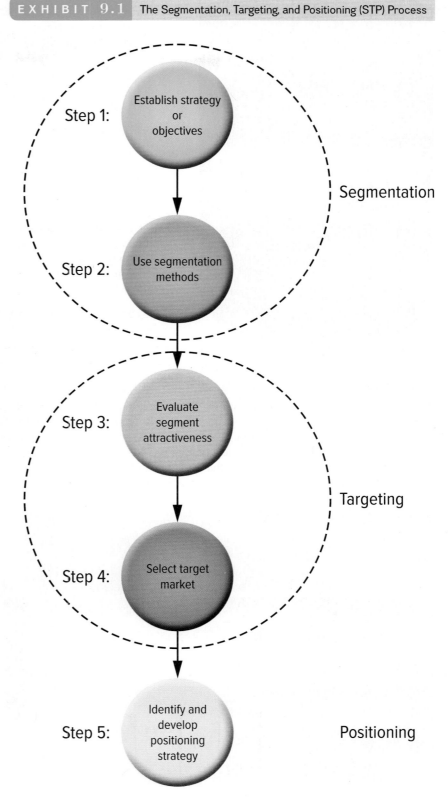

EXHIBIT 9.1   The Segmentation, Targeting, and Positioning (STP) Process

Step 1: Establish strategy or objectives

Step 2: Use segmentation methods

Segmentation

Step 3: Evaluate segment attractiveness

Step 4: Select target market

Targeting

Step 5: Identify and develop positioning strategy

Positioning

To thwart the threat of competition and pursue the opportunity of going after the health-conscious market, Botticelli has introduced a vegan-friendly, soy-based Bolognese sauce.

Courtesy of Botticelli

EXHIBIT 9.2	Methods for Describing Market Segments
Segmentation Method	**Sample Segments**
Geographic	Continent: North America, Asia, Europe, Africa Within the United States: Pacific, mountain, central, south, mid-Atlantic, northeast
Demographic	Age, gender, income, education
Psychographic	Lifestyle, self-concept, self-values
Benefit	Convenience, economy, prestige
Behavioral	Occasion, loyalty

across segments. Marketers use geographic, demographic, psychographic, benefit, and behavioral segmentation methods, as Exhibit 9.2 details.

Food marketers, for instance, divide the traditional pasta sauce landscape into with or without meat, original or light/heart healthy, and marinara versus something else (e.g., Alfredo, pesto). This segmentation method is based on the benefits that consumers derive from the products.

Geographic Segmentation Geographic segmentation organizes customers into groups on the basis of where they live. Thus, a market could be grouped by country, region (northeast, southeast), or areas within a region (state, city, neighborhoods, zip codes). Not surprisingly, geographic segmentation is most useful for companies whose products satisfy needs that vary by region.

Firms can provide the same basic goods or services to all segments even if they market globally or nationally, but better marketers make adjustments to meet the needs of smaller geographic groups.[15] A national grocery store chain such as Safeway or Kroger runs similar stores with similar assortments in various locations across the United States. But within those similar stores, a significant percentage of the assortment of goods will vary by region, city, or even neighborhood, depending on the different needs of the customers who surround each location.

Kellogg's uses demographic segmentation, specifically age, for its breakfast cereals. Lucky Charms, Crunchy Nut, and Corn Pops are for kids; Crispix, Corn Flakes, and Fiber Plus are for adults.

©Daniel Acker/Bloomberg via Getty Images

Demographic Segmentation Demographic segmentation groups consumers according to easily measured, objective characteristics such as age, gender, income, and education. These variables represent the most common means to define segments because they are easy to identify, and demographically segmented markets are easy to reach. As Social & Mobile Marketing 9.1 acknowledges, demographics also can be critical to defining an overall marketing strategy. Kellogg's uses age segmentation for its breakfast cereals: Lucky Charms, Crunchy Nut, and Corn Pops are for kids; Crispix, Corn Flakes, and Fiber Plus are for adults.

Gender plays a very important role in how most firms market products and services.[16] For instance, TV viewing habits vary significantly between men and women. Men tend to channel surf—switching quickly from channel to

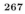

Social & Mobile Marketing 9.1   The Social Sharing Practices of the Teen Segment[i]

According to one retail innovation analyst and "Generation Z expert," for young consumers today, "if it's not shareable, it didn't happen." That notion applies to everything in their lives, including the clothing they wear and the methods they use to purchase those products. Because of these developments, many of the clothing brands and retailers that dominated the market in previous decades are struggling, faced with a distinct lack of appeal to experience-focused, social media–addicted, young sharing consumers.

Stores such as the Gap, J.Crew, and Abercrombie & Fitch still aim to target younger buyers with their clothing offerings, but those shoppers express little interest. Whereas previous generations might have accepted that they needed to keep a few staples in their wardrobe, today's buyers don't want to hold on to a good-old favorite pair of jeans. They want to snap up the latest style, take a picture of how it looks, and share it with their followers and friends. To be able to provide constant content updates on their social media sites, they need a constant flow of new items and clothing to highlight.

Such demands benefit the fast fashion retailers such as Zara, H&M, and Mango that allow consumers to grab the latest styles the very moment that they fly off the design boards. In addition, because they sell products for low prices, even the most frugal young Gen Z buyer can afford to rotate his or her wardrobe nearly constantly. As a result, these fast fashion firms are enjoying the market share that previously would have been held by traditional fashion companies such as the Gap.

The influences stemming from the preferences and practices of these young consumers also is spilling over to older generations and altering the way they shop. Consider the influence of social media usage for example. By its very nature, Pinterest is aspirational, giving users something to aim for in the future. When it comes to clothing, that sort of dream approach means that pinners readily have in mind what they want to wear next. Even older consumers thus are embracing the notion that they need the newest fashions, in constant rotation, so that they can live up to the dream they have pinned on their boards.

The idea of fashion, shopping, and consumption as an experience is a broad and seemingly unstoppable trend. It might have been largely sparked by the latest generation, the Gen Z

Marketers can tap into the aspirational nature of Generation Z consumers by implementing strategies that allow this market to share through social media sites like Pinterest.

©Paul Bradbury/OJO Images RF/Getty Images

teens of today, but it is expanding throughout the generational cohorts. Retailers thus have little choice but to find ways to ensure a shareable experience, not just a good product.

channel—and watch prime-time shows that are action oriented and feature physically attractive cast members. Women, in contrast, tend to view shows to which they can personally relate through the situational plot or characters and those recommended by friends. Print media are similar: A company such as Proactiv, which seeks to appeal to men as well as women who are worried about the condition of their skin, therefore carefully considers the gender-based appeal of different magazines when it purchases advertising space.

However, demographics may not be useful for defining the target segments for other companies. They are poor predictors of the users of activewear such as jogging suits and athletic shoes. At one time, firms such as Nike assumed that activewear would be purchased exclusively by young, active people, but the health and fitness trend has led people of all ages to buy such merchandise. Even relatively inactive consumers of all ages, incomes, and education find activewear to be more comfortable than traditional street clothes.

Using psychographic segmentation, Dove's "Real Beauty Pledge" campaign features photos of "real" rather than "aspirationally" beautiful women.

Source: Unilever

Rethinking some stereotypical ideas about who is buying thus has become a relatively common trend among firms that once thought their target market was well defined.

Psychographic Segmentation Of the various methods for segmenting, or breaking down, the market, psychographic segmentation is the one that delves into how consumers actually describe themselves. Usually marketers determine (through demographics, buying patterns, or usage) into which segment an individual consumer falls. Psychographics studies how people self-select, as it were, based on the characteristics of how they choose to occupy their time (behavior) and what underlying psychological reasons determine those choices.[17] For example, a person might have a strong need for inclusion or belonging, which motivates him or her to seek out activities that involve others, which in turn influences the products he or she buys to fit in with the group. BuzzFeed's segmentation strategy is based on both consumers' behaviors and their interests. Much of the content it creates is aimed specifically at markets that traditionally would have been considered niche or fringe segments. This strategy has been successful because BuzzFeed can not only reach these consumers on more personal levels but also can interact with people who might be outside such niche markets but who appreciate the brand's efforts to interact with and validate those markets.[18] Determining psychographics involves knowing and understanding three components: self-values, self-concept, and lifestyles.

Self-values are goals for life, not just the goals one wants to accomplish in a day. They are the overriding desires that drive how a person lives his or her life. Examples might be the need for self-respect, self-fulfillment, or a specific sense of belonging. This motivation causes people to develop self-images of how they want to be and then images of a way of life that will help them arrive at these ultimate goals. From a marketing point of view, self-values help determine the benefits the target market may be looking for from a product. Sanderson Farms targets consumers whose self-values prioritize saving money rather than worrying about antibiotic use, as Ethical & Societal Dilemma 9.1 reports. The underlying, fundamental, personal need that pushes a person to seek out certain products or brands stems from his or her desire to fulfill a self-value.

People's self-image, or self-concept, is the image people ideally have of themselves.[19] A person who has a goal to belong may see, or want to see, himself as a fun-loving, gregarious type whom people wish to be around. Marketers often make use of this particular self-concept through communications that show their products being used by groups of laughing people who are having a good time. The connection emerges between the group fun and the product being shown and connotes a lifestyle that many consumers seek.

Such tactics need to balance the ideal with the realistic. Advertisements for women's skin care products tend to feature salacious shots of extraordinarily beautiful women. As we know, however, few women reach this ideal, and many of those who do actually think they don't. After some preliminary research in 2000, Unilever's Dove soap brand initiated its "Real Beauty Pledge" campaign. It first placed billboards in the United States, Canada, and the United Kingdom featuring photos of "real" rather than "aspirational" women and two tick-box options such as "flawed?" or "flawless?"; 1.5 million observers texted their vote, and the vote tally appeared on the billboard. Based on this initial campaign, Dove recognized that it hit a raw nerve with many women. Dove's "Real Beauty Pledge" campaign is now the basis of all of its marketing campaigns. The pledge dictates that Dove features real women, portrays them as they are in real life, and works to build girls' self-esteem.[20]

Ethical & Societal Dilemma 9.1 | Using Antibiotics Proudly: Sanderson Farms Distinguishes Its Brand by Going against the Grain[ii]

Antibiotics for poultry are bad, right? That seems to be the consensus, based on retail packaging that touts the products' antibiotic-free status, announcements by chicken suppliers that they will stop using antibiotics in their operations, press releases by restaurant chains promising a lack of antibiotics in their chicken dishes, and demands from consumers for "clean" chicken and egg options. But Sanderson Farms, the nation's third-largest supplier of chicken, contests the very premise and therefore is making its continued insistence on using antibiotics part of its marketing campaign, to set itself apart from its competitors.

The concern about the use of antibiotics focuses specifically on those medications that also are approved for use in humans. The theory suggests that if these antibiotics are used too widely in poultry production, the bacteria they are intended to kill will develop into drug-resistant strains, with resulting threats to human and animal health

About **ANTIBIOTICS**

The **Truth**

The truth is, none of the chicken you buy in the grocery store contains antibiotics. By federal law, all chickens must be clear of antibiotics before they leave the farm.

Sanderson Farms treats its poultry with antibiotics, and it is proud of it!

Source: Sanderson Farms, Inc.

and welfare. The threat to consumers is not the antibiotics themselves; federal regulations require that any products being sold for consumption must be free of antibiotics. Thus, every package of chicken in the grocers' case is antibiotic free, and Sanderson Farms asserts that marketing products on the basis of their lack of antibiotics actually is misleading. In the process of raising the chickens, many producers dose the animals with antibiotics, often in vitro, to reduce the occurrence of disease.

With these clarifications, Sanderson Farms argues that its use of antibiotics is safe and appropriate. It halts the medication well before the animals are prepared for sale. Furthermore, the company argues that there is insufficient scientific evidence to support the link between the use of antibiotics by chicken farms and the increase of drug-resistant bacteria among human populations. Instead, it asserts that companies that promote their antibiotic-free chicken are simply trying to charge more for their products.

Sanderson Farms promises a different approach in its marketing, asserting that by using antibiotics, it can keep its production leaner and more efficient. For example, were it to forgo the use of antibiotics, it says it would need to leave more

space between the cages in which the chickens are kept, which would require building more barns to house them. Such moves would increase costs. It also claims that eliminating antibiotics increases the mortality rates for the animals, such that it is neither environmentally sustainable nor efficient as a production option.

Competitors such as Tyson and Perdue, which are moving toward the complete elimination of human-approved antibiotics from their production lines, instead point to evidence that shows no increase in mortality among chickens left untreated. They also cite reports by the Centers for Disease Control and Prevention that offer initial evidence of a link between antibiotic use in chickens and the rise of drug-resistant bacteria, even if the link has not been proven conclusively.

Some buyers, such as McDonald's and Chick-fil-A, already have committed to doing away with antibiotic-treated chickens in their menus. But for individual consumers, Sanderson Farms believes it has a compelling argument and appeal to make. If Sanderson Farms can explain its perspective on what antibiotic use really means, it thinks customers will be happy to pay less for chicken that is still safe to eat.

Using lifestyle segmentation, Harley-Davidson has four main target markets: On the left is its core segment consisting of men older than 35 years. The ad on the right targets women older than 35 years.

Source: H-D U.S.A, LLC

Lifestyles, the third component of people's psychographic makeup, are the ways we live.[21] If values provide an end goal, and self-concept is the way we see ourselves in the context of that goal, lifestyles are how we live our lives to achieve goals.

One of the most storied lifestyles in American legend is the Harley way of life: the open road, wind in your hair, rebelling against conventions. But the notions of freedom, rebellion, and standing out from a crowd vastly appeal to all sorts of people. In response, Harley-Davidson has shifted its STP methods to define four main target markets: core (men older than 35 years), young adults (both genders, 18–34 years), women (older than 35 years), and diverse (men and women, African American and Hispanic, older than 35 years).[22]

For Millennials, for example, it has partnered with social influencers such as Jessica Haggett, the founder of an all-female motorcycle club, and actor, producer, and model Jason Momoa to be the voice of the company on social media. Furthermore, it is focusing its advertising efforts on popular events such as the X Games and the Ultimate Fighting Championship (UFC.) Harley-Davidson has even introduced a virtual reality game, Crew 2, that allows players to virtually weave through city streets on a motorcycle. It is also expanding the number of stores with its riding academy, which now has almost 250 locations, to teach Millennials how to ride and to make sure they feel comfortable on a motorcycle.[23]

The most widely used psychographic segmentation is the Values and Lifestyles Survey (VALS), owned and operated by Strategic Business Insights (SBI).[24] It examines the intersection of psychology, demographics, and lifestyles. U.S. consumers ages 18 and older are classified into one of the eight segments shown in Exhibit 9.3 based on answers to the VALS survey and proprietary algorithm (www.strategicbusinessinsights.com/vals/presurvey. shtml). The horizontal dimension shows that the majority of consumers have one of three primary motivations: Ideals, Achievement, or Self-Expression. The vertical dimension of the framework indicates level of resources; VALS uses an expanded definition of resources to include not just key demographics such as age and income but measures of curiosity, leadership, information seeking, and interest in experimentation. The consumer groups at the top of the framework have higher resources than those at the bottom.

Consumers buy products and services and engage in activities that bring meaning to their lives. Some consumers are motivated by ideals, others by achievement or by self-expression. Consumers with a primary ideals motivation are guided by knowledge and principles. Consumers motivated by achievement look for products and services that enhance their image of personal success to others. Consumers with a primary motivation of self-expression seek social or physical activity and independence.

VALS enables firms to identify target segments and their underlying motivations to develop strategic initiatives and communications.

VALS is more useful than demographics alone to predict consumer behavior, particularly for not-yet-invented products and services. This is because people who share demographics often have different motivations. Take, for example, Jack and John, both 30-year-old, married college graduates. Demographically they are the same, but Jack is slow to adopt until all new-product issues are resolved; John is confident enough to experiment. Lumping Jack and John together as a target does not make sense because the ways they think are different even though some of their behaviors are the same.

Depending on the marketing objective, psychographics are not always the most appropriate, nor the most cost-effective method by which to segment consumers. With demographics, a firm like Nike can easily identify its customers as, say, men or women and then direct its marketing strategies to each group differently. The problem is that not all men are alike, as we saw with Jack and John. Women are not all alike either! To identify VALS Thinkers or Makers, companies can incorporate the VALS questionnaire in their own surveys or use it as a focus group screener. VALS provides robust segment descriptions using consumer product, lifestyle, and media-use data from GfK MRI's biannual *Survey of the American Consumer* in which the VALS survey is included.[25]

Benefit Segmentation
Benefit segmentation groups consumers on the basis of the benefits they derive from products or services. Because marketing is all about satisfying consumers' needs and wants, dividing the market into segments whose needs and wants are best satisfied by the product benefits can be a very powerful tool.[26] It is effective and relatively easy to portray a product's or service's benefits in the firm's communication strategies.

Hollywood in particular is a constant and effective practitioner of benefit segmentation. Although all movies may seem to provide the same service—entertainment for a couple of hours—film producers know that people visit the theater or rent films to obtain a vast variety of benefits, and market them accordingly. Need a laugh? Try the latest comedy from Adam Sandler or Melissa McCarthy. Want to cry and then feel warm and fuzzy? Go see *Wonder* starring Julia Roberts and Owen Wilson, for by the time you leave the theater, you are likely to feel quite happy: The lead characters will have faced obstacles, overcome them, and ultimately found acceptance.

Behavioral Segmentation
Behavioral segmentation divides customers into groups on the basis of how they use the product or service. Some common behavioral measures include occasion and loyalty.

EXHIBIT 9.3 VALS Framework

US VALS™ Framework

High Resources

Innovators

Ideals	Achievement	Self-Expression
Thinkers	Achievers	Experiencers
Believers	Strivers	Makers

Survivors   Low Resources

The VALS survey places individuals into one of the eight groups. The VALS framework is the visualization of the consumer groups. Consumers with abundant resources—psychological, emotional, and material means and capabilities—are near the top of the framework and those with minimal resources are at the bottom. Consumer groups within a motivation can be targeted together. For instance, a marketer may target Thinkers and Believers together. Do you want to know your VALS type? If you do, take the survey at www.strategicbusinessinsights.com/vals/presurvey.shtml. Simply click on "Take the survey." You will receive your primary and secondary types in real time. To receive an accurate VALS type, your first language must be American English. If you are not a resident of the United States or Canada, residency should be for enough time to know the culture and its idioms.

©2017 by Strategic Business Insights. All Rights Reserved.
www.strategicbusinessinsights.com/vals

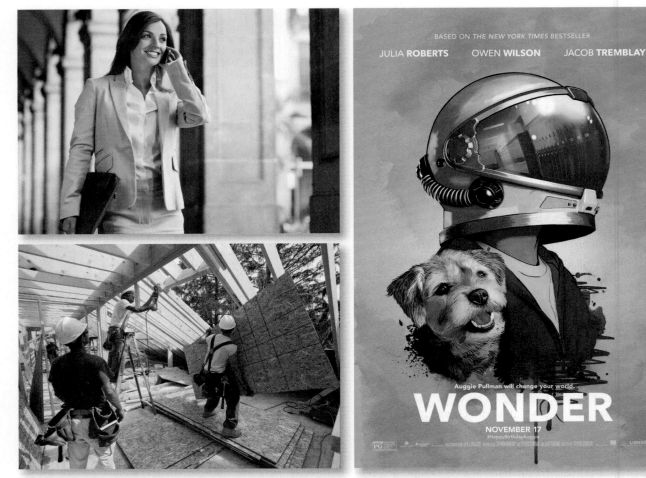

It is just as easy to identify Thinkers (top) as it is Makers (bottom).
SBI uses a proprietary algorithm to score a person's answers to
the VALS questionnaire to determine his or her VALS type.

(Top): ©Sam Edwards/Getty Images; (bottom): ©Huntstock/Getty Images

The movie industry pursues a benefit segmentation strategy.
Want to cry and then feel warm and fuzzy? Go see Wonder
starring Julia Roberts, Owen Wilson, and Jacob Tremblay.

©Lionsgate/Photofest

Restaurants offer loyalty programs because it is less
expensive to retain customers than to attract new ones.

©Eric Audras/Onoky/Superstock

Occasion Behavioral segmentation based on when a product or service is purchased or consumed is called occasion segmentation. Men's Wearhouse uses this type of segmentation to develop its merchandise selection and its promotions. Sometimes men need a suit for their everyday work, but other suits are expressly for special occasions such as a prom or a wedding. Snack food companies such as Frito-Lay also make and promote snacks for various occasions—individual servings of potato chips for a snack on the run but 16-ounce bags for parties.

Loyalty Firms have long known that it pays to retain loyal customers. Loyal customers are those who feel so strongly that the firm can meet their relevant needs best that any competitors are virtually excluded from their consideration; that is, these customers buy almost exclusively from the firm. These loyal customers are the most profitable in the long term.[27] In light of the high cost of finding new customers and the profitability of loyal customers, today's companies are using loyalty segmentation and investing in retention and loyalty initiatives to retain their most profitable customers. From simple, "buy 10 sandwiches, get the 11th free" punch cards offered by local restaurants to the elaborate travel-linked programs run by hotel and airline affiliates, such loyalty segmentation approaches are ubiquitous. Starbucks is using its loyalty programs and mobile apps to enhance value for its customers.

Using Multiple Segmentation Methods Although all segmentation methods are useful, each has its unique advantages and disadvantages. For example, segmenting by demographics and geography is easy because information about who the customers are and where they are located is readily available; however, these characteristics don't help marketers determine their customers' needs. Knowing what benefits customers are seeking or how the product or service fits a particular lifestyle is important for designing an overall marketing strategy, but such segmentation schemes present a problem for marketers attempting to identify specifically which customers are seeking these benefits. Thus, firms often employ a combination of segmentation methods, using demographics and geography to identify and target marketing communications to their customers, then using benefits or lifestyles to design the product or service and the substance of the marketing message. To illustrate, Adding Value 9.1 demonstrates how Nintendo uses both demographic and benefit segmentation strategies.

Adding Value 9.1	Switching the Target Market for the Switch: Nintendo's Pursuit of More Mature Audiences[iii]

Nintendo revolutionized the gaming industry of the 20th century with its Super Nintendo, Nintendo 64, and Game Boy. But in the 21st century, it has been falling short of competitors such as Sony, with its PlayStation, and Microsoft, with its Xbox. For the past decade, Nintendo consistently has suffered the smallest market share among these three options. To compete more directly with them, Nintendo has introduced a new device designed to appeal to multiple target markets—the Switch, which has a handheld console with a distinct operating platform. To source content for the device, Nintendo reached out to various game developers, including those that are known more for games that do not quite match Nintendo's conventional, family-friendly image. The move is intentional, as Nintendo seeks a more mature audience for the Switch by offering games with some violent or risqué content.

With its famous titles, Nintendo has long had a reputation as the console for kids. They can play fun games like Super Mario, and parents do not have to worry as much about their children gaining access to mature games, unlike the concerns they might face with an Xbox or PlayStation console.

But the Switch is different, intended not for the children but for their parents—or at least their older siblings. It features a parental control tool, so if kids come across the device, they cannot access the mature titles. Even the look of the device is distinct from previous Nintendo consoles, presenting a muted color palette rather than the bright, primary colors that appear on the other iterations. Thus, Nintendo hopes to maintain its appeal for children and families, even as it gets the adult members of households to consider adopting the Switch too.

Adding the Switch to a gaming console collection makes sense for many gamers, most of whom already own an existing console or two. If they purchase the newest option from Microsoft or PlayStation, they likely are replacing their old console with a marginally improved version of the same thing, but at a substantial cost in terms of the price. The Switch instead takes a far lower price point, approximately $100 less than either of the other major consoles on the market.

Nintendo's Switch appeals to its traditional kids target market's older siblings and parents.

©leungchopan/Shutterstock

Furthermore, the prospect of adding the Switch, instead of trading in an old console, adds value because customers can justify keeping their existing consoles. In turn, they can still play games exclusive to their old console, even as they enjoy exploring new games on the Switch. Nintendo also is promising them the fun of playing games they knew from their childhood. That is, by rereleasing previously introduced adult games, such as Skyrim, Nintendo is leveraging the nostalgia many people feel for the old-school options. The ability to play these games on a handheld device, instead of traditional consoles, makes the entire experience novel. In this sense, the Switch might be good for game developers too, in that they can re-release their games for the new platform and sell their products to not just new players but also previous customers, who remember the old games fondly.

Using demographic and benefit segmentation together, the Switch appeals to a price-sensitive market that includes children, families, and adults. It is also going after nostalgic users who remember Nintendo from their childhood, while at the same time appealing to new users.

One very popular mixture of segmentation schemes is geodemographic segmentation. Based on the adage "birds of a feather flock together," geodemographic segmentation uses a combination of geographic, demographic, and lifestyle characteristics to classify consumers. Consumers in the same neighborhoods tend to buy the same types of cars, appliances, and apparel and shop at the same types of retailers.

One widely used tool for geodemographic market segmentation is the Tapestry™ Segmentation system developed and marketed by Esri.[28] Tapestry Segmentation classifies all U.S. residential neighborhoods into 65 distinctive segments based on detailed demographic data and lifestyles of people who live in each U.S. block tract (zip code +4).[29] Each block group then can be analyzed and sorted by many characteristics, including income, home value, occupation, education, household type, age, and several key lifestyle characteristics. The information in Exhibit 9.4 describes three Tapestry segments.

Geodemographic segmentation can be particularly useful for retailers because customers typically patronize stores close to their neighborhoods. Thus, retailers can use geodemographic segmentation to tailor each store's assortment to the preferences of the local community. If a toy store discovers that one of its stores is surrounded by Inner City Tenants (Exhibit 9.4), it might adjust its offering to include less expensive toys. Stores surrounded by Top Rung (Exhibit 9.4) would warrant a more expensive stock selection.

EXHIBIT 9.4 Examples of Tapestry

	Segment 01 - *Top Rung*	Segment 18 - *Cozy and Comfortable*	Segment 52 - *Inner City Tenants*
LifeMode Summary Group	L1 *High Society*	L2 *Upscale Avenues*	L8 *Global Roots*
Urbanization Summary Group	U3 *Metro Cities I*	U8 *Suburban Periphery II*	U4 *Metro Cities II*
Household Type	Married-Couple Families	Married-Couple Families	Mixed
Median Age	44.6	41.7	28.8
Income	High	Upper Middle	Lower Middle
Employment	Prof/Mgmt	Prof/Mgmt	Srvc/Prof/Mgmt/Skilled
Education	Bach/Grad Degree	Some College	No HS Diploma; HS; Some Coll
Residential	Single Family	Single Family	Multiunit Rentals
Activity	Participate in public/civic activities	Dine out often at family restaurants	Play football, basketball
Financial	Own stock worth $75,000+	Have personal line of credit	Have personal education loan
Activity	Vacation overseas	Shop at Kohl's	Go dancing
Media	Listen to classical, all-news radio	Listen to sporting events on radio	Read music, baby, fashion magazines
Vehicle	Own/Lease luxury car	Own/Lease minivan	Own/Lease Honda

Source: Esri, "Tapestry Segmentation: The Fabric of America's Neighborhoods."

(Left and middle): ©appleuzr/DigitalVision Vectors/Getty Images; *(right):* ©macrovector/iStock/Getty Images

This kind of segmentation is also useful for finding new locations; retailers identify their best locations and determine what types of people live in the area surrounding those stores, according to the geodemographic clusters. They can then find other potential locations where similar segments reside.

PROGRESS CHECK

1. What are the various segmentation methods?

Step 3: Evaluate Segment Attractiveness

LO9-2 Describe how firms determine whether a segment is attractive and therefore worth pursuing.

The third step in the segmentation process involves evaluating the attractiveness of the various segments. To undertake this evaluation, marketers first must determine whether the segment is worth pursuing, using several descriptive criteria: Is the segment identifiable, substantial, reachable, responsive, and profitable (see Exhibit 9.5)?

Identifiable Firms must be able to identify who is within their market to be able to design products or services to meet their needs. It is equally important to ensure that the segments are distinct from one another because too much overlap between segments means that distinct marketing strategies aren't necessary to meet segment members' needs. As Adding Value 9.2 details, an effective marketing strategy to distinct segments might even offer similar options but with different mascots and colors, if those identifiable segments are connected with particular universities.

Substantial Once the firm has identified its potential target markets, it needs to measure their sizes. If a market is too small or its buying power insignificant, it won't generate sufficient profits or be able to support the marketing mix activities. As China's economy started growing, there were not enough middle-class car buyers to push foreign automakers to design an entry-level vehicle. It was only after that number grew substantially that it became worthwhile for them to market to these identified consumers.

Reachable The best product or service cannot have any impact, no matter how identifiable or substantial the target market is, if that market cannot be reached (or accessed) through persuasive communications and product distribution. The consumer must know that the product or service exists, understand what it can do for him or her, and recognize how to buy it. If Victoria's Secret fails to tell women that it is offering some less luxurious, more affordable options, shoppers will just walk right past the store and buy basic bras from the Macy's store in the same mall.

EXHIBIT 9.5 Evaluation of Segment Attractiveness

Adding Value 9.2   Symbiosis in Your Stay: How Hotels Leverage Their Proximity to Universities[iv]

Orientation. Move-in day. Parents' day. Move-out day. Commencement. Reunion. Over the spans of time that students and their families interact with their colleges or universities, there are innumerable situations in which someone needs an extra room. Whether parents are dropping off their first-year students for their first taste of campus life, picking up their new graduates, or even returning as alumni, they represent a steady, predictable stream of potential revenue for the hotels located close to campus. These clearly identifiable parents and families are vast in number and tend to be highly responsive to offers that highlight their favorite university.

Recognizing the vast opportunity associated with this captive market, hotels are getting better at presenting themselves as virtual extensions of the school. From keeping sports memorabilia in the front lobby to decorating with school colors, these hotels seek to make devoted fans, students, and parents feel connected. One hotel near Boston University has established a dedicated room, the Terrier Suite, to honor the school's mascot. On its walls hang historical photographs of the school, and the minibar has glassware etched with the university emblem. The Nashville Marriott promotes its symbiosis with Vanderbilt University by decorating the lobby with one wall of equations, balanced by another wall of Vandy football helmets.

Beyond décor, hotels also are finding ways to pitch offers to parents that are valuable enough to encourage them to keep coming back for all four (or five or six) years that their students are enrolled in the school. A hotel located next to Bucknell University hands out cards, preprinted with the dates of key events for the upcoming year, such as homecoming or graduation, so that parents can book their next trips well in advance. The Revere Hotel Boston Common is in close proximity to several schools, such as Suffolk University, Tufts University, and Emerson College. For each guest, it determines his or her school loyalty, then hands out welcome packages stuffed with school merchandise, museum passes, and access

To target visitors to Boston University, one hotel features the Terrier Suite, to honor the school's mascot. In addition to terrier décor, on its walls hang historical photographs of the school, and the minibar has glassware etched with the university emblem.
Courtesy of the Hotel Commonwealth

to other local area attractions. It even solicited help designing staff members' uniforms from the design students attending the nearby Massachusetts College of Art and Design.

These moves appear popular among independent hotel operators as well as national chains. They reflect an increasing focus in the hotel industry to address the customer experience, in an effort to enhance customer loyalty and thereby buffer themselves from the dynamic demand they usually face. The targeted group of consumers also is strongly appealing. These parents already might be spending thousands to help pay for their children's educations, suggesting their strong promise for profit for the hotels as well. And ultimately, who can resist a hotel room festooned with balloons and streamers in their school colors?

If you are looking for a luxury SUV, General Motors hopes you will choose a Cadillac.
©Raymond Boyd/Getty Images

Responsive For a segmentation strategy to be successful, the customers in the segment must react similarly and positively to the firm's offering. If, through the firm's distinctive competencies, it cannot provide products or services to that segment, it should not target it. For instance, the Cadillac division of General Motors (GM) has introduced a line of cars to the large and very lucrative luxury car segment. People in this market typically purchase Porsches, BMWs, Audis, and Lexuses. In contrast, GM has been somewhat successful competing for the middle-priced family-oriented car and light truck segments. Thus, even though the luxury car segment meets all the other criteria for a successful segment, GM took a big risk in attempting to pursue this market.

Profitable Marketers must also focus their assessments on the potential profitability of each segment, both current and future. Some key factors to keep in mind in this analysis include market growth (current size and expected growth rate), market competitiveness (number of competitors, entry barriers, product substitutes), and market access (ease of developing or accessing distribution channels and brand familiarity). Some straightforward calculations can help illustrate the profitability of a segment:

$$\text{Segment profitability} = (\text{Segment size} \times \text{Segment adoption percentage} \times \text{Purchase behavior} \times \text{Profit margin percentage}) - \text{Fixed costs}$$

where

Segment size = Number of people in the segment

Segment adoption percentage = Percentage of customers in the segment who are likely to adopt the product/service

Purchase behavior = Purchase price × Number of times the customer would buy the product/service in a year

Profit margin percentage = (Selling price − Average variable costs) ÷ Selling price

Fixed costs = Advertising expenditure, rent, utilities, insurance, and administrative salaries for managers

To illustrate how a business might determine a segment's profitability, consider Camillo's start-up lawn service. He is trying to determine whether to target homeowners or businesses in a small midwestern town. Exhibit 9.6 estimates the profitability of the two segments. The homeowner segment is much larger than the business segment is, but several lawn services with established customers already exist. There is much less competition in the business segment. So, the segment adoption rate for the homeowner segment is only 1 percent, compared with 20 percent for the business segment. Camillo can charge a much higher price to businesses, and they use lawn services more frequently. The profit margin for the business segment is higher as well because Camillo can use large equipment to cut the grass and therefore save on variable labor costs. However, the fixed costs for purchasing and maintaining the large equipment are much higher for the business segment. Furthermore, he would need to spend more money obtaining and maintaining the business customers, whereas he would use less expensive door-to-door flyers to reach household customers. On the basis of these informed predictions, Camillo decides the business segment is more profitable for his lawn service.

This analysis provides an estimate of the profitability of two segments at one point in time. It is also useful to evaluate the profitability of a segment over the lifetime of one of its typical customers. To address such issues, marketers consider factors such as how long the customer will remain loyal to the firm, the defection rate (percentage of customers who switch on a yearly basis), the costs of replacing lost customers (advertising, promotion), whether customers will buy more or less expensive merchandise in the future, and other such factors.

Now that we've evaluated each segment's attractiveness (Step 3), we can select the target markets to pursue (Step 4).

EXHIBIT 9.6	Profitability of Two Market Segments for Camillo's Lawn Service	
	Homeowners	**Businesses**
Segment size	75,000	1,000
Segment adoption percentage	1%	20%
Purchase behavior		
Purchase price	$100	$500
Frequency of purchase	12 times	20 times
Profit margin percentage	60%	80%
Fixed costs	$400,000	$1,000,000
Segment profit	$140,000	$600,000

Step 4: Select a Target Market

LO9-3 Articulate the differences among targeting strategies: undifferentiated, differentiated, concentrated, or micromarketing.

The fourth step in the STP process is to select a target market. The key factor likely to affect this decision is the marketer's ability to pursue such an opportunity or target segment. Thus, as we mentioned in Chapter 2, a firm very carefully assesses both the attractiveness of the target market (opportunities and threats based on the SWOT analysis and the profitability of the segment) and its own competencies (strengths and weaknesses based on the SWOT analysis).

Determining how to select target markets is not always straightforward, as we discuss in more detail next and illustrate in Exhibit 9.7 with several targeting strategies.

| EXHIBIT 9.7 | Targeting Strategies |

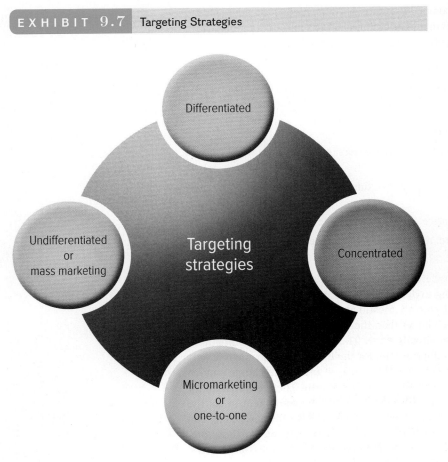

Undifferentiated Targeting Strategy, or Mass Marketing

When everyone might be considered a potential user of its product, a firm uses an **undifferentiated targeting strategy (mass marketing)**. (See Exhibit 9.7.) Clearly, such a targeting strategy focuses on the similarities in needs of the customers as opposed to the differences. If the product or service is perceived to provide similar benefits to most consumers, there simply is little need to develop separate strategies for different groups.

Although not a common strategy in today's complex marketplace, an undifferentiated strategy is used for many basic commodities such as salt or sugar. However, even those firms that offer salt and sugar now are trying to differentiate their products. Similarly, everyone with a car needs gasoline. Yet gasoline companies have vigorously moved from an undifferentiated strategy to a differentiated one by targeting their offerings to low-, medium-, and high-octane gasoline users.

Differentiated Targeting Strategy

Firms using a **differentiated targeting strategy** target several market segments with a different offering for each (again see Exhibit 9.7). Condé Nast has more than 20 niche magazines focused on different

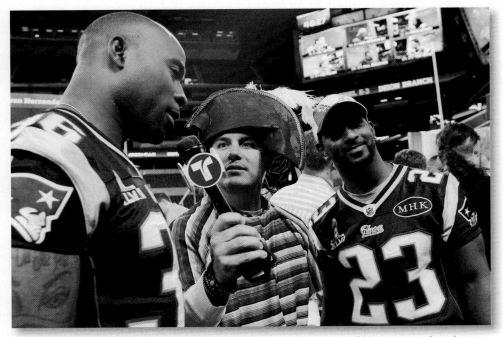

The NFL uses a differentiated targeting strategy to reach Latino and Hispanic markets by partnering with TV networks Telemundo and Univision.

©Kellen Micah/ICON SMI/Newscom

aspects of life—from *Vogue* for fashionistas to *Bon Appétit* for foodies to *GQ* for fashion-conscious men to *The New Yorker* for literature lovers to *Golf Digest* for those who walk the links.

Providing products or services that appeal to multiple segments helps diversify the business and therefore lowers the company's (in this case, Condé Nast's) overall risk. Even if one magazine suffers a circulation decline, the impact on the firm's profitability can be offset by revenue from another publication that continues to do well. But a differentiated strategy is likely to be more costly for the firm.

Firms also embrace differentiated targeting because it helps them obtain a bigger share of the market and increase the market for their products overall. For example, to reach Latino and Hispanic markets, the NFL partnered with television networks Telemundo and Univision. When the NFL wanted to reach more female fans, it created a new clothing line that featured more fashionable and better-fitting clothing for women. More recently the NFL has partnered with Nickelodeon to engage with kids, specifically boys between the ages of 6 and 11 years, with co-branded shows such as *NFL Rush Zone: Season of the Guardians*. In this series, a young football player protects NFL teams from villains, and NFL stars such as Drew Brees and DeMarcus Ware show up to help.[30] Then on Super Bowl Sunday, Nickelodeon airs a competition show in which Nickelodeon stars face off against NFL athletes.[31]

Concentrated Targeting Strategy When an organization selects a single, primary target market and focuses all its energies on providing a product to fit that market's needs, it is using a concentrated targeting strategy. Entrepreneurial start-up ventures often benefit from using a concentrated strategy, which allows them to employ their limited resources more efficiently. Newton Running, for instance, has concentrated its targeting strategy on runners—but not all

Newton Running uses a concentrated segmentation strategy—not all runners, but those who want to improve their running form.

©Newton Running

When women search for pregnancy-related information, P&G is notified and targets advertising exclusively and specifically to these women.

Source: Procter & Gamble

runners. It focuses only on those who prefer to land on their forefeet while running, a style that has been suggested as more natural, efficient, and less injury-prone than the style encouraged by more traditional running shoes with their heel-first construction and substantial cushioning. In comparison, though it also is known for its running shoes, Nike uses a differentiated targeting strategy. It makes shoes for segments that include basketball and football players and skateboarders; it also makes shoes for fashion-conscious white-collar workers with its subsidiary brand Cole Haan. As Adding Value 9.3 explains, Under Armour targets a specific type of runner: those willing to endure awful conditions, just to say they did it.

Micromarketing[32] Take a look at your collection of belts. Have you ever had one made to match your exact specifications? (If you're interested, try www.leathergoodsconnection.com.) When a firm tailors a product or service to suit an individual customer's wants or needs, it is undertaking an extreme form of segmentation called micromarketing or one-to-one marketing.

Procter & Gamble (P&G) uses big data gathered from Google searches to target expectant mothers exclusively. When women begin searching for pregnancy-related information, P&G is notified. Therefore, it can advertise exclusively and specifically to these women, offering advice on diaper bags or showing them which types and sizes of diapers will be most appropriate as their babies grow.[33]

LO9-4 Determine the value proposition.

Step 5: Identify and Develop Positioning Strategy

The last step in developing a market segmentation strategy is positioning. Market positioning involves a process of defining the marketing mix variables so that target customers have a clear, distinctive, desirable understanding of what the product does or represents in comparison with competing products.

The positioning strategy can help communicate the firm's or the product's value proposition, which communicates the customer benefits to be received from a product or service and thereby provides reasons for wanting to purchase it.

To visualize the value proposition, examine the Circles for a Successful Value Proposition framework in part A of Exhibit 9.8.[34] The bottom left circle in part A represents the customer needs and wants, the bottom right circle represents the company's offerings (i.e.,

EXHIBIT 9.8   Circles for a Successful Value Proposition

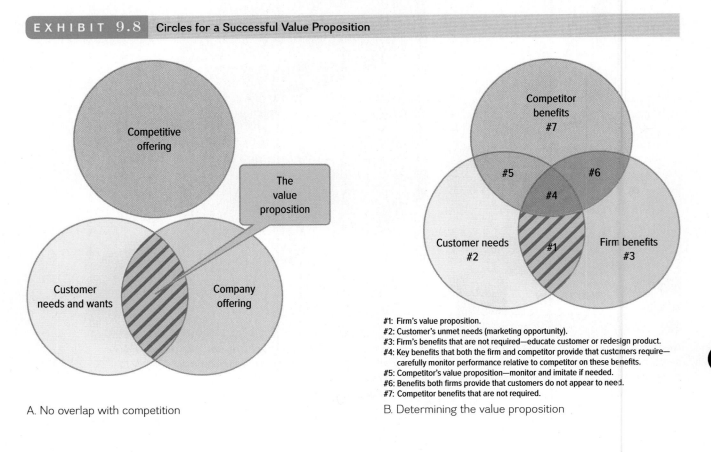

#1: Firm's value proposition.
#2: Customer's unmet needs (marketing opportunity).
#3: Firm's benefits that are not required—educate customer or redesign product.
#4: Key benefits that both the firm and competitor provide that customers require—carefully monitor performance relative to competitor on these benefits.
#5: Competitor's value proposition—monitor and imitate if needed.
#6: Benefits both firms provide that customers do not appear to need.
#7: Competitor benefits that are not required.

A. No overlap with competition

B. Determining the value proposition

Adding Value 9.3 — Are We Still Having Fun? Under Armour's Grueling Advertising Campaign for Runners[v]

During a two-day training camp, held high in the Colorado mountains, Under Armour invited 35 athletes to prove their mettle—and the benefits of Under Armour gear. Outfitted in the latest gear, the participants battled through sleet, snow, and 10,000-foot elevations to prove that they had the heart of a runner.

In the resulting marketing communications, shared mainly through social media and the brand's dedicated sites, the runners describe the harrowing experience, noting just how bad the conditions really were. Some of the international group of athletes had never run at high altitudes before. Others, upon receiving the survival packs that Under Armour provided, stocked with knives and small oxygen tanks, wondered just what they had gotten into. But the spot also offers inspiration and joy, showing exhausted runners hugging in victory after they complete the grueling course.

The spot also ends with a promise for the next adventure, noting that the mountains were nothing compared with the desert that comes next. Thus the brand is setting up a multi-episode communication campaign that seeks to connect with and inspire runners and active people to push themselves to the limits as well. In a parallel social media campaign, it promotes the hashtag #earnyourspot. Thus the chosen few who accept the challenge and earn the right to call themselves runners enjoy a unique status—a situation that Under Armour hopes will rub off on its brand image as well.

GOT WHAT IT TAKES?

Under Armour uses a concentrated targeting strategy in its campaign to reach extreme runners.

Source: Under Armour, Inc.

its capabilities), and the top circle represents the benefits offered by competitors. The best situation is if a company's product or service offering overlaps with customer needs and wants but suffers no overlap with competitors' offerings (Exhibit 9.8). The shaded portion reflects the value proposition, or the intersection of what the customer needs and wants with what the company can offer. Unfortunately, even if the situation depicted in part A of Exhibit 9.8 existed, and the product or service is currently successful, that success would not be sustainable because competitors would attempt to copy the important product or service attributes and therefore begin to encroach on the firm's value proposition. Maintaining a unique value proposition can be sustained in the long term only in monopoly situations or possibly monopolistic competition situations.

In part B of Exhibit 9.8, the intersection of customer needs, the benefits provided by our focal firm, and the benefits provided by a competing firm reveal seven specific spaces where a product or service might be located. Let's look at each one in turn, using the offerings of the airline industry as hypothetical examples to understand each space.

Space 1. Representing the firm's value proposition, this space reveals which customer needs are effectively met by the benefits that the firm provides but not by the benefits provided by competitors. That is, there is no overlap between competitors. When airline customers prefer a cattle-call approach to seating, which allows them to choose their own seats on the plane as long as they get an early check-in, they turn to Southwest, and Southwest alone, for their flights.

Space 2. These customer needs are unmet. It represents an important marketing opportunity in that the firm could create new products or services or augment existing ones to better satisfy these needs. A direct route between two cities that currently are not connected by any airline represents a prime example of such a space.

Space 3. Customers express little need or desire for these company benefits. The firm thus has several options. It might educate customers about the importance and benefits that it provides with this space, to encourage customers to develop a sense of

Audi features the all-wheel-drive Quattro, which is positioned to appeal to those wanting great performance and handling, particularly on snowy and icy roads.

©Lexan/Shutterstock

Salient Attributes

Another common positioning strategy focuses on the product attributes that are most important to the target market. With its all-wheel-drive Quattro, Audi has positioned itself on performance and handling. Targeting a different market, Subaru positions its all-wheel drive slightly differently, instead focusing on safety and handling.

Symbols

A well-known symbol can also be used as a positioning tool. What comes to mind when you think of Colonel Sanders, the Jolly Green Giant, the Gerber Baby, or Tony the Tiger? Or consider the Texaco star, the Nike swoosh, or the Ralph Lauren polo player. These symbols are so strong and well known that they create a position for the brand that distinguishes it from its competition. Many such symbols are registered trademarks that are legally protected by the companies that developed them.

Competition

Firms can choose to position their products or services against a specific competitor or an entire product/service classification. For instance, although most luggage companies focus on building lightweight and functional designs, Saddleback Leather focuses on rugged durability and a classic look. Offering a 100-year guarantee on its products, the owner Dave positions his bags as something "they'll fight over when you're dead."[37] This craftsmanship comes at a cost—its suitcases sell for more than $1,000.

Marketers must be careful, however, that they don't position their product too closely to their competition. If, for instance, their package or logo looks too much like a competitor's, they might be opening

THE
Ultimate Day Pack

Saddleback Leather Co.
"They'll fight over it when you're dead."

How does Saddleback Leather position itself?

Source: Saddleback Leather Company

Adding Value 9.3 | Are We Still Having Fun? Under Armour's Grueling Advertising Campaign for Runners[v]

During a two-day training camp, held high in the Colorado mountains, Under Armour invited 35 athletes to prove their mettle—and the benefits of Under Armour gear. Outfitted in the latest gear, the participants battled through sleet, snow, and 10,000-foot elevations to prove that they had the heart of a runner.

In the resulting marketing communications, shared mainly through social media and the brand's dedicated sites, the runners describe the harrowing experience, noting just how bad the conditions really were. Some of the international group of athletes had never run at high altitudes before. Others, upon receiving the survival packs that Under Armour provided, stocked with knives and small oxygen tanks, wondered just what they had gotten into. But the spot also offers inspiration and joy, showing exhausted runners hugging in victory after they complete the grueling course.

The spot also ends with a promise for the next adventure, noting that the mountains were nothing compared with the desert that comes next. Thus the brand is setting up a multi-episode communication campaign that seeks to connect with and inspire runners and active people to push themselves to the limits as well. In a parallel social media campaign, it promotes the hashtag #earnyourspot. Thus the chosen few who accept the challenge and earn the right to call themselves runners enjoy a unique status—a situation that Under Armour hopes will rub off on its brand image as well.

GOT WHAT IT TAKES?

Under Armour uses a concentrated targeting strategy in its campaign to reach extreme runners.

Source: Under Armour, Inc.

its capabilities), and the top circle represents the benefits offered by competitors. The best situation is if a company's product or service offering overlaps with customer needs and wants but suffers no overlap with competitors' offerings (Exhibit 9.8). The shaded portion reflects the value proposition, or the intersection of what the customer needs and wants with what the company can offer. Unfortunately, even if the situation depicted in part A of Exhibit 9.8 existed, and the product or service is currently successful, that success would not be sustainable because competitors would attempt to copy the important product or service attributes and therefore begin to encroach on the firm's value proposition. Maintaining a unique value proposition can be sustained in the long term only in monopoly situations or possibly monopolistic competition situations.

In part B of Exhibit 9.8, the intersection of customer needs, the benefits provided by our focal firm, and the benefits provided by a competing firm reveal seven specific spaces where a product or service might be located. Let's look at each one in turn, using the offerings of the airline industry as hypothetical examples to understand each space.

Space 1. Representing the firm's value proposition, this space reveals which customer needs are effectively met by the benefits that the firm provides but not by the benefits provided by competitors. That is, there is no overlap between competitors. When airline customers prefer a cattle-call approach to seating, which allows them to choose their own seats on the plane as long as they get an early check-in, they turn to Southwest, and Southwest alone, for their flights.

Space 2. These customer needs are unmet. It represents an important marketing opportunity in that the firm could create new products or services or augment existing ones to better satisfy these needs. A direct route between two cities that currently are not connected by any airline represents a prime example of such a space.

Space 3. Customers express little need or desire for these company benefits. The firm thus has several options. It might educate customers about the importance and benefits that it provides with this space, to encourage customers to develop a sense of

A firm's value proposition is represented by the benefits that a firm provides but that its competitors do not. Airline customers who are looking for a good value and will therefore tolerate a cattle-call approach to seating, which allows them to choose their own seats on the plane as long as they get an early check-in, turn to Southwest for their flights (top). Alternatively, customers who are looking for a spacious, luxurious experience will turn to Singapore Airlines (bottom).

(Top): ©Buskirk Services, Inc./PhotoEdit; (bottom): ©Kyodo News via Getty Images

their need. Alternatively, it could reengineer its approach to stop providing these unwanted benefits, which likely would enable it to save money. For example, when airlines realized that passengers cared little about the appearance of a piece of lettuce underneath the in-flight sandwiches they were served, they saved millions of dollars they had previously spent on unwanted produce.

Space 4. These needs are being met by the benefits of the firm as well as by competitors. Many customers make frequent trips between major cities, such as New York and Washington, DC, and many airlines offer multiple direct flights each day between these hubs. Each firm therefore works to compete effectively, such as by offering convenient flight times or striving to increase its on-time rates to make it easier for customers to compare firms on these specific features.

Space 5. This space constitutes the competitor's value proposition: the needs of customers that are met by benefits a competitor provides but not by the benefits provided by our focal firm. For example, only a few airlines host separate lounges for their best customers; a lower-cost airline cannot compete in this space. However, if more and more customers start to make demands for these benefits, the focal firm needs to monitor developments carefully and match some benefits if possible.

Space 6. Although both the focal firm and its competitors provide these benefits, they somehow are not meeting customer needs. The stringent security screening requirements aim to increase passenger safety, but they also represent a significant inconvenience that many fliers associate with airlines rather than federal regulators. Significant efforts by the focal firm to educate customers about these needs would also benefit competitors, so they likely are lower in the priority list of spending.

Space 7. Finally, some competitor benefits are either undesired or unnecessary among customers. Similar to Space 3, the competitor could invest money to educate customers about the importance of these benefits and highlight their needs through advertising and promotional campaigns. If so, the focal firm should recognize that this need is moving to Space 5. Alternatively, the competitor could reengineer its products to eliminate these benefits, in which case it requires no response from the focal firm.

Regardless of their existing space, firms must constantly and closely monitor their competitors' offerings. If competitors offer features that the firm does not, it is important to determine their importance to customers. Important attributes should be considered for inclusion in the firm's offering—or else they will provide a unique value proposition for competitors.

In Exhibit 9.9, we highlight the elements of developing and communicating a firm's value proposition. The main value proposition components are:

1. Target market
2. Offering name or brand
3. Product/service category or concept
4. Unique point of difference/benefits

Let's focus on a couple of well-known products, Gatorade and 7UP, and their potential value propositions (brackets are added to separate the value proposition components):

EXHIBIT 9.9	Value Proposition Statement Key Elements	
	Gatorade	7UP
Target market	Athletes around the world	Non-cola consumers
Offering name or brand	Gatorade	7UP
Product/service category or concept	Sports drink	Non-caffeinated soft drink
Unique point of difference/ benefits	Represents the heart, hustle, and soul of athleticism and gives the fuel for working muscles, fluid for hydration, and electrolytes to help replace what is lost in sweat before, during, and after activity to get the most out of your body.	Light, refreshing, lemon-lime flavored, and has a crisp, bubbly, and clean taste.

- **Gatorade:**[35] To [athletes around the world] [Gatorade] is the [sports drink] [that represents the heart, hustle, and soul of athleticism and gives the fuel for working muscles, fluid for hydration, and electrolytes to help replace what is lost in sweat before, during, and after activity to get the most out of your body].

- **7UP:**[36] To [non-cola consumers] [7UP] is a [non-caffeinated soft drink] that is [light, refreshing, lemon-lime flavored, and has a crisp, bubbly, and clean taste].

LO9-5 Define positioning, and describe how firms do it.

Positioning Methods

Firms position products and services based on different methods such as the value proposition, salient attributes, symbols, and competition.

Value Proposition Value is a popular positioning method because the relationship of price to quality is among the most important considerations for consumers when they make a purchase decision. But value is in the eyes of the beholder. Some energy bar users buy only KIND bars because they are made with all natural ingredients, have no artificial preservatives or sweeteners, come in a multitude of varieties, including its original nut-based products, fruit snacks, and protein bars, and are a relatively healthy snack option. Consistent with the values of many in its target market, it embraces a conscious marketing perspective. Importantly, it has attempted to provide a better-tasting alternative to competing energy bars like PowerBars. PowerBars, while also healthy and nutritious, appeal to endurance athletes and endurance athlete wannabees by providing high-protein energy bars designed to replenish vital nutrients to tired muscles. Recall from our discussion in Chapter 1, value means different things to different people. Both KIND and PowerBars provide value to their respective target markets.

What are the value propositions for Gatorade and 7UP?

(Left): ©McGraw-Hill Education; (right): ©PhotoTodos/ Shutterstock

KIND and PowerBar both offer their respective target markets a good value. KIND bars (left) are made with natural ingredients, all of which are pronounceable, thus supporting a healthy lifestyle. PowerBars (right) are protein bars designed to improve the performance of athletes.

Audi features the all-wheel-drive Quattro, which is positioned to appeal to those wanting great performance and handling, particularly on snowy and icy roads.

©Lexan/Shutterstock

THE
Ultimate Day Pack

Saddleback Leather Co.
"They'll fight over it when you're dead."

How does Saddleback Leather position itself?

Source: Saddleback Leather Company

Salient Attributes Another common positioning strategy focuses on the product attributes that are most important to the target market. With its all-wheel-drive Quattro, Audi has positioned itself on performance and handling. Targeting a different market, Subaru positions its all-wheel drive slightly differently, instead focusing on safety and handling.

Symbols A well-known symbol can also be used as a positioning tool. What comes to mind when you think of Colonel Sanders, the Jolly Green Giant, the Gerber Baby, or Tony the Tiger? Or consider the Texaco star, the Nike swoosh, or the Ralph Lauren polo player. These symbols are so strong and well known that they create a position for the brand that distinguishes it from its competition. Many such symbols are registered trademarks that are legally protected by the companies that developed them.

Competition Firms can choose to position their products or services against a specific competitor or an entire product/service classification. For instance, although most luggage companies focus on building lightweight and functional designs, Saddleback Leather focuses on rugged durability and a classic look. Offering a 100-year guarantee on its products, the owner Dave positions his bags as something "they'll fight over when you're dead."[37] This craftsmanship comes at a cost—its suitcases sell for more than $1,000.

Marketers must be careful, however, that they don't position their product too closely to their competition. If, for instance, their package or logo looks too much like a competitor's, they might be opening themselves up to a trademark infringement lawsuit. Many private-label and store brands have been challenged for using packaging that appears confusingly similar to that of the national brand leaders in a category. Similarly, McDonald's sues anyone who uses the *Mc* prefix, including McSleep Inns and McDental Services, even though in the latter case there was little possibility that consumers would believe the fast-food restaurant company would branch out into dental services.

Positioning Using Perceptual Mapping

Now that we have identified the various methods by which firms position their products and services, we discuss the actual steps they go through to establish that position. When developing a positioning strategy, firms go through six important steps. But before you read about these steps, examine Exhibits 9.10A through 9.10D on the next page, a hypothetical perceptual map of the soft drink industry. A perceptual map displays, in two or more dimensions, the position of products or brands in the consumer's mind. We have chosen two dimensions for illustrative purposes: sweet versus light taste (vertical) and less natural versus healthy (horizontal). Also, though this industry is quite complex, we have simplified the diagram to include only a few players in the market. The position of each brand is denoted by a small circle, except for the focal brand, Gatorade, which is denoted by a star. The numbered circles denote consumers' ideal points—where a particular market segment's ideal product would lie on the map. The larger the numbered circle, the larger the market size.

Gatorade and Powerade are positioned similarly and compete with each other for customers who seek healthy, sweet drinks.
©Rachel Epstein/PhotoEdit

To derive a perceptual map such as shown in Exhibits 9.10A through 9.10D, marketers follow six steps.

1. **Determine consumers' perceptions and evaluations of the product or service in relation to competitors' product or service.** Marketers determine their brand's position by asking a series of questions about their firm's and the competitors' products. For instance, they might ask how the consumer uses the existing product or services, what items the consumer regards as alternative sources to satisfy his or her needs, what the person likes or dislikes about the brand in relation to competitors, and what might make that person choose one brand over another. Exhibit 9.10A depicts the five products using two dimensions (light taste–sweet taste; and less natural–healthy).

2. **Identify the market's ideal points and size.** On a perceptual map, marketers can represent the size of current and potential markets. For example, Exhibit 9.10B uses differently

EXHIBIT 9.10C Perceptual Map, Chart C

EXHIBIT 9.10D Perceptual Map, Chart D

sized ovals that correspond to the market size. Ideal point 1 represents the largest market, so if the firm does not already have a product positioned close to this point, it should consider an introduction. Point 3 is the smallest market, so there are relatively few customers who want a healthy, light-tasting drink. This is not to suggest that this market should be ignored; however, the company might want to consider a niche market rather than mass market strategy for this group of consumers.

3. **Identify competitors' positions.** When the firm understands how its customers view its brand relative to competitors', it must study how those same competitors position themselves. For instance, Powerade positions itself closely to Gatorade, which means they appear next to each other on the perceptual map and appeal to target market 2 (see Exhibit 9.10C). They are also often found next to each other on store shelves, are similarly priced, and are viewed by customers as sports drinks. Gatorade also knows that its sports drink is perceived to be more like Powerade than like its own Propel Fitness Water (located near target market 3) or Coke (target market 1).

4. **Determine consumer preferences.** The firm knows what the consumer thinks of the products or services in the marketplace and their positions relative to one another. Now it must find out what the consumer really wants—that is, determine the ideal product or service that appeals to each market. For example, a huge market exists for traditional Gatorade, and that market is shared by Powerade. Gatorade also recognizes a market, depicted as the ideal product for segment 4 on the perceptual map, of consumers who would prefer a less sweet, less calorie-laden drink that offers the same rejuvenating properties as Gatorade. Currently, no product is adequately serving market 4.

5. **Select the position.** Continuing with the Gatorade example, the company has some choices to appeal to the "less sweet sports drink" target market 4. It could develop a new product to meet the needs of market 4 (see Exhibit 9.10D, option 1). Alternatively, it could adjust or reposition its marketing approach—its product and promotion—to sell original Gatorade to market 4 (option 2). Finally, it could ignore what target market 4 really wants and hope that consumers will be attracted to the original Gatorade because it is closer to their ideal product than anything else on the market.

6. **Monitor the positioning strategy.** Markets are not stagnant. Consumers' tastes shift, and competitors react to those shifts. Attempting to maintain the same position year after year can spell disaster for any company. Thus, firms must always view the first three steps of the positioning process as ongoing, with adjustments made in step four as necessary.

Despite the apparent simplicity of this presentation, marketers should recognize that changing their firm's positioning is never an easy task.

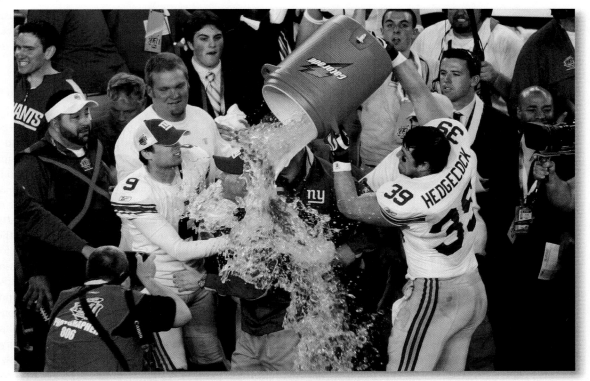

Gatorade uses athletes to compete for target markets in Exhibit 9.10.
©Jim McIsaac/Getty Images

PROGRESS CHECK

1.   What is a perceptual map?
2.   Identify the six positioning steps.

Reviewing Learning Objectives

LO9-1 **Outline the different methods of segmenting a market.**

There is really no one "best" method to segment a market. Firms choose from various methods on the basis of the type of product/service they offer and their goals for the segmentation strategy. For instance, if the firm wants to identify its customers easily, demographic or geographic segmentation likely will work best. But if it is trying to dig deeper into why customers might buy its offering, then psychographic, geodemographic, benefit, or behavioral segmentation (occasion and loyalty) work best. Typically, a combination of several segmentation methods is most effective.

LO9-2 **Describe how firms determine whether a segment is attractive and therefore worth pursuing.**

Marketers use several criteria to assess a segment's attractiveness. First, the customer should be identifiable—companies must know what types of people are in the market so they can direct their efforts appropriately. Second, the market must be substantial enough to be worth pursuing. If relatively few people appear in a segment, it is probably not cost effective to direct special marketing mix efforts toward them. Third, the market must be reachable—the firm must be able to reach the segment through effective communications and distribution. Fourth, the firm must be responsive to the needs of customers in a segment. It must be able to deliver a product or service that the segment will embrace. Finally, the segment must be profitable, both in the near term and over the lifetime of the customer.

LO9-3 **Articulate the differences among targeting strategies: undifferentiated, differentiated, concentrated, or micromarketing.**

Firms use a targeting strategy after they have identified their segments. An undifferentiated strategy uses no targeting at all and works only for products or services that most consumers consider to be commodities. The difference between a differentiated and a concentrated strategy is that the differentiated approach targets multiple segments, whereas the concentrated strategy targets only one. Larger firms with multiple product/service offerings generally use a differentiated strategy; smaller firms or those with a limited product/service offering often use a concentrated strategy. Firms that employ a micromarketing, or one-to-one, marketing strategy tailor their product/service offering to each customer—that is, it is custom-made. In the past, micromarketing was reserved primarily for artisans, tailors, or other craftspeople who would make items exactly as the customer wanted. Recently, however, larger manufacturers and retailers have begun experimenting with custom-made merchandise as well. Service providers, in contrast, are largely accustomed to customizing their offering.

LO9-4 **Determine the value proposition.**

A firm's value proposition communicates the customer benefits to be received from a product or service and thereby provides reasons for the customer to want to purchase it. It consists of the attributes of a product or service that are desired by the target market but not available from competitors. Firms could attempt to offer attributes that are important to its customers, whether or not they are offered by competitors. For attributes that are not important to

its customers, it should either educate its customers about the importance of those attributes, deemphasize them, or not offer those product or service attributes.

LO9-5 **Define positioning, and describe how firms do it.**

Positioning is the *P* in the STP (segmentation, targeting, and positioning) process. It refers to how customers think about a product, service, or brand in the market relative to competitors' offerings. Firms position their products and services according to several criteria. Some focus on their offering's value—customers get a lot for what the product or service costs. Others determine the most important attributes for customers and position their offering on the basis of those attributes. Symbols can also be used for positioning, though few products or services are associated with symbols that are compelling enough to drive people to buy. Finally, one of the most common positioning methods relies on the favorable comparison of the firm's offering with the products or services marketed by competitors. When developing a positioning strategy and a perceptual map, firms go through six steps. First, they determine consumers' perceptions and evaluations of the product or service in relation to competitors. Second, they identify the market's ideal points and market sizes for those products or services. Third, they identify competitors' positions. Fourth, they determine consumer preferences. Fifth, they select the position. Finally, they monitor the positioning strategy.

Key Terms

- behavioral segmentation, 271
- benefit segmentation, 271
- concentrated targeting strategy, 279
- demographic segmentation, 266
- differentiated targeting strategy, 278
- geodemographic segmentation, 274
- geographic segmentation, 266

- ideal point, 285
- lifestyle, 270
- loyalty segmentation, 272
- market positioning, 280
- micromarketing, 280
- occasion segmentation, 272
- one-to-one marketing, 280
- perceptual map, 285
- psychographic segmentation, 268

- psychographics, 268
- self-concept, 268
- self-values, 268
- undifferentiated targeting strategy (mass marketing), 278
- value, 283
- value proposition, 280
- Values and Lifestyles Survey (VALS), 270

Marketing Digitally

1. Go to https://doc.arcgis.com/en/esri-demographics/data/tapestry-segmentation.htm, and identify five segments that you would expect to find in your zip code. Then go to www.esri.com/data/tapestry/zip-lookup, and type in your zip code. Compare the segments that are found in your zip code with your initial prediction. Are they similar or different ? Discuss the extent to which you believe these are accurate descriptions of the main segments of people who reside in your zip code.

2. Go to the VALS website (www.strategicbusinessinsights.com/vals/ustypes.shtml) and review the eight types that VALS uses to segment consumers by clicking on the blue links. What two VALS types do you think Harley-Davidson uses to target young adults? Explain your answer.

Marketing Applications

1. What segmentation methods would you suggest for a small entrepreneur starting her own business selling gourmet chocolates? Justify why you would recommend those methods.

2. You have been asked to identify various segments in the market and then a potential targeting strategy. Describe the segments for a pet supply store, and then justify the best targeting strategy to use.

3. What types of products would you use demographic segmentation for? How about psychographic segmentation? Explain how these products differ.

4. You have been asked to evaluate the attractiveness of a group of identified potential market segments. What criteria will you use to evaluate those segments? Why are these appropriate criteria?

5. A small-business owner is trying to evaluate the profitability of different segments. What are the key factors you would recommend she consider? Over what period of time would you recommend she evaluate?

6. Think about the various soft drinks that you know (e.g., Coca-Cola, Pepsi, 7-Up, Gatorade, Powerade). How do those various brands position themselves in the market?

7. Put yourself in the position of an entrepreneur who is developing a new product to introduce into the market. Briefly describe the product and each component of its value proposition.

8. Think of a specific company or organization that uses various types of promotional material to market its offerings. The web, magazine ads, newspaper ads, catalogs, newspaper inserts, direct-mail pieces, and flyers might all be sources for a variety of promotional materials. Locate two or three promotional pieces for the company and use them as a basis to analyze the segments being targeted. Describe the methods used for segmenting the market reflected in these materials, and describe characteristics of the target market according to the materials. Be sure to include a copy of all the materials used in the analysis.

9. You have been hired recently by a large bank in its credit card marketing division. The bank has relationships with a large number of colleges and prints a wide variety of credit cards featuring college logos, images, and the like. You have been asked to oversee the implementation of a new program targeting first-year college students at the schools with which the bank has a relationship. The bank has already purchased the names and home addresses of the incoming class. You have been told that no credit checks will be required for these cards as long as the student is over 18 years of age. The bank plans a first-day-of-school marketing blitz that includes free hats, T-shirts, and book promotions, as well as free pizza, if the students simply fill out an application. Do you think it is a good idea to target this program to these new students?

Quiz Yourself

1. Which of the following is *not* a criterion that must be met when evaluating segment attractiveness?
   a. Substantial
   b. Reachable
   c. Defined
   d. Responsive
   e. Profitable

2. A firm's value proposition communicates the benefits received from the product or service by customers. Therefore, the value proposition provides the customer with which key piece(s) of information?
   a. The price of the good or service
   b. Where to buy the good or service
   c. How to use the good or service
   d. Reasons to buy the good or service
   e. All of these are correct.

(Answers to these two questions can be found in the Quiz Yourself Answer Key section.)

Chapter Case Study

MERCEDES-BENZ

From Janis Joplin to Jay-Z, The Eagles to Outcast, Kanye West to Mariah Carey, generations of singers and songwriters have been inspired to mention Mercedes-Benz in their lyrics. Whether the brand offers a dreamed-of aspiration that they hope to access someday, or

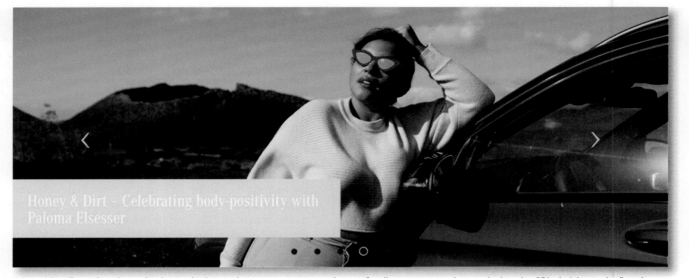

Honey & Dirt - Celebrating body-positivity with
Paloma Elsesser

Mercedes-Benz has launched a multichannel campaign targeted specifically at women that includes the "She's Mercedes" website.

Source: Mercedes

a signal of their wealth and power, Mercedes appeals to the musicians as well as their audiences. When lyricists beg for a Mercedes, or brag about how many sit in their garages, listeners around the world know exactly what they mean.

The diversity of musicians and musical styles represented in the overall list of songs about Mercedes reflects just how effective the car brand has been at establishing a strong image as a luxury vehicle. But simultaneously, Mercedes-Benz also has developed a specific and strategic segmentation, targeting, and positioning approach that allows it to access unique and diverse markets of consumers and potential buyers. With its various models and strategic marketing plan, Mercedes considers ways to segment customers by gender, location, age, and economic strata, among other factors. Then it determines appropriate methods to appeal to each of those segments with dedicated communications, designs, and car models. Let's consider some examples of its STP efforts.

Gender[38] As a function of its "Best Customer Experience" initiative, Mercedes-Benz has launched a multichannel campaign targeted specifically at women. The brand owners expressed their desire to make sure that all customers receive precisely the car buying and owning experience they want. In an attempt to ensure such access and experiences for women, the "She's Mercedes" campaign features a dedicated website, a print magazine, and sponsored events. The events are mostly networking opportunities, and the magazine prominently features successful women (who also own Mercedes, of course) and their efforts to balance work, family, and other commitments. In addition to similar sorts of stories, the website hosts a platform for consumers to share their ideas and impressions.

But the website also features a clever tool designed to target women buyers and position Mercedes as a brand that is friendly to female consumers. Specifically, it gives women the option to use a dedicated configurator—that is, a tool that many car companies provide to help customers build the exact car they want, using virtual tools. On the conventional Mercedes tool, a similar tool allows potential buyers to select their model, color, wheels, audio package, transmission, and so on. On the She's Mercedes site, the configurator instead focuses more on lifestyle questions rather than soliciting preferred drive train sizes. For example, a potential buyer can list her favorite music, hobbies, and travel plans. An algorithm then proposes several models of Mercedes cars that are likely to fit her preferences. She can add options to those models, or else accept the prespecified car that the company has targeted especially for her—or at least segments of consumers like her.

Location[39] Mercedes already is nearly everywhere. But it also develops distinct targeting and positioning strategies in the various locations in which it appears. Thus for example, it notes upward trends in its worldwide sales, but it also acknowledges that sales grew by 14 percent in the United States, 3 percent in Canada, 27 percent in South Korea, 4 percent in Japan, and so on. It also pays particular attention to the BRIC nations (Brazil, Russia, India, and China; see Chapter 8). In all these countries, it has enjoyed strong, double-digit sales growth. Furthermore, Mercedes specifies that in these markets, the luxury car market itself is growing much faster than in other traditional markets. For example, while the U.S. market for luxury automobiles might be growing at a respectable 6 percent annually, India shows promise of increasing by a remarkable 24 percent.

Noting the importance of the Indian luxury car market in particular, Mercedes has developed unique and specific methods to appeal to these consumers. For example, it pursued local production options to avoid the high import taxes and keep the cars affordable. Acknowledging the high "chauffeur share," such that many Indians have drivers to maneuver their cars about, Mercedes made sure to devote attention to the backseats of the high-end sedans it sells there. Similarly, to broaden its appeal in China, where the growing market demands a wider variety of options, Mercedes introduced 15 models in a single year, while also expanding its sales network in that country with 50 new dealerships.[40]

Age[41] When research showed Mercedes that its average customer in the United States was 52 years of age, the company also adopted a more explicit age-based segmentation approach that would help it appeal to younger buyers. Somewhat ironically, its investigation of buyers in their 30s showed that they actually had strongly nostalgic leanings. They liked the idea of Mercedes as a heritage brand. Accordingly, to position the brand as nostalgic, advertising targeting these buyers features glamour shots of the Mercedes legacy, as manifested in row upon row of beautifully designed cars, from the past to the present.

In addition, Mercedes has vastly expanded its product lines to introduce some sportier models and provide a clear contrast to the "boring" sedans that young consumers might associate with the brand. For example, its A-Class is smaller but still powerful, available in hatchback versions, and totally equipped with the latest in smart technology. Noting younger consumers' interest in environmental sustainability, Mercedes also has improved the emissions rate for most of its models and touts its energy-saving innovations.

Economic Strata[42] For luxury carmakers, the lowest-end models in their product lines often represent only a small portion of their sales. Yet these models are critically important when it comes to attracting new customers and, potentially, establishing their lifelong loyalty to the brand. Accordingly, Mercedes has developed some comparatively less option-laden models to lure first-time and unconventional buyers to their dealerships. It introduced its CLA model at a base price of less than $40,000. When consumers realized that they could purchase or lease a Mercedes-Benz for approximately the same monthly price that they would spend for a high-end Toyota or Honda, many of them switched happily.

For the most part, the target market for such models includes young professionals. These consumers earn a steady income that enables them to take on a car payment—but they cannot pay for a new car outright, and the monthly payments must fit their budgets. Mercedes accordingly has enjoyed sales increases due to the introductions of the lower-end models. Furthermore, these purchases are not repeat buys: Approximately 75 percent of CLA purchasers are new to the brand. Such statistics suggest an expanded market for the brands. As these buyers age, advance in their careers, and consider more expensive car purchases, they should be more likely to continue visiting the dealerships that provided them with their very first luxury automobile.

Questions

1. What are the main ways Mercedes-Benz segments its customers? Are there any other methods in this chapter that it might use?

2. How can Mercedes-Benz position itself effectively to appeal to consumers who are (a) men, (b) younger than 30, (c) from China, or (d) very wealthy?

Endnotes

1. John Ballard, "lululemon athletica Pushes Forward with Ambitious Goals for 2020," *The Motley Fool*, December 10, 2017.

2. Adrianne Pasquarelli, "lululemon Woos Men with First Campaign," *Advertising Age*, September 17, 2017.

3. CH Studio, "lululemon Taps Deep Design Expertise to Create New Outerwear for Men," *Cool Hunting*, November 26, 2016.

4. Erik Oster, "lululemon Is Redefining What Strength Means in Its First Campaign for Men," *Adweek*, September 14, 2017.

5. Ibid.

6. Ballard, "lululemon athletica Pushes Forward."

7. Ibid.

8. Lauren Thomas, "lululemon's Laurent Potdevin Sees Huge Potential in Men's Apparel Market, Adds Company Is 'Almost Halfway' to Lofty Sales Goals," *CNBC*, December 7, 2017.

9. Beth Wright, "lululemon Switches Supply Chain Focus to Speed," *just-style*, September 4, 2017.

10. Thomas, "lululemon's Laurent Potdevin Sees Huge Potential."

11. Emily Bary, "Why Men Are Flocking to lululemon," *Barron's Next*, August 28, 2017.

12. www.botticelli-foods.com/index.html.

13. Isaac Thompson, "Botticelli Foods Olive Oil: Sourced from Italy or Tunisia? Pricing Differences?," *World Trade Daily*, July 25, 2012, http://worldtradedaily.com/2012/07/25/botticelli-foods-olive-oil-sourced-from-italy-or-tunisia-pricing-differences/.

14. www.botticelli-foods.com/pastasauces.html.

15. James Agarwal, Naresh K. Malhotra, and Ruth N. Bolton, "A Cross-National and Cross-Cultural Approach to Global Market Segmentation: An Application Using Consumers' Perceived Service Quality," *Journal of International Marketing* 18, no. 3 (September 2010), pp. 18–40.

16. Bill Carter, "ABC Viewers Tilt Female for a Network Light on Sports," *The New York Times*, December 17, 2013, www.nytimes.com; Alex Sood, "The Lost Boys Found: Marketing to Men through Games," *Fast Company*, March 10, 2011, www.fastcompany.com; Jeanine Poggi, "Men's Shopping Shrines," *Forbes*, September 30, 2008, www.forbes.com.

17. David Mothersbaugh and Delbert Hawkins, *Consumer Behavior: Building Marketing Strategy*, 13th ed. (New York: McGraw-Hill Education, 2016).

18. Sami Main, "BuzzFeed Thinks Marketers Will Find More Success with Psychographics Than Demographics," *Adweek*, April 27, 2017.

19. Rosellina Ferraro, Amna Kirmani, and Ted Matherly, "Look at Me! Look at Me! Conspicuous Brand Usage, Self-Brand Connection, and Dilution," *Journal of Marketing Research* 50, no. 4 (2013), pp. 477–88; Keith Wilcox and Andrew T. Stephen, "Are Close Friends the Enemy? Online Social Networks, Self-Esteem, and Self-Control," *Journal of Consumer Research* 40, no. 1 (2013), pp. 90–103.

20. www.dove.com/us/en/stories/about-dove/dove-real-beauty-pledge.html; Nina Bahadur, "Dove 'Real Beauty' Campaign Turns 10: How a Brand Tried to Change the Conversation about Female Beauty," *Huffington Post*, December 6, 2017; Eric Wilson, "Less Ab, More Flab," *The New York Times*, May 22, 2013.

21. Michael R. Solomon, *Consumer Behavior: Buying, Having, and Being*, 10th ed. (Upper Saddle River, NJ: Prentice Hall, 2012).

22. Trefis Team, "Harley-Davidson Works to Reverse the Declining Sales Trend in the Home Market," *Forbes*, February 7, 2017; James M. Hagerty, "Harley, with Macho Intact, Tries to Court More Women," *The Wall Street Journal*, October 31, 2011, http://online.wsj.com.

23. T. L. Stanley, "Harley-Davidson Is Trying to Cultivate Millennials While Catering to Loyalists," *Adweek*, October 2, 2017; Ivan Moreno, "Amid Sales Drop, Harley-Davidson Wants to Teach More Women to Ride," *Chicago Tribune*, December 28, 2017.

24. www.strategicbusinessinsights.com/vals/store/USconsumers/intro.shtml.

25. "The Survey of the American Consumer," http://mri.gfk.com/solutions/the-survey-of-the-american-consumerr/the-survey-of-the-american-consumerr/; Carson J. Sandy, Samuel D. Gosling, and John Durant, "Predicting Consumer Behavior and Media Preferences: The Comparative Validity of Personality Traits and Demographic Variables," *Psychology & Marketing* 30, no. 11 (2013), pp. 937–49.

26. For an interesting take on this issue, see Joseph Jaffe, *Flip the Funnel* (Hoboken, NJ: Wiley, 2010).

27. J. A. Petersen et al., "Unlocking the Power of Marketing: Understanding the Links between Customer Mindset Metrics, Behavior, and Profitability," *Journal of the Academy of Marketing Science*, 2017.

28. Esri, "Tapestry Segmentation Reference Guide" and "Tapestry Segmentation: The Fabric of America's Neighborhood," www.esri.com.

29. Esri, "Lifestyles—Esri Tapestry Segmentation," www.esri.com/data/esri_data/tapestry.

30. Elizabeth Blair, "The NFL's New Target Demographic: Kids," *NPR*, November 29, 2012.

31. John Ourand, "NFL Aims at Younger Fans with Nickelodeon Partnership," *New York Business Journal*, February 3, 2017.

32. Thorsten Blecker, *Mass Customization: Challenges and Solutions* (New York: Springer, 2006).

33. Leonie Roderic, "P&G on How It Will Deliver Personalised Messages at Scale," *Marketing Week*, October 10, 2017.

34. This circular depiction of the value proposition is based on work by John Bers (Vanderbilt University) and adaptation and development of circles of success by Ronald Goodstein (Georgetown University).

35. www.gatorade.com/frequently_asked_questions/default.aspx.

36. www.drpeppersnapplegroup.com/brands/7up/.

37. http://saddlebackleather.com.

38. Mercedes-Benz, "About She's Mercedes," September 15, 2015, www.mercedes-benz.com/en/mercedes-me/inspiration/she/about-shes-mercedes/; Chris Bruce, "Mercedes Wants to Be the Luxury Car for Women," *AutoBlog*, September 16, 2015, www.autoblog.com/2015/09/16/mercedes-luxury-car-for-women/.

39. Joachim Schmidt, "Mercedes-Benz Cars: Sales and Marketing Strategy," March 29, 2012, www.daimler.com/dokumente/investoren/kapitalmarkttage/daimler-irmercedesbenzcarsdivision-dayhungaryschmidt-20120329.pdf.

40. Daimler Chrysler, "Annual Report 2015: Mercedes-Benz Cars," http://ar2015.daimler.com/divisions/mercedes-benz-cars.

41. Vanessa Fuhrmans, German Auto "Makers to Shake Up Luxury Market," *The Wall Street Journal*, January 14, 2013.

42. Mark Clothier, "The Downside of Low-End Luxury Cars," *Bloomberg Businessweek*, July 17, 2014, www.businessweek.com.

i. Mallory Schlossberg, "Instagram and Pinterest Are Killing Gap, Abercrombie, & J. Crew," *Business Insider*, February 14, 2016;

Chantal Fernandez, "J. Crew, Gap, Abercrombie & Fitch: The Trouble with America's Most Beloved Mall Brands," *Business of Fashion*, January 9, 2017.

ii. Stephanie Strom, "Poultry Producer Sanderson Farms Stands Its Ground: It's Proud to Use Antibiotics," *The New York Times*, August 1, 2016; "Sanderson Farms Takes on Misleading Food Labels," press release, August 1, 2016, www.prnewswire.com/news-releases/sanderson-farms-takes-on-misleading-food-labels-300306599.html; Carolyn Heneghan, "Sanderson Farms Wants Healthy—Not Antibiotic-Free—Chicken," *Food Dive*, August 2, 2016.

iii. Takashi Mochizuki, "In Switch, Nintendo Embraces Games with a Rougher Edge for New Console," *The Wall Street Journal*, October 13, 2017; Dave Thier, "The Nintendo Switch's Golden Opportunity," *Forbes*, December 5, 2017; Dave Thier, "The Case for Buying a Nintendo Switch Instead of an Xbox One X," *Forbes*, December 1, 2017; www.nintendo.com/corp/history.jsp; Statista, "Global Unit Sales of Current Generation Video Game Consoles from 2008 to 2016 (in Million Units)," 2017, www.statista.com/statistics/276768/global-unit-sales-of-video-game-consoles/.

iv. Julie Weed, "Hotels Embrace the Campus Nearby," *The New York Times*, May 19, 2014, www.nytimes.com.

v. Adrianne Pasquarelli, "Under Armour Goes above and beyond in Latest Video," *Advertising Age*, August 22, 2016; "Run Camp," www.underarmour.com/en-us/run-challenge.

Quiz Yourself Answer Key

1. Which of the following is *not* a criterion that must be met when evaluating segment attractiveness?

   Answer: (c) Defined

2. A firm's value proposition communicates the benefits received from the product or service by customers. Therefore, the value proposition provides the customer with which key piece(s) of information?

   Answer: (e) All of these are correct.

©Nada Sertic/Shutterstock

LEARNING OBJECTIVES

After reading this chapter, you should be able to:

LO10-1 Identify the five steps in the marketing research process.

LO10-2 Describe the various secondary data sources.

LO10-3 Describe the various primary data collection techniques.

LO10-4 Summarize the differences between secondary data and primary data.

LO10-5 Examine the circumstances in which collecting information on consumers is ethical.

CHAPTER 10

MARKETING RESEARCH

To research a market, every company needs data about it. Marketing research encompasses a range of techniques and options, as this chapter will make clear. But a key direction that modern companies are taking involves leveraging what has come to be known as "big data." These are the data gathered and integrated by advanced technology applications and tools, and they allow even companies that have been researching their markets for literally centuries to gain new insights and understanding of their customers.

Take American Express as an example. To appeal to both customers and merchants, it has long investigated what will make its offers valuable to them. For example, in the 1980s, it relied on what was then called an "expert system" to determine which transactions were most likely to be fraudulent and issue recommendations to human monitors about whether to approve big purchases.[1]

These human analysts also are a long-standing tradition for American Express, which over the years has established a staff of approximately 1,500 data scientists to ensure that it can handle all the marketing research data it gathers.[2] These scientists have a lot more material to work with these days, though, especially as the credit card company shifts its focus from assessments of previous transactions to predictions of future ones.[3] It also is expanding its central offerings: Rather than just providing credit for customers, American Express increasingly sees itself as a provider that facilitates connections between customers and the merchants from which they want to buy.[4]

It therefore gathers data from its customer relationship management systems, websites, and mobile apps to predict what continued customers want. By leveraging these data, American Express alters its offers and promotions virtually in real time, such that each contact with a customer reflects his or her immediately previous activity.[5] For example, it can review customers' purchases and then recommend a local restaurant that they are likely to enjoy, where they can use their card. Location-based services in the American Express app also enable the company to issue real-time coupons according to customers' locations.[6] American Express asserts that it can anticipate the termination of nearly one-quarter of the accounts that will close in any particular quarter too, meaning that it can engage in proactive efforts either to retain the customer or to reduce its own expensive efforts if the customer appears destined to leave.[7] Furthermore, because it inherently and constantly makes in-depth contacts with merchants, as partners in serving their shared customers, it can gather purchase data from their systems. These resulting data span literally millions of businesses and even more customers, meaning that American Express overall makes billions of marketing-related decisions daily.[8] For its merchant partners, the company also offers support for their marketing research analyses. For example, a benchmarking tool allows companies to determine how well they are performing among millions of American Express customers, segmented in various ways, relative to their competitors.

Finally, in an effort that benefits both merchants and customers, American Express leverages its advanced marketing research and data analysis capabilities to anticipate, identify and avoid fraud. Such abilities are particularly valuable in the credit card industry because fraud threatens all members of the market. Therefore, American Express' proprietary machine learning model integrates data from a wide range of sources, coming from both members and merchants, to identify suspicious transactions within milliseconds. For this identification, it relies on comparisons with its vast database of existing purchases. Because it can do so nearly immediately, American Express has saved its markets an estimated $2 billion by avoiding fraudulent transactions.[9] But in addition to saving them money, American Express has developed its fraud detection skills to such an extent that it does not need to contact customers to approve every purchase, which would risk annoying them.[10]

Although some of these applications entail the use of advanced technologies and sophisticated algorithms, the underlying goal is the same as it has always been. American Express seeks to learn all it can about its members, the merchants who serve them, and the markets in which they interact. Then it can be confident that it is offering exactly what each of these actors needs and wants, because its research has told it what those needs and wants are.

Marketing research is a prerequisite of successful decision making. It consists of a set of techniques and principles for systematically collecting, recording, analyzing, and interpreting data that can aid decision makers who are involved in marketing goods, services, or ideas. When marketing managers attempt to develop their strategies, marketing research can provide valuable information that will help them make segmentation, positioning, product, price, place, and promotion decisions.

Firms invest billions of dollars in marketing research every year. The largest U.S.-based marketing research firm, the Nielsen Company, earns annual worldwide revenues of more than $6 billion.[11] Why do marketers find this research valuable? First, it helps reduce some of the uncertainty under which they currently operate. Successful managers know when research might help their decision making and then take appropriate steps to acquire the information they need. Second, marketing research provides a crucial link between firms and their environments, which enables them to be customer oriented because they build their strategies by using customer input and continual feedback. Third, by constantly monitoring their competitors, firms can anticipate and respond quickly to competitive moves.

If you think marketing research is applicable only to corporate ventures, though, think again. Nonprofit organizations and governments also use research to serve their constituencies better. The political sector has been slicing and dicing the voting public for decades to determine relevant messages for different demographics. Politicians desperately want to understand who makes up the voting public to determine how to reach them. But they do not want to know only your political views—they also want to understand your media habits, such as what magazines you subscribe to, so they can target you more effectively.

To do so, they rely on the five-step marketing research process we outline in this chapter. We also discuss some of the ethical implications of using the information that these databases can collect.

LO10-1 Identify the five steps in the marketing research process.

THE MARKETING RESEARCH PROCESS

Managers consider several factors before embarking on a marketing research project. First, will the research be useful; will it provide insights beyond what the managers already know and reduce uncertainty associated with the project? Second, is top management committed to the project and willing to abide by the results of the research? Related to both of these questions is the value of the research. Marketing research can be very expensive, and if the results won't be useful or management does not abide by the findings, it represents a waste of money. Third, should the marketing research project be small or large? A project might involve a simple analysis of data that the firm already has, or it could be an in-depth assessment that costs hundreds of thousands of dollars and takes months to complete.

The marketing research process itself consists of five steps (see Exhibit 10.1). Although we present the stages of the marketing research process in a step-by-step progression, of course research does not always, or even usually, happen that way. Researchers go back and forth from one step to another as the need arises. For example, marketers may establish a specific research objective, which they follow with data collection and preliminary analysis. If they uncover new information during the collection step or if the findings of the analysis spotlight new research needs, they might redefine their objectives and begin again from a new starting point. Another important requirement before embarking on a research project is to plan the entire project in advance. By planning the entire research process prior to starting the project, researchers can avoid unnecessary alterations to the research plan as they move through the process.

Marketing Research Process Step 1: Defining the Objectives and Research Needs

Because research is both expensive and time-consuming, it is important to establish in advance exactly what problem needs to be solved. For example, Marketing Analytics 10.1 details how film studios actively seek to predict potential Oscar winners and thus turn to sophisticated research techniques. In general, marketers must clearly define the objectives of their marketing research project.

Consider a scenario: McDonald's is the global leader in the fast-food market, with more than 36,000 stores in over 100 countries, earning close to $25 billion in annual revenues.[12] But it wants a better understanding of its customers' experience. It also needs to understand how customers view the experience at Wendy's, a main competitor, operating in 30 countries and earning approximately $1.5 billion in annual revenues, even after Wendy's discontinued its breakfast menu.[13] Finally, McDonald's hopes to gain some insight into how it should set a price for and market its latest combo meal of a hamburger, fries, and drink. Any one of these questions could initiate a research project. The complexity of the project that the company eventually undertakes depends on how much time and resources it has available, as well as the amount of in-depth knowledge it needs.

Researchers assess the value of a project through a careful comparison of the benefits of answering some of their questions and the costs associated with conducting the research. When researchers have determined what information they need in order to address a particular problem or issue, the next step is to design a research project to meet those objectives.

EXHIBIT 10.1 The Marketing Research Process

Step 1: Defining the objectives and research needs

Step 2: Designing the research

Step 3: Collecting the data

Step 4: Analyzing the data and developing insights

Step 5: Developing and implementing an action plan

If McDonald's were to do research to better understand its customers' experience, it would study both the McDonald's experience (left) and that of its major competitors, like Wendy's (right).

(Left): ©David Paul Morris/Getty Images; (right): ©Andrew Spear/The New York Times/Redux Pictures

Marketing Research Process Step 2: Designing the Research

The second step in the marketing research project involves design. In this step, researchers identify the type of data needed and determine the research necessary to collect them. Recall that the objectives of the project drive the type of data needed, as outlined in Step 1.

Let's look at how this second step works, using the McDonald's customer experience. McDonald's needs to ask its customers about their McDonald's experience. However, because people don't always tell the whole truth in surveys, the company also may want to observe customers to see how they actually enter the stores, interact with employees, and consume the product. The project's design might begin with available data, such as information that shows that people with children often come into the restaurants at lunchtime and order Happy Meals. Then McDonald's marketing researchers can start to ask customers specific questions about their McDonald's experience.

Marketing Research Process Step 3: Collecting the Data

Data collection begins only after the research design process. Based on the design of the project, data can be collected from secondary or primary data sources. Secondary data are pieces of information that have been collected prior to the start of the focal research project. Secondary data include external as well as internal data sources. Primary data, in contrast, are those data collected to address specific research needs. Some common primary data collection methods include focus groups, in-depth interviews, and surveys.

For our hypothetical fast-food scenario, McDonald's may decide to get relevant secondary data from external providers such as National Purchase Diary Panel and Nielsen. The data might include the prices paid for menu items, sales figures, sales growth or decline in the category,

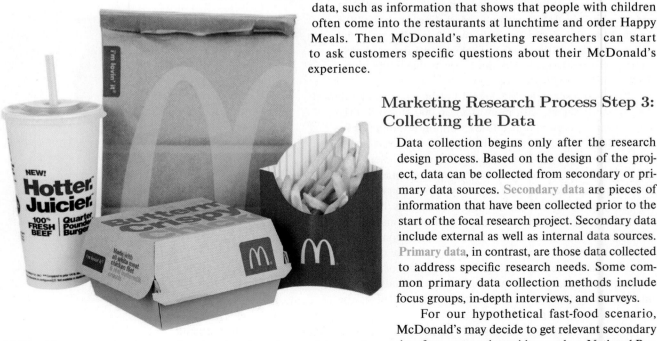

McDonald's assesses its customers' market experience by examining available data and then asks customers about their experience with products such as Value Meals.

©McGraw-Hill Education/Evelyn Nicole Kirksey, photographer

Marketing Analytics 10.1

Big Data and a Big Bear: The Use of Bioanalytics to Predict Box Office Revenues and Award Changes[i]

The success of *The Revenant*, starring Leonardo DiCaprio, became evident soon after its release, with big box office numbers and nominations for prestigious awards. But Fox Studios could have told us that, well before its release, because it implemented a new form of data collection that showed it that audiences found the gritty tale compelling, such that they could barely move in their seats or take their eyes from the screen.

The studio obtained this detailed, specific information not by asking audiences, exactly, but by adopting a method that allowed audiences' physical reactions to give the studio the information. Test audiences in four cities watched a prerelease version of the movie while wearing a fitness tracker that the data analytics firm Lightwave had developed. The tracker gauged their heart rates (10 times per second), bodily movements, body temperatures, and skin conductivity (which signals whether a person's nervous system has taken over, as an automatic response to a stimulus suggesting the need to fight or flee).

The resulting "hundreds of millions of rows of data" revealed exactly when audiences experienced the most excitement, which was mostly when something—bear, arrows, hanging, live burials—threatens the life of the main character. But they also thrill to see icy rivers and chase scenes through majestic landscapes. Thus Lightwave could inform Fox Studios that it had 14 separate "heart-pounding" moments in the film.

Furthermore, the massive data revealed that for nearly half of the film's relatively long running time of 156 minutes, audiences sat quite still, implying that they were transfixed by the story being told on the screens in front of them. That is, rather than wiggling impatiently in their seats or leaving to get a popcorn refill, they kept their eyes glued to the screen.

Combining these data with various other insights, including ratings on review sites, some prognosticators asserted that the key to victory, in the form of both awards acclaim and box office revenues, is sparking strong emotional reactions—even if those emotions tend to be negative. One consultancy took these data to predict, in advance of the Academy Awards, that *The Revenant* had a 64 percent chance of winning the Best Picture Oscar, whereas it gave the actual winner, *Spotlight*, only a 7.2 percent chance.

As this example shows, even massive amounts of research and data cannot predict the future with complete accuracy. Yet the response-tracking technology also informs product development phases, enabling studios to reedit or revise films that fail to capture people's attention. Similar devices also might

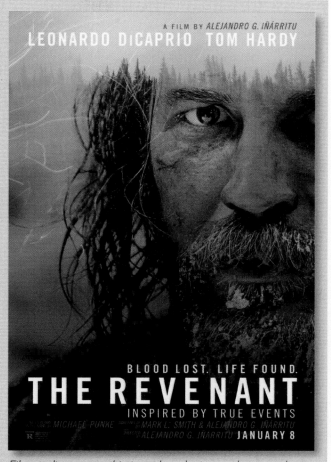

Film studios use sophisticated marketing analytics, such as bioanalytics, to track audiences' physical reactions to films such as The Revenant. *The collected data are expected to predict films' success.*

©Moviestore collection Ltd/Alamy Stock Photo

be used in other entertainment settings, from television shows to concerts to sporting events. The resulting data would give providers vast new insights into what gets people excited—and what doesn't—to help them better meet their demands. And maybe pick up an Oscar or two in the process.

and advertising and promotional spending. McDonald's is likely to gather pertinent data about sales from its franchisees. However, it also wants competitor data, overall food consumption data, and other information about the quick-service restaurant category, which it likely obtains from appropriate syndicated data providers. Based on the data, it might decide to follow up with some primary data using a survey.

No company can ask every customer his or her opinion or observe every customer, so researchers must choose a group of customers who represent the customers of interest, or a sample, and then generalize their opinions to describe all customers with the same characteristics. They may choose the sample participants at random to represent the entire customer market. Or they may choose to select the sample on the basis of some characteristic, such as their age, so they can research how Millennials experience buying Value Meals.

Marketing researchers use various methods of asking questions to measure the issues they are tackling. In our hypothetical McDonald's scenario, assume the research team has developed a questionnaire (see Exhibit 10.2), using a few different types of questions. Section A measures the customer's experience in McDonald's, Section B measures the customer's experience in Wendy's, Section C measures the customer's habits at McDonald's, and Section D measures customer demographics.[14]

EXHIBIT 10.2   A Hypothetical Fast-Food Survey

Please Evaluate Your Experience at McDonald's

A. McDonald's	Strongly Disagree 1	Disagree 2	Neither Agree nor Disagree 3	Agree 4	Strongly Agree 5
McDonald's food tastes good.	☐	☐	☐	☐	☐
McDonald's is clean.	☐	☐	☐	☐	☐
McDonald's has low prices.	☐	☐	☐	☐	☐

B. Wendy's	Strongly Disagree 1	Disagree 2	Neither Agree nor Disagree 3	Agree 4	Strongly Agree 5
Wendy's food tastes good.	☐	☐	☐	☐	☐
Wendy's is clean.	☐	☐	☐	☐	☐
Wendy's has low prices.	☐	☐	☐	☐	☐

C. McDonald's

	Never	1–2 times	3–4 times	More than 5 times
In the last month, how many times have you been to McDonald's?	☐	☐	☐	☐
In the last month, how often did you order breakfast items at McDonald's?	☐	☐	☐	☐
If McDonald's offered breakfast items all the time, how often would you order them outside of normal breakfast times in a typical month?	☐	☐	☐	☐
On average, how much do you spend each visit at McDonald's?	$_____			
What is your favorite item at McDonald's?	_____			

D. Please tell us about yourself

	16 and under	17–24	25–35	36+
What is your age?	☐	☐	☐	☐

	Male	Female		
What is your gender?	☐	☐		

Adding Value 10.1 Did You Hit the Weights or Swim a Lap Today? Your University Wants to Know—For a Good Reason[ii]

When universities and colleges announce the opening of a new sports facility or recreational center, students might feel reassured that their "student activity fees" have gone to good use. But to prove it, the schools are stepping up their efforts to learn exactly how and when students use these services, which enables them to offer the elements that students demand as well as justify their capital expenditures.

By tracking student usage, the schools gather a wealth of valuable data that inform their next steps. For example, students at the University of Florida had begun complaining that their activity fee was too high. When the school reviewed the data showing who was using its health facilities, it realized that graduate students came around 7:00 a.m., when the gym opened, but undergraduates did not. When it moved the opening an hour earlier to 6:00 a.m., undergraduates flooded the facility because they still had enough time to get in a workout, shower, and make their early morning classes. In addition, complaints about the fees dropped off because the students believed they were getting their money's worth.

For North Carolina State University in Raleigh, the usage data showed that far more students were taking fitness classes than were joining intramural sports teams. Thus, the rec center cut back the resources it allocated to intramurals and tripled the number of fitness classes, making sure that it offered what its students wanted, when and where they wanted it.

The GymFlow app available through the University of California Los Angeles shows school administrators how many people are using each section of its gym at different times. In addition, it tabulates exactly how many students and employees—43,734—visited the center in a year. With this information, UCLA was able to show critics that its expenditures were worthwhile. For students, the same app reveals when their favorite piece of equipment is being used by lots of others, as well as when the quiet times are at the facility.

Research at North Carolina State University showed that more students were taking fitness classes than were joining intramural sports teams, so the university tripled the number of fitness classes offered.

©Phovoir/Shutterstock

Purdue went a step beyond tracking usage to link exercise with scholastic performance. When it built a $98 million facility, not everyone thought it was a good idea. But the university was able to demonstrate that students who swiped their ID cards to access the gym also earned higher grade point averages than did students who never came to work out. In a parallel study, a professor investigated the attitudes of participants in one of the gym's kickboxing classes and found that regular participants indicated substantially lower stress levels.

It might seem strange that a school would keep track of when its students are running around the track. But in truth, the information it gathers is valuable for justifying its resource allocations as well as determining future investments in services for students.

Marketing Research Process Step 4: Analyzing the Data and Developing Insights

The next step in the marketing research process—analyzing and interpreting the data—should be both thorough and methodical. To generate meaningful information, researchers analyze and make use of the collected data. Adding Value 10.1 details how universities leverage the data they gain from students' uses of on-campus gyms and facilities to discover new insights into both what students want and how the schools can help them succeed. In this context, data can be defined as raw numbers or other factual information that, on their own, have limited value to marketers. However, when the data are interpreted, they become information, which results from organizing, analyzing, and interpreting data and putting them into a form that is useful to marketing decision makers. For example, a checkout scanner in the grocery store collects sales data about individual consumer purchases. Not until those data are categorized and examined do they provide information about which products and services were purchased together or how an in-store promotional activity translated into sales.

EXHIBIT 10.3   Survey Results for McDonald's and Wendy's

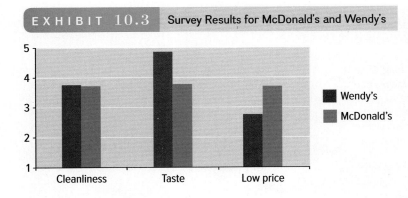

For the McDonald's example, we can summarize the results of the survey (from Exhibit 10.2) in Exhibit 10.3. Both McDonald's and Wendy's scored the same on the cleanliness of their restaurants, but McDonald's had lower prices, whereas Wendy's food tasted better. McDonald's may want to improve the taste of its food, without raising prices too much, to compete more effectively with Wendy's.

Marketing Research Process Step 5: Developing and Implementing an Action Plan

In the final phase in the marketing research process, the analyst prepares the results and presents them to the appropriate decision makers, who undertake appropriate marketing strategies. A typical marketing research presentation includes an executive summary, the body of the report (which discusses the research objectives, methodology used, and detailed findings), the conclusions, the limitations, and appropriate supplemental tables, figures, and appendixes.

In the McDonald's hypothetical scenario, according to the research findings, the company is doing fine in terms of cleanliness (comparable to its competitors) and is perceived to have lower prices, but the taste of its food could be improved. It also found that of those customers who purchased breakfast items relatively frequently (at least three times per month), 35 percent would go for breakfast outside the normal breakfast times frequently. Also, of those who never ordered breakfast items, 25 percent would order breakfast items outside the normal breakfast times occasionally (at least once a month). Using this analysis and the related insights gained, McDonald's might consider hiring some gourmet chefs as consultants to improve the menu and offerings. It then could highlight its efforts to improve the taste of the food and add desired offerings (e.g., breakfast items) through marketing communications and promotions. McDonald's also should consider undertaking additional pricing research to determine whether its lower prices enhance sales and profits or whether it could increase its prices and still compete effectively with Wendy's.

McDonald's marketing research will show how to better compete against Wendy's.
©Michael Neelon/Alamy Stock Photo

Now let's take a closer look at sources of secondary and primary data.

PROGRESS CHECK

1. What are the steps in the marketing research process?
2. What is the difference between data and information?

LO10-2 Describe the various secondary data sources.

SECONDARY DATA

A marketing research project often begins with a review of the relevant secondary data. Secondary data might come from free or very inexpensive external sources such as census data, information from trade associations, and reports published in magazines. Although readily accessible, these inexpensive sources may not be specific or timely enough to solve the marketer's research needs and objectives. Firms also can purchase more specific or applicable secondary data from specialized research firms. Finally, secondary sources can be accessed through internal sources, including the company's sales invoices, customer lists, and other reports generated by the company itself.

In political settings, such secondary data can be critical for candidates running for office. Both major political parties thus have developed proprietary databases that contain vast information about voters, broken down by demographic and geographic information. Before a local politician, canvasser, or poll taker even knocks on doors in a neighborhood, he or she likely knows which houses are inhabited by retirees, who has a subscription to *The Wall Street Journal* or *The New York Times,* for whom the residents said they voted in the last election, or whether they served in the military. All these traits can give hints about the voters' likely concerns, which a good politician can address immediately upon knocking on the door. Such research also can dictate tactics for designing broader campaign materials or to zero in on very specific issues. Social media campaigns are a growing mechanism used to interact with potential voters in a more timely manner than is possible with more traditional methods. Monitoring tweets after a major address by a candidate, for instance, would provide instant feedback and direction for future communications.

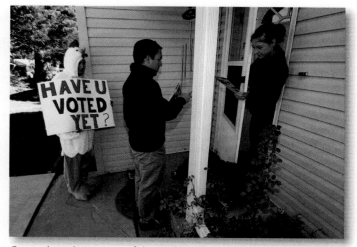

Secondary data are useful to politicians so they know who they are talking to before they knock on any doors.
©Cathleen Allison/AP Photo

Inexpensive External Secondary Data

Some sources of external secondary data can be quickly accessed at a relatively low cost. The U.S. Bureau of the Census (www.census.gov), for example, provides data about businesses by county and zip code. If you wanted to open a new location for a business you are already operating, such data might help you determine the size of your potential market.

Often, however, inexpensive data sources are not adequate to meet researchers' needs. Because the data initially were acquired for some purpose other than the research question at hand, they may not be completely relevant or timely. The U.S. Census is a great source of demographic data about a particular market area, and it can be easily accessed at a low cost. However, the data are collected only at the beginning of every decade, so they quickly become outdated. If an entrepreneur wanted to open a retail flooring store in 2019, for example, the data would already be nine years old, and the housing market likely would be stronger than it was in 2010. Researchers must also pay careful attention to how other sources of inexpensive secondary data were collected. Despite the great deal of data available on the Internet, easy access does not ensure that the data are trustworthy.

Syndicated External Secondary Data

Although the secondary data described previously are either free or inexpensively obtained, marketers can purchase external secondary data called syndicated data, which are available for a fee from commercial research firms such as IRI, the National Purchase Diary Panel, and Nielsen. Exhibit 10.4 contains information about various firms that provide syndicated data.

Consumer packaged-goods firms that sell to wholesalers often lack the means to gather pertinent data directly from the retailers that sell their products to consumers, which makes syndicated data a valuable resource for them. Some syndicated data providers also offer information about shifting brand preferences and product usage in households, which they gather from scanner data, consumer panels—and several other cutting-edge methods.

Scanner data are used in quantitative research obtained from scanner readings of Universal Product Code (UPC) labels at checkout counters. Whenever you go into your local grocery store, your purchases are rung up using scanner systems. The data from these purchases are likely to be acquired by leading marketing research firms such as IRI or Nielsen, which use this information to help leading consumer packaged-goods firms (e.g., Kellogg's, Pepsi, Kraft) assess what is happening in the marketplace. For example, a firm can use scanner data to determine what would happen to its sales if it reduced the price of its least

EXHIBIT 10.4	Syndicated Data Providers and Some of Their Services
Name	**Services Provided**
Nielsen (www.nielsen.com)	With its *Market Measurement Services*, the company tracks the sales of consumer packaged goods, gathered at the point of sale in retail stores of all types and sizes.
IRI (www.iriworldwide.com)	*InfoScan* store tracking provides detailed information about sales, share, distribution, pricing, and promotion across a wide variety of retail channels and accounts.
J.D. Power and Associates (www.jdpower.com)	Widely known for its automotive ratings, it produces quality and customer satisfaction research for a variety of industries.
Mediamark Research Inc. (www.mediamark.com)	Supplies multimedia audience research pertaining to media and marketing planning for advertised brands.
National Purchase Diary Panel (www.npd.com)	Based on detailed records consumers keep about their purchases (i.e., a diary), it provides information about product movement and consumer behavior in a variety of industries.
NOP World (www.nopworld.com)	The *mKids US* research study tracks mobile telephone ownership and usage, brand affinities, and entertainment habits of American youth between 12 and 19 years of age.
Research and Markets (www.researchandmarkets.com)	Promotes itself as a one-stop shop for marketing research and data from most leading publishers, consultants, and analysts.
Roper Center for Public Opinion Research (www.ropercenter.uconn.edu)	The *General Social Survey* is one of the nation's longest running surveys of social, cultural, and political indicators.
Simmons Market Research Bureau (www.smrb.com)	Reports on the products American consumers buy, the brands they prefer, and their lifestyles, attitudes, and media preferences.
Yankelovich (thefuturescompany.com/products/us-yankelovich-monitor/)	The *MONITOR* tracks consumer attitudes, values, and lifestyles shaping the American marketplace.

popular product by 10 percent in a given month. In the test market in which it lowers the price, do sales increase, decrease, or stay the same?

Panel data are information collected from a group of consumers, organized into panels, over time. Data collected from panelists often include their records of what they have purchased (i.e., secondary data) as well as their responses to survey questions that the client gives to the panel firm to ask the panelists (i.e., primary data). Secondary panel data thus might show that when Diet Pepsi is offered at a deep discount, 80 percent of usual Diet Coke consumers switch to Diet Pepsi. Primary panel data could give insights into what they think of each option. We discuss further how marketing researchers use scanner and panel data to answer specific research questions in the primary data section.

Overall, both panel and scanner data, as well as their more advanced methods gathered through social media and online usage patterns, provide firms with a comprehensive picture of what consumers are buying or not buying. The key difference between scanner research and panel research is how the data are aggregated. Scanner research typically focuses on weekly consumption of a particular product at a given unit of analysis (e.g., individual store, chain, region); panel research focuses on the total weekly consumption by a particular person or household.

Internal Secondary Data

Internally, companies also generate a tremendous amount of secondary data from their day-to-day operations. One of the most valuable resources such firms have at their disposal is their rich cache of customer information and purchase history. However, it can

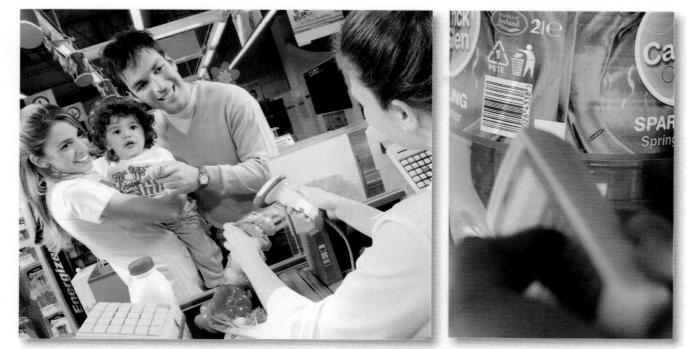

Syndicated external secondary data are acquired from scanner data obtained from scanner readings of UPC codes at checkout counters (left) and from panel data collected from consumers that electronically record their purchases (right).

(Left): ©Glow Images/Getty Images; (right): ©Stephen Barnes/Bowline Images/Alamy Stock Photo

be difficult to make sense of the millions and even billions of pieces of individual data, which are stored in large computer files called data warehouses. For this reason, firms find it necessary to use data mining techniques to extract valuable information from their databases.

Data mining uses a variety of statistical analysis tools to uncover previously unknown patterns in the data or relationships among variables. Some retailers try to customize their product and service offerings to match the needs of their customers. For instance, the UK grocer Tesco uses its loyalty card to collect massive amounts of information about its individual customers. Every time a loyalty card member buys something, the card is scanned and the store captures key purchase data specific to that member. But these specific data are basically useless until Tesco mines and analyzes them to identify, for instance, three income groups: upscale, middle income, and less affluent. With this mined information, Tesco has been able to create appealing private-label product offerings for each group, according to their preferences, and has begun targeting promotions to each customer according to his or her income classification.

Data mining can also enable a home improvement retailer such as Lowe's to learn that 25 percent of the time its customers buy a garden hose, they also purchase a sprinkler. With such information, the retailer may decide to put the garden hoses next to the sprinklers in the store. Outside the retail realm, an investment firm might use statistical techniques to group clients according to their income, age, type of securities purchased, and prior investment experience. This categorization identifies different segments to which the firm can offer valuable packages that meet their specific needs. The firm also can tailor separate marketing programs to each of these segments.

By analyzing the enormous amount of information that they possess about customers, companies have developed statistical models that help identify when a customer is dissatisfied with his or her service. Once the company identifies an unhappy customer, it can follow up and proactively address that customer's issues. By mining customer data and information, the company also reduces its churn levels. Churn is the number of participants who

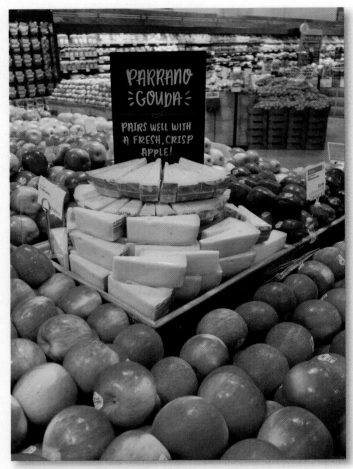

Marketers use data mining techniques to determine what items people buy at the same time so they can be promoted and displayed together.

©McGraw-Hill Education

discontinue use of a service, divided by the average number of total participants. With this knowledge, the company can focus on what it does best and improve potential problem areas. Overall, firms hope to use data mining to generate customer-based analytics that they can apply to their strategic decision making and thereby make good customers better and better customers their best. Adding Value 10.2 examines how data mining is being used in the restaurant industry.

Big Data

The field of marketing research has seen enormous changes in the last few years because of (1) the increase in the amounts of data to which retailers, service providers, and manufacturers have access; (2) their ability to collect these data from transactions, customer relationship management (CRM) systems, websites, and social media platforms that firms increasingly use to engage with their customers;[15] (3) the ease of collecting and storing these data; (4) the computing ability readily available to manipulate data in real time; and (5) access to in-house or available software to convert the data into valuable decision-making insights using analytic dashboards.

To specify this explosion of data, which firms have access to but cannot handle using conventional data management and data mining software, the term big data has arisen in the popular media. Leading firms such as Amazon, Netflix, Google, Nordstrom, Kroger, Tesco, Macy's, American Express, and Walmart already are converting their big data into customer insights—and the list of firms keeps growing.[16]

Amazon may be the poster child for big data. Any Amazon shopper is familiar with its recommendation engine, which notes what the consumer is purchasing, analyzes purchase patterns by similar customers, suggests other items the customer might enjoy, and indicates what other people who bought the focal item also added to their shopping carts.[17] With more than 310 million active customers and billions of pieces of shopping data,[18] Amazon certainly qualifies as a big data user; its item-to-item collaborative filtering helps it determine which relevant products to suggest, generating almost one-third of its sales.[19]

The UK grocery retailer Tesco processes data for each of its products. With 3,500 stores, each stocked with an average of 40,000 products, that's over 100 million data points.[20] Furthermore, each purchased product can feature up to 45 data attributes: Is it Tesco's own brand? An ethnic recipe? Exotic (e.g., star fruit) or basic (e.g., apple)? and so on. On the basis of the attributes of the items customers purchase, Tesco filters them to define who they are, who else lives in their household, and what hobbies they have, then provides specific incentives that match these characteristics.[21]

To enable these efforts, firms such as SAP, Splunk, and GoodData offer a host of software solutions to help firms better integrate their data, visualize them, and then move from data to real-time insights.[22] The suite of options previously were available only to the largest firms, but falling costs mean they are now more accessible to smaller firms.

The big data explosion also stems from the growth of online and social media. In response, Google, Facebook, and Twitter all provide analytic dashboards designed to help their customers understand their own web traffic. In particular, Google has developed tremendous marketing analytical capabilities that it makes available to partner

Adding Value 10.2 | A Big Meal and Some Big Data: The Expanding Uses of Data Mining and Analytics in the Restaurant Industry[iii]

When Damian Mogavero, a restaurant group CFO, realized the vast need for improved data analytics in the restaurant sector, he decided to found a new kind of technology company, Avero. It is dedicated to helping approximately 40,000 restaurants around the world with their data needs. Specifically, Avero collects data from restaurants and provides them with meaningful insights on everything from customer service to menus. Its dedicated server mentoring program helps improve servers' skills and ability. It also provides novel insights into how weather might affect business, which food items are selling the best, and which raw materials represent the most expensive costs for each restaurant.

Although popular, Avero is just one of the many companies offering advanced data analytics support for restaurants. Other systems being developed for the restaurant industry collect the vast information that diners provide with every meal, including the types of food they prefer, with whom they socialize, the time of day they like to eat, how often they eat out rather than at home, and so on. Then they aim to make recommendations for the restaurants to improve their service, such as by ensuring a particular menu item is in stock on the day and time that they can expect consumers to order it. By also integrating information from consumers' social media pages, high-end restaurant managers and hosts can ensure that they recognize diners on sight, and welcome them personally, even if they are not regular customers.

For consumers, such operations offer clear benefits. Being known by restaurant staffers gives consumers a sense of importance. Furthermore, a vegetarian diner would not have to listen to a long list of meat-oriented specials, for example, but instead might receive information about alternative menu options that the chef could create. If the restaurant also uses these data to enhance its operations, consumers likely would enjoy shorter wait times and less chance of popular menu items selling out before they can place their order. For the restaurants, the benefits stem from their ability to provide such services to customers. The results should include reduced operational costs, more streamlined service provision, and increased sales.

But concerns persist, even among these benefits. For consumers, these systems entail gathering substantial amounts of data, with few means to opt out of providing that information. If customers make a reservation and pay with a credit card, the company has a lot of information already, and they can do little to stop a restaurant manager from searching for their name online. Thus privacy concerns are paramount. For restaurants, in addition to being expensive, the systems could lead to an overreliance on data, undermining the personal touch that often leads to service success. Ultimately, personalized service requires a personal touch. Yet that touch might become far more effective if it is underlain by advanced data analytics.

firms. Google helps firms attract customer traffic to their sites through the use of more relevant keywords, the purchase of Google AdWords, and better conversion methods.[23] Using Google Analytics, Puma has gained insights into which online content and products most engaged its web visitors, while also defining where these visitors lived. With these visitor behavioral data in hand, Puma has revised its website (www.Puma.com) to be more dynamic and has created unique identifiers for its various product categories (e.g., PUMA Golf), targeting them in accordance with the home region of the visitor.[24]

PROGRESS CHECK

1. What is the difference between internal and external secondary research?

PRIMARY DATA COLLECTION TECHNIQUES

LO10-3 Describe the various primary data collection techniques.

In many cases, the information researchers need is available only through primary data or data collected to address specific research needs. Depending on the nature of the research problem, the primary data collection method can employ a *qualitative* or a *quantitative* research method. Marketing Analytics 10.2 highlights how Under Armour uses a variety of quantitative data sources to inform its decisions.

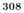

Marketing Analytics 10.2 — The Under Armour Idea of "Connected Fitness"[iv]

With the goal of helping athletes—both professional and weekend warriors—improve their performance, Under Armour seeks to leverage its extensive marketing research and big data capabilities to track and suggest improvements to people's sleep, exercise, and eating habits. In this sense, it is moving beyond functioning as a product company that sells shoes and workout gear, to enter the marketing analytics field to sell the promise of helping customers feel and perform better.

These options derive from a range of data that the company collects from consumers. For example, it purchased several existing health tracking apps (e.g., Endomondo, MapMyFitness), integrating them under its in-house efforts. By combining their capabilities, Under Armour allows its customers to track their sleep patterns, then combine that information with their precise performance on their runs the next morning, for example. The combined data in turn can lead to specific recommendations for how to maximize run time or distance by altering the person's approach to getting to sleep.

But these technology tools are not the only option Under Armour has for collecting customer data. It also uses extensive customer surveys that reveal notable insights. For example, a recent survey indicated that middle-aged male runners (45–54 years) ran approximately 22 percent longer distances than those between the ages of 18 and 24 years. But in addition, nearly half of the long-distance runners surveyed indicated that they struggled to motivate themselves to get started on their runs.

Such research-based insights suggest new ways for Under Armour to interact with customers. For example, it can encourage athletes to link their fitness apps with their friends', so that the running partners can encourage and

Under Armour is more than just an athletic clothing and gear company. It adds customer value by using surveys and data mining techniques to track and suggest improvements to people's sleep, exercise, and eating habits.

©Thearon W. Henderson/Getty Images

motivate each other. It can inspire more casual exercisers, by showing them that even the most dedicated athletes sometimes struggle to get themselves out the door for an exercise regimen. And it hopes to add location-based services soon, such that it might recommend where people can stop on their runs to grab a quick bite to eat or drink—establishing a kind of motivation that sometimes is possible only through snacks. The company firmly believes, based on its research, that these sorts of services and benefits are what customers today are willing to pay for, and it's betting its future on data, rather than on sneakers.

As its name implies, **qualitative research** uses broad, open-ended questions to understand the phenomenon of interest. It provides initial information that helps the researcher more clearly formulate the research objectives. Qualitative research is more informal than quantitative research methods and includes observation, following social media sites, in-depth interviews, and focus groups (see Exhibit 10.5, left side).

Once the firm has gained insights from doing qualitative research, it is likely to engage in **quantitative research**, which are structured responses that can be statistically tested. Quantitative research provides information needed to confirm insights and hypotheses generated via

EXHIBIT 10.5 Qualitative versus Quantitative Data Collection

Qualitative research

- Observation
- In-depth interviews
- Focus groups
- Social media

→ Data collection research ←

Quantitative research

- Experiments
- Survey
- Scanner
- Panel

qualitative research or secondary data. It also helps managers pursue appropriate courses of action. Formal studies such as specific experiments, surveys, scanner and panel data, or some combination of these are quantitative in nature (see Exhibit 10.5, right side). We now examine each of these primary data collection techniques in order.

Observation

Observation entails examining purchase and consumption behaviors through personal or video camera scrutiny, or by tracking customers' movements electronically as they move through a store. For example, researchers might observe customers while they shop or when they go about their daily lives, taking note of the variety of products they use. Observation can last for a very brief period of time (e.g., two hours watching teenagers shop for clothing in the mall), or it may take days or weeks (e.g., researchers live with families to observe their use of products). When consumers are unable to articulate their experiences, observation research becomes particularly useful; how else could researchers determine which educational toys babies choose to play with or confirm details of the buying process that consumers might not be able to recall accurately?

Although traditionally firms might videotape customers' movements, Microsoft's Kinect sensors are providing a less intrusive option. Discreetly embedded in aisles of retail stores, the sensors provide three-dimensional spatial recognition. Thus retailers and their suppliers can unobtrusively track the amount of time people spend in front of a shelf, which products they touch or pick up, the products they return to shelves, and finally what they add to their carts and purchase.[25] The data gathered can be used to improve store layouts because they can identify causes of slow-selling merchandise, such as poor shelf placement. Microsoft has also created smart signage with Kinect sensors that displays different information depending on how far away the customer is to the sign.[26] By studying customers' movements, marketers can also learn where customers pause or move quickly or where there is congestion. This information can help them decide if the layout and merchandise placement is operating as expected, such as whether new or promoted merchandise is getting the attention it deserves.[27]

Observation may be the best—and sometimes the only—method to determine how customers might use a product; therefore it is useful for designing and marketing products. Unilever has found success in developing countries by requiring managers to spend a month living in a village during their first year with the company. By watching customers in rural Thailand, Unilever recognized the fallacy of its assumption that the poorest consumers were interested in buying only necessities. So it worked with retailers to develop stores that offer a wide variety of Unilever products as well as other services such as "food corners" and washing machines. Furthermore, its Platinum store initiative offers an

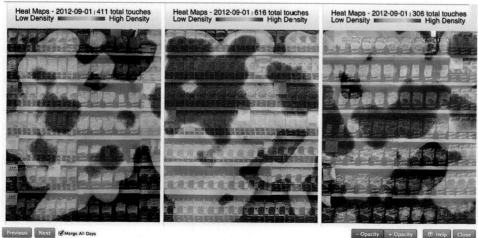

Using Microsoft Kinect sensors, firms such as Shopperception create heatmaps of shopper interactions with the products (touches, pickups, and returns). The red represents the hot zones where shoppers touch the most, yellow less, and blue not at all.

Source: Shopperception

By watching customers in rural Thailand, Unilever recognized the poorest consumers were interested in more than just buying necessities, so it introduced Sunsilk hair products, which are available in many countries throughout the world.

©Agencja Fotograficzna Caro/Alamy Stock Photo

urban shopping experience to rural customers by offering more products, better layouts, and ATMs.[28]

Social Media

Social media sites are a booming source of data for marketers. Marketers have realized that social media can provide valuable information that could aid their marketing research and strategy endeavors. In particular, contributors to social media sites rarely are shy about providing their opinions about the firm's own products or its competitors' offerings. If companies can monitor, gather, and mine these vast social media data, they can learn a lot about their customers' likes, dislikes, and preferences. They then might cross-reference such social media commentary with consumers' past purchases to derive a better sense of what they want. Customers also appear keen to submit their opinions about their friends' purchases, interests, polls, and blogs.

Blogs in particular represent valuable sources of marketing research insights. Marketers are paying attention to online reviews about everything from restaurants to running shoes to recycling. *The Truth About Cars* blog is known for its unflinchingly objective reviews of various makes and models as well as discussions about the industry as a whole, marketing tactics, and global competition, among other topics.[29] Analyzing the content of this and similar blogs provides an excellent source of ideas and information for auto industry executives. Another creative use of social media for marketing research involves building online communities for companies. Sephora's virtual community (an online network of people who communicate about specific topics), Beauty Talk, is a massive beauty forum. It allows customers to ask questions, join groups, live chat with other customers, get advice, and post pictures wearing products. Uploaded customer photos are then linked to the product pages of the featured products. Customers can also filter information based on their interests. This community gives Sephora a lot of data about customer preferences and where the customers need help, and allows the company to address many customer service issues. Therefore, the community lowers customer service costs and heightens customer engagement.[30]

Noting these various opportunities and marketing research sources online, many companies—including Ford Motor Co., PepsiCo, Coca-Cola, and Southwest Airlines—have added heads of social media to their management teams. These managers take responsibility for scanning the web for blogs, postings, tweets, or Facebook posts in which customers mention their experience with a brand. By staying abreast of this continuous stream of

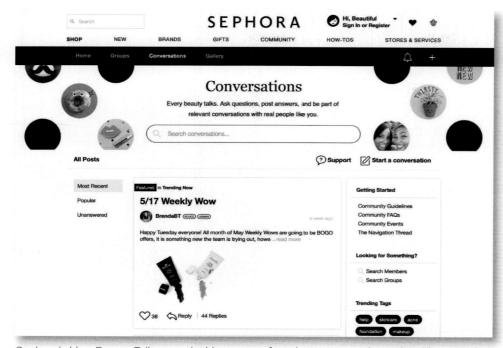

Sephora's blog, Beauty Talk, is a valuable source of marketing research insights. This virtual community allows customers to ask questions, join groups, live chat with other customers, get advice, and post pictures.

Source: Sephora USA, Inc.

information, companies can gather the most up-to-date news about their company, products, and services as well as their competitors. These social media searches allow companies to learn about customers' perceptions and resolve customer complaints they may never have heard about through other channels.

The data gathered through the searches also undergo careful analyses: Are customer sentiments generally positive, negative, or neutral? What sort of intensity or interest levels do they imply? How many customers are talking about the firm's products, and how many focus instead on competitors'? This data analysis is understandably challenging, considering the

When Kraft considered the launch of its South Beach product line, it created a virtual community of health and wellness opinion leaders and women who wanted to lose weight.

©Michael J. Hruby

amount of data available online. However, monitoring consumer sentiments has grown easier with the development of social media monitoring platforms.

Using a technique known as sentiment mining, firms collect consumer comments about companies and their products on social media sites such as Facebook, Twitter, and online blogs. The data are then analyzed to distill customer attitudes toward and preferences for products and advertising campaigns. Scouring millions of sites by combining automated online search tools with text analysis techniques, sentiment mining yields qualitative data that provide new insight into what consumers really think. Companies plugged into this real-time information can become more nimble, allowing for quick changes in a product rollout or a new advertising campaign.[31] Another novel use of social media to collect marketing information is to encourage or even pay people to share their activities in selfies, as Social & Mobile Marketing 10.1 explains.

Social & Mobile Marketing 10.1

Selfies as Data: Relying on a New Form of Self-Reporting to Gauge Consumer Behavior[v]

When marketers search for insights into how and when consumers use their products, they face a few seemingly insurmountable challenges. It is hard to gauge what consumers do in the privacy of their own homes, because it isn't as if a marketer can place a hidden camera in someone's bedroom. They can ask questions, but people often don't tell the full truth about what they do, whether because they're embarrassed to admit what their late-night snacks really consist of, or because they just plain don't remember how they go about the mundane task of brushing their teeth.

But that sort of behavioral information is exactly what marketing researchers need to be able to design new products that can meet people's actual needs, as well as to communicate with those users in the most effective ways. And here's where the selfie—that ubiquitous, popular, seemingly silly form of communication—is making all the difference.

By paying consumers small fees to take selfies as they perform basic, mundane tasks, several service companies are enabling product firms to gain a totally new and far more accurate view of what their customers are doing. For example, Crest asked users registered with the site Pay Your Selfie to take shots of themselves using various Crest-branded products. The collection of thousands of pictures revealed a notable insight that was totally new to Crest: A lot of people brush their teeth between 4:00 and 6:00 p.m. Through a little more analysis with some additional data, the company realized they were getting ready to go out for social events after work. They wanted fresh breath for happy hour! The insight has prompted Crest to initiate a completely new campaign to target and emphasize the benefits of several of its products for just such purposes.

Other selfie requests by other clients of the data gathering service involve other basic tasks, such as cleaning a bathroom or buying a particular brand of candy bar in a store. When a Canadian healthy fast-food chain asked users to depict themselves eating healthy snacks on the go, it was a little surprised by just how many people snapped shots as they ate Snickers bars. This evidence of consumer behavior and consumer perceptions showed the company that people's definitions of healthy are broader than it might have assumed. Snickers might take note of the information as well. Evidently, people see this candy as somehow healthier than other candy bars, a benefit that it could readily leverage in its advertising.

In addition to traditional marketing insights, the selfie-based data can help companies decide appropriate new locations

Paying consumers to take selfies of themselves using products provides new insights into how products are used.

©franckreporter/E+/Getty Images

and market segments for their stores and products. For example, if people mostly show themselves consuming the firm's products in their offices, the company likely should expand into business districts rather than near residential neighborhoods. When a call for selfies of people eating breakfast showed that Millennial contributors were eating a lot of Pop Tarts and Froot Loops, it seems likely that Kellogg's reoriented its advertising budgets to target these older buyers, rather than the young children who have traditionally constituted its target market.

The users who upload their selfies receive a relatively nominal payment: from about 20 cents to $1 for each verified picture. To be verified, the shot needs to complete the assigned task and be visible and appropriate. That last criterion has been an interesting challenge for some companies. As selfie-takers become more and more comfortable with the idea of sharing pictures of themselves performing their everyday tasks, many of them are providing pictures in which toothpaste is running down their chins or they are only partially clothed. Of course, that's information that marketers can use too: 11 percent of the men who participated in the toothpaste task were not wearing shirts in their selfies. What might toothpaste producers learn from that sort of intimate information?

In-Depth Interviews

In an **in-depth interview**, trained researchers ask questions and listen to and record the answers and then pose additional questions to clarify or expand on a particular issue. For instance, in addition to simply watching teenagers shop for apparel, interviewers might stop them one at a time in the mall to ask them a few questions, such as: "We noticed that you went into and came out of Abercrombie & Fitch very quickly without buying anything. Why was that?" If the subject responds that no one had bothered to wait on her, the interviewer might ask a follow-up question like, "Oh? Has that happened to you before?" or "Do you expect more sales assistance there?"

In-depth interviews provide insights that help managers better understand the nature of their industry as well as important trends and consumer preferences, which can be invaluable for developing marketing strategies. Specifically, they can establish a historical context for the phenomenon of interest, particularly when they include industry experts or experienced consumers. They also can communicate how people really feel about a product or service at the individual level. Finally, marketers can use the results of in-depth interviews to develop surveys.

In-depth interviews are, however, relatively expensive and time-consuming. The interview cost depends on the

Although relatively expensive, in-depth interviews can reveal information that would be difficult to obtain with other methods.

©wdstock/Getty Images

length of the interaction and the characteristics of the people included in the sample. If the sample must feature medical doctors, for example, the costs of getting sufficient interviews will be much higher than the costs associated with intercepting teenagers in a mall.

Focus Group Interviews

In focus group interviews, a small group of people (usually 8 to 12) come together for an intensive discussion about a particular topic. Using an unstructured method of inquiry, a trained moderator guides the conversation according to a predetermined, general outline of topics of interest. Researchers usually record the interactions by videotape or audiotape so they can carefully comb through the interviews later to catch any patterns of verbal or nonverbal responses. In particular, focus groups gather qualitative data about initial reactions to a new or existing product or service, opinions about different competitive offerings, or reactions to marketing stimuli, such as a new ad campaign or point-of-purchase display materials.[32]

To obtain new information to help it continue its innovative success derived from its introduction of low-sodium choices, Campbell Soup conducted extensive focus groups with female shoppers who indicated they would buy ready-to-eat soups. The groups clearly revealed the women's top priorities: a nutritious soup that contained the ingredients they would use if they made soup. They wanted, for example, white meat chicken, fresh vegetables, and sea salt. In addition, focus group participants were equally clear about what they did *not* want, such as high fructose corn syrup, MSG, and other ingredients whose names they could not even pronounce.[33]

The growth of online technology, as well as computer and video capabilities, have provided tremendous benefits for focus group research, which now often takes place online. Online focus group firms offer a secure site as a platform for companies to listen in on focus groups and even interact with consumers, without anyone having to travel. The client company not only saves costs but also gains access to a broader range of potential customers who live in various neighborhoods, states, or even countries.

PROGRESS CHECK

1. What are the types of qualitative research?

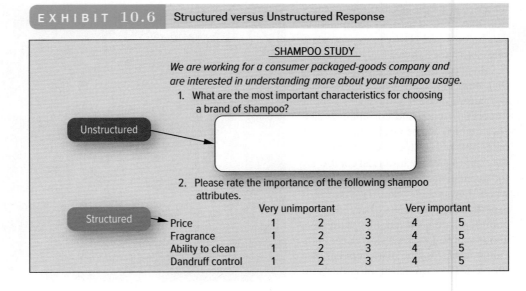

EXHIBIT 10.6   Structured versus Unstructured Response

SHAMPOO STUDY

*We are working for a consumer packaged-goods company and
are interested in understanding more about your shampoo usage.*

1. What are the most important characteristics for choosing
    a brand of shampoo?

Unstructured

2. Please rate the importance of the following shampoo
    attributes.

	Very unimportant			Very important	
Price	1	2	3	4	5
Fragrance	1	2	3	4	5
Ability to clean	1	2	3	4	5
Dandruff control	1	2	3	4	5

Structured

Survey Research

Arguably the most popular type of quantitative primary collection method is a survey—a systematic means of collecting information from people using a questionnaire. A questionnaire is a document that features a set of questions designed to gather information from respondents and thereby accomplish the researchers' objectives. Individual questions on a questionnaire can be either unstructured or structured. Unstructured questions are open ended and allow respondents to answer in their own words. An unstructured question like "What are the most important characteristics for choosing a brand of shampoo?" yields an unstructured response. However, the same question could be posed to respondents in a structured format by providing a fixed set of response categories, such as price, fragrance, ability to clean, or dandruff control, and then asking respondents to rate the importance of each. Structured questions are closed-ended questions for which a discrete set of response alternatives, or specific answers, is provided for respondents to evaluate (see Exhibit 10.6).

Developing a questionnaire is part art and part science. The questions must be carefully designed to address the specific set of research questions. Moreover, for a questionnaire to produce meaningful results, its questions cannot be misleading in any fashion (e.g., open to multiple interpretations), and they must address only one issue at a time.

*Survey research uses questionnaires to collect primary
data. Questions can be either unstructured or structured.*
©Kayte Deioma/PhotoEdit

They also must be worded in vocabulary that will be familiar and comfortable to those being surveyed. The questions should be sequenced appropriately: general questions first, more specific questions next, and demographic questions at the end. Finally, the layout and appearance of the questionnaire must be professional and easy to follow, with appropriate instructions in suitable places. For some tips on what to avoid when designing a questionnaire, see Exhibit 10.7.[34]

Similar to focus groups, marketing surveys can be conducted either online or offline, but online marketing surveys offer researchers the chance to develop a database quickly with many responses. Web surveys have steadily grown as a percentage of all quantitative surveys. Online surveys have a lot to offer marketers with tight deadlines and small budgets.

In particular, the response rates for online surveys are relatively high. Typical response rates run from 1 to 2 percent for mail and 10 to 15 percent for phone surveys. For online surveys,

EXHIBIT 10.7	What to Avoid When Designing a Questionnaire	
Issue	**Good Question**	**Bad Question**
Avoid questions the respondent cannot easily or accurately answer.	When was the last time you went to the grocery store?	How much money did you spend on groceries last month?
Avoid sensitive questions unless they are absolutely necessary.	Do you take vitamins?	Do you dye your gray hair?
Avoid double-barreled questions, which refer to more than one issue with only one set of responses.	1. Do you like to shop for clothing? 2. Do you like to shop for food?	Do you like to shop for clothing and food?
Avoid leading questions, which steer respondents to a particular response, irrespective of their true beliefs.	Please rate how safe you believe a BMW is on a scale of 1 to 10, with 1 being not safe and 10 being very safe.	BMW is the safest car on the road, right?
Avoid one-sided questions that present only one side of the issue.	To what extent do you believe fast food contributes to adult obesity using a five-point scale? 1: Does not contribute 5: Main cause	Fast food is responsible for adult obesity: Agree/Disagree

Source: Adapted from A. Parasuraman, Dhruv Grewal, and R. Krishnan, *Marketing Research*, 2nd ed. (Boston: Houghton Mifflin, 2007), Ch. 10.

in contrast, the response rate can reach 30 to 35 percent or even higher in business-to-business research.[35] It also is inexpensive. Costs likely will continue to fall as users become more familiar with the online survey process. Results are processed and received quickly. Reports and summaries can be developed in real time and delivered directly to managers in simple, easy-to-digest reports, complete with color, graphics, and charts. Traditional phone or mail surveys require laborious data collection, tabulation, summary, and distribution before anyone can grasp their results.

Diverse online survey software, such as Qualtrics, SurveyMonkey, and SurveyGizmo, make it very easy to draft an online survey using questions from existing survey libraries. A survey link can be sent easily in an e-mail to potential respondents or panelists as well as posted on specific sites that are likely to attract the target audience or people who are willing to perform online work. For example, Amazon's Mechanical Turk website (www.mturk .com/) offers a platform where developers can post surveys and connect them with workers who will provide feedback.

Panel-and Scanner-Based Research

As noted previously, panel and scanner research can be either secondary or primary. An example of the use of a panel to collect primary data would be Walmart's subsidiary Asda, which uses an online customer panel, called "Pulse of the Nation," to help determine which products to carry. Asda sends e-mails to each participant with product images and descriptions of potential new products. The customers' responses indicate whether they think each product should be carried in stores. As an incentive to participate, Asda enters respondents automatically in a drawing for free prizes.[36]

Experimental Research

Experimental research (an **experiment**) is a type of quantitative research that systematically manipulates one or more variables to determine which variables have a causal effect on other variables. For example, in our earlier scenario, one thing the hypothetical McDonald's research team was trying

Walmart's UK subsidiary Asda uses an 18,000-customer panel, which it calls "Pulse of the Nation," to help determine which products to carry.
©David Levenson/Alamy Stock Photo

EXHIBIT 10.8	Hypothetical Pricing Experiment for McDonald's				
	1	**2**	**3**	**4**	**5**
Market	**Unit Price**	**Market Demand at Price (in Units)**	**Total Revenue (Col. 1 × Col. 2)**	**Total Cost of Units Sold ($300,000 Fixed Cost + $2.00 Variable Cost)**	**Total Profits (Col. 3 — Col. 4)**
1	$4	200,000	$800,000	$700,000	$100,000
2	5	150,000	750,000	600,000	150,000
3	6	100,000	600,000	500,000	100,000
4	7	50,000	350,000	400,000	(50,000)

to determine was the most profitable price for a new menu combo item (hamburger, fries, and drink). Assume that the fixed cost of developing the item is $300,000 and the variable cost, which is primarily composed of the cost of the food itself, is $2. McDonald's puts the item on the menu at four prices in four markets. (See Exhibit 10.8.) In general, the more expensive the item, the less it will sell. But by running this experiment, the restaurant chain determines that the most profitable price is the second least expensive ($5). These findings suggest some people may have believed that the most expensive item ($7) was too expensive, so they refused to buy it. The least expensive item ($4) sold fairly well, but McDonald's did not make as much money on each item sold. In this experiment, the changes in price likely caused the changes in quantities sold and therefore affected the restaurant's profitability.

Firms are also actively using experimental techniques on Facebook. Once a firm has created its Facebook page, it can devise advertisements and rely on Facebook's targeting options to deliver those ads to the most appropriate customer segments. To make sure the communication is just right, companies can experiment with alternative versions and identify which advertisement is most effective. State Bicycle Co., a manufacturer in Arizona, similarly needed to determine what other interests its customers had and who its main competitors were. Therefore, it tested a range of ads targeting

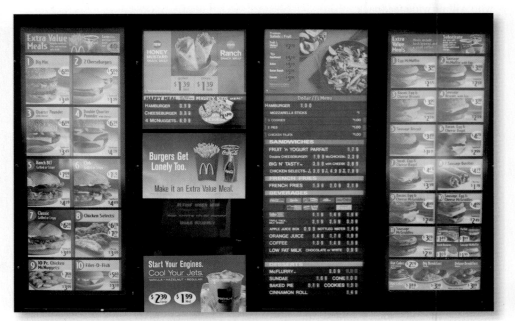

Using an experiment, McDonald's would test the price of new menu items to determine which is the most profitable.

©Mary Altaffer/AP Images

EXHIBIT 10.9 Advantages and Disadvantages of Secondary and Primary Data

Type	Examples	Advantages	Disadvantages
Secondary research	☐ Census data ☐ Sales invoices ☐ Internet information ☐ Books ☐ Journal articles ☐ Syndicated data	☐ Saves time in collecting data because they are readily available ☐ Free or inexpensive (except for syndicated data)	☐ May not be precisely relevant to information needs ☐ Information may not be timely ☐ Sources may not be original, and therefore usefulness is an issue ☐ Methodologies for collecting data may not be appropriate ☐ Data sources may be biased
Primary research	☐ Observed consumer behavior ☐ Focus group interviews ☐ Surveys ☐ Experiments	☐ Specific to the immediate data needs and topic at hand ☐ Offers behavioral insights generally not available from secondary research	☐ Costly ☐ Time-consuming ☐ Requires more sophisticated training and experience to design study and collect data

customers who searched for different bands (e.g., did more Arcade Fire or Passion Pit fans click their link?) and other bicycle manufacturers. With this information, it devised new contests and offerings on its own home page to attract more of the visitors who were likely to buy.[37] Facebook tries to help its corporate clients enhance their own customers' engagement and influence through a variety of options: check-ins, asking for customer comments, sharing information with friends, and so on.[38] It measures all these forms of data, contributing even further to the information businesses have about their page visitors.

LO10-4 Summarize the differences between secondary data and primary data.

Advantages and Disadvantages of Primary and Secondary Research

Now that we have discussed the various secondary and primary data collection methods, think back over our discussion and ask yourself what seem to be the best applications of each and when you would want to go to secondary sources or use primary collection methods. We can see that both primary data and secondary data have certain inherent and distinct advantages and disadvantages. For a summary of the advantages and disadvantages of each type of research, see Exhibit 10.9.

PROGRESS CHECK

1. What are the types of quantitative research?
2. What are the advantages and disadvantages of primary and secondary research?

Facebook analytics help firms increase customer engagement.

Courtesy of True Digital Communications, www.truedigitalcom.com

LO10-5 Examine the circumstances in which collecting information on consumers is ethical.

THE ETHICS OF USING CUSTOMER INFORMATION

As we noted in Chapter 4, upholding strong business ethics requires more than a token nod to ethics in the mission statement. A strong ethical orientation must be an integral part of a firm's marketing strategy and decision making. It is particularly important for marketers to adhere to ethical practices when conducting marketing research. The American Marketing Association provides three guidelines for conducting marketing research: (1) It prohibits selling or fund-raising under the guise of conducting research, (2) it supports maintaining research integrity by avoiding misrepresentation or the omission of pertinent research data, and (3) it encourages the fair treatment of clients and suppliers.[39] Numerous codes of conduct written by various marketing research societies all reinforce the duty of researchers to respect the rights of the subjects in the course of their research. The bottom line: Marketing research should be used only to produce unbiased, factual information.

As technology continues to advance, the potential threats to consumers' personal information grow in number and intensity. Marketing researchers must be vigilant to avoid abusing their access to these data. From charitable giving to medical records to Internet tracking, consumers are more anxious than ever about preserving their fundamental right to privacy. They also demand increasing control over the information that has been collected about them. A potentially troubling ethical issue is how the Roomba robotic vacuums can collect information inside people's homes, as discussed in Ethical & Societal Dilemma 10.1.

Many firms voluntarily notify their customers that any information provided to them will be kept confidential and not given or sold to any other firm. As more firms adopt advanced marketing research technology, such as facial recognition software, they also are working to ensure they receive permission from consumers. **Facial recognition software** is used to detect individuals from a video frame or digital images.[40] For example, Kellogg's used facial recognition software to record participants' faces as they watched three different ads for its Crunchy Nut cereal. It then assessed when they smiled or frowned and their overall positive versus negative response—but only after those participants had agreed to be recorded. Kellogg's was then able to promote the ad that was most widely liked.[41]

Going even deeper than using facial recognition software, **neuromarketing** is the process of examining consumers' brain patterns to determine their responses to marketing communications, products, or services for the purpose of developing marketing tactics or strategies.[42] Such insights would be invaluable for marketers to discover what truly appeals to consumers. For example, based on results of a series of neuromarketing studies, Frito-Lay discovered that shiny potato chip bags invoked feelings of guilt. Therefore, it switched

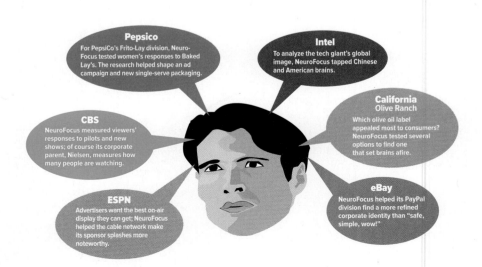

Findings from neuromarketing studies by NeuroFocus.

Ethical & Societal Dilemma 10.1   Vacuuming Up More Than Dirt: The Information Collected by Roomba and Its Potential Uses[vi]

Many consumers leave their house in the morning to go to work or school with their automatic vacuum turned on so that when they arrive home, their floors are pleasantly clean and dirt-free. But to function effectively, these robotic vacuums, such as those sold by iRobot under the brand name Roomba, must develop maps of the layout of people's homes, so that they can avoid bumping into walls or propel themselves down hallways. Is there a privacy concern associated with devices that "vacuum up" that sort of information?

The question became particularly salient when the chief executive of iRobot allegedly noted that the company was working on a deal to share information about consumers' homes with outside companies such as Amazon or Google. The company quickly retracted the assertion, claiming that what the executive really meant was that it may be possible, in the future and only with customers' consent, to share such information. But the genie was out of the proverbial bottle. In response, observers expressed their concerns that as a Roomba learns the layout of the house, it can gather all sorts of other information too. It knows if there are pets in the house, based on the amount of animal hair it encounters; it likely learns if there are children, according to whether it bumps into a lot of toys. With such information, marketers could target specific pet- or child-related offerings to customers. Another opportunity could arise if the Roomba were able to discern that, say, the dining room contained only two chairs. Marketers likely would be very interested in such information because it could prompt them to issue a good deal on a new dining room suite.

The overall layout of the home also might provide information about other consumer characteristics, such as an estimated income level. Combined with location information, these data draw a quite accurate and detailed picture of the consumer—more detailed than some users might be comfortable sharing, whether with iRobot or the marketing partners with which it might someday share the data.

Would you allow a Roomba vacuum cleaner to collect information about the layout of your home, and then sell that information to other companies?

©David Gabis/Alamy Stock Photo

Although iRobot is quick to assure users that it would never share these data without permission, external observers note that the concerns go beyond immediate owners. If a homeowner agrees to share her or his house's layout, but then sells the home, the information already has been shared. The new owner may not agree to such dispersion of the information, but it already has taken place.

In response to such concerns, some customers are deciding to disconnect their vacuum from the Internet altogether. But in turning off the Wi-Fi, they lose the ability to leverage certain features offered by the app, such as remotely scheduling when it runs, customizing cleaning features, or being able to control it through a smart home assistant.

Legal precedent has established that U.S. citizens have a legitimate expectation of privacy within their own homes. But what happens when they invite a robot to make a map of those homes? Are their claims to privacy automatically subverted?

---

its packaging to matte bags and its potato chips sales grew.[43] But as anyone who has ever seen a science fiction movie can imagine, the potential for abuses of such tools are immense. And a key question remains: Do any consumers want marketers reading their brain waves and marketing goods and services to them in a manner that bypasses their conscious thoughts?

Several organizations, including the Center for Democracy & Technology (CDT) and the Electronic Privacy Information Center (EPIC), have emerged as watchdogs over data mining of consumer information. In addition, the Federal Trade Commission plays an important part in protecting privacy and requires companies to disclose their privacy practices to customers on an annual basis.[44] However, as the U.S. federal government has failed to enact comprehensive privacy laws for the Internet, several states are starting to consider legislation. For example, 48 states, the District of Columbia, and several U.S. territories have laws requiring companies to notify customers in cases of security breaches.[45] Although this may be good for the consumer, companies will have to deal with adherence to a complex patchwork of different privacy regulations across the country, making business on the Internet harder to conduct.[46]

Using neuromarketing studies, Frito-Lay discovered that shiny potato chip bags (right) invoked feelings of guilt. Therefore, it switched its packaging to matte bags (left) and its potato chips sales grew.

©McGraw-Hill Education/Evelyn Nicole Kirksey, photographer

PROGRESS CHECK

1. Under what circumstances is it ethical to use consumer information in marketing research?
2. What challenges do technological advances pose for the ethics of marketing research?

Reviewing Learning Objectives

LO10-1 **Identify the five steps in the marketing research process.**

The first step is to define objectives and research needs, which sounds so simple that managers often gloss over it. But this step is crucial to the success of any research project because, quite basically, the research must answer those questions that are important for making decisions. In the second step, designing the research project, researchers identify the type of data that are needed, whether primary or secondary, on the basis of the objectives of the project from Step 1, and then determine the type of research that enables them to collect those data. The third step involves deciding on the data collection process and then collecting the data. The process usually starts with qualitative research methods such as observation, in-depth interviews, or focus groups. The information gleaned from the qualitative research is then used in quantitative research, which may include a survey, an experiment, or the use of scanner and panel data. The fourth step is to analyze and interpret the data and develop insights. The fifth and final step is to develop and implement an action plan. Although these steps appear to progress linearly, researchers often work backward and forward throughout the process as they learn at each step.

LO10-2 **Describe the various secondary data sources.**

External secondary data comprise information that has been collected from outside sources, such as the U.S. Census, the Internet, books, articles, trade associations, or syndicated data services. Internal secondary data can also be derived from internal company records such as sales, customer lists, and other company reports and are analyzed using data mining and big data software.

LO10-3 **Describe the various primary data collection techniques.**

Primary data are collected to address specific research needs. Techniques used for primary qualitative research include observation, social media, in-depth interviews, and focus groups. Techniques used for primary quantitative research include surveys (both offline and online), scanner, panel, and experiments.

LO10-4 **Summarize the differences between secondary data and primary data.**

Compared with primary research, secondary research is quicker, easier, and generally less expensive. However, if you are using secondary data using big data, then the investment in programs supporting secondary data can be expensive. Because secondary research is collected for reasons other than those pertaining to the specific problem at hand, the information may be dated, biased, or simply not specific enough to answer the research questions. Primary research, in contrast, can be designed to answer very specific questions, but it also tends to be more expensive and time-consuming.

LO10-5 **Examine the circumstances in which collecting information on consumers is ethical.**

Marketing researchers should gain permission to collect information on consumers, and it should be for the sole purpose of conducting marketing research endeavors. Information should not be collected under the guise of marketing research when the intent is to sell products or to fund-raise. In addition, marketers must take responsibility for protecting any information they collect.

Key Terms

- big data, 306
- churn, 305
- customer lifetime value (CLV), 327
- data, 301
- data mining, 305
- data warehouses, 305
- experiment, 315
- experimental research, 315
- facial recognition software, 318

Marketing Digitally

1. Go to the website for the marketing research company Kantar (www.kantar.com). Click on "Company News," and then click on one of the recent press releases. What types of research does Kantar conduct, and what types of insights does it develop for its clients?

2. Nielsen provides a wide range of analytical tools and insights that are used by marketing managers across many industries. Go to Nielsen's website (www.nielsen.com) and navigate to the "Insights" section. Choose one of the industries listed (e.g., entertainment) and read the first story. Discuss the key research findings presented in the story. What types of data are presented? How would firms within that industry use these data types and results to develop more effective marketing strategies?

Marketing Applications

1. A large hardware store collects data about what its customers buy and stores these data in a data warehouse. If you were the store's buyer for lawn equipment, what would you want to know from the data warehouse that would help you be a more successful buyer?

2. Identify a nonprofit organization that might use marketing research, and describe one example of a meaningful research project that it might conduct. Discuss the steps it should undertake in this project.

3. Marketing researchers do not always go through the steps in the marketing research process in sequential order. Provide an example of a research project that might not follow this sequence.

4. A sunglasses retailer is trying to determine if there is a significant market for its merchandise in a specific mall location where it is considering opening a store. It has an active Facebook page where customers routinely visit to get coupons and comment on the latest sunglasses offered. How can this retailer use Facebook and Facebook Insights to decide if it should open the new store?

5. A consumer packaged-goods company (e.g., Pepsi) has just developed a new beverage. The company needs to estimate the demand for such a new product. What sources of syndicated data could it explore?

6. A bank manager notices that by the time customers get to the teller, they seem irritated and impatient. She wants to investigate the problem further, so she hires you to design a research project to figure out what is bothering the customers. The bank wants three studies: (a) several focus groups of their customers, (b) observation using a hidden camera, and (c) an online survey of 500 customers. Which studies are qualitative, and which are quantitative?

7. Grocery chains such as Kroger track consumers' purchasing habits through store loyalty cards. These cards collect purchasing data and build consumer profiles. How can grocers such as Kroger use these data to create value for the firm and consumers?

8. Suppose Domino's wants to open a new restaurant. What are some secondary sources of information that might be used to conduct research on potential new locations? Describe how these sources might be used. Describe a method Domino's could use to gather primary research on prospective locations. Do you think Domino's should conduct the primary or secondary source research first? Why?

9. Manuel is planning to launch a new gourmet taco truck and is trying to decide where he should park his truck and what features and prices would entice consumers. He sends a request for proposal to four marketing research vendors, and three respond, as described in the table on the next page. Which vendor should Manuel use? Explain your rationale for picking this vendor over the others.

Vendor A	Vendor B	Vendor C
The vendor that Manuel has used in the past estimates it can get the job done for $200,000 and in two months. The vendor plans to do a telephone-based survey analysis and use secondary data from the U.S. Census.	Manuel's key competitor has used this vendor, which claims that it can get the job done for $150,000 and in one month. This vendor plans to do a telephone-based survey analysis and use secondary data. During a discussion pertaining to its price and time estimates, the vendor indicates it will draw on insights it has learned from a recent report prepared for one of Manuel's competitors.	This well-known vendor has recently started to focus on the restaurant industry. It quotes a price of $180,000 and a time of one month. The vendor plans to conduct a web-based survey analysis and use secondary data.

Quiz Yourself

1. What is the key advantage of primary data?
   a. It is less expensive than secondary data.
   b. It is readily available.
   c. It is collected to address a specific research question.
   d. It is recently collected.
   e. It can be sold by firms.

2. Which step is considered crucial to the marketing research process because it identifies the questions that must be answered?
   a. Setting objectives and research needs
   b. Designing the research project
   c. Collecting data
   d. Analyzing and interpreting the data
   e. Developing and implementing the action plan

(Answers to these two questions can be found in the Quiz Yourself Answer Key section.)

Chapter Case Study

Mc Graw Hill Education **connect**

SWIM, LIFT, PLAY—BUT ALSO DONATE: USING MARKETING RESEARCH TO REDEFINE THE YMCA

Over the years, the YMCA has come to mean different things to different people. Depending on the meanings that people embrace, the charitable organization sometimes struggles to achieve its mission and goals. Accordingly, a key element of its efforts, at both national and local levels, is to conduct ongoing and persistent research into what people perceive when they think of the Y.

Founded in the mid-19th century in response to the new challenges of an industrial society, the YMCA sought to give young men coming to the city for work a place where they could stay safely and for a reasonable rate. In the United States, local YMCAs quickly became known as sources of assistance for new immigrants; though segregated, they also provided meeting places for African Americans and eventually emerged as important rallying sites for the civil rights movement. Once barriers to race and gender fell, the Y embraced its role as a place where every member of the family could find the resources, self-fulfillment, and support that they needed.[47]

Many of those resources historically and still today have focused on exercise and health. Different employees of YMCA facilities have contributed to exercise culture: one originated the term *body building*; others invented games that we now know as volleyball, racquetball, and basketball in Y gymnasiums; and its initiative to help everyone learn to swim led to the vast expansion of public pools and swim classes throughout the nation.

This focus on exercise and health remains a primary element of the reputation of the Y in most Americans' minds. Approximately 13 million adults and 9 million children in the United States turn to their local Y to lift weights, shoot hoops, swim laps, or jog around a track.[48] But the national organization also began to suspect that those purposes were all that

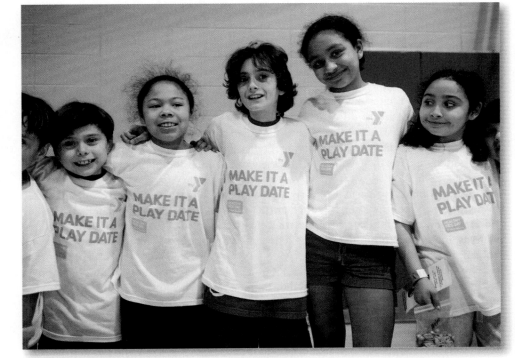

Based on marketing research, the YMCA has been rebranded to the Y, and local branches are encouraged to focus on its core values: caring, honesty, respect, and responsibility.

©Kevin Wolf/AP Images

members, and other stakeholders, were seeing. As the president of the national organization explained, even as membership numbers were climbing, other data related to charitable donations suggested some concerns. That is, people were perceiving the Y "as a gym and swim place. We're also a charity, and that is the missing ingredient. We want people to realize that we're deserving of their charitable donations."[49]

To make that case, the Y (which rebranded in 2010 to take the single-letter moniker, though it also still relies on the longer YMCA acronym to maintain links to its historical functions) relies substantially on research. The goal is to show, with data, facts, figures, and graphics, how programs run by the Y and sponsored by charitable donations actually change lives and improve communities.

For example, a vast survey of consumers across the nation showed that 98 percent of people knew of the YMCA, and 92 percent of them had favorable impressions of it. But only 50 percent indicated that they understood why the Y offered the programs that it did.[50] The national organization considered its mission—to give families resources that they needed to build self-esteem and self-confidence, and thus build communities—evident, but the marketing research showed that these notions were not widespread among people who might use or contribute to their local organizations. In response, it encouraged the local branches (each of which is run autonomously) to emphasize four core values: caring, honesty, respect, and responsibility. It also recommended that local branches consider conducting their own research projects to ensure they were providing the types of resources their local members wanted and needed most.[51]

In other, more targeted, marketing research projects, the national and local arms of the Y also have sought to determine which price points will attract the most members. For example, the Boston branch cited extensive marketing research that showed that if it cut membership fees by 11 percent, it could attract 10,000 new members. The research got it a little bit wrong though: After it reduced the fees, the membership rolls swelled by more than 20,000 users.[52]

Research also has informed which initiatives the Y has made its primary focus for the near future. First, noting extensive academic literature that shows that impoverished students retain less of the education they have received during the summer months, the

Y is expanding a summer camp program in an effort to reduce the well-documented "achievement gap" between children from poor and wealthy families.[53] To support this initiative, the Y also instituted its first national advertising campaign, in which one televised advertisement highlights the various after-school, summer, and meal programs available for children. It also ends with a clear call for contributions to support such programs.[54]

Second, the Y cites national statistics about the number of people with diabetes or prediabetes, as well as scientific evidence that shows that losing even 5 percent of their body weight can help at-risk people avoid becoming diabetic. Accordingly, its second main initiative is to expand its diabetes prevention programs, in collaboration with national health care organizations such as the Centers for Disease Control and Prevention and the "Let's Move" campaign.

Some evidence suggests its efforts are paying off. Visits to the Y's website increased in just the two months after it launched the national advertising campaigns.[55] In addition, the new communications are attracting attention to the Y in various outlets and sources, including a prominent role in a documentary about a swim team for people with autism.[56]

So the Y means a lot of things to a lot of people. The national organization continues to find out what people think of when they think of the Y. In addition, it seeks to learn how it can convince them to think about the Y and its valuable programs as a destination for their charitable donations.

Questions

1. What kinds of marketing research has the Y conducted?

2. Which questions has the Y sought to answer with each different type of marketing research it has conducted?

3. Who are the main stakeholders that the Y is attempting to reach with the information it has gained through its marketing research?

4. Are there other types of marketing research that the Y could conduct in the future to answer other important questions? Give some examples of both the questions it still faces and the research methods it could use to answer them.

Endnotes

1. Thomas H. Davenport and Randy Bean, "How P&G and American Express Are Approaching AI," *Harvard Business Review*, March 31, 2017.

2. Ibid.

3. Eleanor O'Neill, "10 Companies That Are Using Big Data," *CA Today*, September 23, 2016, www.icas.com/ca-today-news/10-companies-using-big-data.

4. Bernard Marr, "American Express Charges into the World of Big Data," *Data Informed*, January 16, 2016, http://data-informed.com/american-express-charges-into-world-big-data/.

5. Alexandra Levit, "Big Data Analytics Doesn't Have to Be Intimidating," *American Express Open Forum*, August 4, 2017, www.americanexpress.com/us/small-business/openforum/articles/big-data-analytics-doesnt-have-to-be-intimidating/.

6. Marr, "American Express Charges into the World of Big Data."

7. O'Neill, "10 Companies That Are Using Big Data."

8. Marr, "American Express Charges into the World of Big Data."

9. Ibid.

10. Davenport and Bean, "How P&G and American Express Are Approaching AI."

11. Nielsen Holding plc, "2015 10-K Annual Report," The Nielsen Company, February 19, 2016.

12. McDonald's Corporation, "About Us," www.mcdonalds.com/us/en-us/about-us.html; McDonald's Corporation, "2016 Annual Report," March 1, 2017.

13. The Wendy's Company, "Wendy's around the World," www.wendys.com/en-us/about-wendys/restaurants-around-the-world; The Wendy's Company, "2016 Annual Report," March 2, 2017.

14. Detailed illustrations of scales are provided in two books: Gordon C. Bruner, *Marketing Scales Handbook: A Compilation of Multi-Item Measures*, vol. 7 (Carbondale, IL/Fort Worth, TX: GCBII Productions, 2013); William O. Bearden, Richard G. Netemeyer, and Kelly L. Haws, *Handbook of Marketing Scales: Multi-Item Measures for Marketing and Consumer Behavior Research* (Thousand Oaks, CA: Sage, 2011).

15. Jeff Kelly, "Big Data: Hadoop, Business, Analytics, and Beyond," *Wikibon*, February 5, 2014, http://wikibon.org.

16. Rachel Wolfson, "Retailers Using Big Data: The Secret behind Amazon and Nordstrom's Success," *Big Data News,* December 11, 2014, www.bigdatanews.com.

17. "How Amazon Is Leveraging Big Data," *BigData Startups,* www.bigdata-startups.com/BigData-startup/amazon-leveraging-big-data/.

18. "Number of Active Amazon Customer Accounts Worldw de from 1st Quarter 2013 to 1st Quarter 2016 (in Millions)," *Statista,* 2018.

19. Wolfson, "Retailers Using Big Data."

20. Bernard Marr, "Big Data at Tesco: Real Time Analytics at the UK Grocery Retail Giant," *Forbes,* November 17, 2016.

21. Tesco, "Your Data Journey," www.tesco.com/help/privacy-and-cookies/privacy-centre/tesco-and-your-data/your-data-journey/; Jenny Davey, "Every Little Bit of Data Helps Tesco Rule Retail," TimesOnline.com, October 4, 2009.

22. Quentin Hardy, "Big Data Picks Up the Pace," *The New York Times,* March 5, 2014, http://bits.blogs.nytimes.com.

23. Google, "Analytic Guide," www.google.com.

24. Amitabh Joshi, "Puma Increased Order Rates to 7.1% via Google Analytics Insights," *Digital Vidya,* March 15, 2016, www.digitalvidya.com/blog/puma-increased-order-rates-to-7-1-via-google-analytics-insights/; Google, "Puma Kicks Up Order Rate 7% with Insights from Google Analytics and Viget," case study, 2013.

25. "Kinect-Enabled Solutions Offer Insights on Retail Customers," Microsoft, January 26, 2016, https://blogs.msdn.microsoft.com/kinectforwindows/2015/01/26/kinect-enabled-solutions-offer-insights-on-retail-customers/; Ronny Max, "12 Technologies to Track People," Navigation, June 1, 2017, www.behavioranalyticsretail.com/7-technologies-to-track-people/.

26. "Retail Signage Gets Smart," Microsoft, May 13, 2015, https://blogs.msdn.microsoft.com/kinectforwindows/2015/05/13/retail-signage-gets-smart/.

27. "Kinect-Enabled Solutions Offer Insights on Retail Customers," Microsoft.

28. Vijay Mahajan, "How Unilever Reaches Rural Consumers in Emerging Markets," *Harvard Business Review,* December 14, 2016, https://hbr.org/2016/12/how-unilever-reaches-rural-consumers-in-emerging-markets.

29. www.thetruthaboutcars.com/.

30. Michael Brenner, "5 Examples of Brilliant Brand Communities That Are Shaping the Online World," Marketing Insider Group, May 1, 2017, https://marketinginsidergroup.com/content-marketing/5-examples-brilliant-brand-communities-shaping-online-world/; www.sephora.com/community.

31. Kristian Bannister, "Understanding Sentiment Analysis: What It Is & Why It's Used," *Brand Watch,* January 26, 2015, www.brandwatch.com/blog/understanding-sentiment-analysis/; Rachael King, "Sentiment Analysis Gives Companies Insight into Consumer Opinion," *Bloomberg Businessweek,* March 1, 2011, www.businessweek.com.

32. Richard A. Krueger and Mary Anne Casey, *Focus Groups: A Practical Guide for Applied Research,* 5th ed. (Thousand Oaks, CA: Sage, 2014).

33. www.campbellsoup.com.

34. Adapted from A. Parasuraman, Dhruv Grewal, and R. Krishnan, *Marketing Research,* 2nd ed. (Boston: Houghton Mifflin, 2007), Ch. 10.

35. Chris Boeckelman, "Everything You Need to Know about Survey Response Rates," *Get Feedback,* January 26, 2017, www.getfeedback.com/blog/better-online-survey-response-rates/; Andrea Fryrear, "3 Ways to Improve Your Survey Response Rates," SurveyGizmo, July 27, 2015, www.surveygizmo.com/survey-blog/survey-response-rates/.

36. https://pulse.asda.com/Portal/faqs.aspx; https://pulse.asda.com; "Asda Wins Vision Critical's European Insight Community Award," press release, Research, September 30, 2013, www.research-live.com/news/.

37. Facebook, "State Bicycle Co.: Building a Strong Customer Base," case study, www.facebook.com/advertising/success-stories/state-bicycle.

38. Facebook, www.facebook.com/business/a/online-sales.

39. Marketingpower.com.

40. www.techopedia.com/definition/26948/facial-recognition-software.

41. E. J. Schultz, "Facial-Recognition Lets Marketers Gauge Consumers' Real Responses to Ads," *Advertising Age,* May 18, 2015, http://adage.com/article/digital/facial-recognition-lets-marketers-gauge-real-responses/298635/.

42. http://dictionary.reference.com/browse/neuromarketing.

43. A. K. Ahuja, "How Big Brands Are Using Neuromarketing to Stay Bold," LinkedIn, October 27, 2017, www.linkedin.com/pulse/how-big-brands-using-neuromarketing-stay-bold-a-k-ahuja; Philip Mahler, "15 Powerful Examples of Neuromarketing in Action," Imotions, March 7, 2017, https://imotions.com/blog/neuromarketing-examples/.

44. https://cdt.org/about/; www.epic.org/; www.ftc.gov/.

45. "Security Breach Notification Laws," National Conference of State Legislators, April 12, 2017, www.ncsl.org/research/telecommunications-and-information-technology/security-breach-notification-laws.aspx.

46. Somini Sengupta, "No U.S. Action, So States Move on Privacy Law," *The New York Times,* October 30, 2013, www.nytimes.com.

47. YMCA, "History," www.ymca.net/history.

48. YMCA, "Organizational Profile," www.ymca.net/organizational-profile.

49. Alina Tugent, "The Y Embarks on Its First National Advertising Campaign," *The New York Times,* January 23, 2016.

50. Aaron K. Olson and B. Keith Simerson, *Leading with Strategic Thinking: Four Ways Effective Leaders Gain Insight, Drive Change, and Get Results* (New York: Wiley, 2015).

51. Foursquare, "What Is a Foursquare Market Research Study?," http://foursquareresearch.com/FourSquare%20Market%20Study%20for%20YMCAs.pdf.

52. Melissa Harris, "Kevin Washington Sets Agenda for YMCA's National Organization," *Chicago Tribune,* November 21, 2014.

53. Ibid.

54. Alina Tugent, "The Y Embarks on Its First National Advertising Campaign," *The New York Times,* January 23, 2016.

55. Adrianne Pasquarelli, "Move Over Clinton and Trump: YMCA Backs a Toddler's Run in New Spot," *Advertising Age,* February 5, 2016.

56. Shanna Belott, "The Best Place for Community Is the One You Grew Up In," *Huffington Post,* February 18, 2016.

i. Dan Tynan, "How 'The Revenant'—and Big Data—Will Change Movies Forever," Yahoo! Finance, January 13, 2016; Matthew Wall, "Can We Predict Oscar Winners Using Data Analytics Alone?," *BBC News,* February 26, 2016.

ii. "Colleges Are Tracking When Students Work Out at Rec Centers," *The Wall Street Journal,* October 28, 2014, http://wsjonline.com.

iii. Karen Stabiner, "To Survive in Tough Times, Restaurants Turn to Data-Mining," *The Wall Street Journal*, August 25, 2017; "How Data Analytics Is Becoming a 'Moneyball' for Restaurants," *CBS News*, February 4, 2017, www.damianmogavero.com/about-damian; www.averoinc.com/products.

iv. John Kell, "How Under Armour Wants to Use Data to Make You Healthier," *Fortune*, April 5, 2016; "Connected Fitness," Under Armour, http://advertising.underarmour.com.

v. Courtney Rubin, "What Do Consumers Want? Look at Their Selfies," *The New York Times*, May 7, 2016; Heather Clancy, "This Marketing Startup Pays People to Take Selfies," *Fortune*, July 13, 2016.

vi. Maggie Astor, "Your Roomba May Be Mapping Your Home, Collecting Data That Could Be Shared," *The New York Times*, July 25, 2017; Alex Hern, "Roomba Maker May Share Maps of Users' Homes with Google, Amazon or Apple," *The Guardian*, July 25, 2017, www.theguardian.com/technology/2017/jul/25/roomba-maker-could-share-maps-users-homes-google-amazon-apple-irobot-robot-vacuum; Allen St. John, "How to Keep a Roomba Vacuum Cleaner from Collecting Data about Your Home," *Consumer Reports*, July 13, 2017, www.consumerreports.org/roomba/how-to-keep-a-roomba-vacuum-cleaner-from-collecting-data-about-your-home/.

Quiz Yourself Answer Key

1. What is the key advantage of primary data?

   Answer: (c) It is collected to address a specific research question.

2. Which step is considered crucial to the marketing research process because it identifies the question that must be answered?

   Answer: (a) Setting objectives and research needs

APPENDIX 10A

USING SECONDARY DATA TO ASSESS CUSTOMER LIFETIME VALUE (CLV)

This appendix examines how secondary data from customer transactions can help determine the value of a customer over time. Specifically, **customer lifetime value (CLV)** refers to the expected financial contribution from a particular customer to the firm's profits over the course of their entire relationship.[1]

To estimate CLV, firms use past behaviors to forecast future purchases, the gross margin from these purchases, and the costs associated with servicing the customers. Some costs associated with maintaining customer relationships include communicating with customers through advertising, personal selling, or other promotional vehicles to acquire their business initially and then retain them over time.

Measures of customer lifetime value typically apply to a group or segment of customers and use available secondary data. A basic formula for CLV, with the assumption that revenues and profits arrive at the start of the year, is as follows:[2]

$$CLV = \frac{\sum_{t=1}^{T} [\text{profit at } t \times \text{retention rate}^{t-1}]}{(1 + i)^{t-1}} - \text{acquisition costs}$$

To implement this CLV formula, we must answer the following questions:

1. How many years (t) can we expect to do business with a customer? The total number of years is denoted by T.
2. What can we expect the annual profits to be from an individual customer or an average customer? These profits are based on sales minus the costs of merchandise and the costs of serving and retaining the customer.

3. What is the retention rate—that is, the average percentage of customers who continue to purchase from the firm from one time period to another? A 90 percent retention rate means that if we have 100 customers in the first year, we will have 90 at the beginning of the second year.

4. What is the discount rate (i)? The discount rate is based on the idea that a dollar is worth less in the future than it is today, so the company can use it to adjust future profits and determine a customer's value today for the customer's purchases in the future. For example, if the discount rate is 10 percent, $100 in profits at the beginning of year 2 are worth only $90.91 [100/(1 + .1)] at the beginning of year 1.

Consider Gregory Missoni, a fairly new client of Very Clean Cleaners who switched from his other dry cleaner because Very Clean sent him $100 worth of coupons in a direct mailing.

Very Clean Cleaners should consider a customer's lifetime value to determine its service levels.

©moodboard/Cultura/Getty Images

Greg just picked up his $200 shirt from Very Clean and found that the dry cleaner had broken a brown button and replaced it with a white button. When he complained, the clerk acted as if it were no big deal. Greg explained to the clerk that it was a very expensive shirt that deserved more careful handling, then asked to speak with the manager. At this point, how important is it for the manager to make sure Greg is satisfied, so that he will continue to bring his dry cleaning to Very Clean Cleaners? To answer this question, the manager uses the following information:

- It cost Very Clean $100 to acquire Greg as a customer. Thus, the acquisition cost is $100.
- Very Clean expects Greg to remain a client for 5 years (time horizon T = 5 years).
- Very Clean expects to make a $1,000 profit each year from Greg's dry cleaning.
- On average, 10 percent of customers defect to another cleaner each year. Therefore, the expected retention rate is 90 percent.
- The discount rate is 10 percent per year (i in this illustration). For simplicity, Very Clean assumes all profits are accrued at the beginning of the year.

Applying the formula, such that CLV equals the profits from years 1–5, less the acquisition costs, we obtain:

$$CLV = \underbrace{\frac{\$1,000 \times (.90)^0}{(1 + .1)^0}}_{\textbf{Year 1}} + \underbrace{\frac{\$1,000 \times (.90)^1}{(1 + .1)^1}}_{\textbf{Year 2}} + \underbrace{\frac{\$1,000 \times (.90)^2}{(1 + .1)^2}}_{\textbf{Year 3}}$$

$$\underbrace{\frac{\$1,000 \times (.90)^3}{(1 + .1)^3}}_{\textbf{Year 4}} + \underbrace{\frac{\$1,000 \times (.90)^4}{(1 + .1)^4}}_{\textbf{Year 5}} - \$100$$

Or

$$CLV = \$1,000 + \$818.2 + \$669.4 + \$547.7 + \$448.1 - \$100 = \$3,383.40$$

Let's see how the formula works. The expected profit from Greg is $1,000 per year. Very Clean assumes profits accrue at the beginning of the year, so the profits for the first year equal $1,000; they are not affected by the retention rate or the discount rate.

However, the retention and discount rates have effects on the profits for the subsequent time periods. In the second year, the retention rate, which Very Clean determined was 90 percent (i.e., 90 percent of customers continue to do business with it) modifies profits, such that expected profits in the second year equal $1,000 × 90% = $900. Moreover, the discount rate is applied such that the profits received in the second year are worth less than if they had been received in the first year. Therefore, the $900 received at the beginning of the second year must be divided by 1.1, which is equivalent to $818.20.

Using similar calculations for the third year, the expected profits adjusted for retention are $1,000 × .9 × .9 = $810. The discount rate then reduces the profit to $810 ÷ $1.1^2 = 669.40 in today's dollars. (Note that the discount rate is squared because it refers to two years in the future.) After calculating the adjusted and discounted profits for the fourth and fifth years in similar fashion, we realize the sum of estimated discounted profits for five years is $3,483.40. However, we still must subtract the $100 spent to acquire Greg, which provides a CLV of $3,383.40.

According to this analysis, it would be a good idea for the manager to take a long-term perspective when evaluating how to respond to Greg's complaint about his button. Greg cannot be viewed as a $2.50 customer, as he would be if Very Clean determined his value based on the cost of laundering his shirt, nor should he be viewed as a $200 customer, based on the cost of the shirt. He actually is worth a lot more than that.

For illustrative purposes, we have simplified the CLV calculations in this example. We assumed that the average profits remain constant at $1,000. But firms usually expect profits to grow over time or else grow, level off, and then perhaps decline. Retention costs, such as special promotions used to keep Greg coming back, also do not appear in our illustration, though such additional costs would reduce annual profits and CLV. Finally, we assume a five-year time horizon; the CLV obviously would differ for longer or shorter periods. For an infinite time horizon, with first period payments upfront, the formula becomes fairly simple:[3]

$$CLV = \text{profits} \times \left[1 + \frac{\text{retention rate}}{(\$1 + \text{discount rate} - \text{retention rate})} \right]$$

$$- \text{acquisition costs}$$

$$= \$1,000 \times \left[1 + \frac{.9}{(1 + .1 - .9)} \right] - \$100$$

$$= \$1,000 \times (1 + 4.5) - \$100$$

$$= \$5,500 - \$100 = \$5,400$$

This illustration thus explains how firms can use secondary data to calculate CLV; it further demonstrates the importance of knowing a customer's lifetime value when executing marketing tactics and strategies.

Endnotes

1. V. Kumar, J. A. Petersen, and R. P. Leone, "How Valuable Is Word of Mouth?," *Harvard Business Review,* October 2007, pp. 139–46; V. Kumar and M. George, "Measuring and Maximizing Customer Equity: A Critical Analysis," *Journal of the Academy of Marketing Science* 35, no. 2 (June 2007), pp. 157–71; V. Kumar, D. Shah, and R. Venkatesan, "Managing Retailer Profitability: One Customer at a Time!," *Journal of Retailing* 82, no. 4 (October 2006), pp. 277–94; V. Kumar, "Profitable Relationships," *Marketing Research: A Magazine of Management and Applications* 18, no. 3 (Fall 2006), pp. 41–46; V. Kumar, "Customer Lifetime Value: A Databased Approach," *Journal of Relationship Marketing* 5, no. 2/3 (2006), pp. 7–35; S. Gupta et al., "Modeling Customer Lifetime Value," *Journal of Service Research* 9 (November 2006), pp. 139–55; V. Kumar,

R. Venkatesan, and W. Reinartz, "Knowing What to Sell, When, and to Whom," *Harvard Business Review*, March 2006, pp. 131–37; W. Reinartz, J. Thomas, and V. Kumar, "Balancing Acquisition and Retention Resources to Maximize Profitability," *Journal of Marketing* 69 (January 2005), pp. 63–79; R. Venkatesan and V. Kumar, "A Customer Lifetime Value Framework for Customer Selection and Resource Allocation Strategy," *Journal of Marketing* 68 (October 2004), pp. 106–25; V. Kumar and J. A. Petersen, "Maximizing ROI or Profitability: Is One Better Than the Other," *Marketing Research: A Magazine of Management and Applications* 16, no. 3 (Fall 2004), pp. 28–34; V. Kumar, G. Ramani, and T. Bohling, "Customer Lifetime Value Approaches and Best Practice Applications," *Journal of Interactive Marketing* 18, no. 3 (Summer 2004), pp. 60–72; J. Thomas, W. Reinartz, and V. Kumar, "Getting the Most Out of All Your Customers," *Harvard Business Review* (July–August 2004), pp. 116–23; W. Reinartz and V. Kumar, "The Impact of Customer Relationship Characteristics on Profitable Lifetime Duration," *Journal of Marketing* 67 (January 2003), pp. 77–99; W. Reinartz and V. Kumar, "The Mismanagement of Customer Loyalty," *Harvard Business Review* (July 2002), pp. 86–97; W. Reinartz and V. Kumar, "On the Profitability of Long Lifetime Customers: An Empirical Investigation and Implications for Marketing," *Journal of Marketing* 64 (October 2000), pp. 17–32.

2. We have made some minor adjustments to the formula suggested by Gupta et al., "Modeling Customer Lifetime Value."

3. S. Gupta and D. R. Lehmann, *Managing Customers as Investments* (Philadelphia, PA: Wharton School Publishing, 2005); Gupta et al., "Modeling Customer Lifetime Value."

VALUE CREATION

Section Four devotes three chapters to how marketing contributes to value creation. Chapters 11 and 12 explore strategies and tactics in the development and management of successful products and their brands. Although many of the concepts involved in developing and managing services are similar to those of physical brands, Chapter 13 addresses the unique challenges of the marketing of services.

Aston Martin ✔
@astonmartin

[Follow] ⌄

Behind the scenes at #AMArtOfLiving in Monaco where @serenawilliams joined us for an exclusive viewing of the Aston Martin Valkyrie!

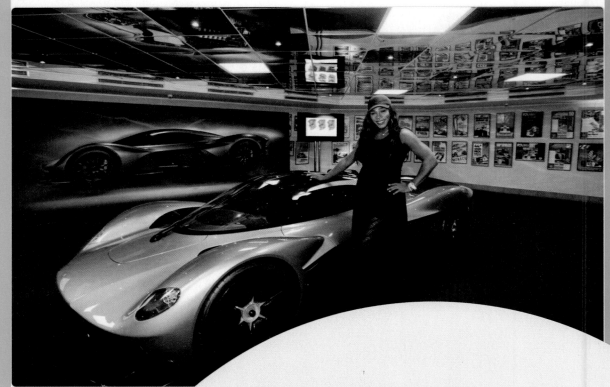

Source: Aston Martin/Twitter

LEARNING OBJECTIVES

After reading this chapter, you should be able to:

LO11-1   Describe the components of a product.

LO11-2   Identify the types of consumer products.

LO11-3   Explain the difference between a product mix's breadth and a product line's depth.

LO11-4   Identify the advantages that brands provide firms and consumers.

LO11-5   Explain the various components of brand equity.

LO11-6   Determine the various types of branding strategies used by firms.

LO11-7   Distinguish between brand extension and line extension.

LO11-8   Indicate the advantages of a product's packaging and labeling strategy.

CHAPTER 11

PRODUCT, BRANDING, AND PACKAGING DECISIONS

Aston Martin has been expertly advertising with celebrity endorsements for years, beginning with its appearance in the 1964 James Bond movie *Goldfinger*. James Bond is still strongly associated with the car, but as the brand has sought to reach different customer segments, it also has pursued some alternative and diversified celebrity endorsements. For example, as Aston Martin looks to gain market share with the wealthy, late 30s, female market of car buyers, it has partnered with tennis star Serena Williams. In June 2017, Williams introduced the latest Aston Martin Valkyrie on social media.

Even still, the brand has not shied away from its traditional market. It remains a luxury car brand renowned for its beautiful designs and British history, such that it also found a great fit in the beautiful face and history-making performance of Tom Brady—who also has lent his endorsement to reputed brands such as TAG Heuer watches, UGG boots, and Under Armour apparel.

The Aston Martin partnership also goes beyond just putting Brady in conventional commercials. Instead, over the course of their long-term partnership, the quarterback will create, or "curate" in the brand's terminology, his own personalized version of the brand's Vanquish S model. A series of videos will document the process, revealing not only the various options available to consumers but also new insights into Brady's own preferences. These preferences clearly revolve around high-performance, luxury cars. Awarded a Chevy Colorado truck when he was named the MVP of Super Bowl XLIX, he turned around and gave it to one of his teammates. Apparently, who needs a truck when you have an Aston Martin?[1]

As a key element of a firm's marketing mix (the four Ps), product strategies are central to the creation of value for the consumer. A **product** is anything that is of value to a consumer and can be offered through a voluntary marketing exchange. In addition to goods, such as soft drinks, or services, such as a stay in a hotel, products might be places (e.g., Six Flags theme parks), ideas (e.g., stop smoking), organizations (e.g., MADD), people (e.g., Oprah Winfrey), or communities (e.g., Facebook) that create value for consumers in their respective competitive marketing arenas.

This chapter begins with a discussion of the complexity and types of products. We then examine how firms adjust their product lines to meet and respond to changing market conditions. Then we turn our attention to branding—why are brands valuable to the firm, and what are the different branding strategies firms use? We also never want to underestimate the value of a product's package and label. These elements should send a strong message from the shelf: Buy me! The final section of this chapter examines packaging and labeling issues.

 L011-1 Describe the components of a product.

COMPLEXITY AND TYPES OF PRODUCTS

Complexity of Products

There is more to a product than its physical characteristics or its basic service function. Marketers involved with the development, design, and sale of products think of physical characteristics and service functions in an interrelated fashion, as depicted in Exhibit 11.1. At the center is the core customer value, which defines the basic problem-solving benefits that consumers are seeking. When Mars manufactures M&M's, Snickers, and other confectionary products, or when Trek designs bicycles, each company's core question is: What are customers looking for? With Mars, is it a sweet, great tasting snack, or is it an energy boost? With Trek, is the bike being used for basic green transportation (a cruiser), or is it for speed and excitement (a road, hybrid, or mountain bike)?

Marketers convert core customer value into an **actual product**. Attributes such as the brand name, features/design, quality level, and packaging are important, but the level of their importance varies, depending on the product. The Trek Madone 9 Series, for instance, is positioned as "see how fastest feels."[2] It features a carbon frame that is light, stiff, and comfortable; an advanced shifting system; and other high-tech features. Not only is it beautiful to look at, but customers can choose from three fits—pro, performance, and touring.

EXHIBIT 11.1 Product Complexity

Actual product
Brand name
Quality level
Packaging
Features/Design
Core customer value
Associated services
Financing
Product warranty
Product support

Photos: (Left): ©Photodisc/Getty Images; (right): ©Michael Blann/Getty Images

The associated services in Exhibit 11.1, also referred to as the augmented product, include the nonphysical aspects of the product, such as product warranties, financing, product support, and after-sale service. The amount of associated services also varies with the product. The associated services for a package of M&M's may include only a customer complaint line, which means they are relatively less important than the associated services for a Trek bicycle. The frame of the Madone 9 Series bicycle is guaranteed for the lifetime of the original owner. Trek sells its bikes only in shops that have the expertise to service them properly. Every possible consumer question is answered on Trek's comprehensive website. Trek even has a financing program that allows customers to purchase new bikes on credit.

The Trek Madone 9 Series is a positioned as "see how fastest feels."
©*overkit/Shutterstock*

When developing or changing a product, marketers start with the core customer value to determine what their potential customers are seeking. Then they make the actual physical product and add associated services to round out the offering.

Types of Products

 LO11-2 Identify the types of consumer products.

Marketers consider the types of products they are designing and selling because these types affect how they will promote, price, and distribute their products. There are two primary categories of products and services that reflect who buys them: consumers or businesses. Chapter 7 discussed products for businesses. Here we discuss consumer products.

Consumer products are products and services used by people for their personal use. Marketers further classify consumer products by the way they are used and how they are purchased.

Specialty Products/Services Specialty products/services are those for which customers express such a strong preference that they will expend considerable effort to search for the best suppliers. Road bike enthusiasts, like those interested in the Trek Madone 9 Series, devote lots of time and effort to selecting just the right one. Other examples might include luxury cars, legal or medical professionals, or designer apparel.

Shopping Products/Services Shopping products/services are products or services for which consumers will spend a fair amount of time comparing alternatives, such as furniture, apparel, fragrances, appliances, and travel. When people need new sneakers, for instance, they often go from store to store shopping—trying on shoes, comparing alternatives, and chatting with salespeople.

Convenience Products/Services Convenience products/services are those products or services for which the consumer is not willing to expend any effort to evaluate prior to purchase. They are frequently purchased commodity items, usually bought with very little thought, such as common beverages, bread, or soap.

Unsought Products/Services Unsought products/services are products or services that consumers either do not normally think of buying or do not know about. Because of their very nature, these products/services require lots of marketing effort and various forms of promotion. When new-to-the-world products are first introduced, they are unsought products. Do you have cold hands and don't know what to do about it? You must not have heard yet of HeatMax HotHands Hand Warmers, air-activated packets that provide warmth for up to 10 hours. Do you have an internship in a less developed country and your regular insurance cannot give you the coverage you may need in case of an emergency? You now can turn to a Medex insurance policy.

A medical professional is a specialty service. Apparel is a shopping product. Soda is a convenience product. Insurance is an unsought service.

(Top left): ©Comstock Images/SuperStock; (top right): ©Big Cheese Photo/SuperStock; (bottom left): ©McGraw-Hill Education/Jill Braaten, photographer; (bottom right): ©numbeos/E-plus/Getty Images

PROGRESS CHECK

1. Explain the three components of a product.
2. What are the four types of consumer products?

L011-3

Explain the difference between a product mix's breadth and a product line's depth.

PRODUCT MIX AND PRODUCT LINE DECISIONS

The complete set of all products and services offered by a firm is called its **product mix**. An abbreviated version of the product mix for Daimler AG, the company that owns Mercedes-Benz, appears in Exhibit 11.2. The product mix typically consists of various **product lines**, which are groups of associated items that consumers tend to use together or think of as part of a group of similar products or services. Daimler's product lines (brands) for consumers include, for example, Mercedes-Benz cars, Mercedes-AMG cars, smart cars, and Mercedes-Benz vans and camper vans.

The product mix reflects the breadth and depth of the company's product lines. A firm's product mix **breadth** represents a count of the number of product lines offered by the firm; the four columns in Exhibit 11.2 depict just four of the lines offered by Daimler AG. Product line **depth**, in contrast, equals the number of products within a product line. Daimler

AG clearly maintains the most products under its Mercedes-Benz line of cars, and it adds more as needed to appeal to various consumers, as Adding Value 11.1 explains.

However, adding unlimited numbers of new products can have adverse consequences. Too much breadth in the product mix becomes costly to maintain, and too many brands may weaken the firm's reputation.[3] If the products are too similar, sales of one brand may cannibalize, or take away sales from the other brand, with no net sales, profit, or market share increase. As described in Adding Value 11.1, the Audi A3 may cannibalize sales from the A4, which is a more expensive model, but looks remarkably like the A3. With more products and product lines, the firm must keep track of trends and developments in various

The Mercedes-Benz product mix includes an assortment of Mercedes-AMG cars (left), smart cars (right), and Mercedes-Benz vans (bottom).
(Left): ©VanderWolf Images/ Shutterstock; (center): ©eans/ Shutterstock; (bottom): ©Grzegorz Czapski/Shutterstock

EXHIBIT 11.2 Abbreviated List of Daimler AG Product Mix

Product Lines			
Mercedes-Benz Cars	**Mercedes-AMG Cars**	**Smart Cars**	**Mercedes-Benz Vans**
A-Class	A-Class	Smart ForTwo	Sprinter
B-Class	C-Class	Smart ForTwo Cabrio	Metro
C-Class	CLA	Smart ForFour	Marco Polo
CLA	CLS		
CLS	E-Class		
G-Class	G-Class		
E-Class	GLA		
GLA	GLC		
GLC	GLE		
GLE	GLS		
GLS	GT		
S-Class	S-Class		
SL	SL		
SLC	SLC		
V-Class			
X-Class			

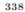

Adding Value 11.1   An Entryway to Luxury: The Latest Entry-Level Models from High-End Car Brands[i]

For luxury carmakers, the lowest-end models in their product lines often represent only a small portion of their sales. Yet these models are critically important when it comes to attracting new customers and, potentially, establishing their lifelong loyalty to the brand. Accordingly, more high-end, traditionally expensive brands have developed comparatively less option-laden alternatives to lure first-time and nontraditional buyers to their dealerships.

The most prominent automobile brand to adopt this strategy was Mercedes-Benz, which introduced its CLA model at a base price of less than $40,000. When consumers realized that they could purchase or lease a Mercedes-Benz for approximately the same monthly price that they would spend for a high-end Toyota or Honda, many of them switched happily. For the most part, the target market for such models includes young professionals. These are consumers who earn a steady income that enables them to take on a car payment but not pay for a new car outright, and their monthly payments must fit their budgets.

Noting the success Mercedes was enjoying, Audi added the A3, for a base price of less than $30,000. With a stated goal of appealing to young, cool, urban drivers, Audi promised that they could "upgrade" from their non-luxury brands, though the differences between the A3 and high-end versions of comparable Hondas or Toyotas have little

to do with actual upgrades to the cars—that is, both likely provide leather interiors and sunroofs. Rather, the key difference is the image benefits that driving a luxury brand offer to consumers.

The lack of distinction in the amenities offered by the luxury brands might constitute a risk too. One test driver, after cruising around in a Mercedes CLA, deemed it similar to the experience of driving a Honda. Such attitudes could readily overturn the distinctive and long-standing advantages that luxury brands have enjoyed. If enough people come to perceive that driving a luxury car is no different from driving a midrange car, those image-based benefits from luxury branding would disappear.

For Mercedes and Audi though, the risks appear subordinate to the potential and realized benefits. Both brands have enjoyed sales increases due to the introductions of these low-end models. Furthermore, these purchases are not repeat buys: Approximately 60 percent of new A3 drivers and 75 percent of CLA purchasers are new to the brands. Such statistics suggest an expanded market for the brands. As these buyers age, advance in their careers, and consider more expensive car purchases, they should be more likely to continue visiting the dealerships that provided them with their very first luxury automobile.

Do the risks outweigh the rewards of Mercedes-Benz and Audi to introduce lower-priced models like the CLA (left) and the A3 (right) to lure first-time buyers?

(Left): ©Tadeas Skuhra/Shutterstock; (right): ©VanderWolf Images/Shutterstock

industries, which might tax its resources. Marketing Analytics 11.1 describes how Macy's uses advanced methods to fine-tune its product lines.

So why do firms change their product mix's breadth or depth?[4]

Increase Depth Firms might add items to address changing consumer preferences or to preempt competitors while boosting sales (see the addition of product A4 in Exhibit 11.3). For Häagen-Dazs brand ice cream, adding new flavors such as Banana Peanut Butter Chip, Honey Salted Caramel Almond, and Midnight Cookies & Cream enables it to appeal to its variety-seeking customers. The product is still essentially the same (ice cream), but the availability of over 45 different flavors significantly increases the product line's depth.[5]

Marketing Analytics 11.1

How Macy's Defines Its Assortment through Analytics[ii]

In the current marketing landscape, it is critical that retailers have a well-developed understanding of their customers. Macy's uses predictive analytics to gain more insight into its customers and improve the buying experience across all channels. Predictive analytics is the use of statistics on data to determine patterns and predict future outcomes and trends. Macy's has been collecting data to create a customer-centric in-store experience for years. Specifically, Macy's uses predictive analytics to create its assortment. The retailer collects data on details such as out-of-stock rates, price promotions, and sell-through rates, then combines those data with stock-keeping unit (SKU) information from each location to segment customers and create personalized store assortments.

As sales continue to shift to digital platforms, Macy's also uses predictive analytics to create an engaging online experience through Macys.com. The company analyzes visit frequency, style preferences, and shopping motivations in its website data, then seeks to apply the insights to ensure that every customer has an enjoyable, effortless shopping experience. Macys.com does more than just use predictive analytics to create personalized purchase suggestions, though. It calculates the likelihood that each customer will spend a specific amount in a particular product category, then uses that information to present the customer with personalized offers on the checkout page. Furthermore, analytics enable Macy's to send registered users of Macys.com even more personalized e-mail offers. For example, it can send up to 500,000 unique versions of the same mailing.

Macy's already has enjoyed significant success as a result of its implementation of advanced predictive analytics. It has continued to experience increases in store sales and online sales, at least partially due to its targeted e-mails. Looking to the future, Macy's plans to improve its online and mobile shopping experiences even further while enhancing the integration of these various shopping platforms to create a seamless experience with just the right product mix.

Macys.com analyzes visit frequency, style preferences, and shopping motivations in its website data to develop promotions like the one pictured here.

Source: Macy's

Häagen-Dazs has increased its product line depth by adding new flavors such as Banana Peanut Butter Chip, Honey Salted Caramel Almond, and Midnight Cookies & Cream.

©McGraw-Hill Education

Decrease Depth From time to time, it is also necessary to delete products within a product line to realign the firm's resources (see the deletion of products B5 and B6 in Exhibit 11.3). The decision is never taken lightly. Generally, substantial investments have been made to develop and manufacture the products. Yet firms often must prune their product lines to eliminate unprofitable or low-margin items and refocus their marketing efforts on their more profitable items. When Procter & Gamble (P&G) announced that it would be merging, eliminating, or selling many of its brands and keeping only the top-performing 70–80 brand names, it may have seemed at first that the historically underperforming Duracell brand would be cut. However, recent merchandising efforts, such as signing an exclusive distribution agreement with Sam's Club, pushed Duracell's annual sales up to $2.3 billion, guaranteeing its continuation as a P&G brand. This quick shift exemplifies the challenges of brand and product line choices: An underperforming brand today might become a superior revenue generator a year later.[6] Thus, marketers need to think very carefully as they decrease the depth of a given product line.

Decrease Breadth Sometimes it is necessary to delete entire product lines to address changing market conditions or meet internal strategic priorities (e.g., deleting product line C in Exhibit 11.3). Thus, the firm drops its line of protein bars and focuses its attention on its energy drinks and vitamin water (product lines A and B).

Increase Breadth Firms often add new product lines to capture new or evolving markets and increase sales (e.g., product line D in Exhibit 11.3). The firm adds a whole new line of yogurt.

EXHIBIT 11.3 Changes to a Product Mix

Product Line A	Product Line B	Product Line C	Product Line D
ENERGY DRINK	VITAMIN WATER	PROTEIN-BAR	YOGURT
A1	B1	C1	D1
A2	B2	C2	D2
A3	B3		D3
A4	B4		D4
	B5		
	B6		

Added depth: New product (A4)

Decreased depth: Dropped B5 & B6

Decreased breadth: Dropped product line C (C1 & C2)

Added breadth: New line (D1, D2, D3 & D4)

BRANDING

A company lives or dies based on brand awareness. Consumers cannot buy products that they don't know exist. Even if the overall brand name is familiar, it won't help sales of individual products unless consumers know what products are available under that name. Sports fans have long been familiar with the rallying cry for Under Armour and its line of athletic gear: "Protect this house." But when the company chose to refresh its tagline, it undertook a massive ad campaign to introduce its new slogan, "I will." In addition to extensive online and outdoor advertising, Under Armour has intensified its branding efforts by signing top athletes from golfer Jordan Spieth, to New England Patriots quarterback Tom Brady, to Washington Nationals baseball star Bryce Harper, who got the biggest endorsement deal for an MLB player.[7]

Under Armour is using its new slogan, "I will," and top athletes like golfer Jordan Spieth in its advertising to help promote its brand.

Source: Under Armour, Inc.

Branding also provides a way for a firm to differentiate its product offerings from those of its competitors. Both Snapple and Tropicana make and sell fruit drinks, yet consumers may choose one over the other because of the associations the brands invoke. As we discuss in more detail subsequently, brand names, logos, symbols, characters, slogans, jingles, and even distinctive packages constitute the various brand elements firms use,[8] which they usually choose to be easy for consumers to recognize and remember. Most consumers know the Nike swoosh and would recognize it even if the word *Nike* did not appear on the product or in an advertisement. Exhibit 11.4 summarizes some of these brand elements.

EXHIBIT 11.4	What Makes a Brand?
Brand Element	**Description**
Brand name	The spoken component of branding, it can describe the product or service characteristics and/or be composed of words invented or derived from colloquial or contemporary language. Examples include Comfort Inn (suggests product characteristics), Apple (no association with the product), or Zillow.com (invented term).
URLs (uniform resource locators) or domain names	Locations of pages on the Internet, which often substitute for the firm's name, such as Toyota (www.toyota.com).
Logos and symbols	Visual branding elements that stand for corporate names or trademarks. Symbols are logos without words. Examples include the McDonald's arches.
Characters	Brand symbols that could be human, anima., or animated. Examples include the Energizer Bunny and Rice Krispies' Snap, Crackle, and Pop.
Slogans	Short phrases used to describe the brand or persuade consumers about some characteristics of the brand. Examples include State Farm's "Like A Good Neighbor" and Dunkin' Donuts' "America Runs On Dunkin'."
Jingles/Sounds	Audio messages about the brand that are composed of words or distinctive music. An example is Intel's four-note sound signature that accompanies the Intel Inside slogan.

Source: Adapted from Keller, Kevin Lane, *Strategic Brand Management,* 4th ed., Upper Saddle River, NJ, Prentice Hall, 2012.

LO11-4 Identify the advantages that brands provide firms and consumers.

Value of Branding for the Customer

Brands add value to merchandise and services, for consumers as well as sellers, beyond physical and functional characteristics or the pure act of performing the service.[9] Let's examine some ways in which brands add value for customers as well as the firm.

Characters like Tony the Tiger help build a brand.
©Sheila Fitzgerald/Shutterstock

LO11-5 Explain the various components of brand equity.

Brands Facilitate Purchases Brands are often easily recognized by consumers and, because brands signify a certain quality level and contain familiar attributes, they help consumers make quick decisions, especially about their purchases.[10] The cola market is a particularly strong example of this benefit. Some people think cola is cola, such that one brand is not too different from another. But branding has made it easy for Pepsi drinkers to find the familiar logo on the store shelf and make it more likely that they simply buy one of Pepsi's other products, should they decide to switch to a diet soda or a flavored version. From promotions, past purchases, or information from friends and family, they recognize the offering before they even read any text on the label, and they likely possess a perception of the brand's level of quality, how it tastes, whether it is a good value, and, most important, whether they like it and want to buy it. Brands enable customers to differentiate one firm or product from another. Without branding, how could we easily tell the difference between Coca-Cola and Pepsi before tasting them?

Brands Establish Loyalty Over time and with continued use, consumers learn to trust certain brands. They know, for example, that they wouldn't consider switching brands and, in some cases, feel a strong affinity to certain brands. Amazon.com has a loyal following because its reputation for service prompts customers to turn to it first.

Brands Protect from Competition and Price Competition Strong brands are somewhat protected from competition from other firms and price competition. Because such brands are more established in the market and have a more loyal customer base, neither competitive pressures on price nor retail-level competition is as threatening to the firm. Lacoste is widely known for its cotton knit shirts. Although many similar brands are available and some retailers offer their own brands, Lacoste is perceived to be of superior quality, garners a certain status among its users, and therefore can command a premium price.

Brands Are Assets For firms, brands are also assets that can be legally protected through trademarks and copyrights and thus constitute a unique form of ownership. Firms sometimes have to fight to ensure their brand names are not being used, directly or indirectly, by others. McDonald's, for instance, has a long history of fighting trademark infringements. It recently won a trademark case with a Singapore-based restaurant chain that wanted to use the term "MACCOFFEE."[11]

Brands Affect Market Value Having well-known brands can have a direct impact on the company's bottom line. The value of a company is its overall monetary worth, comprising a vast number of assets. When the brand loses value, it also threatens other assets. RadioShack was once the first destination for consumers seeking a Walkman or boom box; however, the loss of brand value as it has struggled to maintain relevance as a provider of modern, cutting-edge technology has ultimately led to its demise in bankruptcy.

Lacoste has a superior-quality image that helps protect it from competition and enables it to command relatively high prices.
©Sorbis/Shutterstock

EXHIBIT 11.5		The World's 10 Most Valuable Brands			
2017 Rank	**2015 Rank**	**Brand**	**Country**	**Sector**	**Brand Value (in $ billions)**
1	1	Apple	United States	Technology	$ 184
2	2	Google	United States	Technology	$ 141.7
3	4	Microsoft	United States	Technology	$ 80
4	3	Coca-Cola	United States	Beverages	$ 69.7
5	10	Amazon	United States	Retail	$ 64.8
6	7	Samsung	South Korea	Technology	$ 56.2
7	6	Toyota	Japan	Automotive	$4,550.3
8	N/A	Facebook	United States	Technology	$ 48.2
9	N/A	Mercedes-Benz	Germany	Automotive	$ 47.8
10	5	IBM	United States	Business Services	$ 46.8

Source: From Aimee Picchi, "These Are the World's Most Valuable Brands," *CBS News,* September 25, 2017, www.cbsnews.com/news/brands-most-valuable-in-the-world-interbrand/.

The value of a brand can be defined as the earning potential of that brand over the next 12 months.[12] The world's 10 most valuable brands for 2017 appear in Exhibit 11.5.

Brand Equity for the Owner

The value of a brand translates into brand equity, or the set of assets and liabilities linked to a brand that add to or subtract from the value provided by the product or service.[13] Like the physical possessions of a firm, brands are assets a firm can build, manage, and harness over time to increase its revenue, profitability, and overall value. For example, firms spend millions of dollars on promotion, advertising, and other marketing efforts throughout a brand's life cycle. Marketing expenditures allocated carefully can result in greater brand recognition, awareness, perceived value, and consumer loyalty for the brand, which all enhance the brand's overall equity. Such benefits can be particularly strong if the brand markets itself ethically.

How do we know how good a brand is or how much equity it has? Experts look at four aspects of a brand to determine its equity: brand awareness, perceived value, brand associations, and brand loyalty.

Brand Awareness Brand awareness measures how many consumers in a market are familiar with the brand and what it stands for and have an opinion about it. The more aware of or familiar with it they are, the easier their decision-making process is, which improves the chances of purchase. Familiarity matters most for products that are bought without much thought, such as soap or chewing gum, but brand awareness is also critical for infrequently purchased items or those the consumer has never purchased before. If the consumer recognizes the brand, it probably has attributes that make it valuable.[14] For those who have never purchased a Toyota, the simple awareness that it exists can help facilitate a purchase. Marketers create brand awareness through repeated exposures of the various brand elements (brand name, logo, symbol, character, packaging, or slogan) in the firm's communications to consumers through advertising, publicity, or other methods (see Chapters 17, 18, and 19).

Apple is the world's most valuable brand.
©Jim Young/AFP/Getty Images

These brands are so strong that they have become synonymous with the product itself.
©McGraw-Hill Education

Target has created the retailer/store brand, Goodfellow & Co. for men, which provides well-designed pieces at Target-level prices.

Source: Target

Certain brands gain such predominance in a particular product market over time that they become synonymous with the product itself; that is, the brand name starts being used as the generic product category. Examples include Kleenex tissues, Clorox bleach, Band-Aid adhesive bandages, and the Google search engine. Companies must be vigilant in protecting their brand names because if they are used so generically, over time the brand itself can lose its trademark status. For competitors, this trend similarly is destructive: If everyone with an upset stomach asks for Pepto-Bismol and never considers any alternatives, brands such as Activia suffer smaller chances of making it into customers' shopping baskets. To counteract such concerns, Activia uses well-known celebrities such as Colombian singer Shakira[15] and the first female NFL referee Sarah Thomas in its advertisements to make sure it is recognizable and prominent.[16]

Perceived Value The perceived value of a brand is the relationship between a product's or service's benefits and its cost. Customers usually determine the offering's value in relation to the value of its close competitors. If they believe a less expensive brand is about the same quality as a premium brand, the perceived value of that cheaper choice is high. Merchandise sold by Target and Kohl's is not always perceived to be the highest quality, nor is the apparel the most fashion-forward. But not every customer needs to show up at school looking like they came from a fashion show runway. At the same time, these retailers have created retailer/store brands, such as Target's A New Day for women and Goodfellow & Co. for men, to create well-designed pieces at Target-level prices.[17]

Brand Associations Brand associations reflect the mental and emotional links that consumers make between a brand and its key product attributes, such as a logo and its color, slogan, or famous personality. These brand associations often result from a firm's advertising and promotional efforts. Toyota's hybrid car, the Prius, is known for being economical, a good value, stylish, and good for the environment. But firms also attempt to create specific associations with positive consumer emotions such as fun, friendship, good feelings, family gatherings, and parties. Jingles can establish particularly strong associations, especially when they are catchy and get stuck in consumers' heads. State Farm Insurance continues to rely on the jingle that Barry Manilow wrote for it in the 1970s: In modern advertisements, young customers in trouble sing the phrase "like a good neighbor, State Farm is there," and an agent magically appears on scene.[18]

Because of his vast viral popularity, Grumpy Cat (real name: Tardar Sauce) has been approached by several brands that seek to be associated with him so they can benefit from his entertaining, satirical, and hip image. The feline's naturally unhappy looking mouth now appears across Friskies' prod-

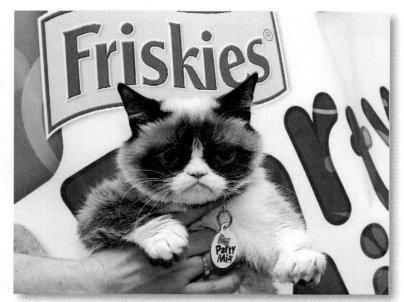

Friskies cat food is associated with its famous "spokesperson," Grumpy Cat.
©Robin Marchant/Getty Images

uct line. Mashable featured Grumpy Cat in its tent at South by Southwest, and a bidding process led to the *Grumpy Cat's Worst Christmas Ever* movie in 2014.

Brand Loyalty Brand loyalty occurs when a consumer buys the same brand's product or service repeatedly over time rather than buying from multiple suppliers within the same category.[19] Therefore, brand-loyal customers are an important source of value for firms. First, firms such as airlines, hotels, long-distance telephone providers, credit card companies, and retailers reward loyal consumers with loyalty or customer relationship management (CRM) programs, such as points customers can redeem for extra discounts or free services, advance notice of sale items, and invitations to special events sponsored by the company. Second, the marketing costs of reaching loyal consumers are much lower because the firm does not have to spend money on advertising and promotion campaigns to attract these customers. Loyal consumers simply do not need persuasion or an extra push to buy the firm's brands. Third, loyal customers tend to praise the virtues of their favorite products, retailers, or services to others. This positive word of mouth reaches potential customers and reinforces the perceived value of current customers, all at no cost to the firm. Fourth, a high level of brand loyalty insulates the firm from competition because, as we noted in Chapter 2, brand-loyal customers do not switch to competitors' brands, even when provided with a variety of incentives.

PROGRESS CHECK

1. How do brands create value for the customer and the firm?
2. What are the components of brand equity?

BRANDING STRATEGIES

Determine the various types of branding strategies used by firms.

LO11-6

Firms institute a variety of brand-related strategies to create and manage key brand assets. The decisions surrounding these strategies are: whether to use manufacturer brands or retailer/store brands, how to name brands and product lines, whether or not to extend the brand name to other products and markets, should the brand name be used with another firm or licensed to another firm, and whether or not the brand should be repositioned.

EXHIBIT 11.6   Who Owns the Brand?

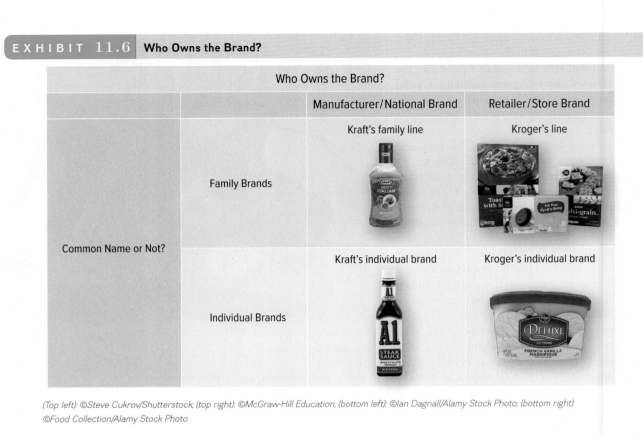

Who Owns the Brand?		Manufacturer/National Brand	Retailer/Store Brand
Common Name or Not?	**Family Brands**	Kraft's family line	Kroger's line
	Individual Brands	Kraft's individual brand	Kroger's individual brand

(Top left): ©Steve Cukrov/Shutterstock; (top right): ©McGraw-Hill Education; (bottom left): ©Ian Dagnall/Alamy Stock Photo; (bottom right): ©Food Collection/Alamy Stock Photo

Brand Ownership

Brands can be owned by any firm in the supply chain, whether manufacturers, wholesalers, or retailers. There are two basic brand ownership strategies: manufacturer brands and retailer/store brands, as Exhibit 11.6 shows. Additionally, the brands can be marketed using a common/family name or as individual brands.

Manufacturer Brands Manufacturer brands, also known as national brands, are owned and managed by the manufacturer. Some famous manufacturer brands are Kraft, Nike, Coca-Cola, KitchenAid, and Sony. With these brands, the manufacturer develops the merchandise, produces it to ensure consistent quality, and invests in a marketing program to establish an appealing brand image. The majority of the brands marketed in the United States are manufacturer brands, and manufacturing firms spend millions of dollars each year to promote their brands. By owning their brands, manufacturers retain more control over their marketing strategy, are able to choose the appropriate market segments and positioning for the brand, and can build the brand and thereby create their own brand equity.

Retailer/Store Brands Retailer/store brands, also called private-label brands, are products developed by retailers. In some cases, retailers manufacture their own products; in other cases they develop the design and specifications for their retailer/store brands and then contract with manufacturers to produce those products. Some national brand manufacturers work with retailers to develop a special version of their standard merchandise offering to be sold exclusively by the retailer.

In the past, sales of store brands were limited. But in recent years, as the size of retail firms has increased through growth and consolidation, more retailers have the scale

Walmart's Jet.com's store brand, Uniquely J, competes against Amazon's store brand, AmazonBasics.

©McGraw-Hill Education

economies to develop private-label merchandise and use this merchandise to establish a distinctive identity. Walmart's Jet.com launched its first private-label brand, Uniquely J, in 2017 which offers a range of products from lemon thyme basil cleaning wipes to organic teriyaki sauce to compete against Amazon's popular private label, AmazonBasics.[2c] Both Costco and Trader Joe's have based their brand identities around their store brands.

Naming Brands and Product Lines

Although there is no simple way to decide how to name a brand or a product line, the more the products vary in their usage or performance, the more likely it is that the firm should use individual brands. For example, General Motors uses several individual brands (Cadillac, Chevrolet, Buick, and GMC), each catering to very different target markets and meeting different needs. Hyundai, on the other hand, uses only one brand because the usage and level of performance are relatively homogeneous across all its cars.

Family Brands A firm can use its own corporate name to brand all its product lines and products; for example, Kraft incorporates the company name into the brand name of its various salad dressings (refer to Exhibit 11.6). When all products are sold under one family brand, the individual brands benefit from the overall brand awareness associated with the family name. Kraft Foods also uses its family brand name prominently on its cheese, pasta, and condiment brands (e.g., Kraft Macaroni & Cheese, Kraft Singles, Kraft Mayo).

Individual Brands A firm can use individual brand names for each of its products. For example, Kraft makes good use of the family branding strategy, but it also allows other products, such as Philadelphia cream cheese, Jell-O, Oscar Mayer, and Planters nuts (Exhibit 11.6) to keep their individual identities, which are not readily regarded as falling under the Kraft umbrella.[21]

Kraft uses a family branding strategy in which several product lines are sold under one name.
©McGraw-Hill Education/Evelyn Nicole Kirksey, photographer

Kraft also uses an individual branding strategy because Velveeta, Classico, Jell-O, Grey Poupon, Heinz, and others are all marketed using separate names.
©McGraw-Hill Education/Evelyn Nicole Kirksey, photographer

Brand and Line Extensions[22]

LO11-7 Distinguish between brand extension and line extension.

A brand extension refers to the use of the same brand name in a different product line. It is an increase in the product mix's breadth.[23] The dental hygiene market, for instance, is full of brand extensions; Colgate and Crest sell toothpaste, toothbrushes, and other dental hygiene products, even though their original product line was just toothpaste. A line extension is the use of the same brand name within the same product line and represents an increase in a product line's depth.

There are several advantages to using the same brand name for new products. First, because the brand name is already well established, the firm can spend less in developing consumer brand awareness and brand associations for the new product.[24] Kellogg's has branched out from the cereal company it once was. Its strategy of branding the corporate name into the product name has allowed it to introduce new products quicker and more easily. Kellogg's Eggo Syrup was a natural extension to its product line of breakfast foods.

Second, if either the original brand or the brand extension has strong consumer acceptance, that perception will carry over to the other product. Ferrari is well known as a brand of luxury sports cars; accordingly, it has leveraged its brand name to introduce clothing offerings emblazoned with its horse logo, which allows enthusiasts to show their devotion to the brand through their apparel. The high cost of luxury cars makes them out of reach for

Ferrari has licensed its brand name to manufacturer-related apparel that appeals to those who can't afford the automobile.
©Alessia Pierdomenico/Bloomberg/ Getty Images

most customers, but clothing-related line extensions give aspirational buyers a pathway to connect with the brand while also helping provide "brand awareness, brand enhancement and, sometimes, brand reinvigoration."[25]

Third, when brand extensions are used for complementary products, a synergy exists between the two products that can increase overall sales. For example, Frito-Lay markets both chips and dips under its Frito-Lay and Tostitos brand names. When people buy the chips, they tend to buy the dips as well.

Not all brand extensions are successful, however. Some can dilute brand equity.[26] **Brand dilution** occurs when the brand extension adversely affects consumer perceptions about the attributes the core brand is believed to hold.[27] Ferrari might be at risk of this effect because it has gone far past clothing to offer brand licenses for sunglasses, perfume and cologne, skis, hotel suites, guitars, phones, LEGOs, leather bags, watches, jewelry boxes, and dice—among other things. It has licensed its logo to 68 different products, prompting Ferrari's chief executive to admit that cars are "almost incidental" to the brand.[28] Here are some examples of unsuccessful brand extensions:[29]

- Lifesavers Soda did well in prelaunch taste tests but didn't in subsequent sales.
- Harley-Davidson's cake decorating kit tried to appeal to the brand's unparalleled consumer loyalty, but it was considered too tame by its consumer base.
- The Virgin Group has successfully entered many markets, from mobile phones with Virgin Mobile to travel with Virgin cruises, but its entry into the wedding dress market with Virgin Brides is just one of the firm's failures.
- Zippo believed that its iconic lighter design would be an appealing design for a woman's perfume. Although the perfume didn't smell like lighter fluid, it turns out lighters aren't something that many women want to associate with perfume.
- Dr Pepper's barbeque marinades hoped to utilize the brand's "one of a kind" image, but it never took off with consumers.

Using a brand extension strategy, Frito-Lay markets chips as well as dips under its Frito-Lay and Tostitos brand names.
©Michael J. Hruby

To prevent the potentially negative consequences of brand extensions, firms should consider the following:

- Marketers should evaluate the fit between the product class of the core brand and that of the extension.[30] If the fit between the product categories is high, consumers will consider the extension credible, and the brand association will be stronger for the extension. Thus, when Starbucks introduced its line of instant coffee, VIA, it made sense to its customers.

- Firms should evaluate consumer perceptions of the attributes of the core brand and seek out similar attributes for the extension because brand-specific associations are very important for extensions.[31] For example, if HP printers were associated with reliability, performance, and value, consumers would expect the same brand-specific attributes in other products that carried the HP brand name.

- To avoid diluting the brand and damaging brand equity, firms should refrain from extending the brand name to too many products and product categories. At its founding, the Kate Spade brand offered aspirational luxury, selling nearly luxury handbags for $2,000 instead of $20,000. Kate Spade sought to expand its reach, opening a range of Kate Spade Saturday stores as well as Jack Spade shops for men to offer lower-priced versions of its designs. Within two years though, the company had decided to close all these stand-alone storefronts and integrate any remaining inventory into its traditional, central line stores.[32]

- Firms should consider whether the brand extension will be distanced from the core brand, especially if the firm wants to use some but not all of the existing brand associations. Marriott has budget, midtier, and luxury hotels. Its luxury hotels, including the Ritz-Carlton, Edition, and Renaissance, do not use the name Marriott at all.[33]

Zippo suffered brand dilution when it extended its brand by introducing a perfume for women. It turns out that women don't associate lighters with perfume.
©McGraw-Hill Education

Brand extensions can be risky. Kate Spade opened Kate Spade Saturday stores to offer lower-priced versions of its designs, but closed them within two years.

©Morgan Dessalles/Abacausa.com/ Newscom

The NBA team, the New Orleans Pelicans (licensor), provides the right to use its brand to apparel manufacturers (licensee) in return for royalty payments.

©Stacy Revere/Getty Images

Co-Branding

Co-branding is the practice of marketing two or more brands together on the same package, promotion, or store. Co-branding can enhance consumers' perceptions of product quality by signaling unobservable product quality through links between the firm's brand and a well-known quality brand. For example, Yum! Brands frequently combines two or more of its restaurant chains, including A&W, KFC, Long John Silver's, Pizza Hut, and Taco Bell, into one store space. This co-branding strategy is designed to appeal to diverse market segments and extend the hours during which each restaurant attracts customers. Yet co-branding also creates risks, especially when the customers of each of the brands turn out to be vastly different.[34] Co-branding may also fail when there are disputes or conflicts of interest between the co-brands.

Brand Licensing

Brand licensing is a contractual arrangement between firms whereby one firm allows another to use its brand name, logo, symbols, and/or characters in exchange for a negotiated fee.[35] Brand licensing is common for toys, apparel, accessories, and entertainment products such as video games. The firm that provides the right to use its brand (licensor) obtains revenues through royalty payments from the firm that has obtained the right to use the brand (licensee). These royalty payments may take the form of upfront, lump-sum licensing fees or be based on the dollar value of sales of the licensed merchandise.

One very popular form of licensing is the use of characters created in books and other media. Such entertainment licensing has generated tremendous revenues for movie studios. Disney, for instance, flooded retail stores with products based on its *Frozen* movie.[36] *Star Wars* memorabilia has been continually successful since the first film was released in the 1970s, and the most recent film releases have led to a massive increase in sales. A long-standing staple of licensing has been major league sports teams that play in the MLB, NBA, NFL, or NHL as well as various collegiate sports teams.

Licensing is an effective form of attracting visibility for the brand and thereby building brand equity while also generating additional revenue. There are, however, some risks associated with it. For the licensor, the major risk is the dilution of its brand equity through overexposure of the brand, especially if the brand name and characters are used inappropriately.[37]

Brand Repositioning

Brand repositioning, or rebranding, refers to a strategy in which marketers change a brand's focus to target new markets or realign the brand's core emphasis with changing market preferences.[38]

Cow Wow repositioned its product from appealing to children (left) to appealing to adult Millennials (right).

Source: Cow Wow Cereal Milk

The cereal-flavored milk Cow Wow seeks to evoke the liquid left over after a breakfast eater finishes all the grains but still has some milk in the bowl. It originally was targeted for children between 5 and 12 years of age, but the company struggled to reach the parents of this target market. After an unexpected endorsement by late-night talk show host Jimmy Kimmel, who described enjoying the flashback to his childhood, Millennials suddenly started seeking out Cow Wow, ready to purchase a fun treat that reminded them of slurping milk from their cereal bowls after they finished their Froot Loops as kids. Thus Cow Wow decided to reposition and transform the product, using regular 1 percent milk and repackaging it in a larger carton with a

Adding Value 11.2   Old Is New Again, for Both Green Vegetables and an Iconic Green Mascot[iii]

He's back, and in a big way! After a multi-year hiatus, B&G Foods is introducing a new generation of consumers to its beloved Jolly Green Giant mascot and hoping to sway both adults and children to adopt its new and existing product lines of frozen and canned vegetables.

With a deeply cinematic approach designed to draw viewers' attention, a new $30 million advertising campaign builds suspense, Spielberg-style, by showing the Giant only indirectly. (Stephen Spielberg famously chose not to reveal the shark until the very end of *Jaws*, in an effort to make moviegoers even more nervous.) His immense shadow darkens buildings, his footsteps mar fields, and characters in the commercial respond with awe at what they, but not the audience, can see. Audiences cannot help but wonder, "What happens next?"

With its slowly unfolding narrative, B&G Foods has also found new channels to air the commercial. Beyond conventional television spots, the marketing communications appear in nontraditional settings such as movie theaters. With these new channels, interest in the brand has expanded vastly and among new segments of the population. The remarkable success of the campaign led B&G Foods to announce plans to continue the approach in 2017, 2018, and 2019, with the addition of new print advertising, as well as mobile pop-up stands to get products in the hands of consumers.

But B&G Foods also is not stopping with advertising. To help keep its brand relevant, it will introduce 15 new vegetable products. Driving its new product generation efforts is the same principle applied to the revamped image of its decades-old

After a multi-year hiatus, the Jolly Green Giant is back with a new marketing campaign.

Source: B&G Foods North America, Inc.

mascot: Old is new again. Familiar dishes such as tater tots have been redesigned to feature a healthier mix of mashed cauliflower and vegetables. Trendy new products such as fire-roasted vegetables are available in the freezer case, next to the traditional bags of broccoli and peas. By leveraging these strategies together, B&G Foods hopes that its revamped product line and updated image of one of the most well-known brand mascots will encourage children to get excited about eating their vegetables and parents to enjoy the compelling and expanded product options.

screw top, to sell to adult Millennial consumers instead of to children.[39] The reemergence of the Jolly Green Giant, as described in Adding Value 11.2, aims to appeal to both cohorts.

Although repositioning can improve the brand's fit with its target segment or boost the vitality of old brands, it is not without costs and risks. Firms often need to spend tremendous amounts of money to make tangible changes to the product and packages as well as intangible changes to the brand's image through various forms of promotion. These costs may not be recovered if the repositioned brand and messages are not credible to consumers or if the firm has mistaken a fad for a long-term market trend. An example of a recent rebranding effort that provoked consumers' disdain was the attempted repositioning of high fructose corn syrup as "corn sugar" as a result of current consumer trends. Not only did the campaign spark a series of legal suits between the corn and sugar industries, but it also failed to convince consumers. Consumption of high fructose corn syrup has continued to decline, and many food manufacturers have cut corn syrup out of their products. For example, Heinz promises that its ketchup avoids high fructose corn syrup, and both Coca-Cola and Pepsi have introduced line extensions based on the promise of being made with "real sugar."[40]

PROGRESS CHECK

1. What are the differences between manufacturer and private-label brands?
2. What is co-branding?
3. What is the difference between brand extension and line extension?
4. What is brand repositioning?

LO11-8 Indicate the advantages of a product's packaging and labeling strategy.

PACKAGING

Packaging is an important brand element that has more tangible or physical benefits than other brand elements have. Packages come in different types and offer a variety of benefits to consumers, manufacturers, and retailers. The **primary package** is the one the consumer uses, such as the toothpaste tube. From the primary package, consumers typically seek convenience in terms of storage, use, and consumption.

The **secondary package** is the wrapper or exterior carton that contains the primary package and provides the UPC label used by retail scanners. Consumers can use the secondary

Kraft's Philadelphia cream cheese changed its packaging from round to oval to ensure front-facing displays that can't spin and fits more into the same shelf space.

©Edible images/Alamy Stock Photo

Morton Salt changed its packaging to celebrate its 100th anniversary.

Source: Mike Mozart/Flickr/CC BY 2.0

package to find additional product information that may not be available on the primary package. Like primary packages, secondary packages add consumer value by facilitating the convenience of carrying, using, and storing the product.

Whether primary or secondary, packaging plays several key roles: It attracts the consumers' attention. It enables products to stand out from their competitors. It offers a promotional tool (e.g., "NEW" and "IMPROVED" promises on labels). Finally, it allows for the same product to appeal to different markets with different sizes, such that convenience stores stock little packages that travelers can buy at the last minute, whereas Costco sells extra-large versions of products.

Firms occasionally change or update their packaging as a subtle way of repositioning the product. A change can be used to attract a new target market and/or appear more up-to-date to its current market. For instance, to help consumers find their preferred taste among the vast variety of flavor options it now sells, Philadelphia cream cheese has undertaken another change—namely, to the packaging of its products. Rather than round tubs—which can easily get spun around on store shelves, such that consumers have trouble seeing exactly which variety is in front of them—the brand introduced an oval tub, to ensure front-facing displays. In addition to preventing spin, the oval shape means that more products can fit into the same shelf space.[41]

Changes also can make consumers feel like they are receiving something tangible in return for paying higher prices, even when the product itself remains untouched. Whether true or not, consumers see new packaging and tend to think that the "new" product may be worth trying. In honor of its 100th birthday, Morton redesigned the packaging of more than 100 individual items to give a clean, modern feel.[42]

An interesting recent development in packaging is a move to sustainable packaging. Sustainable packaging is product packaging that has less of a negative impact on the environment. Leaders in this area of innovation include Coca-Cola, L'Oréal, and P&G. P&G is using the first shampoo bottles that are fully recyclable and made from plastic waste recovered from beaches for its brand Head & Shoulders. Furthermore, these firms attend a sustainable packaging conference that brings together more than 150 firms to discuss new methods to produce environmentally

To answer consumers' call for sustainable packaging, P&G's Head & Shoulders shampoo bottles are fully recyclable and made from plastic waste recovered from beaches.

Source: Procter & Gamble

responsible packaging that is also cost-effective. Ideas from this conference include returnable packaging, use of 3D printing, and flexible packaging. They have also set up a website with information on future conferences and information for the industry at www.sustainability-in-packaging.com.[43]

Packaging can also be used in a far subtler way—namely, to help suppliers save costs. When the costs of producing a product rise significantly, manufacturers are faced with either raising prices—something customers don't usually like—or reducing the amount of product sold in a package. For example, beauty subscription boxes have recently popularized smaller packaging for beauty products, prompting MAC Cosmetics to produce a collection of miniaturized products, Little MAC, with each piece costing only $10 or $12.[44]

Product Labeling

Labels on products and packages provide information the consumer needs for his or her purchase decision and consumption of the product. Because they identify the product and brand, labels are also an important element of branding and can be used for promotion. The information required on them must comply with general and industry-specific laws and regulations, including the constituents or ingredients contained in the product, where the product was made, directions for use, and/or safety precautions.

Many labeling requirements stem from various laws, including the Federal Trade Commission Act of 1914, the Fair Packaging and Labeling Act of 1967, and the Nutrition Labeling Act of 1990. Several federal agencies, industry groups, and consumer watchdogs carefully monitor product labels. The Food and Drug Administration is the primary federal agency that reviews food and package labels and ensures that the claims made by the manufacturer are true.

A product label is much more than just a sticker on the package; it is a communication tool. Many of the elements on the label are required by laws and regulations (i.e., ingredients, fat content, sodium content, serving size, calories), but other elements remain within the control of the manufacturer. Some food companies are responding proactively to the potential of new regulations. In addition, the way manufacturers use labels to communicate the benefits of their products to consumers varies with the product. Many products highlight specific ingredients, vitamin content or nutrient content (e.g., iron), and country of origin. This focus signals to consumers that the product offers these benefits. The importance of the label as a communication tool should not be underestimated.

To combat rising costs, manufacturers like MAC Cosmetics produce a collection of miniaturized products, Little MAC, with each piece costing only $10 or $12.

©McGraw-Hill Education

PROGRESS CHECK

1. Why do firms change packaging?
2. What objectives do product labels fulfill?

Reviewing Learning Objectives

LO11-1 Describe the components of a product.

The product itself is important, but so are its associated services, such as support or financing. Other elements combine to produce the core customer value of a product: the brand name, quality level, packaging, and additional features.

LO11-2 Identify the types of consumer products.

Consumer products tend to be classified into four groups: specialty, shopping, convenience, and unsought products. Each classification involves a different purchase situation and consumer goal.

LO11-3 Explain the difference between a product mix's breadth and a product line's depth.

Breadth, or variety, entails the number of product lines that a company offers. Depth involves the number of categories within one specific product line.

LO11-4 Identify the advantages that brands provide firms and consumers.

Brands play important roles in enabling people to make purchase decisions more easily and encouraging customer loyalty. For firms specifically, they also constitute valuable assets and improve a company's bottom line and help protect against competition.

LO11-5 Explain the various components of brand equity.

Brand equity summarizes the value that a brand adds or subtracts from the offering's value. It comprises brand awareness, or how many consumers in the market are familiar with the brand; brand associations, which are the links consumers make between the brand and its image; and brand loyalty, which occurs when a consumer will only buy that brand's offer. Brand equity also encompasses the concept of perceived value, which is a subjective measure that consumers develop to assess the costs of obtaining the brand.

LO11-6 Determine the various types of branding strategies used by firms.

Firms use a variety of strategies to manage their brands. First, they decide whether to offer manufacturer and/or private-label brands. Second, they have a choice of using an overall family brand or a collection of product line or individual brands. Third, to reach new markets or extend their current market, they can extend their current brands to new products. Fourth, firms can co-brand with another brand to create sales and profit synergies for both. Fifth, firms with strong brands have the opportunity to license their brands to other firms. Finally, as the marketplace changes, it is often necessary to reposition a brand.

LO11-7 Distinguish between brand extension and line extension.

Whereas a brand extension uses the same brand name for a new product that gets introduced into new or the same markets, a line extension is simply an increase of an existing product line by the brand.

LO11-8 Indicate the advantages of a product's packaging and labeling strategy.

Similar to brands, packaging and labels help sell the product and facilitate its use. The primary package holds the product, and its label provides product information. The secondary package provides additional consumer information on its label and facilitates transportation and storage for retailers as well as their customers. Labels have become increasingly important to consumers because they supply important safety, nutritional, and product usage information.

Key Terms

- actual product, 334
- associated services, 335
- augmented product, 335
- brand association, 344
- brand awareness, 343
- brand dilution, 348
- brand equity, 343
- brand extension, 347
- brand licensing, 350
- brand loyalty, 345
- brand repositioning (rebranding), 350
- breadth, 337
- cannibalize, 337
- co-branding, 350
- consumer product, 335
- convenience products/services, 335
- core customer value, 334
- depth, 337
- family brand, 347
- individual brands, 347
- line extension, 347
- manufacturer brands (national brands), 346

Marketing Digitally

1. Visit the Sephora website (www.sephora.com). Explore the Sephora Collection, which is their private-label brand. How does Sephora position this brand in the market vis-à-vis the national brands?

2. Go to BMW's website (www.bmwusa.com) and identify a few recently introduced brand extensions to the marketplace. Discuss whether you believe the brand extension examples you provided will benefit or harm the firm.

Marketing Applications

1. L.L.Bean has a 100 percent satisfaction guaranteed policy on all of its products. What features of a pair of pants from L.L.Bean would be part of the actual product and which would be part of the associated services?

2. Classify each of the following products into either convenience, shopping, specialty, or unsought goods: toothpaste, life insurance, Sharp TV, Eggo waffles, lettuce, Coach handbag, adidas soccer cleats, furniture.

3. Study the following two product mixes. For Product Mix 1: A, B, C, and D are the lines; and for Product Mix 2: X, Y, and Z are the lines.

A	B	C	D
a1	b1	c1	d1
a2	b2	c2	d2
a3	b3	c3	

Product Mix 1

X	Y	Z
x1	y1	z1
x2	y2	z2
x3	y3	z3
x4	y4	

Product Mix 2

Which mix has more *breadth* and why? Which mix is *deeper* and why?

4. Suppose you are the coffee buyer for Kroger's. There is a strong corporate initiative to increase store-label merchandise. Discuss the advantages and disadvantages of offering private-label coffee.

5. Identify a specific brand that has developed a high level of brand equity. What specific aspects of that brand establish its brand equity?

6. Are you loyal to any brands? If so, pick one and explain why you believe you are loyal, beyond that you simply like the brand. If not, pick a brand that you like and explain how you would feel and act differently toward the brand if you were loyal to it.

7. Target owns several private-label brands in different categories, including Mossimo and Xhilaration clothing, Threshold home furniture and decor, and Archer Farms food. Creating all of these brands is complex and expensive. Would it be better for Target to market all of these goods under a "Target" brand? Why do you think Target creates and supports individual brand names instead of using the Target brand?

8. Consumers have become increasingly aware of the amount of packaging that is used for certain products and the possible environmental impact of disposing of packaging materials into the natural environment. Choose a product that you believe should change its packaging. How would you change the packaging? Do you feel these changes would make the product more desirable for consumers?

9. You are the brand manager for a firm that makes herbs, spices, and other food additives. You have had complaints from some of your retail outlets that they are finding empty bottles of pure vanilla extract stashed around the store. Apparently, due to the high (35 percent) alcohol content of pure vanilla extract, people are grabbing the cute little bottles, having a drink, and getting rid of the evidence. Anecdotal evidence from store employees indicates that the majority of the imbibers are teenagers. The cost of placing a tamperproof cap on the extract is a relatively insignificant percentage of the purchase price but will make it more difficult to open, particularly for older customers. Also, there has been a significant rise in sales to retailers as a result of the vanilla "addicts." What should you do?

Quiz Yourself

1. All of the following are elements of a product except
   a. Brand name.
   b. Quality levels.
   c. Packaging.
   d. Warranties.
   e. All of these are elements of a product.

2. Which of the following is a subjective measure of brand equity?

   a. Brand name
   b. Brand awareness
   c. Brand quality
   d. Perceived value
   e. All of these are subjective measures.

(Answers to these questions can be found in the Quiz Yourself Answer Key section.)

Chapter Case Study   connect·

FROM THE COUNTERCULTURE TO THE RUNWAY: HOW DID BIRKENSTOCKS BECOME FASHIONABLE?

Hippies wear them. Rebels, dropouts from conventional consumerism, flower children—all images traditionally associated with Birkenstocks, the clunky, cork-soled sandals that have been issuing forth from German factories for 240 years. Although the company has introduced a few variations, such as a clog or rubberized straps, the look of a Birkenstock is immediately recognizable and little changed from its humble beginnings.[45]

All these features suggest it is a poor candidate as a fashion product. Rather than changing every season, the footwear has stayed largely the same. Rather than focusing on the appearance of the offering, the product design stems solely from considerations of comfort and orthopedic safety. Furthermore, they continue to be made in relatively expensive German factories rather than having production shipped overseas to lower the costs.

Considering these factors, it seems strange that *Vogue* has called Birks "sexy" and *Glamour* named it the shoe of the summer recently. Explanations for this newfound popularity with fashion's elite are varied and unproven. One fashion blogger explained that after years of wearing only uncomfortable, tight, high-heeled shoes, slipping on a pair of Birkenstocks was a life-changing experiment in comfort, so she could not imagine going back. Other fashion leaders, including Manolo Blahnik—known for his sky-high heels and creative shoe designs—has offered his endorsement, asserting that as long as the wearers have nice toes and a good pedicure, the sandals can look nice.

The approval from these fashion leaders has led more and more famous people to name-drop the brand. In popular magazines that feature interviews with trendy celebrities like Keke Palmer and Lorraine Pascale, the Birkenstock name pops up as the shoe of preference on set.[46]

The shift certainly did not result from a conscious effort by Birkenstock though. Rather, it caught the company somewhat by surprise, because it had been doing business the same way it had for more than two centuries. It has a virtually nonexistent marketing budget, does not advertise widely, and did not pursue the endorsements it has received from fashion trendsetters. Its CEO asserts that the popularity is a reaffirmation of a basic, and seemingly outdated, marketing lesson: Build a great product, and people will seek it out on their own.

Still, the company is not immune to the appeal of being known as fashionable. Accordingly, it is happy to tout its mentions in popular media on the

Birkenstock has gone high fashion. Pictured here is British American actress Lily Collins sporting the 240-year-old brand on her feet.
©OPC/ZOJ/WENN/Newscom

Birkenstock website. It also has developed a nice collection of Instagram shots that emphasize its diverse assortment of options. Along with fashion shots of models wearing its silver sandals with high-fashion dresses, it also features hikers in remote locations, sporting its comfortable-looking, well-worn footwear.

The combination of great product and strong branding has been highly effective. Birkenstock's sales have grown by anywhere from 40 percent to 50 percent over the past year in different regions of the world, and it estimates that it will sell 20 million pairs annually by 2020. That's a lot of toes to show.[47]

Questions

1. Visit the company website (www.birkenstockusa.com/) and identify and describe the different product lines that it markets.

2. Describe its product line breadth.

3. Review the different product categories in each of the company's product lines. Which has the greatest depth? Which has the least?

4. How has the company positioned its brand? How does it go about communicating its position?

Endnotes

1. Daniel Bentley, "Aston Martin Drafts Tom Brady for Marketing Push," *Fortune*, May 17, 2017; Robert Klara, "Why Aston Martin Is Marketing Its 'Most Important Car' Ever to Young Female Drivers," *Adweek*, March 3, 2016; "Serena Williams Offers a First Look at the Aston Martin Valkyrie," *Fox News*, June 13, 2017.

2. www.trekbikes.com.

3. Sharon Ng, "Cultural Orientation and Brand Dilution: Impact of Motivation Level and Extension Typicality," *Journal of Marketing Research* 47, no. 1 (February 2010), pp. 186–98.

4. Michael A. Wiles, Neil A. Morgan, and Lopo L. Rego, "The Effect of Brand Acquisition and Disposal on Stock Returns," *Journal of Marketing* 76, no. 1 (2012), pp. 38–58.

5. Laura Knutson, "New Products Amp Up Taste," *General Mills blog*, January 4, 2018, https://blog.generalmills.com/2018/01/new-products-amp-up-taste/; www.haagendazs.us/products.

6. Jack Neff, "As P&G Looks to Cut More Than Half Its Brands, Which Should Go?," *Advertising Age*, August 4, 2014, adage.com.

7. "UA Roster," Under Armour, www.underarmour.com/en-us/ua-roster?cid=PS%7cUS%7cBR%7cggl%7call%7cGoogle-US-All-DSA%7call%7call%7call%7cbroad%7cdg%7c&gclid=EAIaIQobChMI8oPJjO_J2AIV1xSBCh2khAB1EAAYASAAEgLbXvD_BwE&gclsrc=aw.ds; Darren Rovell, "Bryce Harper Signs Biggest Endorsement Deal for MLB Player," *ESPN*, May 4, 2016.

8. Kevin Lane Keller, *Strategic Brand Management: Building, Measuring, and Managing Brand Equity*, 4th ed. (Upper Saddle River, NJ: Prentice Hall, 2012); David A. Aaker, *Building Strong Brands* (New York: Simon & Schuster, 2012).

9. This discussion of the advantages of strong brands is adapted from Keller, *Strategic Brand Management*.

10. Kevin Lane Keller and Donald R. Lehmann, "Assessing Long-Term Brand Potential," *Journal of Brand Management* 17 (2009), pp. 6–17.

11. "McDonald's Just Won a Big Trademark Turf Fight," *Reuters*, July 5, 2016.

12. www.interbrand.com. The net present value of the earnings over the next 12 months is used to calculate the value.

13. Keller, *Strategic Brand Management*; David A. Aaker, *Managing Brand Equity* (New York: Free Press, 1991).

14. R. Huang and E. Sarigöllü, "How Brand Awareness Relates to Market Outcome, Brand Equity, and the Marketing Mix," in T. M. Choi (Ed.), *Fashion Branding and Consumer Behaviors. International Series on Consumer Science* (New York: Springer, 2014).

15. David Kiefaber, "Activia Shows That Inside Shakira's Famous Stomach Are . . . More Shakiras!," *Adweek*, March 18, 2014, www.adweek.com.

16. Jessica Wohl, "Can a Ref Finally Get Activia Past the Jamie Lee Curtis Era?," *Advertising Age*, February 3, 2017, http://adage.com/article/cmo-strategy/activia/307761/.

17. "Countdown's On! Five Things to Know about Target's New Brands Before They Launch This Fall," Target, August 8, 2017, https://corporate.target.com/article/2017/08/new-brands-teaser.

18. Tim Nudd, "Zoinks! State Farm Saves Scooby-Doo and the Gang in Groovy Animated Spot," *Adweek*, October 29, 2013, www.adweek.com.

19. www.marketingpower.com/_layouts/Dictionary.aspx?dLetter=B.

20. Sarah Halzack, "Retail's Secret Weapon Is the Private Label," *Bloomberg*, October 24, 2017; Lauren Hirsch, "Jet Launches Its Own Private Label Brand, Uniquely J," *CNBC*, October 20, 2017, www.cnbc.com/2017/10/20/jet-launches-private-label-brand-uniquely-j.html.

21. www.kraftheinzcompany.com/brands.html.

22. The distinction between brand and line extensions is clarified in Barry Silverstein, "Brand Extensions: Risks and Rewards," *Brandchannel.com*, January 5, 2009.

23. See Alokparna Basu Monga and Deborah Roedder John, "What Makes Brands Elastic? The Influence of Brand Concept and Styles of Thinking on Brand Extension Evaluation," *Journal of Marketing* 74, no. 3 (May 2010), pp. 80–92; Thorsen Hennig-Thurau, Mark B. Houson, and Torsten Heitjans, "Conceptualizing and Measuring the Monetary Value of Brand Extensions: The Case of Motion Pictures," *Journal of Marketing* 73, no. 6

(November 2009), pp. 167–83; Rajeev Batra, Peter Lenk, and Michel Wedel, "Brand Extension Strategy Planning: Empirical Estimation of Brand–Category Personality Fit and Atypicality," *Journal of Marketing Research* 47, no. 2 (April 2010), pp. 335–47.

24. David Aaker, *Aaker on Branding: 20 Principles That Drive Success* (New York: Morgan James, 2014); Aaker, *Building Strong Brands*.

25. Rebecca R. Ruiz, "Luxury Cars Imprint Their Brands on Goods from Cologne to Clothing," *The New York Times*, February 20, 2015.

26. Rosellina Ferraro, Amna Kirmani, and Ted Matherly, "Look at Me! Look at Me! Conspicuous Brand Usage, Self-Brand Connection, and Dilution," *Journal of Marketing Research* 50, no. 4 (August 2013), pp. 477–88; Sanjay Sood and Kevin Lane Keller, "The Effects of Brand Name Structure on Brand Extension Evaluations and Parent Brand Dilution," *Journal of Marketing Research* 49, no. 3 (June 2012), pp. 373–82.

27. Ferraro et al., "Look at Me! Look at Me!"; Sharon Ng, "Cultural Orientation and Brand Dilution: Impact of Motivation Level and Extension Typicality," *Journal of Marketing Research* 47, no. 1 (February 2010), pp. 186–98.

28. Ruiz, "Luxury Cars Imprint Their Brands."

29. Shané Schutte, "6 Worst Brand Extensions from Famous Companies," *Real Business*, June 16, 2014; Emily Marchak, "The Pros and Cons of Sub-Branding and Brand Extension," *Brogan & Partners*, October 13, 2015.

30. Susan Spiggle, Hang T. Nguyen, and Mary Caravella. "More Than Fit: Brand Extension Authenticity," *Journal of Marketing Research* 49, no. 6 (2012), pp. 967–83; Franziska Völckner et al., "The Role of Parent Brand Quality for Service Brand Extension Success," *Journal of Service Research* 13, no. 4 (2010), pp. 379–96.

31. H. Kaur and A. Pandit, "Consumer Evaluation of Brand Extension: Empirical Generalization and Comparative Analysis," *Journal of Empirical Generalisations in Marketing Science* 15, no. 1 (2014); Sood and Keller, "The Effects of Brand Name Structure on Brand Extension Evaluations and Parent Brand Dilution."

32. Kim Bhasin, "For Kate Spade, a Move Downmarket Goes Bust," *Bloomberg Businessweek*, February 5, 2015.

33. www.marriott.com/marriott-brands.mi#ourbrands.

34. Aaker, *Building Strong Brands*.

35. Keller, *Strategic Brand Management*.

36. Rachel Abrams and Gregory Schmidt, "Superhero Movies Create Opportunity for Toymakers," *The New York Times*, February 13, 2015, www.nytimes.com.

37. Denise Lee Yohn, "Think Differently about Protecting Your Brand," *Harvard Business Review*, April 23, 2014.

38. Yi-Lin Tsai, Chekitan S. Dev, and Pradeep Chintagunta, "What's in a Brand Name? Assessing the Impact of Rebranding in the Hospitality Industry," *Journal of Marketing Research* 52, no. 6 (December 2015), pp. 865–78; Mukesh Kumar Mishra and Dibyendu Choudhury, "The Effect of Repositioning on Brand Personality: An Empirical Study on BlackBerry Mobile Phones," *IUP Journal of Brand Management* 10, no. 2 (2013).

39. John Grossman, "A Sweet Breakfast Memory That Connects with the Wrong Market," *The New York Times*, November 12, 2014; John Grossman, "Should Cow Wow Sell to Little Children or Big Children?," *The New York Times*, November 12, 2014; John Grossman, "Cow Wow Picks a Target Audience for Its Flavored Milk," *The New York Times*, November 19, 2014, www.nytimes.com.

40. E. J. Schultz, "Corn and Sugar Industries Battle in Court over Ad Claims," *Advertising Age*, November 3, 2015.

41. E. J. Schultz, "Spread Some Bacon on That Bagel: Kraft's New Philly Flavor," *Advertising Age*, October 8, 2014, http://adage.com.

42. "Morton Salt Girl Birthday Brings Brand Refresh," *Packaging World*, March 12, 2014, www.packworld.com.

43. Lisa McTigue Pierce, "8 Sustainable Packaging Hits of 2017," *Packaging Digest*, December 21, 2017, www.packagingdigest.com/sustainable-packaging/8-sustainable-packaging-hits-of-2017-2017-12-21; www.sustainability-in-packaging.com/.

44. Eleanor Dwyer, "Small Pack Sizes See Growth in the U.S.," *Beauty Packaging*, December 19, 2016, www.beautypackaging.com/contents/view_online-exclusives/2016-12-19/small-pack-sizes-see-growth-in-the-us.

45. Rebecca Mead, "Sole Cycle," *The New Yorker*, March 23, 2015.

46. Birkenstock USA, "Press," www.birkenstockusa.com/press.

47. Ellen Emmerentze Jervell, "Birkenstock Doesn't Care If Fashionistas Stop Wearing Its Sandals," *The Wall Street Journal*, May 11, 2015.

i. Mark Clothier, "The Downside of Low-End Luxury Cars," *Bloomberg Businessweek*, July 17, 2014, www.businessweek.com.

ii. Mark van Rijmenam, "Macy's Is Changing the Shopping Experience with Big Data Analytics," *DataFloq*, March 14, 2014; Nicole Marie Melton, "Macy's Boosts Web Sales, Email Marketing with Predictive Analytics," *FierceRetailT*, May 14, 2014; Joe Keenan, "Customer Retention: Macy's Uses Predictive Analytics to Grow Customer Spend," *Retail Online Integration*, August 2014.

iii. Martha C. White, "Shadows Fall and Jaws Drop for a Jolly Green Icon's Comeback," *The New York Times*, December 4, 2016; Martha White, "At a Theater Near You: Jolly Green Giant," *The Boston Globe*, December 5, 2016; Gina Acosta, "The Jolly Green Giant Gets a Better-for-You Makeover," *Drug Store News*, September 6, 2016.

Quiz Yourself Answer Key

1. All of the following are elements of a product except:
   Answer: (e) All of these are elements of a product.

2. Which of the following is a subjective measure of brand equity?
   Answer: (d) Perceived value

Courtesy of GE FirstBuild

LEARNING OBJECTIVES

After reading this chapter, you should be able to:

LO12-1 Identify the reasons firms create new products.

LO12-2 Describe the different groups of adopters articulated by the diffusion of innovation theory.

LO12-3 Describe the various stages involved in developing a new product or service.

LO12-4 Explain the product life cycle.

CHAPTER 12
DEVELOPING NEW PRODUCTS

On the campus of University of Louisville sits a building that houses FirstBuild, the independent innovation arm of GE Appliances, a Haier company. Founded in 2014, FirstBuild is a clearly distinct entity from its globally known parent, a status that enables it to function with greater agility, risk, and innovative pursuits than would normally be possible for a global firm.

This status is purposeful. Large firms often struggle to innovate as well as small, quick start-ups, but to remain viable, they must find ways to be creative and devise new product and service offerings. To enjoy the benefits of an agile, small firm but the resources of a conglomerate, GE Appliances devised and organized FirstBuild strategically and with great care.

To begin, the company remains small and will not grow much beyond its current size. The approximately two dozen full-time employees include a director, operations manager, marketing manager, and community manager. This latter role is responsible for recruiting a pool of engineers, industrial designers, and scientists who will contribute their expertise, according to an open community structure. Anyone with a new idea is likely to be heard by the small managerial staff, and contributors are free to pursue virtually any interest or ideas they prefer.

The open community structure has several other implications for FirstBuild's innovation process as well. In stark contrast with the careful intellectual property protections that large companies typically impose on their conventional innovation methods and prototypes, visitors to the FirstBuild campus have free access to every project being undertaken. This approach helps the company draw more feedback, and it also necessitates rapid decision making about promising new ideas. If innovations are on display for anyone to copy, then making sure to be first to market becomes an even more pressing goal, thus motivating the company to move quickly and efficiently.

That quick movement is purposefully limited though, such that FirstBuild always begins with a small run of promising products. Once an idea has received approval, it enters into the rapid production process, which typically results in only up to 1,000 units of the new product. These items then are marketed on a "micro scale," and if demand is strong enough, the idea may move on to broader production. The inventor may receive a remuneration offer, equal to some percentage of the total sales revenues for the new product. Although the idea might be produced by GE, using its more conventional marketing and supply chain process, the inventor also retains the right to sell the idea to competitors, giving GE a strong incentive to offer good terms to FirstBuild's most creative innovators.

For the past three years, the firm has held a "hackathon" too—a two-day event in which about 300 people come together to reinvent typical appliances. Participants include engineers, programmers, marketers, and even enthusiasts with no particular scientific background who seek to share their ideas for products, then create them. The 2017 winning team created a sink that included both tap and sparkling water faucets, an ice dispenser, and a fountain for Keurig coffee. Some innovators have come up with products that already appear in the market. The Monogram Pizza Oven is a new entry to GE Appliance's product line, enabling consumers to make restaurant-quality pizzas at home that mimic the taste and texture of pies cooked in brick ovens. The ChillHub refrigerator is one of the smart appliances that GE is bringing to market, offering integrated Wi-Fi, various automatic sensors to check bacteria levels and water quality, and USB stations.[1]

Few three-letter words are more exciting than *new*. It brings forth an image of freshness, adventure, and excitement. Yet *new* also is a complex term when it comes to market offerings because it might mean adding something new to an existing product, introducing a flavor never offered before, or relying on different packaging that provides added value. But the most exhilarating type of new product is something never seen before. Thousands of patent applications pursue this elusive prize: a successful and truly innovative new product.

To think about how once-new products have changed the world, imagine living 200 years ago: You cook meals on a stove fueled by coal or wood; you write out homework by hand (if you are lucky enough to attend school) and by candlelight. To get to school, you hike along unpaved roads to reach a small, cold, basic classroom with just a few classmates who listen to a lecture from a teacher writing on a blackboard.

Today, you finish your homework on a laptop computer with word processing software that appears to have a mind of its own and can correct your spelling automatically. Your climate-controlled room has ample electric light. While you work on your laptop, you also talk with a friend using the hands-free headset of your wireless phone. As you drive to school in your car, you pick up fast food from a convenient drive-through window while browsing and listening to your personal selection of songs playing through your car speakers, connected wirelessly to your iPhone. Your friend calls to discuss a slight change to the homework, so you pull over to grab your iPhone, make the necessary change to your assignment, and e-mail it from your smartphone to your professor. When you arrive at school, you sit in a 200-person classroom, where you can plug in your laptop, take notes on your iPad, or digitally record the lecture. The professor adds notes on the day's PowerPoint presentations using her tablet computer. You have already downloaded the PowerPoint presentations and add similar notes through your own laptop. After class, to complete your planning for a last-minute party, you send out a Facebook invitation to your friends and ask for responses to get a head count. You then text your roommate, telling her to get food and drinks for the right number of people, which she orders through an online grocer that will deliver later in the day.

Our lives are defined by the many new products and services developed through scientific and technological advances and by the added features included in products that we have always used. In this second chapter dealing with the first P in the marketing mix (product), we continue our discussion from the preceding chapter and explore how companies add value to product and service offerings through innovation. We also look at how firms develop new products and services on their own. We conclude the chapter with an examination of how new products and services get adopted by the market and how firms can change their marketing mix as the product or service moves through its life cycle.

 LO12-1 Identify the reasons firms create new products.

WHY DO FIRMS CREATE NEW PRODUCTS?

New market offerings provide value to firms as well as to customers. But the degree to which they do so depends on how new they really are. When we say a "new product/service," we don't necessarily mean that the market offer has never existed before. Completely new-to-the-market products represent fewer than 10 percent of all new product introductions each year. It is more useful to think of the degree of newness or innovativeness on a continuum from truly new-to-the-world—as the Amazon Echo smart speakers are—to slightly repositioned, such as when Kraft's Capri Sun brand of ready-to-drink beverages were repackaged in a bigger pouch to appeal to teens.

Regardless of where on the continuum a new product lies, firms have to innovate. Innovation refers to the process by which ideas are transformed into new offerings, including products, services, processes, and branding concepts that will help firms grow. Without innovation and its resulting new products and services, firms would have only two choices: continue to market current products to current customers or take the same product to another market with similar customers.

Although innovation strategies may not always work in the short run—some estimates indicate that only about 3 percent of new products actually succeed—various overriding and long-term reasons compel firms to continue introducing new products and services, as the following sections describe.

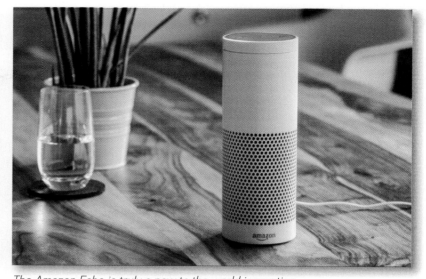

The Amazon Echo is truly a new-to-the-world innovation.
©seewhatmitchsee/Shutterstock

Changing Customer Needs

When they add products, services, and processes to their offerings, firms can create and deliver value more effectively by satisfying the changing needs of their current and new customers or by keeping customers from getting bored with the current product or service offering. Sometimes companies can identify problems and develop products or services that customers never knew they needed. When Apple first introduced its handheld smartphone with advanced camera capabilities, virtually no marketing research provided any hint that consumers wanted one. But with the fervent belief that people would enjoy the convenience of snapping and reviewing a photo or getting online at any particular moment,

The iPhone is an easily accessible, affordable, easy-to-use tool that has changed the phone, camera, communication, and technology markets forever.
©Rawpixel.com/Shutterstock

Ethical & Societal Dilemma 12.1 | "Smart" Toys Raise New Privacy Concerns[1]

Privacy concerns continue to be a hot-button issue for many consumers. As more smart products enter the home, many of wonder just how safe their personal information is from unscrupulous hackers, and even some manufacturers. Laptops and mobile phones are typically the types of devices suspected to cause a breach in security, but a recent announcement from the German telecommunications watchdog group the Federal Network Agency caused new concern for many parents. Could certain smart toys be watching their kids, and thus be used to steal personal data?

The toy at the center of the current controversy is called Cayla. Manufactured by Genesis Toys and distributed by the Vivid Toy group, Cayla connects to consumers' smartphones via a Bluetooth connection. She can interact with children by recording their conversations and responding to certain programmed verbal cues. Although some functions require an Internet connection, many of the conversational abilities do not. The Cayla app offers programming that prevents certain content, and parents can add keywords associated with content they do not want their child to hear.

Yet many adults still see it as a potential menace. Charges have been leveled that the unsecured Bluetooth connection could allow hackers to access Cayla's systems and record the conversations of children (or parents) in the room. Furthermore, some U.S.-based advocacy groups have filed complaints with the Federal Trade Commission, citing concerns about the manufacturer's practice of transmitting and storing all recorded voice data prints. The software company that stores these voice prints, Nuance Communications, has reserved the

Do you believe that the Cayla doll can be an invasion of privacy since it interacts with children by recording their conversations and responding to certain programmed verbal cues?

©Rob Stothard/Getty Images

right to use any data it receives as it chooses in its marketing efforts. Could parents thus hear their children's conversations with their toys broadcast in an advertisement someday?

German telecommunications laws effectively ban Cayla from future sale in Germany, and the Federal Network Agency has urged parents to deactivate any dolls previously purchased. To date, the doll is still available in the United States, though some toy retailers, including Walmart, have decided not to carry the doll online or in stores.

How can a walking stick be improved? 91-year-old Barbara Beskind did it by developing walking sticks that have rockers on the bottoms that users can push off against.

©IDEO

the company's founder and visionary leader, Steve Jobs, insisted on developing the iPhone as an easily accessible, affordable, easy-to-use tool that consumers could enjoy[2]—and thus changed the phone, camera, communication, and technology markets forever. In a similar vein, the Internet has created several new products that take advantage of smartphone capabilities, but at the same time these products have raised some privacy concerns, as detailed in Ethical & Societal Dilemma 12.1.

In other cases, customers enter new stages in their lives that intensify their demand for such innovations. For example, as life expectancy increases due to technology and health care advances, the senior population is increasing at unprecedented rates. The World Health Organization says that 2 billion people will be older than 60 years of age by 2050, and yet most inventors are ignoring this growing market segment. The 91-plus-year-old inventor Barbara Beskind therefore has taken it upon herself to improve one of the most common items used by older adults: the cane. Traditional canes require the user to lean on them, promoting poor posture. Beskind's walking sticks instead have rockers on the bottom that users can push off against, and they are made from modified ski poles. In turn, they promote a proper posture and a more natural walking gait.[3]

On the other end of the age spectrum, the market for products and services targeting athletes and runners seems relatively stable, in the sense that most products have been around for years. But AfterShokz recognized that outdoor sport enthusiasts often wore headphones that blocked their ability to hear cars and other potential hazards while exercising, so it introduced bone conduction headphones, that leave users' ears free.[4] AfterShokz headphones range in price from $50 to $180, which is more expensive than the average headphone price of $34, but if they can appeal to the growing headphone market, this innovation can help the company gain market share.[5]

AfterShokz headphones are an innovative product because they do not block ears from potentially hazardous sounds like cars.
©Hugh Threlfall/Alamy Stock Photo

Market Saturation

The longer a product exists in the marketplace, the more likely it is that the market will become saturated. Without new products or services, the value of the firm will ultimately decline.[6] Imagine, for example, if car companies simply assumed and expected that people would keep their cars until they stopped running. If that were the case, there would be no need to come up with new and innovative models; companies could just stick with the models that sell well. But few consumers actually keep the same car until it stops running. Even those who want to stay with the same make and model often want something new, just to add some variety to their lives. Therefore, car companies revamp their models every year, whether with new features such as advanced GPS or a more powerful engine or by redesigning the entire look of the vehicle. The firms sustain their growth by getting consumers excited about the new looks and new features, prompting many car buyers to exchange their old vehicle years before its functional life is over.

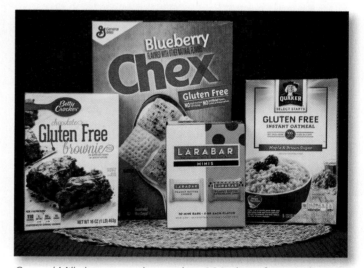

General Mills has created more than 600 gluten-free products in response to the growing market.
©McGraw-Hill Education/Evelyn Nicole Kirksey, photographer

Saturated markets can also offer opportunities for a company that is willing to adopt a new process or mentality. At one point in time, mass marketers would not even consider entering a market that they believed would not earn at least $50 million. But General Mills is looking to niche markets for its future growth. Whereas only 1 percent of the U.S. population suffers from celiac disease—a condition in which ingested gluten damages the digestive system—a much higher percentage of U.S. consumers say they want to reduce or eliminate gluten, a wheat protein, from their diet. As awareness increases, those percentages are growing, such that the U.S. market for gluten-free products could be broadly worth up to $10 billion.[7] General Mills has created more than 600 gluten-free products, including variations on its regular offerings, such as Chex cereals and Oatmeal, as well as Lärabars and Betty Crocker baking mixes.[8]

Managing Risk through Diversity

Through innovation, firms often create a broader portfolio of products, which help them diversify their risk and enhance firm value better than a single product can.[9] If some products in a portfolio perform poorly, others may do well. Firms with multiple products can better withstand external shocks like changes in consumer preferences or intensive competitive activity. For this reason, a firm like Keebler offers many variations of its basic product, cookies, including Animals, Chips Deluxe, E.L. Fudge, Gripz, Sandies, Vanilla Wafers, and Vienna Fingers. This diversification enables Keebler to enjoy more consistent performance than it would with just one kind of cookie.

The Keebler line's risk is lessened by offering many variations of its basic product, cookies.
©Michael J. Hruby

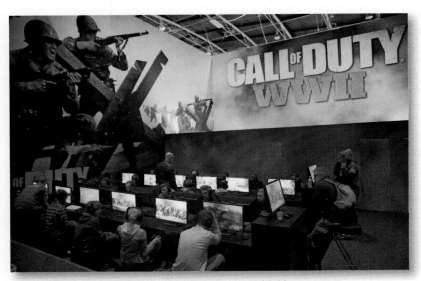

Video games like Call of Duty WWII are "fashionable" because consumers demand new versions. Once they "beat" the game, they want to be challenged with a new experience.

©Chesnot/Getty Images

Fashion Cycles

In industries that rely on fashion trends and experience short product life cycles—including apparel, arts, books, and software markets—most sales come from new products. For example, a motion picture generates most of its theater, DVD, and cable TV revenues within a year of its release. If the same selection of books were always for sale, with no new titles, there would be no reason to buy more. But as Adding Value 12.1 explains, new versions of familiar titles also can be a powerful means to prompt consumers to purchase: Having loved the cartoon version of *Cinderella* as small children, teens and adults might find a new product prompted by a new live-action movie of substantial interest. Consumers of computer software and video games demand new offers because once they have beaten the game, they want to be challenged by another game or experience the most recent version, as the remarkable sales of successive versions of the Call of Duty game exemplify.[10] In the case of apparel, fashion designers produce entirely new product selections a few times per year.

Improving Business Relationships

New products do not always target end consumers; sometimes they function to improve relationships with suppliers. For example, Walmart asked its suppliers for data on all of their products, even the ones not sold by the retail giant. When customers search online or ask in stores for products that Walmart doesn't sell it compiles a list of frequently requested products. With these data from suppliers, Walmart can work quickly with these suppliers to get these products on its shelves. Furthermore, Walmart can use these data to work with suppliers to develop new products that they do not already manufacture.[11]

Even if they succeed in innovating and creating new products, new-to-the-world products are not adopted by everyone at the same time. Rather, they diffuse or spread through a population in a process known as *diffusion of innovation,* which will be discussed next.

PROGRESS CHECK

1. What are the reasons firms innovate?

Adding Value 12.1

No Fairy Godmother Needed: How Disney Is Leveraging Its Inventory of Animated Films to Develop New Live-Action Products[ii]

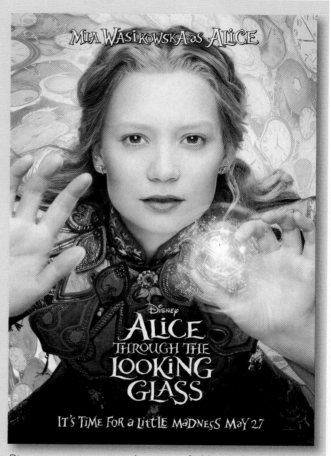

While its partner company Pixar continues to break new ground in animated movies, Walt Disney Pictures is taking a different path. Rather than keep making the sort of well-known, traditional animations that essentially created the movie studio, it is reformulating those tales as live-action films.

One of the first examples was *Cinderella,* whose live-action version hewed closely to Disney's 1950 animated version, from the coach that turns into a pumpkin to the sky blue color of Cinderella's dress at the ball. The goal in making the new version with actors instead of animation was to pay tribute to and resonate with the nostalgic original while still offering something new. That is, the studio's new product strategy is strongly premised in the safe familiarity of well-known and be-loved characters.

The company has embraced this potentially risky strategy wholeheartedly, with many other titles in development or having been recently introduced with similar cartoon-to-live action transformations, including *The Jungle Book, Beauty and the Beast, Dumbo,* and *Pete's Dragon.* It has already introduced a sequel to *Alice in Wonderland* with its *Alice Through the Looking Glass* film.

The source material in many of these cases is both a benefit and a threat to Disney. Because it made fairy-tale films in the early days of movies, it has a strong reputation in this market. When people think *Sleeping Beauty,* they are often imagining the Disney version. Thus, by releasing *Maleficent,* Disney could count on people's knowledge of its previous movie while expanding its reach to more adult audiences.

However, because fairy tales are in the public domain, anyone can make a movie based on the story. Thus Universal Pictures has a new version of *The Little Mermaid* in development, and the movie it ultimately releases does not have to follow the Disney version of the story in any way. This risk may explain Disney's choice to remake some other childhood favorites, such as *Mary Poppins,* for which it owns actual copyrights.

To maximize the profitability of the new films, Disney also leverages its existing access to its target demographic. Store displays of popular *Frozen* toys featured new *Cinderella* paraphernalia immediately adjacent. Before the movie opened, Disney theme parks played up Cinderella's re-emergence. And the trailers preceding Disney movies in theaters for months

Disney creates new products out of old ones by recycling earlier movies like Alice in Wonderland *into new ones like* Alice Through the Looking Glass.

©Moviestore collection Ltd/Alamy Stock Photo

before its release encouraged viewers to consider the new live-action fairy tale for their future entertainment needs.

The goal is to keep audiences—especially young children who love fairy tales—engaged with Disney films, products, and theme park attractions. In this light, one Disney executive explains, "We view the fairy tale space as our arena."

DIFFUSION OF INNOVATION

LO12-2 Describe the different groups of adopters articulated by the diffusion of innovation theory.

The process by which the use of an innovation—whether a product, a service, or a process—spreads throughout a market group, over time and across various categories of adopters, is referred to as **diffusion of innovation**.[12] The theory surrounding diffusion of innovation helps marketers understand the rate at which consumers are likely to adopt a new product or service. It also gives them a means to identify potential markets for their new products or services and predict their potential sales, even before they introduce the innovations.[13]

Truly new product introductions—that is, new-to-the-world products that create new markets—can add tremendous value to firms. These new products, also called **pioneers** or

Apple has released several pioneer products in recent years, including the Apple Watch.

©prykhodov/123RF

breakthroughs, establish completely new markets or radically change the rules of competition as well as consumer preferences in a market.[14] The Apple iPod is a pioneer product. Not only did it change the way people listen to music but it also created an entirely new industry devoted to accessories such as cases, ear buds, docking stations, and speakers. Although Apple offers many of these accessories itself, other companies have jumped on the bandwagon, ensuring that you can strap your iPod to your arm while on the move or insert it into the base of a desk lamp equipped with speakers to get music and light from your desk. And don't forget: The iPod also launched perhaps the most notable other recent pioneer, the iPhone, along with the innovative iTunes service, the iPod Touch, the iPad, and the Apple Watch.[15]

Pioneers have the advantage of being first movers; as the first to create the market or product category, they become readily recognizable to consumers and thus establish a commanding and early market share lead. Studies also have found that market pioneers can command a greater market share over a longer time period than later entrants can.[16]

Yet not all pioneers succeed. In many cases, imitators capitalize on the weaknesses of pioneers and subsequently gain advantage in the market. Because pioneering products and brands face the uphill task of establishing the market alone, they pave the way for followers, who can spend less marketing effort creating demand for the product line and focus directly on creating demand for their specific brand. Also, because the pioneer is the first product in the market, it often has a less sophisticated design and may be priced relatively higher, leaving room for better and lower-priced competitive products.

An important question to ask is, Why is the failure rate for new products so high? One of the main reasons is the failure to assess the market properly by neglecting to do appropriate product testing, targeting the wrong segment, and/or poor positioning.[17] Firms may also overextend their abilities or competencies by venturing into products or services that are inconsistent with their brand image and/or value proposition. We discuss some infamous product failures in Exhibit 12.1.

As the diffusion of innovation curve in Exhibit 12.2 shows, the number of users of an innovative product or service spreads through the population over a period of time and generally follows a bell-shaped curve. A few people buy the product or service at first, then more buy, and finally fewer people buy as the degree of the diffusion slows. These purchasers can be divided into five groups according to how soon they buy the product after it has been introduced: innovators, early adopters, early majority, late majority, and laggards.

Innovators

Innovators are those buyers who want to be the first on the block to have the new product or service. These buyers enjoy taking risks and are regarded as highly knowledgeable. You probably know someone who is an innovator—or perhaps you are one for a particular product or service

Google Glass failed because of privacy concerns, system bugs, and being banned from public spaces.

©Peppinuzzo/Shutterstock

EXHIBIT 12.1 Illustrative Product Failures

Product	Concept	Why It Failed
Google Glass	In 2012, Google announced the next big innovation in wearable technology, Google Glass, glasses with smartphone technology.	Although tech circles were excited about the product, privacy concerns, system bugs, and being banned from public spaces prevented the product from living up to expectations. Development was stopped in 2015.
Heinz EZ Squirt Ketchup	H. J. Heinz Company introduced artificially colored ketchup in 2000 with a narrow nozzle, ideal for drawing on food, in colors such as purple, orange, and teal.	Although initially successful, after three years consumers lost interest either because the colors were not appealing on food, or even worse, when mixed together, it turned brown.
New Coke	In response to growing market pressure, Coca-Cola launched a reformulated version of its classic cola in 1985.	Coke underestimated the consumers' affinity to the original formulation and their unwillingness to change. It was pulled from shelves three months after its introduction.
Sony Betamax	In 1975, Sony bet big on the Betamax, one of the first ever mass-produced home video recording systems.	Unfortunately, the next year JVC launched the VHS player, ensuring a format war similar to the Blu-ray and HD-DVD format wars of 2006.
Harley-Davidson Perfume	After being successful with lighters and T-shirts bearing the Harley logo, Harley-Davidson branched out into its own line of perfumes associated with the motorcycle lifestyle.	Although lighters and T-shirts may resonate with the Harley image, customers were not as attracted to smelling like a motorcycle.
Cheetos Lip Balm	In 2015 Frito-Lay turned its popular Cheetos flavor into lip balm, thinking that fans of the snack would love the flavor as they do other flavored lip balms.	Although people do love the cheesy snack, they didn't want to wear the flavor on their lips all day.
Kellogg's Breakfast Mates	Capitalizing on the convenience market, Kellogg's Breakfast Mates launched a line of cereal products in 1998 that came with cereal, spoon, and milk.	Sometimes a good idea is poorly executed. The milk was usually warm because it did not require refrigeration and the product was not child-friendly, making its appeal very limited.
Apple Newton	Launched in 1993 with a price tag of more than $700, the Apple Newton was one of the first PDAs, which then led the way for the Palm Pilot, BlackBerry, and iPad.	The Newton concept was ahead of its time. Unfortunately, due to its bulky size and ridicule by comedians, the Newton lasted only until 1998.
Colgate Kitchen Entrees	Colgate launched a line of frozen dinners. Apparently the idea was that consumers would enjoy eating a Colgate meal and then using Colgate on their toothbrush afterward.	The association of toothpaste with a chicken stir-fry was something customers did not find appetizing.
Clairol's Touch of Yogurt Shampoo	Clairol marketed a shampoo with a touch of yogurt to improve hair quality.	Consumers were not enticed with the idea of washing their hair with yogurt, something Clairol should have known after its Look of Buttermilk failed in test markets a few years earlier.

Source: Michael Sauter, Samuel Stebbins, Evan Comen, and Thomas Frohlich, "50 Worst Product Flops of All Time," *24/7 Wall St,* April 14, 2017, http://247wallst.com/special-report/2017/04/14/50-worst-product-flops-of-all-time/.

category. For example, the person who stood in line overnight to be sure to get a ticket for the very first showing of the latest superhero movie is an innovator in that context. Those consumers who already fly drones off their back porches are likely innovators too, a development covered in Ethical & Societal Dilemma 12.2. Firms that invest in the latest technology, either to use in their products or services or to make the firm more efficient, also are considered innovators. Typically, innovators keep themselves very well informed about the product category by subscribing to trade and specialty magazines, talking to other experts, visiting product-specific blogs and forums that describe the coolest new products,[18] and attending product-related forums, seminars, and special events. Yet innovators represent only about 2.5 percent of the total market for any new product or service.

EXHIBIT 12.2 Diffusion of Innovation Curve

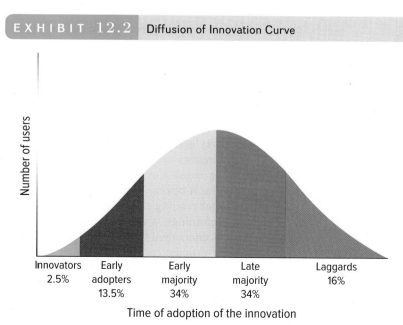

Source: Adapted from Everett M. Rodgers, *Diffusion of Innovation* (New York: Free Press, 1983).

Ethical & Societal Dilemma 12.2   Drones in the Sky, Questions on the Ground[iii]

As some of the hottest gadgets on the market, personal drones are selling in record numbers worldwide. Although the biggest market remains the United States, consumers in Europe and China also find them irresistible, using them for fun, photography, and videography. For more serious-minded and business users, drones also have a variety of critical purposes, from Amazon's proposed package delivery to hurricane and storm tracking efforts to military uses.

Or consider their applications at construction sites. Construction crews now can send drones hundreds of feet in the air to take up-to-the-minute digital images, map the progress of the construction, and identify where to install solar panels or other elements—without requiring any member of the crew to risk life and limb by climbing multiple stories and dangling a tape measure to get the information. Then those data can be shared with managers and clients throughout the world, without requiring them to visit the site itself.

But along with these notable benefits for business and consumers, the uses of drones have created some new privacy and ethical concerns. Unfortunately, drones enable unethical users to capture unsolicited and unwarranted images of others, intruding on the privacy and threatening the safety of some of their subjects. From stories of people spying on their neighbors to a drone that landed on the White House lawn, serious concerns surrounding the use of private drones continue without a clear resolution. Furthermore, evidence that some national governments are seeking to extend their

Drones are among the hottest new products on the market, particularly at gadget retailer Brookstone.
©Kimihiro Hoshino/AFP/Getty Images

uses of drones, to establish massive "armies" of small devices that could swarm battlefields, leads some observers to suggest a serious ethical crisis with potentially global implications.

Thus far in the United States, no legislation or regulations limit the uses of drones by individuals, companies, or government agencies. But the tide may be turning; a recently proposed bill would establish specific privacy protections in relation to drones. The challenge these laws face though is finding a way to impose reasonable privacy limits, without hindering the useful, fun, and effective applications of these innovative devices by ethical businesses and consumers.

These innovators are crucial to the success of any new product or service, though, because they help the product gain market acceptance. Through talking about and spreading positive word of mouth about the new product, they prove instrumental in bringing in the next adopter category, known as early adopters.[19]

Early Adopters

The second subgroup that begins to use a product or service innovation is early adopters. They generally don't like to take as much risk as innovators do but instead wait and purchase the product after careful review. Thus, this market waits for the first reviews of the latest movie before purchasing a ticket, though they likely still go a week or two after it opens. They do not stand in line to grab the first PlayStation VR headset; only after reading the innovators' complaints and praises do they decide whether the new technology is worth the cost. But most of them go ahead and purchase because early adopters tend to enjoy novelty and often are regarded as the opinion leaders for particular product categories.

This group, which represents about 13.5 percent of all buyers in the market, spreads the word. As a result, early adopters are crucial for bringing the other three buyer categories to the market. If the early adopter group is relatively small, the number of people who ultimately adopt the innovation likely will also be small.

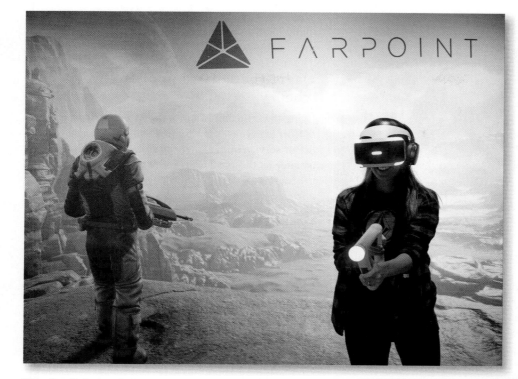

Early adopters for the Play-Station VR headset typically wait for reviews before they purchase.

©Noam Galai/Getty Images for Sony Interactive Entertainment

Early Majority

The early majority, which represents approximately 34 percent of the population, is crucial because few new products and services can be profitable until this large group buys them. If the group never becomes large enough, the product or service typically fails.

The early majority group differs in many ways from buyers in the first two stages. Its members don't like to take as much risk and therefore tend to wait until the bugs are worked out of a particular product or service. This group probably rents the latest *Star Wars* movie during the first week it comes out on video. Thus, early majority members experience little risk because all the reviews are in, and their costs are lower because they're renting the movie instead of going to the theater. When early majority customers enter the market, the number of competitors in the marketplace usually also has reached its peak, so these buyers have many price and quality choices.

Late Majority

At 34 percent of the market, the late majority is the next group of buyers to enter a new product market. When they do, the product has achieved its full market potential. Perhaps these movie watchers wait until the newest movie is available on Netflix. By the time the late majority enters the market, sales tend to level off or may be in decline.

Laggards

Laggards make up roughly 16 percent of the market. These consumers like to avoid change and rely on traditional products until the products are no longer available. In some cases, laggards may never adopt a certain product or service.

The early majority group would probably wait to rent the latest Star Wars *movie until the first week that it is available.*

©Collection Christophel/Alamy Stock Photo

Consumers who are fixated on cleaning will spend substantial amounts for the most technologically advanced machines, like this Dyson Ball Vacuum.

©Hugh Threlfall/Alamy Stock Photo

When the sequel to *Star Wars: The Force Awakens* eventually shows up on their regular television networks, they might watch it.

Using the Diffusion of Innovation Theory

Using the diffusion of innovation theory, firms can predict which types of customers will buy their new product or service immediately after its introduction as well as later as the product is more and more accepted by the market. With this knowledge, the firm can develop effective promotion, pricing, and other marketing strategies to push acceptance among each customer group. Let's consider an example of some everyday products that nearly all of us use at some point.

Although they are not as flashy as the latest iPhone, cleaning supplies are used by everyone. Often the innovators who adopt new cleaning products are the ones who are the most fanatical about cleaning. Firms conduct in-depth research into how people clean their homes to identify such segments. This research finds that some people are so obsessive about cleaning that they spend nearly 20 hours every week doing it, whereas others are so reluctant that they avoid cleaning as much as they can; their average weekly cleaning time is about 2.5 hours.[20] Their options with regard to the products to purchase to assist them in their cleaning tasks are vast, from scrubbers to sprays to vacuums to dusters. Thus, in the vacuum cleaner market, manufacturers recognize that the segment of consumers who will spend substantial amounts for the most technologically advanced, powerful, easy-to-maneuver machines, such as the latest Dyson model, are likely to be the segment of consumers that is most fixated on cleaning.[21] But another segment just wants some basic suction to get the grit out of their rugs.

Relative Advantage If a product or service is perceived to be better than substitutes, then the diffusion will be relatively quick. As advertising for Swiffer products emphasizes, its mops and dusters promise to make cleaning faster, easier, and more efficient. In featuring real families, it seeks to highlight the relative advantage for all types of cleaners. Older people who might once have gotten on their hands and knees to scrub the floor can now rely on the design of the cleaning pads on the end of the mop to get the job done. Their children, who have never been very good at cleaning, can swipe a few surfaces and get the house looking clean before their parents visit. And a man who has lost an arm to cancer can still help his family keep the house clean because the duster does not require him to use a spray or climb a ladder to dust the ceiling fan.[22]

Compatibility A diffusion process may be faster or slower, depending on various consumer features, including international cultural differences. Electrolux's latest bagless vacuums offer a key innovation and solve the age-old problem of how to empty the chamber without having a cloud of particles fly out: compact the dirt into a "pellet." To make the product more compatible with the needs of people in different cultures, it is made in various sizes. The U.S. version offers a carpet nozzle with a motor, to deal with the dirt accumulated in Americans' larger, often carpeted homes. Because in

Products like the Swiffer have a relative advantage over the competition because they make cleaning faster, easier, and more efficient, especially for seniors and other consumers with mobility issues.

Source: Swiffer

Products that are easily observed, like this Blendtec blender that is pulverizing golf balls, enhance the diffusion process.
Source: Will It Blend?/Blendtec/Youtube

many Asian "megacities" consumers live in tiny apartments, Electrolux has introduced a smaller version that is also very quiet.[23]

Observability When products are easily observed, their benefits or uses are easily communicated to others, which enhances the diffusion process. To demonstrate to consumers why they should spend $400 on a blender, Blendtec launched an extensive YouTube campaign titled "Will It Blend?" to demonstrate the effectiveness of the blender. In each video, a spokesperson in a white lab coat blends a different product in the Blendtec—from iPads to golf balls to Justin Bieber's autobiography—and gives visible proof to consumers of the quality of the product. The humor and innovativeness of this product demonstration has caused these videos to go viral, with more than 280 million views and over 880,000 subscribers.[24] Yet some cleaning products face a serious challenge in making their innovations widely observable because few consumers spend a lot of time talking about the products that are of a more personal nature, such as what they use to clean their toilets. Even a great product might diffuse more slowly if people feel uncomfortable talking about what they perceive to be involved in their personal care.

Complexity and Trialability Products that are relatively less complex are also relatively easy to try. These products will generally diffuse more quickly and lead to greater and faster adoption than will those that are not so easy to try. In the cleaning products range, it is far easier to pick up a new spray cleaner at the grocery store to try at home than it is to assess and test a new vacuum. In response, manufacturers seek ways to help people conduct trials. For example, Dyson's displays in national retailers such as Bed Bath & Beyond often include floor space that allows shoppers to run the machine to see how well the roller ball works and watch it pick up dirt.

Knowledge of how a product or service will diffuse is useful for developing marketing strategies. But even before a new product or service is introduced, firms must actually develop those new offerings. In the next section, we detail the process by which most firms develop new products and services and how they introduce them into the market.

PROGRESS CHECK

1. What are the five groups on the diffusion of innovation curve?
2. What factors enhance the diffusion of a good or service?

EXHIBIT 12.3 The Product Development Process

Idea generation	Concept testing	Product development	Market testing	Product launch	Evaluation of results
Development of viable new product ideas.	*Testing of the new product ideas among a set of potential customers.*	*Development of prototypes and/or the product.*	*Testing the actual products in a few test markets.*	*Full-scale commercialization of the products.*	*Analysis of the performance of the new products and making appropriate modifications.*

LO12-3 Describe the various stages involved in developing a new product or service.

HOW FIRMS DEVELOP NEW PRODUCTS

The new product development process begins with the generation of new product ideas and culminates in the launch of a new product and the evaluation of its success. The stages of the new product development process, along with the important objectives of each stage, are summarized in Exhibit 12.3.

Idea Generation

To generate ideas for new products, a firm can use its own internal research and development (R&D) efforts, collaborate with other firms and institutions (R&D consortia), license technology, brainstorm, outsource, research competitors' products and services, and/or conduct consumer research; see Exhibit 12.4. In many cases these practices for identifying new product ideas cascade into other aspects of the product development process. Firms that want to be pioneers rely more extensively on R&D efforts, whereas those that tend to adopt a follower strategy are more likely to scan the market for ideas. Let's look at each of these idea sources.

EXHIBIT 12.4 Sources of New Product Ideas

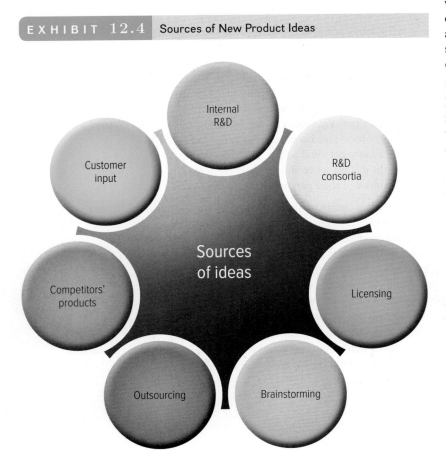

Internal Research and Development
Many firms have their own R&D departments in which scientists and engineers work to solve complex problems and develop new ideas. Historically, firms such as Black and Decker in the consumer goods industry, 3M in the industrial goods industry, and Merck and Pfizer in the pharmaceuticals industry have relied on R&D development efforts for their new products. In the fast-food industry, many chains run vast test kitchens that experiment with various flavors, concepts, and food groups to create potential new offerings. Furthermore, the industry uses its common franchise models to support new product development. For example, Arby's hosts an annual contest for the best menu idea introduced by one of its franchise locations. And in perhaps the most famous example, the Egg McMuffin was created by a franchisee in the early 1970s.[25] In other industries, such as software, music, and motion pictures, product development efforts also

Marketing Analytics 12.1 — Data That Help the Brand and the Customer: GM's Big Data Use[iv]

With its famous brands, such as Chevrolet and Cadillac, General Motors (GM) is a staple in the U.S. car industry. It also was one of the companies hit the hardest by the 2008 recession, following which it filed for bankruptcy and received a government bailout. In 2012, GM announced a new business strategy, a major component of which was more efficient and effective uses of big data. The importance of analytics again came to center stage in 2013, when the company faced legal allegations regarding the recall of the Chevy Cobalt. After the crisis, GM stressed the importance of big data even more and promised that analytics would be at the heart of all its future product development.

In particular, data analytics at GM support the development of new cars. Through GM's newly centralized data warehouse, it can analyze trends in both production and customer behavior. Furthermore, GM manufacturer data can be segmented at the individual vehicle identification number (VIN) level and then analyzed to improve quality and safety. For example, manufacturer data analytics helped GM develop tools that reduce the complexity associated with the mechanics of vehicle design. General Motors also is collecting data about its sales and dealerships and uses these data to create detailed customer profiles. The level of customer insight that these profiles provide enables GM to develop new products that then grant customers sufficient value. For example, GM's applied market information influenced its development of high-efficiency products that help reduce pollution.

All of this is just the start. New "connected cars" are generating even more data for the car industry, and the analyses of these data will likely define the cars found on the roads of the future. Connected cars communicate with the manufacturers

General Motors uses its OnStar system for remote communication with customers and diagnoses of problems. It analyzes the data it collects from its OnStar database to support the development of new cars.

©Bloomberg/Getty Images

directly through 4G or LTE. Currently, there are 9 million of these cars on the road, with 35 million projected by 2020. With its subscription-based, in-car security system, OnStar, GM has an advantage in this effort: It already uses OnStar for remote communication and diagnoses of problems. Thus it gains real-time information, which GM can use to improve its future car designs, even as the predictive diagnosis and preventive maintenance offer customers value by saving them money or preventing them from being stranded by a car that won't start.

---

tend to come from internal ideas and R&D financial investments. According to Marketing Analytics 12.1, General Motors is leveraging the data it gathers from customers as a sort of internal research source to support its designs.

The product development costs for these firms are quite high, but the resulting new product or service is expected to have a good chance of being a technological or market breakthrough. Firms expect such products to generate enough revenue and profits to make the costs of R&D worthwhile. R&D investments generally are considered continuous investments, so firms may lose money on a few new products. In the long run, though, these firms are betting that a few extremely successful new products, often known as blockbusters, can generate enough revenues and profits to cover the losses from other introductions that might not fare so well.

The Samsung ActivWash washing machine was developed using reverse innovation, a new-product development method in which ideas for new products are derived from subsidiaries in less-developed markets. First developed for the Indian market, this top-loading machine is now one of the most popular washers in South Korea.

Source: Samsung

Some global firms also are taking an approach called reverse innovation, as we discussed in Chapter 8. They turn to subsidiaries in less developed markets for new product ideas. Samsung's ActivWash washing machine was designed specifically for the Indian market. However, the top-loading machine is now one of most popular washers in South Korea, where front-loading machines dominated the market previously. The ActivWash machine has become so popular in South Korea that one is sold every two minutes. Unilever's Pureit water purifier was also initially developed for the Indian population; however, it is now available in 13 countries including China, Brazil, and Mexico.[26]

R&D Consortia To develop new product ideas, more and more firms have been joining an R&D consortia, or groups of other firms and institutions, possibly including government and educational institutions, to explore new ideas or obtain solutions for developing new products. Here, the R&D investments come from the group as a whole, and the participating firms and institutions share the results.

In many cases, the consortia involve pharmaceutical or high-tech members, whose research costs can run into the millions—too much for a single company to bear. The National Institutes of Health (NIH) sponsors medical foundations to conduct research to treat rare diseases. The research is then disseminated to the medical community, thus encouraging the development of drugs and therapies more quickly and at a lower cost than would be possible if the research were privately funded.

Licensing In the search for new products, firms buy the rights to use a technology or ideas from other firms through a licensing agreement. This approach saves the high costs of in-house R&D, but it means that the firm is banking on a solution that already exists but has not been marketed.

Brainstorming Firms often engage in brainstorming sessions during which a group works together to generate ideas. One of the key characteristics of a brainstorming session is that no idea can be immediately accepted or rejected. The moderator of the session may channel participants' attention to specific product features and attributes, performance expectations, or packaging. Only at the end of the session do the members vote on the best ideas or combinations of ideas. Those ideas that receive the most votes are carried forward to the next stage of the product development process.

Outsourcing When companies have trouble moving through these steps alone, they turn to outsourcing, a practice in which they hire an outside firm to help generate ideas and develop new products and services. IDEO, a design firm, does not sell ready-made product ideas but rather a service that helps clients generate new product and service ideas in industries such as health care, toys, and computers. IDEO employs anthropologists, graphic designers, engineers, and psychologists whose special skills help foster creativity and innovation. As society keeps moving forward, our homes reflect changing environments and habits. To design the kitchens of the future, IKEA hired IDEO to research how social, technological, and demographic changes will influence how we eat and to develop a full-size prototype kitchen. The prototype included a pantry with see-through containers and cooling technology that respond to RFID stickers. Although the kitchen was not functional, IKEA is using the insights gathered from IDEO research to develop future products.[27]

Competitors' Products A new product entry by a competitor may trigger a market opportunity for a firm, which can use reverse engineering to understand the competitor's product and then bring an improved version to market. Reverse engineering involves taking apart a product, analyzing it, and creating an improved product that does not infringe on the competitor's patents, if any exist. This copycat approach to new product development is widespread and practiced by even the most research-intensive firms. Copycat consumer goods show up in apparel, grocery, and drugstore products as well as in technologically more complex products such as automobiles and computers.

Customer Input Listening to the customer in both B2B and B2C markets is essential for successful idea generation and throughout the product development process.[28] Because

IKEA hired IDEO to research how we eat. This research led to new products like these see-through containers.
©Grzegorz Czapski/Shutterstock

customers for B2B products are relatively few, firms can follow their use of products closely and solicit suggestions and ideas to improve those products either by using a formal approach, such as focus groups, interviews, or surveys, or through more informal discussions. The firm's design and development team then works on these suggestions, sometimes in consultation with the customer. This joint effort between the selling firm and the customer significantly increases the probability that the customer eventually will buy the new product.

Customer input in B2C markets comes from a variety of sources, though increasingly through social media. By monitoring online feedback, whether requested by the firm or provided voluntarily in customer reviews, companies can get better ideas about new products or necessary changes to existing ones. The recent introduction of Green Giant snack chips provides a good example of using inputs from various types of partners. General Mills (which owns the Green Giant brand) heard a pitch for a new vegetable-based snack chip from its supplier, Shearer's Chips. The chip manufacturer developed 10 options for its business customer, General Mills. Then General Mills solicited input from its end consumers to find out which flavors they might like best. Online reviews suggested the need for a much zestier version of the roasted vegetable tortilla chips, which ultimately appeared on store shelves.[29]

In some cases, consumers may not expressly demand a new product even though their behavior demonstrates their desire for it. For example, when marketing researchers observed the popularity of pretzel rolls, the corporate headquarters of several restaurant chains introduced new buns and mandated

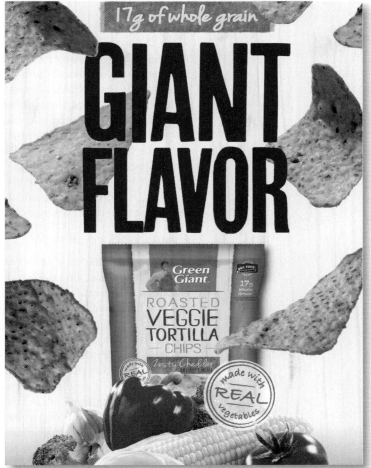

Customers are an important source of new product ideas. General Mills solicited input from consumers to find out which flavors they like best, and Green Giant Roasted Veggie Tortilla Chips was one of the winners.
Source: General Mills

that all their locations carry them. Noting the increasing numbers of vegetarian and vegan eaters, a few chains also have expanded their nonmeat offerings.[30]

Another particularly successful customer input approach is to analyze lead users, those innovative product users who modify existing products according to their own ideas to suit their specific needs.[31] If lead users customize a firm's products, other customers might wish to do so as well. Thus, studying lead users helps the firm understand general market trends that might be just on the horizon. Manufacturers and retailers of fashion products often spot new trends by noticing how innovative trendsetters have altered their clothing and shoes. Designers of high-fashion jeans distress their products in different ways depending on signals they pick up on the street. One season jeans appear with whiskers, the next season they have holes, the next, paint spots.

At the end of the idea-generation stage, the firm should have several ideas that it can take forward to the next stage: concept testing.

Concept Testing

An idea with potential is developed further into a concept, which in this context refers to a brief written description of the product; its technology, working principles, and forms; and what customer needs it would satisfy.[32] A concept might also include visual images of what the product would look like.

Concept testing refers to the process in which a concept statement is presented to potential buyers or users to obtain their reactions. These reactions enable the developer to estimate the sales value of the product or service concept, possibly make changes to enhance its sales value, and determine whether the idea is worth further development.[33] If the concept fails to meet customers' expectations, it is doubtful it would succeed if it were to be produced and marketed. Because concept testing occurs very early in the new product introduction process, even before a real product has been made, it helps the firm avoid the costs of unnecessary product development.

The concept for an electric scooter might be written as follows:

> The product is a lightweight electric scooter that can be easily folded and taken with you inside a building or on public transportation. The scooter weighs 25 pounds. It travels at speeds of up to 15 miles per hour and can go about 12 miles on a single charge. The scooter can be recharged in about two hours from a standard electric outlet. The scooter is easy to ride and has simple controls—just an accelerator button and a brake. It sells for $299.[34]

Concept testing progresses along the research techniques described in Chapter 10. The firm likely starts with qualitative research such as in-depth interviews or focus groups to test the concept, after which it can undertake quantitative research through Internet or mall-intercept surveys. Video clips on the Internet might show a virtual prototype and the way it works so that potential customers can evaluate the product or service. In a mall-intercept survey, an interviewer would provide a description of the concept to the respondent and then ask several questions to obtain his or her feedback.

The most important question pertains to the respondent's purchase intentions if the product or service were made available. Marketers also should ask whether the product would satisfy a need that other products currently are not meeting. Depending on the type of product or service, researchers might also ask about the expected frequency of purchase, how much customers would buy, whether they would buy it for themselves or as a gift, when they would buy, and whether the price information (if provided) indicates a good value. In addition, marketers usually collect some information about the customers so they can analyze which consumer segments are likely to be most interested in the product.

Some concepts never make it past the concept testing stage, particularly if respondents seem uninterested. Those that do receive high evaluations from potential consumers, however, move on to the next step, product development.

Product Development

Product development or product design entails a process of balancing various engineering, manufacturing, marketing, and economic considerations to develop a product's form and features or a service's features. An engineering team develops a product prototype that is based on research findings from the previous concept testing step as well as their own knowledge about materials and technology. A prototype is the first physical form or service description of a new product, still in rough or tentative form, which has the same properties as a new product but is produced through different manufacturing processes—sometimes even crafted individually.[35]

Product prototypes are usually tested through alpha and beta testing. In alpha testing, the firm attempts to determine whether the product will perform according to its design and whether it satisfies the need for which it was intended.[36] Rather than use potential consumers, alpha tests occur in the firm's R&D department. For instance, Ben & Jerry's Ice Cream alpha tests all its proposed new flavors on its own (lucky) employees at its corporate headquarters in Vermont.

In contrast, beta testing uses potential consumers who examine the product prototype in a real-use setting to determine its functionality, performance, potential problems, and other issues specific to its use. The firm might develop several prototype products that it gives to users, then survey those users to determine whether the product worked as intended and identify any issues that need resolution.

The advent of the Internet has made recruiting beta testers easier than ever. Through sites such as OnlineBeta (www.onlinebeta.com), everyday people can sign up to become beta testers for products from companies such as Dell, Kodak, and TomTom. To further automate the beta testing process, YouEye is developing eye tracking technology that works with an individual's webcam. Instead of needing to spend thousands of dollars on eye tracking equipment and having customers come into labs, firms will be able to utilize everyday webcams to track not only what a person attends to on a computer screen but also his or her emotional reactions to these products.[37]

Market Testing

The firm has developed its new product or service and tested the prototypes. Now it must test the market for the new product with a trial batch of products. These tests can take two forms: premarket testing and test marketing.

Is Ben & Jerry's Ice Cream doing alpha or beta testing?
©Nick Wass/AP Images

Premarket Tests Firms conduct premarket tests before they actually bring a product or service to market to determine how many customers will try and then continue to use the product or service according to a small group of potential consumers. One popular proprietary premarket test version is called Nielsen BASES. During the test, potential customers are exposed to the marketing mix variables, such as advertising, then surveyed and given a sample of the product to try.[38] After some period of time, during which the potential customers try the product, they are surveyed about whether they would buy or use the product again. This second survey provides an estimation of the probability of a consumer's repeat purchase. From these data, the firm generates a sales estimate for the new product that enables it to decide whether to introduce the product, abandon it, redesign it before introduction, or revise the marketing plan. An early evaluation of this sort—that is, before the product is introduced to the whole market—saves marketers the costs of a nationwide launch if the product fails.

Sometimes firms simulate a product or service introduction, in which case potential customers view the advertising of various currently available products or services along with advertising for the new product or service. They receive money to buy the product or service from a simulated environment, such as a mock web page or store, and respond to a survey after they make their purchases. This test can determine the effectiveness of a firm's advertising as well as the expected trial rates for the new product.

Test Marketing A method of determining the success potential of a new product, test marketing introduces the offering to a limited geographical area (usually a few cities) prior to a national launch. Test marketing is a strong predictor of product success because the firm can study actual purchase behavior, which is more reliable than a simulated test. A test marketing effort uses all the elements of the marketing mix: It includes promotions such as advertising and coupons, just as if the product were being introduced nationally, and the product appears in targeted retail outlets with appropriate pricing. On the basis of the results of the test marketing, the firm can estimate demand for the entire market. Test marketing is widely used by fast-food chains. Many restaurants roll out new ideas first in Orlando, Florida, a location that attracts a vast range of diverse tourists and thus might offer insights into what various consumers will like.[39]

Test marketing costs more and takes longer than premarket tests do, which may provide an advantage to competitors that could get a similar or better product to market first without test marketing. For this reason, some firms might launch new products without extensive consumer testing and rely instead on intuition, instincts, and guts.[40]

What will be the future of 3D movies? Moviegoers must decide if the experience is worth the higher price.

Product Launch

If the market testing returns with positive results, the firm is ready to introduce the product to the entire market. This most critical step in the new product introduction requires tremendous financial resources and extensive coordination of all aspects of the marketing mix. For any firm, if the new product launch is a failure, it may be difficult for the product—and perhaps the firm—to recover. For example, 3D movie theaters seemed to have reached their peak in the United States in 2010 and then started declining. However, in 2015 the number of movie theaters with 3D screens started to grow and the growth rate accelerated in 2016. There are over 16,000 3D cinema screens in the United States, even though 3D box office sales in 2016 were down 8 percent amid overall box office sales that were up 2 percent. Despite the decline, Hollywood continues to release 3D movies. In 2016, 19 of the top 25 movies were released in

Some products never make it out of the introduction stage, like Kwispelbier, an alcohol-free beer for dogs from the Netherlands.
©Michel Porro/Getty Images

3D, compared to only 14 of the top 25 movies in 2015. But if—as appears to be the case—moviegoers have decided that the realistic, three-dimensional images are not worth the higher ticket price, such investments might be painful for both movie studios and movie theaters.[41]

So what does a product launch involve? First, on the basis of the research it has gathered on consumer perceptions, the tests it has conducted, and competitive considerations, the firm confirms its target market (or markets) and decides how the product will be positioned. Then the firm finalizes the remaining marketing mix variables for the new product, including the marketing budget for the first year.[42] As Adding Value 12.2 details, this early marketing often involves efforts simply to get people to try a new product.

The timing of the launch may also be important, depending on the product.[43] Hollywood studios typically release movies targeted toward general audiences (G- or PG-rated movies) during the summer when children are out of school. New automobile models traditionally are released for sale during September, and fashion products are launched just before the season of the year for which they are intended.

Evaluation of Results

After the product has been launched, marketers must undertake a critical postlaunch review to determine whether the product and its launch were a success or failure and what additional resources or changes to the marketing mix are needed, if any. Many firms use panel data to improve the probability of success during the test marketing phase of a new product introduction. The consumer panel data are collected by panelists scanning in their receipts using a home scanning device. This information is used to measure individual household first-time trials and repeat purchases. Through such data, market demand can be estimated, so the firm can figure out how best to adjust its marketing mix. Some products never make it out of the introduction stage, especially those that seem almost laughable in retrospect. Alcohol-free beer for pets? Harley-Davidson perfume?[44]

For those products that do move on, firms can measure the success of a new product by three interrelated factors: (1) its satisfaction of technical requirements, such as performance; (2) customer acceptance; and (3) its satisfaction of the firm's financial requirements, such as sales and profits.[45] If the product is not performing sufficiently well, poor customer acceptance will result, which in turn leads to poor financial performance.

The new product development process, when followed rationally and sequentially, helps avoid failures. The product life cycle, discussed in the next section, helps marketers manage their products' marketing mix during and after introduction.

Adding Value 12.2

To Get People to Try a New Product, Goodness Knows Encourages Them to Try Something Else New[v]

Convincing people to give a new product a try is nearly always difficult, especially in a crowded product market, such as the one for healthy snack bars. Consumers can choose among vast numbers of granola, fruit, and nut bars, so getting them to switch brands and try the new Goodness Knows line required some creative marketing by its parent brand Mars.

A recent advertising and marketing campaign acknowledges that it can be scary, but also thrilling and wonderful, to try something new. Inviting regular people to try their hand at writing a jingle or acting in a commercial for the Goodness Knows brand, the marketers filmed their efforts, then spliced some examples together for the ultimate marketing campaign.

In so doing, the brand also highlights that first attempts are not always successful. Tone-deaf singers offer up their voices for jingles they have written. Amateur actors deliver the wrong lines, struggle with the pronunciation of "cocoa flavinols," and knock over displays of apples on a soundstage. But these regular people also comment about why they took the risk and how happy they were to try something that they had never done before—an ideal theme for a new product that needs to get people to give it a chance.

Goodness Knows is not totally new; the line began as a local Colorado offering in 2010, then underwent a national rollout in 2015. Its design is distinct. Rather than a single or pair of pressed bars, the packages contain four bite-sized squares, each with a foundation (usually of dark chocolate) that is covered by nuts and fruits. Mars also continues to expand the product line with new flavors. Thus the idea of introducing the brand reflects the staged strategy that Mars is undertaking. It knows that consumers are more familiar with Nature Valley granola bars or KIND bars. Furthermore, Mars' strength has mainly been in the confectionary market, not healthy snacks.

In this $6.8 billion category, General Mills, Clif, Kellogg, and KIND hold most of the market share, accounting for nearly 60 percent of sales among them. Breaking in thus is not an easy proposition, but Goodness Knows remains confident. After all, its philosophy holds that if you don't try, you'll never know whether you might succeed.

WE ASKED PEOPLE TO TRY A LITTLE GOODNESS

To get people to try Mars' new healthy snack bars, Goodness Knows, it filmed people trying to do something new, then spliced some examples together for a great marketing campaign.

Source: Mars, Incorporated

PROGRESS CHECK

1. What are the steps in the new product development process?
2. Identify different sources of new product ideas.

THE PRODUCT LIFE CYCLE

L012-4   Explain the product life cycle.

The product life cycle defines the stages that products move through as they enter, get established in, and ultimately leave the marketplace. It thereby offers marketers a starting point for their strategy planning. The stages of the life cycle often reflect marketplace trends, such as the healthy lifestyle trend that today places organic and green product categories in their growth stages. Exhibit 12.5 illustrates a typical product life cycle, including the industry sales and profits over time. In their life cycles, products pass through four stages: introduction, growth, maturity, and decline. When the product category first launches and innovators start buying the product, the introduction stage begins. In the growth stage, the product gains acceptance, demand and sales increase, and more competitors emerge in the product category. In the maturity stage, industry sales reach their peak, so firms try to rejuvenate their products by adding new features or repositioning them. If these efforts succeed, the product achieves new life.[46] If not, it goes into the decline stage and eventually exits the market.

EXHIBIT 12.5   Product Life Cycle

Not every product follows the same life cycle curve. Many products, such as home appliances, stay in the maturity stage for a very long time. Manufacturers may add features to dishwashers and washing machines, but the mature product category remains essentially the same and seems unlikely to enter the decline stage unless some innovative, superior solution comes along to replace them.

The product life cycle offers a useful tool for managers to analyze the types of strategies that may be required over the life of their products. Even the strategic emphasis of a firm and its marketing mix (the four Ps) strategies can be adapted from insights about the characteristics of each stage of the cycle, as we summarize in Exhibit 12.6.

Let's look at each of these stages in depth.

Introduction Stage

The introduction stage for a new, innovative product or service usually starts with a single firm, and innovators are the ones to try the new offering. Some new-to-the-world products and services that defined their own product category and industry are the telephone (invented by Alexander Graham Bell in 1876), the transistor semiconductor (Bell Laboratories

EXHIBIT 12.6   Characteristics of Different Stages of the Product Life Cycle

	Introduction	Growth	Maturity	Decline
Sales	Low	Rising	Peak	Declining
Profits	Negative or low	Rapidly rising	Peak to declining	Declining
Typical consumers	Innovators	Early adopters and early majority	Late majority	Laggards
Competitors (number of firms and products)	One or few	Few but increasing	High number of competitors and competitive products	Low number of competitors and products

in 1947), the Walkman portable cassette player (Sony in 1979), the Internet browser (Netscape in 1994), the personal digital assistant (Palm in 1996), iTunes (Apple in 2001), Facebook (2004), Blu-ray (Sony in 2006), iPad (Apple in 2010), and Amazon Echo smart speaker (Amazon in 2015). Sensing the viability and commercialization possibilities of some market-creating new product, other firms soon enter the market with similar or improved products at lower prices. The same pattern holds for less innovative products such as apparel, music, and even a new soft drink flavor. The introduction stage is characterized by initial losses to the firm due to its high start-up costs and low levels of sales revenue as the product begins to take off. If the product is successful, firms may start seeing profits toward the end of this stage.

Growth Stage

The growth stage of the product life cycle is marked by a growing number of product adopters, rapid growth in industry sales, and increases in both the number of competitors and the number of available product versions.[47] The market becomes more segmented and consumer preferences more varied, which increases the potential for new markets or new uses of the product or service.[48] Adding Value 12.3 outlines how a couple of entrepreneurs had to take a trial-and-error approach before they ultimately found the segment of the popcorn market that would allow their SkinnyPop brand to grow massively and quickly.

Also during the growth stage, firms attempt to reach new consumers by studying their preferences and producing different product variations—varied colors, styles, or features—which enable them to segment the market more precisely. The goal of this segmentation is to ride the rising sales trend and firmly establish the firm's brand so as not to be outdone by competitors. For example, many food manufacturers are working hard to become the first brand that consumers think of when they consider organic products. Del Monte was the first of the major canned vegetable sellers to go organic. The cans feature bold "organic" banners across the front and promise that no pesticides were used to produce the food items. Even though Del Monte products have been around for more than 100 years, in this growth category the company is a newer entrant in the organic market, so it must work to establish its distinctive appeal.[49]

As firms ride the crest of increasing industry sales, profits in the growth stage also rise because of the economies of scale associated with manufacturing and marketing costs, especially in promotion and advertising. At the same time, firms that have not yet established a stronghold in the market, even in narrow segments, may decide to exit, in what is referred to as an industry shakeout.

Maturity Stage

The maturity stage of the product life cycle is characterized by the adoption of the product by the late majority and intense competition for market share among firms. Marketing costs (e.g., promotion, distribution) increase as these firms vigorously defend their market share against competitors. They also face intense competition on price as the average price of the product falls substantially compared with the shifts during the previous two stages of the life cycle. Lower prices and increased marketing costs begin to erode the profit margins for many firms. In the later phases of the maturity stage, the market has become quite saturated, and practically all potential customers for

Recognizing that shampoo is a mature product category, Alterna and other manufacturers have introduced anti-aging hair products.

©Alterna Haircare

Adding Value 12.3 | Skinny on Ingredients, Thick on Promise: The Growth of SkinnyPop Snacks[vi]

Anyone who has ever wandered Chicago's streets—or flown through its Midway Airport for that matter—likely has at least a vague sense memory of the delicious scent of fresh popcorn, spreading out from the doors of the shops run by the local favorite, Garrett's Popcorn. A tin of Garrett's is a salty, buttery, guilt-inducing pleasure that can be hard to resist in the moment but isn't likely to be a daily snack that health-conscious consumers would stock in their pantries.

Still, when Andrew Friedman and Pam Netzky started up their Wells Street Popcorn brand, their initial goal was to launch a product that could compete with Garrett's. To differentiate themselves, they planned to offer even higher-quality ingredients and promote a sort of luxury version of the local snack. Unlike Garrett's neon-orange cheese corn, for example, Wells Street would offer a version that was milder and less stain-likely. Wells Street products achieved mediocre performance; the founders were able to convince a few high-end, local grocers to stock the products. But the expensive ingredients meant that Wells Street was selling small bags of caramel corn for about $10 each, limiting its expansion opportunities. There just wasn't that big of a market for gourmet popcorn at a high price point, and when another company with a similar product entered the New York market and failed dismally, Netzky and Friedman realized they needed another option.

That option presented itself in the form of customer requests for healthier snacks. Customers liked the flavors of the fancy popcorn, but they hated the artificial ingredients, high levels of saturated fats, and massive amounts of sodium contained in each serving. To come up with an entry into the emerging, "better-for-you" snack market, the founders experimented for months, adjusting the precise recipes and ingredients until they achieved an offering that mimicked the taste of gourmet and movie theater popcorn but did so with "skinny" ingredients. Recognizing that this new product was vastly distinct from, and needed to be marketed separately from, the Wells Street line, Friedman and Netzky launched a new brand, SkinnyPop.

Despite the name, the products are not necessarily lower in calories. Rather, the "skinny" part of the name refers to what goes into the snacks—or perhaps more accurately, what doesn't go into them. Manufactured in a dedicated facility (to avoid any contamination with excluded ingredients), SkinnyPop popcorn contains no gluten, cholesterol, dairy, genetically modified organisms, trans fat, peanuts, or preservatives.

Even once they had the right recipe though, getting SkinnyPop onto grocers' shelves was a struggle. According to Friedman, retailers simply didn't know what to do with the product. Was it a health food? A snack? A natural product? On a visit to

Although it took a lot of trial and error in product development, marketing, and distribution, SkinnyPop is now firmly in the growth phase of the product life cycle.
©Keith Homan/Alamy Stock Photo

one local store, Friedman took advantage of a store manager's vacation, noting that while the manager was gone, "I moved stuff around, put them on the shelves and ran out of the store. Within a couple of days, they were calling to reorder." If you can excuse the pun, the success of the brand just popped from there. Within a year, SkinnyPop had sold $55.7 million in snacks, and then experienced explosive growth of 137.6 percent to earn $132.4 million in sales just a year after that.

The level of growth was so massive and quick that Friedman and Netzky sold their brand to a national company in 2014. And still the brand and its products continue to grow: Currently found in nearly 50,000 retail stores in North America, with plans to double that number before also moving into international markets, SkinnyPop seemingly has no cause to stop.

the product have already adopted the product. Such saturated markets are prevalent in developed countries.

In the United States, most consumer packaged goods found in grocery and discount stores are already in the maturity stage. For example, in the well-established hair care products market, consumer goods companies constantly search for innovations to set themselves apart and extend the time in which they maintain their position in the maturity stage.

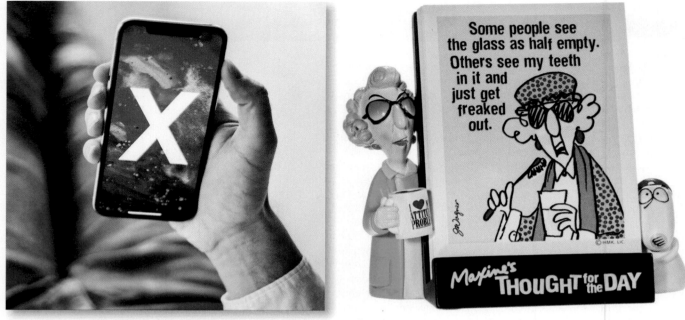

To reach new market segments, Apple reduces the price of older versions of its products when new ones are released.

©Halfpoint/Shutterstock

Hallmark is trying a variety of innovative new products including this "thought for the day" 3D sign featuring beloved card character Maxine.

©McGraw-Hill Education

Observing the popularity of new skin care products, hair care manufacturers have integrated similar product benefits to their products. These companies have introduced anti-aging shampoos and conditioners, prewash hair masks, serums, and multiple-step solutions that go beyond the old mantra of lather, rinse, and repeat.[50]

Firms pursue various strategies during this stage to increase their customer base and/or defend their market share. Other tactics include entry into new markets and market segments and developing new products. (Refer to Growth Strategies in Chapter 2.)

Entry into New Markets or Market Segments

Because a market is saturated, firms may attempt to enter new geographical markets, including international markets (as we discussed in Chapter 8), that may be less saturated. For example, pharmaceutical companies are realizing that they need to turn to BRIC countries for continued growth in the coming years. While the U.S. and European markets are fairly saturated, the BRIC countries are expected to continue to grow. China currently has the fastest-growing market, valued at over $86 billion in 2017.[51]

However, even in mature markets, firms may be able to find new market segments. Apple is well known for releasing new versions of its iPhone and iPad yearly, and development cycles are getting even shorter. Although people still get excited over these new products, they are also beginning to suffer from "device exhaustion," in which they are becoming progressively less likely to continue to upgrade their phones and tablets. As a result, the smartphone and tablet markets appear nearly or completely mature.[52] The market may be mature, but for many people these new versions are prohibitively expensive, even when signing a two-year contract. To expand to these lower-income market segments, Apple doesn't get rid of its older devices when a new one comes along. Instead, it reduces the price on the older versions that are cheaper to produce. As a result, it is able to reach customers that would never be able to afford the latest iPhone model.

Development of New Products

Despite market saturation, firms continually introduce new products with improved features or find new uses for existing products because they need constant innovation and product proliferation to defend market share from intense competition. Firms continually introduce new products to ensure that they are able to retain or grow their respective market shares. Hallmark, which has been the hallmark name for greeting cards for a long time, is trying a variety of innovations. They include customizable greeting cards, mugs and picture frames, and interactive storybooks that can be personalized for various recipients, as well a "thought for the day" 3D sign featuring the beloved card character Maxine.[53]

Decline Stage

Firms with products in the decline stage either position themselves for a niche segment of die-hard consumers or those with special needs or they completely exit the market. The few laggards who have not yet tried the product or service enter the market at this stage. Take vinyl long-playing records (LPs), for example. In an age of Internet-downloaded music files, it may seem surprising that vinyl records are still made and sold. Sales of vinyl LPs had long been declining, but they have enjoyed a resurgence in just the past few years as die-hard music lovers demand the unique sound of a vinyl record rather than the digital sound of CDs and music files. Still, the 5.5 million LPs sold in the United States per year pales in comparison with the 1.26 billion digital downloads.[54] The grooves in vinyl records create sound waves that are similar to those of a live performance, however, which means they provide a more authentic sound, which in turn means nightclub DJs, discerning music listeners, and collectors will always prefer them.[55]

The Shape of the Product Life Cycle Curve

In theory, the product life cycle curve is bell shaped with regard to sales and profits. In reality, however, each product or service category has its own individual shape; some move more rapidly through their product life cycles than others, depending on how different the category is from offerings currently in the market and how valuable it is to the consumer. New products and services that consumers accept very quickly have higher consumer adoption rates very early in their product life cycles and move faster across the various stages.

For example, Microsoft's Xbox Kinect motion sensor transformed gaming by allowing players to ditch traditional controllers. Kinect moved faster than other tech and gaming products through the life cycle curve. Within 60 days of being released, 8 million units were sold, breaking the Guinness World Record for the fastest-selling consumer electronic device. However, just one year later the product seemed to reach maturity, and after two years it reached the decline stage. Although the consumer product moved quickly through the product life cycle, Microsoft has been able to integrate its Kinect motion sensor software into other industrial products such as miniature satellites.[56]

Although most would argue that LPs are in the declining stage of the product life cycle, there has been a resurgence in sales in recent years.

©Keystone/Getty Images

Microsoft's Xbox Kinect moved faster than other tech and gaming products through the life cycle curve. It sold well at first, but reached the decline stage after two years.

©Will Ireland/T3 Magazine via Getty Images

Strategies Based on Product Life Cycle: Some Caveats

Although the product life cycle concept provides a starting point for managers to think about the strategy they want to implement during each stage of the life cycle of a product, this tool must be used with care. The most challenging part of applying the product life cycle concept is that managers do not know exactly what shape each product's life cycle will take, so there is no way to know precisely what stage a product is in. If, for example, a product experiences several seasons of declining sales, a manager may determine that it has moved from the growth stage to decline and so decides to stop promoting the product. As a result, of course, sales decline further. The manager then believes he or she made the right decision because the product continues to follow a predetermined life cycle. But what if the original sales decline was due to a poor strategy or increased competition—issues that could have been addressed with positive marketing support? In this case, the product life cycle decision became a self-fulfilling prophecy, and a growth product was doomed to an unnecessary decline.[57] Fortunately, new research, based on the history of dozens of consumer products, suggests that the product life cycle concept is indeed a valid idea, and new analytical tools now provide rules for detecting the key turning points in the cycle.[58]

PROGRESS CHECK

1. What are the key marketing characteristics of products or services at each stage of the product life cycle?
2. Why might placement decisions for products or services into stages of the product life cycle become a self-fulfilling prophecy?

Reviewing Learning Objectives

LO12-1 **Identify the reasons firms create new products.**

Firms need to innovate to respond to changing customer needs, prevent declines in sales from market saturation, diversify their risk, and respond to short product life cycles, especially in industries such as fashion apparel, arts, books, and software markets, where most sales come from new products. Finally, innovations can help firms improve their business relationships with suppliers.

LO12-2 **Describe the different groups of adopters articulated by the diffusion of innovation theory.**

The diffusion of innovation theory can help firms predict which types of customers will buy their products or services immediately upon introduction, as well as later as they gain more acceptance in the market. Innovators are those buyers who want to be the first to have the new product or service. Early adopters do not take as much risk as innovators do but instead wait and purchase the product after careful

review. The members of the early majority don't like to take risks and therefore tend to wait until the bugs have been worked out of a particular product or service. The late majority are buyers who purchase the product after it has achieved its full market potential. Finally, laggards like to avoid change and rely on traditional products until those products are no longer available. Laggards may never adopt certain products or services.

LO12-3 **Describe the various stages involved in developing a new product or service.**

When firms develop new products, they go through several steps. First, they generate ideas for the product or service using several alternative techniques, such as internal research and development, R&D consortia, licensing, brainstorming, tracking competitors' products or services, or working with customers. Second, firms test their concepts by either describing the idea of the new product or service to potential customers or showing them images of what the product would look like. Third, the design process entails determining what the product or service will actually include and provide. Fourth, firms test market their designs. Fifth, if everything goes well in the test market, the product is launched. Sixth, firms must evaluate the new product or service to determine its success.

LO12-4 **Explain the product life cycle.**

The product life cycle helps firms make marketing mix decisions on the basis of the product's stage in its life cycle. In the introduction stage, companies attempt to gain a strong foothold in the market quickly by appealing to innovators. During the growth stage, the objective is to establish the brand firmly. When the product reaches the maturity stage, firms compete intensely for market share, and many potential customers already own the product or use the service. Eventually, most products enter the decline phase, during which firms withdraw marketing support and eventually phase out the product. Knowing where a product or service is in its life cycle helps managers determine its specific strategy at any given point in time.

Key Terms

- alpha testing, 379
- beta testing, 379
- brainstorming, 376
- concept, 378
- concept testing, 378
- decline stage, 383
- diffusion of innovation, 367
- early adopters, 370
- early majority, 371
- first movers, 368
- growth stage, 383
- innovation, 363
- innovators, 368
- introduction stage, 383
- laggards, 371
- late majority, 371
- lead users, 378
- licensing, 376
- maturity stage, 383
- outsourcing, 376
- pioneers (breakthroughs), 367
- premarket test, 380
- product design, 379
- product development, 379
- product life cycle, 383
- prototype, 379
- R&D consortia, 376
- reverse engineering, 376
- test marketing, 380

Marketing Digitally

1. Visit Tesla's website (www.tesla.com) and explore the range of products it produces. What do its product groups have in common? Which factors have influenced Tesla's creation of its newest products?

2. The automotive industry is constantly adding new and different products and technologies to their cars—above as well as under the hood. Conduct an Internet or library database search and discuss two innovative new automotive technologies that are changing the industry.

Marketing Applications

1. Some people think that a product should be considered "new" only if it is completely new to the market and has never existed before. Describe or give examples of other types of new products.

2. Android Wear is a new category of wearable computing devices that link to Android smartphones. How quickly do you think these products will diffuse among the U.S. population? Describe the types of people that you expect will be in each of the diffusion of innovation stages.

3. What are the advantages and disadvantages for companies that are the first to introduce products that create new markets?

4. Identify and describe the ways that companies generate new product ideas. Which of these ways involve the customer? How can firms assess the value of the ideas that customers generate?

5. Describe an example of a new product or service that is targeted at the college-student market. Using the concept-testing discussion in the chapter, describe how you would conduct a concept test for this product or service.

6. Using the same product or service you used in question 5, use the diffusion of innovation theory to assess how quickly it will diffuse based on its relative advantage, compatibility, observability, complexity, and trialability.

7. How does the Internet help companies gain customer input on their existing and new products?

8. Seventh Generation's products are plant-based and designed to minimize negative environmental impacts. Seventh Generation is considering launching a new infant skin care line. Describe two possible ways that it might conduct initial market testing prior to launching this new product.

9. In which stage of the product life cycle is the iPhone? Was Apple's marketing mix—its 4 Ps—consistent with the product's stage when it released the iPhone X?

10. You have recently been hired by a cosmetics company in the product development group. The firm's brand is a top-selling, high-end line of cosmetics. The head of the development team has just presented research that shows that "tween" girls, aged 11 to 15, are very interested in cosmetics and have the money to spend. The decision is made to create a line of tween cosmetics based on the existing adult line. As the product moves through development you begin to notice that the team seems to lean toward a very edgy and sexual theme for the line, including naming the various lines "envy," "desire," "prowess," and "fatal attraction." You begin to wonder, is this concept too much for girls in the targeted age group?

Quiz Yourself

1. Which of the following is *not* a reason that firms need to innovate?
   a. Changing customer needs
   b. Preventing declining sales
   c. Diversifying risk
   d. Responding to short product life cycles
   e. All of these are reasons that firms need to innovate.

2. The diffusion of innovation stages includes all of the following groups except
   a. Innovators.
   b. Laggards.
   c. Late adopters.
   d. Early majority.
   e. Early adopters.

(Answers to these two questions can be found in the Quiz Yourself Answer Key section.)

Chapter Case Study

Mc Graw Hill Education **connect**

A TOY COMPANY FOR A NEW AGE: HOW MATTEL IS REINVENTING ITSELF FOR MODERN CONSUMERS

To get modern kids engaged with a toy, it likely requires more than conventional products have offered. A simple doll is no longer enough to grab the attention of young consumers who are constantly bombarded with entertainment options through their mobile devices. For Mattel, this trend suggests the need to reinvent itself as a technology, rather than consumer product, company, even as it continues to expand and differentiate its product lines.

With regard to its status, the new CEO of Mattel, who came from a tech background, has proposed that her goal is to define the firm as a "future-proofed kid-experience company" that will focus on digital content, learning activities, and smart toys as its primary value offerings. Mattel will still sell Hot Wheels and Barbie dolls, but the focus will be on how consumers can interact with those products across multiple platforms, not just with the physical items themselves.

At the same time, Mattel recognizes that its focus also needs to be on making the toys fun. Many new technology-driven toys seem to prioritize the technology over the fun, such as the Mattel-owned Fisher-Price Code-a-Pillar, designed to help teach children how to code. Although the idea behind the toy makes sense, few children wanted to play with it. Therefore, Mattel now is seeking to better integrate increased and advanced technology into toys that emphasize storytelling, including Barbie, so that the young consumers can invent and create their own forms of enjoyable play.

These relatively radical shifts come on the heels of some turmoil in Mattel's performance. It fired its previous CEO several years ago and had been functioning under temporary leadership before hiring the current CEO away from Google. Despite a couple of good sales quarters, overall its revenues were falling, and even the conventionally beneficial holiday

New products are the lifeblood of firms like Mattel, so it introduced 15 new Ken dolls featuring three body types, as well as ethnic diversity, various skin tones, clothing, and hairstyles.
©Mandel Ngan/AFP/Getty Images

shopping seasons have been weak in recent years. An excess of inventory after the most recent holidays forced Mattel to offer deep discounts to move the items. Still, its entertainment-related business rose 58 percent in the past year, largely due to the introduction of *Cars 3*–related toys. Such licensed toys offer lower margins than Mattel's original toys, though, so it is in the company's best interest to produce and sell more original product lines, like Barbie.

Accordingly, Mattel has no intentions to stop producing some of its best-known products. Instead, together with its technology orientation, Mattel is seeking to update the image of its dolls, most notably in its introduction of a wider variety of Ken dolls. The 15 new dolls feature three general body types, as well as far greater diversity in apparent ethnicities, skin tones, clothing, and hairstyles. The goal is to appeal better to diverse modern consumers, such as those who might believe that a "man bun" is exactly the kind of style that Barbie's boyfriend needs to sport.

Such diversity initiatives also inform the latest line of 12 dolls, designed to represent the top female wrestlers with the WWE. Thus, young female fans can pose their favorite wrestler Charlotte Flair in a flying leap off the ropes or have Nikki and Brie Bella collaborating to bring down an opponent. This line purposefully and explicitly does not feature any men, encouraging girls to embrace new roles that subvert traditional gender stereotypes.[59]

Question

1. Using the product life cycle, place the products discussed in this case into one of the four stages. Evaluate Mattel's strategy for each of these products based on its current life cycle stage. Using the product development process described in this chapter, choose one of the new products discussed and explain how it might flow through the different steps in the process.

Endnotes

1. Bharat Kapoor, Kevin Nolan, and Natarajan Venkatakrishnan, "How GE Appliances Built an Innovation Lab to Rapidly Prototype Products," *Harvard Business Review*, July 18, 2017; https://firstbuild.com/; Jessica Bard, "GE Appliances FirstBuild Hosts Third Annual Mega Hackathon This Weekend in Louisville," WDRB.com, September 6, 2017, www.wdrb.com/ story/36304402/ge-appliances-firstbuild-hosts-third-annual-mega-hackathon-this-weekend-in-louisville; Mickey Meece, "FirstBuild Hackathon Winning Team Redesigns the Kitchen Sink," *Insider Louisville*, September 11, 2017, https://insiderlouisville.com/business/firstbuild-hackathon-winning-team-redesigns-the-kitchen-sink/.

2. "This Day in History: 2007 Steve Jobs Debuts the iPhone," *History*, January 9, 2017, www.history.com/this-day-in-history/steve-jobs-debuts-the-iphone; Brain Heater, "A Brief History of the iPhone," *Tech Crunch*, June 29, 2017, https://techcrunch.com/gallery/a-brief-history-of-the-iphone/.

3. Timothy Hay, "Technology Innovations That Could Help the Elderly," *The Wall Street Journal*, June 29, 2015.

4. https://aftershokz.com/; Jeff Dengate, "15 Cool New Products from CES 2017," *Runner's World*, January 9, 2017, www.runnersworld.com/electronics/15-cool-new-products-from-ces-2017.

5. https://aftershokz.com/collections/all; Vlad Savov, "Headphones Are Growing More Expensive Because We Demand More of Them," *The Verge*, May 13, 2016, www.theverge.com/circuit-breaker/2016/5/13/11669906/headphones-market-price-worldwide-statistics.

6. Koen Pauwels et al., "New Products, Sales Promotions, and Firm Value: The Case of the Automobile Industry," *Journal of Marketing* 68, no. 4 (2008), p. 142.

7. Elaine Watson, "What's the Size of the US Gluten-Free Prize? $490m, $5bn, or $10bn?," *Food Navigator USA*, February 17, 2014, www.foodnavigator-usa.com.

8. "Going Gluten-Free," General Mills, www.generalmills.com/en/Story-content/Health/GlutenFree.

9. Kalpesh Kaushik Desai and Kevin Lane Keller, "The Effects of Ingredient Branding Strategies on Host Brand Extendibility," *Journal of Marketing* 66, no. 1 (2002), pp. 73–93.

10. Erik Kain, "'Madden NFL 25' Sales Down over Last Year, First Week Still Tops 1M Units," *Forbes*, September 5, 2013, www.forbes.com.

11. Paul Demerr, "Wal-Mart to Suppliers: Help Us Identify New Products to Sell," *Digital Commerce 360*, April 28, 2016, www.digitalcommerce360.com/2016/04/28/wal-mart-suppliers-help-us-identify-new-products-sell/.

12. www.marketingpower.com/_layouts/Dictionary.aspx?dLetter=D.

13. T. Fan, P. N. Golder, and D. R. Lehmann, "Innovation and New Products Research: A State-of-the-Art Review, Models for Managerial Decision Making, and Future Research Directions," in B. Wierenga and R. van der Lans (Eds.), *Handbook of Marketing Decision Models. International Series in Operations Research & Management Science*, vol. 254 (Cham, Switzerland: Springer, 2017); Michael J. Barone and Robert D. Jewell, "The Innovator's License: A Latitude to Deviate from Category Norms," *Journal of Marketing* 77 (January 2013), pp. 120–34.

14. Stanley F. Slater, Jakki J. Mohr, and Sanjit Sengupta, "Radical Product Innovation Capability: Literature Review, Synthesis, and Illustrative Research Propositions," *Journal of Product Innovation Management* 31, no. 3 (May 2014), pp. 552–66; Rosabeth Moss Kanter, *SuperCorp: How Vanguard Companies Create Innovation, Profits, Growth, and Social Good* (New York: Crown Business, 2009); Rajesh K. Chandy, Jaideep C. Prabhu, and Kersi D. Antia, "What Will the Future Bring? Dominance, Technology Expectations, and Radical Innovation," *Journal of Marketing* 67, no. 3 (2003), pp. 1–18; Harald J. van Heerde, Carl F. Mela, and Puneet Manchanda, "The Dynamic Effect of Innovation on Market Structure," *Journal of Marketing Research* 41, no. 2 (2004), pp. 166–83.

15. www.apple.com; Clayton M. Christensen and Michael E. Raynor, *The Innovator's Solution* (Boston: Harvard Business School Press, 2003).

16. Rajan Varadarajan, Manjit S. Yadav, and Venkatesh Shankar, "First-Mover Advantage in the Internet-Enabled Market Environment," in *Handbook of Strategic e-Business Management* (Heidelberg, Germany: Springer, 2014), pp. 157–85; James L. Oakley et al., "Order of Entry and the Moderating Role of Comparison Brands in Brand Extension Evaluation," *Journal of Consumer Research* 34, no. 5 (2008), pp. 706–12; Fernando F. Suarez and Gianvito Lanzolla, "Considerations for a Stronger First Mover Advantage Theory," *Academy of Management Review* 33, no. 1 (2008), pp. 269–70; Ralitza Nikolaeva, "The Dynamic Nature of Survival Determinants in E-commerce," *Journal of the Academy of Marketing Science* 35, no. 4 (2007), pp. 560–71.

17. "Top 10 Reasons for New Product Failure," *The Marketing Fray*, January 7, 2010, www.marketingfray.com.

18. http://smashinghub.com/10-coolest-upcoming-gadgets-of-2011.htm.

19. Barak Libai, Eitan Muller, and Renana Peres, "Decomposing the Value of Word-of-Mouth Seeding Programs: Acceleration versus Expansion," *Journal of Marketing Research* 50, no. 2 (2013), pp. 161–76; Jacob Goldenberg et al., "The Role of Hubs in the Adoption Process," *Journal of Marketing* 73 (March 2009), pp. 1–13.

20. Ellen Byron, "The Cleanest House of All," *The Wall Street Journal*, March 20, 2013, http://online.wsj.com.

21. Carol Matlack, "Electrolux's Holy Trinity for Hit Products," *Bloomberg Businessweek*, October 31, 2013, www.businessweek.com.

22. Gabriel Beltrone, "Most Inclusive Ad Ever? Swiffer Spot Stars Interracial Family, and Dad's an Amputee," *Adweek*, January 21, 2014, www.adweek.com.

23. Matlack, "Electrolux's Holy Trinity for Hit Products."

24. www.youtube.com/user/Blendtec.

25. Charles Passy, "How Fast Food Chains Cook Up New Menu Items," *The Wall Street Journal*, August 24, 2015.

26. Shubham Mukherjee and Nmrata Singh, "Reverse Innovation 2.0: More MNCs Take India's Frugal Engineering Global," *The Times of India*, July 22, 2015, https://timesofindia.indiatimes.com/business/india-business/Reverse-innovation-2-0-More-MNCs-take-Indias-frugal-engineering-global/articleshow/48166102.cms; www.pureitwater.com/IN/.

27. "Designing the Future Kitchen," IDEO Case Study, May 2015, www.ideo.com/case-study/designing-the-future-kitchen.

28. Dominik Mahr, Annouk Lievens, and Vera Blazevic, "The Value of Customer Cocreated Knowledge during the Innovation Process," *Journal of Product Innovation Management* 31, no. 3 (2013), pp. 599–615; Pilar Carbonell, Ana I. Rodríguez-Escudero, and Devashish Pujari, "Customer Involvement in New Service Development: An Examination of Antecedents and Outcomes," *Journal of Product Innovation Management* 26 (September 2009), pp. 536–50; Glen L. Urban and John R. Hauser, "'Listening In' to Find and Explore New Combinations of Customer Needs," *Journal of Marketing* 68, no. 2 (2004), p. 72.

29. Jeff Bellairs, "Innovation and Collaboration Swiftly Launch Green Giant Snack Chips," *Taste of General Mills*, June 19, 2013, www.blog.generalmills.com.

30. Passy, "How Fast Food Chains Cook Up New Menu Items."

31. Michael Nir, *Agile Project Management* (New York: CreateSpace, 2013); Jim Highsmith, *Agile Product Management: Creating Innovative Products* (Boston: Addison-Wesley, 2009); www.betterproductdesign.net; Eric von Hippel, *The Sources of Innovation* (New York: Oxford University Press, 1988); Eric von Hippel, "Successful Industrial Products from Consumers' Ideas," *Journal of Marketing* 42, no. 1 (1978), pp. 39–49.

32. Karl T. Ulrich and Steven D. Eppinger, *Product Design and Development*, 6th ed. (Boston: Irwin/McGraw-Hill, 2015).

33. www.marketingpower.com.

34. Ulrich and Eppinger, *Product Design and Development*.

35. www.marketingpower.com.

36. Ulrich and Eppinger, *Product Design and Development*.

37. Frederic Lardinois, "YouEye Raises $3M for Its Webcam-Based Usability Testing Service with Emotion Recognition," *Tech-Crunch*, May 7, 2013, www.techcrunch.com.

38. http://en-us.nielsen.com/tab/product_families/nielsen_bases.

39. Passy, "How Fast Food Chains Cook Up New Menu Items."

40. Gernot H. Gessinger, *Materials and Innovative Product Development: From Concept to Market* (Oxford: Elsevier, 2009).

41. Motion Picture Association of America, "Theatrical Market Statistics 2016," www.mpaa.org/wp-content/uploads/2017/03/MPAA-Theatrical-Market-Statistics-2016_Final-1.pdf.

42. Product Development Management Association, *The PDMA Handbook of New Product Development,* 3rd ed., Kenneth B. Kahn, ed. (New York: Wiley, 2013).

43. Jan Hendrik Fisch and Jan-Michael Ross, "Timing Product Replacements under Uncertainty—the Importance of Material–Price Fluctuations for the Success of Products That Are Based on New Materials," *Journal of Product Innovation Management,* 2014; Yuhong Wu, Sridhar Balasubramanian, and Vijay Mahajan, "When Is a Preannounced New Product Likely to Be Delayed?," *Journal of Marketing* 68, no. 2 (2004), p. 101.

44. www.walletpop.com/specials/top-25-biggest-product-flops-of-all-time.

45. www.pdma.org/.

46. Theodore Levitt, *Marketing Imagination* (New York: Free Press, 1986).

47. Greg Marshall and Mark Johnston, *Marketing Management,* 3rd ed. (New York: McGraw-Hill Education, 2019).

48. Ibid.; Glen L. Urban and John R. Hauser, *Design and Marketing of New Products,* 2nd ed. (Upper Saddle River, NJ: Prentice Hall, 1993), pp. 120–21.

49. www.organicearthday.org/DelMonteFoods.htm; www.delmonte.com/Products/.

50. Euromonitor International, "A Revival in Hair Care Innovation," August 12, 2013, http://blog.euromonitor.com.

51. "Biggest Pharmaceutical Markets in the World by Country," *World Atlas,* 2017, www.worldatlas.com/articles/countries-with-the-biggest-global-pharmaceutical-markets-in-the-world.html.

52. Wallace Witkowski, "iPhones and Other Portables Suffering from 'Device Exhaustion,' Analyst Says," *The Wall Street Journal,* August 20, 2013, http://blogs.marketwatch.com; Jon Gold, "Is the Smartphone Market Saturated?," *Network World,* July 30, 2015, www.networkworld.com/article/2954568/smartphones/is-the-smartphone-market-saturated.html.

53. www.hallmark.com.

54. Alan Kozzin, "Weaned on CDs, They're Reaching for Vinyl," *The New York Times,* June 9, 2013, www.nytimes.com; Ed Christman, "Digital Music Sales Decrease for First Time in 2013," *BillboardBiz,* January 3, 2014, www.billboard.com.

55. Yvonne Zipp, "As Vinyl Records Get Back in the Groove, Kalamazoo Record Stores See Sales Climb," *MLive,* January 15, 2012, www.mlive.com.

56. Larry Downes and Paul Nunes, "The Faster a New Technology Takes Off, the Harder It Falls," *Wired,* January 3, 2014, www.wired.com/2014/01/why-its-time-to-ditch-the-bell-curve/.

57. Goutam Challagalla, R. Venkatesh, and Ajay Kohli, "Proactive Postsales Service: When and Why Does It Pay Off?," *Journal of Marketing* 73 (March 2009), pp. 70–87; Kevin J. Clancy and Peter C. Krieg, "Product Life Cycle: A Dangerous Idea," *Brandweek,* March 1, 2004, p. 26; Nariman K. Dhalla and Sonia Yuseph, "Forget the Product Life-Cycle Concept," *Harvard Business Review* (January/February 1976), p. 102ff.

58. Jan R. Landwehr, Daniel Wentzel, and Andreas Herrmann, "Product Design for the Long Run: Consumer Responses to Typical and Atypical Designs at Different Stages of Exposure," *Journal of Marketing* 77, no. 5 (2013), pp. 92–107; Peter Golder and Gerard Tellis, "Cascades, Diffusion, and Turning Points in the Product Life Cycle," MSI Report No. 03-120, 2003.

59. Will Jarvis, "Can Ken (with a Man Bun) Help Mattel Bounce Back?," *Advertising Age,* June 20, 2017; "Beyond Barbie: Mattel Plans Digital Transformation," *Advertising Age,* June 14, 2017; Danny Vena, "Mattel Struggles as Barbie Gets Dumped," *The Motley Fool,* July 31, 2017; Sydney Greene, "Girls Can Wrestle, Too: Mattel and WWE Announce New Female Superstar Dolls," *USA Today,* July 21, 2017; Kirsten Korosec, "How Mattel Plans to Win Over Generation Alpha," *Fortune,* July 18, 2017.

i. Kimiko de Freytas-Tamura, "The Bright-Eyed Talking Doll That Just Might Be a Spy," *The New York Times,* February 17, 2017; www.myfriendcayla.com/us-c5ja; Bill Chappell, "Banned in Germany: Kids' Doll Is Labeled an Espionage Device," *NPR,* February 17, 2017.

ii. Ben Fritz, "With 'Cinderella,' Disney Recycles Fairy Tales, Minus the Cartoons," *The Wall Street Journal,* March 10, 2015; Alan French, "Plenty on the Line for Disney's 2016 Live-Action Releases," *Inside the Magic,* February 23, 2016; Drew Mackie, "Here Is a Complete List of All the Disney Classics Being Remade (So Far)," *People,* September 23, 2015.

iii. Sources: Nick Madigan, "Need a Quick Inspection of a 58-Story Tower? Send a Drone," *The New York Times,* August 14, 2018; Amia Srinivasan, "What Termites Can Teach Us," *The New Yorker,* September 17, 2018; April Glaser, "Federal Privacy Laws Won't Necessarily Protect You from Spying Devices," *Recode.net,* March 15, 2017

iv. Chris Murphy, "GM's Data Strategy Pushed to Center Stage," *Information Week,* March 27, 2014; Mark van Rijmenam, "Three Use Cases of How General Motors Applies Big Data to Become Profitable Again," *DataFloq,* August 25, 2014; Jonathan H. Owen, David J. VanderVeen, and Lerinda L. Frost, "General Motors: Using O.R. to Meet Auto Industry Challenges and Provide Value to Customers and the Company," *Informs Online,* December 2013.

v. Jessica Wohl, "Goodness Knows Flubs Are Encouraged in New Mars Ad," *Advertising Age,* January 2, 2011.

vi. Melissa Harris, "Business Is Popping for Healthier Snack," *Chicago Tribune,* February 8, 2012; Ellen Rogan, "SkinnyPop's Success: Lessons I Learned," May 21, 2014; Tomi Kilgore, "5 Things to Know about SkinnyPop-Maker Amplify ahead of Its IPO," *Market Watch,* August 4, 2015; Peter Frost, "SkinnyPop's Parent Company Goes Public, with a 10-Figure Valuation," *Crain's Chicago Business,* August 5, 2015.

Quiz Yourself Answer Key

1. Which of the following is *not* a reason that firms need to innovate?

   Answer: (e) All of these are reasons that firms need to innovate.

2. The diffusion of innovation stages includes all of the following groups except:

   Answer: (c) Late adopters

Design elements: Protein bar: © 4kodiak/Getty Images; icons for Adding Value, Marketing Analytics, & Social & Mobile Marketing boxes: © Molotovcoketail/Getty Images; icon for Ethical & Societal Dilemma box: © McGraw-Hill Education

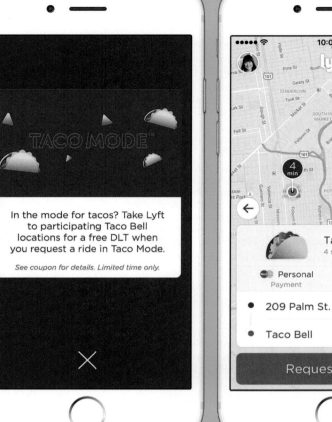

LEARNING OBJECTIVES

After reading this chapter, you should be able to:

LO13-1 Describe how the marketing of services differs from the marketing of products.

LO13-2 Discuss the four gaps in the Service Gaps Model.

LO13-3 Examine the five service quality dimensions.

LO13-4 Explain the zone of tolerance.

LO13-5 Identify three service recovery strategies.

CHAPTER 13

SERVICES: THE INTANGIBLE PRODUCT

Ride-sharing companies already helped create an entirely new service industry. Now Lyft is seeking to innovate in this market yet again, promising not only safe and convenient rides but also snacks for hungry customers. In an early, limited market test with Taco Bell, Lyft will add a "Taco Mode" to its app that enables consumers to order a ride that includes a stop at the nearest outlet of the fast-food restaurant chain. To promote the notion, Taco Bell will provide a customized menu and free Doritos Locos Tacos. On their way to the passenger's destination, drivers will swing through the drive-through, obtain the selected items, and then pass them to the back seat.

In the initial tests, the Taco Mode version of the app will feature taco-related images. Cars eligible to provide the service also will sport Taco Bell logos and carry menus with them. The service will be available between 9:00 p.m. and 2:00 a.m.—prime times for late-night revelers to be craving a snack after an evening out, and also to be needing a safe way home.

Taco Bell is not paying Lyft for these marketing elements. Rather, both brands see the experiment as a potential means to differentiate their offers in the market. If faced with the choice between Uber and Lyft, a hungry passenger might be swayed to select the latter if it means easy access to a burrito and drink. If in a Lyft with a Taco Bell menu on hand, the rider is likely to embrace that fast-food option over competitive choices.

Anecdotal evidence suggests that such deliveries already occur through informal agreements between drivers and passengers. Funny social media accounts detail interactions between friendly drivers and hungry (often inebriated) passengers who share a fast-food feast in the car. Lyft has not set any policies for its drivers regarding whether they must or should obtain food for riders. While some of them clearly are happy to provide the extra service to passengers, others worry about the risks involved, including a messy car that smells like refried beans. Many drivers take particular care to keep their cars impeccable and free of any odors; such status helps improve their ratings. Furthermore, the added service threatens to lower customer satisfaction ratings if drivers get stuck in long drive-through lines or suffer reduced availability during peak hours. In response to these concerns, Lyft emphasizes that participation in Taco Mode is optional for both drivers and customers. If consumers can specify whether they want the option, such as by logging on in Taco Mode, such questions are resolved effectively. That is, customers can self-select into an eating or non-eating Lyft vehicle, increasing the satisfaction of both segments of consumers.

Their satisfaction also seemingly might be enhanced by the experience itself. A convenient ride home is already an appealing option for millions of riders. A safe ride home that also provides a late-night snack extends that experience and convenience even further.[1]

Whereas a service is any intangible offering that involves a deed, performance, or effort that cannot be physically possessed,[2] customer service specifically refers to human or mechanical activities firms undertake to help satisfy their customers' needs and wants. By providing good customer service, firms add value to their products. Although Amazon may have built its reputation on being able to provide a vast range of products, it also has developed capabilities that allow customers to click a link to receive quotes for services, such as electronic installation, home repairs, yard work, or dog walking, from local professionals. Google already provides a service, in the form of its famous search engine, but it also is experimenting with ways to compete in other service spaces. For example, it recently invested heavily in Thumbtack, a platform that allows customers to post their service needs and job offers, then receive bids for those jobs from service providers that have registered with the site.[3]

Exhibit 13.1 illustrates the continuum from a pure service to a pure good. Most offerings lie somewhere in the middle and include some service and some good (i.e., a hybrid of the two). Even those firms that are engaged primarily in selling a good, such as a fast-food restaurant, typically view service as a method to maintain a sustainable competitive advantage. Although Taco Bell is working hard with Lyft to provide excellent customer service, any restaurant needs to provide basic customer service to ensure customers receive what they order and complete their transaction. Therefore, this chapter takes an inclusive view of services as anything from pure service businesses, such as Twitter, to a business that uses service as a differentiating tool to help it sell physical goods.

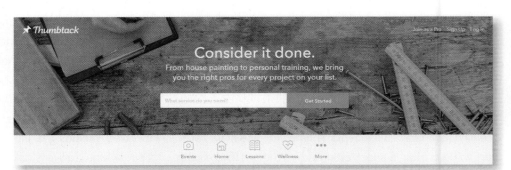

Google has invested in Thumbtack, a platform that allows customers to post their service needs and job offers, then receive bids for those jobs from service providers that have registered with the site.

Source: Thumbtack.com

E X H I B I T 13.1 The Service–Product Continuum

| Doctor | Hotel | Dry cleaners | Restaurant | Apparel specialty store | Grocery store |

Service dominant ←———————————————————————————→ Product dominant

(Doctor): ©Dynamic Graphics/JupiterImages; (Hotel): ©Jose Fuste Raga/Getty Images; (Dry cleaners): ©McGraw-Hill Education/Andrew Resek, photographer; (Restaurant): ©John A. Rizzo/Getty Images; (Apparel): ©Charles Bowman/Alamy Stock Photo; (Grocery store): ©Bill Oxford/Getty Images

Economies of developed countries such as the United States have become increasingly dependent on services. Services account for nearly 80 percent of the U.S. gross domestic product (GDP), a much higher percentage than was true 50, 20, or even 10 years ago.[4] In turn, the current list of *Fortune* 500 companies contains more service companies and fewer manufacturers than it did in previous decades.[5] This dependence and the growth of service-oriented economies in developed countries have emerged for several reasons.

First, it is generally less expensive for firms to manufacture their products in less developed countries. Even if the goods are finished in the United States, some of their components likely were produced elsewhere. In turn, the proportion of service production to goods production in the United States and other similar economies has steadily increased over time.

Second, people place a high value on convenience and leisure. For instance, household maintenance activities, which many people performed themselves in the past, have become more popular and quite specialized. Food preparation, lawn maintenance, house cleaning, pet grooming, laundry and dry cleaning, hair care, and automobile maintenance are all often performed by specialists.

Third, as the world has become more complicated, people are demanding more specialized services—everything from plumbers to personal trainers, from massage therapists to tax preparation specialists, from lawyers to travel and leisure specialists, and even to health care providers. For example, Adding Value 13.1 describes how the firm Cabin is providing a specialized travel option. The aging population in particular has increased the need for health care specialists, including doctors, nurses, and caregivers in assisted living facilities and nursing homes, and many of those consumers want their specialists to provide personalized, dedicated services.

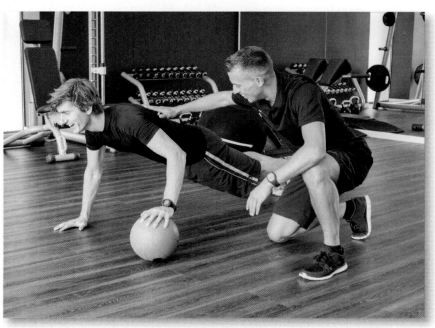

Specialized services like personal training are thriving.
©Photopat/Alamy Stock Photo

Adding Value 13.1   Hotels on Wheels: A Service Innovation[i]

With a new service, the start-up firm Cabin promises an easier travel experience. On its pilot route, from San Francisco to Santa Monica, travelers can board a double-decker bus, bunk down in their own dedicated bed chambers, and wake up at the Southern California beach, with their hotel parked in the lot.

The goal, according to the founder, is to streamline the travel process, which conventionally might involve driving to the airport, boarding a plane, and getting a ride service from the airport to a hotel, and then reversing the multi–service provider process on the way back. By combining several of these elements, Cabin hopes to appeal to travelers who want a simplified experience. But it also offers a nicer setting than conventional buses. The 24 beds on the top of each of Cabin's

double-decker buses are charming pods where people can settle in and sleep comfortably. Downstairs in the buses, Cabin offers social spaces so that travelers can interact if they prefer. Each cabin includes complementary Wi-Fi, outlets, and reading lights. Other amenities include free coffee, water, tea, and earplugs. However, none of the buses currently provide showering facilities, and they are not taking reservations for families with children under the age of 10. At a price point of about $115 between San Francisco and Santa Monica, the service is also cheaper than more conventional travel modes. Although this route is the only one currently in service, the company plans to open new routes as it grows, attracts additional funding, and buys more buses.

Cabin offers a specialized service to travelers. They travel on a double-decker bus with dedicated bed chambers.

Source: Cabin Technologies, Inc.

LO13-1 Describe how the marketing of services differs from the marketing of products.

SERVICES MARKETING DIFFERS FROM PRODUCT MARKETING

The marketing of services differs from product marketing because of the four fundamental differences involved in services: Services are intangible, inseparable, heterogeneous, and perishable.[6] (See Exhibit 13.2.) This section examines these differences and discusses how they affect marketing strategies.

Intangible

As the title of this chapter implies, the most fundamental difference between a product and a service is that services are intangible—they cannot be touched, tasted, or seen like a pure product can. When you get a physical examination, you see and hear the doctor, but the service itself is intangible. This intangibility can prove highly challenging to marketers, especially if they are more accustomed to selling. For instance, it makes it difficult to convey the

EXHIBIT 13.2 Core Differences between Services and Goods

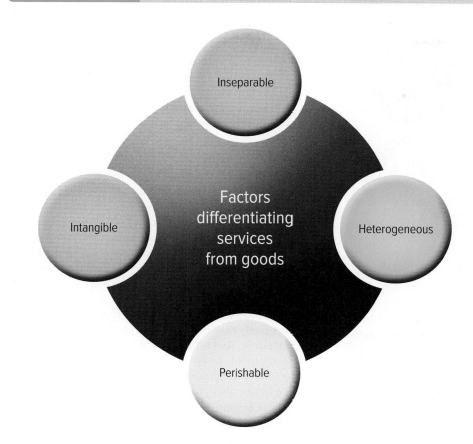

benefits of services—try describing whether the experience of visiting your dentist was good or bad and why. Service providers (e.g., physicians, dentists) therefore offer cues to help their customers experience and perceive their service more positively, such as a waiting room stocked with television sets, beverages, and comfortable chairs to create an atmosphere that appeals to the target market.

A service that cannot be shown directly to potential customers also is difficult to promote. Marketers must creatively employ symbols and images to promote and sell services, as Six Flags does in using its advertising to evoke images of happy families and friends enjoying a roller coaster ride. Professional medical services provide appropriate images of personnel doing their jobs in white coats surrounded by high-tech equipment.

Some services have found excellent ways to make their offerings more tangible to their customers. For example, Carbonite provides simple, affordable, unlimited online backup for individual home computer users as well as small businesses, for which it keeps its services, prices, and customer support well within reach. The basic rate for one home customer is $60 per year; businesses can choose from plans ranging from $270 to $600 a year to cover all company computers. Its software runs invisibly on both Macs and PCs, performing backups automatically. For portable

Because it is difficult to show a service, Six Flags evokes images in its advertising of happy families and friends enjoying a ride at one of its amusement parks.

©Ken James/Bloomberg/Getty Images

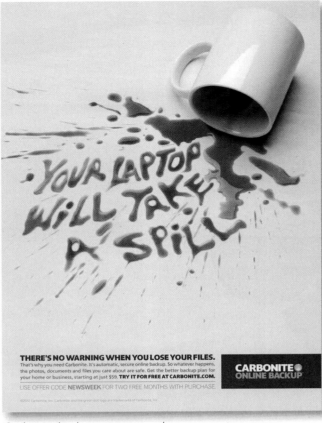

THERE'S NO WARNING WHEN YOU LOSE YOUR FILES.
That's why you need Carbonite. It's automatic, secure online backup. So whatever happens, the photos, documents and files you care about are safe. Get the better backup plan for your home or business, starting at just $59. **TRY IT FOR FREE AT CARBONITE.COM.**
USE OFFER CODE **NEWSWEEK** FOR TWO FREE MONTHS WITH PURCHASE.

**CARBONITE●
ONLINE BACKUP**

Carbonite backs up computer data on remote servers.

Source: Carbonite, Inc.

digital access, the company offers free mobile applications for Apple products as well as Android devices. In addition, it has expanded its capabilities as it has grown, such that it now helps clients in medical professions ensure the security of patients' information. As for security, all files are encrypted, stored on enterprise-grade servers, and kept in state-of-the-art data centers guarded 24 hours a day, 365 days a year. Carbonite thus has firmly established its market position by delivering a reliable, secure, easy-to-use service, combined with reasonable pricing and easily accessible technical support.[7]

Inseparable Production and Consumption

Unlike energy bars that may have been made six months prior to their purchase, services are produced and consumed at the same time; that is, service and consumption are inseparable. When getting a haircut, the customer is not only present but also may participate in the service process. Furthermore, the interaction with the service provider may have an important impact on the customer's perception of the service outcome. If the hairstylist appears to be having fun while cutting hair, it may affect the experience positively.

Because the service is inseparable from its consumption, customers rarely have the opportunity to try the service before they purchase it. And after the service has been performed, it can't be returned. Imagine telling your hairstylist that you want to have the hair around your ears trimmed as a test before he or she does your entire head. Because the purchase risk in these scenarios can be relatively high, service firms sometimes provide extended warranties and 100 percent satisfaction guarantees. The Choice Hotels chain, for instance, states: "When you choose to stay at a Comfort Inn, Comfort Suites, Quality, Clarion, or Sleep Inn hotel, we are committed to making you feel understood, welcome, and important."[8]

Heterogeneous

The more humans are needed to provide a service, the more likely there is to be heterogeneity or variability in the service's quality. A hairstylist may give bad haircuts in the morning because he or she went out the night before. Yet that stylist still may offer a better service than the undertrained stylist working in the next station over. A restaurant, which offers a mixture of services and products, generally can control its food quality but not the variability in food preparation or delivery. If a consumer has a problem with a product, it can be replaced, redone, destroyed, or, if it is already in the supply chain, recalled. In many cases, the problem can even be fixed before the product gets into consumers' hands. An inferior service can't be recalled; by the time the firm recognizes a problem, the damage has been done.

Marketers also can use the variable nature of services to their advantage. A micromarketing segmentation strategy can customize a service to meet customers' needs exactly (see Chapter 9). Exercise facilities might generally provide the same weights, machines, and mats, but at Planet Fitness, customers know that the gym explicitly seeks to offer a laid-back, less intense setting. Planet Fitness actively avoids targeting hard-core gym rats with its service offering. Instead, local storefronts offer pizza nights and bowls of free Tootsie Rolls, varying the details to match the needs and preferences of their local members. Thus each gym seeks to live up to the chain's overall promise to make going to exercise a pleasant experience rather than an intimidation festival.[9]

In an alternative approach, some service providers tackle the variability issue by replacing people with machines. For simple transactions such as getting cash, using an automated teller machine (ATM) is usually quicker and more convenient—and less variable—than

Planet Fitness' service offerings are customized to its customers' needs.
©Bernard Weil/Toronto Star via Getty Images

waiting in line for a bank teller. Many retailers have installed kiosks in their stores: In addition to offering customers the opportunity to order merchandise not available in the store, kiosks can provide routine customer service, freeing employees to deal with more demanding customer requests and problems and reducing service variability. Kiosks can also be used to automate existing store services such as gift registry management, rain checks, credit applications, and preordering service for bakeries and delicatessens.

Perishable

Services are perishable in that they cannot be stored for use in the future. You can't stockpile your membership at Planet Fitness like you could a six-pack of V8 juice, for instance. The perishability of services provides both challenges and opportunities to marketers in terms of the critical task of matching demand and supply. As long as the demand for and supply of the service match closely, there is no problem, but unfortunately this perfect matching rarely

Because services are perishable, service providers like ski areas offer less expensive tickets at night to stimulate demand.
©Buddy Mays/Corbis/Getty Images

occurs. A ski area can be open as long as there is snow, even at night, but demand peaks on weekends and holidays, so ski areas often offer less expensive tickets during off-peak periods to stimulate demand. Airlines, cruise ships, movie theaters, and restaurants confront similar challenges and attack them in similar ways.

Certainly, providing great service is not easy, and it requires a diligent effort to analyze the service process piece by piece. In the next section, we examine what is known as the Service Gaps Model, which is designed to highlight those areas where customers believe they are getting less or poorer service than they should (the gaps) and how these gaps can be closed.

PROGRESS CHECK

1. What are the four marketing elements that distinguish services from products?
2. Why can't we separate firms into just service or just product sellers?

LO13-2 Discuss the four gaps in the Service Gaps Model.

PROVIDING GREAT SERVICE: THE SERVICE GAPS MODEL

Customers have certain expectations about how a service should be delivered. When the delivery of that service fails to meet those expectations, a service gap results. The Service Gaps Model (Exhibit 13.3) is designed to encourage the systematic examination of all aspects of the service delivery process and prescribe the steps needed to develop an optimal service strategy.[10]

EXHIBIT 13.3   Service Gaps Model for Improving Retail Service Quality

Sources: Adapted from Valarie Zeithaml, A. Parasuraman, and Leonard Berry, *Delivering Quality Customer Service* (New York Free Press, 1990); Valarie Zeithaml, Leonard Berry, and A. Parasuraman, "Communication and Control Processes in the Delivery of Service Quality," *Journal of Marketing* 52, no. 2 (April 1988), pp. 35–48.

As Exhibit 13.3 shows, there are four service gaps:

1. The knowledge gap reflects the difference between customers' expectations and the firm's perception of those customer expectations. Firms can close this gap by determining what customers really want by doing research using marketing metrics such as service quality and the zone of tolerance (discussed later).

2. The standards gap pertains to the difference between the firm's perceptions of customers' expectations and the service standards it sets. By setting appropriate service standards, training employees to meet and exceed those standards, and measuring service performance, firms can attempt to close this gap.

3. The delivery gap is the difference between the firm's service standards and the actual service it provides to customers. This gap can be closed by getting employees to meet or exceed service standards when the service is being delivered by empowering service providers, providing support and incentives, and using technology where appropriate.[11]

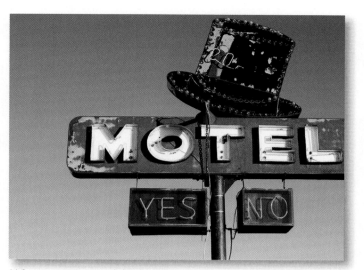

What service gaps did Marcia experience while on vacation at the motel in Maine?

©Sascha Burkard/Getty Images

4. The communication gap refers to the difference between the actual service provided to customers and the service that the firm's promotion program promises. If firms are more realistic about the services they can provide and at the same time manage customer expectations effectively, they generally can close this gap.

As we discuss the four gaps subsequently, we will apply them to the experience that Marcia Kessler had with a motel in Maine. She saw an ad for a package weekend that quoted a very reasonable daily rate and listed the free amenities available at Green Valley Motel: free babysitting services, a piano bar with a nightly singer, a free continental breakfast, a heated swimming pool, and newly decorated rooms. When she booked the room, Marcia discovered that the price advertised was not available during the weekend, and a three-day minimum stay was required. Because of the nice amenities, however, she went ahead. After checking in with a very unpleasant person at the front desk, Marcia and her husband found that their room appeared circa-1950 and had not been cleaned, so they had to wait for several hours before they could use their room. When she complained, all she got was attitude from the assistant manager. Resigned to the fact that they were slated to spend the weekend, she decided to go for a swim. Unfortunately, the water was heated by Booth Bay and stood at around 50 degrees. No one was using the babysitting services because there were few young children at the resort. It turns out the piano bar singer was the second cousin of the owner, and he couldn't carry a tune, let alone play the piano very well. The continental breakfast must have come all the way from the Continent, because everything was stale and tasteless. Marcia couldn't wait to get home.

The Knowledge Gap: Understanding Customer Expectations

An important early step in providing good service is knowing what the customer wants. It doesn't pay to invest in services that don't improve customer satisfaction. To reduce the knowledge gap, firms must understand customers' expectations. To understand those expectations, firms undertake customer research and increase the interaction and communication between managers and employees.

Customers' expectations are based on their knowledge and experiences.[12] Marcia's expectations were that her room at the motel in Maine would be ready when she got there, the swimming pool would be heated, the singer would be able to sing, and the breakfast would be fresh. Not a lot to expect, but in this extreme example, the Green Valley Motel was suffering a severe knowledge gap, perhaps based on its assumption that being on the ocean in Maine was enough. If the resort never understood her expectations, it is unlikely it would ever be able to meet them.

Expectations vary according to the type of service. Marcia's expectations might have been higher, for instance, if she were staying at a Ritz-Carlton rather than the Green Valley Motel. At the Ritz, she might have expected employees to know her by name, be aware of her dietary preferences, and to have placed fresh fruit of her choice and fresh-cut flowers in her room before she arrived. At the Green Valley Motel, she expected easy check-in/check-out, easy access to a major highway, a clean room with a comfortable bed, and a TV, at a bare minimum.

People's expectations also vary depending on the situation. If she had been traveling on business, the Green Valley Motel might have been fine (had the room at least been clean and modern), but if she were celebrating her 10th wedding anniversary, she probably would prefer the Ritz. Thus, the service provider needs to know and understand the expectations of the customers in its target market.

LO13-3 Examine the five service quality dimensions.

Evaluating Service Quality Using Well-Established Marketing Metrics To meet or exceed customers' expectations, marketers must determine what those expectations are. Yet because of their intangibility, the service quality, or customers' perceptions of how well a service meets or exceeds their expectations, is often difficult for customers to evaluate.[13] Customers generally use five distinct service dimensions to determine overall service quality: reliability, assurance, tangibles, empathy, and responsiveness (see Exhibit 13.4). The Broadmoor Hotel in Colorado Springs, Colorado, maintains its five-star rating by focusing on these five service characteristics. In operation for more than a century, the Broadmoor is one of the world's premier resorts.[14] It has received more than 50 consecutive years of five-star ratings from the Forbes Travel Guide—a record unmatched by any other hotel.[15] The aspects of its stellar service quality include:

- **Tangibles** One of the greatest challenges for the Broadmoor in recent years has been updating rooms built in the early part of the 20th century to meet the needs of 21st-century visitors. To accomplish this, it spent millions in improvements, renovating rooms, and adding a new outdoor pool complex.

- **Empathy** One approach used to demonstrate empathy is personalizing communications. Employees are instructed to always address a guest by name, if possible. To accomplish this, employees are trained to listen and observe carefully to determine a guest's name. Subtle sources for this information include convention name tags, luggage ID tags, credit cards, or checks. In addition, all phones within the Broadmoor display a guest's room number and name on a screen.

EXHIBIT 13.4 Dimensions of Service Quality

Reliability:
The ability to perform the service dependably and accurately.

Responsiveness:
The willingness to help customers and provide prompt service.

Assurance:
The knowledge of and courtesy by employees and their ability to convey trust and confidence.

Empathy:
The caring, individualized attention provided to customers.

Tangibles:
The appearance of physical facilities, equipment, personnel, and communication materials.

- **Assurance** The Broadmoor conveys trust by empowering its employees. An example of an employee empowerment policy is the service recovery program. If a guest problem arises, employees are given discretionary resources to rectify the problem or present the customer with something special to help mollify them. For example, if a meal is delivered and there's a mistake in the order or how it was prepared, a server can offer the guest a free item such as a dessert or, if the service was well below expectations, simply take care of the bill. Managers then review each situation to understand the nature of the problem and help prevent it from occurring again.

- **Responsiveness** Every employee is instructed to follow the HEART model of taking care of problems. First, employees must "Hear what a guest has to say." Second, they must "Empathize with them" and then "Apologize for the situation." Fourth, they must "Respond to the guest's needs" by "Taking action and following up."

- **Reliability** Every new Broadmoor employee, before ever encountering a customer, attends a two-and-a-half-day orientation session and receives an employee handbook. Making and keeping promises to customers is a central part of this orientation. Employees are trained always to give an estimated time for service, whether it be room service, laundry service, or simply how long it will take to be seated at one of the resort's restaurants. When an employee makes a promise, he or she keeps that promise. If they don't know the answer to a question, employees are trained to never guess. When an employee is unable to answer a question accurately, he or she immediately contacts someone who can.

Marketing research (see Chapter 10) provides a means to better understand consumers' service expectations and their perceptions of service quality. In Marketing Analytics 13.1, we describe how Kroger uses data to learn about customers' expectations. This research can be extensive and expensive, or it can be integrated into a firm's everyday interactions with customers. Today, most service firms have developed voice-of-customer programs and employ ongoing marketing research to assess how well they are meeting their customers' expectations. A systematic voice-of-customer (VOC) program collects customer inputs and integrates them into managerial decisions.

Marketing Analytics 13.1   Using Analytics to Reduce Wait Time at Kroger[ii]

Shopping for groceries is rarely considered a pleasant task. But what makes the experience so odious? As Kroger found out when it asked customers, the answer is often the long checkout lines. To help alleviate the problem, it began analyzing customer data to find an answer to a simple question: What would happen if it could open up a lane exactly when needed? The answer was that it could significantly improve customer satisfaction. So Kroger developed QueVision.

QueVision combines infrared sensors over store doors and cash registers, predictive analytics, and real-time data feeds from point-of-sale systems to calculate how many registers are needed and what the actual wait times are, all in real time. Wait times appear on a screen at the front of the store. The overall goal of the combined system is to ensure there is never more than one person ahead of any shopper in the checkout line.

This technology has been so successful that it has cut the average wait time for customers from more than 4 minutes to less than 30 seconds. QueVision also has had some unexpected positive consequences, in the form of happier employees. Friendly associates are really important for defining customer-oriented metrics. Although the math might not have predicted it, the cashier friendliness metric, as measured by customer surveys, has improved throughout the company by approximately 24 percent. Shorter lines make customers happy, and when employees encounter happy customers,

Grocery shoppers really hate long checkout lines, so Kroger developed a system to calculate how many registers are needed and what the actual wait times are, all in real time.

©Zuma Press, Inc/Alamy Stock Photo

they're happier too. Kroger also uses its QueVision data in more detailed simulations. It has correlated enough data to keep people moving in the front of stores, including checkout lines, even in stores with unusual layouts. QueVision data also have helped Kroger evaluate new shopping systems, such as self-checkout.

LO13-4 Explain the zone of tolerance.

An important marketing metric to evaluate how well firms perform on the five service quality dimensions (again see Exhibit 13.4) is the zone of tolerance, which refers to the area between customers' expectations regarding their desired service and the minimum level of acceptable service—that is, the difference between what the customer really wants and what he or she will accept before going elsewhere. To define the zone of tolerance, firms ask a series of questions about each service quality dimension that relate to

- The desired and expected level of service for each dimension, from low to high.
- Customers' perceptions of how well the focal service performs and how well a competitive service performs, from low to high.
- The importance of each service quality dimension.

Exhibit 13.5 illustrates the results of such an analysis for Lou's Local Diner, a family-owned restaurant. The rankings on the left are based on a nine-point scale, on which 1 is low and 9 is high. The length of each box illustrates the zone of tolerance for each service quality dimension. For instance, according to the short length of the reliability box, customers expect a fairly high level of reliability (top of the box) and will accept only a fairly high level of reliability (bottom of the box). On the other end of the scale, customers expect a high level of assurance (top of the box) but will also accept a fairly low level (bottom of the box). This difference is to be expected because the customers also were asked to assign an importance score to the five service quality dimensions so that the total equals 100 percent (see bottom of Exhibit 13.5). Looking at the average importance score, we conclude that reliability is relatively important to these customers but assurance is not. So customers have a fairly narrow zone of tolerance for service dimensions that are fairly important to them and a wider range of tolerance for those service dimensions that are less important. Also note that Lou's Local Diner always rates higher than its primary competitor, Square Burger, a national chain, on each dimension.

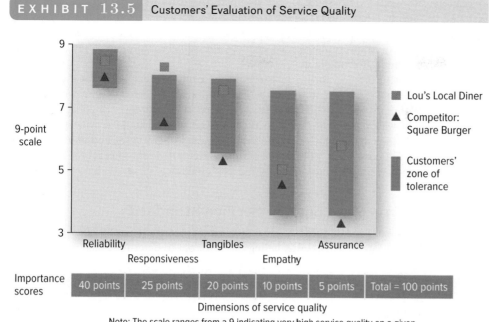

EXHIBIT 13.5 Customers' Evaluation of Service Quality

Note: The scale ranges from a 9 indicating very high service quality on a given service quality dimension to a 1 indicating very low service quality.

Further note that Square Burger scores below the zone of tolerance on the tangibles dimension, meaning that customers are not willing to accept the way the restaurant looks and smells. Lou's Local Diner, in contrast, performs above the zone of tolerance on the responsiveness dimension—maybe even too well. Lou's may wish to conduct further research to verify which responsiveness aspects it is performing so well, and then consider toning down those aspects. For example, being responsive to customers' desires to have a diner that serves breakfast 24 hours a day can be expensive and may not add any further value to Lou's Diner because customers would accept more limited times.

A very straightforward and inexpensive method of collecting consumers' perceptions of service quality is to gather them at the time of the sale. Service providers can ask customers how they liked the service—though customers often are reticent to provide negative feedback directly to the person who provided the service—or distribute a simple questionnaire. Regardless of how information is collected, companies must take care not to lose it, which can happen if there is no effective mechanism for filtering it up to the key decision makers. Furthermore, in some cases, customers cannot effectively evaluate the service until several days or weeks later. Automobile dealers, for instance, often call their customers a week after they perform a service such as an oil change to assess their service quality.

Another excellent method for assessing customers' expectations is making effective use of customer complaint behavior. Even if complaints are handled effectively to solve

Lou's Local Diner always rates higher than its primary competitor, Square Burger, on each service quality dimension.

©McGraw-Hill Education/Gideon Kindall, photographer

customers' problems, the essence of the complaint is too often lost on managers. For instance, an airline established a policy that customer service reps could not discuss any issues involving fees to travel agents with customers. So when a customer calls to complain about these fees, the representative just changes the subject, and management therefore never finds out about the complaint.

Even firms with the best formal research mechanisms in place must put managers on the frontlines occasionally to interact directly with the customers. The late Sam Walton, founder of Walmart, participated in and advocated this strategy, which is known as "management by walking around."[16] Unless the managers who make the service quality decisions know what their service providers are facing on a day-to-day basis, and unless they can talk directly to the customers with whom those service providers interact, any customer service program they create will not be as good as it could be.

The Standards Gap: Setting Service Standards

Getting back to the Green Valley Motel in Maine for a moment, suppose because of a number of complaints or because business was falling off, it set out to determine customers' service expectations and gained a pretty good idea of them. The next step would be to set its service standards accordingly and develop systems to meet the customers' service expectations. How, for instance, can it make sure that every room is cleaned and ready by an optimum time of day in the eyes of the customers, or that the breakfast is checked for freshness and quality every day? To consistently deliver service that meets customers' expectations, firms must set specific, measurable goals. For the Green Valley Motel, the most efficient process might have been to start cleaning rooms at 8:00 a.m. and finish by 5:00 p.m. But many guests want to sleep late, and new arrivals want to get into their room as soon as they arrive, often before 5:00 p.m. So a customer-oriented standard would mandate that the rooms get cleaned between 10:00 a.m. and 2:00 p.m.

Service providers generally want to do a good job as long as they know what is expected of them. Motel employees should be shown, for instance, exactly how managers expect them to clean a room and what specific tasks they are responsible for performing. In general, more employees will buy into a quality-oriented process if they are involved in setting the goals. For instance, suppose an important employee of the motel objects to disposable plastic cups and suggests that actual drinking glasses in the rooms would be classier as well as more ecological. There might be a cost–benefit trade-off to consider here, but if management listens to her and makes the change in this case, it should likely make the employee all the more committed to other tasks involved in cleaning and preparing rooms.

The employees must be thoroughly trained not only to complete their specific tasks but also how to treat guests, and the manager needs to set an example of high service standards, which will permeate throughout the organization. The kind of attitude Marcia got, for instance, when she registered a complaint with the assistant manager at the Green Valley Motel is not a recipe for generating repeat customers and should not be tolerated. For frontline service employees under stress, however, pleasant interactions with customers do not always come naturally. Although people can be taught specific tasks related to their jobs, this is not easily extended to interpersonal relations. But it is simply not enough to tell employees to be nice or do what customers want. A quality goal should be specific, such as: Greet every customer/guest you encounter with "Good morning/afternoon/evening, Sir or Ma'am." Try to greet customers by name.

Service providers, like this room service delivery person at a hotel, generally want to do a good job, but they need to be trained to know what exactly a good job entails.

©Chris Ryan/OJO Images/Getty Images

The Delivery Gap: Delivering Service Quality

The delivery gap is where the rubber meets the road, where the customer directly interacts with the service provider. Even if there are adequate standards in place, the employees are well trained, and management is committed to meeting or exceeding customers' service expectations, there can still be delivery gaps. It could very well have been that Marcia experienced several delivery gaps at the Green Valley Motel. It could have been that the unclean room, the assistant manager's attitude, the unheated swimming pool, the poor piano bar singer, or the stale food resulted from unforeseen or unusual circumstances. Although some of these issues such as an unclean room or the attitude Marcia encountered should have been avoided, it is possible that the motel had a power outage resulting in the unheated swimming pool, the regular piano bar singer was ill, and the breakfast was stale because of a missed delivery. The maid could not vacuum the room because of the lack of power, and the assistant manager felt assaulted on all sides by these problems. But the result was a lost customer. Even if there are no other gaps, a delivery gap always results in a service failure.

Delivery gaps can be reduced when employees are empowered to spontaneously act in the customers' and the firm's best interests when problems or crises are experienced. Such empowerment might have saved the day for Marcia and the Green Valley Motel. Empowerment means employees are supported in their efforts to do their jobs effectively.[17]

Empowering Service Providers In the service context, empowerment means allowing employees to make decisions about how service is provided to customers. When frontline employees are authorized to make decisions to help their customers, service quality generally improves. Empowerment becomes more important when the service is more individualized. Nordstrom provides an overall objective—satisfy customer needs—and then encourages employees to do whatever is necessary to achieve the objective. For example, a Nordstrom shoe sales associate decided to break up two pairs of shoes, one a size 10 and the other a size 10½, to sell to a hard-to-fit customer. Although the other two shoes were unsalable and therefore it made for an unprofitable sale, the customer purchased five other pairs that day and became a loyal Nordstrom customer as a result. Empowering service providers with only a rule like "Use your best judgment" (as Nordstrom does) might cause chaos. At Nordstrom, department managers avoid abuses by coaching and training salespeople to understand what "Use your best judgment" specifically means.

Support and Incentives for Employees To ensure that service is delivered properly, management needs to support the service providers in several ways and give them incentives. This is basic. A service provider's job can often be difficult, especially when customers are unpleasant or less than reasonable. But the service provider cannot be rude or offensive just because the customer is. The old cliché "Service with a smile" remains the best approach, but for this to work, employees must feel supported.

First, managers and coworkers should provide emotional support to service providers by demonstrating a concern for their well-being and standing behind their decisions. Because it can be very disconcerting when, for instance, a server is abused by a customer who believes her food was improperly prepared, restaurant managers must be supportive and help the employee get through his or her emotional reaction to the berating experienced.[18] Such support can extend to empowering the server to rectify the situation by giving the customer new food and a free dessert, in which case the manager must understand the server's decision, not punish him for giving away too much.

Second, service providers require instrumental support—the systems and equipment to deliver the service properly. Many retailers provide state-of-the-art instrumental support for their service providers. In-store kiosks help sales associates provide more detailed and complete product information and enable them to make sales of merchandise that is either not carried in the store or is temporarily out of stock.

Third, the support that managers provide must be consistent and coherent throughout the organization. Patients expect physicians to provide great patient care using state-of-the-art procedures and medications, but because they are tied to managed-care systems (health maintenance organizations [HMOs]), many doctors must squeeze more people into their office hours and prescribe less optimal, less expensive courses of treatment. These conflicting goals can be very frustrating to patients.

Finally, a key part of any customer service program is providing rewards to employees for their excellent service. Numerous firms have developed a service reputation by ensuring that its employees are themselves recognized for recognizing the value the firm places on customer service. The tech company Motley Fool, which offers financial services advice through its website, podcasts, books, and more, uses a unique peer-to-peer employee recognition system. Employees can send "gold" to coworkers who they feel deserve a shout-out. Gold can be given for activities such as helping to develop new services. Employees can then use the gold that they've collected to redeem prizes such as gift cards and travel experiences. Furthermore, Motley Fool has an in-house YouEarnedIt live feed that allows employees to read all the peer-to-peer compliments in real time. Through this program employees reward each other about 35 times a day.[19]

Use of Technology As our chapter opener highlighted, technology has become an increasingly important facilitator for delivering services. Using technology to facilitate service delivery can provide many benefits, such as access to a wider variety of services, a greater degree of control by the customer over the services, and the ability to easily obtain information. Technological advances that help close the delivery gap are expanding. To illustrate, consider Adding Value 13.2 in which we examine how virtual reality is used to help customers get a real sense of a particular experience they are likely to have.

As we discussed in Chapter 5, various markets are being irrevocably altered by the introduction of advanced technologies, including self-service, virtual reality, holograms, and robots. The implications for providing customer service are especially notable. Markets for service robots, for example, are expected to be worth more than $1.5 billion within a few years.[20] The integration of these technologies into service settings, in turn, alters the elements that distinguish services from products. For example, when an automated agent provides the service, it may be less inherently heterogeneous than is the case when humans provide it.[21]

A straightforward way to think about how such advanced technologies are likely to affect the marketing of services in the future is to distinguish them along two dimensions: more traditional interactions with humans, such as with a frontline service person, and interaction with technology, such as a computer or a robot.[22] Combining these two dimensions produces the four-cell matrix shown in Exhibit 13.6.

Each quadrant represents a different type of service interaction. *the Low Tech, Low Effort quadrant* represents traditional service delivery technologies provided by ATMs,

EXHIBIT 13.6 How Technology Is Augmenting the Human Effort

High human effort

Low Tech, High Effort
Skype

High Tech, High Effort
Doctors working with a robot to remotely deliver service

Low technology ⟷ High technology

Low Tech, Low Effort
ATMs
Self-service kiosks

High Tech, Low Effort
Humanoid robots

Low human effort

Adding Value 13.2 — Take a Virtual "Test Drive" before Booking Your Next Trip[iii]

Virtual reality devices and 360-degree videos are quickly becoming widely popular, prompting a variety of players in a wide range of industries to move forward in adopting related technologies as part of their marketing efforts. A particularly prominent example of an industry that has aggressively pursued uses of such technology is the travel industry.

In virtual "test drives" of resorts, events, tourist attractions, and destinations, tourism brands have sought to help generate travelers' interest and boost tourism to the area. From Thailand to Las Vegas, national and local tourism authority organizations realize the value of developing immersive videos that can highlight the beauty of the location and the fun that can be had.

For example, the Tourism Authority of Thailand has capitalized on the country's popular elephant sanctuaries by developing four 360-degree videos that allow users to tour the facilities virtually and see the massive animals as they move about their enclosures. Tourism of Australia also has developed multiple 360-degree films highlighting various aquatic and coastal travel experiences, allowing virtual visitors to enjoy stunning views of the Great Barrier Reef—without ever coming anywhere close to a crocodile! The Las Vegas Convention and Visitors Authority focuses on a different kind of animal: the human sights and sounds captured in 30 different 360-degree videos that simulate drives down the famous Las Vegas Boulevard.

Beyond the tourism agencies, independent airlines and hotels are adopting the technology too. United Airlines has created virtual reality demonstrations showcasing its upscale Polaris business class service. Travelers can virtually tour the space while sitting in special booths set up in the carrier's domestic hubs around the nation.

Marriott Hotels' special "teleporter" booths can be used by guests to view virtual reality destinations accessible from other Marriott Hotels across the globe. It also is initiating a social media blitz of virtual reality videos in a series it calls "In the Moment" to highlight select properties and the "Once-in-a-Lifetime" events that the hotel brand offers to the top members of its reward program. With such virtual access it encourages consumer interest but also offers a recommendation that they become members of its loyalty program, which might enable them to experience the terrific events in person someday.

Even budget-friendly Best Western has gotten in on the action. The company uses Google Street View technology to create 360-degree videos that allow users to tour each of the firm's 2,000 locations. And in Topeka, Kansas, the Evel Knievel Museum enables visitors to experience the daredevil's death-defying stunts without ever putting their lives in danger. Sitting on an actual Harley-Davidson like Knievel's, they can strap on a virtual reality helmet and feel the massive adrenaline rush simulated by the feeling of jumping a line of 18 police cars.

Although not quite as fun as (but still a lot safer than) being there in person, the ability to test drive a property, experience, or location allows consumers to gather more information before deciding where to book their next vacation and what to do once they get there. These new forays into the virtual reality space also allow companies in the travel industry to expand their reach and entice prospective clients.

The Las Vegas Convention and Visitors Authority seeks to attract visitors with 360-degree videos that simulate drives down the famous Las Vegas Boulevard.

©Az Jackson/Getty Images

self-service kiosks, or self-scanning devices, where the effort provided by both humans and technology are low. Accordingly, the inseparability of production and consumption becomes less prominent (refer back to Exhibit 13.2); an ATM can make the cash available at any time, not just when the bank is open.

The Low Tech, High Effort quadrant defines situations in which humans are strongly present, but the role of technology is less so, such as when a patient chats with a medical professional through Skype. The technology facilitates the interaction and can address some of the challenges of service intangibility (again refer back to Exhibit 13.2) by making access to human providers easier.

In contrast, *the High Tech, Low Effort quadrant* describes situations in technology is extremely prominent, but less human effort is required. In this case, the technology

Social & Mobile Marketing 13.1

When Getting It Right Isn't Quite as Fun as Getting It Wrong: The Starbucks Ordering App and the Names on Cups[iv]

When Starbucks introduced its mobile ordering app, there was lots of commentary about what it meant for consumers. They could avoid long lines, specify exactly the drink they wanted, and pop in and out of the store without worrying about being late. In addition, baristas could work more efficiently, balancing out the in-person orders with the printed orders to get drinks ready quickly and accurately.

But there has been another outcome that we might not have predicted. The mobile app allows consumers to type in their names. In stores, the printed label then reproduces those names exactly, so no matter how unusual the spelling of your name, it is going to appear correctly on the cup. That should be a good thing—the company is getting something right. But more and more customers are complaining that they miss the "good old days" when baristas made wild guesses at how to spell their names, then wrote various versions by hand, often with a smiley face or question mark when the name was really tough.

In a way, the errors were part of the fun. There was a game element, as people waited to see just what spelling would appear when their coffee was ready, as well as what pronunciation the barista who had made their latte or mocha would come up with when calling out their names to announce that the drink was ready.

The nostalgia for incorrect name spellings might signal something a little more though. Starbucks has long established itself as a "third place," beyond work or home, where customers could stop and visit for a while, interacting with other customers but also with friendly baristas who even might come to seem like pals. The mobile app eliminates this interaction for the most part. Even if a barista acknowledges a customer who pops in to pick up a preordered drink, their interaction is brief and less personalized. Furthermore, while the mobile app has successfully reduced the length of the queues of coffee drinkers waiting to order, it has increased crowding at the pick-up counter.

For Starbucks, another key question is whether customers ordering through the mobile app spend more or less than those who stand in line to place their orders. In the stores,

Starbucks' success, in part, is based on personal customer service. Although its mobile ordering app is efficient and therefore appeals to both Starbucks and many of its customers, it isn't as personal. Some customers miss the old days when baristas wrote misspelled names on the cups, followed by a smiley face.

©Ronald Martinez/Getty Images

customers are exposed to appealing music playing, such that they might grab the CDs available for sale at the counter. They also might be unable to resist the allure of a pastry or find themselves reminded to grab a bag of coffee beans for home. Such impulse buys may be less likely for customers in a rush, who are trying to get their mobile order as fast as possible. But Starbucks also notes that the mobile app avoids the losses of sales that occurred when busy consumers simply avoided buying anything when faced with long lines at their local shop.

And for every "Eugenia" who misses the fun of seeing her name spelled "Ogenia" or "Ugena," there is a "Sathyarajkumar" who long ago gave up on the idea of having his full name written with any accuracy but still found it frustrating that baristas could not even spell his nickname "Raj" correctly.

deliberately and effectively engages with the consumer. This quadrant includes service technologies like interacting with humanoid service robots, which already appear in some hospitality settings. For example, various hotel chains have added robotic concierges that can answer guests' questions, provide recommendations for nearby restaurants, or deliver room service requests to guests' rooms.[23]

Finally, *the High Tech, High Effort quadrant* represents situations in which both human effort and technology are critical. In these cases, advanced technologies meaningfully supplement people's abilities to provide services. These applications currently appear to be most promising in health care settings, where human doctors can rely on robotic and virtual technologies to reduce the chances of mistakes or process more information, such that together they provide optimal service levels.

Although technological advances can help close the delivery gap, they can cause problems as well. Some customers either do not embrace the idea of replacing a human with a machine for business interactions or have problems using the technology, such as supermarket self-checkout devices that are too challenging for some customers. In other cases, the technology may not perform adequately, such as ATMs that run out of money or are out of order. And for Starbucks, the technology works well but still creates some new challenges, as Social & Mobile Marketing 13.1 explains.

The Communication Gap: Communicating the Service Promise

Poor communication between marketers and their customers can result in a mismatch between an ad campaign's or a salesperson's promises and the service the firm can actually offer. Although firms have difficulty controlling service quality because it can vary from day to day and provider to provider, they have nearly constant control over how they communicate their service package to their customers.

If a firm promises more than it can deliver, customers' expectations won't be met. An advertisement may lure a customer into a service situation once, but if the service doesn't deliver on the promise, the customer will never return. Dissatisfied customers also are likely to tell others about the underperforming service using word of mouth or, increasingly, social media, which have become important channels for dissatisfied customers to vent their frustrations.

The communication gap can be reduced by managing customer expectations and by promising only what you can deliver, or possibly even a little less. Suppose you need an operation, and the surgeon explains, "You'll be out of the hospital in five days and back to your normal routine in a month." You have the surgery and feel well enough to leave the hospital three days later. Two weeks after that, you're playing tennis again. Clearly, you will tend to think your surgeon is a genius. However, regardless of the operation's success, if you had to stay in the hospital for 10 days and it took you two months to recover, you would undoubtedly be upset.

A relatively easy way to manage customer expectations is to coordinate how the expectation is created and the way the service is provided. Expectations typically are created through promotions, advertising, or personal selling. Delivery is another function altogether. If a salesperson promises a client that an order can be delivered in one day, and that delivery actually takes a week, the client will be disappointed. However, if the salesperson coordinates the order with those responsible for the service delivery, the client's expectations likely will be met. As Adding Value 13.3 details, when customers' expectations are exceeded, it can lead to benefits for everyone involved.

Customer expectations can be managed when the service is delivered. Recorded messages tell customers who have phoned a company with a query how many minutes they will have to wait before the next operator is available. Sellers automatically inform online customers of any items that are out of stock. Whether online or in a store, retailers can warn their customers to shop early during a sale because supplies of the sale item are limited. People are generally reasonable when they are warned that some aspect of the service may be below their expectations. They just don't like surprises!

Service Quality and Customer Satisfaction and Loyalty

Good service quality leads to satisfied and loyal customers. As we discussed in Chapter 6, customers inevitably wind up their purchase decision process by undertaking a postpurchase evaluation. This evaluation after the purchase may produce three outcomes: satisfaction, dissonance, and loyalty (see again Exhibit 6.3 in Chapter 6). Dissonance may just

Nordstrom consistently is ranked at the top of customer satisfaction surveys.
©Ben Nelms/Bloomberg via Getty Images

Adding Value 13.3   Luxury Resorts Partner with Auto Manufacturers to Provide a Ride to Remember[v]

Need a ride? Check in to one of the top hotels or resorts in the nation and you may find a luxury car waiting for you. High-end automobile brands such as Lexus, Rolls-Royce, Cadillac, BMW, Mercedes-Benz, and Audi have entered into new and creative agreements with hotels across the country. The automakers loan out a small number of vehicles to the hotel at no cost, and the resorts have a new perk that they can offer guests, in the form of luxury car service or a free car to use for short trips.

With the growing prevalence of such programs, hotels and resorts even can choose a brand and product line that aligns with their property or values. For example, hotels that promote ecotourism or health spas that highlight a connection with nature might request a loan of hybrid vehicles. Resorts in Aspen or other mountainous regions can request sport-utility vehicles, built to perform well even in the most challenging conditions.

The demands from the car companies are typically minor: The hotel must keep the cars visible, promote them to guests, and require drivers to sign a liability waiver. In exchange, the hotels do not have to spend any money needed to purchase vehicles directly for guest-related services.

The benefits to automakers are easy to identify. Each guest who rides in or drives one of the luxury cars is a potential customer, who is in essence taking a test drive while in the happy mood that resort vacations seek to encourage. The automakers' strategic efforts lead them to pursue partnerships mainly with resorts that are likely to attract guests with the income necessary to make luxury car purchases.

Many automobile manufacturers prefer to let the cars speak for themselves, but some have expanded the services offered through the resort, to promote greater interactions with guests. For example, BMW offers a special short-term program, the Resort Driving Tour. Each year, it brings its newest models to resorts during peak season and allows extended test drives. After a six- or eight-week period, the cars disappear from the site, so travelers who miss the tour are out of luck. Audi takes a slightly different approach, seeking to create long-term relationships with each driver, such that it sends written thank-you notes after every experience. The note also contains an offer that can be used on future Audi purchases.

But perhaps the real winners of these experimental new partnerships between hotels and automakers are consumers. For no fee, hotel guests can get where they need to go near their vacation spot, while also living out their dreams of riding in a chauffeur-driven Rolls-Royce or taking in the sights from a sporty coupe. For luxury car lovers, this increasingly popular perk can make any vacation a trip to remember.

Hoteliers interested in exceeding customer expectations offer a luxury car service or a free car to guests to use for short trips.

©J.W.Alker/picture-alliance/dpa/AP Images

be a passing emotion that is overcome; we will discuss recovery from an actual service failure in the next section. Satisfaction, on the other hand, often leads to loyalty.

Assuming that none of the service gaps that we have discussed occur, or at least are not too wide, customers should be more or less satisfied. Surveys of customers that ask them to identify the retailer that provides the best customer service thus often show some consistency. A service provider that does a good job one year is likely to keep customers satisfied the next year too. Some of the best service providers year after year include Amazon, Zappos, L.L.Bean, and Nordstrom.

If a firm not only minimizes but also eliminates any service gaps, customers are likely to exhibit significant loyalty to it. Customers want to continue receiving such superior service and have no desire to go elsewhere for the offerings it provides them.

PROGRESS CHECK

1. Explain the four service gaps identified by the Service Gaps Model.
2. List at least two ways to overcome each of the four service gaps.

SERVICE RECOVERY

LO13-5 Identify three service recovery strategies.

Despite a firm's best efforts, sometimes service providers fail to meet customer expectations. When this happens, the best course of action is to attempt to make amends with the customer and learn from the experience. Of course, it is best to avoid a service failure altogether, but when a failure does occur, the firm has a unique opportunity to demonstrate its customer commitment. Effective service recovery efforts can significantly increase customer satisfaction, purchase intentions, and positive word of mouth, though customers' postrecovery satisfaction levels usually fall lower than their satisfaction level prior to the service failure.

Remember the Green Valley Motel in Maine? It could have made amends with Marcia Kessler after its service failures if it had taken some relatively simple, immediate steps: The assistant manager could have apologized for his bad behavior and quickly upgraded her to a suite and/or given her a free night's lodging for a future stay. The motel could also have given her a free lunch or dinner to make up for the bad breakfast. Alternatively, the assistant manager could have asked Marcia how he could resolve the situation and worked with her to come up with an equitable solution. None of these actions would have cost the motel much money.

Had it used the customer lifetime value approach we described in Chapter 10, the motel would have realized that by not taking action, it lost Marcia as a customer forever. Over the next few years, she could have been responsible for several thousand dollars in sales. Instead, Marcia is now likely to spread negative word of mouth about the motel to her friends, family, and through online review sites, such as Yelp.com, because of its failure to recover. Effective service recovery thus demands (1) listening to the customers and involving them in the service recovery, (2) providing a fair solution, and (3) resolving the problem quickly.[24]

Listening to the Customers and Involving Them in the Service Recovery

Firms often don't find out about service failures until a customer complains. Whether the firm has a formal complaint department or the complaint is offered directly to the service provider, the customer must have the opportunity to air the complaint completely, and the firm must listen carefully to what he or she is saying.

Customers can become very emotional about a service failure, whether the failure is serious (a botched surgical operation) or minor (the wrong change at a restaurant). In many cases, the customer may just want to be heard, and the service provider should give the customer all the time he or she needs to get it out. The very process of describing a perceived wrong to a sympathetic listener or on social media is therapeutic in and of itself. Service providers therefore should welcome the opportunity to be that sympathetic ear, listen carefully, and appear (and actually be) eager to rectify the situation to ensure it doesn't happen again.[25]

When the company and the customer work together, the outcome is often better than either could achieve on their own. This cocreation logic applies especially well to service recovery. A service failure is a negative experience, but when customers participate in its resolution, it results in a more positive outcome than simply listening to their complaint and providing a preapproved set of potential solutions that may satisfy them.

Suppose, for instance, that when you arrived at the airport in San Francisco, your flight had been overbooked and you were bumped. Of course, good customer service required the ticket agent to listen to your frustration and help provide a fair solution. But the most obvious potential solution from the airline's perspective might not have been the best solution for you. It might have been inclined to put you on the next available flight, which would be a red-eye that left at midnight and got you to New York at 6:30 a.m. But if you don't sleep well on planes and you have an important business meeting the next afternoon, the best solution from your perspective would be to have the airline put you up in an airport hotel so you can get a good night's sleep and then put you on an early morning flight that would get you to New York in time for your meeting, well-rested and ready to go. Thus, by working closely with you to understand your needs, the ticket agent would be able to cocreate a great solution to the service failure.

Finding a Fair Solution

Most people realize that mistakes happen. But when they happen, customers want to be treated fairly, whether that means *distributive* or *procedural* fairness.[26] Their perception of what "fair" means is based on their previous experience with other firms, how they have seen other customers treated, material they have read, and stories recounted by their friends.

Distributive Fairness Distributive fairness pertains to a customer's perception of the benefits he or she received compared with the costs (inconvenience or loss). Customers want to be compensated a fair amount for a perceived loss that resulted from a service failure. If, for instance, a person arrives at the airport gate and finds her flight is overbooked, she may believe that taking the next flight that day and receiving a travel voucher is adequate compensation for the inconvenience. But if no flights are available until the next day, the traveler may require additional compensation, such as overnight accommodations, meals, and a round-trip ticket to be used at a later date.[27]

The key to distributive fairness, of course, is listening carefully to the customer. One customer, traveling on vacation, may be satisfied with a travel voucher, whereas another may need to get to the destination on time because of a business appointment. Regardless of how the problem is solved, customers typically want tangible restitution—in this case, to get to their destination—not just an apology. If providing tangible restitution isn't possible, the next best thing is to assure the customer that steps are being taken to prevent the failure from recurring.

Procedural Fairness With regard to complaints, procedural fairness refers to the perceived fairness of the process used to resolve them. Customers want efficient complaint procedures over whose outcomes they have some influence. Customers tend to believe they have been treated fairly if the service providers follow specific company guidelines. Nevertheless, rigid adherence to rules can have deleterious effects. Have you ever returned an item to a store, even a very inexpensive item, and been told that the return needed a manager's approval? The process likely took several minutes and irritated everyone in the checkout line. Furthermore, most managers' cursory inspection of the item or the situation would not catch a fraudulent return. In a case like this, the procedure the company uses to handle a return probably overshadows any potential positive outcomes. Therefore, as we noted previously, service providers should be empowered with some procedural flexibility to solve customer complaints.

A no-questions-asked return policy has been offered as a customer service by many retailers such as L.L.Bean. But because of its high cost as a result of customers abusing the policy, many retailers such as L.L.Bean's competitor REI have modified their return policies.[28] Some large retailers now limit their returns to 90 days, considered a reasonable amount of time for customers to return an item. Others will grant only a store credit based on the lowest selling price for the item if the customer doesn't have a receipt. In addition, for some consumer electronics products that have been opened, customers must pay a 15 percent restocking fee.

Resolving Problems Quickly

The longer it takes to resolve a service failure, the more irritated the customer will become and the more people he or she is likely to tell about the problem. To resolve service failures quickly, firms need clear policies, adequate training for their employees, and empowered employees. Health insurance companies, for instance, have made a concerted effort in recent years to avoid service failures that occur because customers' insurance claims have not been handled quickly or to the customers' satisfaction.

PROGRESS CHECK

1. Why is service recovery so important to companies?
2. What can companies do to recover from a service failure?

Reviewing Learning Objectives

LO13-1 **Describe how the marketing of services differs from the marketing of products.**

Unlike products, services are intangible, inseparable, variable, and perishable. They cannot be seen or touched, which makes it difficult to describe their benefits or promote them. Service providers therefore enhance service delivery with tangible attributes, like a nice atmosphere or price benefits. Services get produced and consumed at the same time, so marketers must work quickly, and they are more variable than products, though service providers attempt to reduce this variability as much as possible. Finally, because consumers cannot stockpile perishable services, marketers often provide incentives to stagger demand.

LO13-2 **Discuss the four gaps in the Service Gaps Model.**

The knowledge gap reflects the difference between customers' expectations and the firm's perception of those customer expectations. Firms need to match customer expectations with actual service through research. The standards gap is the difference between the firm's perceptions of customers' expectations and the service standards it sets. Appropriate service standards and measurements of service performance help close this gap. The delivery gap is the difference between the firm's service standards and the actual service it provides to customers. Closing this gap requires adequate training and empowerment of employees. The communication gap refers to the difference between the actual service provided to customers and the service that the firm's promotion program promises. Firms close the communication gap by managing customer expectations and promising only what they can deliver.

LO13-3 **Examine the five service quality dimensions.**

First, tangibles are the elements that go along with the service, such as the magazines in a doctor's waiting room. Second, empathy entails the provider's recognition and understanding of consumer needs. Third, assurance reflects the service provider's own confidence in its abilities. Fourth, responsiveness means that the provider notes consumers' desires and requests and then addresses them. Fifth, reliability refers to whether the provider consistently provides an expected level of service.

LO13-4 **Explain the zone of tolerance.**

The area between customers' desired service and the minimum level of service they will accept is the zone of tolerance. It is the difference between what the customer really wants and what he or she will accept before going elsewhere. Firms can assess their customers' zone of tolerance by determining the desired and expected level of service for each service dimension, their perceptions of how well the focal service performs and how well a competitive service performs, and the importance of each service quality dimension.

LO13-5 **Identify three service recovery strategies.**

In a best-case scenario, the service never fails. But some failures are inevitable and require the firm to make amends to the customer by (1) listening carefully and involving the customer in the service recovery; (2) finding a fair solution to the problem that compensates the customer for the failure and follows procedures the customer believes are fair; and (3) resolving the problem quickly.

Key Terms

- communication gap, 403
- customer service, 396
- delivery gap, 403
- distributive fairness, 416
- emotional support, 409
- empowerment, 409
- heterogeneity, 400

- inseparable, 400
- instrumental support, 409
- intangible, 398
- knowledge gap, 403
- perishable, 401
- procedural fairness, 416
- service, 396

- service gap, 402
- Service Gaps Model, 402
- service quality, 404
- standards gap, 403
- voice-of-customer (VOC) program, 405
- zone of tolerance, 406

Marketing Digitally

1. What services does Zipcar offer? Go to Zipcar's website (www.zipcar.com) and click on "Getting Started." Evaluate how quick it is to reserve a car in a major city or at a university that has a dedicated Zipcar car pickup/dropoff location.

2. Go to Zappos' website (www.zappos.com) and examine its customer service offerings. Next, go to Reseller Ratings, www.resellerratings.com, and look up Zappos. Based on these reviews, does Zappos have a service gap? If so, how can the company close it?

Marketing Applications

1. Those companies from which you purchase products and services are not pure sellers of services, nor are they pure sellers of products. What services does Home Depot provide? What goods does a health club provide?

2. You have been sitting in the waiting room of your mechanic's shop for more than an hour. With the knowledge that products are different from services, develop a list of the things the shop manager could do to improve the overall service delivery. Consider how the shop might overcome problems associated with the tangibility, separability, heterogeneity, and perishability of services.

3. You have conducted a zone of tolerance analysis for your local pizza restaurant. You find that the lengths of the reliability and responsiveness boxes are much greater than those of the other three service quality dimensions. You also find that the restaurant is positioned above the zone box on reliability but below the box on responsiveness. What should you tell the manager to do?

4. Assume you were hired by the local grocery store to help assess its service quality. How would you go about undertaking this project?

5. What should a restaurant server do when faced with an irate customer who has received undercooked food after a long wait? How can he or she avoid a service failure by being empowered?

6. What types of support and incentives could your university provide advisers to help make them more attentive to students' needs?

7. What mobile apps do you use that help facilitate your transactions with a specific retailer or service provider?

Would you rather use the apps or engage in a face-to-face relationship with a person? How, if at all, would your parents' answer to these two questions differ?

8. A local health club is running a promotional campaign that promises you can lose an inch a month off your waist if you join the club and follow its program. How might this claim cause a communication gap? What should the club do to avoid a service failure?

9. Think about a recent service encounter that you've had when you were dissatisfied with the service quality. What actions did you take? If you complained, what was the result? Was this a satisfactory result for you? If so, why, and if not, how could the service provider have done a better job? If you did not complain, why not? Why do you think consumers choose not to complain?

10. You are hired by a career consulting firm that promises to market new graduates to high-paying employers. The firm provides potential clients with an impressive list of employers. It charges the clients a fee, and then a separate finder's fee if the client gets a position. The firm aggressively markets its services and has a large client base. You learn that the firm simply takes submitted résumés and posts them to a variety of online job search engines. The firm never actually contacts any firms on its clients' behalf. The CEO, himself a recent college grad, tells you that the firm never promises to actually contact potential employers, only that it has access to employers and will distribute clients' résumés. What do you think of the career consulting firm's practices?

Quiz Yourself

1. Which of the following is *not* a characteristic of services?
   a. Intangible
   b. Inseparable
   c. Perishable
   d. Variable
   e. Tangible

2. Which of the following is *not* one of the dimensions of service quality?
   a. Reliability
   b. Responsibility
   c. Assurance
   d. Empathy
   e. All of these are dimensions of service quality.

   (Answers to these two questions can be found in the Quiz Yourself Answer Key section.)

Chapter Case Study

Mc Graw Hill Education **connect**

HOW AI IS REVOLUTIONIZING CUSTOMER SERVICE

Much of the talk surrounding robots in the workforce has centered on robots performing manufacturing jobs or taking the place of cashiers. But the expanding capabilities for artificial intelligence (AI) mean that robots are spreading into other fields, such as sales and marketing. Chatbots—whose software enables them to converse with human counterparts—have been around since 1966,[29] though only recently did they become part of consumers' lives. Early chatbots, such as AOL Instant Messenger's SmarterChild, were not particularly sophisticated, though, limiting both their ability to understand the nuances of human conversation and their appeal in practice.[30]

As AI technology continues to advance, these limits are disappearing. A chatbot designed by Conversica effectively communicates with customers to generate sales. Companies that sign up with Conversica can pick the name and gender of their chatbot. Then, as sales leads come in to the company, the dedicated chatbot gets in touch with the customer via e-mail or text message. If the customer shows interest, this chatbot puts them in contact with a human representative who can close the deal.[31] The use of this tool for the initial contacts frees sales representatives from having to generate leads; they can devote all their time to interacting with customers who are actually interested in buying, instead of wasting time with unproductive cold-calling.

Since its founding in 2007, Conversica has grown to 140 employees who serve more than 1,100 customers in various industries, including automotive, education, finance, insurance, real estate, and technology sectors. Its corporate customers are famous names such as IBM, CenturyLink, and Fiat Chrysler of America.[32] To date, its chatbots have sent approximately 250 million messages.[33]

With this technology, Conversica also collects data that inform its constant efforts to make its software even more efficient. But the data do more than suggest ways to improve the chatbots' communication; they also reveal consumer preferences. For example, using female names from the 1980s and 1990s, such as Ashley and Stephanie, for the chatbots makes them more popular than those with other names. Jennifer is the hardest-working chatbot, according to how many leads it develops; Marie is the most engaging.[34]

At a Connecticut auto dealer, a chatbot named Holly responds within four or five minutes to every potential lead. Approximately 60 percent of these contacted leads then respond, which prompts a connection with human sales associates. The dealer's ultimate goal is to engage customers in some sort of relationship with a sales associate, and Holly has helped it increase this form of customer engagement significantly. Furthermore, customers do not recognize that they have been talking to a chatbot; they often come to the dealership

When enquiring about a new car, you may be communicating with a chatbot—a virtual robot that uses artificial intelligence software that enables it to converse with humans.

©OJO Images/Getty Images

and ask for Holly specifically, though she is never in.[35] Other businesses report that their chatbots have received thank-you cards or flowers.[36]

The success and growing capabilities of chatbot software and AI suggest that Conversica will continue to expand its applications into customer support and service functions, as well as expanding the conversations to languages other than English.

Questions

1. Apply the Service Gaps Model to see how chatbots help provide customer service.
2. What service quality dimensions can chatbots help a firm?

Endnotes

1. Sapna Maheshwari, "It's Late and You've Got the Munchies: Lyft and Taco Bell Have an Idea," *The New York Times*, July 25, 2017; Jessica Wohl, "Taco Bell and Lyft Test a Way to Handle Late Night Cravings Together," *Advertising Age*, July 25, 2017; Eric Larson, "Lyft's New Taco Bell Promo Stinks Worse Than an Old Burrito," *Fortune*, August 1, 2017; Mary Hanbury, "Taco Bell Just Debuted Its Brilliant New Lyft Feature Called 'Taco Mode'—Here's What It's Like," *Business Insider*, July 28, 2017.

2. Valarie A. Zeithaml, Mary Jo Bitner, and Dwayne D. Gremler, *Services Marketing: Integrating Customer Focus across the Firm*, 6th ed. (Burr Ridge, IL: McGraw-Hill/Irwin, 2012).

3. Hilary Stout, "Amazon, Google, and More Are Drawn to Home Services Market," *The New York Times*, April 12, 2015.

4. The World Bank, "Services, etc., Value Added (% of GDP)," https://data.worldbank.org/indicator/NV.SRV.TETC.ZS?locations=US.

5. *Fortune*, "Fortune 500: 2017," http://fortune.com/2017/06/07/fortune-500-companies-list-top/; Mark Perry, "Fortune 500 Firms in 1955 v. 2015; Only 12% Remain, Thanks to the Creative Destruction That Fuels Economic Prosperity," *AEIdeas*, October 12, 2015, www.aei.org/publication/fortune-500-firms-in-1955-vs-2015-only-12-remain-thanks-to-the-creative-destruction-that-fuels-economic-growth/.

6. Valarie A. Zeithaml, Mary Jo Bitner, and Dwayne D. Gremler, *Services Marketing: Integrating Customer Focus across the Firm*, 7th ed. (New York: McGraw-Hill Education, 2017).

7. Ramon Ray, "Carbonite Offers Data Peace of Mind: A Solid Solution for Small Biz," *Business Insider*, January 24, 2012, www.businessinsider.com; "Carbonite Gains from HIPAA Regulations," *Zacks*, March 24, 2014, www.zacks.com; "Pricing," www.carbonite.com.

8. "Special Guest Policies," ChoiceHotels.com.

9. Andrew Adam Newman, "A Gym for People Who Don't Like Gyms," *The New York Times,* January 2, 2013, www.nytimes.com.

10. The discussion of the Service Gaps Model and its implications draws heavily from Michael Levy, Barton A. Weitz, and Dhruv Grewal, *Retailing Management,* 10th ed. (New York: McGraw-Hill Education, 2019). It is also based on the classic work of Valarie A. Zeithaml, A. Parasuraman, and Leonard L. Berry, *Delivering Quality Service: Balancing Customer Perceptions and Expectations* (New York/London: Free Press/ Collier Macmillan, 1990); Valarie Zeithaml, Leonard Berry, and A. Parasuraman, "Communication and Control Processes in the Delivery of Service Quality," *Journal of Marketing* 52, no. 2 (April 1988), pp. 35–48.

11. Zhen Zhu et al., "Fix It or Leave It? Customer Recovery from Self-Service Technology Failures," *Journal of Retailing* 89, no. 1 (2013), pp. 15–29.

12. Velitchka D. Kaltcheva, Robert D. Winsor, and A. Parasuraman, "Do Customer Relationships Mitigate or Amplify Failure Responses?," *Journal of Business Research* 66, no. 4 (2013), pp. 525–32; Ruth N. Bolton et al., "Small Details That Make Big Differences: A Radical Approach to Consumption Experience as a Firm's Differentiating Strategy," *Journal of Service Management* 25, no. 2 (2014), pp. 253–74; Lance A. Bettencourt, Stephen W. Brown, and Nancy J. Sirianni, "The Secret to True Service Innovation," *Business Horizons* 56, no. 1 (2013), pp. 13–22.

13. Zeithaml et al., *Services Marketing,* 2017.

14. The Broadmoor Hotel, www.broadmoor.com.

15. Rich Laden, "Forbes Travel Guide Gives the Broadmoor Its 55th Consecutive Five-Star Rating" *[Colorado Springs] Gazette,* February 2, 2015, http://gazette.com/forbes-travel-guide-gives-the-broadmoor-its-55th-consecutive-five-star-rating/article/1546162.

16. Michael Bergdahl, *The Retail Revolution: How Wal-Mart Created a Brave New World of Business* (New York: Metropolitan Books, 2009); Michael Bergdahl, *The 10 Rules of Sam Walton: Success Secrets for Remarkable Results* (Hoboken, NJ: Wiley, 2006).

17. B. Menguc et al., "The Role of Climate: Implications for Service Employee Engagement and Customer Service Performance," *Journal of the Academy of Marketing Science* 45, no. 3 (2017), pp. 428–51; Steven W. Rayburn, "Improving Service Employee Work Affect: The Transformative Potential of Work Design," *Journal of Services Marketing* 28, no. 1 (2014), pp. 71–81.

18. Jason Colquitt, Jeffery LePine, and Michael Wesson, *Organizational Behavior: Improving Performance and Commitment in the Workplace,* 3rd ed. (Burr Ridge, IL: McGraw-Hill, 2012); Felicitas M. Morhart, Walter Herzog, and Torsten Tomczak, "Brand-Specific Leadership: Turning Employees into Brand Champions," *Journal of Marketing* 73 (September 2009), pp. 122–42.

19. https://careers.fool.com/; Chris Rhatigan, "These 4 Companies Totally Get Employee Recognition," TINYpulse, July 21, 2016, www.tinypulse.com/blog/these-4-companies-totally-get-employee-recognition; "Rewarding Your Employees: Try This New Method," *The Motley Fool,* July 21, 2014, http://culture.fool.com/2014/07/employee-engagement-rewards/.

20. "The Robotics Market Report: The Fast-Multiplying Opportunities in Consumer, Industrial, and Office Robots," *Business Insider,* May 13, 2015, http://uk.businessinsider.com/growth-statistics-for-robots-market-2015-2?r1/4US&IR1/4T (accessed November 10, 2016).

21. Jenny van Doorn et al., "Domo Arigato Mr. Roboto: Emergence of Automated Social Presence in Organizational Frontlines and Customers' Service Experiences," *Journal of Service Research* 20, no. 1 (2017), pp. 43–58.

22. Marcel Heerink et al., "Relating Conversational Expressiveness to Social Presence and Acceptance of an Assistive Social Robot," *Virtual Reality* 14, no. 1 (2010), pp. 77–84.

23. Gina Silva and Jeffrey Thomas DeSocio, "Meet Wally: The Room Service Robot of the Residence Inn Marriott at LAX," *Fox 11 [Los Angeles],* February 17, 2016, www.foxla.com/news/local-news/93131443-story.

24. Zhu et al., "Fix It or Leave It?"; María Leticia Santos-Vijande et al., "An Integrated Service Recovery System (ISRS): Influence on Knowledge-Intensive Business Services Performance," *European Journal of Marketing* 47, no. 5/6 (2013), pp. 934–63.

25. Jorg Finsterwalder, "A 360-Degree View of Actor Engagement in Service Co-Creation," *Journal of Retailing and Customer Services* 40 (2018), pp. 276–78; Christian Grönroos and Päivi Voima, "Critical Service Logic: Making Sense of Value Creation and Co-Creation," *Journal of the Academy of Marketing Science* 41, no. 2 (2013), pp. 133–50; Anne L. Roggeveen, Michael Tsiros, and Dhruv Grewal, "Understanding the Co-Creation Effect: When Does Collaborating with Customers Provide a Lift to Service Recovery?," *Journal of the Academy of Marketing Science* 40, no. 6 (2012), pp. 771–90.

26. Tong Chen et al., "Is High Recovery More Effective Than Expected Recovery in Addressing Service Failure?: A Moral Judgment Perspective," *Journal of Business Research* 82 (2018), pp. 1–9; Kaltcheva et al., "Do Customer Relationships Migrate or Amplify Failure Responses?"

27. Simon Hazee, Yves Van Vaerenbergh, and Vincent Armirotto, "Co-Creating Service after Service Failure: The Role of Brand Equity," *Journal of Business Research* 74 (2017), pp. 101–9; Roggeveen et al., "Understanding the Co-Creation Effect."

28. Amy Martinez, "REI Now Limiting Returns to One Year," *Seattle Times,* June 3, 2013.

29. Carson Biz, "Chatbots Explained: Why the World's Most Powerful Tech Companies Think They're the Biggest Thing Since the iPhone," *Business Insider,* April 9, 2016, www.businessinsider.com/what-are-chatbots-and-who-is-building-them-2016-4/#wait-havent-these-been-around-for-awhile-2; Nicolas Bayerque, "A Short History of Chatbots and Artificial Intelligence," *Venture Beat,* August 15, 2016, https://venturebeat.com/2016/08/15/a-short-history-of-chatbots-and-artificial-intelligence/.

30. Bayerque, "A Short History."

31. Nick Wells, "These AI Bots Are So Believable, They Get More Dates Than You," *CNBC,* July 14, 2017, www.cnbc.com/2017/07/14/these-ai-bots-are-so-believable-they-get-more-dates-than-you.html?utm_source=Daily+Email&utm_campaign=fde2f0b85f-EMAIL_CAMPAIGN_2017_07_15&utm_medium=email&utm_term=0_03a4a88021-fde2f0b85f-248805505.

32. Heather Clancy, "This Cyber 'Sales Assistant' Uses Artificial Intelligence to Hook New Leads," *Fortune,* December 14, 2016, http://fortune.com/2016/12/14/conversica-series-b-funding/; www.conversica.com/.

33. Wells, "These AI Bots Are So Believable, They Get More Dates Than You."

34. Ibid.

35. Ibid.

36. Clancy, "This Cyber 'Sales Assistant' Uses Artificial Intelligence to Hook New Leads."

i. Yuliya Chernova, "Rolling-Hotel Startup Hitting the Road in California," *The Wall Street Journal,* June 28, 2017; www.ridecabin.com/.

ii. "About Kroger," TheKrogerCo.com; Laurianne McLaughlin, "Kroger Solves Top Customer Issue: Long Lines," *InformationWeek,* April 2, 2014.

iii. Jane L. Levere, "Before You Take the Trip: How about a Virtual 'Test Drive'?," *The New York Times,* February 12, 2017; Janet Morrissey, "Virtual Reality Leads Marketers down a Tricky Path," *The New York Times,* March 5, 2017.

iv. Julie Jargon, "Starbucks Spoils the Pun of Serving Up the Rong Gname," *The Wall Street Journal,* May 17, 2016; Trefis Team, "Starbucks' Success with Mobile Order and Pay Is Too Much of a Good Thing," *Forbes,* February 2, 2017.

v. Paul Sullivan, "Here's the Key to Your Suite, and Another to Your Rolls-Royce," *The New York Times,* December 16, 2016; Josh Max, "These 5 Luxury Hotels Provide Guests with Luxury Cars, Too," *Forbes,* September 26, 2016.

Quiz Yourself Answer Key

1. Which of the following is not a characteristic of services?

   Answer: (e) Tangible

2. Which of the following is not one of the dimensions of service quality?

   Answer: (b) Responsibility

VALUE CAPTURE

Section Five contains two chapters on pricing dedicated to capturing value. Chapter 14 examines the importance of setting the right price, the relationship between price and quantity sold, break-even analysis, the impact of price wars, and how the Internet has changed the way people shop. Chapter 15 looks specifically at how to set prices.

LEARNING OBJECTIVES

After reading this chapter, you should be able to:

 LO14-1 List the four pricing orientations.

 LO14-2 Explain the relationship between price and quantity sold.

LO14-3 Explain price elasticity.

 LO14-4 Describe how to calculate a product's break-even point.

 LO14-5 Indicate the four types of price competitive levels.

CHAPTER 14

PRICING CONCEPTS FOR CAPTURING VALUE

When companies use innovation as a key determinant of their pricing strategies, it often involves new products or services. By coming up with something that is new and different, marketers can establish a fresh price position and largely define any prices going forward. But for Kroger, innovation as input for its pricing strategy goes beyond imagining new products for its shelves or services for its shoppers. It means reimagining the very essence of the way that it presents its value promise to consumers.

That is not to say that it never innovates products or services. Its Simple Truth and other private-label brands provide quality comparable to that of national brands, at price points more in line with store brands.[1] Combining new products with service provision, Kroger also has added a meal-kit line to store shelves. Furthermore, Kroger's loyalty program and data analytics capabilities enable it to customize prices to reflect different customers' preferences and prompt purchase behaviors across the various types of shoppers who visit its stores or digital channels.[2] For example, it offers Best Customer Bonuses to reward its most valuable shoppers with price discounts.

But innovation also appears in the form of processes and technologies. For example, in more than 200 Kroger stores across the nation, consumers soon will see a different type of display. Rather than conventional paper tags listing prices, brands, and other information, these stores are piloting the Kroger Edge system that supports digital shelf tags. The electronic signage will detail prices and nutritional information, along with coupons, advertising, and other marketing communications.[3]

The current version of the technology already offers some notable benefits for the grocery retailer. In particular, it can change prices throughout the store with a simple click or two, rather than needing to reprint and replace each individual tag by hand. Such capabilities mean that it can engage in more dynamic pricing, such as lowering the price for a product that seems to be moving slowly. On cold days, it might hype sales of soups; during hot summer months, it can induce more purchases of lemonade by altering the digital displays on the fly. The grocer even could pursue more specific dynamism, such as bumping up the price of beer in the hours right after most people get off work or seeking to earn a little more profit on chicken wings on the morning before a big game.

Beyond these dynamic pricing benefits, the technology also implies that Kroger may gain more leeway in its pricing policies by enhancing the efficiency of its operations. Currently, the grocer needs to pay store employees to walk the aisles and make changes to each shelf tag every time it decides to adjust its prices. Eliminating these expensive tasks by switching to digital shelf tags may mean that the retailer can pass on some of those savings to customers—informed by its individually personalized approach to promotions.[4] In that case, its ability to compete on price with other grocery store chains would improve dramatically.

For consumers, the implemented tags also offer more information and promotions. For now, shoppers need to pick up a handheld device at the store entrance to be able to access the benefits of the tags. In the near future, Kroger anticipates that it will be able to link with shoppers' smartphones and mobile shopping lists.[5] Thus, for example, if a customer is planning on making lasagna that night, her shopping list might include ricotta, noodles, and her family's preferred brand of marinara sauce. As this shopper enters the sauce aisle, the digital tag under the selected marinara sauce will light up, attracting her attention and making it easier for her to find needed products quickly. But Kroger also could program the system to flash the shelf tag under another brand that might offer larger margins or a better value, depending on its knowledge of that customer and her preferences.

This technological innovation offers promise beyond its own stores too. Even as Kroger continues to work on developing a proprietary app to allow people to use their phones to link with the smart tags, it also is planning ways to make its technology available to other retailers, as another source of profit. By collecting vast amounts of data, Kroger sits at the forefront of pricing innovations, and other retailers need to keep up with its abilities. Thus Kroger can define the market with its innovative products, services, and technologies. In turn, it has space and opportunity to devise unique and customized pricing tactics that enable it to compete more effectively with other retailers while also appealing more powerfully to customers.

Although knowing how consumers arrive at their perceptions of value is critical to developing successful pricing strategies, sellers also must consider other factors—which is why developing a good pricing strategy is such a formidable challenge to all firms. Do it right, and the rewards to the firm will be substantial. Do it wrong, and failure will be swift and severe. But even if a pricing strategy is implemented well, consumers, economic conditions, markets, competitors, government regulations, and even a firm's own products change constantly—and that means that a good pricing strategy today may not remain an effective pricing strategy tomorrow.

So much rides on marketers setting the right price that we take two chapters to explain the role of price in the marketing mix. In this chapter we explain what "price" is as a marketing concept, why it is important, how marketers set pricing objectives, and how various factors influence price setting. In the next chapter, we extend this foundation by focusing on specific pricing strategies that capitalize on capturing value.

Imagine that a consumer realizes that to save money on a particular item, she will have to drive an additional 20 miles. She may determine that her time and travel costs are not worth the savings, so even though the price tag is higher at the nearby store, she judges the overall cost of buying the product close by to be lower. To include aspects of price such as this, we may define price as the overall sacrifice a consumer is willing to make to acquire a specific product or service. This sacrifice necessarily includes the money that must be paid to the seller to acquire the item, but it also may involve other sacrifices, whether nonmonetary, such as the value of the time necessary to acquire the product or service, or monetary, such as travel costs, taxes, shipping costs, and so forth, all of which the buyer must give up to take possession of the product.[6] It's useful to think of overall price in this way to see how the narrower sense of purchase price fits in.

Because price is the only element of the marketing mix that does not generate costs but instead generates revenue, it is important in its own right. Every other element in the marketing mix may be perfect, but with the wrong price, sales and thus revenue will not accrue. Consumers generally believe that price is one of the most important factors in their purchase decisions.

Knowing that price is so critical to success, why don't managers put greater emphasis on it as a strategic decision variable? Price is the most challenging of the four Ps to manage, partly because it is often the least understood. Historically, managers have treated price as an afterthought to their marketing strategy, setting prices according to what competitors were charging or, worse yet, adding up their costs and tacking on a desired profit to set the sales price. Prices rarely changed except in response to radical shifts in market conditions. Even today, pricing decisions are often relegated to standard rules of thumb that fail to reflect our current understanding of the role of price in the marketing mix.

In summary, marketers should view pricing decisions as a strategic opportunity to create value rather than as an afterthought to the rest of the marketing mix. Let us now turn to the five basic components of pricing strategies.

THE FIVE Cs OF PRICING

Successful pricing strategies are built around the five critical components (the five Cs) of pricing, found in Exhibit 14.1. We examine these components in some detail because each makes a significant contribution to formulating good pricing policies.[7] To start, the first step is to develop the company's pricing objectives.

Company Objectives

By now, you know that different firms embrace very different goals. These goals should spill down to the pricing strategy, such that the pricing of a company's products and services should support and allow the firm to reach its overall goals. For example, a firm with a primary goal of very high sales growth will likely have a different pricing strategy than will a firm with the goal of being a quality leader.

Each firm then embraces objectives that seem to fit with where management thinks the firm needs to go to be successful, in whatever way it defines success. These specific objectives usually reflect how the firm intends to grow. Do managers want it to grow by increasing profits, increasing sales, decreasing competition, or building customer satisfaction?

Company objectives are not as simple as they might first appear. They often can be expressed in slightly different forms that mean very different things. Exhibit 14.2 introduces

---

EXHIBIT 14.1   The Five Cs of Pricing

EXHIBIT 14.2	Company Objectives and Pricing Strategy Implications
Company Objective	**Examples of Pricing Strategy Implications**
Profit-oriented	Institute a companywide policy that all products must provide for at least an 18 percent profit margin to reach a particular profit goal for the firm.
Sales-oriented	Set prices very low to generate new sales and take sales away from competitors, even if profits suffer.
Competitor-oriented	To discourage more competitors from entering the market, set prices very low.
Customer-oriented	Target a market segment of consumers who highly value a particular product benefit and set prices relatively high (referred to as premium pricing).

some common company objectives and corresponding examples of their implications for pricing strategies. These objectives are not always mutually exclusive, because a firm may embrace two or more noncompeting objectives.

LO14-1 List the four pricing orientations.

Profit Orientation Even though all company methods and objectives may ultimately be oriented toward making a profit, firms implement a profit orientation specifically by focusing on target profit pricing, maximizing profits, or target return pricing.

- Firms usually implement target profit pricing when they have a particular profit goal as their overriding concern. To meet this targeted profit objective, firms use price to stimulate a certain level of sales at a certain profit per unit.

- The maximizing profits strategy relies primarily on economic theory. If a firm can accurately specify a mathematical model that captures all the factors required to explain and predict sales and profits, it should be able to identify the price at which its profits are maximized. Of course, actually gathering the data on all these relevant factors and coming up with an accurate mathematical model is a difficult undertaking. How Amazon maximizes profit is discussed later.

- Other firms are less concerned with the absolute level of profits and more interested in the rate at which their profits are generated relative to their investments. These firms typically turn to target return pricing and employ pricing strategies designed to produce a specific return on their investment, usually expressed as a percentage of sales.

P&G increases sales by introducing new Tide products.
©McGraw-Hill Education/Evelyn Nicole Kirksey, photographer

Sales Orientation Firms using a sales orientation to set prices believe that increasing sales will help the firm more than will increasing profits. Tide laundry detergent might adopt such an orientation selectively when it introduces new products that it wants to establish in the market. A new health club might focus on unit sales, dollar sales, or market share and therefore be willing to set a lower membership fee and accept less profit at first to focus on and generate more unit sales. In contrast, a high-end jewelry store might focus on dollar sales and maintain higher prices. The jewelry store relies on its prestige image, as well as the image of its suppliers, to provoke sales. Even though it sells fewer units, it can still generate high dollar sales levels.

Some firms may be more concerned about their overall market share than about dollar sales per se (though these often go hand in hand) because they believe that market share better reflects their success relative to the market conditions than do sales alone.

A firm may set low prices to discourage new firms from entering the market, encourage current firms to leave the market, and/or take market share away from competitors—all to gain overall market share. For example, as low-cost, no-frills airlines such as Frontier and Spirit have changed travelers' perspectives on what prices are reasonable and necessary to pay, the major airlines such as United, American, and Delta have had to work hard to keep increasing their market share. Delta now offers a Basic Economy fare on most routes that the discount airlines also fly. In exchange for the lower price, passengers lose the right to make changes to their itinerary, and they cannot obtain seat assignments in advance. Both American and United are developing similar economy fares to widen the range of prices that their consumers can access. In addition to lowering the prices they charge consumers, the major carriers are seeking to increase the number of seats in each plane, thus increasing their revenue per flight.[8] However, as airlines expand their capacity, the supply of seats may outstrip demand, making it even more difficult to raise prices. As fuel costs rise, even budget airlines hope to be able to increase ticket prices, but most companies have not been able to successfully do so. In response, both Delta and American have slowed their expansion plans to allow the demand to catch up to the supply so that it may be easier to raise prices.[9]

Yet adopting a market share objective does not always imply setting low prices. Rarely is the lowest-price offering the dominant brand in a given market. Heinz ketchup, Philadelphia cream cheese, Crest toothpaste, and Nike athletic shoes have all dominated their markets, but all are premium-priced brands. On the services side, IBM claims market dominance in human resource outsourcing, but again, it is certainly not the lowest-price competitor.[10] **Premium pricing** means the firm deliberately prices a product above the prices set for competing products so as to capture those customers who always shop for the best or for whom price does not matter. Thus, companies can gain market share by offering a high-quality product at a price that is perceived to be fair by its target market as long as they use effective communication and distribution methods to generate high-value perceptions among consumers. Although the concept of value is not overtly expressed in sales-oriented strategies, it is at least implicit because, for sales to increase, consumers must see greater value.

Competitor Orientation When firms take a **competitor orientation**, they strategize according to the premise that they should measure themselves primarily against their competition. Some firms focus on **competitive parity**, which means they set prices that are similar to those of their major competitors. Another competitor-oriented strategy, **status quo pricing**, changes prices only to meet those of the competition. For example, when Delta increases its average fares, American

Since Frontier and other airlines started offering low-cost, no-frills flights, other airlines have had to work hard to keep increasing market share.
©Blaine Harrington III/Alamy Stock Photo

Adding Value 14.1   "Opulence in Value": The Taco Bell Campaign to Establish Both Its Appeal and Its Low Price[i]

For Taco Bell, value does not mean cheap; rather, value is essential to its very identity and promise to customers. In contrast, for many customers who order off the dollar menus of competing fast-food providers, there is a trade-off between value and satisfaction because the meals tend to be rather small or very basic. For Taco Bell customers, though, this trade-off does not exist: Marketing research showed that they both enjoy value and feel satisfied. To help communicate its positioning and play up the point that it offers both indulgence and value, Taco Bell combines descriptions of the price-based value it offers with clear indications of how innovative, different, and unique its appeals can be. In a sense, it aims to have the best of both worlds.

The most recent example of this effort involves its $1 menu. In response to an announcement by the industry leader McDonald's that it would be issuing expanded menu options for $1, $2, and $3, virtually all fast-food providers initiated their own promotions. For Taco Bell, the effort was not particularly difficult because it already had $1 options available. It is also introducing 20 new items to its $1 menu, such as Nacho Fries.

But in seeking to promote those options, to ensure consumers were well aware of them it avoided a conventional price-based appeal. Instead, it highlighted the ability to find a good food value as a type of status symbol. Citing the "opulence" that can result from finding value, it tells a story in which people who can find a great price are the real leaders of society. Its "Belluminati" advertising campaign showcases smart consumers who know that they can get something special and different from Taco Bell, making them notable members who stand out from the wider market of fast-food eaters.

As the introduction of Nacho Fries exemplifies, Taco Bell also actively innovates in its offerings. Whether in the flavors

To compete with McDonald's low-priced items, Taco Bell is introducing 20 new items to its $1 menu, including Nacho Fries.
©Craig Barritt/Getty Images for Taco Bell

of its taco shells or in the ingredients it piles together in a single "Stacker," the company emphasizes that it is always seeking something different and unique to offer consumers. By combining innovative and limited-time offers—conventional elements that allow companies to raise their prices—with value pricing, Taco Bell hopes to lure many more customers to its stores. Thus far the strategy seems effective: Taco Bell has reported that its dollar menu sales surpassed $500 million in 2017, and its $5 box offer brought in another $1 billion in sales. In this mature market, such a distinct and diverse offer may be the real secret sauce.

Airlines and United often follow with similar increases; if Delta rescinds that increase, its competitors tend to drop their fares too.[11] Value is implicitly considered only in competitor-oriented strategies, but in the sense that competitors may be using value as part of their pricing strategies, copying their strategy might provide value, as shown in Adding Value 14.1 in which Taco Bell responds to McDonald's $1 menu offerings.

Customer Orientation A firm uses customer orientation when it sets its pricing strategy based on how it can add value to its products or services. When CarMax promises a "no-haggle" pricing structure, it exhibits a customer orientation because it provides additional value to potential used car buyers by making the process simple and easy.[12]

Philadelphia brand cream cheese dominates its market and is a premium-priced brand.
©Michael J. Hruby

Firms may offer very high-priced, state-of-the-art products or services in full anticipation of limited sales. These offerings are designed to enhance the company's reputation and image and thereby increase the company's value in the minds of consumers. Paradigm, a Canadian speaker manufacturer, produces what many audiophiles consider to be a high-value product, yet offers speakers priced as low as $278 per pair. However, Paradigm also offers a very high-end speaker for $17,500 per pair. Although few people will spend $17,500 on a pair of speakers, this "statement" speaker communicates what the company is capable of and can increase the image of the firm and the rest of its products—even that $278 pair of speakers. Setting prices with a close eye to how consumers develop their perceptions of value can often be the most effective pricing strategy, especially if it is supported by consistent advertising and distribution strategies.

After a company has a good grasp on its overall objectives, it must implement pricing strategies that enable it to achieve those objectives. As the second step in this process, the firm should look toward consumer demand to lay the foundation for its pricing strategy.

PROGRESS CHECK

1. What are the five Cs of pricing?
2. Identify the four types of company objectives.

Can you tell the difference between the $17,500 and the $278 speakers?

Source: Paradigm Electronics, Inc.

Customers

When firms have developed their company objectives, they turn to understanding consumers' reactions to different prices. The second C of the five Cs of pricing focuses on the customers. Customers want value, and as you likely recall, price is half of the value equation.

LO14-2 Explain the relationship between price and quantity sold.

To determine how firms account for consumers' preferences when they develop pricing strategies, we must first lay a foundation of traditional economic theory that helps explain how prices are related to demand (consumers' desire for products) and how managers can incorporate this knowledge into their pricing strategies. But first read through Adding Value 14.2, which considers how Amazon leverages its renowned algorithms to develop a sophisticated value-based pricing strategy.

Demand Curves and Pricing A demand curve shows how many units of a product or service consumers will demand during a specific period of time at different prices. Although we call them "curves," demand curves can be either straight or curved, as Exhibit 14.3 shows. Of course, any demand curve relating demand to price assumes that everything else remains unchanged. For the sake of expediency, marketers creating a demand curve assume that the firm will not increase its expenditures on advertising and that the economy will not change in any significant way.

Exhibit 14.3 illustrates a classic downward-sloping demand curve for teeth-whitening kits. As price increases, quantity demanded for a product or service will decrease. In the case here, consumers will buy more as the price decreases. We can expect a demand curve similar to this one for many, if not most, products and services.

The horizontal axis in Exhibit 14.3 measures the quantity demanded for the teeth-whitening kits in units and plots it against the various price possibilities

EXHIBIT 14.3 Demand Curve for Teeth-Whitening Kits

Adding Value 14.2 | Changing Once, Changing Twice, Changing 3 Million Times: How Amazon Prices to Win[ii]

On a recent Black Friday (i.e., the day after Thanksgiving, when many retailers make enough profit for the year to exceed their costs, known as getting in the black), Amazon actively changed the prices of one-third of the products in its seemingly endless supply. Try to imagine what that means. Amazon, the marketplace for virtually everything, engaged in literally millions of price changes, on what would already be probably its busiest shopping day. Why?

Here's the thing: It isn't all that unusual for Amazon. Every single day, it changes the prices of 15 to 18 percent of its products. With its famous algorithms and remarkable data warehouses, Amazon evidently believes it has better insights into what consumers will pay at any particular moment for a vast range of products.

Some product categories come in for more changes than others. Some are subject to change every day, others undergo price alterations every third day, another set shifts once a week, and still others experience changes only once or twice a month. Perhaps unsurprisingly, considering its investment in the Kindle, the most frequently changed product category is tablets, for which Amazon changes the prices of 15 percent of its stock every one to two days.

But the really remarkable transitions are the ones that take place around the holidays. Reports from holiday trends indicate that Amazon literally changed more than 3 million prices each and every day in November—of course, with the previously mentioned jump in activity on the day after Thanksgiving.

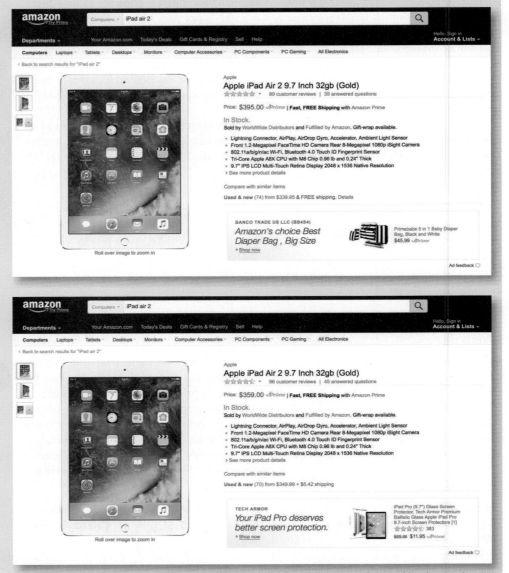

Amazon regularly changes prices of items like the Apple iPad. The iPad was priced at $395 (top), and at $359 (bottom) only a few days later.

Source: Amazon.com, Inc.

Pleased with how well these changes have worked, Amazon promises to continue making them, and perhaps even ramp up its efforts.

indicated on the vertical axis. Each point on the demand curve then represents the quantity demanded at a specific price. So, in this instance, if the price of a kit is $10 per unit ($P_1$), the demand is 1,000,000 units (Q_1), but if the price were set at $15 ($P_2$), the quantity demanded would be only 500,000 units (Q_2). The firm will sell far more teeth-whitening kits at $10 each than at $15 each. Why? Because of the greater value this price point offers.

Knowing the demand curve for a product or service enables a firm to examine different prices in terms of the resulting demand and relative to its overall objective. In our preceding example, the retailer will generate a total of $10,000,000 in sales at the $10 price ($10 × 1,000,000 units) and $7,500,000 in sales at the $15 price ($15 × 500,000 units). In this case, given only the two choices of $10 or $15, the $10 price is preferable as long as the firm wants to maximize its sales in terms of dollars and units. But what about a firm that is more interested in profit? To calculate profit, it must consider its costs, which we cover in the next section.

But not all products or services follow the downward-sloping demand curve for all levels of price depicted in Exhibit 14.3. Consider prestige products or services, which consumers purchase for their status rather than for their functionality. The higher the price, the greater the status associated with it and the greater the exclusivity, because fewer people can afford to purchase it.

French luxury goods manufacturer and retailer Hermès is known for making expensive leather goods. But paying $300,168 for a handbag at auction, which is more than the standard retail price of $280,000, is extraordinary, and not for the casual shopper. Of course, the matte Himalayan crocodile handbag was finished using white-gold hardware set with 245 F-color diamonds.[13]

With prestige products or services, a higher price may lead to a greater quantity sold, but only up to a certain point. The price demonstrates just how rare, exclusive, and prestigious the product is. When customers value the increase in prestige more than the price differential between the prestige product and other products, the prestige product attains the greater value overall.

Hermès uses prestige pricing for its handbags, like this one that sold for more than $300,000 at auction, which is more than $20,000 above the standard retail price.

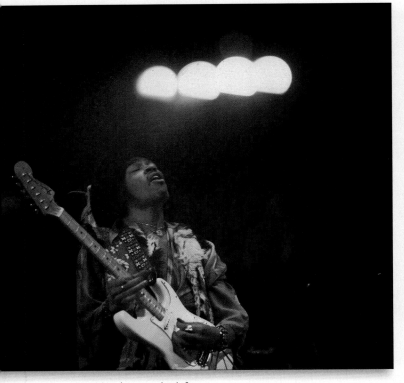

Jimi Hendrix used a left-handed Fender guitar.

©David Redfern/Getty Images

However, prestige products can also run into pricing difficulties. The Fender Telecaster and Stratocaster guitars are absolute necessities for any self-respecting guitar hero, but for hobbyists or students just learning to play, the price of owning a Fender "axe" was simply too much. In response, Fender introduced a separate, budget-priced line of similar guitars under a different brand name, so as not to dilute the prestige of the Fender name. The Squier line, made in Japan with automated manufacturing and less expensive parts, offers a look similar to the famous Fender guitars and performance just a notch below the originals. Today, an American Original 1950s Fender Stratocaster lists for $1,950, which is 13 times as much as a Bullet Strat HT model, which retails for around $150.[14]

Exhibit 14.4 illustrates a demand curve for a hypothetical prestige service, a Club Med vacation. As the graph indicates, when the price increases from $1,000 ($P_1$) to $5,000 ($P_2$), the quantity demanded actually increases from 200,000 (Q_1) to 500,000 (Q_2) units. However, when the price increases to $8,000 ($P_3$), the quantity demanded then decreases to 300,000 (Q_3) units.

Although the firm likely will earn more profit selling 300,000 vacation packages at $8,000 each than 500,000 vacation packages at $5,000 each, we do not know for sure until we bring costs into the picture. However, we do know that more consumers are willing to book the vacation as the price increases initially from $1,000 to $5,000 and that more consumers will choose an alternative vacation as the price increases further from $5,000 to $8,000.

We must consider this notion of consumers' sensitivity to price changes in greater depth.

Price Elasticity of Demand Although we now know something about how consumers react to different price levels, we still need to determine how consumers respond to actual changes in price. These responses vary depending on the product or service. For example, consumers are generally less sensitive to price increases for necessary items, such as milk, because they have to purchase the items even if the price climbs. When the price of milk goes up, demand does not fall significantly, because people still need to buy milk.

EXHIBIT 14.4   Demand Curve for a Club Med Vacation

However, if the price of T-bone steaks rises beyond a certain point, people will buy fewer of them because they can turn to the many substitutes for this cut of meat. Marketers need to know how consumers will respond to a price increase or decrease for a specific product or brand so they can determine whether it makes sense for them to raise or lower prices.

Price elasticity of demand measures how changes in a price affect the quantity of the product demanded. Specifically, it is the ratio of the percentage change in quantity demanded to the percentage change in price. We can calculate it with the following formula:

$$\text{Price elasticity of demand} = \frac{\% \text{ Change in quantity demanded}}{\% \text{ Change in price}}$$

The demand curve provides the information we need to calculate the price elasticity of demand. For instance, what is the price elasticity of demand if we increase the price of our teeth-whitening kit from Exhibit 14.3 from $10 to $15?

$$\% \text{ Change in quantity demanded} = \frac{(500,000 - 1,000,000)}{1,000,000} = -50\%, \text{ and}$$

$$\% \text{ Change in price} = \frac{(\$15 - \$10)}{10} = 50\%, \text{ so}$$

$$\text{Price elasticity of demand} = \frac{-50\%}{50\%} = -1.$$

Thus, the price elasticity of demand for our teeth-whitening kit is −1.

In general, the market for a product or service is price sensitive, or elastic, when the price elasticity is less than −1. Thus, an elasticity of −5 would indicate that a 1 percent decrease in price produces a 5 percent increase in the quantity sold. In an elastic scenario, relatively small changes in price will generate fairly large changes in the quantity demanded, so if a firm is trying to increase its sales, it can do so by lowering prices. However, raising prices can be problematic in this context because doing so will lower sales. To refer back to our grocery examples, a retailer would significantly decrease its sales of steaks by raising its price by a relatively small amount, because T-bones are elastic.

The market for a product is generally viewed as price insensitive, or inelastic, when its price elasticity is greater than −1. For example, an elasticity of −0.50 indicates that a 1 percent increase in price results in one-half a percent decrease in quantity sold. Generally, if a firm must raise prices, it is helpful to do so with inelastic products or services, because in such a market, fewer customers will stop buying or will reduce their purchases. However, if the products are inelastic, lowering prices will not appreciably increase demand; customers just don't notice or care about the lower price.

Consumers are generally more sensitive to price increases than to price decreases.[15] That is, it is easier to lose current customers with a price increase than it is to gain new customers with a price decrease. For instance, a prestige product or service, like our Club Med example in Exhibit 14.4, enjoys a highly inelastic demand curve up to a certain point, so price increases do not affect sales significantly. But when the price reaches that certain point, consumers start turning to other alternatives because the value of the vacation has finally been reduced by the extremely high price.

Ideally, firms could maximize their profits if they charged each customer as much as the customer was willing to pay. The travel industry and airlines realize this benefit particularly well, as Marketing Analytics 14.1 explains. For instance, if a wealthy,

Based on Exhibit 14.4, price increases do not affect sales of the vacation significantly up to a certain point. But after that point, sales decrease because consumers believe it is no longer a good value.

Source: ClubMed

LO14-3 Explain price elasticity.

Consumers are less sensitive to the price of milk than they are to that of steak. When the price of milk goes up, demand does not fall significantly, because people still need to buy milk. However, if the price of steak rises beyond a certain point, people will buy less because they can turn to many substitutes for steak.

(Left): ©Ingram Publishing/SuperStock; (right): ©robynmac/123RF

price-insensitive customer wants to buy a new car, a Ford dealer might like to price a particular car at $40,000, but then price the same car at $35,000 to a more price-sensitive
customer. Such a practice is legal when retailers sell to consumers such as in an eBay auction, but it is permitted only under certain circumstances in B2B settings.[16]

Although charging different prices to different customers is legal and widely used in
some retail sectors, such as automobile and antique dealers, it has not been very practical in

Marketing Analytics 14.1   Airlines Use Price Elasticities to Price Tickets[iii]

The airline industry has been using analytics to influence pricing for decades. Early implementers of data-based pricing
strategies, such as American Airlines, enjoyed a significant
advantage over their competitors who maintained a single, flat
rate for all tickets. By predicting demand for each particular
flight, American Airlines could price different tickets at different rates and ensure that it sold as many tickets as possible.
For example, when its analytics system identified which tickets
might not sell, American Airlines began offering those seats at
a significant discount, but it increased the rates for seats that
were very likely to be purchased.

American Airlines' pricing strategy grew so effective that
every other airline faced an obvious choice: Adopt it or go out
of business. Some of the popularity of data-based pricing is
the result of a key feature that it provides: It allows customers
the freedom to determine the price they will pay. Travelers
well know that they will find vast discrepancies in flight prices,
depending on when they travel (spring break or the off-
season?), when they book (Tuesday nights or Saturday morn-
ings?), and where they want to sit (pay a lot extra for first class,

a little extra for the exit row, or just the base fare for a middle
seat?). Customers can weigh the value of the convenience of
these various factors for themselves and then select the flight
that best fits their own individual needs.

Despite the great deals offered and the resultant benefits
for firms as well as customers, the use of strategic pricing
analytics can require time-consuming hunts for the best deal.
To combat the hassle of searching for airline deals, many service providers have introduced travel booking sites. Some are
specific to a particular airline; others compile pricing information about various flights between two locations to make the
price comparison evident and convenient for the customer.
Kayak.com has taken it a step further and begun implementing
predictive pricing analytics of its own in the form of its price
forecast feature. Kayak takes information from the billions of
requests for travel information that it processes each day and
then predicts whether the price for a given destination on a
particular date is likely to go up or down over the next seven
days. It computes the accuracy of its predictions daily in an
effort to perfect its use of these analytics.

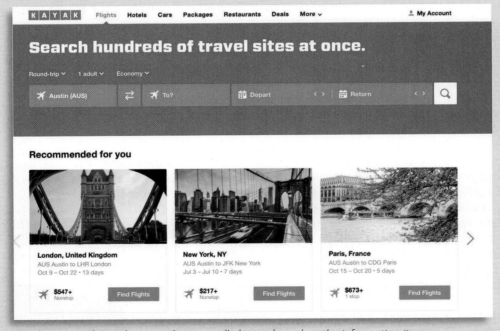

*Kayak.com predicts when travel prices will change based on the information it processes
each day.*

Source: kayak.com

most retail stores until recently. Retailers have increased their use of dynamic pricing techniques due to the information that is available from point-of-sale data collected on Internet purchases and in stores (as we discussed in Adding Value 14.2). Dynamic pricing, also known as individualized pricing, refers to the process of charging different prices for goods or services based on the type of customer; time of the day, week, or even season; and level of demand. Marketing Analytics 14.2 summarizes some of the emerging effects of this pricing strategy.

Factors Influencing Price Elasticity of Demand We have illustrated how price elasticity of demand varies across different products and at different points along a demand curve, as well as how it can change over time. What causes these differences in the price elasticity of demand? We discuss a few of the more important factors next.

Income Effect The income effect refers to the change in the quantity of a product demanded by consumers due to changes in their incomes. Generally, as people's incomes increase, their spending behavior changes: They tend to shift their demand from lower-priced products to higher-priced alternatives. That is, consumers buy hamburger when they're stretching their money but steak when they're flush. Similarly, they may increase the quantity they purchase and splurge on a five-star hotel during their six-day Las Vegas trip rather than three-star lodging over a weekend visit. Conversely, when incomes drop, consumers turn to less expensive alternatives or purchase less.

Substitution Effect The substitution effect refers to consumers' ability to substitute other products for the focal brand. The greater the availability of substitute products, the higher the price elasticity of demand for any given product will be. For example, there are many close substitutes in the laundry detergent category. If Tide raises its prices, many consumers will turn to competing brands (e.g., Arm & Hammer Detergent), because they are more sensitive to price increases when they can easily find lower-priced substitutes. Extremely brand-loyal consumers, however, are willing to pay a higher price, up to a point, because in their minds, Tide still offers a better value than the competing brands do, and they believe the other brands are not adequate substitutes.

Marketing Analytics 14.2   The Ultimate Outcomes of Dynamic Pricing[iv]

In a recent academic study of pricing techniques for Major League Baseball (MLB) games, researchers suggested that rather than creating customer backlash, dynamic pricing for products such as game tickets can lead to customers who are more satisfied, willing to spend more, and more pleased with their purchases. These results thus align with the spreading emergence of dynamic pricing in more and more industries, from ride-sharing services to restaurant reservations.

In the market for sporting events, when services such as StubHub arose to help customers buy and sell unused tickets, MLB and other leagues faced a clear challenge. But shutting down the alternative sales channels quickly proved impossible, so most of them have entered into collaborative agreements with the resale site, to create an official market that offers at least some control for the teams and some protection for customers. On these sites, the individual ticket sellers set the prices such that someone eager to get rid of a pair of seats to this Friday's game likely charges less than another fan who can't decide whether to go or not and thus will sell them only if he or she can get more than face value for the tickets.

Such pricing shifts have long been the practice adopted by scalpers and other gray market providers. By legitimizing the sliding price scale through StubHub sales, teams and their owners started to realize that they needed to rethink some other pricing norms that had long been in place but that perhaps were no longer appropriate.

By charging different prices to customers who buy tickets for specific games at different times, teams can rationalize and increase their revenues. According to the research study, a static price that is carefully chosen actually can be preferable to dynamic pricing, though identifying that optimal static price remains incredibly challenging. If they don't change their prices enough, sellers might leave a lot of revenue on the table.

But overall, the dynamic pricing model offers various benefits for both sellers and buyers. The MLB clubs that have used it have increased their revenues, as well as gathered extensive data about the prices people are willing to pay. The fans have gained greater familiarity with the concept of shifting prices, recognizing that "whether it's with airplanes, professional sports, [or] ride-sharing services, dynamic pricing is here to stay."

Polo/Ralph Lauren has fought the price substitution effect by getting customers to believe that the polo-player logo found on its products makes them unique, different, or extraordinary, compared to other brands.

©Daniel Acker/Bloomberg via Getty Images

Keep in mind that marketing plays a critical role in making consumers brand loyal. And because of this brand loyalty and the lack of what consumers judge to be adequate substitutes, the price elasticity of demand for some brands is very low. For example, Polo/Ralph Lauren sells millions of its classic polo shirts at $85, while shirts of equal quality but without the polo-player logo sell for much less. Getting consumers to believe that a particular brand is unique, different, or extraordinary in some way makes other brands seem less substitutable, which in turn increases brand loyalty and decreases the price elasticity of demand.

Cross-Price Elasticity Cross-price elasticity is the percentage change in the quantity of Product A demanded compared with the percentage change in price in Product B. If Product A's price increases, Product B's price could either increase or decrease, depending on the situation and whether the products are complementary or substitutes. We refer to products such as Mountain Dew and Doritos as complementary products, which are products whose demands are positively related, such that they rise or fall together. In other words, a percentage increase in the quantity demanded for Product A results in a percentage increase in the quantity demanded for Product B.[17] However, if the price for Mountain Dew rises, its demand may decline, but the demand for Sprite will probably increase, so Sprite and Mountain Dew are substitute products because changes in their demand are negatively related. That is, a percentage increase in the quantity demanded for Product A results in a percentage decrease in the quantity demanded for Product B.[18] In addition, shopping engines such as Google Shopping and shopzilla.com have made it much easier for people to shop for substitutable products like consumer electronics, which likely has affected the price elasticity of demand for such products.[19]

Prior to this point, we have focused on how changes in prices affect how much customers buy. Clearly, knowing how prices affect sales is important, but it cannot give us the whole picture. To know how profitable a pricing strategy will be, we must also consider the third C, costs.

PROGRESS CHECK

1. What is the difference between elastic demand and inelastic demand?
2. What are the factors influencing price elasticity?

Costs

To make effective pricing decisions, firms must understand their cost structures so they can determine the degree to which their products or services will be profitable at different prices. In general, prices should *not* be based on costs, because consumers make purchase decisions based on their perceived value; they care little about the firm's costs to produce and sell a product or deliver a service. Although companies incur many different types of costs as a natural part of doing business, there are two primary cost categories: variable and fixed.

Variable Costs Variable costs are those costs, primarily labor and materials, that vary with production volume. As a firm produces more or less of a good or service, the total variable costs increase or decrease at the same time. Because each unit of the product produced incurs the same cost, marketers generally express variable costs on a per-unit basis. Consider a bakery like Entenmann's: The majority of the variable costs are the cost of the ingredients, primarily flour. Each time Entenmann's makes a loaf of bread, it incurs the cost of the ingredients.

In the service industry, variable costs are far more complex. A hotel, for instance, incurs certain variable costs each time it rents a room, including the costs associated with the labor and supplies necessary to clean and restock the room. Note that the hotel does not incur these costs if the room is not booked. Suppose that a particular hotel calculates its total variable costs to be $10 per room; each time it rents a room, it incurs another $10 in variable costs. If the hotel rents out 100 rooms on a given night, the total variable cost is $1,000 ($10 per room × 100 rooms).

In either case, however, variable costs tend to change depending on the quantity produced. If Entenmann's makes 100,000 loaves of bread in a month, it would have to pay a higher price for ingredients on a per-pound basis than if it were producing a million loaves, because the more ingredients it purchases, the less expensive those ingredients become. Similarly, a very large hotel will be able to get a lower per-unit price on most, if not all, the supplies it needs to service the room because it purchases such a large volume. However, as the hotel company continues to grow, it may be forced to add more benefits for its employees or increase wages to attract and keep long-term employees. Such changes will increase its overall variable labor costs and affect the total variable cost of cleaning a room. Thus, though not always the case, variable costs per unit may go up or down (for all units) with significant changes in volume.

Fixed Costs Fixed costs are those costs that remain essentially at the same level, regardless of any changes in the volume of production. Typically, these costs include items such as rent, utilities, insurance, administrative salaries (for executives and higher-level managers), and the depreciation of the physical plant and equipment. Across reasonable fluctuations in production volume, these costs remain stable; whether Entenmann's makes 100,000 loaves or a million, the rent it pays for the bakery remains unchanged.

Total Cost Finally, the total cost is simply the sum of the variable and fixed costs. For example, in one year, our hypothetical hotel incurred $100,000 in fixed costs. We also know that because the hotel booked 10,000 room nights, its total variable cost is $100,000 (10,000 room nights × $10 per room). Thus, its total cost is $200,000.

Next, we illustrate how to use these costs in simple analyses that can inform managerial decision making about setting prices.

Break-Even Analysis and Decision Making

A useful technique that enables managers to examine the relationships among cost, price, revenue, and profit over different levels of production and sales is called break-even analysis. Central to this analysis is the determination of the break-even point, or the point at which the number of units sold generates just enough revenue to equal the total costs. At this point, profits are zero. Although profit, which represents the difference between the total cost and the total revenue (Total revenue or sales = Selling price of each unit sold × Number of units sold), can indicate how much money the firm is making or losing at a single period of time, it cannot tell managers how many units a firm must produce and sell before it stops losing money and at least breaks even, which is what the break-even point does.

How do we determine the break-even point? Exhibit 14.5 presents in graphic format the various cost and revenue information we have discussed. The graph contains three curves (recall that even though they are straight, we still call them curves): fixed costs, total costs, and total revenue. The vertical axis measures the revenue and costs in dollars, and the horizontal axis measures the quantity of units sold. The fixed cost curve will always appear as a horizontal line straight across the graph, because fixed costs do not change over different levels of volume.

The total cost curve starts where the fixed cost curve intersects the vertical axis at $100,000. When volume is equal to zero (no units are produced or sold), the fixed costs of operating the business remain and cannot be avoided. Thus, the lowest point the total costs

LO14-4 Describe how to calculate a product's break-even point.

EXHIBIT 14.5 Break-Even Analysis

can ever reach is equal to the total fixed costs. Beyond that point, the total cost curve increases by the amount of variable costs for each additional unit, which we calculate by multiplying the variable cost per unit by the number of units, or quantity.

Finally, the total revenue curve increases by the price of each additional unit sold. To calculate it, we multiply the price per unit by the number of units sold. The formulas for these calculations are as follows:

$$\text{Total variable costs} = \text{Variable cost per unit} \times \text{Quantity}$$
$$\text{Total costs} = \text{Fixed costs} + \text{Total variable costs}$$
$$\text{Total revenue} = \text{Price} \times \text{Quantity}$$

We again use the hotel example to illustrate these relationships. Recall that the fixed costs are $100,000 and the variable costs are $10 per room rented. If the rooms rent for $50 per night, how many rooms must the hotel rent over the course of a year to break even? If we study the graph carefully, we find the break-even point at 2,500, which means that the hotel must rent 2,500 rooms before its revenues equal its costs. If it rents fewer rooms, it loses money (the pink area); if it rents more, it makes a profit (the gold area). To determine the break-even point in units mathematically, we must introduce one more variable, the **contribution per unit**, which is the price less the variable cost per unit.

In this case,

$$\text{Contribution per unit} = \$50 - \$10 = \$40$$

Therefore, the break-even point becomes

$$\text{Break-even point (units)} = \frac{\text{Fixed costs}}{\text{Contributions per unit}}$$

That is,

$$\text{Break-even point (units)} = \frac{\$100,000}{\$40} = 2,500 \text{ room nights}$$

When the hotel has crossed the break-even point of 2,500 rooms, it will start earning profit at the same rate of the contribution per unit. So if the hotel rents 4,000 rooms—that is, 1,500 rooms more than the break-even point—its profit will be $60,000 (1,500 rooms × $40 contribution per unit).

$$\text{Profit} = (\text{Contribution per unit} \times \text{Quantity}) - \text{Fixed costs}$$
$$\text{Profit} = (\$40 \times 4,000) - \$100,000 = \$60,000$$

Or an alternative formula would be:

$$\text{Profit} = (\text{Price} \times \text{Quantity}) - [\text{Fixed costs} + (\text{Variable costs} \times \text{Quantity})]$$
$$\text{Profit} = (\$50 \times 4,000) - [\$100,000 + (\$10 \times 4,000)]$$
$$\text{Profit} = \$200,000 - (\$100,000 + \$40,000) = \$60,000$$

Let's extend this simple break-even analysis to show how many units a firm must produce and sell to achieve a target profit. Say the hotel wanted to make $200,000 in profit each

In a hotel, the cost of the physical structure, including the lobby, is fixed—it is incurred even if no rooms are rented. The costs of washing the towels and sheets are variable—the more rooms that are rented, the higher the costs.

(Left): ©Africa Studio/Shutterstock; (right): ©design.at.krooogle/Shutterstock

year. How many rooms would it have to rent at the current price? In this instance, we need only add the targeted profit to the fixed costs to determine that number:

$$\text{Break-even point (units)} = \frac{(\text{Fixed costs} + \text{Target profit})}{\text{Contributions per unit}}$$

or

$$7{,}500 \text{ rooms} = \frac{(\$100{,}000 + \$200{,}000)}{\$40}$$

Although a break-even analysis cannot actually help managers set prices, it does help them assess their pricing strategies because it clarifies the conditions in which different prices may make a product or service profitable. It becomes an even more powerful tool when performed on a range of possible prices for comparative purposes. For example, the hotel management could analyze various prices, not just $50, to determine how many hotel rooms it would have to rent at what price to make a $200,000 profit.

Naturally, however, there are limitations to a break-even analysis. First, it is unlikely that a hotel has one specific price that it charges for each and every room, so the price it would use in its break-even analysis probably represents an "average" price that attempts to account for these variances. Second, prices often get reduced as quantity increases, because the costs decrease, so firms must perform several break-even analyses at different quantities. Third, a break-even analysis cannot indicate for sure how many rooms will be rented or, in the case of products, how many units will sell at a given price. It only tells the firm what its costs, revenues, and profitability will be, given a set price and an assumed quantity. To determine how many units the firm actually will sell, it must bring in the demand estimates we discussed previously.

Markup and Target Return Pricing

In many situations, the manufacturer may want to achieve a standard markup—let's say 10 percent of cost. In our example of the teeth-whitening kit, let's assume:

Variable costs per unit:	$8.00
Fixed costs:	$1,000,000.00
Expected sales:	1,000,000 units

The teeth-whitening kit manufacturer would like to calculate the price at which it would make a 10 percent markup.

The formula for calculating a target return price based on a markup on cost is:

$$\text{Target return price} = [\text{Variable costs} + (\text{Fixed costs} \div \text{Expected unit sales})]$$
$$\times [1 \times \text{Target return \% (expressed as a decimal)}]$$

In this example, this would result in the firm charging $9.90.

$$\text{Target return price} = [\$8.00 + (\$1,000,000.00 \div 1,000,000.00)] \times (1 + 0.10)$$
$$\text{Target return price} = \$9.00 \times 1.1 = \$9.90$$

PROGRESS CHECK

1. What is the difference between fixed costs and variable costs?
2. How does one calculate the break-even point in units?

 LO14-5 Indicate the four types of price competitive levels.

Competition

Because the fourth C, competition, has a profound impact on pricing strategies, we use this section to focus on its effect, as well as on how competitors react to certain pricing strategies. There are four levels of competition—monopoly, oligopolistic competition, monopolistic competition, and pure competition—and each has its own set of pricing challenges and opportunities (see Exhibit 14.6).

EXHIBIT 14.6 Four Levels of Competition: Can you match each photo to its respective type of competition?

	Less price competition	More price competition	
	Monopoly One firm controls the market	Oligopoly A handful of firms control the market	Fewer firms
	Monopolistic competition Many firms selling differentiated products at different prices	Pure competition Many firms selling commodities for the same prices	Many firms

In a monopoly, one firm provides the product or service in a particular industry, which results in less price competition. Some near monopolies include SiriusXM radio and Alphabet (parent company of Google). SiriusXM has a monopoly-like position, as it is the only option for satellite radio in the market, and therefore can set its price as it sees fit. However, it is in competition with music streaming sites such as Pandora and Spotify, which keep prices in check. Alphabet has a near monopoly on search engines, controlling 79 percent of the market, and its market share is still rising while its top two competitors control only about 7 percent each.[20] Monopolies are regulated and can be dismantled by the government through antitrust laws to protect customers from paying overly high prices for goods and services.[21]

When a market is characterized by oligopolistic competition, only a few firms dominate. Firms typically change their prices in reaction to competition to avoid upsetting an otherwise stable competitive environment. Examples of oligopolistic markets include the soft drink market and commercial airline travel. Sometimes reactions to prices in oligopolistic markets can result in a price war, which occurs when two or more firms compete primarily by lowering their prices. Firm A lowers its prices; Firm B responds by meeting or beating Firm A's new price. Firm A then responds with another new price, and so on. In some cases though, these tactics result in predatory pricing, which occurs when a firm sets a very low price for one or more of its products with the intent of driving its competition out of business. Predatory pricing is illegal in the United States under both the Sherman Antitrust Act and the Federal Trade Commission Act.

Monopolistic competition occurs when there are many firms competing for customers in a given market but their products are differentiated. When so many firms compete, product differentiation rather than strict price competition tends to appeal to consumers. This is the most common form of competition. Hundreds of firms make sunglasses, thus the market is highly differentiated. Ray-Ban offers its iconic, thick-rimmed, black Wayfarer-style sunglasses. Oakley sells sunglasses that are sporty, with varied lens colors that promise to protect wearers' eyes better when they are engaging in outdoor activities. For consumers looking for more style, fashion designers such as Prada and Gucci have their own sunglasses. Depending on the features, style, and quality, companies compete for very different market segments. By differentiating their products using various attributes, prices, and brands, they create unique value propositions in the minds of their customers.

With pure competition, a large number of sellers offer standardized products or commodities that consumers perceive as substitutable, such as grains, gold, meat, spices, or minerals. In such markets, price usually is set according to the laws of supply and demand. For example, wheat is wheat, so it does not matter to a commercial bakery whose wheat it buys. However, the secret to pricing success in a pure competition market is not necessarily to offer the lowest price, because doing so might create a price war and erode profits. Instead, some firms have brilliantly decommoditized their products. For example, most people feel that all salt purchased in a grocery is the same. But companies like Morton have branded their salt to move into a monopolistically competitive market.

The sunglasses market is characterized by monopolistic competition with hundreds of firms with differentiated products. Ray-Ban's Wayfarer sunglasses (left) are classic, Oakley's sunglasses (middle) are sporty, and Gucci's sunglasses (right) are very, very fashionable.

When a commodity can be differentiated somehow, even if simply by a sticker or logo, there is an opportunity for consumers to identify it as distinct from the rest, and in this case, firms can at least partially extricate their product from a pure competitive market.

PROGRESS CHECK

1. What are the four different types of competitive environments?

How does DeWalt determine the suggested retail price so that all channel members make their required profit?

©S K D/Alamy Stock Photo

Channel Members

Channel members—manufacturers, wholesalers, and retailers—have different perspectives when it comes to pricing strategies. Consider a manufacturer that is focused on increasing the image and reputation of its brand but working with a retailer that is primarily concerned with increasing its sales. The manufacturer may desire to keep prices higher to convey a better image, whereas the retailer wants lower prices and will accept lower profits to move the product, regardless of consumers' impressions of the brand. Unless channel members carefully communicate their pricing goals and select channel partners that agree with them, conflict will surely arise.

Developing a price that allows all channel members to earn their requisite profits requires careful planning. Imagine that the electric tool manufacturer DeWalt is reconsidering the price of its 1/2-inch, 18-volt, Heavy Duty Cordless Drill that it sells through Ace Hardware stores. Using several pricing experiments (as described in Chapter 10), it determines that the profit-maximizing retail price is $100 (see Exhibit 14.7). Ace Hardware is a retailers' cooperative, such that it helps its members achieve economies of scale by buying as a group. In a sense, a retailers' cooperative thus is similar to a

EXHIBIT 14.7   Pricing through the Channels

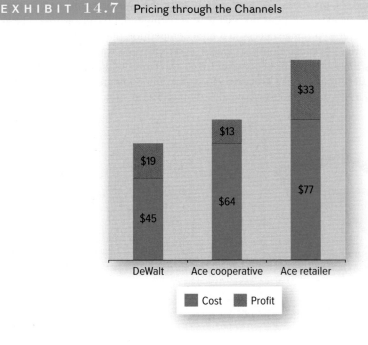

	DeWalt	Ace cooperative	Ace retailer
Profit	$19	$13	$33
Cost	$45	$64	$77

■ Cost   ■ Profit

wholesaler, except that in this case, the retailers have some control over, and sometimes ownership in, the operation of the cooperative. For Ace Hardware to sell the DeWalt drill to consumers for $100, each retail store must purchase it for $77 at most, to be sure it can earn a 30 percent profit margin [$77 cost to retailer + (30 percent profit × $77 = $23 profit) = $100]. The Ace Hardware cooperative in turn requires a 20 percent profit margin on its cost, so it must purchase the drill from DeWalt for $64 [$64 cost to Ace + (20 percent profit × $64 = $13 profit) = $77]. The drill costs DeWalt $45 to produce, leaving DeWalt a profit of $19 ($64 − $45), or 42 percent (19/45), which is slightly above its benchmark profit of 40 percent. As this relatively simple example reveals, determining prices throughout the marketing channel that will enable all channel members to make a reasonable profit requires thought, cooperation, and strong negotiating skills by everyone involved.

Reviewing Learning Objectives

LO14-1 List the four pricing orientations.

A profit-oriented pricing strategy focuses on maximizing, or at least reaching, a target profit for the company. A sales orientation instead sets prices with the goal of increasing sales levels. With a competitor-oriented pricing strategy, a firm sets its prices according to what its competitors do. Finally, a customer-oriented strategy determines consumers' perceptions of value and prices accordingly.

LO14-2 Explain the relationship between price and quantity sold.

Generally, when prices go up, quantity sold goes down. Sometimes, however—particularly with prestige products and services—demand actually increases with price.

LO14-3 Explain price elasticity.

Changes in price generally affect demand; price elasticity measures the extent of this effect. It is based on the percentage change in quantity divided by the percentage change in price. Depending on the resulting value, a market offering can be identified as elastic, such that the market is very price sensitive, or inelastic, in which case the market cares little about the price.

LO14-4 Describe how to calculate a product's break-even point.

Because the break-even point occurs when the units sold generate just enough profit to cover the total costs of producing those units, it requires knowledge of the fixed cost, total cost, and total revenue curves. When these curves intersect, the marketer has found the break-even point.

LO14-5 Indicate the four types of price competitive levels.

In a monopoly setting, one firm controls the market and sets the price. In an oligopolistic competitive market, a few firms dominate and tend to set prices according to a competitor-oriented strategy. Monopolistic competition occurs when there are many firms competing for customers in a given market but their products are differentiated. Finally, pure competition means that consumers likely regard the products offered by different companies as basic substitutes, so the firms must work hard to achieve the lowest price point, limited by the laws of supply and demand.

Key Terms

- break-even analysis, 439
- break-even point, 439
- competitive parity, 429
- competitor orientation, 429
- complementary products, 438
- contribution per unit, 440
- cross-price elasticity, 438
- customer orientation, 430
- demand curve, 431
- dynamic pricing, 437
- elastic, 435
- fixed costs, 439

- income effect, 437
- individualized pricing, 437
- inelastic, 435
- maximizing profits, 428
- monopolistic competition, 443
- monopoly, 443
- oligopolistic competition, 443
- predatory pricing, 443
- premium pricing, 429
- prestige products or services, 433
- price, 426
- price elasticity of demand, 435

- price war, 443
- profit orientation, 428
- pure competition, 443
- retailers' cooperative, 444
- sales orientation, 428
- status quo pricing, 429
- substitute products, 438
- substitution effect, 437
- target profit pricing, 428
- target return pricing, 428
- total cost, 439
- variable costs, 438

Marketing Digitally

1. Several different pricing models can be found on the Internet. Each model appeals to different customer groups. Go to Ebay's website (www.ebay.com) and try to buy this book. What pricing options and prices are available? Do you believe that everyone will choose the least expensive option? Why or why not? Now go to Amazon's website (www.amazon.com). Is there more than one price available for this book? If so, what are those prices? Are different versions available? If you had to buy another copy of this book, where would you buy it and why would you buy it there?

2. Prices can vary depending on many factors including the market and novelty. Etsy allows anyone to sell goods that they've made in its online marketplace. Go to www.etsy.com to learn more about Etsy. Then, search its sellers' shops to find an item in which you are interested. Now, go to www.amazon.com and search for a similar item. Does Amazon offer the same or similar product? Are there price differences between Etsy and Amazon? How do Etsy and Amazon communicate value?

Marketing Applications

1. You and your two roommates are starting a pet grooming service to help put yourselves through college. There are two other well-established pet services in your area. Should you set your price higher or lower than that of the competition? Justify your answer.

2. One roommate believes the most important objective in setting prices for your new pet grooming business is to generate a large profit while keeping an eye on your competitors' prices; the other roommate believes it is important to maximize sales and set prices according to what your customers expect to pay. Who is right and why?

3. Assume you have decided to buy an advertisement in the local newspaper to publicize your new pet grooming service. The cost of the ad is $1,000. You have decided to charge $40 for a dog grooming, and your variable costs are $20 for each dog. How many dogs do you have to groom to break even on the cost of the ad? What is your break-even point if you charge $60 per dog?

4. The local newspaper ad for your pet grooming business isn't helping much, so you decide to post your services on an auction site, where customers can bid for your services. What should the starting price of the auction be?

5. Is there a difference between a $5,900 Loro Piana vicuña sweater and a $150 cashmere sweater from L.L.Bean? Have you ever purchased a higher-priced product or service because you thought the quality was better than that of a similar, lower-priced product or service? What was the product or service? Do you believe you made a rational choice?

6. A soft drink manufacturer opened a new manufacturing plant in the Midwest. The total fixed costs are $100 million. It plans to sell the drinks to retailers for $6 for a package of ten 12-ounce cans. Its variable costs for the ingredients are $4 per package. Calculate the break-even volume. What would happen to the break-even point if the fixed costs decreased to $50 million, or the variable costs decreased to $3 due to declines in commodity costs? What would the break-even volume be if the firm wanted to make $20 million?

7. On your weekly grocery shopping trip, you notice that the price of spaghetti has gone up 50 cents a pound. How will this price increase affect the demand for spaghetti sauce, rice, and Parmesan cheese? Explain your answer in terms of the price elasticity of demand.

8. How do pricing strategies vary across markets that are characterized by monopolistic, oligopolistic, monopolistic competition, and pure competition?

9. Suppose you are in the market for a new Samsung 4K television. You see one advertised at a locally owned store for $300 less than it costs at Best Buy. The salesperson at the local store tells you that the television came from another retailer in a nearby state that had too many units of that model. Explain who benefits and who is harmed from such a gray market transaction: you, Samsung, Best Buy, and the local store.

10. Has the Internet helped lower the price of some types of merchandise? Justify your answer.

11. Imagine that Microsoft has recently developed an innovative technology. Because no other firm has this technology, demand is somewhat inelastic, and therefore Microsoft has some leeway in setting its price. Discuss the factors that Microsoft should consider when setting a market price.

Quiz Yourself

1. As the Vice President of Marketing for her firm, Jana is considering implementing a company wide pricing policy that all products must achieve a target profit margin of 15 percent, so the firm can achieve its overall growth objectives. What type of company objective is this?

   a. Profit orientation

   b. Sales orientation

   c. Competitor orientation

   d. Customer orientation

   e. Market orientation

2. Standardized products and commodities such as grains or chemical products are characteristics of which competitive market form?

   a. Monopoly

   b. Oligopoly

   c. Pure competition

   d. Competitive parity

   e. Monopolistic competition

(Answers to these two questions can be found in the Quiz Yourself Answer Key section.)

Chapter Case Study   connect

PLANET FITNESS: PRICING FOR SUCCESS[22]

How does going completely against the grain of a typical fitness club strategy lead to success? That's the question that Planet Fitness appears uniquely positioned to answer. Most health clubs provide members with vast and seemingly valuable extra amenities such as child care, juice bars and protein supplements, on-staff professional trainers, and a broad range of fitness classes.[23] But many customers find the prices too high because they see little value in some of these amenities. Further reducing the value of traditional gym memberships, many consumers regard the social aspects unpleasant and offputting—whether that means observing others with nearly perfect bodies posturing in the mirror or listening to grunting exercisers huff with every lift.

While its competitors target upscale fitness buffs working on their six-pack abs, Planet Fitness successfully pursues an entirely different market: those who do not really enjoy going to the gym but know they need to do so to stay healthy. These exercisers are unlikely to hit the gym five or six times a week, making conventional gym memberships, which demand yearly contracts and fees of $49 to $95 per month, appear more expensive on a per-visit basis. Planet Fitness' formula is different: At $10 a month, the membership offers good value even if customers get to the club only a couple of times each week.[24]

In combination with its low price point, Planet Fitness promises a clean, friendly, laid-back workout environment featuring brand-name cardiovascular and strength equipment. Although it does not have the high-end amenities its competitors promise (e.g., pools, juice bars), the clubs maintain the key elements its members want: brand-name equipment, unlimited fitness training, flat-screen televisions, and large locker rooms. Its customers know from its advertising that they can expect a nonintimidating workout environment, or, as Planet Fitness promises, "No gymtimidation. No lunks. Just $10 a month."[25] With its foundation in the idea that simple is better,[26] Planet Fitness has become the fastest-growing full-sized fitness club in the United States. Exhibit 14.8 compares the prices of several major gyms.

For those who want a little more, Planet Fitness also offers a premium PF BlackCard membership for $19.99 a month, which promises access to nearly all the clubs in the Planet Fitness chain, unlimited guest privileges, use of tanning and massage chairs, and half-priced drinks.[27]

In addition to these in-club benefits, Planet Fitness' growth has been reinforced by its effective location strategy and marketing efforts that focus on attracting new customers. The low-cost monthly membership makes it easy to draw new members. Because most members come in only a couple of times each week, Planet Fitness also enjoys operating efficiencies and economies of scale, achieved by welcoming a high volume of members on any one day.[28]

EXHIBIT 14.8	Membership Costs of Planet Fitness and Competition in New York City	

Gym	Monthly Cost	Upfront Cost
24 Hour Fitness	$44.99	$99.77
Bally Total Fitness	$29.99	$88.98
LA Fitness	$12.95/wk	$25.90
Planet Fitness	$10.00	$29.00
Snap Fitness	$39.99	$ 0.00

Planet Fitness treats customers like real people. What kind of fitness club offers members pizza on the first Monday of every month, bagels on the first Tuesday, and Tootsie Rolls on a regular basis?[29] The kind of gym that plans to expand to 1,000 locations, with an eventual goal of more than 2,000, and that attracts more than 5 million members and systemwide sales approaching $700 million.[30]

Questions

1. What benefits do customers receive in return for the sacrifice they make when buying a membership at Planet Fitness?

2. How does this benefit–sacrifice ratio give Planet Fitness a competitive advantage in its industry?

3. Given its price strategy, why is it essential for Planet Fitness to continually attract new members? Do its high-end pricing competitors face the same need? Why or why not?

Endnotes

1. Keith Loria, "Kroger's CFO Talks Expansion, Meal Kits, and Private Label Strategy," *Food Dive,* May 15, 2017.

2. Sandy Skrovan, "Kroger's Analytics and Personalized Pricing Keep It a Step Ahead of Its Competitors," *Food Dive,* July 10, 2017.

3. Hayley Peterson, "How Kroger Hopes to Change Grocery Shopping as We Know It," *Business Insider,* January 16, 2018.

4. Skrovan, "Kroger's Analytics and Personalized Pricing Keep It a Step Ahead."

5. Peterson, "How Kroger Hopes to Change Grocery Shopping."

6. R. Suri and M. V. Thakor, "'Made in Country' versus 'Made in County': Effects of Local Manufacturing Origins on Price Perceptions," *Psychology & Marketing* 30, no. 2 (2013), pp. 121–32; R. Suri, K. B. Monroe, and U. Koc, "Math Anxiety and Its Effects on Consumers' Preference for Price Promotion Formats," *Journal of the Academy of Marketing Science* 41, no. 3 (2013), pp. 271–82; Kent B. Monroe, *Pricing: Making Profitable Decisions,* 3rd ed. (New York: McGraw-Hill, 2003); Dhruv Grewal, Kent B. Monroe, and R. Krishnan, "The Effects of Price Comparison Advertising on Buyers' Perceptions of Acquisition Value and Transaction Value," *Journal of Marketing* 62 (April 1998), pp. 46–60.

7. Stephan Liozu, Andreas Hinterhuber, and Toni Somers, "Organizational Design and Pricing Capabilities for Superior Firm Performance," *Management Decision* 52, no. 1 (2014), pp. 54–78; Dhruv Grewal et al., "Evolving Pricing Practices: The Role of New Business Models," *Journal of Product & Brand Management* 20, no. 7 (2011), pp. 510–13.

8. Susan Carey, "Airlines Challenge Low-Cost Foes on Fares," *The Wall Street Journal,* December 29, 2015.

9. Mary Schlangenstein, "Airlines Try and Fail to Raise Fares," *Bloomberg,* February 2, 2018, www.bloomberg.com/news/articles/2018-02-02/airlines-try-and-fail-to-raise-fares-as-fuel-price-threat-looms.

10. "IBM Market Share Leader in Human Resources (HR) Business Transformation Outsourcing, Enterprise Sector," press release, www.ibm.com.

11. Carey, "Airlines Challenge Low-Cost Foes on Fares."

12. www.carmax.com/car-buying-process.

13. Desiree Au, "Who Would Pay $300,000 for a Handbag?," *The New York Times,* June 3, 2016, www.nytimes.com/2016/06/05/fashion/hermes-birkin-most-expensive-bag-ever-sold.html.

14. Fender Electric Guitars, www.fender.com.

15. Monroe, *Pricing.*

16. This type of B2B price discrimination is illegal under the Robinson-Patman Act of 1936. B2B sellers are allowed to charge different prices for merchandise of the same "grade and quality" if (1) the price difference is justified by different costs in manufacture, sale, or delivery (e.g., volume discounts); or (2) the price concession was given in good faith to meet a competitor's price. See www.ftc.gov/tips-advice/ competition-guidance/guide-antitrust-laws/price-discrimination-robinson-patman.

17. www.marketingpower.com/_layouts/Dictionary.aspx?dLetter=C.

18. www.marketingpower.com/_layouts/Dictionary.aspx?dLetter=S.

19. Aurora García-Gallego et al., "On the Evolution of Monopoly Pricing in Internet-Assisted Search Markets," *Journal of Business Research* 67, no. 5 (2014), pp. 795–801; Joan Lindsey-Mullikin and Dhruv Grewal, "Market Price Variation: The Availability of Internet Market Information," *Journal of the Academy of Marketing Science* 34, no. 2 (2006), pp. 236–43.

20. Brian Feroldi, "7 Near-Monopolies That Are Perfectly Legal in America," *The Motley Fool*, July 21, 2017, www.fool.com/investing/2017/07/21/7-near-monopolies-that-are-perfectly-legal-in-amer.aspx.

21. "Guide to Antitrust Laws," United State Federal Trade Commission, www.ftc.gov/tips-advice/competition-guidance/guide-antitrust-laws.

22. This case was written by Jeanne L. Munger (University of Southern Maine) in conjunction with the textbook authors Dhruv Grewal and Michael Levy, as a basis for class discussion rather than to illustrate effective or ineffective marketing practices.

23. "Planet Fitness Continues Successful Growth with Puerto Rico Expansion," press release, www.marketwatch.com/story/.

24. www.planetfitness.com/.

25. Andrew Adam Newman, "A Gym for People Who Don't Like Gyms," *The New York Times*, January 3, 2013, www.nytimes.com.

26. Judith Ohikuare, "The Secret of Planet Fitness's Success," *Inc.*, February 2013, www.inc.com/magazine/.

27. "Planet Fitness Continues Successful Growth."

28. Beth Kowitt, "The Southwest Airlines of the Gym Business," *Fortune*, November 21, 2013, http://features.blogs.fortune.cnn.com/.

29. Newman, "A Gym for People Who Don't Like Gyms."

30. Kowitt, "The Southwest Airlines of the Gym Business."

i. Jessica Wohl, "Taco Bell Gears Up for Value Fight in Fast Food," *Advertising Age*, December 15, 2017; Kristen Monllos, "Taco Bell's Hilarious, Over-the-Top Nod to the Illuminati Isn't Your Average Value Menu Campaign," *Adweek*, December 15, 2017, www.adweek.com/brand-marketing/taco-bells-hilarious-over-the-top-nod-to-the-illuminati-isnt-your-average-value-menu-campaign/; Erica Sweeney, "Taco Bell Weaves a 'Web of Fries' in Fake Film Trailer," *Marketing Dive*, January 26, 2018, www.marketingdive.com/news/taco-bell-weaves-a-web-of-fries-in-fake-film-trailer/515638/; Sarah Witten, "Taco Bell Is Launching Nacho Fries in Bid to Win the Dollar Menu War," *CNBC*, January 3, 2018, www.cnbc.com/2018/01/03/taco-bell-is-launching-nacho-fries-in-bid-to-win-the-dollar-menu-war.html.

ii. Jenn Markey, "Three Things You Need to Know about Amazon's Price Strategy," *Retail Customer Experience*, April 21, 2014, www.retailcustomerexperience.com.

iii. "A Look Back: How Predictive Analytics Transformed the Airline Industry," Cusotra, www.custora.com/university/formarketers/predictive-analytics/basic/predictive-analytics-and-the-airline-industry; "Price Trends & Tips Explanation," Kayak, 2015, www.kayak.com.

iv. Knowledge@Wharton, "Have Customers Accepted Dynamic Pricing?," *RetailWire*, August 18, 2016; "The Promise—and Perils—of Dynamic Pricing," Knowledge@Wharton, February 23, 2016; Jim Pagels, "Dynamic Pricing Can Lower Ticket Revenues If Misused," *Forbes*, February 24, 2015.

Quiz Yourself Answer Key

1. What type of company objective is this?

   Answer: (a) Profit orientation

2. Standardized products and commodities such as grains or chemical products are characteristics of which competitive market form?

   Answer: (c) Pure competition

©Stephen Lovekin/Getty Images for 20th Century Fox

LEARNING OBJECTIVES

After reading this chapter, you should be able to:

LO15-1 Identify three methods that firms use to set their prices.

LO15-2 Describe the difference between an everyday low pricing (EDLP) strategy and a high/low strategy.

LO15-3 Explain the difference between a price skimming and a market penetration pricing strategy.

LO15-4 Identify tactics used to reduce prices to consumers.

LO15-5 Identify tactics used to reduce prices to businesses.

LO15-6 List the pricing practices that are illegal or unethical.

CHAPTER 15

STRATEGIC PRICING METHODS AND TACTICS

The leadership changes at Tiffany & Co., the jewelry line known for its signature blue boxes, are symbolic of the struggles and challenges that many luxury brands face today. Those struggles led to the ouster of one CEO and the reinsertion of another, at least on a temporary basis. Where the brand goes from here is anyone's guess though.

Luxury markets are defined largely by their prices, which are set high specifically to signal their exclusivity and high quality. But high prices limit market growth because only the "lucky few" can afford them. Furthermore, even wealthy shoppers may grow price conscious; overall luxury goods sales recently dropped for the first time since 2009. Several years back, in an attempt to reach more customers, Tiffany expanded its product lines, seeking to attract some customers who could afford to spend a few hundred dollars, but not thousands, on a beautiful trinket or gift for themselves or a loved one.

But by adding a range of lower-priced products, Tiffany risked its reputation for exclusive items and put its luxury status at stake. Nearly half of its sales revenues started coming from items with an average price of $530—really low for a luxury brand. Consumers looking for something special instead started considering brands like Cartier, where "You'd be hard pressed to find anything . . . for $500."

At the same time as it adjusted its pricing strategy, Tiffany & Co. also was spreading its marketing efforts and sales channels. Rather than being available only in the 310 dedicated, branded stores, the products started selling on the fashion website Net-a-Porter and in other boutique retail stores. The marketing campaigns also appeared more widely in various communication channels. As a result, some parties came to believe the famous Tiffany blue was even being overused, saturating every surface instead of maintaining its exclusivity and cachet.

By the same token, when the recently fired CEO sought to limit the use of the blue, critics also assailed the choice as a failure to respect the company's long history and tradition. Such criticisms also arose in response to the announcement that Lady Gaga would be the new face of the brand; unfair comparisons suggested that she was no Audrey Hepburn, the famous actress who helped make the retailer a familiar name by starring in the film version of *Breakfast at Tiffany's*.

Finally, Tiffany & Co. owns much of the production processes it uses to create its goods. Unlike most jewelers, it polishes and finishes its own gemstones, and it maintains agreements with diamond miners to purchase minimum amounts each year. Although this approach helps the company guarantee the quality of its products, it also can create inventory issues. For example, even if it has no pressing need for more diamonds, it must purchase them under the terms of its contract. In that case, Tiffany & Co. could find itself forced to lower prices to clear inventory—a most un-luxury move for a luxury brand.[1]

Coming up with the "right" price is never easy, as this opening example shows. How can a firm determine what consumers are willing to pay and how much firms can charge? To answer such questions, we examine various pricing strategies and tactics in this chapter. We focus on specific considerations for setting pricing strategies, then discuss several specific pricing strategies. We also examine the implications of various pricing tactics—for consumers as well as businesses—and discuss some of the more important legal and ethical issues associated with pricing.

LO15-1 Identify three methods that firms use to set their prices.

CONSIDERATIONS FOR SETTING PRICE STRATEGIES

Firms embrace different objectives, face different market conditions, and operate in different manners. Thus, they employ unique pricing strategies that seem best for the particular set of circumstances in which they find themselves. Even a single firm needs different strategies across its products and services and over time as market conditions change. The choice of a pricing strategy thus is specific to the product/service and target market. Although firms tend to rely on similar strategies when they can, each product or service requires its own specific strategy, because no two are ever exactly the same in terms of the marketing mix. Three different methods that can help develop pricing strategies—cost based, competition based, and value based—are discussed in this section (see Exhibit 15.1).

Cost-Based Methods

As their name implies, cost-based pricing methods determine the final price to charge by starting with the cost. Relevant costs (e.g., fixed, variable, overhead) and a profit are added. Then this total amount is divided by the total demand to arrive at a cost-plus price. For example, assume the fixed costs to produce an item are $200,000, the variable costs add up to $100,000, and the estimated number of units to be produced is 30,000. Then,

$$(\$100,000 + \$200,000) \div 30,000 = \$10$$

EXHIBIT 15.1 Pricing Strategies

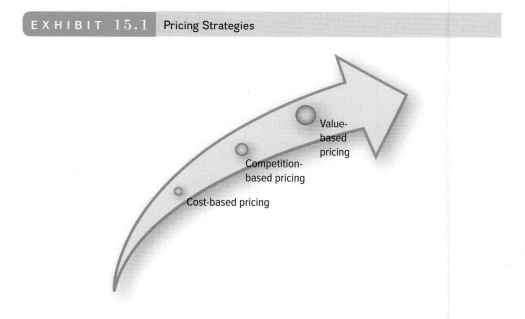

Value-based pricing

Competition-based pricing

Cost-based pricing

Adding Value 15.1   A Price Cut or a Competitive Marketing Tactic? Amazon's Price Drop at Whole Foods Is Both[i]

When Amazon announced that it was purchasing Whole Foods, it also almost immediately announced a big change: The prices at the high-end grocer popularly known as "Whole Paycheck" would drop as soon as the merger was complete. A bunch of organic kale would cost less on Monday than it did on Sunday, simply because on Monday, Amazon would own the grocery chain.

On the first day Amazon took over, customer traffic in Whole Foods stores increased by 31 percent compared with the same day the previous year. Although the spikes were not quite as large in the following weeks, the price cuts still drove increases in store traffic, such that the rates remained higher than they had been for the same weeks the previous year.

The reasons for this strategic move, as well as its advance announcement, are varied, but most observers believe that the primary driver is Amazon's determination to outcompete every other retailer in the market. By announcing the price cuts in advance and lowering the costs required for customers to shop at the popular grocer, Amazon is "putting the rest of the market on notice" that they will need to do better if they hope to survive. Almost immediately, the stock prices of competing retailers such as Kroger and Walmart plummeted, as investors predicted their impending struggles. Their predictions seemingly were borne out: An estimated 10 percent of Trader Joe's consumers visited Whole Foods during the three weeks after the price cuts. During that same time period, 24 percent of new customers visiting Whole Foods were previous Walmart patrons, and another 16 percent previously had been identified as Kroger shoppers.

Yet in some sense, the price cuts were not as dramatic as might have been expected. Avocados and almond milk saw some dramatic cuts, but most product prices decreased by only about 1 percent, or even stayed the same. Among the products with the biggest decreases in price, private-label and in-house bakery items were prominent. These items tend to enjoy higher margins, which makes it much easier for Whole Foods/Amazon to offer price cuts on them. In contrast, products such as frozen foods require a lot aof energy investments and are not as widely popular, so it becomes much harder to cut their prices.

To integrate the businesses, Amazon will introduce a Whole Foods–related rewards program for its Prime members. That is, Prime members will enjoy added discounts at Whole Foods, which Amazon hopes will expand the market for organic products to people who might not have been able to afford them previously. Such market expansions are necessary, especially considering that both Amazon and Whole Foods—regardless of their well-known names—still account for relatively small portions of the grocery market.

which is the total allocated cost per unit when 30,000 units are produced. If the desired markup is 20 percent, we multiply $10 by 1.20 (i.e., by $100 + 20 = 120$ percent) to attain the cost-plus price for this item: $12. This sales price represents a cost-plus-percentage markup.

Cost-based methods do not recognize the role that consumers' or competitors' prices play in the marketplace, though. Although it is relatively simple compared with other methods used to set prices, cost-based pricing requires that all costs be identified and calculated on a per-unit basis. Moreover, the process assumes that these costs will not vary much for different levels of production. If they do, the price might need to be raised or lowered according to the production level. Thus, with cost-based pricing, prices are usually set on the basis of estimates of average costs.

Competition-Based Methods

Recall from Chapter 14 that some firms set prices according to their competitors' prices. But even if they do not have a strict competitor orientation, most firms still know that consumers compare the prices of their products with the different product/price combinations that competitors offer. Thus, using a competition-based pricing method, they may set their prices to reflect the way they want consumers to interpret their own prices relative to competitors' offerings. For example, setting a price very close to a competitor's price signals to consumers that the product is similar, whereas setting the price much higher signals greater features, better quality, or some other valued benefit. Amazon is known for its strong competitive pricing in the online space and now is bringing this strategy into the grocery sector, as shown in Adding Value 15.1.

Value-Based Methods

Value-based pricing methods are approaches to setting prices that focus on the overall value of the product offering as perceived by the consumer. Consumers determine value by comparing the benefits they expect the product to deliver with the sacrifice they will need to

EXHIBIT 15.2	Improvement Value		
Incremental Benefits	**Improved Value**	**Benefit Weight**	**Weighted Factor**
Clarity	20%	0.40	8%
Range	40%	0.20	8%
Security	10%	0.10	1%
Battery life	5%	0.20	1%
Ease of use	30%	0.10	3%
Overall		1.00	21%

make to acquire the product. Of course, different consumers perceive value differently. So how does a manager use value-based pricing methods? We consider two key approaches here: the improvement value and the cost-of-ownership methods. The experimental approach in which different prices are introduced into the marketplace to determine which is the most profitable based on consumer demand was discussed in Chapter 10.

Improvement Value Method With the first method, the manager must estimate the improvement value of a new product or service. This improvement value represents an estimate of how much more (or less) consumers are willing to pay for a product relative to other comparable products. For example, suppose a major telecommunications company has developed a new cell phone. Using any of a host of research methods—such as consumer surveys—the manager could get customers to assess the new product relative to an existing product and provide an estimate of how much better it is; that is, its improvement value.

Exhibit 15.2 illustrates how to calculate the improvement value. Consumers evaluate how much better (or worse) the new cell phone is than an existing product on five dimensions: clarity, range, security, battery life, and ease of use. According to the respondents to the survey, the new cell phone has 20 percent more clarity than the comparison phone has. These consumers also weight the importance of the five attributes by allocating 100 points among them to indicate their relative importance; for the clarity dimension, this weighting is 0.40. When the manager multiplies the improvement weight by the relative importance percentage, clarity (20×0.40) emerges with a weighted factor of 8 percent. The marketer repeats the process for each benefit and sums the weighted factors to arrive at an approximation of the improvement

One way to determine the price of a new product, like a new cell phone model, is to determine the improvement value from the customers' perspective.

©Qi Heng/VCG via Getty Images

value of the new product from customers' points of view. In this illustration, the improvement value is equal to 21 percent, so if the other cell phone costs $100, the firm should be able to charge customers a value-based price as high as $121 ($100 × 1.21).

Cost-of-Ownership Method Another value-based method for setting prices determines the total cost of owning the product over its useful life. Using the cost-of-ownership method, consumers may be willing to pay more for a particular product because, over its entire lifetime, it will eventually cost less to own than will a cheaper alternative.[2]

Consider, for example, that an energy-efficient LED lightbulb costs $3 and is expected to last 6,000 hours. Alternatively, a conventional lightbulb costs $1 but its average life is only 1,500 hours. The LED bulb is expected to last four times longer than a conventional bulb, but it costs three times as much. Using the cost-of-ownership method, and considering the cost per hour, the LED bulb manufacturer could charge $4 for each bulb if it wanted to be equivalent to the cost of the conventional bulb. But research also has indicated that many consumers are reluctant to spend $4 for a bulb when they have been used to getting them for $1, so the manufacturer chose to charge only $3.

Implementing Value-Based Pricing Methods Although value-based pricing methods can be quite effective, they also necessitate a great deal of consumer research to be implemented successfully. Sellers must know how consumers in different market segments will attach value to the benefits delivered by their products. They also must account for changes in consumer attitudes, because the way customers perceive value today may not be the way they perceive it tomorrow.

PROGRESS CHECK

1. What are the three different considerations for setting prices?
2. How can you use value-based methods for setting prices?

PRICING STRATEGIES

A pricing strategy is a long-term approach to setting prices broadly in an integrative effort (across all the firm's products) based on the five Cs of pricing (company objectives, costs, customers, competition, and channel members) discussed in Chapter 14. In this section, we discuss a number of commonly used price strategies: everyday low pricing, high/low pricing, and new product strategies.

Everyday Low Pricing (EDLP)

With an everyday low pricing (EDLP) strategy, companies stress the continuity of their retail prices at a level somewhere between the regular, nonsale price and the deep-discount sale prices their competitors may offer. By reducing consumers' search costs, EDLP adds value; consumers can spend less of their valuable time comparing prices, including sale prices, at different stores. With its EDLP strategy, Walmart communicates to consumers that, for any given group of often-purchased items, its prices will tend to be lower than those of any other company in that market. This claim does not necessarily mean that every item that consumers may purchase will be priced lower at Walmart than anywhere else—in fact, some competitive retailers will offer lower prices on some items. However, for an average purchase, Walmart's prices tend to be lower overall.

LO15-2 Describe the difference between an everyday low pricing (EDLP) strategy and a high/low strategy.

High/Low Pricing

An alternative to EDLP is a high/low pricing strategy, which relies on the promotion of sales, during which prices are temporarily reduced to encourage purchases. A high/low strategy is appealing because it attracts two distinct market segments: those who are not

A high/low pricing strategy relies on the promotion of sales, during which prices are temporarily reduced to encourage purchases.

©Spencer Platt/Getty Images

L015-3 Explain the difference between a price skimming and a market penetration pricing strategy.

price sensitive and are willing to pay the "high" price and more price-sensitive customers who wait for the "low" sale price. High/low sellers can also create excitement and attract customers through the "get them while they last" atmosphere that occurs during a sale.

Sellers using a high/low pricing strategy often communicate their strategy through the creative use of a reference price, which is the price against which buyers compare the actual selling price of the product and that facilitates their evaluation process. The seller labels the reference price as the "regular price" or an "original price." When consumers view the "sale price" and compare it with the provided reference price, their perceptions of the value of the deal increase.[3]

In the photo below, the retailer has provided a card with a reference price which is crossed out to indicate that $59.99 is the regular price of the shirts. In addition, the card highlights the current "sale" price of $39.99. Thus, the reference price suggests to consumers that they are getting a good deal and will save money. Thus, it is crucial that retailers and manufacturers provide genuine advertised reference prices in their ads and signage.

New Product Pricing Strategies

Developing pricing strategies for new products is one of the most challenging tasks a manager can undertake. When the new product is similar to what already appears on the market, this job is somewhat easier, because the product's approximate value has already been established and the value-based methods described earlier in this chapter can be employed. But when the new product is truly innovative, or what we call "new to the world," determining consumers' perceptions of its value and pricing it accordingly become far more difficult.

Two distinct new product pricing strategies are discussed next: penetration pricing and price skimming.

The reference price is $59.99, while the sale price is $39.99. The reference price provides potential customers with an idea of the "regular price" before it was put on sale.

©Mark Kauzlarich/Bloomberg via Getty Images

Penetration Pricing Firms using a penetration pricing strategy set the initial price low for the introduction of the new product or service. Their objective is to build sales, market share, and profits quickly and deter competition from entering the market. The low penetration price is an incentive to purchase the product immediately. Firms using a penetration pricing strategy expect the unit cost to drop significantly as the accumulated volume sold increases, an effect known as the experience curve effect. With this effect, as sales continue to grow, the costs continue to drop.

In addition to offering the potential to build sales, market share, and profits, penetration pricing discourages competitors from entering the market because the profit margin is relatively low. Furthermore, if the costs to produce the product drop because of the accumulated volume, competitors who enter the market later will face higher unit costs, at least until their volume catches up with the early entrant.

A penetration strategy has its drawbacks. First, the firm must have the capacity to satisfy a rapid rise in demand—or at least be able to add that capacity quickly. Second, low price does not signal high quality. Of course, a price below their expectations decreases the risk for consumers to purchase the product and test its quality for themselves. Third, firms should avoid a penetration pricing strategy if some segments of the market are willing to pay more for the product; otherwise, the firm is just "leaving money on the table."

Price Skimming In many markets, and particularly for new and innovative products or services, innovators and early adopters (see Chapter 12) are willing to pay a higher price to obtain the new product or service. This strategy, known as price skimming, appeals to these segments of consumers who are willing to pay the premium price to have the innovation first. This tactic is particularly common in technology markets, where sellers know that customers of the hottest and coolest products will wait in line for hours, desperate to be the first to own the newest version. These innovators are willing to pay the very highest prices to obtain brand-new examples of technology advances and exciting product enhancements. However, after this high-price market segment becomes saturated and sales begin to slow down, companies generally lower the price to capture (or skim) the next most price-sensitive market segment, which is willing to pay a somewhat lower price. For most companies, the price-dropping process can continue until the demand for the product has been satisfied, even at the lowest price points.

New technologies often implement a price skimming strategy. For example, when the Apple Watch was first released, the most affordable option, the Apple Watch Sport, started at $349.[4] Although consumers were slow to embrace the new and expensive technology,

Price skimming is often used for high-demand video games like *Far Cry 5* because fans will pay a higher price to be one of the first to own the newest version.

©Chesnot/Getty Images

enough early adopters purchased the Apple Watches that wearable technology has penetrated wider target markets, and sales for such technologies continue to grow. One reason for this is that prices have dropped. The Apple Watch now starts at $249, and competitors such as Misfit's smartwatches start at just $200.[5]

For price skimming to work though, the product or service must be perceived as breaking new ground in some way, offering consumers new benefits currently unavailable in alternative products. When they believe it will work, firms use skimming strategies for a variety of reasons. Some may start by pricing relatively high to signal high quality to the market. Others may decide to price high at first to limit demand, which gives them time to build their production capacities. Similarly, some firms employ a skimming strategy to try to quickly earn back some of the high research and development investments they made for the new product. Finally, firms employ skimming strategies to test consumers' price sensitivity. A firm that prices too high can always lower the price, but if the price is initially set too low, it is almost impossible to raise it without significant consumer resistance.

Apple uses a price skimming strategy. The Apple Watch Sport (left) started at $349, but now starts at $249, which is still higher than competitors like Misfit (right) that start at just $200.

(Left): ©Alexey Boldin/Shutterstock; (right): ©Olly Curtis/MacFormat Magazine via Getty Image

Furthermore, for a skimming pricing strategy to be successful, competitors cannot be able to enter the market easily; otherwise, price competition will likely force lower prices and undermine the whole strategy. Competitors might be prevented from entering the market through patent protections, their inability to copy the innovation (because it is complex to manufacture, its raw materials are hard to get, or the product relies on proprietary technology), or the high costs of entry.

Skimming strategies also face a significant potential drawback in the relatively high unit costs associated with producing small volumes of products. Therefore, firms must consider the trade-off between earning a higher price and suffering higher production costs. Finally, firms using a skimming strategy for new products must face the consequences of ultimately having to lower the price as demand wanes. Margins suffer, and customers who purchased the product or service at the higher initial price may become irritated when the price falls.

PROGRESS CHECK

1. Explain the difference between EDLP and high/low pricing.
2. What pricing strategies should be considered when introducing a new product?

LO15-4 Identify tactics used to reduce prices to consumers.

PRICING TACTICS

It is important to distinguish clearly between pricing strategies and pricing tactics. A pricing strategy, as we have discussed, is a long-term approach to setting prices broadly in an integrative effort (across all the firm's products) based on the five Cs of pricing (company objectives, customers, costs, competition, and channel members) discussed in Chapter 14. Pricing tactics, in contrast, offer short-term methods to focus on select components of the five Cs. Generally, a pricing tactic represents either a short-term response to a competitive threat (e.g., lowering price temporarily to meet a competitor's price reduction) or a broadly accepted method of calculating a final price for the customer that is short term in nature. We separate our discussion of pricing tactics into those directed at end consumers and those aimed at intermediaries in a business-to-business (B2B) setting.

Pricing Tactics Aimed at Consumers

When firms sell their products and services directly to consumers rather than to other businesses, the pricing tactics they use naturally differ. Some of the tactics aimed directly at consumers—such as markdowns, quantity discounts, seasonal discounts, coupons, rebates, leasing/rental, price bundling, leader pricing, and price lining—continue to be important factors.

Markdowns　Markdowns are the reductions retailers take on the initial selling price of the product or service. An integral component of the high/low pricing strategy we described previously, markdowns enable retailers to get rid of slow-moving or obsolete merchandise, sell seasonal items after the appropriate season, and match competitors' prices on specific merchandise. Retailers must get rid of merchandise that isn't selling, because holding on to such items hurts the retailer's image and ties up money in inventory that could be used more productively elsewhere. Retailers also use markdowns to promote merchandise and increase sales. Particularly when used in conjunction with promotions, markdowns can increase traffic into the store or onto their websites, which many retailers view as half the battle. Once customers are in the store or on their websites, retailers always hope they will purchase other products at regular prices.

Quantity Discounts for Consumers　The most common implementation of a quantity discount at the consumer level is the size discount. Take, for example, three sizes of General Mills' popular cereal Cheerios: 10-, 14-, and 18-ounce boxes are priced at approximately $2.99, $3.99, and $4.49, respectively. The larger the quantity, the less the cost per ounce, which means the manufacturer is providing a quantity discount. The goal of this tactic is to encourage consumers to purchase larger quantities each time they buy. In turn, these consumers are less likely to switch brands and often tend to consume more of the product, depending on the product usage characteristics. Typically, buying a larger package of toilet tissue does not mean consumers will use it faster, but buying a larger box of cereal may encourage them to eat more of it or eat it more often.[6]

Customers get a size discount for buying larger sizes. With Cheerios, the larger the box, the less it costs per ounce.
©Michael J. Hruby

Seasonal Discounts　Seasonal discounts that are offered to consumers are price reductions offered on products and services to stimulate demand during off-peak seasons. You can find hotel rooms, ski lift tickets, snowmobiles, lawn mowers, barbeque grills, vacation packages, flights to certain destinations, and Christmas cards at discounts during their "off" seasons. Some consumers even plan their buying around these discounts, determined to spend the day after Christmas stocking up on discounted wrapping paper and bows for the following year.

Coupons　Coupons offer a discount on the price of specific items when they're purchased. Coupons are issued by manufacturers and retailers in newspapers, on products, on the shelf, at the cash register, over the Internet, and through the mail. Retailers use coupons because they can induce customers to try products for the first time, convert those first-time users to regular users, encourage large purchases, increase usage, and protect market share against competition. However, the impact of coupons on profitability is questionable. Coupon promotions, like all temporary promotions, may be stealing sales from a future period without any net increase in sales. Coupons also may annoy, alienate, and confuse consumers and therefore do little to increase store loyalty. Customers see an ad for a supermarket with a headline reading "Double Coupons" but don't realize there might be conditions, such as a minimum purchase required, or that it may apply only to certain manufacturers.

Recognizing these problems, some retailers have reduced coupon usage and cut the number of days in which customers can redeem coupons. Other retailers, like CVS, are making coupons more attractive to loyal customers by customizing their content to be in line with their unique needs. For instance, if a customer typically spends a small amount during each shopping trip, the customer will receive coupons that encourage larger purchases, such as "buy one, get one free." Unique coupons will also encourage customers to try new brands within categories that they normally purchase, or products that complement their usual *iheartwags.com provides potential customers with instant coupons at Walgreens.*

Source: iheartwags.com

purchases, such as shampoo to customers who purchase hair color.[7]

Internet sites provide customers with several pricing options and instant coupons. For instance, a customer might go to a Walgreens and find the Revlon ColorSilk Luminista hair color for $4.92. A quick search at MyCoupons.com and iheartwags.com, provides her with a $1.00 coupon off at Walgreens. Iheartwags.com provides customers with multiple ways to find and use coupon deals exclusively at Walgreens.

Rebates Rebates provide another form of discounts for consumers off the final selling price. In this case, however, the manufacturer, instead of the retailer, issues the refund as a portion of the purchase price returned to the buyer in the form of cash. A rebate promises savings, usually mailed to the consumer at some later date, only if the consumer carefully follows the rules. The "hassle factor" for rebates thus is higher than for coupons. The consumer must first buy the item during a specified time period, then mail in the required documentation—which usually includes the original sales receipt—and finally wait four to six weeks (or more!) for a check to arrive.

Manufacturers generally like rebates because as much as 90 percent of consumers never bother to redeem them. Manufacturers also embrace this form of price reduction because it lets them offer price cuts to consumers directly. With a traditional wholesale price cut from its vendors, retailers can keep the price on the shelf the same and pocket the difference. Rebates can also be rolled out and shut off quickly. That allows manufacturers to fine-tune inventories or respond quickly to competitors without actually cutting prices. Finally, because buyers are required to fill out forms with names, addresses, and other data, rebates become a great way for vendors to build a customer data warehouse. From the retailer's perspective, rebates are more advantageous than coupons since they increase demand in the same way coupons may, but the retailer has no handling costs.

Leasing/Rentals For some products, discounts, coupons, and rebates may not be sufficient to bring the price within consumers' reach. With a lease or rental, consumers pay a fee to purchase the right to use a product for a specific amount of time. They never actually own the product. Leasing or renting products opens up new, less price-sensitive target markets. Some consumers also like leases or rentals because they get tired of the product before its useful life is over, and they don't have to worry about selling it, trading it, or throwing it away. Car companies have used leasing/rental options for years to appeal to consumers who plan to keep their cars for only a few years and will want to trade in for a new model sooner rather than later. Other industries have recognized that what works for Toyotas and Chevy trucks also works for gowns, handbags, art, and even textbooks.

Price Bundling When you signed up for your high-speed Internet connection, did you also get cable TV and telephone? If so, you probably pay less than if you were to get the three services separately. This practice of selling more than one product for a single, lower price is called price bundling.[8] Firms bundle products or services together to encourage customers to stock up so they won't purchase competing brands, to encourage trial of a new product, or to provide an incentive to purchase a less desirable product or service to obtain a more desirable one in the same bundle.

Leader Pricing Leader pricing is a tactic that attempts to build store traffic by aggressively pricing and advertising a regularly purchased item, often priced at or just above the store's cost. Leader pricing fuels happy hours at restaurants and bars all over the country. At Maison Premiere in Brooklyn, New York, customers down a selection of 25 different kinds of oysters, most priced at $2–$3 per oyster, with $15 glasses of wine.[9] The rationale behind this tactic argues that, to get the great deal on oysters, the consumer will order

Maison Premiere in Brooklyn, New York, uses leader pricing on its oysters to build traffic, but makes a profit on other items customers order.

©Todd Heisler/The New York Times/Redux Pictures

other items that sell at a higher margin. The higher margins and profits on these other items then will more than cover the lower markup on the oysters. Leader pricing can be illegal under some circumstances though, as discussed subsequently in this chapter.

Price Lining When marketers establish a price floor and a price ceiling for an entire line of similar products and then set a few other price points in between to represent distinct differences in quality, the practice is called price lining. Imagine that you need a new dress shirt because you have an important job interview. You go to brooksbrothers.com and find similar-looking shirts for $92 (non-iron), $185 (Egyptian cotton), and $225 (luxury). Which are you going to buy? Are you going to risk the success of the interview by purchasing the least expensive shirt? Probably not. Will the interviewee be able to tell the difference between the $120 Supima cotton and the $298 Sea Island cotton shirt? Probably not. You will probably purchase the middle-quality shirt because you don't want to look cheap, but you really can't afford the highest-priced shirt.[10]

Business Pricing Tactics and Discounts

The pricing tactics employed in B2B settings differ significantly from those used in consumer markets. Among the most prominent are seasonal and cash discounts, allowances, quantity discounts, and uniform delivered versus zone pricing. (See Exhibit 15.3.)

LO15-5 Identify tactics used to reduce prices to businesses.

Seasonal Discounts Unlike seasonal discounts offered to consumers, a seasonal discount to a business is an additional reduction offered as an incentive to retailers to order merchandise in advance of the normal buying season. For instance, Lennox may offer its air conditioner dealers an additional seasonal discount if they place their orders and receive delivery before April 1, prior to the warm months when air conditioner sales are highest. If it can ship earlier in the season, Lennox can plan its production schedules more easily and lessen its finished goods inventory. Its dealers, however, must weigh the benefits of a larger profit because of the discount versus the extra cost of carrying the inventory for a longer period of time.

Cash Discounts A cash discount reduces the invoice cost if the buyer pays the invoice prior to the end of the discount period. Typically, it is expressed in the form of a percentage, such as "3/10, n/30," or "3%, 10 days, net 30," which means the buyer can take a 3 percent discount on the total amount of the invoice if the bill is paid within 10 days of the invoice date; otherwise the full, or net, amount is due within 30 days. Why do B2B sellers offer cash

EXHIBIT 15.3	Business-to-Business Pricing Tactics
Tactic	**Description**
Seasonal discounts	An additional reduction offered as an incentive to retailers to order merchandise in advance of the normal buying season.
Cash discounts	An additional reduction that reduces the invoice cost if the buyer pays the invoice prior to the end of the discount period.
Allowances	Advertising or slotting allowances (additional price reductions) offered in return for specific behaviors. Advertising allowances are offered to retailers if they agree to feature the manufacturer's product in their advertising and promotional efforts. Slotting allowances are offered to get new products into stores or to gain more or better shelf space.
Quantity discounts	Providing a reduced price according to the amount purchased.
Uniform delivered versus zone pricing	Uniform delivered price: shipper charges one rate, no matter where the buyer is located. Zone price: different prices depending on the geographic delivery area.

discounts to customers? By encouraging early payment, they benefit from the time value of money. Getting money earlier rather than later enables the firm to either invest the money to earn a return on it or avoid borrowing money and paying interest on it. In both instances, the firm is better off financially.

Allowances Another pricing tactic that lowers the final cost to channel members is allowances, such as advertising or slotting allowances, offered in return for specific behaviors. An advertising allowance offers a price reduction to channel members if they agree to feature the manufacturer's product in their advertising and promotional efforts. Advertising allowances are legal as long they are available to all customers and not structured in such a way that they consistently and obviously favor one or a few buyers over others. Slotting allowances are fees paid to retailers simply to get new products into stores or to gain more or better shelf space for their products. Some argue that slotting allowances are unethical because they put small manufacturers that cannot readily afford allowances at a competitive disadvantage. Demanding large slotting allowances could be considered a form of bribery—"paying off" the retailer to get preferential treatment.

Quantity Discounts A quantity discount provides a reduced price according to the amount purchased. The more the buyer purchases, the higher the discount and, of course, the greater the value.

A cumulative quantity discount uses the amount purchased over a specified time period and usually involves several transactions. This type of discount particularly encourages resellers to maintain their current supplier because the cost to switch must include the loss of the discount. Recall that we noted that automobile dealers must buy the products they hope to sell to consumers from the manufacturer. They often attempt to meet a quota or a sales goal for a specific time period, such as a quarter or a year, because if they meet those quotas, they earn discounts on all the cars they purchased from the manufacturer, in the form of a cumulative quantity discount. For this very reason, you will often find good deals on cars at the end of a quarter or fiscal year. If the dealership can just sell a few more cars to meet its quota, the cumulative quantity discount earned can be substantial, so taking a few hundred dollars less on those last few cars is well worth the opportunity to receive a check worth many times the amount of the losses.

A noncumulative quantity discount, though still a quantity discount, is based only on the amount purchased in a single order. It therefore provides the buyer with an incentive to purchase more merchandise immediately. Such larger, less frequent orders can save manufacturers order processing, sales, and transportation expenses. For example, a retail store might get a 40 percent discount off the manufacturer's suggested retail price for placing a

$500 order, a 50 percent discount for an order of $501 to $4,999, and a 60 percent discount for an order of greater than $5,000.

Uniform Delivered versus Zone Pricing These pricing tactics are specific to shipping, which represents a major cost for many manufacturers. With a *uniform delivered pricing* tactic, the shipper charges one rate, no matter where the buyer is located, which makes things very simple for both the seller and the buyer. *Zone pricing*, however, sets different prices depending on a geographic division of the delivery areas. For example, a manufacturer based in New York City might divide the United States into seven different zones and use different shipping rates for each zone to reflect the average shipping cost for customers located therein. This way, each customer in a zone is charged the same cost for shipping. Zone pricing can be advantageous to the shipper because it reflects the actual shipping charges more closely than uniform delivered pricing can.

PROGRESS CHECK

1. What are some consumer-oriented pricing tactics?
2. What are some B2B-oriented pricing tactics?

LEGAL AND ETHICAL ASPECTS OF PRICING

LO15-6 List the pricing practices that are illegal or unethical.

With so many different pricing strategies and tactics, it is no wonder that unscrupulous firms find ample opportunity to engage in pricing practices that can hurt consumers. We now take a look at some of the legal and ethical implications of pricing.

Prices tend to fluctuate naturally and respond to varying market conditions. Thus, though we rarely see firms attempting to control the market in terms of product quality or advertising, they often engage in pricing practices that can unfairly reduce competition or harm consumers directly through fraud and deception. A host of laws and regulations at both the federal and state levels attempt to prevent unfair pricing practices, but some are poorly enforced, and others are difficult to prove.

UK-based Tesco wasn't allowed to make the claim that it is "Britain's Biggest Discounter" because it was considered to be misleading. Such a claim probably would be considered puffery in the United States, and therefore would be allowed.
©Alex Segre/Alamy Stock Photo

Deceptive or Illegal Price Advertising

Although it is always illegal and unethical to lie in advertising, a certain amount of "puffery" is typically allowed (see Chapter 19).[11] But price advertisements should never deceive consumers to the point of causing harm. For example, a local car dealer's advertising that it had the "best deals in town" would likely be considered puffery. In contrast, advertising "the lowest prices, guaranteed" makes a very specific claim and, if not true, can be considered deceptive.

Deceptive Reference Prices Previously, we introduced reference prices that create reference points for the buyer against which to compare the selling price. If the reference price is bona fide, the advertisement is informative. If the reference price has been inflated or is just plain fictitious, however, the advertisement is deceptive and may cause harm to consumers. But it is not easy to determine whether a reference price is bona fide. What standard should be used? If an advertisement specifies a "regular price," just what qualifies as regular? How many units must the store sell at this price for it to be a bona fide regular price—half the stock? A few? Just one? Finally, what if the store offers the item at the regular price but customers do not

Is this a legitimate sale, or is the retailer using deceptive reference prices?

©Krisztian Bocsi/Bloomberg via Getty Images

buy any? Can it still be considered a regular price? In general, if a seller is going to label a price as a regular price, the Better Business Bureau suggests that at least 50 percent of the sales have occurred at that price.[12]

Loss-Leader Pricing *Leader pricing* is a legitimate tactic that attempts to build store traffic by aggressively pricing and advertising a regularly purchased item, often priced at or just above the store's cost. Loss-leader pricing takes this tactic one step further by lowering the price *below* the store's cost. No doubt you have seen "buy one, get one free" offers at grocery and discount stores. Unless the markup for the item is 100 percent of the cost, these sales obviously do not generate enough revenue from the sale of one unit to cover the store's cost for both units, which means it has essentially priced the total for both items below cost, unless the manufacturer is absorbing the cost of the promotion to generate volume. In some states, this form of pricing is illegal.

Bait and Switch Another form of deceptive price advertising occurs when sellers advertise items for a very low price without the intent to really sell any. This bait-and-switch tactic is a deceptive practice because the store lures customers in with a very low price on an item (the bait), only to aggressively pressure these customers into purchasing a higher-priced model (the switch) by disparaging the low-priced item, comparing it unfavorably with the higher-priced model, or professing an inadequate supply of the lower-priced item. Again, the laws against bait-and-switch practices are difficult to enforce because salespeople, simply as a function of their jobs, are always trying to get customers to trade up to a higher-priced model without necessarily deliberately baiting them. The key to proving deception centers on the intent of the seller, which is also difficult to prove.

Predatory Pricing

When a firm sets a very low price for one or more of its products with the intent to drive its competition out of business, it is using predatory pricing. Predatory pricing is illegal under both the Sherman Antitrust Act and the Federal Trade Commission Act because it constrains free trade and represents a form of unfair competition. It also tends to promote a concentrated market with a few dominant firms (an oligopoly).

But again, predation is difficult to prove. First, one must demonstrate intent; that is, that the firm intended to drive out its competition or prevent competitors from entering the market. Second, the complainant must prove that the firm charged prices lower than its average cost, an equally difficult task.

The issue of predatory pricing arose recently when a San Francisco taxi company sued Uber for the practice. The taxi company claimed that Uber was using its power as a multibillion-dollar company to undercut its competitors with predatory pricing. It claimed that Uber was actually losing money on UberX and UberXL rides in San Francisco. Furthermore, the complaint also claimed that Uber was artificially raising taxi prices through its UberTaxi service by charging an extra $2 service fee. However, Uber claims that taxis were never its primary competition. Instead, Uber's stance is that its competition has always been private cars. Furthermore, Uber states that its ride-sharing features, such as UberPOOL, lower the cost of the service.[13]

Price Discrimination

There are many forms of price discrimination, but only some of them are considered illegal under the Clayton Act and the Robinson-Patman Act. When firms sell the same product to different resellers (wholesalers, distributors, or retailers) at different prices, it can be considered price discrimination; usually, larger firms receive lower prices.

ADULT	**$11.69**
CHILD (AGE 3-11) / SENIOR (AGE 60 +)	**$8.99**
MILITARY (WITH VALID ID)	**$10.79**
STUDENT (WITH VALID ID MON THROUGH THURS ONLY)	**$10.29**

Is this price discrimination illegal?

©McGraw-Hill Education/Evelyn Nicole Kirksey, photographer

Quantity discounts are a legitimate method of charging different prices to different customers on the basis of the quantity they purchase. The legality of this tactic stems from the assumption that it costs less to sell and service 1,000 units to one customer than 100 units to 10 customers. But quantity discounts must be available to all customers and not be structured in such a way that they consistently and obviously favor one or a few buyers over others.

The Robinson-Patman Act does not apply to sales to end consumers, at which point many forms of price discrimination occur. For example, students and seniors often receive discounts on food and movie tickets, which is perfectly acceptable under federal law. Those engaged in online auctions like eBay are also practicing a legal form of price discrimination, because sellers are selling the same item to different buyers at various prices.

Price Fixing

Price fixing is the practice of colluding with other firms to control prices. Price fixing might be either horizontal or vertical. Whereas horizontal price fixing is clearly illegal under the Sherman Antitrust Act, vertical price fixing falls into a gray area.[14]

Horizontal price fixing occurs when competitors who produce and sell competing products or services collude, or work together, to control prices, effectively taking price out of the decision process for consumers. This practice clearly reduces competition and is illegal. Eighteen pharmaceutical companies have been accused of colluding to fix prices for 15 generic medicines, such as antibiotics, by several U.S. states.[15] As a general rule of thumb, competing firms should refrain from discussing prices or terms and conditions of sale with competitors. If firms want to know competitors' prices, they can look at a competitor's advertisements, its websites, or its stores.

Vertical price fixing occurs when parties at different levels of the same marketing channel (e.g., manufacturers and retailers) agree to control the prices passed on to consumers. Manufacturers often encourage retailers to sell their merchandise at a specific price, known as the **manufacturer's suggested retail price (MSRP)**. Manufacturers set MSRPs to reduce retail price competition among retailers, stimulate retailers to provide complementary services, and support the manufacturer's merchandise. Under federal law manufacturers can enforce MSRPs by developing "take it or leave it" policies. Retailers are allowed to sell products either above or below the MSRP, and manufacturers are allowed to refuse to deal or discontinue dealing with retailers who do not use the MSRP. Although state laws may differ on these regulations, the federal stance is that all manufacturer-imposed pricing programs are evaluated on a case-by-case basis.[16]

According to the U.S. Department of Justice, Apple and several publishing agencies have engaged in vertical price fixing, as outlined in Ethical & Societal Dilemma 15.1.

As these legal issues clearly demonstrate, pricing decisions involve many ethical considerations. In determining their pricing strategies and their pricing tactics, marketers must always balance their goal of inducing customers, through price, to find value and the need to deal honestly and fairly with those same customers. Whether another business or an individual consumer, buyers can be influenced by a variety of pricing methods. It is up to marketers to determine which of these methods works best for the seller, the buyer, and the community.

Ethical & Societal Dilemma 15.1

The Verdict: Apple Conspired to Raise Prices on E-Books[ii]

In a long-running court case, Amazon, Apple, a group of book publishers, and customers fought a tough battle over the price of reading.

Compared with Amazon, Apple was a late entrant to the e-book market. Amazon, with its Kindle devices and well-known reputation as a bookseller (which was how the online giant started), dominated the market of books sold to be read on Kindles as well as on other devices, including Apple's phones and tablets. Amazon also offered great prices, with many popular titles priced at under $10. Faced with this tremendous dominance, Apple believed it needed to find a way to compete. It worked with five major book publishers to decide on a minimum price below which they would not sell. With the agreement, publishers like Simon & Schuster, Penguin, and Macmillan began insisting on higher prices for their titles, and Apple took a percentage of each sale. This pricing method also meant that Amazon had to raise the prices it charged consumers, because it was paying more for the rights to the electronic content.

Amazon immediately brought the situation to the attention of the U.S. Department of Justice, alleging that the agreement represented price fixing and illegal conspiracy. Apple defended its actions vigorously; by entering a market that had been essentially a monopoly, with Amazon as the only seller, Apple asserted that it was increasing competition, not harming it. It also alleged that the effect on the price was not the issue. Whether its entry led to higher or lower prices, the key point—according to Apple's argument—was that, previously, consumers had only one source for e-books, and now they had two, and that was an improvement.

Various levels of the U.S. court system have disagreed with Apple's assertions though, and recently the U.S. Supreme Court refused to hear an appeal. Thus the most recent decision by the lower appellate court stands. That decision establishes that the agreement among Apple and the five big publishers represented collusion. Previously the

Who will ultimately win the Apple–Amazon pricing war? Currently, the Court's decision is that the agreement among Apple and the five big publishers represents collusion.

©Joby Sessions/Computer Arts Magazine/Getty Images

publishers had been forced by Amazon to sell at low prices. The deal with Apple benefited them by allowing them to charge what they wanted. It also benefited Apple, which received a percentage of each sale. But the Court's interest is mostly in the effects on consumers, and for those stakeholders, the conspiracy had negative effects in the form of higher prices.

As a result, Apple is liable to pay a $450 million settlement to e-book consumers. The publishers already had settled with the government.

Gray Market Pricing Channels can be very difficult to manage, and distribution outside normal channels does occur. A gray market employs irregular but not necessarily illegal methods; generally, it legally circumvents authorized channels of distribution to sell goods at prices lower than those intended by the manufacturer.[17] Many manufacturers of consumer electronics therefore require retailers to sign an agreement that demands certain activities (and prohibits others) before the retailers may become authorized dealers. But if a retailer has too many high-definition televisions in stock, it may sell them at just above its own cost to an unauthorized discount dealer. This move places the merchandise in the market at prices far below what authorized dealers can charge and in the long term may tarnish the image of the manufacturer if the discount dealer fails to provide sufficient return policies, support, service, and so forth.

To discourage this type of gray market distribution, many manufacturers have resorted to large disclaimers on their websites, packaging, and other communications to warn consumers that the manufacturer's product warranty becomes null and void unless the item has been purchased from an authorized dealer. Another method is to equalize worldwide prices so the gray market advantage evaporates, as we describe in Ethical & Societal Dilemma 15.2.

Ethical & Societal Dilemma 15.2   Impeding the Gray Market for Luxury Goods[iii]

The euro is lower than it has been in over a decade. As a result, for Asian shoppers seeking Italian designer clothing or French handbags, it is literally worth the cost of flying to Milan and Paris to buy the items there rather than shopping in Shanghai. Prices are nearly always lower in the country of origin, because there are no customs or import duties to pay, and transportation is relatively inexpensive. Currently, prices for Chanel items in China are approximately 63 percent higher than prices for comparable items sold in Paris. When the item is a €4,000 handbag, this difference is great enough that a shopper from Beijing could buy a ticket to Paris, fly over, purchase the bag, and fly home—and still save money compared with buying the item in the local store.

An alternative to a shopping trip to Europe is to buy at home in the gray market. Because of the vast gap between their European and Asian prices, gray market players can readily buy up goods at the lower European cost, increase the price slightly—still remaining below the Asian retail level—and

earn massive profits by selling it in China on the gray market. China's well-known Taobao shopping site is a ready source for such gray market goods.

Although this gray market does move a lot of merchandise, it is not in the best interest of the European luxury goods manufacturers. Their reputation is diminished by having merchandise sold at lower prices through nontraditional channels. Service is nonexistent in such markets, and warranties are null and void. If the gray market thrives, their traditional channels suffer as customers are drawn to the cheaper prices. Ultimately, customers might no longer find value in traditional stores.

In response to these market developments, Chanel has announced it will be raising its retail prices in Europe but cutting them in China. In so doing, it seeks to level the playing field so that the same handbag costs approximately the same amount wherever people buy it. In the end, who benefits from the gray market?

In an attempt to equalize prices across global markets, Chanel is raising its retail prices in Europe but cutting them in China.

©VCG via Getty Images

PROGRESS CHECK

1. What common pricing practices are considered to be illegal or unethical?

Reviewing Learning Objectives

LO15-1 Identify three methods that firms use to set their prices.

The various methods of setting prices have their advantages and disadvantages. The three primary methods are cost based, competition based, and value based. The cost-based techniques are quick and easy but fail to reflect the competitive environment or consumer demand. Although it is always advisable to be aware of what competitors are doing, using competition-based pricing should not occur in isolation without dealing with cost considerations and consumer reactions. Taking a value-based approach to pricing, whether the improvement value, the total-cost-of-ownership approach, or the experimental approach described in Chapter 10 in conjunction with these other methods provides a nicely balanced method of setting prices.

LO15-2 Describe the difference between an everyday low pricing (EDLP) strategy and a high/low strategy.

An everyday low pricing strategy is maintained when a product's price stays relatively constant at a level that is slightly lower than the regular price from competitors using a high/low strategy, and is less frequently discounted. Customers enjoy an everyday low pricing strategy because they know that the price will always be the about the same and will be a better price than the competition's. High/low pricing strategy starts out with a product at one (higher) price, and then discounts the product. This strategy first attracts a less price-sensitive customer who pays the regular price, and then a very price-sensitive customer who pays the low price.

LO15-3 Explain the difference between a price skimming and a market penetration pricing strategy.

When firms use a price skimming strategy, the product or service must be perceived as breaking new ground, or customers will not pay more than what they pay for other products. Firms use price skimming to signal high quality, limit demand, recoup their investment quickly, and/or test people's price sensitivity. Moreover, it is easier to price high initially and then lower the price than vice versa. Market penetration, in contrast, helps firms build sales and market share quickly, which may discourage other firms from entering the market. Building demand quickly also typically results in lowered costs as the firm gains experience making the product or delivering the service.

LO15-4 Identify tactics used to reduce prices to consumers.

Marketers use a variety of tactics to provide lower prices to consumers. The tactics include markdowns, quantity discounts, seasonal discounts, coupons, rebates, leasing or renting, price bundling, leader pricing, and price lining. For example, leader pricing involves retailers pricing certain products or services at very low prices, with the hope that these same customers will also buy other, more profitable items.

LO15-5 Identify tactics used to reduce prices to businesses.

Seasonal discounts give retailers an incentive to buy prior to the normal selling season, cash discounts prompt them to pay their invoices early, and allowances attempt to get retailers to advertise the manufacturer's product or stock a new product. In addition, quantity discounts can cause retailers to purchase a larger quantity over a specific period of time or with a particular order. Finally, zone pricing bases the cost of shipping the merchandise on the distance between the retailer and the manufacturer—the farther away, the more it costs.

LO15-6 List the pricing practices that are illegal or unethical.

There are almost as many ways to get into trouble by setting or changing a price as there are pricing strategies and tactics. Some common legal issues pertain to advertising deceptive prices. Specifically, if a firm compares a reduced price with a "regular" or reference price, it must actually have sold that product or service at the regular price. Bait and switch is another form of deceptive price advertising, where sellers advertise items for a very low price without the intent to really sell any at that price. Collusion among firms to fix prices is always illegal.

Key Terms

- advertising allowance, 462
- bait-and-switch, 464
- cash discount, 461
- competition-based pricing method, 453
- cost-based pricing method, 452

- cost-of-ownership method, 455
- coupons, 459
- cumulative quantity discount, 462
- everyday low pricing (EDLP), 455
- experience curve effect, 457
- gray market, 466

- high/low pricing, 455
- horizontal price fixing, 465
- improvement value, 454
- leader pricing, 461
- lease or rental, 460
- loss-leader pricing, 464

Marketing Digitally

1. Go to www.coupons.com. In which product categories does this website offer coupons? Choose a product from each category.

   - How effective are coupons for selling these types of products? Why?

   - Do any sellers offer rebates through this website? Why or why not?

   - What are the benefits to the seller of using Coupons.com instead of offering coupons in a newspaper?

   - How do you think Coupons.com makes money? For example, consider what companies are advertising on

   the site. Do the same companies who advertise on the site offer coupons?

2. Visit the website for Rent the Runway, renttherunway.com. Navigate to dresses and sort the listings by highest to lowest price and lowest to highest price. What is the difference between how much you would save by renting the highest-priced dresses versus the lowest-priced dresses compared to the associated retail values? What kind of pricing method does Rent the Runway use? Do you agree with how Rent the Runway prices its rentals? If not, how would you create rental prices?

Marketing Applications

1. Suppose you have been hired as the pricing manager for a drugstore chain that typically adds a fixed percentage onto the cost of each product to arrive at the retail price. Evaluate this technique. What would you do differently?

2. Some high-fashion retailers, notably H&M and Zara, sell what some call "disposable fashion"—apparel priced so reasonably low that it can be disposed of after just a few wearings. Here is your dilemma: You have an important job interview and need a new suit. You can buy the suit at one of these stores for $129 or at Brooks Brothers for $500. Of course, the Brooks Brothers suit is of higher quality and will therefore last longer. How would you use the two value-based approaches described in this chapter to determine which suit to buy?

3. A phone manufacturer is determining a price for its product, using a cost-based pricing strategy. The fixed costs are $100,000, and the variable costs are $50,000. If 1,000 units are produced and the company wants to have a 30 percent markup, what is the price of the phone?

4. Identify two stores at which you shop, one of which uses everyday low pricing and another that uses a high/low pricing strategy. Do you believe that each store's chosen strategy is appropriate for the type of merchandise it sells and the market of customers to whom it is appealing? Justify your answer.

5. Almost every time a new-to-the-world electronic device (MP3 player, flat-screen television, digital camera, gaming console, etc.) has been introduced, the firm's marketers have employed a price skimming strategy. Why?

6. What is the difference between a cumulative and a noncumulative quantity discount?

7. Imagine you are the product manager for Neutrogena's sun protection product line and your team developed a new type of sunscreen. Which two B2B pricing tactics would you use to promote it? Why?

8. Coupons and rebates benefit different distribution channel members. Which would you prefer if you were a manufacturer, a retailer, and a consumer? Why?

9. Suppose the president of your university got together with the presidents of all the universities in your athletic conference for lunch. They discussed what each university was going to charge for tuition the following year. Are they in violation of federal laws? Explain your answer.

10. Imagine that you are the newly hired brand manager for a restaurant that is about to open. Both the local newspaper and a gourmet food magazine recently ran articles about your new head chef, calling her one of the best young chefs in the country. In response to these positive reviews, the company wants to position its brand as a premium, gourmet restaurant. Your boss asks what price you should charge for the chef's signature filet mignon dish. Other restaurants in the area charge around $40 for their own filet offerings. What steps might you undertake to determine what the new price should be?

11. You have been hired by a regional supermarket chain as the candy and snack buyer. Your shelves are dominated by national firms such as Wrigley's and Nabisco. The chain imposes a substantial slotting fee to allow new items to be added to their stock selection. Management reasons that it costs a lot to add and delete items, and besides, these slotting fees are a good source of revenue. A small, minority-operated, local firm produces several potentially interesting snack crackers and a line of gummy candy, all with natural ingredients, added vitamins, reduced sugar, and a competitive price—and they also happen to taste great. You'd love to give the firm a chance, but its managers claim the slotting fee is too high. Should your firm charge slotting fees? Are slotting fees fair to the relevant shareholders—customers, stockholders, vendors?

Quiz Yourself

1. In terms of a pricing strategy, _____ adds value by reducing consumers' search costs, while consumers can spend less of their valuable time comparing prices, including sale prices, at different stores.
   a. cost-based pricing
   b. high/low pricing
   c. predatory pricing
   d. everyday low pricing
   e. competitor-based pricing

2. The objective of _____ is to build sales, market share, and profits quickly by providing an incentive to purchase the product immediately.
   a. price lining
   b. price skimming
   c. market penetration pricing
   d. price fixing
   e. experience curve effects

(Answers to these two questions can be found in the Quiz Yourself Answer Key section.)

Chapter Case Study   Mc Graw Hill Education connect·

PIZZA PLAYERS, PIZZA PRICES

For most of us, "pizza wars" suggest the fight over which toppings to put on a shared pie. But in truth, the pizza industry is in the midst of a battle, for which the weapons of choice are mainly pricing tactics. In addition to the small, local pizzerias that appear in nearly every town, there are four major chains that pursue pizza-loving consumers in the United States (see Exhibit 15.4), a massive market in which approximately 1 in 8 people eat pizza on any particular day.[18] Running the gamut from a low-price promise to a higher price and higher quality appeal, these four chains all seek to price their offerings in ways that promise to increase their sales and market share.

How exactly are they doing so? Let's consider their pricing tactics in turn, moving in order from the smallest of the big four (in terms of market share) to the biggest.

Papa John's With its well-known spokespeople, from Peyton Manning and J.J. Watt to the founder himself, "Papa" John Schnatter, Papa John's is a familiar name to many advertising viewers, even though it accounts for only about 6 percent of the national market. Along with these recognizable faces, Papa John's has established a motto and tagline that most consumers can repeat from memory: "Better Ingredients, Better Pizza." In accordance with this focus on quality, Papa John's rarely tries to offer the lowest price in a market.

EXHIBIT 15.4 Top Pizza Chains by Market Share

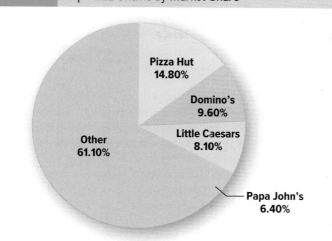

Pizza Hut
14.80%

Domino's
9.60%

Little Caesars
8.10%

Other
61.10%

Papa John's
6.40%

Source: Andrew Alvarez, "BISWorld Industry Report OD4320 Pizza Restaurants in the US," *IBISWorld,* November 2015.

Constantly lowering prices means, according to Schnatter, that "you are either serving ingredients that are not high quality or you're putting less on."[19] Arguing that it is not willing to make such quality-related sacrifices, Papa John's says that it will never seek to reach the $5 pizza threshold that many of its national competitors offer.

But to gain ground, it cannot just ignore the price interests of its consumers. In response, Papa John's promises that if consumers order one large pizza at the regular price, they can get a second for just $.50.[20] The combined deal still remains above that $5 threshold, but it brings the overall cost to consumers more in line with competitors' prices. Furthermore, Papa John's has introduced a quality guarantee: Any consumer dissatisfied with the quality of the pie he or she receives may call the store within a half-hour to complain. That complaint automatically gives them the option of getting another delivery immediately or having their account credited, such that they may receive another pie for free in the future.

Finally, Papa John's seeks to introduce various innovations to get people calling for an order. For example, during a recent one-month promotional run, it offered the Brookie—a combination chocolate chip cookie and brownie—for $6 with any pizza order.[21]

Little Caesars Little Caesars also has a well-known tagline ("Pizza! Pizza!"), but its offer is premised almost completely on convenience. With a different business model than any of the other big players in the market, the restaurant chain promises that its food is "hot and ready," thus eliminating the need to place an order. At the moment a consumer walks in to a store, the pizza will be ready for her or him to take, for just about $5. For a little more, they can upgrade their pie, such as selecting the cheese-stuffed crust or bacon-wrapped deep-dish versions.

In parallel with this relatively simple sales model, Little Caesars embraces a sort of absurdist image. Its advertising often features unrealistic or fantastic sequences, such as when two disembodied heads floated above a pie in a campaign to introduce the new cheese-stuffed crust.[22] To promote the notion that avoiding ordering is more convenient—even though it requires consumers to go out and pick up their food, rather than having it delivered to them at home—another advertising campaign shows a couple desperately trying to remember the password for an online ordering site, typing in name after name of the hundreds of cats who appear to be living in the house with them.

It also likes to play with its "underdog," overlooked status, despite its prominence.[23] In one promotion, it promised an even lower price—free—if any team that was seeded sixteenth in the men's college basketball tournament won in the first round, which would mean that it would have unseated the top ranked team in its division.[24] The risk was relatively low, considering that no team has ever done so. Still, it put the idea in people's minds and offered the chance of a free Hot-N-Ready lunch if the upset occurred. (It didn't.)

Domino's While Papa John's focuses on quality and Little Caesars goes for convenience, Domino's is relying on its delivery reputation and its head start in terms of mobile commerce capabilities to compete more effectively for orders. In the past, Domino's was known for its promise to deliver pizzas in 30 minutes or less, though it ultimately removed the guarantee for safety reasons. Still, it built its reach throughout the market by promising to make it easy for people at home to get their pizza fix. That reputation continues to inform its approach to growth today.

By "utilizing mobile better than their competitors,"[25] Domino's restaurants make it easy for tech-savvy consumers to gain access to the offerings. For example, its well-developed Pizza Tracker app, which is available on all the major mobile platforms, gives users one-touch ordering functions. Then the app keeps consumers apprised of the progress of their pie, constantly updating the expected delivery times. It also has begun experimenting with other mobile channels, such as Snapchat, seeking to find ways to connect with consumers in unexpected, entertaining, and more appealing channels and manners.[26]

In the course of developing these mobile capabilities, Domino's pricing strategy has not changed substantively. As one spokesperson noted, in response to new promotions by Pizza Hut, Domino's does not "play the price or product-of-the-month gimmick game others seem to. The limited-time-only tactic is something we left behind years ago."[27] Instead, since about 2010, Domino's has continued to offer the same baseline: medium cheese pizzas for around $5.99 each. Increasing the size or adding more toppings increases the price, but the pricing is clearly transparent and mostly consistent over time and geographic locations.

Pizza Hut And finally we come to the biggest player, the world's largest pizza chain. Pizza Hut started the most recent pizza war by creating a new pricing and promotion initiative. As long as consumers bought at least one other item (e.g., breadsticks, wings, another pizza), they could get a medium, one-topping pizza for just $5.[28] The promotion is part of the launch of a wider, $5 "flavor menu" that includes multiple options. Similar to single-price menus in other fast-food settings, this approach allows consumers to decide which items they prefer to purchase for their set budget. One consumer might want the variety of wings and pizza, another might need a couple of pizzas to feed multiple people, and yet another could want both a meal and a dessert.

With its more than 15,000 stores, Pizza Hut enjoys vast reach, excellent brand awareness, and a market-leading position. It also asserts that it has been "serving the same great-tasting pizza, at a great value" for its entire history.[29] Yet for several quarters, the performance of the chain had not met the expectations of either its investors or its corporate brand owner, Yum! Brands. To address these concerns, Pizza Hut not only introduced its new price promotion but also adopted a "focused emphasis on making it easier to get a better pizza."[30]

The Rest of the Market Of course, local pizzerias also remain in play. Unlike many local retailers, restaurants offer greatly differentiated options. For consumers who want a basic meal, the large chains offer consistency at a reasonable price, but for those who want something unique and different on their plates, the local pizzeria generally has represented a more appealing option. Patxi's is a chain operating 17 restaurants in California, Colorado, and Washington that is small enough that it can still be considered "local." Unlike its national competitors vying for the five dollars per pie market, Patxi's is a full-service sit-down restaurant that serves gourmet Chicago-style deep dish and New York style pizzas made from fresh, natural ingredients with no preservatives. There is no rushing these pizzas, which can take up to 40 minutes to serve. Pizzas can run up to $28. An order of Brussels sprouts is $14, and salads can run up to $15—a far cry from the basic $5 offering of the national chains.[31]

Besides their relatively low prices, the national chains have also increased the convenience of ordering by using online and mobile systems, which is cutting into the local pizzeria's market. These ordering systems are quick and easy. Consumers do not need to worry about having all their topping preferences ready to shout out quickly, to a harried and possibly rude order taker. Nor do they need to be concerned that someone will mishear their desire for "pepperoncini" and load up their pizza with "pepperoni" instead. Once they plug in their credit card information, those data get stored, so ordering the next time around is

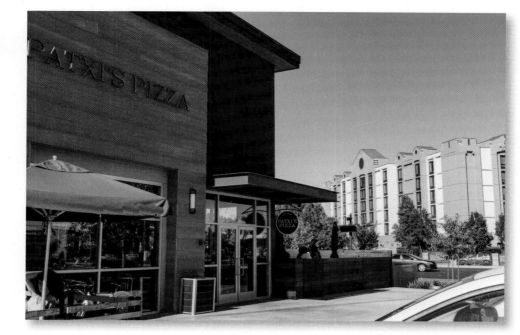

Patxi's is a small pizzeria chain operating in California, Colorado, and Washington. It is a full-service sit-down restaurant serving gourmet pizzas made from fresh, natural ingredients with no preservatives. Its prices are commensurate with its quality.

Courtesy of Patxi

even more convenient and quick. Faced with such efficient systems, many of the small restaurants simply cannot compete on price or fast service.[32]

Most local pizzerias can't afford to establish their own online ordering systems, which would require significant investments in software, technology, and new staff. As an alternative, some restaurants turn to intermediaries like GrubHub or Seamless, which link hungry customers with various food purveyors on a single platform. Such platforms enable online ordering, but they also charge the restaurants a percentage of their sales.

The number of small pizza stores in operation has decreased by nearly 7 percent in recent years. Their best bet to compete with the national chains is to differentiate themselves with great and unusual offerings coupled with an interesting dining experience.

The Results In recent quarters, Papa John's announced a 5 percent growth rate.[33] Little Caesars' sales increased from $2.9 million to $3.4 million over a two-year period.[34] Domino's enjoyed 13 percent revenue growth. Pizza Hut reported flat sales.[35] Will the outcome of the pizza battle change these trends?

Questions

1. Which pricing tactics does each company utilize? Evaluate the effectiveness of each one of these tactics for the particular pizza chain.

2. How might the current price wars change the pricing tactics used by the major pizza chains?

Endnotes

1. Suzanne Kapner, "Tiffany & Co., the Luxury Brand with a Midlife Crisis," *The Wall Street Journal,* July 9, 2017; Ashley Lutz, "Wealthy Shoppers Have a New Attitude That Signals Doom for Tiffany," *Business Insider,* August 24, 2017.

2. Thomas T. Nagle, John E. Hogan, and Joseph Zale, *The Strategy and Tactics of Pricing: A Guide to Growing More Profitability,* 5th ed. (Upper Saddle River, NJ: Pearson, 2010).

3. Abhijit Biswas et al., "Consumer Evaluations of Sale Prices: Role of the Subtraction Principle," *Journal of Marketing* 77, no. 4 (2013), pp. 49–66.

4. Jacob Kastrenakes, "Apple Watch Release Date Is April 24th, with Pricing from $349 to over $10,000," *The Verge,* March 9, 2015, www.theverge.com/2015/3/9/8162455/apple-watch-price-release-date-2015.

5. www.apple.com/watch/compare/; https://misfit.com/smartwatch.

6. Nailya Ordabayeva and Pierre Chandon, "Predicting and Managing Consumers' Package Size Impressions," *Journal of Marketing* 77, no. 5 (2013), pp. 123–37; Xiaoyan Deng and Raji Srinivasan, "When Do Transparent Packages Increase (or Decrease) Food Consumption?," *Journal of Marketing* 77, no. 4 (2013), pp. 104–17; Sha Yang and Priya Raghubir, "Can Bottles Speak Volumes? The Effect of Package Shape on How Much to Buy," *Journal of Retailing* 81, no. 4 (2005), pp. 269–81.

7. Dhruv Grewal, *Retail Marketing Management: The 5 E's of Retailing Today* (Thousand Oaks, CA: Sage Publications, forthcoming).

8. Franklin Shaddy and Ayelet Fishbach, "Seller Beware: How Bundling Affects Valuation," *Journal of Marketing Research* 54, no. 5 (October 2017), pp. 737–51; Marco Bertini and Luc Wathieu, "Research Note: Attention Arousal through Price Partitioning," *Marketing Science* 27, no. 2 (2008), pp. 236–46.

9. Karen Stabiner, "Loss Leaders on the Half Shell," *The New York Times*, February 22, 2014; https://maisonpremiere.com/.

10. https://brooksbrothers.com/.

11. A. Chakraborty and R. Harbaugh, "Persuasive Puffery," *Marketing Science* 33 (2014), pp. 382–400; Alison Jing Xu and Robert S. Wyer Jr., "Puffery in Advertisements: The Effects of Media Context, Communication Norms and Consumer Knowledge," *Journal of Consumer Research*, August 2010.

12. J. Lindsey-Mullikin and R. D. Petty, "Marketing Tactics Discouraging Price Search: Deception and Competition," *Journal of Business Research* 64, no. 1 (2011), pp. 67–73. doi: 10.1016/j.jbusres.2009.10.003.

13. Brian Solomon, "Uber Sued for Predatory Pricing by San Francisco Taxi Company," *Forbes*, November 2, 2016; Kartikay Mehrotra, "Uber Accused of Predatory Pricing by San Francisco Cab Firm," *Bloomberg*, November 2, 2016; Biz Carson, "Uber Book $20 Billion in Rides in 2016, But It's Still Losing Billions," *Business Insider*, April 14, 2017; Dean Baker, "What If Uber Is a Joke?," *The Huffington Post*, April 24, 2017.

14. Daniel M. Garrett, Michelle Burtis, and Vandy Howell, "Economics of Antitrust: An Economic Analysis of Resale Price Maintenance," 2008, www.GlobalCompetitionReview.com; Stephen Labaton, "Century-Old Ban Lifted on Minimum Retail Pricing," *The New York Times*, June 29, 2007.

15. Karen Freifeld, "U.S. States Allege Broad Generic Drug Price-Fixing Collusion," *Reuters*, October 31, 2017; Peter Loftus, "States Expand Price-Fixing Accusations against Generic Drug Companies," *The Wall Street Journal*, October 31, 2017.

16. "Manufacturer-Imposed Requirements," the United States Federal Trade Commission, www.ftc.gov/tips-advice/competition-guidance/guide-antitrust-laws/dealings-supply-chain/manufacturer-imposed.

17. *Merriam-Webster Legal Dictionary*, www.merriam-webster.com/dictionary/gray%20market#legalDictionary.

18. Hollis Johnson, "We Taste-Tested Pizzas from Papa John's, Pizza Hut, and Dominos—Here's Who Does It Best," *Business Insider*, November 13, 2015.

19. Aamer Madhani, "Papa John's Tries New Tack to Challenge Pizza Hut, Domino's for Pizza Supremacy," *USA Today*, January 30, 2016.

20. Fast Food, "2016 Pizza Wars: Who Will Win?," February 12, 2016, www.fastfoodmenuprices.com/2016-pizzawar-who-will-win/.

21. Fast Food, "Papa John's Rings 2016 with the Launching of Its New Dessert," February 12, 2016, www.fastfoodmenuprices.com/2016-pizza-war-who-will-win/.

22. Erik Oster, "Barton F. Graf Hypes Little Caesars Stuffed Crust Deep! Deep! Dish with 'Faces,'" *Adweek*, March 25, 2016, www.adweek.com/agencyspy/barton-f-graf-hypes-little-caesars-stuffed-crust-deep-deep-dish-with-faces/105328.

23. Jonathan Maze, "The Most Underappreciated Growth Restaurant in the Country," *Nation's Restaurant News*, July 22, 2015, http://nrn.com/blog/most-underappreciated-growth-restaurant-country.

24. Brian Manzullo, "Little Caesars Will Give You Free Lunch If No. 16 Seed Scores an Upset," *Detroit Free Press*, March 16, 2016.

25. Rebecca Borison, "Domino's Earns Customer Loyalty with Mobile at the Forefront," *Mobile Commerce Daily*, October 21, 2013, www.mobilecommercedaily.com/domino's-leads-the-mobile-way-for-pizza-chains.

26. Seb Joseph, "Domino's Says Its Snapchat Test Led to a 'Surprising' Surge in Pizza Orders," *Business Insider*, February 18, 2016.

27. Chris Isidore, "Pizza War! Pizza Hut and Papa John's Slash Prices," *CNNMoney*, January 4, 2016.

28. Ibid.

29. Madhani, "Papa John's Tries New Tack to Challenge Pizza Hut, Domino's for Pizza Supremacy."

30. Monica Watrous, "Pizza Hut's Performance Warms Up," *Food Business News*, February 5, 2016, www.foodbusinessnews.net/articles/7479-pizza-hut-s-performance-warms-up.

31. Patxispizza.com.

32. Julie Jargon, "Big Chains Use Web Ordering to Slice Out Bigger Market Share," *The Wall Street Journal,* February 6, 2014, http://online.wsj.com.

33. Isidore, "Pizza War! Pizza Hut and Papa John's Slash Prices."

34. Maze, "The Most Underappreciated Growth Restaurant in the Country."

35. Isidore, "Pizza War! Pizza Hut and Papa John's Slash Prices."

i. Nick Wingfield and David Gelles, "Amazon's Play to Rattle Whole Foods Rivals: Cheaper Kale and Avocado," *The New York Times,* August 28, 2017; Reuters, "Amazon's Whole Foods Price Cuts Are Hurting These 2 Chains the Most," *Fortune,* October 3, 2017; Abha Bhattarai, "Amazon Promised to Make Whole Foods Cheaper. Let's See How That's Going," *The Washington Post,* October 2, 2017.

ii. Adam Liptak and Vindu Goel, "Supreme Court Declines to Hear Apple's Appeal in E-Book Pricing Case," *The New York Times,* March 7, 2016; Reuters, "Supreme Court Rejects Apple e-Books Price-Fixing Appeal," *The New York Times,* March 8, 2016.

iii. Jason Chow and Nadya Masidlover, "Chanel Acts on Prices as Euro Worsens Gray Market," *The Wall Street Journal,* March 17, 2015.

Quiz Yourself Answer Key

1. In terms of a pricing strategy, _____ adds value by reducing consumers' search costs, while consumers can spend less of their valuable time comparing prices, including sale prices, at different stores.

Answer: (d) everyday low pricing

2. The objective of _____ is to build sales, market share, and profits quickly by providing an incentive to purchase the product immediately.

Answer: (c) market penetration pricing

VALUE DELIVERY: DESIGNING THE CHANNEL AND SUPPLY CHAIN

Section Six deals with the value delivery system. It is critical that merchandise is delivered in time to stores to meet customer demand. To achieve this, retailers have initiated many innovative programs with their vendors and have developed sophisticated transportation and warehousing systems. We devote two chapters to value delivery. Chapter 16 takes a look at marketing channels and how to manage the supply chain, while Chapter 17 concentrates on retailing and omnichannel marketing.

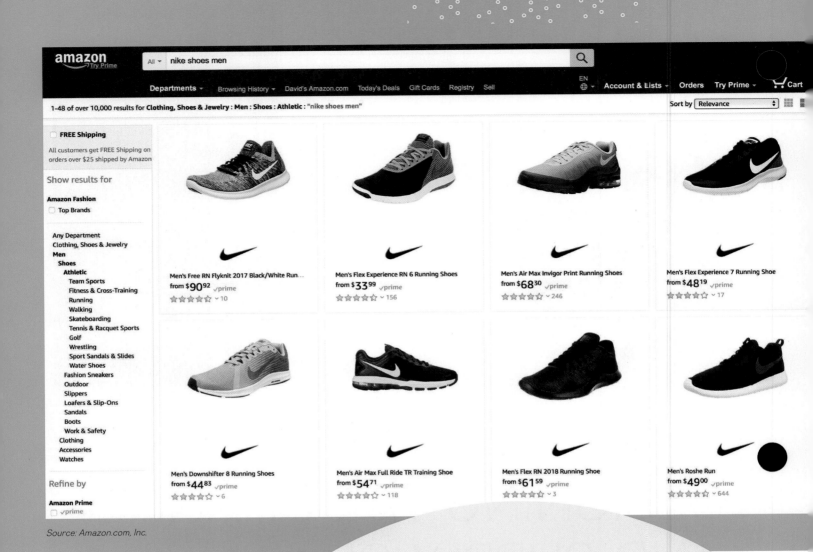

Source: Amazon.com, Inc.

LEARNING OBJECTIVES

After reading this chapter, you should be able to:

LO16-1 Understand the importance of marketing channels and supply chain management.

LO16-2 Understand the difference between direct and indirect marketing channels.

LO16-3 Describe how marketing channels are managed.

LO16-4 Describe the flow of information and merchandise in the marketing channel.

CHAPTER 16

SUPPLY CHAIN AND CHANNEL MANAGEMENT

Once upon a time, popular brand manufacturers held great sway over their physical retail partners. They could insist on certain display rules, demand massive shelf space, and dictate the sale prices of their popular items. Nike, as one of the most popular brands of footwear and athletic apparel, was also among the most demanding, requiring retailers such as Sports Authority and Foot Locker to follow strict rules if they wanted to receive its products in their stores.

Obviously, the arrival of Amazon induced some changes in the retail market, but initially, those changes were not enough to convince Nike that it should sell through the site. For years, Nike has resisted providing products for Amazon to sell its shoppers, with the general sense that its popularity meant that it did not need to rely on an external channel. In addition, manufacturers have relatively less control over the presentation of their products on Amazon, and Nike worried about damage to its brand image and differentiation if its cool shoes and gear were presented in the plain product pages that Amazon uses for all its products.

But what Nike did not realize is that its shoes were going to be on Amazon anyway, whether it provided them directly or not. With the growth of third-party sellers on Amazon, there is plenty of Nike gear to be had through the site—so much so that Nike is the most purchased apparel brand on all of Amazon. There are no laws or regulations that limit people from obtaining goods legally and then reselling them through Amazon. Although Amazon works to police these sellers, to prevent the spread of gray market or counterfeit products, it would be impossible to monitor every one of them.

Thus, Nike was losing sales to Amazon, despite its efforts to spurn any sort of relationship with the retailer. Recognizing that it could not win this battle, Nike decided that it would supply Amazon with a flood of merchandise, in the hope of beating out some of the third-party sellers with which it was competing for customers. In return for receiving the product line, Amazon promised to redouble its efforts to eliminate counterfeit items from its site, and it imposed limitations that would not permit third-party sellers to offer certain Nike products at all. In the aftermath of the pilot program, it appeared as though the strategy was working to cut down on third-party resellers on Amazon.

At the same time, though, Nike is taking on the bots and counterfeiters on its own platforms. With its new SNKRS app, Nike relies on augmented reality to sell specific, widely sought-after sneakers. Beyond just creating an interactive experience with the customer, this program has helped eliminate bots from making purchases.[1]

In this chapter, we discuss the third P in the marketing mix, *place,* which includes all activities required to get the right product to the right customer when that customer wants it. As we noted in Chapter 1, marketing channel management, which also has been called supply chain management, refers to a set of approaches and techniques firms employ to efficiently and effectively integrate their suppliers, manufacturers, warehouses, stores, and transportation intermediaries into a seamless operation in which merchandise is produced and distributed in the right quantities, to the right locations, and at the right time, as well as to minimize systemwide costs while satisfying the service levels their customers require. Students of marketing often overlook or underestimate the importance of place in the marketing mix simply because it happens behind the scenes. Yet marketing channel management adds value because it gets products to customers efficiently, quickly, and at low cost.

LO16-1 Understand the importance of marketing channels and supply chain management.

THE IMPORTANCE OF MARKETING CHANNEL/SUPPLY CHAIN MANAGEMENT

So far in this book we have reviewed the methods companies use to conduct in-depth marketing research, gain insights into consumer and business behaviors, segment markets, select the best target markets, develop new products and services, and set prices that provide good value. But even if firms execute these activities flawlessly, unless they can secure the placement of products in appropriate outlets in sufficient quantities exactly when customers want them, they are likely to fail.

Convincing wholesalers and retailers to carry new products can be more difficult than you might think. Wholesalers are firms that buy products from manufacturers and resell them to retailers; retailers sell products directly to consumers. Consider some familiar examples: Walmart is a massive retailer, and many of its products come from massive partners such as Procter & Gamble (P&G). In this relationship, Walmart certainly needs P&G to supply it with toothpaste, diapers, paper towels, and other consumer goods marketed under P&G's various brand names. But P&G also desperately needs Walmart to agree to stock its products because the retailer represents its largest purchaser, accounting for about $12 billion in annual sales.[2] When P&G introduces a totally new product, such as teeth-whitening strips, it has to convince Walmart to create space in its stores for the innovation without giving up too much space for its other products.[3]

When P&G introduces a totally new product, such as teeth-whitening strips, it has to convince Walmart to create space in its stores for the innovation without giving up too much space for its other products.
©Tom Uhlman/AP Images

For other wholesalers and manufacturers, the effort to convince Walmart to stock their products might be even more challenging because they lack the leverage and power of P&G. For example, Brown Betty Dessert Boutique, a small Philadelphia-based bakery, wanted to put its sweet potato pie in Walmart stores, but first it had to get Walmart to buy what it was selling.[4] Walmart agreed to give them a trial in 300 stores. Walmart also provided no marketing support, but Brown Betty Dessert Boutique agreed to sell its pie under the Patti LaBelle name, which gained national recognition after a viral marketing program.[5] A **viral marketing program** is one that encourages people to pass along a marketing message to other potential consumers. To keep track of sales, it relied on Walmart's Internet-based Retail Link system. Finally, Brown Betty Dessert Boutique, as well as all of Walmart's suppliers, agreed to adhere to strict packaging, labeling, and shipping requirements. And remember, for all this effort, its entry in stores was only a test, and a very expensive gamble! But if it could succeed in Walmart stores, Brown Betty Dessert Boutique would be well on its way to prosperity.

It is not easy to sell to Walmart, but Brown Betty Dessert Boutique, using the name Patti LaBelle, made it in.
©McGraw-Hill Education

In the simplified supply chain in Exhibit 16.1, manufacturers make products and sell them to retailers or wholesalers. The exhibit would be much more complicated if we had included the suppliers of materials to manufacturers; all the various manufacturers, wholesalers, and stores in a typical marketing channel; and digital channels through which customers order products and receive them directly with the assistance of delivery providers such as UPS, FedEx, or the U.S. Postal Service.

Exhibit 16.1 represents a typical flow of manufactured goods: Manufacturers ship to a wholesaler or to a retailer's distribution center (e.g., Manufacturer one and Manufacturer

EXHIBIT 16.1   Simplified Supply Chain

How many companies are involved in making and getting a stove to your kitchen?

©Thinkstock/Alamy Stock Photo

three) or directly to stores (Manufacturer two). In addition, many variations on this supply chain exist. Some retail chains, such as Home Depot or Costco, function as both retailers and wholesalers. They act as retailers when they sell to consumers directly and as wholesalers when they sell to other businesses such as building contractors or restaurant owners. When manufacturers such as Avon sell directly to consumers, they perform production as well as retailing activities. When Lenovo sells computers to a university or business, it engages in a business-to-business (B2B) transaction, but when it sells to students or employees individually, it is a B2C (business-to-consumer) operation.

Marketing Channels Add Value

Why do manufacturers use wholesalers or retailers? Don't these added channel members just cut into their profits? Wouldn't it be cheaper for consumers to buy directly from manufacturers? In a simple agrarian economy, the best supply chain likely does follow a direct route from manufacturer to consumer: The consumer goes to the farm and buys food directly from the farmer. Modern eat-local environmental campaigns suggest just such a process. But before the consumer can eat a fresh steak procured from a local farm, she needs to cook it. Assuming the consumer doesn't know how to make a stove and lacks the materials to do so, she must rely on a stove maker. The stove maker, which has the necessary knowledge, must buy raw materials and components from various suppliers, make the stove, and then make it available to the consumer. If the stove maker isn't located near the consumer, the stove must be transported to where the consumer has access to it. To make matters even more complicated, the consumer may want to view a choice of stoves, hear about all their features, and have the stove delivered and installed.

Each participant in the channel adds value.[6] The components manufacturer helps the stove manufacturer by supplying parts and materials. The stove maker turns the components into the stove. The transportation company gets the stove to the retailer. The retailer stores the stove until the customer wants it, educates the customer about product features, and delivers and installs the stove. At each step, the stove becomes more costly but also more valuable to the consumer.

Unlike distribution centers, fulfillment centers accumulate items one at a time and get them ready to ship to individual customers.

©Daniel Acker/Bloomberg via Getty Images

Marketing Channel Management Affects Other Aspects of Marketing

Every marketing decision is affected by and has an effect on marketing channels. When products are designed and manufactured, how and when the critical components reach the factory must be coordinated with production. The sales department must coordinate its delivery promises with the factory or distribution or fulfillment centers. A **distribution center**, a facility for the receipt, storage, and redistribution of goods to company stores, may be operated by retailers, manufacturers, or distribution specialists.[7] Similar to a distribution center, instead of shipping to stores, **fulfillment centers** are used to ship directly to customers. Furthermore, advertising and promotion must be coordinated with those departments that control inventory and transportation. There is no faster way to lose credibility with customers than to promise deliveries or run a promotion and then not have the merchandise when the customer expects it.

DESIGNING MARKETING CHANNELS

 LO16-2 Understand the difference between direct and indirect marketing channels.

When a firm is just starting out or entering a new market, it doesn't typically have the option of designing the best marketing channel structure—that is, choosing from whom it buys or to whom it sells. A new sporting goods retailer may not have the option of carrying all the manufacturer lines it wants because other competing retailers in its market area might carry the same products. On the other side, a small specialty sporting goods apparel manufacturer may not be able to place its products in major stores such as Dick's Sporting Goods because its line is unproven, and the products might duplicate lines that the retailer already carries. Chapter 17 discusses in more depth how manufacturers choose their retailer partners.

Although there are various constraints on marketing channel partners with regard to the design of the best channel structure, all marketing channels take the form of a direct channel, an indirect channel, or some combination thereof.

Direct Marketing Channel

As shown on the left side of Exhibit 16.2, there are no intermediaries between the buyer and seller in a direct marketing channel. Typically, the seller is a manufacturer, such as when a carpentry business sells bookcases through its own store and online to individual consumers. The seller also can be an individual, such as when a knitter sells blankets and scarves at craft fairs, on Etsy, and through eBay. (Recall our discussion of consumer-to-consumer [C2C] transactions in Chapter 1.) When the buyer is another business, such as when Boeing sells planes to JetBlue, the marketing channel still is direct, but in this case, the transaction is a business-to-business one (see Chapter 7).

Noting that people increasingly use online channels to purchase the consumer goods that it manufactures (e.g., diapers, detergent, paper towels), P&G seeks to enhance its direct-to-consumer online sales. Rather than adding shaving razors to a repeat purchase list on Amazon or at Walmart.com, P&G hopes consumers might buy them directly from it, the manufacturer. In so doing, it might increase its own margins because it would not need to share the revenue with the retailer. It launched its Gillette On Demand so customers can make a one-time purchase or subscribe for monthly razor blade refills.[8] In addition, it can undercut any retailer on price because it would not need to maintain retail stores. For example, even the one-time purchase of Gillette's Mach3 razor blades through its e-commerce site is $7.00, while the same product is $7.35 at Walmart.[9] Considering the long-standing, close relationship between P&G and Walmart, though, such moves might make for some awkward strategy meetings between the two companies in the near future. It also requires P&G to build some new infrastructure, including an $89 million distribution center,

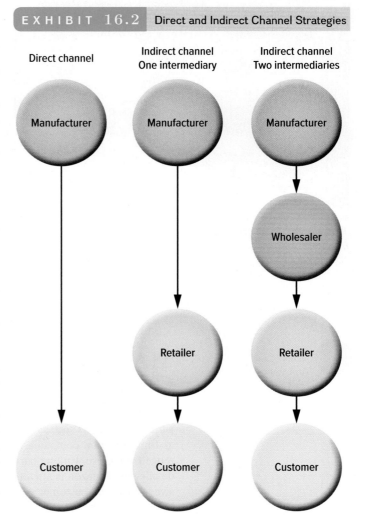

EXHIBIT 16.2 Direct and Indirect Channel Strategies

Ethical & Societal Dilemma 16.1   When Advances in Technology Mean Steps Back for Retail Workers[i]

Artificial intelligence (AI) is everywhere. Its benefits for retailing and consumers are undeniable: Sophisticated AI functions make it possible for retailers to perform inventory analyses more rapidly and accurately, as well as provide accurate and personalized customer service more efficiently. But the expansion of AI throughout retail settings also threatens another critical group: the employees who currently perform those tasks.

The retailing industry employs vast numbers of employees; if those employees' jobs are taken over by AI, the risk is mass unemployment rates. A recent government report suggests that cashiers and drivers are particularly threatened as innovations such as automatic checkouts and driverless cars come closer to reality.

Already, Amazon requires about half as many workers to sell the same amount of merchandise compared with conventional retailers such as Macy's. As it continues to grow, Amazon

plans to reduce these employee requirements even further, by relying on AI that will enable shoppers to place orders on their own, pay for them without any assistance, and have them delivered by drones.

It is impossible to predict the future precisely—some AI applications might never find widespread acceptance, and technologies such as driverless cars still need years of testing before they are safe to use widely. But it also is hard to contest the notion that AI is spreading further and further, such that someday soon, retail workers will have to find other ways to earn a living. If they cannot do so, the vast increase in unemployment rates would threaten the entire economy and depress consumer spending overall.

The solution likely will require new forms of job training, job creation in other sectors, and possibly expanded social safety nets. Unfortunately though, such long-term (and expensive) initiatives are often hard to begin, until it's almost too late.

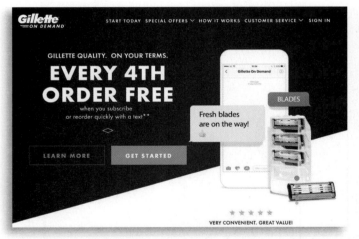

To dissuade customers from purchasing shaving razor blades from online retailers like Amazon or Walmart.com, P&G started Gillette On Demand in which customers can make a one-time purchase or subscribe for monthly razor blade refills directly from the manufacturer.

Source: Procter & Gamble

that it needs to staff and operate so that it can be sure to get the products into customers' homes as quickly as Amazon or Walmart.com promise to do.[0] Finally, such options and the related technology advancements might have implications for the workforce, as Ethical & Societal Dilemma 16.1 notes.

Indirect Marketing Channel

In **indirect marketing channels**, one or more intermediaries work with manufacturers to provide goods and services to customers. In some cases, only one intermediary might be involved. Automobile manufacturers such as Ford and General Motors often use indirect distribution, such that dealers act as retailers, as shown in the middle of Exhibit 16.2. The right side of Exhibit 16.2 reveals how wholesalers are more common when the company does not buy in sufficient quantities to make it cost effective for the manufacturer to deal directly with them—independent book sellers, wine merchants, or independent drugstores, for example. Wholesalers are also prevalent in less developed economies, in which large retailers are rare.

LO16-3 Describe how marketing channels are managed.

MANAGING THE MARKETING CHANNEL AND SUPPLY CHAIN

Marketing channels and supply chains comprise various buying entities such as retailers and wholesalers, sellers such as manufacturers or wholesalers, and facilitators of the exchange such as transportation companies. Similar to interpersonal interactions, their relationships can range from close working partnerships to one-time arrangements. Marketing Analytics 16.1 details how Amazon is attempting to combine all these roles by leveraging its access to massive amounts of customer data. In most cases though, interactions occur across the supply chain because the parties want something from each other: Home Depot wants hammers from

Marketing Analytics 16.1 — Analytics in Support of Anticipatory Shipping by Amazon[ii]

Already well established as an efficient shipper of orders, Amazon continues to seek to do even better. Currently, Amazon receives an order, labels and packages it, loads it onto a delivery truck (run by UPS or the U.S. Postal Service, depending on the day and delivery details), and waits for confirmation that this third-party logistics provider has delivered the product directly to the customer's door. In this traditional process, the online retail giant seeks to improve by adding more warehouses that can provide more customers with overnight or same-day delivery.

But recently, a striking innovation instead aims to reinvent the supply chain completely, to benefit customers as well as itself. That is, Amazon recently applied for and received a patent for its "anticipatory shipping" system, which starts readying packages for delivery before the customer even adds the item to his or her virtual cart. With anticipatory shipping, Amazon boxes and ships out products that it expects customers will want, according to their previous purchases, in the belief that they are likely to order them soon. To determine what to ship, Amazon uses information from customers' previous orders, product searches, shopping cart contents, and previous returns.

This innovation promises to be particularly beneficial for popular books, movies, and games, which people clearly have announced their desire to have in hand the very day they are released. If Amazon can get it to their homes on that same day, it might discourage customers from visiting physical retail locations because their wait times would be even shorter than brick-and-mortar stores can offer. In this sense, Amazon is using big data to predict demand and thus edge out its rivals. However, critics caution that when Amazon's algorithms are incorrect, the necessary returns could grow rapidly to become quite costly. In response, Amazon has suggested that it might simply convert any unwanted deliveries into gifts, thus building goodwill among customers who receive a desirable new order for no cost.

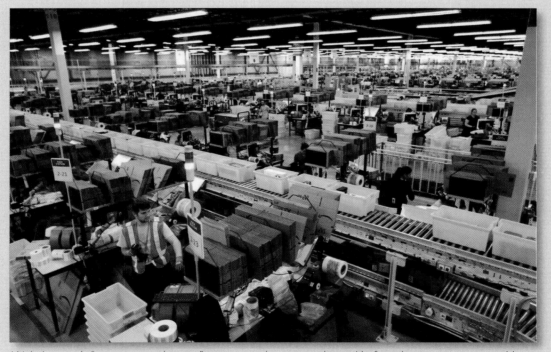

With Amazon's "anticipatory shipping" system, packages are shipped before the customer even adds the item to his or her virtual cart.

©Richard Lautens/Toronto Star via Getty Images

Stanley Black & Decker; Stanley wants an opportunity to sell its tools to the general public; both companies want UPS to deliver the merchandise.

Each member of the marketing channel also performs a specialized role. If one member believes that another has failed to do its job correctly or efficiently, it can replace that member. So, if Stanley isn't getting good service from UPS, it can switch to FedEx. If Home Depot believes its customers do not perceive Stanley tools as a good value, it may buy from another tool company. Home Depot even could decide to make its own tools or use its own

The Home Depot and Stanley Black & Decker have a mutually beneficial partnership. Home Depot buys tools from Stanley because its customers find value in Stanley products. Stanley sells tools to Home Depot because Home Depot has established an excellent market for its products.

Source: Stanley Black & Decker, Inc.

trucks to pick up tools from Stanley. However, anytime a marketing channel member is replaced, the function it has performed remains, so someone needs to complete it.[11]

If a marketing channel is to run efficiently, the participating members must cooperate. Often, however, supply chain members have conflicting goals, and this may result in channel conflict (Exhibit 16.3). For instance, Stanley wants Home Depot to carry all its tools but not the tools of its competitors so that Stanley can maximize its sales. But Home Depot carries a mix of tool brands so it can maximize the sales in its tool category. When supply chain members that buy and sell to one another are not in agreement about their goals, roles, or rewards, **vertical channel conflict** or discord results.

Horizontal channel conflict can also occur when there is disagreement or discord among members at the same level in a marketing channel, such as two competing retailers or two competing manufacturers. Another recent innovation by Amazon, the Vendor Flex program, seeks to lower overall transportation costs but also creates new forms of channel conflict with competitors.[12] As a partner in the Vendor Flex program, P&G agreed to allow Amazon to build fulfillment centers within P&G's own warehouses. The new system thus helped eliminate some of the costs of transporting P&G's products to Amazon's fulfillment centers. But companies such as Target and Walmart, which have enjoyed long-term relationships with P&G, found the move frustrating. Believing that the program was giving its competitor Amazon an unfair advantage, Target reacted vigorously, moving all P&G products from prominent end-cap positions in its stores to less prestigious and less visible locations. Target also stripped P&G of its Category Captain title, meaning Target stopped using P&G as its primary source of advice for planning merchandising strategies within each category.

EXHIBIT 16.3 Vertical versus Horizontal Channel Conflict

Vertical conflict

Manufacturer

Retailer 1   Retailer 2   Retailer 3

Horizontal conflict

Although P&G products are back in end-cap positions in Target stores, the relationship remains strained and P&G has not been reinstated as a Category Captain.[13]

Avoiding vertical channel conflicts demands open, honest communication. Buyers and vendors all must understand what drives the other party's business, their roles in the relationship, each firm's strategies, and any problems that might arise over the course of the relationship. Amazon and P&G recognize that it is in their common interest to remain profitable business partners. Amazon's customers demand and expect to find P&G products on its website; P&G needs the sales generated through Amazon. Amazon cannot demand prices so low that P&G cannot make money, and P&G must be flexible enough to accommodate the needs of this important customer. With a common goal, both firms have the incentive to cooperate because they know that by doing so, each will boost its sales.[14]

Amazon and Procter & Gamble recognize that it is in their common interest to remain profitable business partners.
©Daniel Mihailescu/AFP/Getty Images

Common goals also help sustain the relationship when expected benefits fail to arise. If one P&G shipment fails to reach the Amazon section of one of its fulfillment centers due to an uncontrollable event such as a demand forecasting miscalculation, Amazon does not suddenly call off the whole arrangement. Instead, it recognizes the incident as a simple, isolated mistake and maintains the good working relationship because Amazon knows that both it and P&G are committed to the same goals in the long run.

In this sense, their partnership exhibits both of the nonmutually exclusive ways that exist to manage a marketing channel or supply chain: Coordinate the channel using a vertical marketing system and develop strong relationships with marketing channel partners—topics we now examine.

Managing the Marketing Channel and Supply Chain through Vertical Marketing Systems

Although conflict is likely in any marketing channel, it is generally more pronounced when the channel members are independent entities. Marketing channels that are more closely aligned, whether by contract or ownership, share common goals and therefore are less prone to conflict.

In an **independent (conventional) marketing channel**, several independent members—a manufacturer, a wholesaler, and a retailer—attempt to satisfy their own objectives and maximize their profits, often at the expense of the other members, as we portray in Exhibit 16.4. None of the participants have any control over the others. Before any sort of relationship develops, or in one-time interactions, both parties likely try to extract as much profit from the deal as possible. After the deal is consummated, neither party feels any responsibility to the other.

Over time, though, many parties develop relationships marked by routinized, automatic transactions, such as those that take place between Walmart and P&G. Walmart's customers thus come to expect to find P&G products in stores, and P&G depends on Walmart to purchase a good portion of its output to sell to its own customers. This scenario represents the first phase of a **vertical marketing system**, a marketing channel in which the members act as a unified system, as in Exhibit 16.4. Three types of vertical marketing systems—administered, contractual, and corporate—reflect increasing phases of formalization and control. The more formal the vertical marketing system, the less likely conflict is to ensue.

Administered Vertical Marketing System Walmart's various marketing channel relationships offer examples of different forms of an **administered vertical marketing system**: There is no common ownership or contractual relationships, but the dominant channel member controls or holds the balance of power. Because of its size and relative power,

EXHIBIT 16.4   Independent versus Vertical Marketing Channels

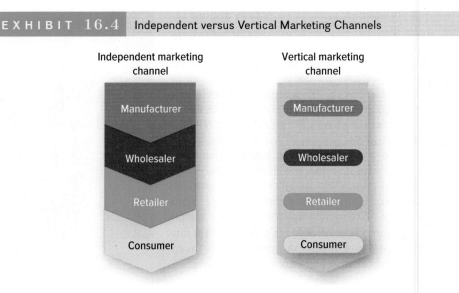

Walmart can easily impose controls on small manufacturers, such as Brown Betty Dessert Boutique, but with large, powerful suppliers such as P&G, the control is more balanced between parties. Power in a marketing channel exists when one firm has the means or ability to dictate the actions of another member at a different level of distribution (Exhibit 16.5). A retailer like Walmart exercises its power over suppliers in several ways.

- With its reward power, Walmart offers rewards, often a monetary incentive, if the wholesalers or manufacturers do what Walmart wants them to do. For example, it might promise to purchase larger quantities if a manufacturer will lower its wholesale price.

- Coercive power arises when Walmart threatens to punish or punishes the other channel member for not undertaking certain tasks, such as if it were to delay payment for a late delivery.

- Walmart may also have referent power if a supplier desperately wants to be associated with Walmart, because being known as an important Walmart supplier enables that supplier to attract other retailers' business. In this sense, P&G might be playing its retailer partners against one another to enhance its own performance.

- If Walmart exerts expertise power, it relies on its vast experience and knowledge to decide how to market a particular supplier's products, without giving the supplier much of a say.

- Because Walmart has vast information about the consumer goods market, it might exert information power over P&G by providing or withholding important market information. At the same time, P&G might have its own information power that it could exert over Walmart, depending on which company has the most or most updated data.

EXHIBIT 16.5   Bases of Power

- Legitimate power is based on getting a channel member to behave in a certain way because of a contractual agreement between the two firms. As Walmart deals with its suppliers, it likely exerts multiple types of power to influence their behaviors. If either party dislikes the way the relationship is going, though, it can simply walk away.

Contractual Vertical Marketing System Over time, members of the supply chain often formalize their relationship by entering into contracts that dictate various terms,[15] such as how much Walmart will buy from P&G each month and at what price, as well as the penalties for late deliveries. In contractual vertical marketing systems like this, independent firms at different levels of the marketing channel join through contracts to obtain economies of scale and coordination and to reduce conflict.[15]

McDonald's is the top franchise opportunity in the United States, according to Entrepreneur *magazine.*

©View Apart/Shutterstock

Franchising is the most common type of contractual vertical marketing system. Franchising is a contractual agreement between a franchisor and a franchisee that allows the franchisee to operate a retail outlet using a name and format developed and supported by the franchisor. Exhibit 16.6 lists the United States' top franchise opportunities. These rankings, determined by *Entrepreneur* magazine, are created using a number of objective measures such as financial strength, stability, growth rate, and size of the franchise system.[17]

In a franchise contract, the franchisee pays a lump sum plus a royalty on all sales in return for the right to operate a business in a specific location. The franchisee also agrees to operate the outlet in accordance with the procedures prescribed by the franchisor. The franchisor typically provides assistance in locating and building the business, developing the

EXHIBIT 16.6   Top 10 Franchises for 2017

Rank	Franchise Name		Number of U.S. Outlets	Start-Up Costs
1	**McDonald's** Burgers, chicken, salads, beverages		13,149	$1M–2.2M
2	**7-Eleven** Convenience stores		7,025	$38K–1.1M
3	**Dunkin' Donuts** Coffee shops		9,141	$229K–1.7M
4	**The UPS Store** Postal, business, printing, and communications services		4,622	$178K–403K
5	**Re/Max LLC** Real estate		3,729	$38K–225K
6	**Sonic Drive-In Restaurants** Burgers, hot dogs, chicken, sandwiches, breakfast, ice cream, beverages		3,212	$1.02M–1.77M
7	**Great Clips** Hair salons		3,945	$137K–258K
8	**Taco Bell** Mexican food		5,535	$525K–2.6M
9	**Hardee's** Burgers, chicken, biscuits		1,749	$1.4M–1.9M
10	**Sport Clips** Men's sports-themed hair salons		1,600	$189K–355K

Source: 2017 Franchise 500 Ranking, Entrepreneur.com.

Tesla represents a corporate vertical marketing system because it manufactures its own cars and it operates its own retail stores.

©Eakrat/Shutterstock

products or services sold, management training, and advertising. To maintain the franchisee's reputation, the franchisor also makes sure that all outlets provide the same quality of services and products.

A franchise system combines the entrepreneurial advantages of owning a business with the efficiencies of vertical marketing systems that function under single ownership (i.e., a corporate system, as we discuss next). Franchisees are motivated to make their stores successful because they receive the profits after they pay the royalty to the franchisor. The franchisor is motivated to develop new products, services, and systems and to promote the franchise because it receives royalties on all sales. Advertising, product development, and system development are all done efficiently by the franchisor, with costs shared by all franchisees.

Corporate Vertical Marketing System In a corporate vertical marketing system, the parent company has complete control and can dictate the priorities and objectives of the marketing channel because it owns multiple segments of the channel, such as manufacturing plants, warehouse facilities, and retail outlets. Adding Value 16.1 highlights how ownership and resulting control lessen potential conflict among segments of the channel.

Tesla Motors, manufacturer of luxury electric automobiles, represents a corporate vertical marketing system because it manufactures its own cars in Fremont, California and it operates its own retail stores in high-foot-traffic locations such as malls and shopping streets.[18] The Tesla Product Specialists that work in these stores are trained to answer questions, not sell cars per se. They could not even sell a car on the spot if they wanted to because there is no inventory on hand. They would, of course, be happy to take an order though. Tesla also owns and operates its own service centers. With this corporate ownership structure, it is able to maintain control of every aspect of Tesla ownership, thus ensuring satisfied and loyal customers.

Managing Marketing Channels and Supply Chains through Strategic Relationships

There is more to managing marketing channels and supply chains than simply exercising power over other members in an administered system or establishing a contractual or corporate vertical marketing system. There is also a human side.

In a conventional marketing channel, relationships between members reflect their arguments over the split of the profit pie: If one party gets ahead, the other party falls behind. Sometimes this type of transaction is acceptable if the parties have no interest in a long-term relationship. But such attitudes can limit the success of the supply chain as a whole.

Therefore, firms frequently seek a strategic relationship, also called a partnering relationship, in which the marketing channel members are committed to maintaining the relationship over the long term and investing in opportunities that are mutually beneficial. In a conventional or administered marketing channel, there are significant incentives to establish a strategic relationship, even without contracts or ownership relationships. Both parties benefit because the size of the profit pie has increased, so both the buyer and the seller increase their sales and profits. These strategic relationships are created explicitly to uncover and exploit joint opportunities, so members depend on and trust each other heavily; share goals and agree on how to accomplish those goals; and are willing to take risks, share confidential information, and make significant investments for the sake of the relationship. Successful strategic relationships require mutual trust, open communication, common goals, interdependence, and credible commitments.

Adding Value 16.1   Milk Is Going Vertical[iii]

Milk is generally thought of as a commodity product: a convenience item, purchased frequently and consumed regularly, sold at low margins. Even though they rarely make much profit on it, grocery retailers realize that they cannot risk being out of milk, because most consumers add a gallon to their shopping baskets on nearly every visit. But at the same time, milk consumption is decreasing, resulting in a downward price trend.

Furthermore, customers have begun to exhibit increasing concerns about where their food comes from. In an effort to ensure quality and still keep prices low, some major U.S. grocery chains are becoming corporate vertical marketing systems by entering the milk processing business. Kroger already processes all of the fresh milk that it sells under its own brand. Walmart plans to open the country's biggest dairy processing plant sometime this year. By taking over this upstream link in the supply chain, retailers can better control their supply of this critical product. Furthermore, when demand decreases, the grocers can shift their production capacity, focusing more on other dairy items such as cheeses or other types of beverages. As one executive noted, in explaining why Albertson's was building a new, 55,000-square-foot production facility, "You can do a lot more in a dairy plant than make dairy."

In addition, by vertically integrating, retailers can cut out existing dairy processers by buying the raw materials directly from farmers. Ultimately, this move may enable retailers to further reduce prices to consumers, even though their short-term investments in building the plants are substantial. For some farmers, this shift may prove beneficial because they gain a new channel in which to sell their products. Such an option would be vastly more appealing than the tactic that some farmers have turned to, when faced with a glut of milk: pouring the excess that they cannot sell right into their fields.

Some major U.S. grocery chains are becoming corporate vertical marketing systems by entering the milk processing business.

©Jason Lugo/Getty Images

For the processors, though, the change in the supply chain looks ominous. They already have been hard pressed by decreasing prices, lower consumption, and the increasing availability of nondairy milk alternatives. Yet the milk business is still worth approximately $8 billion per year. Rather than investing to update their plants to be able to process additional products, most processors have sought to cut costs. Others, including the Dairy Farmers of America cooperative, are investing more in expanding their capabilities to process milk powder or butter. But regardless of their response to the shifts in market demand, these producers realize that retailers' move to create corporate vertical marketing systems will make it more difficult for them to compete effectively.

Mutual Trust Mutual trust holds a strategic relationship together. Trust is the belief that a partner is honest (i.e., reliable, stands by its word, sincere, fulfills obligations) and benevolent (i.e., concerned about the other party's welfare). When vendors and buyers trust each other, they are more willing to share relevant ideas, clarify goals and problems, and communicate efficiently. Information shared between the parties, such as inventory positions in stores, thus becomes increasingly comprehensive, accurate, and timely.

With trust, there's also less need for the supply chain members to constantly monitor and check up on each other's actions because each believes the other won't take advantage, even if given the opportunity. Although it is important in all relationships, monitoring supply chain members becomes particularly pertinent when suppliers are located in less developed countries, where issues such as the use of child labor, poor working conditions, and below-subsistence wages have become a shared responsibility.

Open Communication To share information, develop sales forecasts together, and coordinate deliveries, Walmart and its suppliers maintain open and honest communication. This maintenance may sound easy in principle, but some businesses don't tend to share information with their business partners. But open, honest communication is a key to developing successful relationships because supply chain members need to understand what is driving each other's business, their roles in the relationship, each firm's strategies, and any problems that arise over the course of the relationship.

Common Goals Supply chain members must have common goals for a successful relationship to develop. Shared goals give both members of the relationship an incentive to pool their strengths and abilities and exploit potential opportunities together. Such commonality also offers an assurance that the other partner won't do anything to hinder the achievement of those goals within the relationship.

Walmart and P&G recognize that it is in their common interest to be strategic partners. Walmart needs P&G to satisfy its customers, and P&G recognizes that if it can keep Walmart happy, it will have more than enough business for years to come. With common goals, both firms have an incentive to cooperate because they know that by doing so, both can boost sales. If Walmart needs a special production run of detergent to meet demand following a natural disaster, for example, P&G will work to meet the challenge. If P&G is determined to introduce radically new products, it is in Walmart's best interest to help because it is committed to the same goals in the long run.

Interdependence When supply chain members view their goals and ultimate success as intricately linked, they develop deeper long-term relationships. Interdependence between supply chain members that is based on mutual benefits is key to developing and sustaining the relationship.[19] Walmart's suppliers recognize that without Walmart, their sales would be significantly less. Although it is the more powerful member of most of its supply chains, Walmart also recognizes that it can depend on these suppliers to be a dependable source of supply, thus enabling it to have a very efficient marketing channel.

Credible Commitments Successful relationships develop because both parties make credible commitments to, or tangible investments in, the relationship. These commitments go beyond just making the hollow statement, "I want to be your partner"; they involve spending money to improve the products or services provided to the customer and on information technology to improve supply chain efficiency.[20] As we described previously, Amazon and P&G have worked closely to set up their Vendor Flex program, enabling Amazon to operate fulfillment centers within P&G's own warehouses and thereby lower transportation expenses.[21]

Similar to many other elements of marketing, managing the marketing channel can seem like an easy task at first glance: Put the right merchandise in the right place at the right time. But the various elements and actors involved in a marketing channel create its unique and compelling complexities and require firms to work carefully to ensure they are achieving the most efficient and effective chain possible.

We now turn our attention to how information and merchandise flow through marketing channels.

PROGRESS CHECK

1. What is the difference between an indirect and a direct marketing channel?
2. What are the differences among the three types of vertical marketing systems?
3. How do firms develop strong strategic partnerships with their marketing channel partners?

LO16-4 Describe the flow of information and merchandise in the marketing channel.

MAKING INFORMATION FLOW THROUGH MARKETING CHANNELS

Information flows from the customer to stores, to and from distribution centers, possibly to and from wholesalers, to and from product manufacturers, and then on to the producers of any components and the suppliers of raw materials. To simplify our discussion—and because information flows are similar in other marketing channel links, such as through the Internet and catalogs, as well as in B2B channels—we shorten the supply chain in this section to exclude wholesalers as well as the link from suppliers to manufacturers. Exhibit 16.7

EXHIBIT 16.7   Information Flows

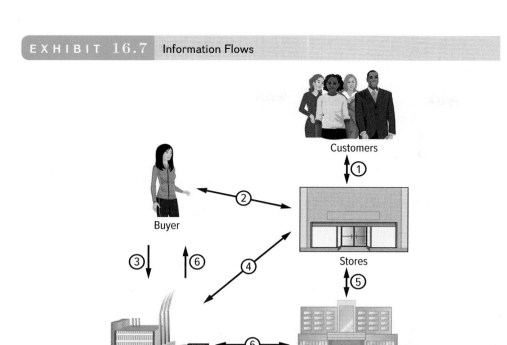

illustrates the flow of information that starts when a customer buys a Sony HDTV at Best Buy. The flow follows these steps:

Flow 1 (Customer to Store): The sales associate at Best Buy scans the Universal Product Code (UPC) tag on the HDTV packaging, and the customer receives a receipt. The UPC tag is the black-and-white bar code found on most merchandise. It contains a 13-digit code that indicates the manufacturer of the item, a description of the item, information about special packaging, and special promotions.[22] In the future, RFID tags, discussed later in this chapter, may replace UPC tags.

Flow 2 (Store to Buyer): The point-of-sale (POS) terminal records the purchase information and electronically sends it to the buyer at Best Buy's corporate office. The sales information is incorporated into an inventory management system and used to monitor and analyze sales and decide to reorder more HDTVs, change a price, or plan a promotion. Buyers also send information to stores about overall sales for the chain, ways to display the merchandise, upcoming promotions, and so on.

Flow 3 (Buyer to Manufacturer): The purchase information from each Best Buy store is typically aggregated by the retailer as a whole, which creates an order for new merchandise and sends it to Sony. The buyer at Best Buy may also communicate directly with Sony to get information and negotiate prices, shipping dates, promotional events, or other merchandise-related issues.

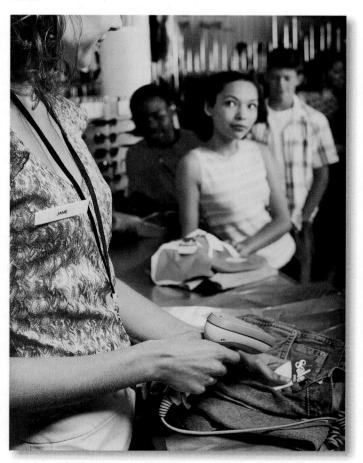

The flow of information starts when the UPC tag is scanned at the point of purchase.

©Digital Vision/Getty Images

Flow 4 (Store to Manufacturer): In some situations, the sales transaction data are sent directly from the store to the manufacturer, and the manufacturer decides when to ship more merchandise to the distribution centers and the stores. In other situations, especially when merchandise is reordered frequently, the ordering process is done automatically, bypassing the buyers. By working together, the retailer and manufacturer can better satisfy customer needs.

Flow 5 (Store to Distribution Center): Stores also communicate with the Best Buy distribution centers to coordinate deliveries and check inventory status. When the store inventory drops to a specified level, more HDTVs are shipped to the store, and the shipment information is sent to the Best Buy computer system.

Flow 6 (Manufacturer to Distribution Center and Buyer): When the manufacturer ships the HDTVs to the Best Buy distribution center, it sends an advanced shipping notice to the distribution center. An advanced shipping notice (ASN) is an electronic document that the supplier sends the retailer in advance of a shipment to tell the retailer exactly what to expect in the shipment. The center then makes appointments for trucks to make the delivery at a specific time, date, and loading dock. When the shipment is received at the distribution center, the buyer is notified and authorizes payment to the vendor.

Data Warehouse

Purchase data collected at the point of sale (information flow 2 in Exhibit 16.7) goes into a huge database known as a data warehouse, similar to those described in Chapter 10. Using the data warehouse, the CEO not only can learn how the corporation is generally doing but also can look at the data aggregated by quarter for a merchandise division, a region of the country, or the total corporation. A buyer may be more interested in a particular manufacturer in a certain store on a particular day. Analysts from various levels of the retail operation extract information from the data warehouse to make a plethora of marketing decisions about developing and replenishing merchandise assortments.

In some cases, manufacturers also have access to this data warehouse. They communicate with retailers by using electronic data interchange (EDI) and supply chain systems known as vendor-managed inventory.

In information flows 3, 4, and 6 in Exhibit 16.7, the retailer and manufacturer exchange business documents through EDI. Electronic data interchange (EDI) is the computer-to-computer exchange of business documents from a retailer to a vendor and back. In addition to sales data, purchase orders, invoices, and data about returned merchandise can be transmitted back and forth. With EDI, vendors can transmit information about on-hand inventory status, vendor promotions, and cost changes to the retailer, as well as information about purchase order changes, order status, retail prices, and transportation routings. Thus EDI enables channel members to communicate more quickly and with fewer errors than in the past, ensuring that merchandise moves from vendors to retailers more quickly.

Vendor-managed inventory (VMI) is an approach for improving marketing channel efficiency in which the manufacturer is responsible for maintaining the retailer's inventory levels in each of its stores.[23] By sharing the data in the retailer's data warehouse and communicating that information via EDI, the manufacturer automatically sends merchandise to the retailer's store or distribution or fulfillment center when the inventory at the store reaches a prespecified level.

In ideal conditions, the manufacturer replenishes inventories in quantities that meet the retailer's immediate demand, which reduces stockouts with minimal inventory. In addition to providing a better match between retail demand and supply, VMI can reduce the vendor's and the retailer's costs. Manufacturer salespeople no longer need to spend time generating orders on items that are already in the stores, and their role shifts to selling new items and maintaining relationships. Retail buyers and planners no longer need to monitor inventory levels and place orders.

MAKING MERCHANDISE FLOW THROUGH MARKETING CHANNELS

Exhibit 16.8 illustrates the merchandise flow steps for a large retailer, such as Best Buy, that relies largely on its physical store operations. The flow of merchandise and pertinent decision variables in an Internet channel are similar, except that orders arrive from customers one at a time and go out in relatively small quantities, so the facility used to store and process these orders—that is, the fulfillment center—works a little differently. In general though, the merchandise flow steps are:

1. Sony to Best Buy's distribution centers, or
2. Sony directly to stores.
3. If the merchandise goes through distribution centers, it is then shipped to stores,
4. and then to the customer.

Making merchandise flow involves first deciding whether the merchandise will go from the manufacturer to a retailer's distribution center or directly on to stores. Once in a distribution center, multiple activities take place before it is shipped on to a store.

Distribution Centers versus Direct Store Delivery

As indicated in Exhibit 16.8, manufacturers can ship merchandise directly to a retailer's stores—direct store delivery (flow 2)—or to their distribution centers (flow 1). Although manufacturers and retailers may collaborate, the ultimate decision is usually up to the retailer and depends on the characteristics of the merchandise and the nature of demand. To determine

EXHIBIT 16.8 Merchandise Flows

which distribution system—distribution centers or direct store delivery—is better, retailers consider the total cost associated with each alternative and the customer service criterion of having the right merchandise at the store when the customer wants to buy it.

There are several advantages to using a distribution center:

- More accurate sales forecasts are possible when retailers combine forecasts for many stores serviced by one distribution center rather than doing a forecast for each store. Consider a set of 50 Target stores, serviced by a single distribution center that each carries Dualit toasters. Each store normally stocks 5 units, for a total of 250 units in the system. By carrying the item at each store, the retailer must develop individual forecasts, each with the possibility of errors that could result in either too much or too little merchandise. Alternatively, by delivering most of the inventory to a distribution center and feeding the stores merchandise as they need it, the effects of forecast errors for the individual stores are minimized, and less backup inventory is needed to prevent stockouts.

- Distribution centers enable the retailer to carry less merchandise in the individual stores, which results in lower inventory investments systemwide. If the stores get frequent deliveries from the distribution center, they need to carry relatively less extra merchandise as backup stock.

- It is easier to avoid running out of stock or having too much stock in any particular store because merchandise is ordered from the distribution center as needed.

- Retail store space is typically much more expensive than is space at a distribution center, and distribution centers are better equipped than stores to prepare merchandise for sale. As a result, many retailers find it cost effective to store merchandise and get it ready for sale at a distribution center rather than in individual stores.

Should Target stock Dualit toasters in distribution centers or keep all its backup stock in stores?

©Lee Hacker/Alamy Stock Photo

But distribution centers aren't appropriate for all retailers. If a retailer has only a few outlets, the expense of a distribution center is probably unwarranted. Also, if many outlets are concentrated in metropolitan areas, merchandise can be consolidated and delivered by the vendor directly to all the stores in one area economically. Direct store delivery gets merchandise to the stores faster and thus is used for perishable goods (meat and produce), items that help create the retailer's image of being the first to sell the latest product (e.g., video games), or fads. Finally, some manufacturers provide direct store delivery for retailers to ensure that their products are on the store's shelves, properly displayed, and fresh. For example, employees delivering Frito-Lay snacks directly to supermarkets replace products that have been on the shelf too long and are stale, replenish products that have been sold, and arrange products so they are neatly displayed.

The Distribution (or Fulfillment) Center

The distribution center performs the following activities: managing inbound transportation; receiving and checking; storing and cross-docking; getting merchandise floor-ready; ticketing and marking; preparing to ship merchandise to stores; and shipping merchandise to stores. Fulfillment centers perform the same functions, but because they deliver directly to customers rather than to stores, they do not have to get merchandise floor-ready. To illustrate these activities being undertaken in a distribution center, we'll continue our example of Sony HDTVs being shipped to a Best Buy distribution center.

Managing Inbound Transportation Traditionally, when working with vendors, buyers focused their efforts on developing merchandise assortments, negotiating prices, and arranging joint promotions. Now, buyers and planners are much more involved in coordinating the physical flow of merchandise to stores. Planners are employees responsible for the financial planning and analysis of merchandise and its allocation to stores. The TV buyer has arranged for a truckload of HDTVs to be delivered to its Houston, Texas, distribution center on Monday between 1:00 and 3:00 p.m. The buyer also specifies how the merchandise should be placed on pallets for easy unloading.

The truck must arrive within the specified time because the distribution center has all of its 100 receiving docks allocated throughout the day, and much of the merchandise on this particular truck is going to be shipped to stores that evening. Unfortunately, the truck was delayed in a snowstorm. The **dispatcher**—the person who coordinates deliveries to the distribution center—reassigns the truck delivering the HDTVs to a Wednesday morning delivery slot and charges the firm several hundred dollars for missing its delivery time. Although many manufacturers pay transportation expenses, some retailers negotiate with their vendors to absorb this expense. These retailers believe they can lower their net merchandise cost and better control merchandise flow if they negotiate directly with trucking companies and consolidate shipments from many vendors. The pressing issue facing those involved in transportation management within firms is whether or not their trucks will be driverless, as shown in Ethical & Societal Dilemma 16.2.

Walmart speeds merchandise from its distribution centers to stores.
©Michael Nagle/Bloomberg via Getty Images

Receiving and Checking Using UPC or RFID Receiving is the process of recording the receipt of merchandise as it arrives at a distribution center. Checking is the process of going through the goods upon receipt to make sure they arrived undamaged and that the merchandise ordered was the merchandise received.

In the past, checking merchandise was a very labor-intensive and time-consuming process. Today, however, many distribution systems using EDI are designed to minimize, if not eliminate, these processes. The advance shipping notice (ASN) tells the distribution center what should be in each carton. A UPC label or radio frequency identification (RFID) tag on the shipping carton that identifies the carton's contents is scanned and automatically counted as it is being received and checked. Radio frequency identification (RFID) tags are tiny computer chips that automatically transmit to a special scanner all the information about a container's contents or individual products. Approximately as large as a pinhead, these RFID tags consist of an antenna and a chip that contains an electronic product code that stores far more information about a product than bar (UPC) codes can. The tags also act as passive tracking devices, signaling their presence over a radio frequency when they pass within a few yards of a special scanner. The tags have long been used in high-cost applications such as automated highway toll systems and security identification badges. As the cost of the tags and implementation technology has decreased, their uses have become more prevalent in retail supply chain applications.

Storing and Cross-Docking After the merchandise is received and checked, it is either stored or cross-docked. When merchandise is stored, the cartons are transported by a conveyor system and forklift trucks to racks that go from the distribution center's floor to its ceiling. Then, when the merchandise is needed in the stores, a forklift driver or a robot goes to the rack, picks up the carton, and places it on a conveyor system that routes the carton to the loading dock of a truck going to the store.

Robots are often used to help prepare merchandise to be shipped to stores.
©David Paul Morris/Bloomberg via Getty Images

Ethical & Societal Dilemma 16.2   Automation Spreading to Yet Another Link in the Supply Chain: Driverless Trucking[iv]

Robots already are doing much of the work in supply chains, from picking orders in warehouses to stocking items on shelves. The trend is expanding out to other stages of the chain too, as the technology supporting self-driving vehicles is being added to the trucks that carry products across the country.

Although driverless vehicles for consumer use seem to have stalled somewhat, their use in the freight and supply chain industry is growing. The reason is the easier task associated with driving long, straight distances, mostly on highways. That is, rather than needing to make multiple turns and stops to run errands, as might be required of a passenger car, long-haul trucks just need to get on the interstate and head down the road. The supporting technology is sufficient to keep them in their lanes and avoid other vehicles in the area. Thus, the market for these trucks is growing rapidly.

This growth also is driven by their benefits: Driverless trucks would save companies both time and money. Labor laws restrict how long truck drivers can drive without taking a break—no more than 11 hours a day without taking an 8-hour break. However, these rules would not apply to driverless trucks, which would be able to be on the road nearly 24 hours a day, every day of the week. In this sense, they could double the efficiency of the transportation industry. Because a major component of shipping costs is labor, driverless trucks also could eliminate a huge part of the expenses involved in shipping, saving companies and their customers thousands of dollars.

The way the fleets will grow remains a matter of some debate, though. Some observers predict that the greatest growth opportunities will come from remote-controlled vehicles, while others anticipate that human operators still will need to sit in the cabs of the trucks, in case of emergency and to handle the local last leg of the trip, at least for the foreseeable future. One start-up company instead envisions groups of autonomous trucks traveling together, like a peloton in bicycle racing, so that they can obtain benefits from drafting off one another.

But ultimately, the goal appears to be fully autonomous trucks performing the delivery step that long-haul drivers currently fulfill. That outcome would mean a radical transformation in the job market, considering that an estimated 3.5 million

The trend toward driverless trucks is moving forward. It costs less money to operate, but also costs jobs.

©Chesky/Shutterstock

people currently work as truck drivers. The potential for vast job losses makes the discussion a political and ethical one as well. However, the trucking industry is highly fragmented, such that it encompasses thousands of relatively small companies. This status makes it difficult to establish labor unions that might protect the drivers' jobs.

Although there is no doubt that these trucks could cause widespread unemployment concerns, other benefits for society might help push them into reality. Automobile accidents involving trucks cause a significant number of fatalities every year, and truck drivers have the highest on-the-job fatality rate of any job. Although driverless technology is still young, it can "learn," such that as it improves and gains experience, the improved driverless trucks will offer significant safety benefits on the road.

Furthermore, in the push for ever more efficient supply chains, technologies that reduce labor costs nearly always win. Thus the future seems likely to feature a lot more empty truck cabs, as well as a lot of people looking for a different job.

Using a **cross-docking distribution center**, merchandise cartons are prepackaged by the vendor for a specific store. The UPC or RFID labels on the carton indicate the store to which it is to be sent. The vendor also may affix price tags to each item in the carton. Because the merchandise is ready for sale, it is placed on a conveyor system that routes it from the unloading dock at which it was received to the loading dock for the truck going to the specific store—hence the name *cross-docked*. The cartons are routed on the conveyor system automatically by sensors that read the UPC or RFID label on the cartons. Cross-docked merchandise is in the distribution center only for a few hours before it is shipped to the stores.

Merchandise sales rate and degree of perishability or fashionability typically determine whether cartons are cross-docked or stored. For instance, because Sony's HDTVs sell so quickly, it is in Best Buy's interest not to store them in a distribution center. Similarly, cross-docking is preferable for fashion apparel or perishable meat or produce.

Getting Merchandise Floor-Ready For some merchandise, additional tasks are undertaken in the distribution center to make the merchandise floor-ready. Floor-ready merchandise is merchandise that is ready to be placed on the selling floor. Getting merchandise floor-ready entails ticketing, marking, and, in the case of some apparel, placing garments on hangers (or maybe attaching RFID chips). For the UK-based grocery chain Tesco, it is essential that products ship in ready-to-sell units so that there is little manipulation or sorting to do at the distribution center or in the stores. To move the store-ready merchandise it receives from suppliers quickly into the store, Tesco demands that products sit on roll cages rather than pallets. Then, store employees can easily wheel them onto the retail floor. The stores' backrooms only have two or three days' worth of backup inventory, and it is important to keep inventory levels low and receive lots of small, accurate deliveries from its suppliers—which also helps cut costs.[24]

Ticketing and Marking Ticketing and marking refers to affixing price and identification labels to the merchandise. It is more efficient for a retailer to perform these activities at a distribution center than in its stores. In a distribution center, an area can be set aside and a process implemented to efficiently add labels and put apparel on hangers. Conversely, getting merchandise floor-ready in stores can block aisles and divert salespeople's attention from their customers. An even better approach from the retailer's perspective is to get vendors to ship floor-ready merchandise, thus totally eliminating the expensive, time-consuming ticketing and marking process.

Preparing to Ship Merchandise to a Store At the beginning of the day, the computer system in the distribution center generates a list of items to be shipped to each store on that day. For each item, a pick ticket and shipping label is generated. The pick ticket is a document or display on a screen in a forklift truck indicating how much of each item to get from specific storage areas. The forklift driver goes to the storage area, picks up the number of cartons indicated on the pick ticket, places UPC shipping labels on the cartons that indicate the stores to which the items are to be shipped, and puts the cartons on the conveyor system, where they are automatically routed to the loading dock for the truck going to the stores. In some distribution and fulfillment centers, these functions are performed by robots.

Shipping Merchandise to Stores Shipping merchandise to stores from a distribution center has become increasingly complex. Most distribution centers run 50 to 100 outbound truck routes in one day. To handle this complex transportation problem, the centers use sophisticated routing and scheduling computer systems that consider the locations of the stores, road conditions, and transportation operating constraints to develop the most efficient routes possible. As a result, stores are provided with an accurate estimated time of arrival, and vehicle usage is maximized.

Customer Store Pickup

Technology advances have changed consumers' expectations of their shopping experience. They want the option of making the purchase online and then picking up in store. Retailers that can offer this option drive additional sales, as customers who come into the store to pick up online orders are more likely to make additional purchases while in store. For retailers to be successful with the buy-online-and-pick-up-in-store option, they need to invest in technology that enables order allocation systems to locate every item in stock so as to fulfill the order in a timely manner.

Consumers have been spoiled by technology that allows them to shop for anything, anywhere, anytime, and they want it delivered now. Multichannel retailers that offer the buy-online-and-pick-up-in-store option will be appealing to these spoiled customers. For this option to be successful, retailers need to ensure that the products that show up as being available online will actually be available in stock and ready for pickup. This requires a high level of accuracy inherent in the retailer's inventory management system.

Walmart offers customer store pickup.
©Danny Johnston/AP Photo

The notification of sales to stores quickly and accurately is crucial for retailers to differentiate themselves. Retailers need to equip themselves with mobile task management technology to deliver outstanding customer experience. Mobile task management technology is a wireless network and a mobile device that receives demand notification and enables a speedy response. This solution allows the associate closest to the ordered item to physically pull it and verify its availability.

For the buy-online-and-pick-up-in-store option to be successful, the retailer must be able to move the product along its supply chain smoothly, effectively, and efficiently with the intention of delivering a single order to an individual customer. That is what enables the retailer to deliver an outstanding in-store pickup experience, and in return, brings the customer back to the store in the future.[25]

Inventory Management through Just-in-Time Inventory Systems

Marketing channel management offers the 21st century's answer to a host of distribution problems faced by firms. As recently as the early 1990s, even the most innovative firms needed 15 to 30 days—or even more—to fulfill an order from the warehouse to the customer. The typical order-to-delivery process had several steps: order creation, usually using a telephone, fax, or mail; order processing, using a manual system for credit authorization and assignment to a warehouse; and physical delivery. Things could, and often did, go wrong. Ordered goods were not available. Orders were lost or misplaced. Shipments were misdirected. These mistakes lengthened the time it took to get merchandise to customers and potentially made the entire process more expensive.

Faced with such predicaments, firms began stockpiling inventory at each level of the supply chain (retailers, wholesalers, and manufacturers), but keeping inventory where it is not needed becomes a huge and wasteful expense. If a manufacturer has a huge stock of items stuck in a warehouse, it not only is not earning profits by selling those items but also must pay to maintain and guard that warehouse.

Therefore many firms, such as H&M, Zara, Mango, and Forever 21, have adopted a practice developed by Toyota in the 1950s. Just-in-time (JIT) inventory systems, also known as quick response (QR) inventory systems in retailing, are inventory management systems that deliver less merchandise on a more frequent basis than in traditional inventory systems.

The firm gets the merchandise just in time for it to be used in the manufacture of another product or for sale when the customer wants it. The benefits of a JIT system include reduced lead time (the amount of time between the recognition that an order needs to be placed and the arrival of the needed merchandise at the seller's store, available for sale), increased product availability, and lower inventory investment.

Reduced Lead Time By eliminating the need for paper transactions, the EDI in the JIT systems reduces lead time. Even better, the shorter lead times further reduce the need for inventory, because the shorter the lead time, the easier it is for the retailer to forecast its demand.

Increased Product Availability and Lower Inventory Investment In general, as a firm's ability to satisfy customer demand by having stock on hand increases, so does its inventory investment; that is, it needs to keep more backup inventory in stock. But with JIT, the ability to satisfy demand can actually increase while inventory decreases. Because a firm like H&M can make purchase commitments or produce merchandise closer to the time of sale, its own inventory investment is reduced. H&M needs less inventory because it's getting less merchandise in each order but receiving those shipments more often. Because firms using JIT order merchandise to cover shorter-term demand, their inventory is reduced even further.

The ability to satisfy customer demand by keeping merchandise in stock also increases in JIT systems as a result of the more frequent shipments. For instance, if an H&M store runs low on a medium-sized red T-shirt, its JIT system ensures a shorter lead time than for those of more traditional retailers. As a result, it is less likely that the H&M store will be out of stock for its customers before the next T-shirt shipment arrives.

Costs of a JIT System Although firms achieve great benefits from a JIT system, it is not without its costs. The distribution function becomes much more complicated with more frequent deliveries. With greater order frequency also come smaller orders, which are more expensive to transport and more difficult to coordinate. Therefore, JIT systems require a strong commitment by the firm and its vendors to cooperate, share data, and develop systems.

PROGRESS CHECK

1. How does merchandise flow through a typical marketing channel?
2. Why have just-in-time inventory systems become so popular?

Reviewing Learning Objectives

 LO16-1 Understand the importance of marketing channels and supply chain management.

Marketing channels allow companies to get their products in the appropriate outlets in sufficient quantities to meet consumer demand. To anticipate this demand, advertising and promotions must be coordinated with the departments that control inventory and transportation. Otherwise, customers would come in seeking a promotion and not find the product.

Without the members in a marketing channel, consumers would be forced to find raw materials, manufacture products, and somehow get them to where they could be used all on their own. Thus, each marketing channel member adds value to the product by performing one or more of these functions. Marketing channel management also creates value for each firm in the chain and helps bind together many company functions, including manufacturing, inventory management, transportation, advertising, and marketing.

LO16-2 Understand the difference between direct and indirect marketing channels.

There are ways by which businesses get their goods to consumers. Using a direct marketing channel, a customer can purchase goods from the manufacturer without needing to go through a retailer or intermediary, generally online (e.g., Ascend speakers) or at company stores (e.g., Apple). More commonly, manufacturers choose to offer their goods to consumers through an intermediary, such as a retailer (e.g.,

Walmart), implementing an indirect marketing channel strategy.

LO16-3 Describe how marketing channels are managed.

The more closely aligned the marketing channel members are with each other, the less likely there will be significant conflict. An administered marketing channel occurs when a dominant and powerful marketing channel member has control over the other members. In a contractual marketing channel (e.g., franchising), coordination and control are dictated by contractual relationships between members. Corporate marketing channels can operate relatively smoothly because one firm owns the various levels of the chains. Marketing channels also can be effectively managed through strong relationships developed with marketing channel partners. To create such relationships, the partners must trust each other, communicate openly, have compatible goals, realize there is benefit in being interdependent, and be willing to invest in each other's success.

LO16-4 Describe the flow of information and merchandise in the marketing channel.

Information flow involves: flow 1 (customer to store), flow 2 (store to buyer), flow 3 (buyer to manufacturer), flow 4 (store to manufacturer), flow 5 (store to distribution center), and flow 6 (manufacturer to distribution center and buyer). Merchandise flow involves flow 1 (manufacturer to retailer distribution centers), flow 2 (manufacturer directly to stores), flow 3 (distribution centers to stores, when shipped first to distribution centers), and flow 4 (retailer to customer).

Key Terms

- administered vertical marketing system, 487
- advanced shipping notice (ASN), 494
- checking, 497
- coercive power, 488
- contractual vertical marketing systems, 489
- corporate vertical marketing system, 490
- cross-docking distribution center, 498
- direct marketing channel, 483
- dispatcher, 497
- distribution center, 482

- electronic data interchange (EDI), 494
- expertise power, 488
- floor-ready merchandise, 499
- franchising, 489
- fulfillment centers, 482
- horizontal channel conflict, 486
- independent (conventional) marketing channel, 487
- indirect marketing channels, 484
- information power, 488
- just-in-time (JIT) inventory systems, 500
- lead time, 501
- legitimate power, 489

- marketing channel management, 480
- mobile task management, 500
- pick ticket, 499
- planners, 496
- power, 488
- quick response (QR) inventory systems, 500
- radio frequency identification (RFID) tags, 497
- receiving, 497
- referent power, 488
- reward power, 488
- strategic or partnering relationship, 490

Marketing Digitally

1. Go to Walmart's corporate website (corporate.walmart.com/our-story/our-business) and read about Walmart's operations, pricing, distribution centers, and fleet in the United States. How do Walmart's distribution centers and supply chain support its mission and marketing strategy?

2. The case study for this chapter examines how Zara International, a division of Inditex, successfully manages its supply chain. Visit Inditex's website (www.inditex.com) and search for "sourcing." How has Inditex created a supply chain that is consistent with the principles of conscious marketing described in Chapter 4.

Marketing Applications

1. Describe marketing channel management by identifying the major activities that it involves. Identify several ways that marketing channel management adds value to a company's offerings, with regard to consumers as well as business partners.

2. In what ways can the flow of information be managed in the supply chain? How can the ready flow of information increase a firm's operating efficiencies?

3. Go to Walmart's corporate website, corporate.walmart.com/our-story/our-business, and read about Walmart's operations, pricing, distribution centers, and fleet in the United States. How do the distribution centers and supply chain support Walmart's mission and marketing strategy?

4. What are the differences between the use of a traditional distribution center and one that relies on cross-docking? Discuss the extent to which one is more efficient than the other, being sure to detail your reasoning.

5. Discuss the advantages to a retailer like Macy's of expending the time and effort to get merchandise floor-ready at either the point of manufacture or in the distribution center rather than having retail store staff members do it in the stores. Provide the logic behind your answer.

6. A just-in-time (JIT) inventory system appears to be an important success factor for retailers like H&M and Forever 21. Choose a local retailer and examine the advantages and disadvantages of its use of a JIT system. Do you believe it should use JIT? Why?

7. Give an example of a retailer that participates in an independent (conventional) supply chain and one involved in a vertical marketing system. Discuss the advantages and disadvantages of each.

8. For each of the following consumer products, identify the type of vertical marketing system used, and justify your answer: (a) Bertolli pasta sold through grocery stores, (b) Krispy Kreme donuts sold through franchises, and (c) www.polo.com by Ralph Lauren.

9. Why might a big company like Lenovo want to develop strategic partnerships with locally owned computer stores? Describe what Lenovo would have to do to maintain such relationships.

10. You are hired as an assistant brand manager for a popular consumer product. One day in an emergency meeting, the brand manager informs the group that there is a problem with one of the suppliers and that he has decided to send you over to the manufacturing facilities to investigate the problem. When you arrive at the plant, you learn that a key supplier has become increasingly unreliable in terms of quality and delivery. You ask the plant manager why the plant doesn't switch suppliers, because it is becoming a major problem for your brand. He informs you that the troubled supplier is his cousin, whose wife has been very ill, and he just can't switch right now. What course of action should you take?

11. Explain how distribution or fulfillment centers use UPC or RFID tags. Which is better? Justify your answer. Why don't all firms use RFID?

Quiz Yourself

1. A _____, which may be operated by retailers, manufacturers, or distribution specialists, is a facility for the receipt, storage, and redistribution of goods to company stores or customers.
   a. logistics center
   b. fulfillment center
   c. distribution center
   d. marketing channel
   e. supply chain

2. When there is disagreement among members at the same level of marketing channels, such as when Best Buy and Lowe's engage in a price war on Maytag appliances, _____ channel conflict can occur.
   a. vertical
   b. independent
   c. competitive
   d. horizontal
   e. administered

(Answers to these two questions can be found in the Quiz Yourself Answer Key section.)

Chapter Case Study

Mc Graw Hill Education **connect**

ZARA DELIVERS FAST FASHION[26]

In the fast fashion retail business strategy, supply chain management processes serve to introduce fashionable merchandise rapidly so that stores can respond immediately to customer demand for merchandise. This was pioneered by Zara, a global specialty apparel chain located in La Coruña, Spain, but it also has been adopted by other retailers, including H&M (headquartered in Sweden), TopShop (UK), and Forever 21 (United States).

The approach is particularly effective for specialty apparel retailers that target fashion-conscious consumers who simply must have the latest looks—but they want to do so on a very limited budget. These shoppers load up on new fast fashions every few weeks instead of purchasing a few higher-priced basics every few months.

To fit with such short cycles and meet customers' demands, the fast fashion process starts with the receipt of timely information from store managers. At Zara, store managers always have their reporting devices literally in hand. These handheld devices, which are linked directly to the company's corporate office in Spain, enable daily reports on what customers are buying (or not) and what they are asking for but not finding.

For example, customers might want a purple version of a pink shirt that they see on the shop floor. Managers immediately pass on the information to the designers in Spain. Those designers then communicate electronically with the factory that produces fabric for shirts. This factory starts up its automated equipment, which is run by assemblers who live in close proximity to the factory. (The undyed fabric comes from Asia, where Zara finds inexpensive sources, and then bulk fabric ships to Spain and Portugal to be manufactured into apparel.) The robots in the company's 14 highly automated factories start cutting out shirts and mixing purple dye. For final construction, a network of small assemblers, located near the factories in Galicia, Spain, and northern Portugal, takes responsibility for making the final product. Finally, to ensure timely delivery, the shirts get shipped by truck to stores in Europe and by air express to stores in the rest of the world. Zara production is so efficient it can get a new product from design to the sales floor in only 10 days.[27] Since Zara now operates in 94 markets, its parent company Inditex works with almost 7,000 factories worldwide to deliver products to stores; however, 60 percent of its clothing is still made in Spain and nearby countries.[28]

THE BENEFITS OF FAST FASHION FOR ZARA

Zara's main advantage over its competitors, such as The Gap, Abercrombie & Fitch, and American Eagle Outfitters, has resulted from its highly responsive and tightly organized supply chain. Unlike these competitors, Zara selects factory locations that are in close geographic proximity to the company's headquarters in Spain. Although this approach increases labor costs, compared with outsourced production in lower-cost countries in Asia, it also improves communication, reduces shipping costs and time, and reduces the time before new fashions appear in stores. It also gives Zara the flexibility to modify its operations in one supply chain function to expedite processes in another, such as pricing or tagging. It might hang merchandise on racks in the warehouse so that store employees can move apparel directly from delivery to the sales floor. And it can do all this because it maintains complete control over the entire process.

Furthermore, instead of shipping new products a few times a season, as many of its competitors do, Zara makes deliveries to every one of its stores twice a week.[29] The purple shirts would be in stores in two weeks—compared with the several months it would take for most department stores and other specialty apparel stores to accomplish the same feat. Because its fast fashion system also ensures shorter lead times, it's less likely that any Zara store will be out of stock before the next sweater shipment arrives. Limiting the stock in stores even can create a sense of scarcity among its customers. If they don't buy now, the item might not be available next time they visit the store. By producing and shipping in these small quantities, Zara can quickly recover from its (rare) fashion faux pas.

Finally, the efficiency of its supply chain means Zara rarely has to discount merchandise that is not selling. At Zara, the number of items that end up marked down is about half the industry average. Furthermore, Zara's clothing is typically more expensive than its competitors; however, customers are more willing to pay full price for clothing they might wait to buy on sale because they know it might not be available for long.[30] Because Zara keeps designs in its stores for only about a month, it introduces around 10,000 new designs and 40,000 new SKUs each year.[31]

MOVING TOO FAST? THE NEGATIVE EFFECTS OF FAST FASHION

Despite some strong signals of success—including a 10 percent increase in same-store sales, and a 12 percent increase in net sales[32]—Zara started to outgrow its own strategy. By their very nature, fashion trends change rapidly and constantly, and so must the merchandise on Zara's shop floors. Faced with disappointed customers, some sales managers ordered extra quantities of hot items to avoid stockouts. Even with this attempt to circumvent the replenishment system, some stores still suffered from stockouts because they received fewer units than they had ordered when overall demand exceeded inventory levels. For some items, Zara even confronted perhaps the most frustrating scenario in a supply chain: Inventory sat unused, eating up storage costs at one location even as another store desperately pleaded for the same inventory to meet its customers' demand.

One way Zara is trying to meet more customer needs is by investing in its in-store pickup for online orders. Zara's fast fashion model is the perfect fit for online shoppers because it can always offer something new. Because Zara designed its ordering platforms for small-store orders, it is able to process online orders in much the same way. Home delivery can create a hurdle; however, by emphasizing in-store pickup, Zara can avoid delivery challenges. One way it is improving in-store pickup is with self-service pickup kiosks that can hold up to 4,000 packages.[33]

As noted among the benefits, the company launches as many as 10,000 new styles annually, with a range of colors and sizes, resulting in hundreds of thousands of SKUs in the system. If we add in replenishment orders, which are received twice weekly, Zara's average shipping total reached nearly 2.5 million items per week, all coming from the company's distribution center. Its legendary supply chain efficiency thus was in danger of a clogged artery.

In response, Zara has adopted some new mathematical processes that turn human experience and mountains of data into actionable information. These models factor in store managers' unique requests for merchandise replenishments, together with historical trends in the sales of the same item. Merchandise display practices have been altered, such as removing all sizes of a garment from the sales floor if a popular size is not available. This practice helps reduce customer frustration, in that they never see an item that might not be

Zara's competitive advantage in specialty apparel retailing is based on its efficient supply chain that delivers fashionable merchandise to its stores frequently.

©Sorbis/Shutterstock

available in their size. It also diminishes shipping; if the medium size is unavailable, the small and large sizes do not get shipped either. Instead, these remaining sizes head toward the stores that still have all sizes in stock so they can be available to customers there.

Furthermore, Zara is making more effective uses of RFID technology. Because Zara manufacturers its own clothing, it can insert RFID tags into the security tags that already appear on each piece of clothing. Thus the very act of inserting the tags becomes viable as a parallel step to the attachment of the security tags. In contrast, retailers that previously tried to insert RFID tags struggled to find efficient methods and had trouble deciding exactly when in the supply chain they should be inserted. Walmart, for example, demanded that suppliers add them, but suppliers balked at the added expense associated with the additional step.[34]

In addition, by including the RFID elements within the security tags, Zara has found a way to reuse the still relatively expensive RFID technology. In previous experiments, the tags left the store with customers who purchased the related item. At Zara, employees remove the security tag as they check out customers, so the RFID chips also stay in the store, available for reuse.

These methods give Zara a distinct advantage. The task of taking inventory has become so much faster and easier—rather than actively scanning each item's bar code, inventory takers simply walk through the store with an RFID device that passively gathers information from each rack—that Zara can perform it every six weeks instead of twice a year, as is common in the industry. In turn, its inventory tracking is drastically more accurate, and it knows exactly what styles and items are selling best (or worst).

Growth, costs, market demand, and technology advances all can push retail executives to rethink their business processes. But truly savvy managers search for ways to optimize operations, even when business is running smoothly. As Zara learned, current approaches will not necessarily work tomorrow.

Questions

1. How does an individual firm like Zara manage a supply chain? How does it get new products from design to store so quickly?

2. What are some of the ways that Zara's supply chain management system has helped create value for its customers? Provide specific examples.

3. What challenges did Zara's focus on supply chain efficiency create? Are all such systems destined to suffer similar growing pains?

Endnotes

1. Laura Stevens and Sara Germano, "Nike Thought It Didn't Need Amazon—Then the Ground Shifted," *The Wall Street Journal,* June 28, 2017; Dennis Green, "Nike Exec: 'We've Elevated the Amazon Experience,'" *Business Insider,* September 14, 2017; Nike, "Nike+ SNKRS Augments the Sneaker Drop," *Nike,* June 23, 2017, https://news.nike.com/news/nike-snkrs-augmented-reality-momofuku-dunk?mid=38660&cp=usns_aff_nike_080113_TnL=HPStwNw&site=TnL5HPStwNw-COg-Zz5dJa.NdwDTJ8nH4dw; Theodore Schleifer, "How Nike Is Fighting Off Bots and Counterfeiters," *Recode,* September 13, 2017, www.recode.net/2017/9/13/16304668/nike-bots-counterfeiters-heidi-oneill-sneakers-retail.

2. Alexander Coolidge, "Walmart's Strategy May Squeeze P&G, Other Suppliers," *Cincinnati Enquirer,* April 13, 2015, www.cincinnati.com/story/money/2015/04/11/walmarts-back-basics-strategy-may-squeeze-pg-suppliers/25632645/.

3. Procter & Gamble, "Recent Innovations," http://us.pg.com/who_we_are/our_approach/our_approach_innovation/recent_innovations.

4. Amy Feldman, "What It Takes to Sell to Walmart: A Senior Buyer Tells All," *Forbes,* May 11, 2017; Kenneth Hilario, "Northern Liberties Woman-Owned Bakery to Close, Shift Focus," *Philadelphia Business Journal,* September 19, 2016.

5. Daphne Howland, "Sales of Wal-Mart's Patti LaBelle Pies Skyrocket after Viral Video," *Marketing Dive,* November 19, 2015.

6. Terry L. Esper et al., "Demand and Supply Integration: A Conceptual Framework of Value Creation through Knowledge Management," *Journal of the Academy of Marketing Science* 38, no. 1 (2010), pp. 5–18.

7. www.marketingpower.com/_layouts/Dictionary.aspx.

8. BI Intelligence, "Procter & Gamble Launches Direct-to-Consumer Subscription Business," *Business Insider,* July 26, 2016; https://ondemand.gillette.com.

9. https://ondemand.gillette.com; www.walmart.com/.

10. Andrew Elliot, "Does P&G Need Retailers Anymore?," *Retail-Wire,* November 3, 2014.

11. George E. Stigler, "The Division of Labor Is Limited by the Extent of the Market," *Journal of Political Economy* 59, no. 3 (1951), pp. 185–93.

12. Dan Berthiaume, "Three Reasons Amazon Is Everyone's Competitor," *Chain Store Age,* November 9, 2015.

13. Jeremy Bowman, "P&G Gets Caught in Rivalry between Amazon and Target," *The Motley Fool,* March 6, 2015; Yuki Noguchi, "Moving In with Manufacturers, Amazon Delivers a New Approach," *NPR,* October 28, 2013.

14. Eugene Kim, "As Amazon's Dominance Grows, Suppliers Are Forced to Play by Its Rules," *CNBC,* December 21, 2017, www.cnbc.com/2017/12/21/as-amazons-dominance-grows-suppliers-are-forced-to-play-by-its-rules.html; Angus Loten and Adam Janofsky, "Sellers Need Amazon, but at What Cost?," *The Wall Street Journal,* January 15, 2015.

15. Tereza Dean, David A. Griffith, and Roger J. Calantone, "New Product Creativity: Understanding Contract Specificity in New Product Introductions," *Journal of Marketing* 80 (March 2016), pp. 39–58.

16. www.marketingpower.com/live/mg-dictionary.

17. "2017 Franchises 500 Ranking," www.entrepreneur.com/franchises/500/2017.

18. www.teslamotors.com/blog/tesla-approach-distributing-and-servicing-cars.

19. Douglas Lambert and Matias Enz, "Issues in Supply Chain Management: Progress and Potential," *Industrial Marketing Management* 62 (April 2017), pp. 1–16; Robert W. Palmatier, Rajiv Dant, and Dhruv Grewal, "A Longitudinal Analysis of Theoretical Perspectives of Interorganizational Relationship Performance," *Journal of Marketing* 71 (October 2007), pp. 172–94.

20. Jiguang Chen, Qiying Hu, and Jing-Sheng Song, "Supply Chain Models with Mutual Commitments and Implications for Social Responsibility," *Production and Operations Management* 26, no. 7 (2017), pp. 1268–83; Erin Anderson and Barton Weitz, "The Use of Pledges to Build and Sustain Commitment in Distribution Channels," *Journal of Marketing Research* 29 (February 1992), pp. 18–34.

21. Matthew Rocco, "WSJ: P&G, Others Share Warehouse Space with Amazon," *Fox Business,* January 25, 2016, www.foxbusiness.com/features/wsj-pg-others-share-warehouse-space-with-amazon.

22. www.marketingpower.com/_layouts/Dictionary.aspx.

23. www.vendormanagedinventory.com.

24. Chris Emond, "Tesco Retail Innovation in the U.K.: Global Analysis Report," *Agriculture and Agri-Food Canada,* June 2016, www.agr.gc.ca/resources/prod/Internet-Internet/MISB-DGSIM/ATS-SEA/PDF/6757-eng.pdf.

25. Jillian Hufford, "Retailers Still Aren't Meeting Customer Standards for Buy Online, Pickup in Store Services," *N Channel,* September 6, 2017, www.nchannel.com/blog/buy-online-pickup-store-bopis/; Jennifer McKevitt, "Wal-Mart Pilots Automated Buy Online, Pickup in Store System," *Supply Chain Dive,* November 2, 2016.

26. Ben Latham, "How Retailers Can Learn from Fast Fashion to Beat the Weather," *RetailWeek,* April 20, 2016; Vertica Bhardwaj and Ann Fairhurst, "Fast Fashion: Response to Changes in the Fashion Industry," *International Review of Retail, Distribution and Consumer Research* 20 (February 2010), pp. 165–73; Felipe Caro et al., "Zara Uses Operations Research to Reengineer Its Global Distribution Process," *Interfaces* 40 (2010), pp. 71–84; Carmen Lopez and Ying Fan, "Case Study: Internationalisation of the Spanish Fashion Brand Zara," *Journal of Fashion Marketing and Management* 13, no. 2 (2009), pp. 279–96.

27. "30 Companies Already Replacing Humans with Robots," *MSN,* March 18, 2017, www.msn.com/en-in/money/photos/30-companies-already-replacing-humans-with-robots/ss-BBy803h#image=30.

28. http://static.inditex.com/.

29. Daphne Howland, "Report: 'Ultra-Fast' Fashion Players Gain on Zara, H&M," *Retail Dive,* May 22, 2017.

30. Susie Poppick, "How Retailers Use Emotion to Make You Spend More," *CNBC,* November 2, 2016.

31. "Zara Clothing Company Supply Chain," *SCM Globe,* 2016, http://blog.scmglobe.com/?page_id=1513.

32. Laura Heller, "Why Zara Is the Most Exciting Retailer Today," *Forbes,* March 15, 2017.

33. Hayley Peterson, "The Next Generation of Walmart's Giant Pickup Towers Could Be Coming to a Zara Store Near You," *Business Insider,* December 12, 2017; Dow Jones Newswire, "How Zara Is Defying a Broad Retail Slump," *Fox Business,* June 14, 2017.

34. Christopher Bjork, "Zara Builds Its Business around RFID," *The Wall Street Journal,* September 17, 2014.

i. *SCDigest,* "Supply Chain News: Goya Foods Shows Path to Success for Mid-Market Companies from New Supply Chain Planning Tools," July 13, 2011, www.scdigest.com.

ii. Taylor Soper, "Amazon's Dominance of Online Shopping Starts with Product Searches, Study Shows," *GeekWire,* October 6, 2015; Greg Besinger, "Amazon Wants to Ship Your Package before You Buy It," *The Wall Street Journal,* January 17, 2014, http://wsjonline.com.

iii. Heather Haddon and Benjamin Parkin, "Retailers Are Bottling Their Own Milk, Raising Pressure on Dairy Companies," *The Wall Street Journal,* October 13, 2017; Phil Lempert, "Walmart Moves into the Dairy Business, Even as Milk Consumption Drops," *Forbes,* August 8, 2017; http://sustainability.kroger.com/supply-chain-our-food-and-products.html.

iv. Tomio Geron, "Driverless Trucks Are Barreling Ahead," *The Wall Street Journal,* July 27, 2017; Ryan Petersen, "The Driverless Truck Is Coming, and It's Going to Automate Millions of Jobs," *Tech Crunch,* April 25, 2016, https://techcrunch.com/2016/04/25/the-driverless-truck-is-coming-and-its-going-to-automate-millions-of-jobs/; National Highway Traffic Safety Administration, "2015 Motor Vehicle Crashes: Overview," *U.S. Department of Transportation,* August 2016, https://crashstats.nhtsa.dot.gov/Api/Public/ViewPublication/812318; Cadie Thompson, "Why Driverless Cars Will Be Safer Than Human Drivers," *Business Insider,* November 16, 2016.

Quiz Yourself Answer Key

1. A _____, which may be operated by retailers, manufacturers, or distribution specialists, is a facility for the receipt, storage, and redistribution of goods to company stores or customers.

   Answer: (c). distribution center

2. When there is disagreement among members at the same level of marketing channels, such as when Best Buy and Lowe's engage in a price war on Maytag appliances, _____ channel conflict can occur.

   Answer: (d). horizontal

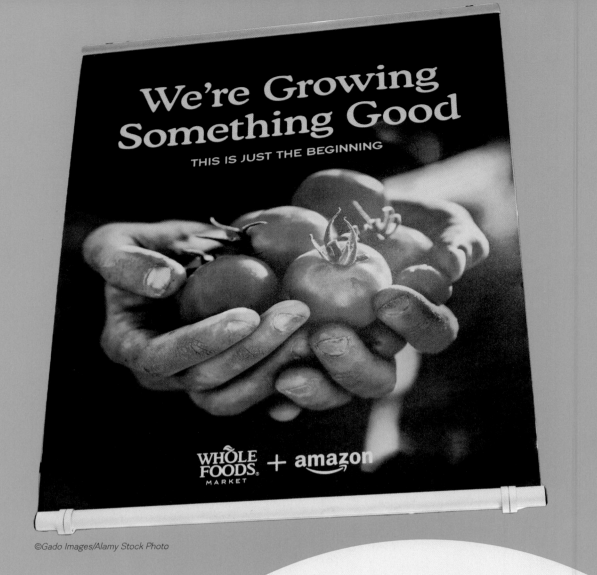

©Gado Images/Alamy Stock Photo

LEARNING OBJECTIVES

After reading this chapter, you should be able to:

LO17-1 Discuss the four factors manufacturers should consider as they develop their strategies for working with retailers.

LO17-2 Outline the considerations associated with choosing retail partners.

LO17-3 List the three levels of distribution intensity.

LO17-4 Describe the various types of retailers.

LO17-5 Describe the components of a retail strategy.

LO17-6 Identify the benefits and challenges of omnichannel retailing.

CHAPTER 17

RETAILING AND OMNICHANNEL MARKETING

Amazon.com has redefined all aspects of the retail market. The e-commerce giant's online presence has forced many brick-and-mortar stores to close locations and move their own operations online to compete. So why would the tech-savvy giant choose to purchase Whole Foods Market Inc., an upscale grocer with 460 retail store locations?

There are a few answers, but "data" are predominant among them. Although Amazon has a firm and enviable grip on how consumers shop online, it struggles to predict consumer behavior in physical store locations. Thus far, its tentative efforts to enter the grocery market, such as its delayed grab-and-go concept store in Seattle and struggling Amazon Pantry service, have remained rare missteps for the company. The purchase of Whole Foods—with its own successful track record of creating and fostering customer loyalty—could provide the answer.

In particular, the consumer data that Amazon will obtain from Whole Foods offer the promise of enhancing, developing, and supporting its newly extended brand. First, Whole Foods will provide Amazon with information about how shoppers behave in physical stores. Everything from impulse purchases to traffic flow patterns will provide valuable insights to Amazon as it seeks to enhance sales at its own brick-and-mortar bookstores and planned grab-and-go convenience stores. As a bonus, 60 percent of Whole Foods shoppers also currently subscribe to Amazon's Prime service, so Amazon already knows that Whole Foods customers represent a viable target segment, displaying the needs and behaviors that shoppers who are in its target market embody.

Second, Whole Foods has successfully built a wide-ranging private-label brand. This experience and expertise will help Amazon better understand how to grow its own private-label brand successfully. It currently produces mostly staples, such as batteries, baby wipes, and computer paper, but there clearly is room for Amazon to leverage its new retail data to expand these offerings.

Third, the new physical store platform will allow Amazon to test a variety of new ideas to see what works and what does not. For example, acquiring Whole Foods means that Amazon gains a space and means to experiment with new forms of payment, such as expanding the use of its Amazon Pay service. The results of these experiments should enable Amazon to devise new ways to encourage greater adoption of this service or any subsequently developed easy pay service—a development that would lead to an even greater stockpile of data.

Ultimately, though, the $13.4 billion purchase of Whole Foods by Amazon still represents a risk. The high-end grocery store has faced increased competition from other grocers, especially as larger chain stores seek to lure shoppers with similar lines of organic products offered at lower prices. Whole Foods' 460 stores also have faced a long stretch of same-store sales declines. With prices that average 20–30 percent higher than other grocers', Whole Foods continues to seek ways to deal with not just declining sales but also a labeling scandal uncovered by the New York Department of Consumer Affairs and growing opposition from both its board and its shareholders about the CEO's plan to remain independent.

Still, the acquisition of Whole Foods and its retail locations suggests that Amazon is dedicated to the idea of competing more aggressively in the retail grocery space and overcoming its early struggles to cross into that market. Purchasing Whole Foods allows Amazon to piggyback on a successful brand and concept.

Fresh leadership and greater purchasing power seemingly might help alleviate many of the woes that Whole Foods has struggled to overcome as an independent retailer.

By adding grocery to its already extensive array of retail offerings, now more than ever Amazon seems poised to compete with Walmart for ultimate dominance in the retail space. Both entities have expanded their operations by acquiring other, smaller, successful brands, then raising the profile of each niche company to help it reach new audiences. For example, Walmart typically has been associated with lower- and middle-income customers in rural areas, but it recently acquired two high-end fashion companies, ModCloth and Bonobos, that are known for their fashion-forward images and significant online retail presence. Through such acquisitions, Walmart clearly is seeking to expand its product offerings and appeal to a new type of affluent consumer. They also allow Walmart to expand its online presence and fashionable image, such that it might compete more directly with Amazon for the same shoppers.

Simultaneously, Amazon's acquisition of Whole Foods seeks to broaden the retailer's appeal and customer base in the grocery market, a sector traditionally dominated by Walmart. As each nips at the heels of the other, the consolidation of retail power behind two mega-brands continues to lead toward what might be an interesting showdown in the retail sector. Which entity will come out on top?[1]

Retailing sits at the end of the supply chain, where marketing meets the consumer.[2] But there is far more to retailing than just manufacturing a product and making it available to customers. It is primarily the retailer's responsibility to make sure that customers' expectations are fulfilled.

M·A·C will use different criteria than will either Coach for Men or Eva's green cosmetics for placing products in retail stores.

©TY Lim/Shutterstock

Retailing is defined as the set of business activities that add value to products and services sold to consumers for their personal or family use. Our definition includes products bought at stores, through catalogs, and over the Internet, as well as services such as fast-food restaurants, airlines, and hotels. Some retailers claim they sell at wholesale prices, but if they sell to customers for their personal use, they are still retailers, regardless of their prices. Wholesalers (see Chapter 16) buy products from manufacturers and resell them to retailers or industrial or business users.

Retailing today is changing, both in the United States and around the world. Manufacturers no longer rule many supply chains as they once did. Retailers such as Walmart (U.S. superstore), Costco (U.S. warehouse club), Kroger (U.S. grocery chain), Schwarz (German conglomerate), Walgreens Boots

EXHIBIT 17.1   Factors for Establishing a Relationship with Retailers

```
1. Choosing     →    2. Identifying   →    3. Developing   →    4. Managing an
   retailing            types of             a retail             omnichannel
   partners             retailers            strategy             strategy
```

Alliance, Inc. (U.S. drugstore/pharmacy), The Home Depot (U.S. home improvement), Carrefour (French hypermarket), Aldi Enkauf (German discount food retailer), Tesco (UK-based food retailer, and Amazon (U.S. e-tailer)[3]—the largest retailers in the world—dictate to their suppliers what should be made, how it should be configured, when it should be delivered, and, to some extent, what it should cost. These retailers are clearly in the driver's seat.

This chapter extends Chapter 16's discussion of supply chain management by examining why and how manufacturers use retailers. The manufacturer's strategy depends on its overall market power and how consistent a new product or product line is with current offerings. Consider the following scenarios:

- Scenario 1: Cosmetics conglomerate Estée Lauder's subsidiary brand M·A·C is introducing a new line of mascara.

- Scenario 2: Coach, well known for its women's handbags, has introduced a line of men's leather goods, apparel, gifts, shoes, and other accessories—products not previously in its assortment.

- Scenario 3: Eva, a young entrepreneur, is launching a new line of environmentally friendly (green) cosmetics.

Each of these scenarios is different and requires the manufacturer to consider alternatives for reaching its target markets through retailers.

Exhibit 17.1 illustrates four factors manufacturers consider to establish their strategies for working with retailers. In choosing retail partners, the first factor, manufacturers assess how likely it is for certain retailers to carry their products. Manufacturers also consider where their target customers expect to find the products because those are exactly the stores in which they want to place their products. The overall size and level of sophistication of the manufacturer will determine how many of the marketing channel functions it performs and how many it will hand off to other channel members. Another aspect in choosing retail partners: The type and availability of the product and the image the manufacturer wishes to portray will determine how many retailers within a geographic region will carry the products.

For the second factor, manufacturers identify the types of retailers that would be appropriate to carry their products. Although the choice is often obvious—such as a supermarket for fresh produce—manufacturers may have a choice of retailer types for some products.

As we discussed in Chapter 16, a hallmark of a strong marketing channel is one in which manufacturers and retailers coordinate their efforts. In the third factor, manufacturers and retailers therefore develop their strategy by implementing retailing's six Ps.

Many retailers and some manufacturers use an omnichannel or multichannel strategy, which involves selling in more than one channel (e.g., store, catalog, and Internet). The fourth factor therefore consists of examining the circumstances in which sellers may prefer to adopt a particular strategy.

Although these factors for establishing a relationship with retailers are listed consecutively, manufacturers may consider them all simultaneously or in a different order.

CHOOSING RETAILING PARTNERS

Imagine, as a consumer, trying to buy a new leather jacket without being able to visit a retailer or buy online. You would have to figure out exactly what size, color, and style of jacket you wanted. Then you would need to contact various manufacturers, whether in

LO17-1 Discuss the four factors manufacturers should consider as they develop their strategies for working with retailers.

 LO17-2 Outline the considerations associated with choosing retail partners.

Coach partners with retailers to help conveniently deliver its products to satisfied customers.

©TY Lim/Shutterstock

person, by phone, or over the Internet, and order the jacket. If the jacket fit you reasonably well but not perfectly, you still might need to take it to a tailor to have the sleeves shortened. You wouldn't find this approach to shopping very convenient.

Most manufacturers like Coach use retailers such as Macy's to undertake partnerships that create value by pulling together all the actions necessary for the greatest possible customer convenience and satisfaction. The store offers a broad selection of purses, leather jackets, scarves, and other accessories that its buyers have carefully chosen in advance. Customers can see, touch, feel, and try on any item while in the store. They can buy one scarf or leather jacket at a time or buy an outfit that works together. Finally, the store provides a salesperson to help customers coordinate their outfits and a tailor to make the whole thing fit perfectly.

When choosing retail partners, manufacturers look at the basic channel structure, where their target customers expect to find the products, channel member characteristics, and distribution intensity.

Channel Structure

The level of difficulty a manufacturer experiences in getting retailers to purchase its products is determined by the degree to which the channel is vertically integrated, as described in Chapter 16; the degree to which the manufacturer has a strong brand or is otherwise desirable in the market; and the relative power of the manufacturer and retailer.

Scenario 1 represents a corporate vertical marketing system. Because M·A·C is made by Estée Lauder and operates its own stores, when the new mascara line is introduced, the stores receive the new line automatically with no decision on the part of the retailer. In contrast, Revlon would have a much more difficult time getting CVS to buy a new mascara line because these supply chain partners are not vertically integrated.

When an established firm such as Coach enters a new market with men's leather goods, apparel, gifts, shoes, and other accessories, as is the case in Scenario 2, it must determine where its customers would expect to find these products and then use its established relationships with women's handbag buyers, the power of its brand, and its overall reputation to leverage its position in this new product area.

Eva (Scenario 3) would have an even more difficult time convincing a retailer to buy and sell her green cosmetics line because she lacks power in the marketplace—she is small and her brand is unknown. She would have trouble getting buyers to see her, let alone consider her line. She might face relatively high slotting allowances just to get space on retailers' shelves. But like Coach in Scenario 2, Eva should consider where the end customer expects to find her products, as well as some important retailer characteristics.

Customer Expectations

Retailers should also know customer preferences regarding manufacturers. Manufacturers, in contrast, need to know where their target market customers expect to find their products and those of their competitors. As we see in the hypothetical example in Exhibit 17.2, Coach currently sells handbags at stores such as Dillard's, Neiman Marcus, and Marshalls as well as in its own stores (red arrows). Its competitor Cole Haan sells at Dillard's and Neiman Marcus (teal arrows). A survey of male Coach customers shows that they would expect to find its products at Saks Fifth Avenue, Dillard's, Neiman Marcus, and its own Coach stores (all of the stores in the light blue box). On the basis of this information,

EXHIBIT 17.2   Coach and Cole Haan Distribution

Coach decides to try selling at Saks Fifth Avenue but to stop selling at Marshalls to better meet customers' expectations.

Customers generally expect to find certain products at some stores but not at others. For example, Estée Lauder would not choose to sell to CVS or Dollar General because its customers would not expect to shop at those stores for high-end cosmetics such as Estée Lauder's. Less expensive cosmetic brands such as Revlon and Maybelline, on the other hand, are sold at CVS and probably even appear as bargain closeouts at Dollar General. But male Coach customers definitely expect to find the brand's clothing offerings at major department stores and at Coach stores.

Channel Member Characteristics

Several factors pertaining to the channel members themselves help determine the channel structure. Generally, the larger and more sophisticated the channel member, the less likely that it will use supply chain intermediaries. Eva will probably use a group of independent salespeople to help sell her line of green cosmetics, whereas a large manufacturer such as Estée Lauder will use its own sales force that already has existing relationships in the industry. In the same way, an independent grocery store might buy merchandise from a wholesaler, but Walmart, the world's largest grocer, only buys directly from the manufacturer. Larger firms often find that by performing the channel functions themselves, they can gain more control, be more efficient, and save money.

Distribution Intensity

When setting up distribution for the first time, as is the case with Eva's green cosmetics (Scenario 3), or introducing a new product line, as is the case with Coach for men (Scenario 2), firms decide the appropriate level of distribution intensity—the number of channel members to use at each level of the marketing channel. Distribution intensity commonly is divided into three levels: intensive, exclusive, and selective.

Intensive Distribution   An intensive distribution strategy is designed to place products in as many outlets as possible. Most consumer packaged-goods companies, such as Pepsi, Procter & Gamble, Kraft, and other nationally branded products found in grocery and discount stores, strive for and often achieve intensive distribution. Pepsi wants its product available everywhere—grocery stores, convenience stores, restaurants, and vending machines. The more exposure the products get, the more they sell.

LO17-3   List the three levels of distribution intensity.

Most consumer packaged-goods companies, such as Pepsi (top), strive for intensive distribution—they want to be everywhere. But cosmetics firms such as Estée Lauder (bottom) use an exclusive distribution strategy by limiting their distribution to a few select higher-end retailers in each region.

(Top): ©Niloo/Shutterstock; (bottom): ©TY Lim/Shutterstock

Exclusive Distribution Manufacturers also might use an *exclusive distribution* policy by granting exclusive geographic territories to one or very few retail customers so that no other retailers in the territory can sell a particular brand. Exclusive distribution can benefit manufacturers by assuring them that the most appropriate retailers represent their products. Luxury goods firms such as Coach limit distribution to a few select, higher-end retailers in each region. The company believes that selling its products to full-line discount stores or off-price retailers would weaken its image.

When supply is limited or a firm is just starting out, providing an exclusive territory to one retailer or retail chain helps ensure enough inventory to provide the buying public an adequate selection. By granting exclusive territories, Eva guarantees her retailers will have an adequate supply of her green cosmetics. This guarantee gives these retailers a strong incentive to market her products. The retailers that Eva uses know there will be no competing retailers to cut prices, so their profit margins are protected. This knowledge gives them an incentive to carry more inventory and use extra advertising, personal selling, and sales promotions.

Selective Distribution Between the intensive and exclusive distribution strategies lies *selective distribution*, which relies on a few selected retail customers in a territory to sell products. Like exclusive distribution, selective distribution helps a seller maintain a particular image and control the flow of merchandise into an area. These advantages make this approach attractive to many shopping goods manufacturers. Recall that shopping goods are those products for which consumers are willing to spend time comparing alternatives, such as most apparel items, home items such as branded pots and pans or sheets and towels, branded hardware and tools, and consumer electronics. Retailers still have a strong incentive to sell the products, but not to the same extent as if they had an exclusive territory.

As we noted in Chapter 16, like any large, complicated system, a marketing channel is difficult to manage. Whether the balance of power rests with large retailers such as Walmart or with large manufacturers such as Procter & Gamble, channel members benefit by working together to develop and implement their channel strategy. In the next section, we explore the different types of retailers with an eye toward which would be most appropriate for each of our scenarios: M·A·C Cosmetics, Coach's products for men, and Eva's new line of environmentally friendly cosmetics.

PROGRESS CHECK

1. What issues should manufacturers consider when choosing retail partners?
2. What are the differences among intensive, exclusive, and selective levels of distribution intensity?

LO17-4 Describe the various types of retailers.

IDENTIFY TYPES OF RETAILERS

At first glance, identifying the types of retailers that Coach and Eva may wish to pursue when attempting to place their new lines seems straightforward. But the choice is not always easy. Manufacturers need to understand the general characteristics of different types of

EXHIBIT 17.3 Types of Retailers

retailers to determine the best channels for their product. The characteristics of a retailer that are important to a food manufacturer may be quite different from those considered valuable by a cosmetics manufacturer. In the next few sections, we examine the various types of retailers, identify some major players, and discuss some of the issues facing each type (Exhibit 17.3).

Food Retailers

The food retailing landscape is changing dramatically. Twenty years ago, consumers purchased food primarily at conventional supermarkets. Now conventional supermarkets account for only slightly more than 60 percent of food sales (not including restaurants).[4] Not only do full-line discount stores such as Walmart and Target offer a full assortment of grocery items in their superstores, but traditional supermarkets also are carrying more nonfood items. Many supermarkets offer pharmacies, health care clinics, banks, and cafés.

The world's largest food retailer, Walmart, attains $247 billion in sales of supermarket-type merchandise.[5] On this measure, it is followed by Costco (United States), Kroger (United States), Carrefour (France), Tesco (United Kingdom), Aeon Co., Ltd. (Japan), and Auchan Holding (France).[6] In North America specifically, the largest supermarket chains in order are Walmart, Kroger, Costco, Albertsons, CVS Health, Loblaw, Target, Publix, and Walgreens Boots Alliance, Inc.[7]

Supermarkets A conventional supermarket is a large, self-service retail food store offering groceries, meat, and produce, as well as some nonfood items such as health and beauty aids and general merchandise.[8] Perishables including meat, produce, baked goods, and dairy products account for just over 60 percent of supermarket sales and typically have higher margins than packaged goods do.[9]

Whereas conventional supermarkets carry about 30,000 SKUs, limited-assortment supermarkets, or extreme-value food retailers, stock only about 1,500 SKUs.[10] The two largest limited-assortment supermarket chains in the United States are Save-A-Lot and Aldi. Rather than carrying 20 brands of laundry detergent, limited-assortment supermarkets offer one or two brands and sizes, one of which is a store brand. By trimming costs, limited-assortment supermarkets can offer merchandise at prices 40 percent lower than those at conventional supermarkets.[11]

Although conventional supermarkets still sell the majority of food merchandise, they are under substantial competitive pressure on multiple sides: from supercenters, warehouse clubs, extreme-value retailers, convenience stores, and even drugstores.[12] All these types of retailers have increased the amount of space they devote to consumables.

To compete successfully against intrusions by other food retailing formats, conventional supermarkets are differentiating their offerings by (1) emphasizing fresh perishables;

Warehouse clubs have expanded their assortment of products in the electronics category and are known for great prices.

©Bloomberg/Contributor/Getty Images

(2) targeting green, ethnic, and Millennial consumers; (3) providing better value with private-label merchandise; (4) adding new value-added services such as online ordering and delivery options; and (5) providing a better shopping experience, such as by adding restaurant options or hosting social events.[13]

Supercenters Supercenters are large stores (185,000 square feet) that combine a supermarket with a full-line discount store. Walmart operates over 3,500 supercenters in the United States,[14] accounting for the vast majority of total supercenter sales—far outpacing its competitors Meijer, SuperTarget (Target), and Fred Meyer (Kroger Co.). By offering broad assortments of grocery and general merchandise products under one roof, supercenters provide a one-stop shopping convenience to customers.

Warehouse Clubs Warehouse clubs are large retailers (100,000 to 150,000 square feet) that offer a limited and irregular assortment of food and general merchandise, little service, and low prices to the general public and small businesses. The largest warehouse club chains are Costco, Sam's Club (Walmart), and BJ's Wholesale Club (operating only on the U.S. East Coast). Customers are attracted to these stores because they can stock up on large packs of basics (e.g., paper towels), mega-sized packaged groceries (e.g., a quart of ketchup), best-selling books and DVDs, fresh meat and produce, and an unpredictable assortment of upscale merchandise and services (e.g., jewelry, electronics, and home decor) at lower prices than are available at other retail stores. Typically, members pay an annual fee of around $50, which amounts to significant additional income for the chains.

Warehouse clubs also have had substantial influences on retailing and its structure. For example, the four biggest warehouse retailers accounted for approximately 8 percent of 2012 retail sales. That's nearly twice as much as e-commerce represented. E-commerce grew from $35 billion to $348 billion in sales between 1992 and 2013; in the same period, warehouse club sales increased from $40 billion to $420 billion. The growth of warehouse clubs appears largely dependent on demand in more heavily populated areas, as the store locations move from distant suburbs into more city centers.[15]

Although both Coach for Men and Eva's products could be sold in warehouse clubs, these retailers probably are not the best choices. Both product lines will have an upscale image, which is inconsistent with any warehouse club. If, however, either firm has overstock merchandise as a result of overestimating demand or underestimating returned merchandise from retailers, warehouse clubs are a potential outlet.

In addition to convenience, 7-Eleven is a trendy place for young consumers in Indonesia to hang out.

©Francis Dean/Corbis/Getty Images

Convenience Stores Convenience stores provide a limited variety and assortment of merchandise at a convenient location in 3,000- to 5,000-square-foot stores with speedy checkout. 7-Eleven is the largest convenience store chain in North America, with 10,000 locations.[16] This type of retailer is the modern version of the neighborhood mom-and-pop grocery or general store. Convenience stores enable consumers to make purchases quickly without having to search through a large store and wait in a lengthy checkout line. Convenience store assortments are limited in terms of depth and breadth, and they charge higher prices than supermarkets do. Milk, eggs, and bread once represented the majority of their sales, but now most sales come from gasoline and cigarettes.

Convenience stores also face increased competition from other retail formats. In response to these competitive pressures, convenience stores are taking steps to decrease their dependency on gasoline sales by offering fresh food and healthy fast food, tailoring assortments to local markets, and making their stores even more convenient to shop. Finally, convenience stores are adding new services, such as financial service kiosks that give customers the opportunity to cash checks, pay bills, and buy prepaid telephone minutes, theater tickets, and gift cards.

Online Grocery Retailers Time-strapped customers are willing to pay more to access options for ordering groceries online and having them delivered (e.g., for a gallon of organic milk, Safeway charges $6.79, and the delivery service Instacart charges $9.95).[17] As a result, online sales of groceries have grown by 25 percent annually.[18] The set of retailers providing online capabilities continues to expand, with Amazon, Walmart, and Kroger joining the long-standing, online-only retailers such as Peapod and FreshDirect.[19] Furthermore, these retailers are joined by companies seeking to add value to the grocery channel by providing delivery services. That is, companies such as Instacart, Amazon Prime Fresh, and Google Express promise to allow customers to place online orders for items from their preferred grocers.[20]

Instacart enables customers to place online grocery orders to be delivered to their homes.

©Peter Dasilva/The New York Times/Redux Pictures

Still, approximately 60 percent of the online orders placed with grocery retailers involve nonfood items such as paper products or cleaning items. In contrast, sales in stores generally feature only around 40 percent nonfood items.[21] Consumers thus rely on online grocers for lower-profit-margin nonperishable items rather than higher-margin fresh fruit or meats. As a result, slim margins continue to be a problem for retailers as well as delivery services. For example, Instacart earns only about $4–$7 per order.[22] Finally, even as customers call for grocery delivery services—and the industry's percentage of total grocery sales is forecasted to double by 2015—online grocery remains much smaller than other online retailing.[23] Part of the reason may be the limited availability of grocery delivery services, which thus far remain accessible mainly in large cities. Delivery costs are also a factor even as the task is outsourced to relatively low-cost individual private contractors. This factor also might reflect a barrier to the industry's growth: Delivering perishable groceries to many customers is a lot easier and more feasible in dense, urban settings than across vast, rural distances. The expansion of this type of food retailing has prompted various other innovations as well, as Marketing Analytics 17.1 describes.

General Merchandise Retailers

The major types of general merchandise retailers are department stores, full-line discount stores, specialty stores, drugstores, category specialists, extreme-value retailers, and off-price retailers.

Department Stores Department stores are retailers that carry a broad variety and deep assortment of merchandise, offer customer services, and organize their stores into distinct departments for displaying merchandise. The list of the largest department store chains in the United States includes Macy's, Kohl's, JCPenney, and Nordstrom.[24] Department stores would be an excellent retail channel for Coach for Men and Eva's new lines.

Even as some observers argue that the era of the department store has come to an end, several retailers have introduced innovative ideas to appeal better to their existing target markets, as well as attract young consumers

Nordstrom's online flash sale site, HauteLook, appeals to its existing customers and attracts younger consumers by offering national brands at substantially discounted prices.

Source: Nordstrom

Marketing Analytics 17.1 | How FreshDirect Figures Out How and When Customers Order[i]

For consumers who do their grocery shopping through electronic channels, such as those maintained by FreshDirect, the device they use may make big differences in the items they order. Accordingly, FreshDirect acknowledges its need to understand where, when, and through which channels its customers are shopping during each interaction with the company.

As a simple example, the grocery delivery service has determined that when people place orders on Saturdays or Sundays, they are usually doing so on their mobile devices. During the workweek though, they largely use computers, suggesting that they are ordering from their desks, during their lunch breaks or in the midst of their workday. This difference means that the mobile site could promote more products that appeal to lazy weekend activities. But the traditional website likely needs to be quick, so that consumers can place their orders before their supervisors notice that they are on a shopping site during work hours.

The company's chief consumer officer offers a range of scenarios in which multichannel and multi-device capabilities are critical for the retailer. In particular, she highlights questions about when and where consumers prefer to find recipes, as well as how they react to potential weather hazards, noting, "Let's say snow is coming. We don't know exactly which day. We need to figure out when's the last time we can fulfill orders this week. Are we going to need to shut down? We know people are panicked and they want their food. So we have to figure out where they are at that moment. Do we need

FreshDirect uses sophisticated analytics to understand its customers' buying behavior so that it can serve them better.

Source: FreshDirect

to give a snow message on their mobile devices? And then coordinate it with what's on the desktop?"

As people's time spent interacting with online and mobile content increases, trends suggest that, conversely, their interactions with each individual seller are getting shorter. Retailers have just a moment to appeal to these quick-moving shoppers, and a key element of that appeal is understanding how they use their various devices in specific ways.

who tend to show preferences for smaller specialty stores. For example, Nordstrom has transformed its image as a high-end destination for only the wealthiest of shoppers by integrating an online flash sale site, HauteLook. There, shoppers can find famous name brands for substantially discounted prices. To make the varied, discounted merchandise available for hands-on buyers too, Nordstrom maintains its Rack stores, as an off-price arm of its retail empire. The number of Nordstrom Rack stores continues to grow.[25] Furthermore, Nordstrom has created strong links between these two "alternative" channels, such that consumers who order the wrong size on HauteLook can return the products to Nordstrom Rack without having to worry about shipping it back.[26]

Full-Line Discount Stores Full-line discount stores are retailers that offer a broad variety of merchandise, limited service, and low prices. The largest full-line discount store chains are Walmart, Target, and Kmart (Sears Holding).

Although full-line discount stores typically might carry men's leather goods, accessories, and cosmetics, they are not good options for Coach for Men or Eva's new green cosmetics line. Customers do not expect higher-end products in full-line discount stores. Rather, they are looking for value prices and are willing to compromise on quality or cachet.

Walmart accounts for approximately two-thirds of full-line discount store retail sales in the United States.[27] Target has experienced considerable growth because its stores offer fashionable merchandise at low prices in a pleasant shopping environment. The retailer has developed an image of cheap chic by offering limited-edition exclusive apparel and cosmetic lines.

Specialty Stores Specialty stores concentrate on a limited number of complementary merchandise categories targeted toward very specific market segments by offering deep but

Social & Mobile Marketing 17.1

Having Fun with Marketing: Sephora's Clever and Slightly Risqué Tactics[ii]

Sephora already has a sophisticated multichannel retailing strategy in place, leveraging its stores, website, and mobile apps in enviable ways to appeal to customers. This status resulted from the beauty brand's consistent efforts to ensure that it appears everywhere its customers go, and those efforts have not slowed down in the slightest, as some of Sephora's latest marketing innovations reveal.

For both its website and its mobile app, Sephora was looking for a fun way to engage its shoppers, and it noted the dating app Tinder as an inspiration. Thus it developed a function that allows consumers to "swipe" on a particular product, shade, or style they like, which narrows down their search options and leads to product recommendations. Scanning through more than 1,000 photographs of products bearing Sephora's private-label brand, users can swipe left on a bright pink lipstick shade or swipe right on a sparkling blue eye shadow, then complete the purchases they prefer without ever leaving the site.

The idea initially was simply to use Tinder as an inspiration, but it seemed to work so well that Sephora also expanded the usage and entered advertising for its new "swipe it, shop it" function onto Tinder itself. People looking for love might also run across branded cards for Sephora, which they can swipe to get taken to the site, register, and receive a free sample.

For consumers who are a little leery of Tinder-like options, Sephora has another, old school–inspired option. By filling in the blanks in a simple "beauty uncomplicator" function on the mobile and Internet sites, users receive a Mad Libs–like response that recommends the kinds of products likely to appeal most to them. For example, if a user's answers to the beauty uncomplicator suggest a strong interest in smoky eyes, the site gathers suggestions for the right shadows, liners, brushes, and mascaras to make it happen.

The promotions of these new facilities appear not just on Tinder and the mobile sites but also in stores. That's part of Sephora's strategy too; it might be fun to play Mad Libs with makeup, but it also wants to ensure that it's fun to come in to stores and play with the makeup in person. As Sephora expands its private-label offerings and initiates its largest advertising campaign in its history, it is approaching the effort with careful forethought. One senior vice president for the brand explains, "This is an example of not just having a marketing campaign, but thinking about a full client experience."

Sephora engages customers with its Tinder-inspired app that enables customers to scan photographs of its private-label products, then purchase those products without leaving the site.

©ferrantraite/E+/Getty Images

---

narrow assortments and sales associate expertise. Although such shops are familiar in brick-and-mortar forms, more retailers also are expanding their online specialty profile as well.

Estée Lauder's M·A·C line of cosmetics sells in the company's own retail specialty stores as well as in some department stores. Certain specialty stores would be excellent outlets for the new lines by Coach for Men and Eva. Customers likely expect to find Coach for Men leather goods and accessories in men's apparel or leather stores. Eva's line of green cosmetics would fit nicely in a cosmetics specialty store such as Sephora, which will likely promote her products to an interested market using innovative marketing tactics, as Social & Mobile Marketing 17.1 predicts.

Drugstores Drugstores are specialty stores that concentrate on pharmaceuticals and health and personal grooming merchandise. Prescription pharmaceuticals represent almost 70 percent of drugstore sales. The largest drugstore chains in the United States are CVS and Walgreens Boots Alliance Inc., which includes Walgreens and Duane Reade in the United States and Boots in the UK.[28]

Drugstores face competition from pharmacies in discount stores and some food retailers and from pressure to reduce health care costs. In response, the major drugstore chains are offering a wider assortment of merchandise such as frequently purchased food items. They also offer services such as convenient drive-through windows and curbside pickup for prescriptions, in-store medical clinics, and even makeovers and spa treatments.[29]

Estée Lauder's M·A·C Cosmetics lines sell in specialty stores.
©Astrid Stawiarz/Getty Images

Dollar General is one of the United States' largest extreme-value retailers. It has small full-line discount stores that offer a limited assortment at very low prices.
©Mark Humphrey/AP Photo

Although Estée Lauder's new line would not be consistent with the merchandise found in drugstores, Eva's green cosmetics may be a welcome addition. Some drugstores have recognized consumer demand for green products, although Eva's cosmetics may be priced higher than its competitors. Eva must decide whether her high-end products will suffer a tarnished image if she sells them in drugstores or whether drugstores could be a good channel for increasing her brand awareness.

Category Specialists Category specialists are big-box retailers or category killers that offer a narrow but deep assortment of merchandise. Most category specialists use a predominantly self-service approach, but they offer assistance to customers in some areas of the stores. For example, the office supply store Staples has a warehouse atmosphere with cartons of copy paper stacked on pallets, plus equipment in boxes on shelves. But in some departments, such as computers, electronics, and other high-tech products, salespeople staff the display area to answer questions and make suggestions. Other prominent category specialists are Men's Warehouse, Best Buy, IKEA, Home Depot, and Bass Pro Shops.

By offering a complete assortment in a category at somewhat lower prices than their competition offers, category specialists can kill a category of merchandise for other retailers, which is why they are frequently called category killers. Using their category dominance, these retailers exploit their buying power to negotiate low prices.

Extreme-Value Retailers Extreme-value retailers are small, full-line discount stores that offer a limited merchandise assortment at very low prices. The largest extreme-value retailers are Dollar General and Dollar Tree (which purchased the Family Stores chain).[30]

Like limited-assortment food retailers, extreme-value retailers reduce costs and maintain low prices by buying opportunistically from manufacturers with excess merchandise, offering a limited assortment, and operating in low-rent locations. They offer a broad but shallow assortment of household goods, health and beauty aids, and groceries.

Many extreme-value retailers target low-income consumers, whose shopping behavior differs from that of typical discount store or warehouse club customers. Although these consumers might demand well-known national brands, they often cannot afford to buy large-sized packages. So vendors such as Procter & Gamble often create special, smaller packages for extreme-value retailers. Also, higher-income consumers are increasingly patronizing these stores for the thrill of the hunt. Some shoppers regard the extreme-value retailers as an opportunity to find some hidden treasure among the household staples.

Extreme-value retailers would not be an obvious consumer choice for Coach for Men or Eva's new lines because these stores are not consistent with the brands' image. But if these manufacturers find themselves in an overstock situation, they could use these retailers to reduce inventory. For the same reason, they might use off-price retailers.

Off-Price Retailers Off-price retailers offer an inconsistent assortment of brand-name merchandise at a significant discount from the manufacturer's suggested retail price

(MSRP). In today's market, these off-price retailers may be brick-and-mortar stores, online outlets, or a combination of both. America's largest off-price retail chains are TJX Companies (which operates TJ Maxx, Marshalls, Winners [Canada], HomeGoods, HomeSense, and Sierra Trading Post), Ross Stores, Burlington, Big Lots Inc., and Overstock.com.

To be able to sell at prices 20 to 60 percent lower than the MSRP,[31] most merchandise is bought opportunistically from manufacturers or other retailers with excess inventory at the end of the season. Therefore, customers cannot be confident that the same merchandise or even type of merchandise will be available each time they visit a store or website. The discounts off-price retailers receive from manufacturers reflect what they do not do as well: They do not ask suppliers to help them pay for advertising, make them take back unsold merchandise, charge them for markdowns, or ask them to delay payments.

Off-price retailers like Big Lots offer an inconsistent assortment of brand-name merchandise at a significant discount from the manufacturer's suggested retail price (MSRP).

©Chris Lee/MCT/Newscom

Service Retailers

The retail firms discussed in the previous sections sell products to consumers. Service retailers, or firms that primarily sell services rather than merchandise, are a large and growing part of the retail industry. Consider a typical Saturday: After a bagel and cup of coffee at a nearby Peet's Coffee and Tea, you go to the Laundromat to wash and dry your clothes, drop off a suit at a dry cleaner, have a prescription filled at a CVS drugstore, and make your way to Jiffy Lube to have your car's oil changed. In a hurry, you drive through a Burger King so you can eat lunch quickly and be on time for your haircut at Supercuts. By midafternoon, you're ready for a workout at your health club. After stopping at home to change your clothes and meet the cleaning service that you hired through Amazon's online referral site to spiff up your apartment, you're off to dinner, a movie, and dancing with a friend. Finally, you end your day with a café latte at Starbucks, having interacted with a dozen service retailers during the day.

There are a wide variety of service retailers, along with some national companies that provide these services. These companies are retailers because they sell goods and services to consumers. However, some are not just retailers. For example, airlines, banks, hotels, and insurance and express mail companies sell their services to businesses as well as consumers.

Several trends suggest considerable future growth in services retailing. For example, the aging population will increase demand for health care services. Younger people are also spending more time and money on health and fitness. Busy parents in two-income families are willing to pay to have their homes cleaned, lawns maintained, clothes washed and pressed, and meals prepared so they can spend more time with their families.

Now that we've explored the types of stores, we can examine how manufacturers and retailers coordinate their retail strategy using the six Ps.

Service retailers, like this nightclub, sell services rather than merchandise.

©Lane Oatey/Blue Jean Images/Getty Images

LO17-5 Describe the components of a retail strategy.

DEVELOPING A RETAIL STRATEGY USING THE SIX Ps

Like other marketers, retailers perform important functions that increase the value of the products and services they sell to consumers. We now examine these functions, classified into the four Ps examined thus far—product, price, promotion, and place. But because so much of the marketing in the retailing world takes place in physical stores, we have added two additional Ps: presentation and personnel.

Product

A typical grocery store carries 30,000 to 40,000 items; a regional department store might carry as many as 100,000. Providing the right mix of merchandise and services that satisfies the needs of the target market is one of retailers' most fundamental activities. Offering assortments gives customers a choice. To reduce transportation costs and handling, manufacturers typically ship cases of merchandise, such as cartons of mascara or boxes of leather jackets, to retailers. Because customers generally do not want or need to buy more than one of the same item, retailers break up the cases and sell customers the smaller quantities they desire.

Given the price of a Coach bag, would you expect to find it in Saks Fifth Avenue or JCPenney?

©Peter Horree/Alamy Stock Photo

Manufacturers don't like to store inventory because their factories and warehouses are typically not available or attractive shopping venues. Consumers don't want to purchase more than they need because storage consumes space. Neither group likes keeping inventory that isn't being used, because doing so ties up money that could be used for something else. Thus, in addition to other values to manufacturers and customers, retailers provide a storage function, though many retailers are beginning to push their suppliers to hold the inventory until they need it. (Recall our discussion of JIT inventory systems in Chapter 16.)

It is difficult for retailers to distinguish themselves from their competitors through the merchandise they carry because competitors can purchase and sell many of the same popular brands. Thus, many retailers have developed **private-label brands** (also called **store brands**), which are products developed and marketed by a retailer and available only from that retailer. For example, if you want Cat & Jack clothing for children, you have to go to Target. Adding Value 17.1 examines how Target is expanding its private-label business.

Price

Price helps define the value of both the merchandise and the service, and the general price range of a particular store helps define its image. Although both Saks Fifth Avenue and

Adding Value 17.1 · Expanding the Product Mix: Target's Extensive Private-Label Plans[iii]

In a strong competitive move, Target is introducing 12 new private-label lines in its stores, offering up appealing clothing and housewares that will be available only there. A couple of lines already have made their mark, suggesting that the retailer has hit on an effective means to compete in modern markets by ensuring that its products are distinctive enough to draw people in to their local stores.

For example, Cat & Jack is a children's wear private label that already has earned $2.2 billion in sales in its first year in the stores. It even ranks among the leading brands in the children's apparel market. Encouraged by the success of this line, Target continues to expand, including through the introduction of several "adaptive apparel" options made specifically to accommodate the needs of children with disabilities.

In another sector, Target has also added a private label it calls A New Day, selling a modern aesthetic for women's clothing with pieces featuring versatile patterns and prints. On the horizon is the line Project 62, which promises to make a midcentury design style available to Target consumers purchasing home goods, and a menswear line called Goodfellow & Co.

The marketing to announce these arrivals is cohesive, in that it highlights that there is "More in Store," rather than specifically targeting any single private-label line. Seeking to ensure that customers realize what they can find under these private labels, Target is promoting them through conventional advertising channels, in-store signage, and special events. The online communications also will provide 360-degree views of the clothing on offer, so that customers can get a sense of the vast range of new product lines before they visit the store.

If you want to purchase Cat & Jack clothing for children, you will have to go to Target since it is one of its private-label brands.
©ZUMA Press Inc./Alamy Stock Photo

Part of Target's confidence in its line extension strategy stems from marketing research that shows that unlike its older customers, young consumers are far less interested in specific, national name brands. Thus, private-label options appeal to them, as long as the product is good. In turn, its announcement of the 12 new private labels sparked approximately 900 million media impressions.

In its effort to "completely reinvent the way we are developing brands and marketing those brands," Target thus seeks to respond to changing markets and continue to appeal to various demographics of customers. Then it hopes that they come to regard the red bulls-eye as the targeted place to find just the products they want and need.

JCPenney are department stores, their images could not be more different. Thus, when Coach considers which of these firms is most appropriate for its new line for men, it must keep in mind customers' perceived images of these retailers' price–quality relationship. The company does not, for instance, want to attempt to sell its new line at JCPenney if it is positioning the line with a relatively high price.

Price must always be aligned with the other elements of a retailer's strategy—that is, product, promotion, and place. A customer would not expect to pay $600 for a Coach for Men briefcase at a JCPenney store, but she might question the briefcase's quality if its price is significantly less than $600 at Neiman Marcus. As we discovered in Chapter 14, there is much more to pricing than simply adding a markup onto a product's cost. Manufacturers must consider at what price they will sell the product to retailers so that both the manufacturer and the retailer can make a reasonable profit. At the same time, both the manufacturer and the retailer are concerned about what the customer is willing and expecting to pay.

Promotion

Retailers and manufacturers know that good promotion, both within the retail environments and in the media, can mean the difference between flat sales and a growing consumer base. Advertising in traditional media such as newspapers, magazines, and television continues to be important to get customers into stores. Increasingly, electronic communications are being used for promotions as well. Some traditional approaches, such as direct mail, are being

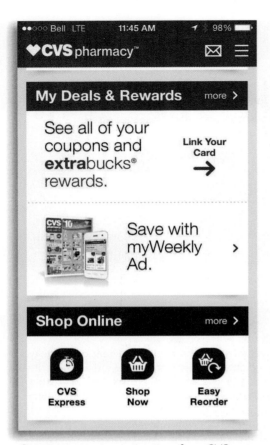

Customers receive promotions from CVS on their mobile devices that can be used immediately in the store.

Source: CVS

reevaluated by retailers, but many are still finding value in sending catalogs to customers and selected mailing lists. Companies also offer real-time promotions on their websites. For example, CVS.com contains in-store and online coupons that customers can use immediately on the website or print to use in the store. Coupons.com offers coupons that customers can use immediately for many grocery store items. Retailers are also investing heavily in **mobile commerce (M-commerce)**—product and service purchases through mobile devices.

A coordinated effort between the manufacturer and retailer helps guarantee that the customer receives a cohesive message and that both entities maintain their images. For example, Coach for Men might work with its most important retailers to develop advertising and point-of-sale signs. It may even help defray the costs of advertising by paying all or a portion of the advertising's production and media costs, an agreement called **cooperative (co-op) advertising**.

Place

Retailers already have realized that convenience is a key ingredient to success, and an important aspect of this success is convenient locations.[32] As the old cliché claims, the three most important things in retailing are location, location, location. Many customers choose stores on the basis of where they are located, which makes great locations a competitive advantage that few rivals can duplicate. For instance, once Starbucks saturates a market by opening in the best locations, Peet's will have difficulty breaking into that same market—where would it put its stores?

In pursuit of better and better locations, retailers are experimenting with different options to reach their target markets. Walgreens has freestanding stores, unconnected to other retailers, so the stores can offer drive-up windows for customers to pick up their prescriptions. Walmart, Staples, and others are opening smaller stores in urban locations to serve those markets better.

Presentation

Retailers invest a lot of time and money in ensuring that the merchandise is appropriately presented in their stores and online. Many retailers and service providers have been able to

To make their locations more convenient, Walgreens has some free-standing stores not connected to other retailers so the stores can offer a drive-up window for customers to pick up their prescriptions.

©McGraw-Hill Education/Andrew Resek, photographer

develop unique images that are based at least in part on their internal environment. These controllable characteristics within the store, known as **atmospherics**,[33] are intended to influence customers' propensity to purchase. As we discussed in Chapter 6, research has shown that, if used in concert with other aspects of a retailer's strategy, the sensory situation—visual (lighting and color), auditory (music), olfactory (smell), tactile (touch), and taste—can positively influence the decision process.[34]

Manufacturers actively work to obtain appropriate placement on shelves and displays in strategic areas such as the point-of-purchase (POP) or the end of aisles. Lighting, color, and music are used to highlight merchandise and create a mood that will attract the store's target markets. The taste and smell of new food items may attract people to try something they normally wouldn't. So, some retailers provide edible samples and encourage pleasant aromas to circulate through the store. Similarly, some retailers offer trunk shows, during which their vendors show their whole line of merchandise on a certain day.

During these well-advertised events, customers are often enticed to purchase that day because they get special assistance from the salespeople and can order merchandise that the retailer otherwise does not carry.

Consider the British outerwear retailer Hunter's new flagship store in Tokyo. This two-story store brings the British countryside to Japan. The first floor evokes a forest with "birch trees" that appear to reach the ceiling. The second floor is themed like a traditional hedge garden, featuring LED-lit hedges. Furthermore, a large screen highlights brand campaigns, recent local and global events, as well as regular weather updates from the UK, which is accompanied by a custom soundscape that includes heavy rain and thunderstorms.[35]

British outerwear retailer Hunter sets a mood to influence sales by invoking a feeling of the British countryside in its flagship store in Tokyo.
©Vince Talotta/Toronto Star via Getty Images

Personnel

Well-trained sales personnel can influence the sale at the point of purchase by educating consumers about product attributes, pointing out the advantages of one item over another, and encouraging multiple purchases, whether in the store, on the phone, or on the Internet. These individuals can also facilitate the sale of products or services that consumers perceive as complicated, risky, or expensive, such as an air conditioning unit, a computer, or a diamond ring. Manufacturers can play an important role in preparing retail sales and service associates to sell their products. Eva thus could conduct seminars or webinars about how to use and sell her new line of green cosmetics and supply printed educational materials to sales associates. Last but not least, sales reps handle the sales transactions.

Each Apple store features a simple layout that enables shoppers to play with the latest gadgets, though the real key to success is the salespeople. Apple keeps its product lines narrow, so salespeople can become familiar with every product in the store. For more technical questions, Apple Geniuses are available and consultations can be scheduled.[36] The company takes nothing for granted when training its employees, such that it uses role-playing scenarios, lists banned words, and specifies exactly how to communicate with agitated customers. Although technical expertise is a must, Apple also looks for salespeople with "magnetic personalities" and trains them in a five-point selling technique: **a**pproach customers warmly, **p**robe politely to assess their needs, **p**resent solutions the customer can do today, **l**isten and resolve worries the customer may still have, **e**nd by giving the customer a warm goodbye and invite them back.[37] See Chapter 20 for a discussion of personal selling.

Traditionally, retailers treated all their customers the same. Today, the most successful retailers concentrate on providing more value to their best customers. The knowledge retailers gain from their store personnel, the Internet browsing and buying activities of customers, and the data they collect on customer shopping habits can be used in customer relationship management (CRM). Using this information, retailers may modify the six Ps of retailing to attempt to increase their share of wallet—the percentage of the customer's purchases made from that particular retailer. For instance, omnichannel retailers use consumer information collected from the customers' Internet browsing and buying behavior to send dedicated e-mails to customers promoting specific products or services. Retailers also may offer special discounts to good customers to help them become even more loyal.

Apple's personnel is a key factor in its stores' success. The salespeople and Apple Geniuses are very knowledgeable.
©Michael Short/Bloomberg via Getty Images

LO17-6 Identify the benefits and challenges of omnichannel retailing.

THE INTERNET AND OMNICHANNEL RETAILING

The addition of the Internet channel to traditional store-based retailers has improved their ability to serve their customers and build a competitive advantage in several ways. According to Social & Mobile Marketing 17.2, IKEA effectively exemplifies these benefits.

First, the addition of an Internet channel has the potential to offer a greater selection of products. Second, an Internet channel enables retailers to provide customers with more personalized information about products and services. Third, it offers sellers the unique opportunity to collect information about consumer shopping behavior—information that they can use to improve the shopping experience across all channels. Fourth, the Internet channel allows sellers to enter new markets economically.

Deeper and Broader Selection

One benefit of adding the Internet channel is the vast number of alternatives retailers can make available to consumers without crowding their aisles or increasing their square footage. Stores and catalogs are limited by their size. By shopping on the Internet, consumers can easily visit and select merchandise from a broader array of retailers. Individual retailers' websites typically offer deeper assortments of merchandise (more colors, brands, and sizes) than are available in stores or catalogs. This expanded offering enables them to satisfy consumer demand for less popular styles, colors, or sizes. Many retailers also offer a broader assortment (more categories) on their websites. Staples.com, for instance, offers soft drinks and cleaning supplies, which are not available in stores, so that its business customers will view it as a one-stop shop.

Social & Mobile Marketing 17.2   In-Store and Online Analytics at IKEA[iv]

IKEA's affordable, ready-to-assemble product line has made it the go-to place for furnishing a new home, apartment, or room. Much of its success stems from its unique store layouts, which force shoppers to walk past virtually every product offered, as displayed in sample rooms that have been modeled to inspire their design ideas. The layout also helps IKEA recognize which sorts of displays of what types of products invoke purchases—a sort of elemental analytics that benefits its strategy. Thus, when IKEA first decided to launch its website, it already recognized the importance of analytics as vital information that would enable it to serve its customers better.

Initially, IKEA's analytics-oriented focus was on website development. With its massive product range, the retailer had to find ways to discover pertinent patterns in consumers' product navigation and selection approaches. As it gathered such information, IKEA could begin to revise its site and successfully design a web page that encouraged customers to slow down during their online browsing, which would lead them to be inspired by new products, design ideas, and other services the company offers, but without ever sacrificing the convenience they demanded.

Having achieved that goal, IKEA turned its focus to increasing its online presence. For this feat, it needed to do more than analyze data that it had gathered from its own site. It needed

IKEA's analytics are used for website development and to improve its social media presence.
©Sergio Dionisio/Bloomberg/Getty Images

data from social networking sites. These social media–derived insights suggest channels and routes for improving consumers' perceptions of the brand. The influences of these analytics on many of IKEA's online actions are evident. For example, when "The Dress" became a vastly and inexplicably trending topic (is it white and gold or black and blue? and why could no one agree?), IKEA rapidly leveraged the social media sensation to plug its products by using the hashtag #TheDress.

Personalization

Another benefit of adding the Internet channel is the ability to personalize promotions and services economically, including heightened service or individualized offerings.

Personalized Customer Service Traditional Internet channel approaches for responding to customer questions—such as FAQ (frequently asked question) pages and offering an 800 number or e-mail address to ask questions—often do not provide the timely information customers are seeking. To improve customer service from an electronic channel, many firms offer live online chats, so that customers can click a button at any time and participate in an instant messaging conversation with a customer service representative. This technology also enables firms to send a proactive chat invitation at specific times to visitors to the site. Verizon Wireless programs its chat windows to appear at the moment a customer chooses a product, because its goal is to upsell these willing buyers to a more expensive plan.[38] Other online retailers use metrics such as the amount of time spent on the site or number of repeat visits to determine which customers will receive an invitation to chat.

Personalized Offering The interactive nature of the Internet also provides an opportunity for retailers to personalize their offerings for each of their customers, based on customers' behavior. Just as a well-trained salesperson would make recommendations to customers prior to checkout, an interactive web page can make suggestions to the shopper about items that he or she might like to see based on previous purchases, what other customers who purchased the same item purchased, or common web viewing behavior.

Some omnichannel retailers are able to personalize promotions and Internet home pages on the basis of several attributes tied to the shopper's current or previous web sessions, such as the time of day, time zone as determined by a computer's Internet address, and assumed gender.[39] However, some consumers worry about this ability to collect information about purchase histories, personal information, and search behavior on the Internet. How will this information be used in the future? Will it be sold to other firms? Will the consumer receive unwanted promotional materials online or in the mail?

Expanded Market Presence

The market for customers who shop in stores is typically limited to consumers living in close proximity to those stores. The market for catalogs is limited by the high cost of printing and mailing them and increasing consumer interest in environmentally friendly practices. By adding the Internet channel, retailers can expand their market without having to build new stores or incur the high cost of additional catalogs. Adding an Internet channel is particularly attractive to retailers that have strong brand names but limited locations and distribution. For example, retailers such as Nordstrom, REI, IKEA, and L.L.Bean are widely known for offering unique, high-quality merchandise. If these retailers had only a few stores, customers would have to travel vast distances to buy the merchandise they carry.

To ensure effective omnichannel retailing practices, modern retailers need to acknowledge modern consumers' preferences. That is, consumers desire a seamless experience when interacting with omnichannel retailers. They want to be recognized by a retailer, whether they interact with a sales associate, the retailer's website, or the retailer's call center by telephone. Customers want to buy a product through the retailer's Internet or catalog channels and pick it up or return it to a local store; find out if a product offered on the Internet channel is available at a local store; and, when unable to find a product in a store, determine if it is available for home delivery through the retailer's Internet channel. Marketing Analytics 17.2 details how Google is trying to help retailers meet these consumer demands.

However, providing this seamless experience for customers is not easy for retailers. Because each of the channels is somewhat different, a critical decision facing omnichannel retailers is the degree to which they should or are able to integrate the operations of the channels.[40] To determine how much integration is best, each retailer must address issues such as integrated CRM, brand image, pricing, and the supply chain.

Marketing Analytics 17.2

Sending Minions to Madison but Jedis to Berkeley: How Google's Search Insights Tool Benefits Retailers[v]

To help retailers determine which products consumers are most interested in at that particular moment and in a specific location, a new service from Google aggregates search data in remarkable detail. The Google Search Insights tool combines the various keywords, keyphrases, and spelling variations that reflect the ways consumers might search for certain products, then combines these data into heat maps that represent local demand.

For example, consumers in Berkeley, California, searching for paraphernalia related to the new movie might search for "Star Wars," "Star Wars: The Force Awakens," "starwars," or some other variation. Google Search Insights aggregates all these millions of searches, then shows that people in Berkeley are way more interested in *Star Wars* than in Minions, whereas online shoppers in Madison, Wisconsin, are focusing their searches on the little yellow Minions rather than on Jedi knights.

In addition to the location, Google can track the popularity of the searches over time and highlight that virtually everyone, everywhere started searching more for *Star Wars* in the immediate aftermath of the release of the first trailer for *The Force Awakens*.

With this location- and time-specific information, retailers can rapidly and appropriately adjust their marketing, inventory levels, and promotions to appeal to what customers want, immediately and locally. In particular, Google links retailers using its Search Insights to its AdWords service, such that they can initiate a new search advertising campaign to respond to emerging demand.

Although Google already offered a version of these analytics, with its Trends service, the new tool provides increased geographic detail and organizes the data according to keywords, rather than products. Furthermore, Search Insights provides information for retailers about whether customers are searching mainly for the pertinent keywords on their mobile devices or through personal computers.

The Google Search Insights tool combines search data into heat maps that represent local demand. Hypothetically, it may show that people in Berkeley are interested in Star Wars *(left)*, whereas shoppers in Madison, Wisconsin, search for Minions *(right)*.

(Left): ©Photo 12/Alamy Stock Photo; (right): ©AF archive/Alamy Stock Photo

Integrated CRM

Effective omnichannel operations require an integrated CRM (customer relationship management) system with a centralized customer data warehouse that houses a complete history of each customer's interaction with the retailer, regardless of whether the sale occurred in a store, on the Internet, or on the telephone.[41] This information storehouse allows retailers to efficiently handle complaints, expedite returns, target future promotions, and provide a seamless experience for customers when they interact with the retailer through multiple channels.

Brand Image

Retailers need to provide a consistent brand image across all channels. For example, Patagonia reinforces its image of selling high-quality, environmentally friendly sports equipment in its stores, catalogs, and website. Each of these channels emphasizes function, not fashion, in the descriptions of Patagonia's products. Patagonia's position about taking

Multichannel retailers like Patagonia sell on the Internet, in catalogs, and in stores.

(Top): Source: Patagonia, Inc; (bottom): ©lentamart/Shutterstock; (right): Source: Patagonia, Inc.

care of the environment is communicated by carefully lighting its stores and using recycled polyester and organic rather than pesticide-intensive cotton in many of its clothes.

Pricing

Pricing represents another difficult decision for omnichannel retailers. Customers expect pricing consistency for the same SKU across channels (excluding shipping charges and sales tax). However, in some cases, retailers need to adjust their pricing strategy because of the competition they face in different channels. For example, to compete effectively against Amazon.com, Barnes & Noble offers lower prices through its Internet channel (www.bn.com) than it offers in its stores.

Retailers with stores in multiple markets often set different prices for the same merchandise to compete better with local stores. Customers generally are not aware of these price differences because they are exposed to the prices only in their local markets. However, omnichannel retailers may have difficulties sustaining these regional price differences when customers can easily check prices on the Internet.

Supply Chain

Omnichannel retailers struggle to provide an integrated shopping experience across all their channels because unique skills and resources are needed to manage each channel.[42] For example, store-based retail chains operate and manage many stores, each requiring the management of inventory and people. With Internet and catalog operations, inventory and telephone salespeople instead are typically centralized in one or two locations. Also, retail distribution centers (DCs) supporting a store channel are designed to ship many cartons of merchandise to stores. In contrast, the DCs supporting a catalog and Internet channel are designed to ship a few items at a time to many individual customers. The difference in shipping orientation for the two types of operations requires a completely different type of distribution center.

Due to these operational differences, many store-based retailers have a separate organization to manage their Internet and catalog operations. But as the omnichannel operation matures, retailers tend to integrate all operations under one organization. Both Walmart and JCPenney initially had separate organizations for their Internet channel but subsequently integrated them with stores and catalogs.

PROGRESS CHECK

1. What are the components of a retail strategy?
2. What are the advantages of traditional stores versus Internet-only stores?
3. What challenges do retailers face when marketing their products through multiple channels?

Reviewing Learning Objectives

L017-1 **Discuss the four factors manufacturers should consider as they develop their strategy for working with retailers.**

When they initiate the decision process for choosing retail partners, manufacturers determine how likely it is that certain retailers would carry their products and whether target customers expect to find their products for sale at those retail locations. Next, manufacturers need to identify types of retailers that would be appropriate locations for their products. After identifying likely and appropriate retailers, manufacturers work with their retailer partners to develop a strategy that comprises the six Ps. Finally, manufacturers, again with their retail partners, must determine which elements of an omnichannel strategy will be effective.

L017-2 **Outline the considerations associated with choosing retail partners.**

Manufacturers often start by noting the basic channel structure, which includes the level of vertical integration, the relative strength of the retailer and the manufacturer, and the strength of the brand. They also consider where their target customers expect to find products, which depends largely on the retailer's image. Channel member characteristics also are important inputs, as is the level of distribution intensity.

L017-3 **List the three levels of distribution intensity.**

Intensive distribution intensity means the product is available virtually everywhere, in as many places as will agree to carry it. In an exclusive distribution

intensity strategy, the manufacturer allows only one retailer (or retail chain) in each area to sell its products. Selective distribution is the middle ground option; several retailers carry the products, but not all of them.

L017-4 **Describe the various types of retailers.**

Retailers generally fall into one of three categories: food retailers, general merchandise retailers, or service retailers. Each of the categories consists of various formats, including supermarkets, supercenters, warehouse clubs, convenience stores, online grocery retailers, department stores, discount stores, specialty retailers, drugstores, category specialists, extreme-value retailers, and off-price stores. Although service retailers primarily sell services, if they sell to consumers, they are still retailers. Service retailers span the gambit from universities to automobile oil change shops.

L017-5 **Describe the components of a retail strategy.**

To develop a coordinated strategy—which represents a key goal for an effective channel partnership between retailers and manufacturers—retailers as well as manufacturers need to consider all of the six Ps in conjunction: product, price, promotion, place, presentation, and personnel.

L017-6 **Identify the benefits and challenges of omnichannel retailing.**

The various types of retail channels—stores, catalogs, and the Internet—all offer their own benefits and limitations, including those related to availability, convenience, and safety, among others. If a retailer adopts an omnichannel strategy, it can exploit the benefits and mitigate the limitations of each channel and help expand its overall market presence. Furthermore, an omnichannel strategy offers the chance to gain a greater share of customers' wallets and more insight into their buying behaviors.

To function in multiple channels, retailers must organize their operations carefully to ensure an integrated customer experience. In particular, they have to have an integrated CRM system, determine how to maintain a consistent brand image across the various channels, whether to charge the same or different prices, and how best to deliver merchandise to multiple channels.

Key Terms

- atmospherics, 526
- big-box retailers, 522
- category killers, 522
- category specialists, 522
- convenience stores, 518
- conventional supermarket, 517
- cooperative (co-op) advertising, 526
- department stores, 519
- distribution intensity, 515
- drugstores, 521

- exclusive distribution, 516
- extreme-value food retailers, 517
- extreme-value retailers, 522
- full-line discount stores, 520
- intensive distribution, 515
- limited-assortment supermarkets, 517
- mobile commerce (M-commerce), 526
- off-price retailers, 522

- omnichannel or multichannel strategy, 513
- online chats, 529
- private-label or store brands, 524
- retailing, 512
- selective distribution, 516
- service retailers, 523
- share of wallet, 527
- specialty stores, 520
- supercenters, 518
- warehouse clubs, 518

Marketing Digitally

1. How do JCrew.com and Gap.com provide value to their customers beyond the physical products they sell? Why would a customer purchase online instead of going to the store? Under what circumstances would the customer prefer a store-based experience?

2. Select a familiar omnichannel retailer. Evaluate its website in terms of how well it provides value to its customers. Do you believe that offering multiple selling channels to customers enhances their shopping experience? How does it help the retailer? Explain your answer.

Marketing Applications

1. Does Reebok pursue an intensive, an exclusive, or a selective distribution intensity strategy? Would you suggest any changes to this strategy?

2. Imagine that you designed a high-end line of clothing and accessories. Which factors should you consider when choosing retail partners? What type of retailer would you choose as a partner? Why?

3. Some argue that retailers can be eliminated from the distribution channel because they only add costs to the final product without creating any value-added services in the process. Do you agree with this perspective? Are consumers likely to make most purchases directly from manufacturers in the near future? Provide justification for your answers.

4. Assume you have been given some money but told that it must be invested in a retailer's stock. In which type of retailer would you choose to invest? Which specific retailer? Provide a rationale for your answers.

5. Provide examples of how P&G may work with Kroger to jointly plan and implement a retail strategy using the six Ps.

6. Why have so many brick-and-mortar retailers adopted an omnichannel strategy?

7. You can purchase apparel at a discount store, specialty store, category specialist, off-price retailer, department store, or Internet-only store. From which of these types of stores do you shop? Explain why you prefer one type store over another.

8. Should Tana, a young entrepreneur who is launching a new line of environmentally friendly (green) cosmetics, sell through a physical store, catalog, or Internet? Explain two key benefits of each channel for her business.

9. Name a retailer from which you have received personalized service, product, or promotion offerings online. What form of personalization did you receive? Did the personalization influence your purchase decision? Explain why or why not.

Quiz Yourself

1. _____ tailor their retail strategies toward very specific market segments by offering deep, yet narrow assortments and sales associate expertise.

    a. Warehouse clubs

    b. Full-line discount stores

    c. Specialty stores

    d. Category specialists

    e. Supercenters

2. Retailers may modify product, price, and/or promotion to attempt to increase their _____, which is the percent-age of a customer's purchases made from that particular retailer.

    a. share of wallet

    b. consumer position

    c. distribution intensity

    d. retail position

    e. share of market

(Answers to these two questions can be found in the Quiz Yourself Answer Key section.)

Chapter Case Study

ASHLEY STEWART[43]

An auditorium full of graduate and undergraduate students was eager to hear what James Rhee, the CEO of Ashley Stewart, the largest plus-size retailer in the United States, would have to say. How did a middle-aged Korean American man turn around a struggling brand that catered primarily to African American women? But Rhee was accustomed to such questions and ready to answer them.

Founded in 1991, Ashley Stewart was named after two distinct style icons: Laura Ashley and Martha Stewart. The founder Joseph Stint sold his shares of the company in 2000. The following decades saw some challenges, such that the company filed for bankruptcy in 2010 and then reorganized again in 2014. But by that point, Rhee—inspired by the brand's promise and its connections to its customers—had resigned from his position on the board as an investor in the retailer to become its CEO.[44] Today, Ashley Stewart maintains just shy of 100 stores in the United States and a global e-commerce platform, helping curvy women around the world find beautiful fashions that fit.

So how did a former high school teacher and hedge fund manager manage the success of a fashion brand?

Ashley Stewart is the largest plus-size retailer in the United States.

©Amy Sussman/Getty Images

Industry Environment and Ashley Stewart's Position Approximately 67 percent of U.S. women wear sizes 14 to 34; however, many companies still don't offer efficient options in this category. Therefore, the plus-size apparel industry accounts for only approximately $20 billion of the $108 billion apparel industry. Still, it is one of the fastest-growing categories in fashion.[45] Whereas once the fashion industry ignored this segment and focused almost exclusively on wearers of smaller sizes, today, retailers cannot ignore this segment. Sales of women's plus-size apparel have increased almost 17 percent from 2013 to 2016.[46]

Just like every other retail setting, women's fashions also have been influenced by the growth of the Internet. As the number of digital shoppers continues to increase, virtually every brand is seeking a space to establish itself in the digital world, to attract attention and expand its reach through traffic to either its website or its stores. At www.ashleystewart.com

customers find bright colors, and stylish models sporting the latest trends. The visually attractive looks for every season also promote web-exclusive collections to customers.

But in the early 2010s, Ashley Stewart did not even have Wi-Fi at its company headquarters. Corporate decisions mostly were based on "gut" perceptions, rather than data. Its e-commerce platform was antiquated. Turnover among employees was high, and the corporate culture was described as fearful,[47] leaving the brand without any real credibility. Following more than a decade of losses, the company seemingly had lost its way: Employees were angry, customers were annoyed, and investors had lost all hope.

But Rhee saw something in the brand. In his own words, he "loved the brand and everything it stood for. Ashley Stewart had been founded to provide plus-size fashion for women in boutiquelike settings in urban neighborhoods across the United States. After listening to our customers, I came to realize that the brand stood for more than that—values like respect, empowerment, and joy. Despite the company's history of failure, I believed that the brand could capitalize on several macro-cyclical trends with a reinvented business model."[48]

A graduate of Harvard Law School, James Rhee had been a high school teacher and private equity investor, with no experience in the fashion industry. So he adopted a teaching-oriented philosophy and applied hedge fund policies to the effort to save the brand.

Rhee's Philosophy Rhee focused on a few core principles that led to the turnaround of the company. He relied on numbers and math, sought to reinvent the company culture, adopted a central focus on the core customer, encouraged continuous innovation, and—perhaps above all—prioritized kindness.[49]

Rhee understood that customers would behave differently on different days, so Ashley Stewart's business model and algorithms would have to adapt to customers' varying behavior. Using sophisticated analytics and data, he improved the flow of goods through the supply chain, which also sped up the arrival of new fashions into stores. Furthermore, Rhee insisted on updated technology in all realms of the business, so that it could offer standardized IT and e-commerce operations. Preferring measures that could not be manipulated, Rhee focused on loyalty, returns on investment and capital, and time assessments. Moreover, "When we were re-writing all of the planning algorithms and business reports, the math and operational discipline was done at the level at which a blue-chip investment firm would operate."[50]

These changes were also part of the reinvented culture, along with physical changes, such as knocking down all the walls in the corporate headquarters to encourage an open-door policy. The company stopped using virtually all of its formal job descriptions. Instead, the goal was a culture that relied on mentoring and teaching, as well as a services-oriented approach. In response to the radical changes, approximately 40 percent of the employees at corporate headquarters left, but those remaining were dedicated to the new culture.[51]

This new services-oriented culture also entailed a reinvigorated focus on the core customer, the "she" who is embodied in the very name Ashley Stewart. In every decision, Ashley Stewart considers what "she" might want and ensures it is respecting "her," such as through enhanced customer service and customer engagement. This "she" is critical to everything associated with Ashley Stewart and part of the reason Rhee even attempted the turnaround: "If this was a business that sold widgets or old expensive neckties for rich guys, I wouldn't have done this."[52] This brand somehow had persisted for decades, without making any consistent profits. It was able to do so simply because "she" loved Ashley Stewart, which provided "her" with beautifully merchandised stores, where each customer is greeted by "Ms. Ashley," the store manager. Once customers found the stores, they stayed loyal to them; Rhee even recounts meeting three generations of women from one family coming together to shop in a place they felt comfortable and respected. With its segmentation and targeting focused primarily on African American plus-size women, Ashley Stewart also provided a safe space for a frequently marginalized population—another reason Rhee was drawn to the sinking brand. When he looked at customers in stores, he observed that their body language signaled more confidence, reminding him of how his mother, who emigrated from

Korea, would exhibit pride and satisfaction when she walked into a Korean store. It was these emotions that he wanted customers at Ashley Stewart, the all-important "her," to feel when they walked into any store.[53]

But a comfortable store is not enough to attract repeat visits by fashionable shoppers if it does not continually offer new looks. Ashley Stewart seeks to get new options in stores within six to eight weeks. Its assortment is extensive and includes clothing, swimwear, shoes, and accessories. Furthermore, noting that larger sizes were stocking out quickly, Ashley Stewart recently added more extended sizes to its collection.[54] Most manufacturers charge retailers more for larger sizes, but Ashley Stewart refuses to pass on this additional cost to its customers, so the fast fashions also remain affordable for consumers.

Outside the stores, innovation also is the hallmark of Ashley Stewart's reinvented website. The brand refers to itself as a real person—that same "she" who is respected throughout the company. With this personalized phrasing, Ashley Stewart connects with other "Neighborhood Girls Gone Global," reminding them of how someone or something local can engage communities all over the world and succeed globally, such as when it promises, "With roots based in New York, my mission has always been to inspire you. . . . I want every woman to cherish her curves. After all, they're what make us sexy, confident, and fabulous. Ashley Stewart is a sisterhood, your best girlfriend next door. Join me—you fit in here."[55] For its 25th anniversary, the retailer hosted a Rock the Block party in Brooklyn, a fun event that garnered more than 15 million social media impressions.

Its social media presence also is marked by its overriding philosophy of kindness, which Rhee calls the company's "core strategic pillar."[56] For example, in a nationwide campaign, the #LoveYourCurvesTour, Ashley Stewart worked to connect with loyal customers by hosting fashion shows, model hunts, and shopping parties in Atlanta, Chicago, Philadelphia, Baltimore, Detroit, and New York. Encouraging women to celebrate their curves, the brand reaffirms its respect and appreciation for its customers. This appreciation also was evident in its #MOMspiration campaign, which encouraged customers to submit pictures of their mothers or daughters that depicted a meaningful memory they shared—perhaps one made while shopping at Ashley Stewart. In its philanthropic efforts, such as #ASGives, it also partners with charities that support local communities, raises money for cancer research, donates clothes and shoes, and grants need-based scholarships. Even in the midst of the company's bankruptcy and reorganization in 2014, Rhee insisted on introducing a generous charitable program during the holiday season, to remind the company of its need to stay true to its core values.

What Does the Future Hold for Ashley Stewart? By most accounts, Rhee's efforts at Ashley Stewart have been a huge success. The corporate culture is healthier. Sales growth has hit double digits over the past few years;[57] e-commerce sales account for 35 percent of total sales.[58] In addition to its robust sales, Ashley Stewart is widely recognized as one of the world's most engaging sites on social media, ranked among the top 10 in terms of its website's active engagement with customers through Facebook.

But the outlook is not all rosy. In its continued efforts to market the brand, Ashley Stewart has run up against rules imposed by Google's AdWords against targeting customers using terms that refer to their body type. Thus, any advertisement that promotes the brand as dedicated to curvy or plus-size women would be rejected from this popular and effective advertising channel. The policy has a respectful aim, yet for a retailer that relies specifically on body type to segment its market, it creates an impossible dilemma.[59]

But facing an auditorium of interested students, James Rhee still predicts the continued success of the brand, as long as "she" continues to embrace the core principles that have gotten her to where she is today.

Questions

1. Describe Ashley Stewart's retail strategy using the six Ps.
2. Who is Ashley Stewart's target market? Could/should that target market be expanded?
3. What are Ashley Stewart's bases for sustainable competitive advantage?

Endnotes

1. Laura Stevens and Heather Haddon, "Big Prize in Amazon-Whole Foods Deal: Data," *The Wall Street Journal*, June 20, 2017; Neil Irwin, "The Amazon-Walmart Showdown That Explains the Modern Economy," *The New York Times*, June 16, 2017; Annie Gasparro and Heather Haddon, "Grocery Pioneer Whole Foods to Join Mass-Market Crowd," *The Wall Street Journal*, June 16, 2017; Farhad Manjoo, "In Whole Foods, Bezos Gets a Sustainably Sourced Guinea Pig," *The New York Times*, June 17, 2017.

2. This chapter draws heavily from Michael Levy, Barton A. Weitz, and Dhruv Grewal, *Retailing Management*, 10th ed. (New York: McGraw-Hill Education, 2019).

3. "2017 Global 250 Chart," *Stores Magazine*, January 2016, https://nrf.com/2017-global-250-chart.

4. "Sales of Food at Home by Type of Outlet Table," USDA Economic Research Service, 2016, www.ers.usda.gov/datafiles/Food_Expenditures/Food_Expenditures/table14.xls.

5. "2016 SN Top 75 U.S. & Canadian Food Retailers & Wholesalers," *Supermarket News*, January 14, 2017, www.supermarketnews.com/top-75-retailers-wholesalers/2016-sn-top-75-us-and-canadian-food-retailers-and-wholesalers; 2017 Global 250 Chart."

6. "2017 Global 250 Chart."

7. "2016 SN Top 75 U.S. & Canadian Food Retailers & Wholesalers."

8. "Conventional Supermarket," TermWiki, http://en.termwiki.com/EN:conventional_supermarket (accessed April 27, 2016).

9. "Supermarket Sales Share in the United States in 2016, by Department," *Statista*, July 2017, www.statista.com/statistics/240580/breakdown-of-us-supermarket-sales-by-department/.

10. Ashley Lutz, "Aldi's Secrets for Selling Cheaper Groceries Than Wal-Mart or Trader Joe's," *Business Insider*, April 8, 2015, www.businessinsider.com/why-aldi-is-so-cheap-2015-4.

11. Ibid.

12. George Anderson, "Supermarkets Continue to Give Ground to Other Channels," *RetailWire*, February 19, 2014, www.retailwire.com/discussion/17340/supermarkets-continue-to-give-ground-to-other-channels.

13. Eliza Barclay, "Grocery Stores Are Losing You. Here's How They Plan to Win You Back," *NPR*, March 30, 2015.

14. http://corporate.walmart.com/our-story/locations/united-states#/united-states.

15. Sarah Halzack, "A Case for Costco and Other Warehouse Clubs Having Transformed Retail More Than Amazon," *Washington Post*, September 2, 2015.

16. Angel Abcede and Greg Lindenberg, "Ranking the Top 40 C-Store Chains: A Year-End Review" *CSP*, www.cspdailynews.com/mergers-acquisition-growth/mergers-acquisitions-news/articles/ranking-top-40-c-store-chains-year-end#page=0.

17. www.safeway.com/.

18. Jim Dudlicek, "Online Grocery Growth Accelerating," *Progressive Grocer*, September 1, 2017, https://progressivegrocer.com/online-grocery-growth-accelerating.

19. "It's a Breakout Year for Online Food Sales," *Digital Commerce*, September 20, 2016, www.digitalcommerce360.com/2016/09/20/its-breakout-year-online-food-sales/.

20. Jillian D'Onfro, "I Tried All the Different Lazy Ways to Get Groceries without Leaving the House—Here's What's Good about Each One," *Business Insider*, March 13, 2016.

21. "The Future of Grocery," *Nielsen*, April 2015, www.nielsen.com/content/dam/nielsenglobal/vn/docs/Reports/2015/Nielsen%20Global%20E-Commerce%20and%20The%20New%20Retail%20Report%20APRIL%202015%20(Digital).pdf.

22. Ronny Kerr, "How Does Instacart Make Money?," *Vator News*, August 2, 2016, http://vator.tv/news/2016-08-02-how-does-instacart-make-money.

23. Jeff Daniels, "Online Grocery Sales Set to Surge, Grabbing 20 Percent of Market by 2025," *CNBC*, January 30, 2017, www.cnbc.com/2017/01/30/online-grocery-sales-set-surge-grabbing-20-percent-of-market-by-2025.html.

24. "Fortune 500," *Fortune*, http://fortune.com/fortune500/.

25. Mary Hanbury, "We Went to Nordstrom's Discount Store and Saw How It Could Be the Future of the Chain," *Business Insider*, March 1, 2018.

26. Kelly Tackett, "An Evolutionary Tale from Nordstrom," *RetailWire*, May 8, 2014.

27. "Sales of the Leading Discount Store Companies Worldwide in 2016 (in Billion U.S. Dollars)," *Statista*, July 2017, www.statista.com/statistics/257983/sales-of-the-leading-discount-store-companies-worldwide/.

28. Adam J. Fein, "2016's Top Retail Pharmacy Chains, According to Drug Store News," *Drug Channels*, July 20, 2017, www.drugchannels.net/2017/07/2016s-top-retail-pharmacy-chains.html.

29. Kate Taylor, "CVS Is Making an Unprecedented Move to Hook Millennial Moms," *Business Insider*, April 19, 2016, www.businessinsider.com/cvs-adds-curbside-pickup-service-2016-4; "12 New In-Store, Online, and Mobile Drugstore Services That Save You Time and Money," *Consumer Reports*, August 2014, www.consumerreports.org/cro/2014/08/new-pharmacy-services/index.htm.

30. Jenna Martin, "Top 10 Stories of 2015: Family Dollar Completes Merger with Dollar Tree," *Charlotte Business Journal*, December 15, 2015, www.bizjournals.com/charlotte/news/2015/12/15/top-10-stories-of-2015-family-dollar-completes.html.

31. www.wikinvest.com/industry/Off-price_Retail.

32. Mukti Behera and Vivek Mishra, "Impact of Store Location and Layout on Consumer Purchase Behavior in Organized Retail," *Anvesha* 10, no. 1 (2017), pp. 10–21; Jennifer Sanchez-Flack et al. "Examination of the Relationship between In-Store Environmental Factors and Fruit and Vegetable Purchasing among Hispanics," *International Journal of Environmental Research and Public Health* 14, no. 11 (2017), p. 1305.

33. The concept of atmospherics was introduced by Philip Kotler, "Atmosphere as a Marketing Tool," *Journal of Retailing* 49 (Winter 1973), pp. 48–64.

34. Anne L. Roggeveen and Dhruv Grewal, "In-Store Marketing: Existing and Emerging Elements," *Handbook of Research on Retailing*, ed. Katrijn Gielens and Els Gijsbrechts, Elgar Publishing, 2018.

35. "Hunter, Tokyo," *Chain Store Age*, April 8, 2016; "5 Creative Ways Stores Are Experimenting with Immersive Retail Experiences," *Shopify*, June 10, 2016; www.hunterboots.com/.

36. Tim Bajarin, "6 Reasons Apple Is So Successful," *Time*, May 7, 2012, http://techland.time.com.

37. Carmine Gallo, "Apple's Secret Employee Training Manual Reinvents Customer Service in Seven Ways," *Forbes*, August 30, 2012.

38. www.verizonwireless.com/smartphones/.

39. Dhruv Grewal, Anne Roggeveen, and Jens Nordfalt, "The Future of Retailing," *Journal of Retailing* 93, no. 1 (2017), pp. 1–6; Elizabeth M. Aguirre et al., "Unraveling the Personalization Paradox: The Effect of Information Collection and Trust-Building Strategies on Online Advertisement Effectiveness," *Journal of Retailing* 91, no. 1 (2015), pp. 34–49; "Sponsored Supplement: Expanding the Reach of Personalization," *Internet Retailer,* March 2010.

40. Christian Homburg, Josef Vollmayr, and Alexander Hahn, "Firm Value Creation through Major Channel Expansions: Evidence from an Event Study in the United States, Germany, and China," *Journal of Marketing,* 2014, http://dx.doi.org/10.1509/jm.12.0179.

41. Hongshuang (Alice) Li and P. K. Kannan, "Attributing Conversions in a Multichannel Online Marketing Environment: An Empirical Model and a Field Experiment," *Journal of Marketing Research* 51 (February 2014), pp. 40–56.

42. Elizabeth Payne, James Peltier, and Victor Barger, "Omni-Channel Marketing, Integrated Marketing Communications and Consumer Engagement: A Research Agenda," *Journal of Research in Interactive Marketing* 11, no. 2 (2017), pp. 185–97; Huqing Yang, Yaobin Lu, Patrick Y. K. Chau, and Sumeet Gupta, "Role of Channel Integration on the Service Quality, Satisfaction, and Repurchase Intention in a Multi-Channel (Online-Cum-Mobile) Retail Environment," *International Journal of Mobile Communications* 15, no. 1 (2017), pp. 1–25.

43. This case was written by Megha Mehta (Babson College), Elisabeth Nevins (Effectual Editorial Services), and Dhruv Grewal (Babson College).

44. James Rhee, "How I Brought Ashley Stewart Back from Bankruptcy," *Harvard Business Review,* July 31, 2015.

45. Shelly Banjo and Rani Molla, "Retailers Ignore Most of America's Women," *Bloomberg Gadfly,* May 10, 2016, www.bloomberg.com/gadfly/articles/2016-05-10/plus-size-could-save-retailers.

46. Ibid.

47. Rhee, "How I Brought Ashley Stewart Back from Bankruptcy."

48. Marianne Wilson, "The Unlikely Champion of Ashley Stewart," *Chain Store Age,* April 20, 2016.

49. Rhee, "How I Brought Ashley Stewart Back from Bankruptcy"; Wilson, "The Unlikely Champion of Ashley Stewart."

50. Wilson, "The Unlikely Champion of Ashley Stewart."

51. Rhee, "How I Brought Ashley Stewart Back from Bankruptcy."

52. Teresa Novellino, "After 2 Bankruptcies in 3 Years, a Reinvented Ashley Stewart Hits the Full-Figured Runway," *New York Business Journal,* June 22, 2015.

53. Robin Givhan, "How a Plus-Size Clothing Label Dug Out of Bankruptcy: Body Pride, Diversity and Instagram," *The Washington Post,* September 1, 2016.

54. Banjo and Molla, "Retailers Ignore Most of America's Women."

55. "About Me," www.ashleystewart.com/aboutus.html.

56. Rhee, "How I Brought Ashley Stewart Back from Bankruptcy."

57. Novellino, "After 2 Bankruptcies in 3 Years."

58. Wilson, "The Unlikely Champion of Ashley Stewart."

59. Maria Carter, "Why Google Rejected This 'Plus-Size' Ad Targeting Gmail Users," *Cosmopolitan,* January 16, 2016.

i. Source: David Orgel, "FreshDirect Targets Multi-Device Strategies," *Supermarket News,* January 20, 2016.

ii. Source: Lauren Johnson, "Sephora Is Driving Mobile Ads with Tinder-Like Features and Digital Mad Libs," *Advertising Age,* July 21, 2016; Scott Davis, "What Hamilton, Sephora and the NFL Have in Common: 2016 Best and Worst Brand Stories," *Forbes,* December 14, 2016; Daphne Howland, "Sephora Launches First-Ever Tinder Ad Campaign," *Retail Dive,* July 22, 2016.

iii. Source: Adrianne Pasquarelli, "Target Kicks Off Aggressive Marketing of New Brands," *Advertising Age,* September 8, 2017; Target, "The Secret to Enviable Style Without Breaking Your Budget? These New, Only-at-Target Brands," July 1, 2017, https://corporate.target.com/article/2017/07/new-brands-announcement; Phil Wahba, "Target Is Ramping Up Store Openings and Remodels in a Bid to Stave Off Walmart," *Fortune,* October 9, 2017; Daphne Howland, "Target Designs Private Label Apparel for Kids with Disabilities," *Retail Dive,* October 19, 2017.

iv. Source: Huge Inc., "Master Plan: IKEA," Huge Inc., 2012; Case Studies, "IKEA and Brandwatch: Embedding Social across the Enterprise," PerformanceIN, March 9, 2015; "IKEA: A Data Matching Love Story," Cream Global, 2012; Matt Kwong, "Building Your Career in Hashtags," *Toronto Star,* March 16, 2015; James Ainsworth, "IKEA Speaks the Language of Emoticons," SmartData Collective, February 12, 2015.

v. Source: Tom Ryan, "Google Tool Offers Local Insights for Merchants," *RetailWire,* October 29, 2015; Angela Moscaritolo, "Discover the Weird Things We Search for on Revamped Google Trends," *PC Magazine,* June 18, 2015.

Quiz Yourself Answer Key

1. _____ tailor their retail strategies toward very specific market segments by offering deep, yet narrow assortments and sales associate expertise.

   Answer: (c). Specialty stores

2. Retailers may modify product, price, and/or promotion to attempt to increase their _____, which is the percentage of a customer's purchases made from that particular retailer.

   Answer: (a). share of wallet

VALUE COMMUNICATION

In Section Seven we explore value communication. Today, value communication methods are more complex because of new technologies that have added e-mail, blogs, Internet, and podcasts to the advertising mix that once utilized only radio, television, newspapers, and magazines to relay messages to consumers. Chapter 18 introduces the breadth of integrated marketing communications. Chapter 19 discusses advertising, public relations, and sales promotions. The text concludes with a discussion of personal selling in Chapter 20.

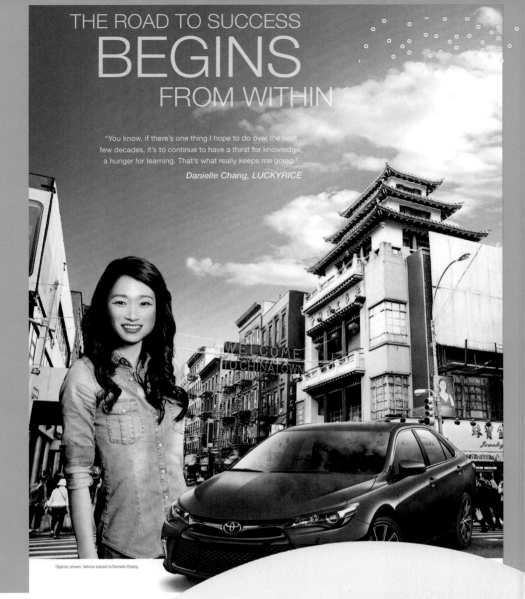

THE ROAD TO SUCCESS
BEGINS
FROM WITHIN

"You know, if there's one thing I hope to do over the next few decades, it's to continue to have a thirst for knowledge, a hunger for learning. That's what really keeps me going."

Danielle Chang, LUCKYRICE

Options shown. Vehicle loaned to Danielle Chang.

LEARNING OBJECTIVES

After reading this chapter, you should be able to:

LO18-1 Identify the components of the communication process.

LO18-2 Explain the four steps in the AIDA model.

LO18-3 Describe the various integrative communication channels.

LO18-4 Explain the methods used to allocate the integrated marketing communications (IMC) budget.

LO18-5 Identify marketing metrics used to measure IMC success.

CHAPTER 18

INTEGRATED MARKETING COMMUNICATIONS

Toyota has been a staple in the automobile industry since it was established 75 years ago. In 2016 Toyota was ranked as the second-largest automobile manufacturer in terms of global sales. Furthermore, its net revenue in 2016 was over $25 billion. One of its best-known cars, the Camry, was launched in the late 1980s and has been a centerpiece of its lineup ever since. However, the dependable Camry has left Toyota with a less than flashy image among customers, until now.[1]

A recent marketing campaign for the Toyota Camry seeks to disrupt and challenge conventional ideas, both in general and for specific customer segments.[2] By creating several distinct advertisements to appeal to different demographic groups, but retaining some consistent elements across all the ads, Toyota aims to establish a new view of the mainstream market that is respectful and transcultural.

The consistent elements in the Camry advertisements include scenes that signal that driving the sedan— long perceived as safe and reliable and thus not a particularly thrilling vehicle option—is actually very exciting. The advertising spots all feature images of the drivers clicking a sport mode button, followed by firing pistons, and then a video of the cars accelerating quickly and taking corners tightly. The featured cars are bright red in color, offering a sense of thrilling excitement. But that's what is similar across the advertisements. Perhaps even more notable is what makes the individual ads different. The actors in the different ads are multiracial, signaling Toyota's attempt at inclusiveness. Moving beyond simple token appearances, though, the commercials also seek to upend stereotypes, in line with the idea of challenging conventional ideas about what the Camry is.

The advertisement featuring an Asian American family, for example, shows a father picking up his daughter from baseball practice. She begins the ride glued to her tablet, but once he starts the music playing and hits the sport mode button, she looks up with joy, prompting an unspoken but affectionate link between them. With these images, Toyota sought to contest the stereotype that Asian fathers can be less demonstrative or involved, and it reiterates the participation of minority families in popular American pastimes such as baseball.

The commercial that appears on Spanish-language channels instead features a single man, driving happily in the sport mode setting, when the dashboard lights up to show that his mother is calling. When he declines the call, the narrative is playing with the stereotypical image that Hispanic children are totally devoted to their parents. With this humorous challenge to this stereotype, Toyota also can highlight just how exciting it is to drive the Camry.

For African American audiences, the male actor featured is found in his bright red car, speeding through streets to the tunes of John Cena's recording "Strut." Although the setting implies that he is just out having an exciting ride, his real goal is to pick up a pizza, which he presumably is about to bring back to his family. So even though he is on a family-oriented errand, by driving the Camry (in sport mode, of course), he can also be hip.

Finally, an advertisement with three separate, parallel stories of people so excited about their driving experiences that they ignore their responsibilities (i.e., a child waiting at school to be picked up, a date, and a business colleague waiting to start a meeting). Each segment features people of different and sometimes indeterminate races. Emphasizing the similarities in their behaviors, Toyota embraces the notion that it calls the "transcultural mainstream," such that a mainstream market no longer implies a problematic focus on white consumers as somehow normative. Rather, Toyota wants to challenge lots of stereotypes—not merely that its cars are boring, but also that society is made up of many, sometimes heterogeneous consumer groups.

Each element of an integrated marketing communications (IMC) strategy must have a well-defined purpose and support and extend the message delivered by all the other elements.

Throughout this book, we have focused our attention on how firms create value by developing products and services. However, consumers are not likely to come flocking to new products and services unless they are aware of them. Therefore, marketers must consider how to communicate the value of a product and/or service—or more specifically, the value proposition—to the target market. A firm must develop a communication strategy to demonstrate the value of its product. We begin our discussion by examining what IMC is, how it has developed, and how it contributes to value creation.

Integrated marketing communications (IMC) represents the promotion dimension of the six Ps. It encompasses a variety of communication disciplines—advertising, personal selling, sales promotion, public relations, direct marketing, and online marketing including social media—in combination to provide clarity, consistency, and maximum communicative impact.[3] Instead of consisting of separated marketing communications channels with no unified control, IMC programs regard each of the firm's marketing communications channels as part of a whole, each of which offers a different means to connect with the target audience. This integration of channels provides the firm with the best means to reach the target audience with the desired message, and it enhances the value story by offering a clear and consistent message.

There are three elements in any IMC strategy: the consumer, the channels through which the message is communicated, and the evaluation of the results of the communication. This chapter is organized around these three elements. In the first section, the focus is on consumers, so we examine how consumers receive communications, whether via media or other methods, as well as how the delivery of that communication affects a message's form and contents. The second section examines the various communication channels that make up the IMC arsenal and how each is used in an overall IMC strategy. The third section considers how the level of complexity in IMC strategies leads marketers to design new ways to measure the results of IMC campaigns.

 LO18-1 Identify the components of the communication process.

COMMUNICATING WITH CONSUMERS

As the number of communication media have increased, the task of understanding how best to reach target consumers has become far more complex. In this section, we examine a model that describes how communications go from the firm to the consumer and the factors

EXHIBIT 18.1 The Communication Process

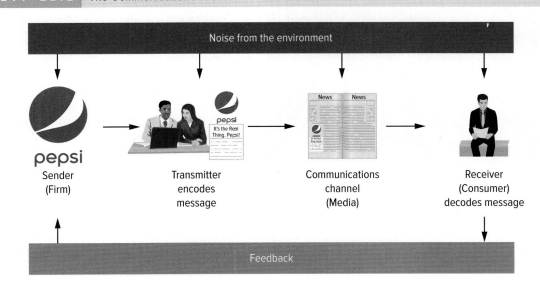

that affect the way the consumer perceives the message. Then we look at how marketing communications influence consumers—from making them aware that a product or service exists to moving them to buy.

The Communication Process

Exhibit 18.1 illustrates the communication process. Let's first define each component and then discuss how they interact.

The Sender The message originates from the sender, who must be clearly identified to the intended audience. As our opening vignette revealed, Pepsi seeks to communicate in new ways with customers, mainly through its packaging and promotional programs. With its emoji campaign and specialized emoji keyboard, for example, Pepsi establishes itself as a source of fun and different emojis that people can use in their daily activities. The Pepsi identity remains clear even with these innovative communications because they consistently highlight its familiar blue, red, and white color scheme and logo images—and also portray happy consumers. Thus people who see and use the newly available emojis know precisely which company made them available. Similarly, when Pepsi introduces new versions—such as the stevia-sweetened True line or the 1893 brand with real sugar—it uses the same color- and shape-based visual reminders that they are Pepsi products, so the sender of the message remains clear and obvious at all times.

The Transmitter The sender works with a creative department, whether in-house or from a marketing (or advertising) agency, to develop marketing communications to highlight the new beverage. With the assistance of its marketing department, Pepsi has developed new mobile and social media tools, together with websites, mobile apps, flyers, in-store displays, and televised

Pepsi emojis encode the message that the iconic drink is associated with fun times and activities when people might likely drink carbonated beverages.

Source: PepsiCo, Inc.

Because the company believes its target market is broad, Pepsi has placed its products in mainstream, popular movies such as Tomorrowland, San Andreas, Jurassic World, Terminator: Genisys, *and* Spider-Man: Homecoming.

Source: Warner Bros. Entertainment Inc

commercials, to tout its brands and what they offer. The marketing department or external agency receives the information and transforms it for use in its role as the **transmitter**.

Encoding **Encoding** means converting the sender's ideas into a message, which could be verbal, visual, or both. Thus the Pepsi emojis signal fun times and activities during which people might be likely to drink carbonated beverages; the grinning face wearing sunglasses and headphones, as if it is ready to head to the beach, is one such emoji.[4] Although a picture can be worth a thousand words, the most important facet of encoding is not what is sent but rather what is received. Consumers must receive information that makes them want to try the new emojis, use Pepsi-linked symbols to communicate with their friends, and continue to purchase new versions of the beverages.

The Communication Channel The **communication channel** is the medium—print, broadcast, the Internet, and so forth—that carries the message. Pepsi could transmit through television, radio, and various print advertisements, but for its emoji campaign, it also made vast and clearly understandable use of social media. The media chosen must be appropriate to connect the sender with the desired recipients. Because the company believes its target market is broad, Pepsi has placed its products in mainstream, popular movies such as *Tomorrowland, San Andreas, Jurassic World, Terminator: Genisys,* and *Spider-Man: Homecoming.*[5] Adding Value 18.1 depicts how Eggo has capitalized on its *Stranger Things* product placement.

Adding Value 18.1   Eleven Loves Eggos; Why Wouldn't Fans of *Stranger Things* Love Them Too?[i]

The hit Netflix series *Stranger Things* is set in the 1980s and also has drawn many comparisons to movies released in that decade. One of the similarities has less to do with style and more to do with the effective use of product placements to create a character, but also create new demand for the product itself. Just as *E.T.: The Extra-Terrestrial* led millions of consumers to start snacking on Reese's Pieces, *Stranger Things* is getting fans to reconsider Eggo waffles.

Kellogg's, which owns the Eggo brand, did not know that its products would appear in the series before it aired. But we can assume it doesn't mind much, considering both the viral marketing benefits it has enjoyed and its response in the lead-up to the second season. In the week prior to the second season's premiere, Eggo mentions on Twitter and Instagram increased almost 150 percent, most of them appearing in the single month before the new season aired.

Then, in addition to granting the series' producers access to its 1980s-era commercials, which they used to promote the upcoming second season, Eggo has developed its own tie-in promotions and products in parallel. In the weeks before Halloween, for example, it provided a list of costume ideas that people could make that integrated empty Eggo boxes. It also published recipes for a nine-course menu that correspond with the nine episodes in the second season, featuring Eggo products, each matched to the title of a different episode.

Does watching Stranger Things *on Netflix make you hungry for Eggo waffles? The Kellogg Company, owner of Eggo, hopes so.*

Source: Netflix

Then at the premiere of the second season, Eggo posted a waffle truck outside the doors, giving attendees a sweet snack. It developed a toaster that can brand waffles with a play on a famous line from the series, which it will send out to influential social media users, along with sample packages of its breakfast foods, in an effort to seed some additional viral marketing.

The Receiver The receiver is the person who reads, hears, or sees and processes the information contained in the message and/or advertisement. The sender, of course, hopes that the person receiving it will be the one for whom it was originally intended. Pepsi wants its message received and decoded properly by a broad population that includes teens, young adults, and families. Decoding refers to the process by which the receiver interprets the sender's message.

Noise Noise is any interference that stems from competing messages, a lack of clarity in the message, or a flaw in the medium. It poses a problem for all communication channels. Pepsi may choose to advertise in newspapers that its target market doesn't read, which means the rate at which the message is received by those to whom it has relevance has been slowed considerably. As we have already defined, encoding is what the sender intends to say, and decoding is what the receiver hears. If there is a difference between them, it is probably due to noise.

Feedback Loop The feedback loop allows the receiver to communicate with the sender and thereby informs the sender whether the message was received and decoded properly. Feedback can take many forms: a customer's purchase of the item, the use of a Pepsi emoji, a complaint or compliment, the redemption of a coupon or rebate, a tweet about the product on Twitter, and so forth.

How Consumers Perceive Communication

The actual communication process is not as simple as the model in Exhibit 18.1 implies. Each receiver may interpret the sender's message differently, and senders often adjust their message according to the medium used and the receivers' level of knowledge about the product or service.

Consumers will perceive this giant billboard differently depending on their level of knowledge and attitude toward the brand.

©imago stock&people/Newscom

Receivers Decode Messages Differently Each receiver decodes a message in his or her own way, which is not necessarily the way the sender intended. Different people shown the same message will often take radically different meanings from it. For example, what does the nearby billboard image convey to you?

If you are a user of this brand, it may convey satisfaction. If you recently went on a diet and gave up your soda, it may convey dismay or a sense of loss. If you have chosen to be a nonuser, it may convey some disgust. If you are a recently terminated employee, it may convey anger. The sender has little, if any, control over what meaning any individual receiver will take from the message.

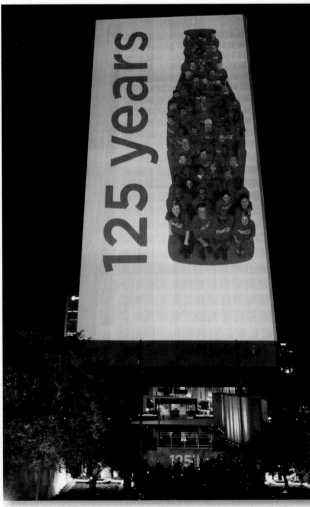

Senders Adjust Messages According to the Medium and Receivers' Traits Different media communicate in varied ways, so marketers make adjustments to their messages and media depending on whether they want to communicate with suppliers, shareholders, customers, the general public, or even specific segments of those groups.[6]

For example, the high-technology firm Analtech sells thin layer chromatography plates to companies that need equipment to determine the ingredients of samples of virtually anything. It is not an easy product to explain and sell to laypeople, particularly when some purchasers might not have a science degree. Therefore, in addition to traditional marketing through trade shows and scientific conferences, Analtech developed a Monty Python–inspired YouTube video (www.youtube.com/watch?v=06gRhDMnPp8) that features a witch who overcomes threats to drown her by proving that the ink in the king's decree is actually from the sheriff's pen. It also highlights points in *CSI* episodes when the television detectives rely on its products. With these more broadly popular appeals, Analtech ensures its messages reach and can be received accurately by a wider audience, with less noise than might occur through more scientific appeals.

LO18-2 Explain the four steps in the AIDA model.

The AIDA Model

Clearly, IMC is not a straightforward process. After being exposed to marketing communications, consumers go through several steps before actually buying or taking some other action. There is not always a direct link between a particular form of marketing communications and a consumer's purchase.

To create effective IMC programs, marketers must understand how marketing communications work. Generally, marketing communications move consumers stepwise through a series of mental stages, for which there are several models. The most common is the AIDA model (Exhibit 18.2),[7] which suggests that **A**wareness leads to **I**nterest, which leads to **D**esire, which leads to **A**ction. At each stage, the consumer makes judgments about whether to take the next step in the process. Customers actually have three types of responses, so the AIDA model is also known as the think, feel, do model. In making a purchase decision, consumers go through each of the AIDA steps to some degree, but the steps may not always follow the AIDA order. For instance, during an impulse purchase, a consumer may feel and do before he or she thinks.

Awareness Even the best marketing communications can be wasted if the sender doesn't gain the attention of the consumer first. Brand awareness refers to a potential customer's ability to recognize or recall that the brand name is a particular type of retailer or product/service. Thus, brand awareness is the strength of the link between the brand name and the type of merchandise or service in the minds of customers.

There are several awareness metrics, including aided recall and top-of-mind awareness. Aided recall is when consumers indicate they know the brand when the name is presented to them. Top-of-mind awareness, the highest level of awareness, occurs when consumers mention a specific brand name first when they are asked about a product or service. For example, Harley-Davidson has top-of-mind awareness if a consumer responds "Harley" when asked about American-made motorcycles. High top-of-mind awareness means that the brand probably enters the evoked set of brands (see Chapter 6) when customers decide to shop for that particular product or service. Manufacturers, retailers, and service providers build top-of-mind awareness by having memorable names; repeatedly exposing their name to customers through advertising, locations, and sponsorships; and using memorable symbols.

As an excellent example of the last method, imagine two smaller circles, sitting on opposite sides atop a larger circle. Did you see Mickey Mouse ears? Did you think of

EXHIBIT 18.2 The AIDA Model

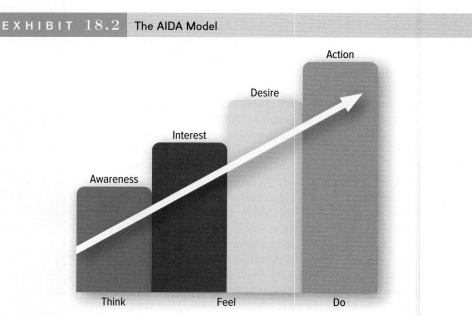

Source: Strong, E. K., *The Psychology of Selling.* New York: McGraw-Hill, 1925.

Disney? In addition, the company has moved on to images brighter than circles to ensure that its name comes easily to the front of young consumers' minds. Whether individual acts—such as Austin Mahone, Selena Gomez, Demi Lovato, and Zendaya—or groups—such as R5, Lemonade Mouth, and Allstar Weekend—Disney starts off its stars with Disney Channel shows, records them on the Disney-owned Hollywood Records label, plays the songs in heavy rotation on Radio Disney and Disney movie soundtracks, organizes concert tours with Disney-owned Buena Vista Concerts, and sells tie-in merchandise throughout Disney stores. Each of these marketing elements reminds the various segments of the target market about both the brand (e.g., One Direction) and its owner, Disney. With this omnichannel approach, Disney gets the same product into more markets than would be possible with a more conservative approach, which further builds top-of-mind awareness for both Disney and its stars.[8]

Is it a car? Or is it a smartphone? Yes.

Now you can synchronize your smartphone with your car and selected apps appear on the display in the centre console.

"Car-Net App-Connect" from Volkswagen.

Think New.

Discover more at www.volkswagen.com/thinknew

Because Volkswagen was suffering as a result of an emissions scandal, it reoriented its marketing campaigns with its new tagline "Think New!"
Source: Volkswagen of America, Inc.

Interest Once the consumer is aware that the company or product exists, communication must work to increase the consumer's interest level. It isn't enough to let people know that the product exists; consumers must be persuaded that it is a product worth investigating. Because Volkswagen was suffering as a result of an emissions scandal, it reoriented its marketing campaigns with its new tagline "Think New!" It also introduced a new mix of family-friendly SUVs and electric vehicles. The cars are designed specifically to appeal to younger car buyers who value high-tech features, such as smartphone integration and easy-to-use interfaces with convenient services such as Apple CarPlay and Google Android Auto. Thus, the ads' messages include attributes that are of interest to the target audience—in this case, young drivers who want a car that is fun to be in, as well as fun to drive.[9] Disney increases interest in an upcoming tour or record by including a mention, whether casual or not, in the stars' television shows. Because the primary target market for the tour is also probably watching the show, the message is received by the correct recipient. As Ethical & Societal Dilemma 18.1 proposes, interest also can be sparked by a little controversy.

Desire After the firm has piqued the interest of its target market, the goal of subsequent IMC messages should move the consumer from "I like it" to "I want it." If Bella Thorne, star of the Freeform (owned by Disney) show *Famous in Love,* appears on *Good Morning America* (on ABC, which is also owned by Disney) to promote an upcoming album or other personal venture, the viewing audience is more likely to tune in to the next episode of *Famous in Love,* watch her old Disney show, *Shake It Up,* or even purchase some of her existing music (produced by Hollywood Records, another subsidiary of Disney).

Action The ultimate goal of any form of marketing communications is to drive the receiver to action. Thus Volkswagen likely aggressively pursues visitors to local dealer websites by following up with phone calls and offering special deals. As long as the message has caught consumers' attention and made them interested enough to consider the product as a means to satisfy a specific desire of theirs, they likely will act on that interest by either searching for the product or making a purchase. If consumers watch Fox's *Empire* or visit Fox's website to

If consumers watch Fox's Empire *or visit Fox's web-site to see what Cookie wore on the show, they might in turn actually purchase the* Empire *original soundtrack on iTunes.*
©Fox Network/Photofest

Ethical & Societal Dilemma 18.1   The Need to Take Risks in IMC[ii]

According to recommendations from a panel of marketing experts, if companies want their communications to resonate and stick with modern customers, they need to run the risk of angering or alienating them too. When marketing campaigns are just regular, "up the middle," or boring, they have little chance of prompting the sorts of behaviors advertisers seek, whether that means getting people to talk or actual sales.

Instead, the goal needs to be to spark interest in the campaign, which then will spark interest in the product or service. Interest might result from an unusual or unexpected presentation—or even a seemingly conventional approach with just a little difference. A key example comes from Honey Maid crackers, which ran a traditional advertising campaign that featured families to communicate a message of wholesomeness. What made the campaign different was the type of families being featured, which included gay parents, single parents, and a multiracial family. For many viewers, the difference was appealing; for those who objected, Honey Maid transformed their often hateful comments into an art piece it could use to further its brand image as wholesome and welcoming.

Rather than challenging biases, other examples are just a little weird, such as a General Electric campaign to introduce

Honey Maid crackers ran an advertising campaign that featured multiracial and other nontraditional families to communicate a message of wholesomeness.
Source: Mondelēz International

an innovation it developed with the social network Quirty, in which an executive gives a foot massage to the inventor of their newly introduced Aros air conditioners. Then there are the fake infomercials directed by the comedy duo behind *Tim & Eric's Bedtime Stories*, which feature the famously distinctive actor Jeff Goldblum hawking GE's new Link LED lightbulbs.

Weird does not work for everybody, but according to these marketing experts, everybody needs to try it. If a marketing communication is not interesting enough to get consumers talking about it, warns one expert, then it is not interesting enough to run.

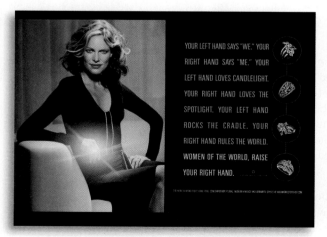

The recurrent presence of De Beers' advertising campaign for diamond jewelry resonates with consumers over time. So, when the occasion arises to buy jewelry for oneself or for a loved one, the consumer will think of diamonds.
Source: DeBeers

see what Cookie wore on the show, they might in turn actually purchase the *Empire* original soundtrack on iTunes.

The Lagged Effect   Sometimes consumers don't act immediately after receiving a form of marketing communications because of the lagged effect—a delayed response to a marketing communications campaign. It generally takes several exposures to a campaign before a consumer fully processes its message.[10] In turn, measuring the effect of a current campaign becomes more difficult because of the possible lagged response to a previous one. The recurrent presence of De Beers' advertising campaign for diamond jewelry resonates with consumers over time. So when the occasion arises to buy jewelry for oneself or for a loved one, the consumer will think of diamonds. But De Beers doesn't know if any particular marketing communication will lead consumers to check out or purchase a new diamond.

Now that we've examined various aspects of the communication process, let's look at how specific media are used in an IMC program.

CHANNELS USED IN AN INTEGRATED MARKETING COMMUNICATIONS STRATEGY

 Describe the various integrative communication channels.

For any communications campaign to succeed, the firm must deliver the right message to the right audience through the right media, with the ultimate goal of profiting from long-term customer relationships rather than just short-term transactions. Reaching the right audience is becoming more difficult, however, as the media environment grows more complicated.

No single channel is necessarily better than another channel; the goal of IMC is to use the channels in conjunction so that the sum exceeds the total of the individual channels. However, advances in technology have led to a variety of new and traditional media channel options for consumers, all of which vie for consumers' attention. Print media have also grown and become more specialized. This proliferation of media has led many firms to shift their promotional dollars from advertising to direct marketing, website development, product placements, and other forms of promotion, all in search of the best way to deliver messages to their target audiences.

We now examine the individual channels of IMC and the way each contributes to a successful IMC campaign (see Exhibit 18.3). The channels can be viewed on two axes: passive and interactive (from the consumer's perspective) and offline and online. Some channels (e.g., advertising, public relations, sales promotion, personal selling, direct and online marketing) are discussed in far more detail in subsequent chapters, so we discuss them here only briefly.

Note that as the marketer's repertoire of IMC channels has expanded, so too have the ways in which marketers can communicate with their customers. So, for instance, direct marketing appears in all four boxes. Firms have expanded their use of these traditional media (e.g., advertising, public relations, and sales promotions) from pure offline approaches to a combination of offline and online.

EXHIBIT 18.3 Channels of an IMC Strategy

Advertising

Perhaps the most visible of the IMC channels, advertising entails the placement of announcements and persuasive messages in time or space purchased in any of the mass media by business firms, nonprofit organizations, government agencies, and individuals who seek to inform and/or persuade members of a particular target market or audience about their products, services, organizations, or ideas.[11] In Chapter 19, we discuss the purpose of advertising and its various types but, for now, note that advertising is extremely effective for creating awareness of a product or service and generating interest. Mass advertising can entice consumers into a conversation with marketers, though it does not necessarily require much action by consumers, which places it on the passive end of the spectrum. Traditionally, advertising has been passive and offline (e.g., television, magazines, newspapers; see Exhibit 18.3), though recently there has been a growth in online advertising and interactive features. Advertising thus must break through the clutter of other messages to reach its intended audience.

Public Relations

Public relations (PR) is the organizational function that manages the firm's communications to achieve a variety of objectives, including building and maintaining a positive image, handling or heading off unfavorable stories or events, and maintaining positive relationships with the media. Like advertising, this tactic is relatively passive in that customers do not have to take any action to receive it. Public relations activities support the other promotional efforts by the firm by generating free media attention, as we discuss further in Chapter 19.

Sales Promotions

Sales promotions are special incentives or excitement-building programs, such as coupons, rebates, contests, free samples, and point-of-purchase (POP) displays, that encourage the purchase of a product or service. Marketers typically design these incentives for use in conjunction with other advertising or personal selling programs. Many sales promotions, such as free samples or POP displays, are designed to build short-term sales. Others, such as contests and sweepstakes, have become integral tactics of some firms' CRM programs as a means to build customer loyalty. We discuss such sales promotions in more detail in Chapter 19.

Personal Selling

Personal selling is the two-way flow of communication between a buyer and a seller that is designed to influence the buyer's purchase decision. Personal selling can take place in various settings: face-to-face, video teleconferencing, on the telephone, or over the Internet. Although consumers don't often interact with professional salespeople, personal selling represents an important channel in many IMC programs, especially in business-to-business (B2B) settings.

The cost of communicating directly with a potential customer is quite high compared with other forms of promotion, but it is simply the best and most efficient way to sell certain products and services. Customers can buy many products and services without the help of a salesperson, but salespeople simplify the buying process by providing information and services that save customers time and effort. In many cases, sales representatives add significant value, which makes the added expense of employing them worthwhile. We devote Chapter 20 to personal selling and sales management.

Direct Marketing

The IMC channel that has received the greatest increase in aggregate spending recently is direct marketing, or marketing that communicates directly with target customers to generate a response or transaction.[12] Direct marketing contains a variety of traditional and new forms of marketing communications initiatives. Traditional direct marketing includes mail and catalogs sent through the mail; direct marketing also includes e-mail and mobile marketing.

Internet-based technologies have had a profound effect on direct marketing initiatives. E-mail, for instance, can be directed to a specific consumer. Firms use e-mail to inform customers of new merchandise and special promotions, confirm the receipt of an order, and indicate when an order has been shipped. Currently available technologies also mean mobile devices can function as a payment medium: Just tap your cell phone, and the transaction occurs in much the same way it occurs with a credit card.

The increased use of customer databases has enabled marketers to identify and track consumers over time and across purchase situations, which has contributed to the rapid growth of direct marketing. Marketers have been able to build these databases, thanks to consumers' increased use of credit and debit cards, store-specific credit and loyalty cards, and online shopping, all of which require the buyer to give the seller personal information that becomes part of its database. Because firms understand customers' purchases better when they possess such information, they can more easily focus their direct marketing efforts appropriately.

Direct marketing retailers try to target their customers carefully so they will be more receptive to their messages. Omaha Steaks, for example, sends e-mail coupons for items that customers have purchased previously, mails slick pictures of gourmet steaks and meal packages to addresses that have received orders in the past, and calls customers personally during likely gift-giving occasions, such as the holidays, to offer to repeat a previous gift order. These different forms of direct marketing demonstrate how this IMC format can vary on both the interactivity and online–offline dimensions of the matrix.

Mobile marketing is marketing through wireless handheld devices such as cellular telephones.[13] Smartphones have become far more than tools to place calls; they offer a kind of mobile computer with the ability to obtain sports scores, weather, music, videos, and text messages as well as purchase merchandise. Marketing success rests on integrating marketing communications with fun, useful apps that are consistent with these consumer attitudes toward mobile devices. In response, firms are steadily improving customers' potential experience with their mobile interface. Exhibit 18.4 highlights four successful mobile marketing campaigns.

Online Marketing

We now examine several electronic media vehicles: websites, blogs, and social media.

Websites Firms have increased their emphasis on communicating with customers through their websites. They use their websites to build their brand image and educate customers about their products or services as well as where they can be purchased. Retailers and some manufacturers sell merchandise directly to consumers over the Internet. For example, in addition to selling merchandise, Office Depot's website hosts a Business Resource Center for its business customers that provides advice, product knowledge, and connections to networking contacts in other businesses. It also provides forms that businesses can use to comply with Occupational Safety and Health Act (OSHA) requirements, check job applicant records,

Cheapflights launched the first search engine that used emojis.

Source: Momondo Group Ltd

EXHIBIT 18.4   Illustrative Mobile Marketing Campaigns

Company	Campaign
Mazda "Don't scroll and drive"	To tackle the problem of being distracted while driving when using a mobile device, Mazda's innovative mobile campaign shows a car racing across the screen, a crash, and then a cracked screen on a cell phone.
BBC Dr. Who Sidekick	When the new season began, the BBC made Dr. Who your mobile sidekick. In the award-winning ad campaign, Dr. Who appears at the bottom of the screen of various high-profile sites. When users clicked on the ad, it would expand and highlight characters on the show.
Cheapflights Emoji search	Cheapflights launched the first search engine that used emojis. It mapped 40 destinations with popular emojis. For example, Sydney, Australia, was represented by a koala; Dublin, Ireland, was represented by a shamrock; and Naples, Italy, was represented with a slice of pizza. The search function was also coupled with a holiday search bot on Facebook Messenger that allowed travelers to search for destinations by weather and currency converter.
Justice League The Gillette League	When DC's Justice League came out, it teamed up with Gillette to create the mobile app "Justice League VR: Join the League Gillette Edition." The app allowed fans to virtually join the League and become a superhero.

Source: Adapted from "5 Best Mobile Campaigns of 2017," *Digital Marketing Institute*, https://digitalmarketinginstitute.com/blog/2017-12-18-5-best-mobile-campaigns-of-2017.

estimate cash flow, and develop a sexual harassment policy; posts workshops for running a business; and summarizes local and national business news. By providing this information, Office Depot reinforces its image as an essential source of products, services, and information for small businesses.

Many firms operate websites devoted to community building. These sites offer an opportunity for customers with similar interests to learn about products and services that support their hobbies and share information with others. Visitors can also post questions seeking information and/or comments about issues, products, and services. Many firms operate websites devoted to community building. These sites offer an opportunity for customers with similar interests to learn about products and services that support their hobbies and share information with others. Visitors can also post questions seeking information and/or comments about issues, products, and services. Social & Mobile Marketing 18.1 shows how an online media site like BuzzFeed is successfully using interactive media by posting interesting videos. Many firms, especially retailers (e.g., Amazon), encourage customers to post reviews of products they have bought or used and even have visitors to their websites rate the quality of the reviews. Research has shown that these online product reviews increase customer loyalty and provide a competitive advantage for sites that offer them.[14]

Blogs   A blog (weblog) contains periodic posts on a common web page. A well-received blog can communicate trends, announce special events, create positive word of mouth, connect customers by forming a community, allow the company to respond directly to customers' comments, and develop a long-term relationship with the company. By its very nature, a blog is supposed to be transparent and

amazon   Try Prime   Hello. Sign in

Departments ⌄   Fire & Kindle ⌄   Prime ⌄   Search

Kitchen & Dining   Best Sellers   Small Appliances   Kitchen Tools   Cookware

Customer Reviews
Presto 03430 Pizzazz Plus Rotating Oven

1,189 Reviews

5 star: (973)
4 star: (138)
3 star: (38)
2 star: (13)
1 star: (27)

Average Customer Review
★★★★☆ (1,189 customer reviews)

Share your thoughts with other customers

[Create your own review]

The most helpful favorable review

377 of 399 people found the following review helpful

★★★★☆ **Mastery of the Cheapie Pizza!**
First of all it's not perfect. The non-stick coating is thin on the pan, and can get scratched off easy. Plus, there's no easy way to clean off the brown, spots you get from baking. All that aside, this is a great device if you like homemade, and frozen varieties of pizza.
I used to try all kinds of tricks to get a frozen pizza to taste good. I'd microwave them...
Read the full review ›

Published on July 29, 2003 by Courtland J. Carpenter

› See more **5 star**, **4 star** reviews

To increase customer loyalty and provide a competitive advantage, firms like Amazon encourage customers to post reviews of products or services they have bought or used.

Source: Amazon.com, Inc.

Social & Mobile Marketing 18.1 — Tasty: A Revolution in Marketing or Just the Latest Example of IMC?[iii]

From one perspective, Tasty—the division of BuzzFeed that is responsible for producing the site's vastly popular, widely viewed videos—is a radically new invention, changing the game and the markets to which it links. From another perspective, though, Tasty is just the latest example of how companies can take a good idea and leverage it across multiple channels to reach consumers wherever they are.

What is new and unique about Tasty? To start, consider that an entire division of the company is dedicated to producing videos, shot from an over-head perspective, of people making food, like "Sliders 4 Ways." This stream of content is hugely popular for BuzzFeed, prompting millions of hits, likes, and views. Its "Cheeseburger Onion Ring" video alone racked up 167 million viewings. Overall, an estimated 1.1 billion views of Tasty content have occurred. Furthermore, Tasty has nearly 90 million followers on Facebook. To support itself, Tasty also makes videos for brands that pay it for its services, so the more popular it is, the more it can attract sellers who will pay to get their products featured.

Such popularity in turn has prompted Tasty to expand its operations to other fields as well, including the publication of a made-to-order cookbook and the development of an app that connects to a small cooktop, which users can program to prepare their food using various cooking methods. This Tasty One Top device thus offers fans their own chance to try sous vide or simmer a pot at home, with the help of the app. By expanding this way, Tasty seemingly is taking a wholly new and innovative route: from an electronic content provider and lifestyle brand to a manufacturer of both physical and electronic products and services.

Tasty, a division of BuzzFeed, produces popular, widely viewed videos, shot from an overhead perspective, of people making food. To make money, Tasty also makes videos for brands that pay for its services.
©Melissa Lyttle/The New York Times/Redux Pictures

The success of Tasty also prompted the Food Network to try its hand at its own version. The new Genius Kitchen has launched with 150 hours of videos, appearing on Facebook and YouTube, as well as Amazon and Apple TV. These videos target the same young consumers whom Tasty has been so successful at reaching, and its content will be similar as well, featuring short videos of hands making original recipes. Genius Kitchen has added a new feature, though: a weekly show starring YouTube personalities Akilah Hughes and Mike Lockyer.

---

contain authors' honest observations, which can help customers determine their trust and loyalty levels. Nowadays, blogs are becoming more interactive as the communication between bloggers and customers has increased. In addition, blogs can be linked to other social media such as the microblog Twitter. See Chapter 3 for further discussion.

Social Media The term social media refers to online and mobile technologies that distribute content to facilitate interpersonal interactions (see Chapter 3). The three most popular facilitators of social media are YouTube, Facebook, and Twitter. In these online sites, consumers review, communicate about, and aggregate information about products, prices, and promotions. These social media also allow users to interact among themselves (e.g., form a community) as well as provide other like-minded consumers (i.e., members of their community) and marketers their thoughts and evaluations about a firm's products or services. Thus, social media help facilitate the consumer decision process (Chapter 6) by encouraging need recognition, information search, alternative evaluation, purchase, and postpurchase reviews.

PROGRESS CHECK

1. What are the different elements of an IMC program?

PLANNING FOR AND MEASURING IMC SUCCESS

We begin this section by examining how marketers set strategic goals before they implement any IMC campaign. After they have established those goals, marketers can set the budget for the campaign and choose the marketing metrics they will use to evaluate whether it has achieved its strategic objectives.

Goals

LO18-4 Explain the methods used to allocate the integrated marketing communications (IMC) budget.

As with any strategic undertaking, firms need to understand the outcome they hope to achieve before they begin. These goals can be short term, such as generating inquiries, increasing awareness, and prompting trial. They can also be long term in nature, such as increasing sales, market share, and customer loyalty. Some other goals are outlined in Exhibit 18.5.

Such goals, both short and long term, should be explicitly defined and measured. Regardless of their measure or changes, though, goals constitute part of the overall promotional plan, which is usually a subsection of the firm's marketing plan. Another part of the promotional plan is the budget.

IT'S A BIG WORLD. GO RUN IT.

Running-shoe manufacturer ASICS devised the "It's a big world. Go run it" campaign to branch out beyond serious runners and to target casual runners.

Source: Asics

Setting and Allocating the IMC Budget

Because all the methods of setting a promotional budget have advantages as well as disadvantages, no one method should be used in isolation.

The **objective-and-task method** determines the budget required to undertake specific tasks to accomplish communication objectives. To use this method, marketers first establish a set of communication objectives, then determine which media best reach the target market and how much it will cost to run the number and types of communications necessary to achieve the objectives. This process—set objectives, choose media, and determine costs—must be repeated for each product or service. The

EXHIBIT 18.5	Illustrative Marketing Goals and Related Campaigns				
Company and Campaign	**Goal**	**Target Market**	**Media Used**	**Outcome**	
ASICS "It's a big world. Go run it."	Branch out beyond serious runner market segment and target casual runners.	Even split males and females, aged 30–49	Television and print ads, online advertising	17% increase in sales	
Columbia Sportswear Company "Tested Tough"	Showcase Columbia's technical innovation ability.	60% males, aged 20–59	Print ads, mobile media, social media, videos, online advertising	11% increase in sales	
Southwest Airlines "Nonstop Love"	To show that Southwest is "an airline with a heart."	Even split males and females, all ages	Television, radio, print, billboard, and in-airport ads	4% increase in revenue	
BMW "#DrivingLuxury"	To highlight the new technology of the redesigned 7 Series sedan.	Mostly men, aged 35 and up	Social media, blog posts, videos	Posts reached up to 13,500 likes on Instagram	

Sources: "ASICS Launches New Global Advertising Campaign, Inspiring People Everywhere to Run with 'It's, a big world. Go run it,'" *PR Newswire*, February 19, 2015; ASICS, 2015 Annual Report, ASICS, February 12, 2016; Karl Greenberg, "Columbia's New Global Campaign Is 'Tested Tough,'" *Marketing Daily*, October 7, 2015; Columbia Sportswear, 2015 Annual Report, Columbia Sportswear, 2016; David Gianatasio, "Southwest Airlines Is Completely, Hopelessly, Head over Heels in Love in New Ads," *Adweek*, July 8, 2014; Southwest Airlines, 2014 Annual Report, March 15, 2015; "BMW's Instagram Influencer Marketing Campaign," Mediakix.

sum of all the individual communication plan budgets becomes the firm's total marketing communications budget. In addition to the objective-and-task method, various *rule-of-thumb methods* can be used to set budgets (see Exhibit 18.6).

These rule-of-thumb methods use prior sales and communication activities to determine the present communication budget. Although they are easy to implement, they have various limitations, as noted in Exhibit 18.6. Clearly, budgeting—not a simple process—may take several rounds of negotiations among the various managers, who are each competing for resources for their own areas of responsibility, to devise a final IMC budget.

Measuring Success Using Marketing Metrics

Once a firm has decided how to set its budget for marketing communications and its campaigns have been developed and implemented, it reaches the point that it must measure the success of the campaigns using various marketing metrics.[15] Each step in the IMC process can be measured to determine how effective it has been in motivating consumers to move to the next step in the buying process. Such measures become particularly challenging when marketing efforts include creative and new forms of communication, as Adding Value 18.2 describes. Furthermore, recall that the lagged effect influences and complicates marketers' evaluations of a promotion's effectiveness as well as the best way to allocate marketing communications budgets. Because of the cumulative effect of marketing communications, it may take several exposures before consumers are moved to buy, so firms cannot expect too much too soon. They must invest in the marketing communications campaign with the idea that it may not reach its full potential for some time. In the same way, if firms cut marketing communications expenditures, it may take time before they experience a decrease in sales.

Traditional Media When measuring IMC success, the firm should examine when and how often consumers have been exposed to various marketing communications. Specifically, the firm uses measures of frequency and reach to gauge consumers' exposure to marketing communications. For most products and situations, a single exposure to a communication is hardly enough to generate the desired response. Therefore, marketers

WELCOME TO THE PACIFIC NORTHWEST. WHERE COUGARS REALLY ARE COUGARS.
GERT BOYLE, CHAIRMAN

Columbia

TESTED TOUGH

SW BROADWAY & TAYLOR

Columbia Sportswear Company's "Tested Tough" campaign's goal is to showcase Columbia's technical innovation ability, here featuring its 93-year-old chairwoman Gert Boyle.
Source: Columbia Sportswear Company

LO18-5 Identify marketing metrics used to measure IMC success.

EXHIBIT 18.6	Rule-of-Thumb Methods	
Method	**Definition**	**Limitations**
Competitive parity	The communication budget is set so that the firm's share of communication expenses equals its share of the market.	Does not allow firms to exploit the unique opportunities or problems they confront in a market. If all competitors use this method to set communication budgets, their market shares will stay approximately the same over time.
Percentage-of-sales	The communication budget is a fixed percentage of forecasted sales.	Assumes the same percentage used in the past, or by competitors, is still appropriate for the firm. Does not take into account new plans (e.g., to introduce a new line of products in the current year).
Available budget	Marketers forecast their sales and expenses, excluding communication, during the budgeting period. The difference between the forecast sales and expenses plus desired profit is reserved for the communication budget. That is, the communication budget is the money available after operating costs and profits have been budgeted.	Assumes communication expenses do not stimulate sales and profit.

Adding Value 18.2   America's Dream Team, Brought to You by Kia[iv]

In North America, spectator sports represent a nearly $64 billion market. Some of that revenue comes from ticket sales to fans who cannot get close enough to the action. But the right to broadcast those sports accounts for an ever-increasing portion of the market's revenue, and as those interests grow, some key priorities are changing too. In particular, the National Basketball Association (NBA) is breaking away from some of its traditional peers by taking a page from soccer and racing leagues: It is considering new sponsorship agreements that place company logos right on the players' uniforms.

Thus far, the new agreement applies only to the uniforms for the 2016 and 2017 All-Star Games, for which the NBA players' uniforms will feature a small, 3.25″ × 1.6″ patch with the name and logo of the automotive brand Kia. Individual teams do not have the league's permission to alter their jerseys similarly, and as of now there are no plans to add advertising patches to regular-season uniforms.

But even in this limited form, the move is still a dramatic change, considering that the NBA—along with its peers, the National Football League, Major League Baseball, and the National Hockey League—has never used them in the past. The uniforms in all these leagues feature logos for the manufacturer of the uniforms, and they often sport commemorative patches to honor important people and personalities who have recently died.

But advertising for other brands has not existed, for several reasons. The uniform manufacturers have resisted it in particular, worried that other ads on the jerseys would compete for consumers' attention. There is also the difficulty of finding an external sponsor that is acceptable to all the teams in the league. In addition, leagues have struggled to define a profit-sharing plan that would be fair. That is, how much of the revenue created by such advertising would go to the league, to the team, or to the players themselves?

For the NBA, Kia's All-Star jersey sponsorship actually was the result of negotiations between the league and Turner Sports, which is the network that owns the broadcast rights for games. When the two parties entered into their most recent

In an unusual partnership between Kia and the NBA, a small Kia logo will appear on players' uniforms, like this one on Anthony Davis, number 23 on the New Orleans Pelicans.
©Justin Sullivan/Getty Images

contract, Turner asked for the right to negotiate with sponsors and sell advertising space on the players' uniforms. In turn, it entered into the two-year marketing agreement with Kia.

Although the NBA and other major sports leagues have little experience with this form of marketing communication, others are far more familiar with it. Drivers as well as their cars are festooned with sponsorship logos in most car-racing leagues. European soccer players also often display logos on their jerseys. One professional—and entrepreneurial—marathon runner sells space on his race kits and bibs to advertisers when he enters big races like the New York Marathon.

Moreover, it isn't as if sponsorships are anything new in sports—on virtually all levels. Another car company, Nissan, recently announced that it had entered into "the widest-reaching sponsorship in the history of collegiate sports." This agreement gives Nissan the rights to place its name and logos in the stadiums of 100 different universities throughout the United States, as well as to use those schools' names in its own advertising.

measure the frequency of exposure—how often the audience is exposed to a communication within a specified period of time.[16] The other measure used to gauge consumers' exposure to marketing communications is reach, which describes the percentage of the target population exposed to a specific marketing communication, such as an advertisement, at least once.[17] Marketing communications managers usually state their media objectives in terms of gross rating points (GRP), which represent reach multiplied by frequency (GRP = Reach × Frequency).

This GRP measure can refer to print, radio, or television, but any comparisons require a single medium. Suppose that Kenneth Cole places seven advertisements in *Vogue* magazine, which reaches 50 percent of the fashion-forward target segment. The total GRP generated by these seven magazine advertisements is 50 reach × 7 advertisements = 350 GRP. Now suppose Kenneth Cole includes 15 television ads as part of the same campaign, run during the program *America's Next Top Model,* which has a rating (reach) of 9.2. The total GRP generated by these 15 advertisements is 138 (9.2 × 15 = 138). However, advertisements typically appear in more than one television program. So, if Kenneth Cole also advertises 12 times during *The Voice,* which earns a rating of 1.8, its GRP would be 1.8 × 12 = 21.6, and the total GRP for both programs would be 138 + 21.6 = 159.6.

Web-Based Media Taken together, firms are spending close to $100.8 billion annually on online advertising, which includes paid search, display ads, e-mail, and sponsorships.[18] Although GRP is an adequate measure for television and radio advertisements, assessing the effectiveness of any web-based communication efforts in an IMC campaign generally requires web-tracking software, which measures how much time viewers spend on particular web pages, the number of pages they view, how many times users click banner ads, which website they came from, and so on. All these performance metrics can be easily measured and assessed using a variety of software, including Google Analytics. Marketing Analytics 18.1 describes how Puma makes use of Google Analytics.

Facebook also helps companies see who has been visiting their fan pages, what those people are doing on the fan pages, and who is clicking their advertisements.[19] By keeping track of who is visiting their fan pages, marketers can better customize the material on their pages by getting to know the people visiting.

When calculating the gross rating points (GRP) of The Voice, *the advertiser would multiply the reach times the frequency.*
©NBC/Photofest

Planning, Implementing, and Evaluating IMC Programs—An Illustration of Google Advertising

Imagine a hypothetical upscale sneaker store in New York City, called Transit, that is modeled after vintage New York City subway trains. Transit's target market is young, well-educated, hip men and women aged 17 to 34 years. The owner's experience indicates the importance of personal selling for this market because these consumers (1) make large purchases and

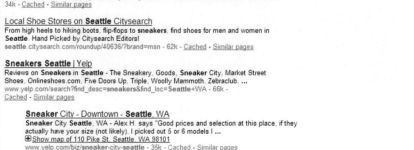

Advertisers pay Google to be listed in the Sponsored Links section in the right-hand column of this screen grab, based on the keywords customers use in their searches.

Source: Alphabet Inc.

Marketing Analytics 18.1   Puma's Use of Google Analytics[v]

The international sports brand Puma offers clothing and accessories alongside its iconic shoes. It enjoys continued success mainly because it has turned to analytics to define its integrated marketing strategies and develop its advertising. When Puma first partnered with Google Analytics, its primary goals were to showcase the breadth of its products online and centralize its online presence. But to compete in the modern age among customers who are accustomed to shopping anywhere at any time, it needed to do more than update its website. Thus, Puma integrated its advertising with its online marketing strategy to devise an overall branded content online strategy.

The insights gained from Google Analytics drive these new advertising and online strategies. For example, Puma launched a new photo-driven site with multiple profiles of famous athletes such as Olympian Usain Bolt and soccer star Mario Balotelli. Instead of traditional web formats, the site weaves the featured apparel together with buy buttons that appear interspersed throughout the content. The new site also was integrated with the brand's "Forever Faster" campaign—a campaign that also featured the same athletes in television commercials and social media campaigns. Although Puma.com is still a relatively small player in the online world, it saw a significant increase in engagement and the number of site visits as a result of these efforts.

Google Analytics also helped Puma develop another aspect of its marketing strategy: By analyzing each product line individually, Puma came to recognize exactly which products and lines were most popular. This analysis in turn revealed the need to improve the visibility of its women's lines. To address this need, Puma decided to add inspirational women to its list of celebrity endorsements, alongside the mostly male athletes it had been featuring. In the hope of reaching more young female customers, for example, Puma named Rihanna as a brand ambassador and creative director of its women's line.

The insights gained from Google Analytics were used to launch a photo-driven site with profiles of famous athletes such as Olympian Usain Bolt and introduce the brand's "Forever Faster" campaign used in television commercials and social media campaigns.

©Jamie McCarthy/Getty Images

(2) seek considerable information before making a decision. Thus, Jay Oliver, the owner, spends part of his communication budget on training his sales associates. Oliver has realized his communication budget is considerably less than that of other sneaker stores in the area. He has therefore decided to concentrate his limited budget on a specific segment and use electronic media exclusively in his IMC program.

The IMC program Oliver has developed emphasizes his store's distinctive image and uses his website, social shopping, and some interesting community-building techniques. Social shopping is the use of the Internet to communicate about product preferences with other shoppers. For instance, he has an extensive customer database as part of his CRM system, from which he draws information for matching new merchandise with his customers' past purchase behaviors. He also has little personal nuggets of information that he or other sales associates have collected on the customers. He then e-mails specific customers information about new products that he believes will be of interest to them. He also encourages customers to use blogs hosted on his website. Customers chat about the hot new sneakers, club events, and races. He does everything with a strong sense of style.

To reach new customers, he is using search engine marketing (SEM). In particular, he is using Google AdWords, a search engine marketing tool offered by Google that allows advertisers to show up in the Sponsored Links section of the search results page based on the keywords potential customers use (see the Sponsored Links section in the right-hand column of the Google screen grab shown earlier).

Oliver must determine the best keywords to use for his sponsored link advertising program. Some potential customers might search using the keywords "sneakers," "sneakers in New York City," "athletic shoes," or other such versions. Using Google AdWords, Oliver can assess the effectiveness of his advertising expenditures by measuring the reach, relevance, and return on investment for each of the keywords that potential customers used during their Internet searches.

To estimate reach, Oliver uses the number of impressions (the number of times the ad appears in front of the user) and the click-through rate (CTR). To calculate CTR, he divides the number of times a user clicks an ad by the number of impressions.[20] For example, if a sponsored link was delivered 100 times and 10 people clicked on it, then the number of impressions is 100, the number of clicks is 10, and the CTR would be 10 percent.

The relevance of the ad describes how useful an ad message is to the consumer doing the search. Google provides a measure of relevance through its AdWords system using a quality score. The quality score looks at a variety of factors to measure how relevant a keyword is to an ad's text and to a user's search query. In general, a high-quality score means that a keyword will trigger ads in a higher position and at a lower cost-per-click.[21] In a search for "sneaker store," the Transit ad showed up fourth, suggesting high relevance.

Using the following formula, Oliver also can determine an ad's return on marketing investment (ROMI):

$$\text{ROMI} = \frac{\text{Gross margin} - \text{Marketing expenditure}}{\text{Marketing expenditure}} \times 100$$

For the two keyword searches in Exhibit 18.8, Oliver finds how much the advertising cost him (Column 3), the sales produced as a result (Column 4), the gross margin in dollars (Column 5), and the ROMI (Column 7). For "sneaker store," the Transit website had a lot more clicks (110) than the clicks received from "New York City sneakers" (40) (see Column 2, Exhibit 18.8). Even though the sales were lower for the keywords "sneaker store" at $35/day, versus $40/day for the keywords "New York City sneakers," the ROMI was much greater for the "sneaker store" keyword combination. In the future, Oliver should continue this keyword

EXHIBIT 18.8 ROMI Assessment

(1) Keyword	(2) Clicks	(3) Marketing Expenditure	(4) Sales	(5) Gross Margin = Sales × Gross Margin% = Sales × 50%	(6) Gross Margin ($) (Col. 5) − Marketing Expenditure (Col. 3)	(7) ROMI = (Col. 6/Col. 3) × 100
Sneaker store	110	$10/day	$70/day	$35/day	$25	250%
New York City sneakers	40	$25/day	$80/day	$40/day	$15	60%

Note: The cost of the sneakers is 50 percent of the sale price.

EXHIBIT 18.9 Program Effectiveness Results

Communication Objective	Question	Before Campaign	Six Months After	One Year After
Awareness (% mentioning store)	What stores sell sneakers?	38%	46%	52%
Knowledge (% giving outstanding rating for sales assistance)	Which stores would you rate outstanding on the following characteristics?	9	17	24
Attitude (% first choice)	On your next shopping trip for sneakers, which store would you visit first?	13	15	19
Visit (% visited store)	Which of the following stores have you been to?	8	15	19

combination, in addition to producing others that are similar to it, in the hope that he will attain an even greater return on investment.

To evaluate his IMC program, Oliver compares the results of the program with his objectives (Exhibit 18.9). To measure his program's effectiveness, he conducted an inexpensive online survey using the questions in Exhibit 18.9, which shows the survey results for one year.

The results show a steady increase in awareness, knowledge of the store, and choice of the store as a primary source of sneakers. This research provides evidence that the IMC program was conveying the intended message to the target audience.

PROGRESS CHECK

1. Why is the objective-and-task method of setting an IMC budget better than the rule-of-thumb methods?
2. How do firms use GRP to evaluate the effectiveness of traditional media?
3. How would a firm evaluate the effectiveness of its Google advertising?

Reviewing Learning Objectives

LO18-1 **Identify the components of the communication process.**

The communication process begins with a sender, which provides the message to a transmitter, which develops or encodes the message for transmission through a communication channel. When a recipient receives the message, it may have been altered by noise in the environment. To find out, the sender needs to receive some form of feedback from the recipient.

LO18-2 **Explain the four steps in the AIDA model.**

Awareness is the first "thinking" step, during which the consumer simply recognizes a brand or product. During the Interest step, the consumer starts to "feel" and become intrigued enough to explore the product or brand. This interest then leads to another feeling, namely, Desire for the marketed item. Finally, to be successful, marketing communication must prompt an Action: a purchase, a commitment,

a recommendation, or whatever else the company is trying to get consumers to do.

LO18-3 **Describe the various integrative communication channels.**

Advertising has long been the primary channel for marketing communication and is still a constant presence, but other media channels have become more and more prominent. For example, direct marketing media options, particularly online options, have increased in recent years. Outbound direct marketing telephone calls have declined, but Internet-based technologies like e-mail and m-commerce have increased. Public relations also has become increasingly important as other media forms become more expensive and as consumers grow more skeptical of commercial messages. With regard to new and electronic media, the wealth of recent options includes websites, corporate blogs, and social media such as YouTube, Facebook, and Twitter.

LO18-4 **Explain the methods used to allocate the integrated marketing communications (IMC) budget.**

Various rule-of-thumb methods rely on prior sales and communication activities to determine the best allocation. For example, the competitive parity method sets the budget so that the share of communication expenses equals the firm's share of the market. The percentage-of-sales method, just as it sounds, uses a fixed percentage of sales as the amount of the budget. In contrast, the objective-and-task method establishes specific communication objectives, identifies which media can best attain those objectives, and then determines the related costs to expend.

LO18-5 **Identify marketing metrics used to measure IMC success.**

Marketers rely on a mix of traditional and nontraditional measures to determine IMC success. Because potential customers generally need to be exposed to IMC messages several times before they will buy, firms estimate the degree to which customers are exposed to a message by multiplying frequency (the number of times an audience is exposed to a message) by reach (the percentage of the target population exposed to a specific marketing communication). Measuring Internet IMC effectiveness requires different measures, such as click-through tracking that measures how many times users click on banner advertising on websites.

Key Terms

- advertising, 550
- AIDA model, 546
- aided recall, 546
- blog (weblog), 552
- brand awareness, 546
- click-through rate (CTR), 559
- communication channel, 544
- decoding, 545
- direct marketing, 550
- encoding, 544
- feedback loop, 545
- frequency, 556
- gross rating points (GRP), 556

- impressions, 559
- integrated marketing communications (IMC), 542
- lagged effect, 548
- mobile marketing, 551
- noise, 545
- objective-and-task method, 554
- personal selling, 550
- public relations (PR), 550
- reach, 556
- receiver, 545
- relevance, 559

- return on marketing investment (ROMI), 559
- rule-of-thumb methods, 555
- sales promotion, 550
- search engine marketing (SEM), 559
- sender, 543
- social media, 553
- social shopping, 559
- top-of-mind awareness, 546
- transmitter, 544
- web tracking software, 557

Marketing Digitally

1. Visit Bluefish's website (bluefish.digital/our-work/timberland-pro-video-content-and-social-media-management/) and read about it's Timberland Pro campaign. What were the goals of the integrated marketing campaign? Which IMC channels were used? How do those channels contribute to the success of the IMC campaign in achieving its stated goals?

Marketing Applications

1. Assume that the contemporary apparel company rag & bone has embarked on a new IMC strategy. It has chosen to advertise on TV during *NBC Nightly News* and in print in *Time* magazine. The message is designed to announce new styles for the season and uses a 17-year-old woman as the model. Evaluate this strategy and, if appropriate, propose an alternative.

2. Using the steps in the AIDA model, explain why a potential consumer in question 1 who views rag & bone's advertising may not be ready to go out and purchase a new pair of jeans.

3. Suppose a snack company introduces a new product called SumSeeds—sunflower seeds with energy boosters

like caffeine, taurine, lysine, and ginseng. How would you expect this product's IMC program to differ from that for regular sunflower seeds sold as snacks?

4. Procter & Gamble sends new parents home from the hospital with a sample of Pampers diapers, and it has started sending Fusion ProGlide razors to each young man in America on his 18th birthday. What are the likely goals of such marketing tactics? How could Procter & Gamble measure how well it has achieved these goals with its free giveaways?

5. Compare and contrast advertising and public relations. How can public relations contribute to a firm's IMC?

6. A hotel runs several advertisements in the student newspaper of a local university, promoting its Sunday brunch menu. The ads increase the number of people visiting its restaurant, but only slightly. Is the campaign necessarily a failure? What other goals might the hotel have for this advertising campaign?

7. Imagine that you work for Puma and are tasked with producing an IMC campaign with a goal of increasing market share by three percent. First, you decide to use traditional and online advertising and public relations to achieve this goal. Finally, you determine the cost of each product to determine the communications budget. What type of IMC budgeting process are you using? Evaluate your strategy compared to a competitive parity budgeting process.

8. You were sitting in the school cafeteria yesterday, and a young man from your marketing class, whom you don't know well, asked if he could sit down. He then started telling you about this very cool new Google app, "WordLens," that allows you to translate signs into different languages in real time using the camera on your smartphone. Although you recognize the merit in the product, you later find out that he works for Google. Do you believe his action constitutes an ethical IMC strategy? How will it affect your attitude toward Google and the potential that you will purchase the product?

Quiz Yourself

1. When designing in-store signage, retailers often develop yellow signs and shelf tags with bold lettering to catch the attention of consumers. The use of visuals in this manner represents the _____ component of the communication process.
   a. communication channel
   b. receiver
   c. feedback
   d. encoding
   e. sender

2. Nathan gauged the level of exposure to his marketing campaign using the percentage of the target population exposed at least once to his advertisement, representing its
   a. reach.
   b. frequency.
   c. relevance.
   d. gross rating points.
   e. return on investment.

(Answers to these two questions can be found in the Quiz Yourself Answer Key section.)

Chapter Case Study

TAKING IMC TO THE MAX: PEPSI MAX AND MODERN COMMUNICATIONS

Pepsi has embraced the communication capabilities of emojis in a big way—you might even say, in a maximal way. Actually, PepsiCo would love it if you used that description, because for its Pepsi Max line of beverages, it actively seeks to establish a consistently cool, cutting-edge perception among consumers, mainly by using integrated marketing campaigns that revolve around the notion of living life "to the max." Let's consider a few of the ways it presents consistent messages across a range of channels.

The very name of the product line provides the foundation for the consistent message. By referring to the carbonated beverage as Pepsi Max, PepsiCo signals that this brand will offer more, greater, and bigger things to consumers. Thus every communication needs to be "to the max" as well—grander, louder, more exciting, more thrilling. In this effort, PepsiCo

Pepsi Max's bus stops allow remarkably realistic videos to play in the windows surrounding the structures. Pepsi Max tapes people's reactions and posts those videos to its YouTube channel.

Source: PepsiCo, Inc.

uses the tagline "Maximum Taste, No Sugar" in combination with hashtags such as #Live-forNow and #Unbelievable on social media.

On its dedicated YouTube channel, Pepsi Max posts videos of people living up to the philosophies embedded in the hashtags, including the "Human Loop the Loop" Damien Walters—a man who seemingly defies gravity (and offers an excellent lesson in centripetal force) in his unbelievable physical feat of running all the way around a vertical loop-the-loop.[22] Other videos on the channel highlight "Amazing Trampoline Tricks" and cool Jump-Cam shots of remarkable feats. The efforts have vastly increased the number of followers and views earned by adrenaline junkies, as well as those who simply find enjoyment in watching seemingly normal people be unbelievable.[23]

Rather than amazing feats by regular people, Pepsi Max's #Maxfootball campaign relies on some of the biggest names in men's soccer, including Sergio Agüero from Man City, James Rodríguez of Real Madrid, Arsenal's Alexis Sánchez, and the goalkeeper David de Gea for Manchester United. In televised advertisements, the players are flashed blue cards (rather than the yellow and red cards that stop play in the game), prompting adventures and fun for the regular people holding them up. One television spot, for example, tells the story of two regular delivery drivers who raise their blue cards and thereby gain magical access to a shooting session with the all-star players, who show off their acrobatic moves and enviable ball-handling skills.[24]

With a linked app, Pepsi Max allows users to enter contests to win similar "Blue Card Experiences," including tickets to the championship game. To increase the coordination across campaigns, the app also features a function that lets users scan the Pepsi emojis on Pepsi Max cans to win other prizes and contest entries.

As if those innovations were not "max" enough, PepsiCo is entering some of the newest channels in unusual ways. Whereas outdoor advertising traditionally has been static and relatively straightforward, Pepsi Max is changing the relationship between this marketing channel and social media. On digital billboards, Pepsi Max posts videos submitted by users to the entertainment network Vine that detail how they #LiveForNow (remember that hashtag?).[25] Drivers passing the billboards thus get to see a quick and exciting video, which they can access again when they get home and log in to their Vine accounts.

With another example of marrying traditional communication forms with modern technology, Pepsi Max also transformed bus stops into adventure zones. Using augmented reality techniques, it has created a system to allow remarkably realistic videos to play in the windows surrounding bus stops. Thus when a rider sits down to wait for the next bus and glances to the right, it appears as though a tiger were literally walking down the street, headed right toward the bus stop. Other videos show a massive meteor ready to obliterate the city street or an alien-looking tentacle grabbing pedestrians nearby.[26] The videos are very short, to avoid truly scaring people, but in those brief moments, more than a few people have experienced some thrilling terror. Of course, Pepsi Max also tapes their reactions and posts those videos to its YouTube channel.

Questions

1. Which channels is Pepsi Max using to communicate its marketing messages? Rank order your impression of how effective they are and justify your answer.

2. How are those various channels integrated?

3. Which IMC channels do these campaigns by Pepsi Max make use of?

Endnotes

1. www.toyota.com; Toyota Motor Company, 2016 Annual Report, Toyota Motor Company, June 24, 2016; Statista, "Leading Motor Vehicle Manufacturers Worldwide in 2016, Based on Global Sales (in Million Units)," 2017, www.statista.com/statistics/275520/ranking-of-car-manufacturers-based-on-global-sales/.

2. Sapna Maheshwari, "Different Ads, Different Ethnicities, Same Car," *The New York Times*, October 12, 2017.

3. J. Craig Andrews and Terence Shimp, *Advertising Promotion and Other Aspects of Integrated Marketing Communications*, 10th ed. (Boston: Cengage Learning, 2018).

4. PepsiCo, "Universal Language," http://design.pepsico.com/pepsimoji.php?v=20#section5.

5. Abe Sauer, "Announcing the 2016 Brandcameo Product Placement Awards," *BrandChannel*, February 24, 2016, http://brand-channel.com/2016/02/24/2016-brandcameo-product-placement-awards-022416/; "Spider-Man: Homecoming (2017) Product Placement Scenes," *Product Placement Blog*, https://productplacementblog.com/tag/spider-man-homecoming-2017/.

6. Andrews and Shimp, *Advertising Promotion and Other Aspects of Integrated Marketing Communications*.

7. E. K. Strong, *The Psychology of Selling* (New York: McGraw-Hill, 1925).

8. Disney, "Music," http://music.disney.com; Phil Gallo, "Disney Music Tops Interscope in Album Market Share, Enters the EDM Fray," *Billboard*, May 10, 2014, www.billboard.com.

9. E. J. Schultz, "Thinking New: Inside Volkswagen's Plans to Become Relevant Again," *Advertising Age*, January 11, 2017.

10. Andrews and Shimp, *Advertising Promotion and Other Aspects of Integrated Marketing Communications*; Christine Köhler et al, "A Meta-Analysis of Marketing Communication Carryover Effects," *Journal of Marketing Research* 54, no. 6 (2017), pp. 990–1008.

11. American Marketing Association, "Advertising," *Dictionary of Marketing Terms*, www.ama.org/resources/Pages/Dictionary.aspx.

12. George E. Belch and Michael A. Belch, *Advertising and Promotion: An Integrated Marketing Communications Perspective*, 11th ed. (New York: McGraw-Hill Education, 2017).

13. Randi Priluck, *Social Media and Mobile Marketing Strategy* (New York: Oxford University Press, 2016); Roger Strom, Martin Vendel, and John Bredican, "Mobile Marketing: A Literature Review on Its Value for Consumers and Retailers," *Journal of Retailing and Consumer Services* 21, no. 6 (2014), pp. 1001–12.

14. Kristopher Floyd et al., "How Online Product Reviews Affect Retail Sales: A Meta-Analysis," *Journal of Retailing* 90, no. 2 (2014), pp. 217–32.

15. Paul Farris et al., *Marketing Metrics: The Manager's Guide to Measuring Marketing Performance*, 3rd ed. (Upper Saddle River, NJ: Pearson Education, 2016); Constantine S. Katsikeas et al., "Assessing Performance Outcomes in Marketing," *Journal of Marketing* 80, no. 2 (2016), pp. 1–20.

16. Susanne Schmidt and Martin Eisend, "Advertising Repetition: A Meta-Analysis on Effective Frequency in Advertising," *Journal of Advertising* 44, no. 4 (2015), pp. 415–28.

17. Laura Lake, "Learn about Market Reach and Why It's Important," *The Balance*, June 26, 2017, www.thebalance.com/what-is-market-reach-2295559.

18. Laurie Sullivan, "Digital Ad Spend to Surpass Traditional in 2018, per Analyst," *Media Post*, January 12, 2018, www.media-post.com/publications/article/312891/digital-ad-spend-to-surpass-traditional-in-2018-p.html.

19. Facebook, "Facebook Pages: Insights for Your Facebook Page," www.facebook.com.

20. Google, "Clickthrough Rate (CTR): Definition," https://support.google.com/adwords/answer/2615875?hl=en.

21. Google, "Quality Score: Definition," https://support.google.com/adwords/answer/140351?hl=en.

22. www.youtube.com/watch?v=OTcdutIcEJ4.

23. "How Pepsi Max's 'Unbelievable' YouTube Channel Helped Increase Market Share," *Think with Google*, November 2014, www.thinkwithgoogle.com/intl/en-gb/case-studies/how-pepsi-maxs-unbelievable-youtube-channel-helped-increase-market-share.html.

24. Tony Connelly, "Pepsi Max Launches Star-Studded Football Ad Campaign to Coincide with Its Emoji Marketing," *The Drum*, February 23, 2016, www.thedrum.com/news/2016/02/23/pepsi-max-launches-star-studded-football-ad-campaign-coincide-its-emoji-marketing.

25. Emma Hall, "Pepsi Max Puts Vine Videos on U.K. Billboards," *Advertising Age*, February 20, 2014.

26. Jessica Gioglio, "Pepsi Max Shocks and Delights Londoners with Augmented Reality Stunt," *Convince and Convert*, n.d.,

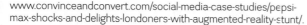

www.convinceandconvert.com/social-media-case-studies/pepsi-max-shocks-and-delights-londoners-with-augmented-reality-stunt/.

i. Sources: Jessica Wohl, "How Eggo Is Playing Up Its Moment in the 'Stranger Things' Spotlight," *Advertising Age*, October 16, 2017; Thomas Barrabi, " 'Stranger Things' Boosts Kellogg's Eggo Waffles on Social Media," *Fox Business*, October 31, 2017; Joe Otterson, " 'Stranger Things' Partners with Eggo, Lyft ahead of Season 2 Premiere," *Variety*, October 25, 2017.

ii. Source: Stuart Elliot, "Marketers Are Urged to Become Fearless," *The New York Times*, September 30, 2014.

iii. Sources: Farhad Manjoo, "How BuzzFeed's Tasty Conquered Online Food," *The Wall Street Journal*, July 27, 2017; Mike Shields, "The Food Network Wants Its Own Version of BuzzFeed's Tasty," *Business Insider*, September 19, 2017, www.businessinsider.com/the-food-networks-parent-company-is-trying-to-take-on-buzzfeed-2017-9.

iv. Sources: Sarah Germano, "NBA to Put Kia Logo on Front of All-Star Jerseys," *The Wall Street Journal*, October 28, 2015; E. J. Schultz, "Nissan Goes Big with College Sports in New Sponsorship Deal," *Advertising Age*, November 6, 2015.

v. Sources: Google Analytics, "Case Study: Puma Kicks Up Order Rate 7% with Insights from Google Analytics and Viget," 2013; Caitlin Carter, "Rihanna Signs on as Puma's New Creative Director," *Music Times*, December 16, 2014; Puma, "Rihanna: Gamechanger," Puma.com; Lucia Moses, "Inside Puma's Branded Content Strategy," *Digiday*, December 15, 2014; Aaron Ricadela, "Puma's Marketing Strategy Is a Whole New Ball Game," *Business World*, September 19, 2014; Larissa Faw, "Puma Adds New Channels to Its 'Forever Faster' Campaign," *Media Post*, August 26, 2014.

Quiz Yourself Answer Key

1. When designing in-store signage, retailers often develop yellow signs and shelf tags with bold lettering to catch the attention of consumers. The use of visuals in this manner represents the _____ component of the communication process.

   Answer: (d) encoding

2. Nathan gauged the level of exposure to his marketing campaign using the percentage of the target population exposed at least once to his advertisement, representing its

   Answer: (a) reach

The People First Warranty*

6 Yrs/72,000 Mi
Bumper-to-Bumper
Limited Warranty

Volkswagen drivers have always put others first, & now we're returning the favor.

Volkswagen

6 years/72,000 miles (whichever occurs first). New Vehicle Limited Warranty on MY2018 VW vehicles, excluding e-Golf. See owner's literature or dealer for warranty exclusions and limitations.

LEARNING OBJECTIVES

After reading this chapter, you should be able to:

LO19-1 Describe the steps in designing and executing an advertising campaign.

LO19-2 Identify three objectives of advertising.

LO19-3 Describe the different ways that advertisers appeal to consumers.

LO19-4 Identify the various types of media.

LO19-5 Identify agencies that regulate advertising.

LO19-6 Describe the elements of a public relations toolkit.

LO19-7 Identify the various types of sales promotions.

CHAPTER 19

ADVERTISING, PUBLIC RELATIONS, AND SALES PROMOTIONS

The history of Volkswagen (VW) features notable images and events, both positive and negative. Although its image and brand personality have remained closely linked to the peace-loving hippie movement, VW also suffered a massive hit to its reputation when the company's attempts to falsify emissions data came to light. The more recent events had serious negative implications for the brand, prompting a new advertising campaign that seeks to skip over the emissions scandal to remind customers that VW has been their "lifelong companion" by showing happy images from more distant decades. Volkswagen hopes the nostalgic campaign will remind customers of their emotional connection to the company.

In particular, and notably, the new advertising campaign never shows any modern VWs. Instead, it highlights old models of the brand's microbus and Beetle. It also features actors dressed as hippies, engaging in altruistic behaviors such as helping push one another's cars out of the mud. It first tested this campaign in Europe in 2016,

as its first major advertising campaign since the "Dieselgate" scandal, before launching it in the United States.

By highlighting this positive, warm image of VW and the people who purchase its cars, the company finds a way to promote the service it has newly started offering, namely, a six-year warranty that exceeds any other bumper-to-bumper warranties offered by other car companies. The tagline reminds viewers that "VW drivers have always put others first; now we are returning the favor."

In emphasizing these ethical notions of collaboration and community, VW also explicitly is avoiding talking about the ways that it failed to live up to those standards. The emissions scandal revealed that the company had found some sneaky workarounds that enabled it to indicate that its vehicles were releasing less pollution into the air than they actually were. Many buyers felt betrayed by the failure and shifted their loyalties to other car companies.

But the brand's sales have already started to rebound, such that now its primary goal is to regain its status and positive image. The advertising encourages that effort, but VW also notes that its real promise to customers comes from the new warranty. By providing a longer, better guarantee than other automobile manufacturers, VW is seeking to reestablish itself as trustworthy and supportive.

It is a relevant strategy, though not one that every company could copy. Volkswagen benefits from its long and well-established image, as well as its close connection to an appealing and nostalgic time in history. The hippies thus appear to be helping, yet again.[1]

Advertising is a paid form of communication delivered through media from an identifiable source about an organization, product, service, or idea designed to persuade the receiver to take some action now or in the future.[2] This definition provides some important distinctions between advertising and other forms of promotion, which we discussed in the previous chapter. First, advertising is not free; someone has paid, with money, trade, or other means, to get the message shown. Second, advertising must be carried by some medium—television, radio, print, the web, T-shirts, sidewalks, and so on. Third, legally, the source of the message must be known or knowable. Fourth, advertising represents a persuasive form of communication designed to get the consumer to take some action. That desired action can range from "ask us questions" to "perceive us as responsive" to "buy more McNuggets for your kids."

Advertising encompasses an enormous industry and clearly is the most visible form of marketing communications—so much so that many people think of marketing and advertising as synonymous. Global advertising expenditures are approximately $584 billion, and almost half that amount is spent in North America. Although expenditures have dropped somewhat, advertising remains virtually everywhere, and predictions are that it will continue to grow.[3]

Yet how many of the advertisements you were exposed to yesterday do you remember today? Probably not more than three or four. As you learned in Chapter 6, perception is a highly selective process. Consumers simply screen out messages that are not relevant to them, and young consumers appear particularly good at doing so. For example, an astounding 92 percent of Millennial consumers indicated that while they watch television, they simultaneously and constantly check their mobile devices.[4] Thus, televised ads are unlikely to capture their attention for long, if at all. Then, if you do notice an advertisement, you may not react to it. Even if you remember the ad, you may not remember the brand or sponsor—or worse yet from the advertiser's point of view, you may remember it as an advertisement for another brand.[5]

As we discussed in Chapter 18, the increasing number of communication channels and changes in consumers' media usage have made the job of advertisers far more difficult.[6] Advertisers continually endeavor to use creativity and various media to reach their target markets. In a public service campaign against domestic violence, the nonprofit organization Women's Aid raised interactive billboards, picturing a battered woman's face and the words "Look At Me." When people walking by stopped to look, facial recognition software embedded in the billboard recognized their actions, and the picture changed, such that the bruises healed. The creative approach not only attracted people's attention but also resonated with the underlying message—namely, that attention to a societal problem can be meaningful for solving the problem.[7]

As a consumer, you are exposed only to the end product—the finished advertisement—but many actions must take place before you actually get to see an ad. In this chapter, we examine the ingredients of a successful advertising campaign from identifying a target audience to creating the actual ad to assessing performance. Although our discussion is generally confined to advertising, much of the process for developing an advertising campaign is applicable to the IMC media vehicles discussed in Chapter 18. We conclude with some regulatory and ethical issues for advertising, then move on to public relations and sales promotions and their use.

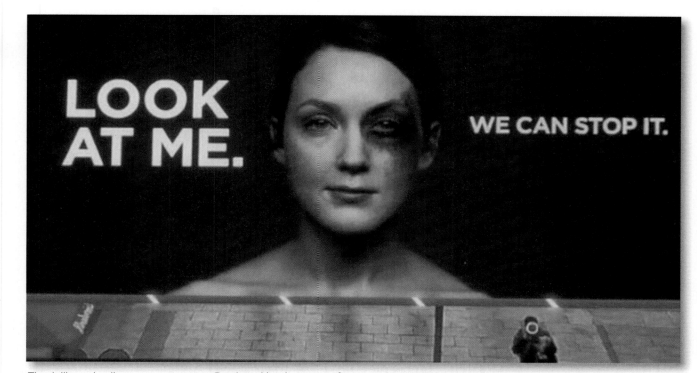

This billboard will get your attention. Produced by the nonprofit organization Women's Aid, this interactive billboard for battered women changes as people walk by and notice. The bruises heal.

Source: WomensAid.org

Designing and carrying out a successful advertising program requires much planning and effort. Exhibit 19.1 shows the key steps in the process, each of which helps ensure that the intended message reaches the right audience and has the desired effect. We examine these steps in the sections that follow.

STEP 1: IDENTIFY TARGET AUDIENCE

LO19-1 Describe the steps in designing and executing an advertising campaign.

The success of an advertising program depends on how well the advertiser can identify its target audience. Firms conduct research to identify their target audience, then use the information they gain to set the tone for the advertising program and help them select the media they will use to deliver the message to that audience.

During this research, firms must keep in mind that their target audience may or may not be the same as current users of the product. For example, Puma knows that FIFA fans likely are at least familiar with its offerings, even if they do not currently purchase sports gear from Puma. Thus some advertisements feature the international football (or

EXHIBIT 19.1 Steps in Planning and Executing an Ad Campaign

Step 1	Step 2	Step 3	Step 4	Step 5	Step 6	Step 7
Identify target audience	Set advertising objectives	Determine the advertising budget	Convey the message	Evaluate and select media	Create advertisements	Assess impact

Puma uses different ads to appeal to different target markets. Jozy Altidore (left) appeals to soccer fans, whereas Selena Gomez (right) attracts teenaged pop music fans.

Source: PUMA NA

soccer) star Jozy Altidore to encourage them to buy more of the brand's products.[8] But teenaged pop music fans might be less likely to pay attention to sporting goods, so Puma also brought in Selena Gomez to put her name on its Phenom line and appear in related advertising.[9]

STEP 2: SET ADVERTISING OBJECTIVES

The objectives of an advertising campaign are derived from the overall objectives of the marketing program and clarify the specific goals that the ads are designed to accomplish. Generally, these objectives appear in the advertising plan, a subsection of the firm's overall marketing plan that explicitly analyzes the marketing and advertising situation, identifies the objectives of the advertising campaign, clarifies a specific strategy for accomplishing those objectives, and indicates how the firm can determine whether the campaign was successful.[10] An advertising plan is crucial because it will later serve as the yardstick against which advertising success or failure is measured.

Generally, in advertising to consumers, the objective is a pull strategy, in which the goal is to get consumers to pull the product into the marketing channel by demanding it. Push strategies also exist and are designed to increase demand by focusing on wholesalers, retailers, or salespeople. These campaigns attempt to motivate the seller to highlight the product, rather than the products of competitors, and thereby push the product to consumers. In this chapter, we focus on pull strategies. Push strategies are examined in Chapters 14, 16, and 20.

All advertising campaigns aim to achieve certain objectives: to inform, persuade, and remind customers. Another way of looking at advertising objectives is to examine an ad's focus. Is the ad designed to stimulate demand for a particular product or service or more broadly for the institution in general? Also, ads can be used to stimulate demand for a product category or an entire industry or for a specific brand, firm, or item. We first look at the broad overall objectives: to inform, persuade, and remind. Then we examine advertising objectives based on the focus of the ad: product versus institutional.

Informative Advertising

LO19-2 Identify three objectives of advertising.

Informative advertising is a communication used to create and build brand awareness, with the ultimate goal of moving the consumer through the buying cycle to a purchase. Such advertising helps determine some important early stages of a product's life cycle (see Chapter 12), particularly when consumers have little information about the specific product

Is this product-focused advertisement designed to inform, persuade, or remind consumers about Pepsi Max?

Source: PepsiCo, Inc.

Lancôme's persuasive ads attempt to motivate consumers to take action: Try the product, switch brands, or continue to buy the product.

©Bill Aron/PhotoEdit

or type of product. Retailers often use informative advertising to tell their customers about an upcoming sales event or the arrival of new merchandise.

Persuasive Advertising

When a product has gained a certain level of brand awareness, firms use persuasive advertising to motivate consumers to take action. Persuasive advertising generally occurs in the growth and early maturity stages of the product life cycle, when competition is most intense, and attempts to accelerate the market's acceptance of the product. In later stages of the product life cycle, persuasive advertising may be used to reposition an established brand by persuading consumers to change their existing perceptions of the advertised product. As Ethical & Societal Dilemma 19.1 describes, Volkswagen is using advertising to try to persuade consumers to trust it again after several recent scandals. Consumer goods firms such as Lancôme often use persuasive advertising to convince consumers to take action—switch brands,[11] try a new product, or even continue to buy the advertised product.

Reminder Advertising

Finally, reminder advertising is a communication used to remind or prompt repurchases, especially for products that have gained market acceptance and are in the maturity stage of their life cycles. Such advertising certainly appears in traditional media, such as television or print commercials, but it also encompasses other forms of advertising. For

Ethical & Societal Dilemma 19.1　Volkswagen Tries to Put Emissions Woes Behind as It Vows to "Think New"ⁱ

Is it possible for Volkswagen to come back from the emissions cheating scandal and resulting betrayal of consumer trust? The company hopes so, and in support of that effort, it plans to "Think New!" That is, Volkswagen has shelved its long-running "Das Auto" tagline in favor of the new phrase, as the company tries to make a fresh start and rebuild its brand.

To win back the trust of auto consumers and stay relevant in the U.S. market, Volkswagen has introduced a new mix of family-friendly SUVs and electric vehicles. The cars are designed specifically to appeal to younger car buyers who value high-tech features, such as smartphone integration and easy-to-use interfaces with convenient services such as Apple CarPlay and Google Android Auto. With this innovative tack, Volkswagen hopes to lure drivers back to drive vehicles that are fun to be in, as well as fun to drive.

Prior to the emissions scandal in 2015, the company heavily relied on its so-called clean diesel vehicles to appeal to environmentally friendly consumers; 20 percent of the company's total U.S. sales featured such vehicles. Losing this market, as well as contending with an overall reduction in VW sales, has made it hard for the company to turn the page and start anew.

It has taken several steps forward in these efforts though. Volkswagen of America has been granted new autonomy from its German headquarters, allowing the company the freedom to respond to the changing market demands in the United States. The company thus hopes to fill a void in its current product line with a new seven-passenger SUV. It also has expressed its goal to emerge as one of the leaders in the electric car market, with ambitious plans to sell 1 million electric cars globally by 2025.

Even with a fresh lineup of cars and SUVs, the road to redemption in the hearts and minds of the American people will be slow to come. The company plans to continue its aggressive spending on advertising, in which it will highlight new vehicle offerings along with a consistent, core message that leverages remaining nostalgia for the brand and outlines what it stands for—as well as where the company wants to go in the future.

Volkswagen is using a new advertising campaign, "Think New," to try to persuade consumers to trust it again after several recent scandals.

Source: Volkswagen of America, Inc.

example, if you decide to buy facial tissue, do you carefully consider all the options, comparing their sizes, prices, and performance, or do you just grab the first thing you see on the shelf? When your grocery store places a display of Kleenex facial tissues on the end of the paper products aisle, it relies on your top-of-the-mind awareness of the Kleenex brand, which the manufacturer has achieved through advertising. That is, Kleenex tissue maintains a prominent place in people's memories and triggers their response without them having to put any thought into it. The advertising and the end cap display thus prompt you and many other consumers to respond by buying a package, just the response Kleenex hoped to attain.

Focus of Advertisements

An ad campaign's objectives determine each specific ad's focus. The ad can be product focused, might have an institutional focus, or could have a public service focus. **Product-focused advertisements** inform, persuade, or remind consumers about a specific product or service. The Kleenex ad shown here is designed to generate sales for Kleenex.

An **institutional advertisement** is a type of advertising that promotes a company, corporation, business, institution, or organization. Unlike product-focused advertisements, it is not intended to sell a particular product or service. An ongoing and well-known institutional advertising campaign promotes GE's Ecomagination.[12] In the past, GE was thought to be one of the world's least "green" companies. Since 2005 GE, through its Ecomagination program, has devoted millions of dollars toward cleaner technologies including water purification technology and lower-emissions aircraft engines, and the development of cleaner energy such as wind and solar power. The program has been so successful that *Fortune* named it as one of the world's top global green brands.[13]

A specific category of institutional advertising is **public service advertising (PSA)**. PSAs focus on public welfare; generally they are sponsored by nonprofit institutions, civic groups, religious organizations, trade associations, or political groups.[14] Like institutionally and product-focused advertising, PSAs also inform, persuade, or remind consumers, but the focus is for the betterment of society. As such, PSAs represent a form of **social marketing**, defined as the application of marketing principles to a social issue to bring about attitudinal and behavioral change among the general public or a specific population segment.

Country music singer Thomas Rhett is the spokesperson for a PSA for "Outnumber Hunger," which was designed to raise awareness of the hunger problem in America.[15] Sponsored by General Mills, Big Machine Label Group, and Feeding America,[16] Rhett has

This ad is designed to remind consumers that when you need tissues, don't think too hard. Just pick up a box of Kleenex.
Image Courtesy of The Advertising Archives

Ecomagination 10 Year Anniversary: Driving Big Impacts for our Customers and Community

Power
~40 GW
Clean Energy Installed

Water
1B Gallons/Day
Wastewater Treated

Transportation
3T Ton
Rail Miles Traveled

The GE Ecomagination program is institutional advertising in that it promotes the company and its "green" programs, not specific products.
Source: General Electric

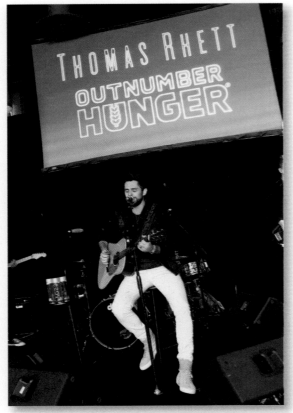

Entertainer Thomas Rhett is the spokesperson for a PSA called Outnumber Hunger, designed to raise awareness of the hunger problem in America.

©Rick Diamond/Getty Images

appeared in special concert events and has been featured on more than 60 General Mills product packages, including Cheerios and Nature Valley. For each General Mills product code entered by its customers at OutnumberHunger.com, five meals are acquired for local Feeding America food banks.[17]

Due to the nature of PSAs, broadcasters often donate free airtime to them. Also, because they often are designed by top advertising agencies for nonprofit clients, PSAs usually are quite creative and stylistically appealing.

Regardless of whether the advertising campaign's objective is to inform, persuade, or remind, with a focus on a particular product or the institution in general, each campaign's objectives must be specific and measurable. For a brand awareness campaign, for example, the objective might be to increase brand awareness among the target market by 50 percent within six months. Another campaign's goal may be to persuade 10 percent of a competitor's customers to switch to the advertised brand. Once the advertising campaign's objectives are set, the firm sets the advertising budget.

STEP 3: DETERMINE THE ADVERTISING BUDGET

The various budgeting methods for marketing communications (Chapter 18) also apply to budgeting for advertising. First, firms must consider the role that advertising plays in their attempt to meet their overall promotional objectives. Second, advertising expenditures vary over the course of the product life cycle. Third, the nature of the market and the product influence the size of advertising budgets. The nature of the market also determines the amount of money spent on advertising. For instance, less money is spent on advertising in B2B (business-to-business) marketing contexts than in B2C (business-to-consumer) markets. Personal selling, as we discuss in Chapter 20, likely is more important in B2B markets.

STEP 4: CONVEY THE MESSAGE

In this step, marketers determine what they want to convey about the product or service. First, the firm determines the key message it wants to communicate to the target audience. Second, the firm decides what appeal would most effectively convey the message. We present these decisions sequentially, but in reality they must be considered simultaneously.

The Message

The message provides the target audience with reasons to respond in the desired way. A logical starting point for deciding on the advertising message is to tout the key benefits of the product or service. The message should communicate its problem-solving ability clearly and in a compelling fashion. In this context, advertisers must remember that products and services solve problems, whether real or perceived. That is, people are not looking for 1/4-inch drill bits; they are looking for 1/4-inch holes to hang a picture on the wall.[18] Because there are many ways to make a 1/4-inch hole, a firm like Stanley Black & Decker must convey to consumers that its drill bit is the best way to get that hole.

Another common strategy differentiates a product by establishing its unique benefits. This distinction forms the basis for the unique selling proposition (USP) or the value proposition (as discussed in Chapter 9), which is often the common theme or slogan in an advertising campaign. A good USP communicates the unique attributes of the product and thereby becomes a snapshot of the entire campaign. Some of the most famous USPs include the following:

Red Bull . . . Gives You Wings

Ford . . . Built Ford Tough

Oreo . . . Milk's Favorite Cookie

TNT . . . Drama.

Kellogg's Corn Flakes Is The Original and Best Cereal

The New York Times . . . All The News That's Fit to Print

Trek . . . Believe in Bikes

Vail . . . Like Nothing On Earth

The selling proposition communicated by the advertising must be not only unique to the brand but also meaningful to the consumer. It furthermore must be sustainable over time, even with repetition.

The Appeal

Advertisers use different appeals to portray their products or services and persuade consumers to purchase them, though advertising tends to combine the types of appeals into two categories: informational and emotional.

Informational Appeals   Informational appeals help consumers make purchase decisions by offering factual information that encourages consumers to evaluate the brand favorably on the basis of the key benefits it provides.[19] Thus, ads for the Sexy Green Car Show in Cornwall, UK, espouse multiple ways in which consumers can educate themselves and act in a more environmentally conscious manner when it comes to their automobiles. This appeal is well suited to this type of product: By informing consumers about a potential source of its competitive advantage, including tangible features and images of science, the advertising copy directly delivers an informational, persuasive message.

Milk's Favorite Cookie

VAIL Like nothing on earth.™

Unique selling propositions like these by Oreo (top) and Vail (bottom) send powerful messages about the benefits of their offerings.

(Top): Source: Mondelēz Global LLC; (bottom): Source: Vail Resorts Management Company

LO19-3   Describe the different ways that advertisers appeal to consumers.

WELCOME TO THE SEXY GREEN CAR SHOW!

WITH THE CLIMATE IN TROUBLE AND OIL EXPENSIVE, CARS NEED TO GET GREENER. FAST.

Driving a more climate-friendly car doesn't mean compromising style, safety or performance:

- There is a beautiful green machine for every pocket and every taste, and a newer car of the same size is generally a greener one. Go shopping with a clean conscience.
- Find out here how new technologies in engines, fuels and bodies are making cars more efficient, and how some neglected old technology is helping out too.
- Visit the Rainforest Biome to see biofuel plants growing.
- Go to the Core for the organic race car, electric car races for schools, and how to green up your driving.
- Get the kids to try Racing Green in the Dome tent next door.
- Don't forget to check your tyre pressures at Lemon car park on the way out!

PROUD TO BE SPONSORED BY

Ads for the Sexy Green Car Show in Cornwall, UK, espouse multiple ways in which consumers can educate themselves and act in a more environmentally conscious manner when it comes to their automobiles.

©Global Warming Images/Alamy Stock Photo

EXHIBIT 19.2	Emotional Appeals in Advertising	
Emotional Appeal	**Company**	**Example**
Fear/safety	National Highway Transportation Safety Administration (NHTSA)	"Secure his future in the correct car seat"
Humor	Orbit Gum	"Don't Let Lunch Meet Breakfast"
Happiness	Instagram	"Stories Are Everywhere"
Love/sex	Mr. Clean	"You Gotta Love a Man Who Cleans"
Comfort	Charmin Ultra Soft	"Embrace Your Softer Side—The Softer, More Cushiony Way to Get Clean"
Nostalgia	Heinz	"Pass the Heinz"

The UK insurance agency John Lewis uses a tender emotional appeal in an ad featuring a little girl dancing to "Tiny Dancer" while almost breaking everything in the room.

Source: John Lewis Home Insurance

Emotional Appeals An emotional appeal aims to satisfy consumers' emotional desires rather than their utilitarian needs. These appeals therefore focus on feelings about the self.[20] The key to a successful emotional appeal is the use of emotion to create a bond between the consumer and the brand. In its advertising, the UK insurance agency John Lewis highlights what really makes homeowner's insurance important, like the daughter in a family who simply must dance to "Tiny Dancer" but whose embellished twirls and leaps put everything in the home at risk of being broken. With both humor and tenderness (see www.youtube.com/watch?v=YqgoUWPx4eE), the advertising gives an emotional appeal to a service that many consumers regard as boring and unappealing.[21] Exhibit 19.2 shows firms and examples of the most common types of emotional appeals: fear/safety, humor, happiness, love (or sex),[22] comfort, and nostalgia.[23]

STEP 5: EVALUATE AND SELECT MEDIA

The content of an advertisement is tied closely to the characteristics of the media that firms select to carry the message, and vice versa. Media planning refers to the process of evaluating and selecting the media mix—the combination of the media used and the frequency of advertising in each medium—that will deliver a clear, consistent, compelling message to the intended audience.[24] For example, Macy's may determine that a heavy dose of television, radio, print, and billboards is appropriate for the holiday selling season between Thanksgiving and the end of the year.

Because the media buy, the actual purchase of airtime or print pages, is generally the largest expense in the advertising budget, marketers must make their decisions carefully. Television advertising is by far the most expensive. To characterize these various types of media, we use a dichotomy: mass and niche media.

LO19-4   Identify the various types of media.

Mass and Niche Media

Mass media channels include outdoor/billboards, newspapers, magazines, radio, and television and are ideal for reaching large numbers of anonymous audience members. Niche media channels are more focused and generally used to reach narrower segments, often with unique demographic characteristics or interests. Specialty television channels (e.g., HGTV) and specialty magazines (e.g., *TransWorld Skateboarding* or *Popstar! Magazine*) all provide examples of niche media. The Internet provides an opportunity to appeal to the masses

Which emotional appeals are these ads from NHTSA, Orbit Gum, and Instagram using?

(Left): Source: US Department of Transportation; (middle): Source: WM. Wrigley Jr. Company; (right): Source: Facebook, Inc.

through ads on the home page of Internet sites such as www.comcast.net or www.yahoo.com or more niched opportunities such as an American Express business card on the *Wall Street Journal* site (www.wsj.com). An example of a more targeted niche media is a direct mailer. As Ethical & Societal Dilemma 19.2 shows, a historical ad that may have been attention getting or funny at the time would now invoke ethical concerns.

Choosing the Right Medium

For each class of media, each alternative has specific characteristics that make it suitable for meeting specific objectives (see Exhibit 19.3).[25] For example, consumers use different media for different purposes, to which advertisers should match their messages. Television is used primarily for escapism and entertainment, so most television advertising relies on a mix of visual and auditory techniques.

Communication media also vary in their ability to reach the desired audience. For instance, radio is a good medium for products such as grocery purchases or fast food because many consumers decide what to purchase either on the way to the store or while in the store.

EXHIBIT 19.3	**Types of Media Available for Advertising**

Medium	Advantages	Disadvantages
Television	Wide reach; incorporates sound and video.	High cost; several channel and program options; may increase awareness of competitors' products.
Radio	Relatively inexpensive; can be selectively targeted; wide reach.	No video, which limits presentation; consumers give less focused attention than TV; exposure periods are short.
Magazines	Very targeted; subscribers pass along to others.	Relatively inflexible; takes some time for the magazine to be available.
Newspapers	Flexible; timely; able to localize.	Can be expensive in some markets; advertisements have short life span.
Internet/mobile	Can be linked to detailed content; highly flexible and interactive; allows for specific targeting.	Becoming cluttered; the ad may be blocked by software on the computer.
Outdoor/ billboard	Relatively inexpensive; offers opportunities for repeat exposure.	Is not easily targeted; has placement problems in some markets; exposure time is very short.
Direct marketing	Highly targeted; allows for personalization.	Cost can vary depending on type of direct marketing used; traditional media, like mail, will be more expensive than newer media.

Ethical & Societal Dilemma 19.2   It's Both Cute and Horrifying: A Historical Ad That Tries to Get Toddlers to Chew More Gum[ii]

A recently unearthed direct-mail piece from around 1938 offers a stellar example of how much marketing ethics has shifted over the years. The advertisement by the Wrigley Company involves a letter addressed to a toddler, suggesting that turning two years old marks the perfect occasion to start chewing gum. It also enclosed a stick of gum for the child to try.

That in itself seems pretty remarkable; sending a stick of gum to a child who might not even have teeth sounds crazy. But the Wrigley Company, and its founder William Wrigley Jr., firmly believed that if the company could catch consumers' attention and loyalty early, it could keep them hooked on Wrigley's gum for their whole lives. To encourage trials, the company sent millions of letters to toddlers across the country, each enclosed with a stick of gum.

The letter also makes several promises that today would not pass the bar for truth in advertising. For example, it claims that gum is good for children's teeth—better than the "modern soft food" they get—and that it can help with the pain of teething. Both these claims are demonstrably untrue, though it is unclear if Wrigley knew that or if the company, at that time, simply did not have the necessary science in hand. That is, many people believed that chewing gum was good for their teeth. Only more recently did we realize that the benefits only outweigh the harms if the gum is free of sugar. Similarly, gum is unlikely to do much for teething toddlers, but it might be better than another old remedy, which recommended putting alcoholic spirits on a toddler's gums to resolve the discomfort.

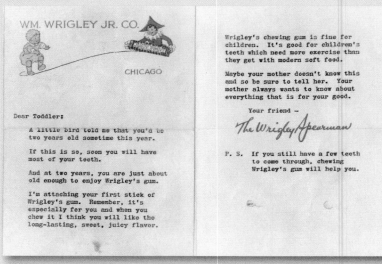

Marketing ethics has shifted considerably since the 1930s when this Wrigley Company direct-mail promotion appeared.

Source: Mars, Incorporated

The funny little direct mailer thus highlights how far marketing has come, but also how it remains similar. Getting consumers to exhibit lifelong loyalty to a product is still a central goal for marketing, and promising remarkable benefits from product consumption is a widespread tactic. But it is rare today to find marketing explicitly targeting toddlers. Increased regulations also demand that product benefit claims be backed up by actual evidence and science.

Because many people listen to the radio in their cars, it becomes a highly effective means to reach consumers at a crucial point in their decision process. Mobile advertising also is becoming more important, as Social & Mobile Marketing 19.1 explains. As we discussed in Chapter 18, each medium also varies in its reach and frequency. Advertisers can determine how effective their media mix has been in reaching their target audience by calculating the total GRP (Reach × Frequency) of the advertising schedule, which we discuss next.

Determining the Advertising Schedule

Another important decision for the media planner is the advertising schedule, which specifies the timing and duration of advertising. There are three types of schedules:

- A continuous schedule runs steadily throughout the year and therefore is suited to products and services that are consumed continually at relatively steady rates and that require a steady level of persuasive and/or reminder advertising. For example, Procter & Gamble advertises its Tide brand of laundry detergent continuously.

- Flighting refers to an advertising schedule implemented in spurts, with periods of heavy advertising followed by periods of no advertising. This pattern generally functions for products whose demand fluctuates, such as suntan lotion, which manufacturers may advertise heavily in the months leading up to and during the summer.

Social & Mobile Marketing 19.1

What Comes Around: Just as Digital Has Pushed Out Traditional, Mobile Is Pushing Out Digital Advertising[iii]

The signs of the growth of mobile advertising, at the expense of digital forms, have long been evident. But the speed with which this shift is occurring seemingly is taking many marketers by surprise, because it is virtually unprecedented.

Consider some of the numbers: In 2018, mobile advertising in the United States was over $70 billion. This represented 75 percent of digital advertising spending, and a 21,775 percentage growth rate from 2008.

Both forms are similar, in the sense that they are clearly distinct from traditional advertising and seek to reach technologically savvy shoppers. But they require unique approaches and marketing plans because a campaign that works well on a user's desktop computer might not function effectively on a tablet or smartphone. Furthermore, mobile advertising offers functionalities and advertising tactics that digital ads cannot provide. Mobile advertising also allows brands and marketers to send timely, location-based communications to consumers at the moment they enter a store or begin a search for a nearby restaurant on their phones.

Another trend occurring apace with this shift is the rise of ad-blocking technology. Apple now allows users to install software to block banner ads in digital channels. Although consumers indicate that they would like the ability to block advertising in mobile settings as well, marketing messages contained within apps continue to be prevalent. In this sense, advertisers might seek to expand their mobile marketing so as to avoid the barriers that consumers can implement on their desktops.

In the longer term, though, the shift to more mobile advertising likely implies the need for new forms of marketing communication, including game-oriented, social content, and informational advertising that does not really look like advertising at all.

- Pulsing combines the continuous and flighting schedules by maintaining a base level of advertising but increasing advertising intensity during certain periods. For example, airlines, hotels, and car rental companies might continuously advertise to ensure brand awareness but might increase the advertising in spikes during certain low-demand periods.

STEP 6: CREATE ADVERTISEMENTS

After the advertiser has decided on the message, type of ad, and appeal, its attention shifts to the actual creation of the advertisement. During this step, the message and appeal are translated creatively into words, pictures, colors, and/or music. (Adding Value 19.1 highlights the pros and cons of using popular music in television advertising campaigns.) Often, the execution style for the ad will dictate the type of medium used to deliver the message. To demonstrate an image, advertisers can use television and magazines. To promote price, they can use newspapers and radio. To appeal to specific target markets, they can use some of the electronic media vehicles described in Chapter 18. When using multiple media to deliver the same message, however, they must maintain consistency across styles—that is, integrated marketing—so that the different executions deliver a consistent and compelling message to the target audience.

How do advertisers go about creating advertisements? They simultaneously consider the objectives of the ad, the targeted customer segment(s), the product or service's value proposition or the unique selling proposition, and how the ad will be coordinated with other IMC elements.

They then go about creating an ad or the ad campaign. Using the print ad for the Ila DUSK personal alarm shown on the right as an example, the first component that the reader generally notices is the visual, and as such it should be eye-catching. The picture of the personal alarm on a chain is attractive and feminine. Although it is not always possible to meet all possible objectives with the visual, other important purposes are to identify the subject of the ad, show the product being used and its unique features, create a favorable impression of the product or advertiser, and arouse the readers' interest in the headline, which is generally noticed second.[26]

The headline is the large type in an ad that is designed to draw attention. In the Ila DUSK personal alarm ad, the headline "ILA PERSONAL ALARM" simply identifies the product. But the subhead, a smaller headline,

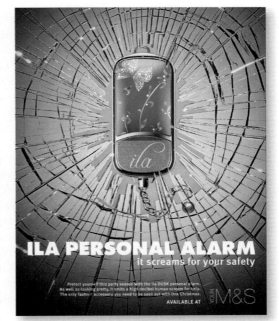

Image Courtesy of The Advertising Archives

Adding Value 19.1   Selling Out or Selling Well? The Use and Choice of Popular Music in Advertising Campaigns[iv]

What's your reaction when one of your favorite songs by one of your favorite bands pops up in a commercial for a brand you might or might not love? Do you groan, annoyed that some hard-rocking rebel or cutting-edge artist has sold the rights to the song for advertising purposes? Or do you smile, pleased to hear your preferred song, and thus feel more affection for the brand being advertised? Obviously, marketers hope that your reaction is the latter one, but in many cases, consumers express attitudes more in line with the former.

The hits keep coming though. During a recent Super Bowl, Acura relied on Van Halen's "Runnin' with the Devil" to introduce the latest model of its NSX sports car. Other advertisers use cover versions of popular songs or seek out relatively unknown artists with a cool sound to add an appropriate vibe to their marketing communications. The various options come with different costs: Licensing a popular song by a well-known musician can cost hundreds of thousands of dollars for a single use with a massive audience, like a Super Bowl commercial. If the brand chooses to use the song in an extended campaign, the licensing costs can easily reach millions. Cover versions of popular songs generally are more affordable, though the songwriter still earns licensing fees. Most affordable of all is new music by unfamiliar artists because many of these musicians are happy mainly for the exposure that the advertising campaign offers them. As it becomes increasingly challenging to succeed in the music industry, such benefits, together with the promise of long-term residual income, make the licensing of music a popular and compelling option for struggling (or not-so-struggling) artists.

Was Van Halen's "Runnin' with the Devil" a good song to accompany a Super Bowl ad to introduce a new model of Acura's NSX sports car?

Source: Acura

But choosing the right song for a marketing campaign involves more than considering the price. If the tone of the song does not match the marketing context, it can create cognitive dissonance. Thus for example, using "Cat's in the Cradle," the melancholy Harry Chapin song about fathers and sons that makes virtually every listener cry, might not have been the best choice for a Nissan advertisement. Furthermore, reactions to songs are intensely personal, which makes it difficult for marketers to predict consumers' reactions. Many people obviously love Van Halen, but there are those for whom the sound of David Lee Roth's voice is deeply annoying. A song might remind an individual listener of a particularly good or particularly bad time in his or her life, with parallel effects on the consumer's perception of the product being advertised with that song. So will the effect be wonderful, or will it be terrible, and how are marketers to predict the answer in advance?

provides more information about the alarm it is selling; specifically, "it screams for your safety." Headlines and subheads should be short and use simple words and include the primary product or service benefits, the name of the brand, and an interest-provoking idea. They should ideally contain an action verb and give enough information for learning even if only the headline is read.

The body copy represents the main text portion of the ad. It is used to build on the interest generated by the visual and headlines, explains in more depth what the headline and subheads introduced, arouses desire for the product, and provides enough information to move the target consumer to action. In this case, the body copy, "Protect yourself this party season with the Ila DUSK personal alarm. As well as looking pretty, it emits a high decibel human scream for help. The only fashion accessory you need to be seen out with this Christmas," tells the story of this product and its use. This particular body copy is necessarily longer than for other products because it requires some explanation—the other ad elements are insufficient to explain and sell the product.

Finally, the ad typically has a number of brand elements that identify the sponsor of the ad, typically through a logo (M&S, which is the logo for Marks & Spencer department store in the United Kingdom) and a unique selling proposition (not found in this ad). Thus the advertiser must convey its message using compelling visuals, headlines, body copy, and identifying brand elements.

Although creativity plays a major role in the execution stage, advertisers must remain careful not to let their creativity overshadow the message. Whatever the execution style, the advertisement must be able to attract the audience's attention, provide a reason for the audience to spend its time viewing the advertisement, and accomplish what it set out to do. In the end, the execution style must match the medium and objectives.

Automobile manufacturers and dealers are among the most active advertisers and use very different messages in their advertising campaigns. Consider, for instance, two well-known car companies that have SUV models, each with very different advertising campaigns.

- **Hyundai Kona.** The brand-new subcompact SUV is designed to appeal to Millennials and first-time car buyers. Therefore, its smaller size than competing SUVs makes it easier to maneuver in cities. Likely advertising outlets include young adult–oriented television spots and social media to get young consumers, who tend to care about technology, attached to the new model.[27]

- **Subaru Outback.** With a focus on dependability, recent ads for the Outback show a family with the same SUV throughout many lifetime milestones. Furthermore, it emphasizes its standard all-wheel drive by showing families driving to outdoor activities, such as hiking. With these appeals, Subaru is focusing largely on TV and magazine spots targeted to families.[28]

These ads for two SUVs stress very different messages. The ad for the Hyundai subcompact SUV, Kona (top), is designed to appeal to Millennials and first-time car buyers who appreciate its small size because they live in urban areas. The ad for the Subaru Outback (bottom) is designed to attract families interested in participating in outdoor activities.

(Top): Source: Hyundai Motor Company; (bottom): Source: Subaru of America, Inc.

STEP 7: ASSESS IMPACT USING MARKETING METRICS

The effectiveness of an advertising campaign must be assessed before, during, and after the campaign has run. **Pretesting** refers to assessments performed before an ad campaign is implemented to ensure that the various elements are working in an integrated fashion and doing what they are intended to do.[29] **Tracking** includes monitoring key indicators such as daily or weekly sales volume while the advertisement is running to shed light on any problems with the message or the medium. **Posttesting** is the evaluation of the campaign's impact after it has been implemented. At this last stage, advertisers assess the sales and/or communication impact of the advertisement or campaign.

Measuring sales impact can be especially challenging because of the many influences other than advertising on consumers' choices, purchase behavior, and attitudes. These influences include the level of competitors' advertising, economic conditions in the target market, sociocultural changes, in-store merchandise availability, and even the weather—all of

EXHIBIT 19.4   Hypothetical Sales History for Red Bull in a Grocery Store Chain

Sales volume is a good indicator of advertising effectiveness for frequently purchased consumer goods in the maturity stage of the product life cycle, such as Red Bull energy drink.
©McGraw-Hill Education/Jill Braaten, photographer

which can influence consumer purchasing behavior. For instance, the sales resulting from even the best ads can be foiled by a lack of merchandise in the stores or a blizzard. Advertisers must try to identify these influences and isolate those of the particular advertising campaign.

For frequently purchased consumer goods in the maturity stage of the product life cycle, such as soda, sales volume offers a good indicator of advertising effectiveness. Because their sales are relatively stable, and if we assume that the other elements of the marketing mix and the environment have not changed, we can attribute changes in sales volume to changes in advertising. Exhibit 19.4 illustrates a hypothetical sales history for Red Bull in a grocery store chain. Using a statistical technique called time-series analysis, sales data from the past are used to forecast the future. The data in Exhibit 19.4 can be decomposed into their basic trend (red), the seasonal influences (orange), and the lift or additional sales caused by the advertising (yellow). In this case, the lift caused by the advertising campaign is substantial.

For other types of goods in other stages of the product life cycle, sales data offer only one of the many indicators that marketers need to examine to determine advertising effectiveness. For instance, in high-growth markets, sales growth alone can be misleading because the market as a whole is growing. In such a situation, marketers measure sales relative to those of competitors to determine their relative market share. Firms find creative ways to identify advertising effectiveness. For example, digital cable allows firms to present a specific advertisement to certain neighborhoods and then track sales by local or regional retailers.

PROGRESS CHECK

1. What are the steps involved in planning an ad campaign?
2. What is the difference between informational, persuasive, and reminder advertising?
3. What are the pros and cons of the different media types?
4. How can the effectiveness of advertising be evaluated?

REGULATORY AND ETHICAL ISSUES IN ADVERTISING

LO19-5 Identify agencies that regulate advertising.

In the United States, the regulation of advertising involves a complex mix of formal laws and informal restrictions designed to protect consumers from deceptive practices.[30] Many federal and state laws, as well as a wide range of self-regulatory agencies and agreements, affect advertising (Exhibit 19.5). The primary federal agencies that regulate advertising activities are the Federal Trade Commission (FTC), the Federal Communications Commission (FCC), and the Food and Drug Administration (FDA). In addition to these agencies, others such as the Bureau of Alcohol, Tobacco, Firearms and Explosives and the U.S. Postal Service regulate advertising to some degree.

The FTC is the primary enforcement agency for most mass media advertising, although occasionally it cooperates with other agencies to investigate and enforce regulations on particular advertising practices. In one recent case, the FTC charged Pure Green Coffee, a Florida company, with false advertising and misrepresentation in its efforts to sell green coffee beans as a weight-loss aid. The company not only promised more benefits of the coffee beans than have been proven but also created fake websites designed to look like news outlets. It also used logos from *The Dr. Oz Show* to imply that the popular television personality endorsed the product.[31]

Many product categories fall under self-regulatory restrictions or guidelines. For example, advertising to children is regulated primarily through self-regulatory mechanisms designed by the National Association of Broadcasters and the Better Business Bureau's Children's Advertising Review Unit. The only formal regulation of children's advertising appears in the Children's Television Act of 1990, which limits the amount of advertising broadcast during children's viewing hours.[32]

Recently, to make matters even more complicated for advertisers, state attorney general offices have begun to inquire into various advertising practices and assert their authority to regulate advertising in their states. The European Union also has increased its regulation of advertising for member nations. Many of these state and European regulations are more restrictive than existing U.S. federal requirements.

The line between what is legal and illegal is more difficult to discern when it comes to puffery, which is the legal exaggeration of praise, stopping just short of deception, lavished on a product. When Match.com claims that it leads to "better first dates," it's puffery because *better* is a subjective measure. But if it claims it produces "more second dates," it must be able to back up its numerical, quantitative assertion. Even cartoon bears must follow the rules: Charmin's

EXHIBIT 19.5	Federal Agencies That Regulate Advertising	
Federal Agency	**General Purpose**	**Specific Jurisdiction**
Federal Trade Commission (FTC) (1914)	Enforces federal consumer protection laws.	Enforces truth in advertising laws; defines deceptive and unfair advertising practices.
Federal Communications Commission (FCC) (1934)	Regulates interstate and international communications by radio, television, wire, satellite, and cable.	Enforces restrictions on broadcasting material that promotes lotteries (with some exceptions); cigarettes, little cigars, or smokeless tobacco products; or that perpetuates a fraud. Also enforces laws that prohibit or limit obscene, indecent, or profane language.
Food and Drug Administration (1930)	Regulates food, dietary supplements, drugs, cosmetics, medical devices (including radiation-emitting devices such as cell phones), biologics (biological issues), and blood products.	Regulates package labeling and inserts, definition of terms such as *light* and *organic*, and required disclosure statements (warning labels, dosage requirements, etc.).
The U.S. Postal Service (USPS) (1971)	Delivers mail and packages.	Regulates advertising that uses the mail and that involves fraud, obscenity, or lotteries.
Bureau of Alcohol, Tobacco, Firearms and Explosives (ATF) (1972)	Regulates manufacturing and sales of alcohol, tobacco, firearms, and explosives.	Regulates the advertising for alcohol, including warning labels, and determines what constitutes false or misleading advertising.

animated spokescharacters need to be drawn with a few pieces of toilet paper on their rears, instead of none, to ensure that Charmin's claims extend only to leaving less toilet paper behind than other brands (puffery), not eliminating the problem altogether (deception).[33]

How do the courts determine what makes an ad deceptive rather than simply puffery? The FTC's position is that it "will not pursue cases involving obviously exaggerated or puffing representations, i.e., those that ordinary consumers do not take seriously."[34] In general, the less specific the claim, the less likely it is considered to be deceptive. In the end, puffery is acceptable as long as consumers know that the firm is stretching the truth through exaggeration.[35]

PUBLIC RELATIONS

As you may recall from Chapter 18, **public relations (PR)** involves managing communications and relationships to achieve various objectives such as building and maintaining a positive image of the firm, handling or heading off unfavorable stories or events, and maintaining positive relationships with the media. In many cases, public relations activities support other promotional efforts by generating free media attention and general goodwill.

Is this ad an example of puffery or deception?

Image Courtesy of The Advertising Archives

Designers, for example, vie to have celebrities, especially those nominated for awards, wear their fashions on the red carpet. Their brands offer intangible benefits, not just

Saoirse Ronan's great popularity meant that she could wear Versace to the Golden Globes (left), then switch to Calvin Klein for the Academy Awards (right), and garner press for both design firms.

(Left): ©Venturelli/WireImage/Getty Images; (right): ©Steve Granitz/WireImage/Getty Images functional benefits. Events such as the Oscars, with its 35 million annual viewers, provide an unparalleled opportunity to showcase the emotional benefits of the brand and make others want to be a part of it. Thus, the celebrities whom designers pursue and offer their items to are those who will sell the most or provide the best iconic images. Saoirse Ronan's great popularity meant that she could wear Versace to the Golden Globes, then switch to Calvin Klein for the Academy Awards, and garner press for both design firms.[36] The placement of designer apparel at media events benefits both the designer and the celebrity. And neither happens by accident. Public relations people on both sides help orchestrate the events to get the maximum benefit for both parties.

Eight-year-old Neftali and singer Yunel Cruz (right) hold up colored-in peppers as they support Chili's "Create-A-Pepper to Fight Childhood Cancer" for St. Jude Children's Research Hospital.
©Taylor Hill/Getty Images

Good PR has always been an important success factor. Yet in recent years, the importance of PR has grown as the costs of other forms of marketing communications have increased. At the same time, the influence of PR has become more powerful as consumers have become increasingly skeptical of marketing claims made in other media.[37] In many instances, consumers view media coverage generated through PR as more credible and objective than any other aspects of an IMC program because the firm does not buy the space in print media or time on radio or television.

Certainly the Chili's restaurant chain conducts plenty of media buys in traditional advertising spaces. But it also has partnered with St. Jude's Children's Research Hospital in one of the most successful examples of cause-related marketing (i.e., commercial activity in which businesses and charities form a partnership to market an image, product, or service for their mutual benefit)[38] in history. For several years, the restaurant has offered customers the opportunity to purchase a paper icon—in the shape of a chili pepper, naturally—that they may color and hang on restaurant walls. Customers also have the option to donate to St. Jude through their tabletop using Ziosk. Chili's is also a platinum sponsor for the St. Jude Walk/Run to End Childhood Cancer. It has raised more than $63 million for St. Jude.[39]

LO19-6 Describe the elements of a public relations toolkit.

Another very popular PR tool is event sponsorship. Event sponsorship occurs when corporations support various activities (financially or otherwise), usually in the cultural or sports and entertainment sectors. Red Bull is a frequent sponsor of various kinds of sports events, such as Red Bull Air Race and numerous extreme sports events (e.g., cliff diving). Some of them are big-name events; the titles of most college football playoff games now include the name of their sponsors (e.g., the Allstate Sugar Bowl). Others are slightly less famous; for example, Rollerblade USA, the maker of Rollerblade in-line skates, sponsors Skate-In-School, a program it developed with the National Association for Sport and Physical Education (NASPE) to promote the inclusion of rollerblading in physical education curricula.

Part of Red Bull's PR toolkit is its event sponsorship of a cliff-diving event.
©James Davies/Alamy Stock Photo

Firms often distribute PR toolkits to communicate with various audiences. Some toolkit elements are designed to inform specific groups directly, whereas others are created to generate media attention and disseminate information. We describe the various elements of a PR toolkit in Exhibit 19.6.

EXHIBIT 19.6 Elements of a Public Relations Toolkit

PR Element	Function
Publications: brochures, special-purpose single-issue publications such as books	Inform various constituencies about the activities of the organization and highlight specific areas of expertise.
Video and audio: programs, public service announcements	Highlight the organization or support cause-related marketing efforts.
Annual reports	Give required financial performance data and inform investors and others about the unique activities of the organization.
Media relations: press kits, news releases, speeches, event sponsorships	Generate news coverage of the organization's activities or products/services.
Electronic media: websites, e-mail campaigns	Websites can contain all the previously mentioned toolbox elements; e-mail directs PR efforts to specific target groups.

PROGRESS CHECK

1. Why do companies use public relations as part of their IMC strategy?
2. What are the elements of a public relations toolkit?

LO19-7 Identify the various types of sales promotions.

SALES PROMOTION

Advertising rarely provides the only means to communicate with target customers. As we discussed in Chapter 18, a natural link appears between advertising and sales promotion. Sales promotions are special incentives or excitement-building programs that encourage consumers to purchase a particular product or service, typically used in conjunction with other advertising or personal selling programs. Many sales promotions, like free samples or point-of-purchase (POP) displays, attempt to build short-term sales; others, such as loyalty programs, contests, and sweepstakes, have become integral components of firms' long-term customer relationship management (CRM) programs, which they use to build customer loyalty.

We present these sales promotion tools next. The tools of any sales promotion can be focused on any channel member—wholesalers, retailers, or end-user consumers. Just as we delineated for advertising, when sales promotions are targeted at channel members, the marketer is employing a push strategy; when it targets consumers themselves, it is using a pull strategy. Some sales promotion tools can be used with either a push or pull strategy. We now consider each of the tools and how they are used.

Types of Sales Promotion

Coupons Coupons offer a discount on the price of specific items when the items are purchased. Coupons are used to stimulate demand and are issued by manufacturers and retailers in newspapers, on products, on the shelf, at in-store kiosks, at the cash register, over the Internet, through the mail, and on mobile devices even when customers are in the store. Some retailers have linked their coupons directly to their loyalty programs. As Marketing Analytics 19.1 describes, the drugstore chain CVS tracks customers' purchases when they use their ExtraCare loyalty card and gives them coupons that are tailored just for them and their unique needs. If a customer typically spends a small amount during each shopping trip, he or she might receive coupons to encourage larger purchases, such as buy one, get one free.

Internet sites also provide customers with instant coupons of their choosing. Imagine a customer who visits her local Walmart and finds a Hot Wheels video game for $29.99. By

This sales promotion deal for Payless ShoeSource is a short-term price promotion that encourages customers to buy a second pair of shoes at one-half off.

Source: Payless Shoe Source, Inc.

Marketing Analytics 19.1 — How CVS Uses Loyalty Data to Define Coupons[v]

In general, loyalty programs offer an effective means to provide more value to customers. In particular, the CVS ExtraCare program represents a flagship loyalty program—it is one of the oldest and largest in the United States. The program has been running for over 20 years; one in every three people in the United States has an ExtraCare card. Thus, more than 90 million households use it in a typical year.

The primary focus of the ExtraCare program has been to provide personalized offers that are relevant to and appreciated by customers while also encouraging their consistent shopping behavior. The program has spread across multiple channels, allowing customers to connect with offers in print, online, or through a mobile app. For example, customers can access the omnichannel MyWeeklyAd program online or from a mobile device, or they can visit coupon kiosks in stores to scan their loyalty program cards and print coupons on the spot.

To support a unique, relevant, and well-appreciated shopping experience that encourages these customers to interact with the program and undertake additional sales, CVS relies heavily on customer data analytics. It collects vast amounts of data on the purchases that each ExtraCare member makes, and then it analyzes those data to uncover interesting or unexpected relationships among the items purchased. For example, customers who buy skin and hair products also purchase cosmetics, though not always at CVS. Furthermore, CVS discovered notable and helpful purchase timing patterns, such as its recognition that people typically buy toothpaste every five weeks.

By using the established relationships among the items that appear together in market baskets, CVS can obtain valuable insights, which in turn inform the personalized offers it sends to customers in an effort to adjust their behaviors. Thus, if an ExtraCare member buys face wash or conditioner, she might receive a coupon for lipstick. If another customer hasn't bought toothpaste in four and a half weeks, he will receive a coupon that provides him with a special incentive to purchase a high-end brand of toothpaste. CVS also uses these analytics to encourage customers to buy more each trip, such that a customer who typically spends $20 may receive a special

Marketing analytics are used to analyze data on the purchases of each ExtraCare customer and uncover interesting or unexpected relationships among items purchased. CVS can then use the information to provide personalized offers that are relevant to and appreciated by customers.

©McGraw-Hill Education/Mark Dierker, photographer

offer if she spends $30 the next time she shops. Finally, the data analytics give CVS important insights into which types of loyalty program offers are most successful—as well as which ones are not. For example, it determined that brand-specific coupons (e.g., for Pantene shampoo) were less effective than promotions geared toward the whole category (i.e., shampoos of various brands).

scanning the bar code using her cell phone, she connects to ShopSavvy.com and finds that the same item at a Target store a mile away is only $19.99. Another scan and a connection to MyCoupons.com provides her with a $10 coupon—which means she's saved $20 in a matter of minutes and just a few clicks.

Some coupons, whether printed from the Internet or sent to mobile phones, also contain information about the customer who uses it.[40] The bar code may identify the customer, his or her Internet address, Facebook page information, and even the search terms the customer used to find the coupon in the first place. These new breeds of coupons may look standard, but they offer up a startling amount of data, which promises benefits for advertisers who want to target their marketing more closely. Traditionally, coupons had low redemption rates and were therefore a relatively inexpensive sales promotion tool, but using customer data to create more targeted promotions has resulted in higher redemption rates, increasing their expense.

Although the Old Spice Guy IMC campaign generated sales, its "buy one, get one free" deals were too costly and therefore diminished the profit impact of the ads.

Source: Procter & Gamble

Deals A deal refers generally to a type of short-term price reduction that can take several forms, such as a featured price, a price lower than the regular price; a certain percentage "more free" offer contained in larger packaging; or a buy one, get one half off offer as shown in the nearby Payless ad. Another form of a deal involves a special financing arrangement such as reduced percentage interest rates or extended repayment terms. Deals encourage customers to try a product because they lower the risk for consumers by reducing the cost of the good.

But deals can also alter perceptions of value—a short-term price reduction may signal a different price–quality relationship than would be ideal from the manufacturer's perspective. In addition, as Old Spice learned, offering too many deals can offset likely gains. Its popular Old Spice Guy campaign attracted consumer attention through funny television commercials and interactive online campaigns, and sales of Old Spice jumped. But the company offered so many buy one, get one free deals at the same time that the potential profit impact of the great ads was essentially eliminated by the costs of the deals.[41]

Premiums A premium offers an item for free or at a bargain price to reward some type of behavior, such as buying, sampling, or testing. These rewards build goodwill among consumers, who often perceive high value in them. Premiums can be distributed in a variety of ways: They can be included in the product packaging, such as the toys inside cereal boxes; placed visibly on the package, such as a coupon for free milk on a box of Cheerios; handed out in the store; or delivered in the mail, such as the free perfume offers Victoria's Secret mails to customers. Furthermore, premiums can be very effective if they are consistent with the brand's message and image and highly desirable to the target market. However, finding a premium that meets these criteria at a reasonable cost can be a serious challenge.

We asked students across the country to create a video about McGraw-Hill Connect and how it has helped them. So many excellent videos came in that it was hard for our panel of judges to decide, but the winners have been posted! Check them out at GetConnectedandWin.com.

Source: McGraw-Hill Education

Contests A contest refers to a brand-sponsored competition that requires some form of skill or effort. McGraw-Hill Education, the publisher of this textbook, held a "Get Connected and Win" contest and a "LearnSmart and Win" contest. Students were asked to share their Connect and LearnSmart learning experiences via videos. The winners received scholarships, iPads, and other prizes.

Sweepstakes A form of sales promotion that offers prizes based on a chance drawing of entrants' names, sweepstakes do not require the entrant to complete a task other than buying a ticket or filling out a form. Often the key benefit of sweepstakes is that they encourage current consumers to consume more if the sweepstakes form appears inside the packaging or with the product. Many states, however, specify that no purchase can be required to enter sweepstakes.

Samples Sampling offers potential customers the opportunity to try a product or service before they make a buying decision. Distributing samples is one of the most costly sales promotion tools but also one of the most effective. Quick-service restaurants and grocery stores frequently use sampling. For instance, Starbucks provides samples of new products to customers. Costco uses so many samples that customers can have an entire meal. Sometimes trial-sized samples come in the mail or are distributed in stores.

Loyalty Programs As part of a sales promotion program, loyalty programs are specifically designed to retain customers by offering premiums or other incentives to customers who make multiple purchases over time. Well-designed loyalty programs encourage consumers to increase their engagement and purchases from a given firm. Such sales promotions are growing increasingly popular and are tied to long-term CRM systems. (Loyalty programs are examined in Chapters 2 and 3.) These programs need to be carefully managed because they can be quite costly.

Point-of-Purchase Displays Point-of-purchase (POP) displays are merchandise displays located at the point of purchase, such as at the checkout counter in a supermarket. Retailers have long recognized that the most valuable real estate in the store is at the POP because they increase product visibility and encourage trial. Customers see products such as a magazine or a candy bar while they are waiting to pay for their purchases and impulsively purchase them. In the Internet version of a POP display, shoppers are stimulated by special merchandise, price reductions, or complementary products that Internet retailers feature on the checkout screen.

Rebates Rebates are a particular type of price reduction in which a portion of the purchase price is returned by the seller to the buyer in the form of cash. Many products, such as consumer electronics, offer significant mail-in rebates that may lower the price of the item significantly. Some companies enjoy the added exposure when they appear on consumer websites such as PriceGrabber.com and NexTag.com, where products are sorted by the price, with links to the retailer's website. The firms garner considerable value from rebates because they attract consumers and therefore stimulate sales, but they may not have to pay off all the rebates offered because consumers don't bother to redeem them.

Product Placement When marketers use product placement, they pay to have their product included in nontraditional situations, such as in a scene in a movie or television program.[42] By doing so, they increase the visibility of their products. Product placement may be subtle, such as when *America's Got Talent* judges are seen drinking Dunkin' Donuts coffee. On HBO's *Silicon Valley,* the industry publication *TechCrunch's* website is not only seen on computer screens in various episodes, but the series also re-created the brand's conference, TechCrunch Disrupt, to pitch its product, and a main character, Erlich, who sells a story to the publication.[43] Although many firms would embrace product placement in hit shows and movies and are willing to pay for it, for Apple, the challenge is a little less stringent. U.S. film and television directors seem to love its sleek white laptops, ear-budded iPods, and ubiquitous iPhones. Thus more than one-third of all top-grossing films at the U.S. box office—129 of 374 movies—have included Apple-branded products in the past decade. Appearances include popular offerings as well as critically acclaimed broadcasts, from an episode of *Modern Family* viewed exclusively through Apple products to more nefarious uses depicted in *Billions.*[44] Apple is also unique in that until recently it claimed it does not pay for product placement beyond supplying the devices, nor does it comment on film appearances. However, in 2017 Apple officially sponsored an episode of *Saturday Night Live* in which its products were featured, and also sponsored Fox's new show, *9-1-1.* An analytics firm that estimates the dollar value of product placements has reported that Apple's five-minute screen time in Disney's *Zootopia* alone was worth about $5 million.[45] Apple seemingly can earn those returns without always paying for the placements, but not all companies are so lucky.

It is not an accident that Damian Lewis is using an iPhone on this episode of Billions. *It is product placement. Even better, Apple does not pay for the placement.*

Source: Showtime Networks Inc.

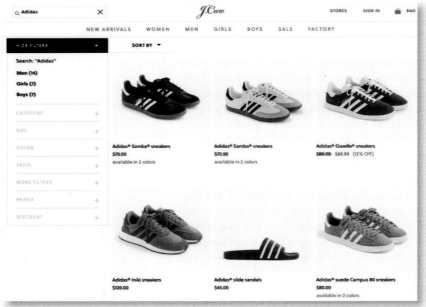

In a cross-promotion campaign, J.Crew has teamed up with several famous brands, including adidas, in its stores and website.

Source: J. Crew

Using Sales Promotion Tools

Marketers must be careful in their use of sales promotions, especially those that focus on lowering prices. Depending on the item, consumers may stock up when items are offered at a lower price, which simply shifts sales from the future to now and thereby leads to short-run benefits at the expense of long-term sales stability. For instance, using sales promotions such as coupons to stimulate sales of household cleaning supplies may cause consumers to stockpile the products and decrease demand for those products in the future. But a similar promotion used with a perishable product such as Dannon yogurt should increase its demand at the expense of competitors like Yoplait.

Many firms are also realizing the value of **cross-promoting**, when two or more firms join together to reach a specific target market. To achieve a successful cross-promotion, the two products must appeal to the same target market and together create value for consumers. J.Crew has teamed up with several famous brands, including Lacoste, Drake's, Timex, New Balance, adidas, and Eastpak, to offer well-known brands in the J Crew stores and website.[46]

The goal of any sales promotion is to create value for both the consumers and the firm. By understanding the needs of its customers, as well as how best to entice them to purchase or consume a particular product or service, a firm can develop promotional messages and events that are of interest to and achieve the desired response from those customers. Traditionally, the role of sales promotion has been to generate short-term results, whereas the goal of advertising was to generate long-term results. As this chapter demonstrates, though, sales promotion as well as advertising can generate both long- and short-term effects. The effective combination of both types of activities leads to impressive results for the firm and the consumers.

PROGRESS CHECK

1. What are various forms of sales promotions?
2. What factors should a firm consider when evaluating a sales promotion?

Reviewing Learning Objectives

 LO19-1 **Describe the steps in designing and executing an advertising campaign.**

Firms (1) identify the target audience, (2) set advertising objectives, (3) determine the advertising budget, (4) convey the message, (5) evaluate and select the media, (6) create the ad, and (7) assess the impact of the ad.

 LO19-2 **Identify three objectives of advertising.**

All advertising campaigns are designed to inform, persuade, or remind customers. Informative advertising is communication used to create and build brand awareness. Persuasive advertising is communication used to motivate consumers to take action. Finally, reminder advertising is communication used to remind or prompt repurchases.

LO19-3 Describe the different ways that advertisers appeal to consumers.

Advertising appeals are either informational or emotional. Informational appeals influence purchase decisions with factual information and strong arguments built around relevant key benefits that encourage consumers to evaluate the brand favorably. Emotional appeals indicate how the product satisfies emotional desires rather than utilitarian needs.

LO19-4 Identify the various types of media.

Firms can use mass media channels like newspapers or television to reach large numbers of anonymous audience members. Niche media, such as cable television and specialty magazines, are generally used to reach narrower segments that have unique demographic characteristics or interests. When choosing media, firms must match their objectives to that channel. Also, certain media are better at reaching a particular target audience than are others.

LO19-5 Identify agencies that regulate advertising.

Advertising is regulated by a plethora of federal and state agencies. The most important federal agencies are the FTC, which protects consumers against general deceptive advertising; the FCC, which has jurisdiction over radio, television, wire, satellite, and cable and covers issues regarding the use of tobacco products and objectionable language; and the FDA, which regulates food, dietary supplements, drugs, cosmetics, and medical devices.

LO19-6 Describe the elements of a public relations toolkit.

A variety of elements compose a firm's public relations toolkit. They include publications, video and audio programs, public service announcements, annual reports, media kits (e.g., press kits), news releases, and electronic media (e.g., websites).

LO19-7 Identify the various types of sales promotions.

Sales promotions are special incentives or excitement-building programs that encourage purchase and include coupons, deals, premiums, contests, sweepstakes, samples, POP displays, rebates, and product placement. They either push sales through the channel, as is the case with contests directed toward retail salespeople, or pull sales through the channel, as coupons and rebates do.

Key Terms

- advertising, 568
- advertising plan, 570
- advertising schedule, 578
- body copy, 580
- brand elements, 580
- cause-related marketing, 585
- contest, 588
- continuous schedule, 578
- coupon, 586
- cross-promoting, 590
- deal, 588
- emotional appeal, 576
- event sponsorship, 585
- flighting, 578
- headline, 579
- informational appeal, 575
- informative advertising, 570

- institutional advertisement, 573
- lift, 582
- loyalty program, 589
- mass media, 576
- media buy, 576
- media mix, 576
- media planning, 576
- niche media, 576
- persuasive advertising, 571
- point-of-purchase (POP) display, 589
- posttesting, 581
- premium, 588
- pretesting, 581
- product placement, 589
- product-focused advertisement, 573

- public relations (PR), 584
- public service advertising (PSA), 573
- puffery, 583
- pull strategy, 570
- pulsing, 579
- push strategy, 570
- rebate, 589
- reminder advertising, 571
- sales promotion, 586
- sampling, 588
- social marketing, 573
- subhead, 579
- sweepstakes, 588
- tracking, 581
- unique selling proposition (USP), 574

Marketing Digitally

1. Go to the website for the Children's Advertising Review Unit (CARU), one of the major self-regulatory bodies for children's advertising, at www.asrcreviews.org. Click on "CARU" and then "About Us—CARU" and examine the activities of CARU. How does this form of regulation complement the more formal regulation of federal and state agencies? Now look under the "Press Releases" link. Choose one of the press releases and discuss what action CARU took against the identified company or group. What was the main issue in the case?

2. Social media, such as Instagram, are some of the newest tools that firms are using in public relations programs. Visit Red Bull's Instagram account and browse through its recent posts. How is Red Bull using Instagram in its public relations program? How does its public relations program impact other aspects of its marketing communications?

Marketing Applications

1. What are the objectives of the Volkswagen ad in the chapter opener? Does the ad have more than one objective? Explain your answer.

2. Using the same ad, explain what kind of appeal it uses.

3. Verizon spends millions of dollars each year on advertising for many different purposes. Provide an example of how it might design an informative ad, a persuasive ad, and a reminder ad.

4. Name a current advertising slogan you believe is particularly effective for developing a unique selling proposition.

5. Bernard's, a local furniture company, target markets to college students with apartments and households of young people purchasing their first furniture items. If you worked for Bernard's, what type of media would you use for your advertising campaign? Justify your answer.

6. Should Bernard's use continuous, pulsing, or flighting for its advertising schedule? Why?

7. Describe one way that marketers can use posttesting to measure the effectiveness of an advertising campaign. For which kind of product is this method most useful? Why is it challenging to track the impact of an advertising campaign?

8. The first step in developing an ad campaign is to identify the target audience. Why is this the starting point for effective advertising? What kind of information is used to identify target audiences?

9. Consider all the diet products that are currently advertised on television today, including weight-loss supplements, weight-loss programs, and fitness equipment. Do you believe that some of these ads overstate what the product or service can actually do? Do you think any of these ads are actually deceptive or puffery?

10. You are invited to your six-year-old niece's birthday party and bring her the new superhero doll being advertised on television. She's thrilled when she unwraps the gift but is in tears a short time later because her new doll is broken. She explains that on TV, the doll flies and does karate kicks, but when she tried to play with the doll this way, it broke. You decide to call the manufacturer, and a representative tells you he is sorry your niece is so upset but that the ad clearly states the doll does not fly. The next time you see the televised ad, you notice very small print at the bottom stating that the doll does not fly. You decide to write a letter to the FTC about this practice. What information should you include in your letter?

Quiz Yourself

1. If Levi's wants to get potential customers to stop buying jeans from Lee and Wrangler, it would use _____ advertising.
   a. informative
   b. persuasive
   c. reminder
   d. push
   e. pull

2. ExxonMobil uses a(n) _____ appeal when it explains technical aspects of its products, such as lithium ion batteries, hydrogen technology, biofuels, and CO_2 capture technologies.
   a. candid
   b. emotional
   c. engineering
   d. informational
   e. contemporary

(Answers to these two questions can be found in the Quiz Yourself Answer Key section.)

Chapter Case Study

MAKING MASTERCARD PRICELESS

How do you pay for books, clothing, groceries, or travel? For many consumers, the answer is Mastercard, which has more than 200 million cards in circulation.[47] Yet despite the credit card's popularity, it lags behind its major competitor, Visa, by over 100 million cards. It is also outstripped by Visa and American Express for both monthly and annual purchases and spending volume.[48] Because Mastercard's primary function is to process transactions between each customer's bank and each merchant's bank, the company must appeal to two customer bases to build market share: the merchants who accept Mastercard for payment and the purchasers who use the card. These audiences are closely related, which implies that a single campaign can target both, likely even for an extended period. However, even the most successful campaigns can grow stale.

In 1997, Mastercard International and the advertising agency McCann Erickson Worldwide launched the emotion-based "Priceless" campaign, which celebrated life's most precious moments with the tagline, "There are some things money can't buy. For everything else, there's Mastercard."[49] The campaign was hugely successful, saving Mastercard from disaster, even in direct competition with the more widely accepted Visa card.[50] However, as consumer values and needs changed and the marketplace evolved, Mastercard faced a new challenge: how to retain customer loyalty and brand identification while reinvigorating its advertising.

Expanding Services to Meet Market Demand

In 1966, a group of California banks created a member-owned association called the Interbank Card Association. This association grew its services, changing its name to Mastercard in 1979 to reflect a commitment to international growth.[51] As it reached new markets across the globe, Mastercard also focused on technology innovation to help make economic transactions faster, more convenient, and more secure. The company acquired interest in the international credit card EuroCard (known today as Europay International), as well as Cirrus, a worldwide interbank network that links Mastercard, Maestro, and Diner's Club credit, debit, and prepaid cards to an international network of ATMs. The company also added fraud/risk management providers to its network of services.

Today Mastercard's technology platform can handle more than 160 million transactions every hour with a 99.9 percent reliability rate,[52] and the company has issued a contactless, or smart, card that communicates with terminals via radio waves. This payment method does not require a signature and can be a card or key fob that is tapped rather than swiped; it also appears as a smartphone app. To provide even more value to customers, the company has added sophisticated consulting and information services that help merchants gain insight into consumer spending, according to their transaction data and in-depth analyses.[53] These efforts have dovetailed with changes in consumer behavior as shoppers have begun relying more on electronic payment options and less on paper-based currency. In 2006, the company transitioned to a new corporate governance and ownership structure and began trading on the New York Stock Exchange.

"Priceless" Revisited

Mastercard began its "Priceless" campaign by identifying its target audience, which in this case focused on consumers. Hoping to persuade shoppers to keep their Mastercard at the top of their wallets, the campaign stressed the relationship between the card and experiences, as opposed to possessions. In early television ads, the narration linked the price of beauty products and new outfits to the "priceless" expression on an ex-boyfriend's face at a reunion, to create positive self-assessment feelings.[54] In another, the cost of tickets, refreshments, and souvenirs at a game was tied to the "priceless" opportunity for meaningful conversation between father and son, to invoke both happiness and love.[55] The "Priceless" campaign included various promotions and competitions in addition to these television spots.

In 2004, "Priceless" print ads took a new tack, weaving well-known retailers into the ads, together with Mastercard's theme. These retailers—which represented another of Mastercard's target audiences—received value from the prominent placement of their names and product images in the ads. Messaging moved from the general to the specific; an ad showing a teenaged rock band playing in a garage that might once have said, "extra-long extension cord, $11; moving them out of the living room: priceless," was modified to indicate that the extension cord was from RadioShack. The result was a form of symbiotic marketing in which well-known brand names helped attract consumer attention to Mastercard ads, and each brand appeared to be endorsing the other.[56]

An endless entrée: £5
A slow spaghetti: £8.50
A leisurely latte: £2.95

A quick bite with a friend: Priceless

There are some things money can't buy, for everything else there's MasterCard

MasterCard

Accepted wherever friends meet and time flies.

The Mastercard "Priceless" IMC campaign has been going strong for more than 20 years, continuously adjusting to appeal to different target markets through multiple media channels.

Source: Mastercard

Magic Moments In July 2011, Mastercard launched an expanded campaign, called "Priceless Cities." This campaign, kicked off initially in New York, offered cardholders special experiences in major cities that could be shared with family and friends.[57] Designed to provide busy consumers with memorable opportunities in the realms of sports, music, entertainment, shopping, travel, arts, culture, and dining out, the campaign touted early opening times at the toy store FAO Schwarz, a safari sleepover at the Bronx Zoo, prime tickets to a Yankees game with an ex-Yankee, and VIP dining experiences designed by a famed chef.[58] The idea, says Mastercard's chief marketing officer, was to transform consumers' perceptions of the card from simply part of a priceless moment to being the force that enables such experiences. In competitive markets, when most competitors focus on deals and discounts, the Mastercard campaign attracted attention by appealing to emotions rather than to wallets and stressing unforgettable experiences rather than cost savings. The campaign forged an additional bond with card users, because it placed Mastercard at the center of these memorable social activities.

The ads ran in more than 100 countries and aired in more than 50 languages, and the overall campaign used print, radio, transit, outdoor advertising, and television. It also included digital platforms to drive home its message, with a new section of the Mastercard website created specifically for the campaign, as well as social media channels such as Facebook and Twitter. Cardholders registered at the site to access special offers; World Elite Mastercard holders got special offers as well as preferred access to the events.

With its continued efforts to keep the campaign fresh and interesting, Mastercard followed up on the Cities function with "Priceless Surprises," an initiative in which famous company endorsers surprised their fans. The resulting advertising, especially a spot in which Justin Timberlake knocked on the door of a woman who claimed to be his biggest fan, led others to believe that using Mastercard could someday lead to a similar surprise.[59]

In 2018, Mastercard is pulling from the social climate to innovate the "Priceless" campaign with "Start Something Priceless." This new spin on the campaign focuses on people believing they can fuel change, and that actions small or large can improve the world. Thus, these ads encourage customers to do the things they've been meaning to do, such as reading or exercising more. The new campaign premiered at the Grammys with a music video in which the artists sing about the struggles they've overcome and ends with the words "Let nothing stop you" across the screen.[60] "Start Something Priceless" is more than an ad campaign; it is a call to action for its customers. As such Mastercard is using the hashtag #StartSomethingPriceless on various social media sites to encourage people to share the passion or purpose they are committed to pursue. As part of the campaign, Mastercard is also taking the call to action with its initiatives that include charities such as the World Food Programme and Stand Up to Cancer. For example, in Paris Mastercard unveiled an interactive billboard that allowed customers to donate meals to hungry children.[61]

Marketers must continuously evaluate their advertising campaigns and update them to ensure they are effectively communicating with their customers. New channels like social marketing can change shopping behaviors, creating opportunities that must be considered as part of any marketing strategy. Thus, as Mastercard continues to demonstrate, even the best ideas need new infusions and innovations to keep appealing to their targets.

Questions

1. What is the primary objective of the "Priceless" campaign?

2. Does the "Priceless" campaign use an informational or an emotional appeal?

3. Given its various target markets, which media are most appropriate for each market?

4. How can Mastercard integrate the "Priceless" campaign into a public relations program?

5. Which sales promotion tactics could Mastercard employ?

Endnotes

1. E. J. Schultz, "VW's Latest Move: A Hippie-Dippy Ad without a New Car in Sight," *Advertising Age*, October 13, 2017; David Gianatasio, "Volkswagen Takes a Trip Back to the 1960s in Nostalgic Ad Saluting Its Free-Spirited Owners," *Adweek*, October 13, 2017; Jennifer Faull, "Volkswagen Gets Nostalgic in Its First Ad Campaign Since the Emissions Scandal," *Business Insider*, February 4, 2016.

2. George E. Belch and Michael A. Belch, *Advertising and Promotion: An Integrated Marketing Communications Perspective*, 11th ed. (New York: McGraw-Hill Education, 2018).

3. "Worldwide Ad Spending: eMarketer's Updated Estimates and Forecast for 2016–2021," eMarketer, October 13, 2017, www.emarketer.com/Report/Worldwide-Ad-Spending-eMarketers-Updated-Estimates-Forecast-20162021/2002145.

4. Christine Birkner, "Millennials' Attention Divided across Devices More Than Any Other Age Group, Study Finds," *Marketing News Weekly*, March 17, 2015, www.ama.org.

5. Da Eun Han, Alastair McClelland, and Adrian Furnham, "The Effects of Programme Context on Memory for Humorous Television Commercials," *Applied Cognitive Psychology* 31, no. 6 (2017), pp. 586–92; Steven Bellman et al., "The Effects of Social TV on Television Advertising Effectiveness," *Journal of Marketing Communications* 23, no. 1 (2014), pp. 73–91; William D. Wells, *Measuring Advertising Effectiveness* (New York: Psychology Press, 2014).

6. Gian Fulgoni and Andrew Lipsman, "Measuring Television in the Programmatic Age: Why Television Measurement Methods Are Shifting toward Digital," *Journal of Advertising Research* 57, no. 1 (2017), pp. 10–14; Markus Pfeiffer and Markus Zinnbauer, "Can Old Media Enhance New Media? How Traditional Advertising Pays Off for an Online Social Network," *Journal of Advertising Research* 50, no. 1 (2010), pp. 42–49.

7. Leonie Roderick, "The Marketing Year: The Top Campaigns of 2015," *Marketing Week*, December 4, 2015, www.marketingweek.com/2015/12/04/the-marketing-year-the-top-campaigns-of-2015/; Adam Davidi, "The Best Ads of 2015: The Professionals Pick Their Favourites," *The Guardian*, December 4, 2015, www.theguardian.com/media-network/2015/dec/04/best-ads-advertising-2015-favourite.

8. Michael Long, "Jozy Altidore Becomes Face of Puma in North America," *Sports Pro*, November 30, 2017, www.sportspromedia.com/news/jozy-altidore-becomes-face-of-puma-in-north-america.

9. https://eu.puma.com/de/en/selena-gomez.

10. Laura Lake, "The Key Differences between Marketing and Advertising," *The Balance*, November 15, 2017, www.thebalance.com/marketing-vs-advertising-what-s-the-difference-2294825 ; Belch and Belch, *Advertising and Promotion*.

11. Paul Suggett, "13 Ways Advertisers Persuade You to Buy," *The Balance*, December 8, 2017, www.thebalance.com/10-ways-advertisers-persuade-you-to-buy-4084767; Amanda Ray, "A Revealing Look at Beauty Advertising," *The Art Institutes*, January 22, 2015, www.artinstitutes.edu/about/blog/a-revealing-look-at-beauty-advertising.

12. "Ecomagination," General Electric, www.ge.com/about-us/ecomagination; Alexander Haldermann, "GE's Ecomagination Turns 10: How a Brand Can Be a Driver for Change," *Huffpost Business*, September 16, 2015.

13. Brian Dumaine, "Is Apple 'Greener' Than Starbucks?," *Fortune*, June 24, 2014.

14. www.marketingpower.com/_layouts/Dictionary.aspx?dLetter=P.

15. "'Backstage'—Outnumber Hunger PSA with Thomas Rhett," *Good NonProfit*, February 9, 2018, https://good-nonprofit.com/non-profit-organizations/feeding-america/backstage-outnumber-hunger-psa-with-thomas-rhett/23819/; www.outnumberhunger.com/.

16. "Big Machine Label Group, General Mills and Feeding America® Partner with Multi-Platinum Artist Thomas Rhett for 2017 Outnumber Hunger Campaign," *PR Newswire*, February 24, 2017, www.prnewswire.com/news-releases/big-machine-label-group-general-mills-and-feeding-america-partner-with-multi-platinum-artist-thomas-rhett-for-2017-outnumber-hunger-campaign-300413397.html.

17. Ashley Halladay, "Thomas Rhett Is Serious about Fighting Hunger," *General Mills*, February 24, 2017, https://blog.generalmills.com/2017/02/thomas-rhett-is-serious-about-fighting-hunger/.

18. Theodore Levitt, *The Marketing Imagination* (New York: Free Press, 1986).

19. Belch and Belch, *Advertising and Promotion*.

20. Katherine White and John Peloza, "Self-Benefit versus Other-Benefit Marketing Appeals: Their Effectiveness in Generating Charitable Support," *Journal of Marketing* 73 (July 2009), pp. 109–24.

21. Adam Davidi, "The Best Ads of 2015: The Professionals Pick Their Favourites," *The Guardian*, December 4, 2015, www.theguardian.com/media-network/2015/dec/04/best-ads-advertising-2015-favourite.

22. John G. Wirtz, Johnny V. Sparks, and Thais M. Zimbres, "The Effect of Exposure to Sexual Appeals in Advertisements on Memory, Attitude, and Purchase Intention: A Meta-analytic Review," *International Journal of Advertising* 37, no. 2 (2017), pp. 168–98; Bruno Tomaselli Fidelis et al., "Sexual Appeal in Print Media Advertising: Effects on Brand Recall and Fixation Time," *Research Journal of Textile and Apparel* 21, no. 1 (2017), pp. 42–58; Jacob Hornik, Chezy Ofir, and Matti Rachamim, "Advertising Appeals, Moderators, and Impact on Persuasion," *Journal of Advertising Research* 57, no. 3 (2017), pp. 305–18.

23. "U.S. Department of Transportation and the Ad Council Kick Off Child Passenger Safety Week with Launch of New PSA Campaign," *Ad Council*, September 15, 2015, www.adcouncil.org/; "Orbit: Lunch Meets Breakfast—Chicken," *Advertising Age*, http://creativity-online.com/work/orbit-lunch-meets-breakfast-chicken/28751; Susannah Breslin, "Mr. Clean Sexes Up P&G's Super Bowl Ad," *Forbes*, January 29, 2017, www.forbes.com; Tim Nudd, "The 10 Best Ads of 2017," *Adweek*, December 10, 2017, www.adweek.com/; https://ca.charmin.com/en-ca/shop-products/toilet-paper/ultra-soft-toilet-paper.

24. *AMA Dictionary*, www.marketingpower.com/_layouts/ Dictionary.aspx?dLetter=M.

25. Some illustrative articles look at the effectiveness of given media: H. Risselada, P. C. Verhoef, and T. H. Bijmolt, "Dynamic Effects of Social Influence and Direct Marketing on the Adoption of High-Technology Products," *Journal of Marketing* 78, no. 4 (2014); Robert Heath, "Emotional Engagement: How Television Builds Big Brands at Low Attention," *Journal of Advertising Research* 49, no. 1 (March 2009), pp. 62–73; Lex van Meurs and Mandy Arist-off, "Split-Second Recognition: What Makes Outdoor Advertising Work?," *Journal of Advertising Research* 49, no. 1 (March 2009), pp. 82–92.

26. William F. Arens, David H. Schaefer, and Michael F. Weigold, *Advertising*, M-Series (Burr Ridge, IL: Irwin/McGraw-Hill, 2012).

27. "Watch the Newest Ads on TV from Hyundai, Subaru, Volvo and More," *Advertising Age*, April 4, 2018, http://adage.com/ article/media/watch-tv-ads-hyundai-subaru-volvo/313001/; Mike Monticello, "2018 Hyundai Kona Wants to Inject Caffeine into the Subcompact SUV Market," *Consumer Reports*, March 26, 2018, www.consumerreports.org/suvs/2018-hyundai-kona-suv-preview/; "Hyundai Kona: New B-Segment SUV," *Auto Trends Magazine*, June 13, 2017, http://autotrends.org/2017/06/13/ hyundai-kona-new-b-segment-suv/; www.hyundaiusa.com/ bluelink/index.aspx.

28. "Watch the Newest Ads on TV"; "Subaru Outback," *Consumer Reports*, www.consumerreports.org/cars/subaru/outback; www.subaru.com/vehicles/outback/index.html.

29. Belch and Belch, *Advertising and Promotion*.

30. Ibid.

31. "FTC Charges Green Coffee Bean Sellers with Deceiving Consumers through Fake News Sites and Bogus Weight Loss Claims," May 19, 2014, www.ftc.gov/news-events/press-releases.

32. "Children's Educational Television," *Federal Communications Commission*, www.fcc.gov/consumers/guides/childrens-educational-television.

33. Irina Slutsky, "Nine Things You Can't Do in Advertising If You Want to Stay on the Right Side of the Law," *Advertising Age*, March 7, 2011, http://adage.com.

34. Bob Hunt, "Truth in Your Advertising: Avoid Puffery?," *Realty Times*, June 20, 2007.

35. Ibid.

36. Barry Samaha, "The Best-Dressed Celebrities at the Oscars 2018," *Forbes*, March 5, 2018, www.forbes.com/; Erika Harwood "All the 2018 Golden Globes Red Carpet Looks," *Vanity Fair*, January 7, 2018, www.vanityfair.com/.

37. Ho Kim and Dominique Hanssens, "Advertising and Word-of-Mouth Effects on Pre-launch Consumer Interest and Initial Sales of Experience Products," *Journal of Interactive Marketing* 37 (2017), pp. 57–74 ; Carl Obermiller and Eric R. Spangenberg, "On the Origin and Distinctness of Skepticism toward Advertising," *Marketing Letters* 11, no. 4 (2000), p. 311.

38. Jackie Huba, "A Just Cause Creating Emotional Connections with Customers," www.inc.com.

39. www.stjude.org/get-involved/other-ways/partner-with-st-jude/ corporate-partners/chili-s-grill-bar.html.

40. Stephanie Clifford, "Web Coupons Know Lots about You, and They Tell," *The New York Times*, April 16, 2010.

41. Jack Neff, "Old Spice Is Killing It on YouTube Again, but Sales Are Down Double-Digits," *Advertising Age*, August 4, 2011, http://adage.com.

42. Eva A. van Reijmersdal, Peter C. Neijens, and Edith G. Smit, "A New Branch of Advertising: Reviewing Factors That Influence Reactions to Product Placement," *Journal of Advertising*

Research 49, no. 4 (December 2009), pp. 429–49; Pamela Mills Homer, "Product Placement: The Impact of Placement Type and Repetition on Attitude," *Journal of Advertising*, Fall 2009.

43. Becca Bleznak, "15 Most Annoying Examples of Product Placement in 2016," *Screen Rant*, September 23, 2016, https:// screenrant.com/awkward-product-placement-movies-tv-2016/.

44. Roger Fingas, "Apple Becoming More Open about Product Placements in TV Shows," *Apple Insider*, March 21, 2018, https://appleinsider.com/articles/18/03/21/apple-becoming-more-open-about-product-placements-in-tv-shows; "Apple Product Placement Scenes," *Product Placement Blog*, https://productplacementblog.com/tag/apple/.

45. Ibid.; "Product Placement Top 10 of 2016," *Concave Brand Tracking*, March 10, 2017, http://concavebt.com/top-10-product-placement-2016/.

46. www.jcrew.com.

47. Alina Comoreanu, "Market Share by Credit Card Network," *WalletHub*, March 7, 2017, www.cardhub.com/edu/market-share-by-credit-card-network/.

48. Ibid.

49. www.youtube.com/watch?v=Q_6stXKGuHo.

50. http://marketingpractice.blogspot.com/2006/11/mastercard-priceless.html.

51. http://mastercard.com/.

52. www.mastercard.com/us/company/en/docs/ CorporateOverview_FINAL.pdf.

53. www.mastercardadvisors.com/.

54. www.youtube.com/watch?v=QJUawVULURM.

55. www.youtube.com/watch?v=Q_6stXKGuHo.

56. Stuart Elliott, "Mastercard Revamps Print Ads," *The New York Times*, August 11, 2004.

57. Stuart Elliott, "Mastercard Brings 'Priceless' to a Pricey Place," *The New York Times*, July 7, 2011; www.creditcardeducation. com/news/mastercard-offers-priceless-city-experiences.html.

58. www.priceless.com/; http://newsroom.mastercard.com/press-releases/priceless-new-york-gives-mastercard-cardholders-privileged-access-to-the-citys-preeminent-experiences/.

59. www.youtube.com/watch?v=vnKnWMapEn8.

60. Ibid.

61. "Make 2018 Your Year of Action: 'Start Something Priceless,'" *Mastercard*, January 18, 2018, https://newsroom.mastercard. com/press-releases/make-2018-your-year-of-action-start-something-priceless-2/; Adrianne Pasquarelli, "Mastercard Puts Altruistic Spin on 'Priceless' Campaign," *Advertising Age*, January 18, 2018, http://adage.com/article/cmo-strategy/master-card-issues-call-action-priceless-campaign/311966/; Kristina Monollos, "Why Mastercard Is Adding a Charitable Aspect to Its Long-Running 'Priceless' Campaign," *Adweek*, January 19, 2018, www.adweek.com/brand-marketing/why-mastercard-is-adding-a-charitable-aspect-to-its-long-running-priceless-campaign/.

i. Sources: E. J. Schultz, "Thinking New: Inside Volkswagen's Plans to Become Relevant Again," *Advertising Age*, January 11, 2017; Stephanie Hernandez McGavin, "Volkswagen Group Leads Automotive Spending on Advertising," *Automotive News*, December 9, 2016; John McCarthy, "Volkswagen Embraces Nostalgia to Rebuild Brand Trust with Ad Requesting VW Memories," *The Drum*, November 9, 2016.

ii. Sources: Rachel Rabkin Peachman, "Is Chewing Gum Good for Toddlers? Or Anyone?," *The New York Times*, April 5, 2017.

iii. Source: Miriam Gottfried, "Publishers Face Moving Target in Mobile," *The Wall Street Journal,* July 7, 2015; John Koetsier, "Mobile Advertising Will Drive 75% of All Digital Ad Spend in 2018: Here's What's Changing," *Forbes,* February 23, 2018.

iv. Source: Michael McCarthy, "Acura Taps Van Halen for a Hard-Driving Super Bowl Commercial," *The New York Times,* January 28, 2016.

v. Source: Elyse Dupré, "CVS/Pharmacy Devotes ExtraCare to Its Loyalty Program," *DM News* 36, no. 8 (2014), pp. 19–22; Stephanie Clifford, "Using Data to Stage-Manage Paths to the Prescription Counter," *The New York Times,* June 19, 2013.

Quiz Yourself Answer Key

1. If Levi's wants to get potential customers to stop buying jeans from Lee and Wrangler, it would use _____ advertising.

   Answer: (b) persuasive

2. ExxonMobil uses a(n) _____ appeal when it explains technical aspects of its products, such as lithium ion batteries, hydrogen technology, biofuels, and CO_2 capture technologies.

   Answer: (d) informational

©Christian Charisius/dpa/picture-alliance/Newscom

LEARNING OBJECTIVES

After reading this chapter, you should be able to:

LO20-1 Describe the value added of personal selling.

LO20-2 Define the steps in the personal selling process.

LO20-3 Describe the key functions involved in managing a sales force.

LO20-4 Describe the ethical and legal issues in personal selling.

CHAPTER 20
PERSONAL SELLING AND SALES MANAGEMENT

Everyone sells something, sometime. But selling well, efficiently, effectively, and with the ability to add value requires thoughtful considerations combined with insights based on experience and perhaps a natural sales ability that gives sellers a good feel for buyers. Personal selling is inevitably personal.

But it also can be greatly improved by advanced analytical technologies. In this sense, IBM's Watson offers one of the best sales tools available today to sellers in virtually any setting. Watson can do much more than beat all comers at *Jeopardy!*[1] In IBM's Watson unit, more than 2,000 employees collaborate on providing software, hardware, and services related to the advanced technology service. With a budget of approximately $100 million, the unit also can fund venture projects to develop apps based on Watson's technology platform.[2]

Leveraging this dedicated support system, Watson gives clients of IBM access to some of the most powerful computing capabilities in the world, all available in the cloud. For example, The North Face uses Watson to enhance the e-commerce experience it provides customers through an "Expert Personal Shopper." When visitors reach www.thenorthface.com/xps, they enounter a series

of questions, asking about what they are shopping for and what needs they hope to meet. Then the digital personal shopper quickly and efficiently comes up with a list of options that are most likely to match their desires. Typically, each interaction with the Watson-powered personal shopper lasts for about two minutes. But by combing through structured and unstructured data—including social media posts and online customer reviews—Watson develops insights that can transform even this quick shopping interaction into a more personalized, more compelling experience.[3]

Supported by these updates and cloud accessibility, Watson also lessens the challenges associated with selling by providing more in-depth and actionable information that salespeople and their managers can use. IBM offers its own use of the tool as a prime example of Watson's benefits and value.[4]

When IBM analyzes sales of its software offerings across industries, customers, or regions, it relies on Watson to inform salespeople about whether customers in the banking or retail sector are more likely to buy a particular software solution, for example. With a few clicks, salespeople in the field also can learn how much of a particular customer's overall budget is devoted to IT software and how much IBM accounts for in that total. With the cloud capabilities, all members of a sales team can access immediately updated information at any time.

Then the analytical capabilities that are inherent to Watson help IBM develop and design new sales initiatives, promotions, and sales plans. For example, by combining historical sales data, budget details, and industry trends, Watson can reveal patterns to sales teams that signal which customers are most likely to respond to which sales campaigns. With this "pattern selling" approach, "The sales patterns can be easily customized for each sales team or for each individual sales rep to help them focus on the customers with the best potential for their specific product lines, for new engagements or for cross-selling and up-selling to existing accounts."[5]

Watson's output is strongly graphical as well, making it easy for salespeople to gain a sense of patterns and trends quickly and easily, without having to perform intricate calculations or analyses on their own. The Watson unit is dedicated to expanding its abilities even further by, for example, providing sales opportunities with new customers and prescriptions for how to sell to new and existing customers in dynamic markets.

Just like advertising, which we discussed in Chapter 19, personal selling is so important to integrated marketing communications that it deserves its own chapter. Almost everyone is engaged in some form of selling. On a personal level, you sell your ideas or opinions to your friends, family, employers, and professors. Even if you have no interest in personal selling as a career, a strong grounding in the topic will help you in numerous career choices. Consider, for instance, Harry Turk, a very successful labor attorney. He worked his way through college selling sweaters to fraternities across the country. Although he loved his part-time job, Harry decided to become an attorney. When asked whether he misses selling, he said, "I use my selling skills every day. I have to sell new clients on the idea that I'm the best attorney for the job. I have to sell my partners on my legal point of view. I even use selling skills when I'm talking to a judge or jury."

THE SCOPE AND NATURE OF PERSONAL SELLING

LO20-1 Describe the value added of personal selling.

Personal selling is the two-way flow of communication between a buyer or buyers and a seller, designed to influence the buyer's purchase decision. Personal selling can take place in various situations: face-to-face, via video teleconferencing, on the telephone, or over the Internet, for example. More than 14 million people are employed in sales positions in the United States,[6] including those involved in business-to-business (B2B) transactions, such as manufacturer's representatives selling to retailers or other businesses, and those completing business-to-consumer (B2C) transactions, such as retail salespeople, real estate agents, and insurance agents. Salespeople are referred to in many ways: sales representatives or reps, account executives, agents. And as Harry Turk found, most professions rely on personal selling to some degree.

Salespeople don't always get the best coverage in popular media. In Arthur Miller's famous play *Death of a Salesman,* the main character, Willie Loman, leads a pathetic existence and suffers from the loneliness inherent in being a traveling salesman.[7] The characters in David Mamet's play *Glengarry Glen Ross* portray salespeople as crude, ruthless, and of questionable character. Unfortunately, these powerful Pulitzer Prize–winning pieces of literature weigh heavily on our collective consciousness and often overshadow the millions of hardworking professional salespeople who have fulfilling and rewarding careers and who add value to their firm and provide value for their customers.

Personal Selling as a Career

Personal or professional selling can be a satisfying career for several reasons. First, many people love the lifestyle. Salespeople are typically out on their own. Although they occasionally work with their managers and other colleagues, salespeople tend to be responsible for planning their own days. This flexibility translates into an easier balance between work and family than many office-bound jobs can offer. Many salespeople now can rely on virtual offices, which enable them to communicate from anywhere and at any time with their colleagues and customers. Because salespeople are evaluated primarily on the results they produce, as long as they meet and exceed their goals, they experience little day-to-day supervision. You might find a salesperson at the gym in the middle of the day, when few other people are there, because no one keeps track of the length of his or her lunch break.

Second, the variety in the job often attracts people to sales. Every day is different, bringing different clients and customers, often in a variety of places. Their issues and problems and the solutions to those problems all differ and require creativity.[8] Third, professional selling and sales management can be a very lucrative career. Sales is among the highest-paying careers for college graduates, and compensation often includes perks such as the use of a company car or bonuses for high performance. A top performer can have a total compensation package of more than $150,000; even starting salespeople can make more than $50,000. Although the monetary compensation can be significant, the satisfaction of being involved in interesting, challenging, and creative work is rewarding in and of itself.

Many salespeople now rely on virtual offices, which enable them to communicate via the Internet with colleagues and customers.
©perfectlab/Shutterstock

Fourth, because salespeople are the frontline emissaries for their firms, they are very visible to management. Furthermore, their performance is fairly straightforward to measure, which means that high-performing salespeople who aspire to management positions are in a good position to be promoted.

The Value Added by Personal Selling

The benefits for salespeople mean that they are expensive for firms. Experts estimate that the average cost of a single B2B sales call is over $500.[9] So why include them in the marketing channel at all? In response to this question, some firms have turned to the Internet and technology to lower the costs of personal selling. Other firms, especially retailers, have made the decision not to use a sales force and thus require customers to perform the sales function on their own. But firms that continue to use personal selling as part of their integrated marketing communications program recognize the value it adds to their product or service mix. That is, personal selling is worth more than it costs. Personal selling adds value by educating customers and providing advice, saving the customer time, making things easier for customers, and building long-term strategic relationships with customers.[10]

Salespeople Provide Information and Advice Imagine how difficult it would be to buy a custom suit, a house, or a car without the help of a salesperson. UPS wouldn't dream of investing in a new fleet of airplanes without the benefit of Boeing's selling team. Boeing's sales team can provide UPS with the technical aspects of the aircraft as well as the economic justification for the purchase. If you need formalwear for your friend's upcoming wedding or a school dance, you might find it helpful to solicit the input of a retail sales associate who can tell you what colors are hot this season, how to tie a bowtie, how each garment tends to fit, what the latest fashions are in formalwear, and how long your dress should be for a function that starts at 6:00 p.m. Certainly you could figure out most of this information on your own, but many customers find value in and are willing to pay for the education and advice that salespeople provide.

Salespeople Save Time and Simplify Buying Time is money! Customers perceive value in time and labor savings. In many grocery and drugstore chains, salespeople employed

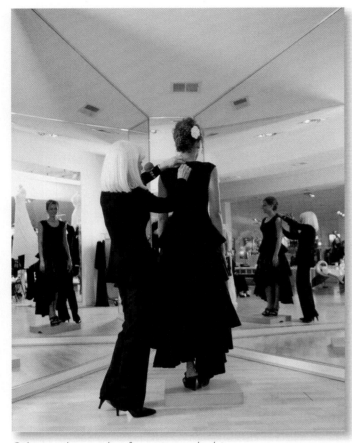

Salespeople provide information and advice.

©Mark Edward Atkinson/Getty Images

by the vendor that supplies the merchandise straighten stock, set up displays, assess inventory levels, and write orders. In some cases, such as bakeries or soft drink sales, salespeople and truck drivers even bring in the merchandise and stock the shelves. These are all tasks that retail employees would otherwise have to do. To appeal to end customers, manufacturers might send salespeople into stores to provide cooking demonstrations or free samples in the case of grocery stores, or trunk or made-to-measure shows in the case of apparel or shoe retailers. In this case, the vendor increases convenience for both its immediate customer (the retailer) and the end consumer.

Salespeople Build Relationships As we discussed in Chapter 16, building strong marketing channel relationships is a critical success factor. Who in the organization is better equipped to manage this relationship than the salesperson, the frontline emissary for the firm? The most successful salespeople are those who build strong relationships with their customers—a rule that holds across all sorts of sales. That is, whether you are selling yourself as a job candidate, a product produced by your company, or a concept to a client, your sale is not successful if it leads to just a one-time transaction. Instead, good salespeople of all stripes consistently take a long-term perspective. This long-term perspective in turn demands effective customer relationship management, a goal that is being transformed with mobile approaches to what has long been a dreaded responsibility of salespeople, as described in Social & Mobile Marketing 20.1.

Building on the relationship concept introduced in Chapter 16, relationship selling refers to a sales philosophy and process that emphasizes a commitment to maintaining the relationship over the long term and investing in opportunities that are mutually beneficial to all parties.[11] Relationship-oriented salespeople work with their customers to find mutually beneficial solutions to their wants and needs. As we described in Chapter 7, colleges often negotiate long-term

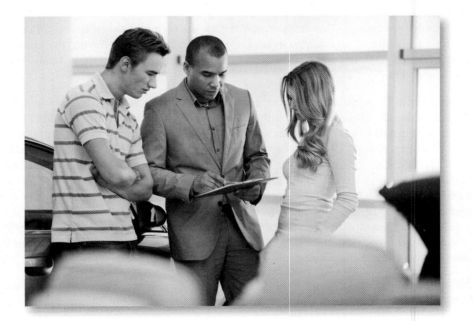

A salesperson's product knowledge and ability to facilitate the sale can make buying a car easy and possibly even enjoyable.

©Kristian Sekulic/Getty Images

Social & Mobile Marketing 20.1 — Managing Relationships While Mobile: Sales Reports from the Field[i]

Effective sales demand in-depth, extensive knowledge about customers, which suggests the need for customer relationship marketing (CRM), a topic we have covered throughout this book. In turn, CRM demands data because these systems cannot work without information being put in to them, for salespeople to take out later, as they need it. But convincing salespeople to take time out of their schedules to file CRM reports (rather than engaging in more lucrative sales efforts) has long been a challenge for managers and companies.

The challenge has been particularly acute for sales reps in the field. Because these sales reps rarely come into the office, the firms cannot support them as well in their efforts to make informed pitches to customers, and sales managers have little insight into what the sales reps are doing, when, how, and with whom. Not only does this leave the firm unable to monitor its employees, but it also makes the calculation of incentives or bonuses more difficult and less accurate, which ultimately could diminish sales performance overall.

In an effort to address these persistent issues, sales companies increasingly are relying on mobile technologies to make the reporting task and updates to the CRM system easy and nearly automatic. Rather than waiting until the end of the day—when they might have forgotten some of the details of an interaction with a client, or might forget to file their report altogether—mobile access to the firm's CRM system means that sales reps can input information immediately, possibly even before they leave the client site.

Some of the best mobile CRM offerings even gather data automatically. For example, mobile apps can gather immediate data about phone calls and e-mails between the sales rep and each client. These data then get cataloged and entered into the CRM system, without the salesperson needing to do anything further. Voice recognition technology also enables them to dictate a summary of their meetings and interactions, without having to fill in forms or write a formal report. All of these technologies in turn help sales managers keep tabs on what sales reps are doing, provide immediate feedback on their successful and unsuccessful efforts, and offer suggestions or training as needed.

With geolocators, the mobile CRM systems also can make recommendations to salespeople in the field, such as when they happen to be in proximity to a customer whose purchase history suggests that this customer might be ready to buy again. Accordingly, the sales reps likely achieve better sales, which benefits them in the form of increased commissions or bonuses. Then they may be more likely to rely on and contribute to the CRM system in other ways. And finally, the increase in sales benefits the firm, which gains not only more sales in the short term but also greatly enhanced data to improve its sales performance in the long term.

agreements with apparel companies to supply their sports teams. Similarly, a Lenovo sales team might be working with your university to provide you with the computer support and security you need during the years you spend working on the school's network.

THE PERSONAL SELLING PROCESS

LO20-2 Define the steps in the personal selling process.

Although selling may appear to be a rather straightforward process, successful salespeople must follow several steps. Depending on the sales situation and the buyer's readiness to purchase, the salesperson might not use every step, and the time required for each step varies with the situation. For example, if a customer goes into The Gap already prepared to purchase some chinos, the selling process will be fairly quick. But if Lenovo is attempting to sell personal computers for the first time to your university, the process may take several months. With this in mind, let's examine each step of the selling process (Exhibit 20.1).

Step 1: Generate and Qualify Leads

The first step in the selling process is to generate a list of potential customers (leads) and assess their potential (qualify). Salespeople who already have an established relationship with a customer will skip this step, and it is not used extensively in retail settings. In B2B situations, however, it is important to work continually to find new and potentially profitable customers.

Salespeople can generate and qualify leads in a variety of ways.[12] They might discover potential leads by talking to current customers, doing research on the Internet, or networking at events such as trade shows, industry conferences, or chamber of commerce meetings. Salespeople can also generate leads through cold calls and social media.

The Internet, and sites such as LinkedIn and Twitter in particular, have been a boon for generating and qualifying leads. Prior to the explosion of Internet use, it was cumbersome to

EXHIBIT 20.1   The Personal Selling Process

Generate and qualify leads

↓

Preapproach

↓

Sales presentation and overcoming reservations

↓

Closing the sale

↓

Follow-up

perform research on products, customers, or competitors. Salespeople would rely on a research staff for this information, and it could take weeks for the research to be completed and sent through the mail. Today, salespeople connect with potential customers through Twitter and LinkedIn. Salespeople curate blogs to draw in customers and generate leads, a process known as inbound marketing. Although these are all important tools, they are unlikely to replace cold calling anytime soon, as many customers still cannot be reached via social media.[13]

Trade shows also offer an excellent forum for finding leads. These major events are attended by buyers who choose to be exposed to products and services offered by potential suppliers in an industry. Consumer electronics buyers always make sure that they attend the annual Consumer Electronics Show (CES) in Las Vegas, the world's largest trade show for consumer technology (www.ces.tech/). The 2017 show was attended by 184,000 people (representing more than 150 countries) such as vendors; developers; and suppliers of consumer-technology hardware, content, technology delivery systems, and related products and services. More than 4,000 vendor exhibits took up more than 2.6 million net square feet of exhibit space, spread over three separate Las Vegas locations, showcasing the very latest products and services. Vendors often use CES to introduce new products, including the first camcorder (1981), high-definition television (HDTV, 1998), Internet protocol television (IP TV, 2005), 3D printers (2014), and virtual reality (2015).[14] In addition to providing an opportunity for retail buyers to see the latest products, the CES conference program features prominent speakers from the technology sector.

Cold calls are a method of prospecting in which salespeople telephone or go to see potential customers without appointments.[15] Telemarketing is similar to a cold call, but it always occurs over the telephone. Sometimes professional telemarketing firms rather than the firm's salespeople make such calls.

However, cold calls and telemarketing have become less popular over time, primarily because their success rate is fairly low. During cold calls, the salesperson is not able to establish the potential customer's specific needs because the receiver of the call is not expecting it and therefore may not be willing to participate in it. Accordingly, these methods can be very expensive. Second, federal as well as state governments are regulating the activities of tele-

Trade shows like the Consumer Electronics Show in Las Vegas are an excellent way to generate and qualify leads.

©Ethan Miller/Getty Images

marketers. Federal rules prohibit telemarketing to consumers whose names appear on the national Do-Not-Call list, which is maintained by the Federal Trade Commission. Even for those consumers whose names are not on the list, the rules prohibit calling before 8:00 a.m. or after 9:00 p.m. (in the consumer's time zone) or after the consumer has told the telemarketer not to call. Federal rules also prohibit unsolicited fax messages, calls, or messages to cell phones.

After salespeople generate leads, they must qualify those leads by determining whether it is worthwhile to pursue them and attempt to turn them into customers. In B2B settings, the costs of preparing and making a presentation are so substantial that the seller must assess a lead's potential. Salespeople consider, for example, whether the potential customer's needs pertain to a product or a service. They should assess whether the lead has the financial resources to pay for the product or service.[16] Clients looking to sell multimillion-dollar properties want real estate agents to qualify potential buyers first. Therefore, the sales agents might create a password-protected website that features floor plans and inside views for the shopping convenience of interested buyers. But to obtain the password, the customer must be prequalified as someone who could actually afford to buy the property. Such qualifications save both the agent and the seller the trouble of showing properties to curious people who could never actually afford to buy.

In a retail setting, though, qualifying potential customers is both dangerous and potentially illegal. Retail salespeople should never judge a book by its cover and assume that a person in the store doesn't fit the store's image or cannot afford to purchase there. Such actions can quickly rise to the level of unethical and illegal discrimination, as recently alleged by several African American shoppers against such well-known retail names as Macy's and Barneys.[17] Although not illegal, imagine the frustration you might feel if you visit an upscale jewelry store to purchase an engagement ring, only to be snubbed because you are dressed in your everyday, casual school clothes.

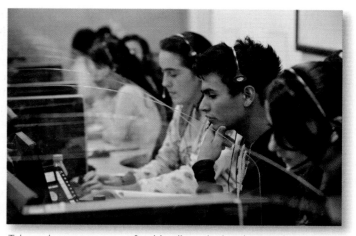

Telemarketing is a type of cold call in which salespeople generate or qualify leads on the telephone.

©Guillermo Legaria/Getty Images

Step 2: Preapproach and the Use of CRM Systems

The **preapproach** occurs prior to meeting the customer for the first time and extends the qualification of leads procedure described in Step 1. Although the salesperson has learned about the customer during the qualification stage, in this step he or she must conduct additional research and develop plans for meeting with the customer. Suppose, for example, a management consulting firm wants to sell a bank a new system for finding checking account errors. The consulting firm's salesperson should first find out everything possible about the bank: How many checks does it process? What system is the bank using now? What are the benefits of the consultant's proposed system compared with the competition? The answers to these questions provide the basis for establishing value for the customer.

When Vonage decided to increase sales of its voice over Internet protocol (VoIP) services to business customers rather than focusing only on consumers, it recognized that it needed information about how these buyers differed from its existing clients. Therefore, it purchased three firms that already function in business markets: Simple Signal, which provides unified communications-as-a-service solutions to small businesses; Telesphere Networks, which offers similar solutions to larger companies; and Vocalocity, which offers cloud-based communication services. Not only do those acquisitions provide it with customer data it can use in its preapproach planning, but they also provide introductions to potential business customers, leading Vonage to predict that it would be able to increase its B2B revenue by 40 percent.[18]

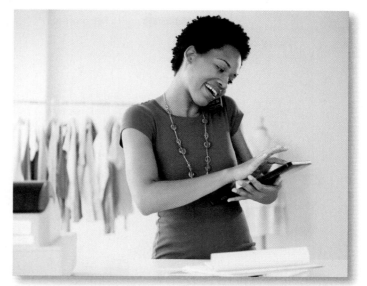

In the past, this customer information, if it was available at all, was typically included in a manual system that each individual salesperson kept, using a notebook or a series of cards. Today, salespeople often can access all this information immediately and conveniently from their firm's customer relationship management (CRM) system.

In most cases, these CRM systems have several components. There is a customer database or data warehouse. Whether the salesperson is working for a retail store or managing a selling team for an aerospace contractor, he or she can record transaction information, customer contact information, customer preferences, and market segment

Salespeople input customer information into their tablets to develop a customer database for CRM systems.

©JGI/Jamie Grill/Getty Images

information about the customer. Once the data have been analyzed and CRM programs developed, salespeople can help implement the programs.

Having done the additional research, the salesperson establishes goals for meeting with the customer. It is important that the salesperson knows ahead of time exactly what should be accomplished. For instance, the consulting firm's salesperson cannot expect to get a purchase commitment from the bank after just the first visit. But a demonstration of the system and a short presentation about how the system would benefit the customer would be appropriate. It is often a good idea to practice the presentation prior to the meeting, using a technique known as **role playing**, in which the salesperson acts out a simulated buying situation while a colleague or manager acts as the buyer. Afterward, the practice sales presentation can be critiqued and adjustments can be made.

Step 3: Sales Presentation and Overcoming Reservations

The Presentation Once all the background information has been obtained and the objectives for the meeting are set, the salesperson is ready for a person-to-person meeting. Let's continue with our bank example. During the first part of the meeting, the salesperson needs to get to know the customer, get the customer's attention, and create interest in the presentation to follow. The beginning of the presentation may be the most important part of the entire selling process because it is when the salesperson establishes exactly where the customer is in the buying process (Exhibit 20.2). (For a refresher on the B2B buying process, see Chapter 7.)

Suppose, for instance, that the bank is in the first stage of the buying process: need recognition. It would not be prudent for the salesperson to discuss the pros and cons of different potential suppliers because doing so would assume that the customer already had reached Step 4 (of the B2B buying process), proposal analysis and customer selection. By asking a series of questions though, the salesperson can assess the bank's need for the product or service and adapt or customize the presentation to match the customer's need and stage in the decision process.[19]

Asking questions is only half the battle; carefully listening to the answers is equally important. Some salespeople, particularly inexperienced ones, believe that to be in control, they must do all the talking. Yet it is impossible to really understand where the customer stands without listening carefully. What if the chief operating officer (COO) says, "It seems kind of expensive"? If the salesperson isn't listening carefully, he or she won't pick up on the subtle nuances of what the customer is really thinking. In this case, it probably means the COO doesn't see the value in the offering.

When the salesperson has gotten a good feel for where the customer stands, he or she can apply that knowledge to help the customer solve its problem or satisfy its need. The salesperson might begin by explaining the features or characteristics of the system that will reduce checking account errors. It may not be obvious, solely on the basis of these features, that the system adds value beyond the bank's current practices. Using the answers to some of the questions the salesperson posed earlier in the meeting, the salesperson can clarify the product's advantages over current or past practices, as well as the overall benefits of adopting the new system.

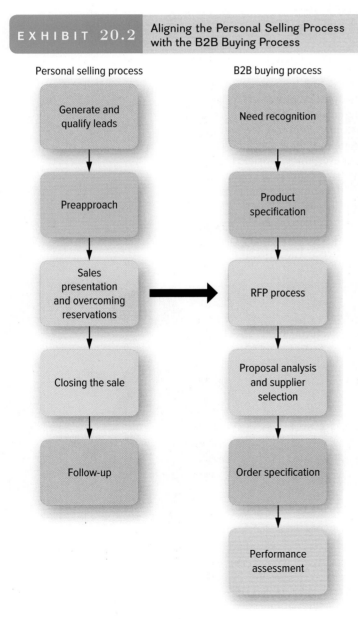

EXHIBIT 20.2   Aligning the Personal Selling Process with the B2B Buying Process

Personal selling process

- Generate and qualify leads
- Preapproach
- Sales presentation and overcoming reservations
- Closing the sale
- Follow-up

B2B buying process

- Need recognition
- Product specification
- RFP process
- Proposal analysis and supplier selection
- Order specification
- Performance assessment

The salesperson might explain, for instance, that the bank can expect a 20 percent improvement in checking account errors and that, because of the size of the bank and number of checks it processes per year, this improvement would represent $2 million in annual savings. Because the system costs $150,000 per year and will take only three weeks to integrate into the current system, it will add significant and almost immediate value.

As this hypothetical example hints, personal selling often relies on an old-fashioned skill: storytelling. Even if they use advanced technologies and Internet-based communication media, salespeople must communicate their messages and sales pitches in ways that resonate with their audience of potential customers. As research in neuroscience continues to affirm, virtually everyone uses at least some level of emotional reaction in determining their choices. To appeal to customers, salespeople thus need to tell a story that engages people's imaginations.[20]

It is important to ask questions at the beginning of a sales presentation to establish where the customer is in the buying process.
©Chris Ryan/OJO Images/agefotostock

Handling Reservations An integral part of the sales presentation is handling reservations or objections that the buyer might have about the product or service. Although reservations can arise during each stage of the selling process, they are very likely to occur during the sales presentation. Customers may raise reservations pertaining to a variety of issues, but they usually relate in some way to value, such as that the price is too high for the level of quality or service.

Good salespeople know the types of reservations buyers are likely to raise. They may know, for instance, that their service is slower than competitors' or that their selection is limited. Although not all reservations can be forestalled, effective salespeople can anticipate and handle some. For example, when the bank COO said the check service seemed expensive, the salesperson was ready with information about how quickly the investment would be recouped.

As in other aspects of the selling process, the best way to handle reservations is to relax and listen, then ask questions to clarify any reservations. For example, the salesperson could respond to the COO's reservation by asking, "How much do you think the bank is losing through checking account errors?" Her answer might open up a conversation about the positive trends in a cost–benefit analysis. Such questions are usually more effective than trying to prove the customer's reservation is not valid, because the latter approach implies the salesperson isn't really listening and could lead to an argument—the last thing a customer usually wants.

Step 4: Closing the Sale

Closing the sale means obtaining a commitment from the customer to make a purchase. Without a successful close, the salesperson goes away empty-handed, so many salespeople find this part of the sales process very stressful. Although losing a sale is never pleasant, salespeople who are involved in a relationship with their customers must view any specific sales presentation as part of the progression toward ultimately making the sale or building the relationship. An unsuccessful close on one day may just be a means of laying the groundwork for a successful close during the next meeting.

Although we have presented the selling process as a series of steps, closing the sale rarely follows so neatly. However, good salespeople listen carefully to what potential customers say and pay attention to their body language. By reading these signals, they can achieve an earlier close. Suppose that our hypothetical bank, instead of being in the first step of the buying process, were in the final step of negotiation and selection. An astute salesperson would pick up on these signals and ask for the sale.

Step 5: Follow-Up

"It ain't over till it's over."

—Yogi Berra[21]

With relationship selling, it is never really over, even after the sale is closed. The attitudes customers develop after the sale become the basis for how they purchase in the future.

The follow-up therefore offers a prime opportunity for a salesperson to solidify the customer relationship through great service quality. Let's apply the five service quality dimensions we discussed in Chapter 13 to understand the follow-up:[22]

- **Reliability.** The salesperson and the supporting organization must deliver the right product or service on time.

- **Responsiveness.** The salesperson and support group must be ready to deal quickly with any issue, question, or problem that may arise.

- **Assurance.** Customers must be assured through adequate guarantees that their purchase will perform as expected.

- **Empathy.** The salesperson and support group must have a good understanding of the problems and issues faced by their customers. Otherwise, they cannot give them what they want.

- **Tangibles.** Because tangibles reflect the physical characteristics of the seller's business, such as its website, marketing communications, and delivery materials, their influence is subtler than that of the other four service quality dimensions. That doesn't mean it is any less important. Retail customers are generally more pleased with a purchase if it is carefully wrapped in nice paper instead of being haphazardly thrown into a crumpled plastic bag. The tangibles offer a signal that the product is of high quality, even though the packaging has nothing to do with the product's actual performance.

When customers' expectations are not met, they often complain—about deliveries, the billing amount or process, the product's performance, or after-sale services such as installation or training (recall the Service Gaps Model from Chapter 13). Effectively handling complaints is critical to the future of the relationship. As we noted in Chapter 13, the best way to handle complaints is to listen to the customer, provide a fair solution to the problem, and resolve the problem quickly.

The best way to nip a postsale problem in the bud is to check with the customer right after he or she takes possession of the product or immediately after the service has been completed. This speed demonstrates responsiveness and empathy. It also shows the customer that the salesperson and the firm care about customer satisfaction. Finally, a postsale follow-up call, e-mail, or letter takes the salesperson back to the first step in the sales process for initiating a new order and sustaining the relationship.

Such efforts are critical, no matter the size of the selling firm. From the moment Barbara Merrill first started her company SukhaMat, to sell the innovative knee pads she had invented along with other yoga products, she recognized the need for personal attention and follow-up efforts. Therefore, she handwrote appreciative notes to each buyer from her home office, assuring them that she would be happy to hear from them with any questions or issues. As

SukhaMat's owner, Barbara Merrill, sends handwritten thank-you notes to each of her customers.

Source: SukhaMat.com

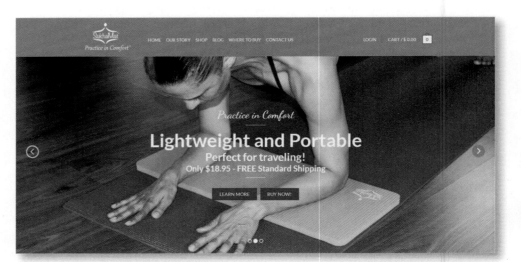

her company grew, with an expanding web presence and sales through Amazon, writing the full notes for each purchase became oppressively time-consuming. Yet she was unwilling to give up the personal link to her customers, so she moved to a printed card, featuring the company's web address (www.sukhamat.com), as well as a personalized address line and signature. Such effort does not go unnoticed by customers; one Amazon review even explains a five-star rating by noting not just that "The SukhaMat is absolutely wonderful. It's just the right thickness and has just the right softness," but also that "P.S.: The handwritten thank-you note from the seller was [an] unexpected and very much appreciated touch."[23]

PROGRESS CHECK

1. Why is personal selling important to an IMC strategy?
2. What are the steps in the personal selling process?

MANAGING THE SALES FORCE

LO20-3 Describe the key functions involved in managing a sales force.

Like any business activity involving people, the sales force requires management. Sales management involves the planning, direction, and control of personal selling activities, including recruiting, selecting, training, motivating, compensating, and evaluating, as they apply to the sales force.

Managing a sales force is a rewarding yet complicated undertaking. As Marketing Analytics 20.1 reveals, it also is dynamic and constantly shifting. In this section, we examine how sales forces can be structured, some of the most important issues in recruiting and selecting salespeople, sales training issues, ways to compensate salespeople, and finally how to supervise and evaluate salespeople.

Sales Force Structure

Imagine the daunting task of putting together a sales force from scratch. Will you hire your own salespeople, or should they be manufacturer's representatives? What will each salesperson's primary duties be: order takers, order getters, sales support? Finally, will they work together in teams? In this section, we examine each of these issues.

Company Sales Force or Manufacturer's Representative

A company sales force comprises people who are employees of the selling company. Independent agents, also known as manufacturer's representatives, or reps, are salespeople who sell a manufacturer's products on an extended contract basis but are not employees of the manufacturer. They are compensated by commissions and do not take ownership or physical possession of the merchandise.

Manufacturer's representatives are useful for smaller firms or firms expanding into new markets because such companies can achieve instant and extensive sales coverage without having to pay full-time personnel. Good sales representatives have many established contacts and can sell multiple products from noncompeting manufacturers during the same sales call. Also, the use of manufacturer's reps facilitates flexibility; it is much easier to replace a rep than an employee and much easier to expand or contract coverage in a market with a sales rep than with a company sales force.

Company sales forces are more typically used for established product lines. Because the salespeople are company employees, the manufacturer has more control over what they do. If, for example, the manufacturer's strategy is to provide extensive customer service, the sales manager can specify exactly what actions a company sales force must take. In contrast, because manufacturer's reps are paid on a commission basis, it is difficult to persuade them to take any action that doesn't directly lead to sales.

Marketing Analytics 20.1   How Technology and Data Are Changing Sales Management, Among Other Things[ii]

The changes brought about by technology, social and mobile media, and massive data are frequent topics of discussion, throughout this book and in general. Another of these shifts is taking place in managerial ranks, where various top and middle managers are discovering that their roles must necessarily change if they want to continue running their businesses effectively and profitably.

In particular, the data-driven analytics that now inform virtually every firm create a flatter organizational hierarchy. Managers' roles even have become obsolete in some cases, such as when an algorithm exists to make operational decisions that previously were the responsibility of a sales manager. Broadly, even firms that are not high-tech in their makeup are becoming tech firms, in some sense.

For example, the insurance provider Liberty Mutual relies on teams that take combined responsibility for sales, information technology, and business tasks. These teams in turn rely heavily on digital collaboration tools, so a conventional sales manager assigned to oversee them would have little to do. Instead, managers in these settings tend to function like coaches or mentors, guiding the teams' existing efforts to complete their diverse, multifunctional job tasks.

Despite some resistance to such radical changes, especially among top executives who might seek to hold tightly to their authority and positions of power, the trends seem clearly to be moving to less hierarchy, fewer managers, more shared authority, and increasing reliance on technological tools. For prospective managers, they also suggest some clear prerequisites: gain some familiarity with agile management, expand information technology and big data skills, and be ready to be flexible when it comes to what the job ultimately will involve.

Salesperson Duties Although the life of a professional salesperson is highly varied, salespeople generally play three important roles: order getting, order taking, and sales support.

Order Getting An *order getter* is a salesperson whose primary responsibilities are identifying potential customers and engaging those customers in discussions to attempt to make a sale. An order getter is also responsible for following up to ensure that the customer is satisfied and to build the relationship. In B2B settings, order getters are primarily involved in new buy and modified new buy situations (see Chapter 7). As a result, they require extensive sales and product knowledge training. The Pepsi salesperson who goes to Safeway's headquarters to sell a special promotion of Pepsi emojis is an order getter.

Order Taking An *order taker* is a salesperson whose primary responsibility is to process routine orders, reorders, or rebuys for products. Colgate employs order takers around the globe who go into stores and distribution centers that already carry Colgate products to check inventory, set up displays, write new orders, and make sure everything is going smoothly.

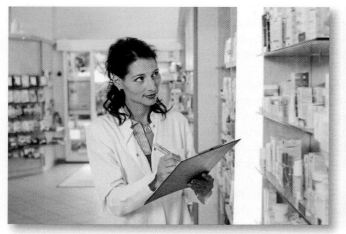

Order takers process routine orders, reorders, or rebuys for products.

©Westend61/Getty Images

Customers like centenarian Ivy Bean can rely on sales support from Best Buy's Geek Squad.

©Bob Collier/PA Wire/AP Images

Sales Support Sales support personnel enhance and help with the overall selling effort. For example, if a Best Buy customer begins to experience computer problems, the company has a Geek Squad door-to-door service as well as support in the store. Those employees who respond to the customer's technical questions and repair the computer serve to support the overall sales process.

Combination Duties Although some salespeople's primary function may be order getting, order taking, or sales support, others fill a combination of roles. For instance, a computer salesperson at Staples may spend an hour with a customer educating him or her about the pros and cons of various systems and then make the sale. The next customer might simply need a specific printer cartridge. A third customer might bring in a computer and seek advice about an operating system problem. The salesperson was first an order getter, next an order taker, and finally a sales support person.

Some firms use selling teams that combine sales specialists whose primary duties are order getting, order taking, or sales support but who work together to service important accounts. As companies become larger and products more complicated, it is nearly impossible for one person to perform all the necessary sales functions.

Recruiting and Selecting Salespeople

When the firm has determined how the sales force will be structured, it must find and hire salespeople. Although superficially this task may sound as easy as posting the job opening on the Internet or running an ad in a newspaper, it must be performed carefully because firms don't want to hire the wrong person. Salespeople are very expensive to train. Among other creative hiring tactics, Zappos' famously considers finding the right people so important that it will pay them to leave after a few weeks if they are not a good fit.[24]

In their critical efforts to find the right person for the job, though, companies must take care to avoid biased practices such as hiring on the basis of stereotypes instead of qualifications. For most people, the picture of someone selling Avon products likely involves a middle-aged woman—namely, the "Avon Lady." But sales revenues for these products continue to provide salespeople a successful living, prompting plenty of women and men to try their hand at selling Avon.[25] Hiring based on misplaced assumptions about gender or other categories can be damaging to the company, as well as discriminatory.

The most important activity in the recruiting process is to determine exactly what the salesperson will be doing and what personal traits and abilities a person should have to do the job well. For instance, the Pepsi order getter who goes to Safeway to pitch a new product will typically need significant sales experience, coupled with great communication and analytical skills. Pepsi's order takers need to be reliable and able to get along with lots of different types of people in the stores, from managers to customers.

Many firms conduct individual and group assessments of candidates in which personality traits, among other criteria, are evaluated.[26] But different firms stress different personality attributes, depending on the requisite traits for the position and the personality characteristics of their most successful salespeople. For instance, impatience is often a positive characteristic for sales because it creates a sense of urgency to close the sale. But for very large, complicated sales targeting large institutions, like the bank in our previous example, an impatient salesperson may irritate the decision makers and kill the deal.

When recruiting salespeople, it helps to possess certain personal traits. What are those personal traits? Managers and sales experts generally agree on the following:[27]

- **Personality.** Good salespeople are friendly, sociable, and, in general, like being around people. Customers won't buy from someone they don't like.

- **Optimism.** Good salespeople tend to look at the bright side of things. Optimism also may help them be resilient—the third trait.

- **Resilience.** Good salespeople don't easily take no for an answer. They keep coming back until they get a yes.

- **Self-motivation.** As we have already mentioned, salespeople have lots of freedom to spend their days the way they believe will be most productive. But if the salespeople are not self-motivated to get the job done, it probably won't get done.

- **Empathy.** Empathy is one of the five dimensions of service quality discussed previously in this chapter and in Chapter 13. Good salespeople must care about their customers, their issues, and their problems.

Sales Training

Even people who possess all these personal traits need training. All salespeople benefit from training about selling and negotiation techniques, product and service knowledge, technologies used in the selling process, time and territory management, and company policies and procedures.

Firms use varied delivery methods to train their salespeople, depending on the topic of the training, what type of salesperson is being trained, and the cost versus the value of the training. For instance, an on-the-job training program is excellent for communicating selling and negotiation skills because managers can observe the sales trainees in real selling situations and provide instant feedback. They can also engage in role-playing exercises in which the salesperson acts out a simulated buying situation and the manager critiques the salesperson's performance.

A much less expensive, but for some purposes equally valuable, training method is the Internet. Online training programs have revolutionized the way training happens in many firms. Firms can provide new product and service knowledge, spread the word about changes in company policies and procedures, and share selling tips in a user-friendly environment that salespeople can access anytime and anywhere. Distance learning and sales training programs through teleconferencing enable a group of salespeople to participate with their instructor or manager in a virtual classroom. And testing can occur online as well. Online sales training may never replace the one-on-one interaction of on-the-job training for advanced selling skills, but it is quite effective and efficient for many other aspects of the sales training task.[28]

Motivating and Compensating Salespeople

An important goal for any effective sales manager is to get to know his or her salespeople and determine what motivates them to be effective. Some salespeople prize their freedom and like to be left alone; others want attention and are more productive when they receive accolades for a job well done. Still others are motivated primarily by monetary compensation.

Technology has changed the lives of salespeople and the delivery methods of sales training. Companies can conduct distance learning and training through videoconferencing.

©Blend Images/Ariel Skelley/Getty Images

Volkswagen may give a free trip to Germany for the salesperson who sells the most Touaregs.
©Stock4B-RF/Getty Images

As Adding Value 20.1 reveals, these motives vary according to the selling context. Great sales managers determine how best to motivate each of their salespeople according to what is most important to each individual. Although sales managers can emphasize different motivating factors, except in the smallest companies, the methods used to compensate salespeople must be fairly standardized and can be divided into two categories: financial and nonfinancial.

Financial Rewards Salespeople's compensation usually has several components. Most salespeople receive at least part of their compensation as a salary, a fixed sum of money paid at regular intervals. Another common financial incentive is a commission, which is money paid as a percentage of the sales volume or profitability. A bonus is a payment made at management's discretion when the salesperson attains certain goals. Bonuses usually are given only periodically, such as at the end of the year. A sales contest is a short-term incentive designed to elicit a specific response from the sales force. Prizes might be cash or other types of financial incentives. For instance, Volkswagen may give a free trip to Germany for the salesperson who sells the most Touaregs.

The bulk of any compensation package is made up of salary, commission, or a combination of the two. The advantage of a salary plan is that salespeople know exactly what they will be paid, and sales managers have more control. Salaried salespeople can be directed to spend a certain percentage of their time handling customer service issues. Under a commission system, however, salespeople have only one objective—make the sale! Thus, a commission system provides the most incentive for the sales force to sell.

Nonfinancial Rewards As we have noted, good salespeople are self-motivated. They want to do a good job and make the sale because it makes them feel good. But this good feeling also can be accentuated by recognition from peers and management. For instance, the internal monthly magazine and blog at the cosmetics firm Mary Kay provides an outlet for not only selling advice but also companywide recognition of individual salespeople's accomplishments.[29]

Nonfinancial rewards should have high symbolic value, as plaques, pens, or rings do. Free trips or days off are also effective rewards. More important than what the reward is, however, is the way it is operationalized. For instance, an award should be given at a sales meeting and publicized in the company newsletter. It should also be done in good

Adding Value 20.1   **When Tupperware Does More Than Store Food: Sales as Empowerment among Indonesian Women[iii]**

Tupperware may have started as an American company, but its primary sales markets have been overseas for years. Germany took top place for a while; today though, the biggest market for the plastic food container systems is Indonesia, where the company earned approximately $200 million in sales last year.

The reasons for its growth in Asia include some familiar notions but also some relatively notable distinctions. For example, a growing middle class leads consumers of virtually every country to look for ways to use their disposable income. Tupperware offers a target that is both fun and practical. In addition, as economies grow and consumers gain access to modern conveniences such as refrigerators, food storage products become a newly discovered need.

But Indonesia is unique in that it has strongly mandated and legally established roles for women that require them to serve as caretakers in their families, while their husbands take the position of head of the household. Required to remain at home to care for their families, many middle-class women seek approved social interactions such as those created by Tupperware parties. Friends can come together to shop and chat, allowing the women a break from their daily routines.

This combination also makes Tupperware an ideal means for women to enter the workforce. Despite conservative social attitudes against women working, the at-home operations enable many of them to make a career out of selling Tupperware and convincing others to do the same. Thus the sales force in Indonesia currently includes about 250,000 women.

The social networks that enable the sales of Tupperware also resonate well in Indonesia, which has a long tradition of *arisans*, or gatherings, in which women pool their money, then award the pot to a different member at each meeting. When

Why is Indonesia Tupperware's biggest market?

Source: Tupperware

the arisans include a Tupperware component, the pot of money usually helps the winner purchase a full set of products, which she would not have been able to afford otherwise.

Finally, the career prospects offered by Tupperware represent a viable means for women to escape poverty. One woman reports earning approximately US$2,400 per month, six times what she and her husband combined earned previously. Thus, whereas "Initially, my husband refused to let me sell Tupperware even part-time. . . . Now he works for me."

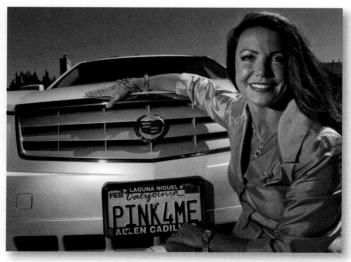

Mary Kay gives high-performing salespeople an award that has both high symbolic value and material value—a pink Cadillac.

©Mindy Schauer/ZUMApress/Newscom

taste, because if the award is perceived as tacky, no one will take it seriously.[30] Mary Kay recognizes salespeople's success with unusually large rewards that have both high symbolic and high material value. Today there are more than 4,000 independent beauty consultants and sales directors with Mary Kay Career Cars, 1,000 of which are the famous pink Cadillac, but it is also possible to gain rewards and recognition such as a set of faux pearl earrings within the first week of becoming a consultant.[31]

Evaluating Salespeople by Using Marketing Metrics

Salespeople's evaluation process must be tied to their reward structure. If salespeople do well, they should receive their rewards the way you do if you do well on your exams and assignments in a class: you earn good grades. However, salespeople should be evaluated and rewarded for only those activities and outcomes that fall under their control. If Nordstrom makes a unilateral decision to put J Brand jeans in all its stores, the J Brand sales representatives responsible for individual Nordstrom stores should not receive credit for making the sale, nor should they get all the windfall commission that would ensue from the added sales.

Consider this guiding principle for how sales managers should evaluate salespeople—evaluate and reward salespeople for what they do and not for what they don't do. The answer is never easy because measures must be tied to performance, and there are many ways to measure performance in a complex job such as selling. For example, evaluating performance on the basis of monthly sales alone fails to consider how profitable the sales were, whether any progress was made to build new business that will be realized sometime in the future, or the level of customer service the salesperson provided. Because the sales job is multifaceted with many contributing success factors, sales managers should use multiple measures.[32]

In business practice, salesperson evaluation measures can be objective or subjective. Sales, profits, and the number of orders represent examples of objective measures. Although each is somewhat useful to managers, such measures do not provide an adequate perspective for a thorough evaluation because there is no means of comparison with other salespeople. For instance, suppose salesperson A generated $1 million last year, but salesperson B generated $1.5 million. Should salesperson B automatically receive a significantly higher evaluation? Now consider that salesperson B's territory has twice as much potential as salesperson A's. Knowing this, we might suppose that salesperson A has actually done a better job. For this reason, firms use ratios such as profit per customer, orders per call, sales per hour, or expenses compared to sales as their objective measures.

Whereas objective measures are quantitative, subjective measures seek to assess salespeople's behavior: what they do and how well they do it. By their very nature, subjective measures reflect one person's opinion about another's performance. Thus, subjective evaluations can be biased and should be used cautiously and only in conjunction with multiple objective measures.

PROGRESS CHECK

1. What do sales managers need to do to manage their sales force successfully?
2. What is the difference between monetary and nonmonetary incentives?

ETHICAL AND LEGAL ISSUES IN PERSONAL SELLING

LO20-4 Describe the ethical and legal issues in personal selling.

Although ethical and legal issues permeate all aspects of marketing, they are particularly important for personal selling. Unlike advertising and other communications with customers, which are planned and executed on a corporate level, personal selling involves a one-to-one, and often face-to-face, encounter with the customer. Therefore, sellers' actions are not only highly visible to customers but also to other stakeholders, such as the communities in which they work.

Ethical and legal issues arise in three main areas. First, there is the relationship between the sales manager and the sales force. Second, in some situations, an inconsistency might exist between corporate policy and the salesperson's ethical comfort zone. Third, ethical as well as legal issues can arise when the salesperson interacts with the customer, especially if that salesperson or the selling firm collects significant information about the customer. To maintain trustworthy customer relationships, companies must take care that they respect customer privacy and respect the information comfort zone—that is, the amount of information a customer feels comfortable providing.

Salespeople must live within their own ethical comfort zone. Should insurance salespeople disclose inadequate hurricane coverage and risk not making the sale?

©Charlie Riedel/AP Photo

The Sales Manager and the Sales Force

Like any manager, a sales manager must treat people fairly and equally in everything he or she does. With regard to the sales force, this fairness must apply to hiring, promotion, supervision, training, assignment of duties and quotas, compensation and incentives, and firing.[33] Federal laws cover many of these issues. For instance, equal employment opportunity laws make it unlawful to discriminate against a person in hiring, promotion, or firing because of race, religion, nationality, sex, or age.

The Sales Force and Corporate Policy

Sometimes salespeople face a conflict between what they believe represents ethical selling and what their company asks them to do to make a sale. Suppose an insurance agent whose compensation is based on commission sells a homeowner's policy to a family that has just moved to New Orleans, an area prone to flooding as a result of hurricanes. Even though the policy covers hurricane damage, it does not cover water damage from hurricanes. If the salesperson discloses the inadequate coverage, the sale might be lost because additional flood insurance is very expensive. What should the salesperson do? Salespeople must live within their own ethical comfort zone. If this or any other situation is morally repugnant to the salesperson, he or she must question the choice to be associated with such a company.[34]

Salespeople also can be held accountable for illegal actions sanctioned by the employer. If the homeowner asks if the home is above the floodplain or whether water damage from flooding is covered by the policy, and it is company policy to intentionally mislead potential customers, both the salesperson and the insurance dealership could be susceptible to legal action.

The Salesperson and the Customer

As the frontline emissaries for a firm, salespeople have a duty to be ethically and legally correct in all their dealings with their customers. Not only is it the right thing to do, it simply means good business. Long-term relationships can deteriorate quickly if customers believe that they have not been treated in an ethically proper manner. Unfortunately, salespeople sometimes get mixed signals from their managers or simply do not know when their behaviors might be considered unethical or illegal. Formal guidelines can help, but it is also important to integrate these guidelines into training programs in which salespeople can discuss various issues that arise in the field with their peers and managers.[35] Most important, however, is for sales managers to lead by example. If managers are known to cut ethical corners in their dealings with customers, it shouldn't surprise them when their salespeople do the same.

PROGRESS CHECK

1. What are three areas of personal selling in which ethical and legal issues are more likely to arise?

Reviewing Learning Objectives

LO20-1 **Describe the value added of personal selling.**

Although the cost of an average B2B sales call is expensive, many firms believe they couldn't do business without their sales forces. Customers can buy many products and services without the help of a salesperson, but in many other cases, it is worth the extra cost built into the price of a product to be educated about the product or get valuable advice. Salespeople can also simplify the buying process and therefore save the customer time and hassle.

LO20-2 **Define the steps in the personal selling process.**

Although we discuss selling in terms of steps, it truly represents a process, and the time spent in each step varies according to the situation. In the first step, the salesperson generates a list of viable customers. During the second step, the preapproach, the salesperson gathers information about the customer and prepares for the presentation. The third step, the sales presentation, consists of a personal meeting between the salesperson and the customer. Through discussion and by asking questions, the salesperson learns where the customer is in the buying process and tailors the discussion around what the firm's product or service can do to meet that customer's needs. During the fourth step, the close, the salesperson asks for the order. Finally, during the follow-up, the salesperson and support staff solidify the long-term relationship by making sure the customer is satisfied with the purchase and addressing any complaints. The follow-up therefore sets the stage for the next purchase.

LO20-3 **Describe the key functions involved in managing a sales force.**

The first task of a sales manager, assuming a firm is starting a sales force from scratch, is to determine whether to use a company sales force or manufacturer's representatives. Then sales managers must determine what the primary selling responsibilities will be—order getter, order taker, or sales support. The sales manager recruits and selects salespeople, but because there are all sorts of sales jobs, the sales manager must determine what it takes to be successful and then go after people with those attributes. In the next step, training, firms can choose between on-the-job and online training. Sales managers are also responsible for motivating and compensating salespeople. Most salespeople appreciate a balance of financial and nonfinancial rewards for doing a good job. Finally, sales managers are responsible for evaluating their salespeople. Normally, salespeople should be evaluated on a combination of objective measures, such as sales per hour, and subjective measures, such as how friendly they appear to customers.

LO20-4 **Describe the ethical and legal issues in personal selling.**

Ethical and legal issues arise in three areas in personal selling. First, ethical and legal issues could arise based on how the sales manager interacts with the sales force. Second, there might be inconsistencies between corporate policy and the salesperson's ethical comfort zone. Finally, ethical and legal issues can arise as the salesperson interacts with customers.

Key Terms

- bonus, 613
- closing the sale, 607
- cold calls, 604
- commission, 613
- company sales force, 609
- inbound marketing, 604
- independent agents, 609
- leads, 603
- manufacturer's representatives (reps), 609
- order getter, 610
- order taker, 610
- personal selling, 600
- preapproach, 605
- qualify, 603
- relationship selling, 602
- role playing, 606
- salary, 613
- sales contest, 613
- sales management, 609
- sales support personnel, 611
- selling teams, 611
- telemarketing, 604
- trade shows, 604

Marketing Digitally

1. Go to Salesforce.com's YouTube channel (www.youtube.com/user/salesforce). Watch a few of the short videos and discuss how the tools described would help you as a salesperson.

2. Go to a job posting website and search for sales jobs in your area. Explore the different sales jobs available. What kind of experience and level of education are preferred? What type of compensation is offered?

Marketing Applications

1. How has your perception of what it would be like to have a career in sales changed since you read this chapter?

2. Your best friend is considering a career in sales. What are the benefits of a sales career that you would share?

3. Kevin started a new job as a car salesperson. What are effective ways that he could generate leads? Justify your answer.

4. Why is it important for salespeople to be good listeners? To be good at asking questions?

5. Suppose you are a salesperson at a high-end jewelry store. What can you do to ensure that your customers are satisfied? Now imagine you are the store manager of the same store; what can you do in your position to guarantee customers remain happy with the service they receive?

6. Imagine you are a salesperson selling office networking systems and are putting together a sales presentation for a new customer. What are important factors to remember when making your sales presentation?

7. What are some of the potentially ethically troubling and illegal situations facing professional salespeople, and how should they deal with them?

8. Why would Gillette use a company sales force, while a small independent manufacturer of organic shaving cream uses manufacturer's representatives?

9. Similar to the way a sales manager evaluates a salesperson, your instructors evaluate your performance to assign you a grade. Choose one of your classes and analyze the advantages and disadvantages of the objective and subjective bases used to evaluate your performance.

10. A customer has the following reservations. How do you respond?
    a. "I really like all the things this copier does, but I don't think it's going to be very reliable. With all those features, something's got to go wrong."
    b. "Your price for this printer is higher than the price I saw advertised on the Internet."

11. Imagine that you have just been hired by the school newspaper to sell ad space. You are asked what you think would be a "fair" compensation package for you. Using the information from the chapter, make a list of all the elements that should be included in your compensation package. How would this compensation package change over time and with continued strong performance?

12. You have taken a summer job in the windows and doors department of a large home improvement store. During sales training, you learn about the products, how to best address customers' needs, and how to sell customers the best product to fit their needs regardless of price point. One day your manager informs you that you are to recommend Smith Windows to every window customer. Smith Windows are more expensive and don't really provide superior benefit except in limited circumstances. The manager is insistent that you recommend Smith. Not knowing what else to do, you recommend Smith Windows to customers who would have been better served by lower-cost windows. The manager rewards you with a sales award. Later the manager tells you that he received an all-expenses-paid cruise for his family from Smith Windows. What, if anything, should you do with this information?

Quiz Yourself

1. When the National Association of Realtors' national awareness campaign emphasizes that Realtors know how to more efficiently market a client's property than an owner can by himself, it is highlighting which value of personal selling?
   a. Matching supply with demand
   b. Saving time and simplifying buying
   c. Building relationships
   d. Reducing marketing costs
   e. Leveraging contacts

2. Although reservations on the part of the buyer can arise during each stage of the selling process, they are very likely to occur during the _____ stage.
   a. generation and qualification of leads
   b. preapproach
   c. sales presentation
   d. closing the sale
   e. follow-up

(Answers to these two questions can be found in the Quiz Yourself Answer Key section.)

ALTA DATA SOLUTIONS: MAKING THE SALE[36]

When Vicki Nguyen reached her office, she had a message from Mike Smith, the regional sales manager, to meet him in his office regarding the Burtell Inc. order. Vicki Nguyen is a senior sales associate for Alta Data Solutions Inc., a firm that markets software and hardware designed for data storage. The Burtell order represents a multimillion-dollar contract for Alta Data Solutions and would help Burtell boost its productivity levels and revenue for the region. To prepare for the meeting, Nguyen reviews her sales call report notes on the Burtell account.

Alta Data Solutions Alta Data Solutions provides software and hardware solutions to large firms and has an established track record for delivering an exceptional standard of quality and high levels of customer service. This excellent reputation allows Alta Data Solutions to charge a substantial premium, ranging from 10 to 20 percent above the market leader.

The data storage software services market has been dominated for two decades by this market leader. Alta Data Solutions holds the second position in the marketplace, with a considerably lower but growing market share. Only one other competitor, an aggressive, small, low-price player, holds a significant market share; this provider has made inroads into the market in the past several years through its aggressive sales tactics.

Alta Data Solutions has just built a new facility and hired 50 new software programmers. Therefore, the company must generate new business to meet its higher financial goals; even more important in the short run, it must keep the new programmers working on interesting projects to retain them.

Burtell Inc. Burtell Inc. is a division of a major U.S.-based consumer products firm. Its purchasing department negotiates contracts for software services and coordinates the interface among a variety of members from different departments. The business environment for consumer products has become highly competitive in recent years, leading to tight budgets and higher levels of scrutiny of the value added by vendors. Competition is fierce, as large numbers of end-user customers are considering vendors that provide the most data analysis with their products.

Burtell Inc. has been consistently buying software development services from the market leader since 1991 and is generally satisfied with its service. A recent change in corporate leadership, however, has increased concerns about its overreliance on one vendor for a particular service. Also, because of the difficult economic climate, the company is concerned about the cost of software services and whether it is necessary to provide such a high service level.

Vicki Nguyen's Call Report A call report is like a diary of sales calls made to a particular client. The notes in Vicki Nguyen's Burtell file pertaining to the current negotiations begun on June 4 read as follows:

> June 4: I contacted Bethany O'Meara, chief purchasing officer at Burtell, to introduce myself to her and get a sense of what their future software needs might be. She told me that the slowed business climate had caused Burtell to institute a program for increased efficiency in operations and that they would be looking to negotiate a new contract for software solutions. She gave me some insights into the technological aspects of their needs.

> June 18: Met with Jon Aaronson, head of R&D, to explain our productivity-enhancing solutions. Went into considerable depth explaining how Alta could service their needs and learned what they were looking for in a provider. I went over some specific product specification issues, but Jon did not seem impressed. But he did ask for a price and told me that the final decision rested with Brad Alexander, the chief financial officer.

What are the key points Vicki Nguyen should make in her presentation?

©Lane Oatey/Blue Jean Images/
Getty Images

July 2: Presented to Bethany O'Meara and Jon Aaronson. They first asked about the price. I gave them a quote of $10 million. They suggested that other services were much cheaper. I explained that our price reflected the latest technology and that the price differential was an investment that could pay for itself several times over through faster communication speeds. I also emphasized our reputation for high-quality customer service. While the presentation appeared to meet their software needs, they did not seem impressed with the overall value. I also sent a copy of the presentation in report form to Brad Alexander and attempted to get an appointment to see him.

July 9: Contacted Jon Aaronson by phone. He told me that we were in contention with three other firms and the debate was heated. He stated that the other firms were also touting their state-of-the-art technology. Discussed a lower price of $7 million. Also encouraged him to visit Alta Data Solutions headquarters to meet with the product manager who oversaw the product development efforts and would manage the implementation of the product. He wasn't interested in making the two-day trip even though it would spotlight our core competencies.

July 15: Received a conference call from Brad Alexander and Jon Aaronson to discuss the price. Brad said the price was still too high and that he could not depreciate that amount over the life of the software and meet target levels of efficiency. He wanted a final quote by August 6.

The Final Pitch   Vicki Nguyen prepared for her meeting with Mike Smith, Alta's regional sales manager, by going over her notes and market data about the competitors. Smith's voicemail had said they'd be meeting to put together their best possible proposal.

Questions

Help Vicki Nguyen prepare her sales presentation.

1.   Who should be at the presentation?
2.   How should she start the meeting?
3.   What are the key points she should make in her presentation?
4.   What reservations should she expect? How should she handle them?

Endnotes

1.   Alex Barinka, "IBM's Watson to Help Rich DBS Clients with 'Jeopardy' Smarts," *Bloomberg Technology*, January 8, 2014, www.bloomberg.com/.

2.   Quentin Harvey, "IBM Plans Big Spending for the Cloud," *The New York Times*, January 17, 2014.

3.   "The North Face, IBM and Fluid Launch New Interactive Shopping Experience Using Artificial Intelligence (AI)," *IBM*, December 14, 2015, www.03.ibm.com/press/us/en/pressrelease/48479.wss.

4.   Source: Debra Pesek, "How IBM Uses Watson Analytics for Pattern Selling," *Watson Analytics* blog, November 17, 2015, https://community.watsonanalytics.com/watson-analytics-blog/how-ibm-uses-watson-analytics-for-pattern-selling/.

5.   Ibid.

6.   Bureau of Labor Statistics, www.bls.gov.

7.   Thomas N. Ingram et al., *Sales Management: Analysis and Decision Making*, 9th ed. (New York: Routledge, 2015).

8.   Ty Swain, "The Complexity of Selling in Today's Marketplace," *OEM Magazine*, May 22, 2018, www.oemmagazine.org/; Dale Carnegie, *How to Win Friends and Influence People* (New York: Pocket, 1998).

9.   http://ultimatelead.com/cost-b2b-sales-call/.

10.   Bill Stinnett, *Think Like Your Customer* (Burr Ridge, IL: McGraw-Hill, 2004).

11.   Aja Frost, "The Ultimate Guide to Relationship Selling," *HubSpot*, January 25, 2018, https://blog.hubspot.com/.

12.   Ingram et al., *Sales Management*.

13.   S. Anthony Iannarino, "The Last Word on Cold Calling versus Social Media," *The Sales Blog*, April 21, 2014, www.thesalesblog.com; Justin Fishaw, "Has LinkedIn Replaced

Cold Calling?," *SocialMediaToday,* August 21, 2013, www.socialmediatoday.com; Ken Krogue, "Cold Calling Is Dead, Thanks to LinkedIn," *Forbes,* August 9, 2013, www.forbes.com.

14. "About CES," www.ces.tech/.

15. American Marketing Association, *AMA Dictionary.*

16. Christine Comaford-Lynch, "A Bad Lead Is Worse Than No Lead at All," *BusinessWeek,* March 26, 2008.

17. J. David Goodman, "Profiling Complaints by Black Shoppers Followed Changes to Stores' Security Policies," *The New York Times,* October 29, 2013, www.nytimes.com.

18. Kate Maddox, "New CMO at Vonage Will Make 'Aggressive' B-to-B Push," *Advertising Age,* April 28, 2015, http://adage.com.

19. Barton A. Weitz, Harish Sujan, and Mita Sujan, "Knowledge, Motivation, and Adaptive Behavior: A Framework for Improving Selling Effectiveness," *Journal of Marketing,* October 1986, pp. 174–91.

20. Dennis Nishi, "To Persuade People, Tell Them a Story," *The Wall Street Journal,* November 9, 2013, http://online.wsj.com.

21. www.quotedb.com/quotes/1303.

22. Ingram et al., *Sales Management.*

23. "Oh, What a Relief," review Amazon.com, May 28, 2015.

24. Benjamin Snyder, "14% of Zappos Staff Left after Being Offered Exit Pay," *Fortune,* May 8, 2015.

25. Lynn Huber, "Can Men Sell Avon?," *Online Beauty Biz,* May 25, 2014, www.onlinebeautybiz.com; Sadie Whitelocks, "I'm an Avon Laddie! Salesman, 21, Is Part of the New Breed of Men Muscling In on Door-to-Door Trade," *Daily Mail,* December 14, 2011, www.dailymail.co.uk.

26. Cut-e Group Hamburg, "The Global Assessment Barometer 2016," https://cdn2.hubspot.net/hubfs/294088/HR2017/ Documenten/Rapporten/Engels/Assessment-barometer- report-cut-e-2016.pdf.

27. Ned Smith, "10 Traits of Successful Salespeople," *Business News Daily,* March 20, 2013, www.businessnewsdaily.com; Steven W. Martin, "Seven Personality Traits of Top Salespeople," *Harvard Business Review,* June 27, 2011, http://blogs.hbr.org; Julie Chang, "Born to Sell?," *Sales and Marketing Management,* July 2003, p. 36.

28. Felicia G. Lassk et al., "The Future of Sales Training: Challenges and Related Research Questions," *Journal of Personal Selling and Sales Management* 32, no. 1 (2012), pp. 141–54.

29. http://blog.marykay.com/; www.shanisoffice.com/ uploads/5/0/9/8/5098161/march_applause_en.pdf.

30. Ingram et al., *Sales Management.*

31. www.marykay.com.

32. Ingram et al., *Sales Management.*

33. Ibid.

34. Nicolas McClaren, "The Personal Selling and Sales Management Ethics Research: Managerial Implications and Research Directions from a Comprehensive Review of the Empirical Literature," *Journal of Business Ethics* 112, no. 1 (January 2013), pp. 101–25; Sean R. Valentine and Connie R. Bateman, "The Impact of Ethical Ideologies, Moral Intensity, and Social Context on Sales-Based Ethical Reasoning," *Journal of Business Ethics* 102, no. 1 (August 2011), pp. 155–68.

35. Omar Itani, Fernando Jaramillo, and Larry Chonko, "Achieving Top Performance While Building Collegiality in Sales: It All Starts with Ethics," *Journal of Business Ethics,* 2017, https://doi.org/10.1007/s10551-017-3598-z; Stephan Castleberry, "Salesperson Ethics," *Journal of Marketing Education* 36, no. 2 (April 2014), pp. 209–16; Casey Donoho and Timothy Heinze, "The Personal Selling Ethics Scale: Revisions and Expansions for Teaching Sales Ethics," *Journal of Marketing Education* 33, no. 1 (April 2011), pp. 107–22.

36. This case was written by Jeanne Munger in conjunction with the textbook authors Dhruv Grewal and Michael Levy as the basis of class discussion rather than to illustrate either effective or ineffective marketing practice. For a discussion of common measures used to evaluate salespeople, see Johnston and Marshall, *Churchill/Ford/Walker's Sales Force Management,* 9th ed. (Boston: McGraw-Hill/Irwin).

i. Source: Oscar Macia, "How Mobile Is Driving the Future of Field Sales," *Sales and Marketing,* March 11, 2016.

ii. Source: Angus Loten and John Simons, "Leadership Evolves among Tech Changes," *The Wall Street Journal,* January 3, 2017; Joe McKendrick, "LinkedIn's Top Jobs of 2017 All Involve Software in One Way or Another," *ZD Net,* January 31, 2017.

iii. Source: Joe Cochrane, "Tupperware's Sweet Spot Shifts to Indonesia," *The New York Times,* February 28, 2015, www.nytimes.com.

Quiz Yourself Answer Key

1. When the National Association of Realtors' national awareness campaign emphasizes that Realtors know how to more efficiently market a client's property than an owner can by himself, it is highlighting which value of personal selling?

   Answer: (b) Saving time and simplifying buying

2. Although reservations on the part of the buyer can arise during each stage of the selling process, they are very likely to occur during the _____ stage.

   Answer: (c) sales presentation

glossary

actual product The physical attributes of a product including the brand name, features/design, quality level, and packaging.

ad-supported apps Apps that are free to download but place ads on the screen when using the program to generate revenue.

administered vertical marketing system A *supply chain* system in which there is no common ownership and no contractual relationships, but the dominant channel member controls the channel relationship.

advanced shipping notice (ASN) An electronic document that the supplier sends the retailer in advance of a shipment to tell the retailer exactly what to expect in the shipment.

advertising A paid form of communication delivered through media from an identifiable source about an organization, product, service, or idea designed to persuade the receiver to take some action now or in the future.

advertising allowance Tactic of offering a price reduction to channel members if they agree to feature the manufacturer's product in their advertising and promotional efforts.

advertising plan A subsection of the firm's overall marketing plan that explicitly analyzes the marketing and advertising situation, identifies the objectives of the advertising campaign, clarifies a specific strategy for accomplishing those objectives, and indicates how the firm can determine whether the campaign was successful.

advertising schedule The specification of the timing and duration of advertising.

affective component A component of *attitude* that reflects what a person feels about the issue at hand—his or her like or dislike of something.

AIDA model A common model of the series of mental stages through which consumers move as a result of marketing communications: *A*wareness leads to *I*nterests, which lead to *De*sire, which leads to *A*ction.

aided recall An awareness metric that occurs when consumers recognize a name (e.g., of a brand) that has been presented to them.

alpha testing An attempt by the firm to determine whether a product will perform according to its design and whether it satisfies the need for which it was intended; occurs in the firm's research and development (R&D) department.

artificial intelligence (AI) Solutions that rely on computer systems to perform tasks that require human intelligence, such as speech recognition, decision making, or translations.

associated services (also called *augmented product*) The nonphysical attributes of the product including product warranties, financing, product support, and after-sale service.

atmospherics The controllable characteristics within the store that are intended to influence customers' propensity to purchase.

attitude A person's enduring evaluation of his or her feelings about and behavioral tendencies toward an object or idea; consists of three components: *cognitive*, *affective*, and *behavioral*.

auditory senses A sensory stimulation that involves hearing and influences the shopping experience, e.g., music.

augmented product See *associated services*.

autocratic buying center A buying center in which one person makes the decision alone, though there may be multiple participants.

Baby Boomers Generational cohort of people born after World War II, between 1946 and 1964.

bait and switch A deceptive practice of luring customers into the store with a very low advertised price on an item (the bait), only to aggressively pressure them into purchasing a higher-priced model (the switch) by disparaging the lower-priced item, comparing it unfavorably with the higher-priced model, or professing an inadequate supply of the lower-priced item.

beacon technology Technology that allows companies to detect where customers (who have enabled the feature) are at each moment through their smartphones.

behavioral component A component of *attitude* that comprises the actions a person takes with regard to the issue at hand.

behavioral segmentation A segmentation method that divides customers into groups based on how they use the product or service. Some common behavioral measures include occasion and loyalty.

benefit segmentation The grouping of consumers on the basis of the benefits they derive from products or services.

beta testing Having potential consumers examine a product prototype in a real-use setting to determine its functionality, performance, potential problems, and other issues specific to its use.

big box retailer Discount stores that offer a narrow but deep assortment of merchandise; see also *category killer*.

big data Data sets that are too large and complex to analyze with conventional data management and data mining software.

blog (weblog) An online diary with periodic posts that allows people to share their thoughts, opinions, and feelings with the entire world; corporate blogs are a new form of marketing communications.

body copy The main text portion of an ad.

bonus A payment made at management's discretion when the salesperson attains certain goals; usually given only periodically, such as at the end of the year.

bottom of the pyramid A term used for economic settings in which consumers earn very low wages.

bounce rate The percentage of times a visitor leaves the website almost immediately, such as after viewing only one page.

brainstorming A group activity used to generate ideas.

brand association The mental links that consumers make between a brand and its key product attributes; can involve a logo, slogan, or famous personality.

brand awareness Measures how many consumers in a market are familiar with the brand and what it stands for; created through repeated exposures of the various brand elements (brand name, logo, symbol, character, packaging, or slogan) in the firm's communications to consumers.

brand dilution Occurs when a brand extension adversely affects consumer perceptions about the attributes the core brand is believed to hold.

brand elements Characteristics that identify the sponsor of a specific ad.

brand equity The set of assets and liabilities linked to a brand that add to or subtract from the value provided by the product or service.

brand extension The use of the same brand name for new products being introduced to the same or new markets.

brand licensing A contractual arrangement between firms, whereby one firm allows another to use its brand name, logo, symbols, or characters in exchange for a negotiated fee.

brand loyalty Occurs when a consumer buys the same brand's product or service repeatedly over time rather than buying from multiple suppliers within the same category.

brand repositioning (rebranding) A strategy in which marketers change a brand's focus to target new markets or realign the brand's core emphasis with changing market preferences.

breadth Number of product lines offered by a firm; also known as variety.

break-even analysis Technique used to examine the relationships among cost, price, revenue, and profit over different levels of production and sales to determine the *break-even point*.

break-even point The point at which the number of units sold generates just enough revenue to equal the total costs; at this point, profits are zero.

breakthroughs See *pioneers*.

business ethics Refers to a branch of ethical study that examines ethical rules and principles within a commercial context, the various moral or ethical problems that might arise in a business setting, and any special duties or obligations that apply to persons engaged in commerce.

business-to-business (B2B) marketing The process of buying and selling goods or services to be used in the production of other goods and services, for consumption by the buying organization, or for resale by wholesalers and retailers.

business-to-consumer (B2C) marketing The process in which businesses sell to consumers.

buyer The buying center participant who handles the paperwork of the actual purchase.

buying center The group of people typically responsible for the buying decisions in large organizations.

cannibalize From a marketing perspective, it is the negative impact on a firm's sales, profits, or market share when one product competes closely with a similar product offered by the same company.

cash discount Tactic of offering a reduction in the invoice cost if the buyer pays the invoice prior to the end of the discount period.

category killer A specialist that offers an extensive assortment in a particular category, so overwhelming the category that other retailers have difficulty competing.

category specialist A retailer that offers a narrow variety but a deep assortment of merchandise.

cause-related marketing Commercial activity in which businesses and charities form a partnership to market an image, a product, or a service for their mutual benefit; a type of promotional campaign.

checking The process of going through the goods upon receipt to ensure they arrived undamaged and that the merchandise ordered was the merchandise received.

choice architecture When evaluating alternatives, the influence that the design of the environment has on how consumers make choices.

churn The number of consumers who stop using a product or service, divided by the average number of consumers of that product or service.

click path Shows how users proceed through the information on a website—not unlike how grocery stores try to track the way shoppers move through their aisles.

click-through rate (CTR) The number of times a user clicks on an online ad divided by the number of impressions.

closing the sale Obtaining a commitment from the customer to make a purchase.

co-branding The practice of marketing two or more brands together, on the same package or promotion.

coercive power A type of marketing channel power that occurs when a member uses threats or punishment of the other channel member for not undertaking certain tasks. Delaying payment for late delivery would be an example.

cognitive component A component of *attitude* that reflects what a person believes to be true.

cold calls A method of prospecting in which salespeople telephone or go to see potential customers without appointments.

commission Compensation or financial incentive for salespeople based on a fixed percentage of their sales.

communication channel The medium—print, broadcast, the Internet—that carries the message.

communication gap A type of *service gap*; refers to the difference between the actual service provided to customers and the service that the firm's promotion program promises.

company sales force The people who are employees of the selling company and are engaged in the selling process.

compensatory decision rule At work when the consumer is evaluating alternatives and trades off one characteristic against another such that good characteristics compensate for bad ones.

competition-based pricing method An approach that attempts to reflect how the firm wants consumers to interpret its products relative to the competitors' offerings; for example, setting a price close to a competitor's price signals to consumers that the product is similar, whereas setting the price much higher signals greater features, better quality, or some other valued benefit.

competitive parity A firm's strategy of setting prices that are similar to those of major competitors.

competitor orientation A company objective based on the premise that the firm should measure itself primarily against its competition.

complementary products Products whose demand curves are positively related, such that they rise or fall together; a percentage increase in demand for one results in a percentage increase in demand for the other.

concentrated targeting strategy A marketing strategy of selecting a single, primary target market and focusing all energies on providing a product to fit that market's needs.

concept Brief written description of a product or service; its technology, working principles, and forms; and what customer needs it would satisfy.

concept testing The process in which a concept statement that describes a product or a service is presented to potential buyers or users to obtain their reactions.

connected effect With regard to the Wheel of Social Media Engagement, the connected effect is an outcome of social media that satisfies humans' innate need to connect with other people.

conscious marketing An approach to marketing that acknowledges four key principles: a higher purpose, stakeholders, conscious leadership, and a conscious culture.

consensus buying center A buying center in which all members of the team must reach a collective agreement that they can support a particular purchase.

consultative buying center A buying center in which one person makes the decision, but he or she solicits input from others before doing so.

consumer decision rules The set of criteria that consumers use consciously or subconsciously to quickly and efficiently select from among several alternatives.

consumer product Products and services used by people for their personal use.

consumer-to-consumer (C2C) marketing The process in which consumers sell to other consumers.

contest A brand-sponsored competition that requires some form of skill or effort.

continuous advertising schedule An advertising schedule that runs steadily throughout the year and therefore is suited to products and services that are consumed continually at relatively steady rates and that require a steady level of persuasive or reminder advertising.

contractual vertical marketing system A system in which independent firms at different levels of the supply chain join together through contracts to obtain economies of scale and coordination and to reduce conflict.

contribution per unit The price less the variable cost per unit. Variable used to determine the break-even point in units.

control phase The part of the strategic marketing planning process when managers evaluate the performance of the marketing strategy and take any necessary corrective actions.

convenience products/services Products or services for which the consumer is not willing to spend any effort to evaluate prior to purchase.

convenience store Type of retailer that provides a limited number of items at a convenient location in a small store with speedy checkout.

conventional supermarket Type of retailer that offers groceries, meat, and produce with limited sales of nonfood items, such as health and beauty aids and general merchandise, in a self-service format.

conversion rate A measure that indicates what percentage of visitors or potential customers click, buy, or donate at the site.

cooperative (co-op) advertising An agreement between a manufacturer and retailer in which the manufacturer agrees to defray some advertising costs.

core customer value The basic problem-solving benefits that consumers are seeking.

corporate blog A website created by a company and often used to educate customers.

corporate social responsibility (CSR) Refers to the voluntary actions taken by a company to address the ethical, social, and environmental impacts of its business operations and the concerns of its stakeholders.

corporate vertical marketing system A system in which the parent company has complete control and can dictate the priorities and objectives of the supply chain; it may own facilities such as manufacturing plants, warehouse facilities, retail outlets, and design studios.

cost-based pricing method An approach that determines the final price to charge by starting with the cost, without recognizing the role that consumers or competitors' prices play in the marketplace.

cost-of-ownership method A value-based method for setting prices that determines the total cost of owning the product over its useful life.

country culture Similar to culture in general, but at a country level. Entails easy-to-spot visible nuances that are particular to a country, such as dress, symbols, ceremonies, language, colors, and food preferences, and subtler aspects, which are trickier to identify.

coupon Provides a stated discount to consumers on the final selling price of a specific item; the retailer handles the discount.

cross-docking distribution center A distribution center to which vendors ship merchandise prepackaged and ready for sale. The merchandise goes to a staging area rather than into storage. When all the merchandise going to a particular store has arrived in the staging area, it is loaded onto a truck, and away it goes. Thus, merchandise goes from the receiving dock to the shipping dock—cross dock.

cross-price elasticity The percentage change in demand for product A that occurs in response to a percentage change in price of product B; see also *complementary products*.

cross-promoting Efforts of two or more firms joining together to reach a specific target market.

crowdsourcing Users submit ideas for a new product or service, and/or comment and vote on the ideas submitted by others.

culture The shared meanings, beliefs, morals, values, and customs of a group of people. It is transmitted by words, literature, and institutions and is passed down from generation to generation and learned over time.

cumulative quantity discount Pricing tactic that offers a discount based on the amount purchased over a specified period and usually involves several transactions; encourages resellers to maintain their current supplier because the cost to switch must include the loss of the discount.

customer excellence Involves a focus on retaining loyal customers and excellent customer service.

customer lifetime value (CLV) The expected financial contribution from a particular customer to the firm's profits over the course of their entire relationship.

customer orientation A company objective based on the premise that the firm should measure itself primarily according to whether it meets its customers' needs.

customer relationship management (CRM) A business philosophy and set of strategies, programs, and systems that focus on identifying and building loyalty among the firm's most valued customers.

customer service Specifically refers to human or mechanical activities firms undertake to help satisfy their customers' needs and wants.

data Raw numbers or facts.

data mining The use of a variety of statistical analysis tools to uncover previously unknown patterns in the data stored in databases or relationships among variables.

data warehouses Large computer files that store millions and even billions of pieces of individual data.

deal A type of short-term price reduction that can take several forms, such as a "featured price," a price lower than the regular price; a "buy one, get one free" offer; or a certain percentage "more free" offer contained in larger packaging; can involve a special financing arrangement, such as reduced percentage interest rates or extended repayment terms.

decider The buying center participant who ultimately determines any part of or the entire buying decision—whether to buy, what to buy, how to buy, or where to buy.

decline stage Stage of the product life cycle when sales decline and the product eventually exits the market.

decoding The process by which the receiver interprets the sender's message.

default An element of choice architecture (the environment) that deals with a "no-action" condition by imposing a choice on a person who fails to make a decision or does not actively opt for a different alternative.

delivery gap A type of *service gap*; the difference between the firm's service standards and the actual service it provides to customers.

demand curve Shows how many units of a product or service consumers will demand during a specific period at different prices.

democratic buying center A buying center in which the majority rules in making decisions.

demographic segmentation The grouping of consumers according to easily measured, objective characteristics such as age, gender, income, and education.

demographics Information about the characteristics of human populations and segments, especially those used to identify consumer markets such as by age, gender, income, and education.

department store A retailer that carries many different types of merchandise (broad variety) and lots of items within each type (deep assortment); offers some customer services; and is organized into separate departments to display its merchandise.

depth The number of categories within a product line.

derived demand The linkage between consumers' demand for a company's output and its purchase of necessary inputs to manufacture or assemble that particular output.

determinant attributes Product or service features that are important to the buyer and on which competing brands or stores are perceived to differ.

differentiated targeting strategy A strategy through which a firm targets several market segments with a different offering for each.

diffusion of innovation The process by which the use of an innovation, whether a product or a service, spreads throughout a market group over time and over various categories of adopters.

digital marketing All online marketing activities, which includes all digital assets, channels, and media spanning not just online but also social media and mobile marketing.

Digital Native See *Generation Z.*

direct investment When a firm maintains 100 percent ownership of its plants, operation facilities, and offices in a foreign country, often through the formation of wholly owned subsidiaries.

direct marketing Sales and promotional techniques that communicate directly with target customers to generate a response or transaction.

direct marketing channel A marketing channel in which there are no intermediaries; the manufacturer sells directly to the buyer.

dispatcher The person who coordinates deliveries to distribution centers.

distribution center A facility for the receipt, storage, and redistribution of goods to company stores or customers; may be operated by retailers, manufacturers, or distribution specialists.

distribution intensity The number of supply chain members to use at each level of the supply chain.

distributive fairness Pertains to a customer's perception of the benefits he or she received compared with the costs (inconvenience or loss) that resulted from a service failure.

distributor A type of reseller or marketing intermediary that resells manufactured products without significantly altering their form. Distributors often buy from manufacturers and sell to other businesses like retailers in a B2B transaction.

diversification strategy A growth strategy whereby a firm introduces a new product or service to a market segment that it does not currently serve.

drugstore A specialty store that concentrates on health and personal grooming merchandise, though pharmaceuticals may represent almost 70 percent of its sales.

duty See *tariff.*

dynamic effect With regard to the Wheel of Social Media Engagement, the *dynamic effect* describes the way in which information is exchanged to network participants through back-and-forth communications in an active and effective manner. It also expands the impact of the network effect by examining how people flow in and out of networked communities as their interests change (see *network effect*).

dynamic pricing Refers to the process of charging different prices for goods or services based on the type of customer; time of the day, week, or even season; and level of demand. Also called *individualized pricing.*

early adopters The second group of consumers in the diffusion of innovation model, after *innovators,* to use a product or service innovation represent about 13.5 percent of the population. They generally don't like to take as much risk as innovators but instead wait and purchase the product after careful review.

early majority A group of consumers in the diffusion of innovation model that represents approximately 34 percent of the population; members don't like to take much risk and therefore tend to wait until bugs are worked out of a particular product or service; few new products and services can be profitable until this large group buys them.

economic situation Macroeconomic factor that affects the way consumers buy merchandise and spend money, both in a marketer's home country and abroad; see also *inflation, foreign currency fluctuations,* and *interest rates.*

elastic Refers to a market for a product or service that is price sensitive; that is, relatively small changes in price will generate fairly large changes in the quantity demanded.

electronic data interchange (EDI) The computer-to-computer exchange of business documents from a retailer to a vendor and back.

emotional appeal An appeal that aims to satisfy consumers' emotional desires rather than their utilitarian needs.

emotional support Concern for others' well-being and support of their decisions in a job setting.

empowerment In the context of service delivery, means allowing employees to make decisions about how service is provided to customers.

encoding The process of converting the sender's ideas into a message, which could be verbal, visual, or both.

esteem needs Part of Maslow's hierarchy, these are needs that enable people to fulfill inner desires.

evaluative criteria Consist of a set of salient, or important, attributes about a particular product.

event sponsorship Popular PR tool that occurs when corporations support various activities (financially or otherwise), usually in the cultural or sports and entertainment sectors.

everyday low pricing (EDLP) A strategy companies use to emphasize the continuity of their retail prices at a level somewhere between the regular, nonsale price and the deep-discount sale prices their competitors may offer.

evoked set Comprises the alternative brands or stores that the consumer states he or she would consider when making a purchase decision.

exchange The trade of things of value between the buyer and the seller so that each is better off as a result.

exchange control The regulation of a country's currency *exchange rate.*

exchange rate The measure of how much one currency is worth in relation to another.

exclusive distribution Strategy in which only selected retailers can sell a manufacturer's brand.

experience curve effect The drop in unit cost as the accumulated volume sold increases; as sales continue to grow, the costs continue to drop, allowing even further reductions in the price.

experiment See *experimental research.*

experimental research (experiment) A type of conclusive and quantitative research that systematically manipulates one or more variables to determine which variables have a causal effect on another variable.

expertise power A type of marketing channel power that occurs when a channel member uses its expertise as leverage to influence the actions of another channel member.

exporting Producing goods in one country and selling them in another.

extended problem solving A purchase decision process during which the consumer devotes considerable time and effort to analyzing alternatives; often occurs when the consumer perceives that the purchase decision entails a lot of risk.

external locus of control Refers to when consumers believe that fate or other external factors control all outcomes.

external search for information Occurs when the buyer seeks information outside his or her personal knowledge base to help make the buying decision.

extreme-value food retailer See *limited-assortment supermarket.*

extreme-value retailer A general merchandise discount store found in lower-income urban or rural areas.

facial recognition software Software that can automatically identify or verify individuals from video or digital images.

family brand A firm's own corporate name used to brand its product lines and products.

feedback loop Allows the receiver to communicate with the sender and thereby informs the sender whether the message was received and decoded properly.

financial risk Risk associated with a monetary outlay; includes the initial cost of the purchase as well as the costs of using the item or service.

first movers Product pioneers that are the first to create a market or product category, making them readily recognizable to consumers and thus establishing a commanding and early market share lead.

fixed costs Those costs that remain essentially at the same level, regardless of any changes in the volume of production.

flighting (advertising schedule) An advertising schedule implemented in spurts, with periods of heavy advertising followed by periods of no advertising.

floor-ready merchandise Merchandise that is ready to be placed on the selling floor immediately.

focus group interview A research technique in which a small group of persons (usually 8 to 12) comes together for an intensive discussion about a particular topic, with the conversation guided by a trained moderator using an unstructured method of inquiry.

food deserts Areas and neighborhoods in which consumers, usually of lower socioeconomic strata, have limited or no access to healthy, affordable, fresh food options.

foreign currency fluctuations Changes in the value of a country's currency relative to the currency of another country; can influence consumer spending.

four Ps See *marketing mix.*

franchisee See *franchising.*

franchising A contractual agreement between a *franchisor* and a *franchisee* that allows the franchisee to operate a business using a name and format developed and supported by the franchisor.

franchisor See *franchising.*

freemium apps Apps that are free to download but include in-app purchases that enable the user to enhance an app or game (see also *in-app purchase*).

frequency Measure of how often the audience is exposed to a communication within a specified period of time.

fulfillment center Warehouse facilities used to ship merchandise directly to customers.

full-line discount store Retailer that offers low prices, limited service, and a broad variety of merchandise.

functional needs Pertain to the performance of a product or service.

gatekeeper The buying center participant who controls information or access to decision makers and influencers.

Generation X (Gen X) Generational cohort of people born between 1965 and 1976.

Generation Y (Gen Y) Generational cohort of people born between 1977 and 2000; biggest cohort since the original postwar baby boom. Also called *Millennials*.

Generation Z (Gen Z) Generational cohort of people born between 2001 and 2014. Also known as *Digital Natives* because people in this group were born into a world that already was full of electronic gadgets and digital technologies, such as the Internet and social networks.

generational cohort A group of people of the same generation—typically have similar purchase behaviors because they have shared experiences and are in the same stage of life.

geodemographic segmentation The grouping of consumers on the basis of a combination of geographic, demographic, and lifestyle characteristics.

geographic segmentation The grouping of consumers on the basis of where they live.

globalization The processes by which goods, services, capital, people, information, and ideas flow across national borders.

glocalization The process of firms standardizing their products globally, but using different promotional campaigns to sell them.

goods Items that can be physically touched.

gray market Employs irregular but not necessarily illegal methods; generally, it legally circumvents authorized channels of distribution to sell goods at prices lower than those intended by the manufacturer.

green marketing A strategic effort by firms to supply customers with environmentally friendly merchandise.

greenwashing Exploiting consumers by disingenuously marketing products or services as environmentally friendly, with the goal of gaining public approval and sales.

gross domestic product (GDP) Defined as the market value of the goods and services produced by a country in a year; the most widely used standardized measure of output.

gross national income (GNI) Consists of GDP plus the net income earned from investments abroad (minus any payments made to nonresidents who contribute to the domestic economy).

gross rating points (GRP) Measure used for various media advertising—print, radio, or television; GRP = Reach × Frequency.

growth stage Stage of the product life cycle when the product gains acceptance, demand and sales increase, and competitors emerge in the product category.

habitual decision making A purchase decision process in which consumers engage with little conscious effort.

headline In an advertisement, large type designed to draw attention.

heterogeneity As it refers to the differences between the marketing of products and services, the delivery of services is more variable.

high/low pricing A *pricing strategy* that relies on the promotion of sales, during which prices are temporarily reduced to encourage purchases.

hit A request for a file made by web browsers and search engines. Hits are commonly misinterpreted as a metric for website success; however, the number of hits typically is much larger than the number of people visiting a website.

horizontal channel conflict A type of channel conflict in which members at the same level of a marketing channel, for example, two competing retailers or two competing manufacturers, are in disagreement or discord, such as when they are in a price war.

horizontal price fixing Occurs when competitors that produce and sell competing products collude, or work together, to control prices, effectively taking price out of the decision process for consumers.

ideal point The position at which a particular market segment's ideal product would lie on a *perceptual map*.

ideas Intellectual concepts—thoughts, opinions, and philosophies.

implementation phase The part of the strategic marketing planning process when marketing managers (1) identify and evaluate different opportunities by engaging in segmentation, targeting, and positioning (see also *segmentation, targeting, and positioning*) and (2) implement the marketing mix using the four Ps.

impressions The number of times an advertisement appears in front of the user.

improvement value Represents an estimate of how much more (or less) consumers are willing to pay for a product relative to other comparable products.

impulse buying A buying decision made by customers on the spot when they see the merchandise.

impulse products Products that are purchased without planning, such as fragrances and cosmetics in a department store and magazines in supermarkets.

in-app purchase A purchase made on a freemium app that enables the user to enhance the app or game.

in-depth interview An exploratory research technique in which trained researchers ask questions, listen to and record the answers, and then pose additional questions to clarify or expand on a particular issue.

inbound marketing Marketing activities that draw the attention of customers through blogs, Twitter, LinkedIn, and other online sources, rather than using more traditional activities that require having to go out to get customers' attention, such as making a sales call.

income effect The change in the quantity of a product demanded by consumers due to a change in their income.

independent agents Salespeople who sell a manufacturer's products on an extended contract basis but are not employees of the manufacturer; also known as *manufacturer's representatives* or *reps*.

independent (conventional) marketing channel A marketing channel in which several independent members—a manufacturer, a wholesaler, and a retailer—each attempts to satisfy its own objectives and maximize its profits, often at the expense of the other members.

indirect marketing channel When one or more intermediaries work with manufacturers to provide goods and services to customers.

individual brands The use of individual brand names for each of a firm's products.

individualized pricing See *dynamic pricing*.

inelastic Refers to a market for a product or service that is price insensitive; that is, relatively small changes in price will not generate large changes in the quantity demanded.

inflation Refers to the persistent increase in the prices of goods and services.

influencer The buying center participant whose views influence other members of the buying center in making the final decision.

information Organized, analyzed, interpreted data that offer value to marketers.

information effect With regard to the Wheel of Social Media Engagement, the *information effect* is the outcome of social media in which relevant information is spread by firms or individuals to other members of their social network.

information encoding stage The first stage in memory development in which consumers transform information that they receive about products and services into storable information.

information power A type of marketing channel power within an administered vertical marketing system in which one party (e.g., the manufacturer) provides or withholds important information to influence the actions of another party (e.g., the retailer).

information storage stage The second stage in memory development that refers to how that knowledge gets integrated and stored with what consumers already know and remember.

informational appeal Used in a promotion to help consumers make purchase decisions by offering factual information and strong arguments built around relevant issues that encourage them to evaluate the brand favorably on the basis of the key benefits it provides.

informative advertising Communication used to create and build brand awareness, with the ultimate goal of moving the consumer through the buying cycle to a purchase.

infrastructure The basic facilities, services, and installations needed for a community or society to function, such as transportation and communications systems, water and power lines, and public institutions like schools, post offices, and prisons.

initiator The buying center participant who first suggests buying the particular product or service.

innovation The process by which ideas are transformed into new products and services that will help firms grow.

innovators Those buyers, representing approximately 2.5 percent of the population, who want to be the first to have the new product or service.

inseparable A characteristic of a service: it is produced and consumed at the same time; that is, service and consumption are inseparable.

institutional advertisement A type of advertising that promotes a company, corporation, business, institution, or organization. Unlike product-focused advertisements, it is not intended to sell a particular product or service.

instrumental support Providing the equipment or systems needed to perform a task in a job setting.

intangible A characteristic of a service; it cannot be touched, tasted, or seen like a pure product can.

integrated marketing communications (IMC) Represents the promotion dimension of the four Ps; encompasses a variety of communication disciplines—general advertising, personal selling, sales promotion, public relations, direct marketing, and electronic media—in combination to provide clarity, consistency, and maximum communicative impact.

intensive distribution A strategy designed to get products into as many outlets as possible.

interest rates The cost of borrowing money; the cost to the customer or the fee the bank charges those customers for borrowing the money.

internal locus of control Refers to when consumers believe they have some control over the outcomes of their actions, in which case they generally engage in more search activities.

internal search for information Occurs when the buyer examines his or her own memory and knowledge about the product or service, gathered through past experiences.

Internet of Things (IoT) When multiple "smart devices" with Internet-connected sensors, such as refrigerators, dishwashers, and coffeemakers, combine the data they have collected to help both consumers and companies consume more efficiently.

introduction stage Stage of the product life cycle when innovators start buying the product.

involvement Consumer's interest in a product or service.

joint venture Formed when a firm entering a new market pools its resources with those of a local firm to form a new company in which ownership, control, and profits are shared.

just-in-time (JIT) inventory system Inventory management system designed to deliver less merchandise on a more frequent basis than traditional inventory systems; the firm gets the merchandise "just in time" for it to be used in the manufacture of another product, in the case of parts or components, or for sale when the customer wants it, in the case of consumer goods; also known as *quick response (QR) inventory system* in retailing.

keyword A phrase that describes the contents of a web page.

keyword analysis An evaluation of what keywords people use to search on the Internet for their products and services.

knowledge gap A type of *service gap;* reflects the difference between customers' *expectations* and the firm's perception of those expectations.

laggards Consumers, representing approximately 16 percent of the population, who like to avoid change and rely on traditional products until they are no longer available. Sometimes laggards never adopt a product or service.

lagged effect A delayed response to a marketing communication campaign.

late majority The last group of buyers to enter a new product market, representing approximately 34% of the population; when they do, the product has achieved its full market potential.

lead time The amount of time between the recognition that an order needs to be placed and the arrival of the needed merchandise at the seller's store, ready for sale.

lead users Innovative product users who modify existing products according to their own ideas to suit their specific needs.

leader pricing Consumer pricing tactic that attempts to build store traffic by aggressively pricing and advertising a regularly purchased item, often priced at or just above the store's cost.

leads A list of potential customers.

learning A person's thought process or behavior that arises from experience and takes place throughout the consumer decision process.

lease or rental A written agreement under which the owner of an item or property allows its use for a specified period of time in exchange for a fee.

legitimate power A type of marketing channel power that occurs if the channel member exerting the power has a contractual agreement with the other channel member that requires the other channel member to behave in a certain way. This type of power occurs in an administered vertical marketing system.

licensing A method used in developing new products in which a firm buys the rights to use a technology or idea from another firm.

lifestyle The way a person lives his or her life to achieve goals.

lift Additional sales caused by advertising.

limited problem solving Occurs during a purchase decision that calls for, at most, a moderate amount of effort and time.

limited-assortment supermarket Retailer that offers only one or two brands or sizes of most products (usually including a store brand) and attempts to achieve great efficiency to lower costs and prices. See also *extreme-value food retailer.*

line extension The use of the same brand name within the same product line; represents an increase in a product line's depth.

locational excellence A method of achieving excellence by having a strong physical location and/or Internet presence.

loss-leader pricing Loss-leader pricing takes the tactic of *leader pricing* one step further by lowering the price below the store's cost.

love needs Part of Maslow's hierarchy, needs are expressed through interactions with others.

loyalty program Specifically designed to retain customers by offering premiums or other incentives to customers who make multiple purchases over time.

loyalty segmentation Strategy of investing in loyalty initiatives to retain the firm's most profitable customers.

macroenvironmental factors Aspects of the external environment that affect a company's business, such as the culture, demographics, social trends, technological advances, economic situation, and political/legal environment (CDSTEP).

manufacturer brands (national brands) Brands owned and managed by the manufacturer.

manufacturer's representatives (reps) See *independent agents.*

manufacturer's suggested retail price (MSRP) The price that manufacturers suggest retailers use to sell their merchandise.

markdowns Reductions retailers take on the initial selling price of the product or service.

market development strategy A growth strategy that employs the existing marketing offering to reach new market segments, whether domestic or international.

market growth rate The annual rate of growth of the specific market in which the product competes.

market penetration strategy A growth strategy that employs the existing marketing mix and focuses on the firm's efforts on existing customers.

market positioning The process of defining the marketing mix variables so that target customers have a clear, distinctive, desirable understanding of what the product does or represents in comparison with competing products.

market segment A group of consumers who respond similarly to a firm's marketing efforts.

market segmentation The process of dividing the market into groups of customers with different needs, wants, or characteristics—who therefore might appreciate products or services geared especially for them.

market share Percentage of a market accounted for by a specific entity.

marketing An organizational function and a set of processes for creating, *capturing,* communicating, and delivering value to customers and for managing customer relationships in ways that benefit the organization and its stakeholders.

marketing channel The set of institutions that transfer the ownership of and move goods from the point of production to the point of consumption; consists of all the institutions and marketing activities in the marketing process.

marketing channel management Also called *supply chain management,* refers to a set of approaches and techniques firms employ to efficiently and effectively integrate their suppliers.

marketing ethics Refers to those ethical problems that are specific to the domain of marketing.

marketing mix (four Ps) Product, price, place, and promotion—the controllable set of activities that a firm uses to respond to the wants of its target markets.

marketing plan A written document composed of an analysis of the current marketing situation, opportunities and threats for the firm, marketing objectives and strategy specified in terms of the four Ps, action programs, and projected or pro forma income (and other financial) statements.

marketing research A set of techniques and principles for systematically collecting, recording, analyzing, and interpreting data that can aid decision makers involved in marketing goods, services, or ideas.

marketing strategy A firm's target market, marketing mix, and method of obtaining a sustainable competitive advantage.

Maslow's hierarchy of needs A paradigm for classifying people's motives. It argues that when lower-level, more basic needs (physiological and safety) are fulfilled, people turn to satisfying their higher-level human needs (social and personal); see also *physiological, safety, love,* and *personal needs.*

mass media Channels that are ideal for reaching large numbers of anonymous audience members; include national newspapers, magazines, radio, and television.

maturity stage Stage of the product life cycle when industry sales reach their peak, so firms try to rejuvenate their products by adding new features or repositioning them.

maximizing profits A profit strategy that relies primarily on economic theory. If a firm can accurately specify a mathematical model that captures all the factors required to explain and predict sales and profits, it should be able to identify the price at which its profits are maximized.

media buy The actual purchase of airtime or print pages.

media mix The combination of the media used and the frequency of advertising in each medium.

media planning The process of evaluating and selecting the *media mix* that will deliver a clear, consistent, compelling message to the intended audience.

memories Psychological factors that affect decision-making that consist of information that has been acquired and stored in the brain, to be available and utilized when needed.

metric A measuring system that quantifies a trend, dynamic, or characteristic.

microblog Differs from a traditional blog in size. Consists of short sentences, short videos, or individual images. Twitter is an example of a microblog.

micromarketing An extreme form of segmentation that tailors a product or service to suit an individual customer's wants or needs; also called *one-to-one marketing*.

Millennials See *Generation Y*.

mission statement A broad description of a firm's objectives and the scope of activities it plans to undertake; attempts to answer two main questions: What type of business is it? What does it need to do to accomplish its goals and objectives?

mobile commerce (M-commerce) Communicating with or selling to consumers through wireless handheld devices such as cellular telephones.

mobile marketing Marketing through wireless handheld devices such as cellular telephones.

mobile task management Mobile task management technology is a wireless network and a mobile device that receives demand notification and enables a speedy response.

modified rebuy In a B2B setting, refers to when the buyer has purchased a similar product in the past but has decided to change some specifications, such as the desired price, quality level, customer service level, options, and so forth.

monopolistic competition Competition that occurs when there are many firms that sell closely related but not homogeneous products; these products may be viewed as substitutes but are not perfect substitutes.

monopoly One firm provides the product or service in a particular industry.

motive A need or want that is strong enough to cause the person to seek satisfaction.

multi-attribute model A compensatory model of customer decision making based on the notion that customers see a product as a collection of attributes or characteristics. The model uses a weighted average score based on the importance of various attributes and performance on those issues.

need recognition The beginning of the consumer decision process; occurs when consumers recognize they have an unsatisfied need and want to go from their actual, needy state to a different, desired state.

negative word of mouth Occurs when consumers spread negative information about a product, service, or store to others.

network effect With regard to the Wheel of Social Media Engagement, the *network effect* is the outcome of social media engagement in which every time a firm or person posts information, it is transferred to the poster's vast connections across social media, causing the information to spread instantaneously.

neuromarketing The process of examining consumers' brain patterns to determine their responses to marketing communications, products, or services for the purpose of developing marketing tactics or strategies

new buy In a B2B setting, a purchase of a good or service for the first time; the buying decision is likely to be quite involved because the buyer or the buying organization does not have any experience with the item.

niche media Channels that are focused and generally used to reach narrow segments, often with unique demographic characteristics or interests.

noise Any interference that stems from competing messages, a lack of clarity in the message, or a flaw in the medium; a problem for all communication channels.

noncompensatory decision rule At work when consumers choose a product or service on the basis of a subset of its characteristics, regardless of the values of its other attributes.

noncumulative quantity discount Pricing tactic that offers a discount based on only the amount purchased in a single order; provides the buyer with an incentive to purchase more merchandise immediately.

nudge One element of the choice architecture (environment) that alters behavior in a predictable way, without forbidding other options or significantly changing any economic incentives.

objective-and-task method An IMC budgeting method that determines the cost required to undertake specific tasks to accomplish communication objectives; process entails setting objectives, choosing media, and determining costs.

observation An exploratory research method that entails examining purchase and consumption behaviors through personal or video camera scrutiny.

occasion segmentation A type of behavioral segmentation based on when a product or service is purchased or consumed.

off-price retailer A type of retailer that offers an inconsistent assortment of merchandise at relatively low prices.

olfactory senses A sensory stimulation that involves smell and influences the shopping experience, e.g., cinnamon rolls.

oligopolistic competition Competition that occurs when only a few firms dominate a market.

omnichannel (multichannel) strategy Selling in more than one channel (e.g., stores, Internet, catalog).

one-to-one marketing See *micromarketing*.

online chat Instant messaging or voice conversation with an online sales representative.

operational excellence Involves a firm's focus on efficient operations, excellent supply chain management, and strong relationships with its suppliers.

opt in A customer privacy issue prevalent in the European Union. Takes the perspective that consumers "own" their personal information. Retailers must get consumers to explicitly agree to share this personal information.

opt out A customer privacy issue prevalent in the United States. Takes the perspective that personal information is generally viewed as being in the public domain and retailers can use it in any way they desire. Consumers must explicitly tell retailers not to use their personal information.

order getter A salesperson whose primary responsibilities are identifying potential customers and engaging those customers in discussions to attempt to make a sale.

order taker A salesperson whose primary responsibility is to process routine orders or reorders or rebuys for products.

organic search The process of listing web page results based on the relevancy of key terms.

organizational culture Reflects the set of values, traditions, and customs that guide a firm's employees' behavior.

outsourcing A practice in which the client firm hires an outside firm to facilitate some aspect of its business. In the context of new product development, the outsourced firm helps its client develop new products or services.

page view The number of times an Internet page gets viewed by any visitor.

paid apps Apps that charge the customer an upfront price to download the app ($0.99 is the most common), but offer full functionality once downloaded.

paid apps with in-app purchase Apps that require the consumer to pay initially to download the app and then offer the ability to buy additional functionality.

paid search A method used by firms to appear higher up in the search results of a search engine. The position on the search page is based on a fee charged by the search engine, and often an additional fee is charged every time a user clicks on the entry.

panel data Information collected from a group of consumers.

partnering (strategic) relationship A supply chain relationship that the members are committed to maintaining long term, investing in opportunities that are mutually beneficial; requires mutual trust, open communication, common goals, and credible commitments. See *strategic relationships*.

penetration pricing strategy A new product or service pricing strategy in which the initial price is set relatively low with the objective of building sales, market share, and profits quickly and to deter competition from entering the market.

perceived value The relationship between a product's or service's benefits and its cost.

perception The process by which people select, organize, and interpret information to form a meaningful picture of the world.

perceptual map Displays, in two or more dimensions, the position of products or brands in the consumer's mind.

performance risk The perceived danger inherent in a poorly performing product or service.

perishable A characteristic of a service: it cannot be stored for use in the future.

personal blog Website created by and usually for individuals, with relatively few marketing implications.

personal selling The two-way flow of communication between a buyer and a seller that is designed to influence the buyer's purchase decision.

persuasive advertising Communication used to motivate consumers to take action.

physical environment The land, the water, the air, and living organisms (flora and fauna).

physiological needs Needs relating to the basic biological necessities of life: food, drink, rest, and shelter. This is part of Maslow's hierarchy.

physiological risk The fear of an actual harm should a product not perform properly.

pick ticket A document or display on a screen in a forklift truck indicating how much of each item to get from specific storage areas.

pioneers New product introductions that establish a completely new market or radically change both the rules of competition and consumer preferences in a market; also called *breakthroughs*.

planner In a retailing context, an employee who is responsible for the financial planning and analysis of merchandise and its allocation to stores.

planning phase The part of the strategic marketing planning process when marketing executives, in conjunction with other top managers (1) define the mission or vision of the business and (2) evaluate the situation by assessing how various players, both in and outside the organization, affect the firm's potential for success.

point-of-purchase (POP) display A merchandise display located at the point of purchase, such as at the checkout counter in a grocery store.

political/legal environment Comprises political parties, government organizations, and legislation and laws.

postpurchase cognitive dissonance The psychologically uncomfortable state produced by an inconsistency between beliefs and behaviors that in turn evokes a motivation to reduce the dissonance; buyers' remorse.

posttesting The evaluation of an IMC campaign's impact after it has been implemented.

power A situation that occurs in a marketing channel in which one member has the means or ability to have control over the actions of another member in a channel at a different level of distribution, such as if a retailer has power or control over a supplier.

preapproach In the personal selling process, occurs prior to meeting the customer for the first time and extends the qualification of leads procedure; in this step, the salesperson conducts additional research and develops plans for meeting with the customer.

predatory pricing A firm's practice of setting a very low price for one or more of its products with the intent to drive its competition out of business; illegal under both the Sherman Antitrust Act and the Federal Trade Commission Act.

predictive analytics The use of statistics on data to determine patterns and predict future outcomes and trends.

premarket test Conducted before a product or service is brought to market to determine how many customers will try and then continue to use it.

premium An item offered for free or at a bargain price to reward some type of behavior, such as buying, sampling, or testing.

premium pricing A competitor-based pricing method by which the firm deliberately prices a product above the prices set for competing products to capture those consumers who always shop for the best or for whom price does not matter.

prestige products or services Products and services that consumers purchase for status rather than functionality.

pretesting Assessments performed before an ad campaign is implemented to ensure that the various elements are working in an integrated fashion and doing what they are intended to do.

price The overall sacrifice a consumer is willing to make—money, time, energy—to acquire a specific product or service.

price bundling Consumer pricing tactic of selling more than one product for a single, lower price than what the items would cost sold separately; can be used to sell slow-moving items, to encourage customers to stock up so they won't purchase competing brands, to encourage trial of a new product, or to provide an incentive to purchase a less desirable product or service to obtain a more desirable one in the same bundle.

price discrimination The practice of selling the same product to different resellers (wholesalers, distributors, or retailers) or to the ultimate consumer at different prices; some, but not all, forms of price discrimination are illegal.

price elasticity of demand Measures how changes in a price affect the quantity of the product demanded; specifically, the ratio of the percentage change in quantity demanded to the percentage change in price.

price fixing The practice of colluding with other firms to control prices.

price lining Consumer market pricing tactic of establishing a price floor and a price ceiling for an entire line of similar products and then setting a few other price points in between to represent distinct differences in quality.

price skimming A strategy of selling a new product or service at a high price that *innovators* and *early adopters* are willing to pay in order to obtain it; after the high-price market segment becomes saturated and sales begin to slow down, the firm generally lowers the price to capture (or skim) the next most price-sensitive segment.

price war A situation [or competition] that occurs when two or more firms compete primarily by lowering their prices.

pricing strategy A long-term approach to setting prices for the firms' products.

pricing tactics Short-term methods, in contrast to long-term *pricing strategies*, used to focus on company objectives, costs, customers, competition, or channel members; can be responses to competitive threats (e.g., lowering price temporarily to meet a competitor's price reduction) or broadly accepted methods of calculating a final price for the customer that is short term in nature.

primary data Data collected to address specific research needs.

primary package The packaging the consumer uses, such as the toothpaste tube, from which he or she typically seeks convenience in terms of storage, use, and consumption.

private-label brand Brand developed and marketed by a retailer and available only from that retailer; also called *store brand*.

procedural fairness Refers to the customer's perception of the fairness of the process used to resolve complaints about service.

product Anything that is of value to a consumer and can be offered through a voluntary marketing exchange.

product design See *product development*.

product development Also called *product design;* entails a process of balancing various engineering, manufacturing, marketing, and economic considerations to develop a product's form and features or a service's features.

product development strategy A growth strategy that offers a new product or service to a firm's current target market.

product excellence Involves a focus on achieving high-quality products; effective branding and positioning is key.

product life cycle Defines the stages that new products move through as they enter, get established in, and ultimately leave the marketplace and thereby offers marketers a starting point for their strategy planning.

product line Group of associated items, such as those that consumers use together or think of as part of a group of similar products.

product mix The complete set of all products offered by a firm.

product placement Inclusion of a product in nontraditional situations, such as in a scene in a movie or television program.

product-focused advertisements Advertisements used to inform, persuade, or remind consumers about a specific product or service.

professional blog Website written by a person who reviews and gives recommendations on products and services.

profit orientation A company objective that can be implemented by focusing on *target profit pricing, maximizing profits,* or *target return pricing.*

prototype The first physical form or service description of a new product, still in rough or tentative form, that has the same properties as a new product but is produced through different manufacturing processes, sometimes even crafted individually.

psychographic segmentation A method of segmenting customers based on how they spend their time and money, what activities they pursue, and their attitudes and opinions about the world in which they live.

psychographics Used in segmentation; delves into how consumers describe themselves; allows people to describe themselves using those characteristics that help them choose how they occupy their time (behavior) and what underlying psychological reasons determine those choices.

psychological needs Pertain to the personal gratification consumers associate with a product or service.

psychological risk Associated with the way people will feel if the product or service does not convey the right image.

public relations (PR) The organizational function that manages the firm's communications to achieve a variety of objectives, including building and maintaining a positive image, handling or heading off unfavorable stories or events, and maintaining positive relationships with the media.

public service advertising (PSA) Advertising that focuses on public welfare and generally is sponsored by nonprofit institutions, civic groups, religious organizations, trade associations, or political groups; a form of *social marketing.*

puffery The legal exaggeration of praise, stopping just short of deception, lavished on a product.

pull strategy A strategy in which the goal is to get consumers to pull the product through the marketing channel by demanding it.

pulsing (advertising schedule) An advertising schedule that combines the continuous and flighting schedules by maintaining a base level of advertising but increasing advertising intensity during certain periods.

purchasing power parity (PPP) A theory that states that if the exchange rates of two countries are in equilibrium, a product purchased in one will cost the same in the other, expressed in the same currency.

pure competition Competition that occurs when different companies sell commodity products that consumers perceive as substitutable; price usually is set according to the laws of supply and demand.

push strategy A strategy designed to increase demand by motivating sellers—wholesalers, distributors, or salespeople—to highlight the product, rather than the products of competitors, and thereby push the product onto consumers.

qualify The process of assessing the potential of sales leads.

qualitative research Informal research methods, including observation, following social media sites, in-depth interviews, and focus groups.

quantitative research Structured responses that can be statistically tested to confirm insights and hypotheses generated via qualitative research or secondary data.

quantity discount Pricing tactic of offering a reduced price according to the amount purchased; the more the buyer purchases, the higher the discount and, of course, the greater the value.

questionnaire A form that features a set of questions designed to gather information from respondents and thereby accomplish the researchers' objectives; questions can be either unstructured or structured.

quick response (QR) inventory system An inventory management system used in retailing; merchandise is received just in time for sale when the customer wants it; see also *just-in-time (JIT) inventory system*.

quota Designates the maximum quantity of a product that may be brought into a country during a specified time period.

R&D consortia A group of firms and institutions, possibly including government and educational institutions, that explore new ideas or obtain solutions for developing new products.

radio frequency identification (RFID) tag Tiny computer chip that automatically transmits to a special scanner all the information about a container's contents or individual products.

reach Measure of consumers' exposure to marketing communications; the percentage of the target population exposed to a specific marketing communication, such as an advertisement, at least once.

rebate A consumer discount in which a portion of the purchase price is returned to the buyer in cash; the manufacturer, not the retailer, issues the refund.

rebranding See *brand repositioning*.

receiver The person who reads, hears, or sees and processes the information contained in the message or advertisement.

receiving The process of recording the receipt of merchandise as it arrives at a distribution center or store.

reference group One or more persons whom an individual uses as a basis for comparison regarding beliefs, feelings, and behaviors.

reference price The price against which buyers compare the actual selling price of the product and that facilitates their evaluation process.

referent power A type of marketing channel power that occurs if one channel member wants to be associated with another channel member. The channel member with whom the others wish to be associated has the power and can get them to do what they want.

regional culture Similar to culture in general, but at a regional level. The influence of the area within a country in which people live.

related diversification A growth strategy whereby the current target market and/or marketing mix shares something in common with the new opportunity.

relational orientation A method of building a relationship with customers based on the philosophy that buyers and sellers should develop a long-term relationship.

relationship selling A sales philosophy and process that emphasizes a commitment to maintaining the relationship over the long term and investing in opportunities that are mutually beneficial to all parties.

relative market share A measure of the product's strength in a particular market, defined as the sales of the focal product divided by the sales achieved by the largest firm in the industry.

relevance In the context of search engine marketing (SEM), it is a metric used to determine how useful an advertisement is to the consumer.

reminder advertising Communication used to remind consumers of a product or to prompt repurchases, especially for products that have gained market acceptance and are in the maturity stage of their life cycle.

request for proposals (RFP) A process through which buying organizations invite alternative suppliers to bid on supplying their required components.

reseller Marketing intermediary that resells manufactured products without significantly altering their form.

retailer/store brands Products developed by retailers. Also called *private-label brands*.

retailers' cooperative A marketing channel intermediary that buys collectively for a group of retailers to achieve price and promotion economies of scale. It is similar to a wholesaler, except that the retailer members have some control over, and sometimes ownership of, the cooperative's operations.

retailing The set of business activities that add value to products and services sold to consumers for their personal or family use; includes products bought at stores, through catalogs, and over the Internet, as well as services like fast-food restaurants, airlines, and hotels.

retrieval set Those brands or stores that the consumer can readily bring forth from memory.

retrieval stage The third stage in memory development in which consumers access desired information.

return on marketing investment (ROMI) The amount of profit divided by the value of the investment. In the case of an advertisement, the ROI is (Sales revenue generated by ad − Ad's cost) ÷ Ad's cost.

reverse engineering Taking apart a competitor's product, analyzing it, and creating an improved product that does not infringe on the competitor's patents, if any exist.

reward power A type of marketing channel power that occurs when the channel member exerting the power offers rewards to gain power, often a monetary incentive, for getting another channel member to do what it wants it to do.

role playing A good technique for practicing the sales presentation prior to meeting with a customer; the salesperson acts out a simulated buying situation while a colleague or manager acts as the buyer.

rule-of-thumb methods Budgeting methods that base the IMC budget on either the firm's share of the market in relation to competition, a fixed percentage of forecasted sales, or what is left after other operating costs and forecasted sales have been budgeted.

safety needs One of the needs in Maslow's hierarchy of needs; pertain to protection and physical well-being.

safety risk See *physiological risk*.

salary Compensation in the form of a fixed sum of money paid at regular intervals.

sales contest A short-term incentive designed to elicit a specific response from the sales force.

sales management The planning, direction, and control of personal selling activities, including recruiting, selecting, training, motivating, compensating, and evaluating, as they apply to the sales force.

sales orientation A company objective based on the belief that increasing sales will help the firm more than will increasing profits.

sales promotions Special incentives or excitement-building programs that encourage the purchase of a product or service, such as coupons, rebates, contests, free samples, and point-of-purchase displays.

sales support personnel Employees who enhance and help with a firm's overall selling effort, such as by responding to the customer's technical questions or facilitating repairs.

sample A group of customers who represent the customers of interest in a research study.

sampling Offers potential customers the opportunity to try a product or service before they make a buying decision.

scanner data A type of syndicated external secondary data used in quantitative research that is obtained from scanner readings of UPC codes at checkout counters.

search engine marketing (SEM) An activity used in online searches to increase the visibility of a firm by using paid searches to appear higher up in search results.

seasonal discount Seasonal discounts that are offered to consumers are price reductions offered on products and services to stimulate demand during off-peak seasons; in contrast, a seasonal discount in B2B settings is a pricing tactic that offers an additional reduction as an incentive to retailers to order merchandise in advance of the normal buying season.

secondary data Pieces of information that have already been collected from other sources and usually are readily available.

secondary package The wrapper or exterior carton that contains the primary package and provides the UPC label used by retail scanners; can contain additional product information that may not be available on the primary package.

segmentation, targeting, and positioning (STP) Firms use these processes to identify and evaluate opportunities for increasing sales and profits.

selective distribution Lies between the intensive and exclusive distribution strategies; uses a few selected customers in a territory.

self-actualization When a person is completely satisfied with his or her life.

self-concept The image a person has of himself or herself; a component of *psychographics*.

self-values Goals for life, not just the goals one wants to accomplish in a day; a component of *psychographics* that refers to overriding desires that drive how a person lives his or her life.

selling teams Combinations of sales specialists whose primary duties are order getting, order taking, or sales support but who work together to service important accounts.

sender The firm from which an IMC message originates; the sender must be clearly identified to the intended audience.

sentiment analysis A technique that allows marketers to analyze data from social media sites to collect consumer comments about companies and their products.

sentiment mining Data gathered by evaluating customer comments posted through social media sites such as Facebook and Twitter.

service Any intangible offering that involves a deed, performance, or effort that cannot be physically possessed; intangible customer benefits that are produced by people or machines and cannot be separated from the producer.

service gap Results when a service fails to meet the expectations that customers have about how it should be delivered.

Service Gaps Model A managerial tool designed to encourage the systematic examination of all aspects of the service delivery process and prescribe the steps needed to develop an optimal service strategy.

service quality Customers' perceptions of how well a service meets or exceeds their expectations.

service retailer A firm that primarily sells services rather than merchandise.

share of wallet The percentage of the customer's purchases made from a particular retailer.

shopping products/services Products or services for which consumers will spend time comparing alternatives, such as apparel, fragrances, and appliances.

showrooming Customers visit a store to touch, feel, and even discuss a product's features with a sales associate, and then purchase it online from another retailer at a lower price.

situation analysis Second step in a marketing plan; uses a SWOT analysis that assesses both the internal environment with regard to its **S**trengths and **W**eaknesses and the external environment in terms of its **O**pportunities and **T**hreats.

situational factors Factors affecting the consumer decision process; those that are specific to the situation that may override, or at least influence, psychological and social issues.

size discount The most common implementation of a quantity discount at the consumer level; the larger the quantity bought, the less the cost per unit (e.g., per ounce).

slotting allowances Fees firms pay to retailers simply to get new products into stores or to gain more or better shelf space for their products.

social marketing The content distributed through online and mobile technologies to facilitate interpersonal interactions.

social media The online and mobile technologies that distribute content to facilitate interpersonal interactions, with the assistance of various firms that offer platforms, services, and tools to help consumers and firms build their connections.

social risk The fears that consumers suffer when they worry others might not regard their purchases positively.

social shopping Using the Internet to communicate about product preferences with other shoppers.

specialty products/services Products or services toward which the customer shows a strong preference and for which he or she will expend considerable effort to search for the best suppliers.

specialty store A type of retailer that concentrates on a limited number of complementary merchandise categories in a relatively small store.

stakeholders The broad set of people who might be affected by a firm's actions, including not just corporate shareholders and customers but also employees (past, current, and prospective) and their families, supply chain partners, government agencies, the physical environment, and members of the communities in which the firm operates (defined either locally or on a global scale).

standards gap A type of *service gap*; pertains to the difference between the firm's perceptions of customers' expectations and the service standards it sets.

status quo pricing A competitor-oriented strategy in which a firm changes prices only to meet those of competition.

store brand Brand developed and marketed by a retailer and available only from that retailer; also called *private-label brand.*

straight rebuy In a B2B setting, refers to when the buyer or buying organization simply buys additional units of products that have previously been purchased.

strategic alliance A collaborative relationship between independent firms, though the partnering firms do not create an equity partnership; that is, they do not invest in one another.

strategic business unit (SBU) A division of the firm itself that can be managed and operated somewhat independently from other divisions and may have a different mission or objectives.

strategic (partnering) relationship A supply chain relationship that the members are committed to maintaining long term, investing in opportunities that are mutually beneficial; requires mutual trust, open communication, common goals, and credible commitments. Also called *partnering relationship.*

structured questions Closed-ended questions for which a discrete set of response alternatives, or specific answers, is provided for respondents to evaluate.

subhead An additional smaller headline in an ad that provides a great deal of information through the use of short and simple words.

substitute products Products for which changes in demand are negatively related; that is, a percentage increase in the quantity demanded for product A results in a percentage decrease in the quantity demanded for product B.

substitution effect Consumers' ability to substitute other products for the focal brand, thus increasing the price elasticity of demand for the focal brand.

supercenter Large store that combines a full-line discount store with a supermarket in one place.

supply chain The group of firms that make and deliver a given set of goods and services.

supply chain management A set of approaches and techniques firms employ to efficiently and effectively integrate their suppliers, manufacturers, warehouses, stores, and transportation intermediaries into a seamless value chain in which merchandise is produced and distributed in the right quantities, to the right locations, and at the right time, as well as to minimize system-wide costs while satisfying the service levels their customers require. Also called *marketing channel management.*

survey A systematic means of collecting information from people that generally uses a *questionnaire.*

sustainable competitive advantage Something the firm can persistently do better than its competitors.

sustainable packaging Product packaging that has less of a negative impact on the environment.

sweepstakes A form of sales promotion that offers prizes based on a chance drawing of entrants' names.

SWOT analysis A method of conducting a situation analysis within a marketing plan in which both the internal environment with regard to its **S**trengths and **W**eaknesses and the external environment in terms of its **O**pportunities and **T**hreats are examined.

syndicated data Data available for a fee from commercial research firms such as Information Resources Inc. (IRI), National Purchase Diary Panel, and Nielsen.

tactile sense A sensory stimulation that involves touch and influences the shopping experience.

target marketing or targeting The process of evaluating the attractiveness of various segments and then deciding which to pursue as a market.

target profit pricing A pricing strategy implemented by firms when they have a particular profit goal as their overriding concern; uses price to stimulate a certain level of sales at a certain profit per unit.

target return pricing A pricing strategy implemented by firms less concerned with the absolute level of profits and more interested in the rate at which their profits are generated relative to their investments; designed to produce a specific return on investment, usually expressed as a percentage of sales.

tariff A tax levied on a good imported into a country; also called a *duty.*

taste sense A sensory stimulation that involves taste and influences the shopping experience, e.g., food and beverages.

telemarketing A method of prospecting in which salespeople telephone potential customers.

test marketing A method of determining the success potential of a new product; it introduces the offering to a limited geographical area prior to a national launch.

ticketing and marking Creating price and identification labels and placing them on the merchandise.

timeliness effect With regard to the Wheel of Social Media Engagement, the *timeliness effect* of social media engagement is concerned with the firm being able to engage with the customer at the right place/time—their ability to do so 24/7 from any location.

top-of-mind awareness A prominent place in people's memories that triggers a response without them having to put any thought into it.

total cost The sum of the *variable* and *fixed costs.*

tracking Assessments that monitor key indicators, such as daily or weekly sales volume, while the advertisement is running to shed light on any problems with the message or the medium.

trade agreement Intergovernmental agreement designed to manage and promote trade activities for specific regions.

trade deficit Results when a country imports more goods than it exports.

trade shows Major events attended by buyers who choose to be exposed to products and services offered by potential suppliers in an industry.

trade surplus Occurs when a country has a higher level of exports than imports.

trading bloc Consists of those countries that have signed a particular trade agreement.

transmitter An agent or intermediary with which the sender works to develop the marketing communications; for example, a firm's creative department or an advertising agency.

triple bottom line A means to measure performance according to economic, environmental, and societal criteria.

undifferentiated targeting strategy (mass marketing) A marketing strategy a firm can use if the product or service is perceived to provide the same benefits to everyone, with no need to develop separate strategies for different groups.

uniform delivered pricing The shipper charges one rate, no matter where the buyer is located.

unique selling proposition (USP) A strategy of differentiating a product by communicating its unique attributes; often becomes the common theme or slogan in the entire advertising campaign.

Universal Product Code (UPC) The black-and-white bar code found on most merchandise. It contains a 13-digit code that indicates the manufacturer of the item, a description of the item, information about special packaging, and special promotions.

universal set All possible choices for a product category.

unrelated diversification A growth strategy whereby a new business lacks any common elements with the present business.

unsought products/services Products or services consumers either do not normally think of buying or do not know about.

unstructured questions Open-ended questions that allow respondents to answer in their own words.

user The person who consumes or uses the product or service purchased by the buying center.

value Reflects the relationship of benefits to costs, or what the consumer *gets* for what he or she *gives*.

value cocreation Customers act as collaborators with a manufacturer or retailer to create the product or service.

value proposition The unique value that a product or service provides to its customers and how it is better than and different from those of competitors.

value-based pricing method An approach that focuses on the overall value of the product offering as perceived by consumers, who determine value by comparing the benefits they expect the product to deliver with the sacrifice they will need to make to acquire the product.

Values and Lifestyles Survey (VALS) A psychographic tool developed by SRI Consulting Business Intelligence; classifies consumers into eight segments: innovators, thinkers, believers, achievers, strivers, experiencers, makers, or survivors.

variable costs Those costs, primarily labor and materials, that vary with production volume.

vendor-managed inventory (VMI) An approach for improving supply chain efficiency in which the manufacturer is responsible for maintaining the retailer's inventory levels in each of its stores.

vertical channel conflict A type of channel conflict in which members of the same marketing channel, for example, manufacturers, wholesalers, and retailers, are in disagreement or discord.

vertical marketing system A supply chain in which the members act as a unified system; there are three types: *administered*, *contractual*, and *corporate*.

vertical price fixing Occurs when parties at different levels of the same marketing channel (e.g., manufacturers and retailers) collude to control the prices passed on to consumers.

viral marketing program A promotional strategy that encourages people to pass along a marketing message to other potential consumers.

virtual community Online networks of people who communicate about specific topics.

visual sense A sensory stimulation that includes colors, lighting, brightness, size, shape, and setup of a retail space and the products within it.

voice-of-customer (VOC) program An ongoing marketing research system that collects customer inputs and integrates them into managerial decisions.

warehouse club Large retailer with an irregular assortment, low service levels, and low prices that often requires membership for shoppers.

web portal An Internet site whose purpose is to be a major starting point for users when they connect to the web.

web-tracking software Software used to assess how much time viewers spend on particular web pages and the number of pages they view.

white papers In a B2B context, white papers are a promotional technique used by B2B sellers to provide information about a product or service in an educational context, thereby not appearing like a promotion or propaganda.

wholesaler Firm engaged in buying, taking title to, often storing, and physically handling goods in large quantities, then reselling the goods (usually in smaller quantities) to retailers or industrial or business users.

zone of tolerance The area between customers' expectations regarding their desired service and the minimum level of acceptable service—that is, the difference between what the customer really wants and what he or she will accept before going elsewhere.

zone pricing The shipper sets different prices depending on a geographic division of the delivery areas.

company index

subject index